## MCSD Certification

To accomplish the MCSD certification, you must pass two required exams and two elective exams. The required courses are Windows Architecture I & II.

The electives from which to choose are quite diverse. A number of popular options are listed here, but consult Microsoft for a current list at: **http://www.microsoft.com/train_cert/**

| Exam | MCSD Course Title Number | Course Number | MCSE Study Guide Title | Required or Elective? |
|------|--------------------------|---------------|------------------------|-----------------------|
| 70-160 | Microsoft Windows Architecture I | TBA | Windows® Architecture I & II MCSD Study Guide Prendergast, 0-7645-3123-9 | R |
| 70-161 | Microsoft Windows Architecture II | TBA | Windows® Architecture I & II MCSD Study Guide Prendergast, 0-7645-3123-9 | R |
| 70-65 | Programming with Microsoft Visual Basic 5.0 | 780 | Visual Basic® 5.0 MCSD Study Guide Dillon & Rotberg, 0-7645-3153-0 | E |

# Windows NT® 4.0 MCSE Study Guide

# WINDOWS NT® 4.0
# MCSE STUDY GUIDE

**Alan R. Carter**

IDG Books Worldwide, Inc.
An International Data Group Company
Foster City, CA ● Chicago, IL ● Indianapolis, IN ● Dallas, TX

Windows NT® 4.0 MCSE Study Guide

Published by
**IDG Books Worldwide, Inc.**
An International Data Group Company
919 E. Hillsdale Blvd., Suite 400
Foster City, CA 94404

www.idgbooks.com (IDG Books Worldwide Web site)

Library of Congress Catalog Card No.: 97-73384

ISBN: 0-7645-3087-9

Printed in the United States of America

10 9 8 7 6 5 4 3

1DD/RY/RS/ZX/IN

Distributed in the United States by IDG Books Worldwide, Inc.

Distributed by Macmillan Canada for Canada; by Contemporanea de Ediciones for Venezuela; by Distribuidora Cuspide for Argentina; by CITEC for Brazil; by Ediciones ZETA S.C.R. Ltda. for Peru; by Editorial Limusa SA for Mexico; by Transworld Publishers Limited in the United Kingdom and Europe; by Academic Bookshop for Egypt; by Levant Distributors S.A.R.L. for Lebanon; by Al Jassim for Saudi Arabia; by Simron Pty. Ltd. for South Africa; by Pustak Mahal for India; by The Computer Bookshop for India; by Toppan Company Ltd. for Japan; by Addison Wesley Publishing Company for Korea; by Longman Singapore Publishers Ltd. for Singapore, Malaysia, Thailand, and Indonesia; by Unalis Corporation for Taiwan; by WS Computer Publishing Company, Inc. for the Philippines; by WoodsLane Pty. Ltd. for Australia; by WoodsLane Enterprises Ltd. for New Zealand. Authorized Sales Agent: Anthony Rudkin Associates for the Middle East and North Africa.

For general information on IDG Books Worldwide's books in the U.S., please call our Consumer Customer Service department at 800-762-2974. For reseller information, including discounts and premium sales, please call our Reseller Customer Service department at 800-434-3422.

For information on where to purchase IDG Books Worldwide's books outside the U.S., please contact our International Sales department at 415-655-3200 or fax 415-655-3295.

For information on foreign language translations, please contact our Foreign & Subsidiary Rights department at 415-655-3021 or fax 415-655-3281.

For sales inquiries and special prices for bulk quantities, please contact our Sales department at 415-655-3200 or write to the address above.

For information on using IDG Books Worldwide's books in the classroom or for ordering examination copies, please contact our Educational Sales department at 800-434-2086 or fax 817-251-8174.

For press review copies, author interviews, or other publicity information, please contact our Public Relations department at 415-655-3000 or fax 415-655-3299.

For authorization to photocopy items for corporate, personal, or educational use, please contact Copyright Clearance Center, 222 Rosewood Drive, Danvers, MA 01923, or fax 508-750-4470.

is a trademark under exclusive license to IDG Books Worldwide, Inc., from International Data Group, Inc.

# ABOUT IDG BOOKS WORLDWIDE

Welcome to the world of IDG Books Worldwide.

IDG Books Worldwide, Inc., is a subsidiary of International Data Group, the world's largest publisher of computer-related information and the leading global provider of information services on information technology. IDG was founded more than 25 years ago and now employs more than 8,500 people worldwide. IDG publishes more than 275 computer publications in over 75 countries (see listing below). More than 60 million people read one or more IDG publications each month.

Launched in 1990, IDG Books Worldwide is today the #1 publisher of best-selling computer books in the United States. We are proud to have received eight awards from the Computer Press Association in recognition of editorial excellence and three from *Computer Currents'* First Annual Readers' Choice Awards. Our best-selling *...For Dummies*® series has more than 30 million copies in print with translations in 30 languages. IDG Books Worldwide, through a joint venture with IDG's Hi-Tech Beijing, became the first U.S. publisher to publish a computer book in the People's Republic of China. In record time, IDG Books Worldwide has become the first choice for millions of readers around the world who want to learn how to better manage their businesses.

Our mission is simple: Every one of our books is designed to bring extra value and skill-building instructions to the reader. Our books are written by experts who understand and care about our readers. The knowledge base of our editorial staff comes from years of experience in publishing, education, and journalism — experience we use to produce books for the '90s. In short, we care about books, so we attract the best people. We devote special attention to details such as audience, interior design, use of icons, and illustrations. And because we use an efficient process of authoring, editing, and desktop publishing our books electronically, we can spend more time ensuring superior content and spend less time on the technicalities of making books.

You can count on our commitment to deliver high-quality books at competitive prices on topics you want to read about. At IDG Books Worldwide, we continue in the IDG tradition of delivering quality for more than 25 years. You'll find no better book on a subject than one from IDG Books Worldwide.

John Kilcullen
CEO
IDG Books Worldwide, Inc.

Steven Berkowitz
President and Publisher
IDG Books Worldwide, Inc.

Eighth Annual
Computer Press
Awards ≥1993

Ninth Annual
Computer Press
Awards ≥1993

Tenth Annual
Computer Press
Awards ≥1994

Eleventh Annual
Computer Press
Awards ≥1995

# The Value of Microsoft Certification

As a computer professional, your opportunities have never been greater. Yet you know better than anyone that today's complex computing environment has never been more challenging.

Microsoft certification keeps computer professionals on top of evolving information technologies. Training and certification let you maximize the potential of Microsoft Windows desktop operating systems; server technologies, such as the Internet Information Server, Microsoft Windows NT, and Microsoft BackOffice; and Microsoft development tools. In short, Microsoft training and certification provide you with the knowledge and skills necessary to become an expert on Microsoft products and technologies—and to provide the key competitive advantage that every business is seeking.

Microsoft offers you the most comprehensive program for assessing and maintaining your skills with our products. When you become a Microsoft Certified Professional (MCP), you are recognized as an expert and are sought by employers industry-wide. Technical managers recognize the MCP designation as a mark of quality—one that ensures that an employee or consultant has proven experience with Microsoft products and meets the high technical proficiency standards of Microsoft products.

As an MCP, you receive many benefits, such as direct access to technical information from Microsoft; the official MCP logo and other materials to identify your status to colleagues and clients; invitations to Microsoft conferences, technical training sessions and special events; and exclusive publications with news about the MCP program.

Research shows that organizations employing MCPs also receive many benefits:

- A standard method of determining training needs and measuring results— an excellent return on training and certification investments

- Increased customer satisfaction and decreased support costs through improved service, increased productivity, and greater technical self-sufficiency

- A reliable benchmark for hiring, promoting, and career planning

- Recognition and rewards for productive employees by validating their expertise
- Retraining options for existing employees, so they can work effectively with new technologies
- Assurance of quality when outsourcing computer services

Through your study, experience, and achievement of Microsoft certification, you will enjoy these same benefits, too, as you meet the industry's challenges.

Nancy Lewis
General Manager
Microsoft Training and Certification

# FOREWORD TO THE MCSE SERIES

Certifications are an effective way of "selling your skills" to prospective employers, since they represent a consistent measurement of knowledge about specific software or hardware products. Because of their expansive product line and tremendous marketing efforts, Microsoft certifications have become the gold standard in the exploding certification industry. As a Microsoft Certified Professional, you are recognized as a "Subject Matter Expert" as defined by objective standards. As a training organization, we recognize the value of offering certification-level training. In fact, approximately 55 percent of students in our Microsoft classes are working toward certification, and I expect that number to continue to rise.

Studies have been conducted that show increased productivity among Microsoft Certified Solutions Developers versus noncertified programmers. Additionally, compensation for Microsoft Certified Systems Engineers and Microsoft Certified Solutions Developers averages higher than for those without certification. For individuals looking for a career in these areas, there is no better metric of legitimacy that can be placed on a resume than Microsoft certification credentials.

Information Systems/Information Technology (IS/IT) decision-makers for ExecuTrain clients worldwide increasingly require certifications for their IS employees. Often, individuals are required to be certified or find that certification was their competitive edge in landing the job. Conventional wisdom and every study you read indicates these trends will continue as technologies become more a part of daily business in corporations.

Microsoft recently certified the 100,000th Microsoft Certified Professional. I expect this number to balloon as corporations make certification part of IS staff job descriptions. I predict certified candidates can expect better-paying jobs and positions with more technical responsibility to match their hard-won certification. Although the number of MCPs rises daily, that population is eclipsed by the more than 200,000 open IT positions reported today. Microsoft tracks these open positions and would like to fill each of them with MCPs. My bet is that if anyone can make the math work, they can.

Kevin Brice
Vice President/General Manager
Technical Training
ExecuTrain Corporation

# CREDITS

**ACQUISITIONS EDITOR**
Anne Hamilton

**DEVELOPMENT EDITORS**
Tracy Thomsic
Ellen Dendy
Kay Keppler

**COPY EDITORS**
Lothlórien Baerenwald
Tracy Brown
Katharine Dvorak
Marcia Baker
Donna Scism

**TECHNICAL EDITOR**
G. Chris Gradwohl, MCT, MCSE, MCIP, CNA

**PROJECT COORDINATOR**
Susan Parini

**GRAPHICS AND PRODUCTION**
Renée Dunn
Todd Klemme
Jude Levinson
Elizabeth Cárdenas-Nelson
Mary Penn
Dina F Quan
Mark Schumann
Deirdre Smith
Elsie Yim

**PROOFREADERS**
Jenny Overmyer
Michelle Croninger

**INDEXER**
Liz Cunningham

**BOOK DESIGN**
Kurt Krames

**COVER DESIGN**
Mike Parsons

## About the Author

Alan R. Carter is a Microsoft Certified Systems Engineer (MCSE), a Microsoft Certified Internet Professional (MCIP), and a Microsoft Certified Trainer (MCT). He teaches Microsoft Official Curriculum courses throughout the U.S. He also participates in the development of new courses and other educational materials. In addition to his Microsoft certifications, Alan is a Certified Network Professional (CNP), a Novell Master Certified Network Engineer (CNE), and a Certified Novell Instructor (CNI). He lives in Kirkland, Washington. He welcomes comments from his readers and can be contacted via the Internet at alan_carter@usa.net.

*To Timothy*

# FOREWORD

When I first met Alan Carter, the author of this book, my understanding of networking was pretty uneven. I knew a great deal about some aspects, but nearly nothing about others. My basic computing fundamentals were sound, but I had not yet taken the step of applying those fundamentals to the big picture of networking.

I met Alan when I signed up for his classes. I had heard a number of very positive comments about his training skills from several of my colleagues, and his experience and certifications constituted a veritable laundry list of acronyms. However, what was important to me was learning to apply networking skills to the computing foundation I had already acquired, and expanding my abilities specifically to Enterprise-level network operating systems. Alan helped me achieve just that.

Alan's vast real-world experience and intimate product knowledge provided the learning context and background I needed to pair up with my more theoretical computing basics. My benchmark for a good instructor is one who can tailor the subject to my needs, provide real-world insight and details to round out my knowledge base, and expand my understanding without simply drilling down to the rote details. Alan's teaching style and provocative discussions do exactly that. He answered my questions just as they were forming on my tongue. He provided compelling real-world examples at every turn, so I never got distracted by the details or lost the big picture.

This is not to say that Alan isn't careful with the details! He is completely familiar with the products and the people who build them. His attention to minutiae makes both his training courses and this book excellent resources for every detail. He understands inside out not only what it takes to pass these difficult exams, but also what real-world skills a certified professional must bring to the table to be effective on the job.

In this book, Alan brings you the same excellence and detail that he does in his training courses. Absolutely every exam objective is covered here — with labs and exercises to reinforce your hands-on experience. More importantly, Alan's vast training experience and product background will provide you with the context you need in the real world, not just on paper. Getting through the Windows NT MCSE exams is no easy task. Fortunately, you've made the right decision in choosing Alan's book to help prepare for these crucial exams.

Donald E. Dillenburg
Senior Network Integrator
Bank of America Northwest
MCSE, CNE, ASE

# PREFACE

Welcome to the MCSE Certification Series! This book is designed to help you acquire the knowledge, skills, and abilities you'll need to pass three of the Microsoft Certified Professional exams:

o Exam No. 70-73: Implementing and Supporting Microsoft Windows NT Workstation 4.0

o Exam No. 70-67: Implementing and Supporting Microsoft Windows NT Server 4.0

o Exam No. 70-68: Implementing and Supporting Microsoft Windows NT Server 4.0 in the Enterprise

If you're *not* planning to take one or more of these exams, but you want to develop a comprehensive working knowledge of the Microsoft Windows NT (referred to mostly from here on out simply as Windows NT or NT) products, then this book is also for you.

This book is designed to be the only book or course you'll need to prepare for and pass the NT exams. However, the goal of this book is *not* to make you into an NT guru. I'll cover NT to the depth of the exam objectives, but not go substantially beyond that point. If, during the course of your study, you find yourself wanting more depth, detail, and advanced technical tidbits, I heartily recommend the following resources:

o *Microsoft Windows NT Workstation Resource Kit for version 4.0* (Microsoft Press, 1996)

o *Microsoft Windows NT Server Resource Kit for version 4.0* (Microsoft Press, 1996)

o *Inside Windows NT* (Microsoft Press, 1993)

o *Inside the Windows NT File System* (Microsoft Press, 1994)

# HOW THIS BOOK IS ORGANIZED

This book is organized into seven major parts, followed by a Resources section that contains appendices and supplemental materials, plus a compact disc. These major parts closely parallel the Microsoft Certified Professional exam objectives for the three Windows NT 4.0 exams.

Within these major parts, each chapter begins with an overview of the topics that will be covered in that chapter. Then pertinent information on each topic is presented. A Key Point Summary follows, summarizing the chapter highlights and reviewing important material. At the end of each chapter are Instant Assessment questions to make sure you understand and can apply what you've read. Additionally, at the end of many chapters there are review activities, and hands-on lab exercises so you can master the specific tasks and skills tested by the exams.

I should explain, at this point, why the preparation guides for the NT Workstation and NT Server exams have been combined into a single book, rather than presented as two separate books. Simply stated, NT is NT. Yes, there are some differences between NT Workstation and NT Server, but the two products are fundamentally the same operating systems. When we talk about NT, we are talking about a coherent body of knowledge. When you learn to perform a task using Windows NT Workstation, it's usually the same as learning the same task on Windows NT Server. Throughout this book, therefore, except where differences are noted, NT refers to *both* NT Workstation and NT Server.

## Part I: Overview

The Overview discusses the basics of Windows NT Workstation and Windows NT Server, including a section on the architecture of Windows NT.

## Part II: Installation and Configuration

This part covers, in detail, installing and configuring Windows NT Workstation and Windows NT Server, including chapters on configuring disks, using Control Panel, deploying Windows NT from a server, and managing printing.

## Part III: Managing Resources

This part explains how to use the features, services, and tools that come with Windows NT. It explains user and group accounts, account policy, auditing, user rights, user profiles, and system policy. It covers managing and optimizing Windows NT Server Directory Services, as well as sharing and securing file systems. It teaches the reader how to access network resources, how to use NT Server tools, and how to back up and restore data.

## Part IV: Connectivity

Connectivity is all about how NT functions in a network setting. Protocols, particularly TCP/IP, are examined. This section discusses the coexistence of Windows NT with Novell NetWare, as well as migrating from a NetWare environment to a Windows NT environment. You will learn how to install and configure Remote Access Server, and also learn about connectivity with Macintosh computers.

## Part V: Running Applications

In this part, I introduce the application environments and explain how to optimize applications to run under Windows NT.

## Part VI: Monitoring and Optimization

This part explores how to monitor and optimize the performance of a specific computer or an entire network. You will learn how to use tools such as Performance Monitor and Network Monitor to gather data. I also examine the basics of capacity planning.

## Part VII: Troubleshooting

From basic to advanced troubleshooting, this part covers it. You'll learn how to approach a troubleshooting situation, as well as which resources to consult when you're stumped by a problem.

## Part VIII: Resources

The supplemental materials at the back of the book contain a wealth of information. In addition to a detailed glossary and thorough index, you'll find the following information in the appendices: exam preparation tips; answers to chapter Instant Assessment questions, Review Activities, and Hands-on Labs; a Mini-Lab Manual that features all of the Hands-on Lab Exercises from the book; Windows NT planning forms; and a description of the compact disc contents. Appendices A, B, and C, which contain the exam objectives for each of the three Windows NT 4.0 exams, also include detailed Exam Objectives Cross-Reference Charts for study purposes.

## CD-ROM

The compact disc included with this book contains the following materials: an electronic version of this book in Adobe Acrobat format; excerpts from *MCSE Career Microsoft®!* (IDG Books Worldwide, 1997); Adobe Acrobat Reader; Microsoft Internet explorer version 3.01; Validate! Windows NT 4.0 Workstation and Server practice exams; Microsoft Training and Certification Offline CD-ROM; *MicroHouse Technical Library* (evaluation copy); and Diskeeper Lite (evaluation copy).

# How to Use This Book

This book can be used either by individuals working independently or by groups in a formal classroom setting.

For best results (and we both know that the only acceptable results are passing scores on the MCSE exams), I recommend the following plan of attack as you use this book. First, read the chapter and the Key Point Summary at the end. Use this summary to see if you've really got the key concepts under your belt. If you don't, go back and reread the section(s) you're not clear on. Then do *all* of the Instant Assessment section questions and review activities at the end of the chapter. Finally, *do* the hands-on lab exercises. Remember, the important thing is to master the tasks that will be tested on the exams. There's really no way to master tasks without seeing the various NT screens over and over again.

note

When you do the hands-on lab exercises and are asked to type something, the text you are instructed to type will be printed in bold, like this: **WORKGROUP**

Important words and concepts appear in italics, and all filenames, folder names, directories, Uniform Resource Locators (URLs), and code appear as monospaced font.

The chapters of this book have been designed to be studied sequentially. In other words, it would be best if you complete Chapter 1 before you proceed to Chapter 2. A few chapters could probably stand alone, but all in all, I recommend a sequential approach. The hands-on lab exercises have also been designed to be completed in a sequential order and often depend on successful completion of the previous labs.

After you've completed your study of the chapters and reviewed the questions and lab exercises in the book, use the compact disc to take the assessment exams and practice tests. The assessment exams and practice tests will help you assess how much you've learned from your study and will also familiarize you with the type of exam questions you'll face when you take the real exams. Once you identify a weak area, you can restudy the corresponding chapters (including the review questions and lab exercises) to improve your knowledge and skills in that area. Use the exam objectives cross-reference charts in the appendices to help you determine on which chapter(s) to redouble your efforts.

## Prerequisites

Although this book is a comprehensive study and exam preparation guide, it does not start at ground zero. I do assume you have the following knowledge and skills at the outset:

1. Basic terminology and basic skills to use a Microsoft Windows product. (This could be Windows 95, Windows for Workgroups, or a Windows NT product.)

2. Basic mouse skills: being able to left-click, right-click, use the pointer, and so on.

3. Networking knowledge or experience equal to the scope required to pass the Microsoft Certified Professional Networking Essentials Exam (Exam No. 70-58).

If you meet these prerequisites, you're ready to begin this book.

If you don't have the basic Windows experience or mouse skills, I recommend you either take a one-day Windows application course or work through a self-study book, such as *Windows 95 for Dummies* (IDG Books Worldwide, 1995), to acquire these skills *before* you begin this book.

If you don't have the networking knowledge or experience, I recommend you use a tool such as *Networking Essentials: Hands-On, Self-Paced Training for Supporting Local and Wide Area Networks* (Microsoft Press, 1996), to obtain this knowledge, and pass the Networking Essentials exam *before* you begin this book.

## How to Determine What You Should Study

Your individual certification goals will ultimately determine which parts of this book you should study. If you want to pass two or three of the Microsoft Certified Professional NT exams, or simply want to develop a comprehensive working knowledge of NT, I recommend you study, in sequential order, the entire book.

If you are preparing for the Implementing and Supporting Microsoft Windows NT Workstation 4.0 exam, I suggest you follow the recommended study plan, shown in Table 1.

If you are preparing for the Implementing and Supporting Microsoft Windows NT Server 4.0 exam, I suggest following the recommended study plan shown in Table 2.

If you are preparing for the Implementing and Supporting Microsoft Windows NT Server 4.0 in the Enterprise exam, I suggest following the study plan shown in Table 3.

| TABLE 1 CHAPTERS AND LABS THAT PREPARE YOU FOR THE IMPLEMENTING AND SUPPORTING MICROSOFT WINDOWS NT WORKSTATION 4.0 EXAM | | |
|---|---|---|
| **CHAPTER NUMBER** | **CHAPTER TITLE** | **RECOMMENDED LABS** |
| 1 | Qverview of Windows NT Workstation and Windows NT Server | None |
| 2 | Installing Windows NT Workstation and Windows NT Server | Lab 2.1, Lab 2.2 |
| 3 | Configuring Disks | Lab 3.3 |
| 4 | Using Control Panel | Lab 4.6 |
| 5 | Server-Based Deployment | Lab 5.7 |
| 6 | Managing Printing | Lab 6.8, Lab 6.9 |
| 7 | Managing User and Group Accounts | Lab 7.10 |
| 9 | Managing User Profiles and System Policy | Lab 9.13 |
| 12 | Sharing and Securing File Systems | Lab 12.18, Lab 12.20 |
| 13 | Accessing Resources on the Network | Lab 13.21, Lab 13.22 |
| 16 | Networking Using TCP/IP | Lab 16.26 |
| 17 | Coexistence with NetWare | Lab 17.29 |
| 19 | Installing and Configuring Remote Access Service (RAS) | Lab 19.32 |
| 21 | Running Applications on Windows NT | Lab 21.34 |
| 22 | Using Performance Monitor | Lab 22.35 |
| 25 | Performance Optimization | Lab 25.37 |
| 26 | The Troubleshooting Process | None |
| 27 | Advanced Troubleshooting Topics | Lab 27.39 |

**TABLE 2** Chapters and Labs That Prepare You for the Implementing and Supporting Microsoft Windows NT Server 4.0 Exam

| CHAPTER NUMBER | CHAPTER TITLE | RECOMMENDED LABS |
| --- | --- | --- |
| 1 | Qverview of Windows NT Workstation and Windows NT Server | None |
| 2 | Installing Windows NT Workstation and Windows NT Server | Lab 2.1, Lab 2.2 |
| 3 | Configuring Disks | Lab 3.3, Lab 3.4 |
| 4 | Using Control Panel | Lab 4.5, Lab 4.6 |
| 5 | Server-Based Deployment | Lab 5.7 |
| 6 | Managing Printing | Lab 6.8, Lab 6.9 |
| 7 | Managing User and Group Accounts | Lab 7.10 |
| 8 | Managing Account Policy, User Rights, and Auditing | Lab 8.11, Lab 8.12 |
| 9 | Managing User Profiles and System Policy | Lab 9.13, Lab 9.14 |
| 12 | Sharing and Securing File Systems | Lab 12.18, Lab 12.19, Lab 12.20 |
| 13 | Accessing Resources on the Network | Lab 13.21 |
| 14 | Using Windows NT Server Tools | Lab 14.23 |
| 15 | Backing Up and Restoring Data | Lab 15.24 |
| 16 | Networking Using TCP/IP | Lab 16.27, Lab 16.28 |
| 17 | Coexistence With NetWare | Lab 17.30 |
| 18 | Migrating to Windows NT from NetWare | None |
| 19 | Installing and Configuring Remote Access Service (RAS) | Lab 19.32 |
| 22 | Using Performance Monitor | Lab 22.35 |
| 25 | Performance Optimization | Lab 25.37 |
| 26 | The Troubleshooting Process | None |
| 27 | Advanced Troubleshooting Topics | None |

**TABLE 3** CHAPTERS AND LABS THAT PREPARE YOU FOR THE IMPLEMENTING AND SUPPORTING WINDOWS NT SERVER 4.0 IN THE ENTERPRISE EXAM

| CHAPTER NUMBER | CHAPTER TITLE | RECOMMENDED LABS |
| --- | --- | --- |
| 1 | Qverview of Windows NT Workstation and Windows NT Server | None |
| 2 | Installing Windows NT Workstation and Windows NT Server | Lab 2.1, Lab 2.2 |
| 3 | Configuring Disks | Lab 3.3, Lab 3.4 |
| 4 | Using Control Panel | Lab 4.5 |
| 5 | Server-Based Deployment | None |
| 6 | Managing Printing | Lab 6.8, Lab 6.9 |
| 7 | Managing User and Group Accounts | Lab 7.10 |
| 8 | Managing Account Policy, User Rights, and Auditing | Lab 8.11, Lab 8.12 |
| 9 | Managing User Profiles and System Policy | Lab 9.13, Lab 9.14 |
| 10 | Managing Windows NT Directory Services | Lab 10.15, Lab 10.16 |
| 11 | Optimizing Windows NT Server Directory Services | Lab 11.17 |
| 12 | Sharing and Securing File Systems | Lab 12.18, Lab 12.19, Lab 12.20 |
| 13 | Accessing Resources on the Network | Lab 13.21, Lab 13.22 |
| 14 | Using Windows NT Server Tools | Lab 14.23 |
| 15 | Backing Up and Restoring Data | Lab 15.24 |
| 16 | Networking Using TCP/IP | Lab 16.25, Lab 16.26, Lab 16.27, Lab 16.28 |
| 17 | Coexistence With NetWare | Lab 17.30, Lab 17.31 |
| 18 | Migrating to Windows NT from NetWare | None |
| 19 | Installing and Configuring Remote Access Service (RAS) | Lab 19.32 |
| 20 | Macintosh Connectivity | Lab 20.33 |
| 22 | Using Performance Monitor | Lab 22.35 |
| 23 | Using Network Monitor | Lab 23.36 |
| 24 | Capacity Planning | None |
| 25 | Performance Optimization | Lab 25.37, Lab 25.38 |
| 26 | The Troubleshooting Process | None |
| 27 | Advanced Troubleshooting Topics | Lab 27.39 |

# HARDWARE AND SOFTWARE YOU'LL NEED

You will need access to various hardware and software to be able to do the hands-on lab exercises in this book. It is extremely important that you do these labs to acquire the skills tested by the Microsoft Certified Professional exams.

If you have the minimum hardware listed below, you will be able to complete *most* of the hands-on lab exercises in this book, and certainly all of the critical exercises. To be able to perform *all* of the labs, however, you will need the additional hardware as well.

**Minimum hardware requirements:**

- Intel-based computer with 486/33 processor, 16MB RAM, and 500MB–1GB available hard disk space
- CD-ROM drive
- Mouse
- VGA monitor and graphics card

 tip
**I strongly recommend that you only use hardware found on the Microsoft Windows NT Hardware Compatibility List, which is shipped with the NT product, or can be accessed via Microsoft's World Wide Web site at** http://www.microsoft.com/ntworkstation, **or at** http://www.microsoft.com/ntserver.

**Optional additional hardware:**

- Additional computer (with the same minimum specifications as the first one)
- Network adapter and cabling (if you have the additional computer listed above)
- Printer
- Tape drive
- Modem and Internet connection (so you can access online resources)

 caution
**Warning! Some of the lab exercises in this book have the potential to erase or corrupt data on existing hard disk drives. Make sure you back up all important data and programs *before* you attempt to perform any of the lab exercises. Or do the labs on a computer that does not contain any vital data or programs.**

**Software requirements:**

o Microsoft Windows NT Workstation 4.0

o Microsoft Windows NT Server 4.0

# ICONS USED IN THIS BOOK

Several different icons used throughout this book draw your attention to matters that deserve a closer look:

Workstation
Server
Enterprise

This icon identifies the MCSE certification exam(s) pertinent to the content adjacent to it. You'll see this icon at the beginning of each chapter and alongside hands-on labs and review activities.

concept link

This icon points you to another place in this book (or to another resource) for more coverage on a given topic. It may point you back to a previous chapter where important material has already been covered, or it may point you ahead to let you know that a concept will be covered in more detail later on.

caution

Be careful here! This icon points out information that can save you a lot of grief. It's often easier to prevent tragedy than to fix it afterwards.

exam
preparation
pointer

This icon identifies important advice for those studying to pass the three Microsoft Certified Professional exams on Windows NT.

in the
real world

I know this will be hard for you to believe, but sometimes things work differently in the real world than books — or software documentation — say they do. This icon draws your attention to the author's real world experiences, which will hopefully help you on the job, if not on the Microsoft Certified Professional exams.

note

This icon points out an interesting or helpful fact, or some other comment that deserves emphasis.

web links

This icon indicates an online resource that you can access to obtain products, utilities, and other worthwhile information.

tip  **Here's a little piece of friendly advice, or a shortcut, or a bit of personal experience that might be of use to you.**

I guess that about wraps up the general comments. From here you can get started on the nuts and bolts of learning about NT and get ready to pass those exams. I wish you great success!

# ACKNOWLEDGMENTS

"No man is an island, entire of itself," wrote John Donne. There's no time when that statement is more true than when you're producing a book like this one. It's a tremendous undertaking — not just by the author, but by scores of other people, too.

With that thought in mind, I'd like to take this opportunity to thank the following people who helped make this book possible:

First of all, thanks to Thomas Willingham, MCSE, MCT for connecting me with IDG Books. Without you, Thomas, this project would have never happened.

Thanks also to fellow authors Martin Matthews and David James Clarke IV for freely sharing your wisdom and advice.

A very hearty thanks to Chris Gradwohl, MCSE, MCT and to Mark Knutson, MCPS, CNE for the many painstaking hours you both spent reviewing this book technically. You guys kept me on my toes, and I appreciate it.

Special thanks to everyone at IDG Books who worked way "above and beyond the call of duty" to get this book into production on schedule, including: Tracy Thomsic, lead development editor; Anne Hamilton, acquisitions editor; Ellen Dendy and Kay Keppler, development editors; Lothlórien Baerenwald, lead copy editor, and Tracy Brown, Katie Dvorak , Marcia Baker, and Donna Scism, copy editors, and the entire graphics and production staff. Many thanks also to Walter Bruce, publishing director, and Brenda McLaughlin, senior vice president and group publisher of the Computer Publishing Group.

I also want to thank my family and friends for their tremendous support during this project. Especially, I thank my wife, Pat, whose hard work helped turn this man's dream of authoring a book into a reality.

The publishers would like to thank Becky Kirsinikas and Holly Heath of the Microsoft ICV program for their prompt responses and information gathering efforts, and the staff at Waggener Edstrom — Joscelyn Zell, Ryan James, and Kelly Stremmel — for providing IDG with crucial help and information.

# Contents at a Glance

# TABLE OF CONTENTS

# Overview

**W**elcome to the wonderful world of NT! Chapter 1 introduces you to Windows NT Workstation 4.0 and Windows NT Server 4.0. First, basic information about these operating systems is presented. Then, foundational NT concepts, such as workgroups and domains, and the basic Windows NT 4.0 architecture, are explained. Finally, an overview of the Windows NT 4.0 user interface wraps up this part.

The key facts and concepts presented in Part I will help you to build a framework that will support you as you read the rest of this book. Mastering these basics will form the foundation of successful exam preparation—no matter which of the three Windows NT 4.0 Microsoft Certified Professional exams you want to pass.

Workstation
Server
Enterprise

# Overview of Windows NT Workstation and Windows NT Server

## About Chapter 1

This chapter explores the basics of Windows NT Workstation 4.0 and Windows NT Server 4.0, and explains how each operating system fits into the overall Microsoft Windows 4.0 operating system family. Ever wondered which operating system to choose for a given situation? Or whether to choose a workgroup or a domain model? These questions are fully explained and answered in this chapter.

Next, this chapter discusses the architecture of Windows NT. Several key NT concepts, such as modular architecture and the virtual memory model, are introduced. Even if you don't aspire to be an NT guru, a basic understanding of this terminology and how Windows NT is structured will serve you well.

Finally, a tour of the Windows NT 4.0 user interface is presented. All of you Windows 95 users will be happy to know that the Windows NT 4.0 interface looks and feels just like the Windows 95 interface.

No matter which of the three Windows NT 4.0 Microsoft Certified Professional exams you're preparing for, you'll want to read this chapter. It provides basic information about Windows NT Workstation 4.0 and Windows NT Server 4.0 that will be invaluable in your exam preparation.

# MICROSOFT WINDOWS 4.0 OPERATING SYSTEMS

This overview of Microsoft Windows NT Workstation and Windows NT Server begins by examining how these operating systems fit into the big picture, the picture that portrays the entire Microsoft Windows 4.0 operating system family. The Microsoft Windows 4.0 operating systems include: Windows 95, Windows NT Workstation, and Windows NT Server. These three operating systems share a common user interface, many common features and utilities, and all are 32-bit operating systems.

Although there are similarities between the three operating systems, each was designed for a different purpose. Allow me to introduce you to each of the three Microsoft Windows 4.0 operating systems.

## Windows 95

Windows 95 is a 32-bit desktop operating system. This operating system requires the least amount of hardware of all the Microsoft Windows 4.0 operating systems. The minimum hardware required to run Windows 95 successfully consists of: an Intel-based computer with a 386DX/20 processor, 8MB of *random-access memory* (RAM), 40MB of available hard disk space, and a VGA graphics card. Windows 95 is the only Windows 4.0 operating system that fully supports Plug and Play architecture.

in the real world  **I know the product documentation says that you only need 4MB of RAM to run Windows 95, but it's been my experience that you need at least 8MB of RAM to achieve any performance at all.**

Windows 95 is compatible with many existing software applications. It supports 16-bit and 32-bit Windows-based applications (including legacy applications designed to run on previous Windows operating systems) and MS-DOS-based applications. You can also run applications that require direct access to the hardware on the Windows 95 operating system.

Windows 95 does not support multiple processors for true multiprocessing. However, it does support preemptive multitasking for Win32 and MS-DOS-based applications.

The Windows 95 operating system provides some, but not a high level of, security. It does not support a local user account database. It does, however, support server-based validation of the logon process.

## Windows NT Workstation

Like Windows 95, Windows NT Workstation is also a 32-bit operating system that is optimized to run as a desktop operating system. It can also be used on personal computers that are networked in a peer-to-peer workgroup configuration, or on a workstation computer that is part of a Windows NT Server domain configuration.

Windows NT Workstation, however, supports fewer hardware platforms than Windows 95 and requires more powerful hardware to run. The minimum hardware required to successfully run Windows NT Workstation consists of an Intel-based computer with a 486/33 processor, 12MB of RAM (16MB recommended), 117MB of free hard disk space, and a VGA graphics card. In order to assure operational success, all hardware must be on the Windows NT *Hardware Compatibility List*

(HCL) that is shipped with the product. Windows NT Workstation provides only minimal support for Plug and Play.

Windows NT Workstation supports most MS-DOS-based applications, most 16-bit and 32-bit Windows-based applications, POSIX 1.*x* applications, and most OS/2 1.*x* applications. It does not support applications that require direct hardware access because this could compromise Windows NT Workstation's security. It also does not support software applications that require a *terminate-and-stay-resident* (TSR) program or a virtual device driver.

Windows NT Workstation is a high-end, powerful operating system that supports multiple processors for true multiprocessing. As with Windows 95, it also supports preemptive multitasking for all software applications that will run on Windows NT Workstation.

The security Windows NT Workstation is capable of providing is greater than the security provided by Windows 95. User logon and authentication are required in order to use the Windows NT Workstation operating system and in order to access local or network resources. Windows NT Workstation supports a local user account database. Alternatively, Windows NT Workstation can be tied into a domain user account database. Windows NT Workstation has been certified for use in C2 secure environments.

## Windows NT Server

Windows NT Server is a powerful 32-bit operating system that is optimized to run on a network file, print, or application server.

Windows NT Server has the most demanding hardware requirements of the three Microsoft Windows 4.0 operating systems. The minimum hardware required to run Windows NT Server consists of an Intel-based computer with a 486/33 processor, 16MB of RAM, 124MB of free hard disk space, and a VGA graphics card. It does not support Plug and Play.

Windows NT Server supports the same software applications as Windows NT Workstation. In addition, Windows NT Server is the operating system of choice for the Microsoft BackOffice products, including SQL Server, Exchange Server, and SNA Server.

An NT Server computer can support several processors to provide powerful multiprocessing capability.

Windows NT Server is a high-security capable operating system. Like Windows NT Workstation, user logon and authentication is required. Security is controlled and administered via a domain directory database.

Of the three Microsoft Windows 4.0 operating systems, Windows NT Server is the only operating system that is optimized for server performance. Its client/server platform provides far more powerful network features than either Windows 95 or Windows NT Workstation.

## Choosing a Desktop Operating System

So which desktop operating system should you choose for a given situation? You would normally *not* choose Windows NT Server as a desktop operating system because it is optimized as a *server* operating system. That leaves you with a choice of either Windows 95 or Windows NT Workstation for your desktop operating system.

The choice you make will be ultimately based on the hardware available to you, software compatibility, and your security needs.

If the hardware available to you is older, not very powerful, or not on the Windows NT Hardware Compatibility List (HCL), you will probably choose Windows 95. However, if you have newer, more powerful hardware that is on the HCL (or if the cost of buying new equipment is not an issue), and if you don't have any software compatibility conflicts, then Windows NT Workstation is the preferred choice.

In terms of software compatibility, the most important fact to determine is whether the applications you plan to use are supported by Windows 95 or Windows NT Workstation. You should test the software you plan to use on both products (or otherwise satisfy yourself that the applications actually work on the operating system you want to use) before you make a decision. If you plan to use older, legacy applications that require direct hardware access, you should choose Windows 95 for your desktop operating system.

If high security is important to you, consider choosing Windows NT Workstation. As long as your hardware is up to it (or if high security is more important to you than the cost of buying new equipment) and the applications you plan to run are compatible, the preferred choice in a desktop operating system, in terms of overall performance, reliability, and security is Windows NT Workstation.

# WORKGROUPS VERSUS DOMAINS

Before this overview of Microsoft Windows NT (from here on referred to as simply Windows NT or NT) can progress much further, it's important that you get good and comfortable with two key concepts: workgroups and domains.

 **Throughout this book, except where differences are noted, Windows NT refers to *both* Windows NT Workstation and Windows NT Server.**

Workgroups and domains are two prevalent methods of grouping networked computers for common purposes. Computers and their users may be grouped based on common usage requirements or on departmental or geographical traits. For example, all the members of an accounting department or all the computers on the third floor of a building may be grouped together.

## Workgroups

A *workgroup* is a logical grouping of networked computers in which one or more of the computers has one or more shared resources, such as a shared folder or a shared printer.

 **The terms *folder* and *directory* are synonymous in the wonderful world of Windows NT. The NT user interface does not use these terms consistently. Sometimes the interface refers to a folder, and sometimes it calls the same (or similar) item a directory.**

In a workgroup environment, the security and user accounts are all maintained individually at each separate computer. Resources and administration are distributed throughout the computers that make up the workgroup. In a workgroup configuration there is no centrally maintained user accounts database, nor any centralized security. Figure 1-1 illustrates how security is distributed throughout a workgroup environment. Notice that security is maintained individually at each separate computer in the workgroup.

Typically, all of the computers in a workgroup run desktop operating systems, such as Windows 95 or Windows NT Workstation.

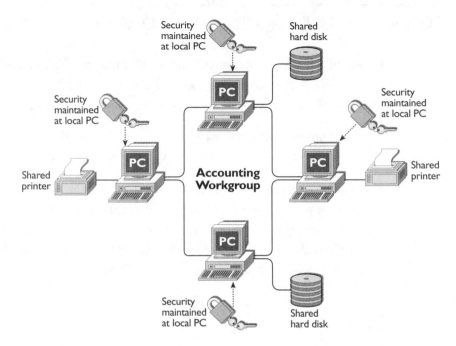

**FIGURE 1-1** **Security in a workgroup environment**

# Domains

A *domain* is a logical grouping of networked computers in which one or more of the computers has one or more shared resources, such as a shared folder or a shared printer, *and* in which all of the computers share a common central domain directory database that contains user account and security information.

One distinct advantage of using a domain (or *domain model*, as it is sometimes called), particularly on a large network, is that administration and security for the entire network can be managed from a centralized location. Figure 1-2 illustrates how security is centralized in a domain environment. Note that the security of all the shared printers and hard disks is maintained at the domain controller.

In a Windows NT domain, at least one of the networked computers is a server computer that runs Windows NT Server. The server computer is configured as a *primary domain controller* (PDC), which maintains the domain directory database. Typically, there is at least one additional server computer that also runs Windows NT Server. This additional computer is usually configured as a *backup domain controller* (BDC). The other computers on the network normally run Windows NT

Workstation or Windows 95 (although they may utilize other operating systems). These non-server computers can share their resources (such as hard disks and printers) on the network, but these shared resources are secured by the domain directory database that is maintained by the PDC.

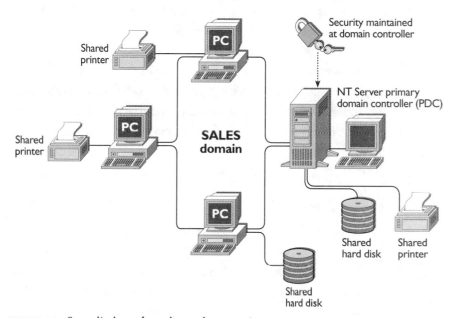

**FIGURE 1-2** Security in a domain environment

# Choosing Between the Workgroup and Domain Models

Choosing the appropriate model of grouping computers and managing shared network resources depends upon the size and security needs of the network.

Often, small- to medium-sized networks (two to twenty computers) can be managed fairly easily by using the workgroup model, with the user of each computer controlling the security to the specific resources that are shared by that user's computer.

In a larger network environment, administration and security become harder to manage; thus, the domain model, which provides centralized account administration and greater security, is usually the preferred choice.

# ARCHITECTURE OF WINDOWS NT

An overview of Windows NT wouldn't be complete without discussing its architecture. If you develop a basic understanding of the operating system's architecture now, you'll have a framework on which to "hang" all of the concepts and facts you learn throughout the rest of this book.

Windows NT uses a modular architecture. This means each component (or module) within the architecture has sole responsibility for the function it is designed to provide. In addition, no other module repeats the functions performed by another. Figure 1-3 illustrates the modular architecture of Microsoft Windows NT 4.0. Notice that the operating system has two pieces, or modes: user mode and kernel mode.

## User Mode

Applications and their subsystems run in *user mode*. This mode is referred to as a less privileged processor mode because it does not have direct access to hardware. User mode applications are limited to assigned memory address spaces and can't directly access other memory address spaces. User mode uses specific *application programming interfaces* (APIs) to request system services from a kernel mode component.

The purpose of separating the applications in user mode from the hardware, of restricting the memory address spaces that applications can access, and of forcing the applications to run all requests for system services through the kernel mode, is to protect against the possibility of an application crashing the system, and also to protect against unauthorized user access.

Examine Figure 1-3 again, and notice that there are several subsystems within user mode. You're now set to explore these subsystems.

### User mode subsystems

There are four main subsystems in user mode: the Win32 Subsystem, the OS/2 Subsystem, the POSIX Subsystem, and the Security Subsystem.

The *Win32 Subsystem* is the primary application subsystem. All 32-bit Windows applications run in the Win32 Subsystem.

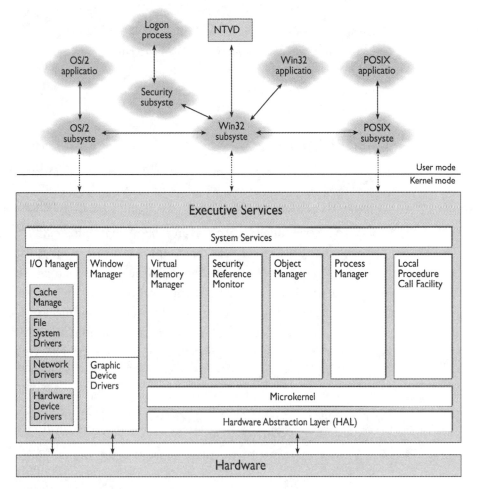

**FIGURE 1-3**  Microsoft Windows NT 4.0 modular architecture

The *OS/2 Subsystem* is required to run OS/2 1.*x* compatible applications. The OS/2 Subsystem obtains its user interface and its screen functions from the Win32 Subsystem, and requests Executive Services in kernel mode to perform all other functions for it. (Executive Services is covered in the next section of this chapter.)

The *POSIX Subsystem* is designed to run POSIX 1.*x* compatible applications. It functions very much like the OS/2 Subsystem. The POSIX Subsystem uses the Win32 Subsystem to provide all of its screen and graphical displays, and it requests Executive Services in kernel mode to perform all other functions for it.

Finally, the *Security Subsystem* supports the logon process. The Security Subsystem also communicates with the Win32 Subsystem.

In addition to the four formal subsystems, an *NT Virtual DOS Machine* (NTVDM) is a feature of user mode. Its function is to run MS-DOS-based and Windows 3.*x*-based (all 16-bit) applications.

# Kernel Mode

*Kernel mode* refers to a highly privileged mode of operation. It is called "highly privileged" because all code that runs in kernel mode can access the hardware directly, and can also access all memory. A process running in kernel mode is not restricted to its own specific address space as is an application running in user mode.

The entire set of services that comprise kernel mode is called Executive Services (or sometimes the Windows NT Executive). Executive Services provide kernel mode services as requested by applications in user mode.

Notice how Figure 1-3 graphically presents the pieces of kernel mode. Observe how they fit together and interact with the hardware and user mode components. Allow me to now introduce you to the components of kernel mode.

### Kernel mode components

Kernel mode is made up of numerous components integral to the Windows NT major operating system functions.

The *I/O Manager* is responsible for all input and output to disk storage subsystems. As it manages input and output, the I/O Manager also serves as a manager and supporter of communication between the various drivers. The I/O Manager can communicate directly with system hardware if it has the appropriate hardware device drivers. Subcomponents of the I/O Manager include a *Cache Manager,* various *file system drivers*, and *network drivers*. Another subcomponent of the I/O Manager is the *hardware device drivers* that perform direct hardware access.

*Window Manager* is responsible for providing all of the graphical user interface. Window Manager communicates directly with the *graphics device drivers*, which in turn communicate directly with the hardware. In Windows NT 3.51, Window Manager and the graphics device drivers were a part of user mode. The developers of Windows NT 4.0 moved this component from user mode to kernel mode. This change enabled faster access to the graphics device drivers and eliminated the need for user applications to switch back and forth between kernel mode and user mode for calls for graphics services.

There are five other kernel mode subsystems: the *Virtual Memory Manager*, the *Security Reference Monitor*, the *Object Manager*, the *Process Manager*, and the *Local Procedure Call Facility*. Each one of these subsystems communicates directly with the Microkernel. The *Microkernel* is the very heart of the NT operating system. It handles interrupts, schedules threads, and synchronizes processing activity. The Microkernel, in turn, communicates with the *Hardware Abstraction Layer* (HAL). The HAL is designed to hide the varying characteristics of hardware so that all hardware platforms appear the same to the Microkernel. As a result, only the HAL, and not the entire Microkernel, needs to address each and every hardware platform. The HAL can communicate directly with the computer's hardware.

Now that you've been introduced to user mode and kernel mode, you're ready to move on to the last major architecture topic: the NT memory model.

## NT Memory Model

Windows NT uses a virtual memory model. *Virtual memory* is the physical space on a hard disk that NT treats as though it were RAM. Virtual memory can also be thought of as an extension of RAM, or "fake" RAM.

The virtual memory model used by NT is a demand-paged system based on a flat, linear, 32-bit address space. Through the use of virtual memory, each application is given access to what *appears* to be 4GB of memory address space. 2GB of the 4GB are reserved for application data, and the remaining 2GB are reserved for NT operating system data.

By using this scheme, the operating system is able to allocate more memory to applications than is actually contained in the computer. The advantage of this is that users can run more applications at one time than the computer's RAM would otherwise physically permit.

The Virtual Memory Manager manages memory in the Windows NT environment by using demand paging. (You may recall that the Virtual Memory Manager is a kernel mode component. It is included in Figure 1-3.) Here's how the Virtual Memory Manager (and demand paging) works: When the Virtual Memory Manager receives a request from an application to retrieve specific pages of memory, it redirects this request to the actual physical location where those pages are stored. This location could be in RAM, or it could be in virtual memory stored in a paging file on the hard disk. If it is in a paging file on the hard disk, the Virtual Memory Manager will move some pages of memory that have not recently been used from RAM to a paging file on the hard disk. It will then recover the pages that were requested by the application from the paging file on the hard disk and move them back into RAM, where the application can access them.

The 32-bit flat addressing scheme used by the NT memory model makes NT compatible with many popular processors, including the MIPS R4000, the PowerPC, the Intel, and the DEC Alpha AXP.

# WINDOWS NT 4.0 INTERFACE

If you're familiar with the Windows 95 user interface, you can probably skip this section. The Windows NT 4.0 interface looks and feels just like the Windows 95 interface.

If this is your first exposure to the Windows 4.0 operating systems, Figure 1-4 shows how the desktop interface looks.

**FIGURE 1-4**  The Windows NT 4.0 desktop

The following is a brief explanation of the Windows NT 4.0 user interface, including the desktop and Windows NT Explorer.

# The Windows NT 4.0 Desktop

After your computer boots Windows NT 4.0, the screen displayed is the desktop. The desktop replaces the Program Manager interface from earlier versions of Windows and Windows NT.

You can create shortcuts to programs you use frequently and place them on the desktop. You can also configure the display properties, such as icon size, background color, screen saver, display resolution, and so on, by right-clicking anywhere on the desktop and then clicking Properties.

There are several icons on the desktop, as well as a taskbar and a Start button.

## *My Computer*

Double-clicking the My Computer icon displays the My Computer dialog box. This dialog box graphically represents every drive on the computer (including network drives, if any), as well as the Control Panel and the Printers folders. If you double-click any icon in the My Computer dialog box, another dialog box is displayed showing the contents of the drive or folder you clicked.

## *Network Neighborhood*

The Network Neighborhood icon is only displayed if you are using a network. If you double-click the Network Neighborhood icon, a dialog box is displayed that contains an icon for your computer and an icon for the entire network. You can expand the icons in this dialog box to show all computers, shared folders, and shared printers on your network.

## *Internet Explorer*

When you double-click the Internet Explorer icon, Microsoft Internet Explorer starts. You can use this application to browse Web pages on the Internet.

## *Recycle Bin*

The Recycle Bin icon is a politically correct '90s version of the Macintosh trash can icon. When you delete files, the files are moved from their original location into the Recycle Bin folder. When you delete items in the Recycle Bin, the items are removed permanently from your computer. Remember to periodically empty your Recycle Bin!

### *My Briefcase*

My Briefcase is a special type of folder that enables you to keep files synchronized between two computers, such as your laptop and your desktop computer.

### *Start button*

The Start button is located on the left side of the taskbar. Clicking the Start button opens a menu that enables you to quickly access programs, recently used documents, settings (such as the Control Panel and Printers folders), and Help. The menu also enables you to run applications from a command line, find a document, and shut down your computer.

### *Taskbar*

The taskbar at the bottom of the desktop contains the Start button, a button for each program that is currently running, and a clock. You can quickly switch between applications by clicking the button that represents the application you want to access. You can configure taskbar properties by right-clicking anywhere on the taskbar, and then selecting Properties. You can easily set the time and date by double-clicking the clock in the taskbar.

### *Close, minimize, and maximize buttons*

At the upper right-hand corner of every window is a button, marked with an X. This button is called the close button and is used to close the window and exit the application.

Many windows have two additional buttons located adjacent to the close button: the minimize and maximize buttons. The minimize button looks like an underscore on a button. Clicking this button will minimize the application to its icon on the taskbar. The maximize button looks like either a single box with a dark line across the top, or like two overlapping boxes, each with a dark line across the top. Clicking the maximize button switches between a small view of the window and a full screen view of the window.

## Windows NT Explorer

You can access any file, folder, printer, or application on your computer or on the network in Windows NT Explorer. Windows NT Explorer replaces File Manager from earlier versions of Windows and Windows NT. Windows NT Explorer is a useful tool for copying, moving, and deleting files.

To access Windows NT Explorer, select Start ⇒ Programs ⇒ Windows NT Explorer.

# Key Point Summary

This chapter covered the basics of the Windows 95, Windows NT Workstation, and Windows NT Server operating systems. You also learned which Windows operating system to choose based on your particular requirements and resources. Chapter 1 also covered several key components of the Windows NT architecture, and the Windows NT user interface.

- *Windows 95* is the best choice for a desktop environment with less sophisticated hardware when backward compatibility for certain legacy applications is required and when minimal security is acceptable. *Windows NT Workstation* is the operating system of choice if you have the hardware platform to support it and don't have any software conflicts, if a high degree of security is important, or if you desire a more powerful desktop operating system. If you want an operating system optimized to function as a server, *Windows NT Server* is the preferred choice.

- A *workgroup* is a collection of networked computers in which administration of user accounts and security of resources are maintained individually, on each separate computer. A *domain* is a group of networked computers in which administration and security for the entire network is managed from a centrally located domain directory database that contains user account and security information.

- The architecture of Windows NT is separated into two modes: *user mode* and *kernel mode*. Applications run in user mode. User mode applications are only able to access their assigned address spaces, and cannot access hardware at all. Code running in kernel mode, in contrast, has direct access to all of memory and direct access to hardware. The NT memory model features a virtual memory system that utilizes demand paging. The Virtual Memory Manager is the kernel mode component that is actually responsible for performing demand paging.

- The *Windows NT 4.0 user interface* looks and feels just like the Windows 95 interface. Several icons appear on the desktop: My Computer, Network Neighborhood, Internet Explorer, Recycle Bin, and My Briefcase. There is also a taskbar at the bottom of the desktop that contains the Start button, a button for each program that is currently running, and a clock. In Windows NT 4.0, Windows NT Explorer replaces File Manager from earlier versions of Windows and Windows NT.

exam preparation pointer

**The Key Point Summaries in this book are excellent exam preparation tools. After you read each one, ask yourself if you have a sound working knowledge of the topics covered. If you don't, go back and reread the section(s) on which you're not clear. Then proceed to the questions in the Instant Assessment section.**

# APPLYING WHAT YOU'VE LEARNED

Now it's time to regroup, review, and apply what you've learned in this chapter. The questions in the following Instant Assessment section bring to mind key facts and concepts. In addition, some of the questions also give you a chance to analyze situations and apply your knowledge of Windows NT to that particular situation.

exam preparation pointer **Take time to answer the questions in the Instant Assessment section at the end of each chapter. They will help you learn to apply the concepts to which you've just been introduced. Keep in mind that your investment now will pay off later when you take the exams!**

## Instant Assessment

1. Your computer has a Pentium processor and 32MB of RAM. It needs to be optimized as a workstation and also capable of true multiprocessing and full 32-bit compatibility. You do *not* have any legacy devices or applications that must be supported. Which Microsoft Windows 4.0 operating system should you choose for your computer?

2. Which Microsoft Windows 4.0 operating system should you choose when you need an operating system that is optimized as a server operating system?

3. You are planning a small network (four computers) for your company. You want the administration and security of the network to be distributed equally among the users of the four computers. Which method of logically grouping computers should you use?

4. Which method of logically grouping computers should you use when you need centralized administration of the network's security and shared resources?

5. Which mode of the Windows NT operating system has direct access to hardware, user mode, or kernel mode?

6. What type of memory model does Windows NT use?

7. Figure 1-5 is a partially filled in model of the Windows NT 4.0 modular architecture. Fill in the missing titles in the chart to solidify your understanding of the Windows NT 4.0 architecture.

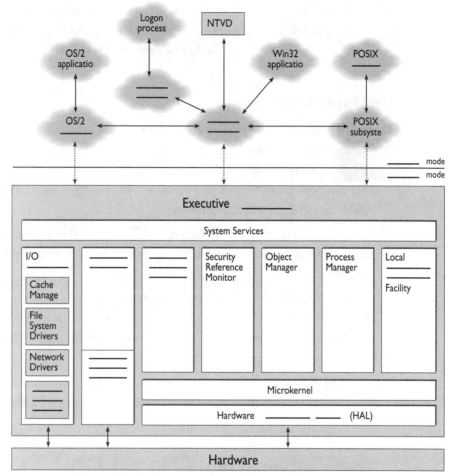

**FIGURE 1-5**   Microsoft Windows NT 4.0 modular architecture activity

concept link   **For answers to the Instant Assessment questions see Appendix D.**

PART

# Installation and Configuration

**II**

This part kicks your exam preparation into high gear. Chapter 2 starts it off with complete information on how to install Windows NT Workstation 4.0 and Windows NT Server 4.0. We also discuss deinstalling Windows NT, as well as how to troubleshoot common installation problems.

After installing NT, Chapter 3 explains configuring a computer's hard disk(s). The various file systems are presented, and disk partitioning is explained.

Next, Chapter 4 explores all of the mini-applications in Control Panel. You may be surprised by what some of these applets can do!

Chapter 5 presents server-based deployment. Ever wonder how to efficiently install Windows NT on multiple computers on a network? This part explains this process in detail.

Finally, Chapter 6 explains how to manage printing with Windows NT. We address key printing terminology, the print process, and creating and connecting to printers. This part also explores configuring, scheduling, and sharing printers, in addition to providing practical information on how to troubleshoot common printing problems.

No matter which of the three Windows NT 4.0 Microsoft Certified Professional exams you're preparing for, you'll want to read every chapter in this part. This part maps directly to the Installation and Configuration section in the exam objectives for each exam. You'll also want to take advantage of the numerous hands-on lab exercises that will help you to learn and practice important skills tested by the exams.

Workstation
Server
Enterprise

# Installing Windows NT Workstation and Windows NT Server

## About Chapter 2

This chapter spells out everything you need to know to install Windows NT Workstation and Windows NT Server, including the hardware requirements. It also includes a very practical preinstallation checklist for gathering all the information you'll need to perform the installation.

Chapter 2 explains how to start an NT installation locally from a CD-ROM drive and over the network using `Winnt.exe` or `Winnt32.exe`. Then it takes you through the entire installation process, step-by-step and phase-by-phase.

Next, this chapter discusses how to deinstall Windows NT, in the event that you want to remove it from a computer.

Finally, this chapter explores troubleshooting solutions to common NT installation problems.

This chapter includes two extensive labs—one that walks you through the process of installing Windows NT Workstation on your own computer, and a second that takes you through the process of installing Windows NT Server and configuring your computer to dual boot between Windows NT Server and Windows NT Workstation.

No matter which of the three Windows NT 4.0 Microsoft Certified Professional exams you're preparing for, you'll want to read this chapter. The information in this chapter covers several objectives listed in the Installation and Configuration and Troubleshooting sections in these exams' objectives.

# HARDWARE REQUIREMENTS FOR INSTALLATION

Before you can install NT, you need to make sure you have the appropriate hardware. To avoid problems, only use hardware that appears on the Windows NT *Hardware Compatibility List* (HCL). The HCL, which is updated periodically, ships with the NT products.

 web links

**You can also access the latest HCL via Microsoft's Web site at** `http://www.microsoft.com/ntworkstation/`, **or** `http://www.microsoft.com/ntserver/`.

If you have hardware that is *not* listed on the HCL, contact the manufacturer of your equipment to see if the correct Windows NT 4.0 drivers for that device can be obtained.

Table 2-1 shows the minimum hardware required for installing Windows NT Workstation and Windows NT Server. The requirements listed apply only to Intel-based platforms. Windows NT can also be installed on DEC Alpha AXP, PowerPC, and MIPS R4000 platforms, but additional hardware may be necessary, depending on the type of processor you plan to use.

**TABLE 2-1** MINIMUM HARDWARE REQUIRED FOR INSTALLATION OF WINDOWS NT

| HARDWARE COMPONENT | WINDOWS NT WORKSTATION | WINDOWS NT SERVER |
|---|---|---|
| Processor | 486/33 | 486/33 |
| Memory | 12MB of RAM | 16MB of RAM |
| Hard disk space | 117MB | 124MB |
| Display | VGA or better | VGA or better |
| Floppy disk drive | 3.5-inch high-density | 3.5-inch high-density |
| CD-ROM drive | Required (If your computer does not have a CD-ROM drive, you can still install NT Workstation by using an over-the-network installation.) | Required (If your computer does not have a CD-ROM drive, you can still install NT Server by using an over-the-network installation.) |
| Network adapter | Optional (Required for over-the-network installation) | Optional (Required for over-the-network installation) |
| Mouse | Optional | Optional |

in the real world

**Table 2-1 shows the *minimum* hardware required for installation purposes only. More hard disk space is needed for applications and data files. Additional memory is required for some applications, and to speed up operations while running applications.**

Do you know exactly what hardware you have in your computer? You can use the *NT Hardware Qualifier* (NTHQ) utility that comes with Windows NT to examine and identify your hardware configuration. NTHQ helps you determine if Windows NT can detect your hardware, and it identifies the hardware settings used for each adapter. To use NTHQ, you must create an NTHQ diskette, which you then use to boot your computer. (You can create an NTHQ diskette with a blank, formatted 3.5-inch floppy diskette by running `Makedisk.bat` from the `\support\hqtool` directory on the Windows NT compact disc.) NTHQ makes a text file you can print to help you complete the preinstallation checklist in the next section of this chapter.

# INFORMATION REQUIRED TO INSTALL WINDOWS NT

A substantial amount of user input is required during the Windows NT installation process. To make the installation go smoother and to avoid the possibility of having to redo it, you should gather all the information you will need before doing the installation. This will enable you to give the appropriate responses as you are prompted by the Windows NT installation program.

## Preinstallation Checklist

To assist you in gathering information about your computer and network environment so you can successfully complete the installation, I have designed a multipart preinstallation checklist for you. A detailed explanation accompanies each checklist item.

 tip **The preinstallation checklist is reproduced *without* the detailed explanations of each item in Appendix G. I encourage you to copy and use this checklist as well as the other planning forms.**

### *Mass storage devices: SCSI, IDE, and CD-ROM adapter information*

You need to know the manufacturer's name, adapter name and model, and hardware settings for each SCSI, IDE, and CD-ROM adapter in your computer. Windows NT automatically detects ESDI and some older IDE controllers, and might display a message during installation stating that there are no adapters present. If you see such a message during installation, it simply means NT didn't detect any adapters that could have a CD-ROM drive attached. Standard IDE adapters are not displayed, but are used by Windows NT. IDE dual-channel PCI adapters are displayed. If your hard disk controller is not displayed, continue with the installation. Your hard disk(s) should appear in the partitioning stage. You can choose to specify manually which adapters you have and skip the automatic detection process.

| SCSI/IDE/CD-ROM Adapter | IRQ | I/O Port | DMA Channel |
|---|---|---|---|
| _____ | ____ | _____ | _____ |
| _____ | ____ | _____ | _____ |
| _____ | ____ | _____ | _____ |
| _____ | ____ | _____ | _____ |

tip **Use the NTHQ utility described in the previous section, "Hardware Requirements for Installation," to examine and identify your hardware configuration, and to print out a text file that will help you complete the preinstallation checklist.**

## Hardware and software components

o **Computer type:** _____

This refers to the type of architecture your PC uses, such as MPS Multiprocessor, IBM PS/2, Standard PC, and so on.

o **Display:** _____

This refers to the video display adapter in your computer. This component setting defaults to Auto Detect. If your display adapter is not on the HCL and you have the NT 4.0 drivers provided by the manufacturer of your display adapter, you can change this setting at the end of Phase 3 of the installation process.

o **Keyboard:** _____

This component's default is a single setting that includes XT, AT, or Enhanced Keyboard (83-104 keys). You can change this setting if you have a different keyboard and the appropriate drivers for it.

o **Keyboard layout:** _____

This setting defaults to U.S. Change this setting if necessary to support
your keyboard layout correctly.

o **Pointing device:** _____

Setup should automatically detect your mouse or other pointing device.
You can change the setting by selecting another pointing device from the
list, or you can supply your own driver from a diskette.

## Upgrade

**Upgrade previous version of Windows?**     Yes_____  No_____

If the Windows NT Setup program detects a previous installation of Windows or
Windows NT on your computer, it will ask if you want to upgrade that version of
Windows or Windows NT to Windows NT 4.0.

Windows 3.*x* and previous versions of Windows NT can be upgraded in this
manner. When you install Windows NT 4.0 in the *same* directory as the previous
Windows installation to perform an upgrade, all application and user preference
settings will be upgraded. You should install Windows NT 4.0 in a *different* directory than the previous Windows installation if you are upgrading from a previous
version of Windows NT and you want to continue to use the previously installed
version. When you install Windows NT 4.0 in a different directory than your previously installed Windows operating system, you must reinstall all applications that
will be used with Windows NT and reconfigure all user preferences within those
applications, such as screen colors, desktop settings, and so on.

 note **When you install Windows NT 4.0 in a different directory than the
original operating system, Windows NT automatically configures
itself to *dual boot* between Windows NT 4.0 and the previously
installed operating system. In addition, Windows NT 4.0 configures
itself to dual boot between Windows NT 4.0 and Windows 3.*x* when
you upgrade from Windows 3.*x* by installing Windows NT 4.0 in the
same directory as Windows 3.*x*.**

Windows 95 and OS/2 cannot be upgraded to Windows NT 4.0 in this manner. You must install Windows NT 4.0 in a different directory than Windows 95 or
OS/2 if you have previously installed either of these operating systems.

If you previously installed Windows 95 and you install Windows NT 4.0 in a different directory, you must reinstall all applications that will be used with Windows NT, and reconfigure all user preferences within those applications. If you previously installed MS-DOS or OS/2 1.*x* and you install Windows NT 4.0 in a different directory, you do not need to reinstall the applications that will be used with Windows NT, nor do you need to reconfigure the user application preferences.

## Hard disk partition information

The space on hard disks is divided into areas called *partitions*. The Windows NT Setup program requires you to choose which partition you will use for the NT installation. Refer to Table 2-1 to make sure the partition you choose has enough available disk space.

| Disk Partition Number | Type of Partition | Available Disk Space |
|:---:|:---:|:---:|
| 1 | _____ | _____ |
| 2 | _____ | _____ |
| 3 | _____ | _____ |

Partition # to be used for installation of Windows NT: _____

Within the Windows NT operating system there are two important, required types of partitions: a *system partition* and a *boot partition*. These two terms are Windows NT jargon for primary and extended partitions that contain specific files and perform specific functions in Windows NT.

- **System Partition:** The *system partition* is located on the active primary partition of the first hard disk in the computer. (This is usually the C: drive.) The system partition contains several files that are required to boot Windows NT, including: `ntldr`, `Ntdetect.com`, `Boot.ini`, and sometimes `Bootsect.dos`, and `Ntbootdd.sys`, depending on the installation type and hardware configuration.

- **Boot Partition:** The *boot partition* can be located on either a primary or extended partition. The boot partition contains the Windows NT installation directory (usually the `Winnt` directory). This partition also contains all of the Windows NT operating system files.

**tip** The names of these two partitions often confuse people. Because of the types of files the partitions contain, many people think the boot partition should be called the system partition, and vice versa. You might find it helpful to make a mental note that these two partitions are named the opposite of what you intuitively think they should be!

In many cases, the system partition and the boot partition are physically located on the same partition of the hard drive. For example, suppose your computer's hard drive contains two partitions: an 800MB primary partition and a 200MB extended partition. If you install Windows NT on the 800MB partition, both the system partition and the boot partition will be physically located on the 800MB partition.

## File system used for installation (choose one)

**FAT** _____     **NTFS** _____

Windows NT supports two file system types: FAT and NTFS.

o **FAT:** The *file allocation table* (FAT) file system is supported by Windows NT and many other operating systems, including: MS-DOS, OS/2, Windows 3.*x*, and Windows 95. Normally, if you want your computer to dual boot between Windows NT and one of these other operating systems (and both operating systems are located on the same hard disk partition), choose the FAT file system. The FAT file system supports neither extended attributes nor file-level security.

o **NTFS:** The *Windows NT file system* (NTFS) is supported only by Windows NT. In general, choose NTFS if you do not want your computer to dual boot between Windows NT and another operating system and you want the added advantages provided by NTFS, including extended attributes and file-level security.

You can select FAT as the file system to be used during installation of Windows NT, and then later choose to convert the file system to NTFS; however, if you choose NTFS as the file system to be used during installation of Windows NT and then later want to convert to FAT, the process isn't so easy. To convert from NTFS to FAT, you need to back up all files, repartition and format the drive, reinstall Windows NT, and restore all the files from backup.

tip **To avoid these time-consuming processes, plan ahead as much as possible when deciding which file system you will use.**

Windows NT 4.0 does not support the *high performance file system* (HPFS) used by OS/2. If you want to install Windows NT 4.0 on a computer that uses HPFS, you must back up all data, repartition and format the computer's drive with FAT or NTFS, and then restore all the files from backup before you can install Windows NT 4.0.

 concept link **For a more in-depth discussion of file systems, see Chapter 3.**

## Installation directory

**Installation directory for new installation:**

_____

In this step you choose in which directory Windows NT 4.0 files will be installed. You may either accept the default directory displayed during setup (usually `c:\winnt`), or type the name of another directory. Be sure the directory you choose has enough free space for the Windows NT 4.0 files.

## Setup options (Windows NT Workstation only)

Choose one:

Typical _____     Portable _____     Compact _____     Custom _____

Four setup options are offered during the installation of Windows NT Workstation: *typical*, *portable*, *compact*, and *custom*. Select one of these four options.

○ **Typical:** You should use the typical setup for most installations. In this option, the Windows NT Setup program presents a list of optional software components that can be added. The typical setup preselects the most popular components by placing a check in the box next to the component; however, you still choose either to accept these preselected components or to modify the list, so the components you want are installed. (See the "Select components" section of this chapter for a listing of the optional software components.) The typical setup partially automates the installation/setup process; therefore, some screens, such as Network Services and Network Bindings, are not displayed during installation. (The Windows NT Setup program accepts and applies the default settings for these options anyway.)

- **Portable:** The portable setup is designed for laptop computers. In this option, the Windows NT Setup program presents the same list of software components as the typical setup option, but preselects different components for the portable setup that are popular for mobile computing. Again, you choose either to accept the preselected components or to modify the list, so the components you want are installed. The portable setup also automates some of the installation/setup process.

- **Compact:** The compact setup is designed for computers where disk space is limited. Only components required by Windows NT are automatically installed. When the list of optional software components that can be added is displayed, setup preselects none of the components. However, as with the typical and portable setup options, you can still override and modify this list. The compact setup also automates some of the installation/setup process.

- **Custom:** The custom setup option is nearly identical to the typical setup, except that none of the installation/setup process is automated. You get to see all of the screens, make all of the choices, and verify all selections before they are implemented.

## Registration

**10 Digit CD Key #:** _____-_____

You need to enter the ten digit CD key number (located on the back of the Windows NT compact disc case) during the Windows NT installation. This entry is required.

## Licensing mode (Windows NT Server only)

**Per server** _____     **Per seat** _____

**Number of client access licenses:** _____

At this point during the installation, a licensing mode must be chosen, and its terms agreed to, in order to continue the installation. Windows NT Server has two licensing modes: *per server* and *per seat*.

- **Per server:** In the per server licensing mode, you must have one client access license for each concurrent connection to the server. For example, if you have 150 client computers (workstations), but only 100 of them would be logged on to the Windows NT Server computer at any one time, then you would need 100 client access licenses. You should enter the number of client access licenses you have purchased for this server in the box next to concurrent connections in the Choose Licensing Mode dialog box.

o **Per seat:** In the per seat licensing mode, you must have one client access license for each client computer that will *ever* connect to a Windows NT Server computer.

in the
real world

**The advantage to using the per seat licensing mode becomes apparent when you have multiple servers on a network. In such a situation, you only have to buy one client access license for each client computer, even if a client computer accesses multiple servers at the same time.**

**For example, suppose you have 500 client computers and 6 Windows NT Server computers on a network, and the client computers access several servers at a time. If you choose the per seat licensing mode, you only need to purchase 500 client access licenses, whereas if you choose the per server licensing mode, you probably need to have more than one client access license per client computer.**

## Computer name

**Computer name:** _____

During installation you need to enter the name your computer will use on the network. The *computer name* is also called a *NetBIOS name,* and can be up to fifteen characters long. All computers on the network *must* use different NetBIOS names. Uniqueness is the key here. If you have a small network, you can probably get by with naming the computers after the characters in your favorite movie, television series, or comic strip. If you have a large network, however, you will probably want to use some type of systematic naming scheme to ensure that each computer has a unique NetBIOS name.

## Server type (Windows NT Server only)

You need to choose the role this server will play on the network. Planning is very important here, because once a server is installed as either a *primary domain controller* (PDC) or a *backup domain controller* (BDC), it *can't* become a stand-alone server or a member server.

Choose one of the following server types:

**caution** ▼ **Careful here! Once a computer is installed as a domain controller in a domain, the domain controller cannot migrate to another domain without a complete reinstall of Windows NT Server.**

o **Primary Domain Controller**

Domain name: _____

Choose *primary domain controller* (PDC) if you want the server to participate in a domain instead of a workgroup, and if you have not already installed any servers in this domain. If you are installing the only server to be used for a small network, you should choose this option.

o **Backup Domain Controller**

Domain name: _____

Administrator's account name: _____

Administrator's password: _____

Choose *backup domain controller* (BDC) if you want the server to participate in a domain instead of a workgroup, and if you have already installed a server in this domain. Additionally, you need to enter the administrator's user account name and password to complete the installation of a BDC.

o **Member Server**

Domain name: _____

Administrator's account name: _____

Administrator's password: _____

Choose member server if you want the server to join a domain but do not want the server to have to expend its resources authenticating user logon requests in the domain. Or, choose member server if you plan to move this server from one domain to another. If you want the server to be a member server in a domain, you will also need to enter the administrator's user account name and password to complete the installation.

o **Stand-Alone Server**

Workgroup name: _____

Choose stand-alone server if you want the server to participate in a workgroup instead of a domain.

**If a stand-alone server later joins a domain, it becomes a member server at that point (and is no longer a stand-alone server). If, at some point after that, this member server no longer participates in a domain (unjoins a domain), it reverts to stand-alone server status.**

## Administrator password

Although you may not want to write down the password on this worksheet, you need to enter an administrator password during the installation process.

## Emergency Repair Disk

**Will an Emergency Repair Disk be created during installation?**    Yes___  No___

Here you choose whether to make an Emergency Repair Disk during the installation process. The Emergency Repair Disk is used to repair Windows NT when its configuration files have been damaged or corrupted. Always make an Emergency Repair Disk. A blank 3.5-inch high-density floppy disk is required during installation to make this disk.

 **You can update your Emergency Repair Disk by using the** `Rdisk.exe` **utility. You should do this every time you change or update your computer's hardware configuration. (You'll get a chance to do this in Lab 3.4.)**

## Select components

This list represents a myriad of optional software components that can be added during the Windows NT installation/setup process. Choose the components you want to install. I've provided explanation for some of the components—others are self-explanatory.

○ **Accessibility options**   Yes___  No___

This component includes options to change the keyboard, sound, video display and mouse attributes for people with mobility, hearing, or visual impairments. This option is either selected or not selected—it has no discrete components.

○ **Accessories**

Calculator ___                    Character Map ___

Clipboard Viewer ___              Clock ___

Desktop Wallpaper ___          Document Templates ___

Imaging ___                    Mouse Pointers ___

Object Packager ___            Paint ___

Quick View ___                 Screen Savers ___

Wordpad ___

- **Communications**

Chat ___                       HyperTerminal ___

Phone Dialer ___

- **Games**

Freecell ___                   Minesweeper ___

Pinball ___                    Solitaire ___

- **Multimedia**

CD Player ___

Jungle Sound Scheme ___        Media Player ___

Musica Sound Scheme ___        Robotz Sound Scheme ___

Sample Sounds ___             Sound Recorder ___

Utopia Sound Scheme ___        Volume Control ___

- **Windows Messaging**

Internet Mail ___              Microsoft Mail ___

Windows Messaging ___

## *Participation on a network*

- **Participate on a network (Windows NT Workstation only)?**   Yes___  No___

  If you are installing Windows NT Workstation, you must choose whether this computer will be part of a network.

- **Wired to the network:** ___

- **Remote access to the network:** ___

  *Wired to the network* means your computer has a direct physical connection to the network and uses either a network adapter or an ISDN adapter. *Remote access to the network* means your computer uses a modem to connect remotely to the network by using Dial-Up Networking to connect to a *Remote Access Service* (RAS) server.

## Microsoft Internet Information Server (Windows NT Server Only)

**Install Microsoft Internet Information Server?**   Yes___ No___

Here you choose whether or not to install *Microsoft Internet Information Server* (IIS). IIS can be used as a *World Wide Web* (WWW) server, a *File Transfer Protocol* (FTP) server, and as a Gopher server.

 **Windows NT 4.0 does not include an FTP server. You must install IIS to get FTP server functionality.**

## Network adapter

**Network adapter manufacturer (if applicable):** _____

**Network adapter name (if applicable):** _____

**Interrupt:** _____   **I/O Port:** _____

You have two choices at this point of the installation: You can enable NT to detect your network adapter (if you have one) automatically, or you can select your network adapter manually from a list displayed by the Windows NT Setup program. Select your network adapter manually by choosing Select from list. If you use this option you have the opportunity to install drivers from a disk supplied by the manufacturer of the network adapter. If you want to install networking but do not have a network adapter, choose *MS Loopback Adapter* from the list. This adapter doesn't have any hardware associated with it — it is a fake adapter that will enable you to install networking services without having a network adapter.

You need to obtain the hardware settings (interrupt and I/O port) for your network adapter, because the Windows NT Setup program may prompt you for them later. (Some drivers automatically detect the network adapter configuration and will not prompt you for input.)

## Network protocols

Each of the protocols below has strengths and weaknesses. Evaluate the needs of your network, and then choose all the protocols you need. NT 4.0 ships with support for TCP/IP, NWLink IPX/SPX Compatible Transport, and NetBEUI.

o **TCP/IP:**   Yes \_\_\_   No \_\_\_

(If Yes, then Windows NT Setup offers you an opportunity to configure TCP/IP by using DHCP.)

**DHCP:**   Yes \_\_\_   No \_\_\_   (If No, fill in information below)

IP address:          _____

Subnet mask:          _____

Default gateway:     _____

DNS server #1:       _____

DNS server #2:       _____

WINS server #1:      _____

WINS server #2:      _____

The *TCP/IP* protocol provides the most capability of the three protocols. It is routable, fast, and has powerful network-wide name resolution capabilities. It can be used on much larger networks than either of the other protocols. TCP/IP is the most commonly supported protocol. It is supported on many operating systems, including Windows NT, Windows 95, UNIX, MS-DOS, Macintosh, and IBM Mainframes. TCP/IP is the protocol used on the Internet.

The main drawback to using TCP/IP is that it requires substantial planning and configuration to implement.

concept link

**For more information on TCP/IP configuration properties, see Chapter 16.**

o **NWLink IPX/SPX Compatible Transport:**   Yes\_\_\_   No\_\_\_

(If Yes) Frame Type: _____

*NWLink IPX/SPX Compatible Transport* is a protocol originally developed by Novell. It was designed for use on Novell NetWare servers. NWLink IPX/SPX is a routable protocol, but has some limitations when used on large NetBIOS-based networks such as Windows NT. It has no name resolution capabilities, so all broadcasts are forwarded across routers.

NWLink IPX/SPX is very easy to configure, and is a good choice for a small, routed network. NWLink IPX/SPX should be used on any network that has NetWare servers on it if Windows NT computers on the network need to access the NetWare servers.

You should choose autodetect for the frame type selection, unless you know which frame types you want to support.

 concept link

**For more information on NWLink IPX/SPX Compatible Transport, coexistence with NetWare, and frame types, see Chapter 17.**

o   **NetBEUI:**   Yes___ No___

The NetBEUI protocol is designed for small, nonrouted networks. It does not require any configuration, and has minimal overhead. NetBEUI is included primarily to provide backward compatibility with earlier networking software that uses NetBEUI as its only protocol.

## Network services

**Network services to add:**

_____

At this point in the installation, several network services are preselected by default, and you cannot deselect them. You can also add additional services by clicking the Select from list command button.

 concept link

**Network services are examined in detail later in this book. Some of the services are covered in Chapter 6, and others are mentioned throughout the chapters in Part IV.**

## Network bindings

**Network bindings to disable:** _____

You have an option to disable and enable *bindings* of various services to protocols, and bindings of protocols to various network adapters. A binding is an association. For example, you might want to associate one protocol with one network adapter, and another protocol with a second network adapter. By default, all services are bound to all protocols that support that service, and all protocols are bound to all network adapters.

 note

**This is an advanced feature. You should accept the default setting unless you have a specific reason to change it.**

## Make this computer a member of

This section applies only to NT Workstation and to NT Server when installed as a stand-alone server.

You *must* choose to participate in either a workgroup or a domain. (See the "Workgroups Versus Domains" section in Chapter 1 for more information on this topic.) Only Windows NT Workstation computers and Windows NT Server computers that are configured as stand-alone servers have this option.

○ **Workgroup:**   Yes_____ No_____

(If Yes) Workgroup name:  _____

If you elect to be a member of a workgroup, only users that have user accounts physically located in this computer's directory database will be able to log on to this computer locally or to access it over the network. You need to supply a workgroup name during installation.

○ **Domain:**   Yes_____ No_____

(If Yes) Domain name: _____

Create a computer account in the domain?   Yes ___ No ___

Administrator's account name: _____

Administrator's password: _____

If you decide to join a domain, two kinds of users will be able to log on to this computer locally or to access it over the network: users that have accounts in this computer's directory database, and users that have accounts in the domain directory database.

You also need to create a computer account in the domain. An administrator can do this before the Windows NT installation using Server Manager on another NT computer in the domain, or, you can create the computer account in the domain during the NT installation process. If you choose to create a computer account in the domain during installation, you need to supply an administrator's user account name and password.

## Internet Information Server (Windows NT Server only)

**Select the publishing directories you want to install:**

World Wide Web publishing directory _____

FTP publishing directory _____

Gopher publishing directory _____

If you elected to install IIS earlier in the Windows NT installation process, you are now asked to choose publishing directories for it. The default directories are acceptable for most installations.

concept link    **For more information on IIS, see Chapter 16 or the *Microsoft Windows NT Server Internet Guide,* which is included in the *Microsoft Windows NT Server Resource Kit for version 4.0* (Microsoft Press, 1996).**

### *Time zone*

**Time zone:** _____

Select the time zone for your location, and choose whether to adjust for daylight saving time.

### *Video adapter display settings*

**Video adapter type:** _____
**Display settings desired:**

_____

You need to know what type of video adapter is installed in your computer and how you want your display to appear. Appearance settings include: Color Palette, Desktop Area (640 by 480, 800 by 600, and so on), Font Size, and Refresh Frequency. Windows NT will preselect some of these settings for you, but you can modify them during or after installation using Control Panel.

# THE INSTALLATION PROCESS

Now that you know the minimum hardware required to install Windows NT and have all the information required to perform the installation, you're ready to move on to the actual installation process.

**My intent is to explain the basic Windows NT installation process. The steps *you* take to perform your installation may be different than the steps listed here, depending on your hardware configuration, any previously installed operating systems on your computer, and so on. This description is only a basic guide—modify it to meet your needs. See Labs 2.1 and 2.2 at the end of this chapter for detailed installation instructions.**

# Starting Setup

Windows NT uses a program called Setup to accomplish the installation. There are three ways to start the installation process: from a CD-ROM drive, by using Winnt.exe, and by using Winnt32.exe. Installation can be done locally, from a CD-ROM drive; or over the network.

## Starting from a CD-ROM drive

To start Setup from a CD-ROM drive, your computer must be configured with a local CD-ROM drive that is on the HCL. Place the Windows NT Workstation or Windows NT Server compact disc in the CD-ROM drive. Then boot the computer from the Windows NT Setup Boot Disk.

## Using Winnt.exe

You can use Winnt.exe to start Setup from an unsupported CD-ROM drive (a CD-ROM drive that is not listed on the HCL), or to start an over-the-network installation. First boot the computer to MS-DOS, and then load either the CD-ROM drivers or network drivers (depending on the type of installation you're doing). Then use Winnt.exe to start Setup.

Winnt.exe has several command-line switches that enable customization of the setup process. Table 2-2 lists these switches and describes their functions. The syntax for the Winnt.exe command is:

```
WINNT [/S[:]sourcepath] [/T[:]tempdrive] [/I[:]inffile
  [/O[X]] [/X | [/F] [/C]] [/B] [/U[:scriptfile]]
  [/R[X]:directory] [/E:command]
```

**TABLE 2-2** WINNT.EXE COMMAND-LINE SWITCHES

| *Switch* | *What the Switch Does* |
|---|---|
| /S[:]sourcepath | Specifies the source location of NT files. You must specify a full path, in the form x:\[path] or \\server\share[\path]. Default sourcepath is the current directory. |
| /T[:]tempdrive | Specifies the drive that contains NT's temporary setup files during installation. If not specified, Setup uses the first drive it finds (that it thinks has enough free space) for the tempdrive. |
| /I[:]inffile | Specifies the filename (no path) of the file containing setup information. Default inffile is DOSNET.INF. |
| /OX | Instructs Setup to create the Setup Boot Disk set. |
| /X | Instructs Setup *not* to create the Setup Boot Disk set. |
| /F | Instructs Setup *not* to verify files as they are copied to the Setup Boot Disk set (during the creation of the Setup Boot Disk set). |
| /C | Instructs Setup to skip the free-space check during the creation of the Setup Boot Disk set. |
| /B | Enables you to install NT without using the Setup Boot Disk set. Requires you to specify the sourcepath by using the /S switch. |
| /U | Allows you to perform an unattended NT installation and use an optional script file. Requires you to specify the sourcepath by using the /S switch. |
| /R | Specifies an optional directory to be installed during installation. |
| /RX | Specifies an optional directory to be copied to the local hard drive during installation. |
| /E | Specifies a command to be executed at the end of the installation/setup process. |
| /UDF | Specifies that a Uniqueness Database File is used during an unattended NT installation. |

tip  **These switches are *not* case-sensitive. You may type them in either upper- or lowercase.**

To illustrate how the switches are used, suppose that you want to install Windows NT from a network drive (named drive K:) without using the Setup Boot Disk set. (This is often referred to as a *floppyless installation*). To accomplish this, use the following command:

```
K:\I386\Winnt /B /S:K:\I386
```

Notice the /B switch is used to permit you to perform a floppyless installation, and the /S switch is used to specify that the sourcepath (the location of the NT files that will be installed on your computer) is a network drive named K:.

 concept link   **For more information on unattended installation/setup, see Chapter 5.**

### Using Winnt32.exe

Winnt32.exe functions in the same way as Winnt.exe, except that Winnt.exe is designed to run on a MS-DOS-based computer, and Winnt32.exe is designed to be used on a Windows NT 3.*x* computer. All Winnt32.exe command-line options are the same as Winnt.exe, with the exception of /F and /C, which are not supported by Winnt32.exe.

## Setup Flow

The installation of Windows NT takes place in four or five phases, depending on whether you install from a CD-ROM or use Winnt.exe. These phases are: the Pre-Copy Phase, Phase 0, and Phases 1-3. During each phase, you perform specific tasks and enter requested information. The Windows NT installation program (Setup) causes the computer to reboot after the Pre-Copy Phase, and again after Phase 0.

Here's a detailed description of what takes place during each phase of the Windows NT installation.

### Pre-Copy Phase (Winnt.exe and Winnt32.exe only)

The Pre-Copy Phase is the initial phase of the installation process. This phase applies only when the Winnt.exe or Winnt32.exe installation option is used. The Windows NT Setup program performs the following tasks:

**1.** Setup creates a set of three floppy disks to use during the installation process. These diskettes are similar to the diskettes used to perform an installation from a CD-ROM drive, except that they point to the directory

that has a copy of the installation files instead of to a CD-ROM drive. The
floppy disks are not created if the /B or /U switches are used.

2. Setup creates a $Win_NT$.~ls folder on the first local drive with enough
   free space, then copies the installation files from the source directory to
   this folder. (The installation program deletes this folder after the
   installation is complete.)

3. Setup prompts you to restart the computer with the Setup Boot Disk.

## Phase 0

Phase 0 begins when you boot the computer with the Setup Boot Disk, or when
you reboot the computer after using Winnt.exe /B. Setup prompts you to take
the following steps during this phase:

1. Confirm all SCSI and CD-ROM adapters, and add drivers for adapters by
   using driver disks supplied by the manufacturer.

2. Agree to the terms of the Windows NT Licensing Agreement.

3. Choose the installation directory. Choose whether to upgrade previously
   installed versions of Windows 3.x or Windows NT, or to install Windows NT
   in a different directory to create a dual boot system, which can boot to
   more than one operating system.

4. Verify the hardware and software components in the computer.

5. Choose the disk partition on which to install Windows NT, and choose the
   type of file system to use on this partition.

Setup will then examine your computer's hard disk for corruption, and then
cause the computer to reboot. After the computer reboots, Setup prompts you to
remove the floppy disk from drive A: if one is there.

## Phase 1

In Phase 1, the NT Setup Wizard starts. Setup gathers more information from you
about your computer and specific installation details. You are prompted to make the
following choices and perform the following tasks during this phase:

1. (Windows NT Workstation only) Choose the setup option type.

2. Enter your name and the name of your organization.

3. Enter your CD key number.

4. (Windows NT Server only) Choose a Licensing mode.

5. Enter your computer name.

6. (Windows NT Server only) Choose a server type.

7. Enter and confirm a password for the Administrator account.

8. Choose whether to create an Emergency Repair Disk. (The Emergency Repair Disk is made at the end of the installation, but you must choose whether or not to make one at this point).

9. Choose the optional components to install.

## *Phase 2*

In Phase 2, Setup installs and configures networking components. To accomplish this, you provide more information and make the following additional choices:

1. Specify how (or if) the computer connects to the network.

 note **If you are installing Windows NT Workstation and you choose no network, Phase 2 will end and Phase 3 will start.**

2. (Windows NT Server only) Choose whether to install Microsoft Internet Information Server (IIS).

3. Indicate which network adapters are installed in your computer.

4. Choose the network protocol(s) you want to use, and enter related information requested depending on the protocol(s) chosen.

5. (Windows NT Server and Windows NT Workstation custom setup option only) Choose additional network services to install.

6. Verify network adapter settings.

7. (Windows NT Server and Windows NT Workstation custom setup option only) Configure network bindings for network services, protocols, and adapters.

8. (Windows NT Server installed as a stand-alone server and Windows NT Workstation only) Choose whether to make your computer part of either a workgroup or a domain. Enter your workgroup or domain name. If you join a domain, create a computer account in the domain and supply the domain administrator's user account name and password.

### Phase 3

In Phase 3, Setup completes the installation. It is very short. You are prompted to do the following:

1. (Windows NT Server only) If you elected to install IIS in an earlier step, you must enter specific IIS setup and publishing directory information now.

2. Configure the date, time, and time zone information.

3. Configure and test the computer's video adapter settings.

 *tip* **You *must* test the display configuration before the Setup Wizard will let you continue the installation process.**

4. Make an Emergency Repair Disk. Then remove this disk from Drive A:.

5. (Installation from CD-ROM only) Remove the Windows NT compact disc from the CD-ROM drive.

6. Restart the computer.

    The Windows NT installation is complete.

# DEINSTALLING WINDOWS NT

If you have incorrectly installed Windows NT, or want to remove it from your computer for any other reason, this section outlines the necessary steps.

## Deinstalling Windows NT from a FAT Partition

If your computer is configured to dual boot between Windows NT and MS-DOS (or to dual boot between Windows NT and Windows 95), it is fairly easy to deinstall Windows NT.

**TO DEINSTALL WINDOWS NT FROM A FAT PARTITION, FOLLOW THESE STEPS:**

**1.** Boot your computer to MS-DOS (or Windows 95) from a floppy disk that has the `Sys.com` utility on it.

**2.** At the command prompt type **Sys a: c:** (and press Enter). This will replace the Windows NT boot sector with the boot sector for your other operating system (MS-DOS or Windows 95).

**3.** Remove the floppy disk from drive A: and reboot the computer. MS-DOS or Windows 95 should start automatically.

**4.** Now that you have disabled NT, you can complete the removal of NT files from your computer. Free up hard disk space by removing `pagefile.sys`, `ntldr`, `Boot.ini`, `Ntdetect.com`, `Bootsect.dos`, and `Ntbootdd.sys`. (Because some of these files have attributes of hidden, system, and read-only, you will have to remove the file attributes before you can delete these files.) You can also remove the entire Windows NT installation folder (usually `C:\Winnt`), and the `\Program files\Windows NT` folder. This completes the deinstallation of Windows NT.

# Deinstalling Windows NT from an NTFS Partition

If you want to deinstall Windows NT from an NTFS partition, you must delete that partition, because no other operating system supports NTFS.

Depending on your situation, to accomplish this you need to either delete an NTFS primary partition, or delete NTFS from an extended partition.

## *Deleting an NTFS primary partition*

There are several ways to delete an NTFS primary partition:

o You can use MS-DOS `Fdisk.exe` from MS-DOS 6.*x*.

o You can use the `Delpart.exe` utility.

**The** Delpart.exe **utility is not included in the basic NT product. However, you can download this free utility from CompuServe (go to the Winnt Forum, Library 4). The filename is** delprt.exe. **You can also get this utility, free, from the Internet by accessing** ftp://ftp.teleprint.ch/pub/ms. **The filename at this location is** delpart.exe.

o   You can use the Windows NT Setup Boot Disk set. Boot the computer from the Setup Boot Disk. Go through the installation process until you get to the disk partition information section. Highlight the NTFS partition you want to delete, and press the D key to delete it. Then press F3 to exit Setup.

Other operating systems also have partitioning utilities that are capable of deleting an NTFS partition.

### Deleting NTFS from an extended partition

You can't use MS-DOS Fdisk.exe to delete NTFS from an extended partition. You must either use Delpart.exe or the Windows NT Setup Boot Disk set, as described above.

# TROUBLESHOOTING COMMON INSTALLATION PROBLEMS

There are many common problems that can cause your installation of Windows NT to fail. Most of these problems occur because of hardware incompatibilities. Most of the time your first troubleshooting step should be to ensure that all of your hardware is on the HCL or is supported by the manufacturer. Table 2-3 lists some common Windows NT installation problems and their possible causes and solutions.

**TABLE 2-3** TROUBLESHOOTING COMMON INSTALLATION PROBLEMS

| PROBLEM: | POSSIBLE CAUSE/SOLUTION: |
|---|---|
| You have the recommended amount of free disk space, but still run out of disk space during installation. | The recommended amount of disk space is based on the expectation that you are using 16K sectors on your hard disk. If you have a very large partition, you could be using 32K or 64K sectors. You would then need significantly more free disk space to complete your installation. |
| A blue screen or STOP message is displayed during installation or after a reboot. | This can be caused by several things. Some of the most common causes are a *corrupt boot sector* or a *boot sector virus,* which you can usually repair by using Fdisk /mbr from MS-DOS (many virus scanners can also repair this error); and *hardware conflicts,* which you can check for by using NTHQ to examine all of your hardware settings. Look for two pieces of hardware with the same I/O port, interrupt, or DMA address. Reconfigure hardware so that there are no hardware conflicts. |
| You can't install from your CD-ROM drive. | This could be caused by an unsupported CD-ROM drive or by an unsupported SCSI adapter. Some SCSI adapters, such as PC card SCSI adapters, are not supported during installation, but you can install the drivers for them after the installation is complete. Try installing using Winnt.exe. |
| You can't join a domain during installation. | Make sure that all network settings, both hardware and software, are correct. Confirm that you have correctly typed in the domain name and the administrator's user account name and password. (All passwords in Windows NT are case-sensitive.) Check the network cable and connections and verify that the PDC is up and accessible on the network. |
| Network services don't start correctly. | Verify that all network adapter and network protocol settings are correct, including interrupt, I/O port, and transceiver type. Confirm that the newly assigned computer name is unique—that it does not match any other computer, domain, or workgroup name used on the network. If you are installing a PDC, ensure that the new domain name is unique—that it does not match any other computer or domain name used on the network. |

# KEY POINT SUMMARY

Chapter 2 covered all of the important topics surrounding the installation and configuration of Windows NT Workstation and Windows NT Server, including the hardware requirements for installation, the information required to perform an installation, the installation process, deinstalling Windows NT, and troubleshooting common Windows NT installation problems.

- It's important that you are thoroughly familiar with the *hardware requirements* for installing Windows NT. Only hardware on the *Windows NT Hardware Compatibility List* (HCL) should be used. You can use the *NTHQ* utility to examine and identify your hardware configuration, and to get a printout of information needed to perform the installation.

- You need a substantial amount of detailed information to install Windows NT. It's a good idea to complete the Preinstallation Checklist to make sure you have all of the information you need *before* you start the installation.

- There are three ways to begin the Windows NT installation process: from a CD-ROM drive, by using `Winnt.exe`, and by using `Winnt32.exe`. Installation can be done locally from a CD-ROM drive or over the network. The installation process takes place in phases:

  - The *Pre-Copy Phase* applies only when the `Winnt.exe` or `Winnt32.exe` installation options are used. In this phase, Setup creates a set of floppy disks to use during the installation process and copies installation files from the source directory to a folder on your computer's hard disk.

  - In *Phase 0,* Setup identifies your computer's hardware, introduces the Windows NT Licensing Agreement, prompts you to choose an installation directory, and prompts you to choose a disk partition and corresponding file system.

  - In *Phase 1,* the NT Setup Wizard starts. You enter more information about your computer and specific installation details. You enter your name, your organization's name, and your CD key number. You choose a setup option type (Windows NT Workstation only). You choose a licensing mode and a server type (Windows NT Server only). You choose whether to create an Emergency Repair Disk. Finally, you select optional software components for installation.

- In *Phase 2,* Setup installs and configures networking components. You select a network connection type. Then you select and configure network adapters, protocols, services, and bindings. You choose whether to make this computer a part of a workgroup or a domain.

- In *Phase 3,* you configure date, time, and time zone information, then configure and test your computer's video display. Setup creates the Emergency Repair Disk. Then the installation is complete.

- It is possible to deinstall Windows NT, both from a file allocation table (FAT) partition and from a Windows NT file system (NTFS) partition. Remember, no other operating system supports NTFS.

- Several common problems can arise during installation that require troubleshooting. Many installation problems occur because of hardware incompatibilities. Most of the time your first troubleshooting step should be to ensure that all of your hardware is on the HCL. Table 2-3 illustrates several common installation problems and their possible causes and solutions.

# APPLYING WHAT YOU'VE LEARNED

Now it's time to regroup, review, and apply what you've learned in this chapter.

The questions in the Instant Assessment section that follows bring to mind key facts and concepts. In addition, the troubleshooting practice exercise in the Review Activity section tests your ability to solve common Windows NT installation problems.

The hands-on lab exercises will really reinforce what you've learned, and allow you to practice some of the tasks tested by the Microsoft Certified Professional exams.

## Instant Assessment

1. What is the minimum processor, amount of RAM, and hard disk space required to install Windows NT Workstation on an Intel-based computer?

2. What is the minimum processor, amount of RAM, and hard disk space required to install Windows NT Server on an Intel-based computer?

3. What is NTHQ and what can it do?

4. When you install Windows NT 4.0 in a different directory than a previously installed operating system, what will Windows NT automatically configure itself to do?

5. Which partition is the active partition that contains the files required to load and boot Windows NT?

6. Which partition contains the Windows NT installation directory (usually Winnt) and all of the Windows NT operating system files?

7. What are the two file system types that Windows NT supports?

8. What is the only operating system that supports NTFS?

9. You want to install Windows NT on an MS-DOS-based computer that does *not* have a local CD-ROM drive. Which of the three methods of starting Setup should you use?

concept link     **For answers to the Instant Assessment questions see Appendix D.**

Workstation
Server
Enterprise

# Review Activity

The following activity tests your ability to troubleshoot common Windows NT installation problems.

### *Installing Windows NT troubleshooting practice exercise*

In each of the following problems, consider the given facts and determine what you think are the possible causes of the problem and what course of action you might take to resolve the problem.

**Problem 1**    You are attempting to install Windows NT. During the installation, the process stops and you see a blue screen containing error information on your display.

**Problem 2**    You are installing Windows NT. You try to join a domain and an error message is displayed stating the domain controller for this domain cannot be located.

concept link     **For answers to the Review Activity see Appendix D.**

# Hands-on Lab Exercises

Now it's time to apply all of this head knowledge by doing a couple of hands-on lab exercises.

exam
preparation
pointer

**These lab exercises are extremely important for your exam preparation. Don't even think about skipping them! There's no substitute for using Windows NT to master the skills that the Microsoft Certified Professional exams test.**

Refer to the "Hardware and Software You'll Need" section in the Preface if you're not sure you have the necessary equipment to do the labs.

caution

**Warning! Some of the lab exercises in this book have the potential to erase or corrupt data on existing hard disk drives. Make sure you back up all important data and programs *before* you attempt to perform any of the lab exercises. Or, better yet, do the labs on a computer that does not contain any vital data or programs.**

## Lab 2.1 *Installing Windows NT Workstation*

The objective of this hands-on exercise is for you to experience the process of installing Microsoft Windows NT Workstation and to develop the skills used to perform this task.

Workstation
Server
Enterprise

note

**For you to complete some of the remaining labs in this book, you will need at least a 10MB partition on your hard disk that will be formatted in a later lab with NTFS. (If you don't partition your hard disk in this manner, you will not be able to do the labs on NTFS security and auditing.) You may create an extended MS-DOS partition for this use. This task should be done *before* MS-DOS is installed, and before you proceed with the rest of this lab. I recommend that you partition your hard drive into two partitions. The first partition should contain *all but* 10MB of the disk's capacity. The extended (second) partition should consist of the remaining 10MB of disk space.**

**I assume, in all of the labs in this book, that drive C: is the large partition, and that drive D: is the 10MB partition. Your actual drive letters may vary from this configuration. If your drives are lettered differently, substitute your drive letters for the ones I use.**

To perform this lab, first install MS-DOS on your computer's hard drive, and load the drivers for your CD-ROM drive. Make sure the Windows NT Workstation compact disc is in your CD-ROM drive. You need one blank, 3.5-inch high-density floppy disk for this lab exercise.

Follow the steps below carefully to perform the installation:

### PRE-COPY PHASE

**1.** Change the default drive to your CD-ROM drive by typing in the CD-ROM drive letter followed by a colon (for example, **D:**). Then press Enter.

**2.** Type **cd I386**, and then press Enter.

**3.** Type **winnt /b**, then press Enter. (This command instructs Setup to perform the Winnt.exe installation without creating the Setup Boot Disk set.)

**4.** When Windows NT Setup asks you to enter the path where NT files are located, press Enter.

**5.** Setup copies files to your hard disk. (This process takes a few minutes. How about a stretch break or a fresh cup of coffee?)

**6.** When the Windows NT Workstation Setup screen appears, press Enter to restart your computer and continue Windows NT Setup.

### PHASE 0

**1.** After a couple of minutes, the Windows NT Workstation Setup screen appears, welcoming you to Setup. Press Enter to set up Windows NT now.

**2.** Setup displays a screen indicating any mass storage devices, such as SCSI adapters, CD-ROM drives, and so on. Some older IDE controllers are not displayed here, but they will still function and be recognized by NT. Specify additional devices by making changes on this screen if you need to. When you have completed all necessary changes, press Enter to continue.

**3.** The Windows NT Licensing Agreement screen appears. Read the licensing agreement, pressing PgDn to view additional screens. When you reach the bottom of the agreement, press F8 to continue setup.

**4.** Setup displays a screen indicating your computer's hardware and software components. Make any changes necessary. When you are finished, highlight "The above list matches my computer" and press Enter.

**5.** If you have a previous version of Microsoft Windows installed on your computer, Setup displays a screen indicating that it has found a previous version. If this screen appears, press N to install Windows NT Workstation in a different directory.

**6.** Setup displays a screen listing your computer's hard disk partitions. Highlight the partition on which you want to install Windows NT, then press Enter. (Make sure the partition you choose has at least 117MB free.)

**7.** Setup asks you to select the type of file system you want on this partition. Highlight "Leave the current file system intact <no changes>," and press Enter.

**8.** Setup displays a location where it will install the NT Workstation files. In the highlighted area, edit the text so that it reads: **\WINNTWKS**. (Don't type the period at the end.) Then press Enter.

**9.** Setup offers to examine your computer's hard disk for corruption. Press Enter to allow this. (This takes a few minutes.)

**10.** Setup displays a screen indicating that this portion of Setup is complete. If you have a floppy disk inserted in drive A:, remove it now. Then press Enter to restart your computer and to continue with setup.

**PHASE 1**

**1.** After your computer reboots, the Windows NT Workstation Setup dialog box appears. Click Next to continue.

**2.** A Setup Options screen appears. Select Custom. Click Next to continue.

**3.** Type in your name, press Tab, then type in the name of your organization. Click Next to continue.

**4.** Type in the ten-digit CD key number from the back of your Windows NT Workstation compact disc case (press Tab after you type the first three digits). Click Next to continue.

**5.** When Setup prompts you to type in a computer name, type **NTW40**. Click Next to continue.

**6.** Type **password** when Setup prompts you to enter an administrator password. Press Tab. Confirm the password by retyping it. Click Next to continue.

**7.** Setup asks you if you want to create an Emergency Repair Disk. Accept the Yes default. Click Next to continue.

**8.** Setup displays a screen indicating you are to Select Components. Add any components that you want to install, but do *not* deselect any components that are selected by default. (I recommend you install FreeCell and all of the games . . . I'm an addict!) Click Next to continue.

**PHASE 2**

**1.** Setup displays a screen indicating that Phase 2, Installing Windows NT Networking, is about to begin. Click Next to continue.

**2.** Select "This computer will participate on a network." Then click the check box next to "Wired to the network." (It's OK to select these options even if you don't have a network adapter in your computer.) Click Next to continue.

**3.** Setup displays the Network Adapters box. If you have a network adapter, click Start Search. Your network adapter should appear in the Network Adapters window. If your network adapter did not appear, or if you do not have a network adapter in your computer, click Select from list. If your network adapter is shown in the list, highlight it and click OK. If your network adapter is not on the list, and you have a driver disk from its manufacturer, highlight any network adapter and click Have Disk. Setup then prompts you to insert this disk. Do so and click OK. Highlight your network adapter from the list and click OK. If you do not have a network adapter, highlight MS Loopback Adapter and click OK. You should now have either the MS Loopback Adapter or your network adapter displayed in the Network Adapters box. Click Next to continue.

**4.** Setup displays the Network Protocols list box. Accept the default selection of TCP/IP Protocol. Click Next to continue.

**5.** Setup displays the Network Services list box. Accept all of the defaults selected in this list box. Click Next to continue.

**6.** Click Next to continue and to have Setup install the selected components.

**7.** Setup prompts you to enter your network adapter card settings. (This screen may not appear for some network adapters.) Verify that the settings shown match the ones that you used when you installed and configured your network adapter. Make changes only as needed. Click Continue.

**8.** A TCP/IP Setup warning screen appears. If you are on a network that has a DHCP server, click Yes. Otherwise, click No.

**9.** The Microsoft TCP/IP Properties dialog box eventually appears if you clicked No in the previous step. *If you are on a network that uses TCP/IP, or if you are connected to the Internet, obtain an IP address, subnet mask, and default gateway from your network administrator.* Otherwise, type an IP address of: **192.168.59.5** and a subnet mask of: **255.255.255.0**.

 caution

**Do *not* use this IP address if you are on a network that uses TCP/IP, or if you are connected to the Internet.**

**10.** Leave the Default Gateway blank. Click OK to continue.

**11.** Setup displays a screen showing network binding information. Click Next to continue.

**12.** Click Next to start the network.

**13.** Setup displays a screen asking you to choose whether your computer will participate in a workgroup or domain configuration. Accept the default selection of Workgroup, and the default workgroup name WORKGROUP. Click Next to continue.

### PHASE 3

**1.** Click Finish to continue the setup process.

**2.** In the drop-down list box under the Time Zone tab, highlight and click your time zone. As an option, you may also click the Date & Time tab and set the correct date and time. Click Close to continue when you are finished.

**3.** Setup displays a screen indicating that it has found your video display adapter. Click OK in the Detected Display dialog box to continue.

**4.** Adjust the display settings to suit your preferences. Click Test. The Testing Mode dialog box appears. Click OK to test. When the Testing Mode dialog box reappears, click Yes if you saw the test bitmap. When the Display Settings dialog box appears, click OK to continue. Click OK in the Display Properties dialog box to complete the installation. (This takes a few minutes.)

**5.** When prompted, label and insert a blank 3.5-inch floppy disk into drive A:. Setup formats this disk and makes it into your Emergency Repair Disk. Click OK to continue. (This takes a couple of minutes.)

**6.** Setup displays a window indicating that Windows NT 4.0 is successfully installed. Remove your newly created Emergency Repair Disk from drive A: (and save it for future use). Also remove the compact disc from your CD-ROM drive. Then click Restart Computer to reboot and start Windows NT Workstation. The setup is complete.

## Lab 2.2 *Installing Windows NT Server and configuring dual boot with Windows NT Workstation*

Workstation
Server
Enterprise

The purpose of this lab exercise is for you to experience the process of installing Microsoft Windows NT Server and to develop the skills used to perform this task. During the installation process you will configure your computer to dual boot between Windows NT Server and Windows NT Workstation.

note  **Before you can successfully perform this lab, you must complete Lab 2.1. You need one blank, 3.5-inch high-density floppy disk for this lab exercise.**

Follow the steps below carefully to perform the installation:

Boot your computer to Windows NT Workstation, and log on as Administrator (remember, the administrator password is *password*). Make sure the Windows NT Server compact disc is in your CD-ROM drive.

### PRE-COPY PHASE

1. Close the Welcome to Windows NT dialog box.
2. Select Start⇒Programs⇒Command Prompt.
3. At the command prompt, change the default drive to your CD-ROM drive by typing in the CD-ROM drive letter followed by a colon (for example, **D:**). Then press Enter.
4. Type **cd I386**, and then press Enter.
5. Type **winnt32 /b**, then press Enter. (This command performs the installation without creating the Setup Boot Disk set.)
6. The Windows NT 4.0 Upgrade/Installation dialog box appears. Click Continue to accept the default path for the location of your Windows NT files.
7. The Installation program copies files to your hard disk. (This process takes a few minutes.)
8. When Setup displays the Windows NT 4.0 Server Installation/Upgrade dialog box, click Restart Computer and continue the installation.

### PHASE 0

1. After a minute or two, when the Windows NT Server Setup screen appears, press Enter to set up Windows NT now.
2. Setup displays a screen showing any mass storage devices, such as SCSI adapters, CD-ROM drives, and so on. Some older IDE controllers are not displayed here, but will still function and be recognized by NT. Specify additional devices by making changes on this screen if you need to. When you have completed all necessary changes, press Enter to continue.
3. The Windows NT Licensing Agreement screen appears. Read the licensing agreement, pressing PgDn to view additional screens. When you reach the bottom of the agreement, press F8 to continue setup.
4. Windows NT Server Setup displays a screen indicating it has found Windows NT Workstation. Press N to cancel upgrade and install a fresh copy of Windows NT.
5. Windows NT Server Setup displays a screen listing your computer's hardware and software components. Make any changes necessary. When you are finished, highlight "The above list matches my computer," and press Enter.

**6.** If you have a previous version of Microsoft Windows installed on your computer, Setup displays a screen stating that it detected a previous version. If this screen appears, press N to install Windows NT Server in a different directory.

**7.** Windows NT Server Setup displays a screen showing your computer's hard disk partitions. Highlight the partition on which you want to install Windows NT Server, then press Enter. (Make sure the partition you choose has at least 124MB free.)

**8.** Windows NT Server Setup asks you to select the type of file system you want on this partition. Highlight "Leave the current file system intact <no changes>," and press Enter.

**9.** Windows NT Server Setup displays the location where it will install the NT Server files. In the highlighted area, edit the text so that it reads: **\WINNTSRV**. (Don't type the period at the end.) Then press Enter.

**10.** Windows NT Server Setup offers to examine your hard disk for corruption. Press Enter to allow this. (This takes a few minutes.)

**11.** Windows NT Server Setup displays a screen that indicates this portion of Setup is complete. If you have a floppy disk inserted in drive A:, remove it now. Then press Enter to restart your computer and to continue with setup.

### PHASE 1

**1.** After your computer reboots and the Windows NT Server Setup dialog box finally appears, click Next to continue.

**2.** Type in your name, press Tab, and then type the name of your organization. Click Next to continue.

**3.** Type in the ten-digit CD key number from the back of your Windows NT Server compact disc case (press Tab after you enter the first three digits). Click Next to continue.

**4.** Select a Licensing mode for the server. Select "Per Server for:" and enter the number of client licenses you purchased. Click Next to continue.

**5.** When prompted to type in a name for your computer, type **PDCLAB**. Click Next to continue.

**6.** Select Primary Domain Controller in the Server Type window. Click Next to continue.

**7.** Type **password** when prompted to enter an administrator password. Press Tab. Confirm the password by retyping it. Click Next to continue.

**8.** Windows NT Server Setup asks if you want to create an Emergency Repair Disk. Accept the Yes default. Click Next to continue.

**9.** Windows NT Server Setup displays a screen prompting you to Select Components. Add any components that you want to install, but do *not* deselect any components that are selected by default. Click Next to continue.

### PHASE 2

**1.** Windows NT Server Setup displays a window indicating that Phase 2, Installing Windows NT Networking, is about to begin. Click Next to continue.

**2.** Accept the default check in the box next to "Wired to the network." (It's OK to select this option even if you don't have a network adapter in your computer.) Click Next to continue.

**3.** Accept the default check in the box next to "Install Microsoft Internet Information Server." Click Next to continue.

**4.** Windows NT Server Setup displays the Network Adapters box. If you have a network adapter, click Start Search. Your network adapter should then appear in the Network Adapters box. If your network adapter did not appear, or if you do not have one in your computer, click Select From List. If your network adapter is shown in the list, highlight it and click OK. If your network adapter is not on the list, and you have a driver disk from its manufacturer, highlight any network adapter and click Have Disk. Setup then prompts you to insert this disk. Insert the disk and click OK. Highlight your network adapter from the list and click OK. If you do not have a network adapter, highlight MS Loopback Adapter and click OK. You should now have either the MS Loopback Adapter or your network adapter displayed in the Network Adapters box. Click Next to continue.

**5.** Windows NT Server Setup displays the Network Protocols list box. Deselect NWLink IPX/SPX Compatible Transport. Ensure that the TCP/IP Protocol is the only protocol selected (it will have a gray check in the check box). Click Next to continue.

**6.** Windows NT Server Setup displays the Network Services list box. Accept all of the defaults selected in this window. Click Next to continue.

**7.** Click Next to have Setup install the selected components.

**8.** Setup prompts you to enter your network adapter card settings. (This screen may not appear for some network adapters.) Verify that the settings shown match the ones you used when you installed and configured your network adapter. Make changes only as needed. Click Continue.

**9.** A TCP/IP Setup warning screen appears. If you are on a network that has a DHCP server, click Yes. Otherwise, click No.

**10.** The Microsoft TCP/IP Properties dialog box appears if you clicked No in the previous step. *If you are on a network that uses TCP/IP, or if you are connected to the Internet, obtain an IP address, subnet mask, and default gateway from your network administrator.* Otherwise, type an IP address of: **192.168.59.5** and a subnet mask of: **255.255.255.0**.

 caution

Do *not* use this IP address if you are on a network that uses TCP/IP, or if you are connected to the Internet.

**11.** Leave the Default Gateway blank. Click OK to continue.

**12.** Windows NT Server Setup displays a screen showing network binding information. Click Next to continue.

**13.** Click Next to start the network.

**14.** Windows NT Server Setup prompts you enter a domain name. Type **LAB** as your domain name. Click Next to continue.

### PHASE 3

**1.** Click Finish to continue the setup process.

**2.** Accept the defaults selected in the Microsoft Internet Information Server 2.0 Setup dialog box. Click OK to continue.

**3.** Click Yes to create the directory.

**4.** Accept the default directories in the Publishing Directories dialog box by clicking OK.

**5.** Click Yes to create the directories.

**6.** Click OK in the Microsoft Internet Information Server 2.0 Setup dialog box. (You won't be configuring the Gopher functionality in this course.)

**7.** Click SQL Server in the Install Drivers dialog box to highlight it. Click OK to continue.

**8.** In the drop-down list box under the Time Zone tab, click your time zone to highlight it. Optionally, click the Date & Time tab and set the correct date and time. When you are finished, click Close to continue.

**9.** Setup displays a screen indicating that it has found your video display adapter. Click OK in the Detected Display dialog box to continue.

**10.** Adjust the display settings to suit your preferences. Click Test. The Testing Mode dialog box appears. Click OK to test. When the Testing Mode dialog box reappears, click Yes if you saw the test bitmap. When the Display Settings dialog box appears, click OK to continue. Click OK in the Display Properties dialog box to complete the installation. (This takes a few minutes.)

**11.** When prompted, label and insert a blank 3.5-inch floppy disk into drive A:. Setup formats and makes this disk into your Emergency Repair Disk. Click OK to continue. (This takes a couple of minutes.)

**12.** Windows NT Setup displays a window indicating that Windows NT 4.0 is successfully installed. Remove your newly created Emergency Repair Disk from drive A: (and save it for future use). Also remove the compact disc from your CD-ROM drive. Then click Restart Computer to reboot and start Windows NT Server. The setup is complete.

At the completion of Labs 2.1 and 2.2, both Windows NT Workstation and Windows NT Server are installed on your computer, and your computer is configured to dual boot between the two operating systems.

Workstation
Server
Enterprise

# Configuring Disks

# About Chapter 3

This chapter explores the basics of configuring a computer's hard disk(s) in a Windows NT environment.

It begins with a discussion of the various file systems that Windows NT supports, namely, FAT and NTFS. The strengths, limitations, and special features of these two file systems are explained. Converting from FAT to NTFS is also covered.

Chapter 3 then presents an in-depth explanation of working with partitions. Disk Administrator, a Windows NT tool used to create and format partitions, is introduced. Then various disk partitioning schemes are explored and compared, including: disk mirroring, stripe sets, stripe sets with parity, and volume sets.

Finally, Chapter 3 provides valuable information on how to recover from a single or multiple disk failure. Updating the Emergency Repair Disk is also covered.

This chapter includes two hands-on labs. In the first lab you use Disk Administrator to manage partitions on your computer's hard disk. In the second you get an opportunity to update your own Emergency Repair Disk.

No matter which of the three Windows NT 4.0 Microsoft Certified Professional exams you're preparing for, you'll want to read this chapter. The information in this chapter covers several objectives listed in the Planning, Installation and Configuration, and Troubleshooting sections in these exams' objectives.

# FILE SYSTEMS

Before you attempt to configure disks in a Windows NT environment, you should have a clear understanding of the different file systems that NT supports. Windows NT 4.0 supports three file systems: the *file allocation table* (FAT) *file system,* the *Windows NT file system* (NTFS), and the *Compact Disc Filing System* (CDFS). Windows NT 4.0 does *not* support the *high performance file system* (HPFS), although earlier versions of NT did. (If you are upgrading from an earlier version of Windows NT that used HPFS, you must convert to NTFS before performing the upgrade.) Table 3-1 shows which file systems are supported by various operating systems.

| **TABLE 3-1** File System Support by Operating System | |
| --- | --- |
| *Operating System* | *File Systems Supported* |
| Windows NT 4.0 | FAT, NTFS, CDFS |
| Windows NT 3.51 (and earlier versions) | FAT, NTFS, CDFS, HPFS |
| Windows 95 | FAT, CDFS |
| Windows 3x and 3.1x | FAT, CDFS |
| OS/2 | FAT, CDFS, HPFS |
| MS-DOS | FAT, CDFS |

# FAT

The *file allocation table* (FAT) *file system* used on Windows NT is a modified version of the FAT file system used by MS-DOS. FAT is the only hard disk file system supported by Windows 3.*x*, Windows 3.1*x*, Windows 95, and MS-DOS. So, if you want to configure a Windows NT computer to dual boot between Windows NT and Windows 3.1*x*, Windows 95, or MS-DOS, your computer's first partition must use the FAT file system.

Don't confuse the FAT file system with the FAT32 file system. Windows NT does not support the FAT32 file system (an enhanced rendition of FAT) that is supported on the original equipment manufacturer (OEM) version of Windows 95 that includes Service Pack 2.

 **Service Pack 2 for Windows 95 is only available on the OEM version of Windows 95, not on the retail version.**

Now it's time to familiarize yourself with the characteristics and features of the FAT file system, including security, naming conventions, speed of access to files, and partition size.

## Security

The FAT file system does *not* support file and folder security in Windows NT. Because file and folder security is not supported on a FAT partition, any user who is logged on locally to a computer has full control of all of the files and folders located in the FAT partition(s) on that computer. This applies only to local access.

However, you can use share permissions to control users' access to shared folders over the network. Share permissions affect only the access of files and folders over the network, not when someone is logged on locally. So, if you need local file and folder security, you should use an NTFS partition instead of a FAT partition.

## Naming conventions

The FAT file system, as used by Windows NT, supports the use of long filenames. This file system permits the full path to a file (including the filename) to be up to 255 characters long.

Filenames can contain any character *except "/ \ [ ] : ; | = , ^ * ?*, and should begin with an alphanumeric character. Filenames can contain spaces and multiple periods, and the characters after the last period are considered the filename extension.

The FAT file system preserves upper- and lowercase in filenames, but filenames are not case-sensitive. Because of this, I can request the file ALAN.DOC by typing **Alan.doc**, **ALAN.DOC**, or **alan.doc**, and Windows NT always retrieves ALAN.DOC.

## Speed of access to files

Access speed to files on a FAT partition is dependent on many factors, including file type, file size, partition size, number of files in a folder, and fragmentation.

Windows NT accesses files on FAT partitions smaller than 500MB faster than it accesses files on other similar-sized file system partitions discussed here. Additionally, NT accesses certain types of files on FAT partitions more efficiently than on partitions formatted with other file systems.

On very large partitions, however, or when there is a large number of files in a folder, Windows NT accesses files on NTFS partitions much faster than it accesses files on a FAT partition of similar size.

Windows NT usually accesses files on a highly fragmented FAT partition slower than it accesses files on an NTFS partition of similar size.

## Partition size

The maximum size of a FAT partition is 4GB. The maximum size of a file in a FAT partition is 4GB.

The FAT file system does *not* support file compression.

# NTFS

The *Windows NT file system* (NTFS) is the most powerful file system supported by Windows NT. Only Windows NT (both Windows NT Workstation and Windows NT Server) supports NTFS—no other operating systems currently support this file system.

When it comes to security, naming conventions, speed of access to files, and partition size, NTFS has its own unique characteristics. Additionally, NTFS has some features not supported by the FAT file system.

## Security

NTFS provides file and folder security for both local and remote users on a network. NTFS is the only file system discussed here that permits the assigning of permissions to individual files and folders.

So how does NTFS security actually work? NTFS security controls access to files on an NTFS partition by utilizing the user's *security identifier* (SID) to determine which files that user can access. (Each file and folder on an NTFS partition has an *access control list* [ACL] associated with it. The ACL is a list that contains user and group SIDs, with the associated privileges of each user and group.)

 concept link    **NTFS and share security are covered in depth in Chapter 12.**

 note    **In addition to the security provided by NTFS, remember that because Windows NT requires a user to log on before accessing files, NT's security is greater than operating systems that don't require the user to log on.**

## Naming conventions

Like the FAT file system, NTFS supports the use of long filenames. Names of files and folders (including extensions) can be up to 255 characters long.

You can use most characters in NTFS file and folder names. However, the characters *? " / \ < > * | :* can't be used.

NTFS preserves upper- and lowercase in filenames. Filenames are not case-sensitive (except when used by a POSIX application). For example, a Win32 application does not distinguish between `Money.DOC`, `MONEY.DOC`, and `money.doc`—it treats all three names as though they were the same file.

The POSIX subsystem, however, is case-sensitive with respect to filenames, because it does not translate a request for a file into all uppercase letters as the Win32 and other subsystems do. A POSIX application treats the filenames in the previous paragraph as though they were three separate files: `Money.DOC`, `MONEY.DOC`, and `money.doc`. You must use a POSIX application if you want to access these three different files — if you attempt to access `Money.DOC` with a Win32 application (no matter how you type the filename) you will normally always retrieve the `MONEY.DOC` file because the Win32 Subsystem translates file requests into all uppercase letters.

### Speed of access to files

NTFS usually provides faster access to files stored on a large partition that contains many files than the FAT file system. NTFS is able to access files in this situation faster than the FAT file system because NTFS uses an enhanced binary tree to locate files. A binary tree search is a faster mechanism for searching through a large number of filenames than the sequential read mechanism used on FAT partitions.

### Partition size

The maximum theoretical size of an NTFS partition is 16 exabytes (an *exabyte* is one billion billion bytes, or a giga-gigabyte). However, when you actually implement NTFS on current standard industry hardware, there is a functional limitation of 2 terabytes.

### Additional features not supported by the FAT file system

NTFS has several other unique attributes and features that are not found in, nor supported by, the FAT file system.

- NTFS supports a compression attribute for each file. You can choose which files to compress and which ones to leave uncompressed. The compression algorithm NTFS uses is similar to the one used by Drivespace in MS-DOS. Using compression provides an approximately 40 to 50 percent increase in hard disk space.

 **Compression can cause some performance degradation on partitions with substantial write activity. Additionally, accessing uncompressed files is faster than accessing compressed files.**

- NTFS is a highly reliable, recoverable file system. It is not necessary to periodically run `Chkdsk.exe` on an NTFS partition.

- Using NTFS greatly reduces fragmentation on partitions. However, files can still become fragmented when their size is increased. Windows NT does not include an NTFS defragmentation utility, but there are several third-party utilities available.

- NTFS maintains a recycle bin for each user.

web links  **If you ever need an NTFS defragmentation utility, a list of third-party products can be found on the Web at** `www.microsoft.com\InfoSource`.

A couple of final facts on NTFS: You can't use NTFS to format floppy disks, and NTFS does not permit you to change media in a removable media drive (such as a Zip drive) without rebooting. (The FAT file system does support changing media without rebooting.)

## CDFS

The *Compact Disc Filing System* (CDFS) supports access to compact discs. It is only used on CD-ROM devices that read and/or write compact discs.

## Converting from FAT to NTFS

In Windows NT you can format a new partition with either FAT or NTFS. But what do you do when you want to change the file system on an existing partition?

You can change an existing FAT partition, and retain the data on it, into an NTFS partition by using `Convert.exe`. This is a fairly simple procedure.

However, it is a one-way process—there is no way to convert an NTFS partition into a FAT partition without first backing up, reformatting the disk, and restoring the data.

To convert a FAT partition into an NTFS partition, use the following syntax:

```
CONVERT drive: /FS:NTFS [/V]
```

The following is an explanation of syntax:

- *Drive*: This specifies the letter of the drive to convert to NTFS.

- /FS:NTFS: This indicates that the file system should be converted to NTFS. This is an outdated switch, because NTFS is the only file system that you can use Convert.exe to switch to in Windows NT 4.0; but its use, in terms of command syntax, is still required.

- /V: This specifies that Convert.exe will run in verbose mode.

    For example, to convert drive D: from FAT to NTFS, use the following command line: **CONVERT D: /FS:NTFS**

 **To successfully use the** Convert.exe **command,** Convert.exe **must be the** *only* **application that accesses the drive you want to change during the conversion process. If Windows NT Explorer accesses the drive you are trying to convert, if you are trying to convert the boot partition, or if your active command prompt has the drive you are trying to convert as its current drive, Windows NT will display an error message stating that** Convert.exe **can't gain exclusive access to the drive.**

**If you can't gain exclusive access to a drive, run** Convert.exe **as shown in the example. The file system conversion will occur when you restart your computer.**

# WORKING WITH PARTITIONS

Before you can format a hard disk with a file system such as FAT or NTFS, you must mark the disk to identify which parts of it will contain a file system (or systems). This is called *partitioning*. A hard disk can be separated into a maximum of four partitions, or one partition can occupy all of the space on a disk.

You may recall that back in Chapter 2, when you installed Windows NT 4.0, you were presented with the option to create a partition on your computer's hard disk. Once Windows NT is installed, the primary tool for creating, formatting, and managing various types of partitions is Disk Administrator. The latter part of this chapter covers how to use Disk Administrator to perform specific tasks on partitions. But first, it's important that you understand the basic types of partitions.

# Partition Types

Windows NT supports two types of partitions: primary and extended. Both types of partitions can coexist on the same hard disk. A disk can have more than one primary partition, but it can have only one extended partition.

## *Primary partitions*

A *primary partition* can occupy all of the space on a disk, or any portion of it. A hard disk can have up to four partitions, and all four can be primary partitions. A primary partition can be formatted as a single logical drive (but not as multiple logical drives).

Any primary partition on the first hard disk in the computer can be designated as the active partition. The active partition is significant because when the computer boots, it attempts to load the operating system from the active primary partition on the first hard disk in the computer.

The Windows NT 4.0 system partition must be located on the active primary partition on the first hard disk in a computer.

 concept link

**Remember the system partition and the boot partition? If your memory needs refreshing, take a peek at Chapter 2, in the "Hard Disk Partition Information" section of the Preinstallation Checklist.**

## *Extended partitions*

There can be only one *extended partition* on a disk. An extended partition can't be marked active, and it can't be used for the system partition of a computer. The Windows NT boot partition, however, can be located on an extended partition.

An extended partition can be formatted as one or more logical drives, where each partition is assigned a different drive letter. Logical drives can be formatted with either FAT or NTFS. You can have one logical drive formatted with FAT, and another logical drive in the same extended partition formatted with NTFS.

Extended partitions are convenient for breaking up a physical disk into more than four logical drives.

# Using Disk Administrator

Windows NT includes a useful tool to manage disks after NT has been installed: Disk Administrator. Disk Administrator can help you create, format, and otherwise manage various types of partitions.

It's good practice to use Disk Administrator only during times when no one else is accessing the server. Some of Disk Administrator's functions take a significant amount of time to complete, and some require the server to be rebooted. This means that service to clients during these times can be seriously slowed or interrupted. Plan to perform disk management tasks during nonbusiness hours whenever possible, just as you would other administration tasks that require the server to be down.

There are two versions of Disk Administrator: the version that ships with Windows NT Workstation, and the version that ships with Windows NT Server. The only difference between the two is the Windows NT Workstation version does not have the Fault Tolerance menu found on the version that ships with Windows NT Server. (Actually, the tool is identical on both operating systems, but Disk Administrator always checks the Registry to determine which NT operating system is being used, and then displays the appropriate menu.)

Figure 3-1 shows a screen shot of the main dialog box of the Windows NT Workstation version of Disk Administrator, and Figure 3-2 shows a screen shot of the main dialog box of the Windows NT Server version of Disk Administrator. Note the Fault Tolerance menu on the NT Server version of the dialog box, which is missing from the dialog box shown for the NT Workstation version.

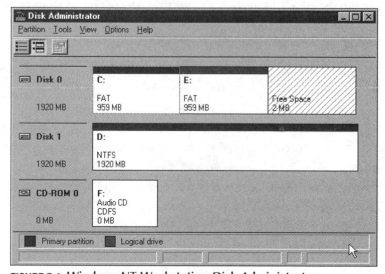

**FIGURE 3-1** Windows NT Workstation Disk Administrator

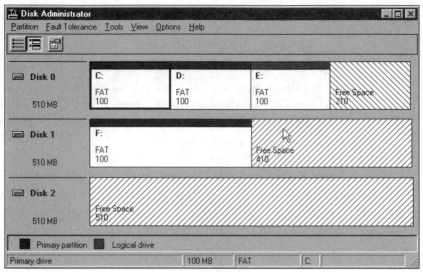

**FIGURE 3-2** Windows NT Server Disk Administrator

The next several sections explain how you can use Disk Administrator to create partitions, format partitions, and establish various disk partitioning schemes, including disk mirroring, stripe sets, stripe sets with parity, and volume sets.

## Creating partitions

You can use Disk Administrator to create partitions on your computer's hard disk.

I've always wished that some text or course would have given me more precise information and detailed instructions on working with Disk Administrator. It's for this reason that I've presented the instructions to perform several disk and partition management tasks in the rest of this chapter in a step-by-step format.

But this doesn't mean I want you to sit down at your computer and create some partitions right now. Even though the descriptions of how to perform these tasks are presented in a step-by-step format, they're meant to be informational — not actual lab exercises. (You can sink your teeth into Lab 3.3: "Managing Partitions" at the end of this chapter soon enough.) What I really have in mind is for you to read through these steps and refer to them when you have a need to do these various disk management procedures.

Here's a look at the basic steps to create and format a primary partition, and the steps to create an extended partition.

**Creating and formatting a primary partition**   In order to create a primary partition on a hard disk, you must have an area of free space on the hard disk.

**The steps in the various how-to sections in the rest of this chapter are meant to be informational, not a lab exercise. (Lab 3.3: "Managing Partitions" is found at the end of this chapter.) If you decide to create a partition on your computer, don't delete or reformat any partition that contains data you don't want to lose. And remember, back up all important data and programs *before* you make any changes to your computer's disk configuration.**

**The steps I've listed to create a primary partition and an extended partition should work as shown about 90 percent of the time. Don't be disconcerted, though, if an extra dialog box or two is displayed. Any number of hardware or system configuration differences can cause a minor deviation from the steps listed. If a different or extra dialog box is displayed, just provide the appropriate response and continue.**

**TO CREATE A PARTITION, FOLLOW THESE STEPS:**

**1.** Start Disk Administrator. (Select Start ⇒ Programs ⇒ Administrative Tools (Common) ⇒ Disk Administrator.)

**2.** If this is the first time you have run Disk Administrator since installing NT, a dialog box appears. If this box appears, click OK to update the system configuration.

**3.** Click a diagonally striped area of the Disk Administrator dialog box marked Free Space.

**4.** Select Partition ⇒ Create.

**5.** Depending on the partitions that already exist on your computer's hard disk, a Confirm dialog box may appear stating that "This operation will result in a disk whose partition scheme may not be compatible with MS-DOS." Click Yes if you want to continue.

**6.** The Create Primary Partition dialog box appears. In the "Create partition of size" text box, enter the size, in MB, that you want the new partition to be. Click OK. The Disk Administrator main dialog box reappears, and the new partition is displayed in a boxed area with the next available drive letter. (If you have several network drives connected, the drive letter might be H:, even though the next local drive letter would be D:. Don't worry, you can fix this later.) The lettering in the box representing the new partition is gray rather than black like all the other partitions shown.

**7.** To complete the partition creation process, select Partition⇒Commit Changes Now.

**8.** Click Yes in the Confirm dialog box to save the changes to your disk.

**9.** Click OK in the Disk Administrator dialog box. This causes the Disk Administrator main dialog box to reappear, and your newly created partition appears in full color with black lettering.

After you've created a partition, you'll usually want to format it.

**TO FORMAT THE PARTITION YOU JUST CREATED, FOLLOW THESE STEPS:**

**1.** Start Disk Administrator (if the Disk Administrator main dialog box is not already displayed).

**2.** Click in the boxed area representing the new partition, and then select Tools⇒Format.

**3.** The Format dialog box (displayed in Figure 3-3) appears. Configure the characteristics you want this partition to have, including the file system type and volume label. (See the detailed discussion following these steps on the various options that are configured in this dialog box.)

**4.** When you are finished, click the Start button. A warning message appears, reminding you that formatting will erase all data on your disk. Only click OK if you want to continue.

**5.** Click OK in the Formatting dialog box that appears after the formatting is complete. Click Close when the Format dialog box reappears.

**6.** The Disk Administrator main dialog box reappears. A file system type (for example FAT, NTFS, and the like) now appears in the boxed area representing your newly created and formatted partition, directly beneath the drive letter of the new partition.

When you format a partition, you have the option to specify several of its characteristics. Figure 3-3 shows a screen shot of the Format dialog box within Disk Administrator.

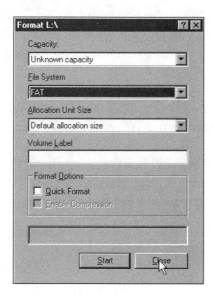

**FIGURE 3-3** Formatting a partition

As Figure 3-3 shows, there are several options in the Format dialog box to be configured:

o **Capacity:** This option displays "Unknown capacity" when you format a new partition. (When you format an existing partition, it displays the size of the partition.) This is an informational item only—no configuration is allowed.

o **File System:** The file system choices available are FAT or NTFS.

o **Allocation Unit Size:** Allocation Unit Size refers to the sector size Disk Administrator uses when it formats a partition. If you chose NTFS as the file system type, you can select the sector size to be used during formatting. Sector sizes in this menu vary from 512KB to 4,096KB.

 note **Although the interface actually refers to the Allocation Unit Size measurements as *bytes*, it means KB.**

**If you want to use a sector size larger than 4,096KB, you must format the partition from the command line using the** Format.exe **command. The** Format.exe **command supports sector sizes up to**

64MB for NTFS partitions. You can type **format** /? **at the command prompt for a complete list of the switches that can be used with the** Format.exe **command. File compression is** *not* **supported when using sector sizes larger than 4,096KB.**

**If you choose FAT as the file system type, you can't set the Allocation Unit Size. You must accept the default Allocation Unit Size, which varies depending on the size of the partition being formatted.**

concept link

**For additional information on Allocation Unit Size, as well as detailed file system information, see Chapter 17 of the** *Microsoft Windows NT Workstation Resource Kit for version 4.0*, **published by Microsoft Press.**

o **Volume Label:** This option permits you to give your partition a name. Type in the text you want to use for the volume label. Configuring this item is optional—an entry is not required in this box.

o **Format Options:**

   o Selecting the *Quick Format* option instructs NT to write only the necessary data to the disk to support a volume, and not to check for bad sectors during formatting.

   o The *Enable Compression* option is only available if you choose NTFS as the file system. (If you choose FAT as the file system, this check box is grayed out.) Selecting this option causes all files and folders placed in this partition to be compressed by default. You can also set this attribute later by using Windows NT Explorer.

**Creating an extended partition**    This section discusses how you can use Disk Administrator to create an extended partition.

**TO USE DISK ADMINISTRATOR (ON EITHER WINDOWS NT WORKSTATION OR WINDOWS NT SERVER) TO CREATE AN EXTENDED PARTITION, FOLLOW THESE STEPS:**

**1.** Start Disk Administrator.

**2.** Click a diagonally striped, boxed area of the Disk Administrator dialog box marked Free Space.

**3.** Select Partition ⇒ Create Extended.

4. The Create Extended Partition dialog box appears. In the "Create partition of size" text box, enter the size, in MB, that you want the extended partition to be. Click OK.

5. Disk Administrator's main dialog box reappears. Notice that the area of free space is still marked Free Space, but the diagonal lines now run from top left to bottom right, which indicate an extended partition. (Free space that is not an extended partition is indicated by diagonal lines that run from top right to bottom left.) Select Partition ⇒ Commit Changes Now.

6. In the Confirm dialog box, click Yes to save the changes to disk. Then click OK to acknowledge that the disks were updated successfully. The Disk Administrator main dialog box reappears.

7. To create a logical drive(s) for this extended partition, select Partition ⇒ Create.

8. When the Create Logical Drive dialog box appears, enter the size you want the drive to be, in MB, in the "Create logical drive of size" text box. Click OK.

9. The Disk Administrator main dialog box reappears. Notice that a logical drive box is displayed at the bottom of this dialog box. Select Partition ⇒ Commit Changes Now.

10. Click Yes in the Confirm dialog box to save the changes to disk. A dialog box appears indicating that the disks were updated successfully, and reminding you to update your Emergency Repair Disk. Click OK. The Disk Administrator main dialog box reappears. The procedure is complete.

# Disk Mirroring

*Disk mirroring* is a fault tolerance method that enables operations to continue when *one* hard disk fails. (Later in this chapter you'll learn how to recover from a single disk failure.)

The term disk mirroring is somewhat of a misnomer. It should be called partition mirroring. Any partition can be mirrored, including the system partition and the boot partition. In disk mirroring, Disk Administrator makes an exact replica of the partition being mirrored on a *separate* hard disk. You can't make a replica of a partition on the same physical disk — the mirror image must be produced on a different hard disk.

Disk mirroring is fairly expensive, as fault tolerance methods go, because twice the normal amount of disk space is required. However, you get a high level of fault tolerance for your money. Disk mirroring is used in situations where the integrity of data is more important than minimizing costs. For example, a financial institution might decide that disk mirroring is cost-effective for their company because the extra safety provided by disk mirroring outweighs the cost of additional disk space.

Disk mirroring does not provide fault tolerance in the event of multiple disk failure, and it does not guarantee continued operations if a server goes down. Disk mirroring is also known as RAID level 1. (RAID stands for *Redundant Array of Inexpensive Disks*.)

Disk mirroring is supported by Windows NT Server, but *not* by Windows NT Workstation.

**TO CREATE A MIRROR SET, FOLLOW THESE STEPS:**

**1.** Start Disk Administrator, and then select (click) the partition you want to mirror. If you don't have any partitions on your hard disk, or you want to create a new partition to mirror, follow the instructions in the "Creating and formatting a primary partition" section earlier in this chapter to create and format a partition. Then do the steps listed here.

**2.** Press and hold Ctrl while you click an area of free space on a different hard disk that is at least as large as the partition you want to mirror.

**3.** Select Fault Tolerance ⇒ Establish Mirror. Figure 3-4 displays the Fault Tolerance menu of the Disk Administrator dialog box. Note that Establish Mirror has been selected and highlighted.

**4.** Disk activity occurs and may continue for quite a while, depending on the size of the partition to be mirrored and the amount of data on that partition. Finally, as Figure 3-5 shows, Disk Administrator displays its main dialog box. Notice that there are now two drives of the same size with the same drive letter, located on different hard disks. The mirrored partitions are highlighted in the color that corresponds to the mirror set box at the bottom of the dialog box. A mirror set has been established.

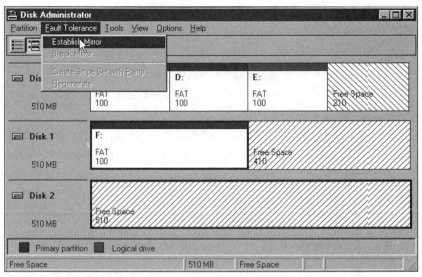

**FIGURE 3-4** Establishing a mirror set

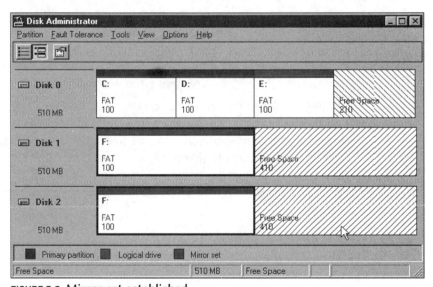

**FIGURE 3-5** Mirror set established

Now that a mirror set is established, a fault tolerance boot disk should be created in case the original disk in the mirror set (the disk that was mirrored) fails.

### Creating a fault tolerance boot disk

A *fault tolerance boot disk* is a floppy disk that enables you to boot your computer in the event that one of the disks in your computer's mirror set fails. The fault tolerance boot disk should be created *before* the disk failure occurs.

If the original disk in a mirror set fails, and if that disk contains the original boot partition, you will not be able to reboot your computer because the Boot.ini file will be pointing at the failed hard disk and partition.

When this happens, you need to use a fault tolerance boot disk that points at the mirrored disk and partition that are still functional to boot your computer.

---

**TO CREATE A FAULT TOLERANCE BOOT DISK, FOLLOW THESE STEPS:**

**1.** Format a 3.5-inch floppy disk by using the Format menu from Windows NT Explorer. This *must* be done in Windows NT, not in Windows 95.

**2.** Copy the ntldr, Ntdetect.com, and Boot.ini files to the floppy disk. Also copy Bootsect.dos to the floppy disk if your computer is configured to dual boot, and copy Ntbootdd.sys to the floppy disk if this file exists in the root of your computer's system partition. (An Ntbootdd.sys file will exist in your system partition only if you have entries in your Boot.ini file that begin with scsi.)

**3.** Edit the Boot.ini file on the floppy disk (not the Boot.ini file on your hard drive) to point at the mirrored disk and partition that still function, instead of at the disk and partition that failed. (The next section of this chapter discusses how to edit the Boot.ini file.)

---

### Editing the Boot.ini file

The Boot.ini file is a read-only file in the root of the active partition on the first hard disk in the computer.

Before you can edit the Boot.ini file, you must remove its read-only attribute.

 caution **Remember, you are editing the** Boot.ini **file that has been copied to a floppy disk, not the** Boot.ini **file on your hard drive.**

You can use Windows NT Explorer to deselect this attribute (which is found in the General tab of the Boot.ini Properties dialog box). After you remove the read-only attribute, you can use any text editor, such as Notepad, to edit the Boot.ini file.

However, before you go on to edit this file, you might want to take a closer look at it to understand its structure and syntax. I've reproduced below a sample Boot.ini file.

**LISTING 3-1** Sample Boot.ini file

```
[boot loader]
timeout=30
default=multi(0)disk(0)rdisk(1)partition(1)\WINNT
[operating systems]
multi(0)disk(0)rdisk(1)partition(1)\WINNT="Windows NT
    Workstation Version 4.00"
multi(0)disk(0)rdisk(1)partition(1)\WINNT="Windows NT
    Workstation Version 4.00 [VGA mode]" /basevideo /sos
C:\="Microsoft Windows"
```

Note that there are two sections to the Boot.ini file: [boot loader] and [operating systems].

The first section, [boot loader], contains two entries. The first entry, timeout, determines how long, in seconds, the boot loader screen (or boot menu) is displayed when the computer boots. The default timeout is thirty seconds. The second entry, default, specifies which operating system loads if no selection is made within the timeout period.

The second section of the Boot.ini file, [operating systems], first lists entries consisting of ARC *(Advanced RISC Computing)* pathnames to various operating systems. Only Windows NT uses ARC pathnames in the Boot.ini file to indicate which partition, physical disk, and folder contains the files used to start the operating system. Next, the drive letter and path to any other operating systems are listed. The operating system named at the end of each operating systems entry, after the = sign (whether it is an ARC pathname entry or not), is displayed in the boot loader screen.

There are two types of ARC pathname entries: multi and scsi. The terms *multi* and *SCSI* refer to the type of hard disk that is listed in the ARC pathname.

note ▮ **The term *scsi* is normally presented in lowercase letters when it is used to indicate a type of file entry. It is normally presented in upper-case letters when it is used to refer to a disk, adapter, or controller.**

All hard disks that can be detected by the computer's BIOS, or by the BIOS on a SCSI adapter, are referred to as *multi*. All hard disks connected to SCSI adapters that do not have their BIOS enabled are referred to as *SCSI*. SCSI disks require a device driver to be loaded before the operating system can access the disk. The Windows NT installation program copies the device driver for a SCSI adapter to the root of the system partition, and renames the file as `Ntbootdd.sys`.

The syntax of operating systems entries that begin with multi is as follows:
`multi(W)disk(X)rdisk(Y)partition(Z)\path`

- **W** is the ordinal number of the adapter. It should always be zero.
- **X** is not used for multi. It is always zero.
- **Y** is the ordinal for the hard disk on the controller. It is always 0 or 1 for disks connected to the primary controller, including SCSI adapters that have their BIOS enabled. It is 0, 1, 2, or 3 on dual channel EIDE controllers.
- **Z** is the partition number. The range of Z is usually 1–4.

The syntax of operating system entries that begin with scsi is as follows:
`scsi(W)disk(X)rdisk(Y)partition(Z)\path`

- **W** is the ordinal number of the adapter.
- **X** is the SCSI ID of the disk.
- **Y** is the logical unit number (LUN) of the disk. It is usually zero.
- **Z** is the partition number. The range of Z is usually 1–4.

Operating systems entries that begin with scsi are typically used in three types of situations:

- When the hard disk containing the system partition is on a SCSI adapter that does *not* have its BIOS enabled
- When the hard disk containing the system partition is on a SCSI adapter *and* has an SCSI ID greater than one
- When the hard disk containing the system partition is on a SCSI adapter *and* there is an IDE or EIDE controller in the system

Now that you understand the structure of the `Boot.ini` file, and the types of entries and syntax used in this file, you're ready to edit it.

Suppose that Figure 3-6 represents a computer that has a newly created mirror set (Disk 1 and Disk 2). The boot partition for this computer is located on the second disk (Disk 1), and uses the drive letter F:. The system partition of this computer (which contains the `ntldr`, `Ntdetect.com`, `Boot.ini`, and `Bootsect.dos` files) is located on the first disk (Disk 0), and uses the drive letter C:. The computer in this example uses a dual-channel EIDE controller.

You want to create a fault tolerance boot disk so you can reboot the computer in the event that Disk 1 fails. You follow the steps outlined in the "Creating a fault tolerance boot disk" section up to the point where you edit the `Boot.ini` file on the floppy disk. The `Boot.ini` file looks like this:

**LISTING 3-2** `Boot.ini` file

```
[boot loader]
timeout=30
default=multi(0)disk(0)rdisk(1)partition(1)\WINNT
[operating systems]
multi(0)disk(0)rdisk(1)partition(1)\WINNT="Windows NT
    Workstation Version 4.00"
multi(0)disk(0)rdisk(1)partition(1)\WINNT="Windows NT
    Workstation Version 4.00 [VGA mode]" /basevideo /sos
C:\="Microsoft Windows"
```

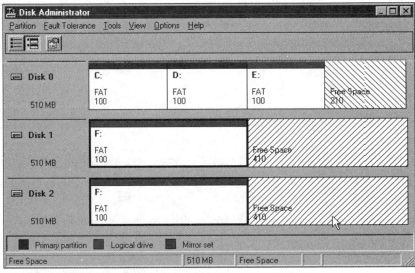

**FIGURE 3-6** New mirror set

In this situation, you must edit the `Boot.ini` file so it points to Disk 2. (The `Boot.ini` file must point to Disk 2 because if Disk 1 fails, Disk 2 will be the only disk in the mirror set that still works.) You remove the `Boot.ini` file's read-only attribute and use a text editor, such as Notepad, to edit the file. The edited version of the `Boot.ini` file on your newly created fault tolerance boot disk is presented here.

**LISTING 3-3** `Boot.ini` file edited for fault tolerance boot disk

```
[boot loader]
timeout=30
default=multi(0)disk(0)rdisk(2)partition(1)\WINNT
[operating systems]
multi(0)disk(0)rdisk(2)partition(1)\WINNT="Windows NT
    Workstation Version 4.00"
multi(0)disk(0)rdisk(2)partition(1)\WINNT="Windows NT
    Workstation Version 4.00 [VGA mode]" /basevideo /sos
C:\="Microsoft Windows"
```

Notice that the ARC pathnames in the operating systems section now point to Disk 2 instead of Disk 1.

Finally, there are several switches you can add at the end of an operating systems entry in the `Boot.ini` file. Table 3-2 lists and describes these switches.

 **note** **These switches are not typically used when creating a fault tolerance boot disk. However, because they are used frequently during troubleshooting, and because this is the only section of this book that addresses the `Boot.ini` file in detail, I've covered the switches here for completeness.**

**TABLE 3-2** BOOT.INI FILE SWITCHES

| SWITCH | DESCRIPTION |
| --- | --- |
| /BASEVIDEO | This switch causes the computer to use the standard VGA driver when it starts, and is useful in troubleshooting video driver problems. |
| /BAUDRATE=nnnn | This switch specifies the baud rate used during debugging, and includes all of the functionality of the /DEBUG switch. |
| /CRASHDEBUG | This switch forces the debugger to load in an inactive state until an error occurs. |

| SWITCH | DESCRIPTION |
|---|---|
| /DEBUG | This switch causes the debugger to be loaded. It can be activated by another computer connected to this computer by a modem or null-modem cable. |
| /DEBUGPORT=comx | This switch specifies which COM port the debugger uses, and includes all of the functionality of the /DEBUG switch. |
| /MAXMEM:n | This switch specifies the maximum amount of memory that Windows NT can use. It is useful for troubleshooting memory problems. |
| /NODEBUG | This switch specifies that the debugger will not run, and that no debugging information will be generated. |
| /NOSERIALMICE= COMx \| COMx,y,z...\| | This specifies that the indicated serial port will not be tested for the presence of a mouse. Use this switch if you have an *uninterruptible power supply* (UPS) or some other device connected to a serial port. |
| /SOS | This switch provides a verbose listing of each device driver as it is loaded during the boot sequence. It is useful for troubleshooting device drivers. |

# Stripe Sets

In a *stripe set*, which is made up of two to thirty-two hard disks, data is stored, a block at a time, evenly and sequentially among all of the disks in the set. Stripe sets are sometimes referred to as disk striping. *Disk striping* alludes to the process wherein a file is written, or striped, one block at a time; first to one disk, then to the next disk, and then to the next disk, and so on, until all of the data has been evenly distributed among all of the disks.

 **Neither the boot nor the system partition can be on a stripe set.**

A stripe set is accessed by using a single drive letter, as if all of its disks were combined into a single drive. A stripe set is created from identical amounts of free space on each of the disks that belong to the set.

Stripe sets provide faster disk access than volume sets or large individual hard disks because the stripe sets store a single file across multiple disks. The various pieces of the file can be read nearly simultaneously from the multiple disks, thus increasing performance. Access speed is the primary advantage and common reason for using a stripe set. The tradeoff or downside to using a stripe set is that the potential disk failure rate is increased because there are more possible points of failure when a file is accessed across several disks.

Stripe sets have no additional cost associated with them because they use the same amount of disk space in which that data would normally be stored. However, stripe sets do not provide any fault tolerance. If one partition or disk in a stripe set fails, all data on the stripe set is lost.

A stripe set (or disk striping) is also known as RAID level 0.

Windows NT Server and Windows NT Workstation both support stripe sets.

---

**TO CREATE A STRIPE SET, FOLLOW THESE STEPS:**

**1.** Start Disk Administrator.

**2.** Click an area of free space on one of your computer's hard disks.

**3.** Press and hold Ctrl while you click one or more additional areas of free space on other hard disks. You can't select more than one area of free space per physical disk.

**4.** Select Partition ⇒ Create Stripe Set.

**5.** The Create Stripe Set dialog box is displayed, as shown in Figure 3-7. Note that it shows the minimum and maximum amount of total space that can be used for the stripe set. The maximum total size is the amount of free space from the smallest area of free space you selected, multiplied by the number of disks you selected. (Remember, in stripe sets, the size of the free space areas on the disks used in the set are identical.) You can either accept this number or type in a smaller value in the "Create stripe set of total size" text box. Click OK to create the stripe set.

**6.** The Disk Administrator main dialog box reappears. Select Partition ⇒ Commit Changes Now. Click Yes to save the changes to disk. Then click OK to acknowledge that the disks were updated successfully.

**7.** The Disk Administrator main dialog box reappears. Figure 3-8 shows the stripe set at this point. Note that the stripe set is created and uses the drive letter H: on Disks 1, 2, and 3, but it still needs to be formatted.

**8.** Follow the directions in the "Creating and formatting a primary partition" section earlier in this chapter to format the stripe set. The stripe set is now complete.

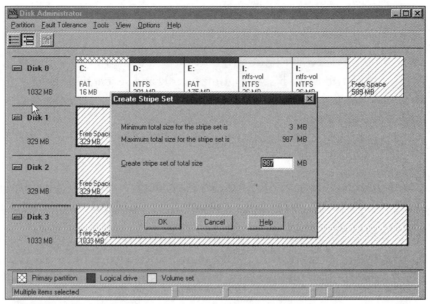

**FIGURE 3-7** Creating a stripe set

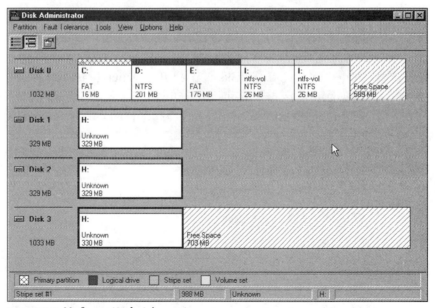

**FIGURE 3-8** Unformatted stripe set

## Stripe Sets with Parity

A *stripe set with parity* is similar to a stripe set, but it provides a degree of fault tolerance which the stripe set cannot. In a stripe set with parity, data is not only distributed a block at a time, evenly and sequentially among all the disks in the set, but parity information is also written across all of the disks in the set.

 **Neither the boot nor the system partition can be on a stripe set with parity.**

A stripe set with parity is made up of three to thirty-two hard disks. Like stripe sets, stripe sets with parity are created from identical amounts of free space on each disk that belongs to the set.

 **Striping with parity, in my experience, is the most common method of fault tolerance. It is less costly than disk mirroring (because data is not replicated on another disk), is faster than disk mirroring, and provides a modest level of data safety.**

A stripe set with parity provides the same read performance as a stripe set, but its write performance is a little slower.

If a single disk in a stripe set with parity fails, the parity information contained in the other disks is used to regenerate the data from the failed disk. (Recovering from a single disk failure in a stripe set with parity is discussed later in this chapter.) You cannot recover your data in a stripe set with parity if more than one disk fails.

Stripe sets with parity (sometimes called *striping with parity*) are also known as RAID level 5.

Stripe sets with parity are supported by Windows NT Server, but not by Windows NT Workstation.

**TO CREATE A STRIPE SET WITH PARITY, FOLLOW THESE STEPS:**

**1.** Start Disk Administrator.

**2.** Click an area of free space on one of your computer's hard disks.

**3.** Press and hold Ctrl while you click two or more additional areas of free space on other hard disks. You can't select more than one area of free space per physical disk.

4. Select Fault Tolerance ⇒ Create Stripe Set with Parity.

5. The Create Stripe Set with Parity dialog box is displayed showing the minimum and maximum amount of space that can be used for the stripe set. The maximum amount is the amount of free space from the smallest area of free space you selected, multiplied by the number of disks you selected. You can either accept this number or type in a smaller value in the "Create stripe set of total size" text box. Click OK to create the stripe set with parity.

6. The Disk Administrator main dialog box reappears. Select Partition ⇒ Commit Changes Now. Click Yes to save the changes to disk. Then click OK to acknowledge that the disks were updated successfully. At this point, the stripe set with parity is created, but still needs to be formatted.

7. To format the stripe set with parity, follow the directions presented earlier in this chapter in the "Creating and formatting a primary partition" section.

8. At the conclusion of the formatting process, Disk Administrator performs additional functions on the newly created stripe set with parity. The Disk Administrator main dialog box reappears. Click any disk that is part of the stripe set with parity to view the status of this process. As Figure 3-9 shows, Disk Administrator indicates that it is INITIALIZING the stripe set with parity. Notice that the stripe set with parity uses the drive letter F: and consists of Disks 1, 2, and 3.

The initializing process takes quite a while. (It may take several minutes to an hour or more, depending on the size of the stripe set with parity.)

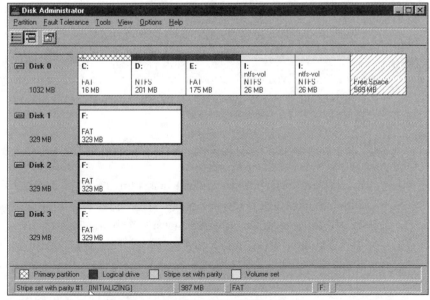

**FIGURE 3-9  Stripe set with parity (INITIALIZING)**

**9.** When the initializing process is finally complete, the Disk Administrator main dialog box changes. Figure 3-10 shows the completed stripe set with parity. Notice at the bottom of the dialog box the stripe set with parity is called HEALTHY.

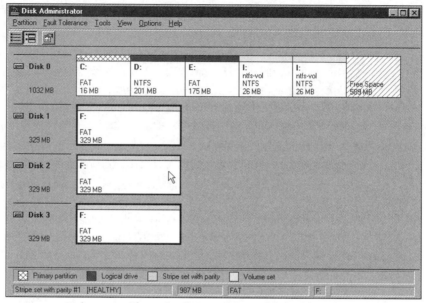

**FIGURE 3-10** **Stripe set with parity (HEALTHY) established**

## Volume Sets

A *volume set* is a combination of free space areas over two to thirty-two hard disks that is treated as a single drive. (The free space areas do not need to be of identical size.)

note 📝 **Neither the boot nor the system partition can be on a volume set.**

The primary purpose and use of a volume set is to access disk space on more than one hard disk by using a single drive letter. A volume set is sometimes used when a drive becomes full and you want to enlarge its capacity.

A volume set is similar to a stripe set. However, a file in a volume set is usually fully contained on a single hard disk, instead of being striped over multiple hard disks.

Volume sets do not involve additional cost, because no additional hard disks are required over the number normally needed to store data.

**Volume sets, like stripe sets, do not perform any fault tolerance function. If one disk in a volume set fails, all data on the volume may be lost, because Windows NT can't access data unless all of the disks that make up the volume set are functional.**

Volume sets are said to be *created* when areas of free space only (not existing volumes) are combined into a volume set. Volume sets are said to be *extended* when an existing NTFS partition is enlarged.

**It's been my experience that extending a volume set is far more common than creating one. It's one way to approach a situation when a drive is filled to capacity and you still need additional space in that volume.**

Windows NT Server and Windows NT Workstation both support volume sets. The following sections explain how to create and extend volume sets.

### TO CREATE A VOLUME SET, FOLLOW THESE STEPS:

1. Start Disk Administrator.
2. Click an area of free space on one of your computer's hard disks.
3. Press and hold Ctrl while you click one or more additional areas of free space on other disks.
4. Select Partition ⇒ Create Volume Set.
5. The Create Volume Set dialog box is displayed showing the minimum and maximum amount of space that can be used for the volume set. Enter the size you want the volume set to be in the "Create volume set of total size" text box. Click OK to create the volume set.
6. The Disk Administrator main dialog box reappears. Select Partition ⇒ Commit Changes Now. Click Yes to save the changes to disk. Then click OK to acknowledge that the disks were updated successfully.
7. The Disk Administrator main dialog box reappears. Figure 3-11 shows the status of the volume set at this point. Note that the volume set, which uses the drive letter F: over Disks 1, 2, and 3 is created, but still needs to be formatted.

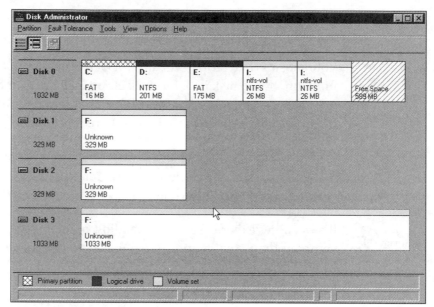

**FIGURE 3-11** Unformatted volume set

8. To format the volume set, follow the directions from the "Creating and formatting a primary partition" section earlier in this chapter. Figure 3-12 displays the completed, formatted volume set.

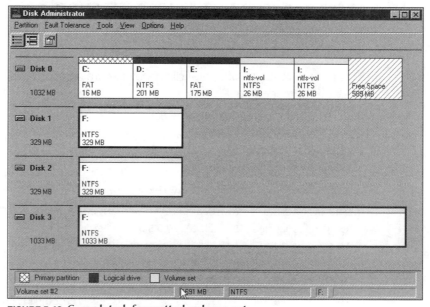

**FIGURE 3-12** Completed, formatted volume set

**TO EXTEND A VOLUME SET, FOLLOW THESE STEPS:**

**1.** Start Disk Administrator.

**2.** Click an NTFS partition on one of your computer's hard disks. (Only NTFS volumes and volume sets can be extended.)

**3.** Press and hold Ctrl while you click one or more additional areas of free space on other disks.

**4.** Select Partition ⇒ Extend Volume Set.

**5.** The Extend Volume Set dialog box is displayed showing the minimum and maximum amount of space that can be used for the total volume set. Enter the size you would like the total volume set to be in the "Create volume set of total size" text box. Click OK to extend the volume set.

**6.** The Disk Administrator main dialog box reappears. The volume set is now extended. You don't have to format extensions to volume sets.

**7.** Exit Disk Administrator and reboot your computer to make the extended volume set effective.

## Comparison of Disk Partitioning Schemes

At this point, you've had a chance to examine four different disk partitioning schemes: disk mirroring, stripe sets, stripe sets with parity, and volume sets.

Table 3-3 compares the fault tolerance, cost, and access speed provided by these four disk partitioning schemes. Note that the most expensive scheme, disk mirroring, also provides the highest level of fault tolerance of the methods listed. As with most things in life, you get what you pay for.

**TABLE 3-3** COMPARISON OF DISK PARTITIONING SCHEMES

| DISK PARTITIONING SCHEME | FAULT TOLERANCE | COST | ACCESS SPEED |
|---|---|---|---|
| Disk mirroring | High | High | Normal (Slowest) |
| Stripe sets with parity | Medium | Medium | Medium–Fast |
| Stripe sets | Low (None) | Low | Fastest |
| Volume sets | Low (None) | Low | Normal (Slowest) |

Now that you're familiar with the various disk partitioning schemes, it's appropriate to discuss how to recover from disk failure when each of these schemes is used.

# RECOVERING FROM DISK FAILURE

So what do you do when it all comes crashing down—when the remote possibility of disk failure that you planned for, but never thought would actually happen, is a painful reality?

This section provides information on how to recover from a single or multiple hard disk failure. Specifically, you'll learn how to recover from disk failure in situations where disk mirroring, stripe sets, stripe sets with parity, and volume sets are used.

exam
preparation
pointer  **Both the Server and the Enterprise exams have an objective on recovering from a fault tolerance failure. Because you are unlikely to get a lot of practice at this in real life, I recommend that you study this section carefully, and revisit it just before you take the exams.**

In some cases your disk configuration may enable you to continue operations (but without any fault tolerance) until you can replace the failed hard disk and restore your fault tolerance configuration.

In cases of stripe set, volume set, or multiple hard disk failure, you must repair the hardware and restore your data from tape to continue operations. If you don't have a tape backup in these situations, Windows NT will *not* be able to recover your data.

concept link  **Tape backup is critically important. For more information on data backup and restoration, see Chapter 15.**

tip  **When you have a disk failure (or a multiple disk failure in the case of disk mirroring or a stripe set with parity), and you don't have a tape backup, you might consider contacting a third-party data recovery service if the data is extremely important or valuable to you. The data recovery service may be able to retrieve some of your data from the failed disk. Be forewarned, however, that this process is expensive and takes time to complete.**

The next several sections explain the detailed steps you can take to recover from disk failure in situations where disk mirroring, stripe sets, stripe sets with parity, and volume sets are involved.

## Disk Mirroring

Sometimes a disk that is part of a mirror set fails. Here's what you can do if that happens.

 caution **The steps in this and other how-to sections in this book are meant to be informational, not a lab exercise. Don't delete or reformat any partition that contains data that you don't want to lose. And remember, back up all important data and programs before you make any changes to your computer's configuration.**

**TO RESTORE YOUR FAULT TOLERANCE DISK CONFIGURATION AFTER ONE DISK IN A MIRROR SET FAILS, FOLLOW THESE STEPS:**

**1.** Boot the computer (by using the fault tolerance boot disk if needed) and then start Disk Administrator.

**2.** Click the disk in the mirror set that is still operational.

**3.** Select Fault Tolerance ➞ Break Mirror. Click Yes in the Confirm dialog box to end mirroring and to create two independent partitions.

**4.** The Disk Administrator main dialog box reappears. Select Partition ➞ Commit Changes Now.

**5.** In the Confirm dialog box, click Yes to save the changes.

**6.** Disk Administrator indicates that the disks were updated successfully. Click OK.

**7.** The Disk Administrator main dialog box reappears. Exit Disk Administrator, shut down the computer, and replace the failed hard disk.

**8.** Restart the computer (by using the fault tolerance boot disk if needed) and then start Disk Administrator.

**9.** Click the partition that you broke the mirror on in Step 3. (This is the good [non-failed] partition that has your data on it.)

**10.** Press and hold Ctrl while you click an area of free space on the new hard disk that is at least as large as the partition you want to mirror.

**11.** From the Fault Tolerance menu, select Establish Mirror.

**12.** The Disk Administrator main dialog box reappears. Disk activity occurs and may last for some time, depending on the size of the partition to be mirrored and the amount of data on that partition. Your mirror set is now reestablished.

# Stripe Sets

Recovering from a failed disk or disks in a stripe set is fairly straightforward.

If you don't have a tape backup of the files on the stripe set, Windows NT can't recover your data. If you have a tape backup, first delete the existing stripe set, and then create a new stripe set. Follow the steps below to recover from a stripe set disk failure.

**TO REPLACE THE FAILED DISK AND DELETE THE EXISTING STRIPE SET (INCLUDING ALL REMAINING DATA ON THE DISKS IN THE SET), FOLLOW THESE STEPS:**

**1.** Replace the failed hard disk or disks. Reboot the computer.

**2.** Start Disk Administrator.

**3.** Click any of the good (non-failed) partitions in the stripe set. (Clicking any good partition in the stripe set highlights all remaining partitions in the set.) Select Partition ⇒ Delete. Click Yes in the Confirm dialog box to delete the partition.

**4.** The Disk Administrator main dialog box reappears. Select Partition ⇒ Commit Changes Now.

**5.** In the Confirm dialog box, click Yes to save the changes.

**6.** Disk Administrator indicates that the disks were updated successfully. Click OK. The Disk Administrator main dialog box reappears.

**THEN, TO CREATE A NEW STRIPE SET (THAT WILL INCLUDE THE NEW DISK) FOLLOW THESE STEPS:**

**1.** To create a new stripe set that will include the new disk, follow the steps presented earlier in this chapter for creating a stripe set.

**2.** Restore all data from tape.

# Stripe Sets with Parity

If you have more than one failed hard disk in a stripe set with parity, follow the steps for recovering from a disk failure in a stripe set (in the previous section). If a single hard disk in your stripe set with parity fails, the following steps explain how to recover.

---

**TO RECOVER FROM A *SINGLE* HARD DISK FAILURE IN A STRIPE SET WITH PARITY, FOLLOW THESE STEPS:**

**1.** Replace the failed disk and reboot the computer.

**2.** Start Disk Administrator.

**3.** Click any portion of the existing stripe set with parity. Press and hold Ctrl while you click the free space area on the new hard disk.

**4.** Select Fault Tolerance⇒Regenerate.

**5.** The Disk Administrator main dialog box reappears. Click any disk that is part of the stripe set with parity. A significant amount of disk activity occurs as the computer regenerates the data on the new hard disk.

   During the regeneration process, various messages are displayed at the bottom of the Disk Administrator dialog box, including: RECOVERABLE, REGENERATING, and HEALTHY. The process is complete when HEALTHY is displayed.

 note   Sometimes it is necessary to reboot the computer during Step 5. For example, if Disk Administrator displays RECOVERABLE for a long period of time (ten minutes or more), you might try rebooting the computer to start the regeneration process.

---

# Volume Sets

Recovering from a failed disk or disks in a volume set is fairly straightforward.

   If you don't have a backup of the files on the volume set, Windows NT can't recover your data. If you have a tape backup, follow these steps to recover from the disk failure.

---

**FIRST, TO DELETE THE EXISTING VOLUME SET (AND ALL REMAINING DATA ON THE DISKS IN THE SET), FOLLOW THESE STEPS:**

**1.** Replace the failed hard disk or disks. Reboot the computer.

**2.** Start Disk Administrator.

**3.** Click any of the good (non-failed) partitions in the volume set. (Clicking any partition in the volume set highlights all remaining partitions in the volume set.) Select Partition ⇒ Delete. Click Yes in the Confirm dialog box to delete the partition.

**4.** The Disk Administrator main dialog box reappears. Select Partition ⇒ Commit Changes Now.

**5.** In the Confirm dialog box, click Yes to save the changes.

**6.** Disk Administrator indicates that the disks were updated successfully. Click OK. The Disk Administrator main dialog box reappears.

**NEXT, CREATE A NEW VOLUME SET (THAT WILL INCLUDE THE NEW HARD DISK) BY FOLLOWING THESE STEPS:**

**1.** To create a new volume set that will include the new hard disk, follow the steps presented earlier in this chapter for creating a volume set.

**2.** Restore all data from tape.

---

# UPDATING THE EMERGENCY REPAIR DISK

The *Emergency Repair Disk* is a floppy disk used to restore the Windows NT Registry to the configuration that existed when the Emergency Repair Disk was created (or updated).

If you have made any changes to your computer's system configuration since the Emergency Repair Disk was created or last updated, those changes will be lost during the emergency repair process. For this reason, you should update your Emergency Repair Disk *every time* you make a change to your computer's system configuration, including any changes to your disk configuration. Windows NT will prompt you to update your Emergency Repair Disk every time you make a change to your disk configuration in Disk Administrator. (You'll have a chance to update your Emergency Repair Disk in Lab 3.4 at the end of this chapter.)

 concept link **This chapter only discusses updating the Emergency Repair Disk. Chapter 27 explains how to use the Emergency Repair Disk to restore the Registry.**

The Emergency Repair Disk is initially created during the installation of Windows NT. To update it at any time after installation (or to create an Emergency Repair disk after installation if one was not created at that time), you must use the `Rdisk.exe` utility.

You won't find the `Rdisk.exe` utility in the Start menu. You will either need to run it from the command line, run it by selecting the Run option from the Start menu, or you can create a shortcut for it on your desktop.

When you run `Rdisk.exe`, a Repair Disk Utility dialog box is displayed. Figure 3-13 shows the first Repair Disk Utility dialog box.

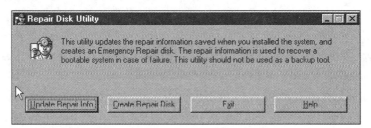

**FIGURE 3-13** The first Repair Disk Utility dialog box

If you click the Update Repair Info command button in the Repair Disk Utility dialog box (and click Yes in the next dialog box displayed to confirm), `Rdisk.exe` will save all of your Registry (with the exception of the Security hive and the Security Accounts Manager [SAM] database) to the `<winntroot>\` `repair` directory. This is the directory that was specified for the installation of Windows NT, usually `C:\winnt`.

 concept link **For additional information on the Windows NT Registry, see Chapter 27, as well as the *Microsoft Windows NT Workstation Resource Kit for version 4.0*, Part V, "Windows NT Registry."**

After `Rdisk.exe` saves your Registry configuration information, it will ask if you want to create an Emergency Repair Disk. Figure 3-14 displays this Repair Disk Utility dialog box. Click Yes to create the Emergency Repair Disk.

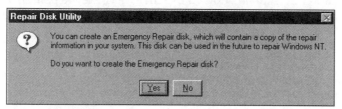

**FIGURE 3-14** Creating (Updating) the Emergency Repair Disk

 **Don't be thrown because** `Rdisk.exe` **asks if you want to create an Emergency Repair Disk when what you're really trying to do is to update it.** `Rdisk.exe` **uses the same process and terminology for both.**

At this point, Repair Disk prompts you to insert a labeled 3.5-inch floppy disk into drive A:. If you have the Emergency Repair Disk you created during the installation of Windows NT, use this disk to create an updated Emergency Repair Disk. If you didn't create an Emergency Repair Disk during installation, insert any blank floppy disk to create an Emergency Repair Disk now.

A second way you can update your Emergency Repair Disk is to use the one command line switch that can be used with `Rdisk.exe`, the `/S` switch. The *s* stands for security. Using the `/S` switch causes the entire Registry, including the Security hive and the SAM database, to be backed up. When you run `Rdisk.exe` with the `/S` switch, `Rdisk.exe` automatically begins saving your Registry information to the repair directory, and then prompts you to create the Emergency Repair Disk.

 **It's a good idea to use the** `Rdisk.exe` **utility with the** `/S` **switch. This will provide you with a backup of the SAM database in addition to the one on your regularly scheduled tape backup.**

 **Another good idea is to write down the Administrator's password when you create a new or updated Emergency Repair Disk. It's very important to know what the Administrator's password is after you have restored the Registry from the Emergency Repair Disk. Personally, I go so far as to write the Administrator's password on the Emergency Repair Disk label.**

To use the `Rdisk.exe` utility with the `/S` switch, select the Run option from the Start menu, and then type **rdisk /s** in the text box within the Run dialog box.

# KEY POINT SUMMARY

This chapter introduced the three file systems that Windows NT supports, as well as partitions and how to work with them, how to recover from disk failure, and how to update the Emergency Repair Disk.

- Windows NT supports the *file allocation table* (FAT) *file system,* the *Windows NT file system* (NTFS), and the *Compact Disc Filing System* (CDFS).
  - The *FAT file system* does not support file and folder security in Windows NT. The FAT file system supports the use of long filenames, and normally permits faster access to files on partitions smaller than 500MB than other file systems. The maximum size of a FAT partition is 4GB. The FAT file system does not support file compression.
  - *NTFS* is the most powerful file system supported by Windows NT. NT is the only operating system that supports NTFS. NTFS provides file and folder security. NTFS, like FAT, supports the use of long filenames. NTFS usually provides faster access to files stored on a large partition that contains a large number of files than the FAT file system. The maximum functional size of an NTFS partition is two terabytes. NTFS supports file compression, and is a highly reliable, recoverable file system. You can use the `Convert.exe` command to convert an existing FAT partition into an NTFS partition. This is a one-way conversion. It is much more difficult to convert an NTFS partition into a FAT partition.
- Marking a disk to identify which parts contain a file system is called *partitioning*. A hard disk can be separated into a maximum of four partitions. Windows NT supports two types of partitions: *primary* and *extended*. The Windows NT 4.0 *system partition* must be located on the active primary partition on the first hard disk in a computer. The *boot partition* can be located on either a primary or extended partition. A hard

disk can have more than one primary partition on it, but can have only one extended partition on it.

o *Disk Administrator* is the Windows NT tool that is used to create, format, and otherwise manage partitions. This chapter includes detailed steps explaining how to use Disk Administrator for creating partitions, formatting partitions, establishing disk mirroring, creating a fault tolerance boot disk (including editing the Boot.ini file), and creating stripe sets, stripe sets with parity, and volume sets. Table 3-3 compares the levels of fault tolerance, cost, and access speed provided by four common disk partitioning schemes: *disk mirroring, stripe sets with parity, stripe sets,* and *volume sets*. Of the four schemes, disk mirroring is the most expensive and provides the highest level of fault tolerance. Stripe sets and volume sets are inexpensive, but neither provide any fault tolerance.

o Specific steps on recovering from single and multiple disk failure in instances of disk mirroring, stripe sets, stripe sets with parity, and volume sets are presented. Tape backup is critically important to this process.

o The Rdisk.exe utility is used to update the Emergency Repair Disk. The *Emergency Repair Disk* is used to restore the Windows NT Registry to the configuration that existed when the Emergency Repair Disk was created (or updated). The Emergency Repair Disk should be updated *every time* you make a change to your computer's system or disk configuration. Rdisk.exe can be run with the /S switch to backup the Security hive and the SAM database.

# Applying What You've Learned

Now it's time to regroup, review, and apply what you've learned in this chapter.

The questions in the following Instant Assessment section bring to mind key facts and concepts.

The two exercises in the Review Activities section focus on planning, and give you a chance to apply your knowledge of disk management to real-world situations.

The hands-on lab exercises will really reinforce what you've learned, and give you an opportunity to practice some of the tasks tested by the Microsoft Certified Professional exams.

## Instant Assessment

1. What are the three file systems supported by Windows NT 4.0?

2. If you want your computer to dual boot between Windows NT 4.0 and Windows 95, which file system must your computer's first partition use?

3. Which is easier to accomplish: converting a FAT partition to NTFS, or converting an NTFS partition to a FAT partition?

4. When a computer boots, from which partition on which disk does it attempt to *begin* the process of loading the operating system?

5. When booting from the hard disk, on which partition must the Windows NT 4.0 system partition be located?

6. How many primary partitions can you have on one disk? How many extended partitions? How many total partitions?

7. Which Windows NT tool is used to create, format, and otherwise manage partitions?

8. Which of the four disk partitioning schemes involves making an exact replica of a partition onto a separate hard disk?

9. When is a fault tolerance boot disk used?

10. What two sections make up the `Boot.ini` file?

11. Which disk partitioning scheme involves the distribution of data, a block at a time, evenly and sequentially, among all of the disks in the set?

12. Which of the four disk partitioning schemes discussed provide no fault tolerance (that is to say, if one disk fails, all data is lost)?

13. Which of the four disk partitioning schemes is the most commonly used method of fault tolerance? Why?

14. Which of the four disk partitioning schemes is the most expensive and provides the highest amount of fault tolerance?

15. Which utility can you use to update your Emergency Repair Disk?

16. After starting Disk Administrator, what's the first main step in recovering from a single disk failure when the disk is part of a mirror set?

T/F

17. The FAT file system supports file and folder security in Windows NT. \_\_\_\_\_

18. The FAT file system supports the use of long filenames. \_\_\_\_\_

19. The FAT file system supports file compression. \_\_\_\_\_

20. NTFS provides file and folder security in Windows NT. \_\_\_\_\_

21. NTFS supports the use of long filenames. \_\_\_\_\_

22. NTFS does not preserve upper- and lowercase in filenames. \_\_\_\_\_

23. The minimum functional size of an NTFS partition is 2 terabytes. \_\_\_\_\_

24. NTFS supports a compression attribute for each file. \_\_\_\_\_

25. NTFS is a highly reliable, recoverable file system. \_\_\_\_\_

26. Using NTFS increases the likelihood of fragmentation on partitions. \_\_\_\_\_

27. You can use NTFS to format a floppy disk. \_\_\_\_\_

concept link   **For answers to the Instant Assessment questions see Appendix D.**

# Review Activities

The following activities test your understanding of disk configuration topics in two different planning exercises.

Workstation
Server
Enterprise

## *File system planning exercise*

Planning involves considering the facts and needs of a given situation *before* you make a choice or commitment to a particular path.

exam
preparation
pointer

**Planning is not only critically important in the real world, it's also tested on the Microsoft Certified Professional exams. In fact, it's a large part of the exam objectives. So, try to start thinking about planning situations, not just as you do this exercise, but throughout the rest of your study and preparation for the exams.**

For each of the following scenarios, consider the given facts and any expressed needs or goals. Then choose the most appropriate file system for each scenario.

**Problem 1**    You want to run Windows NT Workstation on a computer. Your computer's hard disk has one 480MB partition and one 20MB partition. Each folder on the partitions contains a moderate amount of files. You want to optimize access speed to the files. Which file system should you choose?

**Problem 2**   You want your new computer to dual boot between Windows NT Server and MS-DOS. Your computer's 1GB hard drive has only one partition on it. Which file system should you choose?

**Problem 3**   Your computer has two hard disks, and each hard disk has a 4GB partition. There are a large number of files in the folders on these partitions. You want to run Windows NT on this computer and optimize access speed to the files. Which file system should you choose?

**Problem 4**   You plan to install and run Windows NT Server on a computer. Your supervisor informs you that file and folder security are required because of highly sensitive data that is stored on this computer. You also need to be able to utilize file compression because of the amount and size of files on this computer. Which file system should you choose?

concept link   **For answers to the Review Activity see Appendix D.**

## Disk partitioning and fault tolerance planning exercise

This chapter introduced four disk partitioning schemes: disk mirroring, stripe sets with parity, stripe sets, and volume sets.

Server
Enterprise

exam
preparation
pointer

**Both the Server and Enterprise exams test your ability to plan the disk drive configuration for various requirements, including choosing a fault tolerance method.**

**I know this seems like a lot of stuff to memorize, but for experienced network professionals, making these decisions is almost second nature. It should also be second nature to you by the time you take the exams!**

For each of the following scenarios, consider the given facts and any expressed criteria that must be met. Then choose the most appropriate disk partitioning scheme for each scenario.

(Hint: As you may recall, Table 3-3 compares the levels of fault tolerance, cost, and access speed provided by the four schemes.)

**Problem 1**    You are in charge of planning a new server for your company. Management tells you that protection of data is the most important requirement for this new server, more important than speed and even more important than cost. Which disk partitioning scheme should you choose?

**Problem 2**    You are planning a new server for your company's network. The server will contain a large database. Speed of access to files on the database is your primary concern. Fault tolerance is not important, but you do need to minimize costs. Which disk partitioning scheme should you choose?

**Problem 3**    You are planning to add a new server to your organization's network. You want to achieve a moderate amount of fault tolerance *and* minimize costs. Which disk partitioning scheme should you choose?

 concept link    **For answers to the Review Activity see Appendix D.**

# Hands-on Lab Exercises

The following hands-on lab exercises provide you with two different opportunities to use the disk management knowledge you've gained in this chapter.

### Lab 3.3 *Managing Partitions*

Workstation
Server
Enterprise

The objective of this hands-on lab exercise is for you to gain experience using Disk Administrator to manage partitions.

Follow the steps carefully to successfully partition and format the remaining 10MB of your computer's hard drive with an NTFS partition.

 note    **If you didn't leave enough space on your hard disk to perform this, I recommend that you reinstall NT Workstation and NT Server to accommodate this lab. If this is not possible, you should create an NTFS partition somewhere on one of your hard disks so that you can perform the file security labs later in this book.**

 caution    **Don't delete or reformat any partition that contains data that you don't want to lose. As always, make sure you back up all important data and programs *before* you do the lab exercise.**

1. Boot your computer to either Windows NT Server or Windows NT Workstation. Log on as Administrator. (Remember the password? It's *password*.)

2. Close the Welcome to NT dialog box if it appears. (Hint: If you never want to see this dialog box again, the second time it appears, you are given a check box to select if you don't want this box to appear each time you run NT.)

3. Select Start ⇒ Programs ⇒ Administrative Tools (Common) ⇒ Disk Administrator.

4. Disk Administrator displays a dialog box indicating that this is the first time Disk Administrator has been run. Click OK to update the system configuration.

5. If this is the first time Disk Administrator has been run, a Confirm dialog box appears, indicating that no signature is found on Disk 0. Click Yes to write a signature on Disk 0.

6. Click the box that indicates a drive with a 10MB partition (to highlight it), and select Partition ⇒ Delete. (Caution! If this partition is displayed as Free Space, don't do this step. Instead, skip to Step 11.)

7. Click Yes in the Confirm dialog box to delete the partition.

8. Select Partition ⇒ Commit Changes Now.

9. Click Yes in the Confirm dialog box to save the changes to your disk.

10. Click OK to return to the Disk Administrator main dialog box.

11. Click the box that indicates the drive with 10MB of free space (to highlight it), and then select Partition ⇒ Create.

12. A Confirm dialog box appears. Click Yes to continue to create the partition.

13. Click OK in the Create Primary Partition dialog box to create a new partition.

14. Select Partition ⇒ Commit Changes Now.

15. Click Yes in the Confirm dialog box to save the changes to your disk.

16. Click OK to return to the Disk Administrator main dialog box.

17. Click the box that indicates the drive with a 10MB partition (labeled Unknown) to highlight it.

18. Select Tools ⇒ Format.

19. Choose NTFS in the File System drop-down list box, accept all the other defaults, and then click Start.

20. A warning dialog box appears. Click OK to format the drive.

21. A dialog box appears indicating that the format is complete. Click OK.

**22.** Click Close to return to the Disk Administrator main dialog box.

**23.** Select Partition ⇒ Exit to exit Disk Administrator.

Congratulations! You have now formatted the 10MB partition on your computer with NTFS.

### Lab 3.4  *Updating the Emergency Repair Disk*

Server
Enterprise

The purpose of this hands-on lab exercise it to provide you with the skills required to update your Emergency Repair Disk, and to give you experience performing this task.

In order to do this lab, you need the Emergency Repair Disks you created in Labs 2.1 and 2.2 during the original installations of your Windows NT operating systems.

 note **The Emergency Repair Disks for Windows NT Workstation and Windows NT Server are different. If you have both operating systems on the same computer, you need to update both disks.**

Do this lab twice, once from each operating system.

**1.** Boot to Windows NT (either Workstation or Server).

**2.** Select Start ⇒ Run.

**3.** When the Run dialog box appears, type **RDISK** in the drop-down dialog box.

**4.** Click OK to run Rdisk.exe.

**5.** When the Repair Disk Utility dialog box appears, click Update Repair Info.

**6.** Click Yes to update your repair information.

**7.** Rdisk.exe saves your current configuration. This takes a couple of minutes. Click Yes to create the Emergency Repair Disk.

**8.** When prompted, place the Emergency Repair Disk you created in Lab 2.1 (if you are running Windows NT Workstation) or Lab 2.2 (if you are running Windows NT Server) in drive A:. Click OK to create the Emergency Repair Disk. (This process erases your original Emergency Repair Disk and creates a new Emergency Repair Disk with your current system configurations.) It takes a couple of minutes for the Repair Disk Utility to complete this process.

**9.** Click Exit to exit the Repair Disk Utility. Your Emergency Repair Disk is now updated. Remove it from drive A:. (Remember to do this lab again with your other NT operating system.)

Workstation
Server
Enterprise

# Using Control Panel

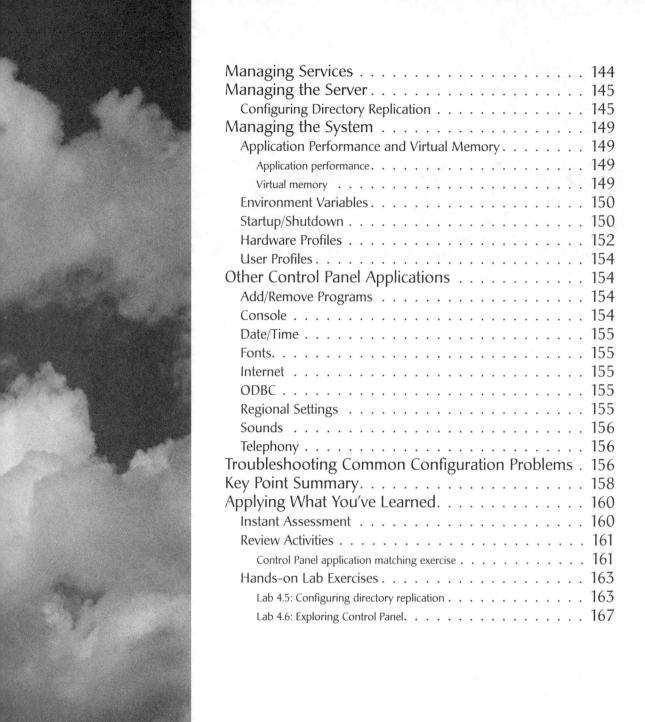

# About Chapter 4

This chapter explores Windows NT Control Panel—a collection of mini-applications that are automatically installed during the installation of Windows NT. After a brief overview, Chapter 4 discusses many of the Control Panel applications that are used to install or configure options, hardware, and hardware drivers.

Next, in-depth coverage of the Network application is presented. A comprehensive list of protocols and services is included in this section. Installing and configuring protocols and services is also covered.

The Server application is explained, with emphasis on configuring directory replication. Then the System application, which is used to configure virtual memory, among other things, is discussed. The chapter then describes briefly the remaining Control Panel applications, and concludes by providing tips for troubleshooting common configuration problems.

This chapter also includes two hands-on labs. In the first lab, you create a logon script and configure directory replication. In the second, you explore and use several Control Panel applications.

This chapter is a "must read" no matter which of the three Windows NT 4.0 Microsoft Certified Professional exams you're preparing for. The information in this chapter covers objectives listed in the Planning, Installation and Configuration, Connectivity, and Troubleshooting sections in these exams' objectives.

# OVERVIEW OF CONTROL PANEL

Windows NT Control Panel is a collection of mini-applications, sometimes called applets. These applications, which are automatically installed during installation of Windows NT Workstation and Windows NT Server, are used to install and/or configure various options, hardware, protocols, and services.

Each Control Panel application is used for a different task. Some software packages and some installable services include their own Control Panel icon, which is displayed in the Control Panel dialog box after the new application or service is installed. (Unless expressly stated otherwise, the information presented about Control Panel applies to both Windows NT Workstation and Windows NT Server.)

You can access Control Panel in several ways:

- Select Start ⇒ Settings ⇒ Control Panel
- Select Control Panel in Windows NT Explorer
- Open the My Computer dialog box and double-click Control Panel

Figure 4-1 shows a screen shot of Control Panel. Notice that there are twenty-seven icons displayed.

**FIGURE 4-1**    Windows NT Server Control Panel

You may have additional icons in Control Panel depending on the services or options you chose to install during installation and setup of Windows NT.

This chapter covers all of the common Control Panel applications, and organizes the applications into sections based on each application's functionality. The basic application functions include: managing peripherals and devices, licensing, networking, managing services, managing the server, managing the system, and miscellaneous other functions. The first function is all about the applications you can use to manage peripherals and hardware devices, and is the topic of the next section.

# MANAGING PERIPHERALS AND DEVICES

This section examines the Control Panel applications that are used to install and/or configure options, hardware, and hardware drivers.

## Accessibility Options

 The *Accessibility Options* application is used to configure the keyboard, sound, and mouse options on a computer to accommodate users that are physically challenged, including persons who have difficulty striking multiple keys simultaneously on a keyboard, persons with hearing disabilities, or persons who have difficulty holding or clicking a mouse.

The Accessibility Options application is available unless you deselected it during the installation of Windows NT, or you performed a compact installation. (Accessibility Options is normally installed by default, but if it's not installed on your computer, you can use the Add/Remove Programs application, discussed later in this chapter, to install it.)

 **Another Control Panel application, Display, can be used to configure the display so that the visibility of some screen elements is enhanced. See the "Display" section later in this chapter.**

## Devices

 The *Devices* application is used to start and stop device drivers, to configure the startup behavior of device drivers, to view the status of a device driver, and to enable or disable a device driver within a hardware profile.

The startup behaviors (or types) available in this application include *boot*, *system*, *automatic*, *manual*, and *disabled*. If you choose boot, system, or automatic, Windows NT starts the device driver automatically every time the computer is booted. If you choose manual, a user (or another device driver) must start the device driver. If you select disabled, the device driver can't be started by a user.

 **Use extreme caution when using the Devices application. Changing the startup type or disabling a device driver, such as Atdisk, can leave your computer in an unbootable state.**

# Display

 The *Display* application is used to configure a computer's desktop background, screen saver options, desktop appearance, Microsoft Plus! options, and display adapter settings. You can also configure the display to use large fonts, large icons, and a high-contrast color scheme to accommodate a visually challenged person. The Display application can also be accessed by right-clicking the desktop and selecting Properties from the menu that appears.

Use the Settings tab to configure your computer's display adapter settings. Figure 4-2 shows the Settings tab of the Display Properties dialog box. Notice the various display options that you can configure, including: Color Palette, Font Size, Desktop Area, and Refresh Frequency.

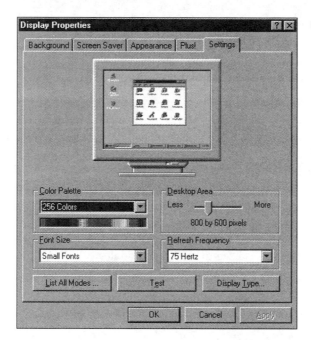

**FIGURE 4-2   The Settings tab**

If you make any changes on the Settings tab, you must test the changes before you can apply them or save them.

# Keyboard

The *Keyboard* application is used to configure specific keyboard features, including speed of character repeat and cursor blink rate, input locale (including keyboard layout), and keyboard type.

The default input locale is English/United States. You can select other languages (localized for use in other countries) by clicking the Add command button on the Input Locales tab, and then scrolling through the drop-down list box.

A list of keyboard layout options is displayed when you click the Properties command button on the Input Locales tab, and then scroll through the drop-down list box. Figure 4-3 illustrates the different U.S. keyboard layouts that can be selected.

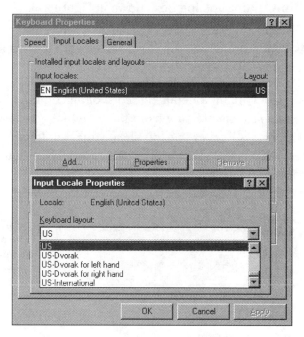

**FIGURE 4-3   United States keyboard layouts**

# Modems

The *Modems* application is used to install and configure modems and to configure dialing properties.

When you install a modem, you can instruct Windows NT to detect your modem automatically, or you can select your modem manually from a list. If you choose to select your modem manually and your modem does not appear on the list, you can choose from the list of standard modem types.

**in the real world**  When you troubleshoot modem connection problems, consider configuring Windows NT to record a log file of your modem connection activity.

To configure Windows NT to record a modem log file follow these steps:

**1.** Double-click Modems in Control Panel.

**2.** Highlight your modem in the Modems Properties dialog box, and then click the Properties command button.

**3.** A specific Modem Properties dialog box is displayed for your particular modem. Click the Connection tab. Then click the Advanced command button to display the Advanced Connection Settings dialog box shown in Figure 4-4.

**4.** At the bottom left corner of the Advanced Connection Settings dialog box, check the check box next to Record a log file. Then click OK and exit the Modems application.

This log file will contain a detailed record of all commands sent to and from your modem starting from the time that you enable this feature. Windows NT saves this log file in your Windows NT installation directory as `ModemLog_your modem name.txt`. You can use any text editor to view this file.

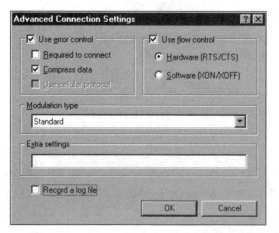

**FIGURE 4-4** Configuring the Modems application to record a log file

You can use the Modems application to configure dialing properties, including the area code you are calling from, the country you are in, special instructions on how to access an outside line, whether to dial using a calling card, instructions on how to disable call waiting, and to specify tone or pulse dialing. To access the Dialing Properties dialog box, double-click Modems in Control Panel, and then click the Dialing Properties command button in the Modems Properties dialog box.

## Mouse

 The *Mouse* application is used to install and configure a mouse or other pointing device. You can choose the mouse button configuration, select a different pointer (this is the arrow on your screen that moves as you move your mouse), and configure pointer speed and double-click speed.

## Multimedia

 The *Multimedia* application is used to install and configure audio/visual devices. You can specify audio record and playback devices, MIDI output configuration, and how a video is shown on your computer's display. The types of devices you can install with this application include sound cards, MIDI devices and instruments, joysticks, video capture devices, and so on.

## PC Card (PCMCIA)

 The *PC Card (PCMCIA)* application is used to install, configure, and manage PC card drivers. However, often PC card drivers are installed and configured by other applications, such as the Modem application (for modem cards), and Network (for network adapters). The PC Card application is a convenient, one-stop application you can use to check the operational status of and resources used by your PC cards.

 **Always shut down and turn off your computer before inserting or removing PC cards. Hot swapping (removing or inserting PC cards while the computer is powered on) is *not* supported by Windows NT.**

Figure 4-5 shows a list of the PC cards that are installed in my laptop computer. Note that in the PC Card (PCMCIA) Devices dialog box, the application detects two PC cards: a Megahertz modem card and a 3Com network adapter. After I click the

Properties button, the MEGAHERTZ CC3288 Properties dialog box is displayed, which shows the device status and other information about the modem card.

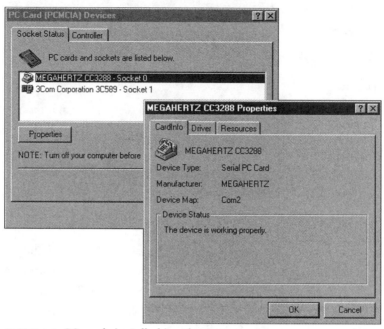

**FIGURE 4-5**  **PC cards installed in a laptop computer**

# Ports

 The *Ports* application is used to add, configure, and manage the serial communication ports (COM ports) in a computer. You can use the Ports application to configure settings for your serial ports, including baud rate, data bits, I/O port address, and interrupt.

# Printers

 The *Printers* application is used to install, configure, manage, and remove printers. It will be covered extensively in Chapter 6.

# SCSI Adapters

 The *SCSI Adapters* application is used to install, configure, and manage SCSI adapters. The SCSI Adapters application looks, feels, and functions much the same as the PC Card (PCMCIA) application (discussed earlier in this chapter). SCSI adapter drivers are usually installed and configured during the installation of Windows NT. The SCSI Adapters application, however, is a convenient tool to add additional SCSI adapters after installation, and to view the operational status, configuration, and resources used by your SCSI adapters.

Figure 4-6 shows the two SCSI adapters installed in my desktop computer (a dual channel IDE controller and an Adaptec SCSI adapter), and the devices connected to each adapter. (Note: Windows NT treats dual channel IDE controllers as SCSI adapters.) After I click the Properties button in the SCSI Adapters dialog box, the IDE CD-ROM dialog box is displayed, which shows the driver status and other information about the IDE controller.

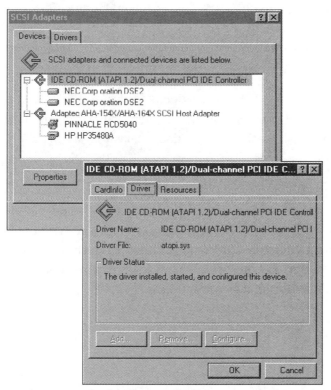

**FIGURE 4-6   SCSI adapters installed in a computer**

## Tape Devices

 The *Tape Devices* application is used to install drivers for tape backup devices and to view the status of tape backup devices connected to your computer. This application functions much like the PC Card (PCMCIA) and SCSI Adapters applications.

You must install a driver for your tape backup device before you can access it in the Windows NT Backup application.

 **Using the Windows NT Backup application is discussed in more detail in Chapter 15.**

## UPS

 The *UPS* application is used to install, configure, and manage an uninterruptible power supply.

 **The UPS application is a basic UPS management tool. Most commercial quality UPS devices include application software that is much more sophisticated than the UPS application that ships with Windows NT. I recommend you use the application software that the manufacturer supplies with your UPS.**

The Windows NT UPS application is adequate for managing an inexpensive UPS that does not include Windows NT-compatible UPS application software.

Figure 4-7 shows the configuration options available in the Windows NT UPS application. Note that you can configure the UPS interface voltages, expected battery life, the name of an executable program to run thirty seconds before shutdown, and other settings.

 **I strongly recommend you use a UPS on any Windows NT Server computer and on any computer that is critical to your operations. A UPS permits an orderly shutdown of your computer to avoid data loss during a power outage.**

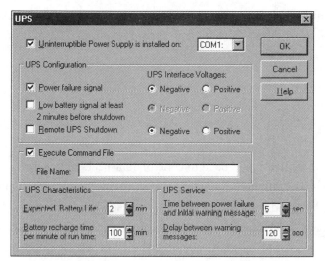

**FIGURE 4-7** Configuring a UPS

 Also remember that UPS batteries don't last forever. Follow the manufacturer's recommendations for battery replacement and maintenance. There's nothing so dissatisfying as finding out that your UPS battery is dead *after* the power fails. I know. I once spent an entire day during a big Seattle windstorm responding to customer calls concerning damaged hardware and lost data problems that were the result of failed UPS batteries.

# LICENSING

 The *Licensing* application (available with Windows NT Server only) is used to manage licensing on your Windows NT Server computer. Normally, a licensing mode (Per Server or Per Seat) is chosen and the number of client access licenses is configured during the installation of Windows NT Server. However, if you purchase additional client licenses, or decide after installation to change your licensing mode, you can use the Licensing application to accomplish this.

 **The Licensing structure of Windows NT is discussed in detail in the "Licensing Mode" section of the Preinstallation Checklist in Chapter 2.**

In addition, you can use the Licensing application to replicate licensing information to a centrally located (enterprise) server on your network.

# NETWORKING

 The *Network* application is used to control all aspects of networking services on the Windows NT computer, including changing the computer/domain/workgroup name, installing and configuring protocols and services, configuring bindings and network access order, and configuring network adapters. The Network application can also be accessed by right-clicking the Network Neighborhood icon and selecting Properties from the menu that appears.

## Changing the Computer/Domain Name of a Domain Controller

Normally you will not change the computer or domain name of a Windows NT Server computer that is configured as a domain controller. However, you may need to change one or both of these names to conform to a naming convention standard that is developed or changed *after* the server is installed. If you want to change a computer or domain name of a domain controller, you can use the Network application to accomplish this.

When you start the Network application on a Windows NT Server that is configured as a domain controller, the Network dialog box is displayed, as shown in Figure 4-8.

Note that the Network dialog box has five tabs: Identification, Services, Protocols, Adapters, and Bindings. The Identification tab is on top initially. If you click the Change command button, the Identification Changes dialog box is displayed, as shown in Figure 4-9.

Notice that in the Identification Changes dialog box you can change the computer name or change the name of the domain.

note  **If you change the domain name of one domain controller in a domain, you *must* change the domain name of all other domain controllers, member servers, and Windows NT Workstation computers in that domain to match the new domain name you assign.**

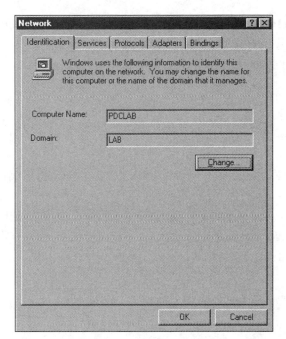

**FIGURE 4-8**  **Starting Network on a Windows NT Server domain controller**

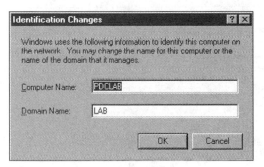

**FIGURE 4-9**  **Making identification changes on a Windows NT Server domain controller**

You *cannot* change a domain controller's domain membership by changing its domain name. For example, if you have two domains on your network named EAST and WEST, you can't move a domain controller from the EAST domain to the WEST domain simply by changing the EAST domain controller's name to WEST. You have to reinstall Windows NT Server to move this domain controller from the EAST domain to the WEST domain. However, if you just want to change the name of the EAST domain to the FAR_EAST domain, you can do this by changing the domain name of all of the domain controllers, member servers, and Windows NT Workstation computers in the EAST domain to FAR_EAST.

## Changing the Computer/Domain/Workgroup Name of a Stand-Alone Server or a Windows NT Workstation Computer

Occasionally you may want to change the computer, domain, or workgroup name, or change the domain membership status of a stand-alone server or a Windows NT Workstation computer. For example, you might change the computer name of a Windows NT Workstation computer that is assigned to a new employee to match the new user's name, instead of the name of the previous employee who used that computer.

When you start the Network application on a stand-alone/member server or on a Windows NT Workstation computer, the Network dialog box is displayed, as shown in Figure 4-10.

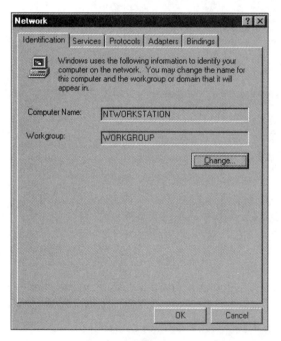

**FIGURE 4-10** **Starting Network on a Windows NT Workstation computer**

Note that the Network dialog box contains five tabs: Identification, Services, Protocols, Adapters, and Bindings. The Identification tab is on top initially. If you click the Change command button, the Identification Changes dialog box is displayed, as shown in Figure 4-11.

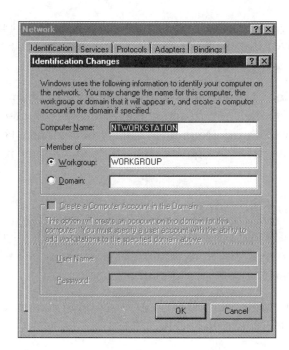

**FIGURE 4-11** Making identification changes on a Windows NT Workstation computer

Notice that in the Identification Changes dialog box you can change the computer name or change the domain or workgroup the computer belongs to. A Windows NT computer must belong to either a workgroup or a domain.

If you select the Workgroup radio button you can accept the workgroup name that is displayed, or, if no name is displayed, you must type in a workgroup name. A Windows NT computer can be a member of any existing workgroup, or it can be the only computer in a new workgroup.

## *Joining a domain*

If you select the Domain radio button, you must either accept the domain name that is displayed or type the name of any existing domain on the network. To be a member of a domain, a Windows NT computer must have a computer account in that domain. If a computer account does not exist in the domain for the computer you are configuring, you must check the Create a Computer Account in the Domain check box, and you must supply the administrator's user account name and password (or any other user account that has the right to add computer accounts to the domain). This entire process is called *joining a domain*.

Once a Windows NT computer has joined a domain, a user can log on to this computer interactively (locally) by using a user account in the domain directory database via a process known as *pass through authentication.*

concept link

**See the section, "Workgroups Versus Domains" in Chapter 1 for more information on how to determine whether a computer should be a member of a workgroup or a member of a domain. For more information on pass through authentication, see Chapter 10.**

## Protocols and Services

Windows NT supports a variety of protocols and services. This section identifies each protocol and service that ships with Windows NT Server and Windows NT Workstation and briefly describes the functionality of each.

concept link

**Many of these protocols and services are covered in more depth in the chapters that make up Part IV.**

Table 4-1 lists and describes the protocols that ship with Windows NT Workstation and Windows NT Server, and Table 4-2 lists and describes the services that ship with Windows NT Workstation and Windows NT Server.

**TABLE 4-1** WINDOWS NT PROTOCOLS

| PROTOCOL | NT WORKSTATION | NT SERVER | DESCRIPTION |
|---|---|---|---|
| AppleTalk Protocol | X | | This protocol enables a Windows NT Workstation computer to connect to AppleTalk network print devices. (AppleTalk is usually associated with Macintosh computers and printers.) Although not listed in the Windows NT Server Network Protocols dialog box, you can install AppleTalk Protocol on a Windows NT Server computer by installing Services for Macintosh. |

| Protocol | NT Workstation | NT Server | Description |
|---|---|---|---|
| DLC Protocol | X | X | This protocol is a datalink protocol. In an NT environment, DLC is primarily used by Windows NT computers to communicate with Hewlett-Packard printers and IBM mainframe computers. |
| NetBEUI Protocol | X | X | This protocol is designed for small, nonrouted networks. It doesn't require any configuration and has minimal overhead. NetBEUI is included with NT 4.0 primarily to provide backward compatibility with earlier networking software that uses NetBEUI as its only protocol. |
| NWLink IPX/SPX Compatible Transport | X | X | This protocol is a routable protocol usually associated with NetWare networks. NWLink is fully supported for Windows NT networking. |
| Point-to-Point Tunneling Protocol | X | X | This protocol is used to provide a secure network communications path between computers over the Internet. |
| Streams Environment | X | X | Some applications require Streams for correct network functionality. I recommend you install Streams Environment only if it is required by an application or service you want to use. |
| TCP/IP Protocol | X | X | Of the protocols listed here, TCP/IP provides the most robust capabilities for Windows NT networking. It is a fast, routable enterprise protocol. TCP/IP is the protocol used on the Internet. TCP/IP is supported by many other operating systems, including Windows 95, Macintosh, UNIX, MS-DOS, and IBM main-frames. Its only drawback is the extensive configuration required to implement it. |

**TABLE 4-2** WINDOWS NT SERVICES

| SERVICE | NT WORKSTATION | NT SERVER | DESCRIPTION |
| --- | --- | --- | --- |
| Client Service for NetWare | X | | This service enables a Windows NT Workstation computer to access files and printers on a NetWare server. |
| DHCP Relay Agent | | X | This service enables a Windows NT Server computer that is functioning as a TCP/IP router to forward DHCP packets to a DHCP server. |
| Gateway (and Client) Services for NetWare | | X | This service enables a Windows NT Server computer to access files and printers on a NetWare server, and enables the NT Server to share NetWare printers and files with its non-NetWare client computers. |
| Microsoft DHCP Server | | X | This service enables a Windows NT Server computer to provide TCP/IP addresses and other TCP/IP configuration information to DHCP-enabled client computers. |
| Microsoft DNS Server | | X | This service is a TCP/IP-based name resolution service. It is used to resolve a host name to its associated IP address. |
| Microsoft Internet Information Server | | X | This service enables a Windows NT Server computer to function as a WWW, FTP, and a Gopher server. It supports unlimited connections. |
| Microsoft Peer Web Services | X | | This service is a limited version of Microsoft Internet Information Server specifically tailored to the Windows NT Workstation operating system. |

| SERVICE | NT WORKSTATION | NT SERVER | DESCRIPTION |
|---|---|---|---|
| Microsoft TCP/IP Printing | X | X | This service enables Windows NT to connect to TCP/IP–based printers that use the *line printer daemon* (LPD). It also enables Windows NT to function as an LPD print server. |
| NetBIOS Interface | X | X | This service is installed by default and is an integral part of Windows NT networking. |
| Network Monitor Agent | X | X | This service enables Performance Monitor to obtain statistics about the network segment. In addition, computers that run the Network Monitor program from Systems Management Server can remotely access computers that use the Network Monitor Agent in order to capture packets from the segment and gather network statistics. |
| Network Monitor Tools and Agent | | X | The Network Monitor that ships with NT Server is a limited version of the Network Monitor that ships with Systems Management Server. The NT version can't connect to remote agents. Also, the NT version uses a non-promiscuous network driver. (This means that Network Monitor captures only packets that are addressed to the computer that is running Network Monitor.) |
| Remote Access Service (RAS) | X | X | This service enables Windows NT to use serial ports and modems as network adapters, for both dial-in and dial-out networking. Windows NT Server supports 256 simultaneous connections. Windows NT Workstation supports only one connection. |

*continued*

**TABLE 4-2** *(continued)*

| SERVICE | NT WORKSTATION | NT SERVER | DESCRIPTION |
|---|---|---|---|
| Remote Boot Service | | X | This service enables client computers that do not have hard drives to load their operating systems across the network from a Windows NT Server computer that is running the Remote Boot Service. |
| RIP for Internet Protocol | | X | This service enables a Windows NT Server computer that is functioning as a TCP/IP router to update its routing tables dynamically based on information from adjacent routers that also run RIP. |
| RIP for NWLink IPX/SPX Compatible Transport | | X | This service enables a Windows NT Server computer to function as an IPX router. |
| RPC Configuration | X | X | This service is installed by default. It enables a program running on a Windows NT computer to contact a program that is running on another Windows NT computer directly. RPC stands for *Remote Procedure Call*. |
| RPC Support for Banyan | X | X | This service is required to support RPC communications on a Banyan Vines network. |
| SAP Agent | X | X | This service is used to advertise services on an IPX-based network. You should install the SAP Agent when you want to connect a Windows NT computer that runs SQL Server or SNA Server to a NetWare network. |

| SERVICE | NT WORKSTATION | NT SERVER | DESCRIPTION |
|---|---|---|---|
| Server | X | X | This service is installed by default. It enables a Windows NT computer to share its files and printers with other computers on the network. |
| Services for Macintosh | | X | This service enables a Windows NT Server computer to share its files and printers with Macintosh client computers. |
| Simple TCP/IP Services | X | X | This service includes client programs such as Character Generator, Daytime, Echo, and Quote of the Day, for simple network protocols. |
| SNMP Service | X | X | This service enables a Windows NT computer to send trap messages to (and be managed by) an SNMP management station. In addition, this service enables Performance Monitor to obtain TCP/IP statistics. (This service used to be called SNMP Agent.) |
| Windows Internet Name Service (WINS) | | X | This service enables a Windows NT Server computer to function as a TCP/IP-based NetBIOS name server. It enables client computers to resolve NetBIOS names to IP addresses. |
| Workstation | X | X | This service enables Windows NT computers to access files and printers located on other computers across the network. This service is essentially the Windows NT client redirector software. |

## Planning for protocols and services

When planning and implementing a Windows NT installation, you should include all of the protocols and services needed to support every type of client computer that is likely to access the server. Sometimes you may want to limit the number of protocols and services used on the network to reduce network traffic. TCP/IP is often the protocol of choice for use in a large, heterogeneous network environment.

# Installing and Configuring Protocols and Services

Once you have determined which protocols and services you want to install, you're ready to begin the installation process. Installing and configuring protocols and services on Windows NT computers are fairly straightforward procedures.

### TO INSTALL A PROTOCOL OR SERVICE, FOLLOW THESE STEPS:

1. Select Start ⇒ Settings ⇒ Control Panel. Double-click Network. Choose either the Protocols or Services tab (depending on which you want to install).

2. Click the Add command button. The Select Network Protocol (or Select Network Service) dialog box appears.

3. Highlight the protocol or service you want to install. Click OK. (If the protocol or service you want to install is not listed, and you have the third-party software you need to install it, click Have Disk and follow the instructions displayed.) The Windows NT Setup dialog box appears.

4. Enter the path to the Windows NT installation source files (such as your Windows NT compact disc), and click Continue. Windows NT copies the files needed to install the protocol or service you selected. The Network dialog box reappears to give you the opportunity to add or configure additional protocols or services. At this point the protocol or service is added, but not yet configured.

5. Click Close. Windows NT examines the newly installed files, and then prompts you to perform any necessary configurations to the protocol or service.

6. Windows NT then prompts you to reboot your computer so that the new settings can take effect.

Occasionally you may need to reconfigure a protocol or service that was previously installed.

**TO CONFIGURE A PROTOCOL OR SERVICE *AFTER* INSTALLATION, FOLLOW THESE STEPS:**

**1.** Select Start ⇒ Settings ⇒ Control Panel. Double-click Network. Choose either the Protocols or Services tab (depending on which you want to configure).

**2.** Highlight the protocol or service you want to configure. Click the Properties command button. A properties dialog box is displayed for the protocol or service you are configuring. Follow the instructions and provide the information requested in this dialog box.

note ▼ The name and content of this dialog box varies, depending on the specific protocol or service you are configuring. The dialog box may contain several tabs which may each need to be configured.

**3.** Click OK when you are finished. The Network dialog box reappears.

**4.** Click OK to complete the configuration. For some configurations, Windows NT will prompt you to reboot your computer so that the configurations can become effective.

## Configuring Bindings and Network Access Order

*Bindings* and *network access order* specify which protocol or service Windows NT will use first when it attempts to connect to another computer.

Bindings and network access order don't have much effect on the speed of performance of the Server service on Windows NT. (The Server service is normally installed by default on both Windows NT Server and Windows NT Workstation computers.) The Server service's performance is not affected because the Server service replies to the client computer that contacted it by using the same protocol the client computer used. For example, if a client computer uses NetBEUI to contact a server, the server will reply by using NetBEUI, even if TCP/IP is the server's first bound protocol.

Bindings and network access order can be very important to the performance of the Workstation service on Windows NT. (The Workstation service is normally installed by default on both Windows NT Server and Windows NT Workstation computers.) The Workstation service's performance can be affected because the Workstation service will try each of the protocols installed, in the order they are bound, when attempting to connect to another computer. For this reason, if a Windows NT computer is primarily used as a client computer (workstation), you should configure the protocols and services that are used most often to be at the top of the bindings and network access order lists.

Figure 4-12 illustrates the network bindings order on a computer. Notice that the WINS Client (TCP/IP) is the first protocol listed for the Workstation service, and that NWLink NetBIOS is listed second.

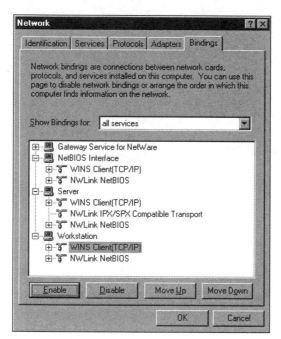

**FIGURE 4-12**  **Bindings order on a Windows NT computer**

Assume that most of the servers you want to connect to from this computer use NWLink NetBIOS. If this is the case, you should move NWLink NetBIOS to the top of the Workstation bindings list. To do this, start the Network application in Control Panel. Select the Bindings tab in the Network dialog box, and then highlight the NWLink NetBIOS Workstation binding, and click the Move Up command button. Click OK to complete the configuration. Windows NT will prompt you to reboot your computer.

The result of this configuration change is shown in Figure 4-13. Notice that NWLink NetBIOS is now the first protocol listed for the Workstation service. Making this configuration change will improve the performance of the Workstation service on this computer.

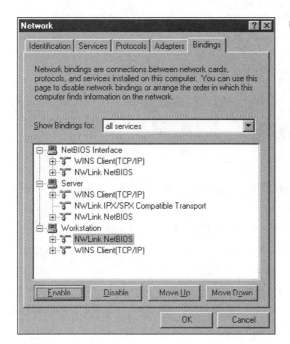

**FIGURE 4-13  Modified Workstation bindings order on a Windows NT computer**

Occasionally you may want to disable network services on one or more network adapters in your server. For example, if you have a server that has two network adapters, one of which is connected to your local network, and the other is connected to the Internet, you might want to disable the Server service on the network adapter that is connected to the Internet so that users on the Internet can't connect network drives to your server. To disable a network binding, start the Network application in Control Panel, select the Bindings tab, highlight the protocol or service on which you want to disable the bindings, and click the Disable command button.

When configuring bindings, the primary emphasis is on ordering protocols. When configuring network access order, the primary emphasis is on ordering network service providers, such as Microsoft Windows Network, or NetWare or Compatible Network. Figure 4-14 shows the network access order on a computer. Notice that Microsoft Windows Network is the first provider listed in the Network Providers list, and that NetWare or Compatible Network is listed second.

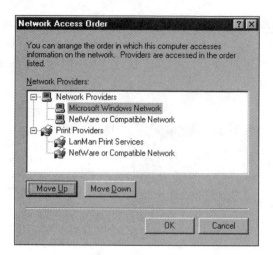

FIGURE 4-14  Network access order on a Windows NT computer

Assume that you use the computer that has the network access order shown in Figure 4-14 primarily to connect to NetWare servers. If this is the case, you should move NetWare or Compatible Network to the top of the Network Providers list. Making this configuration change will improve the performance of the Workstation service on this computer.

To configure network access order, start the Network application in Control Panel. Select the Services tab in the Network dialog box, and then click the Network Access Order command button. Configure the order of Network or Print Providers by highlighting a provider and clicking the Move Up or Move Down command buttons. Click OK. The Services tab in the Network dialog box reappears. Click OK to complete the configuration. Windows NT will prompt you to reboot your computer.

 **The Network Access Order command button appears on the Services tab in the Network dialog box *only* if you have installed more than one network provider, such as Microsoft Windows Network, or NetWare or Compatible Network.**

## Configuring Network Adapters

Occasionally you may need to configure a network adapter. For example, assume that you install an additional card (of any kind) in your computer. You might have to change the settings on your network adapter to resolve an interrupt or an I/O port address conflict between the existing network adapter and the newly installed card.

Configuring a network adapter in Windows NT is usually a two-step process. First, you must configure manually the hardware settings of the network adapter. This can include setting jumpers or switches, or using a manufacturer-supplied configuration program. Second, you must configure the network adapter driver settings used in Windows NT by using the Network application in the Control Panel.

 **note** **Some PC card network adapters are configurable in a single-step process by using the Network application in Control Panel. It would be great if the two steps required to configure most other network adapters were combined into a single step in a future release of Windows NT that fully supports Plug and Play.**

To configure the driver settings for a network adapter, start the Network application in Control Panel. Select the Adapters tab in the Network dialog box. Highlight the adapter you want to configure, and click the Properties command button. An adapter setup dialog box appears. Figure 4-15 shows a setup dialog box for a 3Com Etherlink III network adapter. Notice that you can modify the I/O port address, interrupt, and transceiver type.

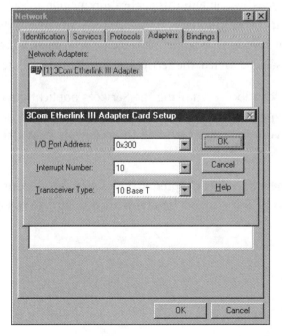

**FIGURE 4-15**  **Configuring a network adapter**

Make any necessary modifications to the settings in the dialog box. Click OK when you are finished. The Adapters tab in the Network dialog box reappears. Click OK to complete the configuration. Windows NT will prompt you to reboot the computer.

 **The options in the adapter setup dialog box vary depending on the specific adapter you select. Some adapters are not configurable at all. For example, to configure the 3Com 3C590 PCI Ethernet adapter, you must boot to DOS and run 3Com's configuration program. There are no configuration options in Windows NT for this adapter.**

# MANAGING SERVICES

 The *Services* application is used to start and stop services, to configure the startup type of services, to view the status of a service, and to enable or disable a service within a hardware profile.

The startup types available in this application include automatic, manual, and disabled. If you choose automatic, Windows NT starts the service automatically every time the computer is booted. If you choose manual, a user must start the service. If you select disabled, the service can't be started by a user.

 **Use extreme caution when using the Services application. Changing the startup type or disabling a service, such as Server or Workstation, can render your computer unable to access (or provide) network resources.**

 **Lab 4.5, at the end of this chapter, includes step-by-step instructions for configuring the startup behavior of the Directory Replicator service.**

# MANAGING THE SERVER

 The *Server* application is used to view user sessions (including the resources that users are accessing), disconnect users from the computer, view the status of shared resources, configure directory replication, and configure administrative alerts. The Server application is included with both NT Workstation and NT Server.

Most of the functions within the Server application are fairly intuitive and straightforward, but directory replication deserves an in-depth discussion.

## Configuring Directory Replication

*Directory replication* was designed to copy logon scripts from a central location (usually the primary domain controller [PDC]) to all domain controllers, thus enabling all users to execute their own logon scripts no matter which domain controller validates their logon. Directory replication is also used extensively by Microsoft Systems Management Server.

 concept link **Directory replication can also be used to replicate system policy. System policy is covered in depth in Chapter 9.**

Replication involves copying all subfolders and their files from the source folder on the source server to the destination folder on all Windows NT computers on the network that are configured as replication destinations.

The source replication folder, by default, is `<winntroot>\system32\repl\export`, where `<winntroot>` is the Windows NT installation folder, which by default is `c:\winnt`. During installation, Windows NT creates a folder named `scripts` in the `export` folder. The `scripts` folder is the default source location for logon scripts.

 note **Logon scripts are batch files. All MS–DOS 5.0 (and earlier versions) batch commands can be used in logon scripts. Logon scripts are covered in more detail in Chapter 9.**

Only subfolders and their files in the `export` folder are replicated. Individual files within the `export` folder are *not* replicated. The `export` folder is shared as the administrative share `REPL$`. This share is not visible in a network browse list.

concept link    **More information on shares is available in Chapter 12.**

The destination replication folder, by default, is `<winntroot>\system32\repl\import`. The `<winntroot>\system32\repl\import\scripts` folder is shared as `NETLOGON`. All client computers look to the `NETLOGON` share on the domain controller that validates their logon for their logon scripts. The `NETLOGON` share is visible in a network browse list.

Replication is configured between source and destination computers. Because of its central location, the primary domain controller (PDC) is usually configured as the source export server, even though any Windows NT Server computer can be configured as the source export server. It seems obvious that the PDC is configured as the export server and that all backup domain controllers (BDCs) are configured as import servers. What is not so obvious is that the PDC should also be configured to import from its *own* `export` folder. In other words, the PDC should be configured to replicate to itself. If the PDC is not configured this way, users that are validated by the PDC won't be able to access their logon scripts.

exam preparation pointer    **Configuring directory replication is a fairly complicated task. The key points you should memorize are listed below. After reading the following steps, I recommend you immediately complete Lab 4.5 at the end of this chapter. (Lab 4.5 contains detailed, step-by-step instructions for configuring directory replication.) Then, come back to this section and review these key points.**

### TO CONFIGURE THE DIRECTORY REPLICATOR SERVICE, FOLLOW THESE STEPS:

**1.** Create and configure a user account for the Directory Replicator service by using User Manager for Domains. This user account must be a member of the Backup Operators group and the Replicator group. In addition, this user account must be granted the "Log on as a service" user right, and must be configured so that its password never expires. Figure 4-16 shows the replication user account being configured in User Manager for Domains. Notice that the user account (Repluser) is a member of the Backup Operators and Replicator groups, as well as the Domain Users group.

note 📝 **WIndows NT Server 4.0 has a fairly significant bug that requires that the user account used by the Directory Replicator service be a member of the Administrators group (in addition to the Backup Operators and Replicator groups) when configuring directory replication between servers. This is not required when configuring directory replication on a single server from its own** export **folder to its own** import **folder.**

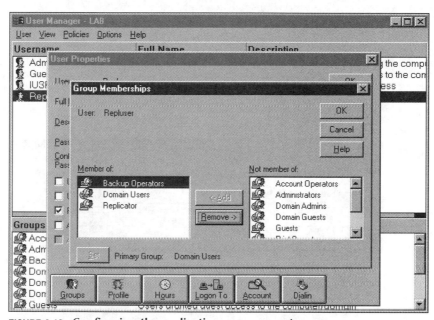

**FIGURE 4-16** **Configuring the replication user account**

2. Configure the startup type of the Directory Replicator service as Automatic, and configure the Directory Replicator service to log on using the user account created in Step 1. (Use the Services applIcation in Control Panel to accomplish this.) Figure 4-17 shows the configuration of the Directory Replicator service on a PDC. Note that the startup type is configured as Automatic, and that the Directory Replicator service is configured to log on as the Repluser account.

3. Configure replication by using the Server application in Control Panel. Figure 4-18 shows a PDC configured for replication. Notice that the PDC (named PDCLAB) is configured to export to all computers in the LAB domain, and that the PDC is configured to import from its own export folder.

**FIGURE 4-17**  Configuring the Directory Replicator service

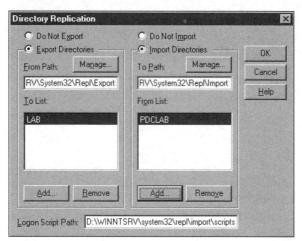

**FIGURE 4-18**  Configuring replication on a PDC

**4.** Stop and restart the Directory Replicator service by using the Services application in Control Panel.

# MANAGING THE SYSTEM

 The *System* application is used to configure foreground application performance, virtual memory, system and user environment variables, startup and shutdown behavior, hardware profiles, and user profiles. Each of these topics is discussed in the following sections.

## Application Performance and Virtual Memory

You can use the System application to set the performance boost for the foreground application and to configure your virtual memory paging file(s).

### *Application performance*

*Foreground application performance* involves giving a higher priority to the application running in the foreground than to other applications. The purpose of assigning a higher priority is to make the foreground application more responsive to the user.

To configure the foreground application priority, double-click the System icon in the Control Panel, and select the Performance tab. Adjust the slide bar for the amount of performance boost you want.

### *Virtual memory*

*Virtual memory* is implemented in Windows NT by the use of paging files.

 concept link    **Virtual memory and paging files are discussed in detail, as you may recall, in the "NT Memory Model" section of Chapter 1.**

You should consider both performance and recoverability when configuring virtual memory paging files.

If you want to configure your system for maximum paging file performance, you should put a small paging file on each physical disk, except on the disk that contains the Windows NT boot partition. This will provide the highest performance for virtual memory.

If you want to configure your system for optimum system recovery, you must put a paging file on the Windows NT boot partition that is at least as large as the amount of RAM in your computer. This paging file is used by Windows NT as a normal paging file, and, additionally, this paging file is required to enable Windows NT to write a `memory.dmp` file when the operating system crashes.

It's up to you to consider the tradeoffs between performance and recoverability, and then to determine the best configuration for your paging files.

You can configure virtual memory paging files by using the System application. On the Performance tab, click the Change command button in the Virtual Memory section. Then configure paging files on each drive as desired.

## Environment Variables

You can use the System application to configure *system* and *user environment variables*. System environment variables apply to all users and to the operating system. User environment variables apply only to a specific user.

To modify a system environment variable, you must be logged on as a user that is a member of the Administrators local group. To modify a user environment variable, you must be logged on as the user whose variable you want to modify.

To configure system and user environment variables, start the System application from the Control Panel, and then select the Environment tab. Highlight the variable you want to modify in the appropriate list box (System or User), edit the value of this variable in the Value text box near the bottom of the dialog box, and then click the Set command button.

To add a new system or user environment variable, highlight any variable in the appropriate list box (System or User), and then type in a new variable name and value in the Variable and Value text boxes near the bottom of the dialog box. Then click the Set command button to create the new variable.

Figure 4-19 shows the layout of the Environment tab within the System application. Notice that the Variable and Value text boxes are located near the bottom of the dialog box.

## Startup/Shutdown

You can use the System application to configure startup and shutdown behavior of Windows NT. Figure 4-20 illustrates the Startup/Shutdown tab within the System application. Notice the System Startup and Recovery options that can be configured.

**FIGURE 4-19** Configuring system and user
environment variables

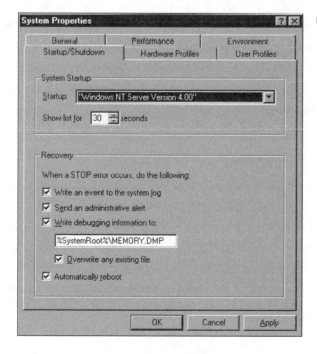

**FIGURE 4-20** Configuring
system startup
and recovery

In the System Startup section of the Startup/Shutdown tab you can configure which operating system will boot by default if no other selection is made from the boot loader menu. You can also configure the length of time the boot loader menu is displayed.

In the Recovery section of the Startup/Shutdown tab you can configure the actions Windows NT takes when a STOP error occurs. A STOP error is an error from which Windows NT cannot recover (in other words, a system crash).

The two most important options you can configure in the Recovery section are the "Write debugging information to" check box and the "Automatically reboot" check box.

The "Write debugging information to" option specifies a file that Windows NT writes the contents of RAM to in the event of a system crash. Remember that Windows NT requires a paging file that is at least as large as the amount of physical RAM on its boot partition in order to create the memory.dmp file.

**In the unlikely event you experience recurrent system crashes, the** memory.dmp **file will be needed when you contact Microsoft Technical Support. Microsoft Technical Support personnel can use a debugger on your** memory.dmp **file to identify and resolve the cause of your system crashes.**

The "Automatically reboot" option, when selected, causes Windows NT to reboot the computer in the event of a system crash. If you select the "Automatically reboot" option, you should also select the "Write an event to the system log" option, so that you will be able to tell, when you view the system log, that the system has crashed and rebooted.

## Hardware Profiles

You can use the System application to create and configure *hardware profiles*. Windows NT creates an initial hardware profile during installation.

The primary reason for creating hardware profiles is to manage the different hardware configurations of laptop computers. (A laptop computer that is used at the office in a docking station has a different hardware configuration than the same laptop computer when it is used at home or on the road without a docking station.) Hardware profiles make it possible to create custom configurations for the same laptop computer that is used both with and without a docking station.

Figure 4-21 shows the Hardware Profiles tab within the System application. Note that you can use the arrows on the right hand side to move profiles up or down in the Available Hardware Profiles list box. Windows NT uses the first profile in this list when no other selection is made during the boot process.

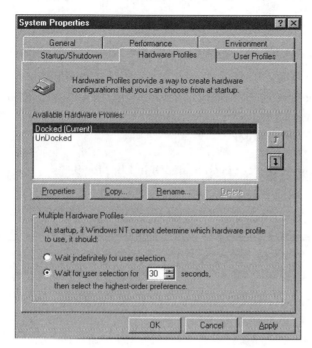

**FIGURE 4-21** Managing hardware profiles

To create a new hardware profile, start the System application from Control Panel, and select the Hardware Profiles tab. Highlight any profile in the Available Hardware Profiles list box, and click the Copy command button. A Copy Profile dialog appears, permitting you to type in a name for your new hardware profile. The new hardware profile now has the same properties as the profile you highlighted and copied. You can configure this new profile as necessary.

To configure a new or existing hardware profile, highlight the profile in the Available Hardware Profiles list box and click the Properties command button. Then select the docking status for this hardware profile, and specify whether this is a network disabled profile. (A network disabled profile prevents any network services from starting on a computer.)

You can also use the Services and Devices applications to enable and disable services and device drivers within each hardware profile.

Once you have created multiple profiles, Windows NT displays the Hardware Profile/Configuration Recovery menu after the boot loader menu when your computer boots to Windows NT. This menu permits you to select the hardware profile you want Windows NT to use. You can configure the length of time this menu is displayed in the Multiple Hardware Profiles section on the Hardware Profiles tab.

## User Profiles

You can use the User Profiles tab within the System application to copy, delete, and change the type of user profiles. The System application is the only application in Windows NT that can copy user profiles. You can't copy user profiles by using Windows NT Explorer.

 concept link    **User profiles are covered in depth in Chapter 9.**

# OTHER CONTROL PANEL APPLICATIONS

Control Panel has several other applications. These applications are all fairly straightforward to use. Each application is briefly discussed in the following sections.

## Add/Remove Programs

 The *Add/Remove Programs* application is used to install and remove third-party software and to add and remove Windows NT optional components.

## Console

 The *Console* application is used to configure how MS-DOS windows appear in Windows NT. You can customize the cursor size, display options (such as window and full screen), font size and type, number of columns and rows, and colors used in each MS-DOS window.

## Date/Time

 The *Date/Time* application is used to configure the date, time, time zone, and optional adjustment for daylight saving time.

You can also access the Date/Time application by double-clicking the clock in the right-hand corner of the taskbar on your desktop.

## Fonts

 The *Fonts* application is used to install, delete, and manage fonts.

## Internet

 The *Internet* application is used to configure whether a proxy server (such as Microsoft Proxy Server) is used when you use applications (such as Microsoft Internet Explorer, FTP.exe, and so on) to access the Internet.

## ODBC

 The *ODBC* application is used to install and remove ODBC drivers. In addition, this application enables you to configure ODBC data sources.

ODBC-enabled applications (such as Microsoft Excel) can use the installed ODBC drivers to connect to data sources (such as Microsoft SQL Server and Microsoft Access).

## Regional Settings

 The *Regional Settings* application is used to configure how certain objects, such as numbers, currency, date, and time are displayed in applications.

You can also use this application to configure your keyboard layout.

## Sounds

The *Sounds* application is used to assign sounds to system events. Some of the Windows NT system events that sounds can be assigned to are exit Windows, new mail notification, empty recycle bin, and many more.

Windows NT supports various sound schemes, including Jungle, Musica, Robotz, and Utopia. You can record new sounds and assign them to the system event you desire. You can also use the Sounds application to select the No Sounds sound scheme if you don't want sounds.

## Telephony

The *Telephony* application is used to configure dialing properties for your computer, such as the area code you are calling from, the country you are in, special instructions on how to access an outside line, whether or not to dial using a calling card, instructions on how to disable call waiting, and to specify tone or pulse dialing. In addition, you can use this application to install, configure, and remove telephony drivers.

# TROUBLESHOOTING COMMON CONFIGURATION PROBLEMS

Configuration problems are common and usually arise in three major areas: hardware, directory replication, and protocols. Troubleshooting configuration problems can be difficult, because it's easy to overlook a simple configuration issue, and to look instead for some complicated (and usually nonexistent) cause.

Some of the most common hardware configuration problems occur when two cards installed in the same computer are configured to use the same interrupt, I/O port address, or DMA address. To resolve this type of problem, you must reconfigure one of the cards to use a nonconflicting setting.

Another common hardware configuration problem occurs when a card is physically configured in one way (via switches or jumpers), and the software driver for that card is configured with different settings. To resolve this type of problem, you must either change the hardware settings or the software driver settings so that both use the same settings.

 in the real world

**Most of the troubleshooting problems I have seen were caused by omitting a step in a configuration process or setting configuration options incorrectly. The successful troubleshooter looks first to make sure that all steps in a configuration process have been completed and to verify that all configuration options are set correctly.**

Directory replication is fairly straightforward to troubleshoot. Verify that each step necessary to configure replication has been properly completed. Ensure that the replication user account is a member of the Backup Operators and Replicator groups, has the "Log on as a service" user right, and is configured so that its password never expires. Make sure the Directory Replicator service is configured to start automatically, and that it is configured to log on by using the replication user account. Verify the password for the replication user account, and ensure that this password is being used by the Directory Replicator service. Verify that the source and destination servers are configured for replication. Finally, make sure to stop and restart the Directory Replicator service on all replication servers.

Troubleshooting protocols can be a detailed, painstaking task.

TCP/IP, for example, is easy to configure improperly. Several settings must be typed on each computer that uses this protocol, including IP address, subnet mask, and default gateway. The best way to prevent configuration problems in a TCP/IP environment is to use a DHCP server to configure TCP/IP automatically on each computer on the network. If you don't use DHCP, you should manually verify that the settings are correctly entered on each computer that experiences a network communications problem.

NWLink IPX/SPX Compatible Transport also has several configuration settings, and thus is prone to human error during protocol configuration. Verify that all of the settings for this (and every) protocol are correctly entered on each computer that experiences a network communications problem.

# KEY POINT SUMMARY

This chapter introduced Control Panel and its numerous applications.

- Many Control Panel applications are used when managing peripherals and devices, including *Accessibility Options*, *Devices*, *Display*, *Keyboard*, *Modems*, *Mouse*, *Multimedia*, *PC Card (PCMCIA)*, *Ports*, *Printers*, *SCSI Adapters*, *Tape Devices*, and *UPS*.

- The *Licensing* application (on Windows NT Server) permits you to change your Windows NT Server licensing mode or to reflect a change in the number of client licenses you have purchased.

- The *Network* application is used to change a computer/domain/workgroup name, to join a domain, to install and configure protocols and services, to configure bindings and network access order, and to configure network adapters. Remember that you can't change a domain controller's domain membership just by changing its domain name.

  - The *protocols and services* that ship with Windows NT Workstation and Windows NT Server are identified and described. Of all the protocols listed, TCP/IP is often the protocol of choice for use in a large, heterogeneous network environment because of its routability, speed, and support by numerous operating systems. When planning a Windows NT installation, you should include all of the protocols and services needed to support every type of client computer that is likely to access the server, keeping in mind that you may need to limit the number of protocols and services used to reduce network traffic.

  - To improve the performance of the Workstation service, *bindings and network access order* should be configured so that the protocol and service that are used most often are listed at the top of their respective lists.

- The *Services* application is used to start and stop services, to configure the startup type of services, to view the status of a service, and to enable or disable a service within a hardware profile.

- The *Server* application is used to view user sessions, disconnect users from the computer, view the status of shared resources, configure directory replication, and configure administrative alerts.

- *Directory replication*, which was designed to copy logon scripts from a central location to all domain controllers, involves copying folders and their files from a source folder on a source server to a destination folder on all Windows NT computers on the network that are configured as replication destinations. Follow these steps to configure the *Directory Replicator service*:

  1. Create and configure a user account for the Directory Replicator service using User Manager for Domains. This account must be a member of the Backup Operators group and the Replicator group. This user account must also be granted the "Log on as a service" user right, and must be configured so that its password never expires.

  2. Configure the startup type of the Directory Replicator service as Automatic (using the Services application). Configure the Directory Replicator service to log on using the user account created in Step 1.

  3. Configure replication by using the Server application. Remember that the PDC should be configured to replicate to itself.

  4. Stop and restart the Directory Replicator service by using the Services application.

- The *System* application is used to configure foreground application performance, virtual memory (paging files), system and user environment variables, startup and shutdown behavior, hardware profiles, and user profiles.

  - Consider both performance and recoverability when configuring paging files.

  - When configuring startup/shutdown behavior, consider selecting the "Write debugging to" and "Automatically reboot" options, so that Windows NT will write the contents of RAM to a `memory.dmp` file (as long as it has a paging file that is at least as large as the amount of RAM on its boot partition) and so that NT will automatically reboot in the event of a system crash.

  - The primary reason for creating hardware profiles is to manage the different hardware configurations of laptop computers.

  - The System application is the only application in Windows NT that can copy user profiles.

- Other applications in Control Panel are briefly described, including *Add/Remove Programs, Console, Date/Time, Fonts, Internet, ODBC, Regional Settings, Sounds, and Telephony*.

o Some tips on troubleshooting common configuration problems are presented. Configuration problems normally arise in three major areas: hardware, directory replication, and protocols. When you troubleshoot, make sure that all steps in a configuration process have been completed and verify that all configuration options are set correctly. Also, verify that hardware devices do not have conflicting interrupt, I/O port addresses, or DMA addresses.

# APPLYING WHAT YOU'VE LEARNED

Now it's time to regroup, review, and apply what you've learned in this chapter.

The questions in the following Instant Assessment section bring to mind key facts and concepts. In addition, the review activity tests your knowledge of specific Control Panel applications.

The hands-on lab exercises will really reinforce what you've learned, and provide you an opportunity to practice several of the tasks tested by the Microsoft Certified Professional exams.

## Instant Assessment

1. What three ways can you access Control Panel?

2. What is the Accessibility Options application used for?

3. Which Control Panel application is used to configure a computer's desktop background, screen saver options, desktop appearance, and Microsoft Plus! options?

4. If you change the domain name of one domain controller in a domain, what else must you do?

5. Which of the protocols that ship with Windows NT is a routable protocol usually associated with NetWare networks?

6. Which of the protocols that ship with Windows NT is usually associated with Macintosh computers and printers?

7. Which of the protocols that ship with Windows NT is a fast, routable enterprise protocol that is used on the Internet and is supported by many operating systems, including Windows NT, Windows 95, Macintosh, UNIX, MS-DOS, and IBM mainframes?

8. When configuring bindings and network access order, where should the protocol and service that are used most often be placed (ordered) on their respective lists to achieve the best Workstation service performance?

9. What are the four tasks that must be accomplished to configure the Directory Replicator service?

10. If you want to configure your Windows NT computer for optimum system recovery, how large must the paging file on your Windows NT boot partition be?

11. What is the only Windows NT application that you can use to copy user profiles?

12. You are troubleshooting what you believe is a configuration problem. What actions should you take?

**T/F**

13. You can't change a domain controller's domain membership by changing its name.                                    _____

 concept link    **For answers to the Instant Assessment questions see Appendix D.**

## Review Activity

The following review activity tests your knowledge of when to use specific Control Panel applications.

Workstation
Server
Enterprise

### *Control Panel application matching exercise*

Do you know which Control Panel application you should use to perform various tasks? Match the letter of the Control Panel application from the list on the left that you should use to perform each task listed on the right. Applications may be used more than once.

**Control Panel Application**

A.  Accessibility Options

B.  Add/Remove Programs

C.  Console

D.  Date/Time

E.  Devices

F.  Display

G.  Fonts

H.  Internet

I.  Keyboard

J.  Licensing

K.  Modems

L.  Mouse

M.  Multimedia

N.  Network

O.  ODBC

P.  PC Card (PCMCIA)

Q.  Ports

R.  Printers

S.  Regional Settings

T.  SCSI Adapters

U.  Server

V.  Services

W.  Sounds

X.  System

Y.  Tape Devices

Z.  Telephony

Zz. UPS

**Task**

1. _____ You want to install the Windows NT games on your Windows NT computer.

2. _____ You want to change the screen saver settings on your Windows NT computer.

3. _____ You want to change your Windows NT Server licensing mode.

4. _____ You want to change your keyboard layout to a US-Dvorak layout.

5. _____ You want to change the computer name of a domain controller.

6. _____ You want to install the TCP/IP Protocol on your Windows NT computer

7. _____ You want to configure bindings and network access order on your Windows NT computer.

8. _____ You want to stop and start the Directory Replicator service.

9. _____ You want to configure the replication import and export options on your Windows NT computer.

10. _____ You want to copy a user profile.

11. _____ You want to create a new hardware profile on your Windows NT computer.

12. _____ You want to configure a paging file on your Windows NT computer.

 concept link    **For answers to the Review Activity see Appendix D.**

# Hands-on Lab Exercises

The following hands-on lab exercises provide excellent opportunities to explore and use the Control Panel applications you've learned about in this chapter.

### Lab 4.5 *Configuring directory replication*

Server
Enterprise

The purpose of this lab is to provide you with hands-on experience and the skills needed to configure and use the Directory Replicator service.

There are seven parts to this lab:

> Part 1: Creating a logon script
> Part 2: Creating a directory replication user account
> Part 3: Configuring the startup type of the Directory Replicator service
> Part 4: Configuring replication
> Part 5: Stopping and restarting the Directory Replicator service
> Part 6: Viewing the replication of the logon script
> Part 7: Testing your logon script

Follow the steps below carefully.

**Part 1: Creating a logon script**

**1.** Boot your computer to Windows NT Server.

**2.** Select Start ⇒ Programs ⇒ Accessories ⇒ Notepad.

**3.** In the Untitled—Notepad dialog box, type the following:

**@echo This is the logon script I created in Lab 4.5.**

**@echo**

**@echo**

**@pause**

(Note: Make sure to type the text *exactly* as it is presented above.)

**4.** Select File ⇒ Save As. Edit the "File name" text box to read as follows:

**c:\winntsrv\system32\repl\export\scripts\logonscript.bat**

**5.** Click Save.

**6.** Exit Notepad.

**Part 2: Creating a directory replication user account**

**1.** Select Start ⇒ Programs ⇒ Administrative Tools (Common) ⇒ User Manager for Domains.

**2.** Select User ⇒ New User in the User Manager dialog box.

**3.** In the New User dialog box, type in the username **Repluser**. Type in a password of **password** (remember that passwords are case-sensitive in Windows NT). Confirm the password by retyping it in the Confirm Password box. Deselect the check box next to User Must Change Password at Next Logon. Select the check box next to Password Never Expires. Click the Groups command button at the lower left-hand corner of the dialog box.

**4.** The Group Memberships dialog box appears. In the "Not member of" text box, highlight Backup Operators and click the Add command button. In the "Not member of" text box, highlight Replicator and click the Add command button. There should be three groups listed in the "Member of" text box: Backup Operators, Domain Users, and Replicator. Click OK.

**5.** The New User dialog box reappears. Click Add. Then click Close.

**6.** The User Manager dialog box reappears. Exit User Manager.

### Part 3: Configuring the startup type of the Directory Replicator service

**1.** Select Start ⇒ Settings ⇒ Control Panel.

**2.** Double-click Services.

**3.** The Services dialog box appears. Highlight Directory Replicator. Click Startup.

**4.** The Service dialog box appears. In the Startup Type section, select the Automatic radio button. In the Log On As section, select the This Account radio button. Click the … command button at the end of the This Account text box.

**5.** The Add User dialog box appears. In the Names list box, highlight Repluser, and click Add. Click OK.

**6.** The Service dialog box reappears. Highlight the asterisks in the Password text box and type **password**. In the Confirm Password text box, highlight the asterisks and type **password**. Click OK.

**7.** A Services dialog box appears indicating that the account LAB\Repluser has been granted the Log On As A Service right. Click OK.

**8.** The Services dialog box reappears. Click Close. The Control Panel dialog box reappears.

### Part 4: Configuring replication

**1.** In Control Panel, double-click Server.

**2.** In the Server dialog box, click Replication.

**3.** The Directory Replication dialog box appears. Click the Export Directories radio button. Click the Add command button at the bottom of the Export Directories section.

**4.** The Select Domain dialog box appears. In the Select Domain list box, click LAB. LAB should now appear in the Domain text box. Click OK.

**5.** The Directory Replication dialog box reappears. LAB should appear in the To List box. Click the Import Directories radio button. Click the Add command button at the bottom of the Import Directories section.

**6.** The Select Domain dialog box appears. In the Select Domain list box, double-click LAB. Click PDCLAB. \\PDCLAB should now appear in the Domain text box. Click OK.

**7.** The Directory Replication dialog box reappears. PDCLAB should appear in the From list box. Click OK to save the directory replication configuration and automatically start the Directory Replicator service.

**8.** In the Server dialog box, click OK. The Control Panel dialog box reappears.

## Part 5: Stopping and restarting the Directory Replicator service

**1.** In Control Panel, double-click Services.

**2.** The Services dialog box appears. In the Service list box, highlight Directory Replicator. Click Stop. A warning message appears, asking if you want to stop the Directory Replicator service. Click Yes.

**3.** A Service Control dialog box appears, indicating that NT is attempting to stop the Directory Replicator service.

**4.** The Services dialog box reappears. Note that the Status column no longer shows "Started" for the Directory Replicator service. Click Start.

**5.** A Service Control dialog box appears, indicating that NT is attempting to start the Directory Replicator service.

**6.** The Services dialog box reappears. Note that the Status column now shows "Started" for the Directory Replicator service. Click Close.

**7.** The Control Panel dialog box reappears. Exit Control Panel.

## Part 6: Viewing the replication of the logon script

**1.** Select Start ⇒ Programs ⇒ Windows NT Explorer.

**2.** Maximize the Exploring dialog box. In the All Folders column on the left, click the + sign next to the `Winntsrv` folder. Then click the + sign next to the `system32` folder. Click the + sign next to the `Repl` folder. Click the + sign next to the `Export` folder. Click the `Scripts` folder. Notice that the `logonscript.bat` file you created in the first part of this lab appears in the Contents window. (Remember that you saved this file in the `c:\winntsrv\system32\repl\export\scripts` folder in the first part of this lab.)

**3.** Click the + sign next to the `Import` folder (in the All Folders column on the left). Click the `Scripts` folder beneath the `Import` folder. Notice that the `logonscript.bat` file has been replicated from the `Export\Scripts` folder to the `Import\Scripts` folder. The Directory Replicator service is now fully functional. Exit Windows NT Explorer.

### Part 7: Testing your logon script

**1.** Select Start⇒Programs⇒Administrative Tools (Common)⇒User Manager for Domains.

**2.** In the User Manager dialog box, select User⇒Properties.

**3.** The User Properties dialog box appears. Click the Profile command button.

**4.** The User Environment Profile dialog box appears. In the Logon Script Name text box, type **logonscript.bat**. (Don't type the period at the end.) Click OK.

**5.** The User Properties dialog box reappears. Click OK.

**6.** Close User Manager.

**7.** Select Start⇒Shut Down. The Shut Down Windows dialog box appears. Click the "Close all programs and log on as a different user" radio button. Then click Yes.

**8.** In the Begin Logon dialog box, press Ctrl + Alt + Delete to log on.

**9.** The Logon Information dialog box appears. Type in your password in the Password text box. Click OK.

**10.** A command prompt window should appear. The logon script you created in part one of this lab has run and appears like the following:

```
This is the logon script I created in Lab 4.5.
ECHO is on.
ECHO is on.
Press any key to continue . . .
```

**11.** Press the spacebar to complete this lab.

 tip **This logon script will appear every time you log on from this point. If you'd like to remove it, start User Manager for Domains, and then double-click the Administrator user. Click Profile. Highlight** `logonscript.bat` **in the User Environment Profile d0ialog box, and**

press Delete. Click OK. In the User Properties dialog box, click OK.
Exit User Manager for Domains.

## Lab 4.6 *Exploring Control Panel*

Workstation
Server

The purpose of this hands-on lab exercise is to provide you the skills required to
use Control Panel applications.

This lab is divided into three parts. You'll use the following Control Panel
applications in the following three sections:

Part 1: Using Add/Remove Programs

Part 2: Using System

Part 3: Becoming familiar with Display, Keyboard, Modems, Mouse,
Ports, SCSI Adapters, Tape Devices, and UPS

Begin this lab by booting your computer to Windows NT Server.

### Part 1: Using Add/Remove Programs

In this part you use Add/Remove Programs to install an optional Windows NT
component.

#### TO INSTALL MAIL, FOLLOW THESE STEPS:

**1.** Select Start ⇒ Settings ⇒ Control Panel.

**2.** Double-click Add/Remove Programs.

**3.** In the Add/Remove Programs Properties dialog box, click the Windows NT
Setup tab. Scroll to the bottom of the Components list box. Click in the
check box next to Windows Messaging. Click the Details command button.
Ensure that the Internet Mail, Microsoft Mail, and Windows Messaging
check boxes are all selected. Click OK.

**4.** In the Windows NT Setup tab in the Add/Remove Programs Properties
dialog box, click OK.

**5.** NT copies files to your hard disk. If prompted, supply the path to your
Windows NT installation source files (usually on your Windows NT compact
disc). This process takes a few minutes.

**6.** The Control Panel dialog box reappears. Windows Messaging (Mail) is now
installed. Exit Control Panel.

**7.** Optional: If you want, you can install games on your computer using the
same steps, except click the check box next to Games (instead of Windows
Messaging) in the Windows NT Setup tab. (Try Pinball if you have a sound
card—it's really fun!)

### Part 2: Using System

In this part you use System to create an additional paging file and create a hardware profile.

#### TO CREATE AN ADDITIONAL PAGING FILE, FOLLOW THESE STEPS:

**1.** Select Start ⟹ Settings ⟹ Control Panel.

**2.** Double-click System.

**3.** Click the Performance tab in the System Properties dialog box. In the Virtual Memory section, click Change.

**4.** The Virtual Memory dialog box appears. Click D: in the Drive list box. In the Paging File Size for Selected Drive section, type **5** in the Initial Size (MB) text box, and type **5** in the Maximum Size (MB) text box. Click Set. Notice that Drive D: now shows a Paging File Size of 5-5 in the list box at the top of the screen. Click OK.

**5.** On the Performance tab click Close.

**6.** Click Yes to restart your computer so the new settings can take effect.

#### TO CREATE A HARDWARE PROFILE, FOLLOW THESE STEPS:

Hardware profiles were originally designed to handle the unique needs of laptop computers. In this lab you create two hardware profiles: docked (connected to the network) and undocked (not connected to the network) to simulate the use of a laptop computer at work and at home.

**1.** Select Start ⟹ Settings ⟹ Control Panel.

**2.** Double-click System.

**3.** Click the Hardware Profiles tab. Highlight Original Configuration (Current) in the Available Hardware Profiles list box. Click the Rename command button.

**4.** In the Rename Profile dialog box, edit the To: text box to read as follows: **Docked**. (Don't type the period at the end.) Click OK.

**5.** The Hardware Profiles tab reappears. Highlight Docked (Current) in the Available Hardware Profiles list box. Click Copy.

**6.** In the Copy Profile dialog box, edit the To: text box to read as follows: **UnDocked**. (Don't type the period at the end.) Click OK.

**7.** The Hardware Profiles tab reappears. Notice that two profiles now appear in the Available Hardware Profiles list box: Docked (Current) and UnDocked. Highlight UnDocked and click the Properties command button.

**8.** In the UnDocked Properties dialog box, click the Network tab. Click the check box next to Network-disabled hardware profile. Click OK.

**9.** The Hardware Profiles tab reappears. Click OK. Exit Control Panel.

**10.** Select Start ⇒ Shut Down. Click the "Restart the computer" radio button in the Shut Down Windows dialog box. Click Yes.

**11.** After you select Windows NT Server 4.0 from the boot loader menu, press the spacebar when the "`Press spacebar now to invoke the Hardware Profile/Last Known Good menu`" appears.

**12.** A Hardware Profile/Configuration Recovery Menu is displayed. You can select a Docked or UnDocked hardware profile at this point. (Select Docked if you are connected to a network; select UnDocked if you are not connected to a network.) Press Enter to continue booting Windows NT Server.

### Part 3: Becoming familiar with Display, Keyboard, Modems, Mouse, Ports, SCSI Adapters, Tape Devices, and UPS

In this part you explore several Control Panel applications. (You may even use a few of these applications to install devices that you have but which may not yet be installed.)

#### DISPLAY

**1.** Select Start ⇒ Settings ⇒ Control Panel.

**2.** Double-click Display.

**3.** In the Display Properties dialog box, click the Screen Saver tab.

**4.** In the Screen Saver drop-down list box, select 3D Pipes (OpenGL). Click the Settings command button.

**5.** In the 3D Pipes Setup dialog box, click the Textured radio button in the Surface Style section. Click the Choose Texture command button.

**6.** In the Choose Texture File dialog box, double-click `lanmannt.bmp`.

**7.** The 3D Pipes Setup dialog box reappears. Click OK.

**8.** The Screen Saver tab reappears. Click Apply. (Your screen saver now consists of 3D Pipes that say "Windows NT Server" on them.)

**9.** Click the Settings tab. In the Desktop Area section, click and hold the slide bar and move it to the right until the display reads "800 by 600 pixels." (Note: If your computer does not support a display setting larger than "640 by 480 pixels", you can click the slide bar, but it won't move.) Continue to Step 10.

**10.** Click the Test command button. Click OK in the Testing Mode dialog box.

**11.** A test screen appears for about five seconds. When the Testing Mode dialog box appears, click Yes if you saw the test bitmap.

**12.** The Settings tab reappears. Click OK to apply your new display settings.

 **If you do not like the appearance of an 800 by 600 display, or your computer can't accommodate this setting, you can change your display settings to any resolution you desire. Follow Steps 9 through 12 to change your display settings.**

### KEYBOARD

**1.** Select Start ⇒ Settings ⇒ Control Panel.

**2.** Double-click Keyboard.

**3.** In the Keyboard Properties dialog box, click the Input Locales tab. Click the Properties command button. Click the drop-down arrow in the Keyboard layout drop-down list box to view the optional keyboard layouts. Notice that US, several Dvorak options, and US-International are listed. Click US, and then click OK.

**4.** In the Input Locales tab in the Keyboard Properties dialog box, click Cancel.

### MODEMS

You don't have to have a modem to complete this section. If you have already installed a modem in your computer using the Modems application in Control Panel, skip this section.

**1.** Select Start ⇒ Settings ⇒ Control Panel.

**2.** Double-click Modems.

**3.** The Install New Modem dialog box appears. Select the check box next to "Don't detect my modem; I will select it from a list." Click the Next command button.

**4.** The Install Modem dialog box appears. Select your modem's manufacturer from the Manufacturers list box. If your manufacturer is not listed, or if you don't have a modem, highlight (Standard Modem Types). Select your modem speed or model in the Models list box, or select Dial-Up Networking Serial Cable between 2 PCs if you don't have a modem. Then click Next.

**5.** The Install New Modem dialog box appears. Click the "Selected ports" radio button.

6. Highlight the COM port to which your modem is connected, or any available COM port (to which your mouse or another device isn't connected) if you don't have a modem. Click Next. Windows NT installs your modem.

7. A dialog box may appear at this point requesting the area code you are in and other information. If this box appears, enter the requested information and continue. If a dialog box does not appear, skip to Step 8.

8. Click the Finish command button.

9. In the Modems Properties dialog box, click the Dialing Properties command button.

10. In the Dialing Properties dialog box, configure the dialing properties for your location. Then click OK.

11. In the Modems Properties dialog box, click Close.

## MOUSE

1. Select Start ⇒ Settings ⇒ Control Panel.

2. Double-click Mouse.

3. In the Mouse Properties dialog box, click each tab and view the configuration options available. Customize your mouse to suit your personal preferences. Click OK to return to Control Panel.

## PORTS

1. Select Start ⇒ Settings ⇒ Control Panel.

2. Double-click Ports.

3. In the Ports dialog box, highlight a COM port, and click Settings.

4. In the Settings dialog box, notice the settings that you can configure for your COM port. Customize your COM port settings as desired. Click Advanced.

5. In the Advanced Settings dialog box, notice the settings that you can configure. Click OK.

6. In the Settings dialog box, click OK.

7. In the Ports dialog box, click Close.

## SCSI ADAPTERS

1. Select Start ⇒ Settings ⇒ Control Panel.

2. Double-click SCSI Adapters.

**3.** View the configuration options available on both the Devices tab and the Drivers tab by clicking each of the tabs. If you have a SCSI adapter but have not yet installed drivers for it, you may want to do so now. You can do this by clicking the Add command button on the Drivers tab and then selecting the appropriate manufacturer and SCSI adapter from the lists displayed. Click OK.

### TAPE DEVICES

**1.** Select Start ⟹ Settings ⟹ Control Panel.

**2.** Double-click Tape Devices.

**3.** View the configuration options available on both the Devices tab and the Drivers tab by clicking each of the tabs. If you have a tape drive but have not yet installed drivers for it, you may want to do so now. You can do this by clicking the Add command button on the Drivers tab and then selecting the appropriate manufacturer and tape device from the lists displayed. Click OK.

### UPS

**1.** Select Start ⟹ Settings ⟹ Control Panel.

**2.** Double-click UPS.

**3.** In the UPS dialog box, view the configuration options available. Click Help.

**4.** Read through the UPS help topics. Exit Windows NT Help.

**5.** If you do not have a UPS, skip to Step 6 now. If you have a UPS but have not yet configured it, you may want to do so now. Configure the settings in the UPS dialog box to match your UPS. Click OK. Stop here if you have a UPS (don't do Step 6).

**6.** Click Cancel in the UPS dialog box. Exit Control Panel.

Workstation
Server
Enterprise

CHAPTER

5

# Server-Based Deployment

# About Chapter 5

This chapter tackles the subject of server-based deployment—the process of automating the installation and setup of Windows NT on multiple computers at a time, either at the factory or on a private network.

First, the chapter addresses what you need to do to prepare for server-based deployment. Complete instructions for this part of the process are outlined.

Next, Chapter 5 introduces *Network Client Administrator*, a Windows NT Server tool you can use to create an installation disk set, or to create a network installation startup disk.

Next, you'll discover how to create answer files and Uniqueness Database Files to fully automate the Windows NT installation and setup process.

Finally, this chapter addresses how to automate the installation of applications during an automated installation of Windows NT. The $OEM$ subfolder and Sysdiff.exe are introduced in this section.

This chapter includes a hands-on lab that will familiarize you with the use of Setup Manager to create an answer file.

This chapter is a "must read," no matter which of the three Windows NT 4.0 Microsoft Certified Professional exams you're preparing for. The information in this chapter covers various objectives listed in the Planning and Installation and Configuration sections in these exams' objectives.

# WHAT IS SERVER-BASED DEPLOYMENT?

*Server-based deployment* is a process that involves automating the installation and setup of Windows NT, other operating systems (Windows 95 and Windows for Workgroups), and applications on multiple computers on a network.

This process is primarily designed for rolling out large networks quickly and efficiently.

exam preparation pointer

**The Windows NT Workstation exam has objectives in both the Planning and Installation and Configuration sections that concern server-based deployment. Because you are unlikely to use server-based deployment very often in real life (unless you manage a large network), I recommend you study this chapter carefully, and revisit it just before you take the Workstation exam. I'd like to tell you to just study one or two sections, but the truth is, the whole chapter's fair game on the exam.**

**Both the Server and Enterprise exams have an objective that concerns configuring a Windows NT Server computer for various types of client computers. This objective ties in to the "Using Network Client Administrator" section of this chapter, and deserves your attention.**

In server-based deployment, source files are placed on a centrally located Windows NT Server computer. Then floppy disks are created which, when run on the computers that need to be set up, cause these computers to automatically connect to the server and to run a partially or fully automated installation and setup routine.

Server-based deployment is commonly used in two types of environments. First, *original equipment manufacturers* (OEMs) use this process to install and configure large numbers of computers at the factory prior to shipping these computers to customers and retail outlets. Second, organizations that install a new network or add several new computers to an existing network use this process to install operating systems and applications on their new computers in an efficient manner.

*tip* **Using server-based deployment can save you a significant amount of time. Consider using it when you have five or more identical installs to perform.**

Before you can use server-based deployment, you must prepare the Windows NT Server computer that will store the source files used in this process.

# PREPARING FOR SERVER-BASED DEPLOYMENT

To prepare your Windows NT Server computer for server-based deployment, you need to place the appropriate files on this server in a prescribed format.

To begin the preparation, copy the `Clients` folder, including all files and subfolders, from your Windows NT Server compact disc to one of the drives on the Windows NT Server computer. This drive must have enough free space to hold the entire contents of the `Clients` folder and the source files for any additional operating systems and applications you want to install using server-based deployment.

Then share the `Clients` folder on the Windows NT Server computer as `CLIENTS`. At this point, if the only operating system you want to deploy is Windows 95, you are finished preparing your Windows NT Server computer. If you want to deploy other operating systems, follow the steps below for *each* operating system you want to deploy.

**TO PREPARE YOUR WINDOWS NT SERVER COMPUTER FOR SERVER-BASED DEPLOYMENT OF WINDOWS FOR WORKGROUPS, FOLLOW THESE STEPS:**

**1.** Create a subfolder in the Clients folder named `Wfw`.

**2.** Create a subfolder in the `Clients\Wfw` folder named `Netsetup`.

**3.** Copy the Windows for Workgroups installation files from your source media (compact disc or floppy disk) to the `Netsetup` folder.

**TO PREPARE YOUR WINDOWS NT SERVER COMPUTER FOR SERVER-BASED DEPLOYMENT OF WINDOWS NT WORKSTATION, FOLLOW THESE STEPS:**

**1.** Create a subfolder in the `Clients` folder named `Winnt`.

**2.** Create a subfolder in the `Clients\Winnt` folder named `Netsetup`.

**3.** Copy the Windows NT Workstation installation files and subfolders from the `I386` folder on your Windows NT Workstation compact disc to the `Netsetup` folder.

**TO PREPARE YOUR WINDOWS NT SERVER COMPUTER FOR SERVER-BASED DEPLOYMENT OF WINDOWS NT SERVER, FOLLOW THESE STEPS:**

**1.** Create a subfolder in the `Clients` folder named `Winnt.srv`.

**2.** Create a subfolder in the `Clients\Winnt.srv` folder named `Netsetup`.

**3.** Copy the Windows NT Server installation files and subfolders from the `I386` folder on your Windows NT Server compact disc to the `Netsetup` folder.

---

Now that you've prepared your Windows NT Server computer, you're ready to use the Network Client Administrator tool to proceed with the server-based deployment process.

# USING NETWORK CLIENT ADMINISTRATOR

*Network Client Administrator* is a Windows NT Server tool that you can use to create an *installation disk set* to install network clients or services on client computers.

You can also use Network Client Administrator to create a *network installation startup disk*. A network installation startup disk, when run on a computer that needs to be set up (the *target computer*), causes the target computer to automatically connect to the server and start an interactive installation/setup routine.

## Creating an Installation Disk Set

You can use Network Client Administrator to create an installation disk set to install network clients or services on client computers.

For example, suppose you want to install TCP/IP on several Windows for Workgroups computers. You can use Network Client Administrator to create a TCP/IP installation disk set, and then use this disk set on each computer on which you want to install TCP/IP.

The network clients and services that you can create an installation disk set for are: Network Client v3.0 for MS-DOS and Windows, Remote Access v1.1a for MS-DOS, TCP/IP 32 for Windows for Workgroups 3.11, LAN Manager v2.2c for MS-DOS, and LAN Manager v2.2c for OS/2.

**TO CREATE AN INSTALLATION DISK SET, FOLLOW THESE STEPS:**

**1.** Boot your computer to Windows NT Server. Select Start⇒ Programs⇒ Administrative Tools (Common)⇒ Network Client Administrator.

**2.** The Network Client Administrator dialog box appears, as shown in Figure 5-1. Notice that the radio button next to Make Network Installation Startup Disk is selected. Click the radio button next to Make Installation Disk Set. Click Continue.

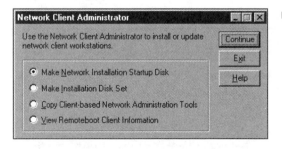

**FIGURE 5-1** Using Windows NT Server Network Client Administrator

**3.** Click the radio button next to Use Existing Shared Directory in the Share Network Client Installation Files dialog box. Type in the name of the Windows NT Server that you are using for server-based deployment for the Server Name. Type **clients** for the Share Name. Click OK.

**4.** In the drop-down list box in the Make Installation Disk Set dialog box, scroll down and select the network client or service for which you want to create an installation disk set. This dialog box is shown in Figure 5-2. Notice that I have selected the TCP/IP 32 for Windows for Workgroups 3.11 network service. Click OK.

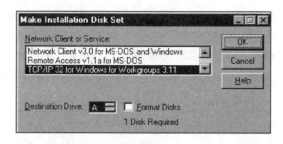

FIGURE 5-2 Creating an installation disk set

5. Windows NT prompts you to insert one to four floppy disks, depending on the network client or service you selected. (These disks will become the installation disk set.) Use blank disks for this procedure, even though NT indicates a specifically named disk should be inserted. Insert a disk and click OK.

6. Windows NT creates the installation disk set.

## Creating a Network Installation Startup Disk

You can use Network Client Administrator to create a network installation startup disk.

For example, suppose you want to install Windows NT Workstation on several new client computers on your network. You can use Network Client Administrator to create a single disk that you can use on each of the new client computers to automatically begin an interactive, over-the-network installation of Windows NT Workstation.

You can create a network installation startup disk that can be used to install any of the following operating systems: Windows for Workgroups, Windows 95, Windows NT Workstation, or Windows NT Server. (A separate disk is required for each different operating system.)

**TO CREATE A NETWORK INSTALLATION STARTUP DISK, FOLLOW THESE STEPS:**

**1.** Boot your computer to Windows NT Server. Select Start ⇒ Programs ⇒ Administrative Tools (Common) ⇒ Network Client Administrator.

**2.** The Network Client Administrator dialog box appears. Ensure the radio button next to Make Network Installation Startup Disk is selected. Click Continue.

**3.** Click the radio button next to Use Existing Shared Directory in the Share Network Client Installation Files dialog box. Type in the name of the Windows NT Server you are using for server-based deployment for the Server Name. Type **clients** for the Share Name. Click OK.

**4.** The Target Workstation Configuration dialog box appears. In the Network Client list box, highlight the client or operating system for which you want to create a network installation startup disk. In the Network Adapter Card drop-down list box, select the network adapter that is installed in the target computer. (The target computer is the computer on which you want to install a new operating system.) Figure 5-3 shows the Target Workstation Configuration dialog box. Notice that Windows NT Workstation and a 3Com EtherLink III network adapter card have been selected. Click OK.

note　You may be wondering, at this point, if the network installation startup disk works only on computers that have identical network adapters installed in them. Yep. That's how it is. You must create a separate network installation startup disk for each network adapter/operating system combination you plan to install.

**5.** A warning message appears, indicating that a license for Windows NT Workstation must be purchased prior to installing and using this operating system. Click OK.

**6.** The Network Startup Disk Configuration dialog box appears. Type in a computer name that will be used by the target computer during the installation process. Type in a user name to be used to log on to the Windows NT Server from the target computer during the installation process. Type in the domain name that the user account is maintained in. Select a network protocol to be used during the installation process. Enter any configuration values needed for this protocol (IP address, subnet mask, default gateway, and so on). Click OK when you are finished. Figure 5-4 shows the Network Startup Disk Configuration dialog box. Note that all text boxes have been completed.

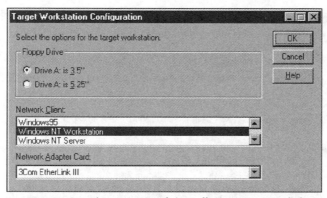

**FIGURE 5-3** Creating a network installation startup disk

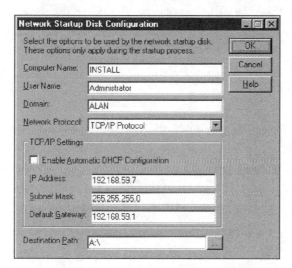

**FIGURE 5-4** Configuring network installation startup disk options

7. The Confirm Network Disk Configuration dialog box appears. Figure 5-5 shows this dialog box. Note that NT requires you to insert a formatted, high-density floppy disk. This disk *must* be formatted as an MS-DOS system disk. (This can be accomplished on any computer that runs MS-DOS by using the FORMAT /s command.) Insert a formatted system disk and click OK to continue.

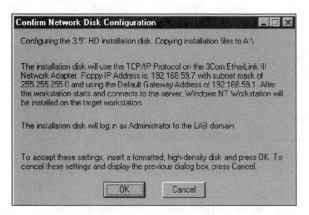

FIGURE 5-5  Confirming network startup disk configuration

**8.** Windows NT creates the over-the-network installation startup disk. The network installation startup disk is now configured for the operating system you selected. To start an interactive installation, boot the target computer by using the network installation startup disk.

To fully automate the Windows NT installation and setup process, you must create an answer file to be used by the Windows NT setup program, and you must edit the `Autoexec.bat` file on the network installation startup disk so that it uses this answer file during the installation. The next section discusses, in detail, automating the Windows NT installation and setup process.

# AUTOMATING SETUP OF WINDOWS NT

Until now, you have learned how to automate the start of an interactive Windows NT installation process by creating a network installation startup disk. Now you'll discover how to create and use answer files (`Unattend.txt`) and Uniqueness Database Files (UDFs) to fully automate the Windows NT installation and setup process.

# Creating and Using Answer Files (Unattend.txt)

*Answer files* are text files that contain stylized responses to the queries posed by the Windows NT Setup program during installation. You can use an answer file, in conjunction with a network installation startup disk (discussed in the previous section), to fully automate the installation of Windows NT on a single computer (that is, perform an unattended installation). The default name for an answer file is Unattend.txt, but you can use any filename you want for your answer files. Listing 5-1 presents a sample answer file.

**LISTING 5-1**  Sample Unattend.txt file

```
[Unattended]
OemPreinstall = yes
NoWaitAfterTextMode = 1
NoWaitAfterGUIMode = 1
FileSystem = ConvertNTFS
ExtendOEMPartition = 0
ConfirmHardware = no
NtUpgrade = no
Win31Upgrade = no
TargetPath = *
OverwriteOemFilesOnUpgrade = no
KeyboardLayout = "US"

[UserData]
FullName = "MCSE Candidate"
OrgName = "MCSE Candidates Company"
ComputerName = NTW2
ProductId = "975-4769754"

[GuiUnattended]
OemSkipWelcome = 1
OEMBlankAdminPassword = 1
TimeZone = "(GMT-08:00) Pacific Time (US & Canada); Tijuana"

[Display]
ConfigureAtLogon = 0
```

```
BitsPerPel = 8
XResolution = 800
YResolution = 600
VRefresh = 60
AutoConfirm = 1

[Network]
DetectAdapters = ""
InstallProtocols = ProtocolsSection
InstallServices = ServicesSection
InstallInternetServer = InternetParamSection
JoinDomain = LAB
CreateComputerAccount = administrator, password

[ProtocolsSection]
TC = TCParamSection

[TCParamSection]
DHCP = no
IPAddress = 192.168.59.7
Subnet = 255.255.255.0
Gateway = 192.168.59.1

[ServicesSection]
```

There are two ways you can create an answer file. You can use any text editor, such as Notepad, to type in all of the appropriate responses in the correct format. Or, you can use Windows NT Setup Manager (Setupmgr.exe) to create an answer file, which is the easiest and preferred method.

concept link

**For additional information on the format and content of answer files, see Appendix A of the *Microsoft Windows NT Workstation Resource Kit for version 4.0* (Microsoft Press, 1996). For detailed, step-by-step instructions for using Setup Manager to create an** Unattend.txt **file, see Lab 5.7 at the end of this chapter.**

To use an answer file, run the Windows NT Setup program (Winnt.exe or Winnt32.exe) with the /U switch.

For example, to use an answer file from the command line, you can type: `Z:\Winnt\Netsetup\Winnt.exe /U:Z:\Winnt\Netsetup\Unattend.txt /S:Z:\Winnt\ Netsetup`

In this example, `Winnt.exe` starts the installation process with the unattended switch (`/U`) to specify that `Winnt.exe` will use a specific answer file (`Z:\Winnt\Netstup\Unattend.txt`). `Winnt.exe` uses the `/S` switch to specify that the source folder for all Windows NT Workstation files is `Z:\Winnt\Netsetup`.

Using the command line is one way to start the installation process with an answer file. Another more efficient way is using the network installation startup disk in conjunction with an answer file to fully automate the installation of Windows NT on a single computer. To do this, you must first edit the `Autoexec.bat` file on the network installation startup disk by using Notepad or any other text editor.

For example, the last line of the `Autoexec.bat` file on a network installation startup disk that has been created for a Windows NT Workstation installation, *before* editing, is normally: `Z:\Winnt\Netsetup\Winnt.exe /B /S:Z:\Winnt\ Netsetup`

To use the startup disk in conjunction with an answer file, you should edit this line so that it reads: `Z:\Winnt\Netsetup\Winnt.exe /U:Z:\Winnt\ Netsetup\Unattend.txt /S:Z:\Winnt\Netsetup`

 **In practice, it often takes several attempts to correctly configure a network installation startup disk and an answer file. I recommend you try these out on a test computer prior to deploying them live on your network.**

Now that you understand what an answer file is and how it is used, it's time to discuss how to create an answer file by using Setup Manager.

## Using Setup Manager

*Windows NT Setup Manager* (`Setupmgr.exe`) is a graphical tool that provides an easy way to create an answer file (`Unattend.txt`) that you can use to install Windows NT in unattended mode.

Setup Manager is located on the Windows NT Server (or Windows NT Workstation) compact disc. You can find it in the `\Support\Deptools\I386` folder (for Intel-based computers). To start Setup Manager, double-click `Setupmgr.exe` in Windows NT Explorer.

When you start Setup Manager, the Windows NT Setup Manager main dialog box appears, as shown in Figure 5-6. Notice that you can choose from three options: General Setup, Networking Setup, and Advanced Setup.

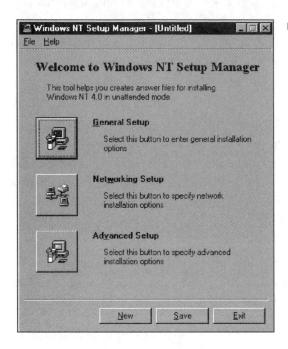

**FIGURE 5-6**  Windows NT Setup Manager main dialog box

The *General Setup* options in Windows NT Setup Manager are used to configure the user information, computer role, installation directory, display settings, time zone, and license mode entries in an answer file.

The *Networking Setup* options in Windows NT Setup Manager are used to configure the adapters, protocols, services, Internet, and modem entries in answer file.

The *Advanced Setup* options in Windows NT Setup Manager are used to configure the file system, mass storage, display driver, keyboard, pointing device, and boot files entries in an answer file.

concept link

**Lab 5.7 takes you through the process of using Setup Manager to create an** Unattend.txt **file.**

# Using Uniqueness Database Files

*Uniqueness Database Files* (UDFs) are text files, similar to answer files, that make it possible for one answer file to be used for the installation of many computers with different identifying characteristics. For example, each computer has a different computer name and user name. A UDF, used in conjunction with a network installation startup disk and an answer file, makes it possible to fully automate the installation of Windows NT on multiple computers on a network.

The UDF is structured like an answer file, and uses the same types of entries that an answer file uses. The UDF has an additional section, named [UniqueIds]. When the appropriate command-line switch is used, selected entries in the UDF replace entries with the same name in the answer file.

The only types of entries you can't use in a UDF are entries that are used during the text-mode portion (Phase 1) of the installation routine. In other words, entries from the following section headings *must* be specified in the answer file — they can't be used in a UDF:

- [Unattended]
- [OEMBootFiles]
- [MassStorageDrivers]
- [KeyboardDrivers]
- [PointingDeviceDrivers]

 **note** **If you have computers with different hard disk controllers, keyboards, or mice, you must use a different answer file for each hardware configuration.**

Listing 5-2 presents a sample UDF named Authors.txt.

**LISTING 5-2**  **Sample UDF,** Authors.txt

```
[UniqueIds]
Wshakespeare = Wshakespeare:UserData
Sclements = Sclements:UserData
Hmelville = Hmelville:UserData

[Wshakespeare:UserData]
FullName = "William Shakespeare"
OrgName = "Playwrights, Inc."
```

```
ComputerName = Willie
ProductId = "975-4769755"

[Sclements:UserData]
FullName = "Samuel Clements"
OrgName = "The Mark Twain Book Company"
ComputerName = Huck
ProductId = "975-4769756"

[Hmelville:UserData]
FullName = "Herman Melville"
OrgName = "A Whale of a Story, Inc."
ComputerName = Moby
ProductId = "975-4769757"
```

Notice in the Authors.txt UDF that the names listed in the [UniqueIds] section map to the other section headings in the UDF.

Using the Authors.txt UDF file as an example, assume that you want to use a UDF, an answer file, and a network installation startup disk to install Windows NT Workstation on Samuel Clements's computer. To configure the network installation startup disk, you must edit the last line of the Autoexec.bat file on this disk so that it reads as follows:

```
Z:\Winnt\Netsetup\Winnt.exe /U:Z:\Winnt\Netsetup\Unattend.txt
/S:Z:\Winnt\Netsetup /UDF:Sclements, Authors.txt
```

This command instructs Winnt.exe to use the entries in the [Sclements:UserData] section of the Authors.txt UDF to replace the entries with the same name in the answer file during the installation. In this case, the user name, organization name, computer name, and product ID specified in the [Sclements:UserData] section of the Authors.txt UDF is used during the installation of Windows NT Workstation; and the user name, organization name, computer name, and product ID specified in the answer file is disregarded.

A UDF can specify that more than one section in a UDF is to be associated with a unique identifier (UniqueId). Continuing along the same line as the previous example, you could specify in the [UniqueIds] section of a UDF that:

```
Wshakespeare = Wshakespeare:UserData, Protocols1
```

This line indicates that the UniqueID Wshakespeare is associated with two sections in the UDF: [Wshakespeare:UserData] and [Protocols1]. The [Wshakespeare:UserData] section contains user specific information, and the

[Protocols1] section contains an alternate list of protocols to be installed on William Shakespeare's computer. During installation, Winnt.exe will use the entries contained in [Wshakespeare:UserData] and [Protocols1] instead of the same-named entries in the answer file.

 concept link **For additional information on UDFs, see Chapter 2 and Appendix A of the *Microsoft Windows NT Workstation Resource Kit*.**

# AUTOMATING APPLICATION INSTALLATION DURING SETUP

In addition to automating the installation of Windows NT, you may also want to automate the installation of various applications at the same time.

In this section, you'll learn how the $OEM$ subfolder and Sysdiff.exe can be used to automatically install applications at the end of the automated installation/setup process.

## The $OEM$ Subfolder

The $OEM$ subfolder is used to store source files that are used to install applications, components, or files that do not ship with Windows NT.

You must create the $OEM$ subfolder—it does not exist as part of Windows NT distribution files.

To create a $OEM$ subfolder to use in conjunction with an automated installation/setup of Windows NT Workstation, create the $OEM$ subfolder in the Clients\Winnt\Netsetup folder.

To create a $OEM$ subfolder to use in conjunction with an automated installation/setup of Windows NT Server, create the $OEM$ subfolder in the Clients\Winnt.srv\Netsetup folder.

You can use the $OEM$ subfolder to store source files of applications that support scripted installation. Scripted installation enables complete installation of an application from a single command line. Most Microsoft applications support scripted installation.

For example, to prepare for automated installation of a scripted application (in conjunction with a Windows NT Workstation automated installation) on your computer's C: drive, first create a $OEM$ subfolder in the Clients\Winnt\ Netsetup folder. Then create a subfolder named C in the $OEM$ folder, and a subfolder named *name_of_application* in the $OEM$\C folder. Then copy the application's source files, including all subfolders, to the Clients\ Winnt\Netsetup\$OEM$\C\*name_of_application* folder. Then, create a Cmdlines.txt file in the $OEM$ subfolder that uses the following syntax:

```
[Commands]
"complete command line to install the application"
```

**note**  **The use of quotation marks to surround the command line is required in the** Cmdlines.txt **file.**

Finally, you must edit the answer file to instruct Winnt.exe to execute the commands in the Cmdlines.txt file. (Otherwise, Winnt.exe ignores the $OEM$ subfolder and all of its contents during automated installation.) Edit the [Unattended] section of the answer file to include the following entry:

```
OemPreinstall = yes
```

concept link  **For additional information on the** $OEM$ **subfolder, see Chapter 2 of the** *Microsoft Windows NT Workstation Resource Kit.*

Applications that don't support scripted installation can be installed by using Sysdiff.exe. Using Sysdiff.exe is discussed in the next section.

## Using Sysdiff.exe

Sysdiff.exe is used to automate the installation of applications that don't support scripted installation and that would otherwise require user interaction during the installation process.

Sysdiff.exe is located on the Windows NT Server (or Windows NT Workstation) compact disc. You can find it in the \Support\Deptools\I386 folder (for Intel-based computers).

Sysdiff.exe can be used to perform these three major functions:

**1.** When run with the /snap switch, it takes a snapshot of a typical target computer's current configuration after Windows NT is installed but before any applications are installed.

**2.** When run with the `/diff` switch after the desired application is installed, it creates a difference file that contains all of the application files and registry changes.

**3.** When run with the `/apply` switch from the `Cmdlines.txt` file, it applies the difference file during an unattended Windows NT installation.

 concept link

**For additional information on using** `Sysdiff.exe`, **see Chapter 2 of the** *Microsoft Windows NT Workstation Resource Kit* **and** *Microsoft TechNet*.

# KEY POINT SUMMARY

Chapter 5 introduced *server-based deployment*, a process that involves automating the installation and setup of Windows NT, other operating systems (Windows 95 and Windows for Workgroups), and applications on multiple computers on a network.

o You must prepare the Windows NT Server computer that you will use for the server-based deployment process by copying the `Clients` folder from the Windows NT Server compact disc to this computer. Then you share the `Clients` folder as `CLIENTS`, and modify this folder depending on the operating system(s) you want to install.

o *Network Client Administrator* is a Windows NT Server tool that you can use to create an installation disk set and a network installation startup disk. An *installation disk set* is used to install network clients or services on client computers. A *network installation startup disk,* when run on a computer that needs to be set up (the target computer), causes the target computer to automatically connect to the Windows NT Server computer and start an interactive installation/setup routine.

o Automating the setup of Windows NT involves creating an *answer file* and *Uniqueness Database File* (UDF) that enable you to fully automate the Windows NT installation and setup process. An answer file is a text file that contains stylized responses to the queries posed by the Windows NT Setup program during installation. The default name for an answer file is `Unattend.txt`. The easiest way to create an answer file is to use Windows

NT Setup Manager (`Setupmgr.exe`). To use an answer file, run the Windows NT Setup program with the /U switch. A Uniqueness Database File (UDF) is a text file, similar to an answer file, that allows one answer file to be used for the installation of many computers that have different identifying characteristics (different computer names, user names, and so on). When used in conjunction with a network installation startup disk and an answer file, a UDF makes it possible to fully automate the installation of Windows NT on multiple computers on a network. If you have computers with different hard disk controllers, keyboards, or mice, you must use a different answer file for each hardware configuration, because these entries can only be specified in an answer file, not in a UDF. When the appropriate command-line switch is used, selected entries in the UDF replace same-named entries in the answer file.

o  In addition to automating the installation of Windows NT, you may want to automate the installation of various applications at the same time. The `$OEM$` subfolder is used to store source files that are used to install scripted applications, components, or files that do not ship with Windows NT. Scripted applications are those that permit complete installation from a single command line. Create the `$OEM$` subfolder in the `Clients\Winnt\Netsetup` folder to use in conjunction with an automated installation of Windows NT Workstation. Create the `$OEM$` subfolder in the `Clients\Winnt.srv\Netsetup` folder to use in conjunction with an automated installation of Windows NT Server.

o  `Sysdiff.exe` is used to automate the installation of applications that don't support scripted installation, and that otherwise would require user interaction during the installation process. `Sysdiff.exe` can be used to perform these three major functions:

  o  When run with the /snap switch, `Sysdiff.exe` takes a snapshot of a typical target computer's current configuration after Windows NT is installed but before any applications are installed.

  o  When run with the /diff switch after the desired application is installed, `Sysdiff.exe` creates a difference file containing all of the application files and Registry changes.

  o  When run with the /apply switch from the `Cmdlines.txt` file, `Sysdiff.exe` applies the difference file during an unattended Windows NT installation.

# APPLYING WHAT YOU'VE LEARNED

Now it's time to regroup, review, and apply what you've learned in this chapter.

The questions in the Instant Assessment section that follows bring to mind key facts and concepts. In addition, some of the questions give you a chance to analyze situations and apply your knowledge of Windows NT to that particular situation.

The hands-on lab exercise will really reinforce what you've learned, and provide you an opportunity to practice several of the tasks tested by the Microsoft Certified Professional exams.

## Instant Assessment

1. What is server-based deployment?

2. What is the primary reason for using server-based deployment?

3. What are the two types of environments in which server-based deployment is commonly used?

4. Which folder must be copied from the Windows NT Server compact disc to the Windows NT Server computer that will be used for server-based deployment?

5. You are preparing a Windows NT Server computer to use in deploying Windows NT Workstation to several client computers. You copy the Clients folder from the Windows NT Server compact disc to one of the drives on the Windows NT Server computer. What two additional subfolders must you create in the Clients folder?

6. You are preparing a Windows NT Server computer to use in deploying Windows NT Server to several other computers. You copy the Clients folder from the Windows NT Server compact disc to one of the drives on the Windows NT Server computer. What two additional subfolders must you create in the Clients folder?

7. You want to install TCP/IP 32 for Windows for Workgroups 3.11 on twenty computers on your network. What can you create, using Network Client Administrator, to help you accomplish this task efficiently?

8. You are rolling out a new network for a company, and want to install Windows NT Workstation on fifty new client computers. What can you

create, using Network Client Administrator, to help you accomplish this task efficiently?

9. What is an answer file?

10. What is the easiest way to create an answer file?

11. What switch must you use with the Windows NT Setup program to ensure that an answer file will be utilized?

12. Where is Windows NT Setup Manager (Setupmgr.exe) located?

13. Fill in the blank: When the appropriate command-line switch is used, selected entries in the UDF _____ same-named entries in the answer file.

14. You want to use UDFs in conjunction with a network installation startup disk and answer files to automate the installation of Windows NT on multiple computers on your network. However, several of the computers on your network have different hard disk controllers and different keyboards. How many different answer files do you need?

15. You want to automate the installation of various applications at the same time you perform an unattended installation of Windows NT. Which subfolder should you use to store source files that will be used to install applications that support scripted installation?

16. What file must you edit to instruct Winnt.exe to execute the commands in the Cmdlines.txt file so that applications will be installed during an unattended installation of Windows NT?

17. What are the three major functions of Sysdiff.exe?

 concept link    **For answers to the Instant Assessment questions see Appendix D.**

## Hands-on Lab Exercise

The following hands-on lab exercise provides an excellent opportunity for you to apply some of the server-based deployment concepts you've learned about in this chapter.

## Lab 5.7 *Creating an answer file using Setup Manager*

Workstation
Server

The purpose of this lab is to familiarize you with the use of Setup Manager to create Unattend.txt files.

There are two parts to this lab:

Part 1: Creating an Unattend.txt file using Setup Manager

Part 2: Viewing the contents of the Unattend.txt file

Begin this lab by booting your computer to Windows NT Server.

Insert your Windows NT Server (or Windows NT Workstation) compact disc in your CD-ROM drive.

Follow the steps below carefully.

### Part 1: Creating an Unattend.txt file using Setup Manager

**1.** Select Start ⇒ Programs ⇒ Windows NT Explorer.

**2.** In the All Folders list box (on the left side of your screen) in Windows NT Explorer, scroll down to My Computer, and then click the + sign next to your CD-ROM drive.

**3.** Click the + sign next to Support, and then click the + sign next to Deptools.

**4.** Click the I386 folder (not the + sign next to it).

**5.** In the Contents of "I386" box (on the right side of your screen), double-click Setupmgr.exe.

**6.** The Windows NT Setup Manager dialog box appears. Click General Setup.

**7.** The General Setup Options dialog box appears. Type in your user name (use **your name**). Press Tab. Type in the name of your organization (use any name . . . how about **MCSE Candidates Company**?). Press Tab. Type in your computer name (use **NTW2** for this lab). Press Tab. For the product ID number, type in **123-4567890**. (Don't type in the period at the end.) Click the General tab.

**8.** Notice the configuration options available in the General tab. Do not select any check boxes. Click the Computer Role tab.

**9.** In the Select the role of the computer drop-down list box, select "Workstation in domain". In the Enter the domain name text box, type **LAB**. Leave the "Enter the computer account" text box blank. Click the Install Directory tab.

**10.** Notice the configuration options available in the Install Directory tab. Do not change any of the options. Click the Display Settings tab.

**11.** Notice the configuration options available in the Display Settings tab. In the Settings section, change the Horizontal Resolution to 800, and change the Vertical Resolution to 600. Click the Time Zone tab.

**12.** In the drop-down list box in the Time Zone tab, select your time zone. Click the License Mode tab.

**13.** A warning message appears, stating that if you want to configure the License Mode, the computer role must be a server. Click OK.

**14.** The General Setup Options dialog box appears. Click OK.

**15.** The Windows NT Setup Manager dialog box reappears. Click Networking Setup.

**16.** The Networking Options dialog box appears. On the General tab, select the radio button next to "Automatically detect and install first adapter". Click the Protocols tab.

**17.** On the Protocols tab, click the Add command button.

**18.** The Adding Protocols dialog box appears. In the drop-down list box, select TCP/IP. Click OK.

**19.** The Networking Options dialog box reappears. Click the Parameters command button.

**20.** The TCP/IP Protocol Parameters dialog box appears. Click the check box next to Do Not Use DHCP. Type an IP Address of **192.168.59.11**. Type a Subnet of **255.255.255.0**. Type a Gateway of **192.168.59.1**. (Don't type a period at the end of any of these.) Click OK to continue.

**21.** The Protocols tab reappears. Click the Services tab.

**22.** The Services tab appears. Click the Add command button.

**23.** The Adding Services dialog box appears. In the drop-down list box, select Remote Access Service (RAS). Click OK.

**24.** The Services tab reappears. Click the Parameters command button.

**25.** The Remote Access Service Parameters dialog box appears. Click the Ports tab.

**26.** On the Ports tab, click the Add command button. (Notice that PortSection1 has moved from the top list box to the bottom list box.)

**27.** Click the Parameters command button.

**28.** The Port Parameters dialog box appears.

**29.** Notice the configuration options available. Do not change any of the options. Click OK.

**30.** The Ports tab reappears. Click OK.

**31.** The Services tab reappears. Click the Modem tab.

**32.** In the COM drop-down list box on the Modem tab, select 1. In the Modem Description list box, type **STANDARD 28800 bps Modem**. (Don't type the period at the end of any of these.) In the Manufacturer text box, type **(Standard Modem Types)**. In the Provider text box, type **Unimodem Service Provider**. (Click the Add command button. Click OK.

**33.** The Windows NT Setup Manager dialog box reappears. Click Advanced Setup.

**34.** The Advanced Options dialog box appears. On the General tab, check the check boxes next to Skip Welcome wizard page and Skip Administrator Password wizard page.

**35.** Click the File System tab.

**36.** Notice the configuration options available on the File System tab. Click the Mass Storage tab.

**37.** Notice the configuration options available on the Mass Storage tab.

 **You only need to specify mass storage devices whose drivers do *not* ship with Windows NT. All other mass storage devices are automatically detected by Windows NT. If you are using a SCSI adapter whose drivers do not ship with NT, click on the Add command button and follow the onscreen directions to add and configure the driver.**

**38.** Click the Display tab.

**39.** Notice the configuration options available on the Display tab. As with mass storage devices, you only need to modify this tab if your display adapter's drivers do not ship with Windows NT. (See the note above.) Click OK.

**40.** The Windows NT Setup Manager dialog box reappears. Select File⇒Save As.

**41.** In the File Name text box, type **C:\Unattend.txt.** (Don't type the period at the end.) Click the Save command button.

**42.** The Windows NT Setup Manager dialog box reappears. Click Exit.

**43.** The Windows NT Explorer dialog box reappears. The `Unattend.txt` file is now created. Continue to Part 2, where you'll view the contents of this file.

### Part 2: Viewing the contents of the `Unattend.txt` file

**1.** In the Windows NT Explorer dialog box, in the All Folders box (on the left side of the screen), click drive C: (not the + sign next to drive C:). In the Contents Of '(C:)' box (on the right side of the screen), scroll down to the bottom. Double-click `Unattend.txt`.

**2.** The `Unattend.txt` file is displayed in Notepad. Examine the contents of this file. (You can print the contents of this file if you desire.) Notice the formatting of the various sections.

**3.** When you are finished, select File⇒Exit.

**4.** Exit Windows NT Explorer.

Workstation
Server
Enterprise

# Managing Printing

## About Chapter 6

This chapter covers printing from A to Z. It begins with a discussion of Windows NT printing terminology, and then quickly moves to the print process, and then to creating and connecting to a printer.

Chapter 6 explores configuring printer properties extensively. You'll learn how to assign a separator page; how to assign forms to paper trays; and how to use Windows NT printer security to assign printer permissions to users and groups, to audit a user or group's printer usage, and to take ownership of a printer. Other topics discussed in this section include printing to multiple ports (printer pools), scheduling printers, setting printer priorities, and sharing printers.

Finally, this chapter concludes with a practical section on troubleshooting common printing problems.

This chapter includes two hands-on labs. In the first lab, you become familiar with the Windows NT `Printers` folder and create and share a local printer. In the second, you install and configure Microsoft TCP/IP Printing.

No matter which of the three Windows NT 4.0 Microsoft Certified Professional exams you're preparing for, you'll want to be sure to read this chapter. This chapter covers printing objectives for all three exams.

# PRINTING TERMINOLOGY

Before you can fully understand printing with Windows NT, you should first understand a few terms.

In Windows NT, the term *printer* does not represent a physical device that produces printed output. Rather, a printer is the software interface between the Windows NT operating system and the device that produces printed output.

 in the real world

**If you are used to working with a different operating system, such as NetWare or UNIX, you may be used to thinking of what Windows NT calls a printer as a combination of a print queue (or print spooler) plus a driver for the device that produces printed output.**

**If you aren't used to working with another operating system, feel free to ignore this note, because it may just be confusing at this point.**

In Windows NT, the term *print device* refers to the physical device that produces printed output—what is more commonly referred to as a "printer."

exam preparation pointer

**Be sure that you know the Windows NT printing terminology cold. Otherwise, you may become confused when taking the exams.**

**Remember: a *printer* is software, and a *print* (or *printing*) *device* is hardware. Beat this into your head with a large wooden mallet!**

Now that you have a grasp of the Windows NT printing terminology, you're ready to move on to the nuts and bolts of printing in Windows NT.

# WINDOWS NT PRINTING OVERVIEW

This section examines the process of printing in Windows NT. It also explains, in detail, the most commonly used print monitors.

## The Print Process

Perhaps the easiest way to understand the Windows NT print process is to follow the steps that occur when a document is printed from an application in Windows NT.

1. A user at a Windows NT computer starts the print process from an application, such as Word, usually by selecting Print from the File menu. This action creates the print job. (A print job is all of the data and commands needed to print a document.)

2. The application hands off the print job to the *Graphics Device Interface* (GDI). (In Windows NT 4.0, the GDI is a kernel mode component.)

3. The GDI initiates a request to the driver for the print device.

4. The driver for the print device converts the application's output (the print job) into either a Windows NT *enhanced metafile* (EMF) or into a RAW format. (The RAW format is ready to print, as is, and no further processing is required.) The driver then returns the converted print job to the GDI.

5. The GDI hands off the print job to the Windows NT spooler.

6. The Windows NT spooler determines whether the print device is managed by the computer that initiated the print job, or by a network-connected computer.

   If the print device is managed by the local computer (the computer that initiated this print job), the spooler copies the print job to a temporary storage area on the computer's hard disk.

   If the print device is managed by a network-connected computer, the spooler hands off the print job to the spooler on the network-connected computer. Then that spooler copies the print job to a temporary storage area on that computer's hard disk.

7. Once the spooler has copied the file to temporary storage, the print job is handed off to the local print provider on the computer that has the print job spooled to its hard disk.

8. The local print provider initiates a request to the print processor to perform any additional conversions needed on the file, such as from EMF to RAW. (When a print device receives a print job, it always receives it in the RAW format.) The print processor then returns the converted print job to the local print provider.

9. The local print provider adds a separator page to the print job (if it's configured to do so) and then hands off the print job to the print monitor.

10. The print monitor communicates directly with the print device and sends the ready-to-print print job to the print device.

11. The print device produces the printed document.

   Figure 6-1 graphically illustrates the steps in the Windows NT print process. Notice that the spooler routes the print job to the local hard disk if the print device is managed by the local computer, and routes the print job to the spooler on the network-connected computer if the print device is managed by the network-connected computer.

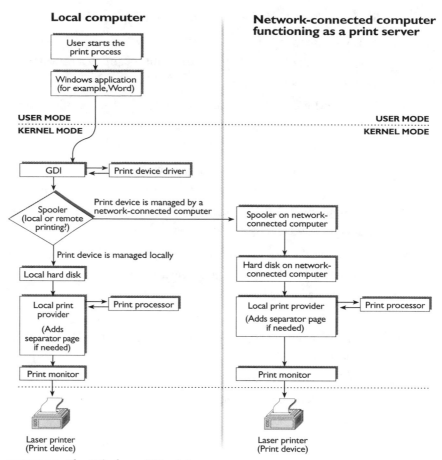

FIGURE 6-1  The Windows NT print process

## *Using EMFs in network printing*

Using Windows NT *enhanced metafiles* (EMFs) can significantly increase the performance of printing across a network for the following reasons:

o  Windows NT creates an EMF faster than it can create a RAW format file.

o  Windows NT splits the overhead of the print process between the local computer (which creates the EMF) and the network-connected computer (which converts the EMF to the RAW format).

This means that the user who creates the print job experiences faster printing than if the RAW format file was created locally on the user's computer.

# CREATING AND CONNECTING TO PRINTERS

There are two ways to install and configure a printer in Windows NT: you can either create a printer, or you can connect to a shared network printer.

Creating a printer involves installing and configuring all of the drivers needed to use a locally managed print device. Connecting to a shared network printer involves installing and configuring all of the drivers needed to use a print device that is managed by another computer on the network. You can either connect to a shared network printer by using the Add Printer Wizard in the Printers folder, or you can use drag-and-drop printing to connect to a shared network printer.

Both creating a printer and connecting to a printer are called "adding a printer," because both processes use the Add Printer Wizard.

## Steps to Create a Printer

This section explains the steps involved in creating a printer in Windows NT by using the Add Printer Wizard.

**TO CREATE A PRINTER IN WINDOWS NT, FOLLOW THESE STEPS:**

1. Open the Printers folder. You can do this in any of the following four ways:

   o Select Start ⇒ Settings ⇒ Printers

   o Double-click My Computer, and then double-click the Printers folder

   o Select Start ⇒ Programs ⇒ Windows NT Explorer, and then click the Printers folder in the All Folders list box

   o Select Start ⇒ Settings ⇒ Control Panel, and then double-click the Printers icon in Control Panel

2. Double-click the Add Printers icon.

3. The Add Printer Wizard dialog box appears. To create a printer, select My Computer, and click Next.

4. Select a port in the Available ports list box. If the port you want to use is not listed, click the Add Port command button and follow the directions given. Click Next.

Figure 6-2 shows the Available ports list box within the Add Printer Wizard. Notice that the LPT1: port is highlighted and selected.

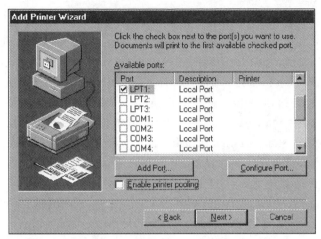

**FIGURE 6-2    Selecting a port for a print device**

**5.** Select the appropriate manufacturer and print device model, and click Next. Figure 6-3 shows the Manufacturers and Printers list boxes.

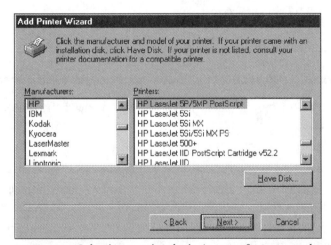

**FIGURE 6-3    Selecting a print device's manufacturer and model**

**6.** Type a printer name, or accept the default. Click Next.

**7.** Choose whether to share the printer. (You can share or stop sharing the printer later if you change your mind. More information is presented in the "Sharing a Printer" section later in this chapter.) Click Next.

**8.** Choose whether to print a test page. Click Finish.

You can modify a printer's properties any time after the printer is created by right-clicking the printer's icon (in the `Printers` folder), and then selecting Properties from the menu that appears.

concept link

**See Lab 6.8 at the end of this chapter for a hands-on exercise in creating a printer.**

## Steps to Connect to a Printer

This section explains the steps involved in connecting to a Windows NT shared network printer using the Add Printer Wizard.

**TO CONNECT TO A WINDOWS NT SHARED NETWORK PRINTER, FOLLOW THESE STEPS:**

**1.** Open the `Printers` folder. (Select Start ⟶ Settings ⟶ Printers.)

**2.** Double-click the Add Printers icon.

**3.** The Add Printer Wizard dialog box appears. To connect to a printer, select Network printer server, and click Next.

**4.** In the Connect to Printer dialog box, do one of the following:

In the Printer text box, type in a complete path to the network printer to which you want to connect, in the form of \\*server_name*\*printer_name*.

Or, use the browse list in the Shared Printers list box to select the network printer to which you want to connect.

Figure 6-4 shows the Connect to Printer dialog box. Notice that when a network printer is selected in the Shared Printers list box, the Add Printer Wizard places the full path to the network printer in the Printer text box.

Then click OK.

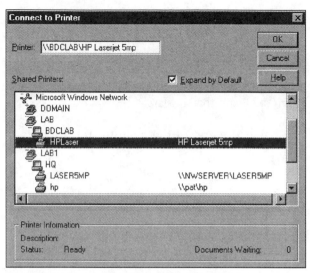

**FIGURE 6-4**    Connecting to a network printer

 When you connect to a shared network printer on a Windows NT computer, your local Windows NT computer automatically copies the necessary printer drivers from the Windows NT computer that hosts the shared printer. If the Windows NT computer that hosts the shared printer does *not* have printer drivers for your version of Windows NT or for your hardware platform (such as Intel, DEC Alpha, MIPS R4000, or PowerPC), then Windows NT prompts you to install printer drivers as the next step in this process.

**5.** In the Add Printer Wizard dialog box, choose whether you want this printer to be your default printer. Click Next.

**6.** Click Finish. You are now connected to a shared network printer.

### Using drag-and-drop printing to connect to a printer

Drag-and-drop printing is an easy way to connect to a shared network printer, because drag-and-drop printing requires less user interaction than using the Add Printer Wizard interactively.

To use drag-and-drop printing to connect to a shared network printer, you must first use My Computer to locate a file that you want to print. Then use Network Neighborhood to locate the shared network printer (or NetWare print queue) that you want to use.

Figure 6-5 shows two windows open on the desktop. Note that one window shows the shares that are available on a network computer named Bdclab, and that the other window contains files in the `Windows` folder. (If you prefer, instead of using My Computer and Network Neighborhood, you can accomplish the same thing by opening two copies of Windows NT Explorer, and then tiling the windows.)

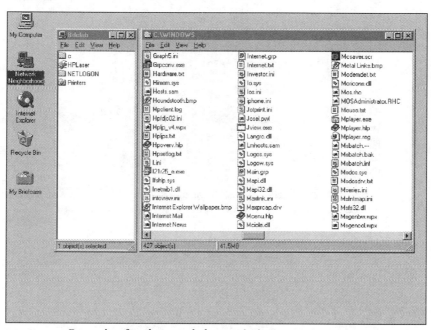

**FIGURE 6-5** Preparing for drag-and-drop printing

To connect to the shared network printer and print your document, drag the file from the open window and drop it on the shared network printer in the other window.

Figure 6-6 shows a document being dropped on the shared printer.

Windows NT displays an information dialog box, which is shown in Figure 6-7. The essence of the dialog box message is that Windows NT must connect to the shared network printer and install drivers on your local Windows NT computer before the document can be printed.

If you click No, Windows NT automatically cancels your print job. If you click Yes, Windows NT automatically connects to the shared network printer, installs local printer drivers, opens the application the document was created in, prints the document, and closes the application.

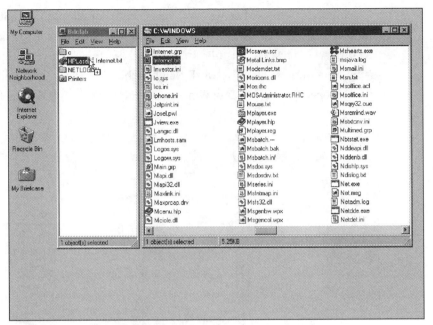

**FIGURE 6-6**    Dragging and dropping a document on a printer

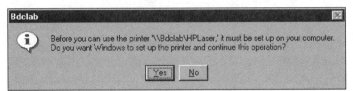

**FIGURE 6-7**    Instructing NT to install local drivers for a shared
network printer

If you click Yes and the Windows NT computer that hosts the shared network
printer does *not* have printer drivers for your version of Windows NT or for your
hardware platform (such as Intel, DEC Alpha, MIPS R4000, or PowerPC), or if you
are dragging and dropping a document to a NetWare print queue, then Windows
NT prompts you to select and install appropriate printer drivers before it
completes the drag-and-drop printing.

note    **Drag-and-drop printing requires that the printer on which you
are dropping files be configured as your default printer. Also,
drag-and-drop printing often produces inconsistent results (for
example, the process may complete normally, but the document will**

not print). Sometimes repeating the process will cause everything to work correctly. Sometimes a printer is created in your `Printers` folder, and sometimes not. Maybe drag-and-drop printing's inconsistencies will be fixed in one of the future service packs for Windows NT 4.0.

# PRINT MONITORS

*Print monitors* are software components that run in kernel mode. In Windows NT, print monitors send ready-to-print print jobs to a print device, either locally or across the network. Print monitors are also called *port monitors*.

When you create a printer, you select the port to which the print device is connected. Each port is associated with one specific print monitor.

This section discusses the most commonly used print monitors. All of the print monitors listed in this section are available in both Windows NT Workstation and Windows NT Server.

## Localmon

The *Localmon print monitor* sends print jobs to print devices that are connected to hardware ports on a local Windows NT computer (local hardware ports include LPT1: and COM1:).

Localmon is the only print monitor that is installed by default during the installation of Windows NT. All other print monitors require that you install additional Windows NT services and/or protocols.

## Hpmon

The *Hpmon print monitor* sends print jobs to a network print device via a Hewlett-Packard JetDirect adapter. The HP JetDirect adapter may either be installed in the print device, or function as a separate external unit.

Hpmon uses the DLC protocol to communicate with HP JetDirect adapters. Most HP JetDirect adapters support multiple protocols, including: TCP/IP, IPX, AppleTalk, and DLC. However, Hpmon can only communicate by using the DLC protocol.

The DLC protocol is a non-routable protocol. A Windows NT computer that uses Hpmon can only communicate with HP JetDirect adapters that are located on the same network segment. In other words, the DLC protocol will not be forwarded by a network router to another network segment.

If your network supports bridging, however, you can use DLC to communicate to an HP JetDirect adapter on any network segment that is connected by a bridge.

The Hpmon print monitor is not installed by default during the installation of Windows NT. Hpmon is installed automatically when you install the DLC protocol. You must install DLC before you can connect to an HP JetDirect adapter using Hpmon.

---

**TO CREATE A PRINTER THAT USES HPMON, FOLLOW THESE STEPS:**

**1.** Install the DLC protocol on your computer. (If you need more information on how to do this, refer to the section on "Installing and Configuring Protocols and Services" in Chapter 4.)

**2.** Open the `Printers` folder. (Select Start ⇒ Settings ⇒ Printers.)

**3.** Double-click the Add Printers icon.

**4.** The Add Printer Wizard dialog box appears. To create a printer, select My Computer, and click Next.

**5.** In the Available ports list box, click the Add Port command button.

**6.** In the Printer Ports dialog box, click the Hewlett-Packard Network Port. Figure 6-8 shows the Printer Ports dialog box. Notice that the Hewlett-Packard Network Port is selected. Click New Port.

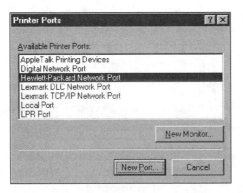

**FIGURE 6-8**  Adding an Hpmon port

**7.** The Add Hewlett-Packard Network Peripheral Port dialog box appears. In the lower Card Address list box, double-click the MAC address of the HP

JetDirect adapter you want to use. The Add Printer Wizard then places this address in the upper Card Address text box. In the Name text box, type a name for the Hpmon port that will be associated with the HP JetDirect adapter you selected.

Figure 6-9 shows the Hewlett-Packard Network Peripheral Port dialog box. Note that the Hpmon port is named after its association with an HP JetDirect adapter. Click the Timers command button.

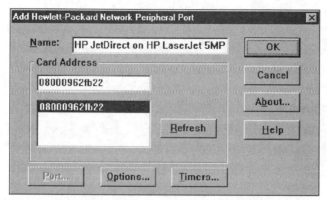

**FIGURE 6-9**    Selecting and configuring an Hpmon port

**8.** The HP Network Peripheral Port Timers dialog box appears. Choose either a *Job Based* or *Continuous* connection.

If you choose *Job Based*, all computers on the network will be able to access the HP JetDirect adapter for printing, because the connection to the HP JetDirect adapter is dropped after each print job. (Only one computer can have a DLC connection to the HP JetDirect adapter at any given time.)

If you choose *Continuous*, Hpmon will monopolize the HP JetDirect adapter and no other computer on the network will be able to use DLC to access the HP JetDirect adapter for printing.

Figure 6-10 shows the HP Network Peripheral Port Timers dialog box. Notice that Continuous Connection is the default selection. Click OK.

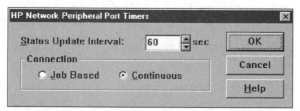

**FIGURE 6-10**    Selecting Job Based or Continuous
                  connection

**9.** Click OK in the Add Hewlett-Packard Network Peripheral Port dialog box.

**10.** Click Close in the Printer Ports dialog box.

**11.** The Add Printer Wizard dialog box, shown in Figure 6-11, reappears. Note that the Hpmon port that you have added is highlighted and selected in the Available ports list box. Click Next.

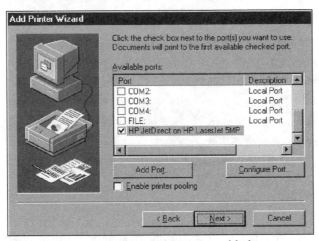

**FIGURE 6-11**    Hpmon/HP JetDirect port added to
available ports list

**12.** Select the appropriate manufacturer and print device model, and click Next.

**13.** Type in a printer name, or accept the default. Click Next.

**14.** Choose whether to share the printer. (You can share or stop sharing the printer later if you change your mind.) Click Next.

**15.** Choose whether to print a test page. Click Finish.

in the
real world

Selecting between a job-based and continuous connection requires some careful planning and consideration.

If a printer isn't shared and you select a continuous connection, only a single user will have access to the HP JetDirect adapter for printing. In this situation, you should generally select a job-based connection.

However, if you share the printer that is associated with the Hpmon port, selecting a continuous connection can make sense. This computer will then function as a print server and manage all print jobs sent to the shared printer. In this situation, all computers on the network that have access to the shared printer, in effect, will have access to the HP JetDirect adapter for printing.

# AppleTalk

The *AppleTalk print monitor* sends print jobs to network print devices that support the AppleTalk protocol. The AppleTalk protocol is normally associated with Apple Macintosh computers.

Before you can connect to an AppleTalk print device, you must install the AppleTalk protocol (on a Windows NT Workstation computer) or Services for Macintosh (on a Windows NT Server computer).

AppleTalk is a routable protocol. A Windows NT computer that uses the AppleTalk print monitor can communicate with any AppleTalk print device on any segment of a routed AppleTalk network.

---

**TO CREATE A PRINTER THAT USES THE APPLETALK PRINT MONITOR, FOLLOW THESE STEPS:**

1. Install the AppleTalk protocol if you are using a Windows NT Workstation computer. Or, install Services for Macintosh if you are using a Windows NT Server computer. (If you need more information on how to do this, refer to the section "Installing and Configuring Protocols and Services" in Chapter 4.)

2. Open the Printers folder. (Select Start ⇒ Settings ⇒ Printers.)

3. Double-click the Add Printers icon.

4. The Add Printer Wizard dialog box appears. To create a printer, select My Computer, and click Next.

5. In the Available ports list box, click the Add Port command button.

6. In the Printer Ports dialog box, click AppleTalk Printing Devices.

   Figure 6-12 shows the Printer Ports dialog box. Notice that AppleTalk Printing Devices is selected. Click New Port.

7. When the Available AppleTalk Printing Devices dialog box appears, highlight the AppleTalk print device you want to use.

   Figure 6-13 shows the Available AppleTalk Printing Devices dialog box, with an HP LaserJet 5P selected. Click OK.

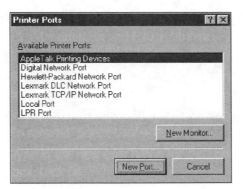

FIGURE 6-12  Adding an AppleTalk port

FIGURE 6-13  Selecting an AppleTalk print device

**8.** A dialog box appears asking if you want to *capture* this AppleTalk print device.

If you choose to capture an AppleTalk print device, it is the same as choosing a continuous connection (discussed in the previous section, "Hpmon"). The AppleTalk print monitor will monopolize the connection to the AppleTalk print device, and no other computer on the network will be able to access the AppleTalk print device. In addition, the AppleTalk print monitor instructs the AppleTalk print device not to advertise itself on the network. This is called *hiding*.

If you choose not to capture an AppleTalk print device, it is the same as choosing a job-based connection (discussed in the previous section, "Hpmon"). All computers on the network will be able to access the AppleTalk print device for printing, because the connection to the print device is dropped after each print job. Only one computer can connect to an AppleTalk print device at any given time.

Click Yes or No.

**9.** Click Close in the Printer Ports dialog box.

**10.** The Available ports list box reappears with your newly created AppleTalk port highlighted and selected. Click Next.

**11.** Select the appropriate manufacturer and print device model, and click Next.

**12.** Type in a printer name, or accept the default. Click Next.

**13.** Choose whether to share the printer. (You can share or stop sharing the printer later if you change your mind.) Click Next.

**14.** Choose whether to print a test page. Click Finish.

# TCP/IP

The *TCP/IP print monitor* sends print jobs to network print devices that both support TCP/IP *and* function as *line printer daemon* (LPD) print servers. TCP/IP and LPD are normally associated with UNIX computers.

 **note**   *Daemon* **is a UNIX term. A UNIX daemon performs the same function as a Windows NT service. Basically, a UNIX daemon is a program that runs in the background and performs an operating system service.**

*Line printer daemon* (LPD) is the print server software used in TCP/IP printing. The client print software used in TCP/IP printing is called *line printer remote* (LPR). To connect to a TCP/IP print server that uses LPD, use a TCP/IP print client that uses LPR.

Before you can connect to a TCP/IP print device, you must install TCP/IP and the Microsoft TCP/IP Printing service on your Windows NT computer.

In addition, to share printers on a Windows NT computer as TCP/IP printers, you must also start the TCP/IP Print Server service. The TCP/IP Print Server service is configured for manual startup by default, so you should configure this service to start automatically.

TCP/IP is a routable protocol. A Windows NT computer that uses the TCP/IP print monitor can communicate with any TCP/IP print device on any segment of a routed TCP/IP network.

**TO CREATE A PRINTER THAT USES THE TCP/IP PRINT MONITOR, FOLLOW THESE STEPS:**

**1.** Install TCP/IP and the Microsoft TCP/IP Printing service. Optionally, you can configure the TCP/IP Print Server service to start automatically if you want to share your printers as TCP/IP printers. (If you need more information on how to do this, refer to the section "Installing and Configuring Protocols and Services" in Chapter 4.)

**2.** Open the `Printers` folder. (Select Start ⇒ Settings ⇒ Printers.)

**3.** Double-click the Add Printers icon.

**4.** The Add Printer Wizard dialog box appears. To create a printer, select My Computer, and click Next.

**5.** In the "Available ports" list box, click the Add Port command button.

**6.** In the Printer Ports dialog box, click LPR Port. (The Lexmark TCP/IP Network Port displayed in this dialog box is for use *only* with Lexmark TCP/IP print devices, and requires you to install additional software.)

Figure 6-14 shows the Printer Ports dialog box. Notice that LPR Port is selected. Then click New Port.

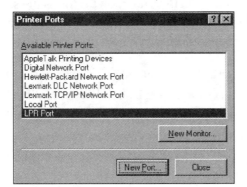

**FIGURE 6-14**  Adding an LPR port

**7.** In the Add LPR compatible printer dialog box, type the host name or IP address of the computer or device that provides the LPD service for the print device you want to use. Depending on your network configuration, this could be the host name or IP address of a UNIX computer, a Windows NT computer, or an HP JetDirect adapter that supports TCP/IP printing.

In addition, type in the name of the printer or print queue on the computer or device providing the LPD service.

Figure 6-15 shows the Add LPD compatible printer dialog box. Notice the IP address of the device providing the LPD service (in this case, an HP JetDirect adapter) and the name of the printer have been entered. Click OK.

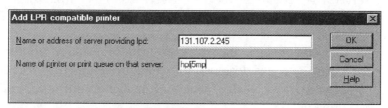

**FIGURE 6-15**   Configuring an LPR port

**8.** In the Printer Ports dialog box, click Close.

**9.** The Add Printer Wizard dialog box, shown in Figure 6-16, reappears. Note that the LPR port that you created is displayed in the form of *IP_address:printer_name,* and is highlighted and selected in the Available ports list box. Click Next.

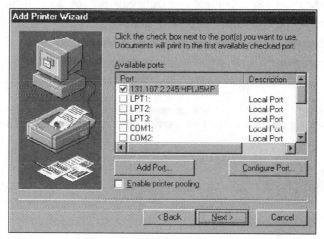

**FIGURE 6-16**   **LPR port added to available ports list**

**10.** Select the appropriate manufacturer and print device model, and click Next.

**11.** Type in a printer name, or accept the default. Click Next.

**12.** Choose whether to share the printer. (You can share or stop sharing the printer later if you change your mind.) Click Next.

**13.** Choose whether to print a test page. Click Finish.

# NetWare

The *NetWare print monitor* sends print jobs to a print queue on a Novell NetWare server. The NetWare server then sends the print job from the print queue to the print device.

 **A *print queue* is the NetWare term for a shared printer. A NetWare print queue is designed to handle print jobs that are ready to send to the print device, and that need no additional conversion or formatting.**

Before you can connect to a NetWare print queue, you must install NWLink IPX/SPX Compatible Transport on your Windows NT computer. In addition, on Windows NT Workstation computers, you must install *Client Service for NetWare* (CSNW); and on Windows NT Server computers, you must install *Gateway Service for NetWare* (GSNW).

NWLink IPX/SPX Compatible Transport is a routable protocol. A Windows NT computer that uses the NetWare print monitor can communicate with any NetWare server on any segment of a routed NetWare network.

**TO CONNECT A WINDOWS NT COMPUTER TO A PRINTER THAT USES THE NETWARE PRINT MONITOR, FOLLOW THESE STEPS:**

**1.** Install NWLink IPX/SPX Compatible Transport on your Windows NT computer. In addition, install Client Service for NetWare (on a Windows NT Workstation computer) or Gateway Service for NetWare (on a Windows NT Server computer), as appropriate. (If you need more information on how to do this, refer to the section "Installing and Configuring Protocols and Services" in Chapter 4.)

**2.** Open the `Printers` folder. (Select Start ⇒ Settings ⇒ Printers.)

**3.** Double-click the Add Printers icon.

**4.** The Add Printer Wizard dialog box appears. To connect to a printer, select Network printer server, and click Next.

**5.** In the Connect to Printer dialog box, do *one* of the following:

In the Printer text box, type in a complete path to the NetWare print queue you want to connect to, in the form of
\\*Netware_server_name*\*print_queue_name*

Or use the browse list in the Shared Printers list box to select the NetWare print queue to which you want to connect.

Figure 6-17 shows the Connect to Printer dialog box. Notice that a NetWare print queue is selected. Then click OK.

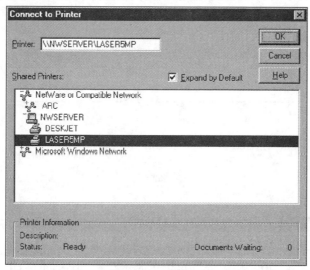

**FIGURE 6-17**   **Connecting to a NetWare print queue**

6. A warning message appears, indicating that the server on which the NetWare print queue resides doesn't have the appropriate printer driver installed. Click OK to install a printer driver on your Windows NT computer.

7. Select the appropriate manufacturer and print device model, and click OK.

8. A dialog box appears asking if you want this printer to be your default printer. Click Yes or No, as appropriate, and then click Next to continue.

9. Click Finish. You are now connected to a NetWare print queue.

# CONFIGURING PRINT SERVER PROPERTIES

A *print server* is a computer (or network device) that manages print jobs and print devices. The Windows NT Spooler service performs many of the functions of a print server. You can configure several of the Spooler service's properties (which Windows NT calls *print server properties*) including the spool folder, forms, and ports.

────────────────────────────⋀────────────────────────────

**TO ACCESS THE PRINT SERVER PROPERTIES DIALOG BOX IN WINDOWS NT WORKSTATION OR WINDOWS NT SERVER, FOLLOW THESE STEPS:**

**1.** Select Start ⇒ Settings ⇒ Printers.

**2.** Then select File ⇒ Server Properties in the Printers dialog box.

────────────────────────────⋀────────────────────────────

The following sections explain how you can configure each of the print server properties.

# Changing the Spool Folder

The *spool folder* is used by the Windows NT Spooler service as a temporary storage area for print jobs waiting to be sent to a print device. The default location for the spool folder is `<winntroot>\System32\Spool\Printers`.

If the partition that contains the spool folder does not have enough free space to store print jobs, you may experience print job failures. On a busy Windows NT Server computer with multiple shared printers, for example, you might need between 25MB and several hundred megabytes of free space for the spool folder, depending on the number, type, and size of print jobs that are spooled on this server.

If you experience print job failures due to a lack of free space for your spool folder, you can specify that a different folder on another partition (that has more free space) be used as your spool folder.

To change your spool folder, click the Advanced tab in the Print Server Properties dialog box. Then, edit the contents of the Spool Folder text box. You can specify any folder in any partition as your spool folder, in the format of `Drive_letter:\Folder\Subfolder`.

Figure 6-18 shows the Advanced tab in the Print Server Properties dialog box. Note the default spool folder location, and the additional options that you can configure on this tab.

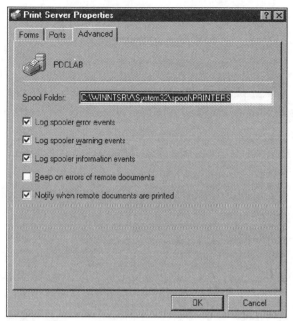

**FIGURE 6-18**   Configuring advanced print server properties

in the
real world

**Many a network administrator has changed the spool folder on a Windows NT computer, only to find out that users can no longer print to shared network printers on this computer.**

**To solve this problem, the administrator must assign permissions so that all users who print to any shared printer on the Windows NT computer have the Change permission to the spool folder. Users that don't have the Change permission to the spool folder won't be able to print to any shared network printer on the Windows NT computer. (Permissions are covered in detail in Chapter 12.)**

## Creating Forms

You can create forms on the Forms tab in the Print Server Properties dialog box. Options that you can configure include form name, paper size, and printer area margins.

Once you've created a form, you can assign that form to a paper tray on a printer. (Assigning a form to a paper tray is covered later in this chapter.) Once a form is assigned to a paper tray, documents that specify that form are automatically printed using that paper tray. This process can be helpful in managing document printing on a network.

For example, suppose a company wants to print all documents that require company letterhead from a specific paper tray. When a user wants to print a document using letterhead paper, the user can select the letterhead form (in the Printer Properties dialog box) in any Windows application when the user creates a print job. Using the Windows NT form capabilities enables the user to print a document on letterhead without necessarily knowing which paper tray in the print device contains the company's letterhead.

Some network administrators create a separate printer for each form and paper tray assignment to ease administration and to enable users to select forms in a more obvious manner.

To create a form, click the Forms tab in the Print Server Properties dialog box. Highlight any existing form in the Forms list box, select the check box next to Create a New Form, and then edit the name of the form, as well as the paper size and printer area margins to meet your new form's specifications. Then click the Save Form command button. The new form is added to the Forms list box, and the old form is not changed or deleted.

Figure 6-19 shows the Forms tab in the Print Server Properties dialog box. Notice that a form called *Letterhead* has been created and now appears in the Forms list box.

## Managing Ports

You can use the Ports tab in the Print Server Properties dialog box to add, delete, and configure ports. (As you recall, creating and configuring ports by using the Add Printer Wizard was discussed in the "Print Monitors" section earlier in this chapter.)

The capabilities of the Ports tab in the Print Server Properties dialog box are identical to those in the Add Printer Wizard with one exception: ports can only be *deleted* from the Ports tab in the Print Server Properties dialog box.

Figure 6-20 shows the Ports tab in the Print Server Properties dialog box. Notice the Delete Port command button.

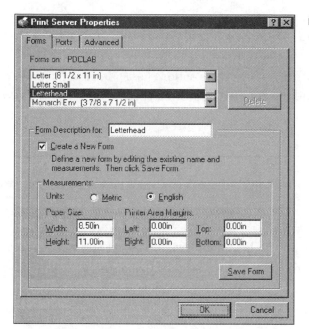

**FIGURE 6-19**   **Creating forms**

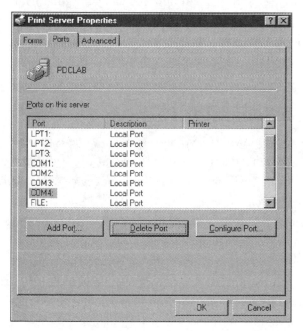

**FIGURE 6-20**   **Managing ports**

# CONFIGURING PRINTER PROPERTIES

In Windows NT you can configure options for a printer in the printer's Properties dialog box. This dialog box is printer specific, and is titled *Printer_name* Properties.

---

**TO ACCESS THE PROPERTIES DIALOG BOX FOR A PRINTER, FOLLOW THESE STEPS:**

**1.** Select Start ⇒ Settings ⇒ Printers.

**2.** In the Printers dialog box, right-click the printer you want to configure.

**3.** Then select Properties from the menu that appears.

---

The following sections explain how you can configure printer properties, including assigning a separator page, assigning forms to paper trays, printer security, printing to multiple ports (printer pools), scheduling printers and setting printer priorities, and sharing a printer.

## Assigning a Separator Page

You can configure Windows NT so that a *separator page* is printed at the beginning of every document. Using separator pages at the beginning of print jobs enables users to locate their print jobs at the print device easily. Separator pages are sometimes called *banner pages*.

You can assign a separator page to a printer by using the Properties dialog box for your printer. To do this, click the Separator Page command button on the General tab in your printer Properties dialog box. In the Separator Page dialog box, type in the full path of the separator page file you want to assign to your printer; or click the Browse command button and double-click the separator page file you want to assign from the Separator Page dialog box. Then click OK in the Separator Page dialog box, and exit the Properties dialog box for your printer.

Figure 6-21 shows the Separator Page dialog boxes. Notice that there are three default separator page files shown: `Pcl.sep`, `Pscript.sep`, and `Sysprint.sep`. The `Pcl.sep` separator page file switches a dual language print device to PCL printing. The `Pscript.sep` separator page file switches a dual language print device to PostScript printing. The `Sysprint.sep` separator page file prints a separator page before each document.

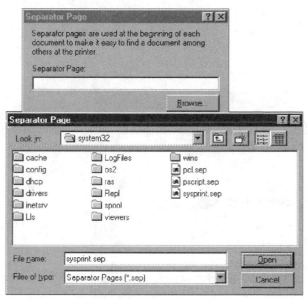

**FIGURE 6-21**    Assigning a separator page to a printer

You can create additional separator page files by editing an existing separator page file and saving it with a different name.

concept link

**For detailed information on editing separator page files and using custom separator pages, search for "Separator pages, printing" in NT Books Online (Start ⇒ Programs ⇒ Books Online — available on Windows NT Server only). Or see Chapter 7 of the *Microsoft Windows NT Workstation Resource Kit for version 4.0* (Microsoft Press, 1996).**

## Assigning Forms to Paper Trays

As discussed in the section on "Creating Forms" section earlier in this chapter, assigning forms to paper trays can be helpful in managing document printing on a network, because once a form is assigned to a paper tray, print jobs that specify that form are automatically printed using that paper tray.

To assign a form to a paper tray, select the Device Settings tab in the Properties dialog box for your printer. Highlight the paper tray to which you want to assign the form, and then select the form you want to assign to this paper tray from the Change Tray Setting list box. Click OK.

Figure 6-22 shows the Device Settings tab in the Properties dialog box for my printer, an HP LaserJet 5MP. Notice that the letterhead form is now assigned to Tray 1.

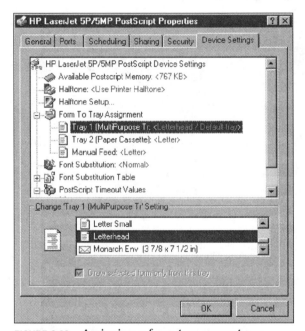

**FIGURE 6-22**    Assigning a form to a paper tray

## Printer Security

You can use Windows NT printer security to control access to a printer by assigning printer permissions to users and groups. Printer security is configured on the Security tab in a printer's Properties dialog box. In addition, you can take ownership of a printer and configure Windows NT to audit printer usage in this dialog box.

Figure 6-23 shows the Security tab in a printer's Properties dialog box. Note the Permissions, Auditing, and Ownership command buttons.

The next sections discuss printer permissions, auditing printers, and taking ownership of a printer.

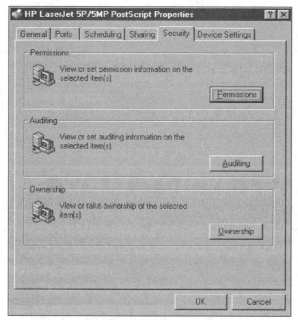

**FIGURE 6-23**   The Security tab in a printer's
Properties dialog box

## Printer permissions

*Printer permissions* control which tasks a user can perform on a specific printer.
Table 6-1 lists and describes the Windows NT printer permissions.

**TABLE 6-1** WINDOWS NT PRINTER PERMISSIONS

| PRINTER PERMISSION | DESCRIPTION AND FUNCTIONALITY |
| --- | --- |
| No Access | A user or group that has the No Access permission cannot access the printer. |
| Print | The Print permission enables users to create print jobs, and also to delete their own print jobs. |
| Manage Documents | The Manage Documents permission enables users to create and delete their own print jobs; as well as pause, restart, delete, and control job settings for all print jobs. |
| Full Control | A user or group that has the Full Control permission can do everything that a user with the Manage Documents permission can do, and can also assign printer permissions, delete printers, share printers, and change printer properties. |

You can assign printer permissions to users and groups. User and group permissions are additive. In other words, if a user has the Print permission, and a group that the user is a member of has Full Control, then the user has Full Control.

There is one exception to this rule. If a user, or any group that a user is a member of, has the No Access permission, then the user's effective permission is always No Access. For example, a user may have the Full Control permission, but a group that the user is a member of may have the No Access permission. The user's effective permission is No Access, and the user cannot access the printer.

concept link     **For more information on user and group accounts, see Chapter 7.**

To assign printer permissions to users and groups, click the Permissions command button on the Security tab in the Properties dialog box for the printer you want to configure. Figure 6-24 shows the default printer permissions assigned to a newly created printer in the Printer Permissions dialog box. Note that by default the Everyone group has the Print permission, which effectively enables all users to create and delete their own print jobs on this printer.

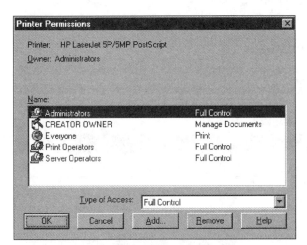

**FIGURE 6-24**    **Assigning printer permissions**

To modify permissions in this dialog box, highlight a user or group, and then select the permission you want to assign to this user or group from the Type of Access drop-down list box. Then click OK, and click OK in your printer's Properties dialog box.

To add a user or group to the Name list box, click the Add command button in the Printer Permissions dialog box. The Add Users and Groups dialog box appears. Select the user(s) and/or group(s) you want to add, then click the Add command button. Then click OK to return to the Printer Permissions dialog box. Click OK, and click OK in your printer's Properties dialog box.

To remove a user or group from the Name list box, highlight the user or group and press Delete. Then click OK. Click OK in your printer's Properties dialog box.

## *Auditing printers*

You can use your printer's Properties dialog box to configure Windows NT to audit a user or group's usage (and/or attempted usage) of a printer. Only members of the Administrators group can configure auditing on a Windows NT computer.

When auditing is enabled, Windows NT adds an entry to the security log in Event Viewer every time an audited user or group exercises (and/or attempts to exercise) an audited permission on a specific printer. To gain a better understanding of auditing printers, how about a walk through the process of configuring printer auditing?

Auditing printers is accomplished in two parts: first, auditing is enabled in User Manager for Domains (or in User Manager on Windows NT Workstation); second, printer auditing is configured in a specific printer's Properties dialog box.

The following sections explain how to perform these tasks.

**TO ENABLE AUDITING IN USER MANAGER, FOLLOW THESE STEPS:**

**1.** Select Start ⇒ Programs ⇒ Administrative Tools (Common) ⇒ User Manager for Domains (or User Manager on a Windows NT Workstation computer).

**2.** In the User Manager dialog box, select Policies ⇒ Audit.

**3.** The Audit Policy dialog box appears. Select the radio button next to Audit These Events. Then select the events you want to be audited. You *must* select the Success and/or Failure check boxes for File and Object Access to audit printer events.

*Success auditing* means that Windows NT will report successful attempts to complete the task or event listed.

*Failure auditing* means that Windows NT will report unsuccessful attempts to complete the task or event listed.

Figure 6-25 shows the Audit Policy dialog box. Note that the radio button next to Audit These Events is selected, and that the Success and Failure check boxes for File and Object Access are checked. Click OK.

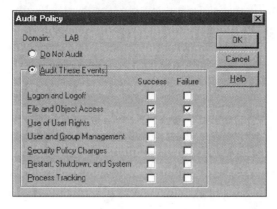

**FIGURE 6-25**  **Enabling auditing of file and object access**

**4.** Exit User Manager for Domains (or User Manger).

**TO CONFIGURE PRINTER AUDITING, FOLLOW THESE STEPS:**

**1.** Select Start ⇒ Settings ⇒ Printers.

**2.** In the Printers dialog box, right-click the printer you want to configure.

**3.** Then select Properties from the menu that appears.

**4.** Click the Security tab in your printer's Properties dialog box.

**5.** Click the Auditing command button.

**6.** The Printer Auditing dialog box appears. You must add the user(s) and/or group(s) you want to audit for this printer to the Name list box. To do this, click the Add command button.

**7.** The Add Users and Groups dialog box appears. Select the user(s) and/or group(s) you want to add, and then click the Add command button. Then click OK to return to the Printer Auditing dialog box.

**8.** The user(s) and/or group(s) you added are now listed in the Name list box. Select the Success and/or Failure check boxes for the print events you want to audit. You *must* select at least one event for print auditing to occur.

Figure 6-26 shows the Printer Auditing dialog box. Notice that the check boxes for Success and Failure auditing of Print events are selected for the Everyone group. Click OK.

**9.** Click OK in your printer's Properties dialog box. Auditing of print events is now enabled and configured.

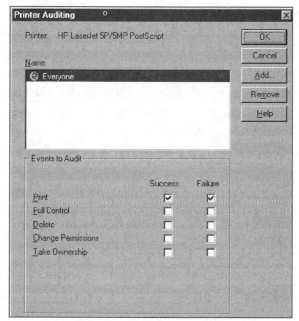

**FIGURE 6-26** Configuring print events to audit

To view the events generated by printer auditing, select Start ⇒ Programs ⇒ Administrative Tools (Common) ⇒ Event Viewer. In the Event Viewer dialog box, select Log ⇒ Security. A list of audited events is displayed. You can double-click any event for a detailed description of the event.

in the real world **Auditing printers can generate a significant number of entries in the security log. I recommend you don't use printer auditing unless you have a specific need to do so.**

### Taking ownership of a printer

The owner of a printer has special status—an owner can assign printer permissions for that printer to any user or group, even if the owner has the No Access permission to that printer. A printer can have only one owner at any given time.

There are two ways to become an owner of a printer: either by creating the printer, or by taking ownership of the printer. By default, the user that creates a printer is the owner of that printer (unless the person who creates a printer is a member of the Administrators group, in which case the Administrators group is the owner of that printer). Only certain users can take ownership of a printer. You must either be a member of the Administrators group or have the Full Control permission to take ownership of a printer.

So why would you ever want to take ownership of a printer? Well, assume that a user on your network (I'll call him Fred) who has the Full Control permission to a printer has inadvertently taken ownership and removed *all* users' printer permissions for that printer. As a result of Fred's faux pas, the network administrator—that's you—(and every other user) now have no permissions for the printer. To be able to resolve the problem and assign yourself and other users permissions to the printer again, you need to first take ownership of the printer.

The process of taking ownership is fairly straightforward. First, log on as Administrator. (You must log on as the user that wants to become the new owner of the printer. Normally this is the administrator, but it can be any user with the Full Control permission to that printer.) In the `Printers` folder, right-click the printer you want to take ownership of, then select Properties from the menu that appears. If you have no permissions to the printer (such as in the previous example), a dialog box appears, indicating that you do not have access to this printer, and that only the Security tab will be displayed. Click OK. On the Security tab, click the Ownership command button. A warning dialog box appears, indicating that you do not have permission to view the current owner, but that you may have permission to change it. Click Yes. The Owner dialog box, shown in Figure 6-27, appears.

Click the Take Ownership command button. Then click OK on the Security tab of the printer's Properties dialog box. You are now the new owner of the printer, and can assign printer permissions for that printer.

## Printing to Multiple Ports (Printer Pools)

When a printer has multiple ports (and multiple print devices) assigned to it, this is called a *printer pool*. Users print to a single printer, and the printer load-balances its print jobs between the print devices assigned to it.

A printer pool is a useful tool when *both* of the following criteria are met:

- All print devices assigned to the printer use the same print device driver. (Usually, this means that identical print devices are used.)

- All print devices assigned to the printer pool are located physically close to each other.

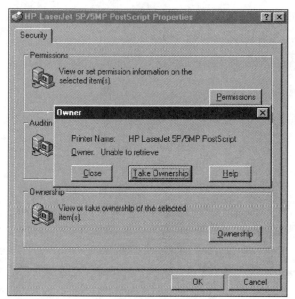

FIGURE 6-27   Taking ownership of a printer

in the real world

**A printer pool can be a good solution when the desired number of printed pages is more output than one print device can produce. When you implement a printer pool, I recommend you use two or more identical print devices, located next to each other. A printer pool is definitely *not* useful if the print devices are located at opposite ends of a building, because users would have to check both locations to find their print jobs.**

To configure multiple ports (and their associated print devices) as a printer pool, first create a printer. Then, from the `Printers` folder, right-click this printer and select Properties from the menu that appears. Click the Ports tab of the printer's Properties dialog box. On the Ports tab, click the check box next to "Enable printer pooling". Then select at least one additional port from the Port list box. Figure 6-28 shows the Properties dialog box for a printer that has been configured as a printer pool. Notice that three ports have been selected, and that the check box next to "Enable printer pooling" is checked.

When a user prints to a printer pool, the print job is sent to the first listed print device in the Port list that is not busy printing another print job. The entire print job is sent to the same port (print device). In a printer pool the print spooler—not the user—determines to which print device the print job will be sent.

**FIGURE 6-28**   Creating a printer pool

# Scheduling Printers and Setting Printer Priorities

Scheduling printers and setting printer priorities are two techniques you can use to help manage the flow of print jobs on your Windows NT network. I will discuss both of these approaches in the following sections.

## Scheduling printers

*Scheduling a printer* means assigning the hours a specific print device is available for use by a specific printer. When scheduling a printer, the hours of availability apply only to the print device, not to the printer. This means that users can print to the printer at any time during the day, and the printer then spools the jobs to the hard disk. However, the print jobs are only sent to the print device during the print device's hours of availability. (If you decide to schedule a printer, be sure to reserve plenty of hard disk space to spool print jobs while they wait for the print device to become available.)

So why would you want to schedule a printer? Well, suppose you are the network administrator for a small, twenty-computer network. The owner of the company recently bought a laser print device for network printing, and doesn't want to spend any more money on print devices. One of the employees occasionally generates a print job that is five to six hundred pages long. This report ties up the one available printer for a long time, frustrating other employees. The large reports are for archival and reference purposes, and are not needed immediately.

You solve the problem this way: first, you create a second printer that prints to the laser print device. Then you schedule the new printer so that it only sends print jobs to the print device during nonbusiness hours. You instruct the employee who creates the large print jobs to use the new printer for the large print jobs. The result is that the employee can generate large print jobs at any time without inconveniencing other employees. The large print jobs are spooled to the hard disk, and then sent to the print device during nonbusiness hours. (Make sure to stock the print device with plenty of paper just before leaving for the evening!)

To schedule a printer, right-click the printer in the `Printers` folder and select Properties from the menu that is displayed. Then select the Scheduling tab from the printer's Properties dialog box. To set the available hours, click the radio button next to From and set the times in the spin boxes next to From and To.

Figure 6-29 shows the Scheduling tab in the HP LaserJet 5MP Properties dialog box. Note that the available hours are from 9:00 p.m. to 5:00 a.m. Print jobs sent to this printer will only be sent to the print device during these non-business hours.

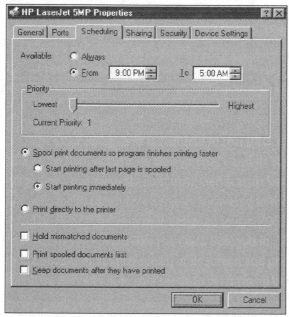

**FIGURE 6-29**   **Scheduling available hours for a print device**

## Setting printer priorities

When more than one printer sends print jobs to the same print device, setting printer priorities may be useful. If two printers are configured to use the same print device, and you configure one of these printers to have a higher priority than the other printer, then all print jobs from the higher priority printer will be sent to the print device before any print jobs from the lower priority printer are sent.

The highest printer priority is 99, and the lowest printer priority is 1. All printers have a priority of 1 by default.

Here's one situation in which setting printer priorities could be beneficial: Suppose you have two printers on a Windows NT Server computer that both send print jobs to the print device connected to LPT1:. One printer is named *sales*, and the other printer is named *managers*. Figure 6-30 shows the *sales* and *managers* Properties dialog boxes. Notice that both printers are configured to use LPT1:.

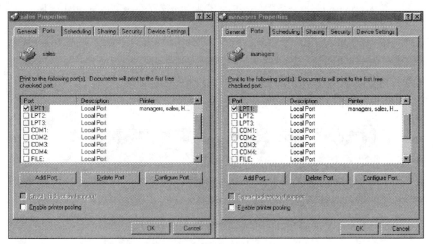

**FIGURE 6-30**  The sales and managers printers

The managers at this company, who think their work is more important than everyone else's, tell you—the network administrator—that they want their print jobs printed before anyone else's.

So what's a network administrator to do? You decide to configure printer security so that everyone can use the *sales* printer, but only members of the Managers group can use the *managers* printer. Then you set the priority on the *managers* printer to a value higher than one. Once this is done, the managers' print jobs will take priority. Suppose that there are one hundred print jobs waiting to print in the *sales* printer, and a manager sends a print job to the *managers* printer. The current print job from the *sales* printer will finish printing, then the manager's print job will be printed, even though there are one hundred other print jobs in the *sales* printer that were generated before the manager's print job.

Figure 6-31 shows the Scheduling tab in the Properties dialog boxes for both the *sales* and *managers* printers. Notice that the *sales* printer is set to a priority of 1 (lowest), and that the *managers* printer is set to a priority of 99 (highest).

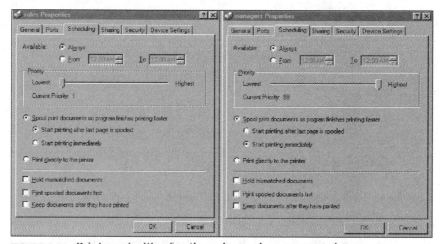

**FIGURE 6-31**   **Printer priorities for the sales and managers printers**

Also notice in Figure 6-31 that the "Start printing after last page is spooled" option is selected for the *sales* printer. This means that print jobs sent to the *sales* printer are not sent to the print device until the *entire* print job has been received by the spooler. Finally, notice that the "Start printing immediately" option is selected for the *managers* printer. This causes print jobs sent to the *managers* printer to be sent to the print device as soon as the spooler *starts* receiving the print job. This setting gives the managers another subtle speed advantage over those who use the *sales* printer.

## Sharing a Printer

The purpose of sharing a printer on a Windows NT computer is to enable users of other computers on the network to connect to and to send print jobs to the shared printer. The computer that hosts the shared printer is called a *print server*. The print server performs all of the spooling, print job management, scheduling, and sending of the final print jobs to the print device.

When you share a printer on your Windows NT computer, the types of computers on the network that can access your shared printer are somewhat dependent upon the protocols and services installed in your computer.

When you install Windows NT, Microsoft Windows Networking is installed by default. If you have not installed any other services and you share a printer on your computer, only computers that support Microsoft Windows Networking can access the shared printer.

If you installed Microsoft TCP/IP Printing *and* started the TCP/IP Print Server service (which is installed with Microsoft TCP/IP Printing), and you share a printer on your computer, then computers that support Microsoft Windows Networking and computers that support TCP/IP printing (such as UNIX computers) can access the shared printer.

If you have installed Services for Macintosh on a Windows NT Server computer and you share a printer on your computer, then computers that support Microsoft Windows Networking and Macintosh computers can access the shared printer. Services for Macintosh can only be installed on a Windows NT Server computer, not a Windows NT Workstation computer.

 concept link

**For more information on sharing printers in a Macintosh environment, see the section "Sharing AppleTalk printers in Windows NT" later in this chapter.**

Microsoft TCP/IP Printing and Services for Macintosh both include components that enable you to share printers. These components are called *print server services*. If you have more than one print server service installed and started on your Windows NT computer, and then you share a printer, the printer is shared on *all* running print server services installed on your computer.

## Installing printer drivers for shared printers

When you share a printer on a Windows NT computer, Windows NT permits you to install alternate printer drivers for other versions of Windows NT and Windows 95. You can also install alternate printer drivers for other Windows NT hardware platforms, such as MIPS R4000, PowerPC, and DEC Alpha.

Installing these drivers enables users of Windows NT and Windows 95 computers on your network to automatically download and install the appropriate printer drivers for their operating systems/hardware platforms when they connect to the shared printer. The advantage of being able to install these alternate printer drivers on a shared printer is that the network administrator is spared the time-consuming task of manually installing printer drivers on every computer on the network.

To install alternate drivers on a shared printer, click the Sharing tab in the shared printer's Properties dialog box. Then select the alternate drivers for the operating systems/hardware platforms you want to install. Click OK when you are finished. Windows NT prompts you for the source media and path for each alternate driver you select.

The source media is your Windows NT Server or Workstation compact disc if you are installing alternate printer drivers for NT 4.0. If you are installing alternate drivers for another version of Windows NT, such as NT 3.51, the source media is the Windows NT Server or Workstation (version 3.51) compact disc. The path is the appropriate platform subdirectory, such as \I386, \MIPS, \PPC, or \Alpha.

When installing alternate printer drivers for Windows 95, a more complex task is indicated. First, copy all of the operating system files from the Windows 95 source media (the Win95 folder on the Windows 95 compact disc) to a folder on your Windows NT computer. Then, in this folder on your Windows NT computer, expand all of the CAB files.

 concept link **For more information on how to expand Windows 95 CAB files, refer to the Windows 95 product documentation and help files.**

When Windows NT prompts you for the source media for the Windows 95 alternate printer drivers, type the path to the folder that contains the expanded Windows 95 source files.

Figure 6-32 shows a shared printer, named *managers*, with alternate printer drivers for Windows 95 and Windows NT 4.0 *x*86 highlighted. The *x*86 indicates that printer drivers for Intel-based computers that run Windows NT 4.0 will be installed.

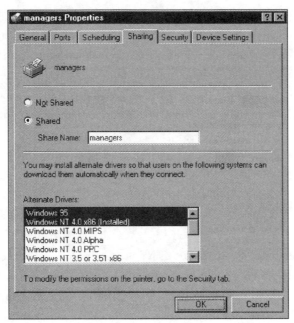

**FIGURE 6-32**   Installing printer drivers for multiple operating systems

## Sharing AppleTalk printers in Windows NT

When a Windows NT Workstation computer that has the AppleTalk protocol installed on it shares a printer, the printer is *not* accessible from Macintosh computers on the network, because Windows NT Workstation does not have any AppleTalk print server capabilities.

This means that if you capture an AppleTalk print device on a Windows NT Workstation computer, and then share the associated printer, Macintosh computers on the network cannot access the AppleTalk print device nor the shared printer. The Macintosh computers can't access the AppleTalk print device, in this situation, because the AppleTalk print monitor has captured (and hidden) the print device. The Macintosh computers can't access the shared printer because Windows NT Workstation is not capable of sharing a printer as an AppleTalk printer.

When a Windows NT Server computer that has Services for Macintosh installed on it shares a printer, the printer *is* accessible from Macintosh computers on the network, because Windows NT Server has full AppleTalk print server capabilities.

Shared printers on a Windows NT Server computer that has Services for Macintosh installed advertise themselves to Macintosh computers on the network as Apple LaserWriters. (An Apple LaserWriter is the original laser print device for Macintosh computers. All Macintosh computers have built-in drivers for the Apple LaserWriter.) This means that a Macintosh computer does not need special drivers to access the shared printer. Windows NT Server converts the PostScript print jobs it receives from Macintosh computers into RAW format print jobs for the print device.

# TROUBLESHOOTING COMMON PRINTING PROBLEMS

Printing problems can occur on a Windows NT network for several reasons. Some of the most common printing problems involve users who do not have the permissions they need to access the printer, or users who have the Full Control permission or the Manage Document permission accidentally deleting documents that belong to other users. A good first step, when troubleshooting printer problems, is to ensure that users have appropriate printer permissions.

Table 6-2 lists some common printing problems, their probable causes, and recommended solutions.

**TABLE 6-2** TROUBLESHOOTING PRINTING PROBLEMS

| PROBLEM | PROBABLE CAUSE/RECOMMENDED SOLUTION |
| --- | --- |
| Print jobs are not being sent from the printer to the print device. A print job with a size of 0 bytes is at the top of the print job list for the printer. Other documents are also listed in the print job list, and users can still send print jobs to the printer. There is plenty of free space on the partition that contains your spool folder. | The most likely cause of this problem is a stalled print spooler. Stop and restart the Spooler service, and printing should resume. |

*continued*

**TABLE 6-2** *(continued)*

| PROBLEM | PROBABLE CAUSE/RECOMMENDED SOLUTION |
|---|---|
| No print events are listed in the security log in Event Viewer. You recently configured success auditing for print events in the Properties dialog box for the printer. Several days have passed, and hundreds of documents have been printed. | The most likely cause of this problem is that the success option for auditing file and object access has not been configured in User Manager for Domains (or User Manager). Auditing of printers requires that auditing of file and object access be configured. To resolve the problem, configure the necessary options in User Manager for Domains (or User Manager). |
| A printer that uses the Hpmon print monitor has stopped sending print jobs to its assigned print device. | This problem usually occurs when another computer on the network is configured to use Hpmon to connect to the print device by using a continuous connection. If you want more than one printer to be able to access a print device by using Hpmon, configure a job-based connection for all printers. |
| You are unable to connect a Windows NT computer to a print device that uses TCP/IP and LPD. | Of the many possible causes for this problem, the most common is an incorrect configuration of a TCP/IP parameter on either the Windows NT computer or on the print device that uses TCP/IP and LPD. Ensure that the IP address, subnet mask, and default gateway parameters on *both* the Windows NT computer and the print device that uses TCP/IP and LPD are set correctly. |
| You experience a paper jam in the middle of an important print job. You want to reprint the entire print job, but it is not possible to reprint the job from the application that created it because you deleted the document after you created the print job. | The cause of the paper jam is not important here, but being able to reprint the entire print job is. To solve this problem, I recommend that you: <br><br>1. Immediately double-click the printer in the Printers folder. <br><br>2. The Printers dialog box appears. Select Document ⇒ Pause. This pauses the print job. <br><br>3. Clear the paper jam at the print device. <br><br>4. Select Document ⇒ Restart to reprint the entire print job. |

| PROBLEM | PROBABLE CAUSE/RECOMMENDED SOLUTION |
|---|---|
| | (Do *not* select Resume from the Document menu, because this will only print the print job from wherever the printer jammed to the end of the document, and the pages jammed in the print device will very likely be lost.) |
| You receive spooler messages indicating that your print job has been spooled with a size of 0 bytes. Figure 6-33 shows a sample error message of this type. | The most probable cause of this problem is that the partition that contains the printer's spool folder does not have enough free space to print the document in question. You should delete some files from this partition, or move the spool folder to a different partition that has more free space. |

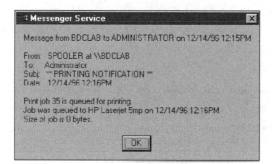

**FIGURE 6-33**    Spooler error message

While troubleshooting is sometimes an art, it is more often a methodical, step-by-step process. If you do not quickly see the cause of your problem, I recommend you check all permissions, as well as hardware and software configuration parameters. Be careful here— it's easy to bypass a configuration parameter that looks correct at first glance but has a small error in it. Be very detail-oriented and methodical when troubleshooting, and you will probably resolve most of the problems you encounter in short order.

# KEY POINT SUMMARY

Chapter 6 introduced many key Windows NT printing topics.

o It is important to have a solid grasp of Windows NT printing terminology, not only for fully understanding printing in NT, but also for passing the Microsoft Certified Professional exams. A *printer* is the software interface between NT and the device that produces printed output. A *print (or printing) device* is the physical device (hardware) that produces the printed output.

o The *print process* begins with the user at an NT computer creating a print job within an application, such as Word. The application then hands off the print job to the *Graphics Device Interface* (GDI). The GDI initiates a request to the driver for the print device. The driver for the print device converts the print job into either a Windows NT *enhanced metafile* (EMF) or into a RAW format. The driver returns the converted print job to the GDI. The GDI hands off the print job to the Windows NT spooler, which determines whether the print device is managed locally or by a network-connected computer. If the print device is managed by the local computer that initiated this print job, the spooler copies the print job to a temporary storage area on the local computer's hard disk. If the print device is managed by a network-connected computer, the spooler hands off the print job to the spooler on the network-connected computer. Then that spooler copies the print job to a temporary storage area on that computer's hard disk. The print job is then handed off to the local print provider on the computer that has the print job spooled to its hard disk. The local print provider calls the print processor to perform any additional necessary conversions. Then the print processor returns the ready-to-print print job to the local print provider. The local print provider adds a separator page to the print job (if it is configured to do so) and then hands off the print job to the print monitor. The print monitor communicates directly with the print device, and sends the ready-to-print print job to the print device, which finally produces the printed output. You may want to refer back to Figure 6-1, which shows a graphical illustration of the Windows NT print process.

o There are two ways of installing and configuring a printer in Windows NT: you can either *create a printer* or *connect to a shared network printer*. Both creating a printer and connecting to a printer are called "adding a

printer," because both processes use the Add Printer Wizard in the
Printers folder. You can also connect to a printer by using drag-and-drop
printing.

- *Print monitors* (also called port monitors) are software components that
  send ready-to-print print jobs to a print device, either locally or across the
  network. Each port is associated with one specific print monitor. The most
  commonly used print monitors are Localmon, Hpmon, AppleTalk, TCP/IP,
  and NetWare.

  - The *Localmon print monitor* sends print jobs to print devices that are
    connected to hardware ports on a local Windows NT computer. It is the
    only print monitor that is installed by default during the installation of
    Windows NT.

  - The *Hpmon print monitor* sends print jobs to a network print device via an
    HP JetDirect adapter. Although HP JetDirect adapters typically support a
    variety of protocols, Hpmon uses only the DLC protocol to communicate
    with HP JetDirect adapters. The DLC protocol is a non-routable protocol,
    although it does support bridging. You must install DLC before you can
    connect to an HP JetDirect adapter using Hpmon. When you configure an
    Hpmon port, you must choose between a job-based and a continuous
    connection. A *job-based connection* enables all computers on the network
    to access the HP JetDirect adapter for printing, because the connection to
    the HP JetDirect adapter is dropped after each print job. A *continuous
    connection* causes Hpmon to monopolize the HP JetDirect adapter, and no
    other computer on the network is able to access the HP JetDirect adapter
    for printing.

  - The *AppleTalk print monitor* sends print jobs to network print devices
    that support the AppleTalk protocol. The AppleTalk protocol is usually
    associated with Apple Macintosh computers. Before you can connect
    to an AppleTalk print device, you must install the AppleTalk protocol
    (on a Windows NT Workstation computer) or Services for Macintosh (on
    a Windows NT Server computer). AppleTalk is a routable protocol.

  - The *TCP/IP print monitor* sends print jobs to network print devices that
    both support TCP/IP *and* function as *line printer daemon* (LPD) print
    servers. TCP/IP and LPD are often associated with UNIX computers. LPD is
    the print server software used in TCP/IP printing, and *line printer remote*

(LPR) is the client print software used in TCP/IP printing. Before you can connect to a TCP/IP print device, you must install TCP/IP and the Microsoft TCP/IP Printing service on your Windows NT computer. In addition, you must start the TCP/IP Print Server service to share printers as TCP/IP printers. TCP/IP is a routable protocol.

o The *NetWare print monitor* sends print jobs to a print queue on a NetWare server. The NetWare server then sends the print job from the print queue to the print device. Before you can connect to a NetWare print queue, you must install NWLink IPX/SPX Compatible Transport on your Windows NT computer. In addition, on Windows NT Workstation computers, you must install Client Service for NetWare; and on Windows NT Server computers, you must install Gateway Service for NetWare. NWLink IPX/SPX Compatible Transport is a routable protocol.

o A *print server* is a computer (or network device) that manages print jobs and print devices. The *Windows NT Spooler service* performs many of the functions of a print server. You can configure several of the Spooler service's properties (which Windows NT calls print server properties), including the spool folder, forms, and ports, by using the Print Server Properties dialog box. If you experience print job failures due to lack of free space on the partition where your spool folder is located, you can specify that a different folder on another partition (that has more free space) be used as your spool folder.

o You can use the Properties dialog box for a specific printer to configure numerous options for the printer, including: assigning a separator page, assigning forms to paper trays, printer security, printing to multiple ports (printer pools), scheduling printers and setting printer priorities, and sharing a printer.

o There are four Windows NT *printer permissions* that control which tasks a user can perform on a specific printer. A user or group with the *No Access* permission cannot access the printer. The *Print* permission enables users to create and delete their own print jobs. The *Manage Documents* permission grants users all the privileges of the Print permission, plus the ability to pause, restart, delete, and control job settings for all print jobs. A user or group that has the *Full Control* permission can do everything a user with the Manage Documents permission can, and in addition, can assign printer permissions, delete printers, share printers, and change printer properties. User and group permissions are additive, with the exception of the No Access permission. *If a user, or any group that a user is a member of, has the No Access permission, then the user's effective permission is always No Access.*

o Windows NT can be configured to audit a user or group's usage (and/or attempted usage) of a printer. Auditing printers is accomplished in two parts: first, auditing is enabled in User Manager for Domains or User Manager; and second, printer auditing is configured in a specific printer's Properties dialog box. You *must* select the Success and/or Failure check boxes for File and Object Access (in User Manager for Domains or User Manager) in order to audit print events.

o The owner of a printer can assign printer permissions for that printer to any user or group, even if the owner has the No Access permission. A printer can have only one owner at any given time. There are two ways to become an owner of a printer: either by creating the printer, or by taking ownership of the printer.

o When a printer has multiple ports (and multiple print devices) assigned to it, this is called a *printer pool*. Users print to a single printer, and the printer load-balances its print jobs between the print devices assigned to it.

o *Scheduling a printer* means assigning the hours that a specific print device is available for use by a printer. *Setting printer priorities* (giving one printer a higher priority to a print device than another printer) can be useful when more than one printer sends print jobs to the same print device. Scheduling printers and setting printer priorities are two techniques you can use to help manage the flow of print jobs on your Windows NT network.

o The purpose of *sharing a printer* is to enable users of other computers on the network to connect to and to send print jobs to that printer. The computer that hosts the shared printer is called a print server. When you share a printer on your Windows NT computer, the types of computers that can access your shared printer are dependent upon the protocols and services installed in your computer. If you have more than one print server service installed on your Windows NT computer, and then you share a printer, the printer is shared on all running print server services installed on your computer.

o   When you share a printer on a Windows NT computer, Windows NT permits you to install *alternate printer drivers* for other versions of Windows NT and Windows 95, and also for other Windows NT hardware platforms, such as MIPS R4000, PowerPC, and DEC Alpha. Installing these alternate drivers enables users of Windows NT and Windows 95 computers on the network to automatically download and install the appropriate printer drivers for their operating systems/hardware platforms when they connect to the shared printer. This process spares the network administrator from having to manually install printer drivers on every computer on the network.

o   AppleTalk printers can be shared in Windows NT. When a Windows NT Server computer that has Services for Macintosh installed on it shares a printer, the printer is accessible from Macintosh computers on the network. However, when a Windows NT Workstation computer that has the AppleTalk protocol installed on it shares a printer, the printer is not accessible from Macintosh computers, because Windows NT Workstation does not have any AppleTalk print server capabilities.

o   Printing problems can occur on a Windows NT network for several reasons. Troubleshooting recommendations for printer problems include: ensuring that users have the permissions they need to access the printer, making sure configuration parameters are correctly set, and using a methodical, step-by-step troubleshooting process.

# APPLYING WHAT YOU'VE LEARNED

Now it's time to regroup, review, and apply what you've learned in this chapter.

The questions in the following Instant Assessment section bring to mind key facts and concepts. In addition, the troubleshooting exercise in the Review Activity section gives you a chance to solve common Windows NT printing problems.

The hands-on lab exercises will really reinforce what you've learned, and provide you the opportunity to practice some of the tasks tested by the Microsoft Certified Professional exams.

## Instant Assessment

1. What is a *printer* in Windows NT terminology?

2. What is a *print device* in Windows NT terminology?

3. Which component in the Windows NT print process determines whether the print device is managed by the local computer that initiated the print job or by a network-connected computer, and routes the print job accordingly?

4. Fill in the blanks: There are two ways to install and configure a printer in Windows NT: you can either _____ a printer or _____ _____ a shared network printer.

5. What is the Windows NT term for software components that send ready-to-print print jobs to a print device?

6. Which print monitor sends print jobs to network print devices that both support TCP/IP and function as LPD print servers?

7. What two things must you install on your Windows NT computer before you can connect to a NetWare print queue by using the NetWare print monitor?

8. Which print monitor sends print jobs to a network print device via an HP JetDirect adapter?

9. What are the characteristics of a job-based connection?

10. What are the characteristics of a continuous connection?

11. Which print monitor uses only the DLC protocol to communicate?

12. If you experience print job failures due to lack of free space on the partition where your spool folder is located, what can you do to resolve the problem?

13. Which Windows NT printer permission, when combined with other permissions, overrides and takes precedence over all other printer permissions?

14. What are the four Windows NT printer permissions?

15. When auditing a printer, what must you select, in User Manager for Domains or User Manager, in order to audit print events?

16. What are the two ways to become an owner of a printer?

17. Which Windows NT printing term is defined as a printer having multiple ports (and multiple print devices) assigned to it?

18. What is the purpose of sharing a printer?

19. What is the advantage of being able to install printer drivers for alternate operating systems/hardware platforms on a shared printer on a Windows NT computer?

**T/F**

20. The DLC protocol is a non-routable protocol that supports bridging. _____

21. AppleTalk, TCP/IP, and NWLink IPX/SPX Compatible Transport are routable protocols. _____

22. When a Windows NT Workstation computer that has the AppleTalk protocol installed on it shares a printer, the printer is not accessible from Macintosh computers on the network, because Windows NT Workstation doesn't have any AppleTalk print server capabilities. _____

concept link 🔗 **For answers to the Instant Assessment questions see Appendix D.**

## Review Activities

The following activity tests your ability to troubleshoot common Windows NT printing problems.

Workstation
Server
Enterprise

### *Windows NT printing troubleshooting exercise*

For each of the following problems, explain what you think are the possible causes of the problem, and what course of action you would take to resolve the problem.

**Problem 1**    Halfway through a print job you discover that the print device's paper tray contains letterhead paper, and you need your document printed on white paper. You want to reprint the entire job, but you have already deleted your document from the spreadsheet application you were using.

**Problem 2**    Several days ago you configured success and failure auditing for print events in the Properties dialog box for your printer. However, no print events are listed in the security log in Event Viewer, even though at least two hundred documents have been printed since you configured auditing.

**Problem 3**　When you attempt to print a document in a word processing application, an error message is displayed, indicating that your print job has been spooled with a print job size of 0 bytes.

concept link  **For answers to the Review Activity see Appendix D.**

## Hands-on Lab Exercises

The following hands-on lab exercises provide you with practical opportunities to apply the knowledge you've gained in this chapter about managing printing.

### Lab 6.8 *Creating and sharing a local printer*

The purpose of this lab is to familiarize you with the Windows NT `Printers` folder and its user interface, and to provide you with the skills necessary to create and share a local printer.

Workstation
Server
Enterprise

To begin this lab, boot your computer to Windows NT Server.

There are two parts to this lab:

Part 1: Creating a local printer

Part 2: Sharing a local printer

#### Part 1: Creating a local printer

1. Select Start ⇒ Programs ⇒ Windows NT Explorer.
2. Highlight (single-click) the `Printers` folder in the All Folders list box. (You might have to scroll down to find this folder.)
3. Double-click the Add Printer icon in the Contents of 'Printers' list box.
4. The Add Printer Wizard appears. Ensure that the radio button next to My Computer is selected. Click Next.
5. Select the check box next to LPT1: in the Available ports list box. Click Next.
6. If you have a print device, select your print device's manufacturer from the Manufacturers list box, and then select your print device's model from the Printers list box. Then click Next. (If you don't have a print device, accept the defaults in the Add Printer Wizard dialog box and click Next.)
7. Type a name for the new printer in the text box, or accept the default name that Windows NT presents. (If your computer has any additional printers installed, you are presented with another option to configure: Select the radio button next to Yes if you want this to be your default printer. Otherwise, select the radio button next to No.) Click Next.

**8.** Ensure that the radio button next to Not shared is selected in the Add Printer Wizard dialog box. Click Next.

**9.** In the Add Printer Wizard dialog box, select the radio button next to Yes to print a test page. Click Finish.

**10.** Windows NT copies files. (Respond to any prompts requesting the location of your Windows NT source files.)

**11.** A dialog box appears indicating that the printer test page is completed. Click Yes.

**12.** The printer is now created. The Windows NT Explorer dialog box reappears. (If you do not have a print device connected to LPT1, an error message eventually appears, indicating that there was an error printing the test page and that the print device is not ready. Click Cancel.) Continue on to Part 2 to share the printer.

### Part 2: Sharing a local printer

**1.** In the Windows NT Explorer dialog box, with the Contents of 'Printers' list box displayed on the right, right-click the printer you just created. Select Sharing from the menu that appears.

**2.** A dialog box with your printer's properties appears. Select the radio button next to Shared. Edit the text box next to Share Name to read: **My Shared Printer**. (Don't type the period at the end.) Don't select any alternate drivers at this time. Click OK.

**3.** A warning message appears (because the share name you typed is longer than eight characters and has spaces in it) indicating that the share name you entered may not be accessible from MS-DOS workstations. Click Yes.

**4.** The Windows NT Explorer dialog box reappears. In the Contents of 'Printers' list box, right-click your printer. Select Properties from the menu that appears.

**5.** In your printer's Properties dialog box, click the Security tab.

**6.** Click Permissions.

**7.** In the Printer Permissions dialog box, notice the default permissions for a newly created printer. Click OK.

**8.** The Printer Permissions dialog box reappears. Click OK. Exit Windows NT Explorer.

### Lab 6.9 *Installing and configuring Microsoft TCP/IP printing*

Workstation
Server
Enterprise

The purpose of this lab is to give you hands-on experience in installing and configuring Microsoft TCP/IP Printing.

Begin this lab by booting your computer to Windows NT Server.

There are two parts to this lab:

Part 1: Installing Microsoft TCP/IP printing

Part 2: Configuring Microsoft TCP/IP printing

#### Part 1: Installing Microsoft TCP/IP printing

1. Select Start ⇒ Programs ⇒ Windows NT Explorer.
2. Click Control Panel in the All Folders list box on the left. In the Contents of 'Control Panel' list box on the right, double-click Network.
3. The Network dialog box appears. Click the Services tab.
4. On the Services tab, click the Add command button.
5. The Select Network Service dialog box appears. Click Microsoft TCP/IP Printing in the Network Service list box. Click OK.
6. A Windows NT Setup dialog box appears, requesting the location of Windows NT source files. Type the path to your Windows NT source files on your Windows NT compact disc (for example, d:\i386) and place your Windows NT compact disc in your CD-ROM drive. Click Continue.
7. Windows NT copies the files to your hard drive. The Services tab reappears. Click Close.
8. Several dialog boxes appear while Windows NT configures the new network service. When the Network Settings Change warning dialog box appears, click Yes to restart your computer.

#### Part 2: Configuring Microsoft TCP/IP Printing

1. Select Start ⇒ Programs ⇒ Windows NT Explorer.
2. Click Control Panel in the All Folders list box on the left. In the Contents of 'Control Panel' list box on the right, double-click Services.
3. Select TCP/IP Print Server from the Service list box. Click the Startup command button.
4. In the Startup Type section of the Service dialog box, select the radio button next to Automatic. Click OK.
5. The Services dialog box reappears. Click the Start command button.

**6.** A Service Control dialog box appears, indicating that Windows NT is attempting to start the service. The Services dialog box reappears. Notice in the Status column that the TCP/IP Print Server service is started. Click Close.

**7.** The Windows NT Explorer dialog box reappears. Exit Windows NT Explorer. Microsoft TCP/IP Printing is now installed and configured.

# Managing Resources

**P**utting it all together and managing what you've got—that's what this part is all about.

First, Chapter 7 explains how to create and manage user accounts. Then, we discuss creating and managing groups—complete with in-depth coverage of local groups and global groups.

Next, Chapter 8 explains managing account policy, followed by step-by-step instructions on how to manage user rights and auditing.

Next, Chapter 9 explores how to manage user profiles, including roaming and mandatory user profiles. It also covers managing Windows NT system policy.

Chapters 10 and 11 are devoted to managing and optimizing Windows NT Directory Services. These chapters cover Windows NT domains and trust relationships extensively.

Finally, Chapters 12 through 15 address sharing and securing file systems, browsing and accessing resources on the network, using Windows NT Server tools, and backing up and restoring data.

Part III maps directly to the Managing Resources section in the exam objectives for each of the three Windows NT 4.0 Microsoft Certified Professional exams. If you're preparing for the Enterprise exam, you'll want to read every chapter in this part. If you're preparing for the NT Workstation 4.0 or NT Server 4.0 exam, consult Appendices A and B to see which chapters are optional.

Workstation
Server
Enterprise

CHAPTER

7

# Managing User and Group Accounts

# About Chapter 7

This chapter could be called, "Everything You Always Wanted to Know About Users and Groups but Were Afraid Someone Would Explain to You in Great Detail."

It starts by taking you through the steps to create a user account, including important tips on naming conventions and passwords. Then it outlines how to configure specific Windows NT user account properties. Other common user account tasks are also explained, including how to copy user accounts, how to apply properties to multiple user accounts, and how to rename and delete user accounts.

The remainder of this chapter focuses on creating and managing groups. Local groups and global groups are discussed and compared extensively. You'll not only find out how to create these groups but also how and when to use them to efficiently organize users and to assign rights and permissions to multiple users. Built-in groups and special groups are also addressed.

This chapter includes one comprehensive hands-on lab. You'll practice creating user accounts, managing user account properties, creating group accounts, assigning user accounts to groups, and creating user account templates.

Chapter 7 is a "must read" no matter which of the three Windows NT 4.0 Microsoft Certified Professional exams you're preparing for. This chapter maps to the "Manage user and group accounts" objective in the Managing Resources section in these exams' objectives.

# CREATING AND MANAGING USER ACCOUNTS

*User accounts* are records that contain unique user information, such as user name, password, and any logon restrictions. User accounts enable users to log on to Windows NT computers or domains.

There are two types of user accounts: built-in accounts, and user accounts that you create. You can configure various user account properties, including group memberships, profile, logon script, logon hours, workstation logon restrictions, account expiration, and dialin permission.

The following sections cover these topics, as well as copying user accounts, applying properties to multiple accounts, and renaming and deleting user accounts.

## Built-in User Accounts

There are two built-in user accounts in Windows NT: *Administrator* and *Guest*. Built-in accounts are created automatically during the installation of Windows NT.

The Administrator account has all of the rights and permissions needed to fully administer a Windows NT computer or a Windows NT domain. The Administrator account can be used to perform numerous tasks, including creating and managing users and groups, managing file and folder permissions, and installing and managing printers and printer security. In addition, members of the Administrators local group have the right to take ownership of any file, folder, or printer. The Administrator account's rights and permissions are due solely to its membership in the Administrators local group.

The Administrator account, because of its powerful capabilities, can pose a security risk to your network if a nonauthorized user is able to guess the password for the account. For this reason, you should consider renaming the Administrator account. (Renaming user accounts is covered later in this chapter.)

The Guest account is designed to permit limited access to network resources to occasional users that don't have their own user account. For example, a client visiting your office might want to connect a laptop computer to the network to print a document. The client can log on using the Guest account. You can specify which network resources are available to this account by assigning the appropriate file, folder, and printer permissions to the Guest account.

The Guest account is disabled by default. If your network contains sensitive data I recommend, for security reasons, you leave the Guest account disabled. Instead of using the Guest account, establish a user account for every person who needs access to network resources.

## Creating a User Account

Every person who uses the network should have a user account. You can create user accounts by using User Manager (on a Windows NT Workstation computer) or User Manager for Domains (on a Windows NT Server computer).

**TO CREATE A USER ACCOUNT, FOLLOW THESE STEPS:**

**1.** Select Start ⇒ Programs ⇒ Administrative Tools (Common) ⇒ User Manager (or User Manager for Domains).

**2.** In the User Manager dialog box, select User⟹New User.

**3.** The New User dialog box, shown in Figure 7-1, appears. Fill in the user name, person's full name (optional), description (this could be a department, location, or job title—it is also optional), and password. Confirm the password by retyping it.

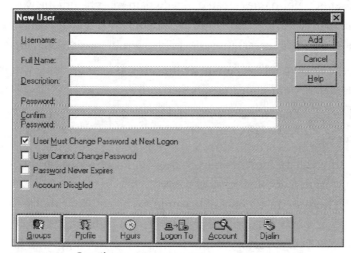

**FIGURE 7-1   Creating a user account**

**4.** Select the check box next to User Must Change Password at Next Logon if you want the user to choose and enter a new password the first time the user logs on. This option is selected by default.

Select the check box next to User Cannot Change Password if you—the network administrator—want to manage user passwords.

Select the check box next to Password Never Expires if you are configuring a user account for a Windows NT service to use when it logs in.

Select the check box next to Account Disabled if you are creating a user template.

**5.** Use the command buttons at the bottom of the New User dialog box to configure group memberships, profile and home folder location, logon hours, logon restrictions, and dialin permission for the new user account. (These options are each discussed in detail later in this chapter.)

**6.** Click the Add command button. Click the Close command button. The new user account is created.

## Naming conventions

When you create user accounts, keep in mind a few simple rules for user account names:

- User account names can be from one to twenty characters long.
- User account names created in a domain must be unique within the domain. User account names created on a non-domain controller (such as a stand-alone server) must be unique within the non-domain controller.
- User account names cannot be the same as a group name within the domain or non-domain controller.
- The following characters may *not* be used in user account names:
  < > ? * + , = | ; : [ ] \ / "

If you have more than a few people in your organization, it's a good idea to plan your user account naming convention.

There are several possible naming schemes you can use. Often, the overall length of a user account name is limited to eight characters (to be compatible with MS-DOS directory name limitations), although this is not mandatory. Common naming schemes include:

A. The first seven letters of the user's first name plus the first letter of the user's last name

B. The first letter of the user's first name plus the first seven letters of the user's last name

C. The user's initials plus the last four digits of the user's employee number

D. Various hybrid combinations of the above schemes

Table 7-1 shows how three user account names would appear using the naming conventions described in A, B, and C above.

**TABLE 7-1** USER ACCOUNT NAMING CONVENTIONS

| FULL NAME | SCHEME A | SCHEME B | SCHEME C |
|-----------|----------|----------|----------|
| Nancy Yates | NancyY | Nyates | NY5500 |
| Robert Jones | RobertJ | Rjones | RJ1234 |
| Jonathan Whitmore | JonathaW | Jwhitmor | JW2266 |

In addition to choosing a naming convention, you should have a way to handle exceptions. It's quite common, for example, for two users to have the same first name and last initial, such as Mike Smith and Mike Sutherland. If you choose to adopt the naming convention described in A above, you would need to have a way to resolve potential duplicate user names. You could resolve the problem by assigning Mike Smith the user account name of MikeS (assuming he was hired before Mike Sutherland), and assigning Mike Sutherland the user account name of MikeSu.

## Passwords

Just a few words about passwords. Everyone knows that using passwords protects the security of the network, because only authorized users can log on.

When user accounts are created, you should have a plan for managing passwords. Will passwords be assigned and maintained by the network administrator? Or will users choose their own passwords?

DILBERT reprinted by permission of United Feature Syndicate, Inc.

in the
real world

**I almost never recommend that the network administrator maintain user passwords, because it can take an enormous amount of administrator time to maintain passwords for users.**

**Normally the only time a network administrator should maintain user passwords is when the highest level of network security is required. The administrator can then assign passwords of the appropriate length and complexity.**

When users maintain their own passwords, it's a good idea to remind them of a few password security basics:

o Don't use your own name or the names of family members or pets as passwords. (This is a common security loophole on most networks.)

o Never disclose your password to anyone. Don't write your password on a sticky note and stick it to your monitor. Other not-so-hot places to store your password are on or under your keyboard, in your top desk drawer, in your Rolodex, or in your briefcase, wallet, or purse.

o Use a sufficiently long password. I recommend using eight or more characters in a password. The longer a password, the more difficult it is to guess. The maximum password length is fourteen characters.

o Use a mix of upper- and lowercase letters, numbers, and special characters. Remember, passwords are case-sensitive.

o If passwords are changed regularly, don't use the same password with an incremental number at the end, such as: Alan01, Alan02, Alan03, and so on. (Don't laugh. This may seem like common sense, but I know several network administrators who actually do this.)

## User Account Properties

User accounts have numerous options that can be configured. These options are called *user account properties.*

User account properties that you can configure include group memberships, profile, logon scripts, logon hours, workstation logon restrictions, account expiration, and dialin permission.

User account properties are configured in the User Properties dialog box in User Manager (on a Windows NT Workstation computer) or in User Manager for Domains (on a Windows NT Server computer).

Figure 7-2 shows the User Properties dialog box for Administrator in User Manager (or User Manager for Domains) on a Windows NT computer configured as a non-domain controller. *Non-domain controllers* include Windows NT Workstation computers and Windows NT Server computers configured as stand-alone or member servers. Notice the Groups, Profile, and Dialin command buttons along the bottom of the dialog box.

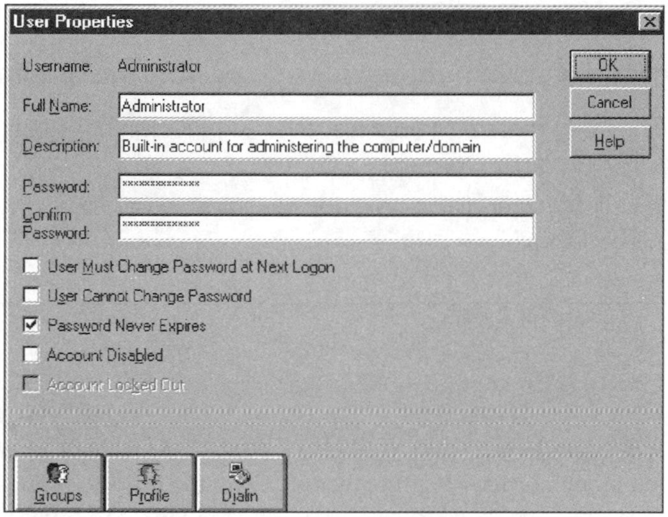

**FIGURE 7-2** Administrator's user properties on a non–domain controller

Figure 7-3 shows the User Properties dialog box for Administrator in User Manager for Domains on a Windows NT Server computer configured as a primary domain controller (PDC). Notice the Groups, Profile, Hours, Logon To, Account, and Dialin command buttons along the bottom of the dialog box. More account properties can be configured on a domain controller than on a non-domain controller.

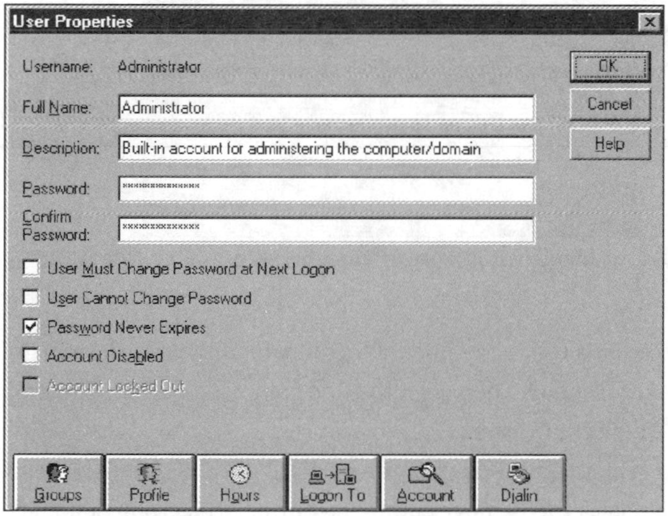

**FIGURE 7-3** Administrator's user properties on a domain controller

---

**TO ACCESS THE USER PROPERTIES DIALOG BOX, FOLLOW THESE STEPS:**

**1.** Select Start ⇒ Programs ⇒ Administrative Tools (Common) ⇒ User Manager
or User Manager for Domains.

**2.** In the User Manager dialog box, double-click any user name in the
Username list box.

---

## Groups

The Groups command button in the User Properties dialog box is used to configure which group(s) a user is a member of. Assigning users to groups is an efficient
way to manage permissions for multiple users. (The subject of groups is covered
in more detail later in this chapter.)

When you click the Groups command button in the User Properties dialog
box, the Group Memberships dialog box appears. Figure 7-4 shows the Group
Memberships dialog box for Administrator.

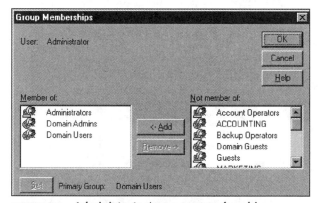

**FIGURE 7-4**   **Administrator's group memberships**

To make a user a member of a group, highlight the desired group in the "Not
member of" list box. Then click the Add command button. The group now appears
in the "Member of" list box.

To remove a user from a group, highlight the group in the "Member of" list
box. Then click the Remove command button. The group no longer appears in the
"Member of" list box.

You can make any number of group membership changes in this dialog box, but you must click OK when you are finished to make the changes effective.

On Windows NT Server domain controllers, there is an option in the Group Memberships dialog box to set a primary group for a user account. The primary group setting concerns file ownership and permissions, and only affects users of Macintosh computers who access files on a Windows NT Server computer and users of Windows NT computers who run POSIX-compliant applications. The default primary group setting is Domain Users. However, you can assign any global group as a user's primary group. In most Windows NT networks, you can simply accept the default setting for this option.

## Profile

The Profile command button in the User Properties dialog box is used to configure the user's environment. You can configure the user profile path, logon script name, and home directory location.

When you click the Profile command button in the User Properties dialog box, the User Environment Profile dialog box appears. Figure 7-5 shows the User Environment Profile dialog box for Administrator.

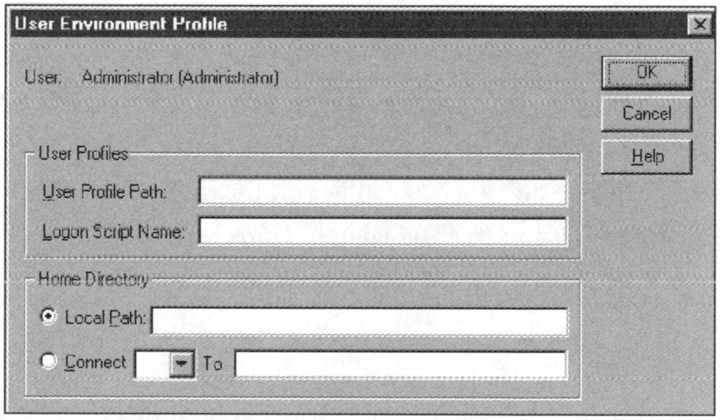

**FIGURE 7-5**    Administrator's environment profile

The user profile path is used to assign a location for the user's profile. A user's profile contains the user's unique desktop settings, such as screen color, screen saver, desktop icons, fonts, and so on. The default location for a user's profile is the `<winntroot>\Profiles\%USERNAME%` folder. User profile paths must include the complete path to the folder that contains the user's profile, in the format of \\*Server_name*\*Share_name*\*Folder*\*Subfolder*. If no path is entered in the User Profile Path text box, Windows NT uses the default location.

 concept link     **Profiles and logon scripts are covered in more detail in Chapter 9.**

The Logon Script Name text box is an optional configuration that enables you to enter the user's logon script filename, if the user has one. *Logon scripts* are batch files that run on a user's computer during the logon process. Many Windows NT installations don't use logon scripts. If you choose to use logon scripts, enter the user's logon script filename in the Logon Script Name text box. You should place a copy of each user's logon script file in the `Netlogon` share on every domain controller in the domain, or use directory replication to replicate the logon script file. Directory replication is covered in detail in Chapter 4.

The Home Directory section of the User Environment Profile dialog box is used to configure either a local home directory on the user's computer, or a server-based home directory.

A *home directory* (either local or server-based) is a user's default directory for the Save As and File Open dialog boxes in most Windows-based applications. Using server-based home directories enables the network administrator to easily backup user-created data files, because the user-created files are stored by default on the server instead of on individual computers. For security reasons, I recommend you place sever-based home directories on an NTFS partition.

If you select the radio button next to Local Path, you can enter the user's home directory in the format of *Drive_Letter:*\*Folder*\*Subfolder*. This assigns a user's home directory to a folder on the user's local computer.

If you want to use a server-based home directory, select the radio button next to Connect. Then select a drive letter to use for the user's home directory. The default drive letter is Z:. Next type a complete path in the form of \\*Server_ name*\*Share_name*\*Folder*\*Subfolder* in the To text box. If the last folder in the path you type in this box does not yet exist, Windows NT will create it.

The most common way of assigning a server-based home directory is to first create a shared folder named `Users` on the server, and then to assign the path \\*Server_name*\Users\%USERNAME% as each user's home directory location. When the %USERNAME% variable is used in a path, Windows NT creates a home directory/folder (that is named using the user's account name) in the `Users` shared folder. Using this variable can simplify administration when creating a large number of user accounts because you can enter the same path for each new user, and Windows NT creates a unique home directory/folder for each user account.

## *Hours*

The Hours command button in the User Properties dialog box is used to configure the hours that a user is allowed to log on. This command button is only available when managing Windows NT Server computers that are configured as domain controllers.

The logon hours configuration only affects the user's ability to access the domain controller—it does not affect a user's ability to log on to a Windows NT Workstation computer or other non-domain controller.

When you click the Hours command button in the User Properties dialog box, the Logon Hours dialog box appears. Figure 7-6 shows the Logon Hours dialog box for Administrator. Notice that by default all hours are available for logon. This is the default for all users, not just Administrator.

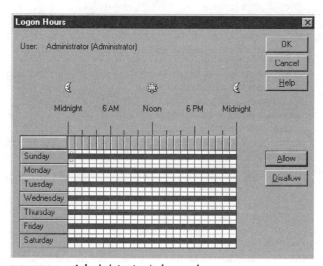

**FIGURE 7-6**    Administrator's logon hours

To modify the user's logon hours, use your mouse to highlight the hours you do *not* want the user to be able to log on, and click the Disallow command button. Or, you can use your mouse to highlight the entire graph, click the Disallow command button, then highlight the hours you *want* the user to be able to log on, and then click the Allow command button.

Figure 7-7 shows modified logon hours for a user named BillT. Notice that BillT can't log on between the hours of midnight and 3:00 a.m. The administrator of BillT's network normally runs a tape backup during these hours, and does not want users to log on and open files (which may not be backed up) during the backup process.

Restricting a user's logon hours does not disconnect a user from a domain controller when the user's logon hours expire. A logon hours restriction only *prevents* a user from logging on to the domain controller during certain specified hours. If you want to forcibly disconnect users when their logon hours expire, additional steps must be taken.

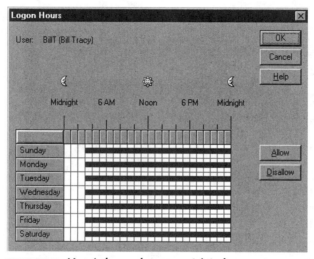

**FIGURE 7-7** User's logon hours restricted

**TO FORCIBLY DISCONNECT ALL USERS FROM THE DOMAIN CONTROLLER(S) WHEN THEIR LOGON HOURS EXPIRE, FOLLOW THESE STEPS:**

**1.** Select Start ⇒ Programs ⇒ Administrative Tools (Common) ⇒ User Manager for Domains.

**2.** Select Policies ⇒ Account in the User Manager dialog box.

**3.** The Account Policy dialog box appears. Select the check box next to "Forcibly disconnect remote users from server when logon hours expire." Click OK.

Figure 7-8 shows the Account Policy dialog box. Notice that the check box next to "Forcibly disconnect remote users from server when logon hours expire" is selected. All settings in the Account Policy dialog box apply to all user accounts in the domain—no individual configurations are possible.

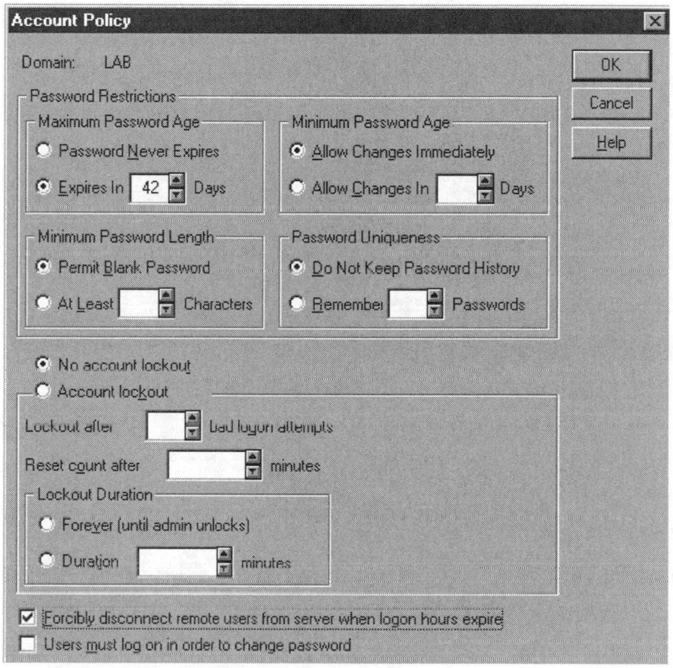

**FIGURE 7-8**   **Disconnecting users from the domain controller when logon hours expire**

## *Logon To*

The Logon To command button in the User Properties dialog box is used to configure the names of computers from which a user can log on to the domain. This command button is only available on Windows NT Server computers that are configured as domain controllers.

When you click the Logon To command button in the User Properties dialog box, the Logon Workstations dialog box appears. Figure 7-9 shows the Logon Workstations dialog box for Administrator. Notice that by default a user may log on to any workstation (computer) on the network. This is the default setting for all users, not just Administrator.

If you want to limit the workstations to which a user can log on, select the radio button next to User May Log On To These Workstations, and then enter the computer name for up to eight workstations. The user will only be able to log on to the domain from the computers entered in this dialog box. Click OK.

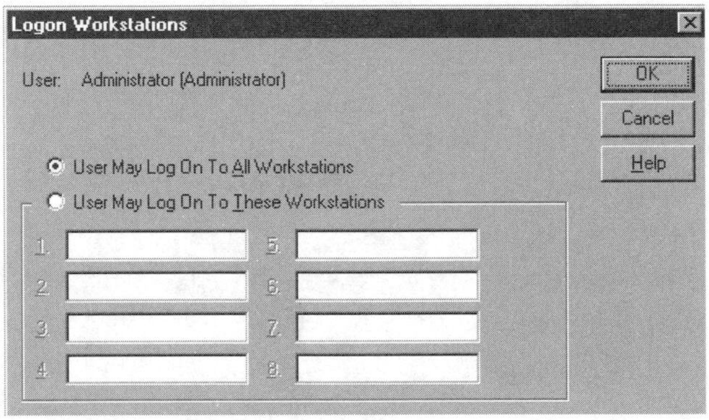

**FIGURE 7-9**   **Configuring logon workstations**

## *Account*

The Account command button in the User Properties dialog box is used to configure account expiration and user account type. This command button is only available on Windows NT Server computers that are configured as domain controllers.

When you click the Account command button in the User Properties dialog box, the Account Information dialog box appears. Figure 7-10 shows the Account Information dialog box for Administrator. Notice that by default a user account never expires. This is the default setting for all users, not just Administrator.

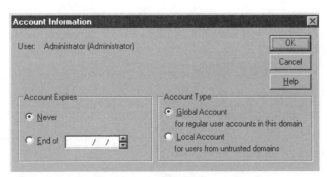

**FIGURE 7-10**   **Configuring account information**

You might want to configure a user account expiration date for an employee working on a temporary or short-term basis. To set an account expiration, select the radio button next to "End of," and then enter the date you want the user's account to expire. Click OK. The user will not be forcibly disconnected from the domain controller when the account expires, but will not be able to log on after the account expiration date. You can't set an account expiration date on the two built-in user accounts, Administrator and Guest.

There are two options for account type: *global account* and *local account*. By default, all user accounts are configured as global accounts. A global account is designed for regular user accounts in this domain. Users can log on to the domain using a global account. Most Windows NT installations only use global accounts.

A local account is designed to enable users from untrusted domains to access resources on the domain controller(s) in this domain. Users can't log on using a local account. (Trust relationships are covered in detail in Chapter 10.)

## Dialin

The Dialin command button in the User Properties dialog box is used to configure dialin permission for a user account. The dialin permission allows a user to log on by using a Dial-Up Networking connection.

When you click the Dialin command button in the User Properties dialog box, the Dialin Information dialog box, which is shown in Figure 7-11, appears. Notice that by default a user account is not granted the dialin permission.

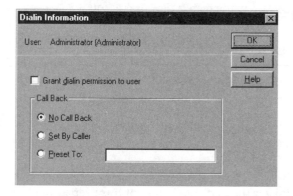

**FIGURE 7-11** Granting dialin permission to a user account

The dialin permission should be granted to every user that needs access to the network by using a Dial-Up Networking connection. For example, traveling sales representatives need to access e-mail and other network resources from their laptop computers, and employees who occasionally work from home may need to be able to dial in to access network resources from their home computers.

To grant a user the dialin permission, select the check box next to Grant dialin permission to user.

There are three options in the Call Back section: No Call Back, Set By Caller, and Preset To. The default setting is No Call Back.

If you select No Call Back, the user can dial in to the server, but the user can't request that the server break the connection and call the user back. Selecting No Call Back ensures that the user dialing in — not the server — is billed for any long distance telephone charges.

If you select Set By Caller, the server prompts the user for a telephone number. The server breaks the connection and calls the user back using this number, and thus the server incurs the bulk of any long distance telephone charges.

If you select Preset To, you must enter a telephone number that the server will always use to call back this user when the user dials in. This setting reduces the risk of unauthorized access to network resources, because the server always calls a preset telephone number, such as a user's home telephone number. An unauthorized user might be able to dial in and guess a password, but will not be able to direct the server to call back at any other number than the number specified in Preset To, and thus will not be able to connect to the network.

## Copying User Accounts

Sometimes the easiest way to create a new user account is to copy an existing user account.

There are basically two ways to accomplish this:

- You can copy any existing user account that has properties that are similar to the desired properties for the new user account, or
- you can create a new user account that will be used as a template to create multiple user accounts with the same set of account properties.

For example, suppose that you want to create a user account to be used by an employee to administer the network. You want this user account to have all of the capabilities of the Administrator account, so you decide to copy the Administrator account. When a user account is copied, all properties of the user account are copied to the new user account, with the exception of user name, full name, password, the account disabled option, and user rights and permissions.

To copy the Administrator user account, highlight Administrator in the Username list box in the User Manager dialog box. Select User ⇒ Copy, and then type in a new user name and password for the new user account. Make any other desired changes in the User Properties dialog box, then click the Add command button. Then click Close. The newly created user has the same account properties as Administrator.

Suppose, instead, that you are setting up a new network and need to create multiple new user accounts for the accountants at a large CPA firm. All of the accountants at this firm have similar network access needs, and their user accounts will have substantially similar properties. You can create a new user account, named Acct_Template, to use as a template to create these new user accounts.

To create a new user account that will be used as a template, select User ⇒ New User in the User Manager dialog box. Assign the user account a name that indicates the type of user account this template will be used to create, such as Acct_Template for the accountants in the previous example. Configure the template user account's group memberships, profile, logon hours, and so on to match the requirements of the user accounts you will create using this template. When you create a user account to be used as a template, I recommend that you select the Account Disabled check box so that no one can log on using this account.

Figure 7-12 shows the User Properties dialog box of a user account that is designed to be used as a template. Note that the Account Disabled check box is selected.

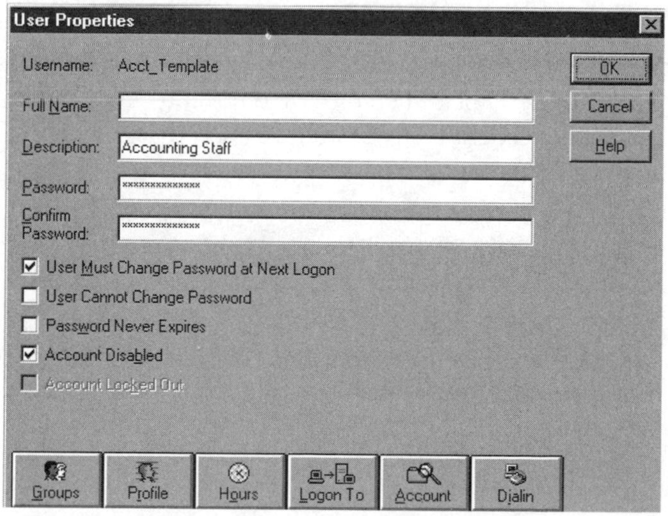

FIGURE 7-12    Configuring a user account to be used as a template

To use a template, highlight the template user account in the User Manager dialog box, then select User ⇒ Copy. Then type in a new user name and password for the new user account. Make any other desired changes in the User Properties dialog box, then click the Add command button. Then click Close.

All properties of the template user account are copied to the new user account, with the exception of user name, full name, password, the account disabled option, and user rights and permissions.

## Applying Properties to Multiple Accounts

Occasionally you might want to apply a property to multiple user accounts.

For example, suppose that you recently installed the *Remote Access Service* (RAS) on one of your network servers, and now you want to grant several users the dialin permission so they can connect to the network from their computers at home.

Another situation where you might want to apply properties to multiple user accounts is right after you create several new user accounts. You can create several bare-bones user accounts, consisting only of user names, full names, and passwords. Then you can select all of the new user accounts, and configure them all at once with identical properties. You can use this method as an alternative to using a user account as a template.

---

**TO APPLY A PROPERTY (OR PROPERTIES) TO MULTIPLE USER ACCOUNTS, FOLLOW THESE STEPS:**

**1.** Highlight the first user account you want to apply a property to in the User Manager dialog box. Then press and hold Ctrl while you click each additional user account that you want to apply that property to. Then select User ⇒ Properties.

**2.** The User Properties dialog box appears. The users you selected in Step 1 are listed in the Users list box. Figure 7-13 shows the User Properties dialog box. Notice that multiple users are displayed in the Users list box.

**3.** Configure the user account property (or properties) as desired. All changes made will apply to all of the users in the Users list box. Then click OK.

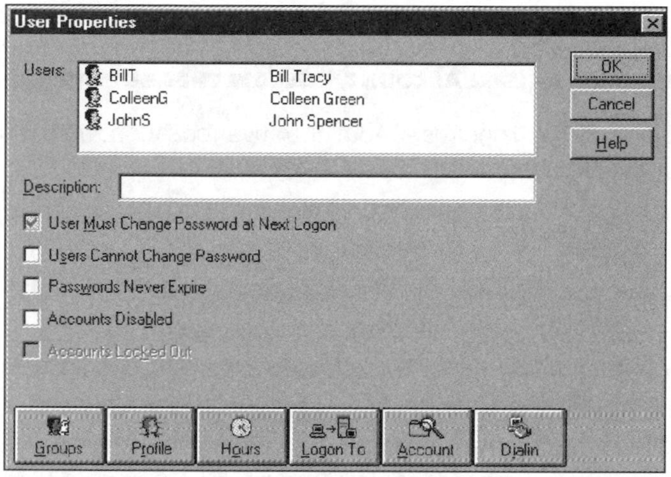

**FIGURE 7-13**   Selecting multiple user accounts

## Renaming and Deleting User Accounts

Occasionally you may want to rename or delete a user account.

Renaming a user account retains all of the account properties, including group memberships, permissions, and rights for the new user of the account. You might want to rename a user account when a new staff member replaces an employee who has left the company.

Deleting a user account is just what it sounds like—the user account is permanently removed, and all of its group memberships, permissions, and rights are lost. Normally you only delete a user account when you never plan to use the account again.

The two built-in accounts, Administrator and Guest, can't be deleted, although they can be renamed. The following section details how to rename and delete a user accout.

**TO RENAME A USER ACCOUNT, FOLLOW THESE STEPS:**

**1.** Select Start ⇒ Programs ⇒ Administrative Tools (Common) ⇒ User Manager (or User Manager for Domains).

**2.** In the User Manager dialog box, highlight the user account that you want to rename. Select User ⇒ Rename.

**3.** Type in the new user name for the user account in the Rename dialog box. Click OK.

**4.** Double-click the renamed user account in the User Manager dialog box.

**5.** The User Properties dialog box appears. Assign (and confirm) a new password to the renamed user account. Select the check box next to User Must Change Password at Next Logon. Click OK.

**6.** Exit User Manager (or User Manager for Domains).

**7.** If the renamed user account has an associated home directory, also rename the home directory using Windows NT Explorer.

**TO DELETE A USER ACCOUNT, FOLLOW THESE STEPS:**

**1.** Select Start ⇒ Programs ⇒ Administrative Tools (Common) ⇒ User Manager (or User Manager for Domains).

**2.** In the User Manager dialog box, highlight the user account you want to delete. Press Delete.

**3.** A warning message appears. Click OK to continue.

**4.** Another warning dialog box appears. Click Yes to delete the user account. The user account is deleted.

**5.** Exit User Manager (or User Manager for Domains).

# CREATING AND MANAGING GROUPS

The remainder of this chapter is dedicated to groups. Using groups is a convenient and efficient way to assign rights and permissions to multiple users.

*Groups* are collections of user accounts. There are four types of groups in Windows NT: *local groups*, *global groups*, *built-in groups*, and *special groups*.

# Local Groups

*Local groups* are primarily used to control access to resources. In a typical Windows NT configuration, a local group is assigned permissions to a specific resource, such as a shared folder or a shared printer. Individual user accounts and global groups (discussed later in this chapter) are made members of this local group. The result is that all members of the local group now have permissions to the resource. Using local groups simplifies the administration of resources, because permissions can be assigned once, to a local group, instead of separately to each user account.

In Windows NT, all domain controllers (within a single domain) maintain identical copies of the same directory database, while each non-domain controller maintains its own separate directory database. All user accounts and group accounts are stored in the directory database in which they are created. For example, if you create a local group in the LAB domain, it is stored in the LAB domain directory database. If you create a local group on a Windows NT Workstation computer, it is stored in the NT Workstation computer's local directory database.

Local groups can be created on any Windows NT computer. A local group in the directory database on a domain controller can be assigned permissions to resources on any domain controller in the domain. However, a local group in the directory database on a domain controller cannot be assigned permissions to resources on any non-domain controller. (Remember that non-domain controllers include stand-alone servers, member servers, and all Windows NT Workstation computers.) A local group in the directory database on a non-domain controller can be assigned permissions to resources only on that computer.

A local group can contain various user accounts and global groups, depending on whether the local group is located in the directory database on a domain controller, on a non-domain controller that is a member of a domain, or on a non-domain controller that is not a member of a domain.

A local group in the directory database on a domain controller can contain individual user accounts and global groups from the domain directory database, and can also contain user accounts and global groups from the directory database of any trusted domain. A *trusted domain* is a domain whose users can access resources in the domain that "trusts" it. Trust relationships are covered in more detail in Chapter 10.

A local group in the directory database on a non-domain controller that is a member of a domain (such as a member server or a Windows NT Workstation computer that is a member of the domain) can contain individual user accounts from the local directory database, user accounts and global groups from the directory database of the member domain, and user accounts and global groups from the directory database of any trusted domain.

A local group in the directory database on a non-domain controller that is *not* a member of a domain (such as a stand-alone server or a Windows NT Workstation computer that is a member of a workgroup) can only contain individual user accounts from the local directory database.

Local groups can't contain other local groups.

The next section explains how local groups are created.

**TO CREATE A NEW LOCAL GROUP, FOLLOW THESE STEPS:**

**1.** Select Start ⇒ Programs ⇒ Administrative Tools (Common) ⇒ User Manager (or User Manager for Domains).

**2.** Highlight any of the groups listed in the Groups list box. (The reason for this is the first user in the Username list box is highlighted by default, and if this user is not unhighlighted, the user will automatically become a member of the new local group you create.) Select User ⇒ New Local Group.

**3.** The New Local Group dialog box appears. In the Group Name text box, type in a name for the new local group. In the Description text box, type a description if you want—such as the name of the resource the group will have permissions to. This text box is optional. Click the Add command button.

**4.** The Add Users and Groups dialog box appears. Highlight the user accounts and/or global groups from the Names list box that you want to make members of the new local group. Then click the Add command button. The names you selected appear in the Add Names list box. Click OK.

**5.** The New Local Group dialog box reappears. Figure 7-14 shows the New Local Group dialog box. Notice that several user accounts and one global group are listed as members of the new local group. Also note that the description reflects the resource to which the new local group has permissions. Click OK.

**6.** The User Manager dialog box reappears. The new local group appears in the Groups list box. Exit User Manager (or User Manager for Domains).

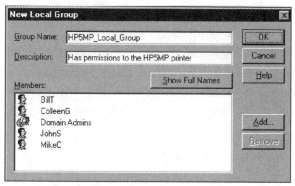

**FIGURE 7-14**    **Creating a new local group**

# Global Groups

*Global groups* are primarily used to organize users that perform similar tasks or have similar network access requirements. In a typical Windows NT configuration, user accounts are placed in a global group, the global group is made a member of one or more local groups, and each local group is assigned permissions to a resource. The advantage of using global groups is ease of administration — the network administrator can manage large numbers of users by placing them in global groups.

Suppose when the network was first installed, the administrator created user accounts, and placed these user accounts in various global groups depending on the users' job functions. Now, the network administrator wants to assign several users permissions to a shared printer on a member server. The administrator creates a new local group on the member server and assigns the new local group permissions to the shared printer. Then the administrator selects, from the domain directory database, the global groups that contain the user accounts that need access to the shared printer. The administrator makes these global groups members of the new local group on the member server. The result is that all domain user accounts that are members of the selected global groups now have access to the shared printer.

A global group can only be created on a domain controller, and can only contain individual user accounts from the domain directory database that contains the global group. Global groups can't contain local groups, other global groups, or user accounts from other domains.

Although it is not a preferred practice, you can assign rights and permissions to global groups. Global groups can be assigned permissions to shared files and folders on domain controllers, member servers, NT Workstation computers that are members of the domain, and computers from trusted domains.

## Creating a new global group

The following section explains how to create a new global group.

**TO CREATE A NEW GLOBAL GROUP, FOLLOW THESE STEPS:**

**1.** Select Start⇒Programs⇒Administrative Tools (Common)⇒User Manager for Domains.

**2.** Highlight any of the groups listed in the Groups list box. (The reason for this is that the first user in the Username list box is highlighted by default, and if this user is not unhighlighted, the user will automatically become a member of the new global group you create.) Select User⇒New Global Group.

**3.** The New Global Group dialog box appears. In the Group Name text box, type in a name for the new global group. In the Description text box, type a description of the group. This text box is optional. Highlight the user accounts from the Not Members list box that you want to make members of the new global group. Then click the Add command button. The names you selected appear in the Members list box. Figure 7-15 shows the New Global Group dialog box. Notice that two user accounts are listed as members of the new global group. Click OK.

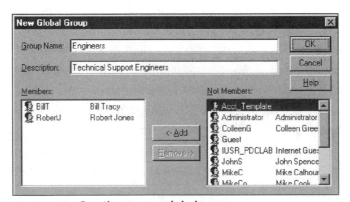

**FIGURE 7-15**  Creating a new global group

**4.** The User Manager dialog box reappears. The new global group appears in the Groups list box. Exit User Manager for Domains.

## Comparison of Local and Global Groups

Local and global groups are complex topics that can be confusing.

exam
preparation
pointer

**Local and global groups are integral parts of many objectives on the three Windows NT 4.0 Microsoft Certified Professional exams. You must know the characteristics and uses of local and global groups—and know them cold—in order to pass the exams—especially the Enterprise exam.**

To help simplify the important information about each type of group, I've prepared a comparison table for you. Table 7-2 summarizes the basic characteristics of local and global groups. Remember that the table is only a summary—you should refer to the detailed descriptions of local and global groups in the previous sections for complete coverage of these topics.

**TABLE 7-2** COMPARISON OF LOCAL AND GLOBAL GROUPS

| CHARACTERISTIC | LOCAL GROUPS | GLOBAL GROUPS |
| --- | --- | --- |
| Primary purpose/use | Used to control access to network resources. | Used to organize users that perform similar tasks or have similar network access requirements. |
| Where created | On any Windows NT computer. | Only on a domain controller. |
| Can contain | User accounts and global groups. (The specific user accounts and global groups that can be contained in a local group depend on the type of computer on which the directory services database that contains the local group in question is located.) | User accounts from the domain directory database that contains the global group. |

*continued*

**TABLE 7-2** *(continued)*

| CHARACTERISTIC | LOCAL GROUPS | GLOBAL GROUPS |
|---|---|---|
| Can't contain | Other local groups. | Local groups, other global groups, or user accounts from other domains. |
| Can be assigned permissions to | Resources on any domain controller in the domain, if the local group is created on a domain controller; otherwise, only resources on the local computer. | Not a preferred practice, but can be assigned permissions to a resource on any computer in the domain, or on any computer in any trusted domain. |

## Built-in Groups

*Built-in groups* are groups with preset characteristics that are automatically created during the installation of Windows NT. The actual built-in groups created during installation depend on whether the computer is configured as a domain controller or a non-domain controller.

The members of built-in local groups have the rights and/or permissions to perform certain administrative tasks. You can assign users to the built-in local groups that most closely match the tasks that the users need to perform. If there isn't a built-in local group that has the rights and/or permissions needed to perform a specific task or access a specific resource, then you can create a local group and assign it the necessary rights and/or permissions to accomplish the task or access the resource.

You can use built-in global groups to organize the user accounts in your domain. As you recall from the previous section, you can also create additional global groups to further organize your domain's user accounts by task or network access requirements.

You can assign permissions to and remove permissions from built-in groups. (An exception is the built-in Administrators group—this group always has full rights and permissions to administer the computer or domain.) You can also assign users to and remove users from built-in groups. Built-in groups can't be renamed or deleted.

The following tables list the various built-in groups on Windows NT domain controllers and non-domain controllers, and give a brief description of each group's purpose or function. The table of built-in groups on domain controllers indicates whether each built-in group is a local or global group. The table of built-in groups on non-domain controllers contains only local groups.

Table 7-3 lists the built-in groups on domain controllers, and Table 7-4 lists the built-in groups on non-domain controllers.

**TABLE 7-3** BUILT-IN GROUPS ON DOMAIN CONTROLLERS

| BUILT-IN GROUP NAME | TYPE OF GROUP | DESCRIPTION |
| --- | --- | --- |
| Administrators | Local | Has full administrative rights and permissions to administer the domain; initially contains the Domain Admins global group. |
| Backup Operators | Local | Has permissions to back up and restore files and folders on all domain controllers in the domain. |
| Guests | Local | Has no initial permissions; initially contains the Domain Guests global group. |
| Replicator | Local | Used by the Windows NT Directory Replicator service. |
| Users | Local | Has no initial permissions; initially contains the Domain Users global group. |
| Account Operators | Local | Can create, delete, and modify user accounts, local groups, and global groups, with the exception of Administrators and Server Operators groups. |
| Printer Operators | Local | Can create and manage printers on any domain controller in the domain. |
| Server Operators | Local | Has permissions to back up and restore files and folders on all domain controllers in the domain; can share folders on any domain controller in the domain. |
| Domain Admins | Global | No initial permissions; initially contains the built-in Administrator user account. |
| Domain Users | Global | No initial permissions; initially contains the built-in Administrator user account; when new user accounts are created, they are automatically made members of this group. |
| Domain Guests | Global | No initial permissions; initially contains the built-in Guest user account. |

| **TABLE 7-4** BUILT-IN LOCAL GROUPS ON NON-DOMAIN CONTROLLERS | |
| --- | --- |
| *BUILT-IN LOCAL GROUP NAME* | *DESCRIPTION* |
| Administrators | Has full administrative rights and permissions to administer the computer; initially contains the built-in Administrator user account. |
| Backup Operators | Has permissions to back up and restore files and folders on the computer. |
| Guests | Has no initial permissions; initially contains the built-in Guest user account. |
| Replicator | Used by the Windows NT Directory Replicator service. |
| Users | Has no initial permissions; when new user accounts are created, they are automatically made members of this group. |
| Power Users | Can create and modify user and group accounts, with the exception of the Administrator user account and the Administrators group; can share folders and printers. |

# Special Groups

*Special groups* are created by Windows NT and are used for specific purposes by the operating system.

These groups don't appear in User Manager or User Manager for Domains. Special groups are only visible in Windows NT utilities that assign permissions to network resources, such as a printer's Properties dialog box, and Windows NT Explorer.

You can assign permissions to and remove permissions from special groups. You can't assign users to special groups, and you can't rename or delete these groups. Special groups are sometimes called system groups.

There are five special groups: *Everyone, Interactive, Network, System,* and *Creator Owner*.

Any user who accesses a Windows NT computer, either interactively or over-the-network, is considered a member of the Everyone special group. This includes all users accessing the computer using authorized user accounts, as well as unauthorized users who accidentally or intentionally breach your system security. If your computer is connected to the Internet, over-the-network also means over-the-Internet. Everyone means *everyone*. You should consider limiting the permissions assigned to the Everyone group to those that you really want everyone to have.

Any user who physically sits at a computer and logs on locally to a Windows NT computer is a member of the Interactive special group. If you want to assign permissions to a resource that is limited to users who have physical access to a computer, consider assigning these permissions to the Interactive group. You are only a member of the Interactive group during the time that you are logged on locally.

Any user who accesses resources on a Windows NT computer over-the-network is a member of the Network special group. If you want to assign permissions to a resource that is limited to users who access the computer over-the-network, consider assigning these permissions to the Network group. You are only a member of the Network group during the time that you access resources on a computer over-the-network.

The System special group is used by the Windows NT operating system. The System special group is not normally assigned any permissions to network resources.

A user who creates a file, folder, or a print job is considered a member of the Creator Owner special group for that object. The Creator Owner special group is used to assign permissions to creators of these objects. For example, by default the Creator Owner special group is assigned the Manage Documents permission to a printer when it is first created, so that creators of print jobs sent to this printer are able to manage their own print jobs.

## Renaming and Deleting Groups

I apologize if you envisioned a time-saving solution when you read the above heading, but unfortunately, the fact of the matter is, you can't rename groups. You can delete user-created groups, but you can't delete built-in or special groups. Deleting a group does not delete the user accounts that the group contains.

**TO DELETE A GROUP, FOLLOW THESE STEPS:**

**1.** Select Start ⇒ Programs ⇒ Administrative Tools (Common) ⇒ User Manager (or User Manager for Domains).

**2.** In the User Manager dialog box, highlight the group you want to delete. Press Delete.

**3.** A warning message appears. Click OK to continue.

**4.** Another warning message is displayed. Click the Yes command button to delete the group.

**5.** The group is deleted. Exit User Manager (or User Manager for Domains).

# KEY POINT SUMMARY

This chapter explored and outlined the properties, creation, and management of user accounts and groups.

- *User accounts* are records that contain unique user information, and enable users to log on to Windows NT. There are two kinds of user accounts: built-in user accounts, and the user accounts that you create. The two built-in user accounts are Administrator and Guest. You can create user accounts by using User Manager (on a Windows NT Workstation computer) or User Manager for Domains (on a Windows NT Server computer). User account names can be up to twenty characters in length, must be unique within the domain, can't be the same as a group name within the domain (or non-domain controller), and may not contain certain special characters. Often a naming convention for user accounts is adopted, along with a way to handle exceptions that would result in two user names being identical. Using passwords protects the security of the network. Normally, users choose their own passwords, although in some high security situations the network administrator may maintain user passwords. Common sense security measures should be taken by users to protect their passwords.

- User accounts have numerous options, called *user account properties,* that can be configured, including: group membership, profile, logon scripts, logon hours, workstation logon restrictions, account expiration, and dialin permission. These properties are configured in the User Properties dialog box in User Manager or User Manager for Domains.

  - The *Groups* command button in the User Properties dialog box is used to configure which group(s) a user is a member of.

- The *Profile* command button in the User Properties dialog box is used to configure the user's environment, including user profile path, logon script name, and home directory location. The variable %USERNAME% is often used when assigning a server-based home directory to many users, because using the variable enables you to enter the same path for multiple users, and yet results in each user having a unique home directory based on their unique user account name.

- The *Hours* command button in the User Properties dialog box is used to configure the hours that a user can log on.

- The *Logon To* command button in the User Properties dialog box is used to configure the names of computers from which a user can log on to the domain.

- The *Account* command button in the User Properties dialog box is used to configure account expiration and user account type. You might want to configure a user account expiration date for a temporary employee. You can't set an account expiration date on the two built-in accounts, Administrator and Guest.

- The *Dialin* command button in the User Properties dialog box is used to configure the dialin permission for a user account. This permission enables a user to log on using a Dial-Up Networking connection. There are three options in the Call Back section: No Call Back (the default setting), Set By Caller, and Preset To.

- The Hours, Logon To, and Account command buttons are only available on Windows NT Server computers that are configured as domain controllers.

- User accounts can be copied using User Manager or User Manager for Domains. You can copy an existing user account that has properties similar to the properties you want the new user account to have, or you can create a new user account that will be used as a template to create multiple user accounts with the same set of account properties.

- You can also use User Manager or User Manager for Domains to apply a property (or properties) to multiple user accounts at the same time. User accounts can also be renamed and deleted, with the exception of the two built-in accounts, Administrator and Guest.

- Using groups is a convenient and efficient way to assign rights and permissions to multiple users.

o *Local groups* are primarily used to control access to resources. Typically, a local group is assigned permission to a specific resource (such as a shared folder or shared printer), and then user accounts and global groups are made members of the local group. As a result, all members of the local group have permission to the resource. Local groups can contain individual user accounts and global groups. (The specific user accounts and global groups that can be contained in a local group depend on the type of computer that the directory services database is located on that contains the local group in question.) Local groups can't contain other local groups. Local groups can be assigned permissions to resources on any domain controller in the domain (if the local group is created on a domain controller); otherwise, local groups can be assigned permissions only to resources on the local computer. Local groups can be created on any Windows NT computer.

o *Global groups* are primarily used to organize users who perform similar tasks or have similar network access requirements. Global groups can contain user accounts from the domain directory database that contains the global group; but global groups can't contain local groups, other global groups, or user accounts from other domains. A global group can only be created on a domain controller.

o There are a number of built-in local and global groups that are automatically created during the installation of Windows NT. Built-in local groups can be used to assign users rights and/or permissions to perform certain administrative tasks. Built-in global groups are used to organize the user accounts in a domain. The actual built-in groups present on a Windows NT computer depend on whether the computer is configured as a domain controller or a non-domain controller. The built-in local groups on domain controllers are: Administrators, Backup Operators, Guests, Replicator, Users, Account Operators, Printer Operators, and Server Operators. The built-in global groups on domain controllers are: Domain Admins, Domain Users, and Domain Guests. The built-in groups on non-domain controllers are: Administrators, Backup Operators, Guests, Replicator, Users, and Power Users. All the built-in groups on non-domain controllers are local groups.

o There are five *special groups* (sometimes called *system groups*) created by Windows NT: Everyone, Interactive, Network, System, and Creator Owner.

You can assign permissions to and remove permissions from special groups, but you can't assign users to special groups.

o You can't rename groups. You can delete user-created groups by using User Manager or User Manager for Domains, but you can't delete built-in or special groups.

# APPLYING WHAT YOU'VE LEARNED

Now it's time to regroup, review, and apply what you've learned in this chapter.

The questions in the following Instant Assessment section bring to mind key facts and concepts.

The hands-on lab exercise will really reinforce what you've learned, and give you an opportunity to practice some of the tasks tested by the Microsoft Certified Professional exams.

## Instant Assessment

1. What are the two built-in user accounts?

2. What Windows NT tool can you use to create user accounts?

3. Name two common user account naming conventions.

4. Which groups can be deleted? Which groups can't be deleted?

5. What are the six command buttons in the User Properties dialog box in User Manager for Domains that can be used to configure various user account properties?

6. What variable is often used when assigning a server-based home directory to many users?

7. Suppose that you wanted to create several new user accounts that all had identical properties. What could you do to accomplish this in an efficient manner?

8. What is the primary purpose of local groups? What is the primary purpose of global groups?

9. Where can local groups be created? Where can global groups be created?

10. Suppose that you want to use groups to assign permissions to a shared folder on your network. How could you accomplish this?

11. List the eight built-in local groups on domain controllers and the three built-in global groups on domain controllers.

12. List the six built-in local groups on non-domain controllers.

13. What are the five special groups in Windows NT?

14. Why is it important to limit the permissions assigned to the Everyone group, especially if your computer is connected to the Internet?

15. Which groups can be renamed?

**T/F**

16. You should pick a name that is familiar to you, such as your own name, or the name of a family member or pet, to use as your password.    ____

 concept link    **For answers to the Instant Assessment questions see Appendix D.**

# Hands-on Lab Exercise

The following hands-on lab exercise provides you with a practical opportunity to apply the knowledge you've gained in this chapter about managing user and group accounts.

### Lab 7.10 *Creating and managing user and group accounts*

Workstation
Server
Enterprise

The purpose of this lab is to give you hands-on experience creating user accounts, assigning home directories, managing user account properties, creating group accounts, and assigning user accounts to groups. You will also create user account templates to help simplify the creation of user accounts.

This lab consists of four parts:

> Part 1: Creating the Users folder
> Part 2: Creating group accounts
> Part 3: Creating user account templates
> Part 4: Creating and managing user accounts

In this lab you'll create users and groups for the local office of a sales organization. Within this organization there are several employees. Table 7-5 shows the organization's employees and their job titles.

**TABLE 7-5** SALES ORGANIZATION EMPLOYEES

| EMPLOYEE | JOB TITLE |
|---|---|
| Pam Rhodes | District Manager |
| John Spencer | Sales Manager |
| Robert Jones | Accounting Manager |
| Colleen Green | Sales Representative |
| Bill Tracy | Sales Representative |
| Mike Calhoun | Sales Representative |
| Nancy Yates | Accounting Staff |
| Mike Cook | Accounting Staff |

The users will select their own passwords when they first access their user accounts. Each user will have a home folder on the primary domain controller named PDCLAB.

Begin this lab by booting your computer to Windows NT Server. Log on as Administrator. (Remember, the password is *password*.)

Follow the steps below carefully.

## Part 1: Creating the Users folder

In this section you create and share a Users folder in Windows NT Explorer. The Users folder will eventually contain a home directory for each user account.

1. Select Start ⇒ Programs ⇒ Windows NT Explorer.

2. In the All Folders list box, highlight the drive on which your NTFS partition is located. (This is probably drive D:.) Select File ⇒ New ⇒ Folder.

3. A folder named New Folder is created and appears in the "Contents of D:." Edit the folder's name so that it is called **Users**. Press Enter.

4. Highlight the Users folder in the Windows NT Explorer dialog box. Select File ⇒ Sharing.

5. In the Users Properties dialog box, select the radio button next to Shared As. Accept the default Share Name of Users. Click OK.

6. Exit Windows NT Explorer. Continue to Part 2.

## Part 2: Creating group accounts

In this section you create three new global groups: Managers, Sales, and Accounting.

**1.** Select Start ⇒ Programs ⇒ Administrative Tools (Common) ⇒ User Manager for Domains.

**2.** Highlight any of the groups listed in the Groups list box. (The reason for this is that the first user in the Username list box is highlighted by default, and if this user is not unhighlighted, the user will automatically become a member of the new global group you create.) Select User ⇒ New Global Group.

**3.** The New Global Group dialog box appears. In the Group Name text box, type in **Managers**. In the Description text box, type in **Managers of the Sales Organization**. Click OK.

**4.** The User Manager dialog box reappears. Select User ⇒ New Global Group.

**5.** The New Global Group dialog box appears. In the Group Name text box, type in **Sales**. In the Description text box, type in **Sales Representatives**. Click OK.

**6.** The User Manager dialog box reappears. Select User ⇒ New Global Group.

**7.** The New Global Group dialog box appears. In the Group Name text box, type in **Accounting**. In the Description text box, type in **Accounting Staff**. Click OK.

**8.** The User Manager dialog box reappears. You have now created three new global groups: Managers, Sales, and Accounting. Continue to Part 3.

## Part 3: Creating user account templates

In this section you create two user account templates, one that will be used to create user accounts for sales representatives, and another that will be used to create user accounts for accounting staff.

**1.** In the User Manager dialog box, select User ⇒ New User.

**2.** The New User dialog box appears. Type the bolded information below in the appropriate text boxes:

- User Name: **Sales_User**
- Full Name: (Leave this box blank.)
- Description: **Sales Representative**
- Password: **newuser**
- Confirm Password: **newuser**

Select the check box next to User Must Change Password at Next Logon. Select the check box next to Account Disabled. Click the Groups command button.

**3.** The Group Memberships dialog box appears. In the "Not member of" list box, highlight Sales. Click the Add command button. (Notice that the Sales group, along with Domain Users, is now listed in the "Member of" list box.) Click OK.

**4.** The New User dialog box reappears. Click the Dialin command button.

**5.** The Dialin Information dialog box appears. Select the check box next to "Grant dialin permission to user." Accept the default of No Call Back in the Call Back section. Click OK.

**6.** The New User dialog box reappears. Click the Profile command button.

**7.** The User Environment Profile dialog box appears. In the Home Directory section, select the radio button next to Connect. Accept the Z: in the drop-down list box. In the To text box, type: **\\PDCLAB\USERS\%USERNAME%**. Click OK.

**8.** The New User dialog box reappears. Click the Add command button.

**9.** The New User dialog box reappears. Type the following bolded information in the appropriate text boxes:

- User Name: **Acct_User**
- Full Name: (Leave this box blank.)
- Description: **Accounting Staff**
- Password: **newuser**
- Confirm Password: **newuser**

Select the check box next to User Must Change Password at Next Logon. Select the check box next to Account Disabled. Click the Groups command button.

**10.** The Group Memberships dialog box appears. In the "Not member of" list box, highlight Accounting. Click the Add command button. (Notice that the Accounting group, along with Domain Users, is now listed in the "Member of" list box.) Click OK.

**11.** The New User dialog box reappears. Click the Hours command button.

**12.** The Logon Hours dialog box appears. Using your mouse, highlight the entire graph. Click the Disallow command button. Using your mouse, highlight the area on the graph that represents 6:00 a.m. to 9:00 p.m. Monday through Friday. Click the Allow command button. Click OK.

**13.** The New User dialog box reappears. Click the Profile command button.

**14.** The User Environment Profile dialog box appears. In the Home Directory section, select the radio button next to Connect. Accept the Z: in the drop-down list box. In the To text box, type: **\\PDCLAB\USERS\ %USERNAME%**. Click OK.

**15.** The New User dialog box reappears. Click the Add command button. Click the Close command button. Notice that your two new user account templates, Sales_User and Acct_User, now appear in the Username list box within the User Manager dialog box. Continue to Part 4.

### Part 4: Creating and managing user accounts

In this section you create user accounts from scratch and also use the user account templates to create user accounts. You assign some of the new user accounts to groups.

**1.** In the User Manager dialog box, select User⇒New User.

**2.** The New User dialog box appears. Type the following bolded information in the appropriate text boxes:

- User Name: **PamR**
- Full Name: **Pam Rhodes**
- Description: **District Manager**
- Password: **newuser**
- Confirm Password: **newuser**

Select the check box next to User Must Change Password at Next Logon. Click the Groups command button.

**3.** The Group Memberships dialog box appears. In the "Not member of" list box, highlight Accounting. Then press and hold Ctrl while you scroll down and click Managers and Sales. Click the Add command button. (The Accounting, Managers, and Sales groups, along with Domain Users, should now be listed in the "Member of" list box.) Click OK.

**4.** The New User dialog box reappears. Click the Add command button.

**5.** The New User dialog box reappears. Type the following bolded information in the appropriate text boxes:

- User Name: **JohnS**
- Full Name: **John Spencer**
- Description: **Sales Manager**
- Password: **newuser**
- Confirm Password: **newuser**

Select the check box next to User Must Change Password at Next Logon. Click the Groups command button.

**6.** The Group Memberships dialog box appears. In the "Not member of" list box, highlight Managers. Then press and hold Ctrl while you click Sales.

Click the Add command button. (The Managers and Sales groups, along with Domain Users, should now be listed in the "Member of" list box.) Click OK.

**7.** The New User dialog box reappears. Click the Add command button.

**8.** The New User dialog box reappears. Type the following bolded information in the appropriate text boxes:

- o User Name: **RobertJ**
- o Full Name: **Robert Jones**
- o Description: **Accounting Manager**
- o Password: **newuser**
- o Confirm Password: **newuser**

Select the check box next to User Must Change Password at Next Logon. Cllck the Groups command button.

**9.** The Group Memberships dialog box appears. In the "Not member of" list box, highlight Accounting. Then press and hold Ctrl while you scroll down and click Managers. Click the Add command button. (The Accounting and Managers groups, along with Domain Users, should now be listed in the "Member of" list box.) Click OK.

**10.** The New User dialog box reappears. Click the Add command button. Click the Close command button.

**11.** The User Manager dialog box reappears. Notice that the three users you just created are in the Username list box. Highlight JohnS, and then press and hold Ctrl while you click PamR and RobertJ. Select User ⇒ Properties.

**12.** The User Properties dialog box appears. Notice the three users you selected are listed in the Users list box. Click the Dialin command button.

**13.** The Dialin Information dialog box appears. Select the check box next to "Grant dialin permission to user." Accept the default of No Call Back in the Call Back section. Click OK.

**14.** The User Properties dialog box reappears. Click the Profile command button.

**15.** The User Environment Profile dialog box appears. In the Home Directory section, select the radio button next to Connect. Accept the Z: in the drop-down list box. In the To text box, type: **\\PDCLAB\USERS\ %USERNAME%**. Click OK.

**16.** The User Properties dialog box reappears. Click OK. You have now granted dialin permission and assigned home folders to JohnS, PamR, and RobertJ.

**17.** The User Manager dialog box reappears. Highlight Sales_User. Select User ⇒ Copy.

**18.** The Copy of Sales_User dialog box appears. Type the following bolded information in the appropriate text boxes:

- User Name: **ColleenG**
- Full Name: **Colleen Green**
- Description: (This is already filled in.)
- Password: **newuser**
- Confirm Password: **newuser**

Select the check box next to User Must Change Password at Next Logon. Click Groups. Notice that the Sales group, as well as Domain Users, is listed in the "Member of" list box. Click OK.

**19.** In the Copy of Sales_User dialog box, click the Dialin command button. In the Dialin Information dialog box, notice that the check box next to "Grant dialin permission to user" is selected. Click OK.

**20.** In the Copy of Sales_User dialog box, click the Add command button.

**21.** The Copy of Sales_User dialog box reappears. Type the following bolded information in the appropriate text boxes:

- User Name: **BillT**
- Full Name: **Bill Tracy**
- Description: (This is already filled in.)
- Password: **newuser**
- Confirm Password: **newuser**

Select the check box next to User Must Change Password at Next Logon. Click the Add command button.

**22.** The Copy of Sales_User dialog box reappears. Type the bolded information below in the appropriate text boxes:

- User Name: **MikeC**
- Full Name: **Mike Calhoun**
- Description: (This is already filled in.)
- Password: **newuser**
- Confirm Password: **newuser**

Select the check box next to User Must Change Password at Next Logon. Click the Add command button. Click the Close command button.

**23.** The User Manager dialog box reappears. Notice that your new users now appear in the Username list box. Highlight the Acct_User. Select User ⇒ Copy.

**24.** The Copy of Acct_User dialog box appears. Type the following bolded information in the appropriate text boxes:

- User Name: **NancyY**
- Full Name: **Nancy Yates**
- Description: (This is already filled in.)
- Password: **newuser**
- Confirm Password: **newuser**

Select the check box next to User Must Change Password at Next Logon. Click the Groups command button. Notice that the Accounting group, in addition to Domain Users, appears in the "Member of" list box. Click OK.

**25.** In the Copy of Acct_User dialog box, click the Hours command button. In the Logon Hours dialog box, notice that this user will be able to log on between 6:00 a.m. and 9:00 p.m. Monday through Friday. Click OK.

**26.** In the Copy of Acct_User dialog box, click the Add command button.

**27.** The Copy of Acct_User dialog box reappears. Type the following bolded information in the appropriate text boxes:

- User Name: **MikeCo**
- Full Name: **Mike Cook**
- Description: (This is already filled in.)
- Password: **newuser**
- Confirm Password: **newuser**

Select the check box next to User Must Change Password at Next Logon. Click the Add command button. Then click the Close command button.

**28.** The User Manager dialog box reappears. Notice that the new users you created appear in the Username list box. Exit User Manager.

Server
Enterprise

# Managing Account Policy, User Rights, and Auditing

# About Chapter 8

This chapter explores the Policies menu in Windows NT User Manager/User Manager for Domains, with emphasis on its three major configurable options: Account Policy, User Rights, and Auditing.

Managing account policy, which applies to all users in the domain, is discussed first. Password restrictions and the account lockout feature are also addressed.

Next, the chapter explains how to manage user rights, which enable users to perform tasks. All the Windows NT user rights are listed and described in this section, followed by detailed, step-by-step instructions for assigning user rights.

Finally, Chapter 8 explores auditing, the Windows NT feature that, when enabled, produces a log of specified events and activities.

This chapter includes two hands-on labs. In the first lab, you implement Windows NT auditing, and then view audit events in the security log in Event Viewer. In the second, you set account policies and configure user rights.

Chapter 8 is optional if you're preparing only for the Workstation exam, but essential if you're preparing for either the Server or Enterprise exams. This chapter maps to the "Manage user and group accounts" objective in the Managing Resources section in the Server and Enterprise exams' objectives.

# MANAGING ACCOUNT POLICY

This chapter focuses on the Policies menu in User Manager (on Windows NT Workstation computers) and User Manager for Domains (on Windows NT Server computers). The Policies menu provides three main configurable options: Account Policy, User Rights, and Auditing. Only members of the Administrators local group have the necessary rights to manage account policy, user rights, and auditing.

The Account Policy dialog box has two main sections: one enables you to configure password restrictions, and another enables you to set the account lockout policy.

Settings in the Account Policy dialog box apply to *all* users in the domain (or to all users on a computer, if it is not a domain controller). You can't set individual account policies.

**TO ACCESS THE ACCOUNT POLICY DIALOG BOX, FOLLOW THESE STEPS:**

**1.** Select Start ⇒ Programs ⇒ Administrative Tools (Common) ⇒ User Manager (or User Manager for Domains).

**2.** In the User Manager dialog box, select Policies ⇒ Account. The Account Policy dialog box appears, as shown in Figure 8-1. Notice the default settings in this dialog box.

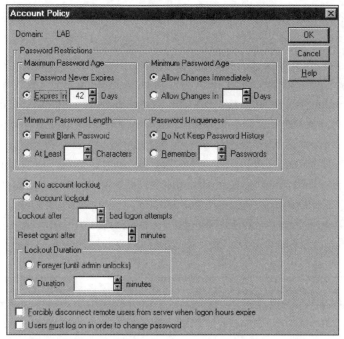

**FIGURE 8-1    The Account Policy dialog box in User Manager for Domains**

# Password restrictions

The Password Restrictions section of the Account Policy dialog box has four configurable options: Maximum Password Age, Minimum Password Age, Minimum Password Length, and Password Uniqueness.

### Maximum Password Age

*Maximum Password Age* determines the maximum number of days a user may use the same password. Two selections are available in this section: Password Never Expires, or Expires In *xx* Days. The default setting is Expires in 42 Days.

When Password Never Expires is selected, users are never required to change their passwords.

When Expires in *xx* Days is selected, Windows NT forces users to change their passwords when the maximum password age setting is exceeded. Normal settings for password expiration are between thirty and ninety days. If users have to change their passwords too frequently, they may be unable to remember their passwords.

If a user's password expires *and* the check box next to "Users must log on in order to change password" (at the bottom of the dialog box) is selected, the user will *not* be able to change his or her own password — the administrator must change the user's password.

in the real world

**I normally recommend administrators do *not* select the check box next to "Users must log on in order to change password," because Windows NT does not give users any warning that their passwords are about to expire. When users attempt to log on after password expiration, they are unable to log on to change their passwords. This situation creates a lot of hassle and extra work for the administrator.**

## Minimum Password Age

*Minimum Password Age* determines the minimum number of days a user must keep the same password. Two selections are available in this section: Allow Changes Immediately, or Allow Changes in *xx* Days. The default setting is Allow Changes Immediately.

If Allow Changes Immediately is selected, users can change their passwords as often as they like, without waiting for any time to pass before selecting a new password.

If Allow Changes in *xx* Days is selected, users must use their passwords for at least the number of days specified before Windows NT lets them change their passwords. Normal settings for Minimum Password Age are from one day to the number of days specified as the Maximum Password Age.

If Minimum Password Age is not set, and Password Uniqueness is set at Remember 8 Passwords, then users are often tempted to bypass the Password Uniqueness setting by changing their passwords nine times, in rapid succession, so they can recycle back to their original, favorite, and easily remembered password.

## Minimum Password Length

*Minimum Password Length* specifies the minimum number of characters required in users' passwords. Two selections are possible in this section: Permit Blank Password, or At Least *xx* Characters.

If Permit Blank Password is selected, users are not required to have a password. This is the default setting.

If At Least *xx* Characters is selected, you can specify the minimum number of characters a user's password must contain. Windows NT will not enable users to choose a password with fewer than the required number of characters. Possible settings for password length are from one to fourteen characters. I recommend you set a minimum of eight characters for Minimum Password Length. With a password length of eight characters or more, (assuming basic password security measures are taken) it's statistically almost impossible for an unauthorized user to guess a password.

### Password Uniqueness

*Password Uniqueness* specifies how many different passwords a user must use before an old password can be reused. Two selections are possible in this section: Do Not Keep Password History, or Remember *xx* Passwords. The default setting is Do Not Keep Password History.

If Do Not Keep Password History is selected, users can cycle back and forth between their two favorite passwords each time they are required to change their passwords.

If Remember *xx* Passwords is selected, users must use at least the number of new passwords specified before they can reuse an old password. Possible settings for Password Uniqueness are between one and twenty-four passwords. Normal settings range between five and twelve passwords.

You can multiply the number of passwords specified in Password Uniqueness times the number of days specified in Minimum Password Age to determine the number of days that must pass before a user can reuse an old password.

concept link  **For more password tips, see the "Passwords" section in Chapter 7.**

## Account lockout

The Account lockout section of the Account Policy dialog box specifies how Windows NT treats user accounts after several successive unsuccessful logon attempts have occurred. The default setting is "No account lockout."

Figure 8-2 shows the Account Policy dialog box. Notice the options in the Account lockout section.

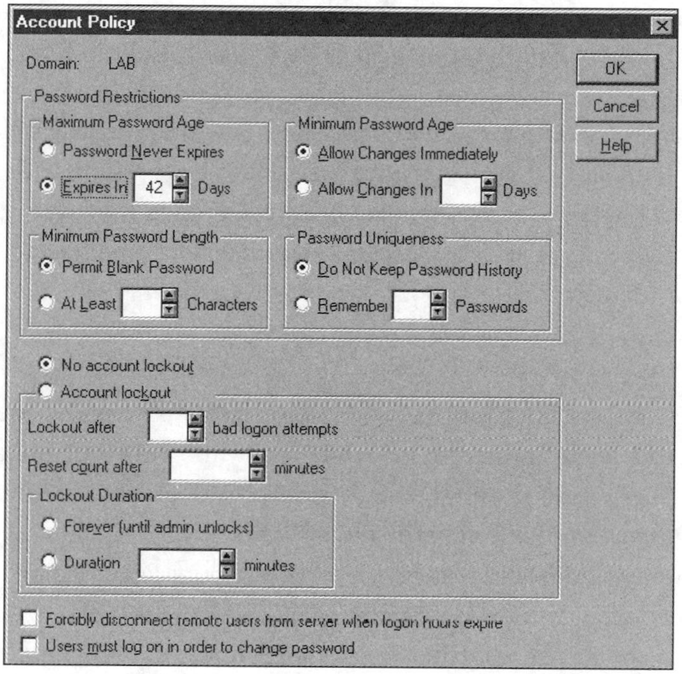

**FIGURE 8-2**     **The Account Policy dialog box in User Manager for Domains**

When "No account lockout" is selected, user accounts are never locked out. This means no matter how many unsuccessful logon attempts a user makes, the user's account is not locked out.

When Account lockout is selected, users are locked out after the specified number of successive bad logon attempts is reached. Several configuration options exist for Account lockout: Lockout after *xx* bad logon attempts, Reset count after *xx* minutes, and Lockout Duration.

Lockout after *xx* bad logon attempts specifies the number of successive unsuccessful logon attempts that are acceptable before Windows NT will lock out an account. The possible settings are from one to 999 bad logon attempts. Normal settings for this configuration are from three to ten bad logon attempts. This counter is reset after each successful logon. Windows NT maintains a separate counter for each user account.

Reset count after *xx* minutes specifies the number of minutes that must pass without a bad logon attempt in order for the bad logon attempts counter to be reset to zero. (Resetting the counter to zero gives users the full number of possible bad logon attempts before account lockout.) The possible settings are from one to 99,999 minutes. Normal settings for this configuration are from thirty to sixty minutes.

Lockout duration specifies how long a user account is locked out after the specified number of bad logon attempts occurs. Two possible settings are in this section: Forever (until admin unlocks), or "Duration *xx* minutes."

If Forever is selected *and* the specified number of bad logon attempts occurs, the administrator must unlock the user account in User Manager (or User Manager for Domains) before the user can log on.

If "Duration *xx* minutes" is selected, user accounts that are locked out (because the specified number of bad logon attempts have been exceeded) are unlocked automatically by Windows NT after the specified number of minutes elapses. The possible settings are from one to 99,999 minutes. Normal settings for this configuration are from thirty to sixty minutes.

Two additional check boxes are in the Account Policy dialog box: "Forcibly disconnect remote users from server when logon hours expire," and "Users must log on to change password." By default, both of these check boxes are *not* selected. The "Forcibly disconnect remote users from server when logon hours expire" check box is only available on Windows NT Server computers configured as domain controllers.

If "Forcibly disconnect remote users from server when logon hours expire" is selected, users whose logon hours expire are automatically disconnected from the domain controllers in the domain. Users are not disconnected from Windows NT Workstation computers, however, or from member servers in the domain.

If "Users must log on in order to change password" is selected, and a user's password expires, the administrator must change the user's password (because the user cannot log on with an expired password).

A configuration conflict arises when the "Users must log on in order to change password" option is set in Account Policy *and* new users are configured so that User Must Change Password at Next Logon. This combination of settings places users in a catch-22 situation: Users can't log on without changing their passwords, and users can't change their passwords without logging on. The administrator can resolve this problem by changing the users' passwords and clearing the check box next to User Must Change Password at Next Logon in the users' Properties dialog box in User Manager (or User Manager for Domains).

# MANAGING USER RIGHTS

*User rights* authorize users and groups to perform specific tasks on a Windows NT computer. User rights are not the same as permissions: user rights enable users to *perform tasks*; whereas permissions enable users to *access objects*, such as files, folders, and printers.

User rights are assigned in the User Rights Policy dialog box in User Manager or User Manager for Domains.

**TO ACCESS THE USER RIGHTS POLICY DIALOG BOX, FOLLOW THESE STEPS:**

**1.** Select Start ⇒ Programs ⇒ Administrative Tools (Common) ⇒ User Manager (or User Manager for Domains).

**2.** In the User Manager dialog box, select Policies ⇒ User Rights.

Figure 8-3 shows the User Rights Policy dialog box. Notice the option to Show Advanced User Rights.

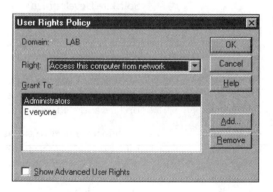

**FIGURE 8-3**   **The User Rights Policy dialog box in User Manager for Domains**

The following sections discuss user rights and advanced user rights and examine how user rights are assigned.

# User Rights

Each *user right* authorizes a user or group to perform a specific task. User rights, unlike account policy, can be assigned to individual users and groups.

User rights are listed in the User Rights Policy Dialog box. You can choose to display regular user rights or a combination of regular and advanced user rights in the Right drop-down list box. The default configuration displays only non-advanced user rights.

Table 8-1 lists and describes each of the Windows NT user rights. The table also indicates whether each right is an advanced user right.

**TABLE 8-1** WINDOWS NT USER RIGHTS

| USER RIGHT | ADVANCED USER RIGHT? | DESCRIPTION |
|---|---|---|
| Access this computer from the network | No | Authorizes a user to access a computer over the network. |
| Act as part of the operating system | Yes | Not normally used by administrators. Used by programmers of Windows NT applications. See Microsoft's Win32 Software Development Kit for more information. |
| Add workstations to domain | No | Authorizes a user to cause workstation computers to join the domain. |
| Back up files and directories | No | Authorizes a user to back up files and folders. This right supersedes permissions on files and folders. |
| Bypass traverse checking | Yes | Authorizes a user to change the current folder on the user's computer to a different folder, even if the user or group has no permissions to the newly selected current folder. |
| Change the system time | No | Authorizes a user to change the time on the Windows NT computer's internal clock. |
| Create a pagefile | Yes | Not normally used by administrators. Used by programmers of Windows NT applications. See Microsoft's Win32 Software Development Kit for more information. |

| USER RIGHT | ADVANCED USER RIGHT? | DESCRIPTION |
|---|---|---|
| Create a token object | Yes | Not normally used by administrators. Used by programmers of Windows NT applications. See Microsoft's Win32 Software Development Kit for more information. |
| Create permanent shared objects | Yes | Not normally used by administrators. Used by programmers of Windows NT applications. See Microsoft's Win32 Software Development Kit for more information. |
| Debug programs | Yes | Not normally used by administrators. Used by programmers of Windows NT applications. See Microsoft's Win32 Software Development Kit for more information. |
| Force shutdown from a remote system | No | This right is not currently implemented. It is reserved for future use. |
| Generate security audits | Yes | Not normally used by administrators. Used by programmers of Windows NT applications. See Microsoft's Win32 Software Development Kit for more information. |
| Increase quotas | Yes | Not normally used by administrators. Used by programmers of Windows NT applications. See Microsoft's Win32 Software Development Kit for more information. |
| Increase scheduling priority | Yes | Not normally used by administrators. Used by programmers of Windows NT applications. See Microsoft's Win32 Software Development Kit for more information. |
| Load and unload device drivers | No | Authorizes a user to load and unload device drivers for the Windows NT operating system. |
| Lock pages in memory | Yes | Not normally used by administrators. Used by programmers of Windows NT applications. See Microsoft's Win32 Software Development Kit for more information. |

*continued*

**TABLE 8-1** *(continued)*

| USER RIGHT | ADVANCED USER RIGHT? | DESCRIPTION |
|---|---|---|
| Log on as a batch job | Yes | Not normally used by administrators. Used by programmers of Windows NT applications. See Microsoft's Win32 Software Development Kit for more information. |
| Log on as a service | Yes | Allows a service or application to log on using a specified user account. (For example, in Chapter 4 you configured the Directory Replicator service to use a specific user account to log on as a service.) |
| Log on locally | No | Authorizes a user to log on locally (interactively at the computer). |
| Manage auditing and security log | No | Authorizes a user to view and change the security log in Event Viewer. Enables a user to configure auditing of files, folders, and printers. Does *not* enable a user to access the Audit Policy dialog box in User Manager. |
| Modify firmware environment values | Yes | Not normally used by administrators. Used by programmers of Windows NT applications. See Microsoft's Win32 Software Development Kit for more information. |
| Profile single process | Yes | Not normally used by administrators. Used by programmers of Windows NT applications. See Microsoft's Win32 Software Development Kit for more information. |
| Profile system performance | Yes | Not normally used by administrators. Used by programmers of Windows NT applications. See Microsoft's Win32 Software Development Kit for more information. |
| Replace a process level token | Yes | Not normally used by administrators. Used by programmers of Windows NT applications. See Microsoft's Win32 Software Development Kit for more information. |

| USER RIGHT | ADVANCED USER RIGHT? | DESCRIPTION |
|---|---|---|
| Restore files and directories | No | Authorizes a user to restore files and folders. This right supersedes permissions on files and folders. |
| Shut down the system | No | Authorizes a user to shut down the Windows NT computer the user is logged on to. |
| Take ownership of files or other objects | No | Authorizes a user to take ownership of files, folders, and printers. |

# Assigning user rights

The assigning of user rights is accomplished in the User Rights Policy dialog box. You can add and remove user rights to and from users and groups in this dialog box.

The following sections describe first how to assign a user right to a user or group, and then how to remove a user right from a user or group.

**TO ASSIGN A USER RIGHT TO A USER OR GROUP, FOLLOW THESE STEPS:**

**1.** In the User Rights Policy dialog box in User Manager (or User Manager for Domains), select the user right you want to assign from the Right drop-down list box. (If you want to assign an advanced user right, first select the check box next to Show Advanced User Rights.)

Figure 8-4 shows the User Rights Policy dialog box. Notice the "Back up files and directories" user right is selected. Click the Add command button.

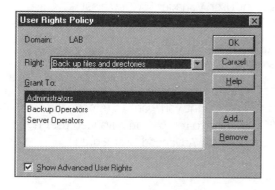

**FIGURE 8-4** Assigning the "Back up files and directories" user right

**2.** The Add Users and Groups dialog box appears. If you want to assign a user right to a user, click the Show Users command button. (Otherwise, only groups are listed.) Scroll down through the Names list box and select the user(s) and/or group(s) to which you want to assign a user right.

Figure 8-5 shows the Add Users and Groups dialog box. Notice both users and groups are displayed in the Names list box (because the Show Users command button has been clicked).

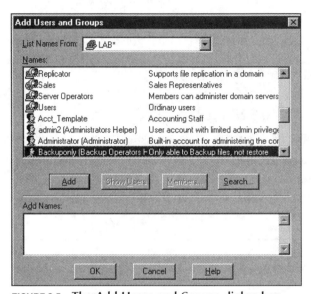

**FIGURE 8-5**   The Add Users and Groups dialog box

Click the Add command button. (Or, instead of first selecting a user or group and then clicking the Add command button, you can double-click each user or group to which you want to assign the user right.) The name(s) you select appear in the Add Names list box. Click OK.

**3.** The User Rights Policy dialog box reappears. Click OK.

**4.** Exit User Manager (or User Manager for Domains).

### TO REMOVE A USER RIGHT FROM A USER OR A GROUP, FOLLOW THESE STEPS:

**1.** In the User Rights Policy dialog box in User Manager (or User Manager for Domains), select the user right you want to remove from the Right drop-down list box. (If you want to remove an advanced user right, first select the check box next to Show Advanced User Rights.)

**2.** Then highlight the user or group you want to remove the user right from in the Grant To list box. Click the Remove command button. Click OK.

**3.** Exit User Manager (or User Manager for Domains).

in the
real world

**Understanding and being able to use Windows NT user rights is important when preparing for the Microsoft Certified Professional exams. Most user rights, however, are not used by administrators in the real world. In my experience, one of the most common "real world" user right assignments is the "Log on locally" user right to users who need to log on interactively to domain controllers.**

# MANAGING AUDITING

When enabled, Windows NT auditing produces a log of specified events and activities that occur on a Windows NT computer. Audited events are written to the security log in Event Viewer. Windows NT auditing is divided into two areas: system access and object access. *System access auditing* is configured by using User Manager or User Manager for Domains. *Object access auditing* is configured in the Properties dialog boxes for files, folders, and printers. By default, auditing is turned off.

The next section explains how to enable system access auditing using the Audit Policy dialog box in User Manager or User Manager Domains.

**TO ACCESS THE AUDIT POLICY DIALOG BOX AND
TO ENABLE AUDITING, FOLLOW THESE STEPS:**

**1.** Select Start ⇒ Programs ⇒ Administrative Tools (Common) ⇒ User Manager (or User Manager for Domains).

**2.** In the User Manager dialog box, select Policies ⇒ Audit.

**3.** The Audit Policy dialog box appears. The default setting for this dialog box is Do Not Audit. To enable auditing, select the radio button next to Audit These Events, *and* select at least one Success or Failure check box.

The Audit Policy dialog box is shown in Figure 8-6. Note the radio button next to Audit These Events is selected, and the Success and Failure check boxes for File and Object Access are checked. Click OK.

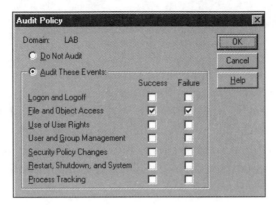

**FIGURE 8-6    Enabling auditing**

**4.** Exit User Manager (or User Manager for Domains).

When a Success check box is selected, Windows NT generates an audit event each time a user successfully performs the audited task.

When a Failure check box is selected, Windows NT generates an audit event each time a user attempts to perform an audited task but fails (usually because of a lack of rights or permissions).

When both success and failure auditing are selected, an audit event is generated each time a user attempts to perform an audited task, whether successfully or unsuccessfully.

Table 8-2 lists and describes the types of audit events that can be selected in the Audit Policy dialog box.

| TABLE 8-2 WINDOWS NT AUDIT EVENTS | |
|---|---|
| *Event* | *Description* |
| Logon and Logoff | A user logs on, logs off, or accesses this Windows NT computer over the network. |
| File and Object Access | A user accesses a file, folder, or printer configured for auditing. |
| | Note: To audit file, folder, or print events, you must enable file and object access auditing *in addition to* |

| Event | Description |
|---|---|
| | file, folder, or printer auditing (which is set in Windows NT Explorer or in a printer's Properties dialog box). |
| Use of User Rights | A user exercises an assigned user right, other than the "Log on locally" or "Access this computer from the network" user rights. |
| User and Group Management | A user account or group is created, changed, or deleted; or, a user account is renamed, disabled, enabled, or its password is changed. |
| Security Policy Changes | The user rights, audit, or trust relationship policies are modified or changed. |
| Restart, Shutdown, and System | A user restarts or shuts down the computer, or a system security or security log event occurs. |
| Process Tracking | An event, such as program activation, some forms of handle duplication, indirect object accesses, or process exit occurs. This event is not often selected for audit by administrators. |

*Tip* **Carefully consider which events you need to audit. If you choose to audit everything, your security log will fill up quickly, primarily with useless information.**

To view audited events in Windows NT, use Event Viewer. The next section describes how to access Event Viewer and view audited events.

**TO ACCESS EVENT VIEWER AND TO VIEW SECURITY LOG EVENTS, FOLLOW THESE STEPS:**

**1.** Select Start ⇒ Programs ⇒ Administrative Tools (Common) ⇒ Event Viewer.

**2.** In the Event Viewer dialog box, select Log ⇒ Security.

**3.** The Security Log dialog box appears.

Figure 8-7 shows a security log in Event Viewer. Notice some events are marked with keys (these designate success events), and some events are marked with locks (these designate unsuccessful events).

Double-click an event you want to view in greater detail.

**4.** The Event Detail dialog box appears. Figure 8-8 shows an Event Detail dialog box. Notice the types of information included in this dialog box.

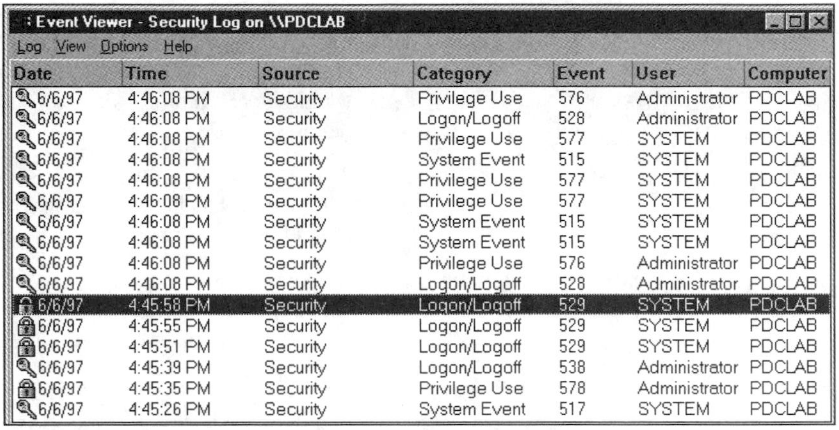

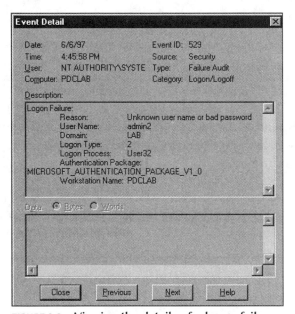

**FIGURE 8-7**    Viewing events in the Security Log dialog box

**FIGURE 8-8**    Viewing the details of a logon failure event

# KEY POINT SUMMARY

This chapter focused on the Policies menu in User Manager and User Manager for Domains, which contains three primary configurable options: *Account Policy, User Rights,* and *Auditing.*

- Only members of the Administrators local group have the necessary rights to manage account policy, user rights, and auditing.

- The Account Policy dialog box in User Manager or User Manager for Domains has two main sections: One allows you to configure password restrictions, and another allows you to set the account lockout policy. Settings in the Account Policy dialog box apply to *all* users in the domain (or to all users on a computer, if it is not a domain controller.)

  - Four configurable options are in the Password Restrictions section of the Account Policy dialog box: Maximum Password Age, Minimum Password Age, Minimum Password Length, and Password Uniqueness.

  - The Account lockout section of the Account Policy dialog box specifies how Windows NT treats user accounts after several successive bad logon attempts have occurred. Several configurations exist for Account lockout: Lockout after *xx* bad logon attempts, Reset count after *xx* minutes, and Lockout Duration (which can either be set to Forever [until admin unlocks], or Duration *xx* minutes).

  - The two additional check boxes in the Account Policy dialog box include: "Forcibly disconnect remote users from server when logon hours expire," and "Users must log on in order to change password." By default, both of these check boxes are *not* selected.

- *User rights* authorize users or groups to perform specific tasks. User rights, unlike account policy, can be assigned to (and removed from) individual users and groups. User rights are not the same as permissions: User rights enable users to *perform tasks*, whereas permissions enable users to *access objects*, such as files, folders, and printers. User rights are assigned in the User Rights Policy dialog box in User Manager or User Manager for Domains.

  - User rights are made up of advanced and non-advanced rights, such as: Access this computer from the network, Add workstations to domain, Back up files and directories, Change the system time, Force shutdown from a remote system, Load and unload device drivers, Log on locally, Manage auditing and security log, Restore files and directories, Shut down the system, and Take ownership of files or other objects.

o  When enabled, *Windows NT auditing* produces a log of specified events and activities that occur on a Windows NT computer. Audited events are written to the security log in Event Viewer. Auditing is configured in the Audit Policy dialog box in User Manager or User Manager for Domains.

   o  When *success auditing* is selected, an audit event is generated every time a user successfully performs the audited task. When *failure auditing* is selected, an audit event is generated each time a user tries to perform an audited task, but fails for some reason. When both success and failure auditing are selected, an audit event is generated every time a user attempts to perform an audited task, whether successfully or unsuccessfully.

   o  The events that can be selected for audit in the Audit Policy dialog box are Logon and Logoff; File and Object Access; Use of User Rights; User and Group Management; Security Policy Changes; Restart, Shutdown, and System; and Process Tracking. Audited events can be viewed in the security log in Event Viewer. Remember: To audit file, folder, or print events you must enable file and object access auditing *in addition to* file, folder, or printer auditing (which is set in Windows NT Explorer or in a printer's Properties dialog box).

# APPLYING WHAT YOU'VE LEARNED

Now it's time to regroup, review, and apply what you've learned in this chapter.

The questions in the following Instant Assessment section bring to mind key facts and concepts.

The hands-on lab exercises reinforce what you learned and give you an opportunity to practice some of the tasks tested by the Microsoft Certified Professional exams.

## Instant Assessment

1. What are the two main configurable sections in the Account Policy dialog box?

2. How can you access the Account Policy dialog box?

3. What is the default setting for Maximum Password Age?

4. What does the Minimum Password Age configuration determine?

5. What are the possible settings for Minimum Password Length? What is a recommended setting for Minimum Password Length?

6. What does the Password Uniqueness configuration specify?

7. What does the Account lockout section of the Account Policy dialog box specify?

8. Only members of which local group have the necessary rights to manage account policy, user rights, and auditing?

9. What is the difference between user rights and permissions?

10. When enabled, what does Windows NT auditing produce?

11. Which Windows NT tool can you use to view audited events?

12. In addition to selecting success and/or failure auditing for File and Object Access in the Audit Policy dialog box, what else must you do before you can audit file, folder, or print events?

13. What are the seven specific event types that can be selected for audit in the Audit Policy dialog box?

**T/F**

14. The settings in the Account Policy dialog box can be configured to apply to individual users.     _____

15. User rights can be assigned to individual users and groups.     _____

 concept link     **For answers to the Instant Assessment questions see Appendix D.**

## Hands-on lab exercises

The following hands-on lab exercises provide excellent opportunities to apply the knowledge you've gained in this chapter about Windows NT account policy, user rights, and auditing.

**Lab 8.11** *Implementing auditing*

Server
Enterprise

The purpose of this lab is to provide you with hands-on experience in using the Windows NT auditing feature.

This lab consists of three parts:

> Part 1: Implementing auditing
> Part 2: Creating audited events
> Part 3: Viewing the security log in Event Viewer

Begin this lab by booting your computer to Windows NT Server. Log on as Administrator.

Perform the following steps carefully.

### Part 1: Implementing auditing

In this part you implement auditing on a Windows NT Server computer.

**1.** Select Start ⇒ Programs ⇒ Administrative Tools (Common) ⇒ User Manager for Domains.

**2.** In the User Manager dialog box, select Policies ⇒ Audit.

**3.** In the Audit Policy dialog box, select the radio button next to Audit These Events, and then select the Success and Failure check boxes for *all* audit events *except* Process Tracking. Click OK.

**4.** Auditing is now implemented. Exit User Manager for Domains. Proceed to Part 2.

### Part 2: Creating audited events

In this part you cause a user to create audited events.

**1.** Select Start ⇒ Shut Down.

**2.** In the Shut Down Windows dialog box, select the radio button next to Restart the computer. Click the Yes command button. The computer shuts down and restarts.

**3.** Reboot the computer to Windows NT Server. Press Ctrl + Alt + Delete to log on. When the Logon Information dialog box appears, type in a user name of **PamR** (replacing Administrator) and a password of **wrongo**. Click OK.

**4.** An error message appears, stating the system could not log you on. Click OK.

**5.** The Logon Information dialog box reappears. Type in a password of **newuser**. Click OK.

6. A message appears, indicating you are required to change your password at first logon. (You may recall you set this configuration when you created this user in Lab 7.10.) Click OK.

7. Type in a new password of **password**. Confirm the new password by retyping it. Click OK.

8. A dialog box appears, indicating your password has been changed. Click OK.

9. Another dialog box appears, indicating the local policy of this system does not enable you to log on interactively. Click OK.

10. The Logon Information dialog box reappears. Type in a user name of **Administrator**, and a password of **password**. Click OK. You have now created several audited events. Continue to Part 3.

## Part 3: Viewing the security log in Event Viewer

In this part you view the security log in Event Viewer to see the audited events you created in Part 2.

1. Select Start ⇒ Programs ⇒ Administrative Tools (Common) ⇒ Event Viewer.

2. Select Log ⇒ Security.

3. Scroll down the list and double-click the first event marked with a lock (not a key) in the left margin. (A lock marks a failure audit event. A key marks a success audit event.)

4. The Event Detail dialog box appears. Notice the event is a logon failure for PamR, because she was not allowed to log on interactively (locally). Click the Close command button.

5. Scroll down and double-click the next event marked with a lock in the left margin.

6. The Event Detail dialog box reappears. This is also a failure audit event. Notice an unexpected error occurred during PamR's attempted logon. Click the Close command button.

7. Scroll down and double-click the next event marked with a lock in the left margin.

8. The Event Detail dialog box appears. This is a logon failure event for PamR, because an incorrect password (wrongo) was entered. Click the Close command button.

9. Double-click various other events, as desired, and view their event details.

10. Exit Event Viewer.

## Lab 8.12 *Managing account policy and user rights*

Server
Enterprise

The purpose of this lab is to provide you with hands-on experience in setting account policy and user rights in Windows NT.

This lab consists of three parts:

Part 1: Setting account policy

Part 2: Creating users and configuring user rights

Part 3: Auditing revisited — clearing the security log in Event Viewer

Begin this lab by booting your computer to Windows NT Server. Log on as Administrator.

Follow the steps carefully.

### Part 1: Setting account policy

In this section you set account policy that affects all users in the domain.

**1.** Select Start ⇒ Programs ⇒ Administrative Tools (Common) ⇒ User Manager for Domains.

**2.** In the User Manager dialog box, select Policy ⇒ Account.

**3.** The Account Policy dialog box appears. Configure the following:

- Configure the Maximum Password Age to Expires in **30** Days.

- Configure the Minimum Password Age to Allow Changes in **5** Days.

- Configure the Minimum Password Length to be At Least **8** Characters.

- Configure Password Uniqueness to Remember (the last) **6** Passwords.

- Select the radio button next to Account lockout.

- Set Lockout after **3** bad logon attempts.

- Set Reset count after **30** minutes.

- Configure Lockout Duration to Forever (until admin unlocks).

- Select the check box next to Users must log on in order to change password.

Figure 8-9 shows the Account Policy dialog box as correctly configured at the close of this step. You can check the configurations you have made against this figure. Click OK.

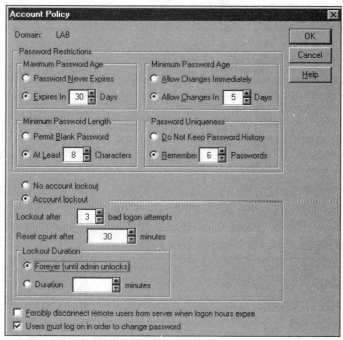

**FIGURE 8-9**   **Account Policy dialog box as correctly configured in Lab 8.12**

**4.** In the User Manager dialog box, select Policies⇸User Rights.

**5.** The User Rights Policy dialog box appears. In the Right drop-down list box, select Log on locally. Click the Add command button.

**6.** The Add Users and Groups dialog box appears. In the Names list box, double-click the Everyone group. (Everyone appears in the Add Names list box.) Click OK. (Granting the "Log on locally" right to the Everyone group enables all users to log on interactively at the Windows NT Server.)

**7.** In the Users Rights Policy dialog box, click OK.

**8.** Exit User Manager.

**9.** Select Start⇸Shut Down. In the Shut Down Windows dialog box, select the radio button next to Close all programs and log on as a different user. Click the Yes command button.

**10.** Press Ctrl + Alt + Delete to log on.

**11.** In the Logon Information dialog box, type in a user name of **JohnS** and a password of **newuser**. Click OK.

**12.** A dialog box appears, indicating you are required to change your password at first logon. (You may recall you set this configuration when you created this user in Lab 7.10.) Click OK.

**13.** The Change Password dialog box appears. Type in a new password of **password**. Confirm the new password by retyping it. Click OK.

**14.** A warning message appears, indicating you do not have permission to change your password. (This is because in the Account Policy dialog box you selected the check box next to "Users must log on in order to change password" *and*, when you created this user, you selected the option for User Must Change Password at Next Logon. *These two options do not work together*.) Click OK.

**15.** The Change Password dialog box appears. Click the Cancel command button.

**16.** The Logon Information dialog box appears. Type in a user name of **PamR** and a password of **wrongo**. Click OK. (Note: In this part of the lab you will attempt to log PamR on several times with an incorrect password to experience the account lockout feature.)

**17.** A warning message appears, indicating the system could not log you on. Click OK.

**18.** Repeat Steps 16 and 17 until a warning message appears, indicating NT is unable to log you on because your account has been locked out. You must contact your network administrator to unlock your account. Click OK. (Next, you will log on as administrator and unlock PamR's user account.)

**19.** In the Logon Information dialog box, type in a user name of **Administrator** and a password of **password**. Click OK.

**20.** Select Start ⇒ Programs ⇒ Administrative Tools (Common) ⇒ User Manager for Domains.

**21.** In the User Manager dialog box, double-click the user account PamR in the Username list box.

**22.** The User Properties dialog box appears. Notice the check box next to Account Locked Out is checked. Deselect this check box. Click OK.

**23.** Double-click PamR again in the Username list box.

**24.** The User Properties dialog box appears. Notice the check box next to Account Locked Out is cleared and grayed out. (The Administrator can't lock out a user account — only the system can.) Click the Cancel command button.

**25.** In the User Manager dialog box, select Policies ⇒ Account.

**26.** In the Account Policy dialog box, deselect the check box next to "Users must log on in order to change password." (This will enable users to change their passwords during logon.) Click OK.

**27.** Continue to Part 2.

## Part 2: Creating users and configuring user rights

In this section you create two special-use user accounts and configure user rights for these new user accounts.

**1.** In the User Manager dialog box, select User ⇒ New User.

**2.** The New User dialog box appears. Type the following bolded text in the appropriate text boxes:

User name: **Admin2**

Full name: **Administrator's Helper**

Description: **User account with limited admin privileges**

Password: **password**

Confirm password: **password**

Deselect the check box next to User Must Change Password at Next Logon. Select the check box next to Password Never Expires. Click the Add command button.

**3.** The New User dialog box reappears. Type the following bolded text in the appropriate text boxes:

User name: **Backuponly**

Full name: **Backup Operator's Helper**

Description: **Only able to back up files, not restore**

Password: **password**

Confirm password: **password**

Deselect the check box next to User Must Change Password at Next Logon. Select the check box next to Password Never Expires. Click the Add command button. Click the Close command button.

**4.** In the User Manager dialog box, select Policies ⇒ User Rights.

**5.** The User Rights Policy dialog box appears. In the Right drop-down list box, select "Log on locally." Click the Add command button.

**6.** The Add Users and Groups dialog box appears. Click the Show Users command button. Double-click Backuponly. Click OK.

**7.** In the Right drop-down list box, select Back up files and directories. Click the Add command button.

**8.** The Add Users and Groups dialog box appears. Click the Show Users command button. Scroll down and double-click Backuponly. Click OK. (The Backuponly user is now able to log on to the Windows NT Server and is able to back up the server's files.)

9. The User Rights Policy dialog box reappears. Using the sequence you used in the previous Steps 7 and 8, grant the following rights to the Admin2 user:

   o Add workstations to domain

   o Back up files and directories

   o Change the system time

   o Log on locally

   o Manage auditing and security log

   o Restore files and directories

   o Shut down the system

   o Take ownership of files or other objects

 **Note: You must go through all the steps for each user right you want to assign. No short cuts exist here.**

Click OK in the User Rights Policy dialog box when you finish.

10. Exit User Manager for Domains. Continue to Part 3.

### Part 3: Auditing revisited — clearing the security log in Event Viewer

In this section you explore the capabilities of the "Manage auditing and security log" user right, and clear the security log in Event Viewer.

1. Press Ctrl + Alt + Delete. Click the Logoff command button. Click OK to close all programs and log off.

2. Press Ctrl + Alt + Delete. In The Logon Information dialog box, type in a user name of **Admin2** and a password of **password**. Click OK. (If a Welcome to Windows NT screen is displayed, click the Close command button.)

3. Select Start ⇒ Programs ⇒ Administrative Tools (Common) ⇒ User Manager for Domains.

4. In the User Manager dialog box, select Policies. Notice all the options in the Policies menu are grayed out. These options are only available to members of the Administrators group — The "Manage auditing and security log" user right does *not* give you the rights needed to set account policy, to configure user rights, or to enable auditing. Exit User Manager for Domains.

5. Select Start ⇒ Programs ⇒ Administrative Tools (Common) ⇒ Event Viewer.

6. In the Event Viewer dialog box, select Log ⇒ Security.

7. Select Log ⇒ Clear All Events.

8. Click Yes in the Clear Event Log dialog box.

9. In the Save As dialog box, type **old security log** in the File name text box. Click the Save command button.

10. Click the Yes command button to clear the security log. The "Manage auditing and security log" user right authorizes a user to view and change the security log in Event Viewer, and enables a user to configure auditing of files, directories, and printers (in Windows NT Explorer, or in a printer's Properties dialog box, and so forth). But this user right does *not* enable a user to access the Audit Policy dialog box in User Manager or User Manager for Domains.

11. Exit Event Viewer.

Workstation
Server
Enterprise

# Managing User Profiles and System Policy

# About Chapter 9

This chapter explores managing user profiles and system policy in a Windows NT environment.

After a quick look at the benefits of using user profiles, the chapter details the contents of a user profile and the steps involved in creating a user profile. Two special types of user profiles—roaming user profiles and mandatory user profiles—are also discussed.

Next, Chapter 9 focuses on managing system policy, which is actually a collection of user, group, and computer policies. The System Policy Editor is introduced. The section wraps up with an explanation of the systematic manner in which system policy is applied, and step-by-step instructions for creating a system policy file.

Finally, this chapter presents a brief discussion of logon scripts and how to assign a logon script to a user.

This chapter includes two hands-on labs. In the first lab, you create and copy user profiles, and configure roaming and mandatory user profiles. In the second, you create and configure both a Windows 95 system policy and a Windows NT system policy.

Chapter 9 is a "must read," no matter which of the three Windows NT 4.0 Microsoft Certified Professional exams you're preparing for. This chapter maps to the various policies and user profiles objectives in the Managing Resources section in these exams' objectives.

# MANAGING USER PROFILES

In Windows NT, a *user profile* is a collection of settings and options that specify a user's desktop and all other user-definable settings for a user's work environment.

Both users and administrators can benefit from user profiles.

Benefits to users include:

o When a user logs on, the same desktop is displayed as when the user last logged off.

o When there's more than one user on the same computer, a customized desktop is displayed for each at logon.

o Roaming user profiles can be saved on a Windows NT Server computer, and thereby apply to a user no matter which Windows NT computer on the network the user logs on at.

Benefits to administrators include:

o Administrators can develop and assign user profiles that are customized, so each user has a desktop and work environment that complies with established company standards, and can assign user profiles that are suitable for the tasks that each particular user needs to perform.

o If desired or necessary, administrators can forcibly prevent certain users from changing any of their desktop or work environment settings by assigning them mandatory user profiles.

o User profiles make it possible for administrators to assign common program items and shortcuts to all users by customizing the All Users profile folder.

The following sections discuss the contents of a user profile, how a user profile is created, customizing the Default User and the All Users profile folders, roaming and mandatory user profiles, and deleting user profiles.

## Contents of a User Profile

Various settings are saved in a user profile. The contents of a user profile include:

o All user-specific settings for Windows NT Explorer, Notepad, Paint, HyperTerminal, Clock, Calculator, and other built-in Windows NT applications;

o  User-specific desktop settings, including: screen saver, background color, background pattern, wallpaper, and other display settings;

o  User-specific settings for applications written to run on Windows NT;

o  User-specific settings for network drive and printer connections;

o  User-specific settings for the Start menu, including program groups, applications, and recently accessed documents.

A user profile is normally stored in a subfolder of the `<winntroot>\Profiles` folder on the local computer. Each user's profile is stored in a separate folder named after the user's account. For example, the Administrator's user profile is stored in the `<winntroot>\Profiles\Administrator` folder. Figure 9-1 shows, in Windows NT Explorer, the location and contents of the Administrator's profile folder.

 note **All user profiles have the same contents as those shown for the Administrator.**

**FIGURE 9-1**  Contents of the Administrator's profile folder

Note in Figure 9-1 that there are several subfolders and files contained in the Administrator's profile folder. Table 9-1 lists and describes each of these folders and files. All users' profile folders (not just the Administrator's) contain the folders and files listed in Table 9-1.

**TABLE 9-1** WINDOWS NT USER PROFILE FOLDER CONTENTS

| FOLDER OR FILE | DESCRIPTION |
| --- | --- |
| Application Data | This folder contains any user-specific application data that an application vendor has chosen to store here. For example, a word processing application could store the user's custom dictionary in this subfolder. Currently, use of this folder is not widely implemented by application vendors. |
| Desktop | This folder contains all shortcuts, files, and folders stored on the user's desktop. |
| Favorites | This folder contains shortcuts from the user's Favorites folder in various applications. For example, when you add an Internet site to your Favorites folder in Internet Explorer, a shortcut to that site is created in this folder. |
| NetHood | This folder contains any shortcuts a user has created to network servers or shared folders. These shortcuts are displayed in the Network Neighborhood dialog box. |
| Personal | This folder contains any shortcuts a user has created to program items. |
| PrintHood | This folder contains any shortcuts a user has created to network printers. These shortcuts are displayed in the Printers dialog box. |
| Recent | This folder contains shortcuts to document files that the user has recently accessed. These shortcuts can be displayed by selecting Start⇒Documents. |
| SendTo | This folder contains shortcuts to folders, briefcases, mail, and so on. These shortcuts are displayed when a user right-clicks any file or folder, and then selects Send To from the menu that appears. |
| Start Menu | This folder contains the Programs folder from a user's Start menu, and any additional shortcuts to programs that the user has created in the Start Menu folder or any of its subfolders. These shortcuts are displayed in the Start menu, or in the Programs folder in the Start menu, depending on where the shortcut was created. |

*continued*

**TABLE 9-1** *(continued)*

| FOLDER OR FILE | DESCRIPTION |
|---|---|
| Templates | This folder contains shortcuts to template items. |
| Ntuser.dat | This file contains all of the Registry settings that are specific to a user account. When a user logs on, the settings in this file are copied to the HKEY_CURRENT_USER Registry settings on the local computer. |
| ntuser.dat.LOG | This file is used by Windows NT to recover the user's original ntuser.dat file if an error occurs while updating the ntuser.dat file. |

## How a User Profile Is Created

A user profile is created in one of two ways: an Administrator can create a user profile for a new user by copying an existing user profile; or if no user profile exists when a user logs on, Windows NT creates a new user profile for the user. The next section explains how an Administrator can create a user profile by copying an existing user profile.

**TO CREATE A USER PROFILE FOR A NEW USER (OR TO OVERWRITE AN EXISTING USER'S PROFILE) BY COPYING AN EXISTING USER PROFILE, FOLLOW THESE STEPS:**

**1.** Select Start ⇒ Settings ⇒ Control Panel.

**2.** Double-click the System icon.

**3.** In the System Properties dialog box, click the User Profiles tab.

**4.** On the User Profiles tab, highlight the existing user profile that you want to copy. Figure 9-2 shows the User Profiles tab in the System Properties dialog box. Notice that the user profile for ColleenG is highlighted. Click the Copy To command button.

**5.** In the Copy To dialog box, type in the full path to the new user's profile folder. For example, to create a new user profile for FrankG, you might type the path `<winntroot>\Profiles\FrankG` in the Copy profile to text box. (Remember, `<winntroot>` is the drive letter and folder in which you installed Windows NT.) Figure 9-3 shows the Copy To dialog box. Notice the user listed in the Permitted to use section of this dialog box. Click the Change command button.

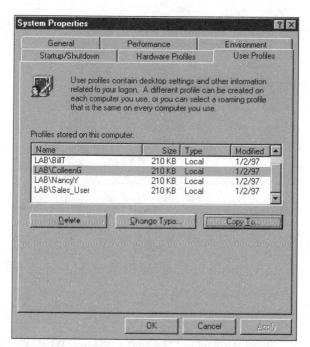

**FIGURE 9-2** Copying an existing user profile

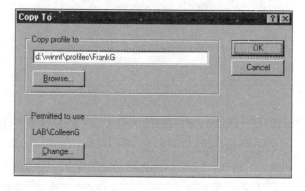

**FIGURE 9-3** Specifying the new user's profile path

**6.** The Choose User dialog box appears. Click the Show Users command button. Scroll down and highlight the new user (FrankG in the previous example), and then click the Add command button. Click OK.

**7.** The Copy To dialog box reappears. Figure 9-4 shows the Copy To dialog box at this point in the process. Notice that FrankG is now permitted to use this profile. Click OK.

**8.** The User Profiles tab reappears. The newly created profile will not appear in the Profiles stored on this computer list box until the new user (FrankG) logs on for the first time. Click OK.

**9.** Exit Control Panel.

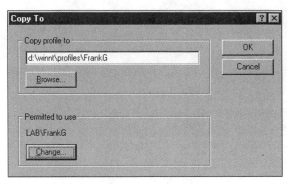

**FIGURE 9-4** New user permitted to use copied profile

 **tip**  **You can't use Windows NT Explorer to copy user profiles. You can only copy user profiles using the System application in Control Panel.**

If no user profile exists when a user logs on, Windows NT creates a new user profile folder for the user by copying the entire contents of the Default User profile folder to a new folder named after the user's account. When Windows NT creates a new user's profile, the new user's initial profile is an exact copy of the Default User profile folder.

The Default User profile folder can also be customized by an Administrator, as described in the next section.

## Customizing the Default User Profile Folder

Administrators can customize the Default User profile folder so new users, at first logon, have the appropriate desktop and work environment settings. For example, you might want to place a shortcut to a network application on the desktop of all new users. Or, you might want to add a shortcut that will appear in the Start menu for all new users.

You can customize the local Default User profile folder on a Windows NT computer, or you can create a domain-wide Default User profile folder for all Windows NT Workstation computers and member servers in a domain. Changes to the local Default User profile folder on a Windows NT computer affect only new users that log on to that computer. The domain-wide Default User profile folder affects all new domain users when they log on to Windows NT Workstation computers (that are domain members) and member servers.

To customize the local `Default User` profile folder on a Windows NT computer, an Administrator can either copy an existing user profile to the local `Default User` profile folder, or create shortcuts in the `Default User` profile subfolders.

---

### TO CREATE SHORTCUTS IN THE DEFAULT USER PROFILE SUBFOLDERS, FOLLOW THESE STEPS:

**1.** Select Start ⇒ Programs ⇒ Windows NT Explorer.

**2.** In the All Folders section of the Exploring dialog box, click the + sign next to the drive letter that you installed Windows NT on. (This is often the C: drive.) Then click the + sign next to the folder in which Windows NT is installed. (This folder is `\Winnt` by default, but you installed Windows NT Server in `\Winntsrv` and Windows NT Workstation in `\Winntwks` in the labs in this book.) Next click the + sign next to the `Profiles` folder, and then click the + sign next to `Default User`. Figure 9-5 shows the `Default User` profile folder in Windows NT Explorer.

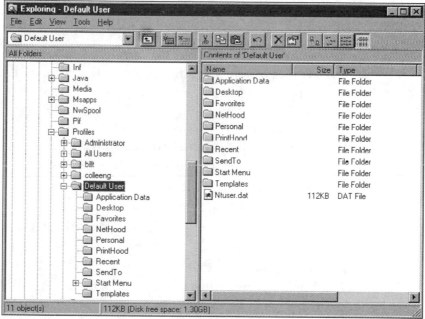

**FIGURE 9-5**  The `Default User` **profile folder**

**3.** Highlight the subfolder of the `Default User` profile folder that you want to create shortcuts in. Select File ⇒ New ⇒ Shortcut

4. In the Create Shortcut dialog box, type in the full path to the application in the Command line text box. Click the Next command button.

5. In the Select a Title for the Program dialog box, type the name of the shortcut the way you want it to appear on the new users' desktops. Click the Finish command button.

6. Repeat Steps 3–5 until you have created all the shortcuts you want in the Default User profile folder. Exit Windows NT Explorer.

To create a domain-wide Default User profile folder for all Windows NT Workstation computers and member servers in a domain, customize and copy an existing user profile to a subfolder named Default User in the <winntroot>\System32\Repl\Import\Scripts folder on the *primary domain controller* (PDC). (Remember, the Import\Scripts folder is shared as Netlogon.)

caution **If you have configured directory replication on your PDC, copy the existing user profile to the** <winntroot>\System32\Repl\Export\Scripts\Default User **folder on the PDC,** *not* **to the** <winntroot>\System32\Repl\Import\Scripts\Default User **folder. If you copy it to the** Import\Scripts **folder and directory replication is configured, the Directory Replicator service will delete any files or folders in the** Import\Scripts **folder that do not exist in the** Export\Scripts **folder.**

To copy an existing user profile, use the steps outlined in the section on "How a User Profile is Created" earlier in this chapter. When choosing the user that is permitted to use this copied profile in the Choose User dialog box, select the Everyone group, and ensure that the Everyone group is listed in the Permitted To Use section of the Copy To dialog box.

After a Default User profile folder is created on the Netlogon share on the PDC, the domain-wide Default User profile folder is available to all Windows NT computers that are members of the domain. When a Windows NT Workstation computer (that is a member of the domain) or a member server is rebooted, it copies the domain-wide Default User profile folder from the PDC to a subfolder named Default User (Network) in its local Profiles folder. This member computer now has two Default User profile folders: one named Default User and one named Default User (Network).

note ✍  **The domain-wide** `Default User` **profile folder is** *not* **copied to the local** `Profiles` **folder on any domain controller in the domain. It is only copied to the local** `Profiles` **folder on non-domain controllers that are members of the domain.**

Figure 9-6 shows the `Profiles` folder and its subfolders on a Windows NT Workstation computer that is a member of the LAB domain. Notice the `Default User` and `Default User (Network)` folders.

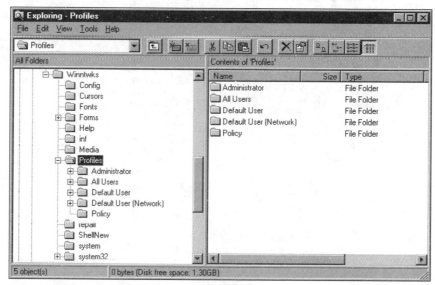

**FIGURE 9-6** Two `Default User` **profile folders on a member computer**

When a user logs on to a member computer that has two `Default User` profile folders by using a *local user account*, and that user does not have a profile folder on this local computer, Windows NT creates a new user profile for the user on the local computer by using the `Default User` profile folder.

When a user logs on to a member computer that has two `Default User` profile folders by using a *user account from the domain*, and that user does not have a profile folder on this local computer, Windows NT creates a new user profile for the user on the local computer by using the `Default User (Network)` profile folder.

# Customizing the All Users Profile Folder

The All Users profile folder is a subfolder of the Profiles folder on all Windows NT computers. The All Users profile folder contains only two subfolders: Desktop and Start Menu. Figure 9-7 shows the All Users profile folder and its subfolders in Windows NT Explorer.

**FIGURE 9-7**  The All Users **profile folder**

The purpose of the All Users profile folder is to enable an administrator to create shortcuts and install applications that are made available to *all*—not just new—users of a particular Windows NT computer. Whenever a user logs on to a Windows NT computer, any shortcuts or applications placed in the Desktop and Start Menu subfolders of the local All Users profile folder appear on the user's desktop and/or Start Menu, as appropriate. Only members of the Administrators group on the local computer can customize the All Users profile folder.

Currently, there is no method to create a domain-wide All Users profile folder on a server. This means that an Administrator must customize the All Users profile folder on each individual Windows NT computer.

To customize the All Users profile folder, follow the same steps you would use to customize the Default User profile folder, except select the All Users profile folder in Windows NT Explorer instead of the Default User profile folder.

## Roaming User Profiles

*Roaming user profiles* are user profiles that are stored on a server. Because these profiles are stored on a server instead of a local computer, they are available to users regardless of which Windows NT computer on the network they log on to.

The benefit of using roaming user profiles is that users retain their own customized desktop and work environment settings even though they may use several different Windows NT computers.

Roaming user profiles are implemented by first creating a shared folder on a server, and then assigning a server-based user profile path to a user account.

**TO IMPLEMENT ROAMING USER PROFILES, FOLLOW THESE STEPS:**

**1.** Choose a server on your network on which to store roaming user profiles. (This is usually the PDC.)

**2.** Create a shared folder on the server. To do this, select Start ⇒ Programs ⇒ Windows NT Explorer.

**3.** In the All Folders section of the Exploring dialog box, highlight one of the drives on the server. (This drive must have enough free space to contain your roaming user profiles.) Select File ⇒ New ⇒ Folder.

**4.** Assign the new folder a name. (I recommend you use the name *Profiles*.) Right-click the newly created folder. Select Sharing from the menu that appears.

**5.** In the Profiles Properties dialog box, select the radio button next to Shared As. Accept the default share name of Profiles in the Share Name text box. Click OK.

**6.** Exit Windows NT Explorer.

**7.** Select Start ⇒ Programs ⇒ Administrative Tools (Common) ⇒ User Manager (or User Manager for Domains).

**8.** In the User Manager dialog box, double-click the user account to which you want to assign a roaming profile.

9. In the User Properties dialog box for that user, click the Profile command button.

10. In the User Profile Path text box in the User Environment Profile dialog box, type in the path to the share that you created in Steps 4 and 5, and append the user name to the end of this path. (For example, on a server named PDCLAB you might use the path `\\pdclab\Profiles\BillT`. If you highlighted multiple users in Step 8, you could use the path `\\server_name\Profiles\%USERNAME%` to assign a unique profile path to each user account. Click OK.

11. In the User Properties dialog box, click OK.

12. Exit User Manager (or User Manager for Domains).

At this point, all you have done is assign a location for the user's roaming user profile. Now the user must log on and log off to create a roaming user profile folder on the server. (When the user logs off, the user's local user profile is saved to the server and becomes the user's roaming user profile.) The roaming user profile is then available to the user from any Windows NT computer to which the user logs on. From this point, every time the user logs off, the user's roaming user profile will be updated with any changes the user has made during the time the user was logged on.

Both new and existing users can be assigned roaming user profiles. If you assign an existing user a roaming user profile, the next time the user logs on and then logs off, the user's local user profile will be copied, intact, at logoff to the server, and will become the user's roaming user profile.

You can also preconfigure a new or existing user's roaming user profile, so that the next time the user logs on, the properties of the preconfigured server-based roaming user profile are applied to the user. The advantage of using preconfigured roaming user profiles is that the administrator can provide users with all the shortcuts and program items users need to perform their day-to-day tasks.

To preconfigure a user's roaming user profile, assign a server-based profile path to a user account, and then copy an existing user profile (that you have customized with all of the shortcuts and applications you want the user to have) to the user's roaming user profile path.

# Mandatory User Profiles

*Mandatory user profiles* are user profiles that, when assigned to a user, cannot be changed by the user. A user can make changes to desktop and work environment settings during a single logon session, but these changes are *not* saved to the mandatory user profile when the user logs off. Each time the user logs on, the user's desktop and work environment settings revert to those contained in the mandatory user profile.

In most cases, an administrator permits users to change and customize their own user profiles. There are instances, however, when you might want to use mandatory user profiles:

o When problem users require a significant amount of administrator time

o When an administrator has a large number of users to administer

Occasionally, a problem user modifies his or her profile so that needed shortcuts and applications are deleted, and the administrator must constantly fix the user's profile by reinstalling the necessary items. After repairing the user's profile, the administrator might choose to assign the user a mandatory user profile. To make an individual user's profile (either local or roaming) a mandatory user profile, rename the user's `Ntuser.dat` file in the user's profile folder as `Ntuser.man`. The mandatory profile becomes effective the next time the user logs on.

Sometimes an administrator needs to create a standardized desktop and work environment for a large number of users with similar job tasks. To accomplish this, the administrator can assign a single, customized mandatory profile to multiple user accounts.

---

**TO ASSIGN A MANDATORY USER PROFILE TO
MULTIPLE USER ACCOUNTS, FOLLOW THESE STEPS:**

**1.** Log on as Administrator. Use User Manager (or User Manager for Domains) to create a new user account. (You will use this user account to create the customized mandatory profile.) Log off.

**2.** Log on as the new user you created in Step 1. Customize desktop and work environment settings as desired. Install shortcuts and applications in the new user's `Start Menu` and `Desktop` folders as desired. (These are subfolders of the user's `Profile` folder.) Log off.

**3.** Log on as Administrator.

**4.** Choose a server on your network on which to store the mandatory user profile. (This is usually the PDC.) In the next steps, you create and share a `Profiles` folder on the server. (If you have already created and shared a `Profiles` folder on your server, skip to Step 10 now.)

**5.** Select Start ⇒ Programs ⇒ Windows NT Explorer.

**6.** In the All Folders section of the Exploring dialog box, highlight one of the drives on the server. (This drive must have enough free space to contain the mandatory user profile.) Select File ⇒ New ⇒ Folder.

**7.** Assign the new folder a name. (I recommend you use the name *Profiles*.) Right-click the newly created folder. Select Sharing from the menu that appears.

**8.** In the Profiles Properties dialog box, select the radio button next to Shared As. Accept the default share name of Profiles in the Share Name text box. Click OK.

**9.** Exit Windows NT Explorer.

**10.** Select Start ⇒ Programs ⇒ Administrative Tools (Common) ⇒ User Manager (or User Manager for Domains).

**11.** In the User Manager dialog box, highlight the first user to whom you want to assign the mandatory user profile. Then press and hold Ctrl while you click each additional user to whom you want to assign the mandatory user profile. When you have selected all the users that you want, select User ⇒ Properties.

**12.** In the User Properties dialog box, click the Profile command button.

**13.** In the User Profile Path text box in the User Environment Profile dialog box, type in the path to the share you created in Steps 7 and 8, and add a subfolder name to the end of this path that describes the group of users the mandatory user profile is being assigned to (such as accountants or sales reps, and so on). An example of a path you might use on a server named PDCLAB when assigning a mandatory profile to several accountants is `\\pdclab\Profiles\accountants`. Click OK.

**14.** In the User Properties dialog box, click OK.

**15.** Exit User Manager (or User Manager for Domains).

**16.** Using the steps to copy a user profile listed in the "How a User Profile is Created" section earlier in this chapter, copy the customized user profile you created in Steps 1 and 2 to the folder specified by the path that you entered in the User Environment Profile dialog box in Step 13. Ensure that the Everyone group is permitted to use the new profile.

**17.** Using Windows NT Explorer, highlight the folder specified by the path you entered in Step 13. Within this folder, rename the `Ntuser.dat` file as `Ntuser.man`. The mandatory profile is assigned, and becomes effective for each assigned user at each user's next logon.

 **If you have a need for the capabilities of mandatory user profiles, consider using a system policy instead. The Windows NT system policy provides the administrator with much more control over users' environment settings than mandatory user profiles. System policy is covered later in this chapter.**

## Deleting User Profiles

You should consider deleting user profiles for user accounts that have been deleted. Deleting a user profile removes the entire user profile folder for the specified user, and also removes any Windows NT Registry entries related to that user profile. Simply deleting the user profile folder by using Windows NT Explorer does *not* completely delete all settings related to the user profile.

**TO DELETE A USER PROFILE, FOLLOW THESE STEPS:**

**1.** Select Start ⇒ Settings ⇒ Control Panel.

**2.** Double-click the System icon in Control Panel.

**3.** Click the User Profiles tab in the System Properties dialog box.

**4.** On the User Profiles tab, highlight the user profile you want to delete. Click the Delete command button.

**5.** In the Confirm Delete dialog box, click the Yes command button.

**6.** On the User Profiles tab, click OK.

**7.** Exit Control Panel.

**exam
preparation
pointer** **Profiles in Windows NT 4.0 have changed significantly from profiles in Windows NT 3.51. Additionally, NT 4.0 now has Windows 95–style system policy. All three exams have objectives covering user profiles. The Server and Enterprise exams also have objectives on system policy. You should become familiar with all of the nuances of user profiles and system policy, when each should be used, which settings take precedence when policies are combined with a user profile, and which settings take precedence when multiple policies apply.**

# MANAGING SYSTEM POLICY

The Windows NT *system policy* file is a collection of user, group, and computer policies. System policy restricts the user's ability to perform certain tasks on any Windows NT computer on the network to which the user logs on. System policy can also be used to enforce certain mandatory display settings, such as wallpaper and color scheme. You can also create a system policy file that applies to users of Windows 95 computers.

System policy, like a mandatory profile, enables an administrator to control the work environment of users on the network. System policy, however, gives the administrator far more configurable options than a mandatory profile. Administrators can use system policy to provide a consistent environment for a large number of users, or to enforce a specified work environment for problem users who demand a significant amount of administrator time.

In addition to enabling the administrator to limit the changes users can make to their work environments, system policy can be used as a security measure to limit access to parts of the network; to restrict the use of specific tools, such as the Registry Editor; and to remove the Run command option from the Start menu.

System policy is managed and configured by using the System Policy Editor. You can use System Policy Editor to create both Windows NT and Windows 95 system policy files. The administrator must create a system policy file—a system policy file is not installed by default.

After a system policy file is created, it should be saved in the `Netlogon` share on each domain controller. When a user logs on to the domain, Windows NT or Windows 95 retrieves the system policy file from the `Netlogon` share on the domain controller that authenticates the user's logon.

Because system policy is comprised of user, group, and computer policies, it can be applied to all users and computers; or it can be applied to individual users, groups, and computers.

## User Policy

A *user policy* is a collection of settings that restrict a user's program and network options and/or enforce a specified configuration of the user's work environment. A user policy is created by an Administrator—it does not exist by default.

There are two types of user policies: an individual user policy and the Default User policy.

An *individual user policy* applies to a single, specific user. Normally, an individual user policy is created only when a user requires a unique policy that differs from any existing Default User or group policy.

The *Default User policy*, contrary to what its name implies, does not exist by default. Rather, it is created when a system policy file is initially created. When the Default User policy is initially created, it doesn't contain any settings that restrict users. The Administrator must configure any desired user restrictions in the Default User policy. The Default User policy applies to a user only if the user does not have an individual user policy.

There are a variety of settings that you can configure in a user policy. Figure 9-8 shows all of the configurable options for a Windows NT individual user policy. The same list of configurable options is available for the Default User policy. Notice the options available in the Desktop and Shell sections.

The actual process of configuring the check boxes in this list is covered in the "Creating a System Policy File" section later in this chapter.

When a user logs on, Windows NT (or Windows 95) permanently overwrites the existing settings in the HKEY_CURRENT_USER section of the Registry on the local computer with the settings contained in the user policy.

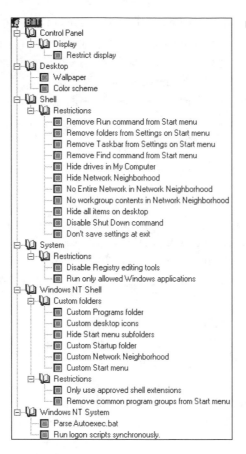

**FIGURE 9-8**  Configurable settings in a Windows NT individual user policy

# Group Policy

A *group policy* is a policy that applies to a group of users. Group policies apply to all users that are members of a group (that has a group policy) and that do not have individual user policies. Group policies have the same configurable options as user policies. Like user policies, group policies don't exist by default — group policies must be created.

A group policy should be created when more than one user requires the same settings. It takes far less time to create one group policy than to create multiple individual user policies.

A user often belongs to multiple groups that have group policies. In this situation, the Administrator can configure group policy priorities. Figure 9-9 shows the Group Priority dialog box in System Policy Editor. Notice the Move Up and Move

Down command buttons that are used to arrange the group priority order. The group at the top of the Group Order list box has the highest priority.

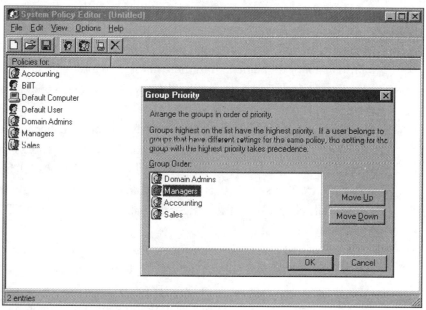

**FIGURE 9-9**   Configuring group priority

Assume that a user named JohnS, a Sales Manager with administrative duties, belongs to three of the groups listed in Figure 9-9: Domain Admins, Managers, and Sales. Also assume that JohnS does *not* have an individual user policy. When JohnS logs on to the domain, the group policy for the Sales group (which has the lowest group priority) is applied first, and then the group policy for the Managers group is applied, and finally the group policy for the Domain Admins group (which has the highest group priority) is applied to JohnS. As each group policy is applied, it overwrites the settings from previously applied group policies. The last group policy applied (the Domain Admins group policy, in this case) takes precedence over the lower priority group policies.

## Computer Policy

A *computer policy* is a collection of settings that specifies a local computer's configuration. A computer policy enforces the specified configuration on all users of a particular Windows NT (or Windows 95) computer. A computer policy is created by an Administrator—it does not exist by default.

There are two types of computer policies: an individual computer policy and the Default Computer policy.

An *individual computer policy* applies to a single, specific computer. Normally, an individual computer policy is created only when a computer requires a unique policy that differs from the Default Computer policy.

The *Default Computer policy*, like the Default User policy, is created when a system policy file is initially created. The Default Computer policy applies to a computer only if the computer does *not* have an individual computer policy.

There are a variety of settings that you can configure in a computer policy. Figure 9-10 shows the configurable options for a Windows NT individual computer policy. The same list of configurable options is available for the Default Computer policy. Notice the options available in the Windows NT System Logon and File system sections.

The actual process of configuring the check boxes in this list is covered in the "Creating a System Policy File" section in this chapter.

When a user logs on, Windows NT (or Windows 95) permanently overwrites the existing settings in the HKEY_LOCAL_MACHINE section of the Registry on the local computer with the settings contained in the computer policy.

## How System Policy Is Applied

A Windows NT system policy is applied to a user or computer in a predefined, systematic manner. When a user logs on, the user's roaming or local profile is applied first, and then the system policy is applied. If settings in the system policy conflict with settings in the user profile, the system policy settings take precedence. System policy is applied in the following sequence:

o If a user has an individual user policy, it is applied.

o If a user does *not* have an individual user policy, and the user is a member of a group that has a group policy, then the group policy (or policies, if the user is a member of multiple groups that have group policies) is applied.

o If a user does *not* have an individual user policy, then the Default User policy is applied. (If a user that does not have an individual user policy has a group policy that conflicts with the Default User policy, then the settings in the Default User policy take precedence.)

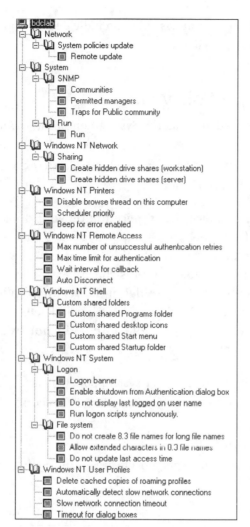

**FIGURE 9-10** **Configurable settings in a Windows NT individual computer policy**

- If the computer the user logs on to has an individual computer policy, it is applied.

- If the computer the user logs on to does *not* have an individual computer policy, then the Default Computer policy is applied.

The end result is that a user has one of the following user/group policy combinations applied: an individual user policy only, a Default User policy only, or a combination of the Default User policy and a group policy (or policies, if the user is a member of multiple groups that have group policies). In addition, the computer to which the user logs on has either an individual computer policy or the Default Computer policy applied.

# Creating a System Policy File

A *system policy file* is created by using the System Policy Editor. After a system policy file is created, it is normally saved in the `Netlogon` share on each domain controller. Only an Administrator can create and save a system policy file to the `NetLogon` share on a domain controller.

 caution **If you have configured directory replication on your domain, copy the system policy file to the** `<winntroot>\System32\Repl\Export\Scripts\` **folder on the PDC,** *not* **to the** `<winntroot>\System32\Repl\Import\Scripts\` **folder that is shared as** `Netlogon`**. If you copy it to the** `Import\Scripts` **folder and directory replication is configured, the Directory Replicator service will delete any files or folders in the** `Import\Scripts` **folder that do not exist in the** `Export\Scripts` **folder.**

The steps for creating a Windows NT system policy file and a Windows 95 system policy file are similar, but have a few important differences.

## *Windows NT system policy*

The following section explains, in detail, how to create and configure a Windows NT system policy file.

**TO CREATE, CONFIGURE, AND SAVE A WINDOWS NT SYSTEM POLICY FILE, FOLLOW THESE STEPS:**

**1.** Select Start⇒ Programs⇒ Administrative Tools (Common)⇒ System Policy Editor.

**2.** In the System Policy Editor dialog box, select Options⇒ Policy Template.

**3.** In the Policy Template Options dialog box, ensure that both the `COMMON.ADM` and `winnt.adm` files are listed. If one of these files is missing, click the Add command button. In the Open Template File dialog box, type **%SystemRoot%\inf\\*filename*** (either `COMMON.ADM` or `winnt.adm`) in the File name text box. Click the Open command button. The Policy Template Options dialog box reappears. (If any files other than

COMMON.ADM and winnt.adm are listed in the Policy Template Options dialog box, highlight the extra file(s), and click the Remove command button.) Click OK.

**4.** In the System Policy Editor dialog box, select File⇒New Policy.

**5.** Two icons are displayed in the System Policy Editor dialog box: Default Computer and Default User. Figure 9-11 shows the System Policy Editor dialog box.

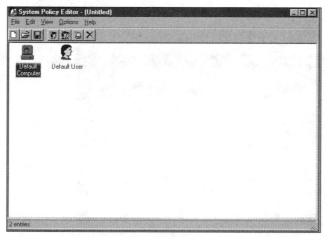

**FIGURE 9-11**   Creating a Windows NT system policy file

**6.** Customize the Default Computer and Default User policies as desired. To customize a policy, double-click the policy icon in the System Policy Editor dialog box. On the Policies tab, click the + sign next to the option that you want to configure. Then configure the check boxes that appear. Each check box has three possible configurations:

o Grayed out—causes the current setting for this option on the local computer to be retained.

o Checked—causes this option to be applied on the local computer.

o Cleared (white)—causes the *opposite* of this option to be applied on the local computer.

Figure 9-12 shows the Policies tab in the Default Computer Properties dialog box. Notice the three check boxes listed under Windows NT Printers. In Figure 9-12, the gray check box next to "Disable browse thread on this computer" causes the current setting for this option on the local computer to be retained. The check in the box next to "Scheduler priority" causes the priority listed in the Settings For Scheduler priority list box to be applied on the local computer. The clear (white) check box next to "Beep for error enabled" causes the "Beep for error" setting to be *disabled* on the local computer. After configuring all check boxes appropriately, click OK.

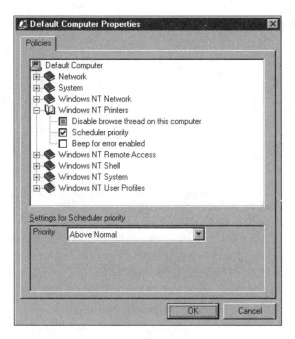

**FIGURE 9-12**  Configuring check boxes for the Default Computer policy

**7.** Create and customize individual user and group policies, and create individual computer policies as desired:

- To create an individual user policy, select Edit⇒Add User in the System Policy Editor dialog box. In the Add User dialog box, type the name of the user you want to create an individual user policy for. Click OK.

- To create a group policy, select Edit⇒Add Group in the System Policy Editor dialog box. In the Add Group dialog box, type the name of the group you want to create a group policy for. Click OK.

- To create an individual computer policy, select Edit⇒Add Computer in the System Policy Editor dialog box. In the Add Computer dialog box, type the name of the computer you want to create an individual computer policy for. Click OK.

To customize your new policies, follow the directions in Step 6.

**8.** After you create and customize all of the user, group, and computer policies, save the system policy file. Select File ⇒ Save As in the System Policy Editor dialog box. Save the file to the `Netlogon` share on all domain controllers as `Ntconfig.pol`. (However, if directory replication is configured on your domain, save the `Ntconfig.pol` file to the `<winntroot>\system32\repl\export\scripts` folder on the PDC instead.)

**9.** Exit System Policy Editor.

---

### *Windows 95 system policy*

To create, configure, and save a Windows 95 system policy file, follow the steps in the previous section on "Windows NT system policy," with the following exceptions:

- In Step 3, substitute the `windows.adm` file for all references to the `winnt.adm` file. In other words, ensure that the `COMMON.ADM` and `windows.adm` file are the only files listed in the Policy Template Options dialog box.

- In Step 8, substitute the `Config.pol` file for all references to the `Ntconfig.pol` file. In other words, save the customized system policy file to the `Netlogon` share on the PDC as `Config.pol`.

Windows 95 system policy can also be configured for load balancing. By default, Windows 95 computers take system policy only from the `Netlogon` share on the PDC. This can place a significant load on the PDC if your network has a large number of Windows 95 computers. To enable Windows 95 computers to take system policy from the domain controller that authenticates the user, configure load balancing for all computer policies (both individual computer policies and the Default Computer policy) in the Windows 95 system policy file.

Figure 9-13 shows load balancing configured for the Windows 95 Default Computer policy. Notice that the check box next to Remote update is checked, and that the check box next to Load balancing (in the Settings For Remote update section) is selected.

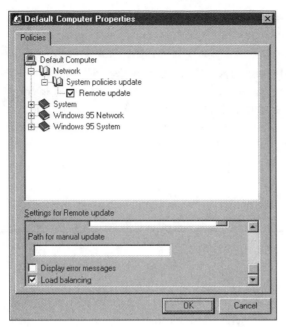

**FIGURE 9-13**   Configuring load balancing for Windows 95 system policy

# LOGON SCRIPTS

A *logon script* is a batch file or executable file that runs during the user's logon process. An administrator can configure logon scripts to connect network drives and printers, or to run a program during logon. Many Windows NT networks don't use logon scripts at all. However, some Microsoft BackOffice products, such as Systems Management Server, use logon scripts extensively.

You can create a logon script by using any text editor, such as Notepad. All MS-DOS 5.0 (and earlier) batch commands can be used in logon scripts. Logon scripts should be saved in the `Netlogon` share on all domain controllers. (Remember, if directory replication is configured on your domain, save the logon script to the `<winntroot>\system32\repl\export\scripts` folder on the PDC instead of the `Netlogon` share on all domain controllers.)

Administrators can assign a unique logon script to each user, or one logon script to multiple users.

**TO ASSIGN A LOGON SCRIPT TO A USER, FOLLOW THESE STEPS:**

1. Select Start ⇒ Programs ⇒ Administrative Tools (Common) ⇒ User Manager (or User Manager for Domains).

2. In the User Manager dialog box, highlight the user(s) you want to assign the logon script to. Select User ⇒ Properties.

3. In the User Properties dialog box, click the Profile command button.

4. In the User Environment Profile dialog box, type the name of the logon script file (*not* the full path) in the Logon Script Name text box. Click OK.

5. In the User Properties dialog box, click OK.

6. Exit User Manager (or User Manager for Domains).

 concept link **For more information on logon scripts, see Logon Scripts and associated topics in the Windows NT Books Online program. Windows NT Books Online is a series of help files that ship with Windows NT Server. To access Books Online on a Windows NT Server computer, select Start ⇒ Programs ⇒ Books Online.**

# KEY POINT SUMMARY

Chapter 9 explored the various types of *user profiles*, and explained the steps involved in creating, customizing, and deleting user profiles. This chapter also covered *Windows NT system policy*, and how system policy is applied and created.

o A *user profile* is a collection of settings and options that specify a user's desktop and all other user-definable settings for a user's work environment. In an environment where user profiles are implemented, when a user logs on, the same desktop is displayed as when the user last logged off, even when more than one user uses the same computer.

  o The contents of a user profile include user-specific settings for: Windows NT Explorer, Notepad, Paint, Calculator, and other built-in NT applications; various display settings; applications written to run on Windows NT; network drive and printer connections; and the Start menu. A user profile is normally stored in a subfolder of the `<winntroot>\Profiles` folder. Each user's profile is stored in a separate folder named after the user's account name.

o  Each user profile folder contains various subfolders and files. Subfolders include: `Application Data`, `Desktop`, `Favorites`, `NetHood`, `Personal`, `PrintHood`, `Recent`, `SendTo`, `Start Menu`, and `Templates`. Files contained in a user profile folder include `Ntuser.dat` and `Ntuser.dat.LOG`.

o  A user profile is created in one of two ways: an Administrator can create a user profile for a new user by using the System application in Control Panel to copy an existing user profile; or if no user profile exists when a user logs on, Windows NT creates a new user profile for the user. *Remember, user profiles are copied by using the System application in Control Panel. You can't use Windows NT Explorer to copy user profiles.*

o  Administrators can customize the `Default User` profile folder so that new users, at first logon, have the appropriate desktop and work environment settings. You can customize the *local* `Default User` profile folder on a Windows NT computer to affect only new users that log on to that computer; or, you can create a *domain-wide* `Default User` profile folder on the `Netlogon` share on the PDC to affect all new domain users when they log on to a member computer.

o  Administrators can customize the `All User` profile folder so that specific shortcuts and applications are made available to *all* users of a particular Windows NT computer. Currently, there is no method available to create a domain-wide `All Users` profile folder on a server.

o  *Roaming user profiles* are user profiles that are stored on a server, and are available to users regardless to which Windows NT computer on the network they log on. Roaming profiles, which can be assigned to new or existing users, make it possible for users to retain their own customized desktop and work environment settings even though they may use different Windows NT computers. Roaming user profiles are implemented by first creating a shared folder on a server, and then assigning a server-based user profile path to a user account. At this point in the process, a location is assigned for the user's roaming user profile, but the roaming user profile is not actually created until the next time the user logs on and logs off. When the user logs off, the user's local profile is saved to the server and becomes the user's roaming profile. From this point on, every time the user logs off, the user's roaming user profile is updated with any changes the user has made during the logon session.

o *Mandatory user profiles*, when assigned to a user, cannot be changed by the user. Although normally administrators permit users to change and customize their own user profiles, administrators may decide to use mandatory user profiles when problem users require a significant amount of administrator time, or when there are a large number of users with similar job tasks to administer. To make an individual user's profile (either local or roaming) a mandatory user profile, rename the user's `Ntuser.dat` file in the user's profile folder as `Ntuser.man`. The mandatory profile becomes effective the next time the user logs on.

o You should consider deleting user profiles for user accounts that have been deleted. Use the System application in Control Panel to delete user profiles, because Windows NT Explorer does not completely delete all settings related to a user profile.

o The *Windows NT system policy file* is an Administrator-created collection of user, group, and computer policies that restrict the user's ability to perform certain tasks on any Windows NT computer to which the user logs on. System policy can also be used to enforce certain mandatory display settings. You can also create a system policy file that applies to users of Windows 95 computers. System policy is created and configured by using System Policy Editor. After a system policy file is created, it should normally be saved in the `Netlogon` share on each domain controller.

o A *user policy* restricts a user's program and network options and/or enforces a specified configuration of the user's work environment. There are two types of user policies: *an individual user policy and the Default User policy*. There are a variety of settings that can be configured in a user policy. When a user logs on, the existing settings in the HKEY_CURRENT_ USER section of the Registry on the local computer are permanently overwritten with the settings contained in the user policy.

o *Group policies* apply to all users that are members of a group (that has a group policy) and that do *not* have individual user policies. If a user belongs to multiple groups that have group policies, an Administrator can configure group policy priorities. When multiple group policies are applied, the group policy of the group that has the *lowest* priority is assigned first. As each next-highest priority group policy is applied, it overwrites settings from previously applied group policies. The last group policy applied takes precedence over the lower priority group policies.

o  There are two types of computer policies: *individual computer policies and the Default Computer policy*. An individual computer policy applies to a single, specific computer. The Default Computer policy applies to a computer only if the computer does *not* have an individual computer policy. When a user logs on, the existing settings in the HKEY_LOCAL_ MACHINE section of the Registry on the local computer are overwritten by the settings contained in the computer policy.

o  When a user logs on, the user's profile is first applied, and then the system policy is applied. If settings in the system policy conflict with settings in the user profile, the system policy settings take precedence. *System policy is applied in the following sequence*:

  o  If a user has an individual user policy, it is applied.

  o  If a user does *not* have an individual user policy, and the user is a member of a group that has a group policy, then the group policy (or policies, if the user is a member of multiple groups that have group policies) is applied.

  o  If a user does *not* have an individual user policy, then the Default User policy is applied. (If a user that does not have an individual user policy has a group policy that conflicts with the Default User policy, then the Default User policy takes precedence.)

  o  If the computer the user logs on to has an individual computer policy, it is applied.

  o  If the computer the user logs on to does *not* have an individual computer policy, then the Default Computer policy is applied.

o  A *logon script* is a batch file or executable file that runs during the user's logon process. Logon scripts can be created with any text editor, such as Notepad. Logon scripts are normally saved in the Netlogon share on all domain controllers. Administrators can assign a unique logon script to each user, or one logon script to multiple users. Many Windows NT networks don't use logon scripts at all.

---

# APPLYING WHAT YOU'VE LEARNED

Now it's time to regroup, review, and apply what you've learned in this chapter.

The questions in the Instant Assessment section that follows bring to mind key facts and concepts.

The hands-on lab exercises will reinforce what you've learned, and give you a chance to practice some of the tasks tested by the Microsoft Certified Professional exams.

## Instant Assessment

1. What is a user profile?

2. Where is a user profile normally stored?

3. What are the subfolders and files contained in a user profile folder?

4. What Windows NT application should you use to copy a user profile?

5. What Windows NT program *can't* you use to copy user profiles?

6. You want all new users, at first logon to a domain member computer, to have the appropriate desktop and work environment settings. What should you do to accomplish this?

7. What is a roaming user profile?

8. What is a logon script?

9. What is a mandatory user profile?

10. Name two situations where the use of mandatory user profiles might be considered.

11. Which file in a user's profile folder must be renamed in order to make the user profile into a mandatory user profile? What must the file be renamed as?

12. What Windows NT application should you use to delete a user profile?

13. What is the Windows NT system policy file?

14. What Windows NT tool is used to create and configure system policy?

15. Where is a system policy file normally saved after it is created?

16. What are the two types of user policies?

17. When multiple group policies are applied, which group policy takes precedence?

18. A user named SusanH has an individual user policy. She is also a member of a group that has a group policy. Which policy is applied to SusanH when she logs on?

19. What are the two types of computer policies?

20. When a user logs on to a Windows NT computer that does *not* have an individual computer policy, what kind of computer policy is applied?

T/F

21. Roaming user profiles can only be assigned to new users. _____

 concept link   **For answers to the Instant Assessment questions see Appendix D.**

## Hands-on Lab Exercises

The following hands-on lab exercises provide you with practical opportunities to apply the knowledge you've gained in this chapter about managing user profiles and Windows NT system policy.

### Lab 9.13 *Implementing user profiles*

Workstation
Server
Enterprise

The purpose of this lab is to give you hands-on experience in creating and copying user profiles, and experience in configuring roaming and mandatory user profiles.

This lab consists of five parts:

Part 1: Creating and sharing a profile's folder
Part 2: Configuring a user profile
Part 3: Copying a user profile
Part 4: Configuring server-based profiles
Part 5: Testing profiles

Begin this lab by booting your computer to Windows NT Server. Log on as Administrator.

Follow the steps below carefully.

### Part 1: Creating and sharing a profile's folder

In this section, you create a shared folder on the PDC that contains users' profiles.

**1.** Select Start ⇒ Programs ⇒ Windows NT Explorer.

**2.** In the All Folders section of the Exploring dialog box, highlight the NTFS volume on your computer—this is most likely drive D:. Select File⇒New⇒Folder.

**3.** In the Contents of the NTFS Volume section, type the new folder name: **Profiles**.

**4.** Right-click the newly created `Profiles` folder. Select Sharing from the menu that appears.

**5.** In the Profiles Properties dialog box, select the radio button next to Shared As. Accept the default Share Name of Profiles. Click OK.

**6.** Notice that a hand appears under the `Profiles` folder in the Exploring dialog box, indicating that it is a shared folder. Exit Windows NT Explorer. Continue to Part 2.

## Part 2: Configuring a user profile

In this section, you configure a profile that will be used by all sales representatives.

**1.** Select Start⇒Programs⇒Administrative Tools (Common)⇒User Manager for Domains.

**2.** In the User Manager dialog box, double-click Sales_User in the Username list box. (You will use this user account to create the profile that you will copy to the user account of each sales representative.)

**3.** In the User Properties dialog box, clear the check boxes next to User Must Change Password at Next Logon and Account Disabled. Select the check box next to Password Never Expires. Click OK.

**4.** Exit User Manager for Domains.

**5.** Select Start⇒Shut Down.

**6.** In the Shut Down Windows dialog box, select the radio button next to "Close all programs and log on as a different user." Click the Yes command button.

**7.** Press Ctrl + Alt + Delete to log on.

**8.** In the Logon Information dialog box, type in a user name of **Sales_User** and a password of **newuser**. Click OK.

**9.** If the Welcome to Windows NT dialog box appears, click the Close command button.

**10.** Right-click the desktop. Select Properties from the menu that appears.

**11.** In the Display Properties dialog box, click the Appearance tab.

**12.** In the Scheme drop-down list box, select the Red, White, and Blue (VGA) scheme. Click the Background tab.

**13.** In the Pattern drop-down list box, select the Scottie pattern. Click OK.

**14.** Right-click the desktop. Select New ⇒ Shortcut from the menus that appear.

**15.** In the Create Shortcut dialog box, type **calc.exe** in the Command line text box. Click the Next command button.

**16.** In the "Select a name for the shortcut" text box, type **Calculator**. Click the Finish command button.

**17.** Right-click the desktop. Select New ⇒ Shortcut from the menus that appear.

**18.** In the Create Shortcut dialog box, type **notepad.exe** in the Command line text box. Click the Next command button.

**19.** In the "Select a name for the shortcut" text box, type **Notepad**. Click the Finish command button.

**20.** Right-click the desktop. Select Arrange Icons ⇒ Auto Arrange from the menus that appear. Notice that the new shortcuts are neatly arranged on your desktop.

**21.** Select Start ⇒ Shut Down.

**22.** In the Shut Down Windows dialog box, select the radio button next to "Close all programs and log on as a different user." Click the Yes command button.

**23.** Press Ctrl + Alt + Delete to log on.

**24.** In the Logon Information dialog box, type in a user name of **Administrator** and a password of **password**. Click OK. Continue to Part 3.

### Part 3: Copying a user profile

In this section, you copy the user profile you created in Part 2 to a profile folder for each sales representative. You also configure one of the sales representative's user profiles as a mandatory user profile.

**1.** Select Start ⇒ Settings ⇒ Control Panel.

**2.** In the Control Panel dialog box, double-click the System icon.

**3.** In the System Properties dialog box, click the User Profiles tab.

**4.** Scroll down the Profiles stored on this computer list box. Select the LAB\Sales_User profile. Click the Copy To command button.

**5.** In the Copy profile to text box, type **\\pdclab\profiles\BillT**. (Don't type the period at the end.) Click the Change command button.

**6.** In the Choose User dialog box, click the Show Users command button. Scroll down the Names list box and select BillT. Click the Add command button. Click OK.

**7.** In the Copy To dialog box, click OK.

**8.** The System Properties dialog box reappears, with LAB\Sales_User highlighted. Click the Copy To command button.

**9.** In the Copy profile to text box, type **\\pdclab\profiles\MikeC**. (Don't type the period at the end.) Click the Change command button.

**10.** In the Choose User dialog box, click the Show Users command button. Scroll down the Names list box and select MikeC. Click the Add command button. Click OK.

**11.** In the Copy To dialog box, click OK.

**12.** The System Properties dialog box reappears, with LAB\Sales_User highlighted. Click the Copy To command button.

**13.** In the Copy profile to text box, type **\\pdclab\profiles\ColleenG**. (Don't type the period at the end.) Click the Change command button.

**14.** In the Choose User dialog box, click the Show Users command button. Scroll down the Names list box and select ColleenG. Click the Add command button. Click OK.

**15.** In the Copy To dialog box, click OK.

**16.** In the System Properties dialog box, click OK.

**17.** Exit Control Panel.

**18.** Select Start ⇒ Programs ⇒ Windows NT Explorer.

**19.** In the All Folders section of the Exploring dialog box, click the + sign next to the NTFS volume (probably drive D:). Click the + sign next to the `Profiles` folder. Highlight the `BillT` folder. In the Contents of BillT section of the dialog box, highlight the `Ntuser.dat` file. Select File ⇒ Rename. Rename the `Ntuser.dat` file as **Ntuser.man**. Press Enter. (Renaming BillT's `Ntuser.dat` file as `Ntuser.man` causes BillT's profile to be a mandatory user profile.)

**20.** Exit Windows NT Explorer. Continue to Part 4.

### Part 4: Configuring server-based profiles

In this section, you configure the user accounts of the sales representatives to use the server-based profiles you created for them in Parts 2 and 3. Additionally, you configure the user accounts of the accounting staff to use roaming user profiles.

**1.** Select Start ⇒ Programs ⇒ Administrative Tools (Common) ⇒ User Manager for Domains.

**2.** In the User Manager dialog box, highlight BillT, and then press and hold Ctrl while you click ColleenG and MikeC in the Username list box. Select User ⇒ Properties.

**3.** In the User Properties dialog box, click the Profile command button.

**4.** In the User Environment Profile dialog box, type **\\pdclab\profiles\ %USERNAME%** in the User Profile Path text box. Click OK. (This step assigns a copied profile to each selected user account.)

**5.** In the User Properties dialog box, click OK.

**6.** In the User Manager dialog box, double-click Sales_User in the Username list box.

**7.** In the User Properties dialog box, select the check box next to Account Disabled. (Remember that in Part 2 you deselected this check box so that you could use the account to create a profile. Now you want to disable the account again so that no one can use it to log on.) Click OK.

**8.** In the User Manager dialog box, highlight MikeCo, and then press and hold Ctrl while you click NancyY. Select User ⇒ Properties.

**9.** In the User Properties dialog box, click the Profile command button.

**10.** In the User Environment Profile dialog box, type **\\pdclab\profiles\ %USERNAME%** in the User Profile Path text box. Click OK. (This step assigns a roaming user profile to MikeCo and NancyY.)

**11.** In the User Properties dialog box, click the Hours command button.

**12.** In the Logon Hours dialog box, highlight the entire chart, so that all hours are selected. Click the Allow command button. (You are changing the hours now in case you're doing this lab during nonbusiness hours. This change permits you to log on as MikeCo or NancyY anytime.) Click OK.

**13.** In the User Properties dialog box, click OK.

**14.** In the User Manager dialog box, select Policies ⇒ User Rights.

**15.** In the User Rights Policy dialog box, select "Shut down the system" from the Right drop-down list box. Click the Add command button.

**16.** In the Names list box (in the Add Users and Groups dialog box), double-click the Everyone group. Click OK.

**17.** In the User Rights Policy dialog box, click OK.

**18.** Exit User Manager for Domains. Continue to Part 5.

### Part 5: Testing profiles

In this section, you try out the sales representatives' profiles, including the mandatory user profile. Additionally, you try out the roaming user profiles for one of the accounting staff.

**1.** Select Start ⇒ Shut Down.

**2.** In the Shut Down Windows dialog box, select the radio button next to "Close all programs and log on as a different user." Click the Yes command button.

**3.** Press Ctrl + Alt + Delete to log on.

**4.** In the Logon Information dialog box, type in a user name of **ColleenG** and a password of **newuser**. Click OK.

**5.** A message appears indicating that you are required to change your password at first logon. Click OK.

**6.** In the Change Password dialog box, type in a new password of **password**, and confirm the new password by retyping it. Click OK.

**7.** A message is displayed, indicating that your password has been changed. Click OK.

**8.** If a Welcome to Windows NT screen appears, deselect the check box next to Show this Welcome Screen next time you start Windows NT, and then click the Close command button.

**9.** Notice that the background pattern (Scottie dogs) and color scheme (Red, white, and blue) that you configured for the Sales_User profile and copied to ColleenG's profile appear on the desktop. Right-click the desktop. Select Properties from the menu that appears.

**10.** In the Display Properties dialog box, select (None) from the Pattern drop-down list box. Select a Wallpaper of lanmannt. Click the Appearance tab.

**11.** In the Scheme drop-down list box, select Rose. Click OK.

**12.** Select Start ⇒ Shut Down.

**13.** In the Shut Down Windows dialog box, select the radio button next to "Close all programs and log on as a different user." Click the Yes command button.

**14.** Press Ctrl + Alt + Delete to log on.

**15.** In the Logon Information dialog box, type in a user name of **ColleenG** and a password of **password**. Click OK.

**16.** Notice that the changes you made to ColleenG's desktop (the rose scheme and the lanmannt wallpaper) appear on the desktop. These settings have been successfully saved to ColleenG's user profile, because her profile is not a mandatory user profile.

**17.** Select Start ⇒ Shut Down.

**18.** In the Shut Down Windows dialog box, select the radio button next to "Close all programs and log on as a different user." Click the Yes command button.

**19.** Press Ctrl + Alt + Delete to log on.

**20.** In the Logon Information dialog box, type in a user name of **BillT** and a password of **newuser**. Click OK.

**21.** A message appears indicating that you are required to change your password at first logon. Click OK.

**22.** In the Change Password dialog box, type in a new password of **password**, and confirm the new password by retyping it. Click OK.

**23.** A message is displayed, indicating that your password has been changed. Click OK.

**24.** If a Welcome to Windows NT screen appears, deselect the check box next to Show this Welcome Screen next time you start Windows NT. Click the Close command button.

**25.** Notice that the background pattern (Scottie dogs) and color scheme (Red, white, and blue) that you configured for the Sales_User profile and copied to BillT's profile appear on the desktop. Right-click the desktop. Select Properties from the menu that appears.

**26.** In the Display Properties dialog box, select Critters from the Pattern drop-down list box. Click the Appearance tab.

**27.** In the Scheme drop-down list box, select Pumpkin (large). Click OK.

**28.** Select Start⇒Shut Down.

**29.** In the Shut Down Windows dialog box, select the radio button next to "Close all programs and log on as a different user." Click the Yes command button.

**30.** Press Ctrl + Alt + Delete to log on.

**31.** In the Logon Information dialog box, type in a user name of **BillT** and a password of **password**. Click OK.

**32.** If a Welcome to Windows NT screen appears, deselect the check box next to "Show this Welcome Screen next time you start Windows NT." Click the Close command button.

**33.** Notice that the desktop changes that you made for BillT's desktop in Steps 26 and 27 were *not* saved to BillT's profile. (This is because in an earlier part of this lab you configured BillT to have a mandatory user profile.) Select Start⇒Shut Down.

**34.** In the Shut Down Windows dialog box, select the radio button next to "Close all programs and log on as a different user." Click the Yes command button.

**35.** Press Ctrl + Alt + Delete to log on.

**36.** In the Logon Information dialog box, type in a user name of **NancyY** and a password of **newuser**. Click OK.

**37.** A Logon Message is displayed, indicating that you are required to change your password at first logon. Click OK.

**38.** In the Change Password dialog box, type in a new password of **password**, and confirm the new password by retyping it. Click OK.

**39.** A message indicating that your password has been changed appears. Click OK.

**40.** If a Welcome to Windows NT screen appears, click the Close command button.

**41.** Right-click the desktop. Select New ⇒ Shortcut from the menus that appear.

**42.** In the Create Shortcut dialog box, type **calc.exe** in the Command line text box. Click the Next command button.

**43.** In the Select a name for the shortcut text box, type **Calculator**. Click the Finish command button.

**44.** Right-click the desktop. Select Arrange Icons ⇒ Auto Arrange.

**45.** Select Start ⇒ Shut Down.

**46.** In the Shut Down Windows dialog box, select the radio button next to "Close all programs and log on as a different user." Click the Yes command button.

**47.** Press Ctrl + Alt + Delete to log on.

**48.** In the Logon Information dialog box, type in a user name of **Administrator** and a password of **password**. Click OK.

**49.** Select Start ⇒ Programs ⇒ Windows NT Explorer.

**50.** In the All Folders section of the Exploring dialog box, click the + sign next to the NTFS volume (probably drive D:). Click the `Profiles` folder. Notice that a profile folder has been created for NancyY. (It Is displayed in the Contents Of Profiles section.) Also notice that there is not a folder for MikeCo, because he has not logged on since you assigned him a roaming profile. Exit Windows NT Explorer.

## Lab 9.14 *Configuring a system policy*

Server
Enterprise

The purpose of this lab is to give you hands-on experience in creating and configuring a Windows 95 system policy; and experience in creating, configuring, and testing a Windows NT system policy.

This lab consists of three parts:

> Part 1: Creating a system policy and configuring load balancing for all Windows 95 computers
>
> Part 2: Creating a system policy for all Windows NT computers
>
> Part 3: Testing the Windows NT system policy

Begin this lab by booting your computer to Windows NT Server. Log on as Administrator.

Follow these steps carefully.

**Part 1: Creating a system policy and configuring
load balancing for all Windows 95 computers**

**1.** Select Start ⇒ Programs ⇒ Administrative Tools (Common) ⇒ System Policy Editor.

**2.** In the System Policy Editor dialog box, select Options ⇒ Policy Template.

**3.** In the Policy Template Options dialog box, click the Add command button.

**4.** In the Open Template File dialog box, type \\**winntsrv\inf\windows.adm** in the File name text box. Click the Open command button.

**5.** The Policy Template Options dialog box reappears. Highlight the `C:\WINNTSRV\INF\Winnt.adm` file. Click the Remove command button. Click OK.

**6.** In the System Policy Editor dialog box, select File ⇒ New Policy.

**7.** Double-click Default Computer.

**8.** On the Policies tab, click the + sign next to Network. Then click the + sign next to System policies update. Select the check box next to Remote update. In the Settings For Remote Update section, select Automatic (use default path) in the Update Mode drop-down list box. Scroll to the bottom of the section, and select the check box next to "Load balancing."

**9.** On the Policies tab, click the + sign next to Windows 95 Network. Then click the + sign next to Microsoft Client for Windows networks. Select the check box next to Log on to Windows NT. In the Settings for Log on to Windows NT section, select the check boxes next to Display domain logon confirmation and Disable caching of domain password. Type **LAB** in the Domain name text box.

**10.** On the Policies tab, click the + sign next to Windows 95 System. Then click the + sign next to Profiles. Select the check box next to "Enable user profiles." Click OK.

**11.** In the System Policy Editor dialog box, double-click Default User.

**12.** On the Policies tab, click the + sign next to Shell. Then click the + sign next to Restrictions. Then select the check boxes next to "Remove Run command from Start menu" and "Don't save settings at exit."

**13.** On the Policies tab, click the + sign next to System. Then click the + sign next to Restrictions. Next, select the check box next to Disable Registry editing tools. Click OK.

**14.** In the System Policy Editor dialog box, select File ⇒ Save As. In the File name text box, type \\**pdclab\repl$\scripts\config**. (Don't type the period at the end.) Click the Save command button.

**15.** In the System Policy Editor dialog box, select File ⇒ Close. Continue to Part 2.

**Part 2: Creating a system policy for all Windows NT computers**

**1.** In the System Policy Editor dialog box, select Options ⇒ Policy Template.

**2.** In the Policy Template Options dialog box, click the Add command button.

**3.** In the Open Template File dialog box, double-click the `Winnt.adm` file.

**4.** In the Policy Template Options dialog box, highlight `C:\WINNTSRV\INF\`
`windows.adm`. Click the Remove command button. Click OK.

**5.** In the System Policy Editor dialog box, select File ⇒ New Policy.

**6.** Double-click Default Computer.

**7.** On the Policies tab, click the + sign next to Windows NT System. Click the
+ sign next to Logon. Then select the check box next to Logon banner.

**8.** On the Policies tab, click the + sign next to Windows NT User Profiles. Then
select the check box next to "Delete cached copies of roaming profiles."

**9.** On the Policies tab, click the + sign next to Windows NT Network. Then
click the + sign next to Sharing. Then select the check box next to "Create
hidden drive shares (server)." Then select the same check box again, so it
turns white (not gray), *without* a check in it. Click OK.

**10.** In the System Policy Editor dialog box, double-click Default User.

**11.** On the Policies tab, click the + sign next to Windows NT System. Then
select the check box next to Parse `Autoexec.bat`. Click OK.

**12.** In the System Policy Editor dialog box, select File ⇒ Save As.

**13.** In the Save As dialog box, type **\\pdclab\repl$\scripts\ntconfig** in the
File name text box. Click the Save command button.

**14.** Exit System Policy Editor.

**15.** Select Start ⇒ Programs ⇒ Windows NT Explorer.

**16.** In the All Folders section of the Exploring dialog box, click the + sign next
to the `Winntsrv` folder. Then click the + sign next to the `System 32`
folder. Next, click the + sign next to the `Repl` folder, and then click the
+ sign next to the `Export` folder. Highlight the `Scripts` folder. Notice
in the Contents of Scripts section that both the policy files you created
(`config.POL` and `ntconfig.POL`) are listed. Click the + sign next to the
`Import` folder. Highlight the `Scripts` folder under `Import`. Wait until
the `ntconfig.POL` file appears (is replicated) to the Contents of Scripts
section.

**17.** Exit Windows NT Explorer. Continue to Part 3.

### Part 3: Testing the Windows NT system policy

**1.** Select Start ⇒ Shut Down.

**2.** In the Shut Down Windows dialog box, select the radio button next to "Close all programs and log on as a different user." Click the Yes command button.

**3.** Press Ctrl + Alt + Delete to log on.

**4.** In the Logon Information dialog box, type in a user name of **Administrator** and a password of **password**. Click OK. (Logging on has implemented the Default Computer and Default User policies. These policies will take effect the next time you log on.)

**5.** Select Start ⇒ Shut Down.

**6.** In the Shut Down Windows dialog box, select the radio button next to "Close all programs and log on as a different user." Click the Yes command button.

**7.** Press Ctrl + Alt + Delete to log on.

**8.** Notice that a logon banner (Important Notice) is displayed. (Remember, you configured a logon banner in Part 2 of this lab.) Click OK.

**9.** In the Logon Information dialog box, type in a user name of **Administrator** and a password of **password**. Click OK. This step completes Lab 9.14.

Enterprise

CHAPTER

# Managing Windows NT Directory Services

# 10

377

# About Chapter 10

This chapter defines and explains Windows NT Directory Services. After a brief overview, trust relationships between domains are discussed extensively. Included in this section are key terms as well as step-by-step instructions for creating one-way and two-way trusts. The chapter then explains the logon process and the part the NetLogon Service plays in this process. Pass-through authentication and synchronization of BDCs with the PDC are also explored.

Next, Chapter 10 outlines the four domain models: the single domain model, the single master domain model, the multiple master domain model, and the complete trust domain model. And finally, the chapter discusses how groups can be used to manage a large number of users in a multiple domain environment.

This chapter includes a review activity on planning as well as two hands-on labs. In the first lab you implement one-way and two-way trust relationships between two domains. In the second, you plan a Directory Services architecture and trust relationship for a given situation. Chapter 10 is optional if you're preparing for the Workstation or Server exams, but essential if you're preparing for the Enterprise exam. This chapter maps to the "Plan the implementation of a directory services architecture" objective in the Planning section in the Enterprise exam's objectives.

# OVERVIEW OF WINDOWS NT DIRECTORY SERVICES

*Windows NT Directory Services* refers to the architecture, features, functionality, and benefits of Windows NT domains and trust relationships. Windows NT Directory Services (often referred to simply as Directory Services), as implemented in Windows NT 4.0, is not X.500-compliant. However, Microsoft plans to release a new version of Windows NT Directory Services, called the *Active Directory*, that will be X.500-compliant in a future release of Windows NT.

The primary benefits of Directory Services, as implemented in NT 4.0, include the following:

o A single user account logon and password are used to gain access to all shared resources on the network. In a Windows NT Directory Services environment, users are not required to remember different user names and passwords for each network resource that they access.

o User and group accounts, as well as shared network resources, can be managed from a central location. Administrators are not required to log on to multiple computers to manage accounts and shared resources.

exam preparation pointer

**The concepts presented in this chapter form the foundation for a large portion of the Windows NT Server 4.0 Enterprise exam. Don't even *think* about attempting to pass this exam until you've completely mastered trusts, domain models, and using groups in a multiple domain environment.**

In the Directory Services architecture, domains contain logical groupings of user and group accounts, computers, and shared resources. A large company might have more than one domain in its Directory Services architecture. The next section examines how trust relationships are used to manage interaction between multiple domains.

# TRUST RELATIONSHIPS

To manage the interaction between multiple domains, trust relationships are necessary. *Trust relationships* enable users from one domain to access shared resources located in other domains.

Without trust relationships, the benefits of single user account logon and centralized administration would not be possible. If no trust relationship exists between two domains, users would have to have user accounts (and passwords) in both domains to access shared resources in both domains.

The terminology used to discuss trusts is sometimes confusing, so the next section is dedicated to explaining and clarifying these terms. Once you've mastered the terminology, trust concepts are much easier to understand.

# Trust Terminology

Two primary terms are used to refer to a trust relationship between two domains: trusting domain and trusted domain.

Trusting domain—The *trusting domain* is the domain that has *resources* to share with user accounts in the trusted domain. The trusting domain trusts the trusted domain.

Trusted domain—The *trusted domain* is the domain that contains the *user accounts* that want to access resources in the trusting domain. The trusted domain is trusted by the trusting domain.

exam
preparation
pointer

**This terminology is used extensively in Microsoft product documentation and on the Microsoft Certified Professional exams. Memorize these terms so that you are clear as to which domain contains the resources and which domain contains the user accounts.**

A trust relationship between two domains is depicted in diagrams by using an arrow to point from the trusting (resource) domain to the trusted (accounts) domain. Remember that the arrow points toward the accounts domain.

Figure 10-1 depicts a trust relationship between the EAST domain and the WEST domain. The EAST domain is the trusted domain, and the WEST domain is the trusting domain. Notice that the arrow points toward the EAST domain, where the user accounts are stored. Users from the EAST domain are able to access shared resources on computers located in the WEST domain.

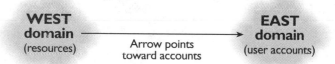

**WEST domain** (resources) — Arrow points toward accounts → **EAST domain** (user accounts)

**FIGURE 10-1**  The WEST domain trusts the EAST domain

Many people are confused by the arrows used to depict trust relationships. It often seems more natural to have the arrow point toward the shared resource, because the resource is the object that users want to access. The opposite is true. The arrow points away from the resource, and the arrow points toward the user accounts. Always follow the arrow to determine the location of the user accounts.

# One-way Trusts

When a single trust relationship exists between two domains, it is called a *one-way* trust.

Figure 10-1 is an example of a one-way trust, in which the WEST domain trusts the EAST domain. In this example, users from the EAST domain are able to access resources in both the EAST and WEST domains. However, the trust is one-way only, and, therefore, users in the WEST domain are able to access resources in the WEST domain only.

It is necessary to configure both domains to establish a trust relationship. Only an Administrator can establish a trust relationship.

## *Steps to create a one-way trust*

Creating a one-way trust is a two-part process. In the first part of the process you configure the trusted domain to allow the trusting domain to trust it. In the second part, you configure the trusting domain to trust the trusted domain.

--------------------------------〈〉--------------------------------

**TO CREATE A ONE-WAY TRUST, FOLLOW THESE STEPS:**

**Part 1**    On a computer in the domain that will be the trusted domain, that is, the domain that contains the user accounts, perform the following steps:

1. Select Start ⇒ Programs ⇒ Administrative Tools (Common) ⇒ User Manager for Domains (*not* User Manager).

2. In the User Manager dialog box, select Policies ⇒ Trust Relationships.

3. In the Trust Relationships dialog box, click the Add command button next to the Trusting Domains list box.

4. In the Add Trusting Domain dialog box, type the name of the trusting domain and an initial password to create the trust relationship. (The other domain will enter this password when the trust relationship is configured on its PDC.) Confirm the password.

   Figure 10-2 shows the Add Trusting Domain dialog box for the EAST domain. In these steps, the EAST domain is being configured to allow WEST domain to trust it. (The EAST domain will be the trusted domain, and the WEST domain will be the trusting domain.)

   Click OK.

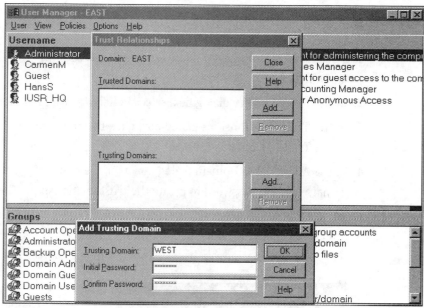

**FIGURE 10-2** Configuring the trusted domain

**5.** In the Trust Relationships dialog box, the name of the trusting domain that you entered in Step 4 appears in the Trusting Domains list box.

Figure 10-3 shows the Trust Relationships dialog box for the EAST domain. Notice that the WEST domain is listed in the Trusting Domains list box. This means the EAST domain allows the WEST domain to trust it.

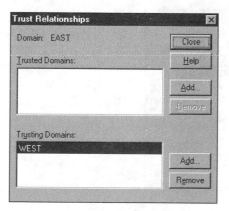

**FIGURE 10-3** Completing the configuration of the trusted domain

Click the Close command button.

**6.** Exit User Manager for Domains.

**Part 2**    On a computer in the domain that will be the trusting domain, that is, the domain that contains the resources, perform the following steps:

1. Select Start⇒Programs⇒Administrative Tools (Common)⇒User Manager for Domains (*not* User Manager).

2. In the User Manager dialog box, select Policies⇒Trust Relationships.

3. In the Trust Relationships dialog box, click the Add command button next to the Trusted Domains list box.

4. In the Add Trusted Domain dialog box, type the name of the trusted domain and the password to create the trust relationship. (The password is the password that was entered in Step 4 in Part 1 of this process.) Click OK.

5. After a few moments a dialog box appears, as shown in Figure 10-4. Notice that the trust relationship has been successfully established. Click OK.

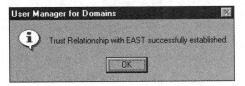

**FIGURE 10-4**  **Trust relationship established**

6. The Trust Relationships dialog box reappears, as shown in Figure 10-5. Notice that the EAST domain is listed in the Trusted Domains list box. This means the WEST domain trusts the EAST domain.

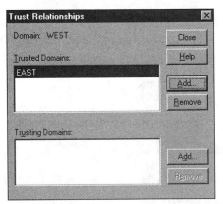

**FIGURE 10-5**  **The WEST domain trusts the EAST domain**

   Click the Close command button.

7. Exit User Manager for Domains.

tip   **I recommend you always configure the trusted domain first, and then configure the trusting domain when establishing a trust relationship. If you configure the domains in the reverse order, the dialog box shown in Figure 10-6 will be displayed. The trust relationship will usually be established within a few minutes.**

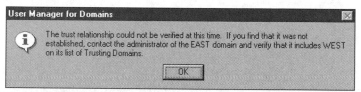

**FIGURE 10-6**   **Result of configuring domains in reverse order when establishing a trust**

## Two-way Trusts

Sometimes it is advantageous to configure two domains to trust each other. For example, you may want to permit users from two different domains to access resources located in both domains.

When two domains trust each other, the configuration is referred to as a *two-way trust*. A two-way trust is really two one-way trusts, and is depicted in diagrams by two arrows between the two domains.

Figure 10-7 shows a two-way trust. Notice that a two-way trust is depicted as two one-way trusts. In this example, a two-way trust exists between the SALES domain and the SERVICE domain. Both domains contain user accounts and resources.

**FIGURE 10-7**   **A two-way trust**

As with one-way trusts, you must configure both domains to establish a two-way trust relationship.

### Steps to create a two-way trust

Assume you want to create a two-way trust between two domains in your company, the SALES domain and the SERVICE domain.

Creating a two-way trust between the SALES domain and the SERVICE domain is a three-step process, as the following section explains.

**TO CREATE A TWO-WAY TRUST, FOLLOW THESE STEPS:**

1. Configure the SALES domain to allow the SERVICE domain to trust it. To do this, follow the steps in Part 1 in the "Steps to create a one-way trust." Figure 10-8 shows the SALES domain configured to allow the SERVICE domain to trust it.

**FIGURE 10-8**  First step in creating a two-way trust

2. Configure the SERVICE domain to trust the SALES domain, and also to allow the SALES domain to trust the SERVICE domain. To do this, follow the steps in Part 2 in the "Steps to create a one-way trust," and then perform the steps in Part 1 in the "Steps to create a one-way trust." Figure 10-9 shows the SERVICE domain configured to trust the SALES domain, and also to allow the SALES domain to trust it.

3. Configure the SALES domain to trust the SERVICE domain. To do this, follow the steps in Part 1 in the "Steps to create a one-way trust." This completes the creation of a two-way trust between the SALES domain and the SERVICE domain. The SALES domain now trusts the SERVICE domain, and the SALES domain allows the SERVICE domain to trust it, as shown in Figure 10-10.

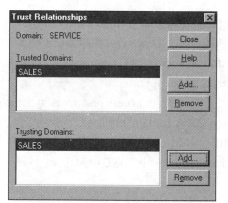

**FIGURE 10-9**  **Second step in creating a two-way trust**

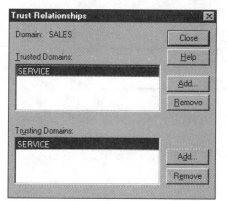

**FIGURE 10-10**  **Two-way trust established between the SALES domain and the SERVICE domain**

# Trusts Are Non-transitive

Trust relationships between domains are *non-transitive*, which means that trusts apply *only* to the domains they are established between (they do not extend to other domains. For example, suppose that the A domain trusts the B domain. Further suppose that the B domain trusts the C domain. Figure 10-11 shows these trust relationships.

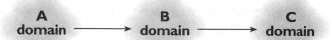

**FIGURE 10-11**  **Trusts between the A, B, and C domains**

At first glance, it might appear that user accounts in the C domain are able to access resources in the A domain. This is *not* the case. A trust relationship does not exist between the A domain and the C domain. Therefore, users in the C domain *can't* access resources in the A domain.

To enable users in the C domain to access resources in the A domain, a trust must be established between the A domain and the C domain. Figure 10-12 shows the three domains after the additional trust is established. Notice that the A domain now trusts the C domain. Users in the C domain can now access resources in the A domain.

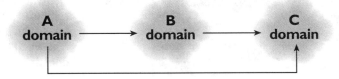

**FIGURE 10-12**   **Trust established between the A domain and the C domain**

# Logging On

When a user logs on to a Windows NT computer or domain, the logon process is managed by the NetLogon Service. The following sections explain the purpose and function of this service, and provide several detailed examples of the logon process.

## The NetLogon Service

The *NetLogon Service* is installed automatically during the installation of Windows NT. The service is configured, by default, to start automatically every time Windows NT is booted.

The NetLogon Service in Windows NT is responsible for managing the logon process, pass-through authentication, and synchronization of the *backup domain controllers* (BDCs) with the *primary domain controller* (PDC) within a domain.

## The logon process

To understand the nuances of the logon process, it's helpful to have an understanding of the Windows NT *Security Accounts Manager* (SAM) database.

Windows NT assigns every user account, group account, and computer account a unique *security identifier* (SID). All account information, including user names, passwords, group memberships, and SIDs are stored in a domain database called the SAM database. This database is created originally on the domain's PDC (and on each local Windows NT computer that is a non-domain controller). The SAM is stored in the `<winntroot>\System32\Config` folder.

> note
> **Several terms are used to refer to the domain SAM. The most commonly used terms include Windows NT Directory Services database, Directory Services database, domain directory database, and directory database. All of these terms are interchangeable and refer to the Security Accounts Manager (SAM) database. I've tried to use *SAM* to refer to the Security Accounts Manager (SAM) database on all non-domain controllers, and the term *Directory Services database* to refer to the common Security Accounts Manager (SAM) database on domain controllers.**

Here's how SIDs, the SAM, and the NetLogon Service interact when you log on to a Windows NT Workstation computer using a local user account:

o You begin the logon process by pressing Ctrl + Alt + Delete. The Logon Information dialog box appears, prompting you to enter a user name and password. If the Windows NT Workstation computer is a member of a domain, an additional Domain drop-down list box is displayed. In the Domain drop-down list box, you can choose to log on using a user account from the domain or using a user account on the local computer. In this example, you are logging on using a user account on the local computer.

o When you click OK in the Logon Information dialog box, Windows NT provides your logon information (user name, password, and domain/local computer name) to the NetLogon Service. The NetLogon Service determines whether you are logging on using a user account on the local computer or a user account from the domain. In this example, you are logging on using a user account on the local computer. The NetLogon Service queries the local SAM to determine if your user account and password is valid. If your user name and password are validated, the NetLogon Service retrieves your user account's SID, and the SIDs for each group of which you are a member. The NetLogon Service combines your user and group SIDs to create an *access token*.

o   The NetLogon Services completes the logon process for you.

For the rest of the logon session, Windows NT uses your access token to determine whether you can access resources. Every time you attempt to access a resource (such as a folder or a printer), Windows NT compares the SIDs in your access token to the SIDs contained in the *access control list* (ACL) for the resource you want to access. If the SIDs in your access token are listed in the ACL for the resource, you are granted access to the resource.

Anytime a user logs on to a Windows NT computer using a user account that is *not* contained in the local computer's SAM, pass-through authentication is used to validate the user.

### Pass-through authentication

*Pass-through authentication* enables a user to log on to a Windows NT computer by using a user account from the domain or from a trusted domain. Without pass-through authentication, the single user account logon/single password feature of Directory Services would not be possible.

Pass-through authentication occurs when a user account can't be validated by the NetLogon Service on the local computer. The NetLogon Service on the local computer forwards (passes-through) the logon request (and logon information) to the NetLogon Service on a Windows NT Server domain controller for validation. The domain controller validates the user account and passes the appropriate SIDs back to the NetLogon Service on the local computer to which the user is logging on. The NetLogon Service on the local computer completes the user's logon and creates the user's access token. The following examples show how pass-through authentication works.

**Example 1: Logging on by using a user account from the domain**    Assume a user logs on to a Windows NT Workstation computer, which is a member of the WEST domain, by using a user account from the WEST domain. Figure 10-13 depicts this scenario.

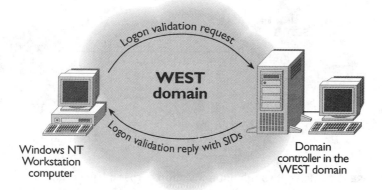

**FIGURE 10-13**   Pass-through authentication in a single domain environment

- The user enters a user name, password, and domain name in the Logon Information dialog box.

- The local NetLogon Service determines that the user account is not in the local computer's SAM, and forwards (passes-through) the logon request to a domain controller (in the WEST domain) for validation.

- The NetLogon Service on the domain controller verifies the user account and password, and retrieves the user and group SIDs for that user account from the Directory Services database.

- Then the NetLogon Service on the domain controller passes the SIDs to the NetLogon Service on the Windows NT Workstation computer, where the local NetLogon Service completes the logon process for the user.

**Example 2: Logging on using a user account from a trusted domain**
Assume a user who normally works in a company's Dallas office is visiting the company's Seattle office. This user logs on to a Windows NT Workstation computer in the SEATTLE domain by using a user account from the DALLAS domain. The SEATTLE domain trusts the DALLAS domain. Figure 10-14 depicts this scenario.

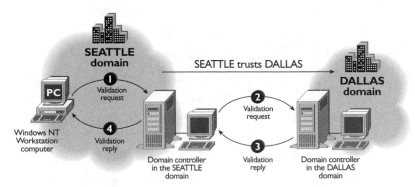

**FIGURE 10-14**   **Pass-through authentication across a trust relationship**

Here are the steps that take place to authenticate the user when the user logs on across a trust:

o  The user begins the logon process at the Windows NT Workstation computer located in the SEATTLE domain by entering a user name, password, and domain name in the Logon Information dialog box. (The user enters a domain name of DALLAS to indicate which domain contains the user's account.) The local NetLogon Service determines that the user account is not in the local computer's SAM, and forwards (passes-through) the logon request to a domain controller in the SEATTLE domain for validation.

o  The NetLogon Service on the domain controller in the SEATTLE domain forwards (passes-through) the logon request to a domain controller in the DALLAS domain for validation.

o  The NetLogon Service on the domain controller in the DALLAS domain verifies the user account and password, and retrieves the user and group SIDs for that user account from the Directory Services database. Then the NetLogon Service on the DALLAS domain controller passes the SIDs to the NetLogon Service on the SEATTLE domain controller.

o  The NetLogon Service on the SEATTLE domain controller passes the SIDs to the NetLogon Service on the Windows NT Workstation computer, where the local NetLogon Service completes the logon process for the user.

note 🖉  **In Windows NT, all pass-through authentication requests and validation replies are sent over the network in an encrypted format.
User names and passwords are never sent over the network in clear
(unencrypted) text. This security feature discourages unauthorized
persons from using network analyzer-type tools in an attempt to
gather password and user account information on a Windows NT
network.**

## Synchronization of BDCs with the PDC

Another function of the NetLogon Service is to periodically copy Directory
Services database update information from the PDC to each BDC in the domain.
This process is called *synchronization*.

To begin the synchronization process, the PDC notifies each BDC that the
Directory Services database on the PDC has been updated. Each BDC then con-
tacts the PDC to obtain the changes necessary to update the BDC's copy of the
PDC's Directory Services database.

concept link   **Managing the synchronization process is covered in more detail in
Chapter 11.**

# DIRECTORY SERVICES ARCHITECTURE

Domains are the basic unit that comprise Directory Services architecture. They
contain logical groupings of user and group accounts, computers, and shared
resources. Domains can be structured and combined in various architectures,
called *domain models*.

Many factors must be considered when planning a Directory Services architecture. Some of these factors include the total number and location of users in
the organization; the number, types, and location of computers and shared
resources; whether centralized or decentralized network management is desired;
and the needs of departments within the organization. The Directory Services
architecture an organization chooses must meet the needs and characteristics of
that organization.

There are four domain models: the single domain model, the single master domain model, the multiple master domain model, and the complete trust domain model. An organization can choose any one of these four models, or it can implement a hybrid combination of two or more models.

## Single Domain Model

The *single domain model* is the most straightforward of the four domain models. It consists of one domain and does not use trust relationships. All user accounts, group accounts, computer accounts, and shared resources are contained in a single domain.

The single domain model is ideal for the small- to medium-sized organization that wants to use centralized network administration. It can by used by organizations that have multiple locations. Although many organizations choose to implement multiple domains when they have multiple locations, it is not a requirement.

The single domain model does have limitations. It can accommodate a maximum of 40,000 user accounts. However, if the domain contains computer accounts and an appropriate number of group accounts, the practical limitation for a single domain is about 26,000 user accounts. If an organization has more than 26,000 user accounts, it should use another domain model. Another limitation of the single domain model is that browsing can be slow if there are a large number of shared resources, or if shared resources are in geographically diverse locations connected by slow WAN links.

## Single Master Domain Model

The *single master domain model* consists of one master domain that contains all user accounts and one or more domains that contain shared resources. This domain model uses one-way trusts from each resource domain to the master domain.

Figure 10-15 depicts the single master domain model. Notice the one-way trust relationships between the domains. The master domain is the trusted domain, and the resource domains are the trusting domains. All user accounts are contained in the master domain.

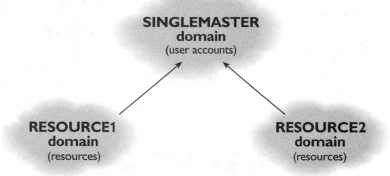

FIGURE 10-15 The single master domain model

The single master domain model is ideal for small- to medium-sized organizations that want to subdivide administration of resources along geographic or departmental lines. This model enables user accounts to be managed centrally, but provides for regional or departmental control over shared resources.

The single master domain model, like the single domain model, is limited to a maximum of 40,000 user accounts.

 concept link **For more information on how to determine the number of user accounts, computer accounts, and group accounts that a domain can accommodate, see Chapter 11.**

## Multiple Master Domain Model

The *multiple master domain model* consists of two or more master domains that contain user accounts and any number of domains that contain shared resources. In this model, a two-way trust is used between each of the master domains, and one-way trusts are used from each resource domain to each and every master domain.

Figure 10-16 depicts the multiple master domain model. Notice the configuration of trust relationships in the diagram.

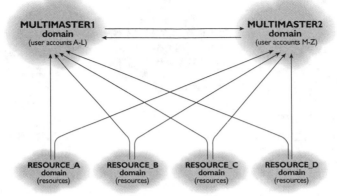

**FIGURE 10-16**   The multiple master domain model

There are various ways to distribute user accounts among the two or more master domains. You can distribute user accounts by any of the following:

o  Division or department

o  Geographic location, such as by city or region

o  Alphabetically, by user account name or by the user's actual name

o  Using any hybrid combination of the aforementioned

The multiple master domain model can be scaled to match any size organization. There is no practical limitation on the number of user accounts an organization can have, because an additional master domain can always be added.

Because of the two-way trust that exists between the master domains, user account administration can be centralized, or it can be distributed among multiple administrators. In the multiple master domain model, management of shared resources can be distributed by geographic location or by department.

This domain model is the preferred model by the majority of large organizations, because of its practicality and scaleability.

## Complete Trust Domain Model

The *complete trust domain model* is a decentralized model that consists of two or more domains that contain user accounts and shared resources. A two-way trust relationship exists between each and every domain.

Figure 10-17 depicts the complete trust domain model. Notice the configuration of trust relationships in the diagram.

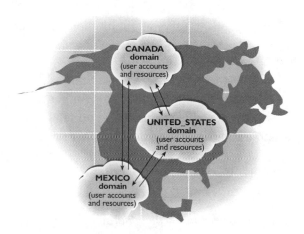

**FIGURE 10-17**  The complete trust domain model

Figure 10-17 shows a total of three domains and six trust relationships. This looks fairly easy to manage upon first glance, but as the number of domains increases, the number of trusts also increases—often to an excessive number. The number of trust relationships required to implement this domain model can be computed by using the formula $n \times (n - 1)$, where $n$ equals the number of domains. A complete trust domain model consisting of four domains requires twelve trust relationships, a complete trust domain model consisting of five domains requires twenty trust relationships, and a complete trust domain model consisting of ten domains requires ninety trust relationships.

Organizations that require decentralized management of user accounts and shared resources can choose the complete trust domain model. However, because of the excessive number of trusts required, this model is *not* recommended.

Besides the number of trusts involved, another drawback of this model is that managers of shared resources must trust administrators of other domains to place only appropriate users in each global group that has permissions to the shared resources they manage.

Because multiple domain environments often involve many users, it's imperative that you understand how to place users into groups appropriately and manage these groups to streamline the administration of your network.

# USING GROUPS TO MANAGE USERS IN A MULTIPLE DOMAIN ENVIRONMENT

The easiest way to manage many users in a multiple domain environment is through groups. Groups enable the administrator to assign rights and permissions to multiple users efficiently.

 concept link **Groups were introduced and discussed in detail in Chapter 7. If it's been a while since you studied Chapter 7, you may want to refresh your understanding of how group accounts are used.**

Groups are commonly used in the following way in a multiple domain environment:

o First, *user accounts* are placed into a *global group* in the trusted domain.

o Next, this global group, which can cross trust relationships to other domains, is made a member of a *local group* in the trusting domain.

o Finally, the local group in the trusting domain is assigned *permissions to a shared resource* in the trusting domain, so that all of the local group's members can access the shared resource.

Figure 10-18 shows how groups are used in a multiple domain environment. Notice the flow of the process: user accounts are made members of a global group in the CALIFORNIA domain. This global group can cross the trust to the ILLINOIS domain. Then the global group is made a member of a local group in the ILLINOIS domain, which is then assigned permissions to a shared printer in the ILLINOIS domain.

Keep in mind that local groups can be assigned permissions only to resources within a single domain. However, global groups can cross trust relationships to other domains. Occasionally a single user account within a domain may be made a member of a local group in another domain. This is possible because user accounts, like global groups, can also cross trust relationships to other domains.

To cement your understanding of how groups can be used to manage users in multiple domain environments, two example applications are presented in the following section.

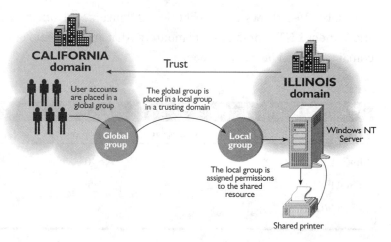

**FIGURE 10-18**   Using groups to manage users in a multiple domain environment

# Example 1: Using Global Groups and Built-in Groups in a Single Master Domain Model

Assume you are an administrator of a Windows NT network that uses the single master domain model. Your organization's domain model is shown in Figure 10-19. Notice the trust relationships between the resource domains and the master domain. Also notice the location of the user accounts.

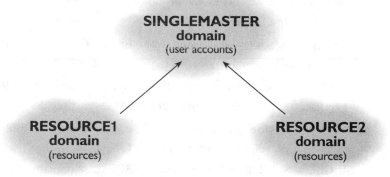

**FIGURE 10-19**   Domain model for Example 1

Table 10-1 shows the distribution of domain controllers, member servers, and Windows NT Workstation computers (that are members of their respective domains) in each of the three domains.

| TABLE 10-1 COMPUTER DISTRIBUTION IN EXAMPLE 1 | | | |
|---|---|---|---|
| *DOMAIN* | *# DOMAIN CONTROLLERS* | *# MEMBER SERVERS* | *# NT WORKSTATIONS* |
| SINGLEMASTER | 3 | 10 | 50 |
| RESOURCE1 | 2 | 5 | 100 |
| RESOURCE2 | 2 | 2 | 100 |

You have been assigned the job of creating a single global group that has rights to restore files to all domain controllers, all member servers, and all Windows NT Workstation computers in all three domains.

You accomplish this task by doing the following:

o Creating one global group, called Restore, in the SINGLEMASTER domain. You assign the appropriate user accounts to this global group.

o Placing the Restore global group in the Backup Operators built-in local group (which has the rights to *restore* as well as backup files) in the SINGLEMASTER, RESOURCE1, and RESOURCE2 domains. (This enables members of the Restore global group to restore files to all of the domain controllers in all three domains.)

o Placing the Restore global group in the Backup Operators built-in local group on *each* member server in the SINGLEMASTER, RESOURCE1, and RESOURCE2 domains. (This enables members of the Restore global group to restore files to all of the member servers in all three domains.)

o Placing the Restore global group in the Backup Operators built-in local group on *each* Windows NT Workstation computer in the SINGLEMASTER, RESOURCE1, and RESOURCE2 domains. (This enables members of the Restore global group to restore files to all of the Windows NT Workstation computers in all three domains.)

# Example 2: Using Global Groups and Built-in Groups in a Multiple Master Domain Model

Assume you are the lead administrator of a Windows NT network that uses the multiple master domain model. Your company's domain model is shown in Figure 10-20. Notice the trust relationships between the resource domains and the master domains. Also notice the location of the user accounts.

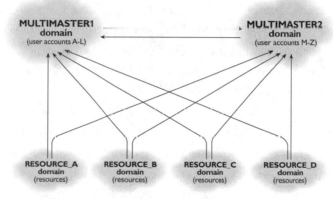

**FIGURE 10-20** Domain model for Example 2

Table 10-2 shows the distribution of domain controllers, member servers, and Windows NT Workstation computers (that are members of their respective domains) in each of the six domains.

| DOMAIN | # DOMAIN CONTROLLERS | # MEMBER SERVERS | # NT WORKSTATIONS |
|---|---|---|---|
| MULTIMASTER1 | 6 | 2 | 25 |
| MULTIMASTER2 | 6 | 2 | 75 |
| RESOURCE_A | 3 | 3 | 100 |
| RESOURCE_B | 4 | 11 | 400 |
| RESOURCE_C | 2 | 7 | 300 |
| RESOURCE_D | 2 | 9 | 350 |

**TABLE 10-2** COMPUTER DISTRIBUTION IN EXAMPLE 2

You have decided that your company needs a global group in each master domain that has rights to restore files to all domain controllers, all member servers, and all Windows NT Workstation computers in all six domains. You accomplish this rather large task by doing the following:

o  Creating a global group called Master1Restore in the MULTIMASTER1 domain, and creating another global group called Master2Restore in the MULTIMASTER2 domain. You assign the appropriate user accounts to these global groups.

o  Placing the Master1Restore and the Master2Restore global groups in the Backup Operators built-in local group (which has the rights to *restore* as well as backup files) in the MULTIMASTER1, MULTIMASTER2, RESOURCE_A, RESOURCE_B, RESOURCE_C, and RESOURCE_D domains. (This enables members of the Master1Restore and Master2Restore global groups to restore files to all of the domain controllers in all six domains.)

o  Placing the Master1Restore and the Master2Restore global groups in the Backup Operators built-in local group on *each* member server in the MULTIMASTER1, MULTIMASTER2, RESOURCE_A, RESOURCE_B, RESOURCE_C, and RESOURCE_D domains. (This enables members of the Master1Restore and Master2Restore global groups to restore files to all of the member servers in all six domains.)

o  Placing the Master1Restore and the Master2Restore global groups in the Backup Operators built-in local group on *each* Windows NT Workstation computer in the MULTIMASTER1, MULTIMASTER2, RESOURCE_A, RESOURCE_B, RESOURCE_C, and RESOURCE_D domains. (This enables members of the Master1Restore and Master2Restore global groups to restore files to all of the Windows NT Workstation computers in all six domains.)

These two examples highlight the use of global groups and built-in local groups in a multidomain environment. They also point out that in a Windows NT network, each member server and each Windows NT Workstation computer has its own SAM, and because of this fact, the local groups on each of these computers must be configured individually.

# KEY POINT SUMMARY

This chapter explained managing Windows NT Directory Services. The following points illuminate the major issues:

o Windows NT Directory Services (Directory Services) is a Microsoft catchall phrase that refers to the architecture, features, functionality, and benefits of Windows NT domains and trust relationships. The primary benefits of Directory Services include a single user account logon and password, and centralized management of user and group accounts. In the Directory Services architecture, domains contain logical groupings of user and group accounts, computers, and shared resources.

o Trust relationships enable users from one domain to access shared resources located in other domains. In a trust relationship between two domains, the trusting domain is the domain that contains the shared resources, and the trusted domain is the domain that contains the user accounts. A trust relationship is depicted in diagrams by an arrow that points from the trusting (resource) domain to the trusted (user accounts) domain. Remember that the arrow points toward the accounts domain.

o When a single trust relationship exists between two domains, it is called a *one-way trust*. Both domains must be configured by an Administrator in order to establish a trust relationship. Trusts are configured in Windows NT by using User Manager for Domains. The trusted domain should be configured first, and then the trusting domain.

o When two domains trust each other, it is called a *two-way trust*. A two-way trust is really two one-way trusts, and is depicted in diagrams by two arrows between the two domains. As with one-way trusts, both domains must be configured by an Administrator in order to establish the two-way trust relationship.

o Trust relationships are non-transitive—they apply only to the domains they are established between. If the A domain trusts the B domain, and the B domain trusts the C domain, user accounts in the C domain *can't* access resources in the A domain because no trust exists between the A domain and the C domain.

o  When a user logs on to a Windows NT computer or domain, the logon process is managed by the NetLogon Service. The NetLogon Service is responsible for managing not only the logon process, but pass-through authentication and synchronization of the BDCs with the PDC, as well.

o  In the logon process, a user enters a user name, password, and domain name in the Logon Information dialog box. The local NetLogon Service determines whether the user account is located in the local computer's Security Accounts Manager (SAM) database. If the user account is found to be valid by the local SAM, the NetLogon Service retrieves the user account's security identifier (SID), and the SIDs for each group that the user is a member of. The NetLogon Service combines the user and group SIDs to create an access token, and then completes the logon process for the user.

o  Anytime a user logs on to a Windows NT computer using a user account that is *not* contained in the local computer's SAM, pass-through authentication is used to validate the user. Pass-through authentication enables a user to log on to a Windows NT computer by using a user account from the domain or from a trusted domain.

o  When a user account can't be validated on the local computer, the NetLogon Service on the local computer forwards (passes-through) the logon request to the NetLogon Service on a Windows NT Server domain controller for validation. The domain controller either validates the user account and passes the appropriate SIDs back to the local NetLogon Service to complete the logon process; or, if the user account resides in a trusted domain, the domain controller forwards (passes-through) the logon request to the NetLogon Service on a Windows NT Server domain controller in the trusted domain for validation. The NetLogon Service on the trusted domain's domain controller validates the user account and passes the appropriate SIDs back to the NetLogon Service on the trusting domain's domain controller, which, in turn, passes the SIDs back to the NetLogon Service on the local computer so that the user's logon can be completed.

o  Domains are the basic unit that comprise Directory Services architecture. Domains can be structured and combined in various architectures, called domain models. Many factors must be considered when planning a

Directory Services architecture, including the number and location of users; the number, types, and location of computers and shared resources; whether centralized or decentralized network management is desired; and the needs of departments within the organization. There are four domain models: the single domain model, the single master domain model, the multiple master domain model, and the complete trust domain model.

o The *single domain model* consists of one domain and does not use trust relationships. All user accounts and shared resources are contained in a single domain. A single domain can accommodate a maximum of 40,000 user accounts; but has a practical limitation of about 26,000 user accounts, assuming that each user has a Windows NT computer.

o The *single master domain model* consists of one master domain that contains all user accounts *and* one or more domains that contain shared resources. This domain model uses one-way trusts from each resource domain to the master domain. This model is ideal for small- to medium-sized organizations that want to mange user accounts centrally but also provide for regional or departmental control over shared resources. The single master domain model, like the single domain model, is limited to 40,000 user accounts.

o The *multiple master domain model* consists of two or more master domains that contain user accounts *and* any number of domains that contain shared resources. A two-way trust is used between each of the master domains, and one-way trusts are used from each resource domain to each and every master domain. This model can be scaled to match any size organization, and has no practical limitation on the number of user accounts, because an additional master domain can always be added. Because of the two-way trust that exists between the master domains, user account administration can be centralized, or it can be distributed among multiple administrators. Management of shared resources is generally distributed by geographic location or by department.

o There are various ways to distribute user accounts among two or more master domains: by division or department, by geographic location, alphabetically, or by using any hybrid combination of the aforementioned.

o The *complete trust domain model* is a decentralized model that consists of two or more domains that contain user accounts and shared resources.

A two-way trust relationship exists between each and every domain. The number of trusts required to implement this model can be computed by using the formula $n \times (n-1)$, where $n$ equals the number of domains. Because of the excessive number of trusts required, this model is not recommended.

o The easiest way to manage many users in a multiple domain environment is by using groups. Groups enable the administrator to assign rights and permissions to multiple users efficiently. Groups are commonly used in the following way in a multiple domain environment:

  o First, user accounts are placed into a global group in the trusted domain.

  o Next, this global group, which can cross trust relationships to other domains, is made a member of a local group in the trusting domain.

  o Finally, the local group in the trusting domain is assigned permissions to a shared resource located in the trusting domain, so that all of the local group's members can access the shared resource.

o Local groups can be assigned permissions only to resources within a single domain.

o In a Windows NT network, each member server and each Windows NT Workstation computer has its own SAM, and because of this fact, the local groups on each of these computers must be configured individually.

# Applying What You've Learned

Now it's time to regroup, review, and apply what you've learned in this chapter.

The questions in the Instant Assessment section that follows bring to mind key facts and concepts. The review activity tests your ability to plan network administration in a multiple master domain environment. The hands-on lab exercises reinforce what you've learned and give you an opportunity to practice some of the tasks tested by the Enterprixe exam.

# Instant Assessment Questions

1. What is Windows NT Directory Services?

2. What are the primary benefits of Windows NT Directory Services?

3. In a trust relationship, which domain is the trusting domain and which domain is the trusted domain?

4. What is a single trust relationship between two domains called?

5. What is the trust relationship of two domains that trust each other called?

6. What Windows NT tool must you use to create a trust relationship?

7. What does the fact that trust relationships are non-transitive mean?

8. Briefly describe the logon process when a user logs on to a Windows NT Workstation computer by using a local user account.

9. What Windows NT feature enables a user to log on to a Windows NT computer using a user account from the domain or from a trusted domain?

10. Briefly describe how pass-through authentication works when a user logs on to a Windows NT Workstation computer, which is a member of a domain, using a user account from the domain.

11. The NetLogon Service periodically replicates Directory Services database update information from the PDC to each BDC in the domain. What is this process called?

12. What factors should be considered when planning a Directory Services architecture?

13. Which domain model consists of two or more master domains that contain user accounts *and* any number of domains that contain shared resources?

14. Which domain model consists of one master domain that contains all user accounts *and* one or more domains that contain shared resources?

15. Which domain model consists of one domain and does not use trust relationships?

16. Which domain model is a decentralized model that consists of two or more domains that contain user accounts and shared resources, and between each domain a two-way trust exists? (Hint: This model can require an excessive number of trust relationships and is not recommended.)

17. You are the administrator for a small company (2,000 users) that wants to use centralized administration of its Windows NT network. You do not require any departmental or geographical control of shared resources. Which domain model would you use?

18. You are the administrator for a large company (60,000 users) that wants to use distributed network administration for the user accounts and shared resources that make up your Windows NT network. Which domain model would you use?

19. Briefly describe how groups are commonly used to manage users in a multiple domain environment.

T/F

20. Both domains must be configured in order to establish a trust relationship.    _____

 concept link    **For answers to the Instant Assessment questions see Appendix D.**

**MCSE**

Enterprise

# Review Activity

## *Planning network administration in a multiple master domain environment exercise*

You manage the administrators of a Windows NT network that uses the multiple master domain model. Your company's domain model is shown in Figure 10-21.

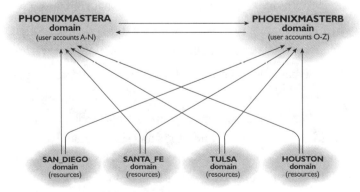

**FIGURE 10-21  Your company's domain model**

Table 10-3 shows the distribution of domain controllers, member servers, and Windows NT Workstation computers (that are members of their respective domains) in each of your company's six domains.

| TABLE 10-3 YOUR COMPANY'S COMPUTER DISTRIBUTION | | | |
|---|---|---|---|
| DOMAIN | # DOMAIN CONTROLLERS | # MEMBER SERVERS | # NT WORKSTATIONS |
| PHOENIXMASTERA | 3 | 2 | 40 |
| PHOENIXMASTERB | 3 | 2 | 25 |
| SAN_DIEGO | 2 | 3 | 150 |
| SANTA_FE | 2 | 6 | 50 |
| TULSA | 2 | 5 | 50 |
| HOUSTON | 2 | 4 | 200 |

As your company's budding Windows NT guru, your job, should you choose to accept it, is to create a global group in each master domain and use existing built-in local groups to enable specific users in the PHOENIXMASTERA and PHOENIXMASTERB domains to fully administer users, groups, and shared resources on all Windows NT computers in all six domains.

The following may help you to plan a solution to this task:

New global group in PHOENIXMASTERA domain: _____

New global group in PHOENIXMASTERB domain: _____

Built-in local group in each domain in which you will place the two new global groups:_____

Built-in local group on every member server in all six domains in which you will place the two new global groups: _____

Built-in local group on every Windows NT Workstation computer in all six domains in which you will place the two new global groups: _____

 concept link    **For answers to the Review Activity see Appendix D.**

## Hands-on Lab Exercises

The following hands-on lab exercises provide an excellent opportunity for you to apply many of the concepts about managing Windows NT Directory Services that you've learned in this chapter.

### Lab 10.15 *Implementing a trust relationship*

Enterprise

**This lab is optional, but only because it requires an additional Intel-based computer with a 486/33 processor, 16MB of RAM, and 500MB – 1GB available hard disk space. You will also need a VGA monitor and graphics card and mouse. A CD-ROM drive for the second computer would be nice, but it's not absolutely necessary if you don't mind taking the CD-ROM drive out of your first computer and installing it in the second for the NT installation portion of this lab. This lab also requires that you use two network adapters and the appropriate cabling to connect the two computers.**

**I can't suggest strongly enough that you go through whatever pain is necessary to beg, borrow, rent, or purchase a second computer to use in this lab (a 486 can be obtained fairly inexpensively), and the benefit you'll receive from experiencing trusts and groups in a multiple domain environment will pay off big when you take the Enterprise exam.**

The objective of this lab is to give you hands-on experience with implementing and testing one-way and two-way trust relationships between two domains.

This lab consists of the following five parts:

Part 1: Installing Windows NT Server 4.0 on a second computer

Part 2: Configuring a one-way trust

Part 3: Testing a one-way trust

Part 4: Configuring a two-way trust

Part 5: Testing a two-way trust

#### Part 1: Installing Windows NT Server 4.0 on a second computer

First install MS-DOS on the second computer's hard drive, and load the drivers for the CD-ROM drive. Make sure that the Windows NT Server compact disc is in the CD-ROM drive.

You will need one blank, 3.5-inch high-density floppy disk for this lab exercise.

Follow the steps below carefully to perform the installation of Windows NT Server 4.0.

### Pre-copy phase

1. Change the default drive to your CD-ROM drive by typing in the CD-ROM drive letter followed by a colon (for example, **D:**), and press Enter.
2. Type **cd i386**, and then press Enter.
3. Type **winnt /b**, and then press Enter. (This command instructs Setup to perform the Winnt.exe installation without creating the Setup Boot Disk set.)
4. When Windows NT Setup asks you to enter the path where NT files are located, press Enter.
5. Setup copies files to your hard disk. (This process takes a few minutes. How about a stretch break or a fresh cup of coffee?)
6. When the Windows NT Server Setup screen appears, press Enter to restart your computer and continue Windows NT Setup.

### Phase 0

1. After a minute or two, when the Windows NT Server Setup screen appears, press Enter to set up Windows NT now.
2. Setup displays a screen showing any mass storage devices, such as SCSI adapters, CD-ROM drives, and so on. Some older IDE controllers will not be displayed here, but they will still function and be recognized by NT. Specify additional devices by making changes on this screen if necessary. When you have completed all necessary changes, press Enter to continue.
3. The Windows NT Licensing Agreement screen appears. Read the licensing agreement, pressing PgDn to view additional screens of the agreement. When you reach the bottom of the agreement, press F8 to continue setup.
4. Windows NT Server Setup displays a screen listing your computer's hardware and software components. Make any changes necessary. When you are finished, highlight "The above list matches my computer," and press Enter.

5. If you have a previous version of Microsoft Windows installed on your computer, Setup displays a screen stating that it detected a previous version. If this screen appears, press **N** to install Windows NT Server in a different directory.

6. Windows NT Server Setup displays a screen showing your computer's hard disk partitions. Highlight the partition on which you want to install Windows NT Server, then press Enter. (Make sure the partition you choose has at least 124MB free.)

7. Windows NT Server Setup asks you to select the type of file system you want on this partition. Highlight "Leave the current file system intact <no changes>," and press Enter.

8. Windows NT Server Setup displays the location where it will install the NT Server files. In the highlighted area, edit the text so that it reads: **\WINNTSRV**. (Don't type in the period at the end.) Then press Enter.

9. Windows NT Server Setup offers to examine your hard disk for corruption. Press Enter to enable this. (This takes a few minutes.)

10. Windows NT Server Setup displays a screen that indicates this portion of Setup is complete. If you have a floppy disk inserted in drive A:, remove it now. Then press Enter to restart your computer and to continue with setup.

### Phase 1

1. After your computer reboots and the Windows NT Server Setup dialog box finally appears, click Next to continue.

2. Type in your name, press Tab, and then type in the name of your organization. Click Next to continue.

3. Type in the ten-digit CD key number from the back of your Windows NT Server compact disc case (press Tab after you enter the first three digits). Click Next to continue.

4. Select a Licensing Mode for the server. Select "Per Server for:" and enter the number of client licenses you purchased. Click Next to continue.

5. When prompted to type in a name for your computer, type **PDCMAINOFFICE**. Click Next to continue.

6. Select Primary Domain Controller in the Server Type window. Click Next to continue.

7. Type **password** when prompted to enter an administrator password. Press Tab. Confirm the password by retyping it. Click Next to continue.

8. Windows NT Server Setup asks you if you want to create an Emergency Repair Disk. Accept the Yes default. Click Next to continue.

**9.** Windows NT Server Setup displays a screen prompting you to Select Components. Add any components that you want to install, but do *not* deselect any components that are selected by default. Click Next to continue.

## Phase 2

**1.** Windows NT Server Setup displays a window indicating that Phase 2, Installing Windows NT Networking, is about to begin. Click Next to continue.

**2.** Accept the default check in the box next to "Wired to the network." Click Next to continue.

**3.** Accept the default check in the box next to "Install Microsoft Internet Information Server." Click Next to continue.

**4.** Windows NT Server Setup displays the Network Adapters box. Click Start Search. Your network adapter should then appear in the Network Adapters box.

If your network adapter did not appear, click Select from list. If your network adapter is shown in the list, highlight it and click OK.

If your network adapter is not on the list, and you have a driver disk from its manufacturer, highlight any network adapter and click Have Disk. Setup then prompts you to insert this disk. Insert the disk and click OK. Highlight your network adapter from the list and click OK.

You should now have your network adapter displayed in the Network Adapters box. Click Next to continue.

**5.** Windows NT Server Setup displays the Network Protocols list box. Deselect NWLink IPX/SPX Compatible Transport. Ensure that the TCP/IP Protocol is the only protocol selected (it will have a gray check in the check box). Click Next to continue.

**6.** Windows NT Server Setup displays the Network Services list box. Accept all of the defaults selected in this window. Click Next to continue.

**7.** Click Next to continue and to have Setup install the selected components.

**8.** Setup prompts you to enter your network adapter card settings. (This screen may not appear for some network adapters.) Verify that the settings shown match the ones that you used when you installed and configured your network adapter. Make changes only as needed. Click Continue to continue.

**9.** A TCP/IP Setup warning screen appears. If you are on a network that has a DHCP server, click Yes. Otherwise, click No.

**10.** The Microsoft TCP/IP Properties dialog box appears if you clicked No in the previous step. *If you are on a network that uses TCP/IP, or if you are connected to the Internet, obtain an IP address, subnet mask, and default gateway from your network administrator.* Otherwise, type an IP address of: **192.168.59.6** and a subnet mask of: **255.255.255.0**.

 **Do *not* use this IP address if you are on a network that uses TCP/IP, or if you are connected to the Internet.**

**11.** Leave the Default Gateway blank. Click OK to continue.

**12.** Windows NT Server Setup displays a screen showing network binding information. Click Next to continue.

**13.** Click Next to start the network.

**14.** Windows NT Server Setup prompts you enter a domain name. Type **MAINOFFICE** as your domain name. Click Next to continue.

### Phase 3

**1.** Click Finish to continue the setup process.

**2.** Accept the defaults selected in the Microsoft Internet Information Server 2.0 Setup dialog box. Click OK to continue.

**3.** Click Yes to create the directory.

**4.** Accept the default directories in the Publishing Directories dialog box by clicking on OK.

**5.** Click Yes to create the directories.

**6.** Click OK in the Microsoft Internet Information Server 2.0 Setup dialog box.

**7.** Click SQL Server in the Install Drivers dialog box to highlight it. Click OK to continue.

**8.** In the drop-down list box under the Time Zone tab, click your time zone to highlight it. Optionally, you may also click the Date & Time tab and set the correct date and time. When you are finished click Close to continue.

**9.** Setup displays a screen indicating that it has found your video display adapter. Click OK in the Detected Display dialog box to continue.

**10.** Adjust the display settings to suit your preferences. Click Test. The Testing Mode dialog box appears. Click OK to test. When the Testing Mode dialog box reappears, click Yes if you saw the test bitmap. When the Display Settings dialog box appears, click OK to continue. Click OK in the Display Properties dialog box to complete the installation. (This takes a few minutes.)

**11.** When prompted, label and insert a blank 3.5-inch floppy disk into drive A:. Setup formats and makes this disk into your Emergency Repair Disk. Click OK to continue. (This takes a couple of minutes.)

**12.** Windows NT Setup displays a window indicating that Windows NT 4.0 is successfully installed. Remove your newly created Emergency Repair Disk from drive A: (and save it for future use). Also remove the compact disc from your CD-ROM drive. Then click Restart Computer to reboot and start Windows NT Server. The setup is complete. Continue on to Part 2.

### Part 2: Configuring a one-way trust

In this section you create users in the MAINOFFICE domain, and configure the LAB domain to trust the MAINOFFICE domain.

Boot both of your computers to Windows NT Server. Log on as Administrator to each one.

Perform the following steps on the computer you named PDCMAINOFFICE (the second computer):

**1.** Select Start ⇒ Programs ⇒ Administrative Tools (Common) ⇒ User Manager for Domains.

**2.** Select User ⇒ New User.

**3.** In the New User dialog box, type the following bolded information in the appropriate text boxes:

User name: **CarmenM**

Full name: **Carmen Martinez**

Description: **Corporate Sales Manager**

Password: **password**

Confirm password: **password**

Clear the check box next to User Must Change Password at Next Logon. Select the check box next to Password Never Expires. Click the Add command button.

**4.** In the New User dialog box, type the following bolded information in the appropriate text boxes:

User name: **HansS**

Full name: **Hans Schmidt**

Description: **Corporate Accounting Manager**

Password: **password**

Confirm password: **password**

Clear the check box next to User Must Change Password at Next Logon. Select the check box next to Password Never Expires. Click the Add command button. Click the Close command button.

**5.** In the User Manager dialog box, select Policies ⇒ Trust Relationships.

6. In the Trust Relationships dialog box, click the Add command button next to the Trusting Domains list box (this is the text box at the bottom of the dialog box).

7. In the Add Trusting Domain dialog box, type the following bolded information in the appropriate text boxes:

   Trusting domain: **LAB**

   Initial password: **password**

   Confirm password: **password**

   Click OK.

8. In the Trust Relationships dialog box, PDCLAB appears in the Trusting Domains list box. Click the Close command button.

9. Exit User Manager for Domains.

Perform the following steps on the computer named PDCLAB (the first computer):

1. Select Start ⇒ Programs ⇒ Administrative Tools (Common) ⇒ User Manager for Domains.

2. In the User Manager for Domains dialog box, select Policies ⇒ Trust Relationships.

3. In the Trust Relationships dialog box, click the Add command button next to the Trusted Domains list box (this is the list box toward the top of the dialog box).

4. In the Add Trusted Domain dialog box, type the following bolded information in the appropriate text boxes:

   Domain: **MAINOFFICE**

   Password: **password**

   Click OK.

5. A message appears, indicating that a trust relationship with MAINOFFICE has been successfully established. Click OK.

6. In the Trust Relationships dialog box, notice that MAINOFFICE appears in the Trusted Domains list box. Click the Close command button.

7. Exit User Manager for Domains. Continue on to Part 3.

**Part 3: Testing a one-way trust**

In this section you verify that the LAB domain trusts the MAINOFFICE domain by assigning a user from the MAINOFFICE domain permissions to a printer in the LAB domain, and by logging on to the PDC in the LAB domain by using a user account from the MAINOFFICE domain. In addition, you attempt to log on to the

PDC in the MAINOFFICE domain by using a user account from the LAB domain, but fail, verifying that the MAINOFFICE domain does *not* trust the LAB domain.

Perform these steps on the computer named PDCLAB (the first computer):

**1.** Select Start ⇒ Settings ⇒ Printers.

**2.** In the Printers dialog box, highlight the printer you created in Lab 6.8. Select File ⇒ Properties.

**3.** In the printer's Properties dialog box, click the Security tab.

**4.** On the Security tab, click the Permissions command button.

**5.** In the Printer Permissions dialog box, click the Add command button.

**6.** In the Add Users and Groups dialog box, click the down arrow in the List Names From drop-down list box. Select MAINOFFICE from the list that appears. Click the Show Users command button. Scroll down the list in the Names list box and highlight CarmenM. Click the Add command button. Click OK.

**7.** In the Printer Permissions dialog box, notice that MAINOFFICE\CarmenM now appears in the Name list box. She has permissions to print to the printer. (You have just verified that the LAB domain trusts the MAINOFFICE domain by successfully assigning CarmenM, a user in the MAINOFFICE domain, permissions to a printer in the LAB domain.) Click OK.

**8.** In the printer's Properties dialog box, click OK.

**9.** Close the Printers dialog box.

**10.** Select Start ⇒ Shut Down.

**11.** In the Shut Down Windows dialog box, select the radio button next to "Close all programs and log on as a different user." Click the Yes command button.

**12.** Press Ctrl + Alt + Delete to log on.

**13.** Click OK in the Important Notice dialog box.

**14.** In the Logon Information dialog box, type the user name, **HansS,** and the password, **password**. Select MAINOFFICE in the Domain drop-down list box. Click OK.

**15.** If the Welcome to Windows NT screen appears, click the Close command button.

**16.** Because HansS, a user in the MAINOFFICE domain, is successful in logging on at the PDC in the LAB domain, you have verified that the LAB domain trusts the MAINOFFICE domain.

**17.** Select Start ⇒ Shut Down.

**18.** In the Shut Down Windows dialog box, select the radio button next to "Close all programs and log on as a different user." Click the Yes command button.

Perform the following steps on the computer named PDCMAINOFFICE (the second computer):

**1.** Select Start ⇒ Shut Down.

**2.** In the Shut Down Windows dialog box, select the radio button next to "Close all programs and log on as a different user." Click the Yes command button.

**3.** Press Ctrl + Alt + Delete to log on.

**4.** In the Logon Information dialog box, click the down arrow in the Domain drop-down list box. Notice that only the MAINOFFICE domain is listed. (This is because the MAINOFFICE domain does *not* trust the LAB domain.) Click the Cancel command button. You have verified that the MAINOFFICE domain does *not* trust the LAB domain. Continue to Part 4.

### Part 4: Configuring a two-way trust

In this section you configure the MAINOFFICE domain to trust the LAB domain. (This completes the creation of a two-way trust between the LAB and MAINOFFICE domains.)

Perform these steps on the computer named PDCLAB (the first computer):

**1.** Press Ctr + Alt + Delete to log on.

**2.** Click OK in the Important Notice dialog box.

**3.** In the Logon Information dialog box, type in a user name of **Administrator**, a password of **password**, and select the LAB domain from the Domain list box. Click OK.

**4.** Select Start ⇒ Programs ⇒ Administrative Tools (Common) ⇒ User Manager for Domains.

**5.** In the User Manager dialog box, select Policies ⇒ Trust Relationships.

**6.** In the Trust Relationships dialog box, click the Add command button next to the Trusting Domains list box (the list box toward the bottom of the dialog box).

**7.** In the Add Trusting Domain dialog box, type the following bolded information in the appropriate text boxes:

Trusting domain: **MAINOFFICE**

Initial password: **password**

Confirm password: **password**

Click OK.

**8.** In the Trust Relationships dialog box, notice that MAINOFFICE appears in the Trusting Domains list box. Click the Close command button.

**9.** Exit User Manager for Domains.

Perform the following steps on the computer named PDCMAINOFFICE (the second computer):

**1.** Press Ctrl + Alt + Delete to log on.

**2.** In the Logon Information dialog box, type in a user name of **Administrator**, a password of **password**, and select the MAINOFFICE domain. Click OK.

**3.** Select Start ⇒ Programs ⇒ Administrative Tools (Common) ⇒ User Manager for Domains.

**4.** In the User Manager dialog box, select Policies ⇒ Trust Relationships.

**5.** In the Trust Relationships dialog box, click the Add command button next to the Trusted Domains list box (this list box is located near the top of the dialog box).

**6.** In the Add Trusted Domain dialog box, type in a domain of **LAB** and a password of **password**. Click OK.

**7.** After a few moments a dialog box appears, indicating that a trust relationship with the LAB domain has been successfully established. Click OK.

**8.** In the Trust Relationships dialog box, notice that the LAB domain appears in the Trusted Domains list box. The MAINOFFICE domain is now configured to trust the LAB domain. Click the Close command button.

**9.** In the User Manager dialog box, select Policies ⇒ User Rights.

**10.** In the User Rights Policy dialog box, select Log on locally from the Right drop-down list box. Click the Add command button.

**11.** In the Add Users and Groups dialog box, double-click the Everyone group in the Names list box. Click OK. (This step enables all users from both the LAB and MAINOFFICE domains to log on locally to this computer.)

**12.** In the User Rights Policy dialog box, click OK.

**13.** Exit User Manager for Domains. Continue to Part 5.


### Part 5: Testing a two-way trust

In this section, you verify that the MAINOFFICE domain trusts the LAB domain by logging on to the PDC in the MAINOFFICE domain by using a user account from the LAB domain. (You already verified that the LAB domain trusts the MAINOFFICE domain.)

Perform the following steps on the computer named PDCMAINOFFICE (the second computer):

1. Select Start ⇒ Shut Down.
2. In the Shut Down Windows dialog box, select the radio button next to "Close all programs and log on as a different user." Click the Yes command button.
3. Press Ctrl + Alt + Delete to log on.
4. In the Logon Information dialog box, type in a user name of **MikeCo**, a password of **newuser**, and select the LAB domain. Click OK.
5. A Logon Message appears, indicating that you are required to change your password at first logon. Click OK.
6. In the Change Password dialog box, type in a new password of **password** and confirm the new password. Click OK.
7. A Change Password dialog box appears, indicating that your password has been changed. Click OK.
8. If a Welcome to Windows NT dialog box appears, click the Close command button.

    Because you were able to log on successfully to the PDC in the MAINOFFICE domain by using a user account from the LAB domain (MikeCo), you verified that the MAINOFFICE domain trusts the LAB domain.

## Lab 10.16 *Planning a Directory Services architecture*

The objective of this lab is to give you hands-on experience in planning a Directory Services architecture and trust relationships in given situations.

Enterprise In each of the following exercises, your job is to:

1. Plan the appropriate Directory Services architecture for the given scenario (single domain model, single master domain model, multiple master domain model, or complete trust domain model).
2. Plan the appropriate trust relationships for the scenario.

**Exercise 1**   An international marketing firm called Worldwide Promotions, Inc., based in New York City, is planning to roll out Windows NT 4.0 in all of its offices worldwide.

Table 10-4 lists Worldwide Promotions' offices, and the number of users at each office.

| **TABLE 10-4** WORLDWIDE PROMOTIONS, INC. | |
|---|---|
| *OFFICE LOCATION* | *NUMBER OF USERS* |
| New York City | 500 |
| Paris | 150 |
| London | 100 |
| Seattle | 100 |
| Mexico City | 50 |
| Total Users | 900 |

A Windows NT network will be installed at each location, and all offices will be connected to the New York City office via a high-speed, digital leased line. The company plans to standardize by using Windows NT Server on all of its servers, and by using Windows NT Workstation on all client computers.

The company's Management Information Systems (MIS) department is located in the New York City office, and wants to manage all of the user accounts in all five locations. On-site network managers at each of the other four offices will manage the security for local network resources at their own respective offices.

Worldwide Promotions maintains a critical database in the New York City office that all users from all locations need to be able to access.

**1.** Which Directory Services architecture would you choose for this situation?

**2.** What trust relationships would you use in this situation, if any?

(You might want to draw out your Directory Services architecture design and trust relationships on a piece of scratch paper.)

**Exercise 2**   An international import company called Import International, Ltd., based in Toronto, Canada, is planning to roll out Windows NT 4.0 in all of its offices worldwide.

Table 10-5 lists Import International, Ltd.'s offices, and the number of users at each office.

| TABLE 10-5 IMPORT INTERNATIONAL, LTD. | |
|---|---|
| *OFFICE LOCATION* | *NUMBER OF USERS* |
| Toronto | 9,000 |
| Los Angeles | 8,000 |
| Tokyo | 7,000 |
| Rio de Janeiro | 6,000 |
| Miami | 6,000 |
| Bombay | 3,000 |
| Johannesburg | 3,000 |
| Sydney | 2,000 |
| Hong Kong | 1,000 |
| Bangkok | 1,000 |
| Total Users | 46,000 |

High-speed, digital leased lines connect the locations, as shown in Figure 10-22.

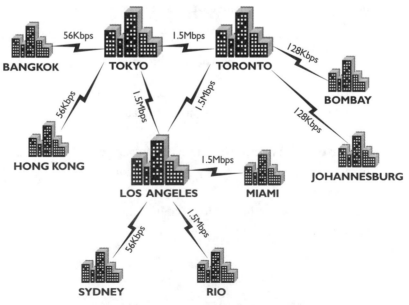

**FIGURE 10-22** Leased lines connecting Import International, Ltd.'s ten offices

A Windows NT network will be installed at each location. Import International plans to standardize by using Windows NT Server on all of its servers, and by using Windows NT Workstation on all client computers.

The company's Data Processing and Computer Services department is located in the Toronto office and wants to manage all of the user accounts for all ten locations. On-site network managers at each of the other nine offices will manage the security for local network resources at their own respective offices.

Personnel travel frequently and log on to computers in various offices when traveling. Users must be able to log on using a single user account from a computer in any Import International office.

Import International maintains three critical databases: one in Toronto, one in Los Angeles, and one in Tokyo. All users from all locations need to be able to access all three of these databases.

1. Which Directory Services architecture would you choose for this situation?

2. What trust relationships would you use in this situation, if any?

(You might want to draw out your Directory Services architecture design and trust relationships on a piece of scratch paper.)

concept link    **For answers to this lab see Appendix D.**

Enterprise

CHAPTER

# 11

# Optimizing Windows NT
# Server Directory Services

# About Chapter 11

This chapter is all about optimizing Windows NT Server Directory Services, particularly in a WAN environment.

First, Chapter 11 takes a quick look at the benefits of optimizing Directory Services. Then, the first step in the optimization process—which consists of determining the size of the Directory Services database—is explored. Next, you'll learn how to determine the appropriate number of master domains for your organization. After this, the chapter explains how to determine the ideal number of domain controllers.

The remainder of the chapter focuses on two primary techniques an administrator can use to optimize Directory Services in a WAN environment. First, the section outlines how to optimize the location of BDCs to reduce logon and authentication traffic across a WAN link. Second, steps to optimize Directory Services synchronization are presented.

This chapter includes one lab. In this lab, you'll plan the optimization of WAN link performance by determining the appropriate number and placement of BDCs throughout a master domain model.

Chapter 11 is optional if you're preparing for the Workstation or Server exams, but essential if you're preparing for the Enterprise exam. This chapter maps to the "Optimize performance for various results" objective in the Monitoring and Optimization section in the Enterprise exam's objectives.

# WHY OPTIMIZE WINDOWS NT SERVER DIRECTORY SERVICES?

*Optimizing Windows NT Server Directory Services* refers to an overall network design and administration process that includes: choosing the appropriate domain model and number of master domains, determining the optimum number of domain controllers, optimizing the location of *backup domain controllers* (BDCs), and optimizing synchronization between a domain's *primary domain controller* (PDC) and BDCs.

The larger your network environment, the greater the likelihood that you need to optimize Directory Services. If you have a small network, or all your *Wide Area Network* (WAN) links are high speed (1Mbps or more), then you may not have a need to optimize Directory Services.

The benefits of optimizing Directory Services include:

o Efficient user logon and authentication

o Efficient use of computer resources

o Efficient synchronization across WAN links

User logon and authentication create network traffic. In a WAN environment, it is normally preferable to keep user logon and authentication traffic from crossing the WAN link, so that the link is freed up for other network traffic. Optimizing Directory Services by choosing the appropriate domain model and optimizing the location of BDCs allows users to logon and access resources quickly and efficiently.

Computers are expensive resources. When Directory Services is optimized, you choose the appropriate type of hardware and optimum number of computers to use as domain controllers in your organization. In this way, you spend neither too much nor too little on your network infrastructure to achieve desired performance levels.

Synchronization of a domain's PDC with its BDCs can create a significant amount of network traffic. When synchronization traffic must cross a WAN link, you can optimize the rate and frequency of synchronization, and limit synchronization traffic to specified time periods during the day.

A first step in optimizing Directory Services is determining the size of the Directory Services database.

# Determining the Size of the Directory Services Database

The size of the Directory Services database is used to make virtually all decisions for optimization of Directory Services, including: determining which domain model is best suited to your needs; how many master domains and domain controllers are required; determining the optimum location of BDCs; and determining the amount, rate, and timing of synchronization traffic.

The recommended maximum size of the Directory Services database is 40MB (40,000KB). Larger databases have been tested, but are not recommended by Microsoft. The Directory Services database contains user accounts, computer accounts, and group accounts.

Each account contained in the Directory Services database requires a specific amount of space:

- Each user account requires 1,024 bytes (1KB). (40,000 user accounts occupy 40MB of disk space. This is where the 40,000 user account limit per domain comes from. However, the 40,000 user account limit does *not* take into account computer accounts or group accounts.)

- Each computer account requires 512 bytes (.5KB).

- Each local group account requires 512 bytes (.5KB) for the group, *plus* 36 bytes for each member of the group.

- Each global group account requires 512 bytes (.5KB) for the group, *plus* 12 bytes for each member of the group.

 tip **The average amount of space required by a group account normally varies between 2KB and 4KB. I recommend that you use a size of 3KB for each group when you calculate the size of the Directory Services database. Using this recommended size is obviously not 100 percent accurate, but it does provide a simple, ball-park estimate to perform the calculation.**

To calculate the size of the Directory Services database, use the following formula: Size of Directory Services database, in KB, = Number of user accounts + (.5 × number of computer accounts) + (3 × total number of groups).

For example, assume that a company has 18,000 users, 18,000 computers, and 300 groups. The size of the company's Directory Services database is calculated as follows:

| | |
|---|---|
| Number of user accounts | 18,000 |
| .5 × number of computer accounts | 9,000 |
| 3 × total number of groups | 900 |
| Total size of Directory Services database: | 27,900KB |

# DETERMINING THE APPROPRIATE NUMBER OF MASTER DOMAINS

Now that you've determined the size of your Directory Services database, you can determine the appropriate number of master domains for your organization.

There are several factors that should be considered when determining the appropriate number of master domains:

o The size of your organization's Directory Services database (as computed in the previous section)

o The hardware capabilities of computers used as domain controllers

o The organizational structure of your organization—i.e., logical department groupings

o The management structure you want to use on your network—centralized or decentralized

o The geographical distribution of your organization's users and computers

When you consider the size of your Directory Services database to determine the number of master domains required, don't forget to take into account future company growth.

 *tip* **When planning a domain architecture, I recommend that the *maximum* size of computed Directory Services database allocated to each master domain be limited to 20,000KB. Depending on the hardware specifications of your domain controllers, your network management needs, the geographic distribution of your network,** or your company's anticipated future growth, you may want to limit each master domain to an *even smaller size* of computed Directory Services database.

The hardware capabilities and specifications of the computers used as domain controllers will significantly affect your determination of the appropriate number of master domains. Table 11-1 shows recommended minimum hardware configurations of domain controllers to accommodate various Directory Services database sizes.

 tip **If you've computed your Directory Services database size and the figure is nearing 40,000KB, I strongly recommend that you don't try to use the single domain or single master domain model.**

| TABLE 11-1  MINIMUM HARDWARE REQUIRED FOR VARIOUS DIRECTORY SERVICES DATABASE SIZES | | |
| --- | --- | --- |
| *DIRECTORY SERVICES DATABASE SIZE* | *MINIMUM CPU REQUIRED* | *MINIMUM RAM REQUIRED* |
| 5MB (5,000KB) | 486DX/33 | 32MB |
| 20MB (20,000KB) | Pentium or RISC | 64MB |
| 40MB (40,000KB) | Pentium Pro or RISC | 128MB |
| Greater than 40MB | Not recommended | |

For example, if your company plans to use Pentium computers with 64MB of RAM for its domain controllers, the maximum Directory Services database size that these computers can accommodate is 20MB per domain. However, this table assumes that domain controllers are used *only* for logon validation and do not perform any other network services (such as WINS, DHCP, hosting shared resources, etc.). If your domain controllers perform multiple functions, you will need more powerful hardware to support the Directory Services database sizes listed in Table 11-1. If more powerful hardware is not available, you must decrease the Directory Services database size that the domain controllers can contain.

Some companies choose their domain structure based on their organization's departmental structure, or by the geographic location of various offices. These factors often have as much influence in determining the number of master domains as do Directory Services database size and hardware limitations. When departmental or regional control over user accounts and resources is desired, master domains are often implemented for these departments or locations.

When a company wants centralized network management, the single master or multiple master domain models are often used. When a more decentralized network management scheme is desired, more master domains are used. If your network structure becomes too decentralized, it may approach the complete trust domain model, which is not recommended.

# DETERMINING THE IDEAL NUMBER OF DOMAIN CONTROLLERS

The minimum recommended number of domain controllers for each domain is one PDC and one BDC. This number of domain controllers accommodates from one to approximately 2,000 users, and is based on a domain controller hardware configuration consisting of a 486/66 CPU with a minimum of 32MB of RAM. (More powerful computers can accommodate more users.)

 **You can configure a Windows NT Server domain with a single PDC and no BDCs. This configuration will work for a small network, but eliminates all of the fault tolerance features of a Windows NT Server domain.**

It is recommended that a BDC be added for every additional 2,000 users, or increment thereof. Using these guidelines, a domain that contains 8,000 users requires one PDC and four BDCs. A domain that contains between 8,001 and 10,000 users requires one PDC and five BDCs.

These guidelines assume that BDCs are used *only* for logon validation, and do not perform any other network services (such as WINS, DHCP, hosting shared resources, etc.). If BDCs perform multiple functions, you need more powerful hardware or additional BDCs to support the number of users recommended in these guidelines.

More BDCs may also be required in a WAN environment to support local user logon validation and authentication at each location. The next section discusses how to optimize Directory Services in a WAN environment.

# OPTIMIZING DIRECTORY SERVICES IN A WAN ENVIRONMENT

Operating a Windows NT network in a WAN environment can present a network administrator with a unique set of challenges.

The WAN environment consists of networks in different locations connected by communications links. WAN links, which consist of dial-up or leased lines, generally vary in speed from 28Kbps to 44Mbps. Because WAN links are typically bottlenecks for network traffic, the administrator needs to ensure that logon and authentication traffic are handled efficiently across the WAN link, and must also ensure that synchronization can occur without tying up the WAN link during peak use times.

There are two primary techniques an administrator can use to optimize Directory Services in a WAN environment: selecting appropriate locations for BDCs to optimize logon and authentication traffic, and optimizing Directory Services database synchronization between the PDC and the BDCs.

## Optimizing Location of BDCs

In a non-WAN environment, the placement of domain controllers is not critical. In a WAN environment, however, because logon and authentication create network traffic, the location of domain controllers is of primary importance.

The PDC should normally be placed in the same location as the network administrator. BDCs should usually be placed in the locations where users log on.

Consider the following example of a company that has two domains: a master domain in San Francisco, which contains all user accounts, and a resource domain in Atlanta. The ATLANTA domain trusts the SAN_FRANCISCO domain, and a 56Kbps WAN link connects the two domains. There are 1,500 users in the San Francisco location, and 1,100 users in the Atlanta location. When users in the Atlanta location log on, a domain controller in the SAN_FRANCISCO domain must validate the logon requests. Because the number of users at the Atlanta location has doubled in size over the past year, users there report that their logon requests take much longer to process than in the past.

Figure 11-1 shows the SAN_FRANCISCO and ATLANTA domains. Notice that all logon requests from users in the ATLANTA domain must flow across the WAN link to the SAN_FRANCISCO domain for validation.

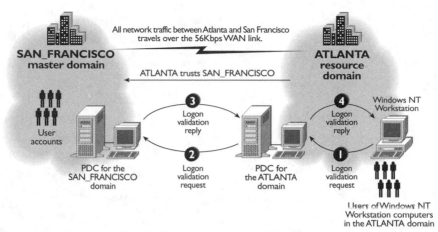

**FIGURE 11-1** **Logon authentication across a slow WAN link**

To resolve the slow logon problem, the company's network administrator decides to place a BDC from the SAN_FRANCISCO domain in the Atlanta office. This results in much faster logons for users in the Atlanta office, because logon validation is now performed locally, instead of across the slow WAN link. Placing a BDC for the SAN_FRANCISCO domain in the Atlanta office also frees up the WAN link, allowing it to handle other network traffic more efficiently.

Figure 11-2 shows the SAN_FRANCISCO and ATLANTA domains with a BDC for the SAN_FRANCISCO domain installed in the Atlanta office. Notice that the logon validation for Atlanta users is all performed locally now, and no longer needs to cross the WAN link.

The key point in optimizing BDC placement is the *location of users* that require logon validation, especially when you want to eliminate logon traffic across a WAN link. Also keep in mind that a BDC can serve up to 2,000 users. If more than 2,000 users are logging on from a remote location, additional remote BDCs are required.

Adding remote BDCs to eliminate logon traffic across a WAN link solves one problem—and to an extent, creates another. Logon traffic across the WAN is eliminated, but because the BDC must periodically update its Directory Services database, and this synchronization with the PDC takes place across the WAN link, synchronization traffic across the WAN link is increased. This synchronization traffic is significantly less than logon validation traffic, but can still create a bottleneck across the WAN link if not managed carefully by the administrator.

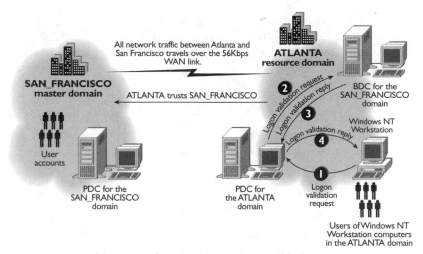

**FIGURE 11-2  Local logon authentication made possible by a remote BDC**

# Optimizing Directory Services Synchronization

*Optimizing Directory Services synchronization* refers to the process of managing the periodic synchronization of Directory Services database changes between the PDC and the BDCs so that other network traffic, particularly traffic across a WAN link, is not hindered.

**TO OPTIMIZE DIRECTORY SERVICES SYNCHRONIZATION, FOLLOW THESE STEPS:**

**1.** Determine the amount of time required each month to perform Directory Services synchronization.

**2.** If the amount of time required for Directory Services synchronization is significant or causes a bottleneck across the WAN link, then one or more of the following measures can be taken:

- Increase the size of the change log
- Modify the ReplicationGovernor value
- Use the Schedule service and the `Regini.exe` program to configure the time of day Directory Services synchronization occurs

These steps are discussed in detail in the following sections.

## Determining synchronization time

The first step in optimizing Directory Services synchronization is determining the amount of time it takes, per month, to synchronize data between a PDC and one BDC (in a given domain) that are separated by a WAN link.

Before you can determine the amount of time synchronization takes, you need to gather the following data:

A. Number of user accounts in the domain

B. The maximum password age, in days

C. Speed of the WAN link, in Kbps

D. Number of BDCs located across the WAN link from the PDC

To estimate the amount of time synchronization takes, you can use the following formula (let A = number of user accounts, etc.):

Synchronization time per month, in hours = $(A \times B/30 + .1A) \times D / (C \times 450)$

> note 📝 **The .1A in this formula represents an estimated number of account changes that occur (including the creation of or change in user accounts, computer accounts, and group accounts; but excluding password changes) in a month. I like to use 10 percent of the total number of users (hence .1A) for this estimate.**

For example, consider the previous example of the SAN_FRANCISCO and ATLANTA domains. The SAN_FRANCISCO domain, which contains all the user accounts, has a total of 2,600 user accounts. The two domains are connected by a 56Kbps WAN link. The SAN_FRANCISCO domain has one remote BDC in the Atlanta location, and, for convenience, assume that the maximum password age is 30 days. The calculation to determine the amount of time it takes each month to synchronize data between the PDC located in San Francisco and its BDC in Atlanta looks like this:

$(A \times B/30 + .1A) \times D / (C \times 450)$ = Synchronization time per month, in hours

$(2,600 \times 30/30 + 260) \times 1 / (56 \times 450)$ =

$(2,860)/(25,200)$ = .11 hours per month

In this example, Directory Services synchronization does not appear to be an issue, because the estimated time it takes is less than seven minutes per month. However, in a multiple master domain model that has a large number of users *and* multiple BDCs from each master domain at multiple remote locations, Directory Services synchronization can consume a significant amount of WAN link bandwidth.

**exam preparation pointer**     **It might appear as though less than roughly two percent of network administrators ever have to worry about managing Directory Services synchronization. However, *everyone* who wants to pass the Enterprise exam should have a solid grasp of how to optimize Directory Services synchronization.**

If Directory Services synchronization is utilizing too much of a WAN link's capacity, an administrator can take various steps to optimize synchronization traffic, including increasing the size of the change log and modifying the ReplicationGovernor value.

### Increasing the size of the change log

The *change log* is a file located on the PDC that contains recent changes to the Directory Services database. The size of this file can be adjusted by changing the value of a setting in the Registry. Sometimes it is beneficial to increase the size of the change log when optimizing Directory Services synchronization.

Synchronization between the PDC and a BDC can be either full or partial.

*Full synchronization* (which is not the norm) involves copying the entire Directory Services database from the PDC to the BDC. Full synchronization only occurs when *all* changes listed in the change log occurred *after* the last synchronization between the PDC and the BDC.

*Partial synchronization* involves copying only the changes listed in the change log that have occurred since the last synchronization between the PDC and the BDC. Because partial synchronization involves copying significantly less data, it is preferred over full synchronization when a slow WAN link is involved.

The change log can contain up to approximately 2,000 account and password changes. In most network environments, this is an adequate size when synchronization occurs at normal intervals. However, the size of the change log may need to be increased if you decide to limit the amount of synchronization data than can be transferred, or the frequency or hours when synchronization traffic across a WAN link can occur.

If the size of the change log is *not* increased and synchronization intervals are too infrequent, then full synchronization (which is not desired because of the large amount of WAN bandwidth used) will occur. This resulting situation may be worse than the one you were attempting to fix.

The change log entry is stored in the Windows NT Registry in: `HKEY_LOCAL_MACHINE\SYSTEM\CurrentControlSet\Services\Netlogon\Parameters\ChangeLogSize`.

The default size of the change log is 65,536 bytes (64KB), and can be configured as large as 4,194,304 bytes (4MB). The average change log entry uses about 32 bytes of space in the change log.

---

**TO INCREASE THE SIZE OF THE CHANGE LOG, FOLLOW THESE STEPS:**

**1.** Select Start ⇒ Run.

**2.** In the Run dialog box, type **Regedt32.exe** in the Open text box. Click OK.

**3.** The Registry Editor dialog box appears. Select Window ⇒ HKEY_LOCAL MACHINE on Local Machine.

**4.** In the Registry Editor dialog box, double-click the SYSTEM folder. Double-click the CurrentControlSet folder. Double-click the Services folder. Double-click the Netlogon folder. Click the Parameters folder. Select Edit ⇒ Add Value.

**5.** In the Add Value dialog box, type **ChangeLogSize** in the Value Name text box. In the Data Type drop-down list box, select REG_DWORD. Figure 11-3 shows the Registry Editor and Add Value dialog boxes. Click OK.

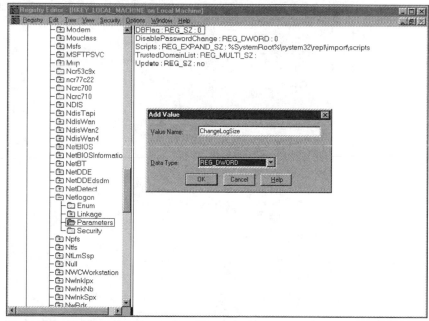

**FIGURE 11-3**  Adding the ChangeLogSize value

**6.** The DWORD Editor dialog box appears. First, select the radio button next to Decimal. Then, in the Data text box, type in a new value for the ChangeLogSize, in bytes. Figure 11-4 shows the DWORD Editor dialog box. Notice that the number entered is twice the default size of the change log (2 × 65,536 = 131,072). Click OK.

FIGURE 11-4   Configuring the ChangeLogSize

**7.** The Registry Editor dialog box reappears, as shown in Figure 11-5. Notice that the ChangeLogSize value appears on the top right-hand side of the dialog box, and that the new value assigned has been converted to hexadecimal. (20,000 is the hexadecimal equivalent of 131,072.) Exit Registry Editor.

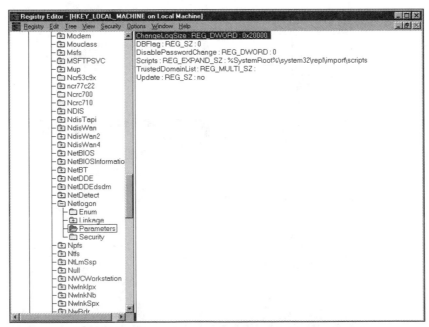

FIGURE 11-5   ChangeLogSize entry successfully added to the Registry

You will need to stop and restart the NetLogon service in order for the new ChangeLogSize value to take effect. (You can do this by using the Services application in Control Panel, or by using the `Net.exe` command-line utility.)

## Modifying the ReplicationGovernor value

The *ReplicationGovernor* is a setting in the Windows NT Registry that controls the size of the synchronization buffer and how frequently the BDC requests Directory Services database updates from the PDC. The value of the ReplicationGovernor can be decreased in order to reduce the frequency and amount of synchronization traffic over a WAN link.

The ReplicationGovernor is configured individually on each BDC, *not* on the PDC.

The acceptable values for the ReplicationGovernor setting are from 0 to 100. The default value for the ReplicationGovernor is one hundred. This means that a maximum buffer size of 128KB is used, and that the BDC requests updates from the PDC (without pausing between requests) until all changes in the change log have been transferred from the PDC to the BDC. After the BDC has received all changes from the PDC, it waits until the PDC notifies it that additional changes to the Directory Services database have occurred. Then the synchronization process begins again.

If a setting of 50 is used, the maximum buffer size is reduced to 64KB. Additionally, during synchronization, the BDC pauses between each request to the PDC so that updates take up only about 50 percent of the WAN link's bandwidth during the synchronization process.

If you decide to decrease the ReplicationGovernor value, you should consider increasing the size of the change log to avoid full synchronization.

If the ReplicationGovernor is set at too low a value, synchronization may never be completed, because changes to the Directory Services database may occur more frequently than the ReplicationGovernor value allows them to be transferred to the BDC. Values lower than 25 percent are not generally recommended.

The ReplicationGovernor entry is stored in the Windows NT Registry in: `HKEY_LOCAL_MACHINE\SYSTEM\CurrentControlSet\Services\Netlogon\Parameters\ReplicationGovernor`.

The steps required to decrease the ReplicationGovernor value are virtually identical to the steps required to increase the size of the change log (listed in the previous section)—just replace all references to ChangeLogSize with ReplicationGovernor, and, when requested, insert the appropriate ReplicationGovernor value.

After changing the ReplicationGovernor value, you will need to stop and restart the NetLogon service in order for the new ReplicationGovernor value to take effect.

### *Controlling when synchronization occurs*

In addition to limiting the size and frequency of synchronization data transfers from the PDC to the BDCs, you can also limit the hours when synchronization can occur.

For example, you might want to limit synchronization traffic over a WAN link to non-business hours, when network traffic on the link is at a minimum.

To accomplish this, you can use the Windows NT Schedule service and the Regini.exe program (from the *Microsoft Windows NT Server Resource Kit for version 4.0*) to set the ReplicationGovernor value to 0 during business hours (so that no synchronization occurs), and to 100 during non-business hours. Every time you change the value of the ReplicationGovernor in the Registry, you need to stop and restart the NetLogon service so that the new ReplicationGovernor value will take effect.

You may also need to increase the size of the change log so that it is large enough to hold all of the changes that occur during the work day.

# KEY POINT SUMMARY

This chapter described optimizing Windows NT Server Directory Services through a comprehensive network design and administration process.

- A first step in optimizing Directory Services is *determining the size of the Directory Services database*. The recommended maximum size of the Directory Services database is 40MB (40,000KB). The Directory Services database contains user accounts, computer accounts, and group accounts. Each component requires a specific amount of space in the database. Each user account requires 1KB, each computer account requires .5KB, each local group requires .5KB *plus* 36 bytes for each member, and each global group requires .5KB *plus* 12 bytes for each member of the group.

- You can calculate the approximate size of the Directory Services database by using the formula: Size of Directory Services database, in KB, = Number of user accounts + (.5 × number of computer accounts) + (3 × total number of groups).

- Several factors should be considered when *determining the appropriate number of master domains*:

  - The size of your organization's Directory Services database

  - The hardware capabilities of computers used as domain controllers

  - The structure of your organization, including organizational/departmental groupings, the centralized or decentralized management structure you want to use for your network, and the geographical distribution of your organization's users and computers

  - Future anticipated growth of the organization

  - The hardware specifications of the computers used as domain controllers significantly impact the determination of the appropriate number of master domains. For example, if your company plans to use Pentium computers with 64MB of RAM for its domain controllers, the maximum Directory Services database size that these computers can accommodate is 20MB per domain. This recommended Directory Services database size assumes that domain controllers are used *only* for logon validation and do not perform any other network services. If your domain controllers perform multiple functions, you will need more powerful hardware to support a given Directory Services database size.

- *The minimum recommended number of domain controllers for each domain is one PDC and one BDC.* This number of domain controllers accommodates from 1 to 2,000 users, and is based on a domain controller hardware configuration consisting of a 486/66 CPU, with a minimum of 32MB of RAM.

- It is recommended that a BDC be added for every additional 2,000 users, or increment thereof. Using these guidelines, a domain that contains between 8,001 and 10,000 users requires one PDC and five BDCs. These guidelines assume that BDCs are used *only* for logon validation, and do not perform any other network services. If BDCs perform multiple functions, you need more powerful hardware or additional BDCs to support the number of users recommended in these guidelines. More BDCs may also be required in a WAN environment to support local logon validation and authentication at each location.

- There are two primary techniques an administrator can use to optimize Directory Services in a WAN environment: selecting appropriate locations for BDCs to optimize logon and authentication traffic, and optimizing Directory Services database synchronization between the PDC and the BDCs.

    - The key point in optimizing BDC placement is the *location of users that require logon validation*, especially when you want to eliminate logon traffic across a WAN link. Also keep in mind that a BDC can serve up to 2,000 users, so if more than 2,000 users are logging on from a remote location, additional remote BDCs are required.

    - *Optimizing Directory Services synchronization* refers to the process of managing the periodic synchronization of Directory Services database changes between the PDC and the BDCs so that other network traffic, particularly traffic across a WAN link, is not hindered.

        - The first step in optimizing Directory Services synchronization is determining the amount of time it takes, per month, to synchronize data between a PDC and the BDCs. If Directory Services synchronization is utilizing too much of a WAN link's capacity, an administrator can take various steps to optimize synchronization traffic.

        - Sometimes it is beneficial to increase the size of the *change log* when optimizing Directory Services synchronization. By default, the change log is 64KB in size, and can contain up to approximately 2,000 account and password changes. This may not be enough if you decide to limit the amount of synchronization data than can be transferred, or the frequency or hours when synchronization traffic across a WAN link can occur. The change log entry is stored in the Windows NT Registry in: `HKEY_LOCAL_MACHINE\SYSTEM\CurrentControlSet\` `Services\Netlogon\Parameters\ChangeLogSize`. The size of the change log can be increased by using Registry Editor.

- The *ReplicationGovernor* is a setting in the Windows NT Registry that controls the size of the synchronization buffer and how frequently the BDC requests Directory Services database updates from the PDC. The value of the ReplicationGovernor can be decreased in order to reduce the frequency and amount of synchronization traffic over a WAN link. The default value for the ReplicationGovernor is one hundred. The ReplicationGovernor is configured individually on each BDC, *not* on the PDC. The ReplicationGovernor entry is stored in the Windows NT Registry in: `HKEY_LOCAL_MACHINE\SYSTEM\CurrentControlSet\` `Services\Netlogon\Parameters\ReplicationGovernor`.

- In addition to limiting the size and frequency of synchronization data transfers to the BDCs, you can also limit the hours when synchronization can occur. For example, you might want to limit synchronization traffic over a WAN link to non-business hours, when network traffic is at a minimum. To accomplish this, you could use the Schedule service and the `Regini.exe` program to set the ReplicationGovernor value to 0 during business hours, and to 100 during non-business hours. Whenever the change log or ReplicationGovernor values are changed, you need to stop and restart the NetLogon service in order for the new value to take effect.

# APPLYING WHAT YOU'VE LEARNED

Now it's time to regroup, review, and apply what you've learned in this chapter.

The following Instant Assessment questions bring to mind key facts and concepts.

The hands-on lab tests your ability to apply the knowledge you've acquired in this chapter on optimizing Windows NT Services.

## Instant Assessment

1. What is the recommended *maximum* size of the Directory Services database?

2. What are the space requirements for each of the components of the Directory Services database?

3. What formula can you use to calculate the size of the Directory Services database?

4. Calculate the approximate size of the Directory Services database for a company that has 21,000 users, 24,000 computers, and 400 groups.

5. Your company has decided to use Pentium computers with 64MB of RAM for its domain controllers. Assuming that the domain controllers are used *only* for logon validation, what is the maximum size of the Directory Services database that can be accommodated by these computers?

6. Your company has decided to use Pentium Pro computers with 128MB of RAM for its domain controllers. Assuming that the domain controllers are used *only* for logon validation, what is the maximum size of the Directory Services database that can be accommodated by these computers?

7. What is the *minimum* recommended number of domain controllers for each domain?

8. Based on a hardware configuration consisting of a 486/66 CPU with 32MB of RAM, up to how many users can each BDC accommodate, assuming that BDCs are used *only* for logon validation and are not used to perform authentication across WAN links?

9. What is the key point in optimizing placement of BDCs, particularly when trying to eliminate logon traffic across a WAN link?

10. By default, what is the size of the change log?

11. Up to how many account and password changes can the change log, by default, contain?

12. Where is the change log entry stored in the Registry?

13. Which Windows NT utility can you use to increase the size of the change log or modify the ReplicationGovernor value?

14. Where is the ReplicationGovernor entry stored in the Registry?

**15.** Whenever you change the size of the change log or modify the ReplicationGovernor value, what must you do before the newly assigned value becomes effective?

**16.** What is the default value for the ReplicationGovernor?

**17.** What does the ReplicationGovernor control?

**18.** On which type of domain controller is the ReplicationGovernor configured?

 concept link    **For answers to the Instant Assessment questions see Appendix D.**

## Hands-on Lab Exercise

The following hands-on lab exercise provides you with an opportunity to use the techniques you've learned in this chapter to optimize Windows NT Directory Services in a WAN environment.

### Lab 11.17 *Optimizing WAN link performance by the appropriate placement of BDCs*

Enterprise

The purpose of this lab is to provide you with hands-on experience in planning the optimization of WAN link performance by determining the appropriate number and placement of BDCs throughout a master domain model.

Your goal, in optimizing WAN link performance, is to optimize for efficient local user logon and authentication.

**Scenario:**   You are planning to implement a master domain model for your company's multilocation Windows NT network. You have chosen to implement the master domain model that is shown in Figure 11-6. Notice that the LAS_VEGAS, SALT_LAKE_CITY, and ALBUQUERQUE domains trust the DENVER domain. Also note that the DENVER domain contains all of the user accounts.

Your company's three remote locations (Las Vegas, Salt Lake City, and Albuquerque) are connected to the Denver office by various-speed WAN links, as shown in Figure 11-7.

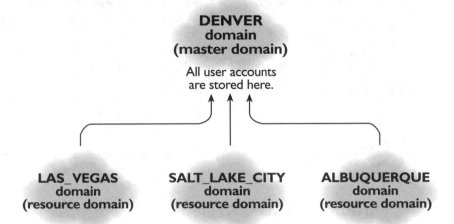

**FIGURE 11-6**  Your company's domain model

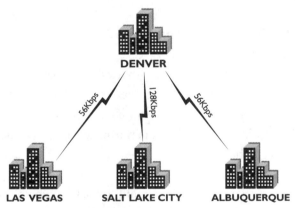

**FIGURE 11-7**  WAN connections between your company's
four locations.

Your company has a different number of users at each of its four locations.
Table 11-2 shows the number of users at each location.

| TABLE 11-2 NUMBER OF USERS, BY LOCATION | |
| --- | --- |
| *LOCATION* | *NUMBER OF USERS* |
| Denver | 4,500 |
| Las Vegas | 2,700 |
| Salt Lake City | 3,800 |
| Albuquerque | 1,200 |

Your company's minimum hardware standard for BDCs is a 486/66 CPU with 32MB of RAM. The BDCs will be used *only* for user logon and authentication purposes.

The PDC will be located in the Denver office.

How many BDCs for the DENVER domain are required in each location to optimize your company's network for efficient local user logon and authentication? (Record your answers below).

**Location**          **# of BDCs**

Denver          _____

Las Vegas          _____

Salt Lake City          _____

Albuquerque          _____

 concept link          **For answers to the hands-on lab exercise see Appendix D.**

Workstation
Server
Enterprise

CHAPTER

# Sharing and Securing File Systems

# 12

# About Chapter 12

This chapter focuses on sharing and securing files and folders on a network. After some introductory information about file and folder attributes, we'll get right to the nitty-gritty of sharing folders. You'll learn how to share a folder and how to modify a share. Share permissions are explained, including how to assign them, and how user and group permissions combine.

Next, we explore NTFS permissions. You'll learn how to assign NTFS permissions to files and folders; how NTFS permissions are applied to new, moved, and copied files and folders; and how NTFS and share permissions interact.

Then this chapter presents tips for planning a strategy for sharing and securing your network resources. Finally, we discuss auditing files and folders on NTFS partitions, and tips for troubleshooting common resource access and permission problems.

This chapter includes three hands-on labs. In the first lab, you'll plan a strategy for sharing and securing resources, and then actually implement that strategy. In the second, you'll establish file and folder auditing. In the third, you'll troubleshoot some common resource access and permission problems.

Chapter 12 is a "must read" no matter which of the three Windows NT 4.0 Microsoft Certified Professional exams you're preparing for. This chapter covers shared resource objectives in the Planning, Managing Resources, and Troubleshooting sections in these exams' objectives.

---

# MANAGING FILE AND FOLDER ATTRIBUTES

Windows NT files and folders have various *attributes*, some of which the administrator can use to provide a limited amount of data protection. For example, administrators often use the read-only file attribute to prevent accidental deletion of files, such as application files. Other file and folder attributes are applied by Windows NT system files automatically during installation.

File attributes can be used on both FAT and NTFS partitions, with the exception of the Compress attribute, which is only available on NTFS partitions.

Table 12-1 lists and describes the five Windows NT file and folder attributes.

**TABLE 12-1** WINDOWS NT FILE AND FOLDER ATTRIBUTES

| ATTRIBUTE | DESCRIPTION |
|---|---|
| Archive | Indicates that the file or folder has been modified since the last backup. |
| | Is applied by the operating system when a file or folder is saved or created, and is commonly removed by backup programs after the file or folder has been backed up. |
| | Is normally not changed by the administrator. |
| Compress | Indicates that Windows NT has compressed the file or folder. |
| | Is only available on NTFS partitions. |
| | Uses the same compression algorithm as the MS–DOS 6.0 DoubleSpace utility. |
| | Can be set on individual files. |
| | Is applied by administrators to control which files and folders will be compressed. |
| Hidden | Indicates that the file or folder can't be seen in a normal directory scan. |
| | Files or folders with this attribute can't be copied or deleted. |
| | Is applied to various files and folders by NT automatically during installation. |
| Read-only | Indicates that the file or folder can only be read. It can't be written to or deleted. |
| | Is often applied by administrators to prevent accidental deletion of application files. |
| System | Indicates that the file or folder is used by the operating system. |
| | Files or folders with this attribute can't be seen in a normal directory scan. |
| | Files or folders with this attribute can't be copied or deleted. |
| | Is applied to various files and folders by NT automatically during installation. |

Any user who can access a file or folder on a FAT partition can modify that file or folder's attributes. Any user who has the Write (W) NTFS permission (or any permission that includes the Write (W) permission) to a file or folder on an NTFS partition can modify that file or folder's attributes. (NTFS permissions are covered later in this chapter.)

On NTFS volumes, when a file or folder has the Read-only attribute, and the file or folder also has the Write (W) NTFS permission for a user or group, the

Read-only attribute takes precedence. The Read-only attribute must be removed before the file can be modified or deleted. The next section describes how to change file or folder attributes, and how to assign file or folder attributes.

---

**TO CHANGE OR ASSIGN FILE OR FOLDER
ATTRIBUTES, FOLLOW THESE STEPS:**

**1.** Select Start ⇒ Programs ⇒ Windows NT Explorer.

**2.** In the Exploring dialog box, highlight the file or folder on which you want to change attributes or to which you want to assign attributes.

**3.** Select File ⇒ Properties. (Or, you can right-click the file or folder, and select Properties from the menu that appears.)

**4.** The *File_name* or *Folder_name* Properties dialog box appears, as shown in Figure 12-1. Notice the System attribute is grayed out and can't be changed using this interface. Also notice the four attributes that are available: Read-only, Archive, Compress, and Hidden.

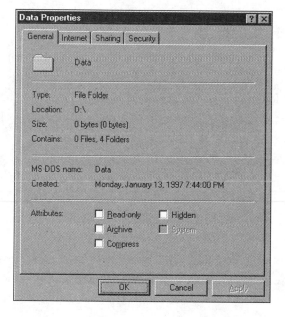

**FIGURE 12-1**   Setting file or folder attributes

**5.** Select the check boxes next to the attributes you want to assign. (Or, clear the check boxes next to attributes you want to remove.) Click OK.

**6.** Exit Windows NT Explorer.

---

# Managing Shared Folders

In Windows NT, folders are *shared* to enable users to access network resources. A folder can't be accessed by users across the network until it is shared or placed within another folder that is shared. Once a folder is shared, users with the appropriate permissions can access the shared folder (and all folders and files that the shared folder contains) over the network.

A shared folder appears in Windows NT Explorer and My Computer as a folder with a hand under it. A shared folder is often referred to as a *share*.

Only members of the Administrators, Server Operators, and Power Users built-in local groups can share folders.

The following sections discuss how to share a folder, shared folder permissions and how to assign them, how to modify a share, how to stop sharing a folder, and administrative shares and how to prevent their automatic creation by Windows NT.

## Sharing a Folder

Only certain users can share folders. Members of the Administrators local group can share folders on any Windows NT computer; members of the Server Operators group can share folders on all Windows NT domain controllers; and members of the Power Users group can share folders on all Windows NT non-domain controllers, including Windows NT Workstation computers.

When a folder is shared, its *entire contents* (including all files and subfolders) are available to users who have the appropriate permissions to the share. Because all files and subfolders are accessible when a folder is shared, you should consider which groups and users need access to folders when you design your server's folder structure.

When sharing a folder, it's a good idea to assign it a share name that is easily recognized by users, and one that appropriately describes the resources contained in the folder. Otherwise, users can become frustrated trying to find the specific network resources they need.

Additionally, keep in mind when you assign a name to a shared folder that a long share name may *not* be readable by all client computers on your network. MS-DOS computers, for example, can only read share names up to eight characters (plus a three-character extension), and Windows 95 computers can only read share names up to twelve characters. Share names in Windows NT can be as long as eighty characters.

You can use either Windows NT Explorer or Server Manager to share folders.

The next sections explain the steps involved in sharing a folder, first by using Windows NT Explorer, and then by using Server Manager.

 note **You can use Windows NT Explorer to share folders only on the local computer; however, you can use Server Manager to share folders both locally and on remote computers.**

### TO SHARE A FOLDER USING WINDOWS NT EXPLORER, FOLLOW THESE STEPS:

**1.** Select Start ⇒ Programs ⇒ Windows NT Explorer.

**2.** In the Exploring dialog box, highlight the folder you want to share. Select File ⇒ Properties. (Or, right-click the folder and select Sharing from the menu that appears. Skip to Step 4.)

**3.** In the *Folder_name* Properties dialog box, click the Sharing tab.

**4.** On the Sharing tab, select the radio button next to Shared As. Either accept the default name in the Share Name text box or type in the name you want to use for the share. Figure 12-2 shows the Sharing tab in the Data Properties dialog box. Note that the radio button next to Shared As is selected.

You can add a descriptive comment about the share in the Comment text box if you so choose. (This is an optional setting.)

If you want to limit the number of users who can connect to this share simultaneously (because of licensing limitations and such) you can configure the User Limit section on the Sharing tab. The default User Limit setting is Maximum Allowed.

Click OK.

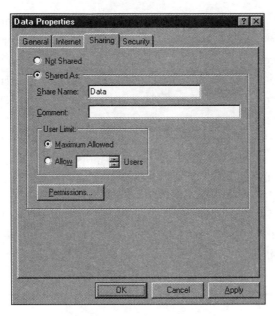

**FIGURE 12-2**  **Using Windows NT Explorer to share a folder**

**5.** The Exploring dialog box reappears. A hand appears under the folder you shared, indicating that it is a shared folder. Exit Windows NT Explorer.

### TO SHARE A FOLDER USING SERVER MANAGER, FOLLOW THESE STEPS:

**1.** Select Start ⇒ Programs ⇒ Administrative Tools (Common) ⇒ Server Manager.

**2.** In the Server Manager dialog box, highlight the computer that contains the folder you want to share. Select Computer ⇒ Shared Directories.

**3.** In the Shared Directories dialog box, click the New Share command button.

**4.** The New Share dialog box appears, as shown in Figure 12-3. Notice the various configuration options in the dialog box.

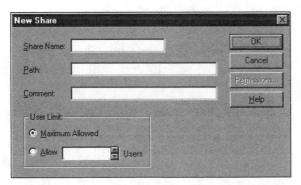

**FIGURE 12-3**  **Using Server Manager to share a folder**

In the Share Name text box, type in the name you want to assign to the new share. Then, in the Path text box, type in the full path to the share, in the form of *Drive_letter:\Folder\subfolder\ . . .* For example, to share the CD-ROM drive on a remote Windows NT computer that uses E: as the drive letter, you would type **E:\** in the Path text box.

You can enter a descriptive comment about the share in the Comment text box if you so choose. If you want to limit the number of users that can connect to this share simultaneously you can configure the User Limit section.

Click OK.

5. The new share appears (with a hand under it) in the Shared Directories dialog box. Click the Close command button.

6. Exit Server Manager.

If you want to restrict user access to the folders that you have shared, you can assign shared folder permissions.

## Shared Folder Permissions

*Shared folder permissions* control user access to shared folders. Shared folder permissions only apply when users connect to the folder over the network—they do not apply when users access the folder from the local computer.

Shared folder permissions (commonly called *share permissions*) apply to the shared folder, its files, and subfolders (in other words, to the *entire* directory tree under the shared folder).

Share permissions are the only folder and file security available on a FAT partition (with the exception of file attributes), and control only over-the-network access to the share—local access is totally unrestricted on a FAT partition.

Table 12-2 lists and describes the Windows NT share permissions, from the most restrictive to the least restrictive.

| **TABLE 12-2** WINDOWS NT SHARE PERMISSIONS | |
| --- | --- |
| *PERMISSION* | *DESCRIPTION* |
| No Access | Permits a user to connect to a share only, but prevents a user from accessing the shared folder and its contents. |
| Read | Permits a user to view file and folder names. |
| | Permits a user to change current folder to a subfolder of the share. |
| | Permits a user to view data in files; and to run application files. |
| Change | Permits a user to perform all tasks included in the Read permission. |
| | Permits a user to create files and folders within the share; to edit data files and save changes; and to delete files and folders within the share. |
| Full Control | Permits a user to perform all tasks included in the Change permission. |
| | Permits a user to change NTFS permissions (discussed later in this chapter)—this only applies to shares on NTFS partitions; and |
| | Permits a user to take ownership of files and folders—this only applies to shares on NTFS partitions. |

Share permissions are assigned by adding a user or group to the permissions list for the share. From an administrative standpoint, it's much more efficient to add groups to the permissions list for a particular share than to add individual users. By default, the Everyone group is granted the Full Control permission to all newly created shared folders.

When assigning permissions to a share, you should consider assigning the most restrictive permission that still allows users to accomplish the tasks they need to perform. For example, on shares that contain applications, consider assigning the Read permission so that users can't accidentally delete application files.

You can assign share permissions by using Windows NT Explorer or Server Manager. The next section explains how to assign share permissions using Windows NT Explorer.

**TO ASSIGN SHARE PERMISSIONS BY USING
WINDOWS NT EXPLORER, FOLLOW THESE STEPS:**

**1.** Select Start ⇒ Programs ⇒ Windows NT Explorer.

**2.** In the Exploring dialog box, highlight the shared folder to which you want to assign permissions. Select File ⇒ Properties.

**3.** In the *Folder_name* Properties dialog box, click the Sharing tab.

**4.** On the Sharing tab, click the Permissions command button.

**5.** The Access Through Share Permissions dialog box appears, as shown in Figure 12-4. Notice that, by default, the Everyone group has Full Control. Click the Add command button.

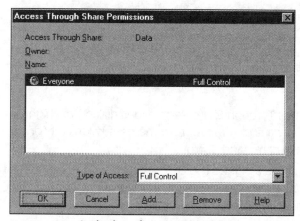

**FIGURE 12-4    Assigning share permissions**

**6.** The Add Users and Groups dialog box appears, as shown in Figure 12-5. Notice that only group names from the WEST domain appear in the Names list box.

If you want to add global groups and users from other trusted domains, click the arrow in the List Names From drop-down list box and select the domain you want. If you want to add individual users, click the Show Users command button. Double-click the group or user you want to add to the permissions list for the share. Then select the appropriate permission from the Type of Access drop-down list box. Click OK.

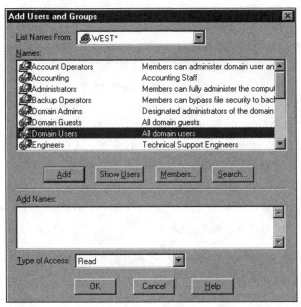

**FIGURE 12-5**    **Adding users and groups to the permissions list for the share**

**7.** In the Access Through Share Permissions dialog box, highlight any users or groups you want to remove from the permissions list for the share. Click the Remove command button.

(Once you have assigned the appropriate user and groups to the permissions list for the share, I recommend you remove the Everyone group from the list, so that only authorized users can access the share.)

Click OK.

**8.** Click OK in the *Folder_name* Properties dialog box.

**9.** Exit Windows NT Explorer.

in the
real world

**If you share folders on a FAT partition, I recommend you assign appropriate share permissions. However, if you share folders on an NTFS partition, I recommend you assign the Domain Users group the Full Control share permission, delete the Everyone group's Full Control share permission, and then manage security by assigning the appropriate NTFS permissions (covered later in this chapter).**

## How user and group permissions combine

It is not uncommon for a user to have permission to a share and to be a member of multiple groups that have different permissions to that share. When this occurs, the user and group permissions are additive, and the *least* restrictive permission is the user's effective permission. For example, a user has the Read permission to a share, and a group that the user is a member of has the Change permission to the share. The user's effective share permission is Change.

The exception to this rule is the No Access permission. *No Access always overrides all other share permissions.* If a user has the Full Control permission, but is a member of a group that has the No Access permission, the user's effective permission is No Access. *No Access always means no access.*

Here are two examples that illustrate how user and group share permissions combine.

**Example 1**   A user, RomanB, manages a shared folder named SalesData that contains Sales Department data. RomanB is a member of three groups. Table 12-3 shows the SalesData share permissions assigned to RomanB and to the three groups of which he is a member.

**TABLE 12-3** ROMANB'S GROUP MEMBERSHIPS AND SHARE PERMISSIONS

| USER OR GROUP | SALESDATA SHARE PERMISSION ASSIGNED |
| --- | --- |
| RomanB | Full Control |
| Sales | Change |
| Everyone | Read |
| Domain Users | Read |

Because share permissions are additive, RomanB's effective permission to the SalesData share is Full Control.

**Example 2**   Until recently, a user, PennyL, was a design analyst in the Marketing Department. She has just been promoted to a management position in the Human Resources Department. PennyL's network has a shared folder named HRData that contains Human Resources Department data, including employee performance reviews. PennyL is a member of three groups. Table 12-4 shows the `HRData` share permissions assigned to the three groups of which PennyL is a member.

| Group | HRData Share Permission Assigned |
|-------|----------------------------------|
| **TABLE 12-4** PennyL's Group Memberships and Their HRData Share Permissions | |
| Managers | Read |
| HR | Change |
| Marketing | No Access |

Because the No Access permission always overrides all other share permissions, PennyL's effective permission to the `HRData` share is No Access. The administrator should remove PennyL from the Marketing group so that she can access the `HRData` share.

# Modifying a Share

After a share is created, you may want to modify its properties. You can assign multiple share names to a share, change the name of a share, or stop sharing a share.

## Assigning multiple share names to a share

To aid different users in locating or recognizing a share, you can assign multiple names to the same share.

For example, a group of technical support engineers might routinely access a share called CIM (CompuServe Information Manager), and less technical personnel at a help desk might access this same share using the name CompuServe.

When you assign an additional name to a share, you can assign a new set of share permissions that apply only to the new share name.

**TO ASSIGN AN ADDITIONAL NAME TO A SHARE, FOLLOW THESE STEPS:**

**1.** Select Start⇒Programs⇒Windows NT Explorer.

**2.** In the Exploring dialog box, highlight the share to which you want to assign an additional name. Select File⇒Properties.

**3.** In the *Folder_name* Properties dialog box, click the Sharing tab.

**4.** On the Sharing tab, click the New Share command button.

**5.** In the New Share dialog box, type in the additional name you want to assign to the share. Type in a descriptive comment if you so choose. Configure the share permissions and user limit as desired. Click OK.

**6.** In the *Folder_name* Properties dialog box, click OK.

**7.** Exit Windows NT Explorer.

## Changing a share name

Occasionally, you may need to change a share name. Perhaps you want to assign a more intuitive share name for users, or you might need to comply with a newly established set of naming conventions.

**TO CHANGE A SHARE NAME, FOLLOW THESE STEPS:**

**1.** Select Start⇒Programs⇒Windows NT Explorer.

**2.** In the Exploring dialog box, highlight the share with the name you want to change. Select File⇒Properties.

**3.** In the *Folder_name* Properties dialog box, click the Sharing tab.

**4.** On the Sharing tab, click the New Share command button.

**5.** In the New Share dialog box, type a new name for the share in the Share Name text box. You should configure the share permissions and user limit to match those assigned to the original share name (assuming no permission or user limit changes are desired). Click OK when you are finished.

**6.** The *Folder_name* Properties dialog box reappears. Click the arrow in the Share Name drop-down list box to display all names assigned to the share. Figure 12-6 shows the Sharing tab in the Data Properties dialog box. Notice that two names are assigned to the Data folder: Data and

Spreadsheets. (In this example, the Data share is being renamed as Spreadsheets because it is a more intuitive name for users to recognize.)

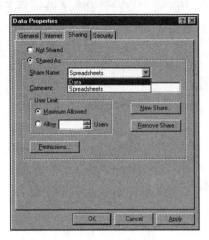

**FIGURE 12-6**  **Changing the name of a share**

Select the original name (not the new name) of the share in the Share Name drop-down list box. Click the Remove Share command button. (This deletes the original share.) Click OK.

**7.** Exit Windows NT Explorer.

## How to stop sharing a folder

You might decide to stop sharing a folder because it is no longer needed, or for other reasons.

**TO STOP SHARING A FOLDER, FOLLOW THESE STEPS:**

**1.** Select Start ⇒ Programs ⇒ Windows NT Explorer.

**2.** In the Exploring dialog box, highlight the share you want to stop sharing. Select File ⇒ Properties.

**3.** In the *Folder_name* Properties dialog box, click the Sharing tab.

**4.** On the Sharing tab, select the radio button next to Not Shared. Then click OK.

**5.** Exit Windows NT Explorer.

# Administrative Shares

Every time you start Windows NT on a computer, NT automatically creates several hidden shares that only members of the Administrators group have permission to access. These shares are referred to as *administrative shares* because they are used by Administrators to perform administrative tasks.

The Windows NT administrative shares are: C$, D$, E$, and so on (one share for the root of each hard disk partition on the computer); and a share named Admin$, which corresponds to the folder in which NT is installed (<winntroot>). The $ at the end of each administrative share causes the share to be hidden from users when they browse the network.

Administrative shares make it possible for an Administrator to connect to any hard drive on a computer and access all of its files and folders, regardless of whether regular shares exist on that hard drive. In this way an Administrator can perform backup, restore, and other administrative functions on a Windows NT computer.

Any share can be configured as a hidden share by placing a $ at the end of its share name. However, hiding a share by appending a $ to the share name does *not* limit user access to the share. The hidden share retains its assigned share permissions. Only access to the hidden *administrative* shares is restricted, by default, to Administrators only.

If you do not want administrative shares available on a Windows NT computer, you can configure NT to prevent the creation of administrative shares.

## Preventing the creation of administrative shares

To configure Windows NT so it does not automatically create administrative shares each time it is started, you can edit the Registry. You can edit the Registry directly using regedt32.exe, or you can use the System Policy Editor to turn off the default administrative shares. The steps below explain how to turn off administrative shares by using the Registry editor, regedt32.exe.

**TO PREVENT THE AUTOMATIC CREATION OF ADMINISTRATIVE SHARES, FOLLOW THESE STEPS:**

**1.** Select Start ⇒ Run.

**2.** In the Open text box, type **Regedt32**. (Don't type the period at the end.)

**3.** In the Registry Editor dialog box, select Window ⇒ HKEY_LOCAL_MACHINE on Local Machine.

4. Double-click the `System` folder under HKEY_LOCAL_MACHINE. Double-click the `CurrentControlSet` folder. Double-click the `Services` folder. Double-click the `LanmanServer` folder, then click the `Parameters` folder.

5. In the window on the right-hand side of the dialog box, double-click AutoShareServer. (If this value is not present, select Edit ⇒ Add Value. In the Add Value dialog box, type **AutoShareServer** in the Value Name text box. In the Data Type drop-down list box, select REG_DWORD. Click OK.)

   (If you are configuring a Windows NT Workstation computer, the value is named AutoShareWks. If this value is not present, select Edit ⇒ Add Value. In the Add Value dialog box, type **AutoShareWks** in the Value Name text box. In the Data Type drop-down list box, select REG_DWORD. Click OK.)

6. In the DWORD Editor dialog box, edit the Data text box so that it has a value of **0** (zero). Click OK.

7. The Registry Editor dialog box reappears. The AutoShareServer REG_DWORD setting (or the AutoShareWks REG_DWORD setting) is changed to 0. Exit Registry Editor.

# MANAGING NTFS FILE AND FOLDER SECURITY

When files and folders are stored on an NTFS volume, NTFS permissions can be assigned to provide a greater level of security than share permissions, because:

o NTFS permissions, unlike share permissions, can be assigned to individual files as well as folders. This gives an administrator a much finer level of control over shared files and folders than is possible by using only share permissions.

o NTFS permissions apply to local users as well as to users who connect to a shared folder over the network. This fills the large security loophole left when files and folders on FAT partitions are secured only by share permissions.

The following sections discuss NTFS permissions, including how they are assigned to files and folders, how NTFS permissions are applied, and how NTFS and share permissions interact.

# NTFS Permissions

*NTFS permissions*, which can only be assigned to files and folders on NTFS volumes, protect data from authorized access when users connect to the share locally or over the network.

The NTFS permissions that can be assigned, and how each permission applies to folders and files, are shown in Table 12-5.

**TABLE 12-5** WINDOWS NT NTFS PERMISSIONS

| PERMISSION | WHEN APPLIED TO A FOLDER, A USER IS ABLE TO . . . | WHEN APPLIED TO A FILE, A USER IS ABLE TO . . . |
|---|---|---|
| Read (R) | View folder attributes, permissions, and owner; view names of files and subfolders. | View file attributes, permissions, owner, and file contents. |
| Write (W) | View folder attributes, permissions, and owner; change folder attributes; add files and subfolders. | View file attributes, permissions, and owner; change file attributes; change file contents. |
| Execute (X) | View folder attributes, permissions, and owner; change the current folder to a subfolder. | View file attributes, permissions, and owner; run the file if it is an executable program. |
| Delete (D) | Delete the folder. | Delete the file. |
| Change Permissions (P) | Assign NTFS permissions to the folder. | Assign NTFS permissions to the file. |
| Take Ownership (O) | Take ownership of the folder. | Take ownership of the file. |

To make the assignment of NTFS permissions easier, Microsoft has created a set of standard directory (folder) permissions, and a set of standard file permissions. These *standard permissions* consist of the most commonly used combinations of NTFS permissions.

Standard permissions are used in most situations. Individual NTFS permissions are typically only used when a unique combination of permissions must be assigned. The individual NTFS permissions are sometimes referred to as *Special Access Directory permissions* and *Special Access File permissions*.

Table 12-6 shows the standard NTFS directory permissions. The permissions specified within the first set of parentheses following the permission name apply to the *folder*, and the permissions specified within the second set of parentheses following the permission name apply to *files* within the folder.

Table 12-7 shows the standard NTFS file permissions. NTFS file permissions apply only to the individual file they are assigned to. Other files in the same folder are *not* affected.

**TABLE 12-6** STANDARD NTFS DIRECTORY (FOLDER) PERMISSIONS

| STANDARD PERMISSION | DESCRIPTION |
|---|---|
| No Access (None) (None) | Prevents access to the folder, and to any file in the folder. When the permission is initially assigned, the administrator can choose whether to apply the permission to existing files and subfolders. |
| List (RX) (Not Specified) | Assigns the Read and Execute permissions to the folder, but no permissions are assigned to any files in the folder. |
| Read (RX) (RX) | Assigns the Read and Execute permissions to the folder and to *new* files created in the folder. When the permission is initially assigned, the administrator can choose whether to apply the permission to all *existing* files and subfolders. |
| Add (WX) (Not Specified) | Assigns the Write and Execute permissions to the folder, but no permissions are assigned to any files in the folder. |
| Add & Read (RWX) (RX) | Assigns the Read, Write, and Execute permissions to the folder, and assigns the Read and Execute permissions to *new* files created in the folder. When the permission is initially assigned, the administrator can choose whether to apply the permission to all *existing* files and subfolders. |
| Change (RWXD) (RWXD) | Assigns the Read, Write, Execute, and Delete permissions to the folder and to *new* files created in the folder. When the permission is initially assigned, the administrator can choose whether to apply the permission to all *existing* files and subfolders. |

| STANDARD PERMISSION | DESCRIPTION |
| --- | --- |
| Full Control (All) (All) | Assigns all NTFS permissions (Read, Write, Execute, Delete, Change Permissions, and Take Ownership) to the folder and to *new* files created in the folder. When the permission is initially assigned, the administrator can choose whether to apply the permission to all *existing* files and subfolders. |

**TABLE 12-7** STANDARD NTFS FILE PERMISSIONS

| STANDARD FILE PERMISSION | DESCRIPTION |
| --- | --- |
| No Access (None) | Prevents access to the file. |
| Read (RX) | Assigns the Read and Execute permissions to the file. |
| Change (RWXD) | Assigns the Read, Write, Execute, and Delete permissions to the file. |
| Full Control (All) | Assigns all NTFS permissions (Read, Write, Execute, Delete, Change Permissions, and Take Ownership) to the file. |

Sometimes a user has a different set of NTFS permissions to a file than to the folder that contains the file. When the user wants to access a file, and the NTFS file and folder permissions conflict, the file permissions are applied. *File permissions take precedence over folder permissions.* For example, if a user has the Change (RWXD) (RWXD) permission to the folder, and has the Read (RX) permission to the file, the user's effective permission to the file is Read (RX).

If a user has permission to access a file, but does *not* have permission to access the folder that contains the file, the user can access the file by typing the file's full path name (in an application, in the Run dialog box, or at the command prompt). The user can't see the file when browsing in Windows NT Explorer.

caution

**The Full Control (All) (All) standard directory permission has a feature that you should be aware of. Because it is designed to support POSIX applications, the Full Control (All) (All) permission allows a user to delete any file in the folder, *even if the user has the No Access (None) standard file permission to the file.* (This is the only exception to the rule that file permissions take precedence over**

**folder permissions.) To prevent this, I recommend that you assign all of the individual (Special Access) NTFS permissions instead of the Full Control (All) (All) standard directory permission.**

As with share permissions, it is not uncommon for a user to have one set of NTFS permissions to a file or folder, and to be a member of multiple groups that have different NTFS permissions to the file or folder. When this occurs, the user and group permissions are additive, and the *least* restrictive combination of permissions applies. The exception to this rule is the No Access permission. *No Access always overrides all other NTFS permissions.*

NTFS permissions are assigned by adding a user or group to the *access control list* (ACL) for the file or folder. From an administrative standpoint, it's much more efficient to add groups to the ACL for a particular file or folder than to add individual users. By default, the Everyone group is granted the Full Control (All) (All) NTFS permission to the root of all newly created NTFS volumes.

## Assigning NTFS Permissions to Files and Folders

A user can assign NTFS permissions to a file or folder only if one or more of the following criteria are met:

o The user is the owner of the file or folder.

o The user has the Change Permissions NTFS permission to the file or folder.

o The user has the Full Control NTFS permission to the file or folder. (The Full Control permission includes the Change Permissions NTFS permission.)

The following sections explain how to assign NTFS permissions—first to a file, and second, to a folder.

**TO ASSIGN NTFS PERMISSIONS TO A FILE, FOLLOW THESE STEPS:**

**1.** Select Start ⇒ Programs ⇒ Windows NT Explorer.

**2.** In the Exploring dialog box, highlight the file to which you want to assign NTFS permissions. (To assign identical permissions to multiple files, highlight more than one file.) Select File ⇒ Properties.

**3.** The *File_name* Properties dialog box appears. Click the Security tab. On the Security tab, click the Permissions command button.

**4.** The File Permissions dialog box appears, as shown in Figure 12-7. Notice the complete path to the file and the owner of the file are listed.

Click the Add command button.

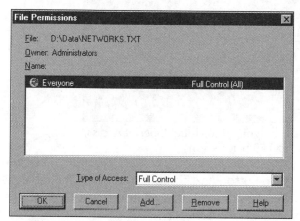

**FIGURE 12-7**    **Assigning NTFS permissions to the Networks.txt file**

**5.** The Add Users and Groups dialog box appears.

To add users or groups from trusted domains, click the arrow in the List Names From drop-down list box, and select the appropriate domain from the list.

To add individual users, click the Show Users command button to display individual users, as well as groups, in the Names list box.

Double-click each user and/or group you want to add to the ACL (permissions list) for the file. Select the NTFS file permission you want to assign from the Type of Access drop-down list box. Click OK.

**6.** The File Permissions dialog box reappears. If you want to assign individual (Special Access) NTFS file permissions (as opposed to the standard NTFS permissions):

**a.** Highlight the user(s) or group(s) to which you want to assign the individual NTFS permissions. Select Special Access from the Type of Access drop-down list box.

**b.** The Special Access dialog box appears, as shown in Figure 12-8. Notice the individual NTFS permissions that can be assigned.

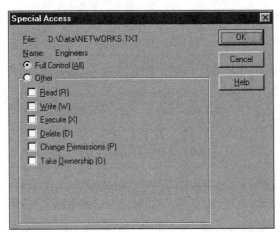

**FIGURE 12-8**    **Assigning individual (Special Access)**
**NTFS permissions**

Select the radio button next to Other. Check the check box next to the individual NTFS permission(s) you want to assign. Click OK. The File Permissions dialog box reappears.

If you want to remove any users or groups from the ACL for the file (such as the Everyone group), highlight the user or group and click the Remove command button.

Figure 12-9 shows the File Permissions dialog box after NTFS permissions have been assigned. Notice the various NTFS permissions assigned, and how they appear in the Name list box. Click OK.

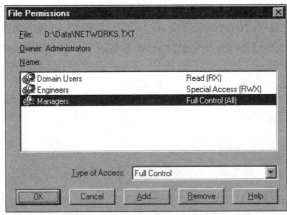

**FIGURE 12-9**    **NTFS permissions assigned to the**
`Networks.txt` **file**

**7.** In the *File_name* Properties dialog box, click OK.

**8.** Exit Windows NT Explorer.

### TO ASSIGN NTFS PERMISSIONS TO A FOLDER, FOLLOW THESE STEPS:

**1.** Select Start⇒Programs⇒Windows NT Explorer.

**2.** In the Exploring dialog box, highlight the folder to which you want to assign NTFS permissions. (To assign identical permissions to multiple folders, highlight more than one folder.) Select File⇒Properties.

**3.** The *Folder_name* Properties dialog box appears. Click the Security tab. On the Security tab, click the Permissions command button.

**4.** The Directory Permissions dialog box appears, as shown in Figure 12-10. Note the two check boxes available. Also note that the check box next to Replace Permissions on Existing Files is selected by default.

Click the Add command button.

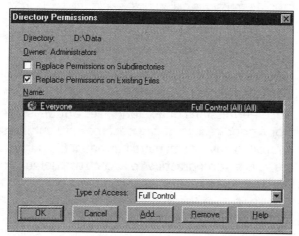

**FIGURE 12-10**    **Assigning NTFS permissions to the**
D:\Data **folder**

**5.** The Add Users and Groups dialog box appears. To add users or groups from trusted domains, click the arrow in the List Names From drop-down list box, and select the appropriate domain from the list.

To add individual users, click the Show Users command button to display individual users, as well as groups, in the Names list box.

Double-click each user and/or group you want to add to the ACL (permissions list) for the folder. Select the NTFS folder permission you want to assign from the Type of Access drop-down list box. Click OK.

**6.** The Directory Permissions dialog box reappears. If you want to assign individual (Special Access) NTFS folder permissions (as opposed to the standard NTFS permissions):

**a.** Highlight the user(s) or group(s) to which you want to assign the individual NTFS permissions. Select Special Directory Access (to assign individual *directory* [folder] permissions) or Special File Access (to assign individual *file* permissions within the folder) from the Type of Access drop-down list box.

**b.** The Special Directory Access (or Special File Access) dialog box appears. Select the radio button next to Other. Then check the check box next to the individual NTFS permission(s) you want to assign. Click OK. The Directory Permissions dialog box reappears.

If you want to remove any users or groups from the ACL for the folder (such as the Everyone group), highlight the user or group and click the Remove command button.

**7.** In the Directory Permissions dialog box, select the check box next to Replace Permissions on Subdirectories if you want these NTFS permissions assigned to all subfolders.

Clear the check box next to Replace Permissions on Existing Files if you do *not* want these NTFS permissions assigned to each existing file within the folder.

note ✏ **The Replace Permissions on Existing Files option is selected by default for a good reason. It can become very cumbersome for an administrator to have to manage individual file permissions. Therefore, it is a good practice to accept the default to Replace Permissions on Existing Files so that all files will have the same permissions as set on the folder. If different permissions are required, a different folder can be created.**

If both check boxes are selected, these NTFS permissions will be assigned to all files within the folder, all subfolders, and their files. If both check boxes are cleared, these NTFS permissions will be assigned only to the folder and to new files created in the folder. Existing subfolders and the files they contain will not be affected.

Figure 12-11 shows the Directory Permissions dialog box after NTFS permissions have been assigned. Notice that both check boxes are selected.

Click OK.

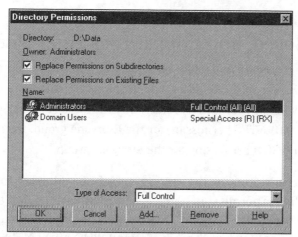

**FIGURE 12-11**　**NTFS permissions assigned to the**
　　　　　　　　D:\Data **folder**

**8.** If you checked the check box next to Replace Permissions on Subdirectories, a warning message appears, asking if you want to replace the security information on all existing subfolders. Click the Yes command button. (If both check boxes were selected, this could take a while. You might want to consider performing this task during nonbusiness hours.)

**9.** In the *Folder_name* Properties dialog box, click OK.

**10.** Exit Windows NT Explorer.

There are a few common administrative practices you should consider when assigning NTFS permissions to files or folders:

○ Consider assigning the most restrictive NTFS permission that still makes it possible for users to accomplish necessary tasks.

○ After assigning the appropriate NTFS permissions, consider removing the Everyone group, which by default is granted the Full Control permission.

○ When you want all users to be able to access a file or folder, consider assigning the NTFS permissions to the Domain Users group instead of to the Everyone group. (The Everyone group includes not only all domain users, but also *anyone* [authorized or not] who can access your network, including those who connect via the Internet.)

## How NTFS Permissions Are Applied to New, Moved, and Copied Files and Folders

When files are created in a folder on an NTFS volume, the new files inherit the NTFS permissions of the folder in which they are created. For example, if you create a new file in the Public folder, and the Public folder has the Change (RWXD) (RWXD) NTFS permission for the Everyone group, the new file inherits the Change (RWXD) permission for the Everyone group.

 **The permissions in the *second* set of parentheses following the NTFS folder permission name are the permissions that are assigned to the new *file*. So, if you create a new file in the Data folder, and the Data folder has the Add & Read (RWX) (RX) NTFS permission for the Domain Users group, the file inherits the Read (RX) permission for the Domain Users group.**

When new subfolders are created on an NTFS volume, they inherit the NTFS permissions of the folder that contains them. For example, if you create a new subfolder in the Data folder, and the Data folder has the Add & Read (RWX) (RX) NTFS permission for the Everyone group, the new subfolder inherits the Add & Read (RWX) (RX) permission for the Everyone group.

*When files or folders are moved or copied, their NTFS permissions often change.* Normally, when files or folders are moved or copied, they inherit the NTFS permissions of the destination folder. The only exception to this rule is when files or folders are *moved* to a new folder on the *same* NTFS volume—in this case, the moved files or folders retain their original NTFS permissions.

The following examples illustrate how NTFS permissions are applied to moved or copied files:

**Example 1: Moving a file to a folder on a different volume**    You *move* the D:\Public\Readme.txt file (that has the Read (RX) NTFS permissions for the Everyone group) to the E:\Data folder (that has the Full Control (All) (All) NTFS permission for the Everyone group). When the file is moved to a folder on a different volume, it inherits the NTFS permissions from the E:\Data folder (the destination folder), so the moved file's permissions are now Full Control (All) for the Everyone group.

**Example 2: Copying a file to a different folder on the same volume**     You *copy* the D:\Data\Busplan.doc file (that has the Read (RX) NTFS permissions for the Managers group) to the D:\Public folder (that has the Change (RWXD) (RWXD) NTFS permissions for the Everyone group). When the file is copied, it inherits the NTFS permissions from the D:\Public folder (the destination folder), so the copied file's permissions are now Change (RWXD) for the Everyone group.

**Example 3: Moving a file to a different folder on the same volume**     You *move* the D:\Data\Busplan.doc file (that has the Read (RX) NTFS permissions for the Managers group) to the D:\Public folder (that has the Change (RWXD) (RWXD) NTFS permissions for the Everyone group). When the file is moved to a folder on the *same* NTFS volume, it retains its original NTFS permissions. In this case, the moved file's NTFS permissions are still Read (RX) for the Managers group.

 tip **Because FAT partitions can't support NTFS permissions, any files that you copy or move to a FAT partition lose all their NTFS permissions, along with the security that those permissions provided.**

## How NTFS and Share Permissions Interact

When users access a share on an NTFS volume over the network, *both* NTFS and share permissions are used to determine the user's effective permission to the file or folder in the share.

When NTFS and share permissions differ, the *most* restrictive permission becomes the user's effective permission to the file or folder in the share. This means that if *either* the NTFS or the share permissions deny a user access, access is denied.

The following examples illustrate how NTFS and share permissions interact:

**Example 1:**     A folder named Documents is shared on an NTFS volume. The Documents share has the Change share permission for the Everyone group, and the files and folders in the share all have the Full Control NTFS permission for the Everyone group. Users who access the Documents share over the network only have the Change permission to the files and folders, because Change is the most restrictive permission.

**Example 2:**   A folder named `Apps` is shared on an NTFS volume. The `Apps` share has the Full Control share permission assigned to the Everyone group, and the files and folders in the share all have the Read NTFS permission for the Everyone group. Users who access the `Apps` share over the network only have the Read permission to the files and folders, because Read is the most restrictive permission.

Remember, share permissions only apply when users connect to a shared folder *over the network*. NTFS permissions are the only permissions that apply to users who log on locally to the computer that contains the share.

# PLANNING STRATEGIES FOR SHARING AND SECURING RESOURCES

There is no one right way to share and secure your network resources. However, there are several common practices that you can use when planning your network sharing-and-securing strategy. Consider using some or all of the following tips to provide security for network resources and to simplify administration.

- Assign share names that are easily recognized by users, that appropriately describe the resources contained in the share; and that are of appropriate length, so that users of all client computers can access the share.

- When assigning permissions, use groups, rather than individual users, when possible, to simplify administration.

- Consider using the Domain Users group instead of the Everyone group when assigning permissions to all users in the domain to close up the security loophole that the Everyone group allows.

- Consider storing important data on NTFS volumes instead of on FAT volumes, because of the greater security possible on NTFS volumes.

- Consider storing operating systems on a separate volume from data files, home folders, and applications. This makes backup, restore, and administration easier.

- Always store data files and application files in different folders. This helps prevent accidental deletion of application files and simplifies backup and restore procedures.

o Consider making it a practice to always assign the most restrictive permission that still allows a user to accomplish the tasks they need to perform.

o Consider assigning administrators the Full Control permission to all shares, with the exception of user's home folders (directories).

o When assigning both share and NTFS permissions, consider assigning the Full Control share permission to the Domain Users group, and using the appropriate NTFS permissions to secure the resource. (After you assign the Domain Users group the Full Control share permission, you can remove the Everyone group's Full Control permission from the share.) This prevents the administrative nightmare of always having to determine the most restrictive combination of share and NTFS permissions for a given user or group to a resource.

## Planning Form: Sharing and Securing Resources

You can use this form to help you plan how to apply share and/or NTFS permissions to shared resources on your network. (Find an enlarged version of this form in Appendix G.)

| Resource: (Include path) | Share Name: | Share Permissions Applied: | | NTFS Permissions Applied: | |
|---|---|---|---|---|---|
| | | User/Group | Permission | User/Group | Permission |
| (Example) D:\Data\Sales | SalesData | Domain Users (Remove Everyone group) | Full Control | Sales | Change |
| | | | | | |
| | | | | | |

# TAKING OWNERSHIP OF FILES AND FOLDERS

The creator of a file or folder is its *owner* (except that when a member of the Administrators group creates a file or folder, the Administrators *group*, not the user, is the owner of the file or folder). The owner of a file or folder can always assign permissions to that file or folder. Only files and folders on NTFS partitions have owners.

Occasionally, you may need to change or assign permissions to a file or folder, but not have the Change Permissions NTFS permission (or the Full Control NTFS permission, which includes the Change Permissions NTFS permission) to the file or folder. Without being the owner of the file or folder or having the Change Permissions NTFS permission, the only way you can accomplish changing or assigning permissions to the file or folder is to *take ownership* of the file or folder.

A common situation where taking ownership becomes necessary is when a user (who created a folder and was its owner) leaves the company, and no one else has the Change Permissions NTFS permission (or the Full Control NTFS permission) to the folder. To change the permissions on the folder, the Administrator must first take ownership of it.

A user can take ownership of a file or folder only if one or more of the following criteria are met:

o The user is a member of the Administrators group.

o The user has the Take Ownership NTFS permission to the file or folder (or has the Full Control NTFS permission, which includes the Take Ownership permission).

o The user has the "Take ownership of files or other objects" user right.

The next section describes the steps involved in taking ownership of a file or folder.

**TO TAKE OWNERSHIP OF A FILE OR FOLDER, FOLLOW THESE STEPS:**

**1.** Select Start ⇒ Programs ⇒ Windows NT Explorer.

**2.** Highlight the file or folder that you want to take ownership of. Select File⇒ Properties.

**3.** The *File_name* or *Folder_name* Properties dialog box appears. Click the Security tab.

**4.** On the Security tab, click the Ownership command button.

**5.** If you currently have no permissions to the file or folder, a warning dialog box appears, as shown in Figure 12-12. Notice that the message asks if you want to try overwriting the current owner.

Click the Yes command button.

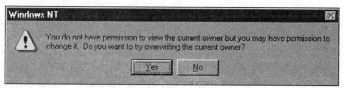

**FIGURE 12-12** Taking ownership warning message

**6.** The Owner dialog box appears, as shown in Figure 12-13. Note that the owner of the folder is listed as "Unable to retrieve."

Click the Take Ownership command button.

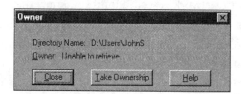

**FIGURE 12-13** Taking ownership of a folder

**7.** If you are taking ownership of a folder, Windows NT displays an informational dialog box, asking if you want to take ownership of all the files and subfolders contained in the selected folder. Click the Yes or No command button, as appropriate. (Yes is usually the appropriate response.)

**8.** If prior to taking ownership you had no permissions to the file or folder, Windows NT displays an informational dialog box, as shown in Figure 12-14. Note that you can choose to grant yourself the Full Control permission to the folder.

Click the Yes command button.

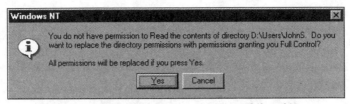

**FIGURE 12-14    Replacing folder permissions while taking ownership**

**9.** The *File_name* or *Folder_name* Properties dialog box reappears. Click OK.

**10.** You are now the owner of the file or folder. Exit Windows NT Explorer.

# AUDITING FILES AND FOLDERS ON NTFS PARTITIONS

You can't be sure that your network is secure until you know that the permissions and other security measures you've put in place haven't been breached. Windows NT auditing makes it possible for you to determine whether unauthorized users have accessed or attempted to access sensitive data.

Windows NT auditing is *only* available on NTFS partitions. You can't audit files or folders that are located on FAT partitions.

Because auditing generates a large amount of data, it's important that you determine what is really necessary to audit. Not only does auditing data take up space in the security log, it also takes administrative time to review the events in the log. In general, if you won't use the information obtained by auditing a given event, you probably shouldn't choose to audit it.

You can choose to audit both successful and unsuccessful (failure) events. For example, you can audit all successful attempts to access a particular program, or you can audit all unsuccessful attempts to access a file that contains confidential data. Success auditing is often performed to gather information about how resources, such as programs and printers, are used. Failure auditing is normally performed to determine whether unauthorized users are attempting to access restricted files or folders. Sometimes success and failure auditing are used simultaneously to determine if any unauthorized users have been successful in breaching the system's security.

When you choose to audit a sensitive resource to determine if your network security has been compromised, consider auditing the Everyone group's success and failure access to the resource. This way, you can track *all* attempts to access the resource, not just attempts made by Domain Users (in other words, the users that you know about).

## Configuring Auditing for Files and Folders on NTFS Partitions

Configuring Windows NT auditing for files and folders on NTFS partitions is a two-part process. First, the audit policy is configured in User Manager or User Manager for Domains. Then, auditing is configured for each file and folder individually using Windows NT Explorer.

Only members of the Administrators group can configure the audit policy. Users with the "Manage auditing and security log" user right can establish file and folder auditing, and view and manage the security log in Event Viewer, but can't set audit policy.

Auditing is configured on an individual computer basis. If you want to audit an event that takes place on a domain controller, such as access to a particular folder, you need to set the audit policy for the domain and configure the folder for auditing on the domain controller. If you want to audit an event that takes place on a non-domain controller, such as access to a particular file, you need to set the audit policy on the non-domain controller and configure the particular file for auditing on the non-domain controller, as well.

The next sections describe how to configure audit policy in User Manager or User Manager for Domains, and then how to configure file or folder auditing in Windows NT Explorer.

**TO CONFIGURE AUDIT POLICY, FOLLOW THESE STEPS:**

**1.** Select Start ⇒ Programs ⇒ Administrative Tools (Common) ⇒ User Manager (or User Manager for Domains).

**2.** In the User Manager dialog box, select Policies ⇒ Audit.

**3.** The Audit Policy dialog box appears, as shown in Figure 12-15. Notice that Success and Failure auditing are selected for File and Object Access.

*You must select File and Object Access auditing to audit files and folders.* If you configure file and folder auditing, but don't configure the audit policy for File and Object Access, no auditing will occur on the files and folders.

Select the radio button next to Audit These Events, and check the check boxes to configure success and/or failure auditing of the events you want to audit. Click OK.

**4.** Exit User Manager (or User Manager for Domains).

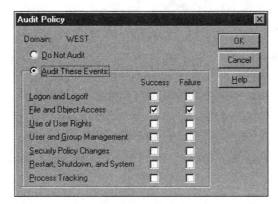

**FIGURE 12-15**    Configuring audit policy

**TO CONFIGURE FILE OR FOLDER AUDITING, FOLLOW THESE STEPS:**

**1.** Select Start ⇒ Programs ⇒ Windows NT Explorer.

**2.** In the Exploring dialog box, highlight the file or folder you want to audit. Select File ⇒ Properties.

**3.** In the *File_name* or *Folder_name* Properties dialog box, click the Security tab.

**4.** On the Security tab, click the Auditing command button.

**5.** In the Directory Auditing dialog box, click the Add command button.

**6.** The Add Users and Groups dialog box appears. If you want to audit global groups and users from other trusted domains, click the down arrow in the List Names From drop-down list box and select the domain you want. If you want to audit individual users, click the Show Users command button. Double-click each of the groups or users whose access or attempted access to this resource you want to audit. Click OK.

**7.** The Directory Auditing dialog box reappears. Select the Success and/or Failure check boxes next to each NTFS permission you want to track for this resource. For example, if you want to know who has viewed or attempted to view a confidential file, you could select Success and Failure auditing for the Read permission.

If you are configuring auditing for a folder, you have the option of choosing to replace the existing auditing configuration on all files and/or subfolders with the settings you are configuring now. Select or deselect the check boxes next to Replace Auditing on Subdirectories and Replace Auditing on Existing Files as desired. Figure 12-16 shows the configured Directory Auditing dialog box for the D:\New Products Research Data folder. Notice that success and failure auditing for the Read permission is configured for the Everyone group.

Click OK.

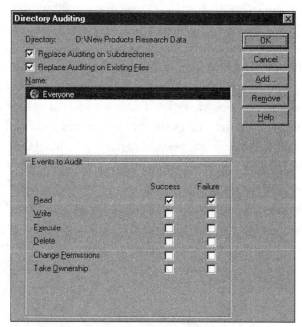

**FIGURE 12-16** Configuring folder auditing

**8.** If you are configuring folder auditing, *and* if you selected the Replace Auditing on Subdirectories check box, a warning dialog box appears, as shown in Figure 12-17.

Click the Yes command button.

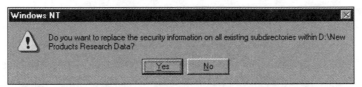

**FIGURE 12-17    Replacing auditing configuration on subfolders**

**9.** The *File_name* or *Folder_name* Properties dialog box reappears. Click OK.

**10.** Exit Windows NT Explorer.

## Using Event Viewer to View Auditing Results

You can use Event Viewer to view the results of the auditing you have configured. Event Viewer has three logs: the system log, the application log, and the security log. The security log contains the data generated by auditing.

You can view the security log in its entirety, or you can filter events by date and type of audit event. You can clear the security log when it is full; and you can save (archive) the log to be viewed at a later date by using Event Viewer, a text editor, or a spreadsheet or database program. You can also configure the size of the log and event log wrapping (how the log handles additional auditing data when it becomes full).

An important consideration, from an administrative standpoint, is scheduling time to regularly view auditing events in the security log. The data gathered by auditing is of no value if it is not used.

The sections that follow explain how to access the security log in Event Viewer and how to filter audit events, how to save (archive) and clear the security log, and how to configure the maximum size of the security log and event log wrapping.

**TO ACCESS THE SECURITY LOG, AND TO FILTER
AND VIEW AUDIT EVENTS, FOLLOW THESE STEPS:**

**1.** Select Start ⇒ Programs ⇒ Administrative Tools (Common) ⇒ Event Viewer.

**2.** In the Event Viewer dialog box, select Log ⇒ Security. This accesses the security log.

Figure 12-18 shows the Security Log dialog box in Event Viewer. Notice that both success and failure events are listed. (Remember, success events are denoted by a key, and failure events are denoted by a lock in the left margin.)

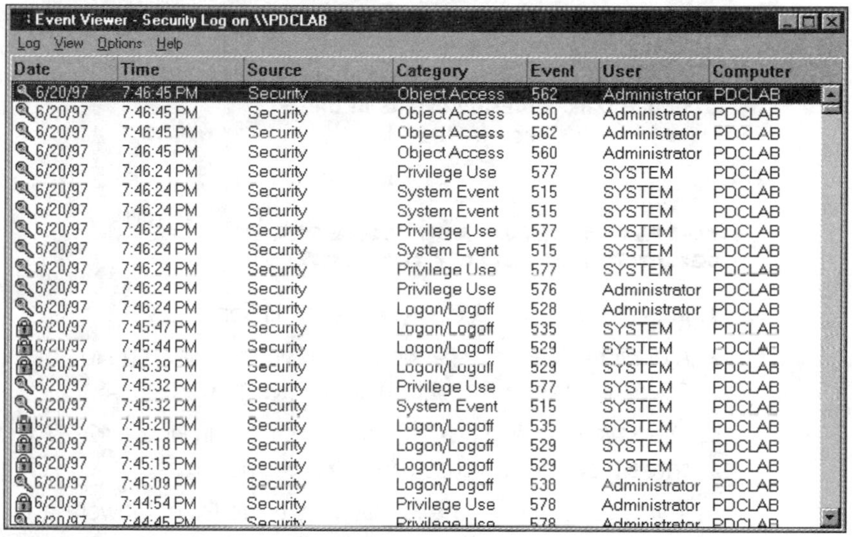

| Date | Time | Source | Category | Event | User | Computer |
|------|------|--------|----------|-------|------|----------|
| 6/20/97 | 7:46:45 PM | Security | Object Access | 562 | Administrator | PDCLAB |
| 6/20/97 | 7:46:45 PM | Security | Object Access | 560 | Administrator | PDCLAB |
| 6/20/97 | 7:46:45 PM | Security | Object Access | 562 | Administrator | PDCLAB |
| 6/20/97 | 7:46:45 PM | Security | Object Access | 560 | Administrator | PDCLAB |
| 6/20/97 | 7:46:24 PM | Security | Privilege Use | 577 | SYSTEM | PDCLAB |
| 6/20/97 | 7:46:24 PM | Security | System Event | 515 | SYSTEM | PDCLAB |
| 6/20/97 | 7:46:24 PM | Security | System Event | 515 | SYSTEM | PDCLAB |
| 6/20/97 | 7:46:24 PM | Security | Privilege Use | 577 | SYSTEM | PDCLAB |
| 6/20/97 | 7:46:24 PM | Security | System Event | 515 | SYSTEM | PDCLAB |
| 6/20/97 | 7:46:24 PM | Security | Privilege Use | 577 | SYSTEM | PDCLAB |
| 6/20/97 | 7:46:24 PM | Security | Privilege Use | 576 | Administrator | PDCLAB |
| 6/20/97 | 7:46:24 PM | Security | Logon/Logoff | 528 | Administrator | PDCLAB |
| 6/20/97 | 7:45:47 PM | Security | Logon/Logoff | 535 | SYSTEM | PDCLAB |
| 6/20/97 | 7:45:44 PM | Security | Logon/Logoff | 529 | SYSTEM | PDCLAB |
| 6/20/97 | 7:45:39 PM | Security | Logon/Logoff | 529 | SYSTEM | PDCLAB |
| 6/20/97 | 7:45:32 PM | Security | Privilege Use | 577 | SYSTEM | PDCLAB |
| 6/20/97 | 7:45:32 PM | Security | System Event | 515 | SYSTEM | PDCLAB |
| 6/20/97 | 7:45:20 PM | Security | Logon/Logoff | 535 | SYSTEM | PDCLAB |
| 6/20/97 | 7:45:18 PM | Security | Logon/Logoff | 529 | SYSTEM | PDCLAB |
| 6/20/97 | 7:45:15 PM | Security | Logon/Logoff | 529 | SYSTEM | PDCLAB |
| 6/20/97 | 7:45:09 PM | Security | Logon/Logoff | 538 | Administrator | PDCLAB |
| 6/20/97 | 7:44:54 PM | Security | Privilege Use | 578 | Administrator | PDCLAB |
| 6/20/97 | 7:44:45 PM | Security | Privilege Use | 578 | Administrator | PDCLAB |

**FIGURE 12-18** Viewing the security log

**3.** To filter security log events by date or type of event, select View ⇒ Filter Events.

**4.** The Filter dialog box appears, as shown in Figure 12-19. Notice the filter configuration options available.

If you need more information on filtering events, click the Help command button. Configure filtering as desired. Click OK.

**5.** To view details for a specific audit event, double-click the event.

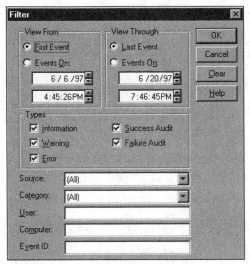

**FIGURE 12-19**    Filtering events in the security log

### TO SAVE (ARCHIVE) AND CLEAR THE SECURITY LOG FOLLOW THESE STEPS:

**1.** In Event Viewer, select Log ⇒ Clear All Events.

**2.** A dialog box appears, asking if you want to save the log before clearing it. Click the Yes command button to save the log.

**3.** The Save As dialog box appears, as shown in Figure 12-20. Notice the three types of files that you can save the log as.

If you want to view the log later by using Event Viewer, save (archive) the log as an Event Log File (*.EVT). If you want to view the log later by using a text editor, save the log as a Text File (*.TXT). If you want to export the file for analysis in a spreadsheet or database program, save the log as a Comma Delimited Text file (*.TXT)

Type in a file name for the log you are saving, then select a type of file in the "Save as type" drop-down list box. Click the Save command button.

**4.** A dialog box appears, asking you to confirm that you want to clear the security log. Click the Yes command button. The log is cleared.

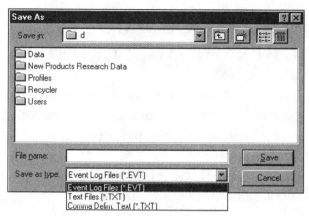

**FIGURE 12-20**    Saving the security log

### TO CONFIGURE THE MAXIMUM SIZE OF THE SECURITY LOG AND EVENT LOG WRAPPING, FOLLOW THESE STEPS:

**1.** Select Log ⇒ Log Settings in the Event Viewer dialog box.

**2.** The Event Log Settings dialog box appears, as shown in Figure 12-21. Notice the available event log wrapping settings. This feature determines how Event Viewer handles new audit events when the security log has reached its maximum size.

Configure the maximum log size as desired. The available range for this setting is from 64KB to 4,194,176KB. The default maximum log size is 512KB.

Select one of the three event log wrapping configuration options. Click OK.

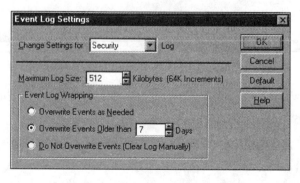

**FIGURE 12-21** Configuring event log settings

# TROUBLESHOOTING COMMON RESOURCE ACCESS AND PERMISSION PROBLEMS

When a user can't access a resource (that he or she is supposed to be able to access), the administrator must determine why this is happening and correct the problem. Most resource access problems are caused by incorrectly configured and/or conflicting permissions.

Here are some recommended troubleshooting tips to help you to determine why a user can't access a shared network resource:

o **Look for conflicting share and NTFS permissions.** Determine which groups the user is a member of (including groups in other domains), and determine the user's effective share permission and effective NTFS permissions to the resource.

o **Look for the No Access permission.** If the user, or any group of which the user is a member, has been assigned the No Access permission to the share or has been assigned the No Access NTFS permission to the resource, the user will not be able to access the resource.

o If you have just assigned the user permission to the resource, and the user can't access the resource, **try having the user log off and log on again,** so the user's access token will be updated.

# KEY POINT SUMMARY

This chapter discussed how to share and secure file systems in a Windows NT environment. The following points illuminate the major issues.

o The Windows NT file and folder attributes are: Archive, Compress, Hidden, Read-only, and System. The file attributes can be used on both FAT and NTFS partitions, with the exception of the Compress attribute, which is only available on NTFS partitions.

- In Windows NT, folders are *shared* to make it possible for users to access network resources. Only members of the Administrators, Server Operators, and Power Users groups can share folders. When a folder is shared, the folder's entire contents, including all files and subfolders (in other words, the entire directory tree under the shared folder), are available to users that have the appropriate permissions to the share. You can use either Windows NT Explorer or Server Manager to share folders.

- *Shared folder permissions* control access to shared folders. Share permissions only apply when users connect to the folder over the network—they do *not* apply when users access the folder from the local computer.

  - The Windows NT share permissions, from most restrictive to least restrictive, are: No Access, Read, Change, and Full Control. Share permissions are assigned by adding a user or group to the permissions list for the share. You can assign share permissions by using Windows NT Explorer or Server Manager.

  - It's not uncommon for a user to be a member of multiple groups that have different permissions to a share. When this occurs, the user and group permissions are additive, and the *least* restrictive permission is the user's effective permission. The exception to this rule is the No Access permission. No Access always overrides other share permissions.

- After a share is created, you may want to modify its properties. You can assign multiple share names to it, change the name of it, or stop sharing it.

- Every time you start Windows NT on a computer, NT automatically creates several hidden shares that only members of the Administrators group have permission to access. These shares are referred to as *administrative shares*. The Windows NT administrative shares are: C$, D$, E$, and so on (one share for the root of each hard disk partition on the computer), and Admin$ (which corresponds to the folder in which NT is installed). The $ at the end of each administrative share causes the share to be hidden from users when they browse the network. Any share can be configured as a hidden share by appending a $ to the share name, but only access to the hidden administrative shares is automatically restricted to Administrators only. If you don't want administrative shares available on a Windows NT computer, you can configure the Registry so that NT does not create these shares each time Windows NT is started.

o When files and folders are stored on an NTFS volume, *NTFS permissions* can be assigned to provide a greater level of security than share permissions. This is because NTFS permissions can be assigned to individual files and folders, and they apply to local users as well as to users who connect to a shared folder over the network.

o The NTFS permissions are: Read (R), Write (W), Execute (E), Delete (D), Change Permissions (P), and Take Ownership (O). The individual NTFS permissions are sometimes referred to as *Special Access Directory permissions* and *Special Access File permissions*. To make the assignment of NTFS permissions easier, Microsoft has created a set of standard directory (folder) permissions and a set of standard file permissions. Standard permissions, which are combinations of the most commonly used NTFS permissions, are used in most situations.

o The standard NTFS directory (folder) permissions are: No Access (None) (None), List (RX) (Not Specified), Read (RX) (RX), Add (WX) (Not Specified), Add and Read (RWX) (RX), Change (RWXD) (RWXD), and Full Control (All) (All). The permissions specified within the first set of parentheses following the permission name apply to the *folder*, and the permissions specified within the second set of parentheses following the permission name apply to *files* within the folder.

o The standard NTFS file permissions are No Access (None), Read (RX), Change (RWXD), and Full Control (All). NTFS file permissions apply only to the individual file to which they are assigned. Other files in the same folder are not affected.

o When a user wants to access a file, and the NTFS file and folder permissions conflict, the file permissions are applied. *File permissions take precedence over folder permissions.*

o As with share permissions, user and group NTFS permissions are additive, and the *least* restrictive combination of permissions applies. The exception to this rule is the No Access permission. No Access always overrides all other NTFS permissions.

o Only a user who is the owner of the file or folder, or who has the Change Permissions or Full Control NTFS permissions, can assign NTFS permissions to the file or folder. NTFS permissions are assigned to files and folders by using Windows NT Explorer.

o When files are created in a folder on an NTFS volume, the new files inherit the NTFS permissions of the folder they are created in. When new subfolders are created on an NTFS volume, the new subfolders inherit the NTFS permissions of the folder that contains the new subfolder.

o When files or folders are moved or copied, their NTFS permissions often change. Normally, when files or folders are moved or copied, they inherit the NTFS permissions of the destination folder. The only exception to this rule is when files or folders are *moved* to a new folder on the *same* NTFS volume—in this case, the moved files or folders retain their original NTFS permissions.

o *When NTFS and share permissions differ, the* **most** *restrictive permission becomes the user's effective permission to the file or folder in the share.* This means that if either the NTFS or the share permissions deny a user access, access is denied.

o The creator of a file or folder is its *owner* (except that when a member of the Administrators group creates a file or folder, the Administrators *group*, not the user, is the owner of the file or folder). Without being the owner of a file or folder or having the Change Permissions NTFS permission, the only way you can change or assign permissions to the file or folder is to *take ownership* of the file or folder.

  o A user must either be a member of the Administrators group, have the Take Ownership NTFS permission to the file or folder (or have the Full Control permission, which includes the Take Ownership permission), or have the "Take ownership of files or other objects" user right in order to take ownership of a file or folder.

o *Windows NT auditing is available only on NTFS partitions.* Success auditing is often performed to gather information about how resources are used. Failure auditing is normally performed to determine whether unauthorized users are attempting to access restricted files or folders.

  o There are two parts involved in configuring auditing: first, the audit policy is configured in User Manager or User Manager for Domains; second, auditing is configured for each file and folder individually by using Windows NT Explorer. Only members of the Administrators group can configure audit policy. When configuring audit policy, you *must* select File and Object Access auditing to audit files and folders. If you configure file and folder auditing, but don't configure the audit policy for File and Object Access, no auditing of files and folders will occur.

o You can view the results of auditing that are contained in the security log in Event Viewer. In Event Viewer, you can filter events by date and type, you can clear the security log when it is full, and you can save (archive) the log to be viewed at a later date. The size of the log and event log wrapping (how the log handles additional auditing data when it becomes full) can also be configured.

o Most resource access problems are caused by incorrectly configured and/or conflicting permissions. Some troubleshooting tips for dealing with resource access problems are:

o Look for conflicting share and NTFS permissions. Determine which groups the user is a member of (including groups in other domains), and determine the user's effective share permission and effective NTFS permissions to the resource.

o Look for the No Access permission.

o If you have just assigned the user permission to the resource, and the user can't access the resource, try having the user log off and log on again.

# APPLYING WHAT YOU'VE LEARNED

Now it's time to regroup, review, and apply what you've learned in this chapter. The Instant Assessment questions bring to mind key facts and concepts. The hands-on lab exercises reinforce what you've learned, and allow you to practice some of the tasks tested by the Microsoft Certified Professional exams.

## Instant Assessment

**1.** What Windows NT file attribute can you use to prevent the accidental deletion of application files?

**2.** What Windows NT file attribute is only available on NTFS partitions?

**3.** On a Windows NT network, what is the purpose of sharing folders?

**4.** List the Windows NT share permissions—from most restrictive to least restrictive.

**5.** When user and group share permissions are combined, which permission always overrides all others?

**6.** A user, JohnZ, belongs to three groups, whose respective share permissions are Change, Read, and Full Control. What is JohnZ's effective share permission?

**7.** A user, PaulS, belongs to two groups, whose respective share permissions are Full Control and No Access. What is PaulS's effective share permission?

**8.** What are the Windows NT administrative shares?

**9.** How can you configure a share to be a hidden share?

**10.** How do NTFS permissions provide a higher level of security than share permissions?

**11.** List the NTFS (individual) permissions.

**12.** What are the standard NTFS folder permissions?

**13.** What are the standard NTFS file permissions?

**14.** When a user wants to access a file, and the NTFS file and folder permissions conflict, which permissions are applied?

**15.** When a file is created in a folder on an NTFS volume, what NTFS permissions does the file have?

**16.** Fill in the blank: Normally, when files or folders are moved or copied, they inherit the NTFS permissions of the _____ folder.

**17.** What NTFS permissions are applied to a file that is *moved* to a different folder on the *same* NTFS volume?

**18.** When NTFS and share permissions differ, which permission becomes the user's effective permission to the file or folder in the share?

**19.** Who is the owner of a file or folder?

**20.** Why would a user want to take ownership of a file or folder?

**21.** What are the two parts involved in configuring auditing?

**22.** What *must* be configured in audit policy in order to audit files and folders?

**23.** Which Windows NT utility is used to examine the results of auditing?

**24.** What is the cause of most resource access problems?

**T/F**

**25.** Only members of the Administrators group can share folders. _____

**26.** When a folder is shared, the folder's entire contents, including
all files and subfolders (i.e., the entire directory tree under the
shared folder) are available to users that have the appropriate
permissions to the share. _____

**27.** User and group NTFS permissions, when combined, are
*not* additive. _____

**28.** Share permissions *don't* apply when a user connects to a
shared folder when sitting at the local computer, but NTFS
permissions *do* apply when a user connects to a shared folder
at the local computer. _____

**29.** Windows NT auditing is only available on FAT partitions. _____

concept link  **For answers to the Instant Assessment see Appendix D.**

# Hands-on Lab Exercises

The following hands-on lab exercises provide you with three practical opportunities to apply the knowledge you've gained in this chapter about sharing and securing file systems.

### Lab 12.18 *Sharing and securing resources*

Workstation
Server
Enterprise

The purpose of this lab is to provide you with hands-on experience in planning a strategy for sharing and securing resources, and in performing the tasks of sharing and securing resources in Windows NT.

This lab consists of three parts:

> Part 1: Planning a strategy for sharing and securing resources
> Part 2: Sharing and securing folders
> Part 3: Establishing NTFS permissions

Begin this lab by booting your computer to Windows NT Server. Log on as Administrator.

Follow the steps below carefully.

### Part 1: Planning a strategy for sharing and securing resources

In this section, you plan a strategy for sharing and securing folders on a Windows NT Server computer given a particular scenario.

**Scenario:** SalesPros, Inc. is a sales organization. (It's the same company you created users and groups for in Lab 7.10). Table 12-8 shows some of SalesPros, Inc.'s employees, their user names, job titles, and respective group membership(s):

**TABLE 12-8** SALESPROS, INC.'S USER AND GROUP ACCOUNTS

| EMPLOYEE | USER NAME | JOB TITLE | GROUP MEMBERSHIP(S) |
|---|---|---|---|
| Pam Rhodes | PamR | District Manager | Managers, Sales, Accounting, Domain Users |
| John Spencer | JohnS | Sales Manager | Managers, Sales, Domain Users |
| Robert Jones | RobertJ | Accounting Manager | Managers, Accounting, Domain Users |
| Colleen Green | ColleenG | Sales Rep | Sales, Domain Users |
| Bill Tracy | BillT | Sales Rep | Sales, Domain Users |
| Mike Calhoun | MikeC | Sales Rep | Sales, Domain Users |
| Nancy Yates | NancyY | Accounting Staff | Accounting, Domain Users |
| Mike Cook | MikeCo | Accounting Staff | Accounting, Domain Users |

The resources to be shared are located on two partitions on a Windows NT Server computer. The C: drive is a FAT partition that contains applications, and the D: drive is an NTFS partition that contains data folders. The following resources exist:

| C: Drive — FAT Partition | D:Drive — NTFS Partition |
|---|---|
| C:\Apps\Word | D:\Data\Managers |
| C:\Apps\Excel | D:\Data\Accounting |
| C:\Apps\Access | D:\Data\Sales |
| | D:\Data\AllUsers |

Use the following criteria for determining your strategy to share and secure resources:

1. All employees need to be able to access all three applications: Word, Excel, and Access. However, employees should *not* be able to save data files to the application folders or to change or delete files in the application folders.

2. Employees should be able to access (create, read, write, and delete files) only the data folders that correspond to the groups to which they belong. For example, only members of the Accounting group should be able to access the D:\Data\Accounting folder. Furthermore, members of the Accounting group should *not* be able to access data folders that correspond to groups of which they are *not* members.

3. All employees need to be able to access (create, read, write and delete files) the D:\Data\AllUsers folder.

4. Members of the Administrators group require Full Control to all shared resources on the NTFS partition.

Plan a strategy for sharing and securing folders by assigning a share name to each resource (folder), and then choosing the appropriate share and/or NTFS permissions for each resource listed.

Use the following worksheet for your answers:

| Resource: (Include path) | Share Name: | Share Permissions Applied: | | NTFS Permissions Applied: | |
|---|---|---|---|---|---|
| | | User/Group | Permission | User/Group | Permission |
| (Example) D:\Data\Sales | SalesData | Domain Users (Remove Everyone group) | Full Control | Sales Administrators | Change Full Control |
| C:\Apps\Word | | | | | |
| C:\Apps\Excel | | | | | |
| C:\Apps\Access | | | | | |
| D:\Data\Managers | | | | | |
| D:\Data\Accounting | | | | | |
| D:\Data\AllUsers | | | | | |

concept link     **For answers to the hands-on lab exercise see Appendix D.**

Continue to Part 2.

## Part 2: Sharing and securing folders

In this section, you create several folders to share, then apply appropriate share permissions to each of the folders.

**1.** Select Start ⇒ Programs ⇒ Windows NT Explorer.

**2.** In the Exploring dialog box, highlight the C: drive (or the drive that contains your FAT partition—this is the drive that you installed Windows NT Server and Windows NT Workstation on). Select File ⇒ New ⇒ Folder.

**3.** The new folder appears in the Name list box. Type in a new folder name of **Apps**. Press Enter. Double-click the Apps folder.

**4.** Select File ⇒ New ⇒ Folder.

**5.** The new folder appears in the Name list box. Type in a new folder name of **Word**. Press Enter.

**6.** Select File ⇒ New ⇒ Folder.

**7.** The new folder appears in the Name list box. Type in a new folder name of **Excel**. Press Enter.

**8.** Select File ⇒ New ⇒ Folder.

**9.** The new folder appears in the Name list box. Type in a new folder name of **Access**. Press Enter.

**10.** Highlight the Word folder in the Name list box. Select File ⇒ Properties.

**11.** In the Word Properties dialog box, click the Sharing tab. Select the radio button next to Shared As. In the Share Name text box, accept the default name of Word. Click the Permissions command button.

**12.** The Access Through Share Permissions dialog box appears. Click the Add command button.

**13.** The Add Users and Groups dialog box appears. Double-click the Domain Users group. In the Type of Access drop-down list box, select Change. Click OK.

**14.** In the Access Through Share Permissions dialog box, highlight the Everyone group. Click the Remove command button. Click OK.

**15.** In the Word Properties dialog box, click OK.

**16.** In the Exploring dialog box, highlight the Excel folder in the Name list box. Select File ⇒ Properties.

**17.** In the Excel Properties dialog box, click the Sharing tab. Select the radio button next to Shared As. In the Share Name text box, accept the default name of Excel. Click the Permissions command button.

**18.** The Access Through Share Permissions dialog box appears. Click the Add command button.

**19.** The Add Users and Groups dialog box appears. Double-click the Domain Users group. In the Type of Access drop-down list box, select Change. Click OK.

**20.** In the Access Through Share Permissions dialog box, highlight the Everyone group. Click the Remove command button. Click OK.

**21.** In the Excel Properties dialog box, click OK.

**22.** In the Exploring dialog box, highlight the Access folder in the Name list box. Select File⇒Properties.

**23.** In the Access Properties dialog box, click the Sharing tab. Select the radio button next to Shared As. In the Share Name text box, accept the default name of Access. Click the Permissions command button.

**24.** The Access Through Share Permissions dialog box appears. Click the Add command button.

**25.** The Add Users and Groups dialog box appears. Double-click the Domain Users group. In the Type of Access drop-down list box, select Change. Click OK.

**26.** In the Access Through Share Permissions dialog box, highlight the Everyone group. Click the Remove command button. Click OK.

**27.** In the Access Properties dialog box, click OK.

**28.** The Exploring dialog box reappears. Notice that all three folders (Word, Excel, and Access) appear in the Name list box, and that all three appear with a hand under the folder, indicating that they are shared folders.

**29.** Highlight the D: drive (or the drive that contains your NTFS partition). Select File⇒New⇒Folder.

**30.** The new folder appears in the Name list box. Type in a new folder name of **Data**. Press Enter. Double-click the Data folder.

**31.** Select File⇒New⇒Folder.

**32.** The new folder appears in the Name list box. Type in a new folder name of **Managers**. Press Enter.

**33.** Select File⇒New⇒Folder.

**34.** The new folder appears in the Name list box. Type in a new folder name of **Accounting**. Press Enter.

**35.** Select File⇒New⇒Folder.

**36.** The new folder appears in the Name list box. Type in a new folder name of **Sales**. Press Enter.

**37.** Select File⇒New⇒Folder.

**38.** The new folder appears in the Name list box. Type in a new folder name of **AllUsers**. Press Enter.

**39.** In the Exploring dialog box, highlight the Managers folder in the Name list box. Select File⇒Properties.

**40.** In the Managers Properties dialog box, click the Sharing tab. Select the radio button next to Shared As. In the Share Name text box, type **ManagersData**. Click the Permissions command button.

**41.** The Access Through Share Permissions dialog box appears. Notice that the Everyone group is listed and has the Full Control share permission. (Because this folder is located on an NTFS partition, you will use NTFS permissions to secure this folder, and accept the default share permission.) Click OK.

**42.** In the Managers Properties dialog box, Click OK.

**43.** A warning message appears, indicating that the new share name may not be accessible from some MS-DOS workstations. (This is because the name you assigned is longer than eight characters). Click the Yes command button.

**44.** In the Exploring dialog box, highlight the Accounting folder in the Name list box. Select File ⇒ Properties.

**45.** In the Accounting Properties dialog box, click the Sharing tab. Select the radio button next to Shared As. In the Share Name text box, type in **AccountingData**. Click OK.

**46.** In the Sharing warning dialog box, click the Yes command button.

**47.** In the Exploring dialog box, highlight the Sales folder in the Name list box. Select File ⇒ Properties.

**48.** In the Sales Properties dialog box, click the Sharing tab. Select the radio button next to Shared As. In the Share Name text box, type in **SalesData**. Click OK.

**49.** In the Sharing warning dialog box, click the Yes command button.

**50.** In the Exploring dialog box, highlight the AllUsers folder in the Name list box. Select File ⇒ Properties.

**51.** In the AllUsers Properties dialog box, click the Sharing tab. Select the radio button next to Shared As. In the Share Name text box, type in **AllUsersData**. Click OK.

**52.** In the Sharing warning dialog box, click the Yes command button.

**53.** The Exploring dialog box reappears. Notice that all four folders (Managers, Accounting, Sales, and All Users) appear in the Name list box, and that all four appear with a hand under the folder, indicating that they are shared folders.

In the next section, you assign NTFS permissions to these folders. Continue to Part 3.

**Part 3: Establishing NTFS permissions**

In this section, you assign the appropriate NTFS permissions to the Managers, Accounting, Sales, and AllUsers folders that you created and shared in Part 2.

1. In the Exploring dialog box, highlight the Managers folder in the Name list box. Select File ⇒ Properties.

2. In the Managers Properties dialog box, click the Security tab. Click the Permissions command button.

3. In the Directory Permissions dialog box, click the Add command button.

4. In the Add Users and Groups dialog box, double-click the Managers group. In the Type of Access drop-down list box, select Change. Click OK.

5. Click the Add command button.

6. In the Add Users and Groups dialog box, double-click Administrators. In the Type of Access drop-down list box, select Full Control. Click OK.

7. In the Directory Permissions dialog box, highlight the Everyone group. Click the Remove command button. Click OK.

8. In the Managers Properties dialog box, click OK.

9. In the Exploring dialog box, highlight the Accounting folder in the Name list box. Select File ⇒ Properties.

10. In the Accounting Properties dialog box, click the Security tab. Click the Permissions command button.

11. In the Directory Permissions dialog box, click the Add command button.

12. In the Add Users and Groups dialog box, double-click the Accounting group. In the Type of Access drop-down list box, select Change. Click OK.

13. Click the Add command button.

14. In the Add Users and Groups dialog box, double-click Administrators. In the Type of Access drop-down list box, select Full Control. Click OK.

15. In the Directory Permissions dialog box, highlight the Everyone group. Click the Remove command button. Click OK.

16. In the Accounting Properties dialog box, click OK.

17. In the Exploring dialog box, highlight the Sales folder in the Name list box. Select File ⇒ Properties.

18. In the Sales Properties dialog box, click the Security tab. Click the Permissions command button.

19. In the Directory Permissions dialog box, click the Add command button.

20. In the Add Users and Groups dialog box, double-click the Sales group. In the Type of Access drop-down list box, select Change. Click OK.

**21.** Click the Add command button.

**22.** In the Add Users and Groups dialog box, double-click Administrators. In the Type of Access drop-down list box, select Full Control. Click OK.

**23.** In the Directory Permissions dialog box, highlight the Everyone group. Click the Remove command button. Click OK.

**24.** In the Sales Properties dialog box, click OK.

**25.** In the Exploring dialog box, highlight the AllUsers folder in the Name list box. Select File ⇒ Properties.

**26.** In the AllUsers Properties dialog box, click the Security tab. Click the Permissions command button.

**27.** In the Directory Permissions dialog box, click the Add command button.

**28.** In the Add Users and Groups dialog box, double-click the Domain Users group. In the Type of Access drop-down list box, select Change. Click OK.

**29.** Click the Add command button.

**30.** In the Add Users and Groups dialog box, double-click Administrators. In the Type of Access drop-down list box, select Full Control. Click OK.

**31.** In the Directory Permissions dialog box, highlight the Everyone group. Click the Remove command button. Click OK.

**32.** In the AllUsers Properties dialog box, click OK. This completes the assigning of NTFS permissions. Exit Windows NT Explorer.

## Lab 12.19 *Establishing file and folder auditing*

Server
Enterprise

The purpose of this lab is to provide you with hands-on experience in establishing file and folder auditing.

This lab consists of two parts:

> Part 1: Establishing file and folder auditing
> Part 2: Testing file and folder auditing

Begin this lab by booting your computer to Windows NT Server. Log on as Administrator.

Follow the steps below carefully.

### Part 1: Establishing file and folder auditing

In this section, you establish file and folder auditing on the Managers, Accounting, Sales, and AllUsers subfolders in the D:\Data folder that you created and shared in Lab 12.18.

In Lab 8.11, you implemented success and failure auditing for File and Object Access by using User Manager for Domains. That was the first step in auditing files and folders. This lab completes the process of establishing auditing on files and folders.

1. Select Start ⇒ Programs ⇒ Windows NT Explorer.

2. In the All Folders section of the Exploring dialog box, click the + sign next to the drive that contains your NTFS partition (usually this is the D: drive). Highlight the `Data` folder. In the Name list box in the Contents of 'Data' section, highlight the `Accounting` folder. Select File ⇒ Properties.

3. In the Accounting Properties dialog box, click the Security tab. Click the Auditing command button.

4. In the Directory Auditing dialog box, click the Add command button. Double-click the Domain Users group. Click OK.

5. In the Directory Auditing dialog box, select the Success and Failure check boxes next to Read, Write, and Execute. Click OK.

6. In the Accounting Properties dialog box, click OK.

7. In the Name list box in the Contents of 'Data' section, highlight the `AllUsers` folder. Select File ⇒ Properties.

8. In the AllUsers Properties dialog box, click the Security tab. Click the Auditing command button.

9. In the Directory Auditing dialog box, click the Add command button. Double-click the Domain Users group. Click OK.

10. In the Directory Auditing dialog box, select the Success and Failure check boxes next to Delete. Click OK.

11. In the AllUsers Properties dialog box, click OK.

12. In the Name list box in the Contents of 'Data' section, highlight the `Managers` folder. Select File ⇒ Properties.

13. In the Managers Properties dialog box, click the Security tab. Click the Auditing command button.

14. In the Directory Auditing dialog box, click the Add command button. Double-click the Domain Users group. Click OK.

15. In the Directory Auditing dialog box, select the Success and Failure check boxes next to Read, Write, Execute, Delete, Change Permissions, and Take Ownership. Click OK.

16. In the Managers Properties dialog box, click OK.

17. In the Name list box in the Contents of 'Data' section, highlight the `Sales` folder. Select File ⇒ Properties.

**18.** In the Sales Properties dialog box, click the Security tab. Click the Auditing command button.

**19.** In the Directory Auditing dialog box, click the Add command button. Double-click the Domain Users group. Click OK.

**20.** In the Directory Auditing dialog box, select the Success and Failure check boxes next to Read, Write, and Execute. Click OK.

**21.** In the Sales Properties dialog box, click OK. Exit Windows NT Explorer. Continue on to Part 2.

### Part 2: Testing file and folder auditing

In this section, you clear the security log in Event Viewer, then log on as NancyY and attempt to access each of the data folders you created and shared in Lab 12.18. Then you use Event Viewer to view the results of the auditing that you established in Part 1.

**1.** Select Start ⇒ Programs ⇒ Administrative Tools (Common) ⇒ Event Viewer.

**2.** In the Event Viewer dialog box, select Log ⇒ Security. Select Log ⇒ Clear All Events. (You are clearing the security log to make room for new auditing events.)

**3.** In the Clear Event Log dialog box, click the No command button, so as to not save the log to a file.

**4.** In the Clear Event Log dialog box, click the Yes command button to clear the security log.

**5.** Exit Event Viewer.

**6.** Select Start ⇒ Shut Down.

**7.** In the Shut Down Windows dialog box, select the radio button next to "Close all programs and log on as a different user." Click the Yes command button.

**8.** Press Ctrl + Alt + Delete to log on.

**9.** Click OK in the Important Notice dialog box.

**10.** Type in a user name of **NancyY**, and a password of **password**. Click OK.

**11.** A warning message may appear, indicating that your password will expire in *xx* days. Click the No command button.

**12.** If a Welcome to Windows NT dialog box appears, clear the check box next to "Show this Welcome Screen next time you start Windows NT." Click the Close command button.

**13.** Select Start ⇒ Programs ⇒ Windows NT Explorer.

14. In the Exploring dialog box, click the plus sign next to the drive that contains your NTFS partition (usually this is the D: drive). Click the plus sign next to the `Data` folder on this drive. Highlight the `Accounting` folder. Notice that there are no files in this folder.

15. Highlight the `AllUsers` folder. Notice that there are no files in this folder.

16. Highlight the `Managers` folder. A dialog box appears, indicating that access has been denied. (This is because NancyY is not a member of the Managers group and does not have the appropriate permission to access this folder.) Click the Cancel command button.

17. Highlight the `Sales` folder. A dialog box appears, indicating that access has been denied. (This is because NancyY is not a member of the Sales group and does not have the appropriate permission to access this folder.) Click the Cancel command button. Exit Windows NT Explorer.

18. Select Start ⇒ Shut Down.

19. In the Shut Down Windows dialog box, select the radio button next to "Close all programs and log on as a different user." Click the Yes command button.

20. Press Ctrl + Alt + Delete to log on.

21. Click OK in the Important Notice dialog box.

22. Type in a user name of **Administrator**, and a password of **password**. Click OK.

23. Select Start ⇒ Programs ⇒ Administrative Tools (Common) ⇒ Event Viewer.

24. In the Event Viewer dialog box, select Log ⇒ Security. Scroll down the log and double-click the first event that lists NancyY in the User column *and* Logon/Logoff in the Category column.

25. The Event Detail dialog box appears. Notice that this is a Success audit of the Logon/Logoff event. Click the Close command button.

26. Scroll down and double-click the event that has a lock (rather than a key) in the left-hand margin, lists NancyY in the User column, *and* Object Access in the Category column. (This should be approximately eleven events down from the one you just viewed.)

27. The Event Detail dialog box appears. Notice that this is a Failure audit event of the Object Access type. (This audit event occurred when NancyY attempted to access the `D:\Data\Sales` folder and was denied access.) Click the Next command button to view the next audit event.

28. Continue clicking on the Next command button to view several more audit events. When you are finished viewing audit events, click the Close command button.

**29.** Exit Event Viewer.

## Lab 12.20  *Troubleshooting resource access and permission problems*

Workstation
Server
Enterprise

The purpose of this lab is to provide you with hands-on experience in troubleshooting some common resource access and permission problems.

For each problem presented, consider the troubleshooting information provided and determine:

**1.** The cause of the problem, and

**2.** What steps you would take to resolve the problem.

**Problem 1**    A user, NancyY, reports that she can't save files to the AccountingData share located on an NTFS volume on a Windows NT computer. You begin the troubleshooting process by using User Manager for Domains and Windows NT Explorer to obtain NancyY's group memberships, and the share and NTFS permissions assigned to the AccountingData share.

Figure 12-22 shows the Group Memberships dialog box, which lists NancyY's group memberships.

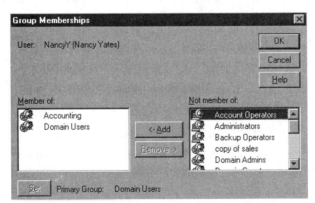

**FIGURE 12-22    Group memberships for NancyY**

Figure 12-23 shows the Access Through Share Permissions dialog box, which lists the share permissions assigned to the AccountingData share.

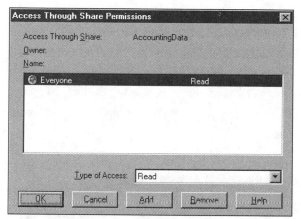

**FIGURE 12-23**   Share permissions for
`AccountingData` **share**

Figure 12-24 shows the Directory Permissions dialog box. This dialog box lists the NTFS permissions assigned to the `D:\Data\Accounting` folder, which is shared as `AccountingData`.

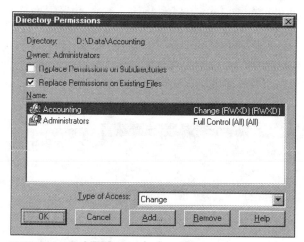

**FIGURE 12-24**   NTFS permissions for
`AccountingData` **share**

What is the cause of the problem?

What would you do to resolve the problem?

**Problem 2**    A user, JohnS, reports he can't access the `ManagersData` share located on an NTFS volume on a Windows NT computer. You begin the trouble-shooting process by using User Manager for Domains and Windows NT Explorer to obtain JohnS's group memberships, and the share and NTFS permissions assigned to the `ManagersData` share.

Figure 12-25 shows the Group Memberships dialog box, which lists JohnS's group memberships.

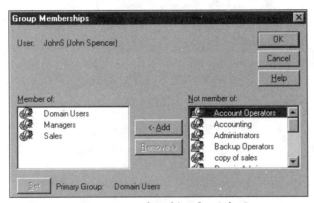

**FIGURE 12-25    Group memberships for JohnS**

Figure 12-26 shows the Access Through Share Permissions dialog box, which lists the share permissions assigned to the `ManagersData` share.

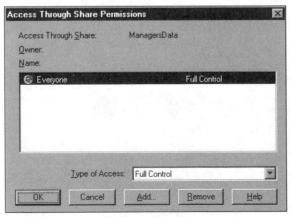

**FIGURE 12-26    Share permissions for**
`ManagersData` **share**

Figure 12-27 shows the Directory Permissions dialog box. This dialog box lists the NTFS permissions assigned to the D:\Data\Managers folder, which is shared as ManagersData.

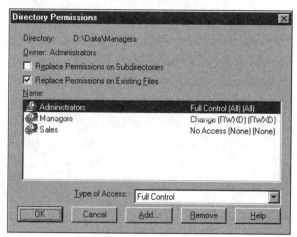

**FIGURE 12-27**   **NTFS permissions for**
ManagersData **share**

What is the cause of the problem?

What would you do to resolve the problem?

 concept link     **For answers to the hands-on lab exercise see Appendix D.**

Workstation
Server
Enterprise

CHAPTER

# Accessing Resources on the Network

# 13

# About Chapter 13

**C**hapter 13 focuses on how to find and access available network resources.

First, this chapter takes an in-depth look at browsing. The various browser roles played by different computers on the network are explained, including domain master browser, master browser, backup browser, potential browser, and non-browser. Then the browsing process is outlined, including browser elections.

Next, Chapter 13 explains how to configure the Computer Browser service, the Windows NT service that manages browsing. Then, the chapter examines how browsing functions on various transport protocols, including NetBEUI, NWLink IPX/SPX Compatible Transport, and TCP/IP.

Finally, this chapter details how to connect to shared network resources using Windows NT Explorer, and how to connect from the command line. Using UNC and FQDN naming conventions is explained.

This chapter includes two hands-on labs. In the first lab, you configure the Windows NT Computer Browser service. In the second, you create and connect to shared network resources.

Chapter 13 is a "must read," no matter which of the three Windows NT 4.0 Microsoft Certified Professional exams you're preparing for. This chapter maps to the "Use various methods to access network resources" objective for the Workstation exam, and maps to the "configure Windows NT Server core services" objective for the Server and Enterprise exams.

# BROWSING

*Browsing* enables users to find out what shared resources are available on the network (including resources in other workgroups and other domains), and facilitates connecting to those resources.

Browsing is managed by the Computer Browser service. The Computer Browser service is installed automatically during the installation of Windows NT (both Workstation and Server). The service is configured, by default, to start every time Windows NT is booted.

The Computer Browser service is responsible for the process of building a list of available network servers—a *browse list*—and for sharing that list with other computers. (Throughout this chapter, the term *network servers* includes all computers that either have shared resources or are capable of sharing their resources.) The Computer Browser service is designed so that not all computers on the network have to maintain a browse list. Certain computers are designated to maintain a browse list, and to provide that list to other computers on the network when they request it. A browse list is displayed when a user attempts to connect a network drive, or views the Network Neighborhood in Windows NT Explorer.

The following sections discuss the roles that various computers play in the browsing process, the actual process of browsing for available network servers, configuring the Computer Browser service, and how browsing works on different transport protocols.

## Browser Roles

To avoid overloading any one computer on the network, the task of maintaining a browse list is distributed among many computers. A hierarchy of browser computers has been established, and each computer plays a different role in this process. The *browser roles* that computers can perform are: domain master browser, master browser, backup browser, potential browser, and non-browser.

Each Windows computer on the network can be designated to perform any of these roles, with the exception of the domain master browser, which is always a function of the *primary domain controller* (PDC) for a domain.

Because each computer on the network does not have to maintain a browse list, processor overhead and network traffic are reduced.

The role each computer performs in the browsing process is determined, in part, by how the computer is configured and, in part, by an election process. (Both configuring computers for browsing and the election process are covered later in this chapter.)

Here's a more in-depth look at the various browser roles.

### Domain master browser

The *domain master browser* performs different functions, depending on whether the network consists of a single subnet or multiple subnets.

If the network has only one subnet, the domain master browser and master browser functions are combined and are performed by a single computer—the PDC. The PDC compiles the browse list of available network servers and makes this list available to the backup browsers.

If the network consists of multiple subnets, the domain master browser maintains a list of available network servers located on *all* subnets in the domain. The domain master browser acquires this information from the master browser on each subnet. The domain master browser makes this list available to the master browser on each subnet, which, in turn, makes the list available to the backup browsers.

There can be only *one* domain master browser in a domain, and it is always the PDC. If the PDC is down, no other computer can assume the role of the domain master browser. If there is no domain master browser, users are only able to browse network resources located on their local subnet.

### Master browser

The *master browser* builds the browse list—the list of available network servers—on its own subnet. Then the master browser passes this list on to the domain master browser, and to the backup browsers on its own subnet.

If a domain spans several subnets, there is a master browser for each subnet.

If multiple workgroups or domains exist on the same subnet, each workgroup or domain has its own master browser for that subnet. (Workgroup browsing is limited to browsing on a single subnet—the master browser for a workgroup can't pass browse list information across a router.) Each workgroup or domain is limited to having only *one* master browser on a subnet.

Any Windows NT Server, Windows NT Workstation, Windows 95, or Windows for Workgroups computer can perform the role of the master browser. However, because the role of master browser requires additional overhead (including CPU time and memory usage), you might consider configuring a more powerful computer to serve as a master browser.

### Backup browser

The *backup browser* receives the browse list from the master browser, and then makes the browse list available to any computer that requests it.

All computers on the network, when they request a copy of the browse list, do so from a backup browser. There can be more than one backup browser on each subnet.

Any Windows NT Server, Windows NT Workstation, Windows 95, or Windows for Workgroups computer can perform the role of the backup browser.

### Potential browser

A computer that does not currently maintain or distribute a browse list, but is capable of doing so, is called a *potential browser*. By default, all Windows NT Server, Windows NT Workstation, Windows 95, and Windows for Workgroups computers are potential browsers.

It is the job of the master browser on a subnet to promote a potential browser to a backup browser should the need arise. Additionally, if the master browser becomes unavailable, a potential browser can be elected to fill the role of the master browser.

### Non-browser

A *non-browser* is a computer that is not capable of maintaining and distributing a browse list. This is either because the computer has been configured to not function as a browser, or the computer's network software does not provide the capability to maintain a browse list.

All MS-DOS and Windows 3.1 client computers are non-browsers. These computers can request a browse list, but can't maintain or distribute such a list.

Any Windows NT Server, Windows NT Workstation, Windows 95, or Windows for Workgroups computer can be configured to be a non-browser. (Configuring Windows NT computers for browsing is discussed later in this chapter.)

## The Browsing Process

The Computer Browser service is responsible for managing the browsing process. Browsing can be thought of as two distinct activities: building and maintaining the browse list, and distributing the browse list to computers that request it. This section discusses what happens during each of these functions.

### How a browse list is built and maintained

1. When a master browser first comes on line, its browse list is empty. To initially build its browse list, the master browser sends a broadcast to all computers on the subnet requesting that all network servers announce their presence. (Remember, for the purpose of discussing browsing in this chapter, network servers include all computers that either have shared resources, or are capable of sharing their resources.)

2. All available network servers respond to this request by announcing their presence within thirty seconds. The master browser incorporates this information into its initial browse list. The master browser then distributes this browse list to the domain master browser and to the backup browsers.

3. After initial creation of the browse list, when a Windows computer that functions as a network server is first booted, it broadcasts its presence to the network. The master browser receives this announcement and places the information in its browse list.

4. During normal operations, a Windows computer that functions as a network server continues to announce its presence to the network every twelve minutes. If the master browser does *not* receive a broadcast from a network server after three consecutive twelve-minute time periods, it removes the computer from its browse list.

   (This is how the master browser maintains its browse list — it assumes that all network servers in its initial browse list are available until it fails to receive a broadcast announcement from a computer for three consecutive twelve-minute periods, at which time it updates its browse list by removing this computer from its list. Therefore, it is possible for a network server to remain on the browse list for some time after it is no longer available to network users.)

5. During normal operations, backup browsers request an updated browse list from the master browser every twelve minutes. If the master browser does not respond to an update request from the backup browser, the backup browser initiates the master browser election process (covered in more detail later in this chapter).

6. During normal operations, the master browser sends an updated browse list to the domain master browser every twelve minutes. The domain master browser, in response, sends an updated domain browse list to the master browser. Additionally, every fifteen minutes, the master browser announces its presence to master browsers of other workgroups and domains located on the same subnet.

## What happens when a user browses the network

1. When a user of a Windows NT computer attempts to access browse information by double-clicking Network Neighborhood or by selecting Tools → Map Network Drive in Windows NT Explorer, the user's computer contacts the master browser and retrieves a list of available backup browsers.

   (This step occurs only the first time a user accesses browse information — the Computer Browser service on the local computer then retains the list of available backup browsers until the computer is rebooted or until the backup browsers on the list are no longer available.)

2. The user's computer then contacts a backup browser to request a list of available network servers. The backup browser processes this request and returns a list of available network servers in the requesting computer's workgroup or domain, plus a list of available workgroups and domains. The user's computer then displays this information for the user.

3. If the user selects an available network server, the user's computer contacts the selected server and requests a list of shared network resources. The selected server then sends a list of shared resources to the requesting computer, which is then displayed for the user.

   If the user selects an available workgroup or domain, the user's computer contacts the master browser in the selected workgroup or domain and requests a browse list. The master browser sends a list of backup browsers for the workgroup or domain to the requesting computer. Then the user's computer contacts a backup browser in the selected workgroup or domain for a list of available network servers, which is then sent by the backup browser to the requesting computer and displayed for the user. The user then selects an available network server, and the user's computer contacts the selected server and requests a list of shared network resources. The selected server then sends a list of shared resources to the requesting computer, which is displayed for the user.

4. The user selects the specific shared resource he or she wants to access from the list that is displayed.

Browser elections are an integral part of building and maintaining browse lists. The browser election process is discussed in the next section.

### Browser elections

A *browser election*, which determines which computer will function as the master browser, takes place when:

o The PDC is booted

o A backup browser is unable to obtain an updated browse list from the master browser

o A computer is unable to obtain a list of backup browsers from the master browser

When one of these events occurs, the computer experiencing the event initiates the browser election process by broadcasting an election packet.

An election packet contains the computer's election criteria value. A computer's election criteria value is based on the computer's operating system, version, and on the computer's current browser role (for example, master browser or backup browser). The more powerful the operating system, the higher its election criteria value. The election criteria value ranking of operating systems, from highest to lowest, is: Windows NT Server, Windows NT Workstation, Windows 95, and Windows for Workgroups. Additionally, newer versions of an operating system have a higher election criteria value than older versions.

For example, Windows NT Server has a higher election criteria value than Windows NT Workstation, which has a higher election criteria value than Windows 95, which has a higher election criteria value than Windows for Workgroups.

Also, Windows NT Server version 4.0 has a higher election criteria value than Windows NT Server version 3.51, which has a higher election criteria value than Windows NT Server version 3.5.

The result of the browser election process is that the computer with the *highest* election criteria value "wins" the election and becomes the master browser.

When a computer initiates the election process by broadcasting an election packet, each browser computer on the subnet (that is, every computer except non-browsers) examines the packet and compares the election criteria value contained in the packet to its own election criteria value. If the computer that receives the packet has an *equal or lower* criteria value than the packet it receives, it takes no action. If the computer that receives the packet has a *higher* criteria value than the packet it receives, it broadcasts its own election packet. This process continues until no further election packets are broadcast. The last computer to send an election packet (the computer with the highest election criteria value) then declares itself as the new master browser.

 note    **Only the master browser is elected. The domain master browser is always the PDC. If the PDC is unavailable, there is *no* domain master browser.**

## Configuring the Computer Browser Service

By default, all Windows 95 and Windows for Workgroups computers are configured as potential browsers. All Windows NT Server and Windows NT Workstation computers that are *not* domain controllers are also configured as potential browsers by default. Additionally, by default, all Windows NT Server domain controllers are configured to maintain a browse list, and to function as a backup or master browser. You can change the default setting for the Computer Browser service on a Windows NT computer, and thereby change the computer's default browser role.

The Computer Browser service on a Windows NT computer is controlled by the following Registry entries in `\HKEY_LOCAL_MACHINE\SYSTEM\CurrentControl Set\Services\Browser\Parameters`:

\MaintainServerList

\IsDomainMaster

The MaintainServerList Registry entry, which specifies whether a computer will maintain a browse list, can be configured with one of the following values:

o No—When this configuration is used, the computer functions as a non-browser.

- Yes—When this configuration is used, the computer maintains a browse list, and will function either as a backup browser or a master browser. This is the default setting for all Windows NT Server domain controllers.

- Auto—When this configuration is used, the computer functions as a potential browser, a backup browser, or a master browser (depending on the outcome of a browser election). This is the default setting for all Windows NT computers that are nondomain controllers.

The IsDomainMaster Registry entry, which specifies whether a computer will initiate an election at startup and gives a computer a higher election criteria value than other computers of equivalent configuration, can be configured with one of the following values:

- True—When this configuration is used, the computer, at startup, initiates a browser election. In addition, the computer is assigned a higher election criteria value than it would normally be assigned, given its operating system, version, and current server role. This higher election criteria value gives the computer an advantage in a browser election, and causes it to become the master browser if all other factors are equal. For example, when this configuration is assigned to a *backup domain controller* (BDC), this BDC will have a higher election criteria value than all other BDCs (assuming that all BDCs use the same versions of Windows NT Server); only the PDC would have a higher election criteria value. Either *True* or *Yes* can be used for this setting.

- False—When this configuration is used, the computer does *not* initiate a browser election at startup, and is *not* assigned a higher election criteria value than other computers with equivalent configurations. Either *False* or *No* can be used for this setting. This is the default setting for all Windows NT computers.

---

**TO CONFIGURE THE COMPUTER BROWSER SERVICE'S REGISTRY SETTINGS, FOLLOW THESE STEPS:**

**1.** Select Start⇒Run.

**2.** In the Run dialog box, type **Regedt32** in the Open drop-down list box. Click OK.

**3.** In the Registry Editor dialog box, select Window ⇒ HKEY_LOCAL_MACHINE on Local Machine.

**4.** Maximize the HKEY_LOCAL_MACHINE on Local Machine window.

**5.** Double-click the `SYSTEM` folder. Under the `SYSTEM` folder, double-click the `CurrentControlSet` folder. Double-click the `Services` folder. Scroll down and double-click the `Browser` folder. Click the `Parameters` folder. Figure 13-1 shows the contents of the `Parameters` folder in the Registry Editor dialog box. Notice the default settings for MaintainServerList and IsDomainMaster on a PDC.

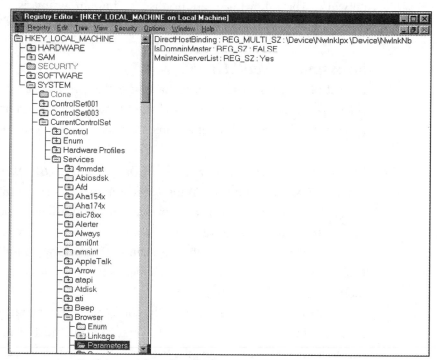

**FIGURE 13-1**    **Registry settings for the Computer Browser service**

**6.** In the right-hand window, double-click either the MaintainServerList or the IsDomainMaster value (depending on the value you want to modify).

**7.** Edit the String Editor dialog box so that it contains the desired value. Click OK.

**8.** Exit Registry Editor. The changes will be effective the next time the computer is booted.

concept link

**For information on configuring the Computer Browser service on Windows 95 or Windows for Workgroups computers, consult the *Microsoft Windows 95 Resource Kit* (Microsoft Press, 1995) or the *Microsoft Windows for Workgroups Resource Kit* (Microsoft Press, 1992).**

# Browsing on Transport Protocols

Browsing functions differently based on the transport protocol in use on the network. The following sections discuss how browsing is implemented on NetBEUI, NWLink IPX/SPX Compatible Transport, and TCP/IP.

### Browsing on NetBEUI

NetBEUI is a nonroutable protocol. Because of the nonroutable nature of this protocol, browsing is always limited to a single subnet. Browsing traffic, and in fact, all network traffic in a NetBEUI environment, cannot be forwarded across a router.

### Browsing on NWLink IPX/SPX Compatible Transport

NWLink IPX/SPX Compatible Transport (commonly associated with NetWare networks) is a routable protocol. All browsing communications on networks that use this protocol consist of NetBIOS broadcasts.

By default, NetWare routers are configured to forward NetBIOS broadcast traffic across up to eight routers. This means that browsing information is automatically forwarded to other subnets.

Third-party routers are usually configured, by default, to *not* forward NetBIOS broadcast traffic (type 20 packets). You must manually configure third-party routers to support the forwarding of NetBIOS broadcast traffic if you want browsing information to be forwarded to other subnets.

If you use Windows NT with routing enabled, *and* use the NWLink IPX/SPX Compatible Transport protocol, you must enable NetBIOS Broadcast Propagation (broadcast of type 20 packets) in order for browsing information to be forwarded across routers to other subnets.

Forwarding NetBIOS broadcasts across routers to other subnets can enable up to eight subnets to function as a single subnet for the purposes of browsing. Forwarding NetBIOS broadcasts can also create a serious increase in the amount of network traffic on all subnets, and should be carefully considered before being implemented.

### *Browsing on TCP/IP*

TCP/IP is a routable protocol. By default, browsing communications on networks that use TCP/IP consist of NetBIOS broadcasts. Because TCP/IP is not normally configured to forward NetBIOS broadcasts, browsing information on networks that use TCP/IP is *not* typically forwarded to other subnets.

However, there are two methods you can use on TCP/IP networks to overcome this limitation and enable browsing information to be forwarded to other subnets. You can use LMHOSTS files, or you can use a WINS server to enable network-wide browsing on TCP/IP networks. Using LMHOSTS files or a WINS server enables the master browser to send and receive browsing information *directly* to and from the domain master browser (on another subnet)—but it does *not* enable forwarding of NetBIOS broadcasts across routers.

Because browsing on a TCP/IP network that uses LMHOSTS files or a WINS server does *not* involve forwarding broadcast traffic, browsing on TCP/IP networks is much more efficient than browsing on networks that use the NWLink IPX/SPX Compatible Transport protocol.

concept link

**For more information on NWLink IPX/SPX Compatible Transport, see Chapter 17. For more information on TCP/IP, see Chapter 16.**

Browsing provides the user with a list of available shared network resources. Once the user knows what resources are available, the user can select a resource, and then connect to the shared folder in order to access the resource.

# CONNECTING TO SHARED FOLDERS

Users must connect to shared folders before they can access the resources they contain.

The following sections discuss how to connect to shared folders, including how to use common naming conventions, Windows NT Explorer, and the command line to connect to shared network resources.

# Naming Conventions

A *naming convention* is an accepted method of identifying individual computers and their resources on the network.

The two common naming conventions used in Windows NT are: *universal naming convention* (UNC), and *fully qualified domain name* (FQDN).

A UNC name consists of a server name and a shared resource name in the following format: `\\Server_name\Share_name`. `Server_name` represents the name of the server that the shared folder is located on. `Share_name` represents the name of the shared folder. A UNC name in this format can be used to connect to a network share. For example, a shared folder named `Public` located on a server named Server1 would have the following UNC name: `\\Server1\Public`.

A UNC name can also specify the name of a subfolder and/or file within the share, using the following format: `\\Server_name\Share_name\Subfolder_name\File_name`. A UNC name in this format can be used to access a specific folder or file, such as a data file on a remote server. For example, a data file named `Salaries.doc` in the `Payroll` folder located in a share named HR on a server named CORP would have the following UNC name: `\\Corp\HR\Payroll\Salaries.doc`.

An FQDN is a fancy term for the way computers are named and referenced on the Internet. FQDNs are often used on networks that use TCP/IP and DNS servers. The format for an FQDN is `Server_name.Domain_name.Root_domain_name`. For example, the FQDN of a server named `Wolf` in a domain named `AlanCarter` in the `com` root domain would be: `wolf.alancarter.com`.

*If your network uses TCP/IP and DNS servers, you can replace the* `Server_name` *in a UNC with an FQDN.* For example, to specify a share named `Books` on a server with an FQDN of `wolf.alancarter.com`, you could use: `\\wolf.alancarter.com\Books`.

Both UNC names and FQDNs can be used to connect to shared network resources in Windows NT Explorer and from the command line.

# Using Windows NT Explorer

Assuming that you have the appropriate permissions, you can connect to any shared network resource by using Windows NT Explorer.

**TO CONNECT TO A SHARED NETWORK RESOURCE BY USING WINDOWS NT EXPLORER, FOLLOW THESE STEPS:**

**1.** Select Start⇒Programs⇒Windows NT Explorer.

**2.** In the Exploring dialog box, right-click Network Neighborhood. Select Map Network Drive from the menu that appears.

**3.** The Map Network Drive dialog box appears, as shown in Figure 13-2. Notice the browsing information available in the Shared Directories list box. In this dialog box, you can use one of two methods to select the network resource to which you want to connect:

- You can type in the UNC name of the resource you want to connect to in the Path text box.

- You can double-click any domain or server shown in the Shared Directories list box to browse the network. If you double-click a domain, a browse list of available network servers in that domain is displayed. If you double-click a server, a browse list of shared folders on that server is displayed. Highlight the shared folder you want to connect to. The UNC name of the shared resource then appears in the Path text box. Click OK.

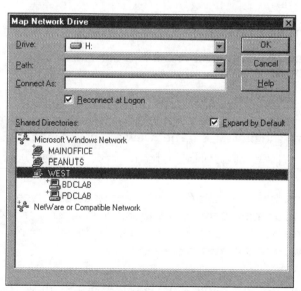

**FIGURE 13-2** **Using Windows NT Explorer to browse the network**

**4.** The resource you select should appear with a drive letter under My Computer in the All Folders section of the Exploring dialog box, indicating that you have successfully connected a network drive to the resource.

**5.** Exit Windows NT Explorer.

---

Once you have connected a drive letter to a shared network resource, the new drive letter appears in Windows NT Explorer, My Computer, and the Open dialog box in standard Windows applications. You can then access the files and folders within the share in the same manner that you access files and folders on your local computer.

## Connecting from the Command Line

You can use the Net.exe utility to browse the network and, assuming that you have the appropriate permissions, to connect to a shared network resource from the command line.

---

**TO BROWSE THE NETWORK FROM THE COMMAND LINE, FOLLOW THESE STEPS:**

**1.** Select Start ⇒ Programs ⇒ Command Prompt.

**2.** To obtain a list of available servers in your domain or workgroup, at the C:\> command prompt, type **net view** and press Enter.

**3.** To obtain a list of all domains on the network, type **net view /domain** and press Enter.

**4.** To obtain a list of available servers in another domain, type **net view /domain:*Domain_name*** and press Enter. (For example, to obtain a list of available servers in the LAB domain, type **net view /domain:lab** and press Enter.)

**5.** To obtain a list of available shares on a network server, type **net view \\\\*Server_name*** and press Enter. (For example, to obtain a list of available shares on a server named PDCLAB, type **net view \\\\pdclab** and press Enter.) To exit the Command Prompt dialog box at any time, type **exit** at the command prompt and press Enter.

---

**TO CONNECT TO A SHARED NETWORK RESOURCE
FROM THE COMMAND LINE, FOLLOW THESE STEPS:**

**1.** Select Start ⇒ Programs ⇒ Command Prompt.

**2.** In the Command Prompt dialog box at the C:\> command prompt, type
**net use *Drive_letter*: \\\\*Server_name*\\*Share_name*** and press Enter. For
example, to connect a drive letter, such as X:, to a share named Data on a
server named Pdclab, type **net use x: \\\\pdclab\\data** and press Enter.

**3.** A message appears indicating that the command completed successfully.

**4.** Exit the Command Prompt dialog box by typing **exit** at the command
prompt and pressing Enter.

Once you have connected a drive letter to a shared network resource, the
new drive letter appears in Windows NT Explorer, My Computer, and the Open
dialog box in standard Windows applications. You can then access the files and
folders within the share in the same manner that you access files and folders on
your local computer.

# KEY POINT SUMMARY

Chapter 13 covered browsing, which permits users to find out what shared resources
are available on the network, and facilitates connecting to those resources. Browsing
is managed by the Computer Browser service, which is responsible for the process of
building a list of available network servers (a browse list), and for sharing that list
with other computers. (For the purposes of this chapter, network servers include all
computers that either have shared resources or are capable of sharing their
resources.) Not every computer on the network has to maintain a browse list, and
because of this fact, processor overhead and network traffic are reduced.

o The task of maintaining a browse list is distributed among many
  computers. *The browser roles* that computers can perform are: domain
  master browser, master browser, backup browser, potential browser, and
  non-browser.

o  If a network has a single subnet, the *domain master browser* and master browser functions are combined, and are performed by a single computer — the PDC. The PDC compiles the browse list and makes this list available to the backup browsers.

o  If a network has multiple subnets, the domain master browser maintains a list of available network servers located on all subnets in the domain, and makes this information available to the master browser on each subnet, which, in turn, makes the information available to the backup browsers.

o  The *master browser* builds the browse list for its own subnet, and distributes this list to the domain master browser and to the backup browsers on its own subnet. Each workgroup or domain is limited to having only *one* master browser on a subnet.

o  The *backup browser* receives the browse list from the master browser, and then distributes the information to any computer that requests it.

o  A computer that does not currently maintain or distribute a browse list, but is capable of doing so, is called a *potential browser*. By default, all Windows NT Server, Windows NT Workstation, Windows 95, and Windows for Workgroups computers are potential browsers.

o  A *non-browser* is a computer that is not capable of maintaining and distributing a browse list, either because it has been configured to not function as a browser, or because the computer's network software does not provide the capability to maintain a browse list.

o  The browsing process consists of two distinct activities: building and maintaining the browse list, and distributing the browse list to computers that request it. There are several steps involved in both of these activities.

o  Because the master browser does not remove a network server from its browse list until *after* it has failed to receive a broadcast announcement from the network server for three consecutive twelve-minute periods, it is possible for a network server to remain on the browse list for some time after it is no longer actually available to network users.

o  A *browser election*, which determines which computer will function as the master browser, takes place when the PDC is booted, when a backup browser is unable to obtain an updated browse list from the master browser, and when a computer is unable to obtain a list of backup browsers from the master browser.

o The computer that initiates the browser election process broadcasts an election packet, which contains the computer's election criteria value. A computer's election criteria value is based on the computer's operating system, version, and on the computer's current browser role. The election criteria value ranking of operating systems, from highest to lowest, is: Windows NT Server, Windows NT Workstation, Windows 95, and Windows for Workgroups. Newer versions of an operating system have a higher election criteria value than older versions. The computer with the *highest* election criteria value, in a browser election, "wins" the election and becomes the master browser. Only the master browser is elected. The domain master browser is always the PDC. If the PDC is unavailable, there is no domain master browser.

o The Computer Browser service on a Windows NT computer is controlled by the MaintainServerList and IsDomainMaster Registry entries that are located in \HKEY_LOCAL_MACHINE\SYSTEM\CurrentControlSet\ Services\Browser\Parameters. The default settings for these entries can be changed by editing the Registry if you want to change a Windows NT computer's default browser role.

o The MaintainServerList entry, which specifies whether a computer will maintain a browse list, can be configured with a value of No, Yes, or Auto. *Yes* is the default setting for all Windows NT Server domain controllers. *Auto* is the default setting for all Windows NT computers that are non-domain controllers.

o The IsDomainMaster entry, which specifies whether a computer will initiate an election at startup, and also gives a computer a higher election criteria value than other computers of equivalent configuration, can be configured with a value of True or False. *False* is the default setting for all Windows NT computers.

o Because of the nonroutable nature of NetBEUI, browsing on a network that uses NetBEUI is limited to a single subnet.

o On networks that use the NWLink IPX/SPX Compatible Transport protocol (a routable protocol), all browsing communications consist of NetBIOS broadcasts. By default, NetWare routers are configured to forward NetBIOS broadcast traffic across up to eight routers, which can enable up to eight subnets to function as a single subnet for the purposes of browsing. However, this can create a serious increase in the amount of network traffic on all subnets.

o On networks that use TCP/IP (a routable protocol), browsing communication, by default, consists of NetBIOS broadcasts. However, because TCP/IP is not normally configured to forward NetBIOS broadcasts, browsing information is typically *not* forwarded to other subnets. This limitation can be overcome by using `LMHOSTS` files or a WINS server, which enables the master browser to send and receive browsing information *directly* to and from the domain master browser (on another subnet), but this is *not* accomplished in the form of a NetBIOS broadcast. When `LMHOSTS` files or a WINS server is used, browsing on a TCP/IP network is much more efficient than browsing on a NWLink IPX/SPX Compatible Transport network, because there is no forwarding of browsing broadcast traffic on the TCP/IP network.

o A naming convention is an accepted method of identifying computers and their resources on the network. The two common naming conventions used in Windows NT are: the *universal naming convention* (UNC), and *fully qualified domain name* (FQDN).

   o A UNC name consists of a server name and a shared resource name in the following format: `\\Server_name\Share_name`. A UNC name can also specify the name of a subfolder and/or file within the share, using the following format: `\\Server_name\Share_name\Subfolder_name\File_name`.

   o An FQDN is a fancy term for the way computers are named and referenced on the Internet. The format for an FQDN is `Server_name.Domain_name.Root_domain_name`. If your network uses TCP/IP and DNS servers, you can replace the `Server_name` in a UNC with an FQDN. Both UNC names and FQDNs can be used to connect to shared network resources in Windows NT Explorer and from the command line.

# Applying What You've Learned

Now it's time to regroup, review, and apply what you've learned in this chapter.

The following Instant Assessment questions bring to mind key facts and concepts.

The hands-on lab exercises will really reinforce what you've learned, and allow you to practice some of the tasks tested by the Microsoft Certified Professional exams.

## Instant Assessment

1. What service manages browsing on Windows NT computers?

2. What is a list of available network servers called?

3. List the five different roles that computers can play in the browsing process.

4. Which computer is always the domain master browser?

5. How many master browsers can each domain have on a subnet?

6. Why are some computers non-browsers?

7. Briefly describe how a browse list is built and maintained.

8. Describe the process that takes place when a user browses the network.

9. You browse the network and are unable to connect to a server that is listed as available on your browse list. What timing issue inherent to the browsing process could account for this problem?

10. Which kind of browser is determined by a browser election?

11. What is contained in an election packet?

12. Which Registry entry specifies whether a given NT computer will be a browser?

13. Which Registry entry specifies whether a given NT computer will initiate a browser election at startup?

14. What type of network traffic does browsing communications consist of on an NWLink IPX/SPX Compatible Transport network?

15. What can you use on a TCP/IP network to enable the master browser to send browsing information *directly* to and from the domain master browser (on another subnet)?

16. Specify the format of a UNC name.

17. Specify the format of an FQDN.

18. If your network uses TCP/IP and DNS servers, what can you replace in a UNC name with an FQDN?

**T/F**

19. Because NetBEUI is a nonroutable protocol, browsing on a
NetBEUI network is limited to a single subnet.          ___

concept link     **For answers to the Instant Assessment questions see Appendix D.**

# Hands-on Lab Exercises

The following hands-on lab exercises provide you with two different opportunities
to apply the knowledge you've gained in this chapter about accessing network
resources.

**Lab 13.21** *Configuring the Computer Browser service*

Workstation
Server
Enterprise

The purpose of this lab is to give you hands-on experience in configuring the
Windows NT Computer Browser service. You will edit the Registry to configure
your Windows NT Computer to force an election when it is booted, in an attempt
to become the master browser for its subnet.

Begin this lab by booting your computer to Windows NT Server. Log on as
Administrator.

**FOLLOW THESE STEPS CAREFULLY:**

1. Select Start ⇒ Run.

2. In the Run dialog box, type **Regedt32** in the Open drop-down list box.
   Click OK.

3. In the Registry Editor dialog box, select Window ⇒ HKEY_LOCAL_MACHINE
   on Local Machine.

4. Maximize the HKEY_LOCAL_MACHINE on Local Machine window.

5. Double-click the SYSTEM folder. Under the SYSTEM folder, double-click the
   CurrentControlSet folder. Double-click the Services folder. Scroll
   down and double-click the Browser folder. Click the Parameters folder.

6. In the right-hand window, double-click the IsDomainMaster value.

7. Edit the String Editor dialog box to read **TRUE**. Click OK. (This step
   configures the computer to force an election on startup, and to attempt
   to become the master browser for its subnet.)

8. Notice in the right-hand window that the IsDomainMaster value is
   changed to TRUE.

**9**. The MaintainServerList value should be Yes. (If it isn't, double-click MaintainServerList and change the value to **Yes** in the String Editor dialog box.)

**10.** Exit Registry Editor. These changes will become effective the next time you boot the computer.

## Lab 13.22 *Accessing network resources*

 **This lab is optional, because it requires an additional networked computer. Additionally, Lab 10.15 must be completed prior to performing this lab. (See Lab 10.15 for specific computer hardware requirements.)**

Workstation
Enterprise

The purpose of this lab is to give you hands-on experience in accessing shared network resources. You will create and then access shared folders by using Windows NT Explorer, and also connect to shared folders from the command line.

This lab consists of three parts:

o Part 1: Configuring shares on the second computer (PDCMAINOFFICE)

o Part 2: Connecting to shared folders by using Windows NT Explorer

o Part 3: Connecting to a shared folder from the command line

Follow the steps in each part carefully.

**Part 1: Configuring shares on the second computer (PDCMAINOFFICE)**
Perform these steps on your second computer (PDCMAINOFFICE) after you have booted the computer to Windows NT Server and logged on as Administrator.

**1.** Select Start⇒Programs⇒Windows NT Explorer.

**2.** In the Exploring dialog box, highlight the Program Files folder. Select File⇒ Properties.

**3.** In the Program Files Properties dialog box, click the Sharing tab.

**4.** On the Sharing tab, select the radio button next to Shared As. Edit the Share Name text box so that it appears as **Programs**. Click OK.

**5.** Highlight the C: drive under My Computer. Select File⇒New⇒Folder.

**6.** Rename the new folder as **Projects**. Press Enter.

**7.** Select File⇒Properties.

**8.** In the Projects Properties dialog box, click the Sharing tab.

9. On the Sharing tab, select the radio button next to Shared As. Accept the default share name of Projects. Click OK.

10. Highlight the C: drive under My Computer. Select File ⟹ New ⟹ Folder.

11. Rename the new folder as **Public**. Press Enter.

12. Select File ⟹ Properties.

13. In the Public Properties dialog box, click the Sharing tab.

14. On the Sharing tab, select the radio button next to Shared As. Accept the default share name of Public. Click OK.

15. Exit Windows NT Explorer. Continue on to Part 2.

### Part 2: Connecting to shared folders by using Windows NT Explorer

Perform these steps on your main computer (NTW40) after booting it to Windows NT **Workstation** and logging on as Administrator.

1. Select Start ⟹ Programs ⟹ Windows NT Explorer.

2. In the Exploring dialog box, right-click Network Neighborhood. Select Map Network Drive from the menu that appears.

3. In the Map Network Drive dialog box, double-click MAINOFFICE in the Shared Directories list box. Double-click PDCMAINOFFICE. Double-click the `Programs` folder.

4. Notice that Programs on 'Pdcmainoffice' appears with a drive letter under My Computer in the All Folders section of the Exploring dialog box. You have successfully connected a network drive to the `Programs` share on PDCMAINOFFICE (the second computer).

5. Select Tools ⟹ Map Network Drive.

6. In the Map Network Drive dialog box, type **\\pdcmainoffice\public** in the Path drop-down list box. Click OK.

7. Notice that Public on 'Pdcmainoffice' appears with a drive letter under My Computer in the All Folders section of the Exploring dialog box. You have successfully connected a network drive to the `Public` share on PDCMAINOFFICE (the second computer.)

8. Exit Windows NT Explorer. Continue on to Part 3.

### Part 3: Connecting to a shared folder from the command line

Perform these steps on your main computer (NTW40) that is running Windows NT Workstation.

1. Select Start ⟹ Programs ⟹ Command Prompt.

2. At the C:\> command prompt, type **net use p:\\pdcmainoffice\projects**

3. Press Enter. Windows NT should indicate that the command completed successfully. This means that you have successfully connected to the `Projects` share on PDCMAINOFFICE (the second computer).

4. At the C:\> command prompt, type **exit** and press Enter.

Server
Enterprise

# Using Windows NT Server Tools

# About Chapter 14

This chapter explores how to manage Windows NT Server computers remotely on your network using Windows NT Server tools.

First, the chapter describes the utilities that make up Windows NT Server tools, and then it explains how to install Windows NT Server tools on Windows 95 computers as well as on Windows NT Workstation computers.

Next, the chapter discusses how a user at a client computer can use Windows NT Server tools to manage an NT Server computer remotely on the network.

The chapter wraps up with an illustrative example of an Administrator who uses Windows NT Server tools (installed on a Windows NT Workstation client computer) to remotely promote a backup domain controller to a primary domain controller.

This chapter includes a comprehensive hands-on lab. In this lab, you install Windows NT Server tools and use NT Server tools to administer a remote server.

Chapter 14 is optional if you're preparing for only the Workstation exam, but essential if you're preparing for either the Server or Enterprise exams. This chapter maps to the "Administer remote servers from various types of client computers" objective in the Managing Resources section in the Server and Enterprise exams' objectives.

# WINDOWS NT SERVER TOOLS

*Windows NT Server tools* are a collection of Windows NT Server utilities that, when installed on a Windows 95 or Windows NT Workstation client computer, make it possible for a user at the client computer to remotely manage an NT Server computer on the network.

The NT Server tools make remote administration of an NT Server computer practical and convenient for many administrators.

Windows NT Server tools are also referred to as *client-based network administration tools*.

Because the NT Server tools, and their installation, differ on Windows 95 and Windows NT Workstation computers, they are discussed separately in the following sections.

## NT Server Tools for Windows 95 Computers

The NT Server tools that can be installed on Windows 95 client computers are: *User Manager for Domains, Server Manager, Event Viewer,* and *security extensions for Windows Explorer* to manage file and printer security on a remote Windows NT Server. These tools are Windows 95 versions of the same tools that ship with Windows NT Server and that are discussed throughout this book.

Table 14-1 shows the NT Server tools that can be installed on Windows 95 client computers and the basic functions that they enable an administrator to perform remotely from the client computer.

**TABLE 14-1** NT SERVER TOOLS FOR WINDOWS 95 CLIENT COMPUTERS

| NT SERVER TOOL | FUNCTIONALITY |
| --- | --- |
| User Manager for Domains | Enables remote management of users, groups, domain security policy, and trust relationships on a Windows NT Server computer. |

*continued*

**TABLE 14-1** *(continued)*

| NT SERVER TOOL | FUNCTIONALITY |
|---|---|
| Server Manager | Enables remote management of shared folders, remote starting and stopping of services, remote management of Directory Replication, remote viewing of which users are accessing shared resources, and remote disconnection of users from shared resources on a Windows NT Server computer. |
| Event Viewer | Enables remote viewing, archiving, and management of the system, security, and application logs in Event Viewer on a Windows NT Server computer. |
| Security tab extensions for Windows Explorer | This feature adds a Security tab to the "file," "foider," or "printer" Properties dialog boxes (tabs that normally exist on NT Server but aren't present on Windows 95 computers); Enables remote management of file, folder, and printer security on a Windows NT Server computer. |

Before you install and run Windows NT Server tools on a Windows 95 client computer, ensure that the computer has the following minimum required hardware and software installed:

**Hardware required:**

o  486DX/33 processor

o  8MB of RAM

o  3MB of available hard disk space on the system partition

**Software required:**

o  Windows 95

o  Client for Microsoft Networks

## Installing NT Server tools on a Windows 95 computer

In addition to the minimum required hardware and software, installing Windows NT Server tools on a Windows 95 client computer requires either a CD-ROM drive on the client computer *and* the Windows NT Server 4.0 compact disc, or access to a shared folder containing a copy of the NT Server tools on an available network server.

You can't pick and choose which NT Server tools to install—they are all installed as a single package. The next section describes how to install NT Server tools on a Windows 95 client computer.

---

**TO INSTALL WINDOWS NT SERVER TOOLS ON A WINDOWS 95 CLIENT COMPUTER (USING A CD-ROM DRIVE), FOLLOW THESE STEPS:**

**1.** Boot the client computer to Windows 95. Place the Windows NT Server 4.0 compact disc in the computer's CD-ROM drive.

**2.** Windows 95 automatically starts the CD-ROM device. Minimize the Windows NT CD-ROM dialog box.

**3.** Select Start ⇒ Settings ⇒ Control Panel.

**4.** The Control Panel dialog box appears. Double-click the Add/Remove Programs icon.

**5.** The Add/Remove Programs Properties dialog box appears. Click the Windows Setup tab.

**6.** On the Windows Setup tab, click the Have Disk command button.

**7.** The Install From Disk dialog box appears. Click the Browse command button.

**8.** The Open dialog box appears. In the Drives drop-down listbox, select the computer's CD-ROM drive. In the Folders list box, double-click the Clients folder. Then scroll down and double-click the Srvtools folder. Double-click the Win95 folder. Srvtools.inf appears in the File Name list box, as shown in Figure 14-1. Click OK.

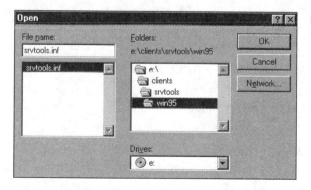

**FIGURE 14-1** Selecting NT Server tools from the CD

**9.** The Install From Disk dialog box reappears, as shown in Figure 14-2. Notice the full path to the NT Server tools. Click OK.

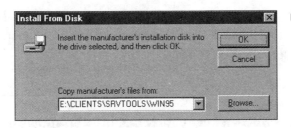

**FIGURE 14-2** Preparing to install NT Server tools from the compact disc

**10.** The Have Disk dialog box reappears. Select the check box next to Windows NT Server Tools in the Components list box. The dialog box's appearance, at this point, is as shown in Figure 14-3. Click the Install command button.

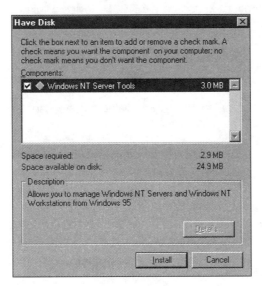

**FIGURE 14-3** Installing NT Server tools

**11.** Windows 95 copies files and updates shortcuts, and then displays the Add/Remove Programs Properties dialog box again, as shown in Figure 14-4. Notice the Components list box shows that the Windows NT Server tools are installed on the computer. Click OK.

**12.** Before the NT Server tools can be used on this computer, you must edit the computer's `autoexec.bat` file. To start this process, select Start⇒ Programs⇒MS-DOS Prompt.

**13.** At the C:\WINDOWS> prompt, type **edit c:\autoexec.bat** and press Enter.

**14.** The contents of the `autoexec.bat` file are displayed. (If you did not previously have an `autoexec.bat` file, the window will be blank.) After the last entry listed, type the following line: **SET PATH=%PATH%;C:\SRVTOOLS** and press Enter. Select File⇒Exit.

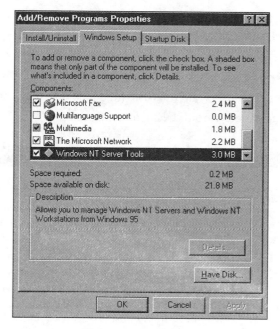

**FIGURE 14-4** NT Server tools installed

**15.** The Save File dialog box appears. Click the Yes command button.

**16.** The C:\WINDOWS> prompt reappears. Type **exit** and press Enter.

**17.** Restart Windows and the new path takes effect. Windows NT Server Tools will appear in the Start ⇒ Programs menu.

 **If you want to install NT Server tools on a Windows 95 computer over the network (instead of using a CD-ROM drive), connect to the shared folder that contains the Windows 95 NT Server tools source files, and select that folder during the installation process.**

## NT Server Tools for Windows NT Workstation Computers

The NT Server tools that can be installed on Windows NT Workstation computers are: *User Manager for Domains, Server Manager, System Policy Editor, Remote Access Admin, DHCP Administrator, WINS Manager,* and *Remoteboot Manager.* These tools are Windows NT Workstation versions of the same tools that ship with Windows NT Server, and that are discussed throughout this book.

Because Event Viewer and Windows NT Explorer are already installed on a Windows NT Workstation computer, they are not part of the NT Server tools add-on package.

Table 14-2 shows the NT Server tools that can be installed on Windows NT Workstation client computers and the basic functions that they enable an administrator to perform remotely from the client computer.

| **TABLE 14-2** NT SERVER TOOLS FOR WINDOWS NT WORKSTATION CLIENT COMPUTERS | |
|---|---|
| *NT SERVER TOOL* | *FUNCTIONALITY* |
| User Manager for Domains | Enables remote management of users, groups, domain security policy, and trust relationships on a Windows NT Server computer. |
| Server Manager | Enable remote management of shared folders, remote starting and stopping of services, remote management of directory replication, remote viewing of which users are accessing shared resources, and remote disconnection of users from shared resources on a Windows NT Server computer. |
| System Policy Editor | Enables remote creation and editing of policy files on a Windows NT Server computer. |
| Remote Access Admin | Enables remote configuration and management of the *Remote Access Service* (RAS) on a Windows NT Server computer. |
| DHCP Administrator | Enables remote configuration and management of the DHCP service on a Windows NT Server computer. |
| WINS Manager | Enables remote configuration and management of the WINS service on a Windows NT Server computer. |
| Remoteboot Manager | Enables remote configuration and management of the Remoteboot service on a Windows NT Server computer. |

Before you can install and run Windows NT Server tools on a Windows NT Workstation client computer, you should ensure that the computer has the following minimum required hardware and software installed:

**Hardware required:**

o  486DX/33 processor

o  12MB of RAM

o  2.5MB of available hard disk space on the system partition

Software required:

- Windows NT Workstation
- Server service
- Workstation service

## Installing NT Server tools on a Windows NT Workstation computer

In addition to the minimum required hardware and software, installing Windows NT Server tools on a Windows NT Workstation client computer requires either a CD-ROM drive on the client computer *and* the Windows NT Server 4.0 compact disc, or access to a shared folder containing a copy of the NT Server tools on an available network server.

You can't pick and choose which NT Server tools to install — they are all installed as a single package. The next section explains how to install NT Server tools on a Windows NT Workstation computer.

**TO INSTALL WINDOWS NT SERVER TOOLS ON A WINDOWS NT WORKSTATION CLIENT COMPUTER (BY USING A CD-ROM DRIVE), FOLLOW THESE STEPS:**

1. Start Windows NT Workstation on the computer. Log on as Administrator. Place the Windows NT Server 4.0 compact disc in the CD-ROM drive.

2. Select Start⇒ Programs⇒ Windows NT Explorer.

3. In the Exploring dialog box, click the + sign next to the CD-ROM drive. Under the CD-ROM drive, click the + sign next to the Clients folder. Click the + sign next to the Srvtools folder. Highlight the Winnt folder. Figure 14-5 shows the Exploring dialog box at this point. Notice the Setup.bat file in the "Contents of Winnt" section.

4. In the "Contents of Winnt" section in the right-hand window, double-click Setup.bat.

5. A window appears, as shown in Figure 14-6, indicating that the Client-based Network Administration Tools have been installed. Press any key to continue.

6. The Exploring dialog box reappears. The Windows NT Server tools are now installed. Continue on to Step 7 to create icons for the server tools.

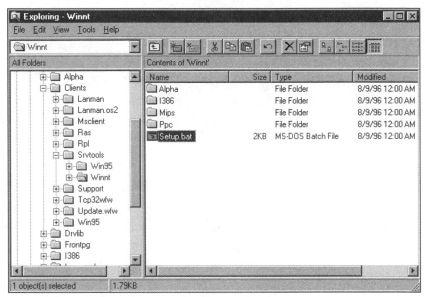

**FIGURE 14-5**   Installing NT Server tools on a Windows NT
Workstation computer

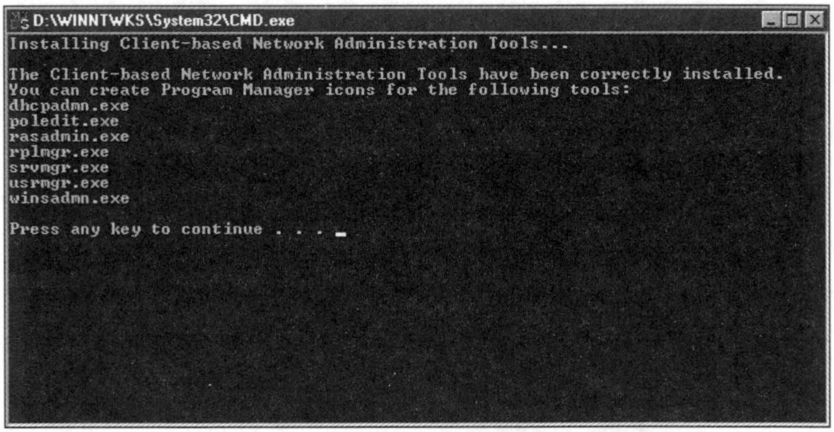

**FIGURE 14-6**   NT Server tools installed on an NT Workstation computer

**7.** In the Exploring dialog box, click the + sign next to the drive on your
computer on which you originally installed Windows NT Workstation (if it is
not already expanded). Often, this is the C: drive. Click the + sign next to
the `<winntroot>` folder. (Remember, `<winntroot>` is the folder in which
Windows NT Workstation is installed.) Click the + sign next to the `Profiles`
folder. Click the + sign next to the `All Users` folder. Click the + sign next
to the Start Menu folder. Click the + sign next to the `Programs` folder.
Highlight the `Administrative Tools (Common)` folder.

8. Select File ⇒ New ⇒ Shortcut.

9. In the Create Shortcut dialog box, type
   **c:\<*winntroot*>\system32\usrmgr.exe** in the command line text box.
   (Replace <*winntroot*> with the name of the folder in which NT
   Workstation is installed.) If Windows NT Workstation is installed on a
   different drive than the C: drive, substitute the correct drive letter in this
   path. Click the Next command button.

10. In the Select A Title For The Program dialog box, type **User Manager for
    Domains** in the Select A Name For The Shortcut text box. Click the Finish
    command button.

11. The Exploring dialog box reappears. Repeat Steps 8–10 to create icons for
    each of the following NT Server tools:

    | Filename: | Shortcut name: |
    |---|---|
    | c:\<*winntroot*>\system32\srvmgr.exe | Server Manager |
    | c:\<*winntroot*>\system32\poledit.exe | System Policy Editor |
    | c:\<*winntroot*>\system32\rasadmn.exe | Remote Access Admin |
    | c:\<*winntroot*>\system32\dhcpadmn.exe | DHCP Administrator |
    | c:\<*winntroot*>\system32\winsadmn.exe | WINS Administrator |
    | c:\<*winntroot*>\system32\rplmgr.exe | Remoteboot Manager |

12. The Exploring dialog box reappears. Exit Windows NT Explorer.

# USING WINDOWS NT SERVER TOOLS TO MANAGE AN NT SERVER COMPUTER

Windows NT Server tools makes it possible for a user at a client computer to
remotely manage an NT Server computer on the network. In effect, NT Server
tools turn an administrator's desktop into an NT Server management station, even
if the administrator's desktop runs Windows 95 or Windows NT Workstation.

For the most part, Windows NT Server tools are used in the same way on a
client computer as they are when they are run on a Windows NT Server computer.
(The main differences on a client computer typically consist of an extra step or
two to select the appropriate domain and/or computer on which the action will be
performed.)

Here's an example of how an Administrator can use Windows NT Server tools (installed on a Windows NT Workstation client computer) to remotely promote a *backup domain controller* (BDC) to a *primary domain controller* (PDC) so that a scheduled upgrade can be performed on the PDC.

## Using Server Manager to Remotely Promote a BDC to a PDC

The Administrator performs the following steps on the Windows NT Workstation client computer, on which NT Server tools have been installed, to remotely promote a BDC on the network to a PDC:

**1.** The Administrator selects Start ⟹ Programs ⟹ Administrative Tools (Common) ⟹ Server Manager. The Server Manager dialog box appears, as shown in Figure 14-7. Note that the computer named BDCLAB is currently a Windows NT 4.0 BDC.

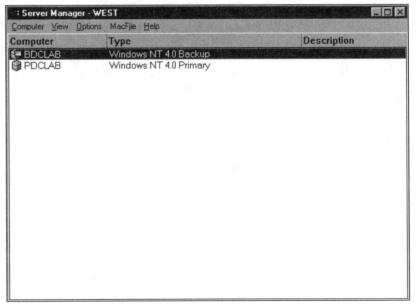

**FIGURE 14-7**    Preparing to promote the BDC

**2.** Next, the Administrator highlights the BDC in the Server Manager dialog box. The administrator selects Computer⇒Promote to Primary Domain Controller, as shown in Figure 14-8. Notice the available options in this menu.

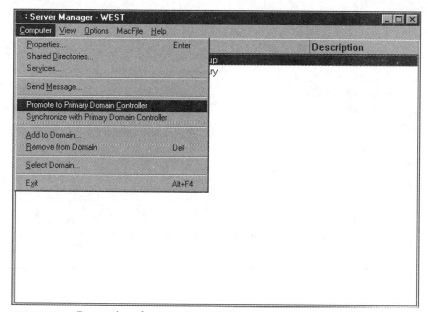

**FIGURE 14-8** Promoting the BDC to a PDC

**3.** Finally, the Administrator confirms that he or she wants to promote the BDC by clicking the Yes command button in the Server Manager warning dialog box. Server Manager remotely promotes the BDC to a PDC, and simultaneously demotes the PDC to a BDC. The process takes a few minutes. Finally, the Server Manager dialog box reappears, as shown in Figure 14-9. Notice that the computer named BDCLAB is now a Windows NT 4.0 primary domain controller (PDC).

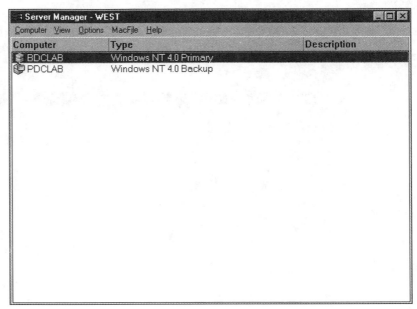

**FIGURE 14-9** BDC promoted to PDC

# KEY POINT SUMMARY

This chapter explored how to manage Windows NT Server computers remotely on a network by using Windows NT Server tools.

o *Windows NT Server tools* are a collection of Windows NT Server utilities that, when installed on a Windows 95 or Windows NT Workstation client computer, enable a user at the client computer to manage an NT Server computer remotely on the network. Windows NT Server tools are also referred to as *client-based network administration tools*.

o The NT Server tools that can be installed on Windows 95 client computers are: *User Manager for Domains, Server Manager, Event Viewer,* and *security extensions for Windows Explorer* to manage file and printer security on a remote Windows NT Server.

- The minimum hardware and software required to install and run NT Server tools on a Windows 95 computer is: a 486DX/33 processor with 8MB of RAM and 3MB of available hard disk space, with Windows 95 and Client for Microsoft Networks installed. Additionally, you need either a CD-ROM drive on the client computer and the Windows NT Server 4.0 compact disc, or you must have access to a shared folder containing a copy of the NT Server tools on an available network server.

- You can't pick and choose which NT Server tools to install—they are all installed as a single package.

- After you install the NT Server tools on a Windows 95 computer, you must edit the computer's `autoexec.bat` file before using the tools.

- The NT Server tools that can be installed on Windows NT Workstation computers are: *User Manager for Domains, Server Manager, System Policy Editor, Remote Access Admin, DHCP Administrator, WINS Manager,* and *Remoteboot Manager.*

  - The minimum hardware and software required to install and run NT Server tools on a Windows NT Workstation computer is: a 486DX/33 processor with 12MB of RAM and 2.5MB of available hard disk space on the system partition, with Windows NT Workstation, the Server service, and the Workstation service installed. Additionally, you need either a CD-ROM drive on the client computer and the Windows NT Server 4.0 compact disc, or you must have access to a shared folder containing a copy of the NT Server tools on an available network server.

  - After you install Windows NT Server tools on a Windows NT Workstation client computer, you need to create icons for the individual server tools.

- NT Server tools, in effect, turn an administrator's desktop into an NT Server management station—even if the administrator's desktop runs Windows 95 or Windows NT Workstation. An example of the process an Administrator goes through to use the Server Manager tool to remotely promote a BDC to a PDC is discussed.

# APPLYING WHAT YOU'VE LEARNED

Now it's time to regroup, review, and apply what you've learned in this chapter.

The following Instant Assessment questions bring to mind key facts and concepts. The hands-on lab exercise reinforces what you've learned, and gives you an opportunity to practice some of the tasks tested by the Microsoft Certified Professional exams.

## Instant Assessment

1. What is the primary purpose of Windows NT Server tools?

2. Which NT Server tools can be installed on a Windows 95 client computer?

3. Which NT Server tools can be installed on a Windows NT Workstation client computer?

4. What is the minimum amount of RAM required to install and run NT Server tools on a Windows 95 client computer? On a Windows NT Workstation client computer?

5. Which NT Server tool should you use to remotely promote a BDC to a PDC?

6. Which NT Server tool should you use to manage a shared folder on an NT Server computer remotely from a Windows 95 client computer?

7. Which NT Server tool should you use to manage users on an NT Server computer remotely from a Windows NT Workstation client computer?

8. Which NT Server tool should you use to share the CD-ROM drive on an NT Server computer remotely from a Windows 95 client computer? (Hint: See the lab at the end of this chapter.)

9. Which NT Server tool should you use to manage file, folder, and printer security on an NT Server computer remotely from a Windows 95 client computer?

concept link  **For answers to the Instant Assessment questions see Appendix D.**

# Hands-on Lab Exercise

The following hands-on lab exercise provides you with a practical opportunity to apply your knowledge of Windows NT Server tools.

**Lab 14.23** *Installing Windows NT Server tools and using NT Server tools to administer a remote server*

Server
Enterprise

The purpose of this lab is to give you hands-on experience in installing Windows NT Server tools, and experience in using NT Server tools to administer a remote server. You install Windows NT Server tools on a Windows NT Workstation computer, and then (optionally) use Windows NT Server tools to administer your second Windows NT Server computer remotely.

This lab consists of two parts:

Part 1: Installing Windows NT Server tools on a Windows NT Workstation computer

Part 2: (Optional) Administering a remote Windows NT Server computer

Follow these steps carefully.

## Part 1: Installing Windows NT Server tools on a Windows NT Workstation computer

**(Perform these steps on your first or primary computer.)**

1. Boot your computer to Windows NT Workstation. Log on as Administrator. Place your Windows NT Server 4.0 compact disc in your CD-ROM drive.

2. Select Start➪Programs➪Windows NT Explorer.

3. In the Exploring dialog box, click the + sign next to your CD-ROM drive. Under your CD-ROM drive, click the + sign next to the Clients folder. Click the + sign next to the Srvtools folder. Highlight the Winnt folder.

4. In the "Contents of Winnt" section in the right-hand window, double-click Setup.bat.

5. A window appears, indicating that the Client-based Network Administration Tools are being installed. When you are prompted to press any key to continue, do so.

6. The Exploring dialog box reappears. The Windows NT Server tools are now installed. Continue to Step 7 to create icons for the various server tools.

**7.** In the Exploring dialog box, click the + sign next to the drive on your computer on which you originally installed Windows NT Workstation (if it is not already expanded). Normally, this is the C: drive. Click the + sign next to the `Winntwks` folder. Click the + sign next to the `Profiles` folder. Click the + sign next to the `All Users` folder. Click the + sign next to the `Start Menu` folder. Click the + sign next to the `Programs` folder. Highlight the `Administrative Tools (Common)` folder.

**8.** Select File ⇒ New ⇒ Shortcut.

**9.** In the Create Shortcut dialog box, type **c:\winntwks\system32\usrmgr.exe** in the Command line text box. (If you installed Windows NT Workstation on a different drive than C:, substitute the correct drive letter in this path.) Click the Next command button.

**10.** In the Select a Title for the Program dialog box, type **User Manager for Domains** in the Select a name for the shortcut text box. Click the Finish command button.

**11.** The Exploring dialog box reappears. Select File ⇒ New ⇒ Shortcut.

**12.** In the Create Shortcut dialog box, type **c:\winntwks\system32\srvmgr.exe** in the Command line text box. (If you installed Windows NT Workstation on a different drive than C:, substitute the correct drive letter in this path.) Click the Next command button.

**13.** In the Select A Title For The Program dialog box, type **Server Manager** in the Select a name for the shortcut text box. Click the Finish command button.

**14.** The Exploring dialog box reappears. Select File ⇒ New ⇒ Shortcut.

**15.** In the Create Shortcut dialog box, type **c:\winntwks\system32\poledit.exe** in the Command line text box. (If you installed Windows NT Workstation on a different drive than C:, substitute the correct drive letter in this path.) Click the Next command button.

**16.** In the Select a Title for the Program dialog box, type **System Policy Editor** in the Select a name for the shortcut text box. Click the Finish command button.

**17.** The Exploring dialog box reappears. Notice the three shortcuts you have just created are listed in the Contents of Administrative Tools (Common). Exit Windows NT Explorer. The icons you have just created will now appear in the Start ⇒ Programs ⇒ Administrative Tools (Common) menu.

Continue to Part 2.

**Part 2: (Optional) Administering a remote Windows NT Server computer**
*Part 2 of this lab is optional,* because it requires an additional networked computer. Additionally, Lab 10.15 and Lab 13.22 must be completed before performing this lab. See Lab 10.15 for specific computer hardware requirements. Begin Part 2 by booting your second computer to Windows NT Server. It is not necessary that you log on.

In the first eight steps of Part 2, you use User Manager for Domains (an NT Server tool that you just installed on your Windows NT Workstation computer) to view users remotely and to add a new user to the MAINOFFICE domain on your second computer.

(Perform these steps from your first or primary computer, booted to Windows NT Workstation. Log on as Administrator.)

**1.** Select Start ⇒ Programs ⇒ Administrative Tools (Common) ⇒ User Manager for Domains.

**2.** The User Manager dialog box appears. Select User ⇒ Select Domain.

**3.** In the Select Domain dialog box, type **MAINOFFICE** in the Domain text box. (This is the domain name of your second computer.) Click OK.

**4.** The User Manager dialog box reappears, this time listing users from the MAINOFFICE domain. Notice that the two users you created in Lab 10.15, CarmenM and HansS, appear in the User Name list box. Select User ⇒ New User.

**5.** Type in your first name and last initial in the User Name text box. (Don't leave a space between the two.) Type in your full name in the Full Name text box. Type in a password of **password**, and confirm the password by retyping it. Clear the check box next to User Must Change Password at Next Logon. Select the check box next to Password Never Expires. Click the Groups command button.

**6.** In the Group Memberships dialog box, highlight Administrators in the Not member of list box. Click the Add command button. Click OK.

**7.** In the New User dialog box, click the Add command button. Click the Close command button.

**8.** The User Manager dialog box reappears. Notice that your name now appears in the list of users in the MAINOFFICE domain. Exit User Manager for Domains.

In the remaining steps in Part 2, you use Server Manager to share the CD-ROM drive on your second computer remotely from your Windows NT Workstation computer.

9. Select Start ⇒ Programs ⇒ Administrative Tools (Common) ⇒ Server Manager.

10. In the Server Manager dialog box, select Computer ⇒ Select Domain.

11. In the Select Domain dialog box, type **MAINOFFICE** in the Domain text box. Click OK.

12. The Server Manager dialog box reappears, this time displaying PDCMAINOFFICE, your second computer, in the Computer list box. Select Computer ⇒ Shared Directories.

13. In the Shared Directories dialog box, click the New Share command button.

14. In the New Share dialog box, type **CDROM** in the Share Name text box, and type the drive letter of the CD-ROM drive on your second computer in the Path text box, for example, **D:\**. Click OK.

    (Note: If you don't have a CD-ROM drive on your second computer, select any other drive letter to share.)

15. The Shared Directories dialog box reappears. Note that CDROM appears in the Shared Directories on \\PDCMAINOFFICE list box, with a hand under it, indicating that it is shared. Click the Close command button.

16. Exit Server Manager.

Server
Enterprise

CHAPTER

# Backing Up and Restoring Data

# 15

# About Chapter 15

This chapter covers the basics of backing up and restoring your Windows NT computer's data.

Chapter 15 begins by explaining the importance of performing and testing regular backups. Various backup types, such as normal, differential, and incremental are considered; and common backup strategies are presented. Security considerations are presented, as well as tape rotation schemes and tips for documenting backups.

Next, the chapter takes you through the steps to perform a backup using Windows NT Backup. Backing up the local Registry is included in this section. Finally, the chapter outlines the steps to perform a restore by using Windows NT Backup.

This chapter includes one hands-on lab that requires the use of a tape drive. In this lab you practice using Windows NT Backup to back up files and folders on your Windows NT computer.

If you're reading this book, it's probably important for you to know how to back up and restore data. That said, this chapter can be considered optional if you're preparing for only the Workstation exam, but is absolutely essential if you're preparing for either the Server or Enterprise exams. This chapter maps to various fault tolerance and Registry backup objectives in the Troubleshooting section in the Server and Enterprise exams' objectives.

# BACKING UP FILES AND FOLDERS

Backing up files and folders is an important part of your network fault tolerance plan. Planning and adhering to a regular backup schedule can make recovering from a corrupt file or a failed hard drive a straightforward, if somewhat painful, task. Failing to make regular backups of your system's critical data can be harmful (or even fatal) to your business and/or to your employment status.

A tape backup is *not* a replacement for other fault tolerance methods, such as disk mirroring and striping with parity. It is an additional safety precaution to use when other fault tolerance methods fail. I don't recommend that you rely solely on disk mirroring, striping with parity, or tape backup. A comprehensive fault tolerance policy typically should include two or more of these strategies.

Always remember that a tape backup is your last line of defense against data loss. If the data on the tape is too old to be of value, or if it is corrupt, or if the tape has been damaged due to fire or other causes, then you have nothing. And having nothing is very hard to explain to upper management.

 in the real world **It's been my sorry duty, on more than one occasion, to have to explain to a client that both disks in a mirrored pair have failed, *and* that their most recent tape backup is corrupt. I can't stress enough the importance of carefully performing regular tape backups and periodically testing the validity of those backups. If you've ever experienced a partial or total disk failure, you know why I'm saying this. Have a hard disk fail on you — and you will never regret the time it takes you to perform backups again.**

This chapter covers the basics about backing up and restoring data, including what to back up, backup types, using Windows NT Backup to perform a backup, using the Schedule service to automate backups, and restoring files and folders.

## What to Back Up

Before you can create a backup strategy, you need to determine which data on your network will be backed up. I recommend that all network data be backed up regularly to tape. This includes operating systems, applications, the Registry, and user-created data files.

In general, operating systems and applications need to be backed up less frequently than user-created data files. You may find it sufficient to back up operating systems and applications once a week, once a month, or even less often. I recommend that you back up operating systems and applications, on separate tapes, initially and every time you modify the operating system or install a new application.

Depending on the importance of the data, user-created data files can be backed up once a week, once a day, once an hour, or at any frequency that meets your organization's needs. When determining which files to back up and how often, the main question you need to ask yourself is *how much data can you afford to lose?* For example, if you decide to back up only once a week, can you afford to lose six days of sales information and other employee-created data?

## Backup Types

Before the specific backup types are presented, a short discussion on the archive attribute, and how the operating system and backup programs use this attribute, is in order.

The *archive attribute* is a marker that the operating system automatically assigns to all files and folders when they are first installed or created. Depending on the backup type, backup programs *remove* the archive attribute from a file or folder to indicate that the file or folder has been backed up. If a file or folder is modified after it is backed up, the operating system reassigns the archive attribute to it.

There are five standard types of backups that you can perform:

o **Normal (full):** A *normal backup* backs up all selected files and folders. It removes the archive attribute from the backed up files and folders. A normal backup is a full, complete backup—it is the backbone of your backup plan or strategy.

o **Differential:** A *differential backup* backs up all selected files and folders that have changed since the last normal (full) backup. A differential backup does *not* remove the archive attribute from any files or folders. A differential backup is a *cumulative* backup since the last normal (full) backup. Because the differential backup does not remove the archive attribute, if a normal backup is performed on Sunday, and differential backups are performed Monday through Friday, Monday's differential backup will contain all changes made to data on Monday; Tuesday's differential backup will contain all changes made to data on Monday and Tuesday, Wednesday's differential backup will contain all changes made to data on Monday, Tuesday, and Wednesday, and so on. A differential backup is often used in between normal backups, because it takes less time to perform a differential backup than a normal backup.

- **Incremental:** An *incremental backup* backs up all selected files and folders that have changed since the last normal or incremental backup. An incremental backup removes the archive attribute from the backed up files and folders. An incremental backup is *not* cumulative like a differential backup. It contains only changes made since the last normal or incremental backup. If a normal backup is performed on Sunday, Monday's incremental backup will contain all changes made to data on Monday; Tuesday's incremental backup will contain all changes made to data only on Tuesday; Wednesday's incremental backup will contain all changes made to data only on Wednesday, and so on. Because less data is backed up, an incremental backup takes even less time to perform than a differential backup.

- **Copy:** A *copy backup* backs up all selected files and folders. It does not remove or otherwise affect the archive attribute. The copy backup can be performed without disrupting the normal backup schedule, because it does not affect the archive attribute. You could use a copy backup to create an extra backup to store off-site.

- **Daily:** A *daily backup* backs up all selected files and folders that have changed during the day the backup is made. It does not remove or otherwise affect the archive attribute.

Companies often use a combination of the standard backup types in their backup strategy.

## Backup Strategies

There are a number of acceptable backup strategies, and three fairly common ones:

- *Perform a normal (full) backup every day.* This is the most time-consuming of the three common strategies. However, should a restore be necessary, only the last normal backup is required, and restore time is generally less than either of the other two strategies.

- *Perform a weekly normal backup and daily differential backups*. As the week progresses, the time required to perform the differential backups increases. However, should a restore be necessary, only two backups will be needed—the most recent normal backup, and the most recent differential backup. (This is because the most recent differential backup contains *all* files and folders that have changed since the last normal backup.) The restore can be accomplished relatively quickly.

- *Perform a weekly normal backup and daily incremental backups*. Incremental backups tend to take about the same amount of time each day, and are considered the fastest backup method. However, should a restore be necessary, multiple backup sets will be required—the most recent normal backup, and *every* incremental backup since the most recent normal backup. (This is because the incremental backups each contain different data and are not cumulative.) The restore will typically take more time than if a differential backup had been used.

When planning your backup strategy, the big trade-off you need to consider is time—the time it takes to perform backups versus the time it takes to restore data.

## Security considerations

When planning your company's backup strategy, there are a few security considerations to take into account:

- If the data is of a sensitive nature, consider physically securing the tape drive and the backup tapes. While your server may require a password and permissions to access confidential data, when a backup tape is taken and restored on another server, your server's security measures are defeated.

- Consider rotating backup tapes to an off-site location. This can prevent or minimize data loss due to a single catastrophic event, such as a theft, fire, flood, or earthquake. Consider using a third-party company that will store your data tapes in a secure, climate-controlled environment.

- If you store backup tapes in a fireproof safe, remember that *fireproof* does not necessarily mean that heat or smoke can't destroy magnetic tapes. Make sure the safe is capable of protecting magnetic media as well as papers and other important items.

o Finally, depending on your organization's security needs, consider who should perform backups. In very high-security environments, consider allowing only administrators to perform backups. In medium-to-low-security situations, consider separating the backup and restore functions by designating certain personnel to perform only backups, and other employees to perform only restores.

## Tape rotation

Most organizations rotate their magnetic tapes in order to reduce the cost of backups. Instead of using a new tape every day, tapes are reused in a systematic manner.

There are probably almost as many tape rotation methods as there are network administrators. Consider the following tape rotation example, which is illustrated in Table 15-1.

| TABLE 15-1 SAMPLE BACKUP TAPE ROTATION SCHEME | | | | |
|---|---|---|---|---|
| MONDAY | TUESDAY | WEDNESDAY | THURSDAY | FRIDAY |
| Tape # 1 | Tape # 2 | Tape # 3 | Tape # 4 | Tape # 5 |
| Tape # 1 | Tape # 2 | Tape # 3 | Tape # 4 | Tape # 6 |
| Tape # 1 | Tape # 2 | Tape # 3 | Tape # 4 | Tape # 7 |
| Tape # 1 | Tape # 2 | Tape # 3 | Tape # 4 | Tape # 8–Archived |

This example requires eight tapes for a four-week period. Tapes one through four are reused each week, with the Monday tape used again the following Monday, and so on. Depending on the amount of data backed up and the tape's capacity, the data from the previous backup can be appended or replaced. The eighth tape is permanently archived and removed from the tape rotation scheme.

When choosing a tape rotation method, consider the following:

o The useful life of a tape. Tapes need to be eventually removed from the rotation scheme and replaced with new tapes. The number of times a magnetic tape can be reused depends on the tape's quality and storage conditions.

- Tape cost versus the cost of lost data. Many tapes are guaranteed for life—but for only the cost of the tape. The cost of lost data is not guaranteed.

- Removing a tape from the rotation schedule weekly, monthly, or quarterly to provide a permanent, long-term archive of your data.

### *Documenting backups*

Documenting your backups will make restoring after a failure a much easier task.

You should consider keeping a backup log book that documents each backup procedure performed. You should record the date and time the backup was performed, a brief description of the data backed up, the name of the person who performed the backup, the tape number used, and its storage location. You can also include a detailed or summarized printed log of the backup. If you have this information readily available, the person performing the restore will be able to quickly identify and locate the most recent backup tape(s) needed.

 **Most backup programs can be configured to create detailed logs that list the individual files and folders backed up. These logs can be quite helpful if a user tells you that he or she has accidentally deleted an important file, and asks you to restore it from tape. A log (either printed, or written to a file on disk) will enable you to locate the appropriate tape needed to restore the file quickly and easily.**

## Performing a Backup Using Windows NT Backup

Windows NT ships with a backup program called *Windows NT Backup*. NT Backup is a basic tape backup program that gives you full capability to back up and restore a Windows NT computer, including the local Registry. It does not back up the Registry on computers other than the one in which the tape device is installed. NT Backup does not provide the extensive scheduling and automation features included in more sophisticated third-party backup programs.

In order to perform a backup, you need a tape drive that is compatible with NT (check the *Windows NT Hardware Compatibility List* [HCL]). If possible, select a tape drive that has the capacity to back up your entire server on a single tape. This is a big help, especially if you perform unattended tape backups.

Before you perform a tape backup using Windows NT Backup, you need to install a tape device and driver, if you haven't already done so, by using the Tape Devices application in Control Panel. Also, make sure that you have the appropriate user rights to perform a backup—you need to either be a member of the Administrators, Backup Operators, or Server Operators groups; or, you need to have the "Back up files and directories" user right assigned to you.

Consider the time of day when performing backups. Because of the utilization of processor and memory during backup, it's normally best to perform backups during the periods of lowest server and/or network usage—often after business hours.

### TO PERFORM A BACKUP USING WINDOWS NT BACKUP, FOLLOW THESE STEPS:

**1.** Place a tape in the tape drive.

**2.** Start ⇒ Programs ⇒ Administrative Tools (Common) ⇒ Backup.

**3.** The Backup dialog box appears. Select Window ⇒ Drives.

**4.** Maximize the Drives dialog box. Select the drive(s) and/or files and/or folders that you want to back up.

- o To back up an entire drive, select the check box next to the drive.

- o To back up individual files and folders, double-click the drive that contains those files and folders, and then select the check boxes next to the files and/or folders that you want to back up. Click the Backup command button.

**5.** The Backup Information dialog box appears, as shown in Figure 15-1. Notice the various backup configuration options available.

- o **Tape Name:** In the Tape Name text box, either accept the default name listed or type in a new name for the tape.

- o **Verify After Backup:** Select the check box next to Verify After Backup if you want Windows NT Backup to verify the files and folders it has backed up. It's a good idea to verify after a backup, even though selecting this option approximately doubles the time the backup takes.

- o **Backup Local Registry:** Select the check box next to Backup Local Registry (if it is not grayed out) if you want Windows NT Backup to include the Registry on the computer that the tape drive is installed on in its backup. In order to back up the Registry, you must select at least one file or folder for backup on the drive on which Windows NT is installed.

- o **Restrict Access to Owner or Administrator:** Select the check box next to Restrict Access to Owner or Administrator if you want Windows NT Backup to only enable the owner of the tape, an Administrator, or a member of the Backup Operators group to read, write, or erase the tape using Windows NT Backup.

- o **Hardware Compression:** Select the check box next to Hardware Compression if you want the backup data compressed as it is backed up, and if your tape backup hardware supports this feature.

- o **Operation:** In the Operation section, you have two options: you can choose to have this backup appended to the last backup on the tape, or you can choose to have Windows NT Backup write over (replace) any existing data on the tape. (Replace is the default operation.)

- o **Backup Set Information:** In the Backup Set Information section, you can type a description of the backup. I recommend that you enter the date, a brief description of the data backed up, and the type of backup performed.

- o **Backup Type:** In the Backup Type drop-down list box, select the backup type you want to perform: Normal, Copy, Differential, Incremental, or Daily.

- o **Log Information:** In the Log Information section, Windows NT Backup shows the location to which it will write a backup log. Modify this location if necessary.

- o **Log Options:** Select the radio button next to one of the three log options, depending on the type of log you want NT Backup to create: Full Detail, Summary Only, or Don't Log. (Summary Only is the default log option.) Click OK.

6. The Backup Status dialog box appears. If the tape has been used before, a Replace Information dialog box appears. These dialog boxes are shown in Figure 15-2. Click the Yes command button to have Windows NT Backup replace the data on the tape with the backup you are preparing to perform.

7. Windows NT Backup performs the backup. (This process takes several minutes to several hours, depending on the amount of data being backed up and your tape drive speed.)

8. The Verify Status dialog box appears if you selected Verify After Backup. Windows NT Backup verifies that all files and folders were backed up correctly. (This process takes approximately the same amount of time as the backup.) Figure 15-3 shows the Verify Status dialog box after the verify has been completed. Notice the information presented in the Summary list box. Click OK after the verify is completed.

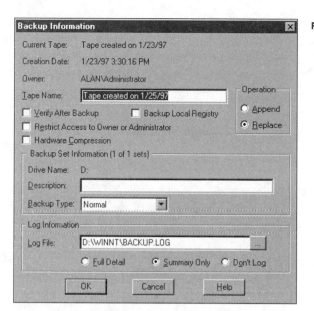

**FIGURE 15-1**   Configurable options in Windows NT Backup

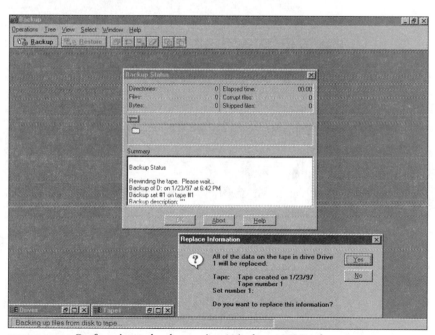

**FIGURE 15-2**   Performing a backup using Windows NT Backup

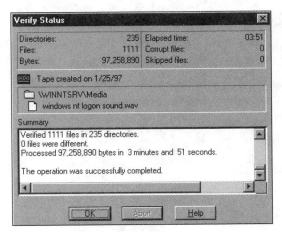

**FIGURE 15-3** Windows
NT Backup
verification
completed

**9.** Exit Windows NT Backup.

## Using the Schedule Service to Automate Backups

You can use the Schedule service in Windows NT to schedule unattended (automated) backups.

To do this, you must first configure the Schedule service to start automatically (by default, it is started manually) by using the Services application in Control Panel.

Then you must use the At.exe command-line utility to schedule and configure the unattended backup. All options of Windows NT Backup can be configured and scheduled by using this utility in conjunction with the NTBackup.exe (Windows NT Backup) utility's command-line switches.

concept link

**A detailed discussion of the command-line syntax and switches is beyond the scope of this book. For more information on the** At.exe **command-line utility, type** at /? **at the command prompt. For more information on the** NTBackup.exe **utility's command-line switches, type** ntbackup /? **at the command prompt. You might also want to check out the Command Scheduler, a graphical scheduler utility on the compact disc that ships with the *Microsoft Windows NT Server Resource Kit* (Microsoft Press, 1996). Command Scheduler is a graphical version of the** At.exe **command-line utility.**

# RESTORING FILES AND FOLDERS

Hopefully, you'll never have to restore files and folders after a catastrophic data loss. Nevertheless, it's a good practice to be comfortable with the process of restoring data to your system, just in case.

For this reason, and also to ensure that your backup tapes contain valid copies of your data files, you should periodically test your backup by performing a trial restore.

The following sections discuss testing your backup with a trial restore and performing a restore using Windows NT Backup.

## Test Your Backup with a Trial Restore

To test the validity of the data contained on a backup tape, you should restore at least one folder that contains several data files to a *different* folder than it was originally backed up from. The folder you restore to is a test folder, and shouldn't contain other files. For example, you could restore the D:\Public folder to D:\Public2 or to E:\Public2. This process verifies that the tape can be read, and that files and folders can be restored from it.

Once you've restored the folder, compare its contents with the original folder (on your hard drive) to find out whether the files are the same by using the Comp.exe command-line utility. If there are no differences between the files compared, then presumably all of the files on the backup tape are valid and not corrupt.

Another resource you can use to compare files is the Windiff.exe graphical utility that ships with the *Microsoft Windows NT Server Resource Kit*. An advantage to using Windiff.exe is that it enables you to specify *multiple files and folders* for comparison; as opposed to Comp.exe, which only enables you to specify a single file at a time for comparison.

## Performing a Restore Using Windows NT Backup

You can use Windows NT Backup to perform a full or partial restore of data from a tape backup created by using NT Backup.

### TO PERFORM A RESTORE USING WINDOWS NT BACKUP, FOLLOW THESE STEPS:

**1.** Place the backup tape that contains the data you want to restore in the tape drive. (If the tape backup consisted of more than one tape, insert the *last* tape in the backup set into the tape drive, because NT Backup wrote a catalog of the backup to this tape.)

**2.** Select Start ⇒ Programs ⇒ Administrative Tools (Common) ⇒ Backup.

**3.** The Backup dialog box appears. Select Window ⇒ Tapes.

**4.** Maximize the Tapes window that is displayed. If you want to perform a full restore, select the check box next to the backup set you want to restore in the right-hand window. If you want to perform a partial restore, double-click the backup set in the right-hand window. Windows NT Backup loads a catalog list of the files and folders in the backup. Then select the check boxes next to the individual files and folders you want to restore.

Click the Restore command button.

**5.** The Restore Information dialog box appears, as shown in Figure 15-4. Notice the available configuration options.

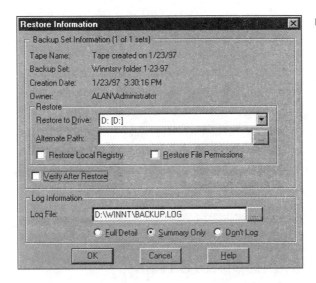

**FIGURE 15-4** Restore options available in Windows NT Backup

○ **Restore to Drive and Alternate Path:** If you want the selected files to be restored to their original drive location, accept the default in the Restore to Drive drop-down list box. Otherwise, you can specify a new drive letter, and then specify a folder that you want the files restored to in the Alternate Path text box. (You might want to do this if you're doing a trial restore to test your backup.)

o **Restore Local Registry:** Select the check box next to Restore Local Registry only if you want the current Registry on your server replaced with the Registry on the backup tape. Use great caution when exercising this option.

o **Restore File Permissions:** Select the check box next to Restore File Permissions if you want to keep the file permissions as they were stored on the tape backup. Otherwise, the restored files will be assigned their file permissions based on the permissions of the folder to which they are restored.

o **Verify After Restore:** Select the check box next to Verify After Restore if you want NT Backup to verify files after it restores them. (Selecting this option approximately doubles the time it takes to perform a restore.)

o **Log Information:** Configure the Log Information section. (The options are the same for performing restores as they are for performing backups.) Click OK.

**6.** The Restore Status dialog box appears. NT Backup rewinds the tape and restores the files and/or folders selected, and verifies the files and folders selected if configured to do so. (This process can take a while.) The Restore Status dialog box, after the restore is completed, is shown in Figure 15-5. Notice the information presented in the Summary list box. Click OK.

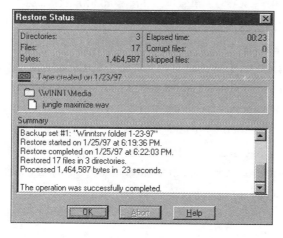

**FIGURE 15-5**  Restore completed

**7.** Exit Windows NT Backup.

# KEY POINT SUMMARY

This chapter covered the importance of backing up files and folders, how to decide which data to back up, and various backup types and strategies. Performing a backup using Windows NT Backup and utilizing the Schedule service were also outlined. Finally, Chapter 15 covered restoring files and folders.

- *Backup is an important part of your network fault tolerance plan.* Backup is not a substitute for other fault tolerance methods, such as disk mirroring and striping with parity, but is an additional safety precaution. A tape backup is your last line of defense against data loss.

- *All network data should be regularly backed up to tape,* including: operating systems, applications, the Registry, and user-created data files. It's a good idea to back up operating systems and applications on separate tapes, and separately from data file backups, to make the restore process easier. Determining the frequency of backup is often based on the answer to the question: How much data can you afford to lose?

- The *archive attribute* is a marker that, when removed from a file or folder, indicates that the file or folder has been backed up.

- There are five standard types of backups:

  - **Normal (full):** Backs up all selected files and folders, and removes the archive attribute from the backed up files and folders.

  - **Differential:** Backs up all selected files and folders that have changed since the last normal backup, and does *not* remove the archive attribute from files or folders. A differential backup is a *cumulative* backup, and because of this fact, takes more time to perform than an incremental backup, but less time to perform than a normal backup.

  - **Incremental:** Backs up all selected files and folders that have changed since the last normal or incremental backup, and removes the archive attribute from the backed up files and folders. An incremental backup is *not* cumulative, and because of this fact, takes less time to perform than a differential backup.

  - **Copy:** Backs up all selected files and folders, and does *not* remove the archive attribute. This backup type can be used without disrupting the normal backup schedule.

- **Daily:** Backs up all selected files and folders that have changed during the day the tape backup is made, and does *not* remove the archive attribute.

- Often, a combination of the standard backup types is used.

- There are three fairly common backup strategies. The trade-off that needs to be considered, when planning a backup strategy, is the time it takes to perform backups versus the time it takes to restore data.

  - One strategy is to perform a normal backup every day. This strategy is time consuming in terms of backup, but requires the least amount of effort should a restore be necessary, because only the most recent normal backup is required.

  - A second strategy is to perform a weekly normal backup and daily differential backups. This strategy takes more backup time than performing daily incremental backups, but requires only the last normal backup and the most recent differential backup should a restore be necessary.

  - A third strategy is to perform a weekly normal backup and daily incremental backups. This strategy takes the least amount of time in terms of backup, and potentially the most amount of time to perform a restore, because the last normal backup, in addition to *all* incremental backups since the last normal backup, are required.

- When planning a backup strategy and procedure, remember to take into account *security considerations*, *tape rotation*, and the *documentation* you should keep on your backups. It is beneficial to keep a detailed logbook that contains the date and time each backup was performed, a brief description of the data backed up, the person who performed the backup, the tape number used, and its storage location. It's also helpful to keep a detailed log of each backup so that individual files can be restored from tape quickly and easily.

- You can use Windows NT Backup to backup and restore data.

- Performing a tape backup requires the use of a tape drive device. Make sure to use a tape drive that is on the HCL, and if possible, one that has the capacity to back up your entire server on a single tape.

- You can use the Schedule service and the At.exe command-line utility in conjunction with Windows NT Backup (NTBackup.exe) command-line switches to configure and schedule unattended backups.

- To ensure that your backup tapes contain valid copies of your data, you should periodically test your backup by performing a trial restore. When performing a trial restore, restore files from a backup tape to a different folder (that is only used as a test folder and that contains no other files). Then compare the files to the original files (on your hard disk) using the Comp.exe command-line utility (or Winndiff.exe, a graphical utility included in the *Microsoft Windows NT Server Resource Kit*). If there are no differences between the files compared, then presumably all of the files on the backup tape are valid, and not corrupt.

# APPLYING WHAT YOU'VE LEARNED

Now it's time to regroup, review, and apply what you've learned in this chapter.

The Instant Assessment questions bring to mind key facts and concepts. The hands-on lab exercise will reinforce what you've learned, and allow you to practice some of the tasks tested by the Microsoft Certified Professional exams.

## Instant Assessment

1. Which Windows NT utility can you use to perform backups and restores?

2. What is the archive attribute, and how can it be affected during backup?

3. Briefly list and describe the five standard types of backups.

4. What two items should be considered when selecting a tape drive device?

5. What should you do periodically to ensure that your backup tapes contain valid copies of your data?

6. Which backup combination listed below, A or B, takes more time *in terms of the amount of time it takes to perform backups*?

   **A.** A weekly normal backup and daily differential backups

   **B.** A weekly normal backup and daily incremental backups

7. Which backup combination listed below, A or B, typically takes more time *in terms of amount of time it takes to perform restores?*

    **A.** A weekly normal backup and daily differential backups

    **B.** A weekly normal backup and daily incremental backups

8. How does selecting the Verify After Backup option in Windows NT Backup affect the amount of time it takes to perform a backup?

9. Which Windows NT Service must be configured before an unattended backup can be performed using Windows NT Backup?

10. What can you do to minimize data loss from a single catastrophic event, such as a theft, fire, flood, or earthquake?

 concept link    **For answers to the Instant Assessment questions see Appendix D.**

## Hands-on Lab Exercise

The following hands-on lab exercise provides you with an opportunity to apply the knowledge you've gained in this chapter about backing up and restoring data.

### Lab 15.24  *Performing a backup*

 note    **This lab is optional because it requires a tape drive.**

Server
Enterprise

The purpose of this lab is to give you hands-on experience using Windows NT Backup to back up files and folders on a Windows NT computer. You will also view the detailed log created during the backup by using Windows NT Explorer and Notepad.

Begin this lab by booting your computer to Windows NT Server. Log on as Administrator. If you haven't already done so, install a driver for your tape drive by using the Tape Devices application in Control Panel. Place a tape in the tape drive.

**FOLLOW THE STEPS BELOW CAREFULLY:**

**1.** Start ⇒ Programs ⇒ Administrative Tools (Common) ⇒ Backup.

**2.** The Backup dialog box appears. Select Window ⇒ Drives.

**3.** Maximize the Drives dialog box. Double-click the C: drive (or the drive that you have installed Windows NT Server on). Select the check box next to the `Winntsrv` folder. (If you wanted to back up the entire C: drive instead of selected folders only, when the Drives dialog box first appears, select the check box next to the C: drive instead of double-clicking it.)

Click the Backup command button.

**4.** The Backup Information dialog box appears. Select the check boxes next to the following: Verify After Backup, Hardware Compression (if the box is not grayed out), and Backup Local Registry.

In the Operation section, ensure that the radio button next to Replace is selected.

In the Description text box, type **Winntsrv folder *current_date* normal backup**.

In the Backup Type drop-down list box, select Normal.

In the Log Information section, select the radio button next to Full Detail.

Click OK.

**5.** The Backup Status dialog box appears. If the tape has been used before, a Replace Information dialog box appears. Click the Yes command button to have Windows NT Backup replace the data on the tape with the backup you are preparing to perform.

**6.** Windows NT Backup performs the backup. (This process takes several minutes.)

**7.** The Verify Status dialog box appears. Windows NT Backup verifies that all files and folders were backed up correctly. (This process also takes several minutes.) After the verify is completed, click OK.

**8.** The Backup - (Drives) dialog box appears. Select Window ⇒ Tapes.

**9.** The Backup - (Tapes) dialog box appears. Double-click the + sign next to the C: in the right-hand window (or the letter of the drive on which you installed Windows NT Server).

**10.** Double-click the `Winntsrv` folder in the left-hand window.

**11.** Windows NT Backup displays the contents of the `Winntsrv` folder from the tape backup that you just created. Notice that, for restore purposes, you can select individual files and subfolders by selecting the check boxes next to the files and subfolders that you want to restore.

Exit Windows NT Backup.

**12.** To view the log for the backup you just created, select Start ⇒ Programs ⇒ Windows NT Explorer.

**13.** In the Exploring dialog box, click the + sign next to the C: drive (or the drive on which you installed Windows NT Server). Highlight the `Winntsrv` folder. In the 'Contents of Winntsrv,' double-click `Backup.log`.

**14.** View the backup log that is displayed in Notepad. Exit Notepad.

**15.** Exit Windows NT Explorer.

# Connectivity

A s the title implies, the emphasis of Part IV is on connectivity—specifically, how Windows NT functions in a network environment.

This part begins with a robust chapter on TCP/IP. Chapter 16 explains IP addressing and routing and introduces the DHCP Relay Agent, WINS, Microsoft DNS Server, and publishing on the Internet. Finally, we discuss some practical suggestions for troubleshooting common TCP/IP connectivity problems.

Chapter 17 explains how Windows NT computers can coexist with NetWare computers. We discuss the NWLink IPX/SPX Compatible Transport protocol, along with several NT services that allow both NT and NetWare to be used on the same network. Chapter 18 then explains how to use the Migration Tool for NetWare to migrate data from a NetWare server to a Windows NT Server computer.

Next, Chapter 19 explores Remote Access Service (RAS). Step-by-step instructions show you how to install and configure RAS, and how to configure Dial-Up Networking connections. Troubleshooting information is also included.

Finally, Chapter 20 covers Macintosh connectivity and the Windows NT Server Services for Macintosh. This chapter is optional unless you're preparing for the Enterprise exam.

This part maps directly to the Connectivity section in the exam objectives for each of the three Windows NT 4.0 Microsoft Certified Professional exams.

Workstation
Server
Enterprise

# Networking Using TCP/IP

# About Chapter 16

This chapter is a concise, practical primer on TCP/IP and related subjects.

After a brief overview of TCP/IP, this chapter discusses IP addressing, including how IP addresses are assigned, and explains the different types of IP routing.

Next, the chapter explains how to install and configure WINS, an NT Server service that provides NetBIOS name resolution to client computers. Then, installing and configuring Microsoft DNS Server, which provides host name resolution to client computers, is covered.

Then the chapter turns its attention to publishing on the Internet. Two Microsoft products, Internet Information Server and Peer Web Services, are featured. Complete steps to install these products are included.

Finally, Chapter 16 presents tips on troubleshooting common TCP/IP connectivity problems.

This chapter boasts four hands-on labs. In these labs, you'll implement WINS and Microsoft DNS Server, configure Internet Information Server, and install and configure Peer Web Services. You'll also install and configure an Internet (TCP/IP) router, and try to identify and resolve some common TCP/IP connectivity problems.

Chapter 16 is a "must read," no matter which of the three Windows NT 4.0 Microsoft Certified Professional exams you're preparing for. This chapter covers numerous exam objectives, including objectives concerning TCP/IP, protocols, network components, multiprotocol routing, Internet Information Server, Internet services, Peer Web Services, and troubleshooting objectives on resolving connectivity problems.

# OVERVIEW OF TCP/IP

The *Transmission Control Protocol/Internet Protocol* (TCP/IP) is a widely used transport protocol that provides robust capabilities for Windows NT networking.

TCP/IP is a fast, routable enterprise protocol that is used on the Internet. TCP/IP is supported by many other operating systems, including: Windows 95, Macintosh, UNIX, MS-DOS, and IBM mainframes. TCP/IP is typically the recommended protocol for large, heterogeneous networks.

Microsoft includes several TCP/IP-based services with Windows NT that enhance networking, including Microsoft DHCP Server, RIP for Internet Protocol, Windows Internet Name Service (WINS), Microsoft DNS Server, Microsoft Internet Information Server, and Peer Web Services. Each of these services is discussed in this chapter.

concept link

**This chapter covers only the basics of TCP/IP that are required for the Workstation, Server, and Enterprise exams. Volumes have been written on this subject! For more information on TCP/IP, see the TCP/IP topics in Books Online, and *TCP/IP MCSE Study Guide*, by Greg Bulette (IDG Books Worldwide, 1997).**

A good place to begin a basic discussion of TCP/IP is with IP addressing—including subnet masks and default gateway addresses.

# IP ADDRESSING

An *IP address* is a 32-bit binary number, broken into four 8-bit sections (often called *octets*), that uniquely identifies a computer or other network device on a network that uses TCP/IP. IP addresses must be unique—*no two computers or other network devices on an internetwork should have the same IP address.* If two computers have the same IP address, one or both of the computers may be unable to communicate over the network. An IP address is *not* the same as a network adapter's hardware (or MAC) address.

Although an IP address is a 32-bit binary number, it is normally represented in a dotted decimal format. Each 8-bit octet is represented by a whole number between 0 and 255. The following numbers are sample IP addresses:

192.168.59.5

172.31.151.1

An IP address contains two important identifiers: a *network ID* and a *host ID*. One portion of each IP address identifies the network segment on which a computer (or other network device) is located. This portion is called the network ID. *All computers located on the same network segment have the same network ID.* The length of the network ID within an IP address is variable and is specified by the subnet mask used in conjunction with the IP address. (Subnet masks are discussed in more detail in the next section.)

The second portion of each IP address identifies the individual computer or network device. This portion is called the host ID. *Each computer or other network device on a given network segment must have a unique host ID.*

To assure that unique IP addresses are used, if you plan to connect your network to the Internet, you should contact your Internet Service Provider or InterNIC to obtain a range of valid IP addresses for your network.

web links  **InterNIC, which manages domain names as well as IP addresses, can be reached by e-mail at** info@internic.net.

## Subnet Masks

A *subnet mask* specifies which portion of an IP address represents the network ID and which portion represents the host ID. A subnet mask allows TCP/IP to determine whether network traffic destined for a given IP address should be transmitted on the local subnet, or whether it should be routed to a remote subnet. *A subnet mask should be the same for all computers and other network devices on a given network segment.*

A subnet mask is a 32-bit binary number, broken into four 8-bit sections (octets), that is normally represented in a dotted decimal format. Each 8-bit section is represented by a whole number between 0 and 255.

A common subnet mask is 255.255.255.0. This particular subnet mask specifies that TCP/IP will use the first three octets of an IP address as the network ID, and will use the last octet as the host ID.

Another common subnet mask is 255.255.0.0. This subnet mask specifies that TCP/IP will use the first two octets of an IP address as the network ID, and use the last two octets as the host ID. (Without getting into too much binary math, an octet number of 255 specifies the *entire* octet is part of the network ID; and an octet number of 0 specifies the *entire* octet is part of the host ID. Numbers *between* 0 and 255 specify that part of the octet corresponds to the network ID, and the remaining part corresponds to the host ID.)

If subnet masks are incorrectly configured, network communications problems due to routing errors may occur. For example, TCP/IP may incorrectly determine that a computer on the local subnet is located on a remote subnet and attempt to route a packet to the remote subnet. In this instance, the computer on the local subnet would never receive the packet intended for it.

# Default Gateway Addresses

A *default gateway address* specifies the IP address of a router on the local network segment. When a computer that uses TCP/IP determines that the computer it wants to communicate with is located on a remote subnet, it sends all network messages intended for the remote computer to the default gateway address, instead of directly to the destination computer. Then the router on the local subnet specified by the default gateway address forwards the messages to the destination computer on the remote subnet, either directly or via other routers.

If a computer's default gateway address does *not* specify a router on the local subnet, then that computer will be *unable* to communicate with computers or other network devices located on other network segments.

When a router is used to connect two network segments, it has two network cards and two IP addresses. Figure 16-1 illustrates how default gateway addresses are used to specify the IP address of a router on the local subnet.

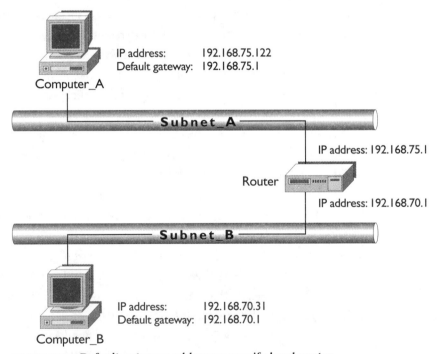

**FIGURE 16-1**   Default gateway addresses specify local router

Notice in Figure 16-1, the default gateway address of Computer_A matches the IP address of its local router, and the default gateway address of Computer_B matches the IP address of its local router.

# ASSIGNING IP ADDRESSES

IP addresses must be configured on each computer when TCP/IP is installed. You can assign an IP address to a Windows NT computer in one of two ways: by configuring a computer to obtain an IP address automatically from a DHCP server, or by manually specifying a computer's IP address configuration.

IP addresses are assigned to Windows NT computers in the Microsoft TCP/IP Properties dialog box. Instructions for accessing and configuring this dialog box are covered later in this chapter.

## Assigning IP Addresses by Using a DHCP Server

The most convenient method for assigning IP addresses to multiple computers, in terms of administration time required, is to configure each of the computers to obtain its IP address from a *Dynamic Host Configuration Protocol* (DHCP) server.

This section discusses the advantages of using a DHCP server, the process of installing and configuring Microsoft DHCP Server, and configuring a client computer to obtain its IP address from a DHCP server.

### *Advantages of using a DHCP server*

Assigning IP addresses by using a DHCP server is the preferred method because:

- Using a DHCP server makes it possible for you to manage IP addresses centrally, thus assuring addresses are valid and *not* duplicated.

- Using a DHCP server reduces the amount of administration time required to manage and maintain IP addresses for each computer on the network.

- Using a DHCP server reduces the likelihood of human error when IP addresses are assigned because no need exists to enter an IP address manually on every individual computer.

○ Using a DHCP server enables you to regain the use of an IP address no longer assigned to a host when the DHCP lease period for this IP address expires.

Before you can assign an IP address to a Windows NT computer by using a DHCP server, you must first install and configure a DHCP server on your network.

## Installing and configuring Microsoft DHCP Server

Microsoft includes a DHCP server product with Windows NT Server. *Microsoft DHCP Server* is an NT Server service that provides centralized management of IP address assignment. Microsoft DHCP Server can be installed on any Windows NT Server computer that has a manually configured IP address for each network adapter installed in it. The next sections explain how to install and configure Microsoft DHCP Server.

### TO INSTALL MICROSOFT DHCP SERVER ON A WINDOWS NT SERVER COMPUTER, FOLLOW THESE STEPS:

**1.** Select Start ⇒ Settings ⇒ Control Panel.

**2.** In the Control Panel dialog box, double-click Network.

**3.** In the Network dialog box, click the Services tab.

**4.** On the Services tab, click the Add command button.

**5.** In the Select Network Service dialog box, highlight Microsoft DHCP Server. Click OK.

**6.** A Windows NT Setup dialog box appears. Ensure the correct path to the Windows NT Server source files (normally the I386 folder on your Windows NT Server compact disc) is displayed in the text box. Edit the text box as necessary. Click the Continue command button.

**7.** Windows NT copies and installs the appropriate files. An informational dialog box appears, indicating all network adapters in this computer must have manually configured IP addresses. (At the end of the DHCP Server installation process, Windows NT prompts you to assign IP addresses manually to the computer's network adapters if you have not already done so.) Click OK.

**8.** The Network dialog box reappears. Click the Close command button. (Manually configure IP addresses only if prompted to do so.)

**9.** Windows NT performs various bindings operations.

**10.** The Network Settings Change dialog box is displayed, indicating you must shut down and restart the computer for the new settings to take effect. Click the Yes command button to restart the computer. You are now ready to configure Microsoft DHCP Server.

### TO CONFIGURE MICROSOFT DHCP SERVER ON A WINDOWS NT SERVER COMPUTER, FOLLOW THESE STEPS:

**1.** Log on as Administrator.

**2.** Select Start ⇒ Programs ⇒ Administrative Tools (Common) ⇒ DHCP Manager.

**3.** The DHCP Manager dialog box appears. Select Server ⇒ Add.

**4.** In the Add DHCP Server to Server List, type the IP address of the computer you installed Microsoft DHCP Server on. Click OK.

**5.** Highlight the IP address you entered in Step 4 in the DHCP Servers list box. Select Scope ⇒ Create.

**6.** In the Create Scope dialog box, enter a starting and ending IP address (in the Start Address and End Address text boxes) to create a scope—a range of IP addresses also called an IP address pool. All IP addresses in the pool must have the same network ID. Enter a subnet mask in the Subnet Mask text box. This subnet mask will be used for all IP addresses assigned from this IP address pool. Figure 16-2 shows a configured Create Scope dialog box. Notice the IP Address Pool configurations. Click OK.

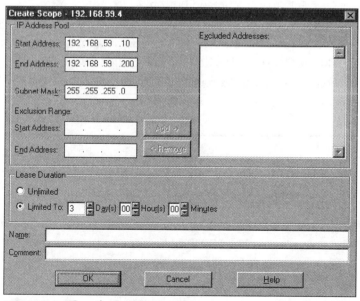

**FIGURE 16-2**   **Creating a DHCP scope**

**7.** The DHCP Manager dialog box appears, indicating the scope has been created, but not yet activated. Click the Yes command button. If a dialog box is displayed indicating no more information is available, click OK to clear it.

**8.** If you want the DHCP Server to assign a predefined default gateway address along with every IP address it assigns from this scope, select DHCP Options⇒Scope in the DHCP Manager dialog box. Continue on to Steps 9, 10, and 11.

If you *don't* want the DHCP server to assign a default gateway address when it assigns IP addresses, skip to Step 12.

**9.** The DHCP Options: Scope dialog box appears. In the Unused Options list box, highlight 003 Router.

 **You can configure several other options in the DHCP Options: Scope dialog box. A detailed discussion of these options is beyond the scope of this book and the objectives for the three Windows NT 4.0 Microsoft Certified Professional exams. For more information on the configurable options in this dialog box, see the various Help screens in DHCP Manager, the *Microsoft Windows NT Server Resource Kit for version 4.0* (Microsoft Press, 1996), and *TCP/IP MCSE Study Guide* (IDG Books Worldwide, 1997).**

Click the Add command button. Click the Value command button. Then click the Edit Array command button.

**10.** The IP Address Array Editor dialog box appears. Type in the IP address of the router you want assigned as the default gateway address in the New IP Address text box. Click the Add command button. Click OK.

**11.** In the DHCP Options: Scope dialog box, click OK.

**12.** Exit DHCP Manager.

## Configuring a computer to obtain an IP address from a DHCP server

Now that you've installed and configured a DHCP server, you're ready to configure a client computer to obtain its IP address from a DHCP server.

**TO CONFIGURE A WINDOWS NT CLIENT COMPUTER TO OBTAIN
AN IP ADDRESS FROM A DHCP SERVER, FOLLOW THESE STEPS:**

**1.** Select Start ⇒ Settings ⇒ Control Panel.

**2.** In the Control Panel dialog box, double-click Network.

**3.** In the Network dialog box, click the Protocols tab.

**4.** On the Protocols tab, double-click the TCP/IP Protocol in the Network
Protocols list box. (Or, if you prefer, highlight the TCP/IP Protocol in the
Network Protocols list box and click the Properties command button.)

**5.** The Microsoft TCP/IP Properties dialog box appears. Ensure the radio
button next to "Obtain an IP address from a DHCP server" is selected.
Figure 16-3 shows the Microsoft TCP/IP Properties dialog box.

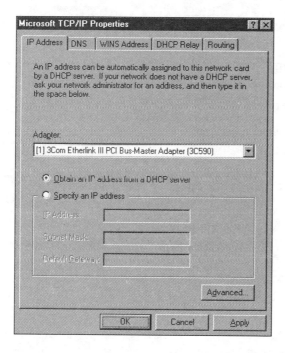

**FIGURE 16-3** Using a DHCP
server to assign
an IP address

**6.** If the radio button next to "Obtain an IP address from a DHCP server"
was *not* selected by default and you selected it, Windows NT displays a
Microsoft TCP/IP warning dialog box, asking if you want to enable DHCP.
Click the Yes command button to continue.

**7.** If only one network adapter is installed in the computer, click OK.

If additional network adapters are installed in the computer you are configuring to obtain IP addresses from a DHCP server, select each adapter (one at a time) from the Adapter drop-down list box, and select the radio button next to "Obtain an IP address from a DHCP server." When you have configured all network adapters, click OK.

**8.** The Network dialog box reappears. Click the Close command button.

**9.** A Network Settings Change dialog box is displayed, indicating you must shut down and restart the computer for the new settings to take effect. Click the Yes command button to restart the computer.

## Assigning IP Addresses Manually

If you don't have a DHCP server, you must assign IP addresses manually. This method is both more time-consuming than using a DHCP server and more prone to error, because an IP address must be manually typed on each individual computer. The following section explains the steps involved in assigning an IP address manually.

### TO ASSIGN AN IP ADDRESS MANUALLY TO A WINDOWS NT COMPUTER, FOLLOW THESE STEPS:

**1.** Select Start ⇒ Settings ⇒ Control Panel.

**2.** In the Control Panel dialog box, double-click Network.

**3.** In the Network dialog box, click the Protocols tab.

**4.** On the Protocols tab, double-click the TCP/IP Protocol in the Network Protocols list box. (Or, if you prefer, highlight the TCP/IP Protocol in the Network Protocols list box and click the Properties command button.)

**5.** The Microsoft TCP/IP Properties dialog box appears. Select the radio button next to "Specify an IP address." Then complete the following text boxes:

- **IP Address:** Enter the IP address you want to assign in the IP Address text box. (The IP address is a mandatory setting.) Press Tab.

- **Subnet Mask:** Either accept the default subnet mask displayed or type in the subnet mask you want to assign in the Subnet Mask text box. (The subnet mask is a mandatory setting.) Press Tab.

- **Default Gateway:** Type in a default gateway address in the Default Gateway text box. (The default gateway setting is optional.)

Figure 16-4 shows a manually configured IP address for a Windows NT Server computer.

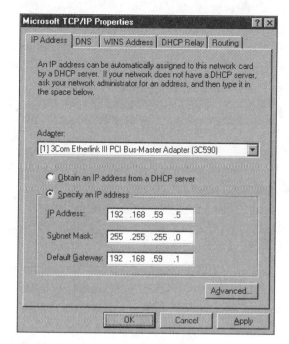

**FIGURE 16-4** **Assigning an IP address manually**

If only one network adapter is installed in the computer, click OK.

If additional network adapters are installed in the computer to which you want to manually assign IP addresses at this time, select each adapter (one at a time) from the Adapter drop-down list box and select the radio button next to "Specify an IP address." Type in an IP address, subnet mask, and default gateway (if desired) for each network adapter. When you have configured IP addresses for all network adapters, click OK.

**6.** The Network dialog box reappears. Click the Close command button.

**7.** A Network Settings Change dialog box is displayed, indicating you must shut down and restart the computer for the new settings to take effect. Click the Yes command button to restart the computer.

# IP ROUTING

*IP routing* is a function of the *Internet Protocol* (IP) that uses IP address information to send data packets from a source computer on one network segment across one or more routers to a destination computer on another network segment. Hardware devices that perform routing are called *routers*.

Windows NT computers that have multiple network adapters (sometimes called *multihomed computers*) can function as IP routers. IP routers are occasionally referred to as *Internet routers*.

Two primary types of routing exist: static and dynamic. These topics are discussed in the next sections.

## Static Routing

*Static routing* is basic, no-frills IP routing. No additional software is necessary to implement static routing in multihomed Windows NT computers.

Static routers are *not* capable of automatically building a routing table. A *routing table* contains a list of network IDs, each of which is associated with the IP address of the router on the network that can forward data packets over the shortest path to the specified destination computer. In a static routing environment, administrators must manually configure the routing table on each individual router. If the network layout changes, the network administrator must manually update the routing tables to reflect the changes.

Both Windows NT Workstation and Windows NT Server multihomed computers can be configured to function as static routers.

**TO CONFIGURE A MULTIHOMED WINDOWS NT COMPUTER TO FUNCTION AS A STATIC ROUTER, FOLLOW THESE STEPS:**

**1.** Select Start ⇒ Settings ⇒ Control Panel.

**2.** In the Control Panel dialog box, double-click Network.

**3.** In the Network dialog box, click the Protocols tab.

**4.** On the Protocols tab, double-click TCP/IP Protocol in the Network Protocols list box.

**5.** The Microsoft TCP/IP Properties dialog box appears. Click the Routing tab.

**6.** On the Routing tab, select the check box next to Enable IP Forwarding.
Figure 16-5 shows the Routing tab in the Microsoft TCP/IP Properties
dialog box. Notice the Enable IP Forwarding check box is selected. Click OK.

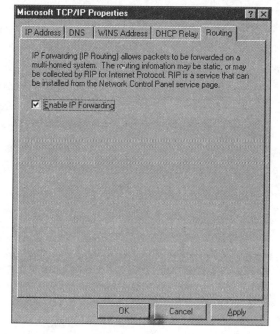

**FIGURE 16-5**  **Implementing static routing**

**7.** In the Network dialog box, click the Close command button.

**8.** A Network Settings Change dialog box appears. Click Yes to restart the
computer and implement the changes you made. After the computer
restarts, static routing will be enabled.

To configure the routing table manually on a Windows NT computer that is
configured as a static router, use the Route.exe command-line utility. For more
information on the Route.exe utility, type **route /help** at the command prompt.

# Dynamic Routing

*Dynamic routing* is intelligent IP routing. Dynamic routing requires the use of
additional software in multihomed Windows NT Server computers.

A dynamic router is capable of automatically building and updating a routing
table. In a dynamic routing environment, administrators needn't configure the

routing table on each individual router manually. As changes are made to the network, dynamic routers automatically adjust their routing tables to reflect these changes.

Periodically, each dynamic router on the network broadcasts packets containing the contents of its routing table. Dynamic routers that receive these packets add the routing table information received to their own routing tables. In this way, dynamic routers can recognize other routers as they are added to and removed from the network. By installing RIP for Internet Protocol, multihomed Windows NT Server computers can be configured to function as dynamic routers. *Routing Information Protocol* (RIP) is the software that allows Windows NT Server computers to share their routing tables dynamically. Dynamic routers that use RIP to share their routing tables are sometimes called *RIP routers*. The next section explains how to install RIP for Internet Protocol.

**TO INSTALL RIP FOR INTERNET PROTOCOL ON A WINDOWS NT SERVER COMPUTER TO ENABLE DYNAMIC ROUTING, FOLLOW THESE STEPS:**

**1.** Select Start⇒ Settings⇒ Control Panel.

**2.** In the Control Panel dialog box, double-click Network.

**3.** In the Network dialog box, click the Services tab.

**4.** On the Services tab, click the Add command button.

**5.** In the Select Network Service dialog box, highlight RIP for Internet Protocol.

Figure 16-6 shows the Select Network Service dialog box. Notice RIP for Internet Protocol is highlighted. Click OK.

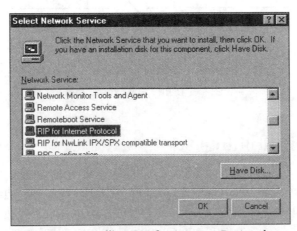

**FIGURE 16-6**    Installing RIP for Internet Protocol

6. A Windows NT Setup dialog box appears. Ensure the correct path to your Windows NT Server source files (usually the I386 folder on your Windows NT Server compact disc) is listed in the text box. Edit the text box as necessary. Click the Continue command button.

7. The Network dialog box reappears.

   Windows NT, in the process of installing RIP for Internet Protocol, has automatically enabled IP forwarding.

   Click the Close command button.

8. Windows NT performs various bindings operations.

9. A Network Settings Change dialog box appears. Click Yes to restart the computer and implement the changes you made. After the computer restarts, dynamic (RIP) routing will be enabled.

## The DHCP Relay Agent

The *DHCP Relay Agent* is a Windows NT Server service that forwards client DHCP configuration requests to a DHCP server on another network segment. The DHCP Relay Agent allows computers on one subnet to receive IP addresses from a DHCP server located on a different subnet.

The DHCP Relay Agent can be installed only on multihomed Windows NT Server computers. The DHCP Relay Agent is normally installed on Windows NT Server computers configured to function as static or dynamic routers. The next section explains how to install the DHCP Relay Agent.

### TO INSTALL THE DHCP RELAY AGENT ON A WINDOWS NT SERVER COMPUTER, FOLLOW THESE STEPS:

1. Select Start ⇒ Settings ⇒ Control Panel.

2. In the Control Panel dialog box, double-click Network.

3. In the Network dialog box, click the Services tab.

4. On the Services tab, click the Add command button.

5. In the Select Network Service dialog box, highlight DHCP Relay Agent. Click OK.

6. A Windows NT Setup dialog box appears. Ensure the correct path to your Windows NT Server source files (usually the I386 folder on your Windows NT Server compact disc) is listed in the text box. Edit the text box as necessary. Click the Continue command button.

7. The Network dialog box reappears. Click the Close command button.

8. Windows NT performs various bindings operations.

9. An Error-Unattended Setup dialog box appears, indicating you must configure the DHCP Relay Agent. Click the Yes command button.

10. The Microsoft TCP/IP Properties dialog box appears. Click the DHCP Relay tab.

11. The DHCP Relay tab appears, as shown in Figure 16-7. Notice no servers are shown in the DHCP Servers list box. Click the Add command button.

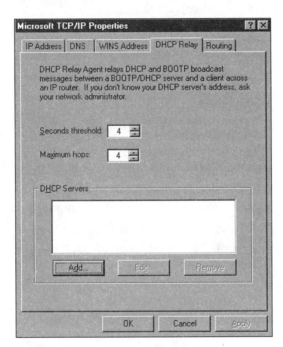

**FIGURE 16-7**  Configuring the DHCP Relay Agent

12. The DHCP Relay Agent dialog box appears, as shown in Figure 16-8.

**FIGURE 16-8**  Adding a server to the DHCP Servers list

Type in the IP address of the DHCP server to which you want the DHCP Relay Agent to forward requests. Click the Add command button.

**13.** The Microsoft TCP/IP Properties dialog box reappears, as shown in Figure 16-9. Notice an IP address is now listed in the DHCP Servers list box. Click OK.

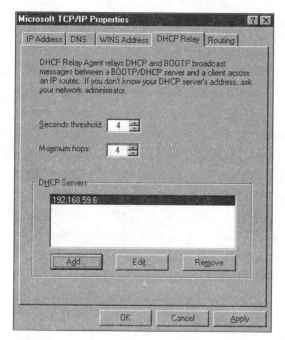

**FIGURE 16-9**   **DHCP Relay Agent successfully configured**

**14.** Windows NT performs various bindings operations.

**15.** A Network Settings Change dialog box appears. Click Yes to restart the computer and implement the changes you made.

# WINDOWS INTERNET NAME SERVICE (WINS)

*Windows Internet Name Service* (WINS) is a Windows NT Server service that provides NetBIOS name resolution services to client computers. A Windows NT Server computer that has WINS installed on it is called a *WINS server*.

A *NetBIOS name* is the computer name assigned during the installation of Windows NT. A NetBIOS name can be up to 15 characters in length. NetBIOS names are used to connect to resources located on other computers when a user browses the network, maps to a network drive, or uses the `Net use` command from the command prompt.

When a user attempts to connect to a computer selected from a browse list by the remote computer's NetBIOS name, the user's computer must first obtain the IP address associated with the remote computer's NetBIOS name. This process is called *NetBIOS name resolution.* Once the user's computer has resolved the remote computer's NetBIOS name to its IP address, it can then establish TCP/IP network communications with the remote computer.

You can perform NetBIOS name resolution in several ways. The two most common methods are manually configuring an `LMHOSTS` file on each individual computer on the network, and installing a WINS server and configuring client computers to use it.

If you use an `LMHOSTS` file (a text file that contains a list of NetBIOS names and their associated IP addresses) to perform NetBIOS name resolution, every time a server is added to or removed from the network, the `LMHOSTS` file on each individual computer on the network must be manually updated.

Installing a WINS server and configuring client computers to use it is the preferred method of handling NetBIOS name resolution on Windows NT networks. When this method is used, the WINS server dynamically updates its NetBIOS name to IP address tables whenever computers are added to or removed from the network.

WINS can only be installed on Windows NT Server computers. On small networks, WINS is often installed on the primary domain controller (PDC). On larger networks, WINS is installed on multiple Windows NT Server computers.

The following section discusses how to install a WINS server and how to configure Windows NT computers to use the WINS server for NetBIOS name resolution.

## Installing and Configuring WINS

Installing and configuring WINS is a two-step process: You must first install WINS on a Windows NT Server computer, and then you must configure each client computer on the network to use the WINS server for NetBIOS name resolution. The next two sections explain how to accomplish these tasks.

**TO INSTALL WINS ON A WINDOWS NT SERVER COMPUTER, FOLLOW THESE STEPS:**

**1.** Select Start ⇒ Settings ⇒ Control Panel.

**2.** In the Control Panel dialog box, double-click Network.

**3.** In the Network dialog box, click the Services tab.

**4.** On the Services tab, click the Add command button.

**5.** The Select Network Service dialog box appears. Scroll down and highlight Windows Internet Name Service. Click OK.

**6.** A Windows NT Setup dialog box appears. Ensure the correct path to your Windows NT Server source files (usually the I386 folder on your Windows NT Server compact disc) is listed in the text box. Edit the text box as necessary. Click the Continue command button.

**7.** Windows NT copies and installs WINS. The Network dialog box reappears. Click the Close command button.

**8.** Windows NT performs various bindings operations.

**9.** A Network Settings Change warning dialog box appears, indicating you need to restart the computer now for the new settings to take effect. Click the Yes command button.

**TO CONFIGURE A WINDOWS NT CLIENT COMPUTER TO USE A WINS SERVER FOR NETBIOS NAME RESOLUTION, FOLLOW THESE STEPS:**

**1.** Select Start ⇒ Settings ⇒ Control Panel.

**2.** In the Control Panel dialog box, double-click Network.

**3.** In the Network dialog box, click the Protocols tab.

**4.** On the Protocols tab, double-click the TCP/IP Protocol in the Network Protocols list box.

**5.** The Microsoft TCP/IP Properties dialog box appears. Click the WINS Address tab.

**6.** The WINS Address tab appears, as shown in Figure 16-10. Notice you can enter IP addresses for a primary and a secondary WINS server.

Type in the IP address for the primary WINS server. If you have multiple WINS servers on your network, you can type in the IP address for a secondary WINS server in case the primary WINS server becomes unavailable. Click OK.

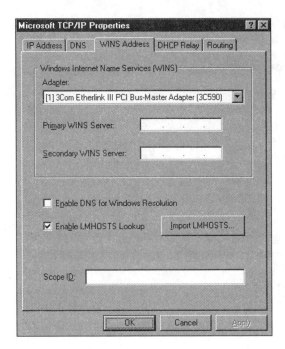

**FIGURE 16-10** Configuring primary and secondary WINS server addresses

**7.** The Network dialog box reappears. Click the Close command button.

**8.** A Network Settings Change warning dialog box appears, indicating you need to restart the computer now for the new settings to take effect. Click the Yes command button.

If you don't want to configure WINS server addresses on each individual computer manually, you can use DHCP Manager to configure a DHCP server to supply the IP address of a primary and a secondary WINS server automatically to computers that obtain their IP address configurations from a DHCP server.

# MICROSOFT DNS SERVER

*Microsoft DNS Server* is a Windows NT Server service that provides host name resolution services to client computers. *DNS* stands for *Domain Name System*. A

Windows NT Server computer that has Microsoft DNS Server installed on it is referred to as a *DNS server*.

A Windows NT computer's host name, by default, is the same as the computer's NetBIOS name (which is the computer name assigned during the installation of NT). Host names are used to access other computers on the network by using TCP/IP-based utilities, such as FTP.exe and Internet Explorer.

When a user attempts to access a World Wide Web server (such as www.microsoft.com) by using Internet Explorer, the user's computer must first obtain the IP address associated with the Fully Qualified Domain Name of the World Wide Web (WWW) server (in this case, www.microsoft.com). This process is called *host name resolution*. Once the user's computer has resolved the Fully Qualified Domain Name of the WWW server to its IP address, it can then establish TCP/IP network communications with the WWW server.

On the Internet, host names are stored in various domains and subdomains that form a hierarchical tree structure called the *Domain Name System* (DNS). (Please note that Internet domains are *not* the same as Windows NT Server domains.) The root of the DNS structure contains several domains with which you may be familiar. These domains are shown in Table 16-1.

**TABLE 16-1** DNS ROOT DOMAINS

| DOMAIN | DESCRIPTION |
| --- | --- |
| com | Commercial organizations, such as pepsi.com |
| gov | Government organizations, such as whitehouse.gov |
| mil | Military organizations, such as army.mil |
| edu | Educational organizations, such as stanford.edu |
| net | Internet Service Providers, such as nsf.net |
| org | Nonprofit organizations, such as metmuseum.org |

Many commercial companies store their host names in a subdomain of the com domain. Examples of subdomains within the com domain include microsoft.com, chevrolet.com, and so forth. Each subdomain is called a *zone*.

When a DNS server is initially installed, you must create a zone in which the DNS server will maintain its host names. A DNS server can have multiple zones. A DNS server stores all zone information, including host names and their associated IP addresses, in a database called a DNS database.

A DNS database is not dynamically created—the network administrator must manually enter host names and their associated IP addresses for each computer on the network.

An alternative to entering every host name and associated IP address manually into a DNS database on a Windows NT Server computer is to configure Microsoft DNS Server to access a WINS server to resolve host names. Because host names on Windows NT networks are usually the same as NetBIOS names, and because the WINS server dynamically updates its NetBIOS name to IP address resolution tables, configuring Microsoft DNS Server to use a WINS server is an efficient way for a network administrator to manage host name resolution without having to enter every host name and associated IP address manually.

The following section covers the steps involved in installing Microsoft DNS Server on a Windows NT Server computer, configuring a zone on Microsoft DNS Server, configuring a Microsoft DNS Server to use WINS Lookup for host name resolution, and configuring client computers to use a DNS server for host name resolution.

## Installing and Configuring Microsoft DNS Server

Installing and configuring Microsoft DNS Server is a three-step process:

- First, you must install Microsoft DNS Server on a Windows NT Server computer.

- Second, you configure a zone on the Microsoft DNS Server. (Optionally, on networks that use DHCP and WINS, you can also configure Microsoft DNS Server to use WINS Lookup for host name resolution.)

- Third, you configure each client computer on the network to use a DNS server for host name resolution.

  Each of these installation and configuration tasks is described in the following sections.

## TO INSTALL MICROSOFT DNS SERVER ON A WINDOWS NT SERVER COMPUTER, FOLLOW THESE STEPS:

**1.** Select Start⇒Settings⇒Control Panel.

**2.** In the Control Panel dialog box, double-click Network.

**3.** In the Network dialog box, click the Services tab.

**4.** On the Services tab, click the Add command button.

**5.** In the Select Network Service dialog box, highlight Microsoft DNS Server. Click OK.

**6.** A Windows NT Setup dialog box appears. Ensure the correct path to your Windows NT Server source files (usually the I386 folder on your Windows NT Server compact disc) is listed in the text box. Edit the text box as necessary. Click the Continue command button.

**7.** Windows NT copies and installs Microsoft DNS Server. The Network dialog box reappears. Click the Close command button.

**8** Windows NT performs various bindings operations.

**9.** A Network Settings Change warning dialog box appears, asking if you want to restart your computer now for the new settings to take effect. Click the Yes command button.

## TO CONFIGURE A ZONE ON A MICROSOFT DNS SERVER, FOLLOW THESE STEPS:

**1.** From the desktop, select Start⇒Programs⇒Administrative Tools (Common)⇒DNS Manager.

**2.** In the Domain Name Service Manager dialog box, select DNS⇒New Server.

**3.** The Add DNS Server dialog box appears. Type the IP address of the Windows NT Server computer you installed Microsoft DNS Server on in the DNS Server text box. Click OK.

**4.** A server appears (indicated by its IP address) in the Server List on the left side of the Domain Name Service Manager dialog box, as shown in Figure 16-11. Notice the Server Statistics.

Right-click the server's IP address. Select Refresh from the menu that appears. Right-click again on the server's IP address. Select New Zone from the menu that appears.

**5.** The Creating new zone for *ip_address* dialog box appears. Select the radio button next to Primary. Click the Next command button.

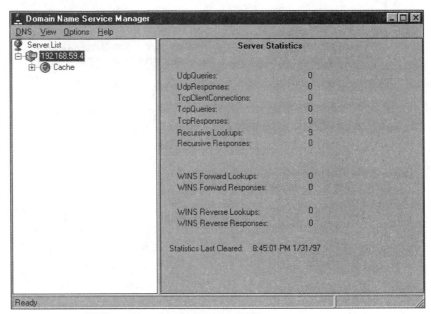

**FIGURE 16-11**    DNS server added to Server List

6. Type the Internet domain name this DNS server will manage in the Zone Name text box—for example, **lab.com**. Type a filename for the file the DNS server will use to store host name and IP address information for the domain in the Zone File text box—for example, **lab.com.dns**. (Don't include the final period.)

Figure 16-12 shows a configured "Creating new zone for 192.168.59.4" dialog box. Notice the zone information that has been entered. Click the Next command button.

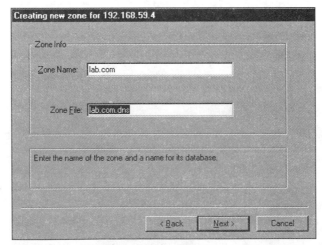

**FIGURE 16-12**    Creating a DNS zone

**7.** Click the Finish command button in the "Creating new zone for *ip_address*" dialog box. The new zone appears in the Domain Name Service Manager dialog box under the Server List for the Windows NT Server computer, as shown in Figure 16-13. Notice the zone information displayed in the dialog box.

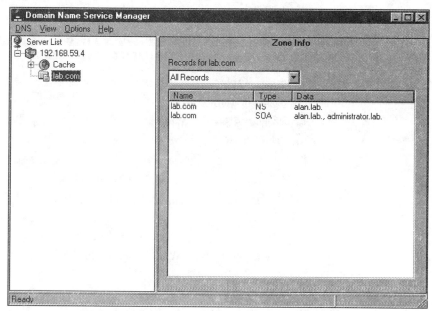

**FIGURE 16-13**    DNS zone created

**8.** This completes the creation of a zone.

If you are *not* using WINS, or if you have computers on your network that don't use WINS, you can manually configure name resolution for those computers now. The following steps explain how to enter computer (host) names and their associated IP addresses manually into the DNS server's database.

**9.** Right-click the new zone. Select New Host from the menu that appears.

**10.** The New Host dialog box appears, as shown in Figure 16-14. Note that you must enter a host name and a host IP address in this dialog box.

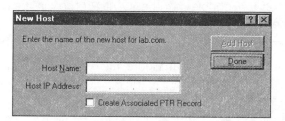

**FIGURE 16-14**    Adding a computer to the DNS server's database

Type in a host name (computer name) and its associated IP address in the Host Name and Host IP Address text boxes. Click the Add Host command button.

11. Repeat Step 10 for every additional computer you want to add to the DNS server's database. When you are finished, click the Done command button.

12. Exit DNS Manager.

### TO CONFIGURE MICROSOFT DNS SERVER TO USE WINS LOOKUP FOR HOST NAME RESOLUTION, FOLLOW THESE STEPS:

1. From the desktop, select Start ⇒ Programs ⇒ Administrative Tools (Common) ⇒ DNS Manager.

2. In the Domain Name Service Manager dialog box, double-click the IP address of the Microsoft DNS Server you want to configure.

3. Right-click the zone for which you want to configure WINS Lookup, and then select Properties from the menu that appears.

4. The "Zone Properties–*zone_name*" dialog box appears. Click the WINS Lookup tab.

5. On the WINS Lookup tab, select the check box next to Use WINS Resolution. In the uppermost WINS Servers text box, type the IP address of the WINS server you want to use for WINS Lookup, and click the Add command button.

   A configured WINS Lookup tab is shown in Figure 16-15. Notice the check box next to Use WINS Resolution is selected and an IP address of a WINS server is listed. Click OK.

6. The Microsoft DNS Server is now configured to use WINS for host name resolution. Exit DNS Manager.

### TO CONFIGURE A WINDOWS NT CLIENT COMPUTER TO USE A DNS SERVER FOR HOST NAME RESOLUTION, FOLLOW THESE STEPS:

1. Select Start ⇒ Settings ⇒ Control Panel.

2. In the Control Panel dialog box, double-click Network.

3. In the Network dialog box, click the Protocols tab.

4. On the Protocols tab, double-click the TCP/IP Protocol in the Network Protocols list box.

5. The Microsoft TCP/IP Properties dialog box appears. Click the DNS tab.

6. The DNS tab appears, as shown in Figure 16-16. Notice, by default, the computer's NetBIOS name is listed in the Host Name text box. Click the Add command button.

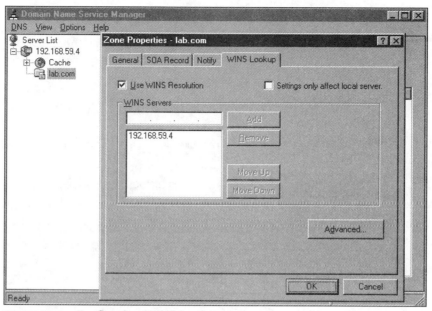

**FIGURE 16-15** Configuring WINS Lookup

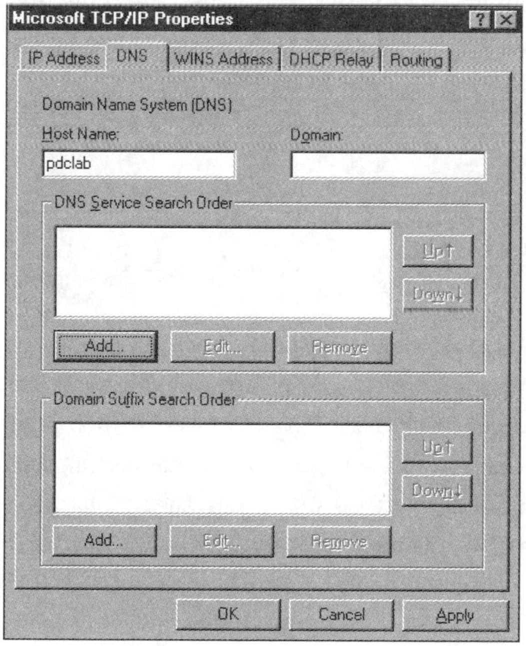

**FIGURE 16-16** Configuring a client computer to use a Microsoft DNS Server for host name resolution

**7.** The TCP/IP DNS Server dialog box appears, as shown in Figure 16-17.

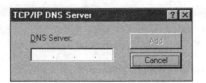

**FIGURE 16-17**   Adding a DNS
server address

Type the IP address of the Microsoft DNS Server. Click the Add command
button.

**8.** The Microsoft TCP/IP Properties dialog box reappears. Click OK.

**9.** The Network dialog box reappears. Click the Close command button.

**10.** A Network Settings Change warning dialog box appears, indicating you
need to restart the computer now for the new settings to take effect.
Click the Yes command button.

If you don't want to configure DNS server addresses manually on each individual client computer, you can use DHCP Manager to configure a DHCP server to
automatically supply the IP address of a DNS server to computers that obtain their
IP address configurations from the DHCP server.

# PUBLISHING ON THE INTERNET

Publishing World Wide Web pages on the Internet is becoming more popular every
day. Many companies and organizations, from small, home-based businesses to
multimillion-dollar concerns, use the Web to advertise their products and services.
Web pages can be made available to anyone who has an Internet connection and a
Web browser, such as Internet Explorer or Netscape Navigator.

Microsoft has two primary tools for publishing on the Internet: Internet
Information Server (for Windows NT Server computers) and Peer Web Services
(for Windows NT Workstation computers). The following sections discuss these
products in detail.

# Microsoft Internet Information Server

*Microsoft Internet Information Server* (IIS) is a Windows NT Server service that provides World Wide Web (WWW), File Transfer Protocol (FTP), and Gopher publishing services.

Internet Information Server uses *Hypertext Transfer Protocol* (HTTP) to publish WWW documents on the Internet. FTP enables users to transfer files between computers on the Internet. The FTP service included with IIS replaces the FTP service included in previous versions of Windows NT Server. Gopher is a complicated publishing service that is not used extensively anymore and is not included in the objectives for the Windows NT 4.0 Microsoft Certified Professional exams.

Internet Information Server (IIS) requires the use of TCP/IP. You *must* have TCP/IP installed in your Windows NT Server computer to install and use IIS. No additional hardware is required to install and use IIS on an internal intranet.

The following sections discuss the basics of IIS, including: connecting your Internet Information Server to the Internet, installing IIS, using Internet Service Manager, configuring the WWW service, and configuring a virtual server.

## Connecting your Internet Information Server to the Internet

If you want to connect your Internet Information Server to the Internet instead of just using it on your company's internal network (intranet), additional hardware is required.

Different hardware is required for different types of Internet connections. When determining the type of Internet connection to use, you should consider how many people will access your Internet Information Server, the frequency and duration of those accesses, and the size of documents and files being accessed.

Table 16-2 shows some of the Internet connection types, their speeds, and the additional hardware each requires.

You may want to consult with your Internet service provider (ISP) when determining the type of connection you need and when configuring the hardware and software used to establish your Internet connection.

**TABLE 16-2** INTERNET CONNECTION TYPES

| CONNECTION TYPE | SPEED | ADDITIONAL HARDWARE REQUIRED |
|---|---|---|
| Modem | 28.8–33.6Kbps | A modem and standard telephone line |
| ISDN | 64–128Kbps | An ISDN adapter card with either an internal or external network terminating unit (NT1), and an ISDN line |
| Digital Leased Line | 56Kbps–44.7Mbps | A router, a DSU/CSU, a network adapter, and a digital leased line – 56Kbps, fractional T1, T1, or T3 |

## Installing Microsoft Internet Information Server

Before installing Microsoft Internet Information Server (IIS), you should install Windows NT Server and TCP/IP. Additionally, you may want to install and configure the computer's Internet connection, including the additional hardware required, before you install IIS.

You can install IIS either during the Windows NT Server installation process or at a later time. The following steps explain how to install IIS on a computer after Windows NT Server and TCP/IP have been installed.

**TO INSTALL MICROSOFT INTERNET INFORMATION SERVER (IIS) ON A WINDOWS NT SERVER COMPUTER, FOLLOW THESE STEPS:**

**1.** Select Start ⇒ Settings ⇒ Control Panel.

**2.** In the Control Panel dialog box, double-click Network.

**3.** In the Network dialog box, click the Services tab.

**4.** On the Services tab, click the Add command button.

**5.** The Select Network Service dialog box appears. Highlight Microsoft Internet Information Server.

Figure 16-18 shows the Select Network Service dialog box. Notice Microsoft Internet Information Server is highlighted. Click OK.

**6.** An Internet Information Server Installation dialog box appears. Ensure the correct path to your Windows NT Server source files (usually the I386 folder on your Windows NT Server compact disc) is listed in the text box. Edit the text box as necessary. Click OK.

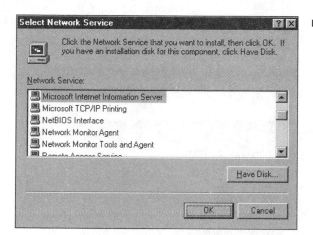

**FIGURE 16-18**  Installing Microsoft Internet Information Server

**7.** A Microsoft Internet Information Server 2.0 Setup dialog box appears. Click OK.

**8.** The Microsoft Internet Information Server 2.0 Setup dialog box appears, as shown in Figure 16-19. Notice the options that can be installed with IIS.

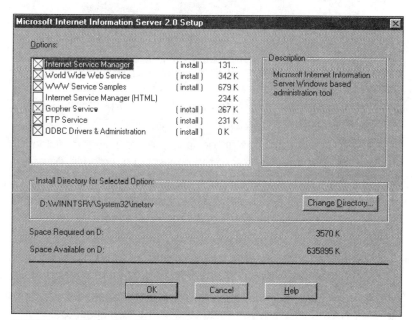

**FIGURE 16-19**  Selecting IIS options

Select all the options you want installed with IIS. Deselect any undesired options. Click OK.

9. If a Microsoft Internet Information Server 2.0 Setup dialog box appears prompting you to confirm the creation of the `inetsrv` folder, click the Yes command button.

10. The Publishing Directories dialog box appears, as shown in Figure 16-20. Note the default publishing directories.

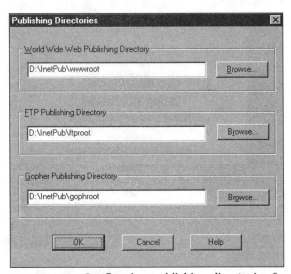

**FIGURE 16-20**    **Configuring publishing directories for the WWW, FTP, and Gopher services**

Configure the publishing directories as desired, or accept the default publishing directories presented. Click OK.

11. If a Microsoft Internet Information Server 2.0 Setup dialog box appears prompting you to create the publishing directories, click the Yes command button.

12. Windows NT installs Microsoft Internet Information Server and the options you selected. (This process takes a few minutes.)

13. If you installed the Gopher service and you have not yet assigned an Internet domain name to the computer, a dialog box appears, indicating you should assign an Internet domain name to your computer. Click OK.

14. If you installed ODBC drivers and administration, a dialog box may appear indicating you need to close Control Panel to continue the ODBC installation. Click OK to close Control Panel.

**15.** The Install Drivers dialog box appears. Highlight the ODBC drivers you want to install, and click OK.

**16.** The Microsoft Internet Information Server 2.0 Setup dialog box appears, indicating IIS was successfully installed. Click OK.

**17.** The Network dialog box reappears. Click the Close command button.

Microsoft Internet Information Server is now installed, and all its services have been started. You needn't restart your computer at this time.

### Using Internet Service Manager

Once you have installed Microsoft Internet Information Server, you can use Internet Service Manager to manage IIS.

*Internet Service Manager* can be used to configure the IIS services, to configure IIS security, and to start and stop the individual IIS services.

Internet Service Manager can be accessed by selecting Start ⇒ Programs ⇒ Microsoft Internet Server (Common) ⇒ Internet Service Manager.

The next section discusses configuring the WWW service.

 **Because configuring the FTP and Gopher services is substantially similar to configuring the WWW service, detailed configuration instructions for the FTP and Gopher services are not included. For more information on the FTP and Gopher services, see the Help screens in Microsoft Internet Service Manager.**

**TO CONFIGURE THE WWW SERVICE, FOLLOW THESE STEPS:**

**1.** Start Internet Service Manager by selecting Start ⇒ Programs ⇒ Microsoft Internet Server (Common) ⇒ Internet Service Manager. Figure 16-21 shows the Microsoft Internet Service Manager dialog box. Notice the WWW service is listed in the Service column and is running.

**2.** To access the Properties dialog box for the WWW service, highlight the computer on the same line as the WWW service, and select Properties ⇒ Service Properties. The WWW Service Properties dialog box appears, as shown in Figure 16-22. Note the configurable options on the Service tab.

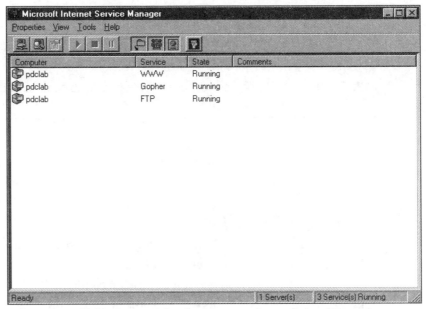

**FIGURE 16-21**     Using Internet Service Manager to configure IIS services

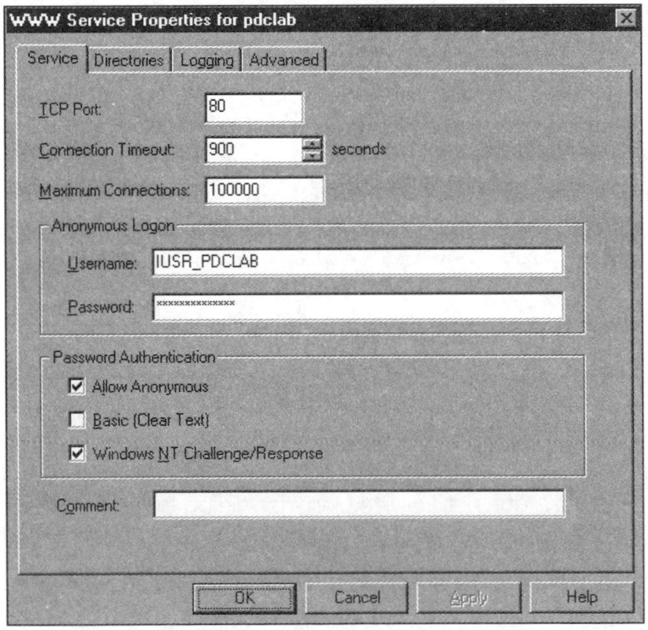

**FIGURE 16-22**     Configuration options on the WWW Service
Properties Service tab

3. Configure options for the WWW service on the Service tab. Many of the options on this tab are security features. The most commonly configured options are:

- **Anonymous Logon:** This section should be configured if the check box next to Allow Anonymous is selected in the Password Authentication section. When a user name and password are entered in the Anonymous Logon section, the user rights and permissions assigned to this user name are applied to all anonymous users of the WWW service. In this way, IIS security is integrated with Windows NT security. The default user name listed is `IUSR_Computer_name`.

- **Password Authentication:** The three options in this section are Allow Anonymous, Basic (Clear Text), and Windows NT Challenge/Response.

  - **Allow Anonymous:** If you select the check box next to Allow Anonymous, anyone with Internet access can access the WWW service on your server anonymously. These users will not be required to supply a user name and password. If you clear the check box next to Allow Anonymous, all users will be required to supply a user name and a password to access the WWW service. The Allow Anonymous option is selected by default.

  - **Basic (Clear Text):** If you select the check box next to Basic (Clear Text), user names and passwords can be sent over the Internet in an unencrypted format. Selecting this option is not normally desirable because it compromises the security of your server. If this check box is cleared, unencrypted user names and passwords will not be accepted by the WWW service. The Basic (Clear Text) option is not selected by default.

  - **Windows NT Challenge/Response:** If you select the check box next to Windows NT Challenge/Response, user names and passwords can be sent over the Internet in an encrypted format. If this check box is cleared, encrypted user names and passwords will not be accepted by the WWW service. This security feature is selected by default and should be used in high-security environments.

4. Configure advanced options for the WWW service as desired on the Advanced tab in the WWW Service Properties dialog box, as shown in Figure 16-23. Note: most of the options on the Advanced tab are used to manage access security for the WWW service.

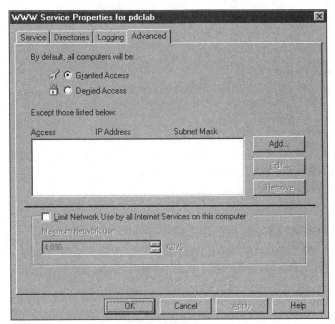

**FIGURE 16-23**    **Configuration options on the WWW Service Properties Advanced tab**

The Advanced tab is primarily used to control access to the WWW service by the IP address of the computer attempting to access the service. The most commonly configured options on the Advanced tab are:

o **Granted Access:** If you select the radio button next to this option, all computers on the Internet will be allowed to access the WWW service *except* those explicitly listed, by IP address, in the following list box. To add computers to the list box, click the Add command button.

o **Denied Access:** If you select the radio button next to this option, all computers on the Internet will be denied access to the WWW service *except* those explicitly listed, by IP address, in the following list box. To add computers to the list box, click the Add command button.

This completes the configuration of the WWW service

**Configuring a virtual server**    A *virtual server* is a pseudo WWW server with its own unique domain name and IP address. To the Internet user accessing the virtual server, a virtual server appears to be a separate server; but in reality, a virtual server is *not* a separate server, but more like an extra shared folder on an Internet Information Server accessed by specifying a different domain name and IP address. A single Internet Information Server can be configured to accommodate multiple virtual servers. Each virtual server is assigned a separate publishing directory.

For example, an Internet service provider could use one Internet Information Server to host virtual servers for several customers. Each customer could have its own domain name, such as www.company_a.com, www.company_b.com, and www.company_c.com, and so forth. To Internet users accessing these companies' WWW services, each domain name appears to be on a separate server.

Configuring a virtual server consists of two parts: first, you must configure an additional IP address for your network adapter; second, you use Internet Service Manager to configure the virtual server. The following sections describe how to accomplish these tasks.

**TO CONFIGURE AN ADDITIONAL IP ADDRESS FOR A NETWORK ADAPTER, FOLLOW THESE STEPS:**

**1.** Select Start ⇒ Settings ⇒ Control Panel.

**2.** In the Control Panel dialog box, double-click Network.

**3.** In the Network dialog box, click the Protocols tab.

**4.** On the Protocols tab, double-click TCP/IP Protocol in the Network Protocols list box.

**5.** The Microsoft TCP/IP Properties dialog box appears. Click the Advanced command button.

**6.** The Advanced IP Addressing dialog box appears. In the Adapter drop-down list box, select the network adapter to which you want to assign an additional IP address. Click the Add command button in the IP Addresses section.

**7.** The TCP/IP Address dialog box appears. Type in the additional IP address and subnet mask you want to assign to the network adapter. Click the Add command button.

**8.** The Advanced IP Addressing dialog box reappears.

Figure 16-24 shows the Advanced IP Addressing dialog box with two IP addresses configured for a single network adapter. Click OK.

**9.** In the Microsoft TCP/IP Properties dialog box, click OK.

**10.** In the Network dialog box, click the Close command button.

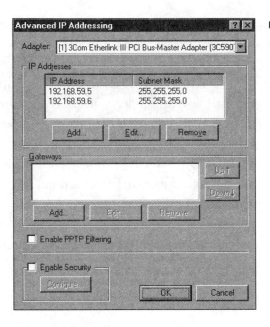

**FIGURE 16-24** Multiple IP addresses assigned to a single network adapter

**11.** A Network Settings Change warning dialog box appears, asking if you want to restart your computer now for the new settings to take effect. Click the Yes command button.

### TO USE INTERNET SERVICE MANAGER TO CONFIGURE THE VIRTUAL SERVER, FOLLOW THESE STEPS:

**1.** Select Start⇒ Programs⇒ Microsoft Internet Server (Common)⇒ Internet Service Manager.

**2.** In the Microsoft Internet Service Manager dialog box, highlight the computer on the same line as the WWW service, and select Properties⇒ Service Properties.

**3.** The WWW Service Properties dialog box appears. Click the Directories tab.

**4.** The Directories tab appears, as shown in Figure 16-25. Note the check box next to Directory Browsing Allowed. When selected, this option permits users to browse all files and folders published by the WWW service. For security reasons, this option is not normally selected. Click the Add command button.

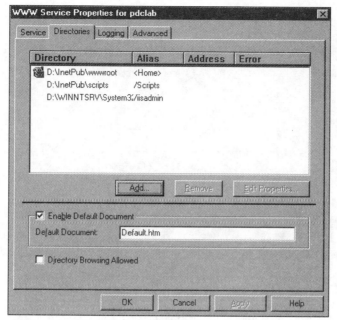

**FIGURE 16-25**    **Configuration options on the WWW Service Properties Directories tab**

**5.** In the Directory Properties dialog box, select the radio button next to Home Directory. In the Directory text box, type the full path to the home directory that will be used by the virtual server, for example: `c:\inetpub\wwwroot_2`. (This directory need *not* be an existing directory—entering a new directory in this text box will cause NT to create it when you click OK.) Then select the check box next to Virtual Server. Type in the additional IP address you assigned to your network adapter in the Virtual Server IP Address text box. Click OK.

Figure 16-26 shows the Directory Properties dialog box configured to implement a virtual server.

**6.** The WWW Service Properties dialog box reappears. The virtual server's home directory and IP address now appear in the list box. Click OK.

**7.** Exit Microsoft Internet Service Manager.

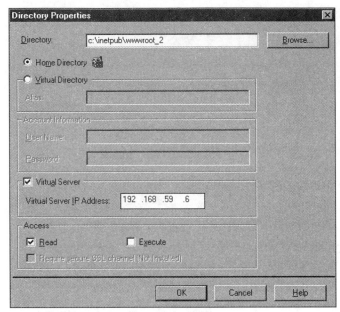

**FIGURE 16-26**    Configuring a virtual server

# Peer Web Services Versus Internet Information Server

*Peer Web Services* is a Windows NT Workstation Internet publishing service. Peer Web Services is substantially the same as Internet Information Server, except Peer Web Services is optimized as a small-scale intranet publishing service for a limited number of users. Additionally, Peer Web Services lacks some of the functionality of IIS — most notably, Peer Web Services cannot accommodate virtual servers and cannot be configured to control access to the WWW service by an IP address.

Peer Web Services can be installed on any Windows NT Workstation computer with TCP/IP installed on it.

Internet Service Manager can be used to configure Peer Web Services in the same way it is used to configure IIS. On a Windows NT Workstation computer, Internet Service Manager is accessed by selecting Start ⇒ Programs ⇒ Microsoft Peer Web Services (Common) ⇒ Internet Service Manager.

## Installing Peer Web Services

Before installing Peer Web Services, you should install Windows NT Workstation and TCP/IP.

**TO INSTALL PEER WEB SERVICES ON A WINDOWS NT WORKSTATION COMPUTER, FOLLOW THESE STEPS:**

**1.** Select Start ⇒ Settings ⇒ Control Panel.

**2.** In the Control Panel dialog box, double-click Network.

**3.** In the Network dialog box, click the Services tab.

**4.** On the Service tab, click the Add command button.

**5.** In the Select Network Service dialog box, highlight Microsoft Peer Web Services. Click OK.

**6.** The Internet Information Server Installation—Files Needed dialog box appears. Ensure the correct source file location is displayed in the text box. (This is normally the I386 folder on the Windows NT Workstation compact disc.) Edit this text box if necessary. Click OK.

**7.** The Microsoft Peer Web Services Setup dialog box appears. Click OK.

**8.** In the Microsoft Peer Web Services Setup dialog box, select all the options you want installed with Peer Web Services. Deselect any undesired options. Click OK.

**9.** When a Microsoft Peer Web Services Setup dialog box appears prompting you to do so, click the Yes command button to create the installation directory.

**10.** The Publishing Directories dialog box appears. Modify the directories if desired, or accept the default publishing directories. Click OK.

**11.** A Microsoft Peer Web Services Setup dialog box appears. Click the Yes command button to create the publishing directories.

**12.** Windows NT copies and installs Peer Web Services. This process takes a few minutes.

**13.** If you installed the Gopher service and have not yet assigned an Internet domain name to the computer, a dialog box appears, indicating you should assign an Internet domain name to your computer. Click OK.

**14.** If you installed ODBC drivers and administration, a Microsoft Peer Web Services Setup dialog box appears, indicating you must close Control Panel before you can install the ODBC drivers. Click OK to close Control Panel.

**15.** If you installed ODBC drivers and administration, the Install Drivers dialog box appears. Highlight the ODBC drivers you want to install, and click OK.

**16.** A dialog box appears, indicating Microsoft Peer Web Services has been installed and set up. Click OK.

**17.** The Network dialog box reappears. Click the Close command button.

# TROUBLESHOOTING COMMON TCP/IP CONNECTIVITY PROBLEMS

There are several common TCP/IP connectivity problems. Most TCP/IP connectivity problems are caused by incorrectly configured TCP/IP settings on the computer that has the problem.

TCP/IP connectivity problems commonly reported by users include:

- A user is unable to access a computer located on another subnet.
- A user is unable to access the Internet.
- A user is unable to access computers on both the local and remote subnets.
- TCP/IP fails to initialize on the user's computer.

When troubleshooting a TCP/IP connectivity problem, carefully check the TCP/IP settings on the computer experiencing the problem, including: IP address, subnet mask, and default gateway:

- **IP address:** Make sure the computer's IP address is *not* a duplicate of another IP address used on the network, and that it is an appropriate IP address for the local subnet (the network ID portion of the IP address must be the same for all computers on the local subnet).
- **Subnet mask:** Ensure the computer's subnet mask is the same subnet mask used by all computers and routers located on that subnet.
- **Default gateway:** Ensure the computer's default gateway address matches the IP address of a router on the local subnet.

Two command-line utilities exist that can help you when you're troubleshooting TCP/IP connectivity problems: Ipconfig.exe and ping.exe.

Ipconfig.exe displays the computer's current IP configuration settings, including IP address, subnet mask, and default gateway. To use Ipconfig.exe, select Start ⇒ Programs ⇒ Command Prompt. At the command prompt, type **ipconfig /all** and press Enter.

Ping.exe verifies network communications between the local computer and any other computer specified on the network. To use ping.exe, select Start ⇒ Programs ⇒ Command Prompt. At the command prompt, type **ping *ip_address*** and press Enter. (The IP address entered is the IP address of the computer with which you are attempting to communicate.) If your computer is able to communicate with the remote computer specified, ping.exe will display four replies from the remote computer's IP address. The following is an example of a successful ping response:

```
Reply from 192.168.59.5: bytes=32 time<10ms TTL=128
Reply from 192.168.59.5: bytes=32 time<10ms TTL=128
Reply from 192.168.59.5: bytes=32 time<10ms TTL=128
Reply from 192.168.59.5: bytes=32 time<10ms TTL=128
```

If your computer is unable to communicate with the remote computer specified, ping.exe usually displays Request timed out four times.

You can ping your own computer's IP address to determine whether TCP/IP is correctly configured and initialized on your local computer. If TCP/IP is correctly configured on your local computer, ping.exe will display four replies from your local computer's IP address.

# KEY POINT SUMMARY

This chapter explored how to network Windows NT using TCP/IP. The following points illuminate the major issues:

- The *Transmission Control Protocol/Internet Protocol* (TCP/IP) is a fast, routable, transport protocol that provides robust capabilities for Windows NT networking. TCP/IP is the protocol used on the Internet. TCP/IP is an enterprise protocol that is supported by many other operating systems. TCP/IP is typically the recommended protocol for large, heterogeneous networks.

- An *IP address* is a 32-bit binary number, broken into four 8-bit sections, which uniquely identifies a computer or other network device on a network that uses TCP/IP. *No two computers or other devices on an internetwork should have the same IP address.* An IP address contains two important identifiers: a *network ID* and a *host ID*. All computers located on the same network subnet have the same network ID. Each computer or other network device on a given network subnet must have a unique host ID.

- A *subnet mask* specifies which portion of an IP address represents the network ID and which portion represents the host ID. A subnet mask allows TCP/IP to determine whether network traffic destined for a given IP address should be transmitted on the local subnet, or whether it should be routed to a remote subnet. *A subnet mask should be the same for all computers on a given network segment.* If subnet masks are incorrectly configured, network communications problems due to routing errors may occur.

- A *default gateway address* specifies the IP address of a router on the local network segment. If a computer's default gateway address does not specify a router on the local subnet, then that computer will be unable to communicate with computers or other network devices located on other network segments.

- IP addresses must be configured on each computer when TCP/IP is installed. You can assign an IP address to a Windows NT computer in one of two ways: by configuring a computer to obtain an IP address from a DHCP server, or by manually specifying a computer's IP address configuration.

- The advantages of using a DHCP server to assign IP addresses are as follows:

  - It allows central management of IP addresses, and assures addresses are valid and not duplicated.

  - It reduces the amount of administration time required to manage and maintain IP addresses for each computer on the network.

  - It reduces the likelihood of human error when IP addresses are assigned, because no need exists to enter an IP address manually on each individual computer.

o *IP routing* is a function of the Internet Protocol (IP) that uses IP address information to send data packets from a source computer on one network segment across one or more routers to a destination computer on another network segment. Windows NT computers with multiple network adapters (called *multihomed* computers) can function as IP routers. The two primary types of routing are static and dynamic.

  o *Static routing* is basic IP routing. No additional software is necessary to implement static routing in multihomed Windows NT computers. Static routers are ***not*** capable of automatically building or updating a routing table, but must be manually configured by a network administrator.

  o *Dynamic routing* is intelligent IP routing. By installing *RIP for Internet Protocol*, a multihomed Windows NT Server computer can be configured to function as a dynamic router. A dynamic router is capable of automatically building and updating its routing table.

o The *DHCP Relay Agent* forwards client DHCP configuration requests to a DHCP server on another network segment, thus allowing computers on one subnet to receive IP addresses from a DHCP server located on another subnet.

o *Windows Internet Name Service* (WINS) provides NetBIOS name resolution services to client computers. *NetBIOS name resolution* is the process of resolving a NetBIOS name to an associated IP address. The two common methods used to perform NetBIOS name resolution include manually configuring an LMHOSTS file on each individual computer on the network, and installing a WINS server and configuring client computers to use it. The second method is the preferred method because the WINS server dynamically updates its NetBIOS name to IP address tables and, therefore, relieves the network administrator from having to enter and update this information on each computer manually.

o Installing and configuring WINS is a two-step process: first, you must install WINS on a Windows NT Server computer, and then you must configure each client computer on the network to use the WINS server for NetBIOS name resolution.

- Microsoft DNS Server provides host name resolution services to client computers. *Host name resolution* is the process of resolving a Fully Qualified Domain Name to an associated IP address. On the Internet, host names are stored in domains and subdomains that form a hierarchical tree structure called the *Domain Name System* (DNS). The root of the DNS structure contains several familiar domains, including: com, gov, mil, edu, net, and org. Each subdomain is called a *zone*.

- When you initially install a DNS server, you must create a zone in which the DNS server will maintain its host names. A DNS server can have multiple zones. A DNS server stores all zone information, including host names and their associated IP addresses, in a database called a *DNS database*. A DNS database is *not* dynamically created—the network administrator must *manually enter* host names and their associated IP addresses for each computer on the network. An alternative to entering every host name and associated IP address manually into a DNS database is to configure Microsoft DNS Server to use a WINS Server to resolve host names.

- Installing and configuring Microsoft DNS Server is a three-step process: First, you install Microsoft DNS Server on a Windows NT Server computer. Second, you configure a zone on the Microsoft DNS Server. (Optionally, on networks that use DHCP and WINS, you can also configure Microsoft DNS Server to use WINS Lookup for host name resolution.) Third, you configure each client computer on the network to use a DNS server for host name resolution.

- Microsoft has two primary tools for publishing on the Internet: *Internet Information Server* for Windows NT Server computers, and *Peer Web Services* for Windows NT Workstation computers. Both of these products require the use of TCP/IP.

- *Internet Information Server* (IIS) provides WWW, FTP, and Gopher publishing services. No additional hardware is required to install IIS on an internal intranet. If you want to connect your IIS to the Internet, however, you need additional hardware to support this connection.

- *Internet Service Manager* is a Windows NT tool you can use to manage IIS. You can use Internet Service Manager to configure the IIS services, configure IIS security, and start and stop the individual IIS services.

- Many of the configuration options on the WWW service enable you to manage security. When configuring password authentication, you can clear the check box next to Basic (Clear Text) and select the check box next to Windows NT Challenge/Response to prevent user names and passwords from being transmitted in an unencrypted format over the Internet. You can control access by IP address. You can ensure directory browsing is not selected, and you can require users to supply user names and passwords by not permitting anonymous users to access the WWW service.

- A *virtual server* is a pseudo WWW server with its own unique domain name and IP address. To the Internet user accessing the virtual server, a virtual server appears to be a separate server; but in reality, a virtual server is not a separate server, but more like an extra shared folder on an Internet Information Server. A single Internet Information Server can be configured to accommodate multiple virtual servers. Before you can configure a virtual server, you must configure an additional IP address for the network adapter in the Windows NT Server computer.

- *Peer Web Services* is a Windows NT Workstation Internet publishing service that is substantially the same as IIS, but is optimized as a small-scale intranet publishing service for a limited number of users. Before installing Peer Web Services, you should install Windows NT Workstation and TCP/IP.

- When troubleshooting a TCP/IP connectivity problem, carefully check the TCP/IP settings on the computer experiencing the problem, including IP address, subnet mask, and default gateway:

  - Make sure the computer's IP address is *not* a duplicate of another IP address used on the network, and that it is an appropriate IP address for the local subnet. (The network ID portion of the IP address must be the same for all computers on the local subnet.)

  - Ensure the computer's subnet mask is the same subnet mask used by all computers and routers located on that subnet.

  - Ensure the computer's default gateway address matches the IP address of a router on the local subnet.

  - Also consider using the `Ipconfig.exe` and `ping.exe` command-line utilities when troubleshooting TCP/IP connectivity problems.

# APPLYING WHAT YOU'VE LEARNED

Now it's time to regroup, review, and apply what you've learned in this chapter.

The questions in the following Instant Assessment section bring to mind key facts and concepts. In addition, some of the questions give you a chance to analyze situations and apply your knowledge of TCP/IP to that situation.

The hands-on lab exercises reinforce what you've learned and provide an opportunity for you to practice several tasks tested by the Microsoft Certified Professional Exams.

## Instant Assessment

1. What does TCP/IP stand for?

2. Which transport protocol is typically recommended for use in large, heterogeneous networks?

3. What is an IP address?

4. What problem can occur if subnet masks are incorrectly configured?

5. What problem will occur if a computer's default gateway address does not specify a router on the local subnet?

6. What are the two methods you can use to assign IP addresses to Windows NT computers?

7. What is IP routing?

8. What are the two primary types of IP routing?

9. What Windows NT service must you install on a multihomed Windows NT Server computer for it to function as a dynamic router?

10. What is the DHCP Relay Agent, and what function does it perform?

11. What is WINS, and what function does it perform for client computers?

12. What service does Microsoft DNS Server provide to client computers?

13. Your company operates in a high-security environment. What steps can you take to secure access to the WWW service on your Microsoft Internet Information Server?

14. How must you configure the network adapter in your computer before you can configure a virtual server?

**15.** What are Microsoft's two primary tools for publishing on the Internet?

**16.** Your company plans to connect its Internet Information Server to the Internet over a fractional T1 leased line. What additional hardware is required to implement the connection?

**17.** You want to connect your Internet Information Server to the Internet using an ISDN line. What additional hardware is required to implement the connection?

**18.** What is a virtual server?

**19.** Which three TCP/IP settings should you check when troubleshooting a computer that has a TCP/IP connectivity problem?

**20.** You want to determine whether TCP/IP is correctly configured and initialized on a Windows NT computer. Which command-line utility can you use to help you determine this?

**21.** You want to verify TCP/IP network communications between two Windows NT Server computers. Which command-line utility can you use to help you determine this?

**22.** You want to display the TCP/IP configuration of a Windows NT computer. Which command-line utility can you use to accomplish this?

|  | T/F |
|---|---|
| **23.** All computers located on the same network segment have the same network ID. | _____ |
| **24.** Each computer or other network device on a given network segment must have the same host ID. | _____ |
| **25.** A subnet mask should be the same for all computers and other network devices on a given network segment. | _____ |
| **26.** Static routers are *not* capable of automatically building and updating a routing table and must be manually configured. | _____ |
| **27.** Dynamic routers are *not* capable of automatically building and updating a routing table and must be manually configured. | _____ |
| **28.** A WINS server dynamically updates its NetBIOS name to IP address tables. | _____ |
| **29.** A DNS database is dynamically created. | _____ |

**concept link** For answers to the Instant Assessment questions see Appendix D.

## Hands-on Lab Exercises

The following hands-on lab exercises provide you with practical opportunities to apply the TCP/IP knowledge you've gained in this chapter.

### Lab 16.25 *Implementing WINS and Microsoft DNS Server*

Enterprise

The purpose of this lab exercise is to give you hands-on experience in installing WINS and DNS Server, and configuring DNS Server to interact with WINS.

This lab consists of two parts:

> Part 1: Installing WINS and Microsoft DNS Server
>
> Part 2: Configuring Microsoft DNS Server to interact with WINS

Begin this lab by booting your computer to Windows NT Server. Log on as Administrator. Place your Windows NT Server compact disc in your CD-ROM drive.

Complete the following steps carefully.

#### Part 1: Installing WINS and Microsoft DNS Server

In this section, you install Windows Internet Name Service (WINS) and Microsoft Domain Name Service (DNS) Server on a Windows NT Server computer.

**1.** Select Start ⇒ Settings ⇒ Control Panel.

**2.** In the Control Panel dialog box, double-click Network.

**3.** In the Network dialog box, click the Services tab.

**4.** On the Services tab, click the Add command button.

**5.** In the Select Network Service dialog box, highlight Microsoft DNS Server. Click OK.

**6.** A Windows NT Setup dialog box appears. Ensure the correct source file location is displayed in the text box at the bottom of the dialog box. (This is probably the I386 folder on your Windows NT Server compact disc.) Edit this text box if necessary. Click the Continue command button.

**7.** Windows NT copies and installs Microsoft DNS Server. The Network dialog box reappears. Click the Add command button.

**8.** The Select Network Service dialog box appears. Scroll down and highlight Windows Internet Name Service. Click OK.

9. A Windows NT Setup dialog box appears. Ensure the correct source file location is displayed in the text box at the bottom of the dialog box. Click the Continue command button.

10. Windows NT copies and installs WINS. The Network dialog box reappears. Click the Close command button.

11. Windows NT performs various bindings operations. A Network Settings Change warning dialog box appears, asking if you want to restart your computer now for the new settings to take effect. Click the Yes command button.

12. Boot your computer to Windows NT Server and log on as Administrator. Continue on to Part 2.

### Part 2: Configuring Microsoft DNS Server to interact with WINS

In this section, you configure Microsoft DNS Server to use WINS to resolve host names to IP addresses.

1. From the desktop, select Start ⇒ Programs ⇒ Administrative Tools (Common) ⇒ DNS Manager.

2. In the Domain Name Service Manager dialog box, select DNS ⇒ New Server.

3. The Add DNS Server dialog box appears. Type **192.168.59.5** in the DNS Server text box. Click OK.

4. Your server appears (indicated by its IP address) in the Server List on the left side of the Domain Name Service Manager dialog box. Right-click your server's IP address. Select Refresh from the menu that appears. Right-click again on your server's IP address. Select New Zone from the menu that appears.

5. The "Creating new zone for 192.168.59.5" dialog box appears. Select the radio button next to Primary. Click the Next command button.

6. Type **lab.com** in the Zone Name text box. Type **lab.com.dns** in the Zone File text box. Click the Next command button.

7. Click the Finish command button in the "Creating new zone for 192.168.59.5" dialog box. The lab.com zone appears in the Domain Name Service Manager dialog box under the Server List for your Windows NT Server computer. Right-click lab.com, and then select Properties from the menu that appears.

8. The "Zone Properties-lab.com" dialog box appears. Click the WINS Lookup tab.

**9.** On the WINS Lookup tab, select the check box next to Use WINS Resolution. In the uppermost WINS Servers text box, type **192.168.59.5** and click the Add command button. Click OK.

**10.** Your DNS Server is now configured to use WINS for host name resolution. Exit DNS Manager.

## Lab 16.26 *Configuring Internet Information Server and installing and configuring Peer Web Services*

The purpose of this lab exercise is to give you hands-on experience in configuring Microsoft Internet Information Server and in installing and configuring Peer Web Services.

Workstation
Enterprise

This lab consists of two parts:

Part 1: Configuring Microsoft Internet Information Server

Part 2: Installing and configuring Peer Web Services

Begin this lab by booting your computer to Windows NT Server. Log on as Administrator.

Complete the following steps carefully.

### Part 1: Configuring Microsoft Internet Information Server

In this section, you configure Microsoft Internet Information Server on your Windows NT Server computer.

**1.** Select Start ⇒ Programs ⇒ Microsoft Internet Server (Common) ⇒ Internet Information Server Setup.

**2.** The Microsoft Internet Information Server 2.0 Setup dialog box appears. Click OK.

**3.** In the next Microsoft Internet Information Server 2.0 Setup dialog box that appears, click the Add/Remove command button.

**4.** Ensure the correct source file location is displayed in the text box. (This is probably the C:\WINNTSRV\system32\inetsrv folder on your Windows NT Server computer.) It should be unnecessary to edit this text box. Click OK.

**5.** In the Microsoft Internet Information Server 2.0 Setup dialog box, *deselect* the check box next to Gopher Service. (This will deinstall the Gopher Service, which is not used in most NT installations.) Click OK.

**6.** The Microsoft Internet Information Server 2.0 Setup dialog box appears. Click the Yes command button to stop the Gopher Publishing Service.

**7.** In the Microsoft Internet Information Server 2.0 Setup dialog box, click OK.

**8.** Select Start ⇒ Programs ⇒ Microsoft Internet Server (Common) ⇒ Internet Service Manager.

**9.** In the Microsoft Internet Service Manager dialog box, double-click the first computer listed in the Computer list box.

**10.** The "WWW Service Properties for pdclab" dialog box appears. Notice the configuration options available on the Service tab. Click the Directories tab.

**11.** On the Directories tab, notice the configuration options available. Click the Logging tab.

**12.** On the Logging tab, notice the configuration options available. Click the Advanced tab.

**13.** Notice the configuration options available. Click OK.

**14.** In the Microsoft Internet Service Manager dialog box, highlight the first computer listed in the Computer list box. Select Properties ⇒ Stop Service.

**15.** Notice the state of the WWW service has changed to Stopped. Select Properties ⇒ Start Service.

**16.** Notice the state of the WWW service has changed to Running. Exit Microsoft Internet Service Manager.

**17.** Double-click Internet Explorer on your desktop.

**18.** The Microsoft Internet Explorer Home Page dialog box appears. Edit the Open text box so it reads **pdclab** and press Enter.

**19.** The Microsoft Internet Information Server home page is displayed. You have successfully configured and accessed the Microsoft Internet Information Server. Exit Internet Explorer.

**20.** Shut down your computer, reboot to Windows NT Workstation, and log on as Administrator. Place the Windows NT Workstation compact disc in your CD-ROM drive. Continue to Part 2.

## Part 2: Installing and configuring Peer Web Services

In this section, you install and configure Peer Web Services on your Windows NT Workstation computer.

**1.** Select Start ⇒ Settings ⇒ Control Panel.

**2.** In the Control Panel dialog box, double-click Network.

**3.** In the Network dialog box, click the Services tab.

**4.** On the Service tab, click the Add command button.

**5.** In the Select Network Service dialog box, highlight Microsoft Peer Web Services. Click OK.

6. The Internet Information Server Installation—Files Needed dialog box appears. Ensure the correct source file location is displayed in the text box. (This is normally the I386 folder on your Windows NT Workstation compact disc.) Edit this text box if necessary. Click OK.

7. The Microsoft Peer Web Services Setup dialog box appears. Click OK.

8. In the Microsoft Peer Web Services Setup dialog box, *deselect* the check box next to Gopher Service. *Select* the check box next to Internet Service Manager (HTML). Click OK.

9. When a dialog box appears prompting you to do so, click the Yes command button to create the installation directory.

10. The Publishing Directories dialog box appears. Click OK to accept the default publishing directories.

11. Windows NT copies and installs Peer Web Services. This process takes a few minutes.

12. If a Microsoft Peer Web Services Setup dialog box appears, indicating you must close Control Panel before you can install the ODBC drivers, click OK to close Control Panel.

    The Install Drivers dialog box appears. Highlight SQL Server, and then click OK.

13. A dialog box appears, indicating Microsoft Peer Web Services has been installed and set up. Click OK.

14. The Network dialog box reappears. Click the Close command button.

15. Exit Control Panel if it is still open.

16. Double-click Internet Explorer.

17. The Microsoft Internet Explorer Home Page appears. Edit the Address text box so it reads: **ntw40** and press Enter.

18. The Microsoft Peer Web Services home page is displayed. Scroll down to the Administrative Tools heading, and click the blue text that reads *click here* in the description under that heading.

19. Internet Service Manager for Peer Web Services appears. This is an HTML version of Internet Service Manager. Exit Internet Explorer.

## Lab 16.27 *Installing and configuring an Internet (TCP/IP) router*

Server
Enterprise

The purpose of this lab exercise is to give you hands-on experience in installing and configuring an Internet (TCP/IP) router on a Windows NT Server computer.

Begin this lab by booting your computer to Windows NT Server. Log on as Administrator. Place your Windows NT Server compact disc in your CD-ROM drive. Complete the following steps carefully.

1. Select Start ⇒ Settings ⇒ Control Panel.

2. In the Control Panel dialog box, double-click Network.

3. In the Network dialog box, click the Adapters tab.

4. On the Adapters tab, click the Add command button.

5. In the Select Network Adapter dialog box, highlight MS Loopback Adapter. Click OK. (You already installed a network adapter when you initially installed Windows NT Server. This step installs a second network adapter that will allow your computer to function as a TCP/IP router.)

6. The MS Loopback Adapter Card Setup dialog box appears. Click OK.

7. The Windows NT Setup dialog box appears. Ensure the correct source file location is displayed in the text box. (This is probably the I386 folder on your Windows NT Server compact disc.) Edit this text box if necessary. Click the Continue command button.

8. The Network dialog box reappears. Click the Services tab.

9. On the Services tab, click the Add command button.

10. In the Select Network Service dialog box, highlight RIP for Internet Protocol. Click OK.

11. The Windows NT Setup dialog box appears. Ensure the correct source file location is displayed in the text box. Click the Continue command button.

12. The Network dialog box reappears. Click the Close command button.

13. Windows NT performs various bindings operations, and then displays the Microsoft TCP/IP Properties dialog box. In the Adapter drop-down list box, select the MS Loopback adapter you installed in Steps 5–7 in this lab. (This is the second adapter in the list.) In the IP Address text box, type **192.168.60.1** and press Tab. In the Subnet Mask text box, type **255.255.255.0** and then click the Routing tab.

14. On the Routing tab, notice the check box next to Enable IP Forwarding is checked. Windows NT automatically selects this check box when RIP for Internet Protocol is installed. Click OK.

15. A Network Settings Change dialog box appears. Click the Yes command button to restart your computer so the new settings can take effect.

caution

**If your computer is connected to a network that uses TCP/IP, you should remove RIP for Internet Protocol after the computer reboots. If you don't do this, it can cause routing problems on your network. (To remove RIP for Internet Protocol, use the Services tab in the Network application in Control Panel.) You will have to reboot your computer again after you remove RIP for Internet Protocol.**

## Lab 16.28 *Identifying and resolving TCP/IP connectivity problems*

Server
Enterprise

The purpose of this lab exercise is to give you hands-on experience in identifying and resolving common TCP/IP connectivity problems.

In each of the following situations:

**1.** Identify the TCP/IP connectivity problem (for example, an invalid or duplicate IP address).

**2.** Describe what you would do to resolve the problem.

**Situation 1**    Several components on a network subnet are configured as shown in Figure 16-27:

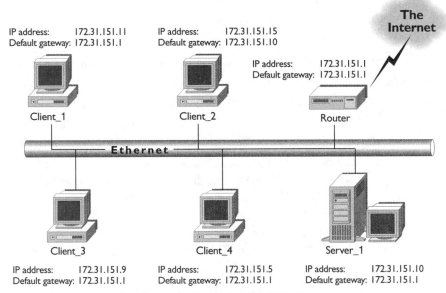

**FIGURE 16-27**    **Network subnet configuration for Situation 1**

What is the TCP/IP connectivity problem in this situation?

What would you do to resolve the problem?

**Situation 2**   Several components on a network subnet are configured as shown in Figure 16-28.

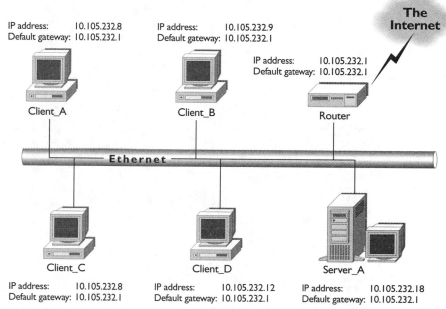

IP address:      10.105.232.8
Default gateway: 10.105.232.1

IP address:      10.105.232.9
Default gateway: 10.105.232.1

IP address:      10.105.232.1
Default gateway: 10.105.232.1

Client_A

Client_B

Router

IP address:      10.105.232.8
Default gateway: 10.105.232.1

IP address:      10.105.232.12
Default gateway: 10.105.232.1

IP address:      10.105.232.18
Default gateway: 10.105.232.1

Client_C

Client_D

Server_A

**FIGURE 16-28**   **Network subnet configuration for Situation 2**

What is the TCP/IP connectivity problem in this situation?

What would you do to resolve the problem?

concept link   **For answers to the hands-on lab exercise see Appendix D.**

Workstation
Server
Enterprise

CHAPTER

# Coexistence With NetWare

# 17

# About Chapter 17

T his chapter is all about protocols and services that increase the interoperability of Windows NT with NetWare.

The chapter describes NWLink IPX/SPX Compatible Transport, which provides protocol compatibility between Windows NT and NetWare computers. Routing this protocol using RIP for NWLink IPX/SPX Compatible Transport is also addressed.

Then the SAP Agent, which advertises a Windows NT computer's services to NetWare client computers, is introduced.

Next, this chapter explores Client Service for NetWare and Gateway Service for NetWare, which enable users of NT computers to access resources on a NetWare server. File and Print Services for NetWare and Directory Services Manager for NetWare are also explained.

Finally, Chapter 17 presents tips on troubleshooting common NetWare connectivity problems.

This chapter includes three hands-on labs. In these labs you'll install and configure NWLink IPX/SPX Compatible Transport, Client Service for NetWare, Gateway Service for NetWare, and RIP for NWLink IPX/SPX Compatible Transport.

Chapter 17 is a "must read" no matter which of the three Windows NT 4.0 Microsoft Certified Professional exams you're preparing for. This chapter covers numerous exam objectives, including objectives concerning network components, the NWLink IPX/SPX Compatible Transport protocol, implementing NT in a NetWare environment, configuring NT for interoperability with NetWare, and troubleshooting objectives on resolving connectivity problems.

# WINDOWS NT IN A NETWARE ENVIRONMENT

Microsoft includes several protocols and services with Windows NT that enable Windows NT computers to coexist with Novell NetWare servers and client computers on the same network.

In a nutshell, these components enable Windows NT computers to utilize the resources on NetWare servers, and, in limited circumstances, can also enable Windows NT Server computers to share their resources with NetWare client computers in a heterogeneous networking environment. These protocols and sevices can be used for long-term integration in a mixed network operating system environment, or for the short-term during a migration from NetWare to Windows NT.

When you consider the large number of existing Novell NetWare networks, particularly when Windows NT was first released, it's not too surprising that Microsoft has developed and included these protocols and services with Windows NT. Solutions that enable both Windows NT and NetWare to be used on the same network were critical to Windows NT's wide acceptance in the network operating system arena.

Microsoft has addressed this challenge by developing various protocols and services that increase the interoperability of Windows NT with NetWare, including:

- NWLink IPX/SPX Compatible Transport
- RIP for NWLink IPX/SPX Compatible Transport
- SAP Agent
- Client Service for NetWare (CSNW)
- Gateway Service for NetWare (GSNW)
- File and Print Services for NetWare (FPNW)
- Directory Services Manager for NetWare (DSMN)

These protocols and services, including their features and how they are used, are discussed in detail in the following sections.

exam preparation pointer

**Chapter 17 contains important information that is tested on all three of the Windows NT 4.0 exams. If you don't regularly use a NetWare server on your network, plan to review this chapter just before you take any of these exams.**

**If you're taking the Workstation exam, you can skip the sections on RIP for NWLink IPX/SPX Compatible Transport and Gateway Service for NetWare.**

**If you're taking either the Server or Enterprise exam, plan on studying the entire chapter.**

**The details in this chapter are *very* important! Plan on doing some brute memorization.**

# NWLink IPX/SPX Compatible Transport

*NWLink IPX/SPX Compatible Transport* is a routable transport protocol typically used in a combined Windows NT and NetWare environment. NWLink IPX/SPX Compatible Transport is Microsoft's version of Novell's IPX/SPX protocol. (*IPX/SPX* is the protocol used on most Novell NetWare networks.) NWLink provides protocol compatibility between Windows NT and NetWare computers. In addition to its functionality in a NetWare environment, NWLink also fully supports Microsoft networking.

NWLink IPX/SPX Compatible Transport, which is included with NT Server and NT Workstation, must be installed on NT Server and NT Workstation computers in order to enable them to communicate over the network with NetWare computers.

There are two important topics that need to be discussed before moving on to the installation of NWLink IPX/SPX Compatible Transport: frame types and network numbers. Because frame types and network numbers must be configured during installation, it's important to have a solid grasp of these basic network concepts.

## Frame types

*Frame types* (also called *frame formats*) are accepted, standardized structures for transmitting data packets over a network. All frame types include certain common components, such as source address, destination address, data field, and cyclic redundancy check—but the various frame types include different combinations of *additional* fields beyond the common components.

Windows NT and NWLink IPX/SPX Compatible Transport support nine different frame types, which are described in Table 17-1.

| **TABLE 17-1** NWLink IPX/SPX Compatible Transport Frame Types | | |
| --- | --- | --- |
| *FRAME TYPE* | *DEFAULT/COMMON USAGE* | *NETWORK ADAPTERS THAT SUPPORT THIS FRAME TYPE* |
| Ethernet 802.2 | Default frame type for NetWare 3.12 and later NetWare versions on Ethernet networks. | Ethernet |

*continued*

**TABLE 17-1** *(continued)*

| FRAME TYPE | DEFAULT/COMMON USAGE | NETWORK ADAPTERS THAT SUPPORT THIS FRAME TYPE |
|---|---|---|
| Ethernet 802.3 | Default frame type for NetWare 3.11 and earlier NetWare versions on Ethernet networks. | Ethernet |
| Ethernet II | Commonly associated with the TCP/IP protocol; not commonly used with NWLink IPX/SPX Compatible Transport. | Ethernet |
| Ethernet SNAP | Commonly associated with the AppleTalk protocol; not commonly used with NWLink IPX/SPX Compatible Transport. | Ethernet, FDDI |
| ARCNET | Default frame type for all versions of NetWare on ARCNET networks. | ARCNET |
| Token-Ring | Default frame type for all versions of NetWare on Token Ring networks. | Token Ring |
| Token-Ring SNAP | Commonly associated with the AppleTalk protocol; not commonly used with NWLink IPX/SPX Compatible Transport. | Token Ring |
| FDDI | Default frame type for NetWare 3.12 and later NetWare versions on FDDI networks. | FDDI |
| FDDI 802.3 | Default frame type for NetWare 3.11 and earlier NetWare versions on FDDI networks. | FDDI |

Before you select a frame type when installing and configuring NWLink IPX/SPX Compatible Transport, you should determine which frame type(s) are already in use on the network. You should select a frame type that *matches* the frame type already in use, or use the Windows NT auto frame type detection feature to automatically select a frame type. You can assign more than one frame type to an individual network adapter.

Frame type mismatching is a common cause of communications problems on networks that use NWLink IPX/SPX Compatible Transport. (This issue is covered in more depth in the "Troubleshooting Common NetWare Connectivity Problems" section in this chapter.)

## Network Numbers

*Network numbers* are 32-bit binary numbers that uniquely identify an NWLink IPX/SPX Compatible Transport network segment for routing purposes. Because network numbers uniquely identify a network segment, they are used by IPX routers to correctly forward data packets from one network segment to another.

Network numbers are only assigned to Windows NT computers that use NWLink IPX/SPX Compatible Transport. Network numbers are assigned during the installation and configuration of NWLink IPX/SPX Compatible Transport.

Network numbers are commonly presented in an eight-digit hexadecimal format. (In a hexadecimal format, the numbers 0 through 9 and the letters A through F can be used.) Don't confuse a network number with a TCP/IP network ID or a computer's MAC (hardware) address.

There are two types of network numbers: network numbers and internal network numbers. A Windows NT computer that uses NWLink IPX/SPX Compatible Transport can have one or more network number(s) and an internal network number, as well.

When NWLink IPX/SPX Compatible Transport is used, a network number is assigned to each network adapter installed in a computer. A network number uniquely identifies the network segment to which the network adapter is connected. (If more than one frame type is assigned to a network adapter, then each frame type is assigned its own network number.) Windows NT can automatically detect and use the network number in use on a network segment. However, you can manually assign any unique eight-digit network number to a network adapter during the configuration of NWLink IPX/SPX Compatible Transport.

An internal network number must be assigned to a Windows NT computer that uses NWLink IPX/SPX Compatible Transport when more than one network adapter is installed in it. (If there is only one network adapter installed in a computer, Windows NT does not require you to assign an internal network number, although you can assign an internal network number if you want.) An internal network number is an additional unique eight-digit network number that is used by the computer's operating system—an internal network number does *not* correspond to a specific network adapter installed in the computer. A Windows NT computer has only one internal network number, regardless of the number of network adapters installed in it.

## Installing and Configuring NWLink IPX/SPX Compatible Transport

Installing and configuring NWLink IPX/SPX Compatible Transport is a fairly straightforward process. You should be prepared to enter the appropriate frame type(s) and network number(s) when prompted. If you have multiple adapters installed in your Windows NT computer, you will also have to assign an internal network number. Finally, only install this protocol at a time when you can shut down and restart the computer.

**TO INSTALL AND CONFIGURE NWLINK IPX/SPX COMPATIBLE TRANSPORT ON A WINDOWS NT COMPUTER, FOLLOW THESE STEPS:**

**1.** Select Start⇒Settings⇒Control Panel.

**2.** In the Control Panel dialog box, double-click Network.

**3.** In the Network dialog box, click the Protocols tab.

**4.** On the Protocols tab, click the Add command button.

**5.** In the Select Network Protocol dialog box, highlight NWLink IPX/SPX Compatible Transport in the Network Protocol list box. Figure 17-1 shows the Select Network Protocol dialog box. Notice NWLink IPX/SPX Compatible Transport is highlighted. Click OK.

**6.** A Windows NT Setup dialog box appears. Ensure that the correct path to your Windows NT Server or Workstation source files (usually the i386 folder on your Windows NT Server or Workstation compact disc) is listed in the text box. Edit the text box as necessary. Click the Continue command button.

**7.** Windows NT installs NWLink IPX/SPX Compatible Transport. The Network dialog box reappears. Click the Close command button.

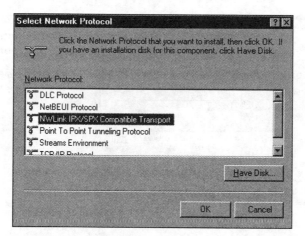

**FIGURE 17-1** Installing NWLink IPX/SPX Compatible Transport

**8.** Windows NT performs various bindings operations.

**9.** If there is more than one network adapter installed in your computer, an NWLink IPX/SPX warning dialog box appears, indicating that you need to configure your computer's internal network number, as shown in Figure 17-2. Click the Yes command button.

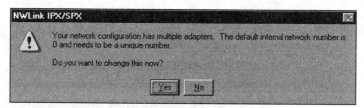

**FIGURE 17-2** Multiple network adapter warning

**10.** The NWLink IPX/SPX Properties dialog box appears, as shown in Figure 17-3. Notice that you can configure the internal network number and the frame type in this dialog box. The configurable options in this dialog box are:

o **Internal Network Number:** Change the Internal Network Number to a unique nonzero hexadecimal number up to eight digits long.

o **Auto Frame Type Detection:** If you want Windows NT to automatically detect and assign a frame type to a network adapter, select the radio button next to Auto Frame Type Detection. Skip to Step 12.

o **Manual Frame Type Detection:** If you want to manually assign a frame type to a network adapter, select the radio button next to Manual Frame Type Detection, and click the Add command button.

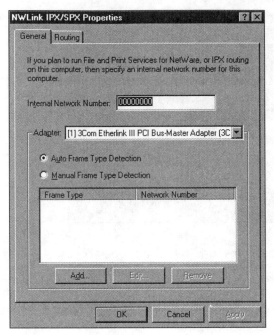

**FIGURE 17-3** Configuring the internal network number

11. If you selected Manual Frame Type Detection, the Manual Frame Detection dialog box appears, as shown in Figure 17-4. Note the Frame Type drop-down list box and the Network Number text box. Select the desired frame type from the Frame Type drop-down list box. Type in a unique nonzero hexadecimal number up to eight digits long in the Network Number text box. Click the Add command button. (Note: All computers on a single subnet should use the same network number.)

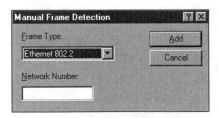

**FIGURE 17-4** Manually assigning a frame type and network number to a network adapter

12. The NWLink IPX/SPX Properties dialog box reappears. If you want to configure a frame type and network number for an additional network adapter(s), select the network adapter from the Adapter drop-down list box, and then follow the instructions in Steps 10 and 11 to configure a frame type and network number for the network adapter.

note ✎ **You can assign multiple frame types and network numbers to an individual network adapter.**

Figure 17-5 shows the NWLink IPX/SPX Properties dialog box after the configuration process is complete. Notice that two frame types and two network numbers are assigned to a single network adapter. Click OK.

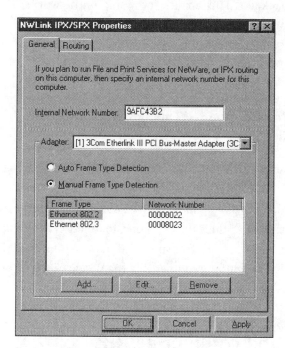

**FIGURE 17-5**   Multiple frame types assigned to a network adapter

**13.** A Network Settings Change dialog box appears, indicating you must shut down and restart the computer in order for the new settings to take effect. Click the Yes command button to restart the computer.

# ROUTING NWLINK IPX/SPX COMPATIBLE TRANSPORT

Windows NT Server computers can be configured to dynamically route NWLink IPX/SPX Compatible Transport. Windows NT can only dynamically route this protocol—there are no static routing configurations available. *Dynamic routing*, as you may recall from Chapter 16, involves the use of intelligent routers that are capable of automatically building and updating their routing tables.

In addition, Windows NT computers that are configured to route NWLink IPX/SPX Compatible Transport can also be configured to forward NetBIOS broadcasts (type 20 packets). This enables browsing on networks that use NWLink IPX/SPX Compatible Transport to cross routers and span multiple subnets. If NWLink IPX/SPX Compatible Transport is *not* configured to forward NetBIOS broadcasts, browsing is limited to a single network segment.

concept link

**To refresh your knowledge of browsing on this protocol, refer to the section "Browsing on NWLink IPX/SPX Compatible Transport" in Chapter 13.**

To implement routing of NWLink IPX/SPX Compatible Transport on a Windows NT Server computer, RIP for NWLink IPX/SPX Compatible Transport must be installed. *RIP for NWLink IPX/SPX Compatible Transport* is the Windows NT Server service that enables the computer to function as a dynamic router for NWLink IPX/SPX Compatible Transport. RIP for NWLink IPX/SPX Compatible Transport can also be configured to enable the Windows NT Server computer to forward NetBIOS broadcasts (type 20 packets).

## Installing and configuring RIP for NWLink IPX/SPX Compatible Transport

Before you install and configure RIP for NWLink IPX/SPX Compatible Transport, NWLink IPX/SPX Compatible Transport should be installed.

When you install and configure RIP for NWLink IPX/SPX Compatible Transport, RIP routing is enabled automatically.

Windows NT Server also installs the SAP Agent (discussed in the next section) automatically when RIP for NWLink IPX/SPX Compatible transport is installed.

Installing and configuring RIP for NWLink IPX/SPX Compatible Transport is not difficult. You should be prepared to choose whether to forward NetBIOS broadcasts when prompted. You will have to shut down and restart the computer at the end of the installation/configuration process.

**TO INSTALL AND CONFIGURE RIP FOR NWLINK IPX/SPX COMPATIBLE TRANSPORT ON A WINDOWS NT SERVER COMPUTER, FOLLOW THESE STEPS:**

**1.** Select Start ⇒ Settings ⇒ Control Panel.

**2.** In the Control Panel dialog box, double-click Network.

**3.** In the Network dialog box, click the Services tab.

**4.** On the Services tab, click the Add command button.

**5.** In the Select Network Service dialog box, highlight RIP for NWLink IPX/SPX Compatible Transport. Figure 17-6 shows the Select Network Service dialog box. Notice that RIP for NWLink IPX/SPX Compatible Transport is highlighted. Click OK.

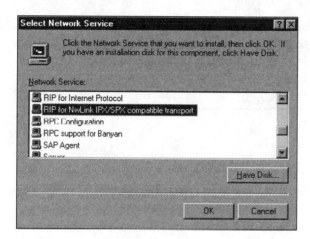

Figure 17-6    Installing RIP for NWLink IPX/SPX Compatible Transport

**6.** A Windows NT Setup dialog box appears. Ensure that the correct path to your Windows NT Server source files (usually the i386 folder on your Windows NT Server compact disc) is listed in the text box. Edit this text box if necessary. Click the Continue command button.

**7.** The RIP for NWLink IPX Configuration dialog box appears, asking if you want to enable NetBIOS Broadcast Propagation, as shown in Figure 17-7. Click the Yes command button if you want to enable forwarding of NetBIOS broadcasts (type 20 packets). Otherwise, click the No command button.

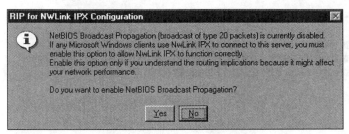

**FIGURE 17-7    Configuring NetBIOS Broadcast Propagation**

**8.** The Network dialog box reappears. RIP routing is automatically enabled by the installation of RIP for NWLink IPX/SPX Compatible Transport. Additionally, the SAP Agent (discussed in the next section) is automatically installed when RIP for NWLink IPX/SPX Compatible transport is installed.

Click the Close command button.

**9.** Windows NT performs various bindings operations.

**10.** A Network Settings Change dialog box appears, indicating that you must shut down and restart the computer in order for the new settings to take effect. Click the Yes command button to restart the computer.

# SAP AGENT

The *Service Advertising Protocol* (SAP) Agent is a Windows NT service that advertises a Windows NT computer's services (such as SQL Server and SNA Server) to NetWare client computers. The SAP Agent requires the use of NWLink IPX/SPX Compatible Transport.

The SAP Agent should be installed when NetWare client computers will access services on a Windows NT computer. The SAP Agent can be installed on both Windows NT Server and Windows NT Workstation computers.

## Installing SAP Agent

If you have already installed RIP for NWLink IPX/SPX Compatible Transport, the SAP Agent is already installed. (Windows NT installs the SAP Agent automatically when RIP for NWLink IPX/SPX Compatible transport is installed.)

NWLink IPX/SPX Compatible Transport should be installed prior to installing the SAP Agent.

If your computer is not functioning as a router but does offer services to NetWare client computers, follow the steps below to install the SAP Agent.

---

**TO INSTALL THE SAP AGENT ON A WINDOWS NT COMPUTER, FOLLOW THESE STEPS:**

**1.** Select Start ⇒ Settings ⇒ Control Panel.

**2.** In the Control Panel dialog box, double-click Network.

**3.** In the Network dialog box, click the Services tab.

**4.** On the Services tab, click the Add command button.

**5.** In the Select Network Service dialog box, highlight SAP Agent.

Figure 17-8 shows the Select Network Service dialog box. Notice that the SAP Agent is highlighted. Click OK.

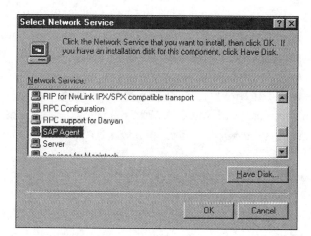

**FIGURE 17-8** **Installing the SAP Agent**

**6.** A Windows NT Setup dialog box appears. Ensure that the correct path to your Windows NT Server or Workstation source files (usually the i386 folder on your Windows NT Server or Workstation compact disc) is listed in the text box. Edit this text box if necessary. Click the Continue command button.

**7.** Windows NT installs the SAP Agent. The Network dialog box reappears. Click the Close command button.

**8.** Windows NT performs various bindings operations.

**9.** A Network Settings Change dialog box appears, indicating that you must shut down and restart the computer in order for the new settings to take effect. Click the Yes command button to restart the computer.

# CLIENT SERVICE FOR NETWARE (CSNW)

*Client Service for NetWare* (CSNW) is a Windows NT Workstation service that, when installed and configured on a Windows NT Workstation computer, enables users to access resources, such as files, folders, and printers, on a NetWare server. CSNW enables access to resources on NetWare 4.*x* servers as well as NetWare 3.*x* servers.

CSNW is included with Windows NT Workstation. CSNW requires the use of NWLink IPX/SPX Compatible Transport.

CSNW makes it possible for users of Windows NT Workstation computers to log in to NetWare 4.*x* *NetWare Directory Services* (NDS), and to browse and access resources in the NDS tree. (NDS is a distributed security database on NetWare 4.*x* servers that enables storage of user names, computer names, and resources in a hierarchical tree structure.) However, you can't manage NDS from a Windows NT Workstation computer running CSNW. To manage NDS, you must run Novell's client software for Windows NT on the Windows NT Workstation computer instead of CSNW.

Additionally, CSNW enables users to run NetWare login scripts during the Windows NT Workstation logon process.

CSNW also supports the use of long filenames on NetWare 3.12 and NetWare 4.1 servers that have the OS/2 name space (OS2.nam) installed, and on NetWare 4.11 servers that have the Long.nam name space installed.

CSNW can be installed on any Windows NT Workstation computer, and should be installed whenever users of the computer want to access resources on NetWare servers.

## Installing Client Service for NetWare

You should install NWLink IPX/SPX Compatible Transport *before* you install CSNW on your Windows NT Workstation computer.

I recommend you only install this service at a time when you can shut down and restart the computer.

---

**TO INSTALL CLIENT SERVICE FOR NETWARE (CSNW) ON A WINDOWS NT WORKSTATION COMPUTER, FOLLOW THESE STEPS:**

**1.** Select Start ⇒ Settings ⇒ Control Panel.

**2.** In the Control Panel dialog box, double-click Network.

**3.** In the Network dialog box, click the Services tab.

**4.** On the Services tab, click the Add command button.

**5.** In the Select Network Service dialog box, highlight Client Service for NetWare. Figure 17-9 shows the Select Network Service dialog box. Note that Client Service for NetWare is highlighted. Click OK.

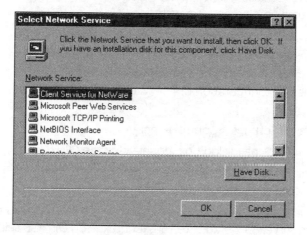

**FIGURE 17-9** Installing Client Service for NetWare

**6.** A Windows NT Setup dialog box appears. Ensure that the correct path to your Windows NT Workstation source files (usually the i386 folder on your Windows NT Workstation compact disc) is listed in the text box. Click the Continue command button.

**7.** Windows NT installs Client Service for NetWare. The Network dialog box reappears. Click the Close command button.

**8.** Windows NT performs various bindings operations.

**9.** A Network Settings Change dialog box appears, indicating that you must shut down and restart the computer in order for the new settings to take effect. Click the Yes command button to restart the computer.

---

# Configuring Client Service for NetWare

You can either configure CSNW the first time you log on after installing CSNW, or you can configure CSNW at a later time by using the CSNW application in Control Panel.

When configuring CSNW, you should be prepared to enter either the name of a preferred NetWare 3.*x* server you want to use or your tree and context for a NetWare 4.*x* server.

**TO CONFIGURE CLIENT SERVER FOR NETWARE (CSNW), FOLLOW THESE STEPS:**

1. The next time you boot your computer after installing CSNW, the Select NetWare Logon dialog box appears. (Note: This dialog box only appears the *first* time you log on after installing CSNW.)

   o If you want to configure CSNW now, skip to Step 4.

   o If you choose to configure CSNW at a later time, click OK in the Select NetWare Logon dialog box. When you decide to initially configure or change the configuration of CSNW, begin the configuration process at Step 2.

2. Select Start ⇒ Settings ⇒ Control Panel.

3. In the Control Panel dialog box, double-click the CSNW icon.

4. The Client Service for NetWare dialog box appears, shown in Figure 17-10. Notice the various configuration options available.

   To configure CSNW, you must select from one of two primary options: Preferred Server, or Default Tree and Context. You can also select print and login script options in this dialog box.

   o **Preferred Server:** Select the radio button next to Preferred Server if you primarily access resources on NetWare 3.*x* servers. Then select the NetWare server of your choice from the Select Preferred Server drop-down list box.

   o **Default Tree and Context:** Select the radio button next to Default Tree and Context if you primarily access resources on NetWare 4.*x* servers. Then enter the tree name and context that contain your NetWare 4.*x* user account in the Tree and Context text boxes. (Note: You have to know this information—browsing is *not* supported in this section.)

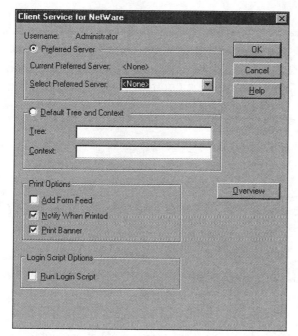

**FIGURE 17-10**  Configuring Client Service for NetWare

o **Print Options:** If you print to a printer on a NetWare server, you can configure the Print Options section of the Client Service for NetWare dialog box. There are three options you can select:

  o **Add Form Feed:** Selecting this check box causes an additional form feed to be sent at the end of each print job. Deselect this check box if an additional blank page is printing at the end of each of your print jobs. By default, this check box is not selected.

  o **Notify When Printed:** Selecting this check box causes a pop-up message to appear on your screen after a print job is sent by the NetWare server to the print device. Clear this check box if you no longer want to receive these messages. This check box is selected by default.

  o **Print Banner:** Selecting this check box causes an additional sheet of paper that identifies the user that initiated the print job (called a *banner page*) to be printed at the beginning of each print job. If you want to save paper, deselect this check box. This check box is selected by default.

o **Login Script Options:** Selecting the check box next to Run Login Script in this section causes the NetWare login script to run during the Windows NT logon process. By default, this check box is not selected.

When you are finished configuring this dialog box, click OK.

**5.** If you are configuring CSNW by using the CSNW application in Control Panel, a Client Service for NetWare dialog box appears, indicating that your configuration changes will take effect the next time you login. Click OK.

**6.** The Control Panel dialog box reappears (if you are configuring CSNW by using the CSNW application in Control Panel). Exit Control Panel.

# GATEWAY SERVICE FOR NETWARE (GSNW)

*Gateway Service for NetWare* (GSNW) is a Windows NT Server service that, when installed and configured on a Windows NT Server computer, provides all of the functionality of Client Service for NetWare (CSNW). Additionally, GSNW enables the Windows NT Server computer to transparently share resources (files, folders, and printers) located on a NetWare server to client computers of the Windows NT Server computer. GSNW accomplishes this by converting the *Server Message Blocks* (SMBs) from the client computers of the Windows NT Server computer into *NetWare Core Protocol* (NCP) requests that are recognized by the NetWare server.

GSNW does *not* enable a Windows NT Server computer to share its resources with NetWare client computers. You should install *File and Print Services for NetWare* (FPNW) if you want to accomplish this. (FPNW is discussed later in this chapter.)

GSNW is included with Windows NT Server. Like CSNW, GSNW requires the use of NWLink IPX/SPX Compatible Transport.

GSNW can be installed on any Windows NT Server computer.

## Installing Gateway Service for NetWare

You should install NWLink IPX/SPX Compatible Transport *before* you install GSNW on your Windows NT Server computer.

I recommend you only install this service at a time when you can shut down and restart the Windows NT Server computer.

**TO INSTALL GATEWAY SERVICE FOR NETWARE (GSNW) ON
A WINDOWS NT SERVER COMPUTER, FOLLOW THESE STEPS:**

**1.** Select Start ⇒ Settings ⇒ Control Panel.

**2.** In the Control Panel dialog box, double-click Network.

**3.** In the Network dialog box, click the Services tab.

**4.** On the Services tab, click the Add command button.

**5.** In the Select Network Service dialog box, highlight Gateway (and Client)
Services For NetWare. Figure 17-11 shows the Select Network Service
dialog box. Note that Gateway (and Client) Services for NetWare is
highlighted. Click OK.

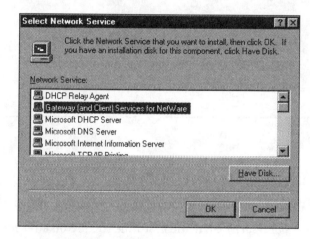

**FIGURE 17-11**   **Installing
Gateway
Service for
NetWare**

**6.** A Windows NT Setup dialog box appears. Ensure that the correct path to
your Windows NT Server source files (usually the 1386 folder on your
Windows NT Server compact disc) is listed in the text box. Click the
Continue command button.

**7.** Windows NT installs Gateway Service for NetWare. The Network dialog box
reappears, as shown in Figure 17-12. Notice that Gateway Service for
NetWare is listed in the Network Services list box. Click the Close
command button.

**8.** Windows NT performs various bindings operations.

**9.** A Network Settings Change dialog box appears, indicating that you must
shut down and restart the computer in order for the new settings to take
effect. Click the Yes command button to restart the computer.

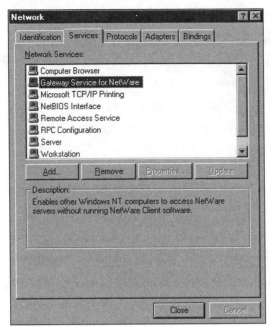

**FIGURE 17-12**  Gateway Service for NetWare installed

# Configuring Gateway Service for NetWare

You can either configure GSNW the first time you log on after installing GSNW, or you can configure GSNW at a later time by using the GSNW application in Control Panel.

When configuring GSNW, you should be prepared to enter either the name of a preferred NetWare 3.*x* server you want to use or your tree and context for a NetWare 4.*x* server.

Pay particular attention to the gateway configuration options, including the user account used to configure the gateway. The user account on the NetWare server *must* be a member of the NTGATEWAY group on the NetWare server, and the NTGATEWAY group *must* have the appropriate NetWare permissions to the share.

The following sections explain the steps necessary to perform some common GSNW configurations. The first section discusses how to configure GSNW, and then how to share a folder on the NetWare server with client computers of the Windows NT Server computer. The second section explains how to share a printer on a NetWare server (with client computers of a Windows NT Server computer) from a Windows NT Server computer that is running GSNW.

---

**TO CONFIGURE GATEWAY SERVICE FOR NETWARE (GSNW) ON A WINDOWS NT SERVER COMPUTER AND SHARE A FOLDER ON THE NETWARE SERVER, FOLLOW THESE STEPS:**

**1.** The next time you boot your computer after installing GSNW, the Select NetWare Logon dialog box appears. (Note: This dialog box only appears the *first* time you log on after installing GSNW.)

   o If you want to configure GSNW now, skip to Step 4.

   o If you choose to configure GSNW at a later time, click OK in the Select NetWare Logon dialog box. When you decide to initially configure or change the configuration of GSNW, begin the configuration process at Step 2.

**2.** Select Start ⇒ Settings ⇒ Control Panel.

**3.** In the Control Panel dialog box, double-click the GSNW icon.

**4.** The Gateway Service for NetWare dialog box appears, as shown in Figure 17-13. Notice the various configuration options available.

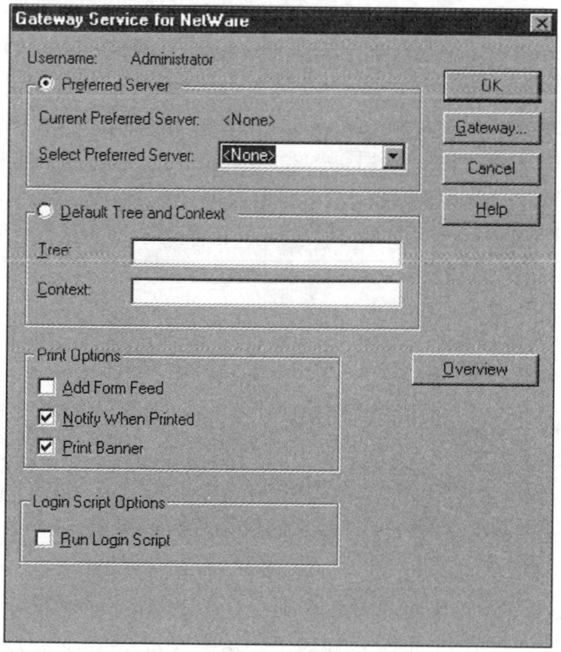

**FIGURE 17-13**    Configuring Gateway Service for NetWare

To configure GSNW, you must select from one of two primary options: Preferred Server, or Default Tree and Context. You can also select print, login script, and gateway options in this dialog box.

- **Preferred Server:** Select the radio button next to Preferred Server if you primarily access resources on NetWare 3.*x* servers. Then select the NetWare server of your choice from the Select Preferred Server drop-down list box.

- **Default Tree and Context:** Select the radio button next to Default Tree and Context if you primarily access resources on NetWare 4.*x* servers. Then enter the tree name and context that contain your NetWare 4.*x* user account in the Tree and Context text boxes. (Note: You have to know this information—browsing is not supported in this section.)

- **Print Options:** If you print to a printer on a NetWare server, you can configure the Print Options section of the Gateway Service for NetWare dialog box. There are three options you can select:

  - **Add Form Feed:** Selecting this check box causes an additional form feed to be sent at the end of each print job. Deselect this check box if an additional blank page is printing at the end of each of your print jobs. By default, this check box is not selected.

  - **Notify When Printed:** Selecting this check box causes a pop-up message to appear on your screen after a print job is sent by the NetWare server to the print device. Clear this check box if you no longer want to receive these messages. This check box is selected by default.

  - **Print Banner:** Selecting this check box causes an additional sheet of paper that identifies the user that initiated the print job (called a banner page) to be printed at the beginning of each print job. If you want to save paper, deselect this check box. This check box is selected by default.

- **Login Script Options:** Selecting the check box next to Run Login Script in this section causes the NetWare login script to run during the Windows NT logon process. By default, this check box is not selected.

- **Gateway:** You can configure the gateway if you want to share resources located on NetWare servers with clients of your Windows NT Server computer. To configure the gateway, proceed to Step 5. If you don't want to configure the gateway at this time, click OK and skip to Step 11.

5. To configure the gateway, click the Gateway command button.

6. The Configure Gateway dialog box appears, as shown in Figure 17-14. Note the check box next to Enable Gateway. You can configure the following items in this dialog box:

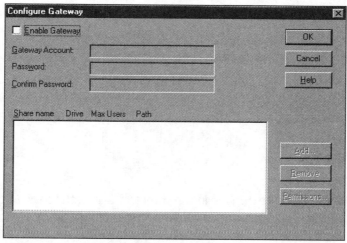

**FIGURE 17-14    Configuring the gateway**

o **Enable Gateway:** Before you can share any resources located on a NetWare server with client computers of your Windows NT Server computer, the check box next to Enable Gateway must be selected. (If you enable the gateway and you login to the NetWare server, GSNW uses two user connections on the NetWare server: one for you, and one for the gateway. When using a five-user client license on the NetWare server, logging in and using the gateway leaves you only three connections.)

o **Gateway Account:** Enter a user account on the NetWare Server that you want to share resources from in the Gateway Account text box. If the user account is on a NetWare 4.*x* server, enter the complete account name, in the format: *.user_name.organizational_unit.organization_name*. This user account *must* be a member of a group on the NetWare server called NTGATEWAY. The gateway won't function correctly if the user account listed in this text box is not a member of this group. Also, the NTGATEWAY group must have the appropriate NetWare permissions to the resources that you want to share by using the gateway.

o **Password and Confirm Password:** Enter the password (and confirm it by retyping it) for the user account on the NetWare Server (that you entered in the Gateway Account text box) in the Password and Confirm Password text boxes. To share a folder from a NetWare server, click the Add command button.

**7.** The New Share dialog box appears, as shown in Figure 17-15. The following options can be configured in this dialog box.

o **Share Name:** Type in the name of the share, as you want it to appear to client computers of the Windows NT Server computer, in the Share Name text box.

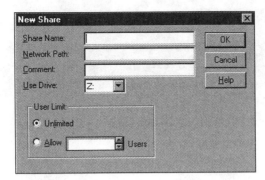

**FIGURE 17-15**  Creating a gateway share

- o **Network Path:** Type in the complete UNC path to the NetWare folder that you are sharing in the Network Path text box. (For more information on UNC paths for NetWare resources, see the section in this chapter on "Using CSNW and GSNW to Access Resources on NetWare Servers.")

- o **Comment:** Type in a comment that will appear in the browse list of the client computers of the Windows NT Server computer. This configuration is optional.

- o **Use Drive:** Select a drive letter that GSNW will use to connect to the NetWare server. This drive letter can't already be in use on this computer.

- o **User Limit:** In the User Limit section, select the radio button next to either Unlimited or Allow *xx* Users. If you select Allow *xx* Users, enter the maximum number of concurrent users that will be allowed to access the share.

   Click OK.

8. The Configure Gateway dialog box reappears. Click the Permissions command button if you want to configure share permissions on the gateway share.

9. The Access Through Share Permissions dialog box appears, as shown in Figure 17-16. Note that this is the standard NT Share Permissions dialog box. Configure the share permissions as desired. (Note: The most restrictive combination of share permissions and NetWare file and folder permissions applies.) Click OK.

10. The Configure Gateway dialog box reappears. Click OK.

11. If you are configuring GSNW by using the GSNW application in Control Panel, a Gateway Service for NetWare dialog box appears, indicating that your configuration changes will take effect the next time you log in. Click OK.

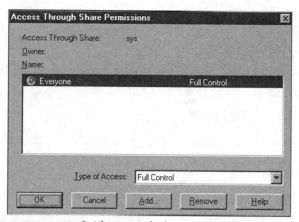

**FIGURE 17-16**    Setting permissions on a gateway share

**12.** The Control Panel dialog box reappears (if you are configuring GSNW by using the GSNW application in Control Panel). Exit Control Panel.

**TO SHARE A PRINTER ON A NETWARE SERVER (WITH CLIENT COMPUTERS OF A WINDOWS NT SERVER COMPUTER) FROM A WINDOWS NT SERVER COMPUTER USING GSNW, FOLLOW THESE STEPS:**

**1.** Enable the gateway, if you haven't already done so, as explained in Steps 5 and 6 in the previous section.

**2.** Select Start ⇒ Settings ⇒ Printers.

**3.** In the Printers dialog box, double-click Add Printer.

**4.** The Add Printer Wizard dialog box appears. Select the radio button next to Network Printer Server. Click the Next command button.

**5.** The Connect to Printer dialog box appears. In the Printer text box, type the UNC path to the NetWare printer. Or, browse the shared network printers in the Shared Printers list box. Click OK.

**6.** A Connect to Printer warning dialog box appears, indicating that you need to install a printer driver. Click OK.

**7.** The Add Printer Wizard dialog box appears. Select the manufacturer and printer model from the list boxes. Click OK.

**8.** The Add Printer Wizard dialog box appears, asking whether you want your Windows-based programs to use this printer as the default printer. Select the appropriate radio button. Click the Next command button.

**9.** Click the Finish command button.

**10.** In the Printers dialog box, highlight the printer you just created. Select File⇒ Properties.

**11.** In the Printer Properties dialog box, click the Sharing tab.

**12.** On the Sharing tab, select the radio button next to Shared. Enter a share name in the Share Name text box. Click OK.

**13.** Close the Printers dialog box.

# Using CSNW and GSNW to Access Resources on NetWare Servers

Resources on NetWare 3.*x* servers and NetWare 4.*x* servers are accessed by using two different types of UNC path names.

To access resources on NetWare 3.*x* servers from Windows NT computers that are running either CSNW or GSNW, you can use standard UNC path names in the format:

`\\server_name\share_name`

For example, to connect to a volume named `SYS` on a NetWare 3.*x* server named `NWSERVER`, use the following UNC path name:

`\\nwserver\sys`

You can use these UNC path names when:

○ Configuring the gateway by using the GSNW application in Control Panel

○ Connecting to a printer by using the Add Printer Wizard

○ Connecting to a shared folder in Windows NT Explorer

To access resources on NetWare 4.*x* servers from Windows NT computers that are running either CSNW or GSNW, you can use UNC path names in the format:

`\\tree_name\volume_name.organizational_unit.organization_` `name\folder_name`

For example, to connect to the `Public` folder in a volume named `NWSERVER_SYS` (on a NetWare 4.*x* server) in the `Sales` organizational unit in the `Widgets` organization in a tree named `CORP`, use the following UNC path name:

`\\corp\nwserver_sys.sales.widgets\public`

You can use these UNC path names when:

- Configuring the gateway by using the GSNW application in Control Panel
- Connecting to a printer by using the Add Printer Wizard
- Connecting to a shared folder in Windows NT Explorer

# FILE AND PRINT SERVICES FOR NETWARE (FPNW)

*File and Print Services for NetWare* (FPNW) is a Windows NT Server service that enables NetWare client computers to transparently access shared files, folders, printers, and applications on a Windows NT Server computer. FPNW is a Windows NT Server add-on product that does *not* ship with Windows NT Server—it must be purchased separately from Microsoft.

No additional software needs to be installed on the NetWare client computers.

FPNW is designed primarily for use during a period of coexistence while migrating from NetWare to Windows NT. FPNW can be used, however, as a long-term solution to allow NetWare client computers to access resources on a Windows NT Server computer. Bear in mind that a Windows NT Server computer running FPNW uses more processor power than a standard Windows NT Server computer, and you may need to compensate for this.

When a NetWare client computer accesses resources on a Windows NT Server computer that has FPNW installed, the NetWare client software treats the Windows NT Server computer, for all intents and purposes, as a NetWare server.

 **note** **A recent release of Novell NetWare client software, called Client32, is unable to access resources on a Windows NT Server computer that runs FPNW. It appears as though Novell has written specific code that prevents its Client32 software from accessing FPNW servers. If you want to implement FPNW, you will have to use NetWare client software that predates Client32.**

concept link   **For more information on FPNW, see the** *Microsoft Windows NT Server 4.0 Resource Kit for Version 4.0* **(Microsoft Press, 1996).**

web links   **Also check out the Microsoft Web site at:**
`www.microsoft.com/ntserver/info/addons4netware.htm`.

# DIRECTORY SERVICES MANAGER FOR NETWARE (DSMN)

*Directory Services Manager for NetWare* (DSMN) is a Windows NT Server service that makes it possible for an administrator to use User Manager for Domains to manage user accounts in the Windows NT domain *and* user accounts on up to thirty-two NetWare 3.12 servers. DSMN also enables users of client computers to use a single user account and password to access resources on both NetWare 3.12 servers and Windows NT computers.

DSMN is a Windows NT Server add-on product that does *not* ship with Windows NT Server—it must be purchased separately from Microsoft.

web links   **For more information on DSMN, check out the Microsoft Web site at:** `www.microsoft.com/ntserver/info/addons4netware.htm`.

# TROUBLESHOOTING COMMON NETWARE CONNECTIVITY PROBLEMS

There are several common NetWare connectivity problems. Most NetWare connectivity problems are caused by incorrectly configuring NWLink IPX/SPX Compatible Transport, CSNW, or GSNW on the computer that is experiencing the problem. Most user-reported problems relate to an inability to connect a Windows NT computer to resources on NetWare servers.

Table 17-2 shows the most common configuration errors that cause NetWare connectivity problems and recommended solutions to these problems.

**TABLE 17-2** COMMON NETWARE CONFIGURATION ERRORS AND RECOMMENDED SOLUTIONS

| CONFIGURATION ERROR | RECOMMENDED SOLUTION |
|---|---|
| Frame type mismatch/network number mismatch | Both the NT client and the NetWare server normally must use the same frame type. Additionally, these computers must use the same network number if they are located on the same network segment. To find out what frame type and network number are being used on the NetWare server, type **config** at the : prompt on the NetWare server. Normally, you can use the NT autodetect feature for frame type selection on an NT computer. However, if you are unable to connect to a resource while using the autodetect feature, try manually configuring the frame type and network number on the NT computer to match those of the NetWare server. Remember, NetWare 3.11 and earlier versions use the Ethernet 802.3 frame type by default on Ethernet networks. NetWare 3.12 and later versions use the Ethernet 802.2 frame type by default on Ethernet networks. |
| Gateway user account is not a member of the NTGATEWAY group on the NetWare server | Make the gateway user account a member of the NTGATEWAY group on the NetWare server. |
| The gateway user account has permissions to access the resource on the NetWare server, but the NTGATEWAY group does not have these permissions | The NTGATEWAY group must have the appropriate permissions to access the shared resource on the NetWare server. Assign permissions to the NTGATEWAY group using the appropriate NetWare administration utility on the NetWare server. Remember that the most restrictive combination of gateway share permissions and NetWare file and folder permissions applies. |
| You have shared a NetWare printer, but have not enabled the gateway | Enable the gateway, even though you are not sharing any files or folders on the NetWare server. |

# KEY POINT SUMMARY

This chapter explored the Windows NT protocols and services that increase the interoperability of Windows NT with NetWare. These components enable Windows NT computers to utilize the resources on NetWare servers, and, in limited circumstances, can also enable Windows NT Server computers to share their resources with NetWare client computers in a heterogeneous networking environment.

o *NWLink IPX/SPX Compatible Transport* is a routable transport protocol that is typically used in a combined Windows NT and NetWare environment, and provides compatibility between Windows NT and NetWare computers. NWLink IPX/SPX Compatible Transport, which is included with NT Server and NT Workstation, must be installed on NT computers in order to enable them to communicate over the network with NetWare computers. NWLink IPX/SPX Compatible Transport can be installed on both Windows NT Server and Windows NT Workstation computers.

o *Frame types* (also called *frame formats*) are accepted, standardized structures for transmitting data packets over a network. A frame type must be configured during the installation and configuration of NWLink IPX/SPX Compatible Transport. It is important that the frame type you select matches the frame type already in use on the network. Frame type mismatching is a common cause of communications problems on networks that use NWLink IPX/SPX Compatible Transport.

o *Network numbers* are 32-bit binary numbers that uniquely identify an NWLink IPX/SPX Compatible Transport network segment for routing purposes. Network numbers are only assigned to Windows NT computers that use NWLink IPX/SPX Compatible Transport, and are assigned during the installation and configuration of this protocol. Network numbers are commonly presented in an eight-digit hexadecimal format.

   o There are two types of network numbers: *network numbers* and *internal network numbers*. A *network number* is assigned to each network adapter installed in the computer. Additionally, an *internal network number* must be assigned to a Windows NT computer when more than one network adapter is installed in it. The internal network number does *not* correspond to a specific network adapter, but rather is used by the computer's operating system. A Windows NT computer has only one internal network number, regardless of the number of network adapters installed in it.

o *RIP for NWLink IPX/SPX Compatible Transport* is a Windows NT Server service, that when installed and configured on a Windows NT Server computer, enables the computer to function as a dynamic router for NWLink IPX/SPX Compatible Transport. RIP for NWLink IPX/SPX Compatible Transport can also be configured to enable a Windows NT Server computer to forward NetBIOS broadcasts (type 20 packets.) When you install and configure RIP for NWLink IPX/SPX Compatible Transport, RIP routing is automatically enabled. Additionally, Windows NT Server automatically installs the SAP Agent when RIP for NWLink IPX/SPX Compatible Transport is installed.

o The *Service Advertising Protocol (SAP) Agent* is a Windows NT service that advertises a Windows NT computer's services (such as SQL Server and SNA Server) to NetWare client computers. The SAP Agent requires the use of NWLink IPX/SPX Compatible Transport. The SAP Agent can be installed on both Windows NT Server and Windows NT Workstation computers.

o *Client Service for NetWare* (CSNW) is a Windows NT Workstation service that allows users to access resources (such as files, folders, and printers) on a NetWare server. CSNW enables access to resources on NetWare 4.*x* servers as well as NetWare 3.*x* servers. CSNW also enables users to run NetWare login scripts during the Windows NT logon process. CSNW is included with Windows NT Workstation, and requires the use of NWLink IPX/SPX Compatible Transport. You can't manage NetWare Directory Services (NDS) from a Windows NT Workstation computer running CSNW. To manage NDS, you must run Novell's client software for Windows NT on the Windows NT Workstation computer *instead* of CSNW.

  o You can configure CSNW the first time you log on after installing CSNW, or you can configure CSNW at a later time by using the CSNW application in Control Panel. When you configure CSNW, you must select from one of two options: *Preferred Server* (if you want to access resources on NetWare 3.*x* servers) or *Default Tree and Context* (if you want to access resources on NetWare 4.*x* servers.) There are also three print options you can configure: Add Form Feed, Notify When Printed, and Print Banner. Finally, you can configure CSNW to run the NetWare login script during the NT logon process.

- *Gateway Service for NetWare* (GSNW) is a Windows NT Server service that provides all of the functionality of CSNW. Additionally, GSNW enables the Windows NT Server computer to transparently share resources (files, folders, and printers) located on a NetWare server to client computers of the Windows NT Server computer. Like CSNW, GSNW requires the use of IPX/SPX Compatible Transport.

    - GSNW does *not* enable, however, a Windows NT Server to share its resources with NetWare client computers. You should install File and Print Services for NetWare (FPNW) if you want to accomplish this.

    - When configuring GSNW, pay particular attention to the gateway configuration options. The user account on the NetWare server *must* be a member of the NTGATEWAY group on the NetWare server, and the NTGATEWAY group *must* have the appropriate NetWare permissions to the gateway share.

- To access resources on NetWare 3.*x* servers from Windows NT computers that are running either CSNW or GSNW, use standard UNC path names in the format: `\\server_name\share_name`.

- To access resources on NetWare 4.*x* servers from Windows NT computers that are running either CSNW or GSNW, use UNC path names in the format: `\\tree_name\volume_name.organizational_unit.organization_name\folder_name`.

- *File and Print Services for NetWare (FPNW)* is a Windows NT Server service that enables NetWare client computers to transparently access shared files, folders, printers, and applications on a Windows NT Server computer. FPNW is an NT Server add-on product—it does not ship with NT Server and must be purchased separately from Microsoft.

- *Directory Services Manager for NetWare* (DSMN) is a Windows NT Server service that makes it possible for an administrator to use User Manager for Domains to manage user accounts in the Windows NT domain *and* user accounts on up to thirty-two NetWare 3.12 servers. This service also enables users of client computers to use a single user account and password to access resources on both NetWare 3.12 servers and Windows NT computers. DSMN is an NT Server add-on product—it does not ship with NT Server and must be purchased separately from Microsoft.

○ Most NetWare connectivity problems are caused by incorrectly configuring NWLink IPX/SPX Compatible Transport, CSNW, or GSNW on the computer that is experiencing the problem. Most user-reported problems relate to an inability to connect to resources on NetWare servers. The most common configuration errors that cause NetWare connectivity problems include: frame type mismatch and/or network number mismatch, the gateway user account is not a member of the NTGATEWAY group, the NTGATEWAY group does not have the necessary permissions to access the resource, and the gateway is not enabled.

# APPLYING WHAT YOU'VE LEARNED

Now it's time to regroup, review, and apply what you've learned in this chapter.

The Instant Assessment questions bring to mind key facts and concepts.

The hands-on lab exercises will really reinforce what you've learned, and give you the opportunity to practice some of the tasks tested by the Microsoft Certified Professional exams.

## Instant Assessment

1. Which routable transport protocol is typically used in a combined Windows NT and NetWare environment because it provides compatibility between Windows NT and NetWare computers?

2. What are frame types?

3. What frame type configuration error is a common cause of NetWare connectivity problems?

4. What is a network number?

5. What are the two types of network numbers?

6. Which Windows NT Server service, when installed and configured on a Windows NT Server computer, enables the computer to function as a dynamic router for NWLink IPX/SPX Compatible Transport?

7. What conversion does GSNW perform to enable client computers of a Windows NT Server computer to access resources on a NetWare server?

8. What does the SAP Agent do?

9. Which Windows NT Workstation service enables users to access resources (such as files, folders, and printers) on NetWare servers?

10. What are two common configuration errors that cause NetWare connectivity problems?

11. Which Windows NT Server add-on product enables an administrator to use User Manager for Domains to manage user accounts in the Windows NT domain *and* user accounts on up to thiry-two NetWare 3.12 servers?

12. What are the three print options you can configure in CSNW?

13. Which Windows NT Server service enables users to access resources (such as files, folders, and printers) on NetWare servers, and also permits resources located on a NetWare server to be transparently shared with client computers of the Windows NT Server computer?

14. Which Windows NT Server add-on product enables NetWare client computers to transparently access shared files, folders, printers, and applications on a Windows NT Server computer?

15. When configuring the gateway using GSNW, of what group on the NetWare server must the gateway user account on the NetWare server be a member?

16. What UNC path name format must you use to access resources on NetWare 3.*x* servers from Windows NT computers that are running either CSNW or GSNW?

17. What UNC path name format must you use to access resources on NetWare 4.*x* servers from Windows NT computers that are running either CSNW or GSNW?

**T/F**

18. GSNW does *not* allow a Windows NT Server computer to share its resources with NetWare client computers.    _____

19. CSNW and GSNW both require the use of NWLink IPX/SPX Compatible Transport.    _____

20. You can manage NDS from a Windows NT Workstation computer running CSNW.    _____

21. RIP for NWLink IPX/SPX Compatible Transport can be configured to forward NetBIOS broadcasts (type 20 packets).    _____

 concept link **For answers to the Instant Assessment questions see Appendix D.**

# Hands-on Lab Exercises

The following hands-on lab exercises provide you with practical opportunities to apply the knowledge you've gained in this chapter about the protocols and services that increase the interoperability of Windows NT with NetWare.

## Lab 17.29 *Installing and configuring NWLink and Client Service for NetWare*

Workstation

The purpose of this lab exercise is to give you hands-on experience in installing and configuring NWLink IPX/SPX Compatible Transport, and also in installing and configuring Client Service for NetWare on a Windows NT Workstation computer.

This lab consists of two parts:

Part 1: Installing NWLink and Client Service for NetWare

Part 2: Configuring Client Service for NetWare and NWLink

Begin this lab by booting your computer to Windows NT Workstation. Log on as Administrator. Place your Windows NT Workstation compact disc in your computer's CD-ROM drive.

Follow these steps carefully.

### Part 1: Installing NWLink and Client Service for NetWare

In this section, you install NWLink IPX/SPX Compatible Transport and Client Service for NetWare on a Windows NT Workstation computer.

1. Select Start ⇒ Settings ⇒ Control Panel.
2. In the Control Panel dialog box, double-click Network.
3. In the Network dialog box, click the Protocols tab.
4. On the Protocols tab, click the Add command button.
5. In the Select Network Protocol dialog box, highlight NWLink IPX/SPX Compatible Transport in the Network Protocol list box. Click OK.
6. A Windows NT Setup dialog box appears. Ensure that the correct path to your Windows NT Workstation source files (usually the i386 folder on your Windows NT Workstation compact disc) is listed in the text box. Edit the text box as necessary. Click the Continue command button.

**7.** Windows NT installs NWLink IPX/SPX Compatible Transport. The Network dialog box reappears. Click the Services tab.

**8.** On the Services tab, click the Add command button.

**9.** In the Select Network Service dialog box, highlight Client Service for NetWare. Click OK.

**10.** A Windows NT Setup dialog box appears. Ensure that the correct path to your Windows NT Workstation source files (usually the i386 folder on your Windows NT Workstation compact disc) is listed in the text box. Click the Continue command button.

**11.** Windows NT installs Client Service for NetWare. The Network dialog box reappears. Click the Close command button.

**12.** Windows NT performs various bindings operations.

**13.** A Network Settings Change dialog box appears, indicating that you must shut down and restart the computer in order for the new settings to take effect. Click the Yes command button to restart the computer. Continue to Part 2.

### Part 2: Configuring Client Service for NetWare and NWLink

In this section you configure Client Service for NetWare and NWLink IPX/SPX Compatible Transport on a Windows NT Workstation computer.

**1.** When the computer restarts, reboot to Windows NT Workstation. Log on as Administrator.

**2.** When the Select NetWare Logon dialog box appears, click OK.

**3.** Select Start⇒Settings⇒Control Panel.

**4.** In the Control Panel dialog box, double-click the CSNW icon.

**5.** The Client Service for NetWare dialog box appears.

- If your computer is connected to a network that has a NetWare server, configure the Select Preferred Server option, or Default Tree and Context option, as appropriate. (Obtain the appropriate configuration settings from your network administrator.) Configure the Print Options and Login Script Options as desired or as instructed by your network administrator.

- If your computer is *not* connected to a network that has a NetWare server, ensure that the radio button next to Preferred Server is selected, and accept the default Select Preferred Server option of <None>.

   Click OK.

**6.** The Control Panel dialog box reappears. Double-click Network.

**7.** In the Network dialog box, click the Protocols tab.

8. On the Protocols tab, double-click NWLink IPX/SPX Compatible Transport.

9. The NWLink IPX/SPX Properties dialog box appears. In the Frame Type drop-down list box, select Ethernet 802.2. In the Network Number text box, type **12345678** (if you are connected to a network that uses IPX, obtain an appropriate network number from your network administrator). Click OK.

10. The Network dialog box reappears. Click the Close command button.

11. A Network Settings Change dialog box appears, indicating that you must shut down and restart the computer in order for the new settings to take effect. Click the Yes command button to restart the computer.

## Lab 17.30 *Installing and configuring NWLink and Gateway Service for NetWare*

Server
Enterprise

The purpose of this lab exercise is to give you hands-on experience in installing and configuring NWLink IPX/SPX Compatible Transport, and also in installing and configuring Gateway Service for NetWare on a Windows NT Server computer.

This lab consists of two parts:

Part 1: Installing NWLink and Gateway Service for NetWare

Part 2: Configuring Gateway Service for NetWare

Begin this lab by booting your computer to Windows NT Server. Log on as Administrator. Place your Windows NT Server compact disc in your computer's CD-ROM drive.

Follow these steps carefully.

### Part 1: Installing NWLink and Gateway Service for NetWare

In this section, you install NWLink IPX/SPX Compatible Transport and Gateway Service for NetWare on a Windows NT Server computer. Additionally, you configure NWLink IPX/SPX Compatible Transport.

1. Select Start ⇒ Settings ⇒ Control Panel.

2. In the Control Panel dialog box, double-click Network.

3. In the Network dialog box, click the Protocols tab.

4. On the Protocols tab, click the Add command button.

5. In the Select Network Protocol dialog box, highlight NWLink IPX/SPX Compatible Transport in the Network Protocol list box. Click OK.

**6.** A Windows NT Setup dialog box appears. Ensure that the correct path to your Windows NT Server source files (usually the i386 folder on your Windows NT Server compact disc) is listed in the text box. Edit the text box as necessary. Click the Continue command button.

**7.** Windows NT installs NWLink IPX/SPX Compatible Transport. The Network dialog box reappears. Click the Services tab.

**8.** On the Services tab, click the Add command button.

**9.** In the Select Network Service dialog box, highlight Gateway (and Client) Services for NetWare. Click OK.

**10.** A Windows NT Setup dialog box appears. Ensure that the correct path to your Windows NT Server source files (usually the i386 folder on your Windows NT Server compact disc) is listed in the text box. Click the Continue command button.

**11.** Windows NT installs Gateway Service for NetWare. The Network dialog box reappears. Click the Close command button.

**12.** Windows NT performs various bindings operations.

**13.** An NWLink IPX/SPX warning dialog box appears, indicating that you need to configure your computer's internal network number. Click the Yes command button.

**14.** The NWLink IPX/SPX Properties dialog box appears. Change the Internal Network Number to **87654321.** Select the radio button next to Manual Frame Type Detection, and click the Add command button.

**15.** In the Manual Frame Detection dialog box, select Ethernet 802.2 from the Frame Type drop-down list box. Type in a Network Number of **12345678** (If you are connected to a network that uses IPX, obtain an appropriate network number from your network administrator.) Click the Add command button.

**16.** In the NWLink IPX/SPX Properties dialog box, click OK.

**17.** A Network Settings Change dialog box appears, indicating that you must shut down and restart the computer in order for the new settings to take effect. Click the Yes command button to restart the computer. Continue to Part 2.

### Part 2: Configuring Gateway Service for NetWare

In this section, you configure Gateway Service for NetWare on a Windows NT Server computer.

**1.** When the computer restarts, reboot to Windows NT Server. Log on as Administrator.

**2.** When the Select NetWare Logon dialog box appears, click OK.

**3.** Select Start ⇒ Settings ⇒ Control Panel.

**4.** In the Control Panel dialog box, double-click the GSNW icon.

**5.** The Gateway Service for NetWare dialog box appears.

- o If your computer is connected to a network that has a NetWare server, configure the Select Preferred Server option, or Default Tree and Context option, as appropriate. (Obtain the appropriate configuration settings from your network administrator.) Configure the Print Options and Login Script Options as desired or as instructed by your network administrator.

- o If your computer is *not* connected to a network that has a NetWare server, ensure that the radio button next to Preferred Server is selected, and accept the default Select Preferred Server option of <None>.

Click the Gateway command button.

**6.** The Configure Gateway dialog box appears. Notice the various options in this dialog box. Click OK.

**7.** The Gateway Service for NetWare dialog box reappears. Click OK.

**8.** The Control Panel dialog box reappears. Exit Control Panel.

**Lab 17.31** *Installing and configuring RIP for NWLink*
*IPX/SPX Compatible Transport*

**MCSE**

**Enterprise**

The purpose of this lab exercise is to give you hands-on experience installing and configuring RIP for NWLink IPX/SPX Compatible Transport.

Begin this lab by booting your computer to Windows NT Server. Log on as Administrator. Place your Windows NT Server compact disc in your computer's CD-ROM drive.

Follow these steps carefully.

**1.** Select Start ⇒ Settings ⇒ Control Panel.

**2.** In the Control Panel dialog box, double-click Network.

**3.** In the Network dialog box, click the Services tab.

**4.** On the Services tab, click the Add command button.

**5.** In the Select Network Service dialog box, highlight RIP for NWLink IPX/SPX Compatible Transport. Click OK.

**6.** A Windows NT Setup dialog box appears. Ensure that the correct path to your Windows NT Server source files (usually the i386 folder on your Windows NT Server compact disc) is listed in the text box. Edit this text box if necessary. Click the Continue command button.

7. The RIP for NWLink IPX Configuration dialog box appears, asking if you want to enable NetBIOS Broadcast Propagation. Click the Yes command button.

8. The Network dialog box reappears. Click the Protocols tab.

9. On the Protocols tab, double-click NWLink IPX/SPX Compatible Transport.

10. The NWLink IPX/SPX Properties dialog box appears. Click the Routing tab.

11. On the Routing tab, notice that the check box next to Enable RIP Routing is selected. Windows NT automatically enables RIP routing when it installs RIP for NWLink IPX/SPX Compatible Transport. Click OK.

12. The Network dialog box reappears. Click the Close command button.

13. Windows NT performs various bindings operations.

14. A Network Settings Change dialog box appears, indicating that you must shut down and restart the computer in order for the new settings to take effect. Click the Yes command button to restart the computer.

caution

If your computer is connected to a network that uses IPX, you should remove RIP for NWLink IPX/SPX Compatible Transport after the computer restarts unless you want your computer to function as a RIP router. If you don't remove RIP for NWLink IPX/SPX Compatible Transport, it will create additional broadcast traffic on your network. (To remove RIP for NWLink IPX/SPX Compatible Transport, use the Services tab in the Network application in Control Panel.) You will have to reboot your computer again after you remove RIP for NWLink IPX/SPX Compatible Transport.

Server
Enterprise

# Migrating to Windows NT from NetWare

# About Chapter 18

**T**his chapter is all about migration. No, we're not talking about flying south for the winter. What we're talking about is converting from Novell NetWare to Microsoft Windows NT, and the process of copying accounts, files, and folders from the NetWare server to the Windows NT Server computer.

Chapter 18 takes you through this migration process from start to finish. It explains how to start the Migration Tool for NetWare; how to select the source NetWare server and destination Windows NT Server computer; and how to configure the way user accounts, group accounts, files, and folders will be migrated. Next, the process of performing one or more trial migrations is outlined. Then the actual migration is performed. Finally, Chapter 18 explains how NetWare client computers must be configured after the migration to enable them to access the Windows NT Server computer.

This chapter is optional if you're preparing for only the Workstation exam, but essential if you're preparing for either the Server or Enterprise exams. This chapter maps to the "Configure Windows NT Server for interoperability with NetWare servers by using various tools . . . including Migration Tool for NetWare" objective for the Server and Enterprise exams.

# MIGRATING TO WINDOWS NT FROM NETWARE

When an organization decides to replace one or more of its Novell NetWare servers with a Windows NT Server computer, a *migration* to Windows NT from NetWare is performed. The migration process involves copying user and group accounts, files, and folders from the NetWare server(s) to the Windows NT Server computer.

Microsoft supplies an administrative tool with Windows NT Server, called the *Migration Tool for NetWare*, that makes migrating to Windows NT from NetWare possible. The Migration Tool for NetWare can be used to migrate user accounts, group accounts, files, and folders from NetWare 2.*x*, 3.*x*, and 4.*x* servers to a Windows NT Server computer. You can choose to migrate only users, only files, only groups, or any combination of the three.

The migration process involves the following steps:

- Starting the Migration Tool for NetWare
- Selecting the source NetWare server and destination Windows NT Server computer
- Configuring how user and group accounts will be migrated
- Configuring how files and folders will be migrated
- Performing one or more trial migrations to test your configurations
- Performing an actual migration
- Configuring NetWare client computers to access the Windows NT Server computer

Each of these steps is discussed in the sections that follow.

# MIGRATION TOOL FOR NETWARE

You don't have to install the Migration Tool for NetWare—it is automatically installed on a Windows NT Server computer during the installation process.

However, before you can use the Migration Tool for NetWare, several prerequisites must be satisfied:

o NWLink IPX/SPX Compatible Transport must be installed and configured on the Windows NT Server computer.

o Gateway Service for NetWare (GSNW) must be installed and configured on the Windows NT Server computer.

o The user who performs the migration must have Administrator privileges on the Windows NT Server computer, and must also have Supervisor privileges on the NetWare server(s).

o An NTFS partition must be configured on the Windows NT Server computer and must be specified as the destination volume if you want to retain file permissions on migrated files.

o If you are migrating from a NetWare 4.*x* server, the NetWare server must be configured for bindery emulation.

When planning a migration from NetWare to Windows NT, it's helpful to know exactly what can and can't be migrated. Table 18-1 lists this information.

**TABLE 18-1** WHAT CAN AND CAN'T BE MIGRATED

| WHAT CAN BE MIGRATED | WHAT CAN'T BE MIGRATED |
| --- | --- |
| User accounts and their properties | User account passwords |
| Group accounts and their properties | Print servers, print queues, and their configurations—all printing must be configured manually on the Windows NT Server computer *after* the migration is complete |
| Files and their permissions | Workgroup managers and user account managers |
| Folders (directories) and their permissions | Application-defined bindery objects |
|  | Login scripts—NetWare login scripts don't run on client computers of Windows NT Server computers |

# Using the Migration Tool for NetWare

Using the Migration Tool for NetWare is fairly straightforward. The following section explains how to start and use this tool.

**TO START THE MIGRATION TOOL FOR NETWARE ON A WINDOWS NT SERVER COMPUTER, AND TO SELECT THE SOURCE AND DESTINATION SERVERS, FOLLOW THESE STEPS:**

**1.** Select Start⇒ Programs⇒ Administrative Tools (Common)⇒ Migration Tool for NetWare.

**2.** The Migration Tool for NetWare dialog box appears with the Select Servers For Migration dialog box on top of it, as shown in Figure 18-1. Notice that you must configure a source and destination server before you can continue.

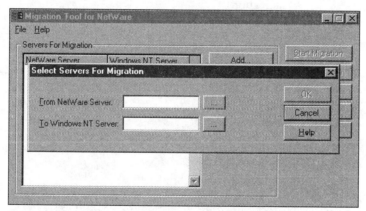

FIGURE 18-1   Starting the Migration Tool for NetWare

Fill in the following text boxes:

○ **From NetWare Server**—Type in the name of the NetWare server to be migrated in the From NetWare Server text box, or click the ... command button to browse for the NetWare server to be migrated.

○ **To Windows NT Server**—Type in the name of the Windows NT Server computer that will be the destination for the user accounts, group accounts, files, and folders that will be migrated in the To Windows NT Server text box. Or, click the ... command button to browse for the destination Windows NT Server computer.

Click OK.

**3.** The Migration Tool for NetWare dialog box appears, as shown in Figure 18-2. Note that the NetWare Server and Windows NT Server list boxes display the source and destination servers.

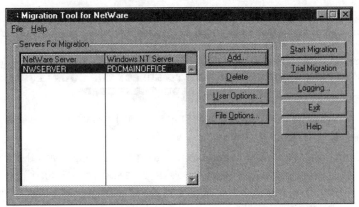

**FIGURE 18-2**    **Source and destination servers configured for migration**

- o  If you want to add additional source and/or destination servers, click the Add command button.

- o  If you want to delete a server pair from the Servers For Migration list box, highlight the pair of servers you want to delete and click the Delete command button.

- o  To configure user and group account migration options, click the User Options command button. (Specific configuration of user options is discussed in the next section.)

- o  To configure file and folder migration options, click the File Options command button. (Specific configuration of file options is discussed in a later section in this chapter.)

The next sections discuss the remaining steps in the migration process, including configuring the Migration Tool for NetWare to migrate user and group accounts, configuring the Migration Tool for NetWare to migrate files and file permissions, and performing a trial migration.

## Migrating user and group accounts

An important consideration is determining how duplicate user and group account names will be treated during the migration. If you are migrating more than one

NetWare server, it is likely that users have accounts on more than one NetWare server. This is because each NetWare server maintains its own user account database, much like a stand-alone Windows NT Server computer.

An efficient way to deal with duplicate user and group account names is to create a mapping file. A *mapping file* specifies every source NetWare user and group account name that is being migrated, and specifies a corresponding user or group account name that will be created on the destination Windows NT Server computer during the migration for each specified NetWare user or group. A mapping file can also specify unique passwords for all user accounts being migrated. The following section explains how to configure user and group account migration options.

## TO CONFIGURE USER AND GROUP ACCOUNT OPTIONS IN MIGRATION TOOL FOR NETWARE, FOLLOW THESE STEPS:

1. After starting Migration Tool for NetWare and configuring the source and destination servers, click the User Options command button in the Migration Tool for NetWare dialog box.

2. The User and Group Options dialog box appears, as shown in Figure 18-3. Notice the check boxes next to Transfer Users and Groups and Use Mappings in File.

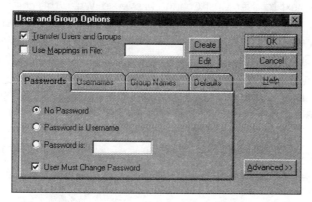

**FIGURE 18-3** Configuring options for migrating users and groups

There are several configurable options in this dialog box:

- **Transfer Users and Groups:** Select the check box next to Transfer Users and Groups if you want to migrate user and group accounts from the NetWare server. Clear this check box if you don't want to migrate user and group accounts. This check box is selected by default.

- **Use Mappings in File:** Select the check box next to Use Mappings in File if you want to use a mapping file to migrate user and group accounts. You don't need to select this check box if you are only migrating one NetWare server and you want to retain the same user and group account names on the NT Server computer that were used on the NetWare server. This check box is not selected by default.

  For more information on creating a mapping file, click the Help command button in the User and Group Options dialog box.

- **Passwords tab:** Because NetWare user passwords can't be migrated, you can choose from one of three password options to be applied to the migrated user accounts:

  - **No Password:** Select the radio button next to No Password if you want user accounts to be migrated without passwords. This option is selected by default.

  - **Password is Username:** Select the radio button next to Password is Username if you want each migrated user account to have a password consisting of the user account name.

  - **Password is:** Select the radio button next to Password is if you want to specify one password that will be assigned to all user accounts that are migrated. If you select this option, type in the password you want to be assigned.

  - **User Must Change Password:** In addition to choosing from the three radio buttons on the Passwords tab, you can select the check box next to User Must Change Password. When this check box is selected, users whose user accounts are migrated will have to change their password the first time they log on to the Windows NT Server computer. This check box is selected by default.

3. To configure user name options, click the Usernames tab in the User and Group Options dialog box. The Usernames tab appears, as shown in Figure 18-4. There are four radio buttons you can choose from to configure how duplicate user account names will be handled:

  - **Log Error:** Selecting this radio button causes an error to be logged to a log file when a duplicate user account is encountered during the migration process. Once a user account is migrated, each additional occurrence of an identical user account name will be logged to a log file but will not be migrated. This radio button is selected by default.

  - **Ignore:** Selecting this radio button causes duplicate user account names to be ignored during the migration process. Once a user account is migrated, each additional occurrence of an identical user account name will be ignored.

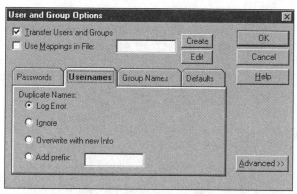

**FIGURE 18-4**  Configuring options for duplicate user account names

○ **Overwrite with new info:** Selecting this radio button causes Windows NT to overwrite existing user account information with the account information from the duplicate user account(s) encountered during migration.

○ **Add prefix:** Selecting this radio button causes a prefix to be added to duplicate user account names encountered during the migration process.

**4.** To configure group name options, click the Group Names tab in the User and Group Options dialog box. The Group Names tab appears, as shown in Figure 18-5. Notice the options available for handling duplicate group names encountered during the migration process.

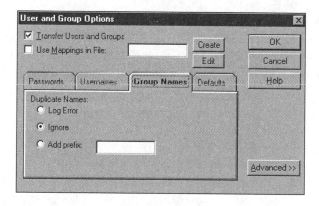

**FIGURE 18-5**  Configuring options for duplicate group account names

You can choose from three duplicate name options: Log Error, Ignore, and Add prefix. These options have the same effect as the identical options on the Usernames tab, except that they are applied to group accounts rather than to user accounts.

**5.** To configure defaults, click the Defaults tab. The Defaults tab appears, as shown in Figure 18-6. Notice the three check boxes on the tab. Select or deselect the defaults options check boxes, as appropriate:

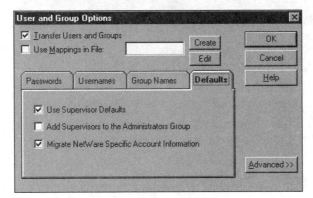

**FIGURE 18-6** Configuring default account migration options

- **Use Supervisor Defaults**—To migrate global NetWare account policy settings, such as password length and expiration, to the Windows NT Server account policy, select the check box next to Use Supervisor Defaults. This check box is selected by default.

caution

If you are *not* migrating to a "clean" Windows NT Server computer that was installed expressly for the purpose of migration, use caution here—selecting this check box can cause your existing Windows NT Server account policy to be overwritten.

- **Add Supervisors to the Administrators Group**— Selecting the check box next to Add Supervisors to the Administrators Group causes the NetWare Supervisor user account, and all NetWare user accounts with Supervisor equivalence, to be added to the Administrators group on the Windows NT Server computer. This check box is *not* selected by default.

- **Migrate NetWare Specific Account Information**— If you select the check box next to Migrate NetWare Specific Account Information, all user account properties, such as group memberships, will be migrated to equivalent properties on the Windows NT Server computer. (Note: Not all NetWare account properties have equivalent properties in Windows NT. Account properties with no equivalents will not be migrated.)

**6.** When you have finished configuring all user and group account options, click OK to return to the Migration Tool for NetWare dialog box.

## *Migrating files and folders*

When migrating files from a NetWare server to a Windows NT Server computer, the files must be migrated to an NTFS partition on the Windows NT Server computer for the file permissions to be retained.

NetWare file and folder permissions are *not* the same as Windows NT file and folder permissions. During migration, each NetWare file and folder permission is translated into its closest equivalent Windows NT permission. For more information on how NetWare file and folder permissions are applied during the migration process, select the Help menu in the Migration Tool for NetWare dialog box.

By default, certain files and folders on the NetWare server are *not* migrated. Hidden files, system files, and the contents of the \SYSTEM, \MAIL, \LOGIN, and \ETC directories are not migrated. You can override these defaults, however, by configuring the file options in the Migration Tool for NetWare. The next section explains how to configure file and folder migration options.

 tip **Because potentially large volumes of data are transferred during a migration, you should consider performing the migration during nonbusiness hours, so that network performance is not impaired.**

---

**TO CONFIGURE FILE MIGRATION OPTIONS IN MIGRATION TOOL FOR NETWARE, FOLLOW THESE STEPS:**

**1.** After starting Migration Tool for NetWare, configuring the source and destination servers, and configuring user options (if desired), click the File Options command button in the Migration Tool for NetWare dialog box.

**2.** The File Options dialog box appears, as shown in Figure 18-7. Note the check box next to Transfer Files.

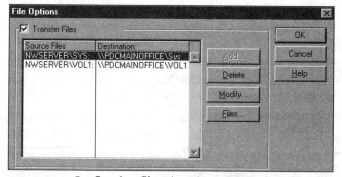

FIGURE 18-7   Configuring file migration options

- If you *don't* want to migrate files, clear the check box next to Transfer Files. This check box is selected by default.
- To modify, delete, or add NetWare volumes on the source NetWare server to be transferred during the migration, select the Modify, Delete, or Add command buttons, as appropriate.
- If you want to select or deselect specific files and/or folders for migration, highlight the source NetWare volume in the Source Files list box, and click the Files command button.
- If you don't want to select or deselect specific files, click OK to return to the Migration Tool for NetWare dialog box. You are finished configuring file migration options.

**3.** The Files To Transfer dialog box appears, as shown in Figure 18-8. Notice the check boxes next to each file and folder.

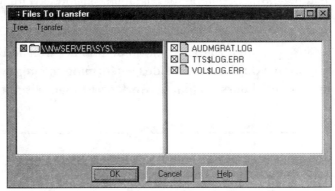

**FIGURE 18-8**    **Selecting individual files and folders for migration**

There are two primary configurable options in this dialog box—Tree and Transfer.

- **Tree options:** To expand your view of subdirectories and files on the volume you have selected, select Tree and then choose the appropriate option from the menu that appears. The Tree options are: Expand One Level, Expand Branch, Expand All, and Collapse Branch.

  Figure 18-9 shows the Files To Transfer dialog box after the Tree ⇒ Expand All option has been selected. Note that the full tree is expanded and displayed on the left side of the dialog box.

  To select or deselect individual files or folders to be migrated, select or deselect the check box next to the file or folder, as appropriate.

- **Transfer options:** To migrate hidden or system files (which are not migrated by default), select Transfer ⇒ Hidden Files or Transfer ⇒ System Files, as appropriate, in the Files To Transfer dialog box.

When you finish configuring the files to transfer, click OK.

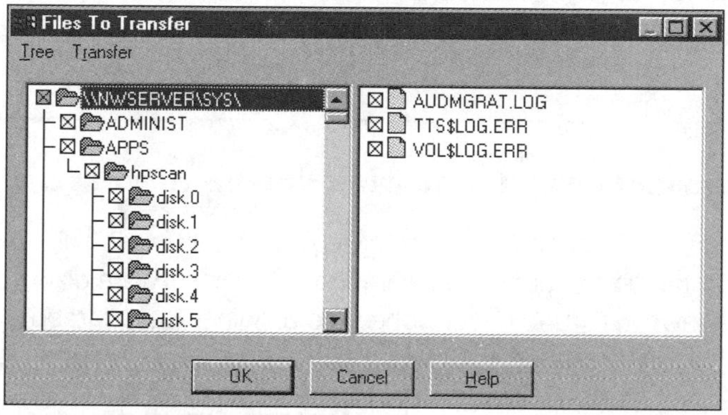

**FIGURE 18-9**  **Expanded tree view**

**4.** The File Options dialog box reappears. Repeat Steps 2 to 3 to configure file options on the remaining volumes as desired. When you finish configuring file options on all volumes selected for migration, click OK to return to the Migration Tool for NetWare dialog box.

This completes the configuration of file options. You can save your completed migration configurations for use at a later time by selecting File ⇒ Save Configuration.

Now you're ready to proceed with a trial migration to test your configurations.

# PERFORMING TRIAL MIGRATIONS AND AN ACTUAL MIGRATION

The Migration Tool for NetWare enables you to perform one or more trial migrations that simulate a migration without actually completing the migration process.

The purpose of performing trial migrations is to test your migration configurations and to resolve any errors that occur *before* the actual migration is performed. The Migration Tool for NetWare can be configured so that errors that occur during a trial (or actual) migration are written to a log file and/or displayed on screen. It is recommended that you perform as many trial migrations as necessary until you are satisfied that no critical errors will occur during the actual migration. The next section discusses the steps involved in performing a trial migration.

**TO PERFORM A TRIAL MIGRATION, FOLLOW THESE STEPS:**

**1.** Start the Migration Tool for NetWare. After configuring all user, group, and file migration options, the Migration Tool for NetWare dialog box appears, as shown in Figure 18-10. Notice the Logging, Trial Migration, and Start Migration command buttons.

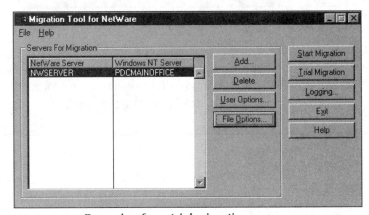

FIGURE 18-10    Preparing for a trial migration

To configure error logging options, click the Logging command button. Figure 18-11 shows the Logging dialog box.

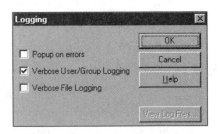

FIGURE 18-11    Configuring logging options

Notice the three logging configuration options available, and select the options you want applied during the trial migration:

○ **Popup on errors:** Selecting this check box causes the migration process to pause and to display a message on the screen when an error occurs during the migration process. This check box is not selected by default.

This option can require extensive amounts of user intervention, and can significantly increase the amount of time involved in a trial migration.

o **Verbose User/Group Logging:** Selecting this check box causes all user and group migration errors to be written to the log file, in addition to recording a complete list of users and groups migrated. This check box is selected by default.

o **Verbose File Logging:** Selecting this check box causes all file and folder migration errors to be written to the log file, in addition to recording a complete list of files migrated. This check box is not selected by default.

When you are finished configuring logging options, click OK.

**2.** In the Migration Tool for NetWare dialog box, click the Trial Migration command button to begin a trial migration.

**3.** A Verifying Information dialog box appears, as shown in Figure 18-12.

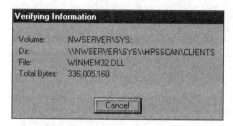

**FIGURE 18-12  Trial migration in process—part 1**

After some time, the Converting dialog box appears, as shown in Figure 18-13.

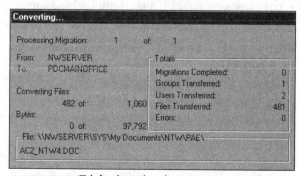

**FIGURE 18-13  Trial migration in process—part 2**

**4.** At the completion of the trial migration, the Transfer Completed dialog box appears, as shown in Figure 18-14. Notice the summary migration statistics presented.

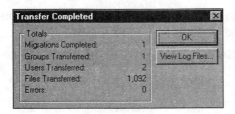

**FIGURE 18-14**  Trial migration
completed

If errors are displayed in the Totals section of the Transfer Completed
dialog box, you can click the View Log Files command button to view the
three logs created during the trial migration: `Error.LOG`, `Summary.LOG`,
and `LogFile.LOG`. When you are finished viewing the log files, close the
LogView dialog box. Click OK in the Transfer Completed dialog box.

5. The trial migration is complete. Resolve any errors that occurred, such as
   duplicate user or group account names, or disk space limitations on the
   destination Windows NT Server computer. Perform additional trial
   migrations as necessary.

 note

**Some migration errors are more serious than others. You might
choose to ignore some errors and clean up the Windows NT Server
after the migration. Sometimes performing a migration in this way
involves less work than eliminating all migration errors.**

**Not all errors are detected by a trial migration. Some errors will be
detected only when the migration utility performs the actual
migration.**

When you are satisfied with the results of a trial migration, you can click the
Start Migration command button in the Migration Tool for NetWare dialog box to
perform an actual migration. The process of performing an actual migration is the
same as performing a trial migration.

If you're not ready to perform an actual migration at this time, select File⇒
Save Configuration to save your current settings for later use in an actual migration.

# CONFIGURING NETWARE CLIENT COMPUTERS TO ACCESS THE WINDOWS NT SERVER COMPUTER AFTER MIGRATION

After the migration is performed, the existing NetWare client computers must be reconfigured to enable them to access the Windows NT Server computer.

If the existing NetWare client computers will no longer access any NetWare servers, their NetWare client software should be removed and a Microsoft redirector (Microsoft client software that enables client computers to access resources on the Windows NT Server computer) should be installed on each of the client computers.

Examples of Microsoft client software include: Network Client v3.0 for MS-DOS and Windows, TCP/IP 32 for Windows for Workgroups 3.11, and LAN Manager v2.2c for OS/2. Microsoft client software is included with Windows for Workgroups, Windows 95, Windows NT Workstation, and Windows NT Server.

If the existing NetWare client computers will continue to access NetWare servers, and will also access the Windows NT Server computer, their NetWare client software should be left intact, and a Microsoft redirector should be installed on each of the client computers.

# KEY POINT SUMMARY

This chapter explored migrating from NetWare to Windows NT. The following points illuminate the major issues:

o When an organization decides to replace one or more of its Novell NetWare servers with a Windows NT Server computer, a *migration* to Windows NT from NetWare is performed. The migration process entails copying user accounts, group accounts, files, and folders from the NetWare server(s) to the Windows NT Server computer. Microsoft supplies an administrative tool with NT Server, called the *Migration Tool for NetWare*, that makes migrating to Windows NT from NetWare possible.

- Migration involves several steps:
  - Starting and configuring the Migration Tool for NetWare
  - Selecting the source NetWare server and destination Windows NT Server computer
  - Configuring how user and group accounts will be migrated
  - Configuring how files and folders will be migrated
  - Performing a trial migration to test your configurations
  - Performing an actual migration
  - Configuring NetWare client computers to access the Windows NT Server computer
- Several prerequisites that must be satisfied *before* a migration can successfully be performed:
  - NWLink IPX/SPX Compatible Transport and Gateway Service for NetWare must be installed and configured on the Windows NT Server computer.
  - The user who performs the migration must have Administrator privileges on the Windows NT Server computer, and must also have Supervisor privileges on the NetWare server(s).
  - An NTFS partition must be configured on the Windows NT Server computer and must be specified as the destination volume if you want to retain file permissions on migrated files.
  - If you are migrating from a NetWare 4.*x* server, the NetWare server must be configured for bindery emulation.
- User and group accounts and their properties, and files and folders and their permissions *can* be migrated. User account passwords; print servers and print queues and their configurations; workgroup managers and user account managers; application-defined bindery objects; and login scripts *cannot* be migrated.
- An important consideration when migrating user and group accounts is determining how duplicate user and group account names will be treated during the migration. An efficient way to handle duplicate user and group account names is to create a mapping file. A *mapping file* specifies every

source NetWare user and group account name that is being migrated, and specifies a corresponding user or group account name that will be created on the destination Windows NT Server computer, during the migration, for each specified NetWare user or group.

o When migrating files from a NetWare server to a Windows NT Server computer, the files must be migrated to an NTFS partition on the Windows NT Server computer for the file permissions to be retained. By default, hidden files, system files, and the contents of the \SYSTEM, \MAIL, \LOGIN, and \ETC directories are *not* migrated. You can override these defaults, however, by configuring the file options in the Migration Tool for NetWare.

o The purpose of performing trial migrations is to test migration configurations and to resolve any errors that occur *before* the actual migration is performed. The Migration Tool for NetWare can be configured so that errors that occur during a trial (or actual) migration are written to a log file and/or displayed on screen. Perform as many trial migrations as necessary until you are satisfied that no critical errors will occur during the actual migration. When you are satisfied with the results of a trial migration, the actual migration can be performed. The process of performing an actual migration is identical to performing a trial migration.

o After the migration is performed, the existing NetWare client computers must be reconfigured to enable them to access the Windows NT Server computer. A Microsoft redirector (Microsoft client software) must be installed on each NetWare client computer to enable it to access resources on the Windows NT Server computer.

# APPLYING WHAT YOU'VE LEARNED

Now it's time to regroup, review, and apply what you've learned in this chapter. The following Instant Assessment questions bring to mind the key facts and concepts presented in Chapter 18.

## Instant Assessment

1. What are the steps involved in performing a migration from NetWare to Windows NT?

2. Which Windows NT protocol and which Windows NT Server service must be installed and configured on the Windows NT Server before a migration is performed?

3. What privileges must the user who performs the migration have?

4. What type of partition must be configured on the Windows NT Server computer and specified as the destination volume if you want to retain file permissions on migrated files?

5. What items can be migrated?

6. What items cannot be migrated?

7. What type of file can you use to efficiently manage duplicate user and group account names during a migration?

8. What should you always do before you perform an actual migration?

9. Which Windows NT Server tool should you use to accomplish a migration from Novell NetWare to Windows NT?

10. How must you reconfigure existing NetWare client computers *after* a migration is performed to enable them to access resources on the Windows NT Server computer?

 concept link **For answers to the Instant Assessment questions see Appendix D.**

Workstation
Server
Enterprise

CHAPTER

# Installing and Configuring
# Remote Access Service (RAS)

# 19

RAS Overview . . . . . . . . . . . . . . . . . . . . . . 707
 RAS Connection Types. . . . . . . . . . . . . . . . . 708
 Connection Protocols Supported by RAS . . . . . . . . . 709
  Serial Line Internet Protocol (SLIP) . . . . . . . . . . . 710
  Point-to-Point Protocol (PPP) . . . . . . . . . . . . . . 710
  Point-to-Point Multilink Protocol. . . . . . . . . . . . . 711
  Point-to-Point Tunneling Protocol (PPTP) . . . . . . . . . 711
 Transport Protocols Supported by RAS . . . . . . . . . . 711
 RAS NetBIOS Gateway. . . . . . . . . . . . . . . . . 712
 RAS Name Resolution . . . . . . . . . . . . . . . . . 713
Installing and Configuring RAS. . . . . . . . . . . . . . 713
 Installing RAS . . . . . . . . . . . . . . . . . . . . . 713
 Configuring Modems and Ports . . . . . . . . . . . . . 714
 Configuring Protocols and Encryption . . . . . . . . . . 716
  Configuring NetBEUI . . . . . . . . . . . . . . . . . . 719
  Configuring TCP/IP . . . . . . . . . . . . . . . . . . . 720
  Configuring IPX (NWLink IPX/SPX Compatible Transport) . . . . . 722
 Completing the RAS Installation. . . . . . . . . . . . . 724
Using Remote Access Admin to
Manage the RAS Server . . . . . . . . . . . . . . . . 725
 Assigning Dialin Permission and
 Configuring Call Back Security. . . . . . . . . . . . . . 726
Configuring Dial-Up Networking Connections . . . . 729
 Configuring and Using Phonebook Entries . . . . . . . . 729
  Configuring basic properties . . . . . . . . . . . . . . 731
  Configuring server properties. . . . . . . . . . . . . . 734
  Configuring script properties . . . . . . . . . . . . . . 736
  Configuring security properties . . . . . . . . . . . . . 737
  Configuring X.25 connection properties . . . . . . . . . 738

# About Chapter 19

The focus of this chapter is on Remote Access Service (RAS), the Windows NT service that enables dial-up network connections between a RAS server and a Dial-Up Networking client computer.

First, the chapter explains the various RAS connection types, and the connection and transport protocols supported by RAS. The RAS NetBIOS gateway and RAS name resolution are also introduced.

Next, the steps to install and configure RAS are outlined. Then the chapter discusses how to use Remote Access Admin to manage a RAS server.

Next, Chapter 19 details how to configure Dial-Up Networking connections. Dial-Up Networking is the client/dial out component of RAS. Configuring Dial-Up Networking to connect to the Internet is also addressed.

Finally, Chapter 19 presents tips on troubleshooting common RAS problems.

This chapter includes a review activity that will give you practice troubleshooting RAS problems. It also includes a hands-on lab, during which you'll install and configure RAS on a Windows NT Server computer, and then install RAS and configure Dial-Up Networking on a Windows NT Workstation computer.

Chapter 19 is a "must read," no matter which of the three Windows NT 4.0 Microsoft Certified Professional exams you're preparing for. This chapter maps to the Dial-Up Networking objective for the Workstation exam, and to the RAS objectives for the Server and Enterprise exams.

# RAS OVERVIEW

*Remote Access Service* (RAS) is a Windows NT service that enables dial-up network connections between a RAS server and a Dial-Up Networking client computer. RAS includes software components for both the RAS server and the Dial-Up Networking client in a single Windows NT service.

exam
preparation
pointer

**RAS is a complex topic. Even Administrators who manage RAS servers on a daily basis are well advised to study the details and nuances presented in this chapter before taking any of the three Windows NT exams. Become familiar with the various dialog boxes and configuration options. I recommend you review this chapter just prior to taking any of the NT exams.**

RAS enables users of remote computers to use the network as though they were directly connected to it. Once the dial-up connection is established, there is no difference in network functionality, except the speed of the link is often much slower than a direct connection to the LAN.

RAS is an important networking function in light of today's highly mobile workforce. With RAS and Dial-Up Networking, users can connect to their company's network from home, from a hotel room, or from a client's remote office.

RAS can be installed on both Windows NT Server and Windows NT Workstation computers. On Windows NT Server computers, RAS can support up to 256 simultaneous dial in connections. On Windows NT Workstation computers, however, RAS only supports a single dial in connection. For this reason, a Windows NT Workstation computer is not typically used as a RAS server.

Client computers that run MS-DOS, Windows 3.1$x$, Windows for Workgroups, Windows 95, and Windows NT can be configured as Dial-Up Networking or RAS client computers. These clients can all connect to a Windows NT RAS server.

RAS supports multiple connection types, connection protocols, and transport protocols. These features are discussed in the following sections.

## RAS Connection Types

Dial-Up Networking client computers can connect to a RAS server by using a variety of connection types, including:

- a standard telephone line (also called a *Public Switched Telephone Network* or PSTN) and modem
- ISDN
- X.25
- Point-to-Point Tunneling Protocol (PPTP)

Probably the most common connection type is a standard analog telephone line (also called *plain old telephone service* or POTS) and modem. This service is inexpensive and widely available.

Many modems are supported by Windows NT. You can determine if your modem is supported by checking the *Windows NT Hardware Compatibility List* (HCL), or by trying to have Windows NT autodetect your modem. Unsupported modems can generally be used by adding an entry for that modem to the Modem.inf file in the

`<Winntroot>\System32\Ras` folder. (Instructions for adding a new entry to this file are contained in the file.)

*Integrated Services Digital Network* (ISDN) is a digital, dial-up telephone service that supports much faster data transmission rates than a standard analog telephone line. The standard ISDN connection is called an ISDN *Basic Rate Interface* (BRI) line. An ISDN BRI line consists of three separate data channels. Two of these channels (called *B channels*) support telephone or data communications at a rate of 64Kbps. The third channel is called a *D channel*, and is used to establish and maintain the connection. If both B channels are used together, data transmission rates of up to 128Kbps can be supported.

ISDN lines must be installed at both the dial-up server and Dial-Up Networking client locations. Additionally, an ISDN adapter card with either an internal or external network terminating unit (NT1) must be installed in the dial-up server and in the Dial-Up Networking client. (The ISDN adapter card takes the place of a modem.) Finally, you may need a *Service Provider Identification* (SPID) number to configure the ISDN adapter cards. If needed, you can obtain the SPID from the telephone company that provides your ISDN service.

*X.25* is a packet-switching protocol that is used on dial-up or leased lines. X.25 is available in most countries. An X.25 connection requires a fair amount of hardware, including an X.25 adapter card, with either a built-in or external *Packet Assembler/Disassembler* (PAD) in the dial-up server and in the Dial-Up Networking client. Additionally, access to an X.25 packet-switched network is required at both the dial-up server and the Dial-Up Networking client locations.

*Point-to-Point Tunneling Protocol* (PPTP) is not a physical connection type. Rather, it is a virtual network connection that is "tunneled" inside of an existing TCP/IP network connection. RAS encryption can be used with PPTP to provide a secure, private connection over a public TCP/IP network, such as the Internet. Because PPTP uses an existing TCP/IP network connection, no additional hardware is required.

# Connection Protocols Supported by RAS

RAS communications can be carried out over several connection protocols. These protocols provide the data-link connectivity for Dial-Up Networking in much the same way as Ethernet, ARCNET, or Token Ring provide the data-link connectivity on a local area network. Each of these protocols has different features and capabilities. The connection protocols commonly used by RAS include: Serial Line Internet Protocol (SLIP), Point-to-Point Protocol (PPP), Point-to-Point Multilink Protocol, and Point-to-Point Tunneling Protocol (PPTP). These protocols are discussed in the following sections.

### Serial Line Internet Protocol (SLIP)

The *Serial Line Internet Protocol* (SLIP) is an older connection protocol, commonly associated with UNIX computers, that only supports one transport protocol—TCP/IP. SLIP connections don't support NWLink IPX/SPX Compatible Transport or NetBEUI.

The version of SLIP supported by Windows NT 4.0 requires a static IP address configuration at the client computer—dynamic IP addressing is not supported. Additionally, password encryption is not supported by this version of SLIP. A script file is usually required to automate the connection process when SLIP is used.

Windows NT RAS can't be used as a SLIP server. Only the Dial-Up Networking portion of RAS (the client side) supports SLIP. This means that only dial out SLIP connections are supported—such as when a Dial-Up Networking client computer dials out to connect to a UNIX SLIP server. (The Dial-Up Networking client computer, in this case, can be either a Windows NT Server or Windows NT Workstation computer that has RAS installed on it.)

### Point-to-Point Protocol (PPP)

*Point-to-Point Protocol* (PPP) is a newer connection protocol that was designed to overcome the limitations of SLIP. PPP is currently the industry standard remote connection protocol, and is recommended for use by Microsoft.

PPP connections support multiple transport protocols, including: TCP/IP, NWLink IPX/SPX Compatible Transport, and NetBEUI. Additionally, PPP supports dynamic server-based IP addressing (such as DHCP).

PPP supports password encryption, and the PPP connection process does not usually require a script file.

PPP is supported over both dial in and dial out connections. Windows NT computers that have RAS installed on them can function either as Dial-Up Networking clients or as RAS servers when using PPP.

### Point-to-Point Multilink Protocol

*Point-to-Point Multilink Protocol* is an extension of PPP. Point-to-Point Multilink Protocol combines the bandwidth from multiple physical connections into a single logical connection. This means that multiple modem, ISDN, or X.25 connections can be bundled together to form a single logical connection with a much higher bandwidth than a single connection can support.

In order to implement Point-to-Point Multilink Protocol, multiple modems and telephone lines (or multiple ISDN adapter cards and lines; or multiple X.25 adapters, PADs, and connections) are required at *both* the RAS server and at the Dial-Up Networking client locations. Additionally, both sides of the connection must be configured to use Point-to-Point Multilink Protocol.

### Point-to-Point Tunneling Protocol (PPTP)

*Point-to-Point Tunneling Protocol* (PPTP) permits a virtual private encrypted connection between two computers over an existing TCP/IP network connection. The existing TCP/IP network connection can be over a LAN or over a Dial-Up Networking TCP/IP connection (including the Internet). All standard transport protocols are supported within the PPTP connection, including NWLink IPX/SPX Compatible Transport, NetBEUI, and TCP/IP.

A primary reason for choosing to use PPTP is that it supports the RAS encryption feature over standard, unencrypted TCP/IP networks, such as the Internet.

## Transport Protocols Supported by RAS

All Windows NT standard transport protocols are supported by RAS. Client computers can connect to a RAS server by using:

- NetBEUI
- TCP/IP
- IPX—Including NWLink IPX/SPX Compatible Transport

The DLC protocol is *not* supported by RAS.

Client computers can use one or more of these transport protocols on a RAS connection. For example, a client computer that needs to access a NetWare server and a UNIX host via a RAS server can use both NWLink IPX/SPX Compatible Transport and TCP/IP during a single RAS session.

A RAS server acts as a router for client computers that use TCP/IP or IPX, enabling these clients to access other computers on the network via the RAS server's routing functionality. Access to NetBIOS-based resources (such as shared folders and printers, Lotus Notes servers, SQL Servers, and SNA Servers) and protocol-specific resources (such as NetWare servers and World Wide Web servers) is possible because of the RAS server's routing capability. The RAS server can only route protocols that are installed on the RAS server. For example, if a client computer has NWLink IPX/SPX Compatible Transport installed, but the RAS server doesn't, the client computer won't be able to access IPX-based resources, such as a NetWare server.

A RAS server acts as a NetBIOS gateway for client computers that use the NetBEUI protocol.

## RAS NetBIOS Gateway

The *RAS NetBIOS gateway* is a function of the RAS server. The RAS NetBIOS gateway enables client computers that use NetBEUI to access shared resources on other servers located on the RAS server's local network. These other servers can use TCP/IP, NWLink IPX/SPX Compatible Transport, or NetBEUI. In a nutshell, the RAS NetBIOS gateway performs protocol translation for the remote NetBEUI client computer so it can access shared resources on the RAS server's local network.

Only NetBIOS-based services (such as shared folders and printers, Lotus Notes servers, SQL Servers, and SNA Servers) can be accessed by NetBEUI client computers via the RAS NetBIOS gateway. Protocol-specific services (such as NetWare servers and World Wide Web servers) can't be accessed by NetBEUI client computers via the RAS NetBIOS gateway.

Even though RAS enables up to 256 simultaneous connections, the NetBIOS gateway has a maximum connection limit of 250 simultaneous connections. This is a NetBIOS limitation, not a RAS limitation.

## RAS Name Resolution

The same methods that are used for NetBIOS name resolution and browsing functionality on a Windows NT network are supported by RAS and are used by Dial-Up Networking client computers that connect to a RAS server. Supported NetBIOS name resolution methods include:

- NetBIOS broadcasts
- WINS servers
- DNS servers
- LMHOSTS files
- HOSTS files

---

# INSTALLING AND CONFIGURING RAS

Before installing RAS, you should install and configure all of the transport protocols you plan to use on the RAS server. Also, you should install and configure at least one connection device, such as a modem, ISDN adapter card, or X.25 adapter card in the Windows NT computer that you plan to install RAS on. Or, you can install the Point-to-Point Tunneling Protocol (PPTP).

 **note** **If you don't install a connection device or PPTP before installing RAS, the RAS installation program will prompt you to do so during installation.**

The following sections explore the various steps involved in installing RAS, including configuring modems, ports, protocols, and encryption.

## Installing RAS

This section explains how to install RAS on a Windows NT computer.

**TO INSTALL RAS ON A WINDOWS NT COMPUTER, FOLLOW THESE STEPS:**

**1.** Select Start ⇒ Settings ⇒ Control Panel.

**2.** In the Control Panel dialog box, double-click Network.

**3.** In the Network dialog box, click the Services tab.

**4.** On the Services tab, click the Add command button.

**5.** In the Select Network Service dialog box, highlight Remote Access Service, as shown in Figure 19-1. Click OK.

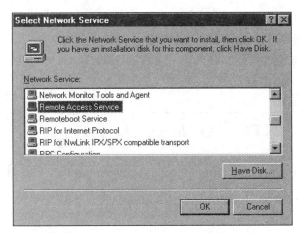

**FIGURE 19-1** Installing RAS

**6.** A Windows NT Setup dialog box appears. Ensure the correct path to your Windows NT Server or Windows NT Workstation source files (usually the `I386` folder on your Windows NT Server or Windows NT Workstation compact disc) is listed in the text box. Edit this text box if necessary. Click the Continue command button.

**7.** Windows NT copies source files.

After copying the RAS source files, Windows NT prompts you to configure modems and ports. These tasks are explained in the following section.

## Configuring Modems and Ports

Configuring modems and ports is an integral part of the RAS installation and configuration process.

## TO CONFIGURE MODEMS AND PORTS, FOLLOW THESE STEPS:

**1.** After Windows NT copies source files, the Add RAS Device dialog box appears, as shown in Figure 19-2. Notice that a Sportster modem is listed in the RAS Capable Devices drop-down list box. Select the modem, ISDN adapter card, X.25 adapter card, or PPTP virtual LAN connection that you installed prior to beginning the RAS installation from the RAS Capable Devices drop-down list box. Click OK.

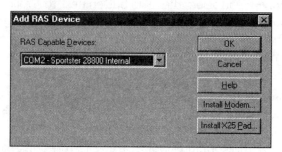

**FIGURE 19-2**   Adding a RAS device/port

**2.** The Remote Access Setup dialog box appears, as shown in Figure 19-3.

To add additional RAS ports, click the Add command button.

To remove a listed port, highlight the port and click the Remove command button.

To configure a port's dial in/dial out properties, highlight the port and click the Configure command button.

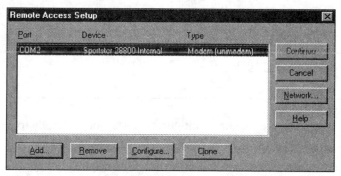

**FIGURE 19-3**   Managing a RAS port

**3.** The Configure Port Usage dialog box appears, as shown in Figure 19-4. Note the three port usage options available.

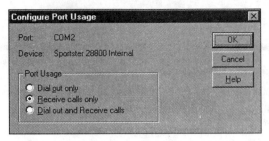

**FIGURE 19-4** Configuring dial in/dial out port settings

Choose one of three options for the port:

- **Dial out only:** If you select the radio button next to "Dial out only," the port will *only* be available for use by the Dial-Up Networking client. Selecting this radio button for *all* ports effectively selects a client-only role for this computer. This computer won't be able to function as a RAS server if this radio button is selected for all ports.

- **Receive calls only:** If you select the radio button next to "Receive calls only," the port will *only* be available for use by the RAS server. Selecting this radio button for *all* ports effectively selects a RAS server-only role for this computer. This computer won't be able to function as a Dial-Up Networking client if this radio button is selected for all ports.

- **Dial out and Receive calls:** If you select the radio button next to "Dial out and Receive calls," the port will be available for use by both the RAS server and the Dial-Up Networking client. This computer will be able to function both as a RAS server and as a Dial-Up Networking client.

  Click OK.

 note    **Each port is configured individually. If one port is configured to dial out only, another can be configured to receive calls only or to dial out and receive calls.**

**4.** The Remote Access Setup dialog box reappears. Add and configure additional ports as desired.

When you are finished configuring ports, you are ready to configure the RAS network settings for both the RAS server and the Dial-Up Networking client. The next section explains how these network settings, including protocols and encryption, are configured.

## Configuring Protocols and Encryption

The next part of the RAS installation/configuration process involves configuring protocols and encryption.

**TO CONFIGURE PROTOCOLS AND ENCRYPTION, FOLLOW THESE STEPS:**

**1.** After configuring RAS ports, the Remote Access Setup dialog box reappears. Click the Network command button.

**2.** The Network Configuration dialog box appears, as shown in Figure 19-5. Notice the Dial out Protocols and Server Settings sections.

*This is the primary RAS configuration dialog box.* In this dialog box, select dial out protocols (if you configured any ports for dial out usage), configure dial in protocols and RAS server settings (if you configured any ports for dial in usage), select RAS encryption features, and enable the RAS server side of Point-to-Point Multilink Protocol connections, if desired.

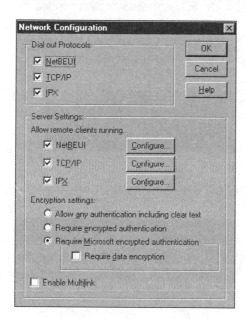

**FIGURE 19-5 Configuring protocols and security**

 note  Configuration options selected in the Network Configuration dialog box are global settings that apply to *all* ports. No individual port protocol or encryption settings are available.

o **Dial out Protocols:** If you configured any ports for dial out usage, you can select any or all of three dial out protocols: NetBEUI, TCP/IP, and/or IPX (NWLink IPX/SPX Compatible Transport). If you *didn't* configure any ports for dial out usage, these options are grayed out and not available. All installed protocols are selected by default.

○ **Server Settings: Allow remote clients running:** If you configured any ports for dial in (RAS server) usage, you can select any or all of three dial in protocols: NetBEUI, TCP/IP, and/or IPX (NWLink IPX/SPX Compatible Transport). If you didn't configure any ports for dial in usage, the Server Settings configuration section is not displayed. All installed protocols are selected by default.

You can configure individual protocol-specific options for each of the three protocols in this section. (Configuring each of these protocols is discussed in detail later in this chapter.)

○ **Server Settings: Encryption settings:** Select one of the three possible password authentication encryption options:

  ○ **Allow any authentication including clear text:** If you select the radio button next to "Allow any authentication including clear text," the RAS server will authenticate user passwords in clear text or in any encryption format supported by the RAS server. Selecting this radio button, in effect, enables the Dial-Up Networking client to determine the level of password encryption.

  ○ **Require encrypted authentication:** If you select the radio button next to "Require encrypted authentication," Dial-Up Networking clients will be required to send encrypted user passwords in any encryption format supported by the RAS server. The RAS server won't authenticate user passwords that are sent in clear text.

  ○ **Require Microsoft encrypted authentication:** If you select the radio button next to "Require Microsoft encrypted authentication," Dial-Up Networking clients must send user passwords that are encrypted using Microsoft encrypted authentication. The RAS server won't authenticate user passwords sent in clear text or in any encryption format other than Microsoft encrypted authentication. This is the most secure password authentication option, and is selected by default. If the "Require Microsoft encrypted authentication" radio button is selected, the "Require data encryption" check box is available.

  ○ **Require data encryption:** If you select this check box, in addition to requiring Microsoft encrypted password authentication, the RAS server requires that all data sent to the RAS server from the Dial-Up Networking client be transmitted in an encrypted format. This check box is not selected by default. Currently, only Windows NT Dial-Up Networking clients support data encryption. If you want to use the RAS server to establish secure, private PPTP connections, ensure that you select the radio button next to "Require Microsoft encrypted authentication" *and* the check box next to "Require data encryption."

- **Server Settings: Enable Multilink:** Selecting the check box next to Enable Multilink enables the RAS server side of Point-to-Point Multilink Protocol connections. Selecting this check box enables the RAS server to support Multilink connections if requested to do so by the Dial-Up Networking client computer. This check box is not selected by default, and is not available on Windows NT Workstation computers. Don't click the OK command button just yet—you still need to configure the dial in protocol(s) you selected. Configuring these three dial in protocols (NetBEUI, TCP/IP, and IPX) is explained in detail in the next three sections.

## Configuring NetBEUI

Once you have selected dial out protocol(s) in the Server Settings section of the Network Configuration dialog box, you are ready to configure the protocols.

If you selected NetBEUI as a dial out protocol, it must be configured.

**TO CONFIGURE NETBEUI, FOLLOW THESE STEPS:**

**1.** Click the Configure command button next to NetBEUI in the Server Settings section of the Network Configuration dialog box.

**2.** The RAS Server NetBEUI Configuration dialog box appears, as shown in Figure 19-6. Notice the two configuration options available.

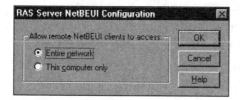

**FIGURE 19-6**   Configuring RAS server NetBEUI options

Choose one of the two possible NetBEUI configuration options:

- **Entire network:** If you select the radio button next to "Entire network," the RAS server's NetBIOS gateway will be enabled, and remote NetBEUI clients will be able to access shared resources on all servers on the RAS server's local network, even servers that use TCP/IP or NWLink IPX/SPX Compatible Transport. This radio button is selected by default.

o **This computer only:** If you select the radio button next to "This computer only," the RAS server's NetBIOS gateway will be disabled, and remote NetBEUI clients will only be able to access shared resources located on the RAS server. This option is sometimes used in high security environments to prevent unauthorized access to other computers on the corporate network.

 **Selections made in this dialog box apply to *all* Dial-Up Networking client computers that access the RAS server using NetBEUI. You either choose to allow all remote NetBEUI client computers to access the entire network, or you choose to allow all remote NetBEUI client computers to access *only* the RAS server.**

**3.** Click OK to return to the Network Configuration dialog box.

## Configuring TCP/IP

If you selected TCP/IP as a dial out protocol, it must be configured.

**TO CONFIGURE TCP/IP, FOLLOW THESE STEPS:**

**1.** Click the Configure command button next to TCP/IP in the Server Settings section of the Network Configuration dialog box.

**2.** The RAS Server TCP/IP Configuration dialog box appears, as shown in Figure 19-7. Notice the options to configure IP address assignment for remote Dial-Up Networking clients.

 **Selections made in this dialog box apply to *all* Dial-Up Networking client computers that access the RAS server using TCP/IP.**

In the Allow remote TCP/IP clients to access section, choose one of the two possible TCP/IP configuration options:

o **Entire network:** If you select the radio button next to "Entire network," the RAS server will function as a router for Dial-Up Networking client computers, and remote TCP/IP clients will be able to access resources on all servers that use TCP/IP on the RAS server's local network. This radio button is selected by default.

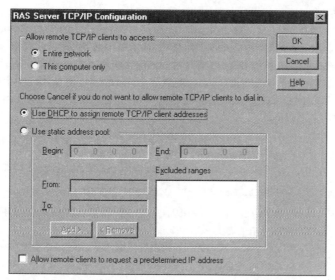

**FIGURE 19-7** Configuring RAS server TCP/IP options

- **This computer only:** If you select the radio button next to "This computer only," the RAS server will not function as a router for Dial-Up Networking client computers, and remote TCP/IP clients will only be able to access resources located on the RAS server. This option is sometimes used in high security environments to prevent unauthorized access to other computers on the corporate network.

**3.** The remainder of this dialog box is concerned with the assignment of IP addresses to remote Dial-Up Networking client computers that use TCP/IP. Choose one of the two primary IP address assignment options:

- **Use DHCP to assign remote TCP/IP client addresses:** If you select the radio button next to "Use DHCP to assign remote TCP/IP client addresses," the RAS server will request an IP address for the remote TCP/IP client from the DHCP server on its local network when the remote TCP/IP client connects to the RAS server. This option should be selected if a DHCP server is available. This radio button is selected by default.

- **Use static address pool:** If you select the radio button next to "Use static address pool," the RAS server will assign an IP address to the remote TCP/IP client from the range of IP addresses specified in the Begin and End text boxes.

Even though "Use DHCP to assign remote TCP/IP client addresses" is the default option, I recommend that you use a specific address pool for RAS IP address assignments. When you use DHCP, the IP address is assigned to a specific client for the length of the lease, whereas if you use an IP address pool, the IP address is only assigned to the client during the connection time period.

If you want to exclude specific IP addresses from the range, type the IP address (or range of IP addresses) you want to exclude in the From and To text boxes, and then click the Add command button. The excluded IP addresses will appear in the Excluded Ranges list box.

**4.** Select the "Allow remote clients to request a predetermined IP address" check box when remote TCP/IP clients have been configured so that their Dial-Up Networking software requests a specific IP address from the RAS server. This option is not selected by default, and is not commonly used.

**5.** Click OK to return to the Network Configuration dialog box.

## *Configuring IPX (NWLink IPX/SPX Compatible Transport)*

If you selected IPX (NWLink IPX/SPX Compatible Transport) as a dial out protocol, it must be configured.

### TO CONFIGURE IPX, FOLLOW THESE STEPS:

**1.** Click the Configure command button next to IPX in the Server Settings section of the Network Configuration dialog box.

 References to IPX in the various RAS configuration dialog boxes include NWLink IPX/SPX Compatible Transport and other versions of IPX.

**2.** The RAS Server IPX Configuration dialog box appears, as shown in Figure 19-8. Notice the network number configuration options.

 Selections made in this dialog box apply to *all* Dial-Up Networking client computers that access the RAS server by using IPX.

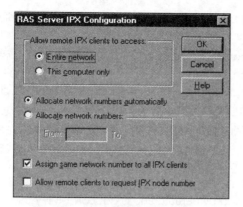

**FIGURE 19-8**   Configuring RAS server IPX options

In the "Allow remote IPX clients to access" section, choose one of the two possible configuration options:

- **Entire network:** If you select the radio button next to "Entire network," the RAS server will function as a router for Dial-Up Networking client computers, and remote IPX clients will be able to access resources on all servers that use IPX on the RAS server's local network. This radio button is selected by default.

- **This computer only:** If you select the radio button next to "This computer only," the RAS server will not function as a router for Dial-Up Networking client computers, and remote IPX clients will only be able to access resources located on the RAS server. This option is sometimes used in high security environments to prevent unauthorized access to other computers on the corporate network.

3. The remainder of this dialog box concerns the assignment of network numbers and node numbers to remote IPX client computers. Select one of the two primary network number assignment options:

- **Allocate network numbers automatically:** If you select the radio button next to "Allocate network numbers automatically," the RAS server assigns a network number that is not currently in use to a remote IPX client computer when it connects to the RAS server. This radio button is selected by default.

- **Allocate network numbers:** If you select the radio button next to "Allocate network numbers," the RAS server assigns a network number from the specified range of numbers listed in the From and To text boxes to a remote IPX client computer when it connects to the RAS server. You must specify a range of network numbers in the From and To text boxes if you select this radio button.

Two additional check boxes are available in this section, regardless of the network number allocation method you selected above:

o **Assign same network number to all IPX clients:** If you select the check box next to "Assign same network number to all IPX clients," the RAS server assigns the same network number to all remote IPX client computers. This check box is selected by default.

o **Allow remote clients to request IPX node number:** Select the check box next to "Allow remote clients to request IPX node number" when remote IPX clients have been configured so that their Dial-Up Networking software requests a specific IPX node number from the RAS server. This option is not selected by default, and is not commonly used.

4. Click OK to return to the Network Configuration dialog box.

## Completing the RAS Installation

Once you have completed all configurations in the Network Configuration dialog box, you are ready to complete the RAS installation.

**TO COMPLETE THE RAS INSTALLATION, FOLLOW THESE STEPS:**

1. In the Network Configuration dialog box, click OK.

2. The Remote Access Setup dialog box reappears. Click the Continue command button.

3. Windows NT installs RAS. If you selected the IPX dial in protocol, the RIP for NWLink IPX Configuration dialog box appears, as shown in Figure 19-9.

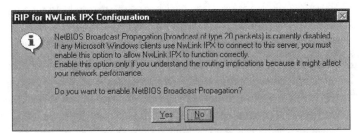

**FIGURE 19-9**   **Configuring NetBIOS Broadcast Propagation**

o Select the Yes command button if remote IPX clients will be accessing shared NetBIOS resources on servers (that use IPX) on the RAS server's local network. Selecting the Yes command button causes RAS to automatically forward NetBIOS broadcasts from IPX clients.

o Select the No command button if remote IPX clients will only be accessing resources on the RAS server, and/or will only be accessing resources on NetWare servers on the RAS server's local network. Selecting the No command prevents the RAS server from automatically forwarding NetBIOS broadcasts from IPX clients.

4. A Setup Message is displayed, indicating that RAS has been successfully installed. Click OK.

5. The Network dialog box reappears. Click the Close command button.

6. Windows NT performs various bindings operations.

7. A Network Settings Change dialog box appears, indicating that you must shut down and restart the computer in order for the new settings to take effect. Click the Yes command button to restart the computer.

---

# USING REMOTE ACCESS ADMIN TO MANAGE THE RAS SERVER

*Remote Access Admin* is a Windows NT administrative tool that is primarily used to start and stop the Remote Access Service (RAS), to assign the dialin permission to users, and to configure a call back security level for each user. Remote Access Admin can also be used to view COM port status and statistics, to disconnect users from individual ports, and to remotely manage RAS on other Windows NT computers.

Remote Access Admin is available on all Windows NT computers that have RAS installed, and is also available on Windows NT Workstation computers that have Windows NT Server Tools installed.

To access Remote Access Admin, select Start ⇒ Programs ⇒ Administrative Tools (Common) ⇒ Remote Access Admin.

When you start Remote Access Admin, the Remote Access Admin dialog box appears, as shown in Figure 19-10. Notice the RAS server condition and other information displayed.

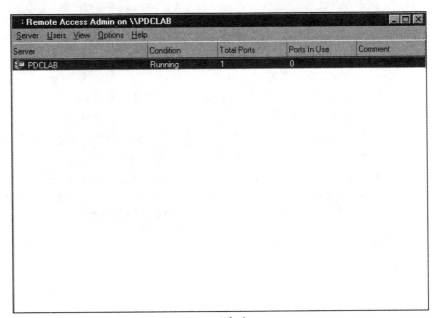

**FIGURE 19-10    Starting Remote Access Admin**

To start, stop, or pause RAS on a server, highlight the server in the Server list box and select the appropriate option from the Server menu, as shown in Figure 19-11.

In addition to starting, stopping, or pausing RAS, Remote Access Admin is also used to manage the assignment of the dialin permission and to configure call back security. These tasks are discussed in the next section.

## Assigning Dialin Permission and Configuring Call Back Security

Before remote users can dial in and connect to a RAS server, they must be assigned the dialin permission. Until this permission is assigned to at least one user account, RAS connections and RAS functionality can't be established.

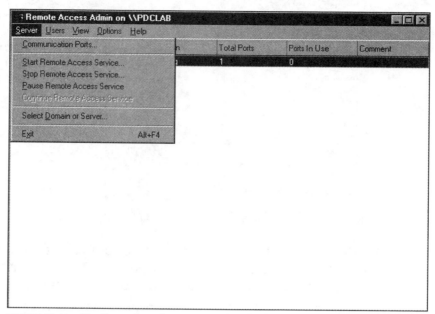

**FIGURE 19-11**   Starting, stopping, or pausing RAS

## TO ASSIGN THE DIALIN PERMISSION TO USERS AND TO CONFIGURE CALL BACK SECURITY, FOLLOW THESE STEPS:

**1.** Select Start ⇒ Programs ⇒ Administrative Tools (Common) ⇒ Remote Access Admin to start Remote Access Admin. In the Remote Access Admin dialog box, select Users ⇒ Permissions.

**2.** The Remote Access Permissions dialog box appears, as shown in Figure 19-12. Notice the Grant All command button.

- o To assign the dialin permission to *all* users, click the Grant All command button.

- o To remove the dialin permission from *all* users, click the Revoke All command button.

- o To assign the dialin permission to an *individual* user account, highlight the user account in the Users list box, then select the check box next to Grant dialin permission to user.

note   **The dialin permission and call back security can also be configured by selecting the Dialin command button in the User Properties dialog box in User Manager or User Manager for Domains. (See Chapter 7 to refresh yourself on how to use User Manager to manage the dialin permission for user accounts.)**

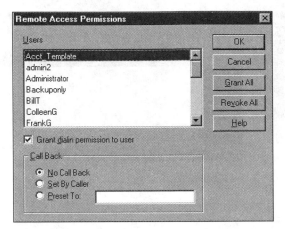

**FIGURE 19-12** Assigning the dialin permission and configuring call back security

3. **Call back security** is configured on an individual user basis in the Remote Access Permissions dialog box. To configure call back security, highlight the user account, then select one of the following three options:

   o **No Call Back:** If you select the radio button next to No Call Back, the user can dial in to the RAS server, but the user can't request that the RAS server break the connection and call the user back. Selecting this option ensures that the user dialing in—not the server—is billed for any long-distance telephone charges. Selecting this option provides no security other than user account and password authentication. This radio button is selected by default.

   o **Set By Caller:** If you select the radio button next to Set By Caller, the RAS server prompts the remote user for a telephone number to dial back. The RAS server then breaks the connection and dials the user back at the number specified by the remote user. This setting is typically used when remote employees must make a long-distance call to connect to the RAS server. Selecting this radio button enables the company, rather than the remote employee, to incur the bulk of the long-distance telephone charges. There is no real security (other than user account and password authentication) provided when this option is selected, because the RAS server will dial back to *any* telephone number specified by a user, whether authorized or unauthorized.

   o **Preset To:** If you select the radio button next to Preset To, you must also specify a telephone number that the RAS server will always use to call back whenever this remote user dials in.  This configuration provides the highest amount of call back security, because only a predetermined telephone number (such as an employee's home telephone number) will be used by the RAS server. Unauthorized remote users calling from a different location, even if they can provide a valid user name and password, won't be able to maintain a connection, because the RAS server will break the connection and call back only the prespecified number.

**4.** When you have finished configuring call back security, click OK to return to the Remote Access Admin dialog box.

**5.** Exit Remote Access Admin.

# CONFIGURING DIAL–UP NETWORKING CONNECTIONS

*Dial-Up Networking* is the client/dial out component of RAS. The Dial-Up Networking accessory is installed during the RAS installation. Dial-Up Networking enables Windows NT computers to connect to dial-up servers, and to establish network connections through those servers. Dial-up servers include: Windows NT RAS servers; UNIX computers that are configured as SLIP or PPP servers; and any other computers, routers, or front-end processors that are configured as SLIP or PPP servers.

Before the Dial-Up Networking functionality on a Windows NT computer can be used, RAS must be installed and configured, and at least one of the computer's RAS ports must be configured for dial out usage. Additionally, you must create at least one phonebook entry that contains various dialing information and instructions. Phonebook entries are created by using the Windows NT Dial-Up Networking accessory, and are explained in detail in the next section.

## Configuring and Using Phonebook Entries

Phonebook entries contain all of the information and instructions required by Dial-Up Networking to connect to a dial-up server. You can select, create, or edit a phonebook entry by using the Dial-Up Networking accessory.

To access the Dial-Up Networking accessory, select Start → Programs → Accessories → Dial-Up Networking. Figure 19-13 shows the Dial-Up Networking dialog box.

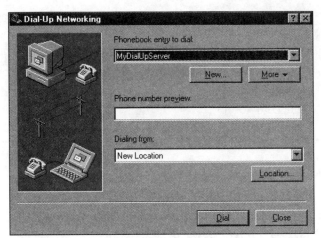

**FIGURE 19-13**    The Dial-Up Networking accessory main dialog box

To use an existing phonebook entry to connect to a dial-up server, select the phonebook entry you want to use from the "Phonebook entry to dial" drop-down list box. Then select your current location from the "Dialing from" drop-down list box. Then click the Dial command button.

To create a new phonebook entry, click the New command button in the Dial-Up Networking dialog box. The New Phonebook Entry dialog box appears, as shown in Figure 19-14. Notice the five configuration tabs in this dialog box: Basic, Server, Script, Security, and X.25.

*tip*  **To configure the Telephony settings for the location you are dialing from, use the Telephony application in Control Panel; or, click the Location command button in the Dial-Up Networking dialog box. (Telephony settings include your area code, country, number used to access an outside line, and calling card settings for each location that you configure.)**

**The Telephony application is decidedly more user friendly than the Location Settings dialog box in Dial-Up Networking.**

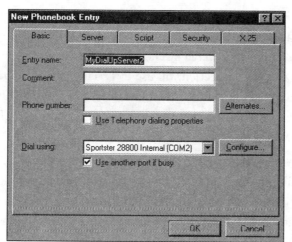

**FIGURE 19-14**  Creating a new phonebook entry

 **note** The first time the you start Dial-Up Networking, a dialog box appears stating that the phonebook is empty.

To complete the new phonebook entry, select the appropriate configuration options on the various tabs in the New Phonebook Entry dialog box. Each of the five configuration tabs are discussed in detail in the following sections.

**note** If you are editing an existing phonebook entry (rather than creating a new phonebook entry) the five configuration tabs — Basic, Server, Script, Security, and X.25 — are the same. The only difference is that the dialog box is titled Edit Phonebook Entry instead of New Phonebook Entry.

## Configuring basic properties

The Basic tab in the New Phonebook Entry dialog box is used to configure the phonebook entry name, the phone number to be used, and the modem/port to be used to establish the connection to the dial-up server. The Basic tab contains several configurable options:

o **Entry name:** Type in a name that describes the connection in the "Entry name" text box. The default name is MyDialUpServer. Entry name is a mandatory setting.

o **Comment:** You can enter a comment about the phonebook entry in the Comment text box if you want to. This entry is optional.

o **Phone number:** Type in the phone number to be dialed to access the dial-up server in the "Phone number" text box. Alternate phone numbers for the dial-up server can be entered by clicking the Alternates command button. If this dial-up connection will use PPTP, enter the IP address of the RAS server in the "Phone number" text box instead of a phone number. (Remember, PPTP tunnels its connection *inside* of an existing TCP/IP network connection.)

o **Use Telephony dialing properties:** If you select the check box next to "Use Telephony dialing properties", Dial-Up Networking will use your location telephony settings (area code, number to dial to get an outside line, and so on) when dialing the phone number entered in the "Phone number" text box to establish a connection. If you don't select this check box, the location telephony settings won't be used—only the phone number listed in the "Phone number" text box will be used. This check box is not selected by default.

o **Dial using:** Select the modem, other connection device, or PPTP RAS port you want to use for this connection from the "Dial using" drop-down list box. After you highlight your selection, click the Configure command button to configure the modem, device, or port. Modems can also be configured by using the Modems application in Control Panel.

o **Use another port if busy:** Select the check box next to "Use another port if busy" if you want Dial-Up Networking to use a different port to establish a connection if the primary port you selected is busy.

### Configuring a Multilink connection

When you need more throughput than a single line can provide, you might consider using multiple lines to establish a Point-to-Point Multilink Protocol connection.

**TO CONFIGURE A POINT-TO-POINT MULTILINK PROTOCOL CONNECTION, FOLLOW THESE STEPS:**

**1.** Select the Multiple Lines option from the "Dial using" drop-down list box, as shown in Figure 19-15. Notice that the "Phone number" text box is grayed out when the Multiple Lines option is selected.

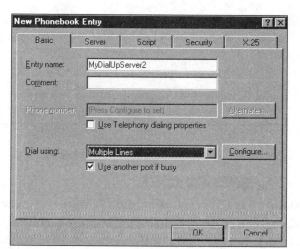

**FIGURE 19-15**   Configuring a Multilink connection

**2.** To configure the phone numbers to be dialed to establish the Multilink connection, click the Configure command button. The Multiple Line Configuration dialog box appears, as shown in Figure 19-16. Notice the text in the dialog box that indicates that multiple lines simultaneously connected to a PPP Multilink server behave like a single, faster connection.

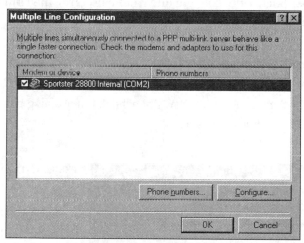

**FIGURE 19-16**   Selecting the modems, devices, or ports to be used in a Multilink connection

**3.** Select two or more modems, devices, or ports from those listed, and individually configure a phone number for each by highlighting the modem, device, or port and clicking the Phone numbers command button. Click OK when you are finished to return to the Basic tab in the New Phonebook Entry dialog box.

note    **To establish a Multilink connection, both the Dial-Up Networking client and the RAS server must be configured to support Multilink. Both Windows NT Workstation and Windows NT Server Dial-Up Networking can support dial out Multilink connections. Only Windows NT Server (with RAS installed) can support dial in Multilink connections.**

caution    **Call back security should normally *not* be configured on RAS servers that support Multilink connections. The reason for this is that only one phone number can be stored in the call back configuration, and if the RAS server breaks the connection and calls this number back, only a single line will be used for the connection. This effectively eliminates any Multilink functionality.**

### Configuring server properties

To configure server properties, including dial-up server type and network protocols, click the Server tab in the New Phonebook Entry dialog box. The Server tab appears, as shown in Figure 19-17.

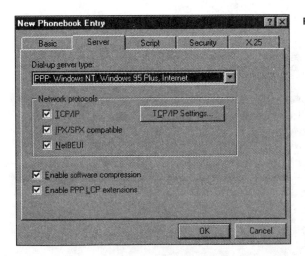

**FIGURE 19-17**  Configuring dial-up server type and network protocols

Select from the many options presented on the Server tab:

o **Dial-up server type:** Select the type of dial-up server you want to connect to from the "Dial-up server type" drop-down list box.

o **Network protocols:** Select the transport protocols that you want to use for this dial-up connection. Protocols available include TCP/IP, (NWLink) IPX/SPX Compatible (Transport), and NetBEUI. You can select more than one protocol. All installed protocols are selected by default.

o **TCP/IP Settings:** If you select TCP/IP, click the TCP/IP Settings command button to configure TCP/IP settings for this connection. The PPP TCP/IP Settings dialog box appears, as shown in Figure 19-18. Notice that you can either accept a server assigned IP address, or specify an IP address.

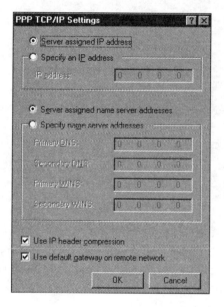

**FIGURE 19-18**    **Configuring TCP/IP address assignment options**

o **Enable software compression:** Select the check box next to "Enable software compression" if you want the Dial-Up Networking software to compress all data before it is transmitted to the RAS server. You should disable modem compression if you select this option. This check box is selected by default.

o **Enable PPP LCP extensions:** Select the check box next to "Enable PPP LCP extensions" if you want to enable the newer PPP features. Deselect this check box only if you are unable to connect with it selected. This check box is selected by default.

### Configuring script properties

To configure script properties, click the Script tab in the New Phonebook Entry dialog box. The Script tab appears, as shown in Figure 19-19. Notice that only "After dialing" script options are shown. To configure script options that will be used prior to dialing, click the Before dialing command button.

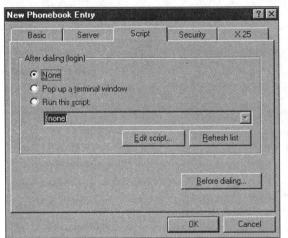

**FIGURE 19-19**  Configuring Dial–Up Networking scripts

Scripts are often used to connect to dial-up servers that require interactive logon sequences, and/or have special menu options that must be selected during the connection process. Scripts are typically associated with SLIP servers, or with servers that support both SLIP and PPP.

By default, this tab is configured so that Dial-Up Networking will *not* use a script. Unless you are connecting to a dial-up server that requires the use of a script, you do not need to configure this tab.

To configure script properties, select one of the three script options:

o **None:** If you select the radio button next to None, no script or pop-up terminal will be used. This option is selected by default.

o **Pop up a terminal window:** Select the radio button next to "Pop up a terminal window" if you don't want to create or use a script, but you still need to make interactive selections during the logon process. Experienced users often select this option to determine which settings need to be placed in a script file.

o **Run this script:** Select the radio button next to "Run this script" to automate the connection process to a dial-up server that requires the use of a script. If you select this option, either select a script from the drop-down list box or click the Edit script command button to create a new script file. When you click the Edit script command button, a copy of the Switch.inf file is displayed by the Notepad text editor. The Switch.inf file includes instructions for creating new script files.

## Configuring security properties

To configure security, including password authentication and encryption options, click the Security tab in the New Phonebook Entry dialog box. The Security tab appears, as shown in Figure 19-20. Notice that the authentication and encryption options are similar to the Server Settings that are configured for dial in connections during the installation of RAS.

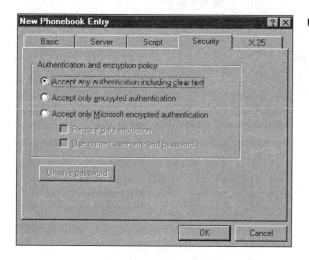

**FIGURE 19-20** Configuring password authentication and encryption options

Options selected in this dialog box will be applied to the Dial-Up Networking client only, not to the RAS server.

Select one of the three authentication and encryption policy options:

o **Accept any authentication including clear text:** If you select the radio button next to "Accept any authentication including clear text", Dial-Up Networking will connect to a dial-up server using the lowest password authentication option accepted by the server. For example, if the dial-up server is configured to enable any authentication including clear text, and this option is selected, Dial-Up Networking transmits the password to the dial-up server by using clear text. This option is selected by default.

o **Accept only encrypted authentication:** If you select the radio button next to "Accept only encrypted authentication", Dial-Up Networking will not be able to connect to a dial-up server that does not support some form of encrypted authentication.

o **Accept only Microsoft encrypted authentication:** If you select the radio button next to "Accept only Microsoft encrypted authentication", Dial-Up Networking will not be able to establish a connection with a dial-up server unless that server supports Microsoft encrypted authentication. You must select this option if you want to use data encryption. If you select this option, two additional check boxes are available:

  o **Require data encryption:** If you select the check box next to "Require data encryption", the Dial-Up Networking client will encrypt all data sent over this connection. You should select this check box if you are configuring a PPTP connection. This check box is only available if you selected the radio button next to Accept only Microsoft encrypted authentication. This check box is not selected by default.

  o **Use current username and password:** If you select the check box next to "Use current username and password", Dial-Up Networking will not prompt you for a user name or password when establishing a connection with the dial-up server. This check box is only available if you selected the radio button next to "Accept only Microsoft encrypted authentication". This check box is not selected by default.

### Configuring X.25 connection properties

To configure an X.25 connection, click the X.25 tab in the New Phonebook Entry dialog box. The X.25 tab appears, as shown in Figure 19-21.

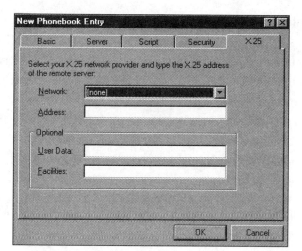

**FIGURE 19-21**  Configuring X.25 settings

Contact your X.25 provider to obtain the information you should use to configure this dialog box. You should obtain the network provider type (such as CompuServe, InfoNet, or Transpac), and X.25 address to be used.

# CONFIGURING DIAL–UP NETWORKING TO CONNECT TO THE INTERNET

There are several circumstances when you might want to use Dial-Up Networking to connect your Windows NT computer to the Internet:

- When users need to access the Internet to perform research, browse Web pages, and so on.

- When you want to connect your Windows NT WWW server (that is also a Dial-Up Networking client) to the Internet, and you expect only a few concurrent users to access your WWW server.

- When you want to establish a TCP/IP connection to the Internet so that you can use PPTP to access a remote RAS server over the Internet.

To establish a Dial-Up Networking connection to the Internet, you normally need to use the services of an *Internet service provider* (ISP). The ISP has a local network connection directly to the Internet. The ISP uses dial-up servers, such as RAS servers, SLIP servers, or front-end processors to enable remote users to connect to the Internet via the ISP's network.

Before you can establish a connection to the Internet via your ISP, you need to know how to configure your Dial-Up Networking client so that it is compatible with the ISP's dial-up server. Configuration information you should obtain from your ISP includes:

o  Type of dial-up server used by the ISP (SLIP or PPP connection protocol)

o  Whether the ISP's dial-up server supports software compression

o  Whether you will specify an IP address when you connect to the ISP, or the ISP's dial-up server will assign you an IP address

o  Whether the ISP will provide the IP address of a DNS server during the connection process

o  Whether the ISP's dial-up server uses IP header compression (IP header compression is also referred to as Van Jacobson header compression or VJ header compression)

o  Type of modem you will be connecting to at the ISP and recommended settings that you should use for your modem

o  The phone number you should use to connect to the ISP

# Configuring PPTP Security

If your RAS server is connected to the Internet via a router and an ISP, and you want to allow only PPTP connections to your server, you can configure TCP/IP to only accept PPTP packets. To accomplish this, a TCP/IP PPTP option, called *PPTP filtering*, must be individually configured for each network adapter installed in the RAS server that has a routed connection to the Internet.

**TO CONFIGURE PPTP FILTERING FOR A
NETWORK ADAPTER, FOLLOW THESE STEPS:**

**1.** Select Start ⇒ Settings ⇒ Control Panel.

**2.** In Control Panel, double-click the Network application.

**3.** In the Network dialog box, click the Protocols tab.

**4.** On the Protocols tab, double-click the TCP/IP Protocol in the Network Protocols list box.

**5.** In the Microsoft TCP/IP Properties dialog box, click the Advanced command button.

**6.** The Advanced IP Addressing dialog box appears, as shown in Figure 19-22. Notice the check box next to Enable PPTP Filtering. Select the network adapter you want to configure from the Adapter drop-down list box. Then select the check box next to Enable PPTP Filtering. Click OK.

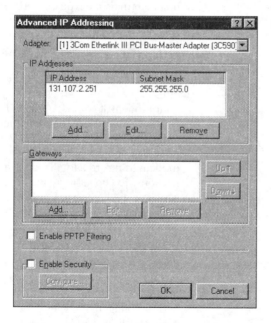

**FIGURE 19-22**     **Enabling PPTP filtering for a network adapter**

**7.** In the Microsoft TCP/IP Properties dialog box, click OK.

**8.** In the Network dialog box, click the Close command button.

**9.** A Network Settings Change dialog box appears, indicating that you must shut down and restart the computer in order for the new settings to take effect. Click the Yes command button to restart the computer.

# TROUBLESHOOTING COMMON RAS PROBLEMS

Most common RAS problems reported by users involve an inability to connect to a RAS server, a third-party SLIP server, or a front-end processor from a Dial-Up Networking client computer.

Table 19-1 shows some common causes of RAS connection problems, and recommended solutions.

| **TABLE 19-1** COMMON CAUSES OF RAS PROBLEMS AND RECOMMENDED SOLUTIONS | |
|---|---|
| *COMMON CAUSES OF RAS PROBLEMS* | *SUGGESTED/RECOMMENDED SOLUTIONS* |
| Modem configuration or compatibility problem | If you suspect that your modem is the problem, first determine the type of modem to which you are attempting to connect; and then reconfigure your modem settings to the most compatible option, or as recommended by your ISP. If you are using an unsupported modem (for example, one that is not on the HCL), verify that your settings in the `Modem.inf` file are appropriate for your modem. If you have selected RAS software compression, ensure that your modem is not configured to compress data. If you are still unable to connect, you can configure your modem to record a log file of all attempted connections. To configure a modem log file, use the Modems application in Control Panel to access your modem's Properties dialog box. Select the Connection tab and then the Advanced Connection Settings dialog box. |
| Password authentication problem | If you suspect a password authentication problem, configure Dial-Up Networking to accept any authentication including clear text, and/or configure the RAS server to enable any authentication including clear text. (Note: Clear text passwords are usually required by SLIP servers.) |

| Common Causes of RAS Problems | Suggested/Recommended Solutions |
| --- | --- |
| TCP/IP configuration problem | If you suspect a TCP/IP configuration problem, contact the manager of the dial-up server you are attempting to connect to and determine the dial-up server's TCP/IP configuration. Configure Dial-Up Networking so that the client's TCP/IP configuration settings match those of the dial-up server. |
| Dial-Up Networking configuration problem | Verify that you have chosen the appropriate dial-up server type (SLIP or PPP connection type) by contacting the manager of the dial-up server, if necessary. |
| Script problem | If you are using a script and your modem makes contact with the dial-up server, but you are *not* able to successfully complete a connection to the dial-up server, try editing your script file or try using a pop-up terminal window instead of the script file. |

# KEY POINT SUMMARY

This chapter focused on *Remote Access Service (RAS)* — a Windows NT service that enables dial-up network connections between a RAS server and a Dial-Up Networking client computer.

- Dial-Up Networking client computers can connect to a RAS server by using a variety of connection types, including: a standard telephone line and modem, ISDN, X.25, and Point-to-Point Tunneling Protocol (PPTP).

  - The most common connection type is a standard analog telephone line and modem. This service is inexpensive and widely available.

  - ISDN is a digital, dial-up telephone service that supports faster data transmission rates than a standard telephone line. An ISDN Basic Rate Interface (BRI) line consists of two B channels and a D channel. If both B channels are used together, data can be transmitted at up to 128Kbps.

- o X.25 is a packet-switching protocol that is used on dial-up or leased lines. This service is available in most countries, and requires a fair amount of hardware to implement.

- o PPTP is not a physical connection type. Rather, it is a virtual network connection that is "tunneled" inside of an existing TCP/IP network connection. RAS encryption can be used with PPTP to provide a secure, private connection over a public TCP/IP network, such as the Internet.

- o RAS communications can be carried out over several connection protocols, including: Serial Line Internet Protocol (SLIP), Point-to-Point Protocol (PPP), Point-to-Point Multilink Protocol (PPMP), and Point-to-Point Tunneling Protocol (PPTP).

  - o *SLIP* is an older connection protocol, commonly associated with UNIX computers, that supports only the TCP/IP transport protocol.

  - o PPP is a newer connection protocol designed to overcome the limitations of SLIP. *PPP is currently the industry standard remote connection protocol,* and is recommended for use by Microsoft. PPP supports password encryption, multiple transport protocols (including TCP/IP, NWLink IPX/SPX Compatible Transport, and NetBEUI), and dynamic, server-based IP addressing.

  - o *Point-to-Point Multilink Protocol* combines the bandwidth from multiple physical connections into a single logical connection.

  - o *PPTP* supports the RAS encryption feature over standard, unencrypted TCP/IP networks, such as the Internet. PPTP supports all standard transport protocols, including: NWLink IPX/SPX Compatible Transport, NetBEUI, and TCP/IP.

- o All Windows NT standard transport protocols are supported by RAS. Client computers can connect to a RAS server by using: NetBEUI, TCP/IP, or NWLink IPX/SPX Compatible Transport. The DLC protocol is *not* supported by RAS. A RAS server acts as a router for client computers that use TCP/IP or NWLink IPX/SPX Compatible Transport, enabling these clients to access other computers on the network via the RAS server's routing capability.

o The *RAS NetBIOS gateway* enables client computers that use NetBEUI to access shared resources on other servers located on the RAS server's local network. The RAS NetBIOS gateway performs protocol translation for the remote NetBEUI client computers. Only NetBIOS-based services (such as shared folders and printers, Lotus Notes servers, SQL Servers and SNA Servers) can be accessed by NetBEUI client computers via the RAS NetBIOS gateway. The NetBIOS gateway has a maximum connection limit of 250 simultaneous connections.

o RAS supports the following NetBIOS name resolution methods: NetBIOS broadcasts, WINS servers, DNS servers, LMHOSTS files, and HOSTS files.

o Before installing RAS, you should install and configure all of the transport protocols you plan to use, and you should also install and configure at least one connection device, such as a modem or ISDN adapter card.

o RAS is installed using the Services tab in the Network application in Control Panel. Many items are configured during the RAS installation, including: modems, ports, protocols, password encryption, and enabling Multilink. All settings in the Network Configuration dialog box are global settings that apply to all ports. When each protocol is configured, you must choose whether to allow remote clients connecting via that protocol access to all computers on the RAS server's local network (Entire network), or to limit remote clients' access to only the RAS server (This computer only).

o *Remote Access Admin* is a Windows NT administrative tool that is commonly used to start, stop, and pause RAS; to assign the dialin permission to users; and to configure call back security. Before remote users can establish a dial-up connection with a RAS server, they must be assigned the dialin permission. (The dialin permission can also be assigned by selecting the Dialin command button in the User Properties dialog box in User Manager or User Manager for Domains.) Call back security is configured on an individual user basis in Remote Access Admin. The Preset To configuration offers the highest level of call back security.

o *Dial-Up Networking* is the client/dial out component of RAS. The Dial-Up Networking accessory is installed during the RAS installation. Before Dial-Up Networking functionality on a Windows NT computer can be used, RAS must be installed and configured, and at least one of the computer's RAS ports must be configured for dial out usage. Additionally, you must create at least one phonebook entry that contains dialing information and instructions. Phonebook entries are created, edited, and selected by using the Dial-Up Networking accessory.

- When a new phonebook entry is created (or an existing phonebook entry is edited) by using the Dial-Up Networking accessory, there are five tabs on which configurations can be made: Basic, Server, Script, Security, and X.25. The phonebook entry name, phone number to be used, and modem/port to be used are configured on the Basic tab. A Multilink connection can also be configured on the Basic tab. The dial-up server type and network protocols are configured on the Server tab. Scripts, which are typically associated with SLIP servers, are configured on the Script tab. Password authentication and encryption policy is configured on the Security tab. X.25 connection settings are configured on the X.25 tab.

- To establish a Dial-Up Networking connection to the Internet, you normally need to use the services of an Internet service provider (ISP). Configuration information you should obtain from your ISP includes the following:

  - Type of dial-up server used by the ISP (SLIP or PPP connection protocol)

  - Whether the ISP's dial-up server supports software compression

  - Whether you will specify an IP address when you connect to the ISP, or the ISP's dial-up server will assign you an IP address

  - Whether the ISP will provide the IP address of a DNS server during the connection process

  - Whether the ISP's dial-up server uses IP header compression (IP header compression is also referred to as Van Jacobson header compression or VJ header compression)

  - Type of modem to which you will be connecting at the ISP and recommended settings that you should use for your modem

  - The phone number you should use to connect to the ISP

- If your RAS server has a routed connection to the Internet, you can configure *PPTP filtering* so that TCP/IP will only accept PPTP packets. To accomplish this, use the Network application in Control Panel.

o Most common RAS problems reported by users involve an inability to connect to a RAS server, a third-party SLIP server, or a front-end processor from a Dial-Up Networking client computer. Common causes of RAS connection problems are: modem compatibility or configuration problems, password authentication problems, TCP/IP configuration problems, Dial-Up Networking configuration problems, and script problems.

# Applying What You've Learned

Now it's time to regroup, review, and apply what you've learned in this chapter.

The questions in the Instant Assessment section that follows bring to mind key facts and concepts. In addition, the review activity gives you an opportunity to test your troubleshooting skills.

The hands-on lab exercise will really reinforce what you've learned, and give you an chance to practice some of the tasks tested by the Microsoft Certified Professional exams.

## Instant Assessment

1. What is the "server component" of RAS called?

2. What is the "client component" of RAS called?

3. Up to how many simultaneous dial in connections can RAS support on a Windows NT Server computer?

4. How many simultaneous dial in connections can the RAS NetBIOS gateway support on a Windows NT Server computer?

5. List the four types of connection types that Dial-Up Networking client computers can use to connect to a RAS server.

6. List the four connection protocols that RAS communications can be carried out over.

7. Which connection protocol is older, commonly associated with scripts and with UNIX computers, and supports only the TCP/IP transport protocol?

8. Which connection protocol is newer, is currently the industry standard, and supports multiple transport protocols (including TCP/IP, NWLink IPX/SPX Compatible Transport, and NetBEUI)?

9. Describe the Point-to-Point Multilink Protocol.

10. What is PPTP?

11. Which transport protocols are supported by RAS?

12. What does the RAS NetBIOS gateway do?

13. Which NetBIOS name resolution methods does RAS support?

14. Assuming that RAS and Dial-Up Networking are installed and configured, what must be assigned before remote users can establish a dial-up connection with a RAS server?

15. What entries in Dial-Up Networking contain dialing information and instructions that are used to establish the connection to the dial-up server?

16. List three configuration information items you should obtain from your Internet service provider (ISP) before you establish a Dial-Up Networking connection to the Internet.

17. Which Windows NT tool should you use to configure RAS call back security, and which configuration option offers the highest level of security?

concept link  **For answers to the Instant Assessment questions see Appendix D.**

## Review Activity

Server
Enterprise

The following activity gives you a chance to apply your RAS knowledge in two common real-life troubleshooting situations.

### *Troubleshooting common RAS problems*

The purpose of this review activity is to give you experience in troubleshooting common RAS problems.

In each of the situations below, propose a solution to the reported problem.

**Problem 1**   A user reports that he can't establish a connection with the dial-up server from his Dial-Up Networking client computer. You suspect a modem problem.

Recommend a course of action to solve the reported problem:

**Problem 2**    A user reports that she is unable to connect to a SLIP server from her Dial-Up Networking client computer. The phonebook entry on the user's computer is configured as shown in Figure 19-23.

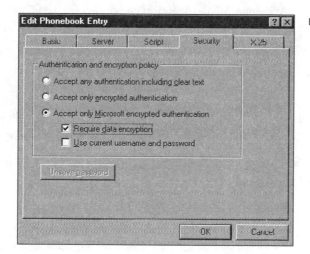

**FIGURE 19-23**   Password authentication configuration for Dial-Up Networking client computer in Problem 2

Recommend a course of action to solve the reported problem:

 concept link    **For answers to the Review Activity see Appendix D.**

## Hands-on Lab Exercise

The following hands-on lab exercise provides you with an opportunity to apply the RAS knowledge you've gained in this chapter.

## Lab 19.32 *Installing and Configuring RAS and Dial-Up Networking*

Workstation
Server
Enterprise

The purpose of this lab is to give you hands-on experience in installing and configuring RAS on a Windows NT Server computer, and in installing RAS and configuring Dial-Up Networking on a Windows NT Workstation computer.

This lab consists of two parts:

Part 1: Installing and configuring RAS (on a Windows NT Server computer)

Part 2: Installing RAS and configuring Dial-Up Networking (on a Windows NT Workstation computer)

Begin this lab by booting your computer to Windows NT Server. Log on as Administrator. Place your Windows NT Server compact disc in your CD-ROM drive. Follow the steps below carefully.

**Part 1: Installing and configuring RAS (on a Windows NT Server computer)**
In this section, you install and configure RAS on your Windows NT Server computer.

**1.** Select Start ⇒ Settings ⇒ Control Panel.

**2.** In the Control Panel dialog box, double-click Network.

**3.** In the Network dialog box, click the Services tab.

**4.** On the Services tab, click the Add command button.

**5.** In the Select Network Service dialog box, highlight Remote Access Service. Click OK.

**6.** A Windows NT Setup dialog box appears. Ensure that the correct path to your Windows NT Server source files (usually the i386 folder on your Windows NT Server compact disc) is listed in the text box. Edit this text box if necessary. Click the Continue command button.

**7.** Windows NT copies source files. The Add RAS Device dialog box appears. Select the modem that you installed in Lab 4.6 from the RAS Capable Devices drop-down list box. Click OK.

**8.** The Remote Access Setup dialog box appears. Click the Configure command button.

**9.** The Configure Port Usage dialog box appears. Select the radio button next to "Dial out and Receive calls". Click OK.

**10.** The Remote Access Setup dialog box reappears. Click the Network command button.

11. The Network Configuration dialog box appears. Select the check box next to Enable Multilink at the bottom of the dialog box. Click the Configure command button next to the TCP/IP option in the Server Settings section.

12. The RAS Server TCP/IP Configuration dialog box appears. Click the radio button next to "Use static address pool". In the Begin text box, enter an IP address of **192.168.58.1**, and in the End text box, enter an IP address of **192.168.58.255**. Click OK.

13. The Network Configuration dialog box reappears. Click the Configure command button next to the IPX option in the Server Settings section.

14. The RAS Server IPX Configuration dialog box appears. Notice that IPX clients are configured, by default, to access the entire network. Click OK.

15. The Network Configuration dialog box reappears. Click OK.

16. The Remote Access Setup dialog box reappears. Click the Continue command button.

17. Windows NT installs and configures RAS. If the RIP for NWLink IPX Configuration dialog box appears, asking if you want to enable NetBIOS Broadcast Propagation, click the Yes command button.

18. A Setup Message dialog box appears, indicating that RAS has been successfully installed. Click OK.

19. The Network dialog box reappears. Click the Close command button.

20. Windows NT performs various bindings operations.

21. A Network Settings Change dialog box appears, indicating that you must shut down and restart the computer in order for the new settings to take effect. Click the Yes command button to restart the computer.

22. Reboot your computer to Windows NT Server. Log on as Administrator. If the Control Panel dialog box appears, close it.

23. Select Start ⇒ Programs ⇒ Administrative Tools (Common) ⇒ Remote Access Admin.

24. The Remote Access Admin dialog box appears. Notice that RAS is running on your server. Select Users ⇒ Permissions.

25. The Remote Access Permissions dialog box appears. Click the Grant All command button to assign the dial in permission to all user accounts.

26. The Remote Access Admin warning dialog box appears, asking you to confirm that you want to grant the dialin permission to all users. Click the Yes command button.

27. The Remote Access Permissions dialog box reappears. Click OK.

28. The Remote Access Admin dialog box reappears. Close Remote Access Admin. Continue on to Part 2.

## Part 2: Installing RAS and configuring Dial-Up Networking (on a Windows NT Workstation computer)

In this section, you install RAS and configure Dial-Up Networking on your Windows NT Workstation computer.

Begin this section by booting your computer to Windows NT Workstation. Log on as Administrator. Place your Windows NT Workstation compact disc in your CD-ROM drive.

1. Select Start ⇒ Settings ⇒ Control Panel.

2. In the Control Panel dialog box, double-click Network.

3. In the Network dialog box, click the Services tab.

4. On the Services tab, click the Add command button.

5. In the Select Network Service dialog box, highlight Remote Access Service. Click OK.

6. A Windows NT Setup dialog box appears. Ensure that the correct path to your Windows NT Workstation source files (usually the I386 folder on your Windows NT Workstation compact disc) is listed in the text box. Edit this text box if necessary. Click the Continue command button.

7. Windows NT copies source files. If you have already installed a modem using Windows NT Workstation, skip to Step 13.

   If you haven't installed a modem, the Remote Access Setup dialog box appears, indicating that there are no RAS capable devices to add. Click the Yes command button to invoke the modem installer.

8. The Install New Modem dialog box appears. Select the check box next to "Don't detect my modem; I will select it from a list". Click the Next command button.

9. The Install New Modem dialog box appears. Ensure that (Standard Modem Types) is highlighted in the Manufacturers list box, and that Dial-Up Networking Serial Cable between 2 PCs is selected in the Models list box. Click the Next command button.

10. The next Install New Modem dialog box appears. Ensure that the radio button next to "Selected ports" is selected. Highlight a serial port from the list box (such as COM1 or COM2). Click the Next command button.

11. The Location Information dialog box appears. Type in your area code in the "What area (or city) code are you in now" text box. Click the Next command button.

12. Click the Finish command button in the Install New Modem dialog box.

13. The Add RAS Device dialog box appears. Select a modem from the RAS Capable Devices drop-down list box. Click OK.

**14.** The Remote Access Setup dialog box appears. Click the Configure command button.

**15.** The Configure Port Usage dialog box appears. Select the radio button next to "Dial out and Receive calls". Click OK.

**16.** The Remote Access Setup dialog box reappears. Click the Continue command button.

**17.** The RAS Server TCP/IP Configuration dialog box appears. Click the radio button next to "Use static address pool". In the Begin text box, enter an IP address of **192.168.58.1**, and in the End text box, enter an IP address of **192.168.58.255**. Click OK.

**18.** The RAS Server IPX Configuration dialog box appears. Click OK.

**19.** Windows NT installs and configures RAS. If the RIP for NWLink IPX Configuration dialog box appears, asking if you want to enable NetBIOS Broadcast Propagation, click the Yes command button.

**20.** A Setup Message dialog box appears, indicating that RAS has been successfully installed. Click OK.

**21.** The Network dialog box reappears. Click the Close command button.

**22.** Windows NT performs various bindings operations.

**23.** A Network Settings Change dialog box appears, indicating that you must shut down and restart the computer in order for the new settings to take effect. Click the Yes command button to restart the computer.

**24.** Reboot the computer to Windows NT Workstation. Log on as Administrator.

**25.** If the Control Panel dialog box appears, close it.

**26.** Select Start ⇒ Programs ⇒ Accessories ⇒ Dial-Up Networking.

**27.** A Dial-Up Networking dialog box appears, indicating that the phonebook is empty. Click OK.

**28.** The New Phonebook Entry Wizard appears. Accept the default of MyDialUpServer in the "Name the new phonebook entry" text box. Click the Next command button.

**29.** The Server dialog box appears. Select the check boxes next to "I am calling the Internet" and "Send my plain text password, if that's the only way to connect". Click the Next command button.

**30.** The Phone Number dialog box appears. Type **555-5425** in the "Phone number" text box. Click the Next command button.

**31.** Click the Finish command button in the New Phonebook Entry Wizard dialog box.

**32.** The Dial-Up Networking dialog box reappears. Exit Dial-Up Networking.

Enterprise

CHAPTER

# Macintosh Connectivity

# 20

# About Chapter 20

This chapter is all about Services for Macintosh, a Windows NT Server service that provides support for Macintosh client computers on a Windows NT Server network.

After presenting an overview of Macintosh client computer connectivity and Services for Macintosh, this chapter outlines how to install Services for Macintosh on a Windows NT Server computer. Next is an explanation of how to create a Macintosh-accessible volume on a Windows NT Server computer, so that Macintosh client computers can access the files contained in that volume. Following that is a discussion of how to enable password encryption for Macintosh client computers.

Finally, the chapter addresses Macintosh printing. This section explains how to share Windows NT printers with Macintosh client computers, as well as how to connect a Windows NT Server computer to an AppleTalk print device.

This chapter includes one hands-on lab. In this lab, you install and configure Services for Macintosh on your Windows NT Server computer.

Chapter 20 contains some valuable and interesting information, but is optional reading unless you're preparing for the Enterprise exam. This chapter maps to the protocol objectives (which include AppleTalk) and the "Configure a Windows NT Server computer for various types of client computers . . . including Macintosh" objective for the Enterprise exam.

# OVERVIEW OF MACINTOSH CLIENT CONNECTIVITY AND SERVICES FOR MACINTOSH

Many mixed operating system networks include Macintosh client computers. Macintosh client computers use the AppleTalk protocol to communicate with servers and network-connected print devices that support the AppleTalk protocol.

Windows NT Server provides support for Macintosh client computers via *Services for Macintosh*. Services for Macintosh is a Windows NT Server (not Workstation) service.

Services for Macintosh allows:

o Macintosh client computers to connect to Macintosh-accessible volumes on a Windows NT Server computer

o Macintosh client computers to access shared printers on a Windows NT Server computer

o A Windows NT Server computer to connect to network-connected print devices that support the AppleTalk protocol

o A Windows NT Server computer to function as an AppleTalk router

The remaining sections in this chapter cover installing Services for Macintosh, creating a Macintosh-accessible volume, password encryption for Macintosh client computers, and Macintosh printing.

# INSTALLING SERVICES FOR MACINTOSH

Services for Macintosh can be installed on any Windows NT Server computer that has 2MB of free disk space.

Services for Macintosh also requires that a supported network adapter be installed in the Windows NT Server computer. Supported network adapter types include LocalTalk, Ethernet, Token Ring, and FDDI. Services for Macintosh does *not* support ARCNET network adapters.

---

## TO INSTALL SERVICES FOR MACINTOSH ON A WINDOWS NT SERVER COMPUTER, FOLLOW THESE STEPS:

**1.** Select Start ⇒ Settings ⇒ Control Panel.

**2.** In the Control Panel dialog box, double-click the Network application.

**3.** In the Network dialog box, click the Services tab.

**4.** On the Services tab, click the Add command button.

**5.** In the Select Network Service dialog box, highlight Services for Macintosh, as shown in Figure 20-1. Click OK.

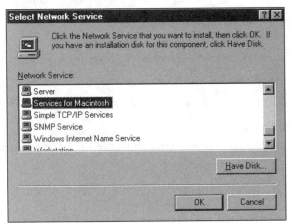

**FIGURE 20-1**  Installing Services for Macintosh

**6.** A Windows NT Setup dialog box appears. Ensure the correct path to your Windows NT Server source files (usually the I386 folder on your Windows NT Server compact disc) is listed in the text box. Edit this text box if necessary. Click the Continue command button.

**7.** Windows NT Server copies source files and installs Services for Macintosh.

**8.** The Network dialog box reappears. Click the Close command button.

**9.** Windows NT Server performs various bindings operations.

**10.** The Microsoft AppleTalk Protocol Properties dialog box appears, as shown in Figure 20-2. Notice that in this dialog box you can select a default network adapter and a default AppleTalk zone for this computer.

   o **Default Adapter:** Select the network adapter installed in the Windows NT Server computer that connects to the network segment that Macintosh client computers are connected to.

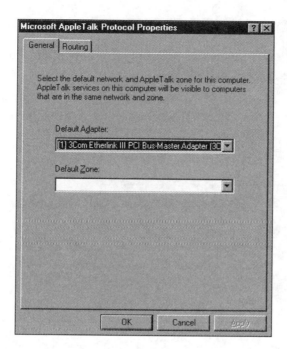

**FIGURE 20-2**   Configuring a default AppleTalk network adapter and zone

- **Default Zone:** A zone is a Macintosh term for a logical grouping of computers, much like a Windows NT workgroup. Select the zone that you want Services for Macintosh to be a part of. If no zones are listed, you can create a zone by configuring AppleTalk routing.

**11.** To configure AppleTalk routing, click the Routing tab, shown in Figure 20-3. There are several configurable options on the Routing tab:

- **Enable Routing:** To enable AppleTalk routing, select the check box next to Enable Routing.

- **Use this router to seed the network:** If you select the check box next to Enable Routing, the "Use this router to seed the network" check box becomes available. If no zones were listed on the General tab, select this check box to create a zone (or zones) on your AppleTalk network.

- **To create a zone:** If you select the check box next to "Use this router to seed the network", you will also need to enter a Network Range. Then click the Add command button to create a zone. The Add Zone dialog box appears. Type in the name of the zone you want to add.

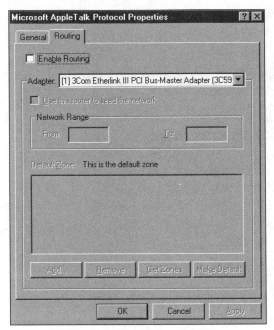

**FIGURE 20-3** Configuring AppleTalk routing

Figure 20-4 shows the Add Zone dialog box after a new zone name has been entered.

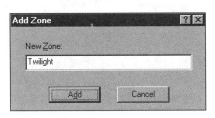

**FIGURE 20-4** Creating a zone

Click the Add command button. The Routing tab reappears, as shown in Figure 20-5. Notice that the first zone I created is listed as the default zone. Add additional zones as needed. Click OK.

**12.** A Network Settings Change dialog box appears, indicating that you must shut down and restart the computer for the new settings to take effect. Click the Yes command button to restart the computer.

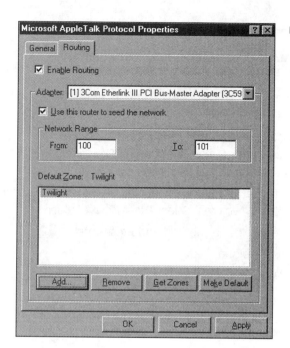

**FIGURE 20-5** AppleTalk routing configured

# CREATING A MACINTOSH–ACCESSIBLE VOLUME

A *Macintosh-accessible volume* is a folder on an NTFS partition (on a Windows NT Server computer) that permits Macintosh client computers to access the files contained in that folder. Services for Macintosh must be installed on the Windows NT Server computer before Macintosh-accessible volumes can be created.

After Macintosh-accessible volumes are created, they can also be shared with other types of client computers, such as Windows 95, Windows NT Workstation, and MS-DOS computers, so users of all these client computers can access the same files.

Macintosh-accessible volumes can be created by using Server Manager or File Manager. Macintosh-accessible volumes can be shared with other types of client computers by using Windows NT Explorer, Server Manager, or File Manager.

## TO CREATE A MACINTOSH-ACCESSIBLE VOLUME BY USING SERVER MANAGER, FOLLOW THESE STEPS:

**1.** If the folder you want to use as a Macintosh-accessible volume already exists, skip to Step 5.

If the folder you want to use as a Macintosh-accessible volume does *not* yet exist, select Start⇒Programs⇒Windows NT Explorer to create the folder.

**2.** The Exploring dialog box appears. In the All Folders list box, highlight the drive letter of the NTFS volume on which you want to create the Macintosh-accessible volume. Select File⇒New⇒Folder.

**3.** Rename the New Folder as desired and press Enter.

**4.** Exit Windows NT Explorer.

**5.** Select Start⇒Programs⇒Administrative Tools (Common)⇒Server Manager.

**6.** The Server Manager dialog box appears. Highlight your server in the list box and select MacFile⇒Volumes, as shown in Figure 20-6.

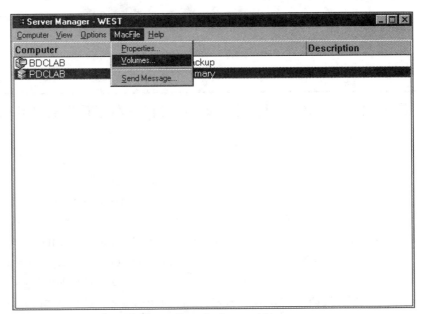

**FIGURE 20-6**   Macintosh file options in Server Manager

**7.** The Macintosh-Accessible Volumes dialog box appears, as shown in Figure 20-7. Notice that the `Microsoft UAM Volume` is listed in the Volumes list box. This volume is automatically created by Windows NT

Server during the installation of Services for Macintosh. Click the Create Volume command button.

**FIGURE 20-7** Managing Macintosh–accessible volumes

**8.** The Create Macintosh-Accessible Volume dialog box appears, as shown in Figure 20-8.

**FIGURE 20-8** Creating a Macintosh-accessible volume

Type entries in the appropriate text boxes:

- **Volume Name:** Enter the name of the volume as you want it to appear to Macintosh client computers.

- **Path:** Enter the complete local path to the folder that will be used as the Macintosh-accessible volume. For example, `D:\`, or `D:\MACFILES`, and so on.

 **note** You can specify an entire drive as a Macintosh-accessible volume. However, if you do this you *won't* be able to create additional Macintosh-accessible volumes on this drive within the existing Macintosh-accessible volume.

- **Password:** Enter the password that users of Macintosh client computers must specify to access this volume. This entry is optional.

- **Confirm Password:** Retype the password.

- **Volume Security:**
  - **This volume is read-only:** Select the check box next to "This volume is read-only" if you don't want users of Macintosh client computers to be able to save or delete files in this volume. This check box is not selected by default.
  - **Guests can use this volume:** Clear the check box next to "Guests can use this volume" if you want to only allow users with Windows NT user accounts to access this volume. This check box is selected by default.

  Click the Permissions command button if you want to assign Macintosh file and folder permissions to the Macintosh-accessible volume.
  Click OK.

9. The Macintosh-Accessible Volumes dialog box reappears. Click the Close command button.

10. The Server Manager dialog box reappears. Exit Server Manager.

If you want to share a Macintosh-accessible volume on a Windows NT Server computer with Windows 95, Windows NT Workstation, and/or MS-DOS client computers, use Windows NT Explorer, Server Manager, or File Manager to share the folder that contains the Macintosh-accessible volume.

# PASSWORD ENCRYPTION FOR MACINTOSH CLIENT COMPUTERS

By default, Macintosh client computers send passwords in clear text when they connect to a server. A Windows NT Server computer that has Services for Macintosh installed on it can permit this. However, clear text passwords can pose a network security risk because an unauthorized person could use a protocol analyzer to capture clear text passwords.

Services for Macintosh includes a *User Authentication Module* (UAM) that allows Macintosh client computers to send encrypted passwords when connecting to a Windows NT Server computer. Windows NT Server automatically creates the Microsoft UAM Volume (that contains the UAM) on the NT Server computer's first NTFS partition when Services for Macintosh is installed. If you are concerned about password security, you may want to enable password encryption on your Macintosh client computers.

**TO ENABLE PASSWORD ENCRYPTION ON A MACINTOSH CLIENT COMPUTER, FOLLOW THESE STEPS:**

**1.** From the Macintosh client computer, connect to the `Microsoft UAM Volume` located on the Windows NT Server computer.

**2.** From the Macintosh desktop, double-click the `Microsoft UAM Volume`.

**3.** Drag the `AppleShare` Folder from the `Microsoft UAM Volume` and drop it on the `System` Folder on the Macintosh client computer. (This installs the UAM on the Macintosh client computer.)

**4.** Restart the Macintosh client computer.

This procedure must be performed on *every* Macintosh client computer that you want to enable password encryption on.

concept link

**For more information on the Microsoft UAM, see the** `ReadMe.UAM` **text file located in the** `AppleShare` **Folder in the** `Microsoft UAM Volume`.

# MACINTOSH PRINTING

Services for Macintosh facilitates the integration of Windows NT and Macintosh printing environments.

When a Windows NT Server has Services for Macintosh installed on it:

o The Windows NT Server computer's shared printers are accessible from Macintosh client computers.

o The Windows NT Server computer can connect to network-connected AppleTalk print devices. (Additionally, after connecting, the NT Server computer can share these AppleTalk print devices with all client computers that access the Windows NT Server computer.)

The next two sections discuss sharing a Windows NT printer with Macintosh client computers and connecting to an AppleTalk print device.

## Sharing a Windows NT Printer with Macintosh Client Computers

When a Windows NT Server computer that has Services for Macintosh installed on it shares a printer, the printer is accessible to Macintosh client computers (as well as other client computers of the Windows NT Server computer).

 tip **You don't have to reshare existing shared printers after installing Services for Macintosh to make them available to Macintosh client computers. Services for Macintosh makes *all* shared printers available to Macintosh client computers.**

A shared printer (on a Windows NT Server computer that has Services for Macintosh installed) advertises itself on the AppleTalk network as an Apple LaserWriter print device.

Macintosh client computers treat the shared printer as if it were an Apple LaserWriter print device. Apple LaserWriter is the original laser print device for Macintosh computers. All Macintosh computers have built-in drivers for the Apple LaserWriter. This means that Macintosh client computers don't need special drivers to access the shared printer on the Windows NT Server computer.

Macintosh client computers send print jobs formatted for an Apple LaserWriter (i.e., in PostScript) to the shared printer on the Windows NT Server computer. The Windows NT Server computer converts the PostScript print jobs it receives from Macintosh client computers into RAW format print jobs for the print device.

 concept link **For detailed instructions on how to share a printer, refer to the "Sharing a Printer" section in Chapter 6.**

## Connecting to an AppleTalk Print Device

Before you can connect a Windows NT Server computer to an AppleTalk print device, you must install Services for Macintosh.

A Windows NT Server computer can connect to any AppleTalk print device on any segment of a routed AppleTalk network.

To connect a Windows NT Server computer to an AppleTalk print device, create a printer that specifies the AppleTalk print device as its print destination. Creating this printer establishes a connection between the Windows NT Server computer and the AppleTalk print device. The next section explains, in more detail, how to accomplish this task.

**TO CONNECT A WINDOWS NT SERVER COMPUTER TO AN APPLETALK PRINT DEVICE, FOLLOW THESE STEPS:**

**1.** Select Start ⇒ Settings ⇒ Printers.

**2.** The Printers dialog box appears. Double-click the Add Printer icon.

**3.** The Add Printer Wizard dialog box appears. To create a printer, select My Computer, and click Next.

**4.** In the Available ports list box, click the Add Port command button.

**5.** In the Printer Ports dialog box, highlight AppleTalk Printing Devices. Figure 20-9 shows the Printer Ports dialog box. Notice that AppleTalk Printing Devices is highlighted. Click the New Port command button.

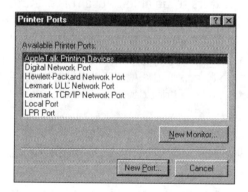

**FIGURE 20-9**  Adding an AppleTalk port

**6.** When the Available AppleTalk Printing Devices dialog box appears, double-click the AppleTalk zone that contains the print device you want to use. Or, if no zones are listed, highlight the AppleTalk print device you want to use.

Figure 20-10 shows the Available AppleTalk Printing Devices dialog box, with an HP LaserJet 5P selected. Click OK.

**7.** A Windows NT dialog box appears, asking if you want to capture this AppleTalk print device.

If you choose to *capture* an AppleTalk print device, the AppleTalk print monitor will monopolize the connection to the AppleTalk print device, and no other computer on the network will be able to access the AppleTalk print device. Additionally, the AppleTalk print monitor will instruct the AppleTalk print device *not* to advertise itself on the network. This is called *hiding.*

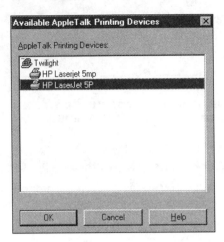

**FIGURE 20-10**    Selecting an AppleTalk print device

  *tip*

**When you capture an AppleTalk print device, you should share the printer you're creating if you want to allow Macintosh (and other) client computers to be able to use this print device. If you *don't* share the printer, only the user sitting at the Windows NT Server computer will be able to access the AppleTalk print device.**

If you choose *not to capture* an AppleTalk print device, all computers on the network will be able to access the AppleTalk print device for printing, because the connection to the print device will be dropped after each print job.

Click the Yes or No command button.

**8.** The Printer Ports dialog box reappears. Click the Close command button.

**9.** The Add Printer Wizard dialog box reappears. The Available Ports list box shows the newly created AppleTalk port highlighted and selected, as shown in Figure 20-11. Click the Next command button.

**10.** In the Add Printer Wizard dialog box, select the appropriate manufacturer and print device model. Click the Next command button.

**11.** In the Add Printer Wizard dialog box, type in a printer name, or accept the default. Click the Next command button.

**12.** In the Add Printer Wizard dialog box, choose whether or not to share the printer. (You can share or stop sharing the printer later if you change your mind.) If you choose to share the printer, accept the default share name or type in a new share name. Click the Next command button.

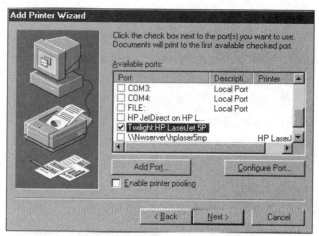

**FIGURE 20-11**  AppleTalk port created and selected

**13.** In the Add Printer Wizard dialog box, choose whether or not to print a test page. Click the Finish command button.

**14.** The Printers dialog box reappears with the newly created printer displayed in it. Close the Printers dialog box.

# KEY POINT SUMMARY

This chapter presented the basics of Macintosh connectivity. The following points illuminate the major issues.

- Macintosh client computers use the AppleTalk protocol to communicate with servers and network-connected print devices that support the AppleTalk protocol. Windows NT Server provides support for Macintosh client computers via Services for Macintosh. Services for Macintosh is a Windows NT Server service.

- Services for Macintosh allows:

  - Macintosh client computers to connect to Macintosh-accessible volumes on a Windows NT Server computer

  - Macintosh client computers to access shared printers on a Windows NT Server computer

- o A Windows NT Server computer to connect to network-connected print devices that support the AppleTalk protocol

  - o A Windows NT Server computer to function as an AppleTalk router

- o Services for Macintosh can be installed on any Windows NT Server computer that has 2MB of free disk space. Services for Macintosh also requires that a supported network adapter be installed in the Windows NT Server computer. Supported network adapter types include LocalTalk, Ethernet, Token Ring, and FDDI. Services for Macintosh does *not* support ARCNET network adapters.

- o A Macintosh-accessible volume is a folder on an NTFS partition (on a Windows NT Server computer) that permits Macintosh client computers to access files in that folder. After Macintosh-accessible volumes are created, they can also be shared with other types of client computers, such as Windows 95, Windows NT Workstation, and MS-DOS computers, so users of all of these client computers can access the same files. Macintosh-accessible volumes can be created by using Server Manager or File Manager.

- o By default, Macintosh client computers send passwords in clear text when they connect to a server. A Windows NT Server computer that has Services for Macintosh installed on it can permit this. However, clear text passwords can pose a network security risk because an unauthorized person could use a protocol analyzer to capture them.

- o Services for Macintosh includes a User Authentication Module (UAM) that allows Macintosh client computers to send encrypted passwords when connecting to a Windows NT Server computer. Windows NT Server automatically creates the `Microsoft UAM Volume` (that contains the UAM) when Services for Macintosh is installed.

- o When a Windows NT Server computer that has Services for Macintosh installed on it shares a printer, the printer is accessible to Macintosh client computers (as well as other client computers of the Windows NT Server computer). You don't have to reshare existing shared printers after installing Services for Macintosh to make them available to Macintosh client computers—Services for Macintosh makes *all* shared printers available to Macintosh client computers. A shared printer (on a Windows NT Server computer that has Services for Macintosh installed) advertises itself on the AppleTalk network as an Apple LaserWriter print device.

o To connect a Windows NT Server computer (that has Services for Macintosh installed on it) to an AppleTalk print device, create a printer that specifies the AppleTalk print device as its print destination. Creating this printer establishes a connection between the Windows NT Server computer and the AppleTalk print device.

# APPLYING WHAT YOU'VE LEARNED

Now it's time to regroup, review, and apply what you've learned in this chapter.

The Instant Assessment questions bring to mind key facts and concepts. The hands-on lab exercise reinforces what you've learned, and allows you to practice some of the tasks tested by the Enterprise exam.

## Instant Assessment

1. What four network activities does Services for Macintosh allow?

2. List the types of network adapters supported by Services for Macintosh.

3. What type of network adapter is *not* supported by Services for Macintosh?

4. Which transport protocol is used by Macintosh client computers to connect to servers and network-connected print devices?

5. On what type of volume must a Macintosh-accessible volume be created?

6. Which Windows NT Server tool can you use to create a Macintosh-accessible volume?

7. By default, in what manner do Macintosh client computers send passwords when connecting to a Windows NT Server computer?

8. What component is included in Services for Macintosh that allows Macintosh client computers to send encrypted passwords when connecting to a Windows NT Server computer?

9. How does a shared printer (on a Windows NT Server computer that has Services for Macintosh installed) advertise itself on the AppleTalk network?

10. What should you do to connect a Windows NT Server computer (that has Services for Macintosh installed on it) to an AppleTalk print device?

T/F

**11.** Services for Macintosh can be installed on a
Windows NT Workstation computer.                              _____

concept link  **For answers to the Instant Assessment questions see Appendix D.**

# Hands-on Lab Exercise

The following hands-on lab exercise provides you with an opportunity to apply the
knowledge you've gained in this chapter about Macintosh connectivity.

## Lab 20.33 *Installing and configuring Services for Macintosh*

Enterprise

The purpose of this lab exercise is to give you hands-on experience in installing
and configuring Services for Macintosh on a Windows NT Server computer.

This lab consists of two parts:

Part 1: Installing and configuring Services for Macintosh

Part 2: Configuring a Macintosh-accessible volume

Begin this lab by booting your computer to Windows NT Server. Log on as
Administrator. Place your Windows NT Server compact disc in your computer's
CD-ROM drive.

Follow the steps below carefully.

### Part 1: Installing and configuring Services for Macintosh

In this section, you install and configure Services for Macintosh on a Windows NT
Server computer.

**1.** Select Start ⇒ Settings ⇒ Control Panel.

**2.** In the Control Panel dialog box, double-click the Network application.

**3.** In the Network dialog box, click the Services tab.

**4.** On the Services tab, click the Add command button.

**5.** In the Select Network Service dialog box, highlight Services for Macintosh.
Click OK.

**6.** A Windows NT Setup dialog box appears. Ensure that the correct path to
your Windows NT Server source files (usually the I386 folder on your
Windows NT Server compact disc) is listed in the text box. Edit this text
box if necessary. Click the Continue command button.

7. Windows NT copies source files and installs Services for Macintosh.

8. The Network dialog box reappears. Click the Close command button.

9. Windows NT performs various bindings operations.

10. The Microsoft AppleTalk Protocol Properties dialog box appears. Click OK to continue.

11. A Network Settings Change dialog box appears, indicating that you must shut down and restart the computer for the new settings to take effect. Click the Yes command button to restart the computer.

12. Reboot your computer to Windows NT Server. Log on as Administrator. If the Control Panel dialog box appears, close it. Continue to Part 2.

## Part 2: Configuring a Macintosh-accessible volume

In this section, you configure a Macintosh-accessible volume on an NTFS partition on a Windows NT Server computer.

1. Select Start ⇒ Programs ⇒ Windows NT Explorer.

2. The Exploring dialog box appears. Highlight your D: drive (or the drive where your NTFS volume is located) in the All Folders list box. Select File ⇒ New ⇒ Folder.

3. In the Contents of D: list box, rename the New Folder **Macfiles** and press Enter.

4. Exit Windows NT Explorer.

5. Select Start ⇒ Programs ⇒ Administrative Tools (Common) ⇒ Server Manager.

6. The Server Manager dialog box appears. Highlight your server in the list box and select MacFile ⇒ Volumes.

7. The Macintosh Accessible Volumes dialog box appears. Click the Create Volume command button.

8. The Create Macintosh-Accessible Volumes dialog box appears. Type the following bolded information in the appropriate text boxes:

Volume Name—**MACFILES**

Path—**D:\MACFILES** (Or if your NTFS volume is located on another drive, use the drive letter for your NTFS volume.)

Password—Leave this text box blank.

Confirm Password—Also leave this text box blank.

Click OK.

**9.** The Macintosh-Accessible Volumes dialog box reappears. Notice that MACFILES appears in the Volumes list box as a shared Macintosh volume. Click the Close command button.

**10.** The Server Manager dialog box reappears. Exit Server Manager.

# Running Applications

No matter how powerful an operating system is, it must be capable of consistently running the applications we use in order for us to be satisfied with it. Windows NT 4.0 is designed to run applications created for several different types of operating system environments. Part V discusses these various operating system environments, as well as the various hardware platforms on which Windows NT 4.0 supports applications.

Chapter 21 explains how Windows NT distributes processor time to an application based on that application's priority. We discuss using the Start command and configuring foreground application priority boost.

Finally, Chapter 21 explores how to use Windows NT Task Manager, and presents valuable information on troubleshooting common application problems.

The information in Part V maps directly to the Running Applications section in the exam objectives for the Implementing and Supporting Microsoft Windows NT Workstation 4.0 exam only. This part is optional if you're preparing for either of the other two Windows NT 4.0 Microsoft Certified Professional exams.

 Workstation

# About Chapter 21

This chapter explores the various application environments supported by Windows NT 4.0, as well as some techniques for customizing application performance.

Chapter 21 begins by explaining that Windows NT 4.0 is designed to run applications created for many different operating system environments, including MS-DOS, Win16, Win32, POSIX, and OS/2. Next, the chapter presents the various hardware platforms on which Windows NT 4.0 supports applications.

Following that is an exploration of application priorities, and how to use the Start command to start applications at various priorities. Configuring foreground application priority boost is also explained.

Next, the chapter details how to use Windows NT Task Manager to perform various tasks, such as stopping an application, viewing performance statistics, and changing an application's base priority.

Finally, Chapter 21 presents tips on troubleshooting common application problems.

This chapter includes a review activity that will give you practice troubleshooting application problems. It also includes a hands-on lab during which you'll configure foreground application responsiveness and start applications at various priorities on your Windows NT Workstation computer.

This chapter contains some valuable and interesting information, but is optional reading unless you're preparing for the Workstation exam. The information in this chapter covers both objectives in the Running Applications section in the Workstation exam's objectives.

# APPLICATION ENVIRONMENTS

Windows NT 4.0 is designed to run applications created for several different types of operating system environments. Windows NT supports these different application types by using multiple environment *subsystems*. These subsystems each include the *application programming interface* (API) of the operating system or environment that the subsystem is designed to support. The subsystems enable applications to run in the Windows NT environment as if they were running in the operating system environment they were designed for.

The application types and operating system environments supported by Windows NT 4.0 include:

- MS-DOS applications (MS-DOS environment)
- 16-bit Windows applications, such as those written for Windows 3.*x* and Windows for Workgroups (Win16 environment)
- 32-bit Windows applications, such as those written for Windows NT and Windows 95 (Win32 environment)
- POSIX applications (POSIX environment)
- OS/2 applications, such as those written for OS/2 1.*x* (OS/2 environment)

Each of these environments is discussed in the following sections.

## MS-DOS Environment

Applications designed for the MS-DOS environment are typically legacy applications that use a character-based, command-line interface. A *character-based, command-line interface* is one that relies on keyboard input rather than mouse input. Additionally, the screen display does *not* necessarily match the printed output— it's not *What You See Is What You Get* (WYSIWYG). Many utilities designed for MS-DOS are still useful even though they haven't been rewritten for use in the Windows graphical environment.

Windows NT 4.0 includes support for MS-DOS applications via a subsystem called an *NT Virtual DOS Machine* (NTVDM). An NTVDM emulates an Intel 486 computer running the MS-DOS operating system. NTVDM support is included for all hardware platforms supported by Windows NT 4.0, including Intel 486 and higher, DEC Alpha, PowerPC, and MIPS R4000.

Most MS-DOS applications are supported by Windows NT in an NTVDM. However, MS-DOS applications that make direct calls to hardware are *not* supported by Windows NT. These applications will not run correctly in a Windows NT environment.

Each MS-DOS application runs in its own separate NTVDM. Because each application runs in its own separate NTVDM, if an MS-DOS application crashes, other applications are *not* affected.

Windows NT 4.0 enables multiple NTVDMs to be run. Because each MS-DOS application runs in a separate NTVDM, Windows NT can preemptively multitask multiple MS-DOS applications. In *preemptive multitasking*, the operating system allocates processor time between applications. Because Windows NT, *not* the application, allocates processor time between multiple applications, one application can be preempted by the operating system, and another application allowed to run. When multiple applications are alternately paused and then allocated processor time, they appear to run simultaneously to the user.

NTVDMs have three threads. (A *thread* is the smallest unit of processing that can be scheduled by the Windows NT Schedule service. All applications require at least one thread.) Two of these threads are used to maintain the NTVDM environment. The third thread is used by the application. An application that runs in an NTVDM is referred to as a singled-threaded application (because only *one* thread is used by the application).

Some MS-DOS applications require environmental settings that would normally be configured in the MS-DOS computer's `Autoexec.bat` or `Config.sys` files. For example, a path to the application may need to be specified, or a *terminate-and-stay-resident (TSR)* program may need to be loaded prior to starting the application. To provide the same environmental settings in a Windows NT environment, you can edit the `Autoexec.nt` and/or `Config.nt` files to include any necessary instructions. Settings contained in the `Autoexec.nt` and `Config.nt` files are executed each time an NTVDM is started. These files are edited in the same manner as you would edit an `Autoexec.bat` or `Config.sys` file. The `Autoexec.nt` and `Config.nt` files are stored in the `<winntroot>\System32` folder.

# Win16 Environment

Win16 environment applications consist of 16-bit Windows applications designed for Windows 3.x and Windows for Workgroups. These applications are graphical applications that accept input from both a mouse and keyboard. Often the screen display matches the printed output (WYSIWYG).

Windows NT provides support for 16-bit Windows applications via a special subsystem called *WOW*, for *Win16-on-Win32*. The WOW subsystem emulates an Intel 486 computer running MS-DOS and Windows 3.1. The WOW subsystem runs in an NTVDM called the *Win16 NTVDM*. Because NTVDMs are supported on all Windows NT platforms, Windows NT supports Win16 applications on all hardware platforms supported by Windows NT.

Most 16-bit Windows applications are supported by Windows NT. However, 16-bit Windows applications that make undocumented calls to the operating system or that require specific device drivers that make direct calls to hardware may not run correctly on Windows NT.

By default, when multiple Win16 applications are run at the same time, they all run in a single Win16 NTVDM. This means that, by default, all Win16 applications share the same memory space and the Win16 NTVDM's single thread. Because the Win16 applications share the same memory space, if one application crashes, other Win16 applications may also crash. Because multiple Win16 applications share a single NTVDM's thread, Windows NT *can't* preemptively multitask multiple Win16 applications.

To prevent a rogue Win16 application from crashing all of your other Win16 applications, and to allow Win16 applications to be preemptively multitasked, Windows NT permits Win16 applications to be run in separate NTVDMs. This is referred to as *running Win16 applications in separate memory spaces*.

## *Running Win16 applications in separate memory spaces*

Windows NT allows the user to run a 16-bit Windows application in its own separate memory space. When a Win16 application is configured to run in its own separate memory space, Windows NT assigns that application its own Win 16 NTVDM when the application is run.

Running Win16 applications in separate memory spaces has advantages and disadvantages. Advantages include:

o When a Win16 application running in a separate memory space crashes, other applications are *not* affected.

o Windows NT can preemptively multitask Win 16 applications when they are run in separate memory spaces.

Disadvantages include:

o More RAM and system resources are used when Win 16 applications are run in separate memory spaces.

o Some Win 16 applications that use shared memory instead of Object Linking and Embedding (OLE) or Dynamic Data Exchange (DDE) to communicate with other Win 16 applications may not work correctly when run in separate memory spaces.

There are two methods you can use to run a Win16 application in a separate memory space: You can configure the properties of the shortcut to the application, or you can use a batch file that uses the `Start/separate` command.

Configuring the properties of the shortcut to the Win16 application is the easiest and most commonly used method of configuring a Win16 application to run in a separate memory space.

---

**TO CONFIGURE THE PROPERTIES OF THE SHORTCUT TO A WIN16 APPLICATION, FOLLOW THESE STEPS:**

**1.** On the desktop or in Windows NT Explorer, right-click the shortcut to the Win16 application. Select Properties from the menu that appears.

**2.** The application's Properties dialog box appears. Click the Shortcut tab.

**3.** The Shortcut tab appears, as shown in Figure 21-1. Notice the Run in Separate Memory Space check box.

 note **If the Run in Separate Memory Space check box is selected and grayed out, the application is a Win32 (not a Win16) application, and will always be run in a separate memory space.**

If the Run in Separate Memory Space check box is available, select it. The application is now configured to run in a separate memory space. Click OK.

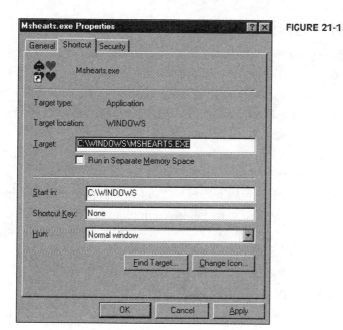

**FIGURE 21-1** Configuring a Win16 application to run in a separate memory space

# Win32 Environment

The Win32 environment is Windows NT's native application environment. It is the preferred and fastest environment for running applications on Windows NT 4.0, because no emulation or workarounds are required. Win32 environment applications consist of 32-bit Windows applications written specifically for Windows NT and/or Windows 95. Windows NT provides support for Win32 applications via the *Win32 subsystem*. Windows NT supports the Win32 subsystem on all hardware platforms supported by Windows NT.

Win32 applications are *source-compatible* across all supported hardware platforms. This means that Win32 applications must be recompiled for each hardware platform in order to be run on that platform.

Each Win32 application runs in its own separate memory space. Because of this, if a Win32 application crashes, other applications are *not* affected. Windows NT can preemptively multitask multiple Win32 applications.

# POSIX Environment

*Portable Operating System Interface for Computing Environments* (POSIX) was developed as a set of accepted standards for writing applications for use on various UNIX computers. POSIX environment applications consist of applications developed to meet the POSIX standards. These applications are sometimes referred to as *POSIX-compliant applications*.

Windows NT provides support for POSIX-compliant applications via the *POSIX subsystem*. Windows NT supports the POSIX subsystem on all hardware platforms supported by Windows NT. To fully support POSIX-compliant applications, at least one NTFS partition is required on the Windows NT computer.

POSIX applications are source-compatible across all supported hardware platforms. This means that POSIX applications must be recompiled for each hardware platform in order to run on that platform.

Each POSIX application runs in its own separate memory space. Because of this, if a POSIX application crashes, other applications are *not* affected. Windows NT can preemptively multitask POSIX applications.

# OS/2 Environment

OS/2 environment applications consist of 16-bit, character-based applications designed for OS/2 version 1.x. Applications designed for other versions of OS/2, including OS/2 2.x, 3.x, and Presentation Manager applications, are *not* supported by Windows NT. Microsoft has developed an add-on product that allows Windows NT to support OS/2 1.x Presentation Manager applications. This product is not included with Windows NT—it must be purchased separately from Microsoft.

Windows NT provides support for OS/2 applications via the *OS/2 subsystem*. It supports the OS/2 subsystem only on Intel 486 and higher platforms. Windows NT does *not* support the OS/2 subsystem on any other hardware platforms.

However, some OS/2 applications, called *real-mode applications,* can be run in an MS-DOS environment. Because Windows NT supports MS-DOS NTVDMs on *all* hardware platforms that it supports, real-mode OS/2 applications can be run in an NTVDM on any of these platforms by using the `Forcedos.exe` command to start the application.

Each OS/2 application runs in its own separate memory space. This means that if an OS/2 application crashes, other applications are *not* affected. Windows NT can preemptively multitask OS/2 applications.

# APPLICATION SUPPORT ON DIVERSE HARDWARE PLATFORMS

Windows NT 4.0 supports several different types of applications on various hardware platforms. Not all application types are supported on every hardware platform.

Some types of applications are source-compatible across hardware platforms. As mentioned previously, this means that the application must be recompiled for each hardware platform that you want to run it on. For example, to run a POSIX 1.*x* compliant application on both the Intel and DEC Alpha platforms, the application must be compiled separately for each processor type.

Table 21-1 shows the support provided by Windows NT 4.0 for different application types on diverse hardware platforms. Each hardware platform is based on a different type of processor.

**TABLE 21-1** APPLICATION SUPPORT ON WINDOWS NT 4.0 COMPUTERS WITH VARIOUS PROCESSORS

| APPLICATION TYPE | HOW THE APPLICATION RUNS IN WINDOWS NT (BROKEN DOWN BY PROCESSOR TYPE) | | | |
| --- | --- | --- | --- | --- |
| | *INTEL 486 OR HIGHER* | *DEC ALPHA* | *POWERPC* | *MIPS R4000* |
| MS–DOS and Win16 | Runs in a Virtual DOS Machine (NTVDM) | Runs in Intel 486 emulation mode | Runs in Intel 486 emulation mode | Runs in Intel 486 emulation mode |
| Win32 | Runs in Win32 subsystem; source code must be recompiled for Intel processor | Runs in Win32 subsystem; source code must be recompiled for DEC Alpha processor | Runs in Win32 subsystem; source code must be recompiled for PowerPC processor | Runs in Win32 subsystem; source code must be recompiled for MIPS R4000 processor |

*continued*

| **TABLE 21-1** *(continued)* | | | | |
| --- | --- | --- | --- | --- |
| APPLICATION TYPE | HOW THE APPLICATION RUNS IN WINDOWS NT (BROKEN DOWN BY PROCESSOR TYPE) | | | |
| | INTEL 486 OR HIGHER | DEC ALPHA | POWERPC | MIPS R4000 |
| POSIX | Runs in POSIX subsystem; source code must be recompiled for Intel processor | Runs in POSIX subsystem; source code must be recompiled for DEC Alpha processor | Runs in POSIX subsystem; source code must be recompiled for PowerPC processor | Runs in POSIX subsystem; source code must be recompiled for MIPS R4000 processor |
| OS/2 1.x character-based | Runs in OS/2 subsystem; only OS/2 1.x character-based applications are supported— additional software is required to support other OS/2 applications | No OS/2 application support; however, real-mode OS/2 applications can be run in an MS-DOS NTVDM by using the Forcedos.exe command to start the application | No OS/2 application support; however, real-mode OS/2 applications can be run in an MS-DOS NTVDM by using the Forcedos.exe command to start the application | No OS/2 application support; however, real-mode OS/2 applications can be run in an MS-DOS NTVDM by using the Forcedos.exe command to start the application |

# APPLICATION PRIORITIES

The Windows NT Schedule service uses application priorities to determine which applications receive the most processor time. Applications that have a high priority receive more processor time than applications with a low priority.

An *application priority* is a number between 0 and 31 that is assigned to an application when it is started. By default, most user applications are assigned a priority of 8, the normal priority. A user application can be assigned a priority between 0 and 15. These applications can be written to a paging file.

A real-time or kernel mode application can be assigned a priority between 16 and 31. Real-time applications *can't* be written to a paging file. When running, these applications are always stored in RAM.

Windows NT can dynamically raise and lower application priorities based on changing conditions in the computer. Most application priority changes are beyond the user's control, and are managed by the operating system. However, the base priority assigned to an application can be set by the user, and the foreground application can be assigned a one- or two-point boost in priority by the user.

## Starting Applications at Various Priorities

In Windows NT, the Start command is used to start applications at various priorities. The Start command can be used in batch files and from the command prompt. The Start command *can't* be used in shortcuts to applications.

Six switches are commonly used with the Windows NT Start command. These switches are listed and described in Table 21-2.

| **TABLE 21-2** WINDOWS NT START COMMAND SWITCHES | |
| --- | --- |
| *SWITCH* | *DESCRIPTION* |
| /low | Starts the application with a base priority of **4**. |
| /normal | Starts the application with a base priority of **8**. This is the priority that is normally assigned to most user applications. Windows NT typically starts user applications with a base priority of 8 when no other priority is specified. |
| /high | Starts the application with a base priority of **13**. |
| /realtime | Starts the application with a base priority of **24**. An application with this priority *can't* be written to a paging file. Applications started at the real-time base priority can slow the performance of the operating system itself. The real-time base priority should be used with extreme caution and is not recommended for most applications. |
| /min | Does *not* affect the base priority of an application. It starts an application in a minimized window. This switch can be used in conjunction with a priority switch and/or the /separate switch. |
| /separate | Does *not* affect the base priority of an application. It starts a Win16 application in a separate memory space. |

For example, to start User Manager at a high priority and in a minimized window, the following command is used at the command prompt:
`Start /min /high Usrmgr.exe`

**in the real world**

**It's been my experience that the `Start` command often doesn't work properly unless it is run from the application's default folder. For example, to start User Manager, the `Start` command should be run from the `<winntroot>\System32` folder.**

**If you are unable to change an application's base priority by using the `Start` command, even from the application's default folder, you may need to use Windows NT Task Manager to change the application's base priority after it is started. (Task Manager is covered later in this chapter.)**

## Configuring Foreground Application Priority Boost

Normally it is desirable to give the application running in the foreground (the active application) a higher priority than applications running in the background. By default, Windows NT assigns a two-point priority boost to the foreground application.

You can boost the foreground application's priority by zero, one, or two points. The foreground application priority boost is *applied* to an application when it becomes the foreground application, and is *removed* from that application when the application is minimized or when another application becomes the foreground application. Once the foreground application priority boost is configured, that boost is applied to the foreground application from then on until the foreground application priority boost is changed.

The System application in Control Panel is used to configure the amount of boost a foreground application is assigned by Windows NT, as the next section explains.

## TO CHANGE THE FOREGROUND APPLICATION'S PRIORITY BOOST, FOLLOW THESE STEPS:

**1.** Select Start ⇒ Settings ⇒ Control Panel.

**2.** In Control Panel, double-click the System icon.

**3.** The System Properties dialog box appears. Click the Performance tab.

**4.** The Performance tab appears, as shown in Figure 21-2. Notice that the boost slide bar is set at Maximum, by default.

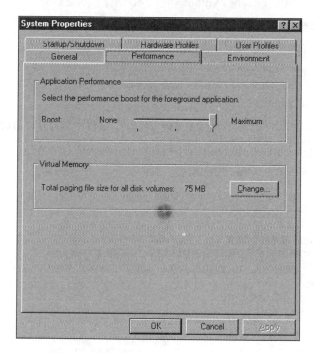

**FIGURE 21-2**   Configuring foreground application performance boost

Use the boost slide bar in the Application Performance section to choose one of three possible settings:

- **None**—No foreground application priority boost is applied.
- **Middle Setting**—A one-point application priority boost is applied to the foreground application.
- **Maximum**—A two-point application priority boost is applied to the foreground application. This is the default setting. Click OK.

**5.** The Control Panel dialog box reappears. Exit Control Panel.

# Using Windows NT Task Manager

*Windows NT Task Manager* is a Windows NT administrative utility that can be used to start and stop applications; to view performance statistics, such as memory and CPU usage; and to change a process's base priority.

There are three different ways to access Task Manager:

- By pressing Ctrl + Alt + Delete, and then clicking the Task Manager command button in the Windows NT Security dialog box;
- By right-clicking a blank space on the taskbar (on the Windows NT desktop), and then selecting Task Manager from the menu that appears;
- By selecting Start ⇒ Run, and then typing **taskmgr** in the Run dialog box.

## Using Task Manager to Stop an Application

Task Manager is often used to stop or end an application that has crashed and has stopped responding to user input.

### TO USE TASK MANAGER TO STOP OR END AN APPLICATION OR PROCESS, FOLLOW THESE STEPS:

**1.** Start Task Manager (press Ctrl + Alt + Delete, and then click the Task Manager command button in the Windows NT Security dialog box).

**2.** The Windows NT Task Manager dialog box appears, as shown in Figure 21-3. Notice that the Applications tab is on top, by default. Highlight the application you want to stop. Click the End Task command button. Exit Task Manager.

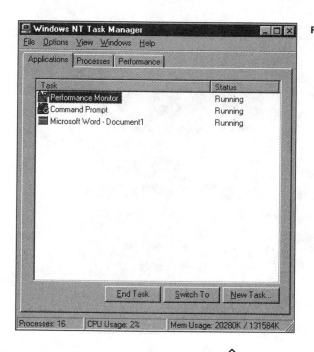

**FIGURE 21-3** Using Task Manager to stop (end) an application

## Using Task Manager to View Performance Statistics

You can also use Task Manager to view performance statistics for your Windows NT computer.

**TO USE TASK MANAGER TO VIEW STATISTICS, FOLLOW THESE STEPS:**

**1.** Start Task Manager.

**2.** The Windows NT Task Manager dialog box appears. Click the Performance tab.

**3.** The Performance tab appears, as shown in Figure 21-4. Notice the CPU Usage and Memory Usage graphs. When you are finished viewing performance statistics, exit Task Manager.

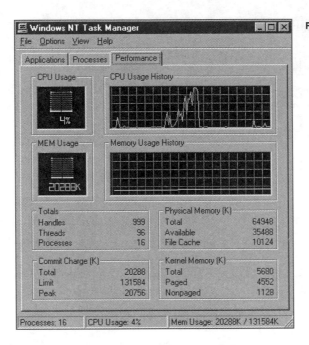

**FIGURE 21-4** Viewing performance statistics in Task Manager

# Using Task Manager to Change an Application's Base Priority

Task Manager can also be used to view individual application and process statistics, and to set an application or process's base priority.

**TO VIEW PROCESS STATISTICS OR TO CHANGE AN APPLICATION OR PROCESS'S BASE PRIORITY BY USING TASK MANAGER, FOLLOW THESE STEPS:**

**1.** Start Task Manager.

**2.** The Windows NT Task Manager dialog box appears. Click the Processes tab.

**3.** The Processes tab appears, as shown in Figure 21-5. Notice the various statistics displayed. Maximize the Task Manager dialog box. Select View ⇒ Select Columns.

**4.** The Select Columns dialog box appears, as shown in Figure 21-6. Note the various process statistics that you can choose to display in Task Manager. Select the check box next to Base Priority. Click OK.

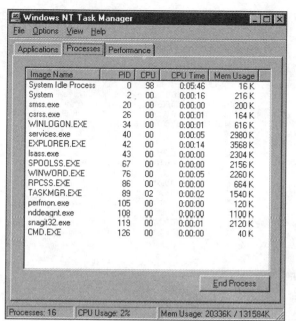

**FIGURE 21-5** Using Task Manager to view process statistics

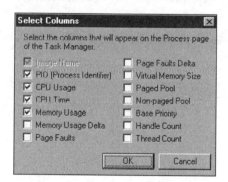

**FIGURE 21-6** Selecting process information to be displayed in Task Manager

**5.** The Processes tab in the Windows NT Task Manager dialog box reappears, as shown in Figure 21-7. Note the new column that displays the base priority for each process. Also note that `perfmon.exe` (Performance Monitor) currently has a base priority of High.

Right-click the application or process for which you want to change the base priority. From the menu that appears, select the base priority (Realtime, High, Normal, or Low) that you want to assign to the application or process.

Figure 21-8 shows the process of selecting menu options to assign a base priority of Realtime to the `perfmon.exe` (Performance Monitor) process.

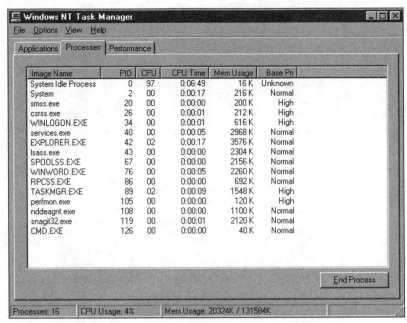

**FIGURE 21-7** Viewing a process's base priority in Task Manager

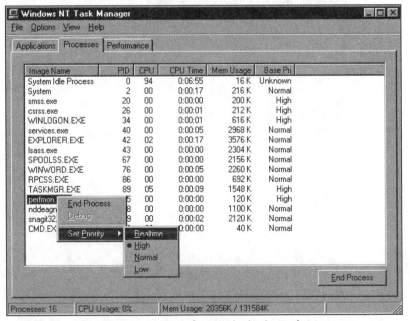

**FIGURE 21-8** Changing a process's base priority in Task Manager

6. A Task Manager Warning dialog box appears, indicating that changing the base priority of a process may have undesirable results. Click the Yes command button to continue.

7. The Processes tab in the Windows NT Task Manager dialog box reappears, as shown in Figure 21-9. Notice that `perfmon.exe` (Performance Monitor) now has a base priority of Realtime. Exit Task Manager.

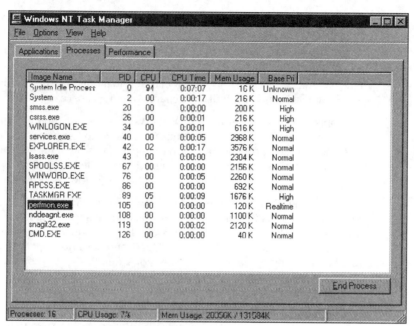

**FIGURE 21-9**    **Base priority of** `perfmon.exe`
**(Performance Monitor) changed**

# TROUBLESHOOTING COMMON APPLICATION PROBLEMS

Occasionally you may experience problems when running an application on Windows NT. Some application problems have workarounds, and others can't be solved easily because they involve applications that simply aren't compatible with Windows NT.

Table 21-3 shows some common applications problems and recommended solutions.

| **TABLE 21-3** TROUBLESHOOTING APPLICATION PROBLEMS IN WINDOWS NT | |
| --- | --- |
| *PROBLEM* | *RECOMMENDED SOLUTION* |
| An application crashes and no longer responds to user input. | Use Task Manager to stop (end) the application. (This is sometimes called killing the application.) |
| A 16-bit Windows (Win16) application often crashes, which results in all other Win16 applications locking up. | Use Task Manager to stop (end) all of the Win16 applications that are running. Configure the application that often crashes to run in its own separate memory space. |
| An application that makes a direct call to the hardware does not function properly on your Windows NT computer. | Windows NT does not support applications that make direct calls to hardware. Run this application on the operating system for which it was originally designed, or rewrite the application to function correctly in a Windows NT environment. |
| An OS/2 or POSIX application makes calls to APIs that aren't supported by Windows NT. The application doesn't function properly on your Windows NT computer. | Windows NT does not support calls to OS/2 Presentation Manager APIs (unless you have the special add-on product that supports Presentation Manager), and does not support many POSIX extensions. Run this application on the platform for which it was originally designed, or rewrite the application to function correctly in a Windows NT environment. |
| A standard Win32 application won't run on your PowerPC (or DEC Alpha, or MIPS R4000) computer. | Purchase a PowerPC (or DEC Alpha, or MIPS R4000) version of the application, or recompile the application for the PowerPC (or DEC Alpha, or MIPS R4000) platform. Win32 applications are source-compatible, and must be recompiled for each individual hardware platform. |

# KEY POINT SUMMARY

This chapter explored the various application environments supported by Windows NT 4.0, as well as some techniques for customizing application performance. Windows NT 4.0 is designed to run applications created for several different types of operating system environments. Windows NT supports these different application types via multiple environment subsystems.

- The application types and operating system environments supported by Windows NT 4.0 include:

  - MS-DOS applications (MS-DOS environment)

  - 16-bit Windows applications, such as those written for Windows 3.*x* and Windows for Workgroups (Win16 environment)

  - 32-bit Windows applications, such as those written for Windows NT and Windows 95 (Win32 environment)

  - POSIX applications (POSIX environment)

  - OS/2 applications, such as those written for OS/2 1.*x* (OS/2 environment)

- *MS-DOS applications* are supported in Windows NT 4.0 by a subsystem called an *NT Virtual DOS Machine (NTVDM)*. An NTVDM emulates an Intel 486 computer running MS-DOS. Each MS-DOS application runs in its own separate NTVDM. Because of this, if an MS-DOS application crashes, other applications are *not* affected. Windows NT can preemptively multitask multiple MS-DOS applications.

- NTVDMs have three threads, although only *one* of these threads is used by the application. A *thread* is the smallest unit of processing that can be scheduled by the Windows NT Schedule service.

- You can edit the `Autoexec.nt` and/or `Config.nt` files to include any necessary MS-DOS environmental settings that would normally be configured in the MS-DOS computer's `Autoexec.bat` or `Config.sys` files.

- *Win16 applications* are 16-bit Windows applications designed for Windows 3.*x* and Windows for Workgroups. Windows NT 4.0 provides support for 16-bit Windows applications via a subsystem called WOW (short for Win16-on-Win32). WOW emulates an Intel 486 computer running MS-DOS *and* Windows 3.1. The WOW subsystem runs in an NTVDM called the Win16 NTVDM.

- By default, when multiple Win16 applications are run at the same time, they all run in a single Win16 NTVDM. This means that, by default, all Win16 applications share the same memory space and the Win16 NTVDM's single thread. Because applications share the same memory space, if one application crashes, other Win16 applications may also crash. Because multiple Win16 applications share an NTVDM's single thread, Windows NT *can't* preemptively multitask multiple Win16 applications.

o To prevent a rogue Win16 application from crashing other Win16 applications, Windows NT permits a Win16 application to be configured to *run in its own separate memory space.* The advantages of running Win16 applications in separate memory spaces are (1) when an application crashes, other applications are not affected, and (2) Windows NT can preemptively multitask Win16 applications when they are configured to run in separate memory spaces. Disadvantages of running Win16 applications in separate memory spaces are (1) more RAM and system resources are used in this configuration, and (2) some Win16 applications may not work correctly when run in separate memory spaces.

   o There are two methods you can use to run a Win16 application in a separate memory space: You can configure the properties of the shortcut to the application (this is the easiest and most commonly used method); or you can use a batch file that uses the `Start/separate` command.

o The *Win32 environment* is Windows NT's native application environment, and is supported on Windows NT via the Win32 subsystem. Win32 applications are 32-bit Windows applications written for Windows NT and/or Windows 95. Win32 applications are *source-compatible* across all supported hardware platforms, which means that Win32 applications must be recompiled for each hardware platform in order to be run on that platform. Each Win32 application runs in its own separate memory space. Because of this, if a Win32 application crashes, other applications are *not* affected. Windows NT can preemptively multitask multiple Win32 applications.

o *POSIX environment* applications that are written to meet POSIX standards are called POSIX-compliant applications. Windows NT provides support for POSIX-compliant applications via the POSIX subsystem. To fully support POSIX-compliant applications, at least one NTFS partition is required on the Windows NT computer. POSIX applications are source-compatible across all supported hardware platforms, which means that POSIX applications must be recompiled for each hardware platform in order to run on that platform. Each POSIX application runs in its own separate memory space. If a POSIX application crashes, other applications are *not* affected. Windows NT can preemptively multitask POSIX applications.

o *OS/2 environment* applications consist of 16-bit character-based applications designed for OS/2 version 1.*x*. Presentation Manager and OS/2 2.*x* and 3.*x* applications are *not* supported by Windows NT. Windows NT only supports the OS/2 subsystem on Intel 486 and higher platforms. Each OS/2 application runs in its own separate memory space. If an OS/2 application crashes, other applications are *not* affected. Windows NT can preemptively multitask OS/2 applications.

o Windows NT 4.0 supports several different types of applications on various hardware platforms. Supported hardware platforms include the Intel 486 processor, the DEC Alpha processor, the PowerPC processor, and the MIPS R4000 processor.

o An *application priority* is a number between 0 and 31 that is assigned to an application when it is started. Applications that have a high priority receive more processor time than applications with a low priority. Most user applications are assigned a priority of 8, the normal priority. In Windows NT, the `Start` command is used to start applications at various priorities. The six switches commonly used with the `Start` command are: `/low`, `/normal`, `/high`, `/realtime`, `/min`, and `/separate`. The `Start` command can be used in batch files and from the command prompt.

o You can configure the *foreground application priority boost* by zero, one, or two points by using the System application in Control Panel.

o *Windows NT Task Manager* can be used to start and stop (end) applications, to view performance statistics, and to change a process's base priority. There are three ways to access Task Manager:

   o By pressing Ctrl + Alt + Delete, and then clicking the Task Manager command button in the Windows NT Security dialog box.

   o By right-clicking a blank space on the taskbar (on the Windows NT desktop), and then selecting Task Manager from the menu that appears.

   o By selecting Start ⇒ Run, and then typing **taskmgr** in the Run dialog box.

o Occasionally you may experience problems when running an application on Windows NT. Some application problems have workarounds, and others can't be solved easily because they involve applications that simply aren't compatible with Windows NT.

# Applying What You've Learned

Now it's time to regroup, review, and apply what you've learned in this chapter.

The following Instant Assessment questions bring to mind key facts and concepts. In addition, the review activity provides an opportunity to test your troubleshooting skills.

The hands-on lab exercise will really reinforce what you've learned, and give you a chance to practice some of the tasks tested by the Workstation exam.

## Instant Assessment

1. What subsystem in Windows NT 4.0 supports MS-DOS applications?

2. Describe the concept of preemptive multitasking as it applies to Windows NT.

3. What is a thread?

4. Which two files can you edit on a Windows NT computer to include any necessary MS-DOS environmental settings that would normally be configured in the MS-DOS computer's Autoexec.bat and/or Config.sys files?

5. By default, when multiple Win16 applications are run at the same time on a Windows NT computer, where do they run?

6. What can you do to prevent a rogue Win16 application from crashing other Win16 applications?

7. What is the Start/separate command used for?

8. What is the native Windows NT application environment?

9. What does the phrase "source-compatible across all hardware platforms" mean?

10. What is required on a Windows NT computer to fully support POSIX-compliant applications?

11. What number represents a normal Windows NT user application priority?

12. What would you type at the command prompt on a Windows NT computer to start Notepad in a minimized window with an application priority of 13 (high).

13. What Windows NT application can you use to change the foreground application priority boost?

**14.** What are the three ways you can access Windows NT Task Manager?

**15.** What kinds of applications does the Windows NT OS/2 environment support?

|  | **T/F** |
|---|---|
| **16.** On Windows NT computers, each MS-DOS application runs in its own separate NTVDM. | ___ |
| **17.** Each Win32 application runs in its own separate memory space. | ___ |
| **18.** If one Win32 application crashes, all other Win32 applications also crash. | ___ |
| **19.** Win32 applications and POSIX applications are *not* source-compatible across all supported hardware platforms on Windows NT. | ___ |

 concept link    **For answers to the Instant Assessment questions see Appendix D.**

## Review Activity

The following activity gives you a chance to apply your knowledge of running applications on Windows NT computers in two real-life troubleshooting situations.

Workstation    *Troubleshooting common application problems*

The purpose of this exercise is to give you experience in troubleshooting common application problems on Windows NT computers. For each of the following problems, recommend a solution.

**Problem 1**    An application has crashed on your Windows NT computer, and won't respond to any input from the mouse or keyboard. What should you do?

**Problem 2**    You try to run a POSIX-compliant application compiled for a DEC Alpha processor on your Intel Pentium Pro/200MHz computer that is running Windows NT, but the application won't run properly. What should you do?

concept link    **For answers to the Review Activity see Appendix D.**

# Hands-on Lab Exercise

The following hands-on lab exercise provides you with a practical opportunity to apply the knowledge you've gained in this chapter.

## Lab 21.34  *Starting applications at various priorities*

Workstation

The purpose of this lab exercise is to give you hands-on experience in configuring foreground application responsiveness and in starting applications at various priorities on a Windows NT Workstation computer.

This lab consists of two parts:

> Part 1: Using the System application to configure foreground application responsiveness

> Part 2: Using the Start command and Task Manager to start applications at various priorities

Begin this lab by booting your computer to Windows NT Workstation. Log on as Administrator. Place your Windows NT Workstation compact disc in your computer's CD-ROM drive.

Follow the steps below carefully.

### Part 1: Using the System application to configure foreground application responsiveness

In this section, you use the System application in Control Panel to change foreground application responsiveness on a Windows NT Workstation computer. Additionally, you install games on your computer (if you haven't already done so).

**1.** Select Start ⇒ Settings ⇒ Control Panel.

**2.** The Control Panel dialog box appears. Double-click the System icon.

**3.** The System Properties dialog box appears. Click the Performance tab.

**4.** The Performance tab appears. Notice the Application Performance section on this tab. Move the Boost slide bar to the middle, halfway between None and Maximum. (This configures a performance boost of one point for the foreground application.) Move the Boost slide bar back to Maximum. (This configures a performance boost of 2 points for the foreground application.) Click OK.

**5.** The Control Panel dialog box reappears. If you have already installed games (including Pinball) on your Windows NT Workstation computer, close Control Panel, skip the remaining steps in this section, and continue on to Part 2. If you haven't yet installed games on your Windows NT Workstation computer, double-click the Add/Remove Programs icon, and continue on to step 6.

**6.** The Add/Remove Programs Properties dialog box appears. Click the Windows NT Setup tab.

**7.** The Windows NT Setup tab appears. Select the check box next to Games in the Components list box. Click OK.

**8.** The Add/Remove Programs Properties—Copying Files dialog box appears. If the Files Needed dialog box appears, ensure that the correct path to the source files (usually the I386 folder on your Windows NT Workstation compact disc) is presented in the "Copy files from" text box. Edit this text box as necessary. Click OK.

**9.** Windows NT Workstation copies files.

**10.** The Control Panel dialog box reappears. Close Control Panel.

Continue on to Part 2.

### Part 2: Using the Start command and Task Manager to start applications at various priorities

In this section, you use the Start command and Windows NT Task Manager to start applications at various priorities on a Windows NT Workstation computer.

**1.** Select Start ⇒ Programs ⇒ Command Prompt.

**2.** The Command Prompt dialog box appears. At the command prompt, type **cd \winntwks\system32** and press Enter.

**3.** At the C:\WINNTWKS\system32> command prompt, type **start /low usrmgr.exe** and press Enter.

**4.** User Manager starts. Press Ctrl + Alt + Delete.

**5.** The Windows NT Security dialog box appears. Click the Task Manager command button.

**6.** The Windows NT Task Manager dialog box appears. Click the Processes tab.

**7.** The Processes tab appears. Select View ⇒ Select Columns.

**8.** The Select Columns dialog box appears. Deselect the check boxes next to PID (Process Identifier) and CPU Usage. Select the check box next to Base Priority. Click OK.

**9.** The Processes tab in the Windows NT Task Manager dialog box reappears. Find USRMGR.EXE in the list box. Notice that USRMGR.EXE has a base priority of Low. Click the Applications tab.

**10.** The Applications tab appears. Highlight User Manager and click the End Task command button at the bottom of the dialog box. (This action stops User Manager). Minimize (*don't* close) Windows NT Task Manager.

**11.** At the `C:\WINNTWKS\system32>` command prompt, type **start /realtime usrmgr.exe** and press Enter.

**12.** User Manager starts. Maximize Task Manager, and click the Processes tab.

**13.** The Processes tab appears. Notice that `USRMGR.EXE` now has a base priority of Realtime. Highlight `USRMGR.EXE` and click the End Process command button.

**14.** A Task Manager Warning dialog box appears. Click the Yes command button. (This action stops User Manager.)

**15.** Minimize (*don't* close) Windows NT Task Manager.

**16.** At the `C:\WINNTWKS\system32>` command prompt, type **start /realtime perfmon.exe** and press Enter.

**17.** Performance Monitor starts. Maximize Task Manager.

**18.** The Processes tab appears. Notice that `perfmon.exe` has a base priority of High. (The `/realtime` switch does *not* always work with all applications. Performance Monitor always starts with a base priority of High, no matter which priority is assigned with the `Start` command.)

Right-click `perfmon.exe`. Select Set Priority ⇒ Realtime from the menu that appears.

**19.** A Task Manager Warning dialog box appears. Click the Yes command button.

**20.** In the Windows NT Task Manager dialog box, notice that `perfmon.exe` now has a base priority of Realtime. (This is how you can change the priority of applications that don't respond correctly to the priority setting specified by the `Start` command.)

Highlight `perfmon.exe` and click the End Process command button.

**21.** A Task Manager Warning dialog box appears. Click the Yes command button.

**22.** Minimize (*don't* close) Windows NT Task Manager.

**23.** At the `C:\WINNTWKS\system32>` command prompt, type **cd "\program files\windows nt\pinball"** and press Enter.

**24.** At the `C:\Program Files\Windows NT\PINBALL>` command prompt, type **start /realtime pinball** and press Enter.

**25.** The Pinball game starts. Notice that your computer is locked up and won't respond to keyboard or mouse input. As you can see, not all programs should be run at real-time priority. In this case, when Pinball is set at real-time priority, it utilizes all available system resources, so that even the operating system is unable to function properly. Press the Restart button on your computer, or power off your computer.

# Monitoring and Optimization

This part explores how to monitor and optimize the performance of your Windows NT computer or Windows NT network by using various Windows NT tools.

This part begins with Chapter 22, which explains how to use Performance Monitor, a Windows NT tool that can identify performance problems, determine current usage of resources, track performance trends over time, predict future usage of resources, and determine how configuration changes affect performance.

Next, Chapter 23 explains how to use Network Monitor, a Windows NT Server administrative tool that enables you to capture, view, and analyze network packets.

Then, Chapter 24 examines the fundamentals of capacity planning. We explore both capacity planning your server and capacity planning your network.

Finally, Chapter 25 presents practical information on performance optimization, focusing on what you can do to increase performance on your system and how to resolve bottlenecks.

Part VI maps directly to the Monitoring and Optimization section in the exam objectives for each of the three Windows NT 4.0 Microsoft Certified Professional exams. If you're preparing for the Enterprise exam, you'll want to read every chapter in this part. If you're preparing for the NT Workstation 4.0 or NT Server 4.0 exam, consult Appendices A and B to see which chapters are optional.

Workstation
Server
Enterprise

CHAPTER

## Using Performance Monitor

# 22

# About Chapter 22

The focus of this chapter is on Performance Monitor, a Windows NT tool that can be used to identify bottlenecks, determine usage of system resources, track performance trends over time, predict future usage of system resources, and determine how system configuration changes affect system performance.

The chapter begins by explaining Performance Monitor objects, instances, and counters. Then it details how to install the SNMP Service and Network Monitor Agent to obtain various objects and their counters. It also describes how to enable the PhysicalDisk and LogicalDisk objects and their counters.

The remainder of the chapter is all about using Performance Monitor to gather and view statistics. Each of the four Performance Monitor views—Chart view, Alert view, Report view, and Log view—are explored.

This chapter includes one hands-on lab. In this lab, you'll install Network Monitor Agent and SNMP Service, use Performance Monitor Chart view and Alert view, create a Performance Monitor log file, and import a Performance Monitor log file into Report view and Chart view.

Chapter 22 is a "must read," no matter which of the three Windows NT 4.0 Microsoft Certified Professional exams you're preparing for. This chapter maps to the "Monitor performance" objectives in the Monitoring and Optimization section in these exams' objectives.

# What Is Performance Monitor?

*Performance Monitor* is a Windows NT tool that ships with both Windows NT Workstation and Windows NT Server. You don't need to install Performance Monitor—it's installed automatically when you install Windows NT.

Performance Monitor has several uses. It can be used to:

- Identify performance problems and/or bottlenecks
- Determine current usage of system resources
- Track performance trends over time
- Predict future usage of system resources (capacity planning)
- Determine how system configuration changes affect system performance

Performance Monitor is often used when there's a problem to be resolved, but it can also be used for planning purposes.

The rest of this chapter discusses the basics of how to use Performance Monitor.

concept link

**This chapter covers only the basics of monitoring performance. Advanced use of Performance Monitor for system capacity planning is discussed in Chapter 24. Using Performance Monitor to detect common bottlenecks is featured in Chapter 25.**

A good place to start when discussing Performance Monitor is with an explanation of Performance Monitor objects, instances, and counters—the things Performance Monitor can measure.

# Performance Monitor Objects, Instances, and Counters

The system components that Performance Monitor can measure, such as processor, memory, and physical disk, are called *objects*.

If a system has more than one of a particular object, such as multiple processors or multiple physical disks, there is said to be more than one *instance* of that object. Some objects, such as memory, do not have instances. This is because there can't be more than one of the particular object.

Each instance of an object can be measured in different ways. Each possible measurement of an object is called a *counter*. For example, the PhysicalDisk object has multiple possible counters, including Disk Reads/sec (second), Disk Writes/sec, % Disk Time, % Disk Read Time, and % Disk Write Time. Each counter is selected individually. An object can be selected multiple times with a different counter for each selection, as shown in Figure 22-1. Notice the Performance Monitor report shows multiple counters selected for the PhysicalDisk object.

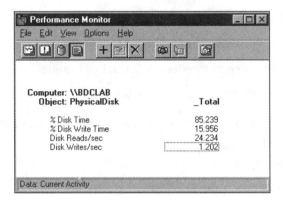

**FIGURE 22-1** Measuring multiple counters for a single object

Many different objects and counters can be measured in Performance Monitor. Table 22-1 shows some of the most commonly used Performance Monitor objects and counters.

| **TABLE 22-1** COMMONLY USED PERFORMANCE MONITOR OBJECTS AND COUNTERS | | |
|---|---|---|
| *OBJECT* | *COUNTER* | *DESCRIPTION* |
| Memory | Pages/sec | This counter measures how often data is written to and read from the paging file. I use this counter to obtain an overall view of how memory is utilized by Windows NT. |
| | | A consistently high number (greater than 2–3) indicates that the current amount of RAM may be insufficient for the computer. |
| Network Segment | % Network utilization | This counter measures the total network utilization on a given network segment as a percentage of the maximum amount of network traffic possible on that segment. |

| OBJECT | COUNTER | DESCRIPTION |
|--------|---------|-------------|
| | | A consistently high number (a number approaching 100 percent) may indicate that there is too much traffic on that network segment, and that an additional network adapter may need to be installed in the server or a router installed to further segment the network. |
| PhysicalDisk | Avg. Disk Queue Length | This counter measures the average number of disk reads and writes waiting to be performed. |
| | | A consistently high number (greater than 2–3) may indicate that a faster hard disk and/or hard disk controller, or a different disk configuration (such as a stripe set or a stripe set with parity) may be required for adequate system performance. |
| PhysicalDisk | % Disk Time | This counter measures the percentage of time the disk performs reads and writes. |
| | | A consistently high number (a number approaching 100 percent) may indicate that a faster hard disk and/or hard disk controller, or a different disk configuration (such as a stripe set or a stripe set with parity) may be required for adequate system performance. |
| Processor | % Processor Time | This counter measures the percentage of time that the processor is actively used by processes other than the Idle process. (The *Idle process* can be defined as the time the processor spends waiting to be assigned tasks.) |
| | | A consistently high number (a number approaching 100 percent) may indicate that a faster processor (or an additional processor) may be required for adequate system performance. |
| Server | Bytes Total/sec | This counter measures the total amount of network utilization of a Windows NT Server computer. Specifically, it measures the total number of bytes sent to and received from all network adapters in the Windows NT computer by the Server process. |
| | | The measurement can be used to compare utilization of two similar servers for load balancing purposes. It can also be used in conjunction with other measurements to determine network segment utilization. |

Not all Performance Monitor objects and counters are available when Windows NT is first installed. For example, the Transport Control Protocol (TCP) object is not available until the *Simple Network Management Protocol* (SNMP) service is installed, and the Network Segment object is not available until the Network Monitor Agent is installed. Additionally, some objects and counters must be enabled before they can be effectively used in Performance Monitor.

The following sections explain how to add and enable certain Performance Monitor objects and counters.

## Installing the SNMP Service to Obtain TCP/IP Objects and their Counters

By default, Performance Monitor does *not* make available TCP/IP objects and their counters, even when TCP/IP is installed and configured on the Windows NT computer. The SNMP Service must be installed before you can monitor TCP/IP objects and counters in Performance Monitor.

Installing the SNMP Service adds four objects and their counters to Performance Monitor:

o  IP (Internet Protocol)

o  ICMP (Internet Control Message Protocol)

o  TCP (Transport Control Protocol)

o  UDP (User Datagram Protocol)

These four objects and their counters are used by developers to optimize network usage of applications, and by administrators of large networks to troubleshoot and optimize TCP/IP network traffic.

**TO INSTALL THE SNMP SERVICE ON A WINDOWS NT COMPUTER, FOLLOW THESE STEPS:**

**1.** Select Start ⇒ Settings ⇒ Control Panel.

**2.** The Control Panel dialog box appears. Double-click the Network icon.

**3.** The Network dialog box appears. Click the Services tab.

**4.** The Services tab appears. Click the Add command button.

**5.** The Select Network Service dialog box appears. Highlight SNMP Service, as shown in Figure 22-2. Click OK.

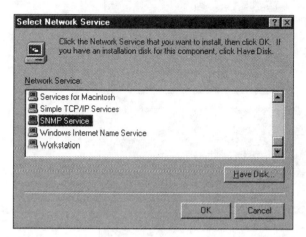

**FIGURE 22-2** Installing the SNMP Service

**6.** A Windows NT Setup dialog box appears. Ensure that the correct path to your Windows NT Workstation or Windows NT Server source files (usually the i386 folder on your Windows NT Workstation or Windows NT Server compact disc) is listed in the text box. Edit this text box if necessary. Click the Continue command button.

**7.** Windows NT copies source files and installs the SNMP Service.

**8.** The Microsoft SNMP Properties dialog box appears, as shown in Figure 22-3. Notice the three tabs available: Agent, Traps, and Security. Configure the SNMP Service as desired. Click OK.

note 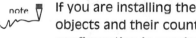 **If you are installing the SNMP Service only to obtain TCP/IP objects and their counters for use in Performance Monitor, no configuration is required.**

**9.** The Network dialog box reappears. Click the Close command button.

**10.** Windows NT performs various bindings operations.

**11.** A Network Settings Change dialog box appears, indicating that you must shut down and restart the computer for the new settings to take effect. Click the Yes command button to restart the computer.

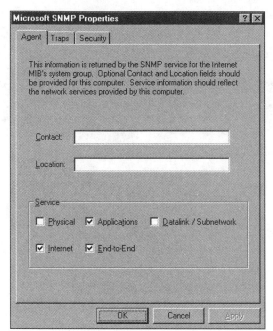

**FIGURE 22-3**  Configuring SNMP Properties

## Installing Network Monitor Agent to Obtain the Network Segment Object and its Counters

By default, the Network Segment object and its counters are *not* available in Performance Monitor. The Network Monitor Agent must be installed to make this object and its counters available.

The counters that are installed with the Network Segment object include: % Broadcast Frames, % Network Utilization, Total Bytes Received/second, and Total Frames Received/second.

The Network Segment object has an instance for each network adapter installed in the Windows NT computer. You can monitor counters for each instance of the Network Segment object. In other words, you can monitor network traffic on each network segment that your Windows NT computer is connected to.

The Network Segment object and its counters are used by network administrators to determine network utilization on individual network segments. In addition, this object and its counters are often used for network capacity planning. The following section explains how to install Network Monitor Agent to obtain the Network Segment object and its counters.

**TO INSTALL NETWORK MONITOR AGENT ON A
WINDOWS NT COMPUTER, FOLLOW THESE STEPS:**

**1.** Select Start⇒Settings⇒Control Panel.

**2.** The Control Panel dialog box appears. Double-click the Network icon.

**3.** The Network dialog box appears. Click the Services tab.

**4.** The Services tab appears. Click the Add command button.

**5.** The Select Network Service dialog box appears. Highlight Network Monitor Agent, as shown in Figure 22-4. Click OK.

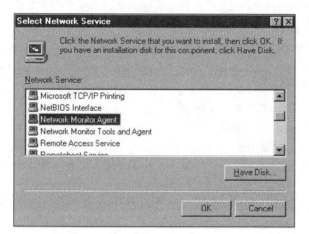

**FIGURE 22-4** Installing the Network Monitor Agent

**6.** A Windows NT Setup dialog box appears. Ensure that the correct path to your Windows NT Workstation or Windows NT Server source files (usually the i386 folder on your Windows NT Workstation or Windows NT Server compact disc) is listed in the text box. Edit this text box if necessary. Click the Continue command button.

**7.** Windows NT copies source files and installs the Network Monitor Agent.

**8.** The Network dialog box reappears. Click the Close command button.

**9.** Windows NT performs various bindings operations.

**10.** A Network Settings Change dialog box appears, indicating that you must shut down and restart the computer for the new settings to take effect. Click the Yes command button to restart the computer.

# Enabling the PhysicalDisk and LogicalDisk Objects and their Counters

By default, the PhysicalDisk and LogicalDisk objects and their counters are installed, but *not* enabled. Although you can select these objects and their counters in Performance Monitor, until they are enabled, the counters will always display a value of zero.

The reason these objects and their counters are not enabled by default is that monitoring these objects can cause up to a one-and-a-half-percent increase in processor utilization on an Intel 486 computer. On a Pentium computer, enabling these objects and their counters usually causes a negligible (less than one half of one percent) increase in processor utilization.

The Windows NT `Diskperf.exe` command-line utility is used to enable the PhysicalDisk and LogicalDisk objects and their counters. You must reboot the computer after running `Diskperf.exe` before these objects and their counters will be usable in Performance Monitor.

Table 22-2 shows how the `Diskperf.exe` command-line utility can be used to enable and disable the PhysicalDisk and LogicalDisk objects and their counters.

**TABLE 22-2** THE WINDOWS NT DISKPERF.EXE COMMAND

| *DISKPERF.EXE COMMAND* | *DESCRIPTION* |
| --- | --- |
| `diskperf-y` | Enables the PhysicalDisk and LogicalDisk objects and their counters. |
| `diskperf-ye` | Enables the PhysicalDisk and LogicalDisk objects and their counters for stripe sets and stripe sets with parity. |
| `diskperf-n` | Disables the PhysicalDisk and LogicalDisk objects and their counters. |

The remainder of this section explains how to enable the PhysicalDisk and LogicalDisk objects and their counters by using the `Diskperf.exe` command-line utility.

**TO USE DISKPERF.EXE TO ENABLE THE PHYSICALDISK
AND LOGICALDISK OBJECTS AND THEIR COUNTERS,
FOLLOW THESE STEPS:**

**1.** Select Start ⇒ Programs ⇒ Command Prompt.

**2.** The Command Prompt dialog box appears. At the command prompt, type **diskperf -y** and press Enter.

**3.** The `Diskperf.exe` command displays a message, as shown in Figure 22-5. Notice that you must reboot the computer before these changes will become effective. At the command prompt, type **exit** and press Enter.

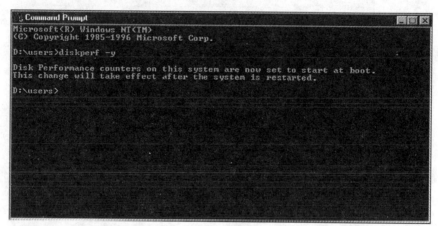

**FIGURE 22-5**   Using `Diskperf.exe` to enable disk performance objects and counters

**4.** Shut down and restart the computer.

# USING PERFORMANCE MONITOR TO GATHER AND VIEW STATISTICS

Now that you have a basic understanding of the Performance Monitor objects and their counters, you're ready to use the Performance Monitor tool.

In this section, you'll learn how to start Performance Monitor and how to use the "views" within Performance Monitor to gather and view statistics on a Windows NT computer's performance.

To start Performance Monitor, select Start ⇒ Programs ⇒ Administrative Tools (Common) ⇒ Performance Monitor.

The Performance Monitor dialog box appears, as shown in Figure 22-6. Notice that no objects are monitored when Performance Monitor is first started.

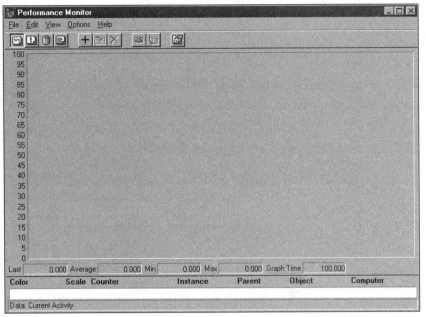

**FIGURE 22-6    Starting Performance Monitor**

There are four possible views in Performance Monitor: Chart, Alert, Report, and Log. By default, Performance Monitor starts in Chart view. The other views can be selected from the View menu, as shown in Figure 22-7.

The following sections explain how to use each of the four Performance Monitor views.

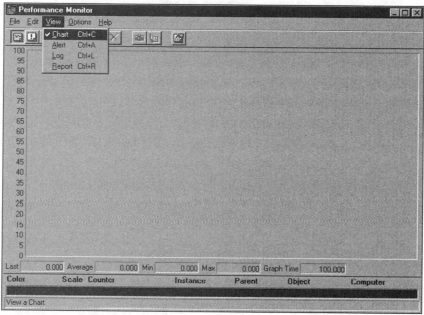

**FIGURE 22-7** The four views available in Performance Monitor

## Chart View

The Performance Monitor Chart view displays activity in a graphical format. It can be used to view current performance activity, or to view archived performance activity from a Performance Monitor log file. (Log files are discussed later in this chapter.)

Before you can view performance statistics in a Performance Monitor chart, you must first select one or more objects and their counters to be measured and displayed in a Chart view.

To select objects and their counters to be displayed in a Performance Monitor chart, you need to access the Add to Chart dialog box. You can access this dialog box in one of two ways: selecting Edit ⇒ Add To Chart, or clicking the **+** command button in the toolbar at the top of the Performance Monitor dialog box.

The Add to Chart dialog box is shown in Figure 22-8. Notice that you can select objects, counters, and instances in this dialog box.

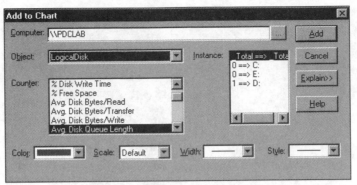

**FIGURE 22-8**   Selecting objects, counters, and instances in the
Add to Chart dialog box

**TO SELECT OBJECTS AND COUNTERS (IN THE ADD TO CHART
DIALOG BOX) TO BE DISPLAYED IN A PERFORMANCE
MONITOR CHART, FOLLOW THESE STEPS:**

**1.** In the Computer text box, type in the name of the computer you want to
monitor the performance of in the format \\*computer_name*, for
example, \\PDCLAB. (The name of the computer you are running
Performance Monitor on is displayed by default.) You can browse for the
computer you want to monitor by clicking the ... command button to the
right of the Computer text box.

 note   **You can view objects and counters from more than one
computer on a single Performance Monitor chart.**

**2.** Select the object you want to monitor from the list in the Object drop-
down list box.

**3.** Select the instance of the object you selected in Step 2 (if an instance is
available for this object) from the Instance list box.

**4.** Select a counter to be monitored for the object you selected in Step 2
from the Counter list box.

 tip   **When you are configuring the Add to Chart dialog box, you
can click the Explain command button at any time to display
a detailed description of the highlighted object and counter
combination. This description is displayed in the Counter
Definition box at the bottom of the Add to Chart dialog box,
as shown in Figure 22-9.**

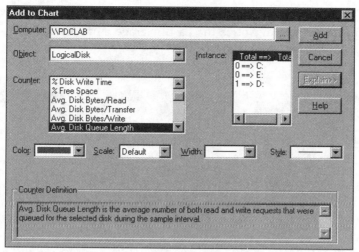

**FIGURE 22-9**   Obtaining a counter definition by clicking the
Explain command button

The Explain command button is also available in the Add to Alert,
Add to Report, and Add To Log dialog boxes.

**5.** In the Color drop-down list box, select the color you want Performance
Monitor to use to display the counter's activity in the chart.

**6.** In the Scale drop-down list box, accept the default or select the multiplier
you want Performance Monitor to apply to the counter's measurement in
the chart. For example, if the counter's activity normally varies between 0
and 1, you might select a scale setting of 100.0. This will enable you to
view a larger picture of the counter's activity in the chart.

Normally the default scale setting is the appropriate setting for the
selected counter.

**7.** In the Width drop-down list box, select the line width you want
Performance Monitor to use to display the counter's activity in the chart.

**8.** In the Style drop-down list box, select the style of the line you want
Performance Monitor to use to display the counter's activity in the chart.

**9.** When you have configured all of the settings for a particular object,
instance, and counter combination, click the Add command button to
begin displaying the counter's activity on the Performance Monitor chart.

**10.** Repeat Steps 1–9 if you want to add additional objects, instances, and
counter combinations to your Performance Monitor chart.

**11.** When you are finished adding counters to your chart, click the Done
command button to return to the Performance Monitor Chart view.

Figure 22-10 shows a Performance Monitor chart with several objects and counters selected. Notice the Last, Average, Min, Max, and Graph Time boxes toward the bottom of the chart.

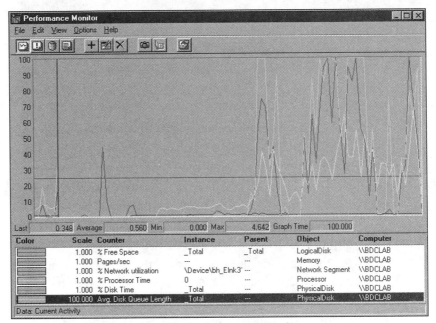

**FIGURE 22-10    Viewing a chart in Performance Monitor**

When you highlight any counter in the section at the bottom of the dialog box, that counter's statistics are displayed in the Last, Average, Min, Max, and Graph Time boxes directly below the chart. Table 22-3 explains the statistics displayed in each of these text boxes.

**TABLE 22-3** STATISTICS DISPLAYED IN PERFORMANCE MONITOR CHART VIEW

| STATISTIC | DESCRIPTION |
| --- | --- |
| Last | This is the most recent measurement of the counter. |
| Average | This is an average of the counter's measurement over the period of time represented by the chart. |

| Statistic | Description |
|-----------|-------------|
| Min | This is the lowest (minimum) measurement of the counter during the period of time represented by the chart. |
| Max | This is the highest (maximum) measurement of the counter during the period of time represented by the chart. |
| Graph Time | This is the number of seconds represented by the entire chart. This is the total amount of time it takes Performance Monitor to graph from one side of the chart to the other. |

If you have difficulty determining which line on the chart represents the highlighted counter, you can press Ctrl + H to highlight that counter's line. Press Ctrl + H again to stop highlighting the counter's line on the chart.

To export a Performance Monitor chart for review at a later time in a spreadsheet or database application, select File ⇒ Export Chart. You can export the chart data in either a tab separated value (tsv) file, or a comma separated value (csv) file.

## Alert View

The Performance Monitor Alert view is used to display an alert when a monitored counter's value exceeds or drops below a prespecified value.

Performance Monitor has no preset alerts. Alerts must be created in Alert view by selecting one or more counters to be monitored, and by entering a threshold value for each counter. When this threshold value is exceeded or falls below a minimum level (depending on how the alert is configured), an alert is triggered.

To access Alert view in Performance Monitor, select View ⇒ Alert.

To add counters to be monitored in Alert view you need to access the Add to Alert dialog box. You can access this dialog box in one of two ways: either by selecting Edit ⇒ Add To Alert, or by clicking the **+** command button in the toolbar at the top of the Performance Monitor dialog box.

The Add to Alert dialog box is shown in Figure 22-11. Notice that you can select objects, counters, and instances in this dialog box. The next section explains how to create an alert by using this dialog box.

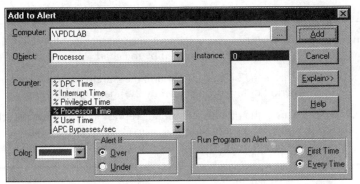

**FIGURE 22-11** **Selecting objects, counters, and instances in the Add to Alert dialog box**

## TO CREATE AN ALERT BY USING THE ADD TO ALERT DIALOG BOX, FOLLOW THESE STEPS:

**1.** In the Computer text box, type in the name of the computer you want to monitor using the format \\*computer_name,* for example, \\PDCLAB. (The name of the computer on which you are running Performance Monitor is displayed by default.) You can browse for the computer you want to monitor by clicking the ... command button to the right of the Computer text box.

**2.** Select the object you want to monitor from the list in the Object drop-down list box.

**3.** Select the instance of the object you selected in Step 2 (if an instance is available for this object) from the Instance list box.

**4.** Select a counter to be monitored for the object you selected in Step 2 from the Counter list box.

**5.** In the Color drop-down list box, select the color of dot you want Performance Monitor to use next to the text description when displaying the alert.

**6.** In the Alert If section:

o Select the radio button next to Over if you want Performance Monitor to generate an alert when the counter being monitored *exceeds* the value you specify.

o Select the radio button next to Under if you want Performance Monitor to generate an alert when the counter being monitored *drops below* the value you specify.

In the text box in the Alert If section, type in a number for the value you want Performance Monitor to use as the threshold value.

**7.** If you want Performance Monitor to run a program automatically when an alert is generated, type the full path to the program in the "Run Program on Alert" text box.

o If you want this program to be run only the first time an alert is generated for this counter, select the radio button next to First Time.

o If you want this program to be run every time an alert is generated for this counter, select the radio button next to Every Time.

**8.** When you have configured all of the settings for a particular object, instance, and counter combination, click the Add command button to begin monitoring the counter.

**9.** Repeat Steps 1–8 if you want to create additional alerts.

**10.** When you are finished creating alerts, click the Done command button.

Figure 22-12 shows a Performance Monitor alert. Notice the Alert Legend at the bottom of the dialog box. In this situation, I configured Performance Monitor to generate an alert when the amount of free space on my computer's hard disk dropped below thirty percent.

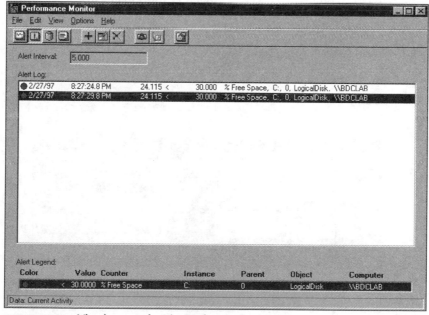

**FIGURE 22-12**   Viewing an alert in Performance Monitor

By default, Performance Monitor measures each specified counter in five second intervals, and compares each measurement with the threshold value. If the threshold value is exceeded or falls below a minimum level (depending on how the alert is configured), Performance Monitor generates an alert. If the threshold value is consistently exceeded or consistently falls below a minimum level, an alert will be generated every five seconds. You can change the alert interval by selecting Options ⇒ Alert (in the Alert view) and then configuring the Alert Options dialog box that appears.

## Report View

The Performance Monitor Report view displays activity in a report format. It can be used to view current performance activity, or to view archived performance activity from a Performance Monitor log file. (Log files are discussed later in this chapter.)

To access Report view in Performance Monitor, select View ⇒ Report.

Before you can view Performance Monitor statistics in Report view, you must select one or more objects and their counters to be measured and displayed in the report.

To select objects and their counters to be displayed in a Performance Monitor report, you need to access the Add to Report dialog box. You can access this dialog box in one of two ways: selecting Edit ⇒ Add To Report, or clicking the **+** command button in the toolbar at the top of the Performance Monitor dialog box.

The Add to Report dialog box is shown in Figure 22-13. Notice that there are fewer options in this dialog box than are in the Add to Chart and Add to Alert dialog boxes.

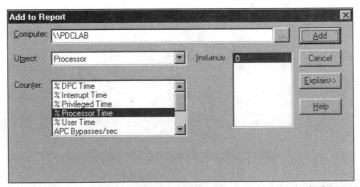

**FIGURE 22-13**  Selecting objects and counters to be included in a Performance Monitor report

**TO SELECT OBJECTS AND COUNTERS (IN THE ADD TO REPORT DIALOG BOX) TO BE INCLUDED IN A PERFORMANCE MONITOR REPORT, FOLLOW THESE STEPS:**

1. In the Computer text box, type the name of the computer you want to monitor using the format \\*computer_name,* for example, \\PDCLAB. (The name of the computer on which you are running Performance Monitor is displayed by default.) You can browse for the computer you want to monitor by clicking the ... command button to the right of the Computer text box.

2. Select the object you want to monitor from the list in the Object drop-down list box.

3. Select the instance of the object you selected in Step 2 (if an instance is available for this object) from the Instance list box.

4. Select a counter to be monitored for the object you selected in Step 2 from the Counter list box.

5. When you have selected an object, instance, and counter combination, click the Add command button to begin displaying the counter's activity in a Performance Monitor report.

6. Repeat Steps 1–5 if you want to add additional objects, instances, and counter combinations to your Performance Monitor report.

7. When you are finished adding counters to your report, click the Done command button to return to the Performance Monitor Report view.

Figure 22-14 shows a Performance Monitor report with several objects and counters selected.

The value displayed for each counter in the report represents the *most recent measurement* for each counter. This number is not an average, minimum, or maximum value, but simply the most recent measurement of each counter. Performance Monitor, by default, updates the report every five seconds. You can change the report interval by selecting Options ⇒ Report (in Report view) and then configuring the Report Options dialog box that appears.

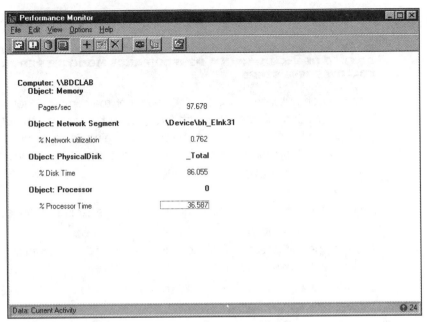

**FIGURE 22-14**   Viewing a report in Performance Monitor

# Log View

The Performance Monitor Log view is used to save statistics gathered by Performance Monitor to a log file. The Performance Monitor log file can be viewed at a later time in Chart, Alert, or Report view.

To access Performance Monitor Log view, select View ⇒ Log.

Before you can create a log file, you must select one or more objects to be monitored. To select objects, you need to access the Add To Log dialog box. You can access this dialog box in one of two ways: selecting Edit ⇒ Add To Log, or clicking the + command button in the toolbar at the top of the Performance Monitor dialog box.

The Add To Log dialog box is shown in Figure 22-15. Notice you can only select a computer and the objects to be monitored in this dialog box. The next section explains how to select objects for a Performance Monitor log in this dialog box.

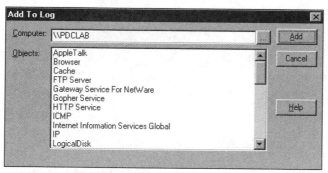

**FIGURE 22-15**     Selecting objects to be monitored for a
Performance Monitor log

**TO SELECT OBJECTS TO BE MONITORED (IN THE ADD TO LOG DIALOG BOX) FOR A PERFORMANCE MONITOR LOG, FOLLOW THESE STEPS:**

**1.** In the Computer text box, type in the name of the computer you want to log using the format \\*computer_name,* for example, \\PDCLAB. (The name of the computer on which you are running Performance Monitor is displayed by default.) You can browse for the computer you want to monitor by clicking the ... command button to the right of the Computer text box.

**2.** Select the objects you want to monitor from the list in the Objects drop-down list box. (You can select more than one object at a time.)

note    You *can't* select individual counters for the objects you select. *All* counters for the selected object will be monitored and logged.

**3.** Click the Add command button.

**4.** Repeat Steps 1–3 until all computers and objects that you want to select have been selected.

**5.** Click the Done command button to return to Performance Monitor Log view.

**6.** In the Performance Monitor dialog box (Log view), select Options ⇒ Log.

**7.** The Log Options dialog box appears, as shown in Figure 22-16.

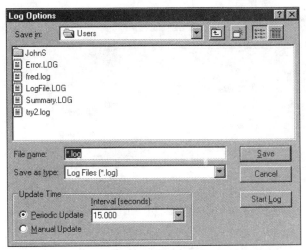

**FIGURE 22-16** **Starting a Performance Monitor log**

Use the Explorer view in the top half of the Log Options dialog box to select the folder in which you want to store the log file.

**8.** In the "File name" text box, type in a name for the log file that uses the .log extension.

**9.** In the Interval (seconds) drop-down list box, select the interval, in seconds, that you want Performance Monitor to use for measuring the selected objects and logging their activity.

Click the Start Log command button to begin logging.

Performance Monitor begins monitoring the selected objects and logging the statistics it gathers to the log file. It will continue to collect and log this data until you stop the process.

Figure 22-17 shows Performance Monitor in the process of collecting data for the log file. Notice the Status and File Size text boxes.

**10.** When you have collected all the data you want and are ready to stop the logging process, select Options ⇒ Log.

**11.** The Log Options dialog box appears. Click the Stop Log command button. The Performance Monitor log file has been created. Performance Monitor Log view reappears.

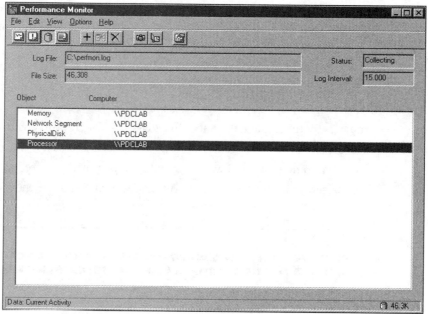

FIGURE 22-17   Logging data to a Performance Monitor log file

The next section explains how to import the log file you've created into Performance Monitor Chart, Alert, or Report views.

## Viewing data from log files

Performance Monitor log files can be viewed in Performance Monitor Chart, Alert, and Report views.

To change Performance Monitor's input from current activity to activity archived in a log file, select Options ⇒ Data From. The Data From dialog box appears, as shown in Figure 22-18.

FIGURE 22-18   Changing Performance Monitor's input type from current activity to activity archived in a log file

Select the radio button next to Log File and type in the complete path to the Performance Monitor log file you want to view data from. (You can browse for the file name by clicking the ... command button.) Click OK.

The Performance Monitor dialog box reappears. Select the type of view from the View menu (Chart, Alert, or Report) that you want to use to view log file data.

Once you have selected the view that you want to use, you must select objects, counters, and instances to be viewed. The steps to create a chart, alert, or report from a log file are the same as those used to create a chart, alert, or report from current activity. However, only the objects which were logged are available for selection in the Add to Chart, Add to Alert, and Add to Report dialog boxes.

---

**FOR EXAMPLE, TO VIEW A PERFORMANCE MONITOR REPORT CONSISTING OF DATA FROM A LOG FILE, FOLLOW THESE STEPS:**

**1.** Start Performance Monitor. Select View ⇒ Report.

**2.** Select Options ⇒ Data From.

**3.** In the Data From dialog box, select the radio button next to Log File, and type in the complete path to the Performance Monitor log file you want to use. Click OK.

**4.** Select Edit ⇒ Add To Report.

**5.** The Add to Report dialog box appears. Select the computer, object, instance, and counter you want to view in the report. Click the Add command button.

**6.** Repeat Step 5 until you have selected all of the counters you want to view in the report. Click the Done command button to view the report.

---

When you have finished viewing data from a log file, you should change Performance Monitor's input back to current activity. To change Performance Monitor's input from log file to current activity, select Options ⇒ Data From. In the Data From dialog box, select the radio button next to Current Activity and click OK.

# KEY POINT SUMMARY

This chapter focused on how to use Performance Monitor. The following points highlight the major issues.

- *Performance Monitor* is a Windows NT tool that can be used to identify performance problems and/or bottlenecks, determine current usage of system resources, track performance trends over time, predict future usage of system resources (capacity planning), and determine how system configuration changes affect system performance.

- The system components that Performance Monitor can measure, such as processor, memory, and physical disk, are called *objects*. If there is more than one of a particular object in the system (such as multiple processors or multiple physical disks) there is said to be more than one *instance* of that object. Some objects, such as memory, do not have instances, because there can't be more than one of the particular object. Each instance of an object can be measured in different ways. Each possible measurement of an object is called a *counter*.

- Commonly used Performance Monitor objects and counters include:

| Object | Counter(s) |
|---|---|
| Memory | Pages/sec |
| Network Segment | % Network utilization |
| PhysicalDisk | Avg. Disk Queue Length, % Disk Time |
| Processor | % Processor Time |
| Server | Bytes Total/sec |

- Not all Performance Monitor objects and counters are available when Windows NT is first installed. For example, TCP/IP-related objects (and their related counters) are not available until the *SNMP Service* is installed, and the Network Segment object (and its counters) is not available until the *Network Monitor Agent* is installed. Additionally, some objects and their counters must be enabled by using the `Diskperf.exe` command before they can be effectively used to monitor performance.

- Performance Monitor has four possible views: Chart, Alert, Report, and Log.

  - *Chart view* displays activity in a graphical format. One or more objects and their counters must be selected (in the Add to Chart dialog box) to be measured and displayed in Chart view. Chart view not only displays a graph of activity, but also displays several statistics for each counter, including: *Last, Average, Min, Max, and Graph Time.*

  - *Alert view* is used to display an alert when a monitored counter's value exceed or drops below a prespecified value. Alerts must be created in Alert view by selecting one or more counters to be monitored and by entering a threshold value that will trigger an alert.

  - *Report view* displays activity in a report format. One or more objects and their counters must be selected (in the Add to Report dialog box) to be measured and displayed in Report view. The value displayed for each counter in the report represents the *most recent measurement* for each counter (not average, minimum, or maximum values).

  - *Log view* is used to save statistics gathered by Performance Monitor to a Performance Monitor log file. The log file can be viewed at a later time in Chart, Alert, or Report view. One or more objects must be selected to be monitored and their activity logged to a file. The Start Log command button (in the Log Options dialog box) is used to begin logging, and the Stop Log command button is used to stop the logging process.

- To view data from Performance Monitor log files in Performance Monitor Chart, Alert, and Report views, you must change Performance Monitor's input from current activity to log file. Then you select the type of view (Chart, Alert, or Report) and proceed as though you were creating a chart, alert, or report of current activity. When you finish viewing data from a log file, you should change Performance Monitor's input back to current activity.

# Applying What You've Learned

Now it's time to regroup, review, and apply what you've learned in this chapter. The following Instant Assessment questions bring to mind key facts and concepts.

The hands-on lab exercise reinforces what you've learned, and gives you an opportunity to practice some of the tasks tested by the Microsoft Certified Professional exams.

## Instant Assessment

1. What command button do you click to cause Performance Monitor to *end* the process of gathering data for a Performance Monitor log file?

2. List five uses of Performance Monitor.

3. What are the system components that Performance Monitor can measure, such as processor and memory, called?

4. What is each possible measurement of a Performance Monitor object called?

5. When does more than one instance of a Performance Monitor object exist?

6. You want to obtain an overall view of how memory is being used on a particular Windows NT computer. Which Performance Monitor object and counter should you use?

7. You want to measure the percentage of time that the processor is actively used by processes (other than the Idle process) on a Windows NT computer. Which Performance Monitor object and counter should you use?

8. You want to measure the percentage of total network utilization on a given network segment as a percentage of the maximum amount of network traffic possible on that segment. Which Performance Monitor object and counter should you use?

9. You want to measure the total amount of network utilization on a particular Windows NT Server computer. Which Performance Monitor object and counter should you use?

10. What must you install on your Windows NT computer before the IP, TCP, ICMP, and UDP objects (and their counters) are available for use in Performance Monitor?

11. What must you install on your Windows NT computer before the Network Segment object (and its counters) is available for use in Performance Monitor?

12. What should you type at the command prompt to enable the PhysicalDisk and LogicalDisk Performance Monitor objects and their counters?

13. What are the four possible views in Performance Monitor?

14. Besides a graph, what other statistics are presented for a highlighted counter in Performance Monitor Chart view?

15. What value must you enter in the Alert If section of the Add to Alert dialog box for a Performance Monitor alert to be created?

16. What command button do you click to cause Performance Monitor to *begin* the process of gathering data for a Performance Monitor log file?

17. When Performance Monitor's input is current activity, what value is displayed for each selected counter in Performance Monitor Report view?

18. What is Performance Monitor Log view used for?

**T/F**

19. You can view either current performance activity or archived performance activity from a Performance Monitor log file in Performance Monitor Report view.                                         ___

20. Performance Monitor is a Windows NT tool that is shipped with Windows NT Server but *not* with Windows NT Workstation.     ___

21. Before you can view data from a Performance Monitor log file, you must change Performance Monitor's input from log file to current activity.                                                 ___

concept link      **For answers to the Instant Assessment questions see Appendix D.**

# Hands-on Lab Exercise

The following hands-on lab exercise provides you with an opportunity to apply the knowledge you've gained in this chapter about Performance Monitor.

## Lab 22.35 *Using Performance Monitor*

Workstation
Server
Enterprise

The purpose of this hands-on lab exercise is to provide you with experience in using Performance Monitor on a Windows NT computer.

This lab consists of four parts:

Part 1: Adding objects and counters by installing Network Monitor Agent and SNMP Service, and enabling the PhysicalDisk and LogicalDisk objects and their counters using `Diskperf.exe`

Part 2: Using Performance Monitor Chart view and Alert view

Part 3: Creating a Performance Monitor log file

Part 4: Importing a Performance Monitor log file into Report view and Chart view

Begin this lab by booting your computer to Windows NT Server. Log on as Administrator. Place your Windows NT Server compact disc in your computer's CD-ROM drive.

 **note** 🦜 **If you are preparing *only* for the NT Workstation exam, you might want to perform this lab on your Windows NT Workstation computer (instead of your Windows NT Server computer). The steps are the same regardless of whether you use Windows NT Server or Windows NT Workstation.**

Follow these steps carefully.

### Part 1: Adding objects and counters by installing Network Monitor Agent and SNMP Service, and enabling the PhysicalDisk and LogicalDisk objects and their counters by using Diskperf.exe

In this section, you check for the existence of Performance Monitor objects. Then you install Network Monitor Agent and SNMP Service on your Windows NT Server computer. Finally, you use `Diskperf.exe` to enable the PhysicalDisk and LogicalDisk objects and their disk counters on your Windows NT Server computer.

**1.** Select Start ⇒ Programs ⇒ Administrative Tools (Common) ⇒ Performance Monitor.

**2.** The Performance Monitor dialog box appears. Select View ⇒ Chart.

**3.** Click the **+** command button located in the toolbar at the top of the dialog box.

**4.** The Add to Chart dialog box appears. Click the down arrow in the Object drop-down list box. Look for each of the following objects: ICMP, IP, Network Segment, TCP, and UDP. Notice that *none* of these objects appear in the Object drop-down list box. Click the Cancel command button.

**5.** The Performance Monitor dialog box reappears. Exit Performance Monitor.

**6.** Select Start ⇒ Settings ⇒ Control Panel.

**7.** The Control Panel dialog box appears. Double-click the Network icon.

**8.** The Network dialog box appears. Click the Services tab.

**9.** The Services tab appears. Click the Add command button.

**10.** The Select Network Service dialog box appears. Highlight Network Monitor Agent. Click OK.

**11.** A Windows NT Setup dialog box appears. Ensure that the correct path to your Windows NT Server source files (usually the i386 folder on your Windows NT Server compact disc) is listed in the text box. Edit this text box if necessary. Click the Continue command button.

**12.** Windows NT copies source files and installs Network Monitor Agent.

**13.** The Network dialog box reappears. Click the Add command button.

**14.** The Select Network Service dialog box appears. Highlight SNMP Service. Click OK.

**15.** A Windows NT Setup dialog box appears. Ensure that the correct path to your Windows NT Server source files (usually the I386 folder on your Windows NT Server compact disc) is listed in the text box. Edit this text box if necessary. Click the Continue command button.

**16.** Windows NT copies source files and installs the SNMP Service.

**17.** The Microsoft SNMP Properties dialog box appears. Click OK.

**18.** The Network dialog box reappears. Click the Close command button.

**19.** Windows NT performs various bindings operations.

**20.** A Network Settings Change dialog box appears. Click the No command button.

**21.** The Control Panel dialog box reappears. Exit Control Panel.

**22.** Select Start ⇒ Programs ⇒ Command Prompt.

**23.** The Command Prompt dialog box appears. At the command prompt, type **diskperf -y** and press Enter.

Notice that Windows NT indicates that disk performance counters on your computer are now set to start at boot, and will become effective after the computer is restarted.

**24.** At the command prompt, type **exit** and press Enter.

**25.** The Windows NT desktop reappears. Select Start ⇒ Shut Down.

**26.** In the Shut Down Windows dialog box, select the radio button next to "Restart the computer". Click the Yes command button.

**27.** Reboot the computer to Windows NT Server. Log on as Administrator. Continue to Part 2.

### Part 2: Using Performance Monitor Chart view and Alert view

In this section, you install games (if you haven't already done so) on your Windows NT Server computer, and use Performance Monitor Chart view and Alert view to chart server performance and to create an alert.

**1.** If you have already installed games (including Solitaire and Pinball) on your Windows NT Server computer, skip to Step 8.

If you have *not* already installed games on your Windows NT Server computer, select Start ⇒ Settings ⇒ Control Panel, and continue to Step 2.

**2.** The Control Panel dialog box appears. Double-click the Add/Remove Programs icon.

**3.** The Add/Remove Programs dialog box appears. Click the Windows NT Setup tab.

**4.** The Windows NT Setup tab appears. Select the check box next to Games. (Or if you have one or two games installed but Solitaire or Pinball is *not* yet installed, deselect and then reselect this check box.) Click OK.

**5.** The Add/Remove Programs Properties—Copying Files dialog box appears.

If the Files Needed dialog box appears, ensure that the correct path to your Windows NT Server source files (usually the I386 folder on your Windows NT Server compact disc) is listed in the "Copy files from" text box. Edit the text box as necessary. Click OK.

**6.** Windows NT installs games.

**7.** The Control Panel dialog box reappears. Exit Control Panel.

**8.** Select Start ⇒ Programs ⇒ Administrative Tools (Common) ⇒ Performance Monitor.

**9.** The Performance Monitor dialog box appears. Select View ⇒ Chart.

**10.** Click the **+** command button located in the toolbar at the top of the dialog box.

**11.** The Add to Chart dialog box appears. Click the down arrow in the Object drop-down list box. Look for each of the following objects: ICMP, IP, Network Segment, TCP, and UDP. Notice that after installing Network Monitor Agent and the SNMP Service (which you did in Part 1), all of these objects now appear in the Object drop-down list box.

Click Memory in the Object drop-down list box. Select Pages/sec from the Counter list box. Click the Add command button.

**12.** Click the down arrow in the Object drop-down list box. Click Processor in the Object drop-down list box. Select % Processor Time from the Counter list box. Click the Add command button.

**13.** Click the down arrow in the Object drop-down list box. Click PhysicalDisk in the Object drop-down list box. Select % Disk Time from the Counter list box. Click the Add command button.

**14.** Click the down arrow in the Object drop-down list box. Click Server in the Object drop-down list box. Select Bytes Total/sec from the Counter list box. Click the Add command button. Click the Done command button.

You have just configured the four most commonly used Performance Monitor counters that monitor server performance.

**15.** The Performance Monitor dialog box reappears. In the list box at the bottom of the dialog box, highlight % Processor Time in the Counter column. Note the color assigned to the % Processor Time counter.

**16.** Move your mouse rapidly in a sweeping circular pattern on your mouse pad for several (at least five) seconds. Notice the increase in % Processor time usage, as depicted on the graph, from just moving your mouse.

**17.** Minimize (*don't* close) Performance Monitor.

**18.** Select Start ⇒ Programs ⇒ Accessories ⇒ Games ⇒ Solitaire.

**19.** Play Solitaire for a minute or two.

(If you've never played Solitaire before, select Help ⇒ Contents to find out how to play.)

When you finish playing, exit Solitaire, and quickly select Performance Monitor from the taskbar.

**20.** The Performance Monitor dialog box appears. Notice the counters and their levels during your Solitaire game, as depicted on the Performance Monitor chart.

**21.** Highlight Pages/sec (in the Counter column). Press Delete.

Highlight % Disk Time (in the Counter column). Press delete.

Highlight Bytes Total/sec (in the Counter column). Press Delete.

Highlight % Processor Time (in the Counter column). Press Delete.

**22.** Select Edit ⇒ Add To Chart.

**23.** The Add to Chart dialog box appears. Click the down arrow in the Object drop-down list box. Click LogicalDisk in the Object drop-down list box. Select % Free Space from the Counter list box. Highlight 0==>C: in the Instance list box. Click the Add command button. Click the Done command button.

**24.** The Performance Monitor dialog box reappears. Write the number that appears in the Last box here: _____

**25.** Add 5 to the number that you entered in Step 24, and write the resulting number here: _____

**26.** Highlight % Free Space (in the Counter column), and press Delete.

**27.** Select View ⇒ Alert.

**28.** The Alert View appears. Select Edit ⇒ Add To Alert.

**29.** The Add to Alert dialog box appears. Click the down arrow in the Object drop-down list box. Click LogicalDisk in the Object drop-down list box. Select % Free Space from the Counter list box. Select 0==>C: in the Instance list box. Select the radio button next to Under in the Alert If section. Type the number you entered in Step 25 in the text box in the Alert If section. Click the Add command button. Click the Done command button.

**30.** The Performance Monitor dialog box reappears. Every five seconds an alert should appear in the Alert Log list box, indicating that the % Free Space on your C: drive has fallen below the level that you entered in the previous step.

Press Delete to stop logging this alert.

Continue to Part 3.

### Part 3: Creating a Performance Monitor log file

In this section, you create a Performance Monitor log file. (You will view the data in this Performance Monitor log file in Part 4.)

**1.** In the Performance Monitor dialog box, select View ⇒ Log.

**2.** Select Edit ⇒ Add To Log.

**3.** The Add To Log dialog box appears. Highlight Memory in the Objects list box. Click the Add command button.

**4.** Highlight PhysicalDisk in the Objects list box. Click the Add command button.

5. Highlight Processor in the Objects list box. Click the Add command button.

6. Highlight Server in the Objects list box. Click the Add command button. Click the Done command button.

7. The Performance Monitor dialog box reappears. Select Options ⇒ Log.

8. The Log Options dialog box appears. In the File Name text box, type **practice.log**. Select **1** from the Interval (Seconds) drop-down list box. Click the Start Log command button.

9. Minimize (*don't* close) Performance Monitor.

10. Select Start ⇒ Programs ⇒ Accessories ⇒ Games ⇒ Pinball.

11. Play one game of Pinball.

    (Hold down the space bar for a couple of seconds and then release it to launch the ball. The z key on the keyboard controls the left flipper. The ? key on the keyboard controls the right flipper.)

    When you finish playing, exit Pinball, and quickly select Performance Monitor from the taskbar.

12. The Performance Monitor dialog box reappears. Select Options ⇒ Log.

13. The Log Options dialog box appears. Click the Stop Log command button. Continue to Part 4.

### Part 4: Importing a Performance Monitor log file into Report view and Chart view

In this section, you import the Performance Monitor log file you created in Part 3 into Performance Monitor Report view and Chart view.

1. In the Performance Monitor dialog box, select View ⇒ Report.

2. Select Options ⇒ Data From.

3. The Data From dialog box appears. Select the radio button next to Log File. Type **practice.log** in the text box. Click OK.

4. Select Edit ⇒ Add to Report in the Performance Monitor dialog box.

5. The Add to Report dialog box appears. Click the down arrow in the Object drop-down list box. Notice that only four objects appear in this list, because you only chose to log four objects when you created the log file. Click Memory. Select Pages/sec in the Counter list box. Click the Add command button.

6. Click the down arrow in the Object drop-down list box. Click PhysicalDisk. Select % Disk Time in the Counter list box. Click the Add command button.

7. Click the down arrow in the Object drop-down list box. Click Processor. Select % Processor Time in the Counter list box. Click the Add command button.

8. Click the down arrow in the Object drop-down list box. Click Server. Select Bytes Total/sec in the Counter list box. Click the Add command button. Click the Done command button.

9. The Performance Monitor dialog box reappears.

   The report displayed shows the last value measured for each of the four counters you selected, from the time you initially created the log file until after you finished your Pinball game and clicked on the Stop Log command button in Performance Monitor.

   Now let's look at the same four counters (for the same time period) in a Chart view (instead of a Report view).

10. Select View ⇒ Chart.

11. Select Options ⇒ Data From.

12. The Data From dialog box appears. Select the radio button next to Log FIle. Ensure that **practice.log** appears in the text box. Click OK.

13. Select Edit ⇒ Add To Chart in the Performance Monitor dialog box.

14. The Add to Chart dialog box appears. Click the down arrow in the Object drop-down list box. Click Memory. Select Pages/sec in the Counter list box. Click the Add command button.

15. Click the down arrow in the Object drop-down list box. Click PhysicalDisk. Select % Disk Time In the Counter list box. Click the Add command button.

16. Click the down arrow in the Object drop-down list box. Click Processor. Select % Processor Time in the Counter list box. Click the Add command button.

17. Click the down arrow in the Object drop-down list box. Click Server. Select Bytes Total/sec in the Counter list box. Click the Add command button. Click the Done command button.

18. The Performance Monitor dialog box reappears.

    The chart displayed shows the values for each of the four counters you selected, from the time you initially created the log file until after you finished your Pinball game and clicked on the Stop Log command button in Performance Monitor.

19. Exit Performance Monitor.

Enterprise

---

**Using Network Monitor**

CHAPTER

23

---

# About Chapter 23

The focus of Chapter 23 is on Network Monitor, a Windows NT Server administrative tool that enables you to monitor your network's performance by capturing, viewing, and analyzing network packets.

After a brief overview, the chapter outlines the steps to install Network Monitor on a Windows NT Server computer.

Next, the chapter presents in-depth coverage of how to use Network Monitor to capture network packets. Starting and stopping a capture, configuring a capture filter, and saving captured data are covered.

Finally, once a capture has been performed, Chapter 23 explains how you can use Network Monitor to view and analyze the captured packets.

This chapter includes one hands-on lab. In this lab you'll install and use Network Monitor on your own Windows NT Server computer.

Chapter 23 contains some great information, but can be considered optional reading unless you're preparing for the Enterprise exam. This chapter maps to the "Monitor network traffic by using Network Monitor" objective for the Enterprise exam.

# WHAT IS NETWORK MONITOR?

*Network Monitor* is a Windows NT Server administrative tool that makes it possible for you to capture, view, and analyze network traffic (packets). Network Monitor doesn't ship with Windows NT Workstation.

Network Monitor can be used to view network statistics, such as: percent of network utilization, number of frames per second, number of broadcasts per second, and so forth. This packet analysis tool is useful in troubleshooting network problems and protocol problems. It is also useful to determine current network utilization, as well as for trend analysis and network capacity planning.

Network Monitor is capable of capturing entire *packets* (also referred to as *frames*) from the network, and of analyzing the contents of each of these packets. Packets can be viewed and interpreted when captured, or saved to disk for later analysis.

The version of Network Monitor that ships with NT Server 4.0 is designed to capture only packets addressed to, or sent from, the Windows NT Server computer running Network Monitor. A more robust version of Network Monitor ships with Microsoft Systems Management Server.

The primary difference between the two versions of Network Monitor is the capability of each product to use the promiscuous mode of the computer's network adapter: The version of Network Monitor that ships with NT Server 4.0, by default, is *not* used in promiscuous mode; the version that ships with System Management Server, by default, *is* used in promiscuous mode.

*Promiscuous* refers to a network adapter's ability to receive packets not addressed to that network adapter. A *non promiscuous network adapter* can only receive packets addressed to that network adapter. A *promiscuous network adapter* can receive any packets transmitted on the local network segment. Whether a network adapter functions in promiscuous mode depends upon the design of the network adapter (most network adapters are capable of functioning in promiscuous mode) and the driver used for the network adapter.

The following sections explain how to install Network Monitor, and how to use Network Monitor to capture and view network packets.

# INSTALLING NETWORK MONITOR

Network Monitor consists of two parts: the *Network Monitor Tools*, and the *Network Monitor Agent*. Both parts are installed together using the Network application in Control Panel.

If the Network Monitor Agent is already installed, *it must be removed* before you can install the combination Network Monitor Tools and Agent.

Network Monitor requires a network adapter that uses an NDIS 4.0 driver. Check the Windows NT Hardware Compatibility List *(HCL)* to see which network adapters are supported.

### TO INSTALL NETWORK MONITOR ON A WINDOWS NT SERVER COMPUTER, FOLLOW THESE STEPS:

1. Select Start ⟹ Settings ⟹ Control Panel.
2. In the Control Panel dialog box, double-click the Network icon.
3. In the Network dialog box, click the Services tab.
4. If Network Monitor Agent is *not* installed on the computer, skip to Step 6.

   If Network Monitor Agent *is* installed on the computer, you must remove it to install Network Monitor. On the Services tab, highlight Network Monitor Agent in the Network Services list box. Click the Remove command button.
5. A warning dialog box appears. Click the Yes command button to continue. Windows NT removes Network Monitor Agent.
6. On the Services tab, click the Add command button.
7. In the Select Network Service dialog box, highlight Network Monitor Tools and Agent, as shown in Figure 23-1. Click OK.
8. A Windows NT Setup dialog box appears. Ensure the correct path to your Windows NT Server source files (usually the i386 folder on your Windows NT Server compact disc) is listed in the text box. Edit this text box if necessary. Click the Continue command button.
9. Windows NT copies source files and installs Network Monitor Tools and Agent.
10. The Network dialog box reappears. Click the Close command button.
11. Windows NT performs various bindings operations.

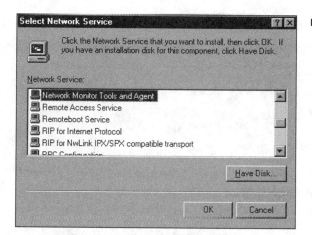

**FIGURE 23-1** **Installing Network Monitor**

**12.** A Network Settings Change dialog box appears, indicating you must shut down and restart the computer for the new settings to take effect. Click the Yes command button to restart the computer.

# USING NETWORK MONITOR TO CAPTURE NETWORK PACKETS

Network Monitor can be used both to capture and view network packets. The next few sections focus on capturing network packets. Before you actually use Network Monitor, it's a good idea to take an introductory look at the look and feel of its primary interface.

To access Network Monitor, from the Windows NT Server desktop, Select Start ⇒ Programs ⇒ Administrative Tools (Common) ⇒ Network Monitor.

The Network Monitor main dialog box is shown, after a capture has been performed, in Figure 23-2. (Until a capture is performed, no statistics appear in this dialog box. The process of capturing is explained in the following sections.) Notice this dialog box is called the Capture Window, and four different scrolling list boxes are contained within it. Each of these scrolling list boxes is called a *pane* (as in a window pane).

Graph pane          Session Stats pane          Total Stats pane          Station Stats pane

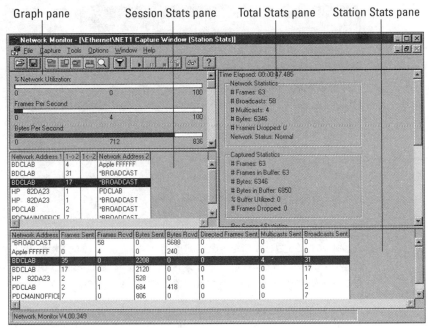

**FIGURE 23-2**   The Network Monitor Capture Window dialog box

Each of the four panes in the Network Monitor Capture Window dialog box displays different data and has a unique name. The four panes are: the Graph pane, the Total Stats pane, the Session Stats pane, and the Station Stats pane.

The *Graph pane,* which is the scrolling list box located at the upper left corner of the dialog box, displays five bar graphs. Each of these graphs depicts various network packet statistics, including: % Network Utilization, Frames Per Second, Bytes Per Second, Broadcasts Per Second, and Multicasts Per Second.

Figure 23-3 shows an entire Graph pane, with all five bar graphs displayed.

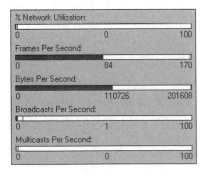

**FIGURE 23-3**   The Graph pane in the Network Monitor Capture Window

The *Total Stats pane,* which is the scrolling list box located at the upper right corner of the dialog box, displays five different types of statistics in five different sections. The sections listed are: Network Statistics, Captured Statistics, Per Second Statistics, Network Card (MAC) Statistics, and Network Card (MAC) Error Statistics.

Figure 23-4 shows an entire Total Stats pane, with all five sections displayed.

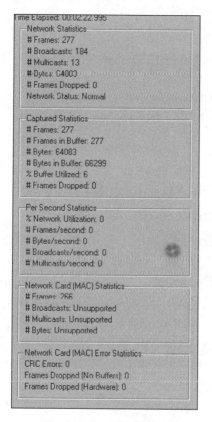

**FIGURE 23-4** **The Total Stats pane in the Network Monitor Capture Window**

The *Session Stats pane,* which is the scrolling list box located in the middle of the left side of the dialog box, displays a summary of packets transmitted between pairs of computers or network devices on the local network segment. Each computer or device in this section is listed as a network address or a computer name.

Two statistics columns are shown between the pairs of network addresses/ computer names. The first statistics column displays the number of packets sent (during the capture period) from the computer or network device in the Network Address 1 column to the corresponding computer/device in the Network Address 2 column. The second statistics column displays the number of packets sent (during the capture period) from the computer/device in the Network Address 2 column to the corresponding computer/ device in the Network Address 1 column.

The *Station Stats pane,* which is the scrolling list box located across the bottom of the dialog box, displays several statistics associated with each computer/ network device that transmitted and/or received at least one packet captured from the local network segment during the capture period. Statistics shown include: Frames Sent, Frames Received, Bytes Sent, Bytes Received, Directed Frames Sent, Multicasts Sent, and Broadcasts Sent.

Now that you have an understanding of the primary Network Monitor interface, you're ready to learn how to use Network Monitor to capture packets and view captured data.

## Configuring Network Monitor to Capture Using Promiscuous Mode

By default, the version of Network Monitor that ships with Windows NT Server 4.0 uses a special mode of the NDIS 4.0 driver, called *"local capture only."*

"Local capture only" is used primarily for two reasons: It minimizes the amount of processor utilization (promiscuous mode can use as much as 30 percent of total processor utilization), and it increases network security (not everyone should be able to capture and read all packets on the network segment).

Some NDIS 4.0 drivers don't correctly implement the "local capture only" mode. These drivers can capture packets sent *to* the Windows NT Server computer, but *not* the packets sent *by* the Windows NT Server computer. To remedy this situation and to allow Network Monitor to capture packets sent both to and sent by the Windows NT Server computer, Network Monitor must be reconfigured to use the promiscuous mode of the NDIS 4.0 driver.

A by-product of forcing Network Monitor to use promiscuous mode is that Network Monitor can then capture *all* packets transmitted on the local network segment (instead of only packets addressed to or from the Windows NT Server computer on which Network Monitor is running). Being able to capture all packets transmitted on the local network segment can be useful when you are trying to troubleshoot a network problem or perform other network analysis tasks. The next section explains how to configure Network Monitor to capture using promiscuous mode.

**in the real world**

Microsoft only supports the use of promiscuous mode for the version of Network Monitor that ships with Systems Management Server. However, Microsoft recommends using promiscuous mode in conjunction with the version of Network Monitor that ships with NT Server 4.0 when an NDIS 4.0 driver doesn't correctly implement the "local capture only" mode.

Practically speaking, though, you can force Network Monitor to use almost any network adapter in promiscuous mode. If you do this, you will put more load on your processor, but you can capture all packets sent on the local network segment.

**caution**

One final word of caution on this—using the NT Server 4.0 version of Network Monitor in promiscuous mode (except to remedy a situation where a network adapter doesn't correctly implement the "local capture mode") might be considered a violation of the Windows NT Server licensing agreement.

---

**TO CONFIGURE NETWORK MONITOR TO USE THE PROMISCUOUS MODE OF THE NDIS 4.0 DRIVER:**

1. Select Start⇒Run from the Windows NT Server desktop.
2. The Run dialog box appears. Type **regedt32** in the Open drop-down list box. Click OK.
3. The Registry Editor dialog box appears. Select Windows⇒ HKEY_LOCAL_MACHINE on Local Machine.
4. Double-click the + sign next to SYSTEM. Double-click the + sign next to CurrentControlSet. Double-click the + sign next to Services. Double-click the + sign next to bh. Highlight the Linkage folder.
5. Find the Bind value (located in the right-hand part of the dialog box).

   Figure 23-5 shows the Registry Editor dialog box at this point. Notice the Bind value is highlighted on the right side of the dialog box.

   Note the portion of the entry for the Bind value that *directly follows* the first\Device\listing in the entry. (In the example shown, this is Elnk31.) Write down this information for future use.

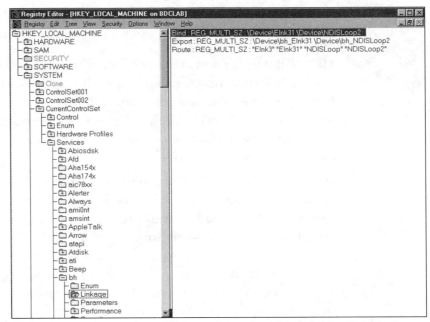

**FIGURE 23-5**   **Using Registry Editor to determine Network Monitor bindings**

6. Highlight the `Parameters` folder.

7. Select Edit⇒Add Key.

8. The Add Key dialog box appears. Type **ForcePmode** in the Key Name text box. Leave the Class text box blank. Figure 23-6 shows the Add Key dialog box correctly configured. Click OK.

9. The Registry Editor dialog box reappears. Click the `ForcePmode` folder you just created.

10. Select Edit⇒Add Value.

11. The Add Value dialog box appears. In the Value Name text box, type the value you noted in Step 5. (For example, Elnk31.) In the Data Type drop-down list box, select REG_DWORD. Figure 23-7 shows the Add Value dialog box correctly configured. Click OK.

12. The DWORD Editor dialog box appears. In the Data text box, type **1**. (Don't type the period at the end.) Click OK.

13. The Registry Editor dialog box reappears, as shown in Figure 23-8. Notice the new value has been added to the Registry (at the upper right side of the dialog box). Close the Registry Editor.

14. Shut down and restart your computer for this Registry setting to become effective.

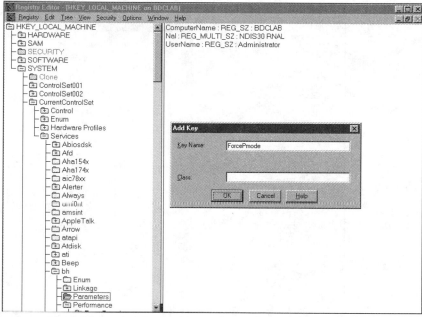

**FIGURE 23-6** Adding a key to the Network Monitor Registry settings

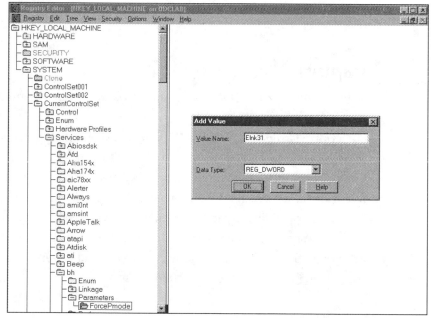

**FIGURE 23-7** Adding a value to the Network Monitor Registry settings

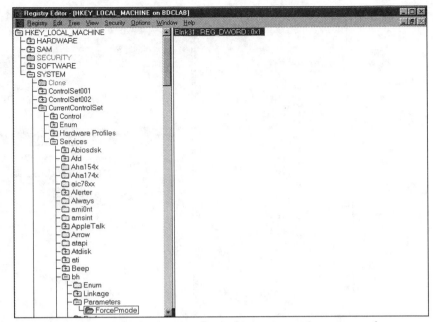

**FIGURE 23-8**   Network Monitor configured to use promiscuous mode

# Capturing Packets

Network Monitor does *not* produce any statistics or other useful data until a capture is performed.

During a *capture,* Network Monitor receives packets transmitted on the local network segment and stores these packets either in memory or in a capture file. Capture files can be used for later analysis. The process of capturing doesn't interfere with packets reaching their intended destinations on the network.

If you are doing capacity planning or troubleshooting network access problems, you should consider performing a capture during a time of peak network activity. To troubleshoot other problems, you should perform a capture during the time when those problems most often occur.

To perform a capture, you must manually start and stop a capture in Network Monitor.

Three ways exist to *start* a capture in Network Monitor:

- Selecting Capture ⇒ Start

- Pressing F10

- Clicking the Start Capture icon on the toolbar (this icon appears as a single right arrow, much like a play button on a CD or cassette tape player)

Once started, capturing continues until you stop the process.

There are three ways to *stop* a capture in Network Monitor:

- Selecting Capture ⇒ Stop

- Pressing F11

- Clicking the Stop Capture icon on the toolbar (this icon appears as a single small square, much like a stop button on a CD or cassette tape player)

During the capture process, statistics in the four Network Monitor panes are updated continuously. You can view these statistics as they change to get a general impression of how the network is being used.

If you don't want to view statistics during the capture process, select Capture ⇒ Dedicated Capture Mode before you begin the capture process. Selecting the *Dedicated Capture Mode* can save processor time on a computer that performs multiple server functions on the network. After you select the Dedicated Capture Mode, start the capture as you normally would. During the capture period, the Network Monitor dialog box will be minimized, and the Dedicated Mode dialog box will be displayed, as shown in Figure 23-9. Notice the only statistic displayed is the total number of frames captured, and that you can stop and pause the capture by using this dialog box.

When you stop a Dedicated Mode capture, all statistics are immediately updated and displayed in the four panes of the Network Monitor Capture Window dialog box.

Because a large number of packet statistics may be displayed in the Network Monitor Capture Window dialog box, you might want to use a capture filter to limit the type of network packets that will be captured by Network Monitor.

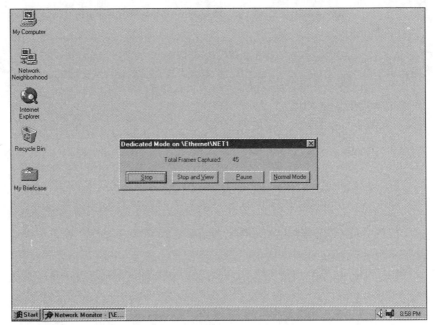

**FIGURE 23-9** Network Monitor performing a capture in Dedicated Mode

## *Configuring a capture filter*

By default, Network Monitor's *capture filter* is configured to capture *all* packets addressed to or sent by the Windows NT Server computer. However, you can specify which packets transmitted on the network segment will be captured by configuring a capture filter.

You can configure a capture filter so that:

- o Only packets using certain protocols are (or are not) captured

- o Only packets to or from specified computers or network devices are (or are not) captured

- o Only packets containing specific byte patterns are captured

- o Any combination of the previous

**TO CONFIGURE A CAPTURE FILTER, FOLLOW THESE STEPS:**

**1.** In Network Monitor, select Capture⇒Filter. (Or press F8, or click the Edit Capture Filter icon in the toolbar—this icon appears as a funnel.)

**2.** The Capture Filter dialog box appears, as shown in Figure 23-10. Notice the default capture filter is displayed.

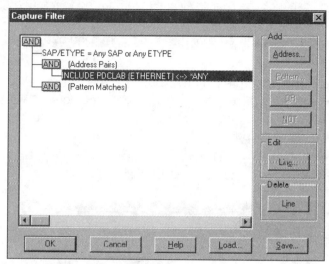

**FIGURE 23-10**    Default capture filter settings

**3.** To configure a capture filter to capture packets by protocol, double-click SAP/ETYPE = Any SAP or Any ETYPE in the Capture Filter dialog box.

**4.** The Capture Filter SAPs and ETYPEs dialog box appears, as shown in Figure 23-11.

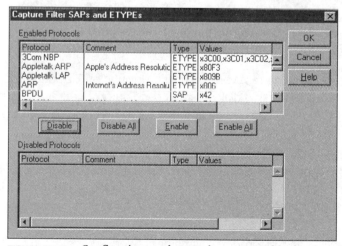

**FIGURE 23-11**    Configuring packets to be captured by protocol

Highlight the protocol(s) you want to exclude in the Enabled Protocols list box. Click the Disable command button.

Or, you can click the Disable All command button to exclude all protocols, and then highlight the protocol(s) you want to include in the Disabled Protocols list box. Then click the Enable command button.

Click OK.

5. To configure a capture filter to capture packets by their associated computer name or network address, highlight (Address Pairs) in the Capture Filter dialog box. Click the Address command button in the Add section of the dialog box.

6. The Address Expression dialog box appears, as shown in Figure 23-12. Note the Station 1 and Station 2 list boxes.

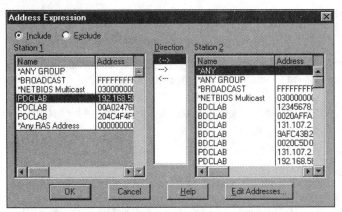

**FIGURE 23-12    Configuring packets to be captured by network address or computer name**

First, select the radio button next to Include or Exclude at the top of the Address Expression dialog box, depending on whether you want to capture or exclude from capturing packets associated with a particular pair of computer names or network addresses.

Then select a computer name or network address from the Station 1 list box. Then, select a direction arrow in the Direction list box to indicate whether the computer name or network address highlighted in the Station 1 list box is the packets' source address (--->), destination address (<--- ), or can be either (<-->).

Finally, select a computer name or network address from the Station 2 list box. Click OK.

The new address appears in the Capture Filter dialog box. Network Monitor enables you to configure up to three address pairs in a single capture filter.

**7.** If you have configured Network Monitor to use promiscuous mode, and you want to configure a capture filter to capture all packets transmitted on the local network segment, highlight INCLUDE computer_name [Ethernet] <--> *ANY in the Capture Filter dialog box, and then click the Line command button in the Delete section of this dialog box. This will instruct Network Monitor not to filter by computer name or network address, but to instead capture all packets.

Figure 23-13 shows the resulting Capture Filter dialog box after this configuration is made. Compare this figure to Figure 23-10. Notice the capture filter in Figure 23-13 no longer restricts capturing by computer name or network address, because the INCLUDE *computer_name* [Ethernet] <--> *ANY entry under (Address Pairs) has been removed.

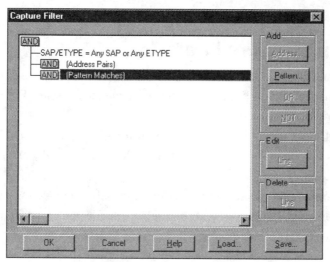

**FIGURE 23-13**   **Configuring Network Monitor to capture all packets transmitted on the local network segment**

**8.** To configure a capture filter to capture packets by a specific byte pattern contained in those packets, highlight (Pattern Matches) in the Capture Filter dialog box and click the Pattern command button in the Add section of the dialog box.

**9.** The Pattern Match dialog box appears, as shown in Figure 23-14. Configure the Offset (in hex) and Pattern text boxes. Click OK.

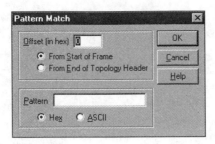

**FIGURE 23-14**   Configuring packets to be captured by byte pattern

 note   Configuring a capture filter by byte pattern is normally only done by advanced users of Network Monitor. Detailed knowledge of packet construction is required to configure a pattern match filter.

**10.** The Capture Filter dialog box reappears. Click OK.

## Saving Captured Data

After you finish performing a capture, you can save the captured data to a file for later analysis if you like. To save captured data to a file, select File ⇒ Save As in the Network Monitor main dialog box.

Also, when you exit Network Monitor, the Save File dialog box appears, prompting you to save captured data to a file at that time if you haven't previously done so.

To view the saved file at a later time, select File ⇒ Open in the Network Monitor main dialog box, and then select the file you saved from the Open File dialog box.

# USING NETWORK MONITOR TO VIEW CAPTURED PACKETS

Captured packets are of no use until you view them and interpret the statistics and information displayed.

You can use two primary dialog boxes to view captured data in Network Monitor: the Capture Window dialog box, and the Capture Summary dialog box. The view you choose depends on the type of information you seek.

The *Capture Window* dialog box (the Network Monitor main dialog box) displays general network activity statistics. This dialog box is useful for determining current network utilization, the type and number of packets being sent over the network, and which computers are generating (or receiving) the most network traffic. These statistics can be used for troubleshooting, for trend analysis, and for capacity planning purposes.

The *Capture Summary* dialog box displays a listing of all packets captured, and enables individual packet contents to be viewed and analyzed. This dialog box is used for capacity planning and troubleshooting. For example, you can use this dialog box to establish a baseline of the amount of network traffic that maintains browser information on a network segment or subnet. This baseline can help with capacity planning your network.

 concept link **Capacity planning is discussed in more detail in Chapter 24.**

In addition to being useful for capacity planning, the Capture Summary dialog box can be useful when troubleshooting protocol and network adapter driver problems.

The following sections explain how to view and interpret captured data by using the Capture Window and Capture Summary dialog boxes.

## Using the Capture Window Dialog Box

The Capture Window dialog box is the Network Monitor main dialog box, and is shown in Figure 23-15. As previously mentioned, this dialog box has four panes: the Graph pane, the Total Stats pane, the Session Stats pane, and the Station Stats pane.

The following sections explain how to use the Capture Window dialog box in Network Monitor to perform some of the most common network analysis tasks on captured data.

Graph pane          Session Stats pane     Total Stats pane     Station Stats pane

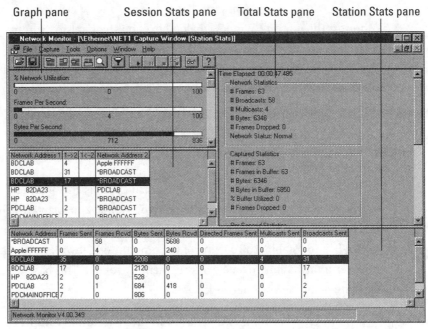

**FIGURE 23-15**    The Network Monitor Capture Window dialog box

## *Determining current network utilization*

One way to determine the current utilization of a network segment is to start a capture in Network Monitor, and then watch the % Network Utilization bar graph in the Graph pane *during the entire capture period*. This graph displays only the most recent one-second's worth of network activity, so you must view it during the entire capture period to get a feel for overall network utilization. A high number on the graph (any number consistently over 50%) may indicate too many computers are on the segment being analyzed.

Another way to determine the overall utilization of a network segment during the entire capture period is to view the Network Statistics section in the Total Stats pane *after* the capture is completed. You can derive a great deal of information from the statistics displayed. For example, you can determine the average number of bytes transmitted per second by dividing the number of bytes shown by the number of seconds shown in the Time Elapsed statistic at the top of the Total Stats pane. If the average number of bytes per second is greater than 50 percent of the segment's total capacity (an Ethernet 10BaseT segment, for example, has a maximum capacity of 10Mbps or 1,250,000 bytes per second), this may indicate too many computers are on the segment being analyzed.

## Replacing network addresses with computer names

Sometimes analysis of data is simplified when you can easily identify the computer whose statistics are displayed in Network Monitor.

To view computers by their computer names instead of their network (MAC) addresses, first select Capture ⇒ Find All Names in the Network Monitor Capture Window dialog box, as shown in Figure 23-16.

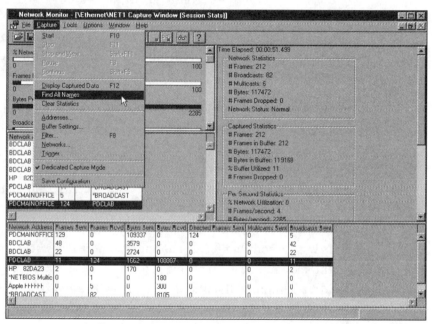

**FIGURE 23-16**    Finding NetBIOS names (computer names) in the captured data

A Find All Names dialog box appears, indicating how many NetBIOS (computer names) were found in the captured data. Click OK to replace the network addresses in the Session Stats and Station Stats panes with computer names.

 note    **Not *all* network addresses are replaced with computer names — only the network addresses whose associated computer names were transmitted and captured during the capture period will be replaced.**

### *Sorting columns to determine which computer is generating the most network traffic*

You can sort any of the columns in the Session Stats and Station Stats panes to determine which computer is sending (or receiving) the most of a specific type of network traffic.

 **Sorting a column only produces a list of those computers whose packets were captured during the capture period. If you filtered the capture, some Network Monitor statistics, particularly the statistics in the Session Stats and Station Stats panes, are complete *only* for those computers, protocols, and byte patterns you specified for capture.**

**Also, if you are *not* using Network Monitor in promiscuous mode, your capture data will *not* include all packets sent on the network segment.**

For example, you can sort the Frames Sent column in the Station Stats pane to determine which computer on the network segment sent the most packets during the capture period. Similarly, you can sort the Broadcasts Sent column in the Station Stats pane to determine which computer sent the most broadcasts during the capture period. You can also sort the Frames Received column in the Station Stats pane to determine which computer received the most packets during the capture period. All the other columns can be sorted, as well, to determine which computer was responsible for generating the most bytes sent, most directed frames sent, most multicasts sent, and so forth.

To sort a column, right-click the column header (for example, Frames Sent). Select Sort Column from the menu that appears, as shown in Figure 23-17.

Network Monitor sorts the column in descending order, with the largest number appearing at the top of the column.

## Using the Capture Summary Dialog Box

To access the Capture Summary dialog box select Capture ⇒ Display Captured Data from the Network Monitor Capture Window (main dialog box).

The Network Monitor Capture Summary dialog box appears, as shown in Figure 23-18. Notice the dialog box lists, by frame number, all the packets captured by Network Monitor during the capture period.

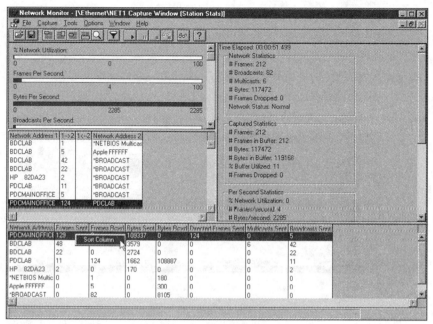

**FIGURE 23-17**    Sorting a column in Network Monitor

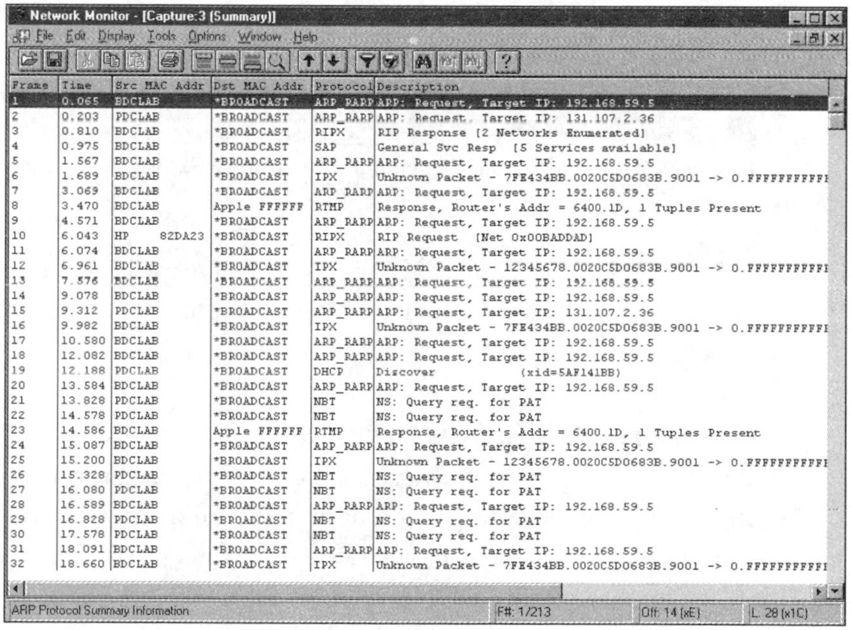

**FIGURE 23-18**    The Capture Summary dialog box

You can double-click any frame listed in this dialog box to obtain detailed information about the contents of that packet. Figure 23-19 shows the packet details view. Notice that middle pane in the dialog box shows protocol decode information, and the bottom pane shows, in hexadecimal, the entire contents of the packet.

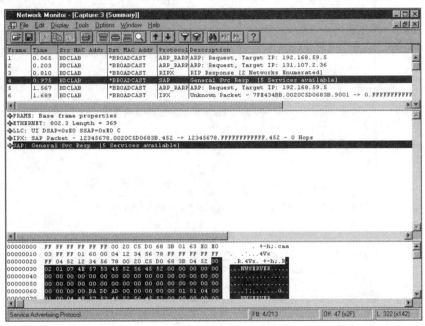

**FIGURE 23-19**    Viewing packet detail in the Capture Summary dialog box

Because a large number of packets may be displayed in the Capture Summary dialog box, you might want to use a display filter to limit the number of captured packets displayed.

## Configuring a display filter

By default, Network Monitor's *display filter* is configured to display *all* packets captured in the Capture Summary dialog box. You can specify which captured packets will be displayed in this dialog box, however, by configuring a display filter.

You can configure a display filter so that:

o Only packets using certain protocols are (or are not) displayed

o Only packets to or from specified computers or network devices are (or are not) displayed

○ Only packets containing specific byte patterns are displayed

○ Any combination of the previous

For example, if you want to view all network packets containing browser information, you can configure a display filter so only packets containing the Browser protocol are displayed.

Likewise, if you are troubleshooting an IP address assignment problem, and your network uses DHCP to assign IP addresses, you can configure a display filter so only packets containing the DHCP protocol are displayed.

## TO CONFIGURE A DISPLAY FILTER, FOLLOW THESE STEPS:

**1.** In the Network Monitor Capture Summary dialog box, select Display ⇒ Filter. (Or press F8.)

**2.** The Display Filter dialog box appears, as shown in Figure 23-20. Notice the default settings. Configure the display filter as desired. Click OK.

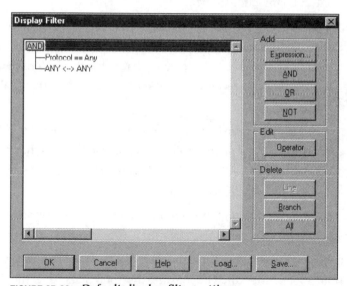

**FIGURE 23-20**  Default display filter settings

 note  Configuring a display filter is similar to configuring a capture filter. (The steps for configuring a capture filter are presented earlier in this chapter.)

# KEY POINT SUMMARY

Chapter 23 explored Network Monitor, a Windows NT Server administrative tool that enables you to capture, view, and analyze network packets. This packet analysis tool is useful in troubleshooting network problems and protocol problems. It can also be used to determine current network utilization, for trend analysis, and for network capacity planning.

- The version of Network Monitor that ships with Windows NT Server 4.0 is designed to capture only packets addressed to, or sent from, the Windows NT Server computer running Network Monitor. A more robust version of Network Monitor ships with Microsoft Systems Management Server. The main difference between the two versions in the ability of each product to use the promiscuous mode of the computer's network adapter: The NT Server 4.0 version, by default, *can't* be used in promiscuous mode; the Systems Management Server version, by default, *is* used in promiscuous mode.

- *Promiscuous* refers to a network adapter's ability to receive packets not addressed to that network adapter. A *non-promiscuous* network adapter can only receive packets addressed to that network adapter. A *promiscuous* network adapter can receive any packet transmitted on the local network segment.

- Network Monitor consists of two parts: the *Network Monitor Tools,* and the *Network Monitor Agent.* Both parts are installed together by using the Network application in Control Panel. Network Monitor requires a network adapter that uses an NDIS 4.0 driver.

- To access Network Monitor, from the Windows NT Server desktop, Select Start⇒Programs⇒Administrative Tools (Common)⇒Network Monitor.

- The Network Monitor main dialog box is called the *Capture Window,* which contains four panes: the Graph pane, the Total Stats pane, the Session Stats pane, and the Station Stats pane.

- By default, the version of Network Monitor that ships with Windows NT Server 4.0 uses a special mode of the NDIS 4.0 driver, called "local capture only." Some NDIS 4.0 drivers don't correctly implement the "local capture only" mode. These drivers can capture packets sent *to* the Windows NT

Server computer, but *not* the packets sent *by* the Windows NT Server computer. To remedy this situation and to enable Network Monitor to capture packets both sent to and sent by the Windows NT Server computer, the Registry must be edited to configure Network Monitor to use the promiscuous mode of the NDIS 4.0 driver.

- A by-product of forcing Network Monitor to use promiscuous mode is Network Monitor can then capture *all* packets transmitted on the local network segment (instead of only packets addressed to or from the Windows NT Server computer on which Network Monitor is running).

- Network Monitor does *not* produce any statistics or other useful data until a capture is performed. During a capture, Network Monitor receives packets transmitted on the local network segment and stores these packets either in memory or in a capture file. Capture files can be used for later analysis. The process of capturing doesn't interfere with packets reaching their intended destinations on the network.

- To perform a capture, you must manually start and stop a capture in Network Monitor. You can either choose to view statistics in the Network Monitor Capture Window dialog box as they are gathered, or you can select the *Dedicated Capture Mode to not* view data while it is gathered and to ease processor load during the capture process.

- By default, Network Monitor's capture filter is configured to capture *all* packets addressed to or sent by the Windows NT Server computer. However, you can configure a capture filter to specify which packets transmitted on the network segment will be captured.

  - You can configure a *capture filter* so that:
    - Only packets using certain protocols are (or are not) captured
    - Only packets to or from specified computers or network devices are (or are not) captured
    - Only packets containing specific byte patterns are captured
    - Any combination of the previous.

- After you finish performing a capture, you can save the captured data to a file for later analysis if you like.

- Two primary dialog boxes in Network Monitor are used to view captured data: the Capture Window dialog box, and the Capture Summary dialog box.

- The *Capture Window* dialog box (the Network Monitor main dialog box) displays general network activity statistics in its four panes. In addition to being able to determine current network utilization in this dialog box, you can replace network addresses with NetBIOS (computer names); this will make it easier to identify the computer whose statistics you are analyzing. You can also sort columns to determine which computer is sending (or receiving) the most of a specific type of network traffic.

- The *Capture Summary* dialog box displays a listing of all packets captured, and enables individual packet contents to be viewed and analyzed. This dialog box is useful for both capacity planning and troubleshooting. To access this dialog box, from the Network Monitor Capture Window (main dialog box) select Capture ⇒ Display Captured Data.

- By default, Network Monitor's display filter is configured to display *all* packets that are captured in the Capture Summary dialog box. However, you can configure a display filter to specify which captured packets will be displayed in this dialog box.

- You can configure a display filter so that:

  - Only packets using certain protocols are (or are not) displayed

  - Only packets to or from specified computers or network devices are (or are not) displayed

  - Only packets containing specific byte patterns are displayed

  - Any combination of the previous

- To configure a display filter, in the Network Monitor Capture Summary dialog box, select Display ⇒ Filter, or press F8. Configuring a display filter is similar to configuring a capture filter.

# APPLYING WHAT YOU'VE LEARNED

Now it's time to regroup, review, and apply what you've learned in this chapter. The following Instant Assessment questions bring to mind key facts and concepts.

The hands-on lab exercise will reinforce what you've learned and give you an opportunity to practice some of the tasks tested by the Enterprise exam.

## Instant Assessment

1. Which Windows NT packet analysis tool is useful for troubleshooting network problems and protocol problems; and also for determining current network utilization, trend analysis, and network capacity planning?

2. Define the term *promiscuous* as it refers to a network adapter.

3. Which two parts make up Network Monitor?

4. You want to install Network Monitor on your Windows NT Server computer. This computer already has the Network Monitor Agent installed. What must you do before you can install Network Monitor?

5. What hardware is specifically required to use Network Monitor?

6. How can you access Network Monitor from the NT Server desktop?

7. List the four panes found in the Network Monitor Capture Window dialog box.

8. Which special mode of the NDIS 4.0 driver does the Windows NT version of Network Monitor use, by default?

9. What must be performed *before* statistics can be displayed in Network Monitor?

10. By default, which packets are captured by Network Monitor?

11. What can you do if you want to specify or restrict the type of packets Network Monitor captures?

12. When configuring a capture filter, what types of criteria can you specify Network Monitor use to determine whether packets will be included in or excluded from capturing?

13. When can you save captured data to a file?

14. Which two dialog boxes in Network Monitor are the primary dialog boxes used to *view* captured packets?

15. You want to determine current network utilization. What are two ways you can do this by using Network Monitor?

16. How do you sort a column in the Capture Window dialog box?

17. You use Network Monitor to perform a capture and you are currently viewing the captured packets in the Capture Summary dialog box. You decide you *only* want to view packets containing the IPX protocol. What should you do to accomplish this?

                                                                          **T/F**

18. Network Monitor is a Windows NT tool that ships with *both* Windows NT Workstation and Windows NT Server.                    _____

19. By default, the Windows NT version of Network Monitor is *not* used in promiscuous mode.                                      _____

concept link    **For answers to the Instant Assessment questions see Appendix D.**

# Hands-on Lab Exercise

The following hands-on lab exercise provides you with an opportunity to apply the knowledge you've gained in this chapter about Network Monitor.

### Lab 23.36 *Installing and using Network Monitor*

Enterprise

The purpose of this hands-on lab exercise is to provide you with the experience of installing and using Network Monitor on a Windows NT Server computer.

note    ***This lab is optional* because it requires that a network adapter be installed in your Windows NT Server computer. Also, if you have a second computer that is network-connected to your first computer, you can use this computer in Part 2 of this lab.**

This lab consists of two parts:

    Part 1: Installing Network Monitor
    Part 2: Using Network Monitor

Begin this lab by booting your computer to Windows NT Server. Log on as Administrator. Place your Windows NT Server compact disc in your computer's CD-ROM drive.

Complete the following steps carefully.

**Part 1: Installing Network Monitor**

In this section, you install Network Monitor on your Windows NT Server computer. Then you edit the Registry to force the network adapter in your computer to operate in promiscuous mode.

**1.** Select Start ⇒ Settings ⇒ Control Panel.

**2.** In the Control Panel dialog box, double-click the Network icon.

**3.** In the Network dialog box, click the Services tab.

**4.** On the Services tab, highlight Network Monitor Agent in the Network Services list box. Click the Remove command button.

**5.** A warning dialog box appears. Click the Yes command button to continue. Windows NT removes Network Monitor Agent.

**6.** On the Services tab, click the Add command button.

**7.** In the Select Network Service dialog box, highlight Network Monitor Tools and Agent. Click OK.

**8.** A Windows NT Setup dialog box appears. Ensure the correct path to your Windows NT Server source files (usually the I386 folder on your Windows NT Server compact disc) is listed in the text box. Edit this text box if necessary. Click the Continue command button.

**9.** Windows NT copies source files and installs Network Monitor Tools and Agent.

**10.** The Network dialog box reappears. Click the Close command button.

**11.** Windows NT performs various bindings operations.

**12.** A Network Settings Change dialog box appears. Click the No command button.

**13.** Close Control Panel.

**14.** Select Start ⇒ Run.

**15.** The Run dialog box appears. Type **regedt32** in the Open drop-down list box. Click OK.

**16.** The Registry Editor dialog box appears. Select Windows ⇒ HKEY_LOCAL_MACHINE on Local Machine.

**17.** Double-click the + sign next to SYSTEM. Double-click the + sign next to CurrentControlSet. Double-click the + sign next to Services. Double-click the + sign next to bh. Highlight the Linkage folder.

**18.** Find the Bind value (located in the right-hand part of the dialog box). In the space provided, write the entry for the Bind value that directly follows the *first* \Device\ portion of the entry. (For example, Elnk31.).

**19.** Highlight the `Parameters` folder.

**20.** Select Edit⟹Add Key.

**21.** The Add Key dialog box appears. Type **ForcePmode** in the Key Name text box. Leave the Class text box blank. Click OK.

**22.** The Registry Editor dialog box reappears. Click the ForcePmode folder.

**23.** Select Edit⟹Add Value.

**24.** The Add Value dialog box appears. In the Value Name text box, type the value you wrote in Step 18. For example, elnk31. In the Data Type drop-down list box, select REG_DWORD. Click OK.

**25.** The DWORD Editor dialog box appears. In the Data text box, type **1**. (Don't type the period at the end.) Click OK.

**26.** The Registry Editor dialog box reappears. Close the Registry Editor.

**27.** Select Start⟹Shut Down.

**28.** In the Shut Down Windows dialog box, click the radio button next to "Restart the computer". Click the Yes command button.

**29.** Reboot your computer to Windows NT Server. Log on as Administrator.

Continue to Part 2.

### Part 2: Using Network Monitor

In this section you use Network Monitor on your Windows NT Server computer to capture and view packets.

 **If you have a second computer and it is network-connected to your first computer, boot both computers before you do this part of the lab. (Boot the first [primary] computer to Windows NT Server, and boot the second computer to Windows NT Workstation.)**

**If you don't have a second computer, you can still do this part of the lab, but you won't be able to capture as much data.**

**1.** Select Start⟹Programs⟹Administrative Tools (Common)⟹Network Monitor.

**2.** The Network Monitor dialog box appears. Maximize this dialog box. Also maximize the Capture Window (Station Stats) within the Network Monitor dialog box.

**3.** Select Capture⟹Filter.

**4.** A Capture Filter dialog box appears. Click OK.

**5.** The Capture Filter dialog box appears. Highlight the entry *under* AND (Address Pairs). Click the Line command button in the Delete section of this dialog box. (This allows Network Monitor to capture all packets transmitted on the local network segment.) Click OK.

**6.** The Network Monitor dialog box reappears. Select Capture ⇒ Start to start capturing packets.

**7.** Wait approximately 1-2 minutes to allow Network Monitor time to capture data. While this process is taking place, notice the % Network Utilization, Frames Per Second, and Bytes Per Second bar graphs in the Network Monitor dialog box.

**8.** Select Capture ⇒ Stop to stop capturing packets.

**9.** Select Capture ⇒ Find All Names.

**10.** A Find All Names dialog box appears. Click OK.

**11.** To determine which computer is sending the most packets on the network segment, right-click Frames Sent (the Frames Sent column header) in the bottom section of the Network Monitor dialog box. Select Sort Column from the menu that appears. The computer on the network segment that sent the most packets during the capture period should appear at the top of the list in this section of the dialog box.

**12.** Right-click each of the other column headers (Frames Rcvd, Bytes Sent, Bytes Rcvd, Directed Frames Sent, Multicasts Sent, and Broadcasts Sent) and sort each column, one at a time. Notice the results of each sort.

**13.** Select Capture ⇒ Display Captured Data.

**14.** The Capture (Summary) dialog box appears. Select Display ⇒ Filter.

**15.** The Display Filter dialog box appears. Double-click Protocol == Any.

**16.** The Expression dialog box appears. Notice you can filter the display of captured packets by address, by protocol, or by protocol property. Click OK.

**17.** The Display Filter dialog box reappears. Click OK.

**18.** The Capture (Summary) dialog box reappears. Double-click any packet displayed in this dialog box to view its details. Do this several times.

**19.** When you are finished viewing packet details, exit Network Monitor.

**20.** A Save File dialog box appears. Click the No command button.

**21.** A Save Address Database dialog box appears. Click the No command button.

Enterprise

# Capacity Planning

# About Chapter 24

**C**hapter 24 explores the fundamentals of capacity planning, a process that includes determining current usage of a server's or network's resources, as well as tracking their utilization over time to predict future usage and any additional equipment that will be required to meet projected needs.

This chapter begins by defining the basic steps involved in capacity planning: establishing a baseline, gathering data over time, and using data to predict future utilization. Then it explains how to perform each of these tasks.

Next, this chapter explains how to capacity plan your server. This section suggests specific tools and techniques you can use to determine if your server's performance is adequate for now, and, if it is, to determine when the server will need upgrading.

Next, the chapter explains how to capacity plan your network, either for overall network utilization, or for a specific type of network traffic. Specific Performance Monitor counters and Network Monitor statistics are suggested.

Chapter 24 contains some interesting and worthwhile information, but can be considered optional reading unless you're preparing for the Enterprise exam. This chapter maps to the "Establish a baseline for measuring system performance" objective in the Monitoring and Optimization section for the Enterprise exam.

# FUNDAMENTALS OF CAPACITY PLANNING

*Capacity planning* is the process of determining current usage of server and/or network resources, and tracking utilization over time to predict future usage and the additional hardware that will be required to meet projected levels of utilization. Capacity planning can be performed on a single computer, such as a network server, or it can be performed on an entire network. Capacity planning enables you to plan for your organization's future needs and growth.

Two methods are commonly used to perform capacity planning. One method involves determining current server/network utilization to predict future utilization. The second method involves simulating the expected future utilization using various tools. These tools, which are sometimes called *stress test tools*, can simulate specified levels of server utilization and/or network traffic to determine how current hardware responds to expected future levels of use.

Because the second method requires the use of special tools that *don't* ship with Windows NT, and, therefore, aren't part of the Windows NT 4.0 Certified Professional exam objectives, this chapter focuses on the first method of capacity planning.

The two primary Windows NT administrative tools that can be used for capacity planning are Performance Monitor and Network Monitor. Additionally, Windows NT Diagnostics provides some statistics that can be useful for capacity planning.

The basic steps involved in capacity planning are:

o Establishing a baseline

o Gathering data over time

o Using this data to predict future utilization and future hardware requirements

The following sections explain each of these basic capacity planning steps. Additionally, this chapter recommends specific statistics to use when capacity planning a server and when capacity planning a network.

## Establishing a Baseline

Establishing a baseline is the equivalent of determining the status quo—you gather data to determine current server and/or network utilization and performance. Determining the current situation is the first step in predicting what the future environment might be like.

You can use Performance Monitor and Network Monitor to gather data about your server's memory, processor, and disk. You can also obtain statistics about the network in general and about how a particular server utilizes the network specifically. The data you gather in this step will form an initial baseline of data about your server and/or network.

You should consider gathering data at various times to obtain an overall picture of utilization. For example, consider collecting data during business hours, when network usage is at its peak and production is heavy. Also consider collecting data during nonbusiness hours when network utilization levels should be lower. You might also consider gathering data over several days in a week, or perhaps over several days in a month to take into account normal cyclical business highs and lows. Taking several samples over a limited period of time normally provides the most accurate initial picture of your server and/or network environment.

## Gathering Data Over Time

Once you've established a baseline of data, the next step in capacity planning is to continue gathering data over time to obtain additional statistics that can later be used for trend analysis.

A reasonable period of time for data gathering depends on many factors, including:

- The amount of time you can afford to allocate to capacity planning tasks
- How fast your organization is growing
- External requirements, such as equipment budget deadlines
- The changing skill levels of users in your organization (because more skilled users tend to create more data)
- The nature of your organization, particularly if your company experiences seasonal peaks and lows during the course of its operating cycle

Perhaps the most important consideration is that data should be gathered frequently enough so that you can perform reliable trend analysis to predict future utilization.

## Using Data to Predict Future Utilization

Once you've established a baseline and gathered data over time, you're ready to analyze that data to predict future utilization, and the hardware that will be required to meet those utilization levels.

Often the raw data, in and of itself, isn't extremely useful for trend analysis. It is usually beneficial to export the gathered data in a format acceptable to standard analysis tools (such as spreadsheets and databases). For example, Performance Monitor enables you to export data directly to a comma-separated value or tab-separated value file. These types of files can be imported directly into most spreadsheets and databases.

Once you have imported the data into a spreadsheet or database, you can chart it, graph it, or otherwise manipulate it to obtain meaningful results.

In most instances, the data gathered over the last several months can be used to graph growth trends in server/network utilization. This growth trend graph can be extended to predict future server/network utilization. When the extended graph indicates that future utilization of a specific resource will approach or exceed maximum capacity, additional hardware may be required to meet anticipated needs.

Up to this point, gathering data for capacity planning has been discussed in general terms. Now let's look at the specific types of data and statistics that are most useful for capacity planning your server, and for capacity planning your network.

# CAPACITY PLANNING YOUR SERVER

Capacity planning your server involves using Performance Monitor and Network Monitor to gather server and network statistics over time to establish a baseline and to provide additional data for trend analysis. You can analyze these statistics to determine if the server's performance is adequate now, and, if it is, to determine approximately when the server will need to be upgraded, and what hardware will be required to maintain its performance.

tip  **When planning for future utilization, plan for more disk space, more memory, more network bandwidth, and more processor power than is indicated by your statistical analysis alone. Trend analysis is helpful, but may not take into account that as time passes, operating systems and applications become more complex and require more system resources.**

The two primary methods you can use to gather statistics using Performance Monitor are running Performance Monitor individually on each server to be monitored, and running Performance Monitor on a single, centralized Windows NT computer to monitor several servers simultaneously.

You can run Performance Monitor individually on each server to be monitored on the network. Be aware that when Performance Monitor is run on the computer being monitored, the memory, disk, and processor statistics obtained may be above normal levels because of the running of Performance Monitor itself.

You can also run Performance Monitor on a single, centralized Windows NT Server or Workstation computer to monitor several servers on the network simultaneously. When Performance Monitor is run on a different computer than the computer being monitored, the memory, disk, and processor statistics are accurate for the computer being monitored, but the network utilization statistics may be above normal levels. This is due to the sending of Performance Monitor statistics across the network to the centralized Windows NT computer from the servers being monitored.

When using Network Monitor, keep in mind that the version of Network Monitor that ships with Windows NT Server 4.0 can only be run on the computer being monitored—you *can't* monitor a remote computer by using this version of Network Monitor. If you want to monitor computers remotely, consider using the version of Network Monitor that ships with Microsoft Systems Management Server.

The four components that are of critical importance when capacity planning your server are memory, processor, disk, and network. Here's a closer look at each of these critical server components, and the specific statistics that you can use to monitor each.

# Memory

Gathering statistics about a server's memory utilization is an important step when capacity planning your server. I recommend using the following counter to obtain this data:

o **Memory Pages/sec:** This Performance Monitor counter is the primary counter that is used to monitor memory usage for capacity planning or troubleshooting purposes. It measures the amount of 4KB memory pages that are read from or written to the paging file during a one-second time period.

This counter is selected for monitoring in the Add to Chart, Add to Alert, Add to Report, and Add To Log dialog boxes in Performance Monitor. The Add to Chart dialog box is shown in 24-1. Notice that Memory is selected in the Object drop-down list box, and that Pages/sec is selected in the Counter list box.

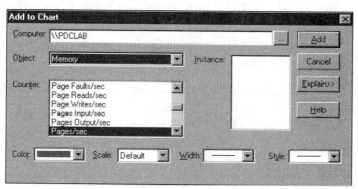

**FIGURE 24-1**    Selecting the Memory Pages/sec counter in Performance Monitor

o **Interpreting the results of this counter:** A consistently low number for this counter (less than 2) indicates that the computer most likely has sufficient memory. A consistently high number for this counter (more than 2-3) may indicate that the computer does *not* have sufficient RAM.

Memory is probably the most important component of a server. Insufficient RAM can cause excessive disk and processor utilization. When it appears that the computer's disk, processor, and memory are all functioning at or near maximum capacity, try adding additional RAM *first.* This usually alleviates some of the disk and processor load because paging is significantly reduced when RAM is added.

When in doubt, add RAM before proceeding to the more expensive processor and disk upgrades.

## Processor

Gathering information about your server's processor performance is also important. I recommend using the following counters:

- **Processor % Processor Time:** This performance counter is the primary counter used to monitor processor utilization on a single-processor computer for capacity planning or troubleshooting purposes. It measures the percent of the time that the processor is actively used by processes other than the Idle process.

  This counter is selected for monitoring in the Add to Chart, Add to Alert, Add to Report, and Add To Log dialog boxes in Performance Monitor. The Add to Chart dialog box is shown in Figure 24-2. Notice that Processor is selected in the Object drop-down list box, and that % Processor Time is selected in the Counter list box.

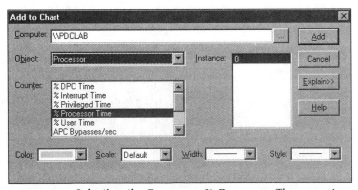

**FIGURE 24-2**    Selecting the Processor % Processor Time counter in Performance Monitor

- **System % Total Processor Time:** This is an additional Performance Monitor counter you can use to monitor overall processor utilization on a multiprocessor computer. It measures the percent of the time that all processors in the computer are actively used by processes other than the Idle process. Figure 24-3 shows this counter being selected in the Add to Chart dialog box.

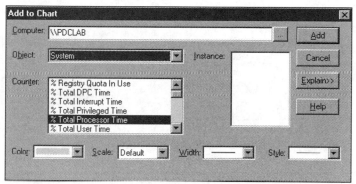

**FIGURE 24-3**    Selecting the System % Total Processor Time counter in Performance Monitor

- **Interpreting the results of these counters:** A consistently low number for either of these counters (less than 60%) indicates that the computer most likely has sufficient processor power. A consistently high number for either of these counters (approaching 100%) may indicate that the computer does *not* have sufficient processor power. Before upgrading your computer's processor(s), check memory utilization first. Upgrade RAM, if necessary, *before* upgrading your processor(s).

## Disk

There are three primary counters that can be used to monitor disk utilization on a server.

- **PhysicalDisk Avg. Disk Queue Length:** This Performance Monitor counter measures the average number of disk reads and writes waiting to be performed.

This counter is selected for monitoring in the Add to Chart, Add to Alert, Add to Report, and Add To Log dialog boxes in Performance Monitor. The Add to Chart dialog box is shown in Figure 24-4. Notice that PhysicalDisk is selected in the Object drop-down list box, that Avg. Disk Queue Length is selected in the Counter list box, and that Total is selected in the Instance list box.

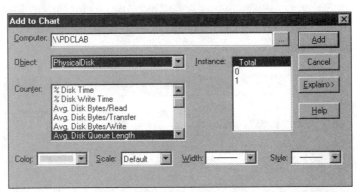

**FIGURE 24-4**    Selecting the PhysicalDisk Avg. Disk Queue Length counter in Performance Monitor

o   **Interpreting the results of this counter:** A consistently high number for this counter (greater than 2–3) may indicate that a faster hard disk and/or hard disk controller is required for adequate system performance.

o   **PhysicalDisk % Disk Time:** This Performance Monitor counter measures the percentage of time that the disk performs reads and writes. Figure 24-5 shows this counter being selected in the Add to Chart dialog box.

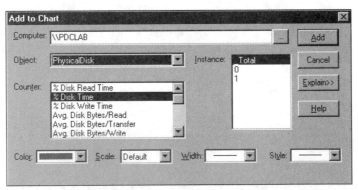

**FIGURE 24-5**    Selecting the PhysicalDisk % Disk Time counter in Performance Monitor

- **Interpreting the results of this counter:** A consistently high number for this counter (between 70% and 100%) may indicate that a faster hard disk and/or hard disk controller is required for adequate system performance.

- **LogicalDisk % Free Space:** This Performance Monitor counter measures the percentage of unused disk space. Figure 24-6 shows this counter being selected in the Add to Chart dialog box. Notice that LogicalDisk is selected in the Object drop-down list box, that % Free Space is selected in the Counter list box, and that Total ==> Total is selected in the Instance list box.

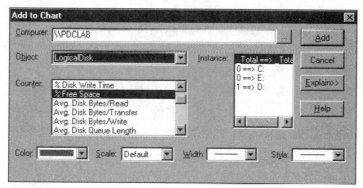

**FIGURE 24-6** Selecting the LogicalDisk % Free Space counter in Performance Monitor

- **Interpreting the results of this counter:** A consistently high or gradually increasing number for this counter (approaching 100%) indicates that the server does *not* have sufficient disk space available. An additional disk, or a replacement disk that has more capacity, may be required.

## Network

There are two primary Performance Monitor counters for monitoring network utilization.

- **Network Segment % Network utilization:** This Performance Monitor counter measures the total network utilization on a given network segment as a percentage of the maximum amount of network traffic possible on that segment. If your server is connected to more than one network segment, each segment should be monitored.

This counter is selected for monitoring in the Add to Chart, Add to Alert, Add to Report, and Add To Log dialog boxes in Performance Monitor. The Add to Chart dialog box is shown in Figure 24-7. Notice that Network Segment is selected in the Object drop-down list box, that % Network utilization is selected in the Counter list box, and that the first network adapter on the server is selected in the Instance list box.

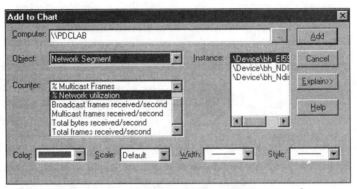

**FIGURE 24-7**   Selecting the Network Segment % Network Utilization counter in Performance Monitor

- **Interpreting the results of this counter:** A consistently high number for this counter (between 60% and 100%) may indicate that there are too many computers (or too much network traffic) on the network segment, and that an additional network adapter may need to be installed in the server, or a router may need to be installed on the network to further segment the network.

- **Server Bytes Total/sec:** This Performance Monitor counter can be used in place of the Network Segment % Network Utilization counter if the Network Monitor Agent is not installed on the server. This counter measures the total amount of bytes sent to and received by the server. If this server is the only server on the network segment (and the server is only connected to one network segment), the measurement obtained from this counter approximates the total network utilization on that network segment. (The counter is said to approximate total network utilization because it is assumed that most network traffic is to and from the server.)

  Figure 24-8 shows this counter being selected in the Add to Chart dialog box.

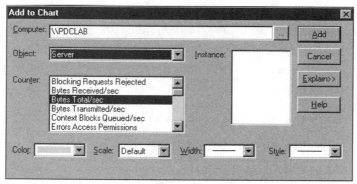

**FIGURE 24-8**    Selecting the Server Bytes Total/sec counter in Performance Monitor

- **Interpreting the results of this counter:** A consistently high number for this counter (approaching the maximum number of bytes that can be sent on the network segment in one second) may indicate that there are too many computers (or too much network traffic) on the network segment, and that an additional network adapter may need to be installed in the server, or a router may need to be installed on the network to further segment the network.

Network Monitor can also be used to monitor network usage. You can view the Network Statistics section in the Total Stats pane after a capture is completed. Using the information presented in this section, you can determine the average number of bytes transmitted per second by dividing the number of bytes shown by the number of seconds shown in the Time Elapsed statistic at the top of the Total Stats pane.

If the average number of bytes per second approaches the segment's maximum capacity (an Ethernet 10BaseT segment, for example, has a maximum capacity of 10Mbps or 1,250,000 bytes per second), this may indicate that there are too many computers or too much network traffic on the segment being analyzed.

# CAPACITY PLANNING YOUR NETWORK

Capacity planning your network involves using Performance Monitor and Network Monitor to gather network statistics over time to establish a baseline and to provide additional data for trend analysis. You can analyze these statistics to determine if the network's performance is adequate now, and if it is, to determine approximately when the network will need to be upgraded.

Capacity planning a network typically falls into one of two categories: capacity planning *overall* network utilization, or capacity planning for a *specific type* of network traffic.

## Capacity Planning Overall Network Utilization

There are two primary Performance Monitor counters for monitoring overall network utilization: Network Segment % Network utilization, and Server Bytes Total/sec.

 concept link

**Detailed information about these counters is presented in the "Network" section earlier in this chapter.**

Network Monitor can also be used to monitor network usage. The Network Statistics section in the Total Stats pane provides various network utilization statistics.

You can use these Performance Monitor and Network Monitor statistics to determine your network's overall baseline performance, and also for trend analysis that will indicate when the network should be upgraded to meet projected overall network utilization needs.

## Capacity Planning for a Specific Type of Network Traffic

You might occasionally want to perform capacity planning for a specific type of network traffic, such as browsing, name resolution, or broadcasts. For example, if you are planning a new WAN link, you might be concerned about the amount of browsing traffic that will exist on the WAN link once it is installed.

To begin the process of capacity planning your new WAN link for browsing traffic, configure Network Monitor to capture and analyze all browsing traffic on an existing network. Once the browsing packets are captured, Network Monitor is used to determine how large each of these packets is, how many browsing packets are transmitted per workstation and per server on the network, and how frequently browsing packets are transmitted.

Once you have determined the amount of browsing traffic that each workstation and server generates over a given time period, you can use this information, in conjunction with your planned network configuration (including the number of workstations and servers that will be used on each side of the WAN link) to project how much browsing traffic will be sent over the new WAN link.

Network Monitor is the primary tool for capacity planning specific types of network traffic, because you can configure it to capture and display only the types of network traffic you want to analyze. Our example features browsing, but you can use Network Monitor to analyze virtually any type of network traffic, including: WINS and DNS name resolution traffic, broadcast traffic, NetBIOS multicast traffic, IP address assignment traffic (DHCP), Directory Services synchronization traffic, and so on.

 **note** **To use Network Monitor for this type of capacity planning, you may need to use the version of Network Monitor that ships with Systems Management Server. (The version that ships with Windows NT Server 4.0 is designed to only capture packets sent to and from the Windows NT Server computer that is running Network Monitor.)**

 concept link **For more information on how to use Network Monitor, see Chapter 23.**

# Key Point Summary

This chapter introduced the basics of capacity planning. The following points highlight the major issues.

- *Capacity planning* is the process of determining current usage of server and/or network resources, as well as tracking utilization over time to predict future usage and the additional hardware that will be required to meet projected needs. Capacity planning can be performed on a single computer, such as a network server, or it can be performed on an entire network.

- Performance Monitor and Network Monitor are the two primary Windows NT tools that can be used for capacity planning.

- The basic steps involved in capacity planning are establishing a baseline, gathering data over time, and using this data to predict future utilization and future hardware requirements.
  - Establishing a baseline determines the status quo. Consider gathering several samples of data during both business and nonbusiness hours when establishing an initial baseline. Once you've established a baseline, continue gathering data over time to obtain additional statistics that can later be used for trend analysis.
  - Finally, use the data you've gathered to predict future utilization. It is usually beneficial to export this data to a comma-separated value or tab-separated value file, which can then be imported directly into most spreadsheets and databases for trend analysis.
- Capacity planning your server involves using Performance Monitor and Network Monitor to gather server and network statistics over time. These statistics, when analyzed, help you to determine if the server's performance is adequate now, and, if it is, to determine approximately when the server will need to be upgraded.
- The two primary methods you can use to capacity plan your server by using Performance Monitor are running Performance Monitor individually on each server to be monitored; and running Performance Monitor on a single, centralized Windows NT computer to monitor several servers simultaneously.
  - When Performance Monitor is run individually on each server to be monitored, the memory, disk, and processor statistics produced may be above normal levels due to the running of Performance Monitor itself. When Performance Monitor is run on a single, centralized computer, network utilization statistics may be above normal levels due to the sending of statistics across the network to the centralized computer running Performance Monitor.
- The four components that are of critical importance when capacity planning your server are memory, processor, disk, and network.
  - *Memory:* The primary Performance Monitor counter used to monitor memory utilization is Memory Pages/sec. A consistently high number for this counter (greater than 2-3) may indicate that the server doesn't have sufficient RAM.

- *Processor:* The primary Performance Monitor counter used to monitor processor utilization on a single-processor computer is Processor % Processor Time. The primary Performance Monitor counter used to monitor processor utilization on a multi-processor computer is System % Total Processor Time. A consistently high number for either of these counters (approaching 100%) may indicate that the computer doesn't have sufficient processor power.

- *Disk:* The three primary Performance Monitor counters used to monitor disk utilization on a server are: PhysicalDisk Avg. Disk Queue Length, PhysicalDisk % Disk Time, and LogicalDisk % Free Space. The first two counters indicate whether the speed of the disk is adequate, and the third counter indicates whether the disk has sufficient capacity.

- *Network:* The two primary Performance Monitor counters used to monitor network utilization are Network Segment % Network utilization and Server Bytes Total/sec. A consistently high number for either of these counters may indicate there are too many computers or too much network traffic on the network segment. Network Monitor can also be used to provide network usage statistics.

- Capacity planning your network involves using Performance Monitor and Network Monitor to gather network statistics over time. These statistics, when analyzed, help you determine if the network's performance is adequate now, and if it is, determine approximately when the network will need to be upgraded.

- Capacity planning a network typically falls into one of two categories: capacity planning *overall* network utilization, or capacity planning for a *specific type* of network traffic.

  - When capacity planning overall network utilization, two primary Performance Monitor counters are used. These counters are Network Segment % Network utilization and Server Bytes Total/sec. Network Monitor can also be used to monitor network usage.

  - When capacity planning for a specific type of network traffic, such as browsing, name resolution, or broadcasts, Network Monitor is often used. You can configure Network Monitor to capture and display only the specific type of network traffic you want to analyze.

# APPLYING WHAT YOU'VE LEARNED

Now it's time to regroup, review, and apply what you've learned in this chapter.

The following Instant Assessment questions will bring to mind key capacity planning facts and concepts that you've learned in this chapter.

## Instant Assessment

1. What is capacity planning?

2. What are the three basic steps in capacity planning?

3. When establishing a baseline, when should you consider collecting data?

4. Performance Monitor enables you to export data directly to two types of files that can be imported directly into most spreadsheets and databases. What are these two types of files called?

5. What are the two primary methods that you can use to gather server and network statistics by using Performance Monitor?

6. What is the primary Windows NT administrative tool used when capacity planning for a specific type of network traffic?

7. List two categories of network capacity planning.

8. List the four components that are of critical importance when capacity planning a Windows NT server.

9. What is the primary Performance Monitor counter used to monitor memory usage for capacity planning purposes?

10. Which Performance Monitor counter is used to monitor processor utilization on a single-processor computer?

11. List three Performance Monitor counters that can be used to monitor disk utilization.

12. What is the primary Performance Monitor counter used to monitor network utilization?

**T/F**

13. Running Performance Monitor on a single, centralized
    Windows NT computer to monitor several servers on
    the network simultaneously can increase the network
    utilization statistics above normal levels.                        _____

14. Running Performance Monitor on each individual
    server to be monitored can increase the memory, disk,
    and processor statistics of these computers above normal
    levels due to the running of Performance Monitor itself.           _____

concept link  **For answers to the Instant Assessment questions see Appendix D.**

Workstation
Server
Enterprise

CHAPTER

# Performance Optimization

# 25

# About Chapter 25

This chapter is all about getting the fastest server and/or network response out of your hardware and software combination. The technical term for this is performance optimization.

Because bottlenecks slow down system performance, Chapter 25 begins by explaining how to identify a bottleneck. Specific Performance Monitor counters are recommended.

The remainder of this chapter focuses on practical things you can do to resolve bottlenecks and optimize system performance. Various techniques, including adding RAM, optimizing paging files, optimizing or upgrading disks, upgrading or adding a processor, optimizing the server, and optimizing network traffic are discussed.

This chapter includes two hands-on labs. In the first lab, you'll get practical experience in analyzing Performance Monitor statistics in order to identify a bottleneck. In the second, you'll make recommendations to optimize server and/or network performance for a given situation.

This chapter is a "must read" no matter which of the three Windows NT 4.0 Microsoft Certified Professional exams you're preparing for. This chapter maps to the "Identify and resolve a given performance problem" and "Optimize system performance" objectives for the Workstation exam, to the "Identify performance bottlenecks" objective for the Server and Enterprise exams, and to the "Optimize performance for various results" objective for the Enterprise exam.

# WHAT IS PERFORMANCE OPTIMIZATION?

*Performance optimization* is the process of modifying server and/or network hardware and software configurations with the intent of speeding up server and/or network response.

Performance optimization is performed for several reasons:

- To get the most performance out of existing hardware
- When planning for a new server or network
- In response to user or administrator observations of slow system performance

Performance optimization should be performed with a specific goal in mind. Your primary goal might be to provide the fastest possible file services to client computers. Or your goal might be to remedy slow system response by identifying the problem and implementing a solution. In short, your goal can be almost anything that focuses on improving efficiency and speed of system performance.

For most network administrators, performance optimization usually means resolving user reports of slow system performance. Determining the cause of the slow performance is referred to as *identifying a bottleneck*. This chapter focuses on identifying bottlenecks, as well as on ways to optimize system performance and to resolve bottlenecks.

# IDENTIFYING BOTTLENECKS

A *bottleneck* is the component in the system that is slowing system performance. In a networking environment, the bottleneck is the part of the system that is performing at peak capacity while other components in the system are not. In other words, if it weren't for the limiting component, the rest of the system could go faster.

When you are attempting to identify the bottleneck in your system, use Performance Monitor to measure performance of the server's memory, processor, and disk. You can also use Performance Monitor and/or Network Monitor to gather statistics about your network that may help you identify network bottlenecks.

The following tables contain Performance Monitor counters that may help you in identifying bottlenecks. Table 25-1 shows the counters you can use to monitor the server's memory.

**TABLE 25-1** PERFORMANCE MONITOR MEMORY COUNTERS

| OBJECT | COUNTER | DESCRIPTION AND HOW TO INTERPRET |
|--------|---------|----------------------------------|
| Memory | Pages/sec | Measures the amount of 4KB memory pages that are read from or written to the paging file during a one-second time period. This counter is used to obtain an overall view of how memory is utilized by Windows NT. If the server does not have enough memory, then excessive paging will occur. A consistently high number for this counter (greater than 2–3) indicates that the current amount of RAM may be insufficient for the computer. |
| Paging File | % Usage | This counter measures the percentage of paging file utilization. A consistently high percentage for this counter (approaching 100%) may indicate that you should add RAM to the system or enlarge the paging file. Enlarging the paging file won't speed up the system – only adding RAM will do that. |

Table 25-2 shows the counters you can use to monitor the server's processor.

**TABLE 25-2** PERFORMANCE MONITOR PROCESSOR COUNTERS

| OBJECT | COUNTER | DESCRIPTION AND HOW TO INTERPRET |
|--------|---------|----------------------------------|
| Processor | % Processor Time | Measures the percentage of time that the processor is actively being used by processes other than the Idle process. This counter only measures one processor – if your system has multiple processors, use the System % Total Processor Time counter instead. A consistently high number for this counter (approaching 100%) may indicate that a faster processor (or an additional processor) may be required for adequate system performance. Check the memory counters *before* upgrading your processor – if the memory counters are consistently high, you might just need more RAM. |

| OBJECT | COUNTER | DESCRIPTION AND HOW TO INTERPRET |
|---|---|---|
| System | % Total Processor Time | This counter measures the percentage of time that *all* processors in the computer are actively being used by processes other than the Idle process. A consistently high number for this counter (approaching 100%) may indicate that faster processors (or an additional processor) may be required for adequate system performance. Check the memory counters *before* upgrading your processor(s)—if the memory counters are consistently high, you might just need more RAM. |

Table 25-3 shows the counters you can use to monitor the server's disk.

**TABLE 25-3** PERFORMANCE MONITOR DISK COUNTERS

| OBJECT | COUNTER | DESCRIPTION AND HOW TO INTERPRET |
|---|---|---|
| PhysicalDisk | Avg. Disk Queue Length | This counter measures the average number of disk reads and writes waiting to be performed. A consistently high number for this counter (greater than 2–3) may indicate that a faster hard disk and/or disk controller, or a different disk configuration (such as a stripe set or a stripe set with parity) may be required for adequate system performance. Check the memory counters *before* upgrading your disk(s)—if the memory counters are consistently high, you might just need more RAM. |
| PhysicalDisk | % Disk Time | This counter measures the percentage of time that the disk is actually busy performing reads and writes. A consistently high number for this counter (approaching 100%) may indicate that a faster hard disk and/or disk controller, or a different disk configuration (such as a stripe set or a stripe set with parity) may be required for adequate system performance. Check the memory counters *before* upgrading your disk(s)—if the memory counters are consistently high, you might just need more RAM. |

*continued*

**TABLE 25-3** *(continued)*

| OBJECT | COUNTER | DESCRIPTION AND HOW TO INTERPRET |
|---|---|---|
| LogicalDisk | % Free Space | This counter measures the percentage of unused disk space. A consistently high or gradually increasing number for this counter (approaching 100%) indicates that the server does *not* have sufficient disk space available. An additional disk or a replacement disk that has more capacity may be required. |

Table 25-4 shows the counters you can use to monitor the network.

**TABLE 25-4** PERFORMANCE MONITOR NETWORK COUNTERS

| OBJECT | COUNTER | DESCRIPTION AND HOW TO INTERPRET |
|---|---|---|
| Network Segment | % Network utilization | This counter measures the total network utilization on a given network segment as a percentage of the maximum amount of network traffic possible on that segment. A consistently high number for this counter (approaching 100%) may indicate that there are too many computers or too much network traffic on that network segment. An additional network adapter may need to be installed in the server, or a router may need to be installed on the network to further segment the network. |

| OBJECT | COUNTER | DESCRIPTION AND HOW TO INTERPRET |
|--------|---------|---------------------------------|
| Server | Bytes Total/sec | This counter measures the total amount of network utilization of a Windows NT Server computer. Specifically, it measures the total number of bytes sent to and received from all network adapters in the Windows NT computer by the Server process. *This counter should only be used to measure network utilization when there is only one server on a network segment, and there is only one network adapter in that server.* A consistently high number for this counter (approaching the maximum number of bytes that can be sent on the network segment in one second) may indicate that there are too many computers or too much network traffic on that network segment. An additional network adapter may need to be installed in the server, or a router may need to be installed on the network to further segment the network. |

Once you've interpreted the Performance Monitor and Network Monitor statistics and have identified the bottleneck in your system, you're ready to take steps to resolve that bottleneck. The next section covers ways to optimize performance and to resolve bottlenecks.

 concept link

**To refresh yourself on how to use Performance Monitor, see Chapter 22; for details on how to use Network Monitor, see Chapter 23.**

# OPTIMIZING PERFORMANCE AND RESOLVING BOTTLENECKS

Performance optimization involves getting the most speed out of your existing hardware and software combination. It can also involve adding to or upgrading specific components to resolve bottlenecks.

You don't have to make a large number of configuration or Registry setting changes to optimize the performance of Windows NT. Windows NT is designed to automatically tune itself for providing the best performance it can with the hardware resources available in the computer. For example, Windows NT automatically adjusts the amount of memory assigned to cache, the amount of memory assigned to buffering network packets, and prioritizes processor allocation as needed.

However, the administrator can modify hardware and software configurations to optimize system performance and to resolve bottlenecks. You can add RAM, optimize paging files, optimize or upgrade disks, upgrade or add a processor, optimize the server, and optimize network traffic. Depending on your situation, implementing one or more of these options may improve your system's performance or resolve a bottleneck.

## Adding RAM

Perhaps the single most inexpensive and effective upgrade you can make to your server is to add additional RAM. I've never heard an administrator whine that he or she "just had too much RAM in his or her server." You can *never* have too much RAM.

**Operating systems and applications are constantly being updated and revised. Each new version seems to need more RAM and a faster processor just to perform basic tasks.**

Adding RAM can reduce how often the server reads or writes virtual memory pages to or from the paging file on the hard disk. This is called *reducing paging*. Because paging uses both processor time and disk time, when paging is reduced, the performance of the processor and the disk can also be improved.

When RAM is added to the server, Windows NT automatically increases the allocation of RAM made available to the disk cache. The disk cache temporarily stores user requested files from the hard disk. Because the disk doesn't need to be accessed when a file is retrieved from the cache, files in the cache are more quickly available to users than files on the disk. Thus, increasing the size of the cache can improve disk performance because the number of disk accesses is reduced.

## Optimizing Paging Files

The best method for optimizing a paging file is adding more RAM. The more RAM in the computer, the less paging activity will occur.

That said, there are a few additional things you can do to optimize paging file performance. If the Performance Monitor Paging File % Usage and Paging File % Usage Peak counters indicate that the paging file is being used a consistently high percentage of the time, you might consider trying one of the following:

o Place the paging file on the physical disk in your system that has the least amount of activity.

- Place the paging file on a stripe set, or a stripe set with parity.
- Place multiple, smaller paging files on multiple physical disks in your system.
- Place the paging file on any other partition than the system partition.

caution

**If you have configured Windows NT to create a memory dump file** (memory.dmp) **when a stop error occurs, you *must* have a paging file on the system partition that is at least as large as the amount of RAM in the computer. If the paging file isn't large enough or has been moved from the system partition, a memory dump file won't be created.**

The next section explains how to move and configure paging files.

### TO MOVE AND/OR CONFIGURE THE PAGING FILE(S) ON YOUR WINDOWS NT COMPUTER, FOLLOW THESE STEPS:

**1.** Select Start ⇒ Settings ⇒ Control Panel.

**2.** In the Control Panel dialog box, double-click the System icon.

**3.** In the System Properties dialog box, click the Performance tab.

**4.** On the Performance tab, click the Change command button in the Virtual Memory section.

**5.** The Virtual Memory dialog box appears, as shown in Figure 25-1. Notice that *all* logical drives are listed in the Drive list box, regardless of whether a paging file exists on each drive.

   - **To move a paging file to another disk,** create a new paging file on the disk to which you want to move the paging file (see instructions on how to create a paging file in the next step), and then reconfigure the original paging file with an initial size and maximum size of 0.

   - **To configure or create an additional paging file**, highlight the logical drive you want to configure or create the paging file on in the Drive list box.

     Next, configure the Initial Size and Maximum Size of the paging file in the Paging File Size for Selected Drive section of the dialog box. Click the Set command button.

   When you're finished configuring paging files, click OK.

**6.** The System Properties dialog box reappears. Click the Close command button.

**7.** A System Settings Change dialog box appears, indicating that you must restart your computer before the new settings will take effect. Click the Yes command button to restart your computer.

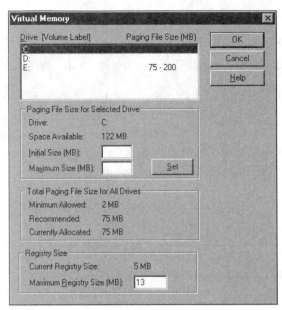

**FIGURE 25-1** Configuring a paging file

 When deciding how large to make your paging files, check out the Total Paging File Size for All Drives section of the Virtual Memory dialog box. This section shows the minimum required paging file size, as well as the recommended and currently allocated sizes. Be aware that the numbers shown in this section are totals for all paging files on your system, not recommended settings for each individual paging file.

## Optimizing and/or Upgrading Disks

Optimizing disks is the process of speeding up hard disk response. Upgrading disks involves either adding to or replacing the existing disk(s) in a computer.

Consider optimizing disks when planning for a new Windows NT Server computer that will perform a specific task, such as file services.

Consider optimizing and/or upgrading disks when you determine, through performance monitoring, that the Windows NT computer's disk is a bottleneck to system performance. Before you upgrade a disk(s), ensure that memory (RAM) is *not* the bottleneck in your system.

You can increase disk performance by doing the following:

- Defragmenting the hard disk(s) in your computer
- Upgrading to a faster disk controller and/or a faster hard disk(s)
- Configuring a stripe set with parity across three or more disks
- Configuring a stripe set across two or more disks

 **note** **Configuring disk mirroring does not necessarily improve disk performance. However, it does significantly improve fault tolerance.**

## Upgrading and/or Adding a Processor

When you determine, through performance monitoring, that the Windows NT computer's processor is a bottleneck to system performance, you should consider upgrading and/or adding a processor to the computer.

Before you upgrade and/or add a processor, ensure that memory (RAM) is *not* the bottleneck in your system.

The following are ways to improve processor performance, all of which involve replacing and/or adding hardware:

- Replacing the existing processor with a faster processor
- Replacing the existing motherboard and processor with a faster motherboard and processor
- Upgrading from a single processor system to a multiprocessor system
- Adding a processor to a multiprocessor system

## Optimizing the Server

Optimizing your server enables you to get the most out of what you've got.

There are four primary ways to optimize a server. You can optimize a server by doing the following:

- Configuring load balancing across multiple servers
- Disabling unused services, protocols, and drivers
- Scheduling large, server-intensive tasks for nonpeak hours
- Optimizing the Server service

The following sections explain each of these server optimization methods in detail.

### Configuring load balancing across multiple servers

Configuring load balancing across multiple servers involves spreading server tasks among more than one server so that no one server is overburdened.

Say you have two servers that are primarily used for file and print services. One of these servers is functioning near peak capacity, while the other server is hardly being used. To improve overall server performance, consider moving a portion of the busy server's files to the other server. This will reduce some of the load on the busy server, and "balance the load" with the second server.

### Disabling unused services, protocols, and drivers

Another way to improve server performance is to disable unused services, protocols, and drivers. Each installed service, protocol, and driver uses processor time and memory space. Also, some services and protocols generate additional network traffic. If an installed service, protocol, or driver is no longer being used, consider removing the service, protocol, or driver; or, consider configuring the service, protocol, or driver to start manually (instead of automatically) when Windows NT starts.

### Scheduling server-intensive tasks for nonpeak hours

Another way to improve server performance is to schedule large, server-intensive tasks to be performed during nonpeak hours.

For example, if you must update a large database or generate a large report on a daily basis, and it is *not* critical that this task be done during business hours, consider scheduling the task to run after business hours (and before the tape backup is run for the night). If the task *must* be done during business hours, consider scheduling it to run during a period of lower activity, such as during a lunch hour.

### Optimizing the Server service

Finally, you can optimize the Server service for the type of tasks the server normally performs, and for the number of client computers that normally access the server.

 **note**    You *can't* configure the Server service on a Windows NT Workstation computer.

The Server service has the following four possible optimization options:

- **Minimize Memory Used:** Select this option when less than ten users will be accessing the Windows NT Server computer at the same time, and a user will sit at the server and use the server as his or her desktop computer.

- **Balance:** Select this option when less than sixty-four users will be accessing the Windows NT Server computer at the same time. This option is also a good choice when the server is used for file and print services as well as by a distributed application that performs its own memory caching, such as Microsoft SQL Server.

- **Maximize Throughput for File Sharing:** Select this option when more than sixty-four users will be accessing the Windows NT Server computer at the same time, and when the server is primarily used as a file and print server. *This is the default option for Windows NT Server*, and is a good selection whenever the server functions primarily as a file and print server, even if there are fewer than sixty-four users.

- **Maximize Throughput for Network Applications:** Select this option when more than sixty-four users will be accessing the Windows NT Server computer at the same time, and when the server is primarily used for a distributed application that performs its own memory caching, such as SQL Server. This is a good selection whenever the server functions primarily as an application server, even if there are fewer than sixty-four users.

 tip **If a Windows NT Server computer is primarily used as a WINS server, a DHCP server, or is the PDC for a large network, configuring the Server service to Maximize Throughput For Network Applications should yield the best server performance.**

---

**TO OPTIMIZE THE SERVER SERVICE ON A WINDOWS NT SERVER COMPUTER, FOLLOW THESE STEPS:**

**1.** Select Start ⇒ Settings ⇒ Control Panel.

**2.** In the Control Panel dialog box, double-click the Network icon.

**3.** In the Network dialog box, click the Services tab.

**4.** On the Services tab, highlight Server in the Network Services list box. Click the Properties command button.

5. The Server dialog box appears, as shown in Figure 25-2. Notice the four options available for optimizing the Server service. Select the radio button next to the option that will provide the best performance for your server. Click OK.

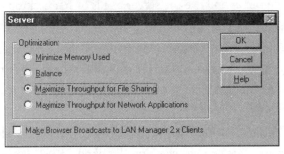

**FIGURE 25-2**   **Optimizing the Server service**

6. In the Network dialog box, click the Close command button.

7. A Network Settings Change dialog box appears, indicating that you must restart your computer before the new settings will take effect. Click the Yes command button to restart your computer.

## Optimizing Network Traffic

There are two common situations when optimizing network traffic may be beneficial: when there is too much traffic on a network segment, and when a server is on the wrong side of a WAN link from the client computers it services.

When Performance Monitor and/or Network Monitor indicates a high percentage of network utilization on a network segment, you might consider further segmenting that network segment. You can accomplish this by adding an additional network adapter to the server, or by installing a router on the network.

When users of client computers report slow response time from a server that is physically located on the other side of a WAN link, consider one of the following options:

o  *Move* the server to the other side of the WAN link so client computers can access the server directly, without having to send network traffic across the WAN link.

o *Add* an additional server of the appropriate type (BDC, DHCP, or WINS) on the other side of the WAN link to service the client computers on that side of the link and to minimize WAN traffic.

For example, when users access a server for logon authentication, IP address assignment, or NetBIOS name resolution across a WAN link (such as a BDC, a DHCP server, or a WINS server), and slow server response time is reported, consider placing an additional server of the appropriate type on the same side of the WAN link as the client computers that need to access that type of server. Placing the server physically close to the client computers will improve server response time and reduce WAN link traffic.

 concept link

**For more information on optimizing Directory Services traffic across a WAN link, including logon authentication and Directory Services synchronization, see Chapter 11.**

# KEY POINT SUMMARY

Chapter 25 described *performance optimization* — the process of modifying server and/or network hardware and software configurations with the intent of speeding up server and/or network response. This chapter provided information on how to best optimize performance, including identifying and resolving bottlenecks.

o For most network administrators, performance optimization most often means resolving user reports of slow system performance. Determining the cause of the slow performance is referred to as identifying a bottleneck. A *bottleneck* is the component in the system that is slowing system performance. In a networking environment, the bottleneck is the part of the system that is performing at peak capacity while other components in the system are *not* working at peak capacity. In other words, if it weren't for the limiting component, the rest of the system could go faster.

o To identify the bottleneck in your system, use Performance Monitor to measure performance of the server's memory, processor, and disk. You can also use Performance Monitor and/or Network Monitor to gather statistics about your network that may help you identify network bottlenecks. Once you've interpreted the statistics and have identified the bottleneck in your system, you're ready to take steps to resolve that bottleneck.

o Performance optimization involves getting the most speed out of your existing hardware and software combination. It can also involve adding to or upgrading specific components to resolve bottlenecks.

o Adding RAM is often the single most inexpensive and effective upgrade you can make to your server. A beneficial by-product of adding RAM is that processor and disk performance may be improved, as well, because paging is reduced and the disk cache size is increased when RAM is added.

o The best method for optimizing a paging file is adding more RAM. Additionally, you can place the paging file on the disk that has the least amount of activity, on a stripe set or a stripe set with parity, on a partition other than the system partition, or place multiple, smaller paging files on multiple disks in the system. To move the paging file to a different disk or partition, or to configure and/or add additional paging files, use the System application in Control Panel.

o Consider optimizing disks when planning for a new Windows NT Server computer that will perform a specific task, such as file services. Consider optimizing and/or upgrading disks when you determine that the disk is a bottleneck to system performance. Before you upgrade a disk(s), ensure that RAM is *not* the bottleneck in your system.

o You can increase disk performance by defragmenting the hard disk(s) in your computer, upgrading to a faster disk controller and/or a faster hard disk(s), configuring a stripe set with parity across three or more disks, or configuring a stripe set across two or more disks.

o When you determine that the processor is a bottleneck to system performance, you should consider upgrading and/or adding a processor to the computer. Before you upgrade and/or add a processor, ensure that RAM is *not* the bottleneck in your system.

   o To improve processor performance, consider replacing the existing processor with a faster processor, replacing the existing motherboard and processor with a faster motherboard and processor, upgrading from a single processor system to a multiprocessor system, or adding a processor to a multiprocessor system.

o There are four primary ways to optimize a server. You can optimize a server by: configuring load balancing across multiple servers; disabling unused services, protocols, and drivers; scheduling large, server-intensive tasks during nonpeak hours; and by optimizing the Server service. The Server service is optimized by using the Network application in Control Panel.

o There are two common situations when optimizing network traffic may be beneficial: when there is too much traffic on a network segment, and when a server is on the wrong side of a WAN link from the client computers that it services.

o When Performance Monitor and/or Network Monitor indicates a high percentage of network utilization on a network segment, consider further segmenting that network segment.

o When users of client computers report slow response time from a server that is physically located on the other side of a WAN link, consider either moving the server to the other side of the WAN link, or adding an additional server of the appropriate type (BDC, DHCP, or WINS) on the other side of the WAN link.

# APPLYING WHAT YOU'VE LEARNED

Now it's time to regroup, review, and apply what you've learned in this chapter.

The Instant Assessment questions bring to mind key facts and concepts.

The hands-on lab exercises will really reinforce what you've learned, and give you an opportunity to practice some of the tasks tested by the Microsoft Certified Professional exams.

## Instant Assessment

1. What is performance optimization?

2. In a networking environment, what is a bottleneck?

3. Which two Windows NT tools can you use to help identify a bottleneck in your Windows NT system?

4. Which four components should you monitor when attempting to identify a bottleneck in your Windows NT system?

5. What is perhaps the single most inexpensive and effective upgrade that you can make to your Windows NT Server computer?

6. Name one beneficial by-product of adding RAM to a Windows NT Server computer.

7. You decide you want to move the paging file on your Windows NT computer to a different disk. Which Control Panel application should you use to move/configure the paging file?

8. You determine that the disk is the bottleneck in your Windows NT Server computer. List three ways to increase disk performance.

9. You determine that the processor is the bottleneck in your Windows NT Server computer. List three ways to improve processor performance.

10. List four ways to optimize a Windows NT Server computer.

11. Users of client computers report slow server response time for logon authentication from a BDC that is located on the other side of a WAN link. What should you do to improve server response time?

concept link  **For answers to the Instant Assessment questions see Appendix D.**

## Hands-on Lab Exercises

The following hands-on lab exercises provide you with practical opportunities to apply the knowledge you've gained in this chapter about performance optimization.

### Lab 25.37 *Finding and resolving bottlenecks*

Workstation
Server
Enterprise

The purpose of this lab exercise is to give you experience in analyzing Performance Monitor statistics in order to identify the bottleneck in a system, and also to give you experience in making recommendations to resolve a bottleneck.

Each problem below presents a situation and a set of statistics. In the space provided, supply the requested response to the problem.

**Problem 1**    Users of your network report slow response times when accessing files from a Windows NT Server computer. The server has a 486/66MHz processor with 20MB of RAM and a 2GB IDE hard disk. You run Performance Monitor on that server and obtain the statistics shown in the following table:

| Object | Counter | Statistic |
|---|---|---|
| Processor | % Processor Time | 55% |
| Memory | Pages/sec | 125 |
| PhysicalDisk | % Disk Time | 85% |
| Network Segment | % Network utilization | 15% |

There is enough money left in your annual equipment budget to enable you to do any *one* of the following:

o Upgrade the processor to a Pentium 166MHz processor

o Upgrade memory to 64MB of RAM

o Upgrade to a faster hard disk and a faster hard disk controller

o Install a second network adapter in the server and segment the network

Which upgrade would you perform, and why?

_____

_____

_____

_____

**Problem 2**  Users of your network report slow response times when accessing files from a Windows NT Server computer. The server has a Pentium 100MHz processor with 64MB of RAM and a 4GB SCSI hard disk. You run Performance Monitor on that server and obtain the following statistics:

| Object | Counter | Statistic |
|---|---|---|
| Processor | % Processor Time | 15% |
| Memory | Pages/sec | 4 |
| PhysicalDisk | % Disk Time | 90% |
| Network Segment | % Network utilization | 15% |

There is enough money left in your annual equipment budget to enable you to do any *one* of the following:

o Upgrade to a multiprocessor system with 2 Pentium PRO 200MHz processors

- o Upgrade memory to 128MB of RAM
- o Upgrade to a hardware-based RAID 5 (disk striping with parity) disk subsystem
- o Install a second network adapter in the server to segment the network

    Which upgrade would you perform, and why?

_____

_____

_____

_____

concept link                    For answers to the hands-on lab exercise see Appendix D.

## Lab 25.38 *Optimizing Windows NT performance*

Enterprise

The purpose of this lab exercise is to give you experience in analyzing a Windows NT Server network, and to make recommendations to optimize server and/or network performance for a given situation.

Assume that you are an outside consultant, hired to optimize server/network performance for a company. Each problem below presents a situation and what your customer wants to accomplish. In the space provided, supply the requested response to each problem.

**Problem 1** Your client has three networks, each located in a different city. The three networks are connected by WAN links, as shown in Figure 25-3.

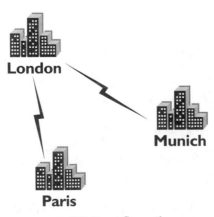

**London**

**Munich**

**Paris**

FIGURE 25-3   WAN configuration for Problem 1

The company uses a master domain model for its Windows NT network. The master domain is located in London, and resource domains are located in Paris and Munich.

Servers are currently installed as follows:

**London**   PDC for LONDON domain

7 BDCs for LONDON domain

1 BDC for PARIS domain

1 BDC for MUNICH domain

4 WINS servers

**Paris**   PDC for PARIS domain

3 BDCs for PARIS domain

**Munich**   PDC for MUNICH domain

2 BDCs for MUNICH domain

The company wants you to make recommendations for minimizing the amount of logon authentication and NetBIOS name resolution traffic sent across their WAN links. What recommendations would you make to accomplish these two tasks?

_____

_____

_____

**Problem 2**   Your client wants you to optimize the Server service on a Windows NT Server computer. The computer functions as the PDC for a large network. The PDC is used primarily to manage the Directory Services database, and also functions as a DHCP server for clients on its local network segment.

How would you optimize the Server service on this Windows NT Server computer?

_____

 concept link   **For answers to the hands-on lab excercise see Appendix D.**

# Troubleshooting

I t happens to the best of us. Sooner or later, something on our computer or network doesn't work the way we expected it to, and we end up having to troubleshoot it. From basic to advanced troubleshooting, this part covers it.

Chapter 26 begins with an overview of troubleshooting, followed by an in-depth discussion of the troubleshooting process. Next, numerous resources for troubleshooting Windows NT are recommended. You'll even find step-by-step instructions on how to use some of these resources.

Chapter 27 is devoted entirely to advanced Windows NT troubleshooting, including such complex topics as troubleshooting the boot sequence, using the Registry editors, and diagnosing and interpreting those dreaded blue screens.

No matter which of the three Windows NT 4.0 Microsoft Certified Professional exams you're preparing for, you'll want to read both of the chapters in this part. Part VII maps directly to the Troubleshooting section in the exam objectives for each of the three exams.

Workstation
Server
Enterprise

CHAPTER

# The Troubleshooting Process

# 26

# About Chapter 26

**H**ave you ever wondered where to begin when faced with a tough troubleshooting problem? Or wondered where to get help when you just couldn't find a workable solution? Chapter 26 holds the answers to these questions and more.

After a brief overview of troubleshooting, this chapter explains my recommended five-step approach to troubleshooting.

The process basically boils down to gathering information, defining the problem, listing the probable causes of the problem, identifying possible solutions and attempting to fix the problem, and finally, resolving and documenting the problem.

The last half of this chapter is jam-packed with resources that can help you when you're troubleshooting basic or advanced Windows NT problems. You'll be introduced to Microsoft TechNet, the Microsoft Technical Support Web site, the Microsoft Download Service, as well as several additional troubleshooting resources.

Chapter 26 is a "must read" no matter which of the three Windows NT 4.0 Microsoft Certified Professional exams you're preparing for. This chapter maps to nearly all of the Troubleshooting objectives for these exams.

# OVERVIEW OF TROUBLESHOOTING

Some say that troubleshooting is a science. Others say it's a fine art. I guess it's really a bit of both—a methodical approach to solving a problem that's devised from a person's base of knowledge, experience, and intuition.

Perhaps the best preparation for becoming an outstanding troubleshooter is to gain an in-depth understanding of how what you're troubleshooting works—in this case, Windows NT in a workstation, server, or enterprise environment. In addition to understanding Windows NT, you also need to have an intimate understanding of networking and PC hardware. This combined knowledge will form the backbone of your troubleshooting capability.

You can gain this understanding and knowledge in several ways. This book is a great place to start. You can also attend classes, read other books, and work in the Windows NT networking world. One of the best ways to obtain understanding and knowledge is through on-the-job experience.

When you're faced with a tough troubleshooting problem, remember that you're probably *not* the first or only person who's ever had this problem. Don't be afraid to call your friends, colleagues, and professional contacts. Troubleshooting a critical system at 2:00 a.m. is no time to be a Lone Ranger. (Okay, maybe you shouldn't call your friends *then*.) Above all, especially if you've never encountered a problem like it before, use *all* of the troubleshooting resources and technical references available to you—your problem and its solution are probably out there; you just have to find them.

Finally, there's no substitute for experience. If you've seen the problem before, hopefully a little light will come on, and you will remember how you solved it before.

# THE TROUBLESHOOTING PROCESS

There are many effective troubleshooting methods. Different people use different methods to arrive at the same solution.

While there may not be one "best" troubleshooting method out there, there are some basic steps you can take to simplify and organize the troubleshooting process.

The basic steps I use when troubleshooting Windows NT are:

- Gather information
- Define the problem
- List probable causes
- Identify possible solutions and attempt to fix the problem
- Resolve and document the problem

The following sections discuss each of these steps in detail.

## Gather Information

The troubleshooting process typically starts by a user reporting a problem to you. In this step, you gather specific information that will help you identify the problem.

Talk to the user(s) who is experiencing the problem. Ask a lot of questions.

Specifically, find out:

- What *exactly* is the problem?

  Sometimes it's painstakingly difficult and time-consuming to identify the problem. A user's description of a problem, such as "I can't get on the network," can mean anything from "I can't log on" to "I can't get my e-mail." Be patient with the user, and encourage him or her to be as specific as possible.

- If the problem is experienced regularly, *when* does the problem occur?

- If an error message was displayed, *what* did the message say?

  Ask the user to write the error message down verbatim, if possible. A paraphrased or otherwise interpreted error message can be extremely difficult to research in a knowledge base.

- Did the user correctly perform all necessary steps to complete the task?

  Consider walking the user through the correct steps to see if you can recreate the problem.

- Has whatever is not working now *ever* worked before?

- If it did work before, when did it *stop* working?

- What has changed since the last time it worked?

This may be the single most important question you can ask. I usually ask this question several times during the troubleshooting process. Often, problems are created by users, administrators, or consultants who have changed, fixed, optimized, or otherwise fiddled with a perfectly good, functional system.

## Define the Problem

Once you've gathered information, you're ready to define the problem. Sometimes the problem is glaringly obvious from the information you've gathered. Other times, you'll need to piece together bits and pieces of information from various users before you can identify the problem.

Identifying the problem as accurately as you can is an important step, because all of your efforts to resolve the problem, from that point, will be based on this diagnosis.

## List Probable Causes

Once you've defined the problem, make a list of all the hardware and software components, configurations, and common user errors that could be a probable cause of the problem. Don't overlook the obvious here. Is it plugged in? Is it turned on? Is the computer cabled to the network?

Sometimes it's difficult to identify probable causes. For example, if an application fails and Windows NT displays an obscure error message, you might have to do extensive research just to come up with one or more probable causes of the problem.

After you've listed all the probable causes you can, place the items on your list in order, from the most likely cause of the problem to the least likely cause of the problem. If your intuition or experience tells you that one or two of the items may be the culprit, place these at the top of your list.

## Identify Possible Solutions and Attempt to Fix the Problem

Starting at the top of your list, identify possible solutions for the first one or two probable causes.

Many causes, by their very nature, imply a solution. For example, if you suspect that the cause of the problem is a bad network cable, it's fairly obvious that replacing the network cable should resolve the problem. Other causes, such as a hardware component that's not on the Hardware Compatibility List (HCL), may involve significant amounts of research to come up with a workable solution.

Next, starting at the top of your list of probable causes, implement one of the possible solutions that you identified for the most likely cause of the problem. This may involve repairing, replacing, or reconfiguring the suspected offending component or remedying the suspected user error.

Test the system after this step to determine whether the problem is fixed. If this change *doesn't* fix the problem, restore the system to its original configuration and proceed to the next item on the list. Continue this process until you are satisfied that you have identified the cause and solution to the problem.

 **tip** **Don't change more than one component at a time or you may have a difficult time determining what's broken and what isn't.**

## Resolve and Document the Problem

Once you have positively identified the problem's cause and solution, permanently implement the solution. If the solution to the problem is a configuration change, no more work is required here—you have already implemented a permanent fix to the problem. However, if you determined that a segment of network cable in a wall (or ceiling) was defective by temporarily bypassing this segment, you will have to have the cable segment in the wall (or ceiling) replaced to fix the situation permanently.

Test the system again to make sure the problem is really fixed, and that you have not created any new problems in the system. If the problem only occurred at specific times, test the system during those times to ensure that the problem has been remedied.

Once you're satisfied that you have resolved the problem, document the problem, the date it occurred, and its solution in a trouble log. This will aid you and other engineers in your company if and when this problem reoccurs.

 **in the real world** **I can't tell you how many times I've spent four hours solving a problem, only to remember afterward that I had solved the exact same problem six months or a year before. If I'd documented the problem the first time, I would have saved myself four hours of troubleshooting the second time around.**

# RESOURCES FOR TROUBLESHOOTING

Several resources are available to help you when you're troubleshooting Windows NT. Use these resources—they are your friends.

Using outside resources enables you to draw on the experience of others. Typically, you won't be the first person to have encountered a particular problem. If others have had this same problem before you, it is likely that this problem (and its solution) is documented in a knowledge-base resource.

Troubleshooting resources come in many flavors. Knowledge bases are often chock full of white papers, configuration hints and tips, and problem-specific troubleshooting information. If you have a modem and/or an Internet connection, you can access download services and FTP sites to obtain the latest patches, fixes, drivers, and white papers. You can also access technical support forums via modem or the World Wide Web. On these forums you can post a question, and other professionals may read it and reply to you.

The next sections discuss some of the most helpful and common Windows NT troubleshooting resources: *Microsoft TechNet*, the Micro House Technical Library, the Microsoft Technical Support Web site, the Microsoft Download Service, and other troubleshooting resources.

## Microsoft TechNet

*Microsoft TechNet* is an invaluable knowledge base—I recommend using it as your first and primary troubleshooting resource. *TechNet* is published monthly by Microsoft on multiple compact discs. In my opinion, the price of an annual subscription is money well spent.

*TechNet* includes a complete set of all Microsoft operating system Resource Kits (currently in a help file format), the entire Microsoft Knowledge Base, and supplemental compact discs full of patches, fixes, and drivers (so you don't have to spend time downloading them).

*TechNet* is particularly helpful when troubleshooting a specific problem. When Microsoft Technical Support helps a client troubleshoot a problem, that problem and its solution are documented. All significant problems and their solutions are then placed in the *TechNet* resource. *TechNet* includes thousands of problems and their respective solutions.

Using *TechNet* is fairly straightforward. Figure 26-1 shows the opening dialog box for *TechNet*. Notice the categories that are displayed in the Entire Contents list box.

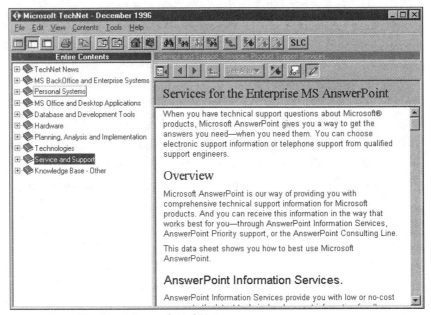

**FIGURE 26-1**    Starting *Microsoft TechNet*

You can search the entire contents of *TechNet*, or a specific subset of the contents for information on a specific topic. To begin a search, click the Query icon (which appears in the toolbar as a pair of binoculars). The Query dialog box appears, as shown in Figure 26-2.

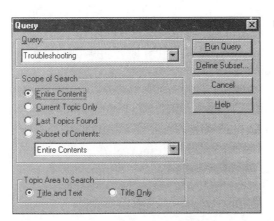

**FIGURE 26-2**    Performing a search in *Microsoft TechNet*

Type the topic you want information on in the Query drop-down list box. Be as specific as you can. Even when you are specific, don't be surprised to see numerous articles that include the words you searched for. You can include multiple words in your query, and you can use the logical operators AND, OR, and NOT within the query. If you need more information on constructing a query, click the Help command button in this dialog box. When you're ready to execute the search, click the Run Query command button.

I can't recommend this resource highly enough. When you're troubleshooting, think *TechNet* first.

 *tip* **You can order *Microsoft TechNet* by calling (800) 344 2121 in the U.S. If you're a Microsoft Certified Professional or an MCSE, discounts or special promotions may be offered for first-year subscriptions.**

## Micro House Technical Library

The *Micro House Technical Library* is a useful CD-ROM-based set of encyclopedias that contains hardware configuration information. This resource can be particularly helpful when you need to configure a specific hardware device, such as a motherboard, I/O card, or network adapter.

Have you ever lost the documentation for a hard drive (or any other piece of hardware)? I have. If you have access to the *Micro House Technical Library*, it could save you a lengthy phone call to product support to obtain jumper switch settings and other configuration information.

An evaluation copy of this product is included on the compact disc that accompanies this book. The *Micro House Technical Library* can be purchased from Micro House International. Their phone number for sales (in the U.S.) is 1-800-926-8299.

## Microsoft Technical Support Web Site

Microsoft Technical Support has its own site on the World Wide Web. You can access this site by first accessing the Microsoft Support home page at: `http://www.microsoft.com/support/`. Figure 26-3 shows the Microsoft Support home page.

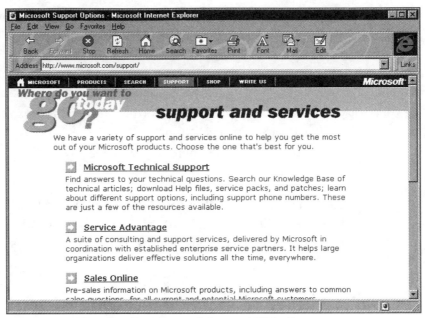

**FIGURE 26-3**   Accessing the Microsoft Support Web site

Click the Microsoft Technical Support link to access the Microsoft Technical Support home page. A list of several topics/options is displayed on the Technical Support home page, including:

o  Knowledge Base

o  Troubleshooting Wizards

o  Frequently Asked Questions

o  Help Files, Service Packs, and Other Files

o  Support Options and Phone Numbers

o  Submit a Question to a Support Engineer

You can search the Knowledge Base; use the troubleshooting wizards; download service packs, patches, and drivers; or post a question for a support engineer. You can also obtain a phone number to access Microsoft Technical Support engineers directly.

 note    **Be aware that Microsoft charges a fee for most calls to their Technical Support engineers.**

The Microsoft Technical Support Web site is a great resource, especially if you don't have *TechNet*.

# The Microsoft Download Service

The Microsoft Download Service is a *bulletin board service* (BBS). Through this BBS, you can download patches, fixes, and drivers.

You can access the Microsoft Download Service by using the Windows NT HyperTerminal application. The phone number for the Microsoft Download Service is (425)-936-6735.

The modem settings for accessing the Microsoft Download Service are:

- Data bits = 8
- Parity = 0
- Stop bits = 1
- Flow control = 0

When you first connect to the Microsoft Download Service, a welcome screen appears asking you to enter your full name. After you've entered your name, you'll be prompted to enter the city and state from which you are calling. A scrolling screen containing new user information is displayed. Finally, the main screen appears, as shown in Figure 26-4.

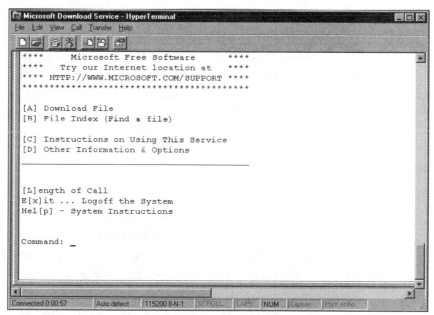

**FIGURE 26-4**  The Microsoft Download Service main menu

At the main menu, type **B** to access the file index and to search for a file.

Most of the files you can access from the Microsoft Download Service are the same files available on the *TechNet* compact discs and from the Microsoft Technical Support Web site. This resource can be helpful, but it is the least user friendly of the three Microsoft resources mentioned in this chapter.

# Additional Troubleshooting Resources

Other troubleshooting resources are available, including online service forums, Microsoft Solution Providers, a Microsoft FTP site, Internet search tools, and professional contacts and colleagues.

Many online services host forums where you can post a question that will be read by many people, a few of whom may even respond with some free advice.

Some helpful forums include:

o The MS WinNT Forum, the MS Win32 Forum, and the NT Workstation Forum on CompuServe

o The Windows NT Workstation Forum and the Windows NT Server Forum on MSN (The Microsoft Network)

Other resources may be as close as your telephone. For example, when I worked for a national computer reseller, I could send a voice mail message requesting help with a specific problem to all the engineers in the company, nationwide. That one call would usually generate five to ten responses within twenty-four hours.

Microsoft Solution Providers usually have multiple MCSEs on staff. These consultants, who are typically available for an hourly fee, can assist you not only with troubleshooting but also with system design and implementation.

Microsoft has another site on the Internet for those who use FTP to download files. You can access this site at ftp.microsoft.com. This site has most of the same files that you can access by using *TechNet*, the Microsoft Technical Support Web site, and the Microsoft Download Service.

Several other Internet sites contain Windows NT information. You can find these sites using Internet search tools such as AltaVista, Lycos, and Yahoo!.

Last but not least, don't forget your professional contacts and colleagues. Many times someone you've worked with or met at a conference will have just the bit of information you need to solve a problem. You might consider joining a professional organization or users group where you can meet and network with other industry professionals.

**tip** **If you want people to share their time and expertise with you willingly, it's a good idea if you're willing to do the same yourself.**

# Key Point Summary

This chapter defined and described the troubleshooting process. The following points highlight the major issues:

- Troubleshooting is a methodical approach to solving a problem. The best preparation for becoming an outstanding troubleshooter is to understand intimately what you're troubleshooting—in this case, Windows NT, and the computer hardware and networking environment in which it runs.

- The basic steps suggested for troubleshooting are:
    - Gather information
    - Define the problem
    - List probable causes
    - Identify possible solutions and attempt to fix the problem
    - Resolve and document the problem

- Several resources can help you when you're troubleshooting Windows NT, including knowledge bases, Web sites, download services, and others.

- *Microsoft TechNet* is a CD-ROM-based knowledge base. It contains a complete set of all the Microsoft Resource Kits, the entire Microsoft Knowledge Base, and supplemental compact discs full of patches, fixes, and drivers.

- The Micro House Technical Library is a CD-ROM-based set of encyclopedias that contains hardware configuration information.

- The Microsoft Technical Support Web site, which can be accessed at http://www.microsoft.com/support/, is also a great resource. On this site you can search the Microsoft Knowledge Base, use troubleshooting wizards, download service packs, patches, and drivers, obtain support telephone numbers, or post a question for a support engineer.

- The Microsoft Download Service is a BBS. Through this service you can download patches, fixes, and drivers.

- Additional troubleshooting resources include online service forums, Microsoft Solution Providers, a Microsoft FTP site, Internet search tools, and professional contacts and colleagues.

# APPLYING WHAT YOU'VE LEARNED

Now it's time to regroup, review, and apply what you've learned in this chapter.

The questions in the following Instant Assessment section will bring to mind key troubleshooting facts and concepts.

## Instant Assessment

1. What is troubleshooting?

2. List the five basic steps suggested for troubleshooting.

3. Which troubleshooting resource is published monthly by Microsoft in a multiple compact disc format?

4. What Microsoft Web site can you access to use troubleshooting wizards, download help files and service packs, and post a question to a support engineer?

5. Which Microsoft troubleshooting resource is a bulletin board service (BBS)?

concept link  **For answers to the Instant Assessment questions see Appendix D.**

Workstation
Server
Enterprise

# Advanced Troubleshooting Topics

# About Chapter 27

Chapter 27 explores a number of advanced Windows NT trouble-shooting topics.

This chapter begins with a discussion of the Windows NT boot sequence, and recommends solutions to several common boot sequence problems. Included in this section are detailed instructions for performing the Emergency Repair process.

Next, this chapter explains how to use Event Viewer, which can be used to determine why a service or driver failed during system startup. Windows NT Diagnostics, which enables you to view detailed configuration information, is also covered.

Next, this chapter outlines the structure of the Windows NT Registry, and explains how to use the Registry editors to search and modify the Registry.

Various other advanced troubleshooting issues are explored, including diagnosing and interpreting blue screens, configuring a memory dump, configuring Dr. Watson for Windows NT, and configuring a computer for remote debugging.

This chapter includes one comprehensive hands-on lab. You'll get to practice advanced Windows NT troubleshooting techniques, including: using Windows NT Diagnostics, using the Registry editors, configuring a memory dump, and starting and configuring Dr. Watson for Windows NT.

Chapter 27 is a "must read" no matter which of the three Windows NT 4.0 Microsoft Certified Professional exams you're preparing for. This chapter maps to many of the Troubleshooting objectives for these exams.

# TROUBLESHOOTING THE BOOT SEQUENCE

The *boot sequence* refers to the process of starting Windows NT, including initializing all of its services and completing the logon process. There are several common problems that can occur during the boot sequence, and in order to successfully troubleshoot them, you need to have an understanding of the steps that occur during the boot sequence.

The following sections identify and explain the steps that occur during the boot sequence, list common boot sequence problems and recommended solutions, and discuss how to perform the Emergency Repair process, which is a solution to several common boot sequence problems.

## Overview of the Boot Sequence

The Windows NT boot sequence consists of a sequential series of steps, beginning with powering on the computer and ending with completion of the logon process. Understanding the individual steps that make up the boot sequence will help you to troubleshoot problems that may occur during this process.

The boot sequence steps vary according to the hardware platform you are using. The boot sequence steps discussed in this section apply to the Intel platform only.

The Windows NT boot sequence (Intel platform) is as follows:

1. **Power On Self Test:** The *Power On Self Test* (POST) is performed by the computer's BIOS every time the computer is powered on to test for the existence of specific components, such as processor, RAM, and video adapter. If any errors are detected during this phase, an error message or onscreen diagnostics is typically displayed.

2. **Initial Startup:** In this step, the computer's BIOS attempts to locate a startup disk, such as a floppy disk, or the first hard disk in the computer.

   If the startup disk is the first hard disk, the BIOS reads the *Master Boot Record* from the startup disk, and the code in the Master Boot Record is run. The Master Boot Record then determines which partition is the active partition, and loads sector 0 (also called the partition boot sector) from the active partition into memory. Then the code contained in sector 0 is run. This causes the Ntldr file to be loaded into memory from the root folder of the active partition. Ntldr is then run.

If the startup disk is a floppy disk, the code from sector 0 on the floppy disk is loaded into memory. Then the code contained in sector 0 is run. This causes Ntldr to be loaded into memory from the root folder of the floppy disk. Ntldr is then run.

3. **Selecting an operating system:** Ntldr switches the processor into a 32-bit flat memory mode. Ntldr then initializes the appropriate minifile system (either FAT or NTFS) to enable Ntldr to locate and load the Boot.ini file. Ntldr uses the Boot.ini file to create the *boot loader screen*.

A typical Window NT 4.0 boot loader screen appears as follows:

```
OS Loader V4.00

Please select the operating system to start:

        Windows NT Server Version 4.00
        Windows NT Server Version 4.00 [VGA mode]
        MS-DOS

Use ↑ and ↓ to move the highlight to your choice.
Press Enter to choose.

Seconds until highlighted choice will be started automatically: 30
```

At this point, either the user selects an operating system from the boot loader menu, or the default operating system is automatically started after a specified number of seconds has elapsed.

If an operating system *other* than Windows NT is selected, the Bootsect.dos file is loaded into memory and run, and the appropriate operating system is started. (If an operating system other than Windows NT is selected, the remaining steps of the Windows NT boot sequence do not apply.)

If Windows NT is selected, Ntldr loads Ntdetect.com and executes it.

4. **Detecting hardware:** Ntdetect.com searches for computer ID, bus type (ISA, EISA, PCI, or MCA), video adapter, keyboard, serial and parallel ports, floppy disk(s), and pointing device (mouse).

As it checks, the following is displayed onscreen:

```
NTDETECT V4.0 Checking Hardware . . .
```

Ntdetect.com creates a list of the components it finds and passes this information to Ntldr.

5. **Selecting hardware profile and loading the kernel:** Ntldr displays the
following message:

```
OS Loader V4.0
Press spacebar now to invoke Hardware Profile/Last Known Good menu.
```

Ntldr gives you approximately three to five seconds to press the spacebar. If
you press the spacebar at this time, the Hardware Profile/Last Known Good
menu is displayed as shown:

```
Hardware Profile/Configuration Recovery Menu
This menu enables you to select a hardware profile
to be used when Windows NT is started.

If your system is not starting correctly, then you may switch to a
previous system configuration, which may overcome startup problems.
IMPORTANT: System configuration changes made since the last
successful startup will be discarded.

                Original Configuration
                Some other hardware profile

Use the up and down arrow keys to move the highlight
to the selection you want. Then press Enter.
To switch to the Last Known Good Configuration, press 'L'.
To Exit this menu and restart your computer, press F3.

Seconds until highlighted choice will be started automatically: 5
```

If you press **L** while this screen is displayed, the Last Known Good control
set will be used, and any configuration changes made during the last logon
session will be discarded.

If you don't press the spacebar and have only one hardware profile, the
default hardware profile is loaded.

If you don't press the spacebar and have more than one hardware profile,
the Hardware Profile/Configuration Recovery Menu is displayed.

Once you've selected a hardware profile, Ntldr loads Ntoskrnl.exe and
executes the Windows NT kernel.

6. **Kernel initialization:** When the kernel starts, a screen similar to the following is displayed:

```
Microsoft (R) Windows NT (TM) Version 4.0 (Build 1381)
1 System Processor (32 MB Memory)
```

This screen indicates that the kernel has successfully started.

7. **Initializing device drivers:** At this point, the kernel loads either the default control set or, if you selected the Last Known Good Configuration, it loads the Last Known Good control set. Then the kernel initializes all of the device drivers listed in the control set.

8. **Initializing services:** The kernel loads and starts the services listed in the control set being used.

9. **Logon process:** The Begin Logon dialog box is displayed, prompting the user to press Ctrl + Alt + Delete to log on. Then the user logs on, supplying an appropriate user name and password.

Once a user has successfully logged on, the boot sequence is complete, and the control set currently in use is copied to the Last Known Good Configuration.

## Troubleshooting Common Boot Sequence Problems

There are many common problems that can occur during the Windows NT boot sequence. Table 27-1 lists these problems, along with their possible causes and recommended solutions.

**TABLE 27-1** TROUBLESHOOTING THE WINDOWS NT BOOT SEQUENCE

| PROBLEM | POSSIBLE CAUSE | RECOMMENDED SOLUTION |
|---------|----------------|----------------------|
| An error message is displayed during the POST. | This message most likely indicates a hardware failure. | Use the error message (or onscreen diagnostics) displayed to determine the offending hardware device. Repair, replace, or reconfigure the hardware device as necessary. |

| PROBLEM | POSSIBLE CAUSE | RECOMMENDED SOLUTION |
|---------|----------------|----------------------|
| An error message, such as "Invalid partition table" or "Missing operating system" is displayed after the POST. | This type of error message often indicates that either sector 0 of the active partition is damaged, or that important operating system files (such as `Ntldr`) are missing. | Perform the Emergency Repair process (as explained in the next section of this chapter) and select the Inspect boot sector option during this process. If you suspect that there are missing files, also select the Verify Windows NT system files option during the Emergency Repair Process. |
| After you select MS-DOS from the boot loader menu, the following error is displayed: "I/O error accessing boot sector . . . " | This message indicates that `Ntldr` can't find the `Bootsect.dos` file. | Restore this file from tape; or, perform the Emergency Repair process, selecting the Inspect boot sector option during the process. |
| During the boot sequence, NT displays a message indicating that it cannot find a specific file, such as `Ntoskrnl.exe` or `Ntldr`. | There are two possible causes for this problem: the specified file is missing or corrupt, or the `Boot.ini` file does not specify the correct path to system files. | To restore a missing or corrupt file (except for the `Boot.ini` file), perform the Emergency Repair process, selecting the Verify Windows NT system files option during the process. If the `Boot.ini` file is missing, perform the Emergency Repair Process, selecting the Inspect startup environment option during the process, which will create a new `Boot.ini` file. To repair a `Boot.ini` file, do one of the following: |

o  Boot to MS-DOS and edit the `Boot.ini` file (assuming that the `Boot.ini` file is on a FAT partition)

o  Create a Windows NT boot diskette with the appropriate `Boot.ini, Ntldr, Ntdetect.com,` and `Bootsect.dos` files on it. Use this diskette to boot the computer to Windows NT, and then edit the `Boot.ini` file

o  Reinstall Windows NT (this is definitely *not* the preferred option).

*continued*

**TABLE 27-1** *(continued)*

| PROBLEM | POSSIBLE CAUSE | RECOMMENDED SOLUTION |
|---------|---------------|---------------------|
| Your Windows NT computer crashes during a power outage. When you reboot the computer, a blue screen is displayed during the boot sequence. | The most likely cause of this problem is a corrupt file. Power outages can easily corrupt files on the hard disk. | Perform the Emergency Repair process, selecting the Inspect boot sector and Verify Windows NT system files options during the process. |
| You make several configuration changes and then reboot your Windows NT computer. A blue screen is displayed during the boot sequence. | The most likely cause of this problem is the configuration changes made during the last logon session. | Reboot the computer, and select the Last Known Good Configuration during the boot sequence. If this does *not* repair the problem, perform the Emergency Repair process, selecting the Inspect Registry files option during the process. |
| A STOP error (blue screen) is displayed during the device driver or service initialization steps of the boot sequence. | The most probable causes of this error are a corrupt Registry entry, a corrupt device driver, or a corrupt service file. | Perform the Emergency Repair process, selecting the Inspect Registry files and Verify Windows NT system files options during the process. |

### Performing the Emergency Repair Process

Sometimes the only way to restore a malfunctioning Windows NT system to an operable state is to perform the Emergency Repair process. The Emergency Repair process is primarily used when you are unable to successfully boot your Windows NT computer.

The Emergency Repair process involves using the Windows NT Setup Boot Disk set, the Windows NT compact disc, and the Emergency Repair disk created during (or after) the installation process to repair a damaged or corrupt Windows NT installation.

 note    **If you didn't create an Emergency Repair disk during (or after) the Windows NT installation, an Emergency Repair disk from any other**

Windows NT installation on the same hardware platform (such as Intel) can be used for *most* repair options, but *can't* be used to inspect Registry files. Also see the following caution.

caution *Never* replace or repair the Registry with an Emergency Repair disk from another computer. Only repair the Registry using that specific computer's Emergency Repair Disk. Using another computer's Emergency Repair Disk can damage your computer's Windows NT installation, possibly to the point where it won't even start. This is because Registry entries are specific for an individual computer's hardware, software, policy, and user account information. No two computers have identical Registries.

The Emergency Repair process has four different repair options. During the Emergency Repair process, you are prompted to select one or more of these options. These four options are detailed in Table 27-2.

**TABLE 27-2** WINDOWS NT EMERGENCY REPAIR PROCESS REPAIR OPTIONS

| REPAIR OPTION | DESCRIPTION |
|---|---|
| Inspect Registry files | This option enables you to select any or all of the Registry files for replacement, including: |
| | o `System` (System configuration) |
| | o `Software` (Software information) |
| | o `Default` (Default user profile) |
| | o `Ntuser.dat` (New user profile) |
| | o `Security` (Security policy) |
| | o `SAM` (Security Accounts Manager user accounts database) |
| | All selected files will be replaced during the Emergency Repair process. |
| Inspect startup environment | Selecting this option causes Emergency Repair to verify the files in the Windows NT system partition, including: `Ntldr`, `Ntdetect.com`, `Ntbootdd.sys`, and `Boot.ini`. If any of these files are missing or corrupt, they will be replaced. |

*continued*

**TABLE 27-2** *(continued)*

| REPAIR OPTION | DESCRIPTION |
|---|---|
| Verify Windows NT system files | Selecting this option causes Emergency Repair to verify the files in the Windows NT `install` folder, and to replace any missing or corrupt files from the Windows NT compact disc. |
| Inspect boot sector | Selecting this option causes Emergency Repair to verify that sector 0 on the active partition (also called the partition boot sector) contains the code to start `Ntldr`. If the partition boot sector is corrupt, Emergency Repair will repair it if the partition boot sector is the active partition on the first hard disk in the computer. |

**TO PERFORM THE EMERGENCY REPAIR PROCESS, FOLLOW THESE STEPS:**

**1.** Start the computer using the Windows NT Setup Book Disk. Ensure that the Windows NT compact disc is in the computer's CD-ROM drive.

**2.** Insert Windows NT Setup Disk #2 when prompted.

**3.** When prompted to choose whether to repair an existing installation or to install a new copy of Windows NT, press **R** to start the Emergency Repair process.

**4.** The Emergency Repair menu is displayed. By default, all four options listed in Table 27-2 are selected. Deselect any options that you don't want to perform. When you're finished selecting options, select Continue from the menu.

**5.** Insert Windows NT Setup Disk #3 when prompted.

**6.** Insert the Emergency Repair Disk when prompted.

**7.** When the Emergency Repair process is completed, remove the floppy disk and reboot the computer to Windows NT.

If the Emergency Repair process doesn't repair your system, you may need to reinstall Windows NT.

**If you don't have the Windows NT Setup Boot Disk set, you can create one on an MS-DOS or Windows NT computer that has a CD-ROM drive.**

**To create the Windows NT Setup Boot Disk set, place the Windows NT compact disc in the computer's CD-ROM drive. Then, from an MS-DOS command prompt, type winnt /ox and press Enter to create the disk set. Or, on a Windows NT computer, type winnt32 /ox at the command prompt and press Enter to create the disk set.**

# USING EVENT VIEWER

*Event Viewer* is a Windows NT administrative tool that is used to view the system, security, and application logs. These logs contain success, failure, and informational messages generated by the operating system, auditing, and applications.

The most common troubleshooting application of Event Viewer is determining why a service or device driver failed during system startup. After booting the computer, Windows NT notifies the user of such a failure by displaying a Service Control Manager warning dialog box. Figure 27-1 shows a typical Service Control Manager warning dialog box.

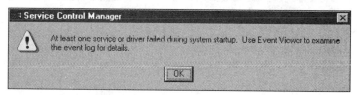

**FIGURE 27-1**    **Notification of service or driver failure during startup**

When a Service Control Manager warning is displayed, you can use the Event Viewer system log to determine which service or driver failed, and to view a detailed description of the failure. This information will often help you to determine the cause of the failure and an appropriate solution.

**TO ACCESS THE SYSTEM LOG IN EVENT VIEWER, FOLLOW THESE STEPS:**

1. Select Start ⇒ Programs ⇒ Administrative Tools (Common) ⇒ Event Viewer.

2. The Event Viewer dialog box appears. If the system log is not displayed, select Log ⇒ System.

3. The Event Viewer System Log dialog box appears, as shown in Figure 27-2. Notice the many stop errors listed in the dialog box.

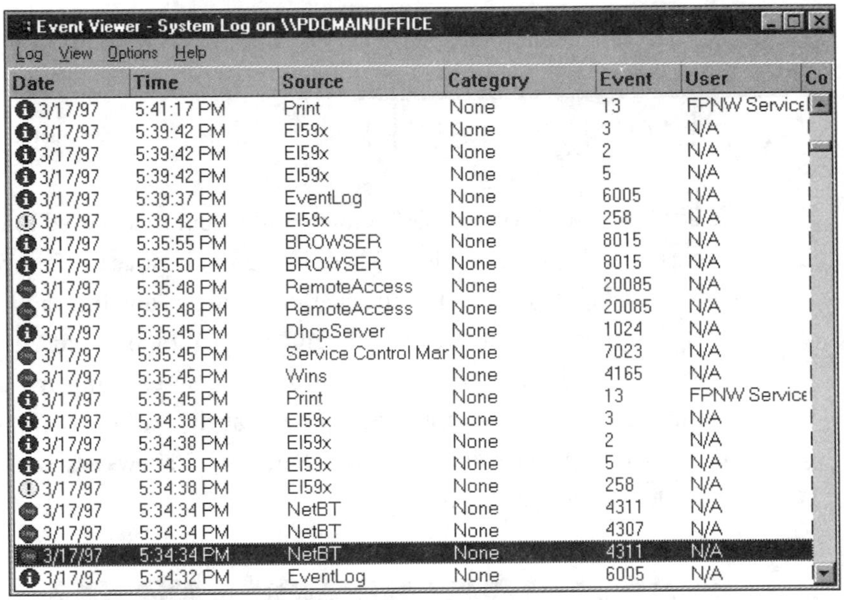

**FIGURE 27-2**   Viewing the system log in Event Viewer

A stop error in the system log is identified by a red stop sign preceding the event on the left-hand side of the dialog box. A *stop error* indicates that the service or driver listed in the Source column was unable to initialize correctly during system startup.

Examining stop error event details is the key to troubleshooting failed services or drivers. When multiple stop errors are listed, it's usually best to start your troubleshooting by examining the *oldest* stop error in the list first. The oldest stop error is the *first* stop error that occurred during the boot process — it is also the last stop error on the system log list. This stop error is probably the cause of all the later stop errors listed.

To view stop error event detail, double-click the stop error in the system log in Event Viewer. When you double-click the stop error, the Event Detail dialog box is displayed, as shown in Figure 27-3. Notice the description of the stop error in the Description text box.

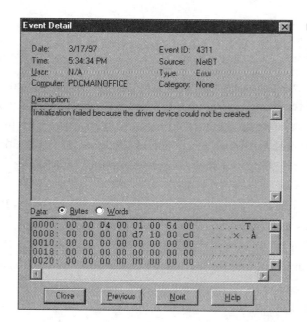

**FIGURE 27-3** Viewing stop error event detail

The stop error detailed in Figure 27-3 indicates that initialization of the NetBT service failed because the driver device could not be created.

Sometimes the event detail provides specific information that can be used to correct the problem. Other times, further investigation using a resource such as *TechNet* may be necessary. (When using *TechNet*, I recommend searching by the complete text listed in the Event Detail Description box.)

In this case, further research determined that the NetBT device driver was corrupt, and needed to be replaced. To solve the problem, I restored the device driver from tape. Incidentally, fixing the NetBT service stop error repaired all of the other stop errors in the list.

**Remember, when using Event Viewer for troubleshooting, *always* view the Event Detail for the *last* stop error in the list (the event that happened *first* chronologically during the boot process) first. Resolving this error will often take care of most or all of the other stop errors listed.**

# USING WINDOWS NT DIAGNOSTICS

*Windows NT Diagnostics* is a Windows NT administrative tool that enables you to view detailed system configuration information and statistics. This tool can help you troubleshoot system configuration problems. It is also very useful for determining service and device driver dependencies. Windows NT Diagnostics does not actually diagnose anything—it simply displays your current system configuration information.

To access Windows NT Diagnostics, at the desktop select Start ⇒ Programs ⇒ Administrative Tools (Common) ⇒ Windows NT Diagnostics.

The Windows NT Diagnostics dialog box appears, as shown in Figure 27-4. Notice the nine different tabs in this dialog box: Version, System, Display, Drives, Memory, Services, Resources, Environment, and Network.

The various tabs in Windows NT Diagnostics contain different options and are used for different purposes:

o **Version:** The Version tab, shown in Figure 27-4, displays this Windows NT installation's version, build number, and service pack number. It also displays the serial number and registered owner. Clicking the Print command button on any Windows NT Diagnostics tab will print details contained on *all* of the tabs in Windows NT Diagnostics. This list can be quite extensive.

o **System:** The System tab, which is shown in Figure 27-5, displays the type of *Hardware Abstraction Layer* (HAL) being used; BIOS information, including BIOS date and manufacturer; and a specific processor description for each processor in the computer.

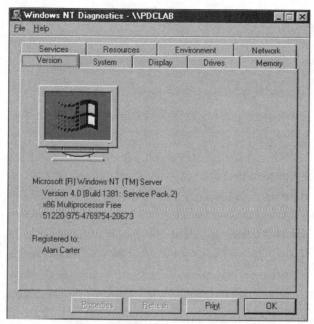

**FIGURE 27-4**   The Windows NT Diagnostics initial
dialog box

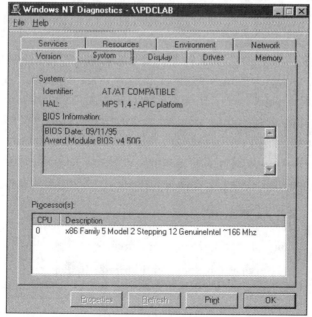

**FIGURE 27-5**   The System tab in Windows NT
Diagnostics

○ **Display:** The Display tab, shown in Figure 27-6, displays the display adapter configuration and the Windows NT display driver in use.

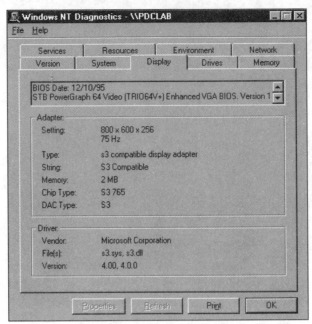

**FIGURE 27-6**   The Display tab in Windows NT Diagnostics

○ **Drives:** The Drives tab, shown in Figure 27-7, displays all drives connected to this Windows NT computer, including network connected drives, if any. You can double-click any drive listed to view specific drive properties, including number of bytes free, number of bytes in use, and total number of bytes. You can also view specific file system information about the drive, such as file system type.

○ **Memory:** The Memory tab, shown in Figure 27-8, displays various statistics on memory and paging file(s) in this computer. You can use these statistics to help you determine if the computer has enough memory and large enough paging files for optimum performance.

○ **Services:** The Services tab, shown in Figure 27-9, displays the status of all services and device drivers installed on this Windows NT computer. Using this tab is a quick way to determine whether a particular service is running.

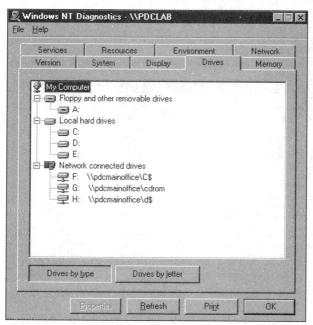

**FIGURE 27-7** The Drives tab in Windows NT Diagnostics

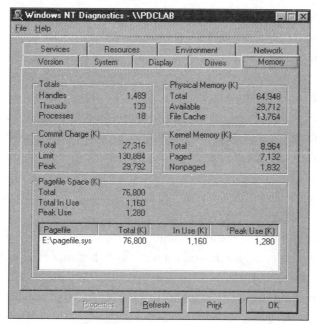

**FIGURE 27-8** The Memory tab in Windows NT
Diagnostics

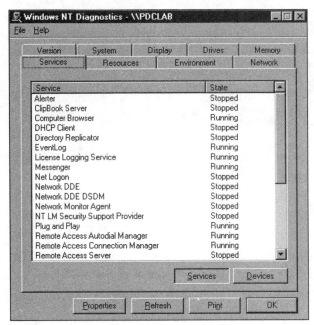

**FIGURE 27-9**    The Services tab in Windows NT
Diagnostics

You can double-click any service or device driver to obtain detailed information about that service or driver.

I use this feature primarily to determine service dependencies and group dependencies for a specific service or driver — it's a lot quicker and easier than searching the Registry. *Service dependencies* show which services and drivers must be running before the service in question can start. *Group dependencies* show which groups of services or drivers must be running before the service in question can start. Once you have determined what the service and group dependencies for a particular service or driver are, you can then verify that all of these services and drivers (that are required to be running *before* a particular service or driver can start) are, in fact, running.

To determine service and group dependencies, double-click the service or driver you want to research, and then click the Dependencies tab in the Service Properties dialog box that is displayed. Figure 27-10 shows the Dependencies tab for the Computer Browser service. Notice the services that must be running before the Computer Browser service can start.

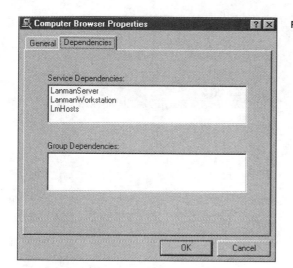

**FIGURE 27-10**   **Using Windows NT Diagnostics to determine service and group dependencies**

o **Resources:** The Resources tab, shown in Figure 27-11, displays the *interrupt requests* (IRQs) used by various devices in this computer. You can use this information to troubleshoot interrupt conflicts. You can also click the I/O Port, DMA, and Memory command buttons to obtain listings of all devices in this computer, by the I/O Port addresses, DMA addresses, and Memory addresses that they use. You can click the Devices command button for a listing of all devices in this computer.

o **Environment:** The Environment tab, shown in Figure 27-12, displays the system environment variables, such as the path, in use on this Windows NT computer. To obtain a list of environment variables for the user that is currently logged on to this computer, click the Local User command button.

o **Network:** The Network tab, shown in Figure 27-13, displays various network information, such as domain name and computer name. If you click the Transports or Settings command buttons, additional network configuration is displayed.

If you click the Statistics command button, numerous network utilization statistics are displayed, as shown in Figure 27-14. These statistics are not updated automatically—you must click the Refresh command button each time you want to update these statistics. These network statistics are sometimes helpful when troubleshooting network problems.

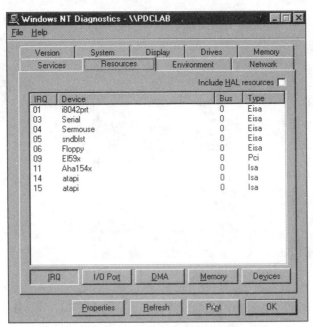

**FIGURE 27-11**    The Resources tab in Windows NT
Diagnostics

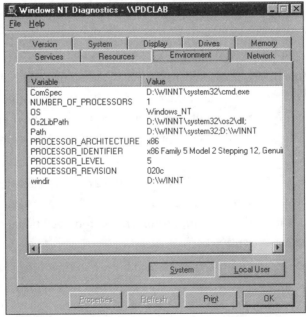

**FIGURE 27-12**    The Environment tab in Windows NT
Diagnostics

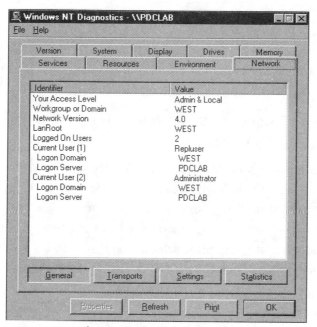

**FIGURE 27-13**   The Network tab in Windows NT Diagnostics

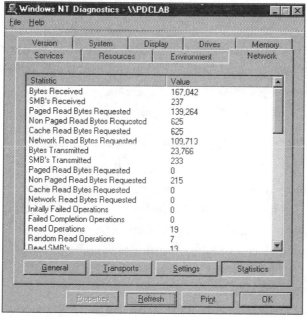

**FIGURE 27-14**   Viewing network utilization statistics in Windows NT Diagnostics

# USING THE REGISTRY EDITORS

Registry editors are tools that enable you to search and modify the Windows NT Registry. There are two primary tools for editing the Windows NT Registry:

o Windows NT Registry Editor (`regedt32.exe`)

o Windows 95 Registry Editor (`regedit.exe`)

Additionally, you can use the Windows NT System Policy Editor (`poledit.exe`) to modify a limited number of settings in the Registry. However, you can't use System Policy Editor to search the Registry.

The Registry editors are primarily used for three types of tasks:

o To change Registry settings which can't be changed with any other user interface (such as Control Panel)

o To modify the Registry as directed by *TechNet* or by Microsoft Technical Support to resolve a particular problem or to provide a particular feature

o To troubleshoot various startup problems

The focus of this section is on using the Registry editors for troubleshooting purposes. Specifically, you'll learn how to use the Registry editors to determine service and group dependencies of various Windows NT services and device drivers.

Before explaining the specifics of how to use the Registry editors, it will be helpful for you to understand the basics of how the Windows NT Registry is structured.

## Registry Structure Overview

The Windows NT Registry is a database that contains all of the information required to correctly configure an individual Windows NT computer, its user accounts, and its applications. Registries are unique to each computer—you shouldn't use the Registry from one computer on another computer. The Registry is organized in a tree structure consisting of five subtrees and their keys and value entries. Within the subtrees, keys are similar to folders in a file system, and value entries are similar to files.

Figure 27-15 shows the five subtrees within the Windows NT Registry.

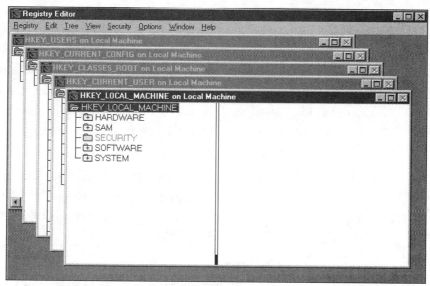

**FIGURE 27-15**    The five subtrees in the Windows NT Registry hierarchy

Each subtree in the Registry contains different types of information:

o **HKEY_LOCAL_MACHINE:** This subtree contains various configuration information specific to the local computer, including: hardware, software, device driver, and services startup configurations. Windows NT accesses this information during system startup and uses it to correctly configure the computer.

 When troubleshooting Windows NT, check the HKEY_LOCAL MACHINE subtree *first*, because this subtree contains most of the service and driver configuration information for the operating system.

o **HKEY_CURRENT_USER:** This subtree contains the entire user profile for the user that is currently logged on. This includes the user's individual desktop settings, network drive and printer connections, and so on.

o **HKEY_CURRENT_CONFIG:** The subtree contains the hardware configuration currently being used by Windows NT. This subtree consists of a replica of the keys and values stored in `HKEY_LOCAL_MACHINE\ System\CurrentControlSet\HardwareProfiles\Current`.

○ **HKEY_CLASSES_ROOT:** This subtree contains all of the associations between applications and their specific filename extensions. For example, files ending in .doc are associated with Microsoft Word. This association is what makes it possible for you to double-click a .doc file and have Word start automatically and open that file. This subtree also contains all of the *object linking and embedding* (OLE) information used by various Windows applications, and consists of a replica of the keys and values stored in HKEY_LOCAL_MACHINE\Software\Classes.

○ **HKEY_USERS:** This subtree contains the user profile for the user that is currently logged on (the current user profile), as well as the default user profile. The current user profile is a replica of the keys and values stored in HKEY_CURRENT_USER.

In the Windows NT Registry, various keys and their values are grouped together and stored in a single file. This file is called a hive. All of the Windows NT Registry hives are stored in the <winntroot>\System32\Config folder.

Table 27-3 shows the six hives and their respective Windows NT Registry locations.

**TABLE 27-3** WINDOWS NT REGISTRY HIVES

| HIVE FILE NAME | LOCATION IN THE REGISTRY |
| --- | --- |
| SAM | HKEY_LOCAL_MACHINE\SAM |
| Security | HKEY_LOCAL_MACHINE\Security |
| Software | HKEY_LOCAL_MACHINE\Software |
| System | HKEY_LOCAL_MACHINE\System and HKEY_CURRENT_CONFIG |
| Ntuser.dat | HKEY_CURRENT_USER |
| Default | HKEY_USERS\.DEFAULT |

Now that you've got a basic understanding of the Windows NT Registry structure, you're almost ready to begin using the Registry editors. But first, it's important to back up the Registry before you use a Registry editor to modify it.

# Backing Up the Registry

*Always* back up the Registry before you use the Registry editors to modify it—if you don't, you could end up with a system that won't boot.

There are three primary tools you can use to back up the Windows NT Registry:

o The Windows NT Backup program

o The Regback.exe utility included in the *Microsoft Windows NT Workstation Resource Kit*

o The Rdisk.exe utility

When you back up the Registry using the Windows NT Backup program, you must choose to back up at least one file on the boot partition, and you must select the check box next to the Backup Local Registry option.

When you back up the Registry using the Rdisk.exe utility, two backup copies are made. First, Rdisk makes a backup copy of the Registry and stores it in the <winntroot>\Repair folder. Then Rdisk prompts you to insert a floppy disk (which will become the Emergency Repair Disk), and copies the contents of the <winntroot>\Repair folder to the floppy disk. This process is known as *updating the Emergency Repair Disk*. Be sure to update your computer's Emergency Repair Disk every time you make a successful configuration change to your Windows NT computer.

 tip
**Always run Rdisk using the /s switch, because using this switch will cause the SAM and Security hives to be backed up. If you *don't* use the /s switch, these two hives won't be backed up.**

 in the real world
**It's a good idea to write the Administrator's current password on the Emergency Repair Disk when you create or update this disk. The reason for this practice is when you restore the Registry from the Emergency Repair Disk, Emergency Repair replaces whatever the Administrator's current password is with the password that was in effect when the Emergency Repair Disk was created or last updated. If the password has changed since that time, and the old password isn't written down or remembered, the Administrator won't be able to log on after the Registry is restored.**

# Searching the Registry

Now that you understand the structure of the Windows NT Registry and the importance of backing it up before you modify it, you can begin using the Registry editors to search and modify the Registry.

As mentioned previously, there are two primary tools you can use to edit the Windows NT Registry: the Windows NT Registry Editor (regedt32.exe) and the Windows 95 Registry Editor (regedit.exe).

I recommend you use the Windows 95 Registry Editor (regedit.exe) for searching the Windows NT Registry, because this editor can search the Registry by key, by value, or by the data contained in the value. As a Registry search tool, I find this editor more effective than the Windows NT Registry Editor, which can only search the Registry by key. You can manually wade your way through the various Registry folders and subfolders by using the Windows NT Registry Editor, and you can use this editor to modify any Registry value—it's just more cumbersome to use as a search tool than the Windows 95 Registry Editor.

> **note** While the Windows 95 Registry Editor is a better search tool, the Windows NT Registry Editor has a couple of features not included in the Windows 95 version, including the capability to connect to and edit a remote Windows NT computer's Registry, and the capability to set security on various Registry keys.

Suppose that you recently bought a used computer that came with Windows NT installed. You want to change the Registry so that your name (not the previous owner's) is displayed as the registered owner. You are unsure where in the Registry this data is stored. However, you know the previous owner's name.

In this example, you could use the Windows 95 Registry Editor (regedit.exe) to search and modify the Registry.

To access the Windows 95 Registry Editor, select Start ⇒ Run. Type **regedit** in the Open drop-down list box in the Run dialog box, as shown in Figure 27-16, and click OK.

The Registry Editor dialog box appears, as shown in Figure 27-17. Notice the various subtrees displayed in this dialog box.

> **note** Notice the HKEY_DYN_DATA subtree in the Registry Editor dialog box. This subtree only exists on Windows 95 computers. So, while this subtree is shown, it can't be opened when editing a Windows NT Registry.

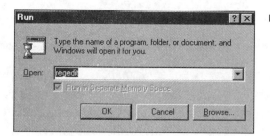

**FIGURE 27-16** **Starting the Windows 95 Registry Editor**

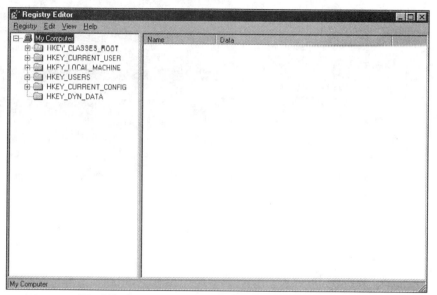

**FIGURE 27-17** The Windows 95 Registry Editor dialog box

Now that the Registry Editor is started, you can use it to search the Registry for the previous owner's name.

 **The following example shows you how to search the Windows NT Registry for values that contain the previous owner's name. *However, you can use these same steps to search the Registry for any key, value, or data.***

**TO SEARCH THE WINDOWS NT REGISTRY, FOLLOW THESE STEPS:**

**1.** Select Edit⟹Find in the Registry Editor dialog box.

**2.** The Find dialog box appears, as shown in Figure 27-18. Notice that three check boxes give you the option of searching by keys, values, and/or data. (You can select any or all of these options.) Type in the previous owner's name in the "Find what" text box, and click the Find Next command button.

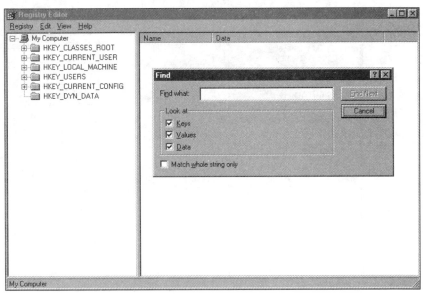

**FIGURE 27-18** Configuring the search parameters

**3.** Registry Editor searches the Registry. Registry Editor displays the first instance of the previous owner's name, as shown in Figure 27-19. Notice that the complete path to the key that contains this value is shown across the bottom of the Registry Editor dialog box.

If you want to edit the displayed value, double-click the value and edit the value's data in the Edit String dialog box that appears. Figure 27-20 shows the Edit String dialog box. Click OK when you're finished.

**4.** The Registry Editor dialog box reappears. To search for additional instances of the previous owner's name, select Edit⟹Find Next. Registry Editor searches the Registry again and displays the next instance it finds of the previous owner's name.

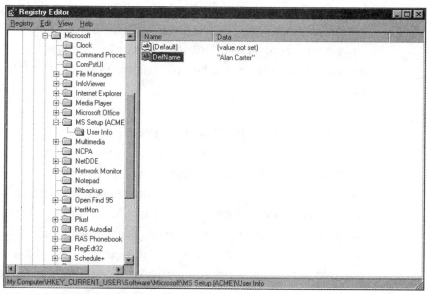

**FIGURE 27-19**    **Registry Editor displays search results**

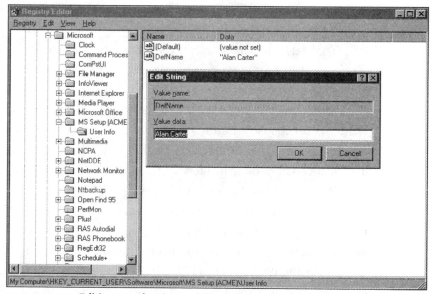

**FIGURE 27-20**    **Editing a value in Registry Editor**

**5.** Repeat Steps 3 and 4 as needed to replace all instances of the previous owner's name.

**6.** Exit Registry Editor when your search is completed.

Another common type of search that is performed in Registry Editor is a search for a specific service or driver, with the intent of determining the service and group dependencies of that service or driver. The next section explains how to perform such a search, and how to determine the dependencies of the service or driver.

## Finding service and group dependencies

As mentioned previously, *service dependencies* show which services and drivers must be running before a particular service (or driver) can start. *Group dependencies* show which groups of services or drivers must be running before the service (or driver) in question can start. For troubleshooting purposes, once you have determined what the service and group dependencies for a particular service (or driver) are, you can then verify that all of these services and drivers (that are required to be running *before* a particular service or driver can start) are, in fact, running.

The easiest way to determine a particular service's or driver's service and group dependencies is using the Services tab in Windows NT Diagnostics, as described earlier in this chapter.

That said, you can search the Windows NT Registry to locate a particular service or driver for the purpose of determining that service's or driver's service and group dependencies.

Although you can use either Registry editor to find dependencies, only the Windows NT Registry Editor (`regedt32.exe`) presents this information in a usable format. (The Windows 95 Registry Editor presents service and group dependencies in hexadecimal format.)

If you don't know the name of the Registry key that is used to store a particular service's or driver's information, you can use the Windows 95 Registry Editor to find the key in the Registry, and then use the Windows NT Registry Editor to view the data. For example, you probably wouldn't think to look for Registry entries for the WINS Client (TCP/IP) service in a key named NetBT, but that's exactly where they are. If you didn't know this up front, you'd have to use the Windows 95 Registry Editor to determine the name of the key in which this service's entries are stored before using the Windows NT Registry Editor to view the specific data.

All service and driver Registry entries are stored in subkeys of `HKEY_LOCAL_MACHINE\System\CurrentControlSet\Services`.

Suppose you want to use a Registry editor to determine service and group dependencies of the Messenger service. (You want to do this because Event Viewer indicates that the Messenger service failed to start because a dependency service of the Messenger service was not running.)

## TO USE THE WINDOWS NT REGISTRY EDITOR TO DETERMINE SERVICE AND GROUP DEPENDENCIES, FOLLOW THESE STEPS:

**1.** Start the Windows NT Registry Editor by selecting Start⇒Run from the desktop, and by then typing **regedt32** in the Open drop-down list box in the Run dialog box. Then click OK.

**2.** If the HKEY_LOCAL_MACHINE window is not displayed, select Window⇒ HKEY_LOCAL_MACHINE on Local Machine.

**3.** The HKEY_LOCAL_MACHINE window is displayed. Double-click the SYSTEM folder. Double-click the CurrentControlSet folder. Double-click the Services folder.

**4.** Highlight the service or driver for which you want to determine service and group dependencies. In the example, this is the Messenger service. Various Registry entries for the highlighted service or driver are displayed on the right-hand side of the window, as shown in Figure 27-21. Notice the DependOnGroup and DependOnService entries.

**FIGURE 27-21** Viewing the Messenger service's Registry entries

You can ignore the REG_MULTI_SZ: portion of the DependOnGroup and DependOnService entries—REG_MULTI_SZ just identifies the type of data that will be placed in the Registry, in this case, multiple string values.

In this example, notice that the Messenger service's DependOnGroup entry does not contain any data (other than the ignored REG_MULTI_SZ). This means this service has no group dependencies.

Also notice that the Messenger's service DependOnService entry lists the LanmanWorkstation and NetBios services as its service dependencies. This means the Messenger service will not start if the LanmanWorkstation (Workstation) and the NetBios services are not running.

5. When you've finished determining a service's dependencies, exit Registry Editor.

# DIAGNOSING AND INTERPRETING BLUE SCREENS

Windows NT displays a blue screen when it encounters a STOP error from which it cannot recover. Facing a blue screen is a daunting task for any network administrator. However, it's not as scary if you understand the basics of what is displayed when this happens.

It's also beneficial for you to understand blue screen contents when you contact Microsoft Technical Support personnel. If you have a basic idea what's going on, it will be easier for you to communicate with Technical Support, and may result in faster problem resolution.

If you encounter a blue screen, I recommend that you write down the blue screen's contents exactly as they are displayed on the screen. The blue screen contains information that is absolutely required by Microsoft Technical Support before they can help you troubleshoot the problem.

Most blue screens are caused by corrupt drivers or by drivers developed for a previous version of Windows NT. Most of the blue screens I have personally experienced have been the result of installing third-party drivers intended for Windows NT 3.51 on a Windows NT 4.0 computer.

Listing 27-1 shows a blue screen that I generated on my Windows NT Server computer. (In case you're wondering, I generated this blue screen by installing a HAL file that was intended for use on a computer that uses a different bus architecture than mine.) Blue screens normally appear as white lettering on a blue background, thus the term "blue screen." For ease in reading, I've reproduced this blue screen with black lettering on a white background.

There are three primary sections in this displayed blue screen : the STOP error and description, a list of loaded drivers, and a stack dump (including the operating system's build number).

o **STOP error and description:** The first line at the top of the screen displays the STOP error and several hexadecimal values. The first hexadecimal value (in this case, 0x00000079) indicates the error code for the STOP error. (The error code is sometimes referred to as a *BugCheck code*.) To determine what this error code means, you'll need a resource, such as the *Microsoft Windows NT Device Developer's Kit*. In this example, error code 79 indicates a mismatched HAL. The error code is probably the first piece of information that Microsoft Technical Support will want from you.

o **List of loaded drivers:** The second main section of the screen, which begins with the headers Dll, Base, DateStmp, and Name, contains a list of drivers that have been loaded into memory.

o **Build number and stack dump:** The third main section of the screen begins with the headers Address, dword dump, Build [1381], and Name. This section contains the build number of the operating system (in this case, 1381). It also contains the contents of the operating system's stack. A stack is a temporary storage area used by the operating system.

Depending on your Windows NT configuration, additional information may be displayed on a blue screen. Additional lines might include information as to whether a serial port is currently being used for remote debugging purposes, and information might be displayed regarding the status of creation of the memory dump file (memory.dmp).

**LISTING 27-1** Sample blue screen

```
*** STOP: 0x00000079 (0x00000003,0x00000000,0x00000002,0x00000000)

CPUID:GenuineIntel  5.2.c  irql:1   SYSVER  0xf0000565

Dll Base DateStmp - Name                Dll Base DateStmp - Name
80100000 32add131 - ntoskrnl.exe        80010000 31ee6c55 - hal.dll
80001000 32b1cf7b - atapi.sys           80007000 328ce233 - SCSIPORT.SYS
8001b000 31f05449 - aha154x.sys         801d5000 3290d07e - Disk.sys
801d9000 32a88067 - CLASS2.SYS          801dd000 32a89744 - Ntfs.sys


Address  dword dump   Build [1381]                    - Name
80147d8c 80147fb3 80147fb3 8014b500 801c1aa4 00000000 80087000 - ntoskrnl.exe
80147d90 8014b500 8014b500 801c1aa4 00000000 80087000 00000000 - ntoskrnl.exe
80147d94 801c1aa4 801c1aa4 00000000 80087000 00000000 80144974 - ntoskrnl.exe
80147da4 80144974 80144974 80144f20 00000003 00003f9d 00000001 - ntoskrnl.exe
80147da8 80144f20 80144f20 00000003 00003f9d 00000001 0000009e - ntoskrnl.exe
80147ec0 80144d20 80144d20 80144f20 80145010 00000000 00000000 - ntoskrnl.exe
80147ec4 80144f20 80144f20 80145010 00000000 00000000 00000000 - ntoskrnl.exe
80147ec8 80145010 80145010 00000000 00000000 00000000 00000000 - ntoskrnl.exe
80147f7c 80147fb5 80147fb5 00000001 801c750e 00000001 80147fe4 - ntoskrnl.exe
80147f84 801c750e 801c750e 00000001 80147fe4 80147fe4 80147fe4 - ntoskrnl.exe
80147f8c 80147fe4 80147fe4 80147fe4 80147fe4 80147fe8 00010101 - ntoskrnl.exe
80147f90 80147fe4 80147fe4 80147fe4 80147fe8 00010101 01000101 - ntoskrnl.exe
80147f94 80147fe4 80147fe4 80147fe8 00010101 01000101 01010101 - ntoskrnl.exe
80147f98 80147fe8 80147fe8 00010101 01000101 01010101 01010101 - ntoskrnl.exe
80147fc0 80118efd 80118efd 00000000 ffdff120 0000020c 8014813c - ntoskrnl.exe
80147fd0 8014813c 8014813c 801c7193 80144f20 80148104 00000000 - ntoskrnl.exe
80147fd4 801c7193 801c7193 80144f20 80148104 00000000 80147dac - ntoskrnl.exe
80147fd8 80144f20 80144f20 80148104 00000000 80147dac 8014813c - ntoskrnl.exe
80147fdc 80148104 80148104 00000000 80147dac 8014813c 801c721a - ntoskrnl.exe
80147fe4 80147dac 80147dac 8014813c 801c721a 00000000 80087000 - ntoskrnl.exe
80147fe8 8014813c 8014813c 801c721a 00000000 80087000 80036c00 - ntoskrnl.exe
81047fec 801c721a 801c721a 00000000 80087000 80036c00 801c6678 - ntoskrnl.exe
80147ffc 801c6678 801c6678 80144f20 00000000 00000000 00000000 - ntoskrnl.exe
80148000 80144f20 80144f20 00000000 00000000 00000000 00000000 - ntoskrnl.exe
80148080 80140764 80140764 00000000 00000000 00000000 00000000 - ntoskrnl.exe
80148124 80147ff8 80147ff8 00000000 ffffffff 80139074 80142a80 - ntoskrnl.exe
80148130 80139074 80139074 80142a80 00000000 00000000 801c5e50 - ntoskrnl.exe
80148134 80142a80 80142a80 00000000 00000000 801c5e50 80144d20 - ntoskrnl.exe
80148140 801c5e50 801c5e50 80144d20 80144f20 80148160 ffdff120 - ntoskrnl.exe
80148144 80144d20 80144d20 80144f20 80148160 ffdff120 00000000 - ntoskrnl.exe
80148148 80144f20 80144f20 80148160 ffdff120 00000000 80087000 - ntoskrnl.exe
8014814c 80148160 80148160 ffdff120 00000000 80087000 0000000e - ntoskrnl.exe
```

# CONFIGURING A MEMORY DUMP

Sometimes Microsoft Technical Support won't be able to help you quickly resolve a blue screen. Microsoft may need to analyze the contents of the memory dump file created when the blue screen occurred.

To ensure that Windows NT will create a memory dump file when a STOP error occurs, you can use the System application in the Control Panel to make sure Windows NT is appropriately configured.

**TO CONFIGURE WINDOWS NT TO CREATE A MEMORY DUMP FILE (MEMORY.DMP), FOLLOW THESE STEPS:**

**1.** Select Start ⇒ Settings ⇒ Control Panel.

**2.** In the Control Panel dialog box, double-click the System icon.

**3.** The System Properties dialog box appears. Click the Startup/Shutdown tab.

**4.** The Startup/Shutdown tab appears, as shown in Figure 27-22. Notice the Recovery section in this dialog box.

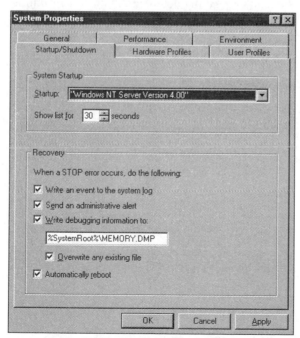

**FIGURE 27-22**   Configuring Windows NT recovery options

Ensure that the check boxes next to "Write debugging Information to" and "Overwrite any existing file" are selected.

Ensure that the text box in the Recovery section contains the following: `%SystemRoot%\MEMORY.DMP`

Click OK.

5. Exit Control Panel. You should shut down and restart your computer for these changes to become effective.

---

**note**    **To create a `memory.dmp` file, Windows NT requires a paging file on the boot partition of the system disk that is at least as large as the amount of RAM in the computer.**

There are two utilities that you can use to examine the `memory.dmp` file: `Dumpchk.exe`, and `Dumpexam.exe`. Both utilities can be found on the Windows NT compact disc in the `Support\Debug\i386` folder. Normally these utilities are used as directed by Microsoft Technical Support.

The `Dumpchk` utility is used to check the `memory.dmp` file to ensure that it can be correctly read by a kernel debugger. Microsoft recommends that you use the `Dumpchk` utility before you send the `memory.dmp` file to Microsoft Technical Support for debugging. If you have to send the `memory.dmp` file to Microsoft via the Internet or a modem, use a compression utility (such as PKZIP or WinZip) to compress the file before you send it.

The `Dumpexam` utility is used to analyze the `memory.dmp` file and extract specific types of information from this file. The `Dumpexam` utility then places this information in a text file, usually `memory.txt`. The `memory.txt` file is normally small enough to be e-mailed directly to Microsoft Technical Support, or you can print it out and fax it.

# CONFIGURING DR. WATSON FOR WINDOWS NT

*Dr. Watson for Windows NT* is a tool that is used to debug application errors. Dr. Watson detects application errors as they occur, analyzes the error, and logs error information to a log file.

Additionally, Dr. Watson for Windows NT can be configured to create an application dump file that can be analyzed by a more sophisticated application debugger. You might use this application dump file feature at the request of your application developer if you're having application problems.

Windows NT automatically starts Dr. Watson when an application error occurs. By default, Dr. Watson is configured to create an application dump file. You may want to ensure that Dr. Watson is configured correctly, or change Dr. Watson's configuration. Before you can configure Dr. Watson for Windows NT, you must start Dr. Watson manually from the Run dialog box.

**TO MANUALLY START DR. WATSON FOR WINDOWS NT AND TO ENSURE THAT DR. WATSON IS CONFIGURED CORRECTLY, FOLLOW THESE STEPS:**

**1.** From the Windows NT desktop, select Start ⇒ Run.

**2.** The Run dialog box appears. In the Open drop-down list box, type **drwtsn32** and click OK.

**3.** The Dr. Watson for Windows NT dialog box appears, as shown in Figure 27-23. Notice that, by default, Dr. Watson is configured to create a log file and to dump application memory to a file named user.dmp when an application fails.

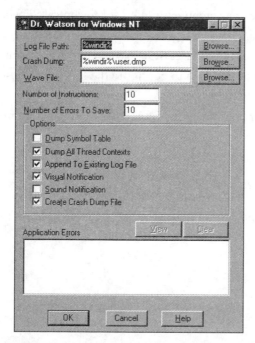

**FIGURE 27-23**  Configuring Dr. Watson for Windows NT

Ensure that the Crash Dump text box reads as follows:
`%windir%\user.dmp.`

Ensure that the check boxes next to: Dump All Thread Contexts, Append To Existing Log File, Visual Notification, and Create Crash Dump File are selected.

Click OK. Windows NT closes Dr. Watson for Windows NT automatically.

# CONFIGURING A COMPUTER FOR REMOTE DEBUGGING

Occasionally Microsoft Technical Support may not be able to resolve a problem by analyzing a blue screen or by analyzing a memory dump file. In this situation, Microsoft may need to remotely connect to the computer experiencing the problem and actively debug the computer. The tool that Microsoft Technical Support uses to remotely debug the computer is the *Kernel Debugger*.

Three computers are involved in the debugging process: the computer being debugged (the *target computer*), an additional Windows NT computer at your site (the *host computer*), and a computer at Microsoft Technical Support.

Both the target and host computers need to be running the same version of Windows NT, and you need to connect the two computers using a null-modem cable.

Normally it will be your job to configure the target and host computers at your site for the debugging session. Ask Microsoft Technical Support if they want you to configure your computers for remote debugging before proceeding with the steps listed below.

## Configuring the Target Computer

This section explains how to configure the target computer at your site for remote debugging.

**TO CONFIGURE THE TARGET COMPUTER FOR REMOTE DEBUGGING, FOLLOW THESE STEPS:**

1. Connect one end of the null-modem cable to the COM2 port on the target computer. (If you only have one COM port, or if you have a serial mouse connected to COM2, connect the null-modem cable to COM1.)

2. Edit the `Boot.ini` file on the target computer by adding `/DEBUG` to the end of the ARC pathname that you use to boot the computer.

   The following is a `Boot.ini` file that has been correctly configured for remote debugging:

   ```
   [boot loader]
   timeout=30
   default=multi(0)disk(0)rdisk(1)partition(1)\WINNT
   [operating systems]
   multi(0)disk(0)rdisk(1)partition(1)\WINNT="Windows NT
        Server Version 4.00" /DEBUG
   multi(0)disk(0)rdisk(1)partition(1)\WINNT="Windows NT
        Server Version 4.00 [VGA mode]" /basevideo /sos
   C:\="Microsoft Windows"
   ```

3. Shut down and reboot the target computer to Windows NT.

## Configuring the Host Computer

This section explains how to configure the host computer at your site for a remote debugging session.

**TO CONFIGURE THE HOST COMPUTER, FOLLOW THESE STEPS:**

1. Connect the other end of the null-modem cable to any available COM port on the host computer.

2. Place the Windows NT compact disc in the host computer's CD-ROM drive. Select Start ⇒ Programs ⇒ Command Prompt.

**3.** At the Command Prompt, type in the drive letter of the CD-ROM drive followed by a colon (for example, D:) and press Enter.

Type **\support\debug\expndsym.cmd** *<your_CD-ROM_drive_letter:>* *<full_path_to_your_Windows_NT_installation>* and press Enter. For example, on a Windows NT computer that has a CD-ROM on drive D:, and has Windows NT installed in c:\winnt, the command would be as follows: \support\debug\expndsym.cmd d: c:\winnt. (Don't type the period at the end.)

This command line installs the Windows NT debugger and all of the Windows NT symbol files required by the debugger.

 **If you've installed any service packs on your Windows NT host computer, you must also install all of the symbol files from the service pack(s) at this point.**

**4.** Install and configure RAS on the host computer if it is not already installed and configured. Don't configure RAS to use the COM port to which the null-modem cable is connected. You must configure RAS with at least one dial in port so that Microsoft Technical Support can remotely access this computer. (Installing and configuring RAS is covered in Chapter 19.)

Note: If you don't want to install RAS on the host computer, RAS can be installed on another Windows NT computer on the same network as the host computer.

**5.** Just before Microsoft Technical Support connects to the host computer via a RAS connection, select Start ⇒ Programs ⇒ Command Prompt, and type the following commands at the Command Prompt (Press Enter after each command):

**set nt_debug_port=com1** (or the COM port on the host computer that the null-modem cable is connected to, if not COM1)

**set nt_debug_baud_rate=19200**

**set nt_symbol_path=c:\winnt\symbols** (or the path to your Windows NT installation, if not c:\winnt)

**set nt_log_file_open=c:\debug.log**

**remote /s "i386kd -v" debug**

At this point, all of the environment variables required for remote debugging are configured on the host computer, and the Remote.exe utility and the debugger are running.

**6.** After Microsoft Technical Support connects to the host computer via RAS, the Microsoft technician will type remote /c *host_computer_name* debug at a command prompt on a computer at the Microsoft site to connect to the debugger on the host computer.

# KEY POINT SUMMARY

exam
preparation
pointer

**Many of the topics in this chapter are very dry. You will hopefully not need to use this information very often. However, you should study this entire chapter carefully before you take any of the Windows NT 4.0 Certified Professional exams.**

Chapter 27 covered advanced troubleshooting topics, including solutions to common boot sequence problems; how and when to use the Event Viewer and Windows NT diagnostics; how to search and modify the Registry; how to interpret blue screens, and how to set up and use memory dumps, Dr. Watson, and remote debugging.

o The boot sequence refers to the process of starting Windows NT, including initializing all of its services and completing the logon process. To successfully troubleshoot problems that can occur during this process, you need an understanding of the steps that occur during the boot sequence. The steps in the Windows NT boot sequence (for the Intel platform only) are:

- o Power On Self Test (POST)
- o Initial Startup
- o Selecting an operating system
- o Detecting hardware
- o Selecting hardware profile (or Last Known Good Configuration) and loading the kernel
- o Kernel initialization
- o Initializing device drivers
- o Initializing services
- o Logon process

o Table 27-1, Troubleshooting the Windows NT Boot Sequence, lists many common problems that can occur during the boot sequence, along with their possible causes and recommended solutions. Refer to this table now and review it. Review it again just before taking any of the three Windows NT exams. Note that the Emergency Repair process is part of many solutions to boot sequence problems.

o The *Emergency Repair process* involves using the Windows NT Setup Boot Disk set, the Windows NT compact disc, and the Emergency Repair disk created during (or after) the installation process to repair a damaged or corrupt Windows NT installation. There are four different repair options in the Emergency Repair Process. You can select one or more of these options: Inspect Registry files, Inspect startup environment, Verify Windows NT system files, and Inspect boot sector.

o *Event Viewer* is a Windows NT administrative tool used to view the system, security, and application logs. When a Service Control Manager warning message is displayed during bootup, indicating that a service or driver failed to start, you can use the Event Viewer system log to determine which service or driver failed, and to view a detailed description of the failure. When examining stop errors in the system log, it's usually most efficient to examine the event that took place first—the last event in the list—first. Solving the oldest error often solves all other errors listed.

o *Windows NT Diagnostics* is a Windows NT administrative tool that enables you to view detailed system configuration information and statistics. This tool can help you troubleshoot system configuration problems, and also help you determine service and device driver dependencies. The Services tab in Windows NT Diagnostics is particularly useful for determining service and group dependencies for a specific service or driver.

o *Registry editors* are tools that enable you to search and modify the Windows NT Registry. There are two primary tools for editing the Windows NT Registry: the Windows NT Registry Editor (`regedt32.exe`) and the Windows 95 Registry Editor (`regedit.exe`). Before getting into the specifics of how to use the Registry editors, it's helpful to have a basic understanding of how the Windows NT Registry is structured.

- The Windows NT Registry is a database that contains all of the information required to correctly configure an individual Windows NT computer, its user accounts, and applications. The Registry is organized in a tree structure consisting of five subtrees and their keys and value entries. The five subtrees of the Registry are: HKEY_LOCAL_MACHINE, HKEY_CURRENT_USER, HKEY_CURRENT_CONFIG, HKEY_CLASSES_ROOT, and HKEY_USERS. The HKEY_LOCAL_MACHINE subtree is the most helpful subtree in terms of troubleshooting because it contains most of the service and driver configuration information for the operating system.

- *Always* back up the Registry before you use the Registry editors to modify it. You can use the Windows NT Backup program, the `Regback.exe` utility, or the `Rdisk.exe` utility to back up the Registry on your Windows NT computer. If you use `Rdisk`, always run this utility using the `/s` switch, so that the `SAM` and `Security` hives will be backed up.

- Use the Windows 95 Registry Editor to search the Registry, because this editor can search the Registry by key, by value, or by the data contained in the value. The Windows NT Registry, on the other hand, can only search the Registry by key. To access the Windows 95 Registry Editor, select Start⇒ Run from the desktop. Then type **regedit** in the Open drop-down list box in the Run dialog box, and click OK.

- *Service dependencies* show which services and drivers must be running before a particular service (or driver) can start. *Group dependencies* show which groups of services or drivers must be running before the service (or driver) in question can start. For troubleshooting purposes, once you have determined what the service and group dependencies for a particular service (or driver) are, you can then verify that all of these services and drivers (that are required to be running *before* a particular service or driver can start) are, in fact, running.

- The easiest way to determine a particular service's or driver's service and group dependencies is to use Windows NT Diagnostics. However, you can also determine dependencies by using the Windows NT Registry Editor (`regedt32.exe`). To access the Windows NT Registry Editor, select Start⇒ Run from the desktop. Then type **regedt32** in the Open drop-down list box in the Run dialog box, and click OK.

- All service and driver Registry entries are stored in subkeys of
  `HKEY_LOCAL_MACHINE\System\CurrentControlSet\Services`

- Windows NT displays a *blue screen* when it encounters a STOP error from
  which it can't recover. Most blue screens are caused by corrupt drivers or
  by drivers developed for a previous version of Windows NT. There are three
  primary sections in a blue screen: the STOP error (including error code or
  BugCheck code) and description, a list of loaded drivers, and a stack dump
  (including the operating system's build number).

- You can use the System application in Control Panel to ensure that
  Windows NT is correctly configured to create a *memory dump file*
  (`memory.dmp`) when a STOP error occurs. There are two utilities that you
  can use to examine the memory dump file: `Dumpchk.exe` and
  `Dumpexam.exe`.

- *Dr. Watson for Windows NT* is a tool used to debug application errors.
  Windows NT automatically starts Dr. Watson when an application error
  occurs. By default, Dr. Watson is configured to create an application
  dump file.

- Occasionally, Microsoft Technical Support may need to remotely connect to
  a computer experiencing a problem and actively debug the computer. Three
  computers are involved in the debugging process: the computer being
  debugged (the target computer), an additional Windows NT computer at
  your site (the host computer), and a computer at Microsoft Technical
  Support. Both the target and host computers need to be running the same
  version of Windows NT, and you need to connect the two computers by
  using a null-modem cable. Normally, you will be responsible for configuring
  the target and host computers at your site for the debugging session.

## APPLYING WHAT YOU'VE LEARNED

Now it's time to regroup, review, and apply what you've learned in this chapter.
The review questions in the following Instant Assessment section bring to
mind key facts and concepts. In addition, some of the questions give you a chance

to analyze a situation and apply your troubleshooting knowledge of Windows NT to that particular situation.

The hands-on lab exercise will reinforce what you've learned, and provide an opportunity for you to practice some of the tasks tested by the Microsoft Certified Professional exams.

## Instant Assessment

1. Briefly list the nine major steps in the Windows NT boot sequence.

2. Your Windows NT computer crashes during a power outage. When you reboot the computer, a blue screen is displayed during the boot sequence. What is the most likely cause of this problem, and what should you do to resolve it?

3. You make several configuration changes and then reboot your Windows NT computer. A blue screen is displayed during the boot sequence. What is the most likely cause of this problem, and what should you do to resolve it?

4. What does the Emergency Repair process involve?

5. You receive a Service Control Manager warning message that indicates that a service or device driver failed during system startup. Which Windows NT administrative tool should you use to obtain more information about the failure?

6. When using the system log in Event Viewer for troubleshooting, for which stop error should you view the Event Detail first?

7. What are service dependencies and group dependencies?

8. Which tab in Windows NT Diagnostics is useful for determining service and group dependencies for a specific service or driver?

9. Name the two Registry editors.

10. When you are troubleshooting Windows NT, which subtree in the Registry should you normally check first?

11. What should you always do to the Registry before you modify it?

12. Which switch must you use with the `Rdisk` utility if you want the `SAM` and `Security` hives to be backed up?

13. Which of the two Registry editors is a better tool for searching the Registry, and why?

14. Which of the two Registry editors is more useful for viewing the service and group dependencies of a particular service?

15. When does Windows NT display a blue screen?

16. What are the three main sections in a blue screen?

17. Which Control Panel application can you use to ensure that Windows NT is configured to create a memory dump file (`memory.dmp`) when a STOP error occurs?

18. Which Windows NT tool is used to debug application errors?

 concept link    **For answers to the Instant Assessment questions see Appendix D.**

# Hands-on Lab Exercise

The following hands-on lab exercise provides you with a practical opportunity to apply the Windows NT troubleshooting knowledge you've gained in this chapter.

### Lab 27.39 *Troubleshooting Windows NT*

Workstation
Enterprise

The purpose of this lab exercise is to give you experience in using advanced Windows NT troubleshooting techniques.

This lab consists of four parts:

Part 1: Using Windows NT Diagnostics
Part 2: Using the Registry editors
Part 3: Configuring a memory dump
Part 4: Starting and configuring Dr. Watson for Windows NT

Begin this lab by booting your computer to Windows NT Server. Log on as Administrator.

Follow these instructions carefully.

### Part 1: Using Windows NT Diagnostics

In this section you use Windows NT Diagnostics to examine your Windows NT Server system configuration and to view service dependencies and group dependencies.

**1.** Select Start ⇒ Programs ⇒ Administrative Tools (Common) ⇒ Windows NT Diagnostics.

**2.** The Windows NT Diagnostics dialog box appears. Click the System tab.

**3.** The System tab appears. Notice the BIOS and CPU information displayed on this tab. Click the Display tab.

**4.** The Display tab appears. Notice the display adapter and driver settings. Click the Drives tab.

**5.** The Drives tab appears. Click the + sign next to Local hard drives. Highlight drive D: (or the letter of your NTFS drive, if not D:). Click the Properties command button.

**6.** The Properties dialog box appears. Notice the statistics on the number of bytes free, used, and total that are presented. Click OK. Click the Memory tab.

**7.** The Memory tab appears. Notice the memory and pagefile statistics displayed. Click the Network tab.

**8.** The Network tab appears. Notice the various network information that is displayed. Click the Statistics command button. Notice the statistics that are displayed. These statistics are not updated automatically—you must click the Refresh command button to update these statistics. Click the Resources tab.

**9.** The Resources tab appears. Notice that you can obtain Interrupt (IRQ), I/O Port, DMA, and memory information on this tab. Click the Devices command button. Double-click Floppy in the Device list box.

**10.** The Floppy Properties dialog box appears. Notice the resource settings displayed. Click OK. Click the Services tab.

**11.** The Services tab appears. Click the Devices command button.

**12.** In the Device list box, scroll down and double-click Parallel.

**13.** The Parallel Properties dialog box appears. Click the Dependencies tab.

**14.** The Dependencies tab appears. Notice the Service Dependencies and Group Dependencies listed. In the space provided, write down the following, as shown on your monitor:

Service Dependencies: _____

Group Dependencies: _____

Click OK.

**15.** The Services tab reappears. Click the Services command button.

**16.** Double-click the Server service.

**17.** The Server Properties dialog box appears. Click the Dependencies tab.

**18.** The Dependencies tab appears.

In the space provided, write down the following, as shown on your monitor: Service Dependencies: _____

Group Dependencies: _____

Click OK.

**19.** The Services tab reappears. Click OK. Proceed to Part 2.

### Part 2: Using the Registry editors

In this section you use the `Regedit.exe` and `Regedt32.exe` Registry editors to search the Registry, and to view service dependencies and group dependencies.

**1.** Select Start⇒Run.

**2.** The Run dialog box appears. In the Open drop-down list box, type **regedit** and click OK. (This starts the Windows 95 Registry Editor.)

**3.** The Registry Editor dialog box appears. Select Edit⇒Find.

**4.** The Find dialog box appears. In the Find what text box, type **WINS Client**. Ensure that the check boxes next to Keys, Values, and Data are checked. Click the Find Next command button.

**5.** Registry Editor searches the Registry. (This may take a few minutes.) The Registry Editor dialog box reappears. Notice that the Title value is highlighted on the right-hand side of the screen. Also notice that the Registry location of the highlighted value is displayed across the bottom of the dialog box.

**6.** Select Edit ⇒ Find Next.

**7.** Registry Editor searches the Registry. The Registry Editor dialog box reappears. Notice that a different value, DeviceDesc, is highlighted. Again, notice that the Registry location of this value is displayed across the bottom of the dialog box.

**8.** Exit Registry Editor.

**9.** Select Start⇒Run.

**10.** The Run dialog box appears. In the Open drop-down list box, type **regedt32** and click OK. (This starts the Windows NT Registry Editor.)

**11.** The Registry Editor dialog box appears. Select Window⇒ HKEY_LOCAL_MACHINE on Local Machine.

**12.** Maximize the Registry Editor dialog box and the HKEY_LOCAL_MACHINE on Local Machine window.

**13.** Double-click the `SYSTEM` folder.

**14.** Double-click the `CurrentControlSet` folder.

**15.** Double-click the `Services` folder.

**16.** Scroll down and highlight the `Parallel` folder. Notice the DependOnGroup and DependOnService entries on the right-hand side of the dialog box.

In the space provided, write down the entries that follow these values: (You can ignore the REG_MULTI_SZ: portion of the entries—this just identifies the type of data that will be placed in the Registry, in this case, multiple string values.)

DependOnGroup: _____

DependOnService: _____

Notice that the DependOnGroup and DependOnService values are the same as the Group Dependencies and Service Dependencies that you found using Windows NT Diagnostics in Step 14 in Part 1 of this lab.

**17.** On the left side of the Registry Editor dialog box, scroll up and highlight the `LanmanServer` folder. Notice the DependOnGroup and DependOnService entries on the right-hand side of the dialog box.

In the space provided, write down the entries that follow these values: (You can ignore the REG_MULTI_SZ: portion of the entries.)

DependOnGroup: _____

DependOnService: _____

Notice that the DependOnGroup and DependOnService values are the same as the Group Dependencies and Service Dependencies that you found using Windows NT Diagnostics in Step 18 in Part 1 of this lab.

Also notice the DisplayName value on the right-hand side of the dialog box. The LanmanServer service is the same as the Server service.

**18.** Exit Registry Editor. Proceed to Part 3.

## Part 3: Configuring a memory dump

In this section you use the System application in Control Panel to ensure that Windows NT Server is correctly configured to automatically dump memory when a STOP error occurs.

Then you use the System application to configure Windows NT Workstation to automatically dump memory when a STOP error occurs.

**1.** Select Start ⇒ Settings ⇒ Control Panel.

**2.** The Control Panel dialog box appears. Double-click the System icon.

**3.** The System Properties dialog box appears. Click the Startup/Shutdown tab.

**4.** The Startup/Shutdown tab appears. In the Recovery section of the dialog box, ensure that all check boxes are selected. Also ensure that the text box reads as follows: `%SystemRoot%\MEMORY.DMP`. Click OK.

**5.** Exit Control Panel.

**6.** Select Start ⇒ Shut Down.

**7.** In the Shut Down Windows dialog box, click the radio button next to "Restart the computer." Click the Yes command button.

**8.** Reboot your computer to Windows NT Workstation. Log on as Administrator.

**9.** Select Start ⇒ Settings ⇒ Control Panel.

**10.** The Control Panel dialog box appears. Double-click the System icon.

**11.** The System Properties dialog box appears. Click the Startup/Shutdown tab.

**12.** The Startup/Shutdown tab appears. In the Recovery section of the dialog box, select all of the check boxes. Also ensure that the text box reads as follows: `%SystemRoot%\MEMORY.DMP`. Click OK.

**13.** A System Control Panel Applet dialog box appears, indicating that the Alerter service is not running. Click OK.

**14.** A System Settings Change dialog box appears. Click the No command button (don't reboot your computer at this time).

**15.** The Control Panel dialog box reappears. Double-click the Services icon.

**16.** The Services dialog box appears. Highlight the Alerter service. Click the Startup command button.

**17.** The Service dialog box appears. In the Startup Type section, select the radio button next to Automatic. Click OK.

**18.** In the Services dialog box, click the Close command button.

**19.** Exit Control Panel. Proceed to Part 4.

### Part 4: Starting and configuring Dr. Watson for Windows NT

In this section you manually start Dr. Watson for Windows NT, and verify that Dr. Watson is configured to automatically dump application memory when an application fails.

**1.** Select Start ⇒ Run.

**2.** The Run dialog box appears. In the Open drop-down list box, type **drwtsn32** and click OK.

**3.** The Dr. Watson for Windows NT dialog box appears. Notice that, by default, Dr. Watson is configured to create a log file and to dump application memory to a file named user.dmp when an application fails.

Ensure that the Crash Dump text box reads as follows:

```
%windir%\user.dmp
```

Ensure that the check boxes next to: Dump All Thread Contexts, Append To Existing Log File, Visual Notification, and Create Crash Dump File are selected.

Click OK. Window NT closes Dr. Watson for Windows NT automatically.

# Resources

# Microsoft Windows NT Workstation 4.0 Exam Objectives

## EXAM 70-73: IMPLEMENTING AND SUPPORTING MICROSOFT WINDOWS NT WORKSTATION 4.0

This appendix consists of four parts:

- The first part contains portions of Microsoft's *Preparation Guide for Exam 70-73: Implementing and Supporting Microsoft Windows NT Workstation 4.0,* including a complete list of this exam's objectives.

- The second part lists the basic facts for this exam, including the number of questions, passing score, and time allowed to take the exam.

- The third part is an exhaustive exam objectives cross-reference chart for study purposes. Every exam objective is linked to the corresponding materials (text and labs) in this book.

- The fourth part is a quick-reference chart listing the chapters and labs in this book that you should read and study to prepare for the exam.

**This exam information is current as of the date this book went to press, but is subject to change by Microsoft at any time. You can ensure that you have the most current version of this exam's objectives by accessing the Microsoft Training and Certification Web site at:** `www.microsoft.com/train_cert/`

## Credit Toward Certification

A passing score on this exam counts as core credit toward *Microsoft Certified Systems Engineer* certification and as core credit toward *Microsoft Certified Product Specialist* certification.

## Skills Measured

The *Implementing and Supporting Microsoft Windows NT Workstation 4.0* certification exam measures your ability to implement, administer, and troubleshoot information systems that incorporate Windows NT Workstation. Before taking the exam, you should be proficient in the following job skills.

## Exam Objectives

### Planning

- Create unattended installation files.
- Plan strategies for sharing and securing resources.
- Choose the appropriate file system to use in a given situation. File systems and situations include: NTFS, FAT, HPFS, security, and dual-boot systems.

### Installation and Configuration

- Install Windows NT Workstation on an Intel platform in a given situation.
- Set up a dual-boot system in a given situation.
- Remove Windows NT Workstation in a given situation.

- Install, configure, and remove hardware components for a given situation. Hardware components include network adapter drivers, SCSI device drivers, tape device drivers, UPS, multimedia devices, display drivers, keyboard drivers, and mouse drivers.
- Use Control Panel applications to configure a Windows NT Workstation computer in a given situation.
- Upgrade to Windows NT Workstation 4.0 in a given situation.
- Configure server-based installation for wide-scale deployment in a given situation.

## Managing Resources

- Create and manage local user accounts and local group accounts to meet given requirements.
- Set up and modify user profiles.
- Set up shared folders and permissions.
- Set permissions on NTFS partitions, folders, and files.
- Install and configure printers in a given environment.

## Connectivity

- Add and configure the network components of Windows NT Workstation.
- Use various methods to access network resources.
- Implement Windows NT Workstation as a client in a NetWare environment.
- Use various configurations to install Windows NT Workstation as a TCP/IP client.
- Configure and install Dial-Up Networking in a given situation.
- Configure Microsoft Peer Web Services in a given situation.

## Running Applications

- Start applications on Intel and RISC platforms in various operating system environments.
- Start applications at various priorities.

## *Monitoring and Optimization*

- o Monitor system performance by using various tools.
- o Identify and resolve a given performance problem.
- o Optimize system performance in various areas.

## *Troubleshooting*

- o Choose the appropriate course of action to take when the boot process fails.
- o Choose the appropriate course of action to take when a print job fails.
- o Choose the appropriate course of action to take when the installation process fails.
- o Choose the appropriate course of action to take when an application fails.
- o Choose the appropriate course of action to take when a user cannot access a resource.
- o Modify the registry using the appropriate tool in a given situation.
- o Implement advanced techniques to resolve various problems.

# EXAM FACTS

| | |
|---|---|
| Number of questions on this exam: | 51 |
| Passing score: | 705 |
| Time allowed to take exam: | 90 minutes |

# EXAM OBJECTIVES CROSS-REFERENCE CHART FOR STUDY PURPOSES

Table A-1 lists the stated objectives for Exam 70-73, Implementing and Supporting Microsoft Windows NT Workstation 4.0, in a cross-reference chart for study purposes. Use this table to help you determine the specific chapters in this book that you should study, as well as the labs that you should perform, to prepare for the exam.

| **TABLE A-1** NT WORKSTATION 4.0 EXAM OBJECTIVES CROSS-REFERENCE CHART | | |
|---|---|---|
| *EXAM OBJECTIVE* | *CHAPTER(S)* | *LAB(S) (IF APPLICABLE)* |
| **Planning** | | |
| Create unattended installation files. | Chapter 5, pages 183–189 | Lab 5.7 |
| Plan strategies for sharing and securing resources. | Chapter 12, pages 478–479 | Lab 12.18 |
| Choose the appropriate file system to use in a given situation. File systems and situations include NTFS, FAT, HPFS, security, and dual-boot systems. | Chapter 3, pages 69–75 | Review Activity, pages 110–111 |
| **Installation and Configuration** | | |
| Install Windows NT Workstation on an Intel platform in a given situation. | Chapter 2, pages 27–50<br><br>Chapter 5, pages 175–189 | Lab 2.1 |

*continued*

**TABLE A-1** *(continued)*

| EXAM OBJECTIVE | CHAPTER(S) | LAB(S) (IF APPLICABLE) |
|---|---|---|
| Set up a dual-boot system in a given situation. | Chapter 2, pages 31, 48<br><br>Chapter 3, page 70–71 | Lab 2.2 |
| Remove Windows NT Workstation in a given situation. | Chapter 2, pages 50–52 | None |
| Install, configure, and remove hardware components for a given situation. Hardware components include network adapter drivers, SCSI device drivers, tape device drivers, UPS, multimedia devices, display drivers, keyboard drivers, and mouse drivers. | Chapter 4, pages 119–127, 142–144 | Lab 4.6 |
| Use Control Panel applications to configure a Windows NT Workstation computer in a given situation. | Chapter 4, pages 117–156 | Lab 4.6 |
| Upgrade to Windows NT Workstation 4.0 in a given situation. | Chapter 2, pages 31–32, 48 | None |
| Configure server-based installation for wide-scale deployment in a given situation. | Chapter 5, pages 175–198 | Lab 5.7 |
| *Managing Resources* | | |
| Create and manage local user accounts and local group accounts to meet given requirements. | Chapter 7, pages 261–282, 285–301 | Lab 7.10 |
| Set up and modify user profiles. | Chapter 9, pages 335–350 | Lab 9.13 |

| EXAM OBJECTIVE | CHAPTER(S) | LAB(S) (IF APPLICABLE) |
|---|---|---|
| Set up shared folders and permissions. | Chapter 12, pages 454–465, 478–479 | Lab 12.18 |
| Set permissions on NTFS partitions, folders, and files. | Chapter 12, pages 466–482 | Lab 12.18 |
| Install and configure printers in a given environment. | Chapter 6, pages 201–243, 246–256 | Lab 6.8<br>Lab 6.9 |
| *Connectivity* | | |
| Add and configure the network components of Windows NT Workstation. | Chapter 4, pages 128–144 | |
| | Chapter 6, pages 217–220 | Lab 6.9 |
| | Chapter 16, pages 585–595, 612–626 | Lab 16.26 |
| | Chapter 17, pages 645–653, 658–662, 670–671 | Lab 17.29 |
| Use various methods to access network resources. | Chapter 13, pages 515–537 | Lab 13.22 |
| Implement Windows NT Workstation as a client in a NetWare environment. | Chapter 17, pages 645–653, 658–662, 670–671 | Lab 17.29 |
| Use various configurations to install Windows NT Workstation as a TCP/IP client. | Chapter 2, pages 40–42, 49 | Lab 2.1 |
| | Chapter 6, pages 217–220 | Lab 6.9 |
| | Chapter 16, pages 585–595 | |

*continued*

**TABLE A-1** *(continued)*

| EXAM OBJECTIVE | CHAPTER(S) | LAB(S) (IF APPLICABLE) |
|---|---|---|
| Configure and install Dial-Up Networking in a given situation. | Chapter 19, pages 707–725, 729–741 | Lab 19.32 |
| | Chapter 4, pages 121–123, 156 | Lab 4.6 |
| Configure Microsoft Peer Web Services in a given situation. | Chapter 16, pages 612–626 | Lab 16.26 |
| ***Running Applications*** | | |
| Start applications on Intel and RISC platforms in various operating system environments. | Chapter 21, pages 779–805 | None |
| Start applications at various priorities. | Chapter 21, pages 786–789 | Lab 21.34 |
| ***Monitoring and Optimization*** | | |
| Monitor system performance by using various tools. | Chapter 22, pages 809–845 | Lab 22.35 |
| | Chapter 21, page 791 | |
| | Chapter 27, pages 952–959 | |
| Identify and resolve a given performance problem. | Chapter 25, pages 903–915 | Lab 25.37 |
| Optimize system performance in various areas. | Chapter 25, pages 907–915 | None |
| ***Troubleshooting*** | | |
| Choose the appropriate course of action to take when the boot process fails. | Chapter 27, pages 941–949 | None |
| | Chapter 26, pages 925–938 | |

| Exam Objective | Chapter(s) | Lab(s) (if applicable) |
|---|---|---|
| Choose the appropriate course of action to take when a print job fails. | Chapter 6, pages 243–245 | Review Activity, pages 252–253 |
| | Chapter 26, pages 925–938 | |
| Choose the appropriate course of action to take when the installation process fails. | Chapter 2, pages 52–53 | Review Activity, page 56 |
| | Chapter 26, pages 925–938 | |
| Choose the appropriate course of action to take when an application fails. | Chapter 21, pages 795–796 | Review Activity, page 801 |
| | Chapter 26, pages 925–938 | |
| Choose the appropriate course of action to take when a user cannot access a resource. | Chapter 12, page 490 | Lab 12.20 |
| | Chapter 26, pages 925–938 | |
| Modify the registry using the appropriate tool in a given situation. | Chapter 27, pages 960–970 | Lab 27.39 |
| | Chapter 13, pages 521–524 | Lab 13.21 |
| Implement advanced techniques to resolve various problems. | Chapter 27, pages 939–989 | Lab 27.39 |

# Quick Reference — Chapters and Labs That Prepare You for the Windows NT Workstation 4.0 Exam

Table A-2 lists the specific chapters you should read and study, as well as the labs you should perform, to prepare for Exam 70-73, Implementing and Supporting

Microsoft Windows NT Workstation 4.0. With the exception of Chapter 1, which provides basic Windows NT information, each of these chapters and labs corresponds directly to the exam objectives listed in the previous section.

**TABLE A-2** CHAPTERS AND LABS THAT PREPARE YOU FOR THE WINDOWS NT WORKSTATION 4.0 EXAM

| CHAPTER NUMBER | CHAPTER TITLE | APPLICABLE LAB(S) IN THIS CHAPTER |
|---|---|---|
| Chapter 1 | Overview of Windows NT Workstation and Windows NT Server | None |
| Chapter 2 | Installing Windows NT Workstation and Windows NT Server | Lab 2.1, Lab 2.2, Review Activity: Installing Windows NT troubleshooting practice exercise |
| Chapter 3 | Configuring Disks | Lab 3.3 Review Activity: File system planning exercise |
| Chapter 4 | Using Control Panel | Lab 4.6 |
| Chapter 5 | Server-Based Deployment | Lab 5.7 |
| Chapter 6 | Managing Printing | Lab 6.8, Lab 6.9, Review Activity: Windows NT printing troubleshooting exercise |
| Chapter 7 | Managing User and Group Accounts | Lab 7.10 |
| Chapter 9 | Managing User Profiles and System Policy | Lab 9.13 |
| Chapter 12 | Sharing and Securing File Systems | Lab 12.18, Lab 12.20 |
| Chapter 13 | Accessing Resources on the Network | Lab 13.21, Lab 13.22 |
| Chapter 16 | Networking Using TCP/IP | Lab 16.26 |
| Chapter 17 | Coexistence with NetWare | Lab 17.29 |

| CHAPTER NUMBER | CHAPTER TITLE | APPLICABLE LAB(S) IN THIS CHAPTER |
|---|---|---|
| Chapter 19 | Installing and Configuring Remote Access Service (RAS) | Lab 19.32 |
| Chapter 21 | Running Applications on Windows NT | Lab 21.34, Review Activity: Troubleshooting common application problems |
| Chapter 22 | Using Performance Monitor | Lab 22.35 |
| Chapter 25 | Performance Optimization | Lab 25.37 |
| Chapter 26 | The Troubleshooting Process | None |
| Chapter 27 | Advanced Troubleshooting Topics | Lab 27.39 |

# Microsoft Windows NT Server 4.0
## Exam Objectives

## EXAM 70-67: IMPLEMENTING AND SUPPORTING MICROSOFT WINDOWS NT SERVER 4.0

This appendix consists of four parts:

- The first part contains portions of Microsoft's *Preparation Guide for Exam 70-67: Implementing and Supporting Microsoft Windows NT Server 4.0*, including a complete list of this exam's objectives.

- The second part lists the basic facts for this exam, including the number of questions, passing score, and time allowed to take the exam.

- The third part is an exhaustive exam objectives cross-reference chart for study purposes. Every exam objective is linked to the corresponding materials (text and labs) in this book.

- The fourth part is a quick-reference chart listing the chapters and labs in this book that you should read and study to prepare for the exam.

**This exam information is current as of the date this book went to press, but is subject to change by Microsoft at any time. You can ensure that you have the most current version of this exam's objectives by accessing the Microsoft Training and Certification Web site at:** `www.microsoft.com/train_cert/`

## Credit Toward Certification

A passing score on this exam counts as core credit toward *Microsoft Certified Systems Engineer* certification and as core credit toward *Microsoft Certified Product Specialist* certification.

## Skills Measured

The *Implementing and Supporting Microsoft Windows NT Server 4.0* certification exam measures your ability to implement, administer, and troubleshoot information systems that incorporate Windows NT Server 4.0 in a simple computing environment. A simple computing environment is typically a homogeneous LAN. It might include one or more servers, a single domain, and a single location; and it might have file-sharing and print-sharing capabilities. Before taking the exam, you should be proficient in the following job skills.

## Exam Objectives

### Planning

- Plan the disk drive configuration for various requirements. Requirements include choosing a file system and choosing a fault-tolerance method.
- Choose a protocol for various situations. Protocols include TCP/IP, NWLink IPX/SPX Compatible Transport, and NetBEUI.

### Installation and Configuration

- Install Windows NT Server on Intel-based platforms.
- Install Windows NT Server to perform various server roles. Server roles include primary domain controller, backup domain controller, and member server.

- Install Windows NT Server by using various methods. Installation methods include CD-ROM, over-the-network, Network Client Administrator, and express versus custom.

- Configure protocols and protocol bindings. Protocols include TCP/IP, NWLink IPX/SPX Compatible Transport, and NetBEUI.

- Configure network adapters. Considerations include changing IRQ, IObase, memory addresses, and configuring multiple adapters.

- Configure Windows NT Server core services. Services include Directory Replicator, License Manager, and other services.

- Configure peripherals and devices. Peripherals and devices include communication devices, SCSI devices, tape device drivers, UPS devices and UPS service, mouse drivers, display drivers, and keyboard drivers.

- Configure hard disks to meet various requirements. Requirements include allocating disk space capacity, providing redundancy, improving performance, providing security, and formatting.

- Configure printers. Tasks include adding and configuring a printer, implementing a printer pool, and setting print priorities.

- Configure a Windows NT Server computer for various types of client computers. Client computer types include Windows NT Workstation, Microsoft Windows 95, and Microsoft MS-DOS-based.

## Managing Resources

- Manage user and group accounts. Considerations include managing Windows NT user accounts, managing Windows NT user rights, managing Windows NT groups, administering account policies, and auditing changes to the user account database.

- Create and manage policies and profiles for various situations. Policies and profiles include local user profiles, roaming user profiles, and system policies.

- Administer remote servers from various types of client computers. Client computer types include Windows 95 and Windows NT Workstation.

- Manage disk resources. Tasks include copying and moving files between file systems, creating and sharing resources, implementing permissions and security, and establishing file auditing.

## *Connectivity*

- Configure Windows NT Server for interoperability with NetWare servers by using various tools. Tools include Gateway Service for NetWare and Migration Tool for NetWare.

- Install and configure Remote Access Service (RAS). Configuration options include configuring RAS communications, configuring RAS protocols, configuring RAS security, and configuring Dial-Up Networking clients.

## *Monitoring and Optimization*

- Monitor performance of various functions by using Performance Monitor. Functions include processor, memory, disk, and network.

- Identify performance bottlenecks.

## *Troubleshooting*

- Choose the appropriate course of action to take to resolve installation failures.

- Choose the appropriate course of action to take to resolve boot failures.

- Choose the appropriate course of action to take to resolve configuration errors.

- Choose the appropriate course of action to take to resolve printer problems.

- Choose the appropriate course of action to take to resolve RAS problems.

- Choose the appropriate course of action to take to resolve connectivity problems.

- Choose the appropriate course of action to take to resolve resource access problems and permission problems.

- Choose the appropriate course of action to take to resolve fault-tolerance failures. Fault-tolerance methods include tape backup, mirroring, stripe set with parity, and disk duplexing.

# EXAM FACTS

Number of questions on this exam:    55

Passing score:    764

Time allowed to take exam:    90 minutes

# EXAM OBJECTIVES CROSS-REFERENCE CHART FOR STUDY PURPOSES

Table B-1 lists the stated objectives for Exam 70-67, Implementing and Supporting Microsoft Windows NT Server 4.0, in a cross-reference chart for study purposes. Use this table to help you determine the specific chapters in this book that you should study, as well as the labs that you should perform to prepare for the exam.

**TABLE B-1** NT SERVER 4.0 EXAM OBJECTIVES CROSS-REFERENCE CHART

| EXAM OBJECTIVE | CHAPTER(S) | LAB(S) (IF APPLICABLE) |
|---|---|---|
| **Planning** | | |
| Plan the disk drive configuration for various requirements. Requirements include choosing a file system and choosing a fault-tolerance method. | Chapter 3, pages 69–99 | Review Activities, pages 110–112 |
| Choose a protocol for various situations. Protocols include TCP/IP, NWLink IPX/SPX Compatible Transport, and NetBEUI. | Chapter 2, pages 40–42<br><br>Chapter 4, pages 132–137<br><br>Chapter 16, pages 585–586<br><br>Chapter 17, pages 645–653 | None |

*continued*

**TABLE B-1** *(continued)*

| Exam Objective | Chapter(s) | Lab(s) (if applicable) |
|---|---|---|
| ***Installation and Configuration*** | | |
| Install Windows NT Server on Intel-based platforms. | Chapter 2, pages 27–50 | Lab 2.2 |
| | | Lab 10.15 |
| Install Windows NT Server to perform various server roles. Server roles include primary domain controller, backup domain controller, and member server. | Chapter 2, pages 36 – 37, 49 Chapter 4, pages 128–132 | Lab 2.2 Lab 10.15 |
| Install Windows NT Server using various methods. Installation methods include CD-ROM, over-the-network, Network Client Administrator, and express versus custom. | Chapter 2, pages 45–47 Chapter 5, pages 175–189 | Lab 2.2 Lab 10.15 Lab 5.7 |
| Configure protocols and protocol bindings. Protocols include TCP/IP, NWLink IPX/SPX Compatible Transport, and NetBEUI. | Chapter 4, pages 132–142 Chapter 16, pages 586–589, 592-595 Chapter 17, pages 650–653 | Lab 16.27 Lab 17.30 |
| Configure network adapters. Considerations include changing IRQ, IObase, memory addresses, and configuring multiple adapters. | Chapter 4, pages 127–128, 144 – 148 | Lab 2.2 Lab 16.27 |
| Configure Windows NT Server core services. Services include Directory Replicator, License Manager, and other services. | Chapter 4, pages 127–128, 144 – 148 Chapter 13, pages 521–524 Chapter 25, pages 912-914 | Lab 4.5 Lab 13.21 |
| Configure peripherals and devices. Peripherals and devices include communication devices, SCSI devices, tape device drivers, UPS devices and UPS service, and mouse drivers, display drivers, and keyboard drivers. | Chapter 4, pages 119 – 127 | Lab 4.6 |

| EXAM OBJECTIVE | CHAPTER(S) | LAB(S) (IF APPLICABLE) |
| --- | --- | --- |
| Configure hard disks to meet various requirements. Requirements include allocating disk space capacity, providing redundancy, improving performance, providing security, and formatting. | Chapter 3, pages 69–99 | Lab 3.3<br><br>Review Activities, pages 110–112 |
| Configure printers. Tasks include adding and configuring a printer, implementing a printer pool, and setting print priorities. | Chapter 6, pages 201–243 | Lab 6.8<br><br>Lab 6.9 |
| Configure a Windows NT Server computer for various types of client computers. Client computer types include Windows NT Workstation, Microsoft Windows 95, and Microsoft MS-DOS-based. | Chapter 5, pages 175–182 | None |
| **Managing Resources** | | |
| Manage user and group accounts. Considerations include managing Windows NT user accounts, managing Windows NT user rights, managing Windows NT groups, administering account policies, and auditing changes to the user account database. | Chapter 7, pages 261–301<br><br>Chapter 8, pages 305–331 | Lab 7.10<br><br>Lab 8.11<br><br>Lab 8.12 |
| Create and manage policies and profiles for various situations. Policies and profiles include local user profiles, roaming user profiles, and system policies. | Chapter 9, pages 335–359 | Lab 9.13<br><br>Lab 9.14 |
| Administer remote servers from various types of client computers. Client computer types include Windows 95 and Windows NT Workstation. | Chapter 14, pages 541–558 | Lab 14.23 |

*continued*

**TABLE B-1** *(continued)*

| Exam Objective | Chapter(s) | Lab(s) (if applicable) |
|---|---|---|
| Manage disk resources. Tasks include copying and moving files between file systems, creating and sharing resources, implementing permissions and security, and establishing file auditing. | Chapter 12, pages 451–489 | Lab 12.18<br><br>Lab 12.19 |

### Connectivity

| | | |
|---|---|---|
| Configure Windows NT Server for interoperability with NetWare servers by using various tools. Tools include Gateway Service for NetWare and Migration Tool for NetWare. | Chapter 17, pages 645–658, 662–672<br><br>Chapter 18, pages 685–704 | Lab 17.30 |
| Install and configure Remote Access Service (RAS). Configuration options include configuring RAS communications, configuring RAS protocols, configuring RAS security, and configuring Dial-Up Networking clients. | Chapter 19, pages 707–741 | Lab 19.32 |

### Monitoring and Optimization

| | | |
|---|---|---|
| Monitor performance of various functions by using Performance Monitor. Functions include processor, memory, disk, and network. | Chapter 22, pages 809–845 | Lab 22.35 |
| Identify performance bottlenecks. | Chapter 25, pages 903–921 | Lab 25.37 |

### Troubleshooting

| | | |
|---|---|---|
| Choose the appropriate course of action to take to resolve installation failures. | Chapter 2, pages 52–53<br><br>Chapter 26, pages 925–938 | Review Activity, page 56 |

| EXAM OBJECTIVE | CHAPTER(S) | LAB(S) (IF APPLICABLE) |
|---|---|---|
| Choose the appropriate course of action to take to resolve boot failures. | Chapter 27, pages 941–949 | None |
| | Chapter 26, pages 925–938 | |
| Choose the appropriate course of action to take to resolve configuration errors. | Chapter 4, pages 156–157 | None |
| | Chapter 26, pages 925–938 | |
| Choose the appropriate course of action to take to resolve printer problems. | Chapter 6, pages 243–245 | Review Activity, pages 252–253 |
| | Chapter 26, pages 925–938 | |
| Choose the appropriate course of action to take to resolve RAS problems. | Chapter 19, pages 742–743 | Review Activity, pages 748–749 |
| | Chapter 26, pages 925–938 | |
| Choose the appropriate course of action to take to resolve connectivity problems. | Chapter 16, pages 626–627 | Lab 16.28 |
| | Chapter 17, pages 672–673 | |
| | Chapter 26, pages 925–938 | |
| Choose the appropriate course of action to take to resolve resource access problems and permission problems. | Chapter 12, page 490 | Lab 12.20 |
| | Chapter 26, pages 925–938 | |
| Choose the appropriate course of action to take to resolve fault-tolerance failures. Fault-tolerance methods include tape backup, mirroring, stripe set with parity, and disk duplexing. | Chapter 3, pages 100–107 | Lab 3.4 |
| | Chapter 15, pages 559–579 | Lab 15.24 |
| | Chapter 27, pages 946–949, 963 | |
| | Chapter 26, pages 925–938 | |

# QUICK REFERENCE — CHAPTERS AND LABS THAT PREPARE YOU FOR THE WINDOWS NT SERVER 4.0 EXAM

Table B-2 lists the specific chapters you should read and study, as well as the labs that you should perform, to prepare for Exam 70-67, Implementing and Supporting Microsoft Windows NT Server 4.0. With the exception of Chapter 1, which provides basic Windows NT information, each of these chapters and labs corresponds directly to the exam objectives listed in the previous section.

**TABLE B-2** CHAPTERS AND LABS THAT PREPARE YOU FOR THE WINDOWS NT SERVER 4.0 EXAM

| CHAPTER NUMBER | CHAPTER TITLE | APPLICABLE LAB(S) IN THIS CHAPTER |
|---|---|---|
| Chapter 1 | Overview of Windows NT Workstation and Windows NT Server | None |
| Chapter 2 | Installing Windows NT Workstation and Windows NT Server | Lab 2.1 (Note: Lab 2.1 is not required to meet the exam objectives covered in this chapter; however, it is required to perform some of the later labs.) Lab 2.2, Review Activity: Installing Windows NT troubleshooting practice exercise |
| Chapter 3 | Configuring Disks | Lab 3.3, Lab 3.4, Review Activities: File system planning exercise, Disk partitioning and fault tolerance planning exercise |
| Chapter 4 | Using Control Panel | Lab 4.5, Lab 4.6 |
| Chapter 5 | Server-Based Deployment | Lab 5.7 |

| CHAPTER NUMBER | CHAPTER TITLE | APPLICABLE LAB(S) IN THIS CHAPTER |
|---|---|---|
| Chapter 6 | Managing Printing | Lab 6.8, Lab 6.9, Review Activity: Windows NT printing troubleshooting exercise |
| Chapter 7 | Managing User and Group Accounts | Lab 7.10 |
| Chapter 8 | Managing Account Policy, User Rights, and Auditing | Lab 8.11, Lab 8.12 |
| Chapter 9 | Managing User Profiles and System Policy | Lab 9.13, Lab 9.14 |
| Chapter 12 | Sharing and Securing File Systems | Lab 12.18, Lab 12.19, Lab 12.20 |
| Chapter 13 | Accessing Resources on the Network | Lab 13.21 |
| Chapter 14 | Using Windows NT Server Tools | Lab 14.23 |
| Chapter 15 | Backing Up and Restoring Data | Lab 15.24 |
| Chapter 16 | Networking Using TCP/IP | Lab 16.27, Lab 16.28 |
| Chapter 17 | Coexistence with NetWare | Lab 17.30 |
| Chatper 18 | Migrating to Windows NT from NetWare | None |
| Chapter 19 | Installing and Configuring Remote Access Service (RAS) | Lab 19.32, Review Activity: Troubleshooting common RAS problems |
| Chapter 22 | Using Performance Monitor | Lab 22.35 |
| Chapter 25 | Performance Optimization | Lab 25.37 |
| Chapter 26 | The Troubleshooting Process | None |
| Chapter 27 | Advanced Troubleshooting Topics | None |

# Microsoft Windows NT Server 4.0 in the Enterprise Exam Objectives

## EXAM 70-68: IMPLEMENTING AND SUPPORTING MICROSOFT WINDOWS NT SERVER 4.0 IN THE ENTERPRISE

This appendix consists of four parts:

- The first part contains portions of Microsoft's *Preparation Guide for Exam 70-68: Implementing and Supporting Microsoft Windows NT 4.0 Server,* including a complete list of this exam's objectives.

- The second part lists the basic facts for this exam, including the number of questions, passing score, and time allowed to take the exam.

- The third part is an exhaustive exam objectives cross-reference chart for study purposes. Every exam objective is linked to the corresponding materials (text and labs) in this book.

- The fourth part is a quick-reference chart listing the chapters and labs in this book that you should read and study to prepare for the exam.

**web links** **This exam information is current as of the date this book went to press, but is subject to change by Microsoft at any time. You can ensure that you have the most current version of this exam's objectives by accessing the Microsoft Training and Certification Web site at:** www.microsoft.com/train_cert/

## Credit Toward Certification

A passing score on this exam counts as core credit toward *Microsoft Certified Systems Engineer* certification.

## Skills Measured

The *Implementing and Supporting Microsoft Windows NT Server 4.0 in the Enterprise* certification exam measures your ability to implement, administer, and troubleshoot information systems that incorporate Windows NT Server 4.0 in an enterprise computing environment. An enterprise computing environment is typically a heterogeneous WAN. It might include multiple servers and multiple domains, and it might run sophisticated server applications. Before taking the exam, you should be proficient in the following job skills.

## Exam Objectives

### Planning

- Plan the implementation of a directory services architecture. Considerations include selecting the appropriate domain model, supporting a single logon account, and allowing users to access resources in different domains.
- Plan the disk drive configuration for various requirements. Requirements include choosing a fault-tolerance method.
- Choose a protocol for various situations. Protocols include TCP/IP, TCP/IP with DHCP and WINS, NWLink IPX/SPX Compatible Transport Protocol, Data Link Control (DLC), and AppleTalk.

## Installation and Configuration

- Install Windows NT Server to perform various server roles. Server roles include primary domain controller, backup domain controller, and member server.

- Configure protocols and protocol bindings. Protocols include TCP/IP, TCP/IP with DHCP and WINS, NWLink IPX/SPX Compatible Transport Protocol, DLC, and AppleTalk.

- Configure Windows NT Server core services. Services include Directory Replicator and Computer Browser.

- Configure hard disks to meet various requirements. Requirements include providing redundancy and improving performance.

- Configure printers. Tasks include adding and configuring a printer, implementing a printer pool, and setting print priorities.

- Configure a Windows NT Server computer for various types of client computers. Client computer types include Windows NT Workstation, Windows 95, and Macintosh.

## Managing Resources

- Manage user and group accounts. Considerations include managing Windows NT user accounts, managing Windows NT user rights, managing Windows NT groups, administering account policies, and auditing changes to the user account database.

- Create and manage policies and profiles for various situations. Policies and profiles include local user profiles, roaming user profiles, and system policies.

- Administer remote servers from various types of client computers. Client computer types include Windows 95 and Windows NT Workstation.

- Manage disk resources. Tasks include creating and sharing resources, implementing permissions and security, and establishing file auditing.

## Connectivity

- Configure Windows NT Server for interoperability with NetWare servers by using various tools. Tools include Gateway Service for NetWare and Migration Tool for NetWare.

- Install and configure multiprotocol routing to serve various functions. Functions include Internet router, BOOTP/DHCP Relay Agent, and IPX router.
- Install and configure Internet Information Server.
- Install and configure Internet services. Services include World Wide Web, DNS, and Intranet.
- Install and configure Remote Access Service (RAS). Configuration options include configuring RAS communications, configuring RAS protocols, and configuring RAS security.

## Monitoring and Optimization

- Establish a baseline for measuring system performance. Tasks include creating a database of measurement data.
- Monitor performance of various functions by using Performance Monitor. Functions include processor, memory, disk, and network.
- Monitor network traffic by using Network Monitor. Tasks include collecting data, presenting data, and filtering data.
- Identify performance bottlenecks.
- Optimize performance for various results. Results include controlling network traffic and controlling server load.

## Troubleshooting

- Choose the appropriate course of action to take to resolve installation failures.
- Choose the appropriate course of action to take to resolve boot failures.
- Choose the appropriate course of action to take to resolve configuration errors. Tasks include backing up and restoring the registry and editing the registry.
- Choose the appropriate course of action to take to resolve printer problems.

- Choose the appropriate course of action to take to resolve RAS problems.

- Choose the appropriate course of action to take to resolve connectivity problems.

- Choose the appropriate course of action to take to resolve resource access and permission problems.

- Choose the appropriate course of action to take to resolve fault-tolerance failures. Fault-tolerance methods include: tape backup, mirroring, and stripe set with parity.

- Perform advanced problem resolution. Tasks include diagnosing and interpreting a blue screen, configuring a memory dump, and using the Event Log service.

# EXAM FACTS

| | |
|---|---|
| Number of questions on this exam: | 51 |
| Passing score: | 784 |
| Time allowed to take exam: | 90 minutes |

# EXAM OBJECTIVES CROSS–REFERENCE CHART FOR STUDY PURPOSES

Table C-1 lists the stated objectives for Exam 70-68, Implementing and Supporting Microsoft Windows NT Server 4.0 in the Enterprise, in a cross-reference chart for study purposes. Use this table to help you determine the specific chapters in this book that you should study, as well as the labs that you should perform, to prepare for the exam.

| TABLE C-1 NT SERVER IN THE ENTERPRISE EXAM OBJECTIVES CROSS-REFERENCE CHART | | |
|---|---|---|
| *EXAM OBJECTIVE* | *CHAPTER(S)* | *LAB(S) (IF APPLICABLE)* |
| **Planning** | | |
| Plan the implementation of a directory services architecture. Considerations include selecting the appropriate domain model, supporting a single logon account, and enabling users to access resources in different domains. | Chapter 10, pages 379–423<br><br>Chapter 1, pages 9–11 | Review Activity, pages 408–409<br><br>Lab 10.15<br><br>Lab 10.16 |
| Plan the disk drive configuration for various requirements. Requirements include choosing a fault-tolerance method. | Chapter 3, pages 69–99 | Review Activity, pages 111–112 |
| Choose a protocol for various situations. Protocols include TCP/IP, TCP/IP with DHCP and WINS, NWLink IPX/SPX Compatible Transport Protocol, Data Link Control (DLC), and AppleTalk. | Chapter 2, pages 40–42<br><br>Chapter 4, pages 132–137<br><br>Chapter 6, pages 211–215<br><br>Chapter 16, pages 585–595, 601–604<br><br>Chapter 17, pages 645–653<br><br>Chapter 20, pages 757 | None |
| **Installation and Configuration** | | |
| Install Windows NT Server to perform various server roles. Server roles include primary domain controller, backup domain controller, and member server. | Chapter 2, pages 36–38, 49<br>Chapter 4, pages 128–132 | Lab 2.2<br><br><br>Lab 10.15 |
| Configure protocols and protocol bindings. Protocols include TCP/IP, TCP/IP with DHCP and WINS, NWLink IPX/SPX Compatible Transport Protocol, DLC, and AppleTalk. | Chapter 4, pages 132–142<br><br>Chapter 16, pages 585–595, 601–604<br><br>Chapter 17, pages 650–653<br><br>Chapter 20, pages 757–761 | <br><br>Lab 16.25<br>Lab 16.27<br><br>Lab 17.30<br><br>Lab 20.33 |

| Exam Objective | Chapter(s) | Lab(s) (if applicable) |
| --- | --- | --- |
| Configure Windows NT Server core services. Services include Directory Replicator and Computer Browser. | Chapter 4 pages 144–148<br><br>Chapter 13, pages 521–524<br><br>Chapter 25, pages 912–914 | Lab 4.5<br><br>Lab 13.21 |
| Configure hard disks to meet various requirements. Requirements include providing redundancy and improving performance. | Chapter 3, pages 69–99 | Lab 3.3<br><br>Review Activities, pages 110–112 |
| Configure printers. Tasks include adding and configuring a printer, implementing a printer pool, and setting print priorities. | Chapter 6, pages 201–243 | Lab 6.8<br>Lab 6.9 |
| Configure a Windows NT Server computer for various types of client computers. Client computer types include Windows NT Workstation, Windows 95, and Macintosh. | Chapter 5, pages 175–182<br><br>Chapter 20, pages 755–774 | <br><br>Lab 20.33 |
| **Managing Resources** | | |
| Manage user and group accounts. Considerations include managing Windows NT user accounts, user rights, and groups; administering account policies; and auditing changes to the user account database. | Chapter 7, pages 261–301<br><br>Chapter 8, pages 305–331 | Lab 7.10<br><br>Lab 8.11<br>Lab 8.12 |
| Create and manage policies and profiles for various situations. Policies and profiles include local user profiles, roaming user profiles, and system policies. | Chapter 9, pages 335–359 | Lab 9.13<br><br>Lab 9.14 |
| Administer remote servers from various types of client computers. Client computer types include Windows 95 and Windows NT Workstation. | Chapter 14, pages 539–558 | Lab 14.23 |

*continued*

**TABLE C-1** *(continued)*

| EXAM OBJECTIVE | CHAPTER(S) | LAB(S) (IF APPLICABLE) |
|---|---|---|
| Manage disk resources. Tasks include creating and sharing resources, implementing permissions and security, and establishing file auditing. | Chapter 12, pages 451 – 489 | Lab 12.18<br>Lab 12.19 |

### Connectivity

| EXAM OBJECTIVE | CHAPTER(S) | LAB(S) (IF APPLICABLE) |
|---|---|---|
| Configure Windows NT Server for interoperability with NetWare servers by using various tools. Tools include Gateway Service for NetWare and Migration Tool for NetWare. | Chapter 17, pages 645 – 658, 662 – 672<br><br>Chapter 18, pages 685 – 704 | Lab 17.30 |
| Install and configure multiprotocol routing to serve various functions. Functions include Internet router, BOOTP/DHCP Relay Agent, and IPX router. | Chapter 16, pages 596 – 601<br><br>Chapter 17, pages 653 – 656 | Lab 16.27<br><br>Lab 17.31 |
| Install and configure Internet Information Server. | Chapter 16, pages 612 – 624 | Lab 16.26 |
| Install and configure Internet services. Services include World Wide Web, DNS, and Intranet. | Chapter 16, pages 604 – 624 | Lab 16.25<br>Lab 16.26 |
| Install and configure Remote Access Service (RAS). Configuration options include RAS communications, RAS protocols, and configuring RAS security. | Chapter 19, pages 707 – 729, 740 – 741 | Lab 19.32 |

### Monitoring and Optimization

| EXAM OBJECTIVE | CHAPTER(S) | LAB(S) (IF APPLICABLE) |
|---|---|---|
| Establish a baseline for measuring system performance. Tasks include creating a database of measurement data. | Chapter 24, pages 881 – 899 | None |

| Exam Objective (applicable) | Chapter(s) | Lab(s) (if |
|---|---|---|
| Monitor performance of various functions by using Performance Monitor. Functions include processor, memory, disk, and network. | Chapter 22, pages 809–845<br><br>Chapter 24, pages 885–893 | Lab 22.35 |
| Monitor network traffic by using Network Monitor. Tasks include collecting data, presenting data, and filtering data. | Chapter 23, pages 847–879<br><br>Chapter 24, pages 893–895 | Lab 23.36 |
| Identify performance bottlenecks. | Chapter 25, pages 903–921 | Lab 25.37 |
| Optimize performance for various results. Results include controlling network traffic and controlling server load. | Chapter 11, pages 427–447<br><br>Chapter 25, pages 901–921 | Lab 11.17<br><br><br>Lab 25.38 |

### Troubleshooting

| Exam Objective (applicable) | Chapter(s) | Lab(s) (if |
|---|---|---|
| Choose the appropriate course of action to take to resolve installation failures. | Chapter 2, pages 52–53<br><br>Chapter 26, pages 925–938 | Review Activity, page 56 |
| Choose the appropriate course of action to take to resolve boot failures. | Chapter 27, pages 941–949<br><br>Chapter 26, pages 925–938 | None |
| Choose the appropriate course of action to take to resolve configuration errors. Tasks include backing up and restoring the registry and editing the registry. | Chapter 4, pages 156–157<br><br>Chapter 15, pages 566–576<br><br>Chapter 27, pages 946–949, 960–970<br><br>Chapter 26, pages 925–938 | Lab 3.4<br><br>Lab 15.24<br><br>Lab 27.39 |
| Choose the appropriate course of action to take to resolve printer problems. | Chapter 6, pages 243–245<br><br>Chapter 26, pages 925–938 | Review Activity, pages 252–253 |
| Choose the appropriate course of action to take to resolve RAS problems. | Chapter 19, pages 742–743<br><br>Chapter 26, pages 925–938 | Review Activity, pages 748–749 |

*continued*

**TABLE C-1** *(continued)*

| EXAM OBJECTIVE | CHAPTER(S) | LAB(S) (IF APPLICABLE) |
|---|---|---|
| Choose the appropriate course of action to take to resolve connectivity problems. | Chapter 16, pages 626–627 | Lab 16.28 |
| | Chapter 17, pages 672–673 | |
| | Chapter 26, pages 925–938 | |
| Choose the appropriate course of action to take to resolve resource access problems and permission problems. | Chapter 12, page 490 | Lab 12.20 |
| | Chapter 26, pages 925–938 | |
| Choose the appropriate course of action to take to resolve fault-tolerance failures. Fault-tolerance methods include tape backup, mirroring, and stripe set with parity. | Chapter 3, pages 100–107 | Lab 3.4 |
| | Chapter 15, pages 559–579 | Lab 15.24 |
| | Chapter 27, pages 946–949, 963 | |
| | Chapter 26, pages 925–938 | |
| Perform advanced problem resolution. Tasks include diagnosing and interpreting a blue screen, configuring a memory dump, and using the Event Log service. | Chapter 27, pages 939–989 | Lab 27.39 |

# QUICK REFERENCE – CHAPTERS AND LABS THAT PREPARE YOU FOR THE WINDOWS NT SERVER 4.0 IN THE ENTERPRISE EXAM

Table C-2 lists the specific chapters you should read and study, as well as the labs that you should perform, to prepare for Exam 70-68, Implementing and Supporting Microsoft Windows NT Server 4.0 in the Enterprise. With the exception of Chapter 1, which provides basic Windows NT information, each of these chapters and labs corresponds directly to the exam objectives listed in the previous section.

**TABLE C-2** CHAPTERS AND LABS THAT PREPARE YOU FOR THE WINDOWS NT SERVER 4.0 IN THE ENTERPRISE EXAM

| CHAPTER NUMBER | CHAPTER TITLE | APPLICABLE LAB(S) IN THIS CHAPTER |
|---|---|---|
| Chapter 1 | Overview of Windows NT Workstation and Windows NT Server | None |
| Chapter 2 | Installing Windows NT Workstation and Windows NT Server | Lab 2.1 (Note: Lab 2.1 is not required to meet the exam objectives covered in this chapter; however, it is required to perform some of the later labs.) |
| | | Lab 2.2, Review Activity: Installing Windows NT troubleshooting practice exercise |
| Chapter 3 | Configuring Disks | Lab 3.3, Lab 3.4, Review Activities: File system planning exercise, Disk partitioning and fault tolerance planning exercise |
| Chapter 4 | Using Control Panel | Lab 4.5 |
| Chapter 5 | Server-Based Deployment | None |
| Chapter 6 | Managing Printing | Lab 6.8, Lab 6.9, Review Activity: Windows NT printing troubleshooting exercise |
| Chapter 7 | Managing User and Group Accounts | Lab 7.10 |
| Chapter 8 | Managing Account Policy, User Rights, and Auditing | Lab 8.11, Lab 8.12 |
| Chapter 9 | Managing User Profiles and System Policy | Lab 9.13, Lab 9.14 |
| Chapter 10 | Managing Windows NT Directory Services | Lab 10.15, Lab 10.16, Review Activity: Planning network administration in a multiple master domain environment exercise |
| Chapter 11 | Optimizing Windows NT Server Directory Services | Lab 11.17 |
| Chapter 12 | Sharing and Securing File Systems | Lab 12.18, Lab 12.19, Lab 12.20 |

*continued*

**TABLE C-2** *(continued)*

| *Chapter Number* | *Chapter Title* | *Applicable Lab(s) in This Chapter* |
| --- | --- | --- |
| Chapter 13 | Accessing Resources on the Network | Lab 13.21, Lab 13.22 |
| Chapter 14 | Using Windows NT Server Tools | Lab 14.23 |
| Chapter 15 | Backing Up and Restoring Data | Lab 15.24 |
| Chapter 16 | Networking Using TCP/IP | Lab 16.25, Lab 16.26, Lab 16.27, Lab 16.28 |
| Chapter 17 | Coexistence with NetWare | Lab 17.30, Lab 17.31 |
| Chapter 18 | Migrating to Windows NT from NetWare | None |
| Chapter 19 | Installing and Configuring Remote Access Service (RAS) | Lab 19.32, Review Activity: Troubleshooting common RAS problems |
| Chapter 20 | Macintosh Connectivity | Lab 20.33 |
| Chapter 22 | Using Performance Monitor | Lab 22.35 |
| Chapter 23 | Using Network Monitor | Lab 23.36 |
| Chapter 24 | Capacity Planning | None |
| Chapter 25 | Performance Optimization | Lab 25.37, Lab 25.38 |
| Chapter 26 | The Troubleshooting Process | None |
| Chapter 27 | Advanced Troubleshooting Topics | Lab 27.39 |

# Answers to Instant Assessment Questions, Review Activities, and Hands-on Labs

## CHAPTER 1: OVERVIEW OF WINDOWS NT WORKSTATION AND WINDOWS NT SERVER

### Answers to Instant Assessment

1. Windows NT Workstation

2. Windows NT Server

3. Workgroup

4. Domain

5. Kernel mode

6. A virtual memory model

7. See Figure D-1 (on the following page) for answers.

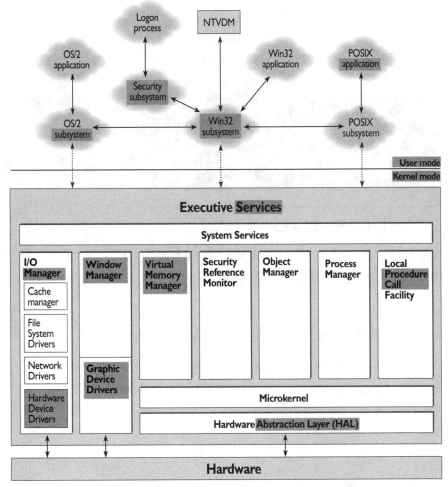

**FIGURE D-1** Answers to Windows NT 4.0 modular architecture review activity

# Chapter 2: Installing Windows NT Workstation and Windows NT Server

## Answers to Instant Assessment

1. 486/33 processor with 12MB of RAM and 117MB of free hard disk space

2. 486/33 processor with 16MB of RAM and 124MB of free hard disk space

3. The NTHQ is the NT Hardware Qualifier utility. It is used to examine and identify a computer's hardware configuration.

4. Windows NT 4.0 will automatically configure itself to dual boot between Windows NT 4.0 and the previously installed operating system.

5. The system partition

6. The boot partition

7. FAT and NTFS

8. Windows NT

9. `Winnt.exe`

# Answers to Review Activity

## *Installing Windows NT troubleshooting practice exercise*

**Problem 1**    Some possible causes of this problem are hardware conflicts (or incompatibilities), a corrupt boot sector, or a boot sector virus.

Possible courses of action you could take to resolve this problem include using the NTHQ to examine your hardware configuration, checking for two pieces of hardware with the same settings (same I/O Port, interrupt, and so on) and reconfiguring hardware if conflicts are found, and repairing the boot sector by using `Fdisk/mbr` from MS-DOS or by using a virus detection utility.

**Problem 2**    Probably the most common cause of this problem is that the domain name or the Administrator's user account name or password has been typed incorrectly, or typed in the wrong case. *Remember that all passwords in Windows NT are case-sensitive.* Is the Caps Lock key on? Other possible causes of this problem are incorrect network hardware or software settings, a bad cable or connection, or a PDC that is inaccessible.

Possible courses of action you could take to resolve this problem include: retyping the domain name, Administrator's user account name or password (making sure to use the proper case and making sure the Caps Lock key is turned off); and ensuring that all network hardware and software settings are correct. You might also check the network cable and connections, and verify that the PDC is up and accessible on the network.

## CHAPTER 3: CONFIGURING DISKS

### Answers to Instant Assessment

1. The FAT (File Allocation Table) file system, the Windows NT file system (NTFS), and the Compact Disc Filing System (CDFS)

2. The FAT file system

3. Converting a FAT partition to NTFS

4. From the active primary partition on the first hard disk in the computer

5. On the active primary partition on the first hard disk in the computer

6. You can have up to four primary partitions on one disk, only one extended partition, and a maximum total of four partitions on a disk.

7. Disk Administrator

8. Disk mirroring

9. A fault tolerance boot disk is used to boot a computer after one hard disk in a mirrored set fails.

10. The boot loader section and the operating systems section

11. Stripe sets

12. Stripe sets and volume sets

13. Striping with parity, because it is faster and cheaper than disk mirroring, and provides a modest level of data safety

14. Disk mirroring

15. Rdisk.exe

16. Break the mirror

17. False

18. True

19. False

20. True

21. True

22. False

**23.** False

**24.** True

**25.** True

**26.** False

**27.** False

# Answers to Review Activities

## File system planning exercise

**Problem 1**   The FAT file system is probably the best choice for this scenario, because it enables NT to access files on partitions smaller than 500MB faster than it could by using NTFS.

**Problem 2**   You must use the FAT file system in this situation in order to accommodate both NT and MS-DOS.

**Problem 3**   NTFS is probably the best choice for this scenario. NTFS usually provides faster access to files stored on a large partition that contains a large number of files than the FAT file system provides.

**Problem 4**   NTFS is the obvious choice for this scenario because it is the only file system supported by Windows NT 4.0 that provides the required file and folder security and also supports file compression.

## Disk partitioning and fault tolerance planning exercise

**Problem 1**   Disk mirroring is the best answer because it provides the most fault tolerance of the four disk partitioning schemes.

**Problem 2**   A stripe set is the best answer because it provides the fastest access speed to files.

**Problem 3**   A stripe set with parity is the best choice, because it provides moderate fault tolerance and a moderate price tag.

# CHAPTER 4: USING CONTROL PANEL

## Answers to Instant Assessment

1. Select Start ⟹ Settings ⟹ Control Panel, or Select Control Panel in Windows NT Explorer, or Open the My Computer dialog box, then double-click Control Panel.

2. The Accessibility Options application is used to configure the keyboard, sound, and mouse options on a computer to accommodate users that are physically challenged, including persons who have difficulty striking multiple keys simultaneously on a keyboard, persons with hearing disabilities, or persons who have difficulty holding or clicking a mouse.

3. Display

4. You must change the domain name of all other domain controllers member servers, and Windows NT Workstation computers in that domain to match the new domain name that you have assigned.

5. NWLink IPX/SPX Compatible Transport

6. AppleTalk Protocol

7. TCP/IP Protocol

8. The protocol and service used most often should be at the *top* of their respective lists.

9. Here are the four steps to configure the Directory Replicator service:

   o Create and configure a user account for the Directory Replicator service by using User Manager for Domains. This account must be a member of the Backup Operators group and the Replicator group. This user account must also be granted the "Log on as a service" user right, and must be configured so that its password never expires.

   o Configure the startup type of the Directory Replicator service as Automatic (by using the Services application). Configure the Directory Replicator service to log on using the user account created in Step 1.

- Configure replication by using the Server application. Remember that the PDC should be configured to replicate to itself.
- Stop and restart the Directory Replicator service by using the Services application.

10. At least as large as the amount of RAM in your computer

11. System

12. Make sure that all steps in a configuration process have been completed, verify that all configuration options are set correctly, and ensure that hardware devices do not have conflicting interrupt, I/O port address, or DMA addresses.

13. True

## Answers to Review Activity

### *Control Panel application matching exercise*

The correct answers are:

1. B
2. F
3. J
4. I
5. N
6. N
7. N
8. V
9. U
10. X
11. X
12. X

# CHAPTER 5: SERVER-BASED DEPLOYMENT

## Answers to Instant Assessment

1. Server-based deployment involves automating the installation and setup of Windows NT and/or other operating systems (Windows 95 and Windows for Workgroups) and applications on multiple computers on a network.

2. To save time

3. First, original equipment manufacturers (OEMs) use server-based deployment to install and configure large numbers of computers at the factory. Second, organizations that install a new network or add several new computers to their existing network use server-based deployment to efficiently perform these tasks.

4. The `Clients` folder

5. You must create a subfolder in the `Clients` folder named `Winnt`. Then you must create a subfolder in the `Clients\Winnt` folder named `Netsetup`.

6. You must create a subfolder in the `Clients` folder named `Winnt.srv`. Then you must create a subfolder in the `Clients\Winnt.srv` folder named `Netsetup`.

7. An installation disk set

8. A network installation startup disk

9. An answer file is a text file that contains stylized responses to the queries posed by the Windows NT Setup program during installation.

10. By using Windows NT Setup Manager (`Setupmgr.exe`)

11. The `/U` switch

12. Setup Manager is located on the Windows NT Server (or Windows NT Workstation) compact disc. You can find it in the `\Support\Deptools\i386` folder (on Intel-based computers).

13. Replace

14. You need a different answer file for *each* hardware configuration, so you need as many answer files as you have different hardware configurations.

15. The `$OEM$` subfolder

**16.** The answer file

**17.** When run with the /snap switch, Sysdiff.exe takes a snapshot of a typical target computer's current configuration after Windows NT is installed but before any applications are installed.

When run with the /diff switch after the desired application is installed, Sysdiff.exe creates a difference file that contains all of the application files and registry changes.

When run with the /apply switch from the Cmdlines.txt file, Sysdiff.exe applies the difference file during an unattended Windows NT installation.

# CHAPTER 6: MANAGING PRINTING

## Answers to Instant Assessment

**1.** A printer is the software interface between Windows NT and the device that produces the printed output.

**2.** A print (or printing) device is the physical hardware device that produces the printed output.

**3.** The spooler

**4.** Create, connect to

**5.** Print monitors

**6.** The TCP/IP print monitor

**7.** NWLink IPX/SPX Compatible Transport, plus: Client Service for NetWare (on a Windows NT Workstation computer) or Gateway Service for NetWare (on a Windows NT Server computer)

**8.** Hpmon

**9.** A job-based connection enables all computers on the network to access an HP JetDirect adapter for printing, because the connection to the HP JetDirect adapter is dropped after each print job.

10. A continuous connection does not permit any other computer on the network to access an HP JetDirect adapter for printing, because the Hpmon print monitor monopolizes the HP JetDirect adapter when a continuous connection is used.

11. Hpmon

12. You can specify that a different folder on another partition (that has more free space) be used as your spool folder.

13. No Access

14. No Access, Print, Manage Documents, Full Control

15. You must select the Success and/or Failure check boxes for File and Object Access.

16. By creating a printer

    By taking ownership of a printer

17. A printer pool

18. The purpose of sharing a printer is to enable users of other computers on the network to connect to and send print jobs to that printer.

19. The advantage is that the network administrator is spared the time-consuming task of manually installing printer drivers on every computer on the network.

20. True

21. True

22. True

## Answers to Review Activity

### *Windows NT printing troubleshooting exercise*

**Problem 1**    To reprint the entire print job:

1. Immediately double-click the printer in the `Printers` folder.

2. When the printer's dialog box appears, select Document ⇒ Pause.

3. Make sure that the correct paper is in the paper tray.

4. Select Document ⇒ Restart to reprint the entire print job.

**Problem 2**  The most likely cause of this problem is that the success and failure options for auditing file and object access have not been configured in User Manager for Domains or User Manager. Auditing of printers requires that auditing of file and object access be configured.

To solve the problem, configure these options in User Manager for Domains or User Manager. Print events should begin to appear in the security log in Event Viewer.

**Problem 3**  The most likely cause of this problem is that the partition that contains the printer's spool folder doesn't have enough free space.

To solve the problem, you can delete some files from this partition, or move the spool folder to a different partition that has more free space.

# CHAPTER 7: MANAGING USER AND GROUP ACCOUNTS

## Answers to Instant Assessment

1. Administrator and Guest
2. User Manager (on a Windows NT Workstation computer) or User Manager for Domains (on a Windows NT Server computer)
3. Use the first seven letters of the user's first name, plus the first letter of the user's last name.

   Use the first letter of the user's first name, plus the first seven letters of the user's last name.
4. You can delete user-created groups, but you can't delete built-in or special groups.
5. Groups, Profile, Hours, Logon To, Account, and Dialin
6. %USERNAME%

7. Create a user account to be used as a template.

8. The primary purpose of local groups is to control access to resources.

   The primary purpose of global groups is to organize users that perform similar tasks or have similar network access requirements.

9. Local groups can be created on any Windows NT computer.

   A global group can only be created on a domain controller.

10. First, create a local group and assign the local group permission to the shared folder. Then, make individual user accounts and/or global groups members of the local group that you created. The result is that all members of the local group will have permission to the shared folder.

11. The built-in local groups on domain controllers are: Administrators, Backup Operators, Guests, Replicator, Users, Account Operators, Printer Operators, and Server Operators.

    The built-in global groups on domain controllers are: Domain Admins, Domain Users, and Domain Guests.

12. The built-in local groups on non-domain controllers are: Administrators, Backup Operators, Guests, Replicator, Users, and Power Users.

13. The five special groups are: Everyone, Interactive, Network, System, and Creator Owner.

14. It's important to limit the permissions assigned to the Everyone group, especially if your computer is connected to the Internet, because everyone includes all users accessing your computer by using authorized user accounts, as well as unauthorized users who accidentally or intentionally breach your system security—this even includes individuals who access your computer via the Internet.

15. No groups can be renamed.

16. False

# CHAPTER 8: MANAGING ACCOUNT POLICY, USER RIGHTS, AND AUDITING

## Answers to Instant Assessment

1. The Password Restrictions section, and the Account lockout section

2. Select Start ⇒ Programs ⇒ Administrative Tools (Common) ⇒ User Manager (or User Manager for Domains).

   Then, in the User Manager dialog box, select Policies ⇒ Account.

3. Expires in 42 Days

4. The Minimum Password Age configuration determines the minimum number of days a user must keep the same password.

5. The possible settings are from one to fourteen characters.

   The author's recommended setting is a minimum of eight characters.

6. The Password Uniqueness configuration specifies how many different passwords a user must use before an old password can be reused.

7. The Account lockout section of the Account Policy dialog box specifies how Windows NT treats user accounts after several successive unsuccessful logon attempts have occurred.

8. The Administrators local group

9. User rights allow users to perform certain tasks; whereas permissions allow users to access objects, such as files, folders, and printers.

10. Auditing produces a log of specified events and activities that occur on a Windows NT computer.

11. Event Viewer

12. You must also configure file, folder, or printer auditing (which is set in Windows NT Explorer or in a printer's Properties dialog box.)

13. Logon and Logoff; File and Object Access; Use of User Rights, User and Group Management; Security Policy Changes; Restart, Shutdown, and System; and Process Tracking

14. False

15. True

# CHAPTER 9: MANAGING USER PROFILES AND SYSTEM POLICY

## Answers to Instant Assessment

1. In Windows NT, a user profile is a collection of settings and options that specify a user's desktop environment and all other user-definable settings for a user's work environment.

2. A user profile is normally stored in a subfolder of the `<winntroot>\ Profiles` folder.

3. The subfolders contained in a user profile folder include: `Application Data`, `Desktop`, `Favorites`, `NetHood`, `Personal`, `PrintHood`, `Recent`, `SendTo`, `Start Menu`, and `Templates`. The files contained in a user profile folder include `Ntuser.dat` and `ntuser.dat.LOG`.

4. The System application in Control Panel

5. Windows NT Explorer

6. Create a domain-wide `Default User` profile folder on the `Netlogon` share on the PDC.

7. A roaming user profile is a user profile that is stored on a server, and is available to a user regardless of which Windows NT computer on the network the user logs onto. Roaming profiles enable users to retain their own customized desktop and work environment settings even though they may use different Windows NT computers.

8. A logon script is a batch file or executable file that runs during a user's logon process.

9. A mandatory user profile is a user profile that, when assigned to a user, cannot be changed by the user.

10. When "problem users" require a significant amount of administrator time
    When an administrator has a large number of users with similar job tasks to administer

11. The `Ntuser.dat` file must be renamed as `Ntuser.man`.

12. The System application in Control Panel

13. The Windows NT system policy file is an Administrator-created collection of user, group, and computer policies that restrict the user's ability to perform certain tasks on any Windows NT computer that the user logs on to. System policy can also be used to enforce certain mandatory display settings.

14. System Policy Editor

15. In the `Netlogon` share on each domain controller

16. Individual user policies and the Default User policy

17. The last group policy applied (which is the group policy of the group that has the highest priority)

18. SusanH's individual user policy

19. Individual computer policies and the Default Computer policy

20. The Default Computer policy

21. False

# CHAPTER 10: MANAGING WINDOWS NT DIRECTORY SERVICES

## Answers to Instant Assessment

1. Windows NT Directory Services is a Microsoft catchall phrase that refers to the architecture, features, functionality, and benefits of Windows NT domains and trust relationships.

2. The primary benefits of Windows NT Directory Services are:

   A single user account logon and password are used to gain access to all shared resources on the network; and,

   User and group accounts, as well as shared network resources, can be managed from a central location.

3. The *trusting* domain is the domain that contains the shared resources, and the *trusted* domain is the domain that contains the user accounts.

4. A one-way trust

**5.** A two-way trust

**6.** User Manager for Domains

**7.** Trust relationships are non-transitive—which means that they apply only to the domains they are established between.

**8.** In the logon process, a user enters a user name, password, and domain name in the Logon Information dialog box. The local NetLogon Service determines whether the user account is located in the local computer's Security Accounts Manager (SAM) database. If the user account is found to be valid by the local SAM, the NetLogon Service retrieves the user account's security identifier (SID), and the SIDs for each group that the user is a member of. The NetLogon Service combines the user and group SIDs to create an access token, and then completes the logon process for the user.

**9.** Pass-through authentication

**10.** During the logon process, a user enters a user name, password, and domain name in the Logon Information dialog box. The local NetLogon Service determines whether the user account is located in the local computer's Security Accounts Manager (SAM) database. When a user account can't be validated on the local computer (as is the case in this situation, where a user account from the domain is used), the NetLogon Service on the local computer forwards (passes-through) the logon request to the NetLogon Service on a Windows NT Server domain controller for validation. The domain controller validates the user account and passes the appropriate SIDs back to the local NetLogon Service to complete the logon process.

**11.** Synchronization

**12.** Factors to consider when planning a Directory Services architecture include: the number and location of users; the number, types and location of computers and shared resources; whether centralized or decentralized network management is desired; and the needs of various departments within the organization.

**13.** Multiple master domain model

**14.** Single master domain model

**15.** Single domain model

**16.** Complete trust domain model

**17.** Probably the single domain model

**18.** Probably the multiple master domain model (neither the single domain model nor the single master domain model will accommodate more than 40,000 user accounts)

**19.** Groups are commonly used in the following way in a multiple domain environment:

- First, *user accounts* are placed into a *global group* in the trusted domain;

- Next, this *global group*, which can cross trust relationships to other domains, is made a member of a *local group* in the trusting domain;

- Finally, the *local group* in the trusting domain is assigned *permissions to a shared resource*, so that all of its members can access the shared resource.

**20.** True

## Answers to Review Activity

### *Planning network administration in a multiple master domain environment exercise*

*Note: The two new global groups can have any names you want to assign.*

New global group in PHOENIXMASTERA domain: **PhoenixAdminA**

New global group in PHOENIXMASTERB domain: **PhoenixAdminB**

Built-in local group in each domain in which you will place the two new global groups:

**Administrators** — (This allows members of the PhoenixAdminA and PhoenixAdminB global groups to fully administer users, groups, and shared resources on the domain controllers in all six domains.)

Built-in local group on every member server in all six domains in which you will place the two new global groups:

**Administrators** — (This allows members of the PhoenixAdminA and PhoenixAdminB global groups to fully administer users, groups, and shared resources on the member servers in all six domains.)

Built-in local group on every Windows NT Workstation computer in all six domains in which you will place the two new global groups:

**Administrators**—(This allows members of the PhoenixAdminA and PhoenixAdminB global groups to fully administer users, groups, and shared resources on the Windows NT Workstation computers in all six domains.)

# Answers to Lab

## Lab 10.16: Planning a Directory Services architecture

*Note: The answers to these exercises are suggested solutions only. There are often many ways to design a Directory Services architecture for a given situation. What is important is that you understand the Directory Services architecture models and trust relationships.*

### Exercise 1

**1.** Given the scenario, the most appropriate Directory Services architecture is the *single master domain model*. Using a single master domain model enables the MIS department in New York City to manage all user accounts for all locations, and also enables the local network managers total control over local network resources. Network managers at one location will not be able to manage resources from other locations.

A single domain model could be used. However, the drawback to using the single domain model in this situation is that network managers at each location would be able to manage resources from all other locations, as well.

**2.** To create the single master domain model for this situation, I would create five domains named NYC, PARIS, LONDON, SEATTLE, and MEXICO_CITY. NYC would be the master domain, and would contain all user accounts for all locations.

I would then create the following one-way trust relationships:

    SEATTLE trusts NYC
    MEXICO_CITY trusts NYC
    LONDON trusts NYC
    PARIS trusts NYC

Figure A-2 is a diagram that depicts the trust relationships recommended for this single master domain model:

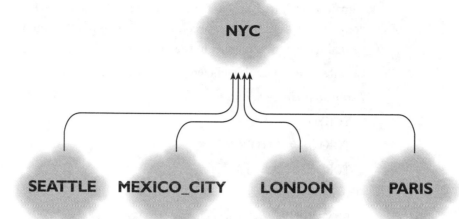

**FIGURE D-2** **Recommended trust relationships for Worldwide Promotions, Inc.**

**Exercise 2**

**1.** Given the scenario, the most appropriate Directory Services architecture is the *multiple master domain model*. This model is the only practical model that will accommodate 46,000 users. Using a multiple master domain model enables the Data Processing and Computer Services department in Toronto to manage all user accounts for all locations, and also enables the local network managers total control over local network resources.

A complete trust domain model could be used. However, the drawback to using the complete trust domain model in this situation is that the number of trust relationships needed is excessive and cumbersome.

**2.** To create the multiple master domain model for this situation, I would create ten domains named TORONTO, LA, TOKYO, RIO, MIAMI, BOMBAY, JOHANNESBURG, SYDNEY, HK, and BANGKOK.

TORONTO, LA, and TOKYO will be the master domains. The TORONTO domain will contain user accounts for TORONTO, BOMBAY, and JOHANNESBURG. The LA domain will contain user accounts for LA, SYDNEY, RIO, and MIAMI. The TOKYO domain will contain user accounts for TOKYO, BANGKOK, and HK.

Because Import International, Ltd. will be using the multiple master domain model, user accounts contained in the TORONTO, LA, and TOKYO domains (for example, user accounts for all users in the company) can all be maintained by personnel in the TORONTO office.

I would then create the following trust relationships:

*Two-way trusts between:*

    TOKYO  <-->  LA

    TOKYO  <-->  TORONTO

    TORONTO  <-->  LA

*One-way trusts:*

    BANGKOK trusts TOKYO, LA, and TORONTO

    HK trusts TOKYO, LA, and TORONTO

    SYDNEY trusts TOKYO, LA, and TORONTO

    MIAMI trusts TOKYO, LA, and TORONTO

    RIO trusts TOKYO, LA, and TORONTO

    JOHANNESBURG trusts TOKYO, LA, and TORONTO

    BOMBAY trusts TOKYO, LA, and TORONTO

Figure D-3 is a diagram that depicts the trust relationships recommended for this multiple master domain model:

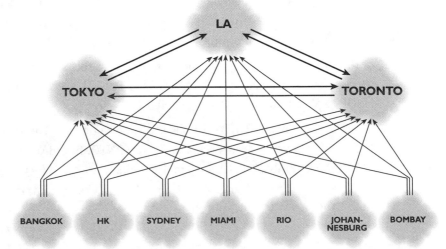

**FIGURE D-3 Recommended trust relationships for Import International, Ltd.**

# CHAPTER 11: OPTIMIZING WINDOWS NT SERVER DIRECTORY SERVICES

## Answers to Instant Assessment

1. 40MB (40,000KB)

2. Each user account requires 1,024 bytes (1KB).

   Each computer account requires 512 bytes (.5KB).

   Each local group account requires 512 bytes (.5KB) for the group, *plus* 36 bytes for each member of the group.

   Each global group account requires 512 bytes (.5KB) for the group, *plus* 12 bytes for each member of the group.

3. Size of Directory Services database, in KB, = Number of user accounts + (.5 × number of computer accounts) + (3 × total number of groups)

4. 

| | |
|---|---:|
| Number of user accounts | 21,000 |
| .5 × number of computer accounts | 12,000 |
| 3 × total number of groups | 1,200 |
| Total size of Directory Services database: | 34,200KB |

5. 20MB (20,000KB)

6. 40MB (40,000KB)

7. 1 PDC and 1 BDC

8. 2,000

9. The key point in optimizing BDC placement is the location of users that require logon validation, especially when you want to eliminate logon traffic across a WAN link.

10. 64KB

11. Approximately 2,000

12. The change log is stored in the Windows NT Registry in:
    `HKEY_LOCAL_MACHINE\SYSTEM\CurrentControlSet\Services`
    `\Netlogon\Parameters\ChangeLogSize`

13. Registry Editor

14. The ReplicationGovernor is stored in the Windows NT Registry in:
    `HKEY_LOCAL_MACHINE\SYSTEM\CurrentControlSet\Services`
    `\Netlogon\Parameters\ReplicationGovernor`

15. Stop and restart the NetLogon service

16. 100

17. The ReplicationGovernor controls the size of the synchronization buffer and how frequently the BDC requests Directory Services database updates from the PDC.

18. The ReplicationGovernor is configured individually on each BDC, *not* on the PDC.

# Answers to Lab

## *Lab 11.17: Optimizing WAN link performance by the appropriate placement of BDCs*

| CORRECT NUMBER OF BDCs, BY LOCATION | |
| --- | --- |
| *LOCATION* | *# OF BDCs* |
| Denver | 3 |
| Las Vegas | 2 |
| Salt Lake City | 2 |
| Albuquerque | 1 |

Remember, the goal of this lab is to optimize the WAN for *efficient local user logon and authentication*. To do this, you must eliminate logon and authentication traffic from the WAN links. The numbers of BDCs in the answer are based on the fact that each BDC can accommodate up to 2,000 users.

# CHAPTER 12: SHARING AND SECURING FILE SYSTEMS

## Answers to Instant Assessment

1. Read-only

2. Compress

3. The purpose of sharing folders is to make it possible for users to access network resources.

4. No Access, Read, Change, and Full Control

5. No Access

6. Full Control

7. No Access

8. The Windows NT administrative shares are the hidden shares that Windows NT automatically creates every time you start NT on a computer. Only members of the Administrators group have permission to access these shares. The administrative shares are: C$, D$, E$, and so on (one share for the root of each hard disk partition on the computer), and Admin$ (which corresponds to the folder that NT is installed in).

9. Any share can be configured as a hidden share by appending a $ to the share name.

10. NTFS permissions provide a greater level of security than share permissions because:

    NTFS permissions can be assigned to individual files and folders, and

    NTFS permissions apply to local users as well as to users who connect to a shared folder over-the-network.

11. The NTFS permissions are: Read (R), Write (W), Execute (E), Delete (D), Change Permissions (P), and Take Ownership (O).

12. The standard NTFS directory (folder) permissions are: No Access (None) (None), List (RX) (Not Specified), Read (RX) (RX), Add (WX) (Not Specified), Add and Read (RWX) (RX), Change (RWXD) (RWXD), and Full Control (All) (All).

13. The standard NTFS file permissions are No Access (None), Read (RX), Change (RWXD), and Full Control (All).

14. File permissions

15. The new file inherits the NTFS permissions of the folder that contains the new file.

16. Destination

17. The file retains its original NTFS permissions.

18. The *most* restrictive permission

19. The user who created it (except that when a member of the Administrators group creates a file or folder, the Administrators *group*, not the user, is the owner of the file or folder)

20. A user might want to take ownership of a file or folder if the user wanted to assign or change permissions on the file or folder, but wasn't the owner of the file or folder and didn't have the Change Permissions NTFS permission (or the Full Control permission, which includes the Change Permissions NTFS permission) to the file or folder.

21. First, the audit policy is configured in User Manager or User Manager for Domains. Then, auditing is configured for each file and folder individually by using Windows NT Explorer.

22. You must select success and/or failure auditing of File and Object access in order to audit files and folders.

23. Event Viewer

24. Most resource access problems are caused by incorrectly configured and/or conflicting permissions.

25. False

26. True

27. False

28. True

29. False

# Answers to Labs

## *Lab 12.18: Sharing and securing resources*

Suggested answer:

| Resource | Share Name | Share Permissions Applied | | NTFS Permissions Applied | |
|----------|-----------|----------|----------|----------|----------|
| | | User/Group | Permission | User/Group | Permission |
| D:\Data\Sales | SalesData | Domain Users | Full Control | Sales<br>Admin-istrators | Change<br>Full Control |
| C:\Apps\Word | Word | Domain Users | Read | N/A | N/A |
| C:\Apps\Excel | Excel | Domain Users | Read | N/A | N/A |
| C:\Apps\Access | Access | Domain Users | Read | N/A | N/A |
| D:\Data\ Managers | ManagersData | Domain Users | Full Control | Managers<br>Admin-istrators | Change<br>Full Control |
| D:\Data\ Accounting | AccountingData | Domain Users | Full Control | Accounting<br>Admin-istrators | Change<br>Full Control |
| D:\Data\ All Users | AllUsersData | Domain Users | Full Control | Domain Users<br>Admin-istrators | Change<br>Full Control |

### Lab 12.20: Troubleshooting resource access and permission problems

The following are the causes and suggested solutions to resolve the given problems.

**Problem 1**   The cause of the problem is that the Everyone group is assigned the Read permission for the `AccountingData` share. *When share permissions combine with NTFS permissions, the most restrictive permission applies.* Even though NancyY is a member of the Accounting group and the Accounting group has the NTFS Change permission, NancyY's effective permission is limited to the Read permission because of the share permission.

To resolve the problem, assign the Everyone group the Full Control share permission for the `AccountingData` share. Access to this share will then be controlled by NTFS permissions.

**Problem 2**   The cause of the problem is that JohnS is a member of the Sales group, which has been assigned the No Access NTFS permission for the `D:\Data\Managers` folder. Even though JohnS is appropriately a member of the Managers group, which has been assigned the NTFS Change permission for the `D:\Data\Managers` folder, *when the NTFS No Access permission is assigned to any group the user is a member of, the user's effective permission is always No Access.*

To resolve the problem, remove the Sales group from the Name list box in the Directory Permissions dialog box.

# CHAPTER 13: ACCESSING RESOURCES ON THE NETWORK

## Answers to Instant Assessment

1. The Computer Browser service
2. A browse list
3. Domain master browser, master browser, backup browser, potential browser, and non-browser
4. The PDC

**5.** One

**6.** Computers can be non-browsers either because they are configured to not function as a browser, or because their network software does not provide them with the capability to maintain a browse list.

**7.** How a browse list is built and maintained:

- When a master browser first comes online, its browse list is empty. To build its browse list initially, the master browser sends a broadcast to all computers on the subnet requesting that all network servers announce their presence. (Remember for the purpose of discussing browsing in this chapter, *network servers include all computers that either have shared resources, or are capable of sharing their resources*.)

- All available network servers respond to this request by announcing their presence, within thirty seconds. The master browser incorporates this information into its initial browse list. The master browser then distributes this browse list to the domain master browser and to the backup browsers.

- After initial creation of the browse list, when a Windows computer that functions as a network server is first booted, it broadcasts its presence to the network. The master browser receives this announcement and places the information in its browse list.

- During normal operations, a Windows computer that functions as a network server continues to announce its presence to the network every twelve minutes. If the master browser does *not* receive a broadcast from a network server after three consecutive twelve-minute time periods, it removes the computer from its browse list.

- (This is how the master browser maintains its browse list — it assumes that all network servers in its initial browse list are available until it fails to receive a broadcast announcement from a computer for three consecutive twelve-minute periods, at which time it updates its browse list by removing this computer from its list. Therefore, it is possible for a network server to remain on the browse list for some time after it is no longer available to network users.)

- During normal operations, backup browsers request an updated browse list from the master browser every twelve minutes. If the master browser does not respond to an update request from the backup browser, the backup browser initiates the master browser election process (covered in more detail in the next section of this chapter).

- During normal operations, the master browser sends an updated browse list to the domain master browser every twelve minutes. The domain master browser, in response, sends an updated domain browse list to the master browser. Additionally, every fifteen minutes, the master browser announces its presence to master browsers of other workgroups and domains located on the same subnet.

8. When a user browses the network:

- When a user of a Windows NT computer attempts to access browse information by double-clicking Network Neighborhood or by selecting Tools ⇒ Map Network Drive in Windows NT Explorer, the user's computer contacts the master browser and retrieves a list of available backup browsers.

- (This step occurs only the first time a user accesses browse information—the Computer Browser service on the local computer then retains the list of available backup browsers until the computer is rebooted or until the backup browsers on the list are no longer available.)

- The user's computer then contacts a backup browser to request a list of available network servers. The backup browser processes this request and returns a list of available network servers in the requesting computer's workgroup or domain, plus a list of available workgroups and domains. The user's computer then displays this information to the user.

- If the user selects an available network server, the user's computer contacts the selected server and requests a list of shared network resources. The selected server then sends a list of shared resources to the requesting computer, which is then displayed for the user.

- If the user selects an available workgroup or domain, the user's computer contacts the master browser in the selected workgroup or domain and requests a browse list. The master browser sends a list of

> backup browsers for the workgroup or domain to the requesting computer. Then the user's computer contacts a backup browser in the selected workgroup or domain for a list of available network servers, which is then returned by the backup browser to the requesting computer and displayed for the user. The user then selects an available network server, and the user's computer contacts the selected server and requests a list of shared network resources. The selected server then sends a list of shared resources to the requesting computer, which is displayed for the user.
>
> o The user selects the specific shared resource he or she wants to access from the list that is displayed.

9. Because the master browser does not remove a network server from its browse list until *after* it has failed to receive a broadcast announcement from the network server for three consecutive twelve-minute periods, *it is possible for a network server to remain on the browse list for some time after it is no longer available to network users*. This could result in a situation where a user sees a resource on a browse list that is no longer available.

10. The master browser

11. The computer's election criteria value

12. The MaintainServerList entry, which is located in \HKEY_LOCAL_MACHINE\ SYSTEM\CurrentControlSet\Services\Browser\Parameters

13. The IsDomainMaster entry, which is located in \HKEY_LOCAL_MACHINE\ SYSTEM\CurrentControlSet\Services\Browser\Parameters

14. NetBIOS broadcasts

15. LMHOSTS files or a WINS server

16. \\Server_name\Share_name\Subfolder_name\File_name

17. Server_name.Domain_name.Root_domain_name

18. You can replace the Server_name in a UNC with an FQDN (if your network uses TCP/IP and DNS servers).

19. True

# CHAPTER 14: USING WINDOWS NT SERVER TOOLS

## Answers to Instant Assessment

1. The primary purpose of Windows NT Server tools is to enable a user at a client computer to manage an NT Server computer remotely on the network.

2. The Windows NT Server tools that can be installed on a Windows 95 client computer are: User Manager for Domains, Server Manager, Event Viewer, and security extensions for Windows Explorer to manage file and printer security on a remote Windows NT Server.

3. The Windows NT Server tools that can be installed on a Windows NT Workstation computer are: User Manager for Domains, Server Manager, System Policy Editor, Remote Access Admin, DHCP Administrator, WINS Manager, and Remoteboot Manager.

4. The minimum RAM required to install and run NT Server tools on a Windows 95 computer is 8MB.

   The minimum RAM required to install and run NT Server tools on a Windows NT Workstation computer is 12MB.

5. Server Manager

6. Server Manager

7. User Manager for Domains

8. Server Manager

9. Windows Explorer—use the added Security tabs on the file, folder, and printer Properties dialog boxes

# CHAPTER 15: BACKING UP AND RESTORING DATA

## Answers to Instant Assessment

1. Windows NT Backup

2. The archive attribute is a marker that the operating system automatically assigns to all files and folders when they are first installed or created. Depending on the backup type, backup programs *remove* the archive attribute from a file or folder to indicate that the file or folder has been backed up. If a file or folder is modified after it has been backed up, the operating system reassigns the archive attribute to it.

3. There are five standard types of backups:

   **Normal (full):** backs up all selected files and folders, and removes the archive attribute from the backed up files and folders.

   **Differential:** backs up all selected files and folders that have changed since the last normal backup, and does *not* remove the archive attribute from files or folders. A differential backup is a *cumulative* backup, and because of this fact, takes more time to perform than an incremental backup, but less time to perform than a normal backup.

   **Incremental:** backs up all selected files and folders that have changed since the last normal or incremental backup, and removes the archive attribute from the backed up files and folders. An incremental backup is *not* cumulative, and because of this fact, takes less time to perform than a differential backup.

   **Copy:** backs up all selected files and folders, and does *not* remove the archive attribute. This backup type can be used without interrupting the normal backup schedule.

   **Daily:** backs up all selected files and folders that have changed during the day the tape backup is made, and does *not* remove the archive attribute.

4. When selecting a tape drive device, you should consider both of the following:

> Be sure to select a tape drive that is on the Hardware Compatibility List, and,

> If possible, select a tape drive that has the capacity to back up your entire server on a single tape.

5. Perform a trial restore

6. A

7. B

8. Selecting the verify option approximately doubles the time it takes to perform a backup.

9. The Schedule service

10. Store a current normal (full) backup off-site—preferably at a location that is secure and that has a controlled-climate environment.

# CHAPTER 16: NETWORKING USING TCP/IP

## Answers to Instant Assessment

1. Transmission Control Protocol/Internet Protocol

2. TCP/IP

3. An IP address is a 32-bit binary number, broken into four 8-bit octets, that uniquely identifies a computer or other network device on a network that uses TCP/IP. An IP address is normally represented in a dotted decimal format, with each octet being represented by a whole number between zero and 255. An IP address contains two important identifiers: a network ID and a host ID.

4. If subnet masks are incorrectly configured, network communications problems due to routing errors may occur. For example, TCP/IP may incorrectly determine that a computer on the local subnet is located on a remote subnet, and attempt to route a packet to the remote subnet. In this

instance, the computer on the local subnet would never receive the packet intended for it.

5. If a computer's default gateway address does not specify a router on the local subnet, then that computer will *not* be able to communicate with computers or other network devices located on other network segments.

6. You can assign an IP address to a Windows NT computer in one of two ways: by configuring a computer to obtain an IP address from a DHCP server, or by manually specifying a computer's IP address configuration.

7. IP routing is a function of the Internet Protocol (IP) that uses IP address information to send data packets from a source computer on one network segment across one or more routers to a destination computer on another network segment.

8. Static and dynamic

9. RIP for Internet Protocol

10. The DHCP Relay Agent is a Windows NT Server service that forwards client DHCP configuration requests to a DHCP server on another network segment. The DHCP Relay Agent enables computers on one subnet to receive IP addresses from a DHCP server that is located on a different subnet.

11. Windows Internet Name Service (WINS) is a Windows NT Server service that provides NetBIOS name resolution services to client computers.

12. Microsoft DNS Server provides host name resolution services to client computers.

13. Steps you can take to increase security include:

When configuring password authentication, you can clear the check box next to Basic (Clear Text) and select the check box next to Windows NT Challenge/Response to prevent user names and passwords from being transmitted in an unencrypted format over the Internet.

You can control access by IP address.

You can ensure that directory browsing is not selected.

You can require that users supply user names and passwords by not enabling anonymous users to access the WWW service.

**14.** You must assign and configure an additional IP address to the network adapter in your computer.

**15.** Internet Information Server and Peer Web Services

**16.** A router, a DSU/CSU, a network adapter, and a fractional T1 leased line

**17.** An ISDN adapter card with either an internal or external network terminating unit (NT1) and an ISDN line

**18.** A virtual server is a pseudo WWW server that has its own unique domain name and IP address. To the Internet user accessing the virtual server, a virtual server appears to be a separate server; but in reality, a virtual server is *not* a separate server, but more like an extra shared folder on an Internet Information Server. A single Internet Information Server can be configured to accommodate multiple virtual servers.

**19.** IP address, subnet mask, and default gateway

**20.** `ping.exe`

**21.** `ping.exe`

**22.** `Ipconfig.exe`

**23.** True

**24.** False

**25.** True

**26.** True

**27.** False

**28.** True

**29.** False

## Answers to Lab

### *Lab 16.28: Identifying and resolving TCP/IP connectivity problems*

**Situation 1**    The problem in this situation is that Client_2 has an incorrect default gateway. (It is incorrect because it specifies Server_1's IP address.) If left in its current configuration, users of Client_2 won't be able to access the Internet.

To resolve the problem, Client_2's default gateway should be changed to match the router's IP address: 172.31.151.1

**Situation 2**   The problem in this situation is that Client_A has the same IP address as Client_C. Duplicate IP addresses are *not* permitted.

To resolve the problem, either Client_A's or Client_C's IP address should be changed so that it is a *unique* IP address.

# Chapter 17: Coexistence With NetWare

## Answers to Instant Assessment

1. NWLink IPX/SPX Compatible Transport

2. Frame types (also called frame formats) are accepted, standardized structures for transmitting data packets over a network.

3. Frame type mismatching

4. A network number is a 32-bit binary number that uniquely identifies an NWLink IPX/SPX Compatible Transport network segment for routing purposes. Network numbers are commonly presented in an 8-digit hexadecimal format.

5. Network numbers and internal network numbers

6. RIP for NWLink IPX/SPX Compatible Transport

7. It converts Server Message Blocks (SMBs) into NetWare Core Protocol (NCP) requests that are recognized by the NetWare server.

8. The SAP Agent is a Windows NT service that advertises a Windows NT computer's services (such as SQL Server and SNA Server) to NetWare client computers.

9. Client Service for NetWare (CSNW)

10. The correct answer consists of any two of the following common configuration errors that cause NetWare connectivity problems:

   o the NTGATEWAY group does not have the necessary permissions to access the resource

   o the gateway is not enabled

- frame type mismatch and/or network number mismatch
- the gateway user account is not a member of the NTGATEWAY group

11. Directory Services Manager for NetWare (DSMN)

12. Add Form Feed, Notify When Printed, and Print Banner

13. Gateway Service for NetWare (GSNW)

14. File and Print Services for NetWare (FPNW)

15. NTGATEWAY

16. *\\server_name\share_name*

17. *\\tree_name\volume_name.organizational_unit.*
    *organization_name\folder_name*

18. True

19. True

20. False

21. True

# CHAPTER 18: MIGRATING TO WINDOWS NT FROM NETWARE

## Answers to Instant Assessment

1. The migration process involves several steps:

   - Starting and configuring the Migration Tool for NetWare
   - Selecting the source NetWare server and destination Windows NT Server computer
   - Configuring how user and group accounts will be migrated
   - Configuring how files and folders will be migrated
   - Performing a trial migration to test your configurations
   - Performing an actual migration

- Configuring NetWare client computers to access the Windows NT Server computer

2. NWLink IPX/SPX Compatible Transport and Gateway Service for NetWare

3. The user who performs the migration must have Administrator privileges on the Windows NT Server computer, and must also have Supervisor privileges on the NetWare server(s).

4. An NTFS partition

5. User and group accounts and their properties, and files and folders and their permissions

6. User account passwords, print servers and print queues and their configurations, workgroup managers and user account managers, application defined bindery objects, and login scripts

7. A mapping file

8. Perform a trial migration

9. Migration Tool for NetWare

10. A Microsoft redirector (Microsoft client software) must be installed on each NetWare client computer to enable it to access resources on the Windows NT Server computer.

---

# CHAPTER 19: INSTALLING AND CONFIGURING REMOTE ACCESS SERVICE (RAS)

## Answers to Instant Assessment

1. RAS, or the RAS server

2. Dial-Up Networking

3. 256

4. 250

5. Standard analog telephone line and modem, ISDN, X.25, and Point to Point Tunneling Protocol (PPTP)

6. Serial Line Internet Protocol (SLIP), Point-to-Point Protocol (PPP), Point-to-Point Multilink Protocol, and Point-to-Point Tunneling Protocol (PPTP)

7. SLIP

8. PPP

9. Point-to-Point Multilink Protocol is an extension of PPP. Point-to-Point Multilink Protocol combines the bandwidth from multiple physical connections into a single logical connection. This means that multiple modem, ISDN, or X.25 connections can be bundled together to form a single logical connection with a much higher bandwidth than a single connection can support.

10. Point-to-Point Tunneling Protocol (PPTP) permits a virtual private encrypted connection between two computers over an existing TCP/IP network connection. The existing TCP/IP network connection can be over a local area network or over a dial-up networking TCP/IP connection (including the Internet).

    All standard transport protocols are supported within the Point-to-Point Tunneling Protocol connection, including NWLink IPX/SPX Compatible Transport, NetBEUI, and TCP/IP.

    A primary reason for choosing to use PPTP is that it supports the RAS encryption feature over standard, unencrypted TCP/IP networks, such as the Internet.

11. RAS supports the following transport protocols: NetBEUI, TCP/IP, and NWLink IPX/SPX Compatible Transport.

12. The RAS NetBIOS gateway is a function of the RAS server. The RAS NetBIOS gateway enables client computers that use NetBEUI to access shared resources on other servers located on the RAS server's local network. These other servers can use TCP/IP, NWLink IPX/SPX Compatible Transport, or NetBEUI. In a nutshell, the RAS NetBIOS gateway performs protocol translation for the remote NetBEUI client computer so that it can access shared resources on the RAS server's local network.

**13.** The NetBIOS name resolution methods supported by RAS include: NetBIOS broadcasts, WINS servers, DNS servers, `LMHOSTS` files, and `HOSTS` files.

**14.** Remote users must be assigned the dialin permission before they can establish a dial-up connection with a RAS server.

**15.** Phonebook entries

**16.** Any three of the following:

- Type of dial-up server used by the ISP (SLIP or PPP connection protocol)

- Whether the ISP's dial-up server supports software compression

- Whether you will specify an IP address when you connect to the ISP, or the ISP's dial-up server will assign you an IP address

- Whether the ISP will provide the IP address of a DNS server during the connection process

- Whether the ISP's dial-up server uses IP header compression (IP header compression is also referred to as Van Jacobson header compression or VJ header compression)

- Type of modem you will be connecting to at the ISP and recommended settings that you should use for *your* modem

- The phone number you should use to connect to the ISP

**17.** RAS call back security is configured by using Remote Access Admin. (It can also be configured by using User Manager or User Manager for Domains.) Call back security is configured on an individual user basis. The Preset To configuration option offers the highest level of call back security.

## Answers to Review Activity

### *Troubleshooting common RAS problems*

**Problem 1**    First, determine the type of modem to which the user is attempting to connect; then reconfigure the user's modem settings to the most compatible option, or as recommended by the manager of the dial-up server the user is attempting to connect to.

If the user is using an unsupported modem (i.e., one that is *not* on the Hardware Compatibility List), verify that the settings in the user's `Modem.inf` file are appropriate for the modem.

Determine whether the user's computer is configured for RAS software compression—if it is, ensure that the modem is configured to *not* compress data.

If the user is still unable to connect, configure the modem to record a log file of all attempted connections.

**Problem 2**    Because SLIP servers normally require clear text passwords, try changing the authentication and encryption policy configuration on the Dial-Up Networking client computer. Select the radio button next to "Accept any authentication including clear text" on the Security tab of the Edit Phonebook Entry dialog box (instead of the current configuration of "Accept only Microsoft-encrypted authentication").

# Chapter 20: Macintosh Connectivity

## Answers to Instant Assessment

1. Services for Macintosh allows:
   - Macintosh client computers to connect to Macintosh-accessible volumes on a Windows NT Server computer
   - Macintosh client computers to access shared printers on a Windows NT Server computer
   - A Windows NT Server computer to connect to network-connected print devices that support the AppleTalk protocol
   - A Windows NT Server computer to function as an AppleTalk router
2. LocalTalk, Ethernet, Token Ring, and FDDI
3. ARCNET
4. AppleTalk
5. An NTFS volume

6. You can use either Server Manager or File Manager to create a Macintosh-accessible volume.

7. In clear text

8. A User Authentication Module (UAM)

9. As an Apple LaserWriter

10. To connect a Windows NT Server computer (that has Services for Macintosh installed on it) to an AppleTalk print device, create a printer that specifies the AppleTalk print device as its print destination.

11. False

# CHAPTER 21: RUNNING APPLICATIONS ON WINDOWS NT

## Answers to Instant Assessment

1. The NT Virtual DOS Machine (NTVDM)

2. In preemptive multitasking, the operating system allocates processor time between applications. Because Windows NT, *not* the application, allocates processor time between multiple applications, one application can be preempted by the operating system, and another application allowed to run. When multiple applications are alternately paused and then allocated processor time, they appear to run simultaneously to the user.

3. A thread is the smallest unit of processing that can be scheduled by the Windows NT Schedule service.

4. `Autoexec.nt` and `Config.nt`

5. By default, when multiple Win16 applications run at the same time on a Windows NT computer, they all run in a single Win16 NTVDM.

6. You can configure the rogue Win16 application to run in its own separate memory space.

7. The `Start/separate` command is one method you can use to run a Win16 application in its own separate memory space.

8. The Win32 environment

9. This means that an application must be *recompiled* for each hardware platform to be run on that platform.

10. At least 1 NTFS partition

11. 8

12. `start/min/high notepad.exe`

13. The System application in Control Panel

14. The three ways you can access Windows NT Task Manager are:

    - By pressing Ctrl + Alt + Delete, and then clicking the Task Manager command button in the Windows NT Security dialog box.

    - By right-clicking a blank space on the taskbar (on the Windows NT desktop), and then selecting Task Manager from the menu that appears.

    - By selecting Start ⇒ Run, and then typing **taskmgr** in the Run dialog box.

15. OS/2 environment applications supported consist of 16-bit character-based applications designed for OS/2 version 1.*x*. OS/2 2.*x*, 3.*x*, and Presentation Manager applications are *not* supported by Windows NT.

16. True

17. True

18. False

19. False

# Answers to Review Activity

## *Troubleshooting common application problems*

**Problem 1**   Use Task Manager to end the application.

I recommend that you access Task Manager by using Ctrl + Alt + Delete in this type of situation, because sometimes all other forms of input are unsuccessful when an application has crashed.

**Problem 2**   Recompile the application to run on an Intel platform.

# CHAPTER 22: USING PERFORMANCE MONITOR

## Answers to Instant Assessment

1. The Stop Log command button in the Log Options dialog box

2. Performance Monitor is used to:

   o identify performance problems and/or bottlenecks,

   o determine current usage of system resources,

   o track performance trends over time,

   o predict future usage of system resources (capacity planning), and

   o determine how system configuration changes affect system performance.

3. Objects

4. A counter

5. There is more than one instance of a Performance Monitor object when there is *more than one* of that particular object (such as a physical disk or a processor) in the system.

6. Memory         —         Pages/sec

7. Processor       —         % Processor Time

8. Network Segment  —   % Network utilization

9. Server          —         Bytes Total/sec

10. The SNMP Service

11. The Network Monitor Agent

12. **diskperf-y**

13. Chart, Alert, Report, and Log

14. Last, Average, Min, Max, and Graph Time

15. A *threshold value* that will cause Performance Monitor to generate an alert if the specified counter *exceeds* or *drops below* this value (depending on whether the Over or Under radio button is selected)

16. The Start Log command button in the Log Options dialog box

**17.** The most recent measurement for each selected counter

**18.** Performance Monitor Log view is used to save statistics gathered by Performance Monitor to a log file. The Performance Monitor log file can be viewed at a later time in a Chart, Alert, or Report view.

**19.** True

**20.** False

**21.** False

# CHAPTER 23: USING NETWORK MONITOR

## Answers to Instant Assessment

**1.** Network Monitor

**2.** Promiscuous refers to a network adapter's ability to receive packets that are *not* addressed to that network adapter. A non-promiscuous network adapter can only receive packets that are addressed to that network adapter. A promiscuous network adapter can receive any packets transmitted on the local network segment.

**3.** The Network Monitor Tools and Network Monitor Agent

**4.** You must remove the Network Monitor Agent.

**5.** Network Monitor requires a network adapter that uses an NDIS 4.0 driver.

**6.** Select Start ⇒ Programs ⇒ Administrative Tools (Common) ⇒ Network Monitor.

**7.** The Graph pane, the Total Stats pane, the Session Stats pane, and the Station Stats pane

**8.** "Local capture only"

**9.** A capture

**10.** All packets addressed to or sent by the Windows NT Server computer that is running Network Monitor

**11.** Configure a capture filter.

**12.** You can configure a capture filter so that:

- Only packets that use certain *protocols* are (or are not) captured,
- Only packets to or from *specified computers or network devices* are (or are not) captured,
- Only packets that contain specific *byte patterns* are captured,
- Or any combination of the above.

**13.** *After* a capture is performed

**14.** The Capture Window dialog box (the Network Monitor main dialog box) and the Capture Summary dialog box

**15.** One way to determine the current utilization of a network segment is to start a capture in Network Monitor, and then watch the % Network Utilization bar graph in the Graph pane *during the entire capture period*. This graph displays only the most recent second's worth of network activity, so you must view it during the entire capture period to get a feel for overall network utilization. A high number on the graph (any number consistently over 60%) may indicate that there are too many computers or too much network traffic on the segment being analyzed.

Another way to determine the overall utilization of a network segment during the entire capture period is to view the Network Statistics section in the Total Stats pane *after* the capture is completed. You can derive a great deal of information from the statistics displayed. For example, you can determine the average number of bytes transmitted per second by dividing the number of bytes shown by the number of seconds shown in the Time Elapsed statistic at the top of the Total Stats pane. If the average number of bytes per second is greater than fifty percent of the segment's total capacity (an Ethernet 10BaseT segment, for example, has a maximum capacity of 10 Mbps or 1,250,000 bytes per second), this may indicate that there are too many computers or too much network traffic on the segment being analyzed.

**16.** To sort a column, right-click the column header (for example, Frames Sent). Select Sort Column from the menu that appears.

**17.** Configure a display filter that specifies that only packets that use IPX be displayed.

**18.** False

**19.** True

---

# CHAPTER 24: CAPACITY PLANNING

## Answers to Instant Assessment

1. Capacity planning is the process of determining current usage of server and/or network resources, as well as tracking utilization over time, to predict future usage and the additional hardware that will be required to meet the projected levels of utilization. Capacity planning can be performed on a single computer, such as a network server; or it can be performed on an entire network.

2. Establishing a baseline, gathering data over time, and using this data to predict future utilization and future hardware requirements

3. You should consider gathering data at *various times* to obtain an overall picture of utilization. For example, consider collecting data during business hours, when network usage is at its peak and production is heavy. Also consider collecting data during nonbusiness hours when network utilization levels should be lower. You might also consider gathering data over several days in a week, or perhaps over several days in a month to take into account normal cyclical business highs and lows. Taking several samples over a limited period of time normally provides the most accurate initial picture of your server and/or network environment.

4. Comma-separated value files and tab-separated value files

5. You can run Performance Monitor individually on each server to be monitored; or, you can run Performance Monitor on a single, centralized Windows NT computer and simultaneously monitor several servers on the network.

6. Network Monitor

7. Capacity planning overall network performance, and capacity planning for a specific type of network traffic

8. Memory, processor, disk, and network

9. Memory Pages/sec

10. Processor % Processor Time

11. PhysicalDisk Avg. Disk Queue Length, PhysicalDisk % Disk Time, and LogicalDisk % Free Space

12. Network Segment % Network utilization

13. True

14. True

# CHAPTER 25: PERFORMANCE OPTIMIZATION

## Answers to Instant Assessment

1. Performance optimization is the process of modifying server and/or network hardware and software configurations with the intent of *speeding up* server and/or network response.

2. A bottleneck is the component in the system that is slowing system performance. The bottleneck in a networking environment is the part of the system that is performing at peak capacity while other components in the system are *not* working at peak capacity. In other words, if it weren't for the limiting component, the rest of the system could go faster.

3. Performance Monitor and Network Monitor

4. Memory, processor, disk, and network

5. Adding RAM

6. A beneficial by-product of adding RAM is that processor and disk performance may be improved, as well, because paging is reduced and the disk cache size is increased when RAM is added.

7. The System application in Control Panel

8. Any three of the following:

    o Defragment the hard disk(s) in your computer

    o Upgrade to a faster disk controller and/or a faster hard disk(s)

    o Configure a stripe set with parity across three or more disks

    o Configure a stripe set across two or more disks

**9.** Any three of the following:

- Replace the existing processor with a faster processor
- Replace the existing motherboard and processor with a faster motherboard and processor
- Upgrade from a single-processor system to a multi-processor system
- Add a processor to a multi-processor system

**10.** The four ways to optimize a Windows NT Server computer are:

- Configuring load balancing across multiple servers
- Disabling unused services, protocols, and drivers
- Scheduling large, server-intensive tasks during nonpeak hours
- Optimizing the Server service

**11.** Either move the BDC to the other side of the WAN link, so it is physically close to the client computers that it services; or, add an additional BDC on the other side of the WAN link.

## Answers to Labs

### Lab 25.37: Finding and resolving bottlenecks

**Problem 1**    The statistics in this problem seem to indicate that the processor, memory and disk all need upgrading. However, if you upgrade RAM to 64MB, the amount of paging would be significantly reduced. Reducing paging would also decrease the % Processor Time and % Disk Time statistics to reasonable levels. This server should probably have all of the possible upgrades presented, *but adding memory (RAM) is the best choice if only one upgrade can be performed.*

**Problem 2**    The statistics in this problem seem to indicate that the *disk* is the biggest bottleneck to optimum system performance. If only one of the possible upgrades can be performed, upgrading to a hardware-based RAID 5 disk subsystem should yield the most significant increase in disk performance for this server.

### Lab 25.38: Optimizing Windows NT performance

**Problem 1** *Add* a BDC for the LONDON domain at the Paris location, and *add* a BDC for the LONDON domain at the Munich location.

Additionally, *move* one of the WINS servers from London to Paris, and *move* a second WINS server from London to Munich.

This places the servers that perform logon authentication and NetBIOS name resolution physically close to the users that access them, thereby improving server response time and minimizing traffic across the WAN links.

**Problem 2** Optimize the Server service to *Maximize Throughput for Network Applications*.

# CHAPTER 26: THE TROUBLESHOOTING PROCESS

## Answers to Instant Assessment

1. Troubleshooting is a methodical approach to solving a problem. The approach is often the result of a person's knowledge, experience, and intuition.

2. The five basic steps suggested for troubleshooting are:
   - Gather information
   - Define the problem
   - List probable causes
   - Identify possible solutions and attempt to fix the problem
   - Resolve and document the problem

3. *Microsoft TechNet*

4. Microsoft Technical Support Web site, at:
   http://www.microsoft.com/support/

5. Microsoft Download Service

# Chapter 27: Advanced Troubleshooting Topics

## Answers to Instant Assessment

1. The nine major steps in the Windows NT boot sequence are:
   - Power On Self Test (POST)
   - Initial Startup
   - Selecting an operating system
   - Detecting hardware
   - Selecting hardware profile (or Last Known Good Configuration) and loading the kernel
   - Kernel initialization
   - Initializing device drivers
   - Initializing services
   - Logon process

2. The most likely cause of this problem is a corrupt file. Power outages can easily corrupt files on the hard disk.

   To resolve the situation, perform the Emergency Repair process, selecting the Inspect boot sector and Verify Windows NT system files options during the process.

3. The most likely cause of this problem is the configuration changes made during the last logon session.

   To resolve the situation, reboot the computer, and select the Last Known Good Configuration during the boot sequence.

   If this does *not* repair the problem, perform the Emergency Repair process, selecting the Inspect Registry files option during the process.

4. The Emergency Repair process involves using the Windows NT Setup Boot Disk set, the Windows NT compact disc, and the Emergency Repair disk created during (or after) the installation process to repair a damaged or corrupt Windows NT installation.

5. Event Viewer (specifically, the system log in Event Viewer)

6. View the Event Detail for the *last* stop error in the list (the event that happened *first* chronologically during the boot process) *first*. Resolving this error will often take care of most or all of the other stop errors listed.

7. *Service dependencies* show which services and drivers must be running before the service in question can start. *Group dependencies* show which groups of services or drivers must be running before the service in question can start. Once you have determined what the service and group dependencies for a particular service or driver are, you can then verify that all of these services and drivers (that are required to be running *before* a particular service or driver can start) are, in fact, running.

8. The Services tab

9. Windows NT Registry Editor (`regedt32.exe`) and Windows 95 Registry Editor (`regedit.exe`)

10. HKEY_LOCAL_MACHINE

11. Back it up

12. `/s`

13. The Windows 95 Registry Editor (`regedit.exe`) is a better tool for *searching* the Windows NT Registry because this editor can search the Registry by key, by value, or by data contained in the value. As a Registry search tool, this editor is more effective than the Windows NT Registry Editor, which can only search the Registry by key. You can manually wade your way through the various folders and subfolders in the Windows NT Registry Editor, and you can edit any Registry value, it's just more cumbersome to use as a search tool than the Windows 95 Registry Editor.

14. The Windows NT Registry Editor (`regedt32.exe`)

15. Windows NT displays a blue screen when it encounters a STOP error that it cannot recover from.

16. There are three primary sections in a blue screen: the STOP error (including error code or BugCheck code) and description, a list of loaded drivers, and a stack dump (including the operating system's build number).

17. The System application

18. Dr. Watson for Windows NT

# Mini-Lab Manual

Table E-1 lists all the lab exercises in this book, including the number and title of each lab, and the chapter in which the lab is presented.

**TABLE E-1** HANDS-ON LAB EXERCISES IN THIS BOOK

| LAB NUMBER | LAB TITLE | CHAPTER |
| --- | --- | --- |
| 2.1 | Installing Windows NT Workstation | 2 |
| 2.2 | Installing Windows NT Server and configuring dual boot with Windows NT Workstation | 2 |
| 3.3 | Managing Partitions | 3 |
| 3.4 | Updating the Emergency Repair Disk | 3 |
| 4.5 | Configuring directory replication | 4 |
| 4.6 | Exploring Control Panel | 4 |
| 5.7 | Creating an answer file using Setup Manager | 5 |
| 6.8 | Creating and sharing a local printer | 6 |
| 6.9 | Installing and configuring Microsoft TCP/IP Printing | 6 |
| 7.10 | Creating and managing user and group accounts | 7 |

*continued*

**TABLE E-1** *(continued)*

| LAB NUMBER | LAB TITLE | CHAPTER |
|---|---|---|
| 8.11 | Implementing auditing | 8 |
| 8.12 | Managing account policy and user rights | 8 |
| 9.13 | Implementing user profiles | 9 |
| 9.14 | Configuring a system policy | 9 |
| 10.15 | Implementing a trust relationship *(Note: This lab is optional because it requires an additional computer.)* | 10 |
| 10.16 | Planning a Directory Services architecture | 10 |
| 11.17 | Optimizing WAN link performance by the appropriate placement of BDCs | 11 |
| 12.18 | Sharing and securing resources | 12 |
| 12.19 | Establishing file and folder auditing | 12 |
| 12.20 | Troubleshooting resource access and permission problems | 12 |
| 13.21 | Configuring the Computer Browser service | 13 |
| 13.22 | Accessing network resources *(Note: This lab is optional because it requires an additional computer.)* | 13 |
| 14.23 | Installing Windows NT Server tools and using NT Server tools to administer a remote server *(Note: Part 2 of this lab is optional because it requires an additional computer.)* | 14 |
| 15.24 | Performing a backup *(Note: This lab is optional because it requires a tape drive.)* | 15 |
| 16.25 | Implementing WINS and Microsoft DNS Server | 16 |
| 16.26 | Configuring Internet Information Server and installing and configuring Peer Web Services | 16 |
| 16.27 | Installing and configuring an Internet (TCP/IP) router | 16 |
| 16.28 | Identifying and resolving TCP/IP connectivity problems | 16 |
| 17.29 | Installing and configuring NWLink and Client Service for NetWare | 17 |
| 17.30 | Installing and configuring NWLink and Gateway Service for NetWare | 17 |

## Hands-on Lab Exercises

Following are all the lab exercises that appear in this book. We've pulled them together for you in this Mini-Lab Manual to help prepare you for the certification exams. These lab exercises are extremely important to your exam preparation. Don't even think about skipping them! There's no substitute for using Windows NT to master the skills that the Windows NT 4.0 Microsoft Certified Professional exams will test you on.

Refer to the "Hardware and software you'll need" section in this Appendix if you're not sure you have the necessary equipment to do the labs.

 **Warning! Some of the lab exercises in this book have the potential to erase or corrupt data on existing hard disk drives. Make sure you back up all important data and programs *before* you attempt to perform any of the lab exercises. Or, better yet — do the labs on a computer that does not contain any vital data or programs.**

 **The answers to all of the labs that contain questions can be found in Appendix D.**

### Hardware and software you'll need

You will need access to various hardware and software to be able to do the hands-on lab exercises in this book.

If you have the minimum hardware listed below, you will be able to complete *most* of the hands-on lab exercises in this book, and certainly all of the critical exercises. To perform all of the labs, however, you will need the optional additional hardware, as well.

### Minimum hardware requirements

- Intel-based computer with 486/33 processor, 16MB RAM, and 500MB-1GB available hard disk space
- CD-ROM drive
- Mouse
- VGA monitor and graphics card

 *tip* **I strongly recommend you only use hardware found on the Microsoft Windows NT Hardware Compatibility List (HCL), which is shipped with the NT Product, or can be accessed via Microsoft's World Wide Web site at** http://www.microsoft.com/ntworksta-tion **or** http://www.microsoft.com/ntserver.

### Optional additional hardware

- Additional computer (with the same minimum specifications as the first one)
- Network adapter and cabling (if you have the additional computer listed above)
- Printer
- Tape drive
- Modem and Internet connection (so you can access the various online resources)

### Software required

- Microsoft Windows NT Workstation 4.0
- Microsoft Windows NT Server 4.0

### Lab 2.1 *Installing Windows NT Workstation*

The objective of this hands-on exercise is for you to experience the process of installing Microsoft Windows NT Workstation and to develop the skills used to perform this task.

Workstation
Server
Enterprise

**For you to complete some of the remaining labs in this book, you will need at least a 10MB partition on your hard disk that will be formatted in a later lab with NTFS. (If you don't partition your hard disk in this manner, you will not be able to do the labs on NTFS security and auditing.) You may create an extended MS-DOS partition for this use. This task should be done *before* MS-DOS is installed, and before you proceed with the rest of this lab. I recommend you partition your hard drive into two partitions. The first partition should contain *all but* 10MB of the disk's capacity. The extended (second) partition should consist of the remaining 10MB of disk space.**

**I assume, in all of the labs in this book, that drive C: is the large partition, and that drive D: is the 10MB partition. Your actual drive letters may vary from this configuration. If your drives are lettered differently, substitute your drive letters for the ones I use.**

To perform this lab, first install MS-DOS on your computer's hard drive, and load the drivers for your CD-ROM drive. Make sure the Windows NT Workstation compact disc is in your CD-ROM drive. You need one blank, 3.5-inch high-density floppy disk for this lab exercise.

Follow the steps below carefully to perform the installation.

#### PRECOPY PHASE

1. Change the default drive to your CD-ROM drive by typing in the CD-ROM drive letter followed by a colon (for example, **D:**). Then press Enter.

2. Type **cd I386**, and then press Enter.

3. Type **winnt /b**, and then press Enter. (This command instructs Setup to perform the `Winnt.exe` installation without creating the Setup Boot Disk set.)

4. When Windows NT Setup asks you to enter the path where NT files are located, press Enter.

5. Setup copies files to your hard disk. (This process takes a few minutes. How about a stretch break or a fresh cup of coffee?)

6. When the Windows NT Workstation Setup screen appears, press Enter to restart your computer and continue Windows NT Setup.

### PHASE 0

1. After a couple of minutes, the Windows NT Workstation Setup screen appears, welcoming you to Setup. Press Enter to set up Windows NT now.

2. Setup displays a screen indicating any mass storage devices, such as SCSI adapters, CD-ROM drives, and so on. Some older IDE controllers are not displayed here, but they will still function and be recognized by NT. Specify additional devices by making changes on this screen if necessary. When you have completed all changes, press Enter to continue.

3. The Windows NT Licensing Agreement screen appears. Read the licensing agreement, pressing PgDn to view additional screens. When you reach the bottom of the agreement, press F8 to continue setup.

4. Setup displays a screen indicating your computer's hardware and software components. Make any necessary changes. When you are finished, highlight "The above list matches my computer" and press Enter.

5. If you have a previous version of Microsoft Windows installed on your computer, Setup displays a screen indicating that it has found a previous version. If this screen appears, press N to install Windows NT Workstation in a different directory.

6. Setup displays a screen listing your computer's hard disk partitions. Highlight the partition on which you want to install Windows NT, and then press Enter. (Make sure the partition you choose has at least 117MB free.)

7. Setup asks you to select the type of file system you want on this partition. Highlight "Leave the current file system intact <no changes>" and press Enter.

8. Setup displays a location where it will install the NT Workstation files. In the highlighted area, edit the text so that it reads: **\WINNTWKS**. (Don't type the period at the end.) Press Enter.

9. Setup offers to examine your computer's hard disk for corruption. Press Enter to allow this. (This takes a few minutes.)

10. Setup displays a screen indicating that this portion of Setup is complete. If you have a floppy disk inserted in drive A:, remove it now. Then press Enter to restart your computer and to continue with setup.

### PHASE 1

1. After your computer reboots, the Windows NT Workstation Setup dialog box appears. Click Next to continue.

**2.** A Setup Options screen appears. Select Custom. Click Next to continue.

**3.** Type in your name, press Tab, and then type in the name of your organization. Click Next to continue.

**4.** Type in the ten-digit CD key number from the back of your Windows NT Workstation compact disc case (press Tab after you type the first three digits). Click Next to continue.

**5.** When Setup prompts you to type in a computer name, type **NTW40**. Click Next to continue.

**6.** Type **password** when Setup prompts you to enter an administrator password. Press Tab. Confirm the password by retyping it. Click Next to continue.

**7.** Setup asks you if you want to create an Emergency Repair Disk. Accept the Yes default. Click Next to continue.

**8.** Setup displays a screen indicating you are to Select Components. Add any components that you want to install, but do *not* deselect any components that are selected by default. (I recommend you install Freecell and all of the games . . . I'm an addict!) Click Next to continue.

**PHASE 2**

**1.** Setup displays a screen indicating that Phase 2, Installing Windows NT Networking, is about to begin. Click Next to continue.

**2.** Select "This computer will participate on a network." Then click to check the box next to "Wired to the network." (It's okay to select these options even if you don't have a network adapter in your computer.) Click Next to continue.

**3.** Setup displays the Network Adapters box. If you have a network adapter, click Start Search. Your network adapter should appear in the Network Adapters window. If your network adapter did not appear, or if you do not have a network adapter in your computer, click Select from list. If your network adapter is shown in the list, highlight it and click OK. If your network adapter is not on the list, and you have a driver disk from its manufacturer, highlight any network adapter and click Have Disk. Setup then prompts you to insert this disk. Do so and click OK. Highlight your network adapter from the list and click OK. If you do not have a network adapter, highlight MS Loopback Adapter and click OK. You should now have either the MS Loopback Adapter or your network adapter displayed in the Network Adapters box. Click Next to continue.

**4.** Setup displays the Network Protocols list box. Accept the default selection of TCP/IP Protocol. Click Next to continue.

5. Setup displays the Network Services list box. Accept all of the defaults selected in this list box. Click Next to continue.

6. Click Next to continue and to have Setup install the selected components.

7. Setup prompts you to enter your network adapter card settings. (This screen may not appear for some network adapters.) Verify that the settings shown match the ones that you used when you installed and configured your network adapter. Make changes only as needed. Click Continue.

8. A TCP/IP Setup warning screen appears. If you are on a network that has a DHCP server, click Yes. Otherwise, click No.

9. The Microsoft TCP/IP Properties dialog box eventually appears if you clicked No in the previous step. *If you are on a network that uses TCP/IP, or if you are connected to the Internet, obtain an IP address, subnet mask, and default gateway from your network administrator.* Otherwise, type an IP address of: **192.168.59.5** and a subnet mask of: **255.255.255.0**.

 caution

**Do *not* use this IP address if you are on a network that uses TCP/IP, or if you are connected to the Internet.**

10. Leave the Default Gateway blank. Click OK to continue.

11. Setup displays a screen showing network binding information. Click Next to continue.

12. Click Next to start the network.

13. Setup displays a screen asking you to choose whether your computer will participate in a workgroup or domain configuration. Accept the default selection of Workgroup, and the default workgroup name WORKGROUP. Click Next to continue.

**PHASE 3**

1. Click Finish to continue the setup process.

2. In the drop-down list box under the Time Zone tab, highlight and click your time zone. As an option, you may also click the Date & Time tab and set the correct date and time. Click Close to continue when you are finished.

3. Setup displays a screen indicating that it has found your video display adapter. Click OK in the Detected Display dialog box to continue.

4. Adjust the display settings to suit your preferences. Click Test. The Testing Mode dialog box appears. Click OK to test. When the Testing Mode dialog box reappears, click Yes if you saw the test bitmap. When the Display Settings dialog box appears, click OK to continue. Click OK in the Display Properties dialog box to complete the installation. (This takes a few minutes.)

**5.** When prompted, label and insert a blank 3.5-inch floppy disk into drive A:. Setup formats this disk and makes it into your Emergency Repair Disk. Click OK to continue. (This takes a couple of minutes.)

**6.** Setup displays a window indicating that Windows NT 4.0 is successfully installed. Remove your newly created Emergency Repair Disk from drive A: (and save it for future use). Also remove the compact disc from your CD-ROM drive. Then click Restart Computer to reboot and start Windows NT Workstation. The setup is complete.

## Lab 2.2 *Installing Windows NT Server and configuring dual boot with Windows NT Workstation*

Workstation
Server
Enterprise

The purpose of this lab exercise is for you to experience the process of installing Microsoft Windows NT Server and to develop the skills used to perform this task. During the installation process, you will configure your computer to dual boot between Windows NT Server and Windows NT Workstation.

note

**Before you can successfully perform this lab, you must complete Lab 2.1. You need one blank, 3.5-inch high-density floppy disk for this lab exercise.**

Follow the steps below carefully to perform the installation:

Boot your computer to Windows NT Workstation, and log on as Administrator (remember: the administrator password is *password*). Make sure the Windows NT Server compact disc is in your CD-ROM drive.

### PRECOPY PHASE

**1.** Close the Welcome to Windows NT dialog box.

**2.** Select Start ⇒ Programs ⇒ Command Prompt.

**3.** At the command prompt, change the default drive to your CD-ROM drive by typing in the CD-ROM drive letter followed by a colon (for example, **D:**). Then press Enter.

**4.** Type **cd I386**, then press Enter.

**5.** Type **winnt32 /b**, then press Enter. (This command performs the installation without creating the Setup Boot Disk set.)

**6.** The Windows NT 4.0 Upgrade/Installation dialog box appears. Click Continue to accept the default path for the location of your Windows NT files.

**7.** The Installation program copies files to your hard disk. (This process takes a few minutes.)

**8.** When Setup displays the Windows NT 4.0 Server Installation/Upgrade dialog box, click Restart Computer and continue the installation.

### PHASE 0

**1.** After a minute or two, when the Windows NT Server Setup screen appears, press Enter to set up Windows NT now.

**2.** Setup displays a screen showing any mass storage devices, such as SCSI adapters, CD-ROM drives, and so on. Some older IDE controllers are not displayed here, but will still function and be recognized by NT. Specify additional devices by making changes on this screen if you need to. When you have completed all necessary changes, press Enter to continue.

**3.** The Windows NT Licensing Agreement screen appears. Read the licensing agreement, pressing PgDn to view additional screens. When you reach the bottom of the agreement, press F8 to continue setup.

**4.** Windows NT Server Setup displays a screen indicating it has found Windows NT Workstation. Press N to cancel upgrade and install a fresh copy of Windows NT.

**5.** Windows NT Server Setup displays a screen listing your computer's hardware and software components. Make any changes necessary. When you are finished, highlight "The above list matches my computer," and press Enter.

**6.** If you have a previous version of Microsoft Windows installed on your computer, Setup displays a screen stating that it detected a previous version. If this screen appears, press N to install Windows NT Server in a different directory.

**7.** Windows NT Server Setup displays a screen showing your computer's hard disk partitions. Highlight the partition on which you want to install Windows NT Server, then press Enter. (Make sure the partition you choose has at least 124MB free.)

**8.** Windows NT Server Setup asks you to select the type of file system you want on this partition. Highlight "Leave the current file system intact <no changes>," and press Enter.

**9.** Windows NT Server Setup displays the location where it will install the NT Server files. In the highlighted area, edit the text so that it reads: **\WINNTSRV**. (Don't type the period at the end.) Then press Enter.

**10.** Windows NT Server Setup offers to examine your hard disk for corruption. Press Enter to allow this. (This takes a few minutes.)

**11.** Windows NT Server Setup displays a screen that indicates this portion of Setup is complete. If you have a floppy disk inserted in drive A:, remove it now. Then press Enter to restart your computer and to continue with setup.

### PHASE 1

**1.** After your computer reboots and the Windows NT Server Setup dialog box finally appears, click Next to continue.

**2.** Type in your name, press Tab, then type in the name of your organization. Click Next to continue.

**3.** Type in the ten-digit CD key number from the back of your Windows NT Server compact disc case (press Tab after you enter the first three digits). Click Next to continue.

**4.** Select a Licensing mode for the server. Select "Per Server for:" and enter the number of client licenses you purchased. Click Next to continue.

**5.** When prompted to type in a name for your computer, type **PDCLAB**. Click Next to continue.

**6.** Select Primary domain controller in the Server Type window. Click Next to continue.

**7.** Type **password** when prompted to enter an administrator password. Press Tab. Confirm the password by retyping it. Click Next to continue.

**8.** Windows NT Server Setup asks if you want to create an Emergency Repair Disk. Accept the Yes default. Click Next to continue.

**9.** Windows NT Server Setup displays a screen prompting you to Select Components. Add any components that you want to install, but do *not* deselect any components that are selected by default. Click Next to continue.

### PHASE 2

**1.** Windows NT Server Setup displays a window indicating that Phase 2, Installing Windows NT Networking, is about to begin. Click Next to continue.

**2.** Accept the default check in the box next to "Wired to the network." (It's okay to select this option even if you don't have a network adapter in your computer.) Click Next to continue.

**3.** Accept the default check in the box next to "Install Microsoft Internet Information Server." Click Next to continue.

4. Windows NT Server Setup displays the Network Adapters box. If you have a network adapter, click Start Search. Your network adapter should then appear in the Network Adapters box. If your network adapter did not appear, or if you do not have one in your computer, click Select From List. If your network adapter is shown in the list, highlight it and click OK. If your network adapter is not on the list, and you have a driver disk from its manufacturer, highlight any network adapter and click Have Disk. Setup then prompts you to insert this disk. Insert the disk and click OK. Highlight your network adapter from the list and click OK. If you do not have a network adapter, highlight MS Loopback Adapter and click OK. You should now have either the MS Loopback Adapter or your network adapter displayed in the Network Adapters box. Click Next to continue.

5. Windows NT Server Setup displays the Network Protocols list box. Deselect NWLink IPX/SPX Compatible Transport. Ensure that the TCP/IP Protocol is the only protocol selected (it will have a gray check in the check box). Click Next to continue.

6. Windows NT Server Setup displays the Network Services list box. Accept all of the defaults selected in this window. Click Next to continue.

7. Click Next to have Setup install the selected components.

8. Setup prompts you to enter your network adapter card settings. (This screen may not appear for some network adapters.) Verify that the settings shown match the ones you used when you installed and configured your network adapter. Make changes only as needed. Click Continue.

9. A TCP/IP Setup warning screen appears. If you are on a network that has a DHCP server, click Yes. Otherwise, click No.

10. The Microsoft TCP/IP Properties dialog box appears if you clicked No in the previous step. *If you are on a network that uses TCP/IP, or if you are connected to the Internet, obtain an IP address, subnet mask, and default gateway from your network administrator.* Otherwise, type an IP address of: **192.168.59.5** and a subnet mask of: **255.255.255.0**.

 caution **Do *not* use this IP address if you are on a network that uses TCP/IP, or if you are connected to the Internet.**

11. Leave the Default Gateway blank. Click OK to continue.

12. Windows NT Server Setup displays a screen showing network binding information. Click Next to continue.

13. Click Next to start the network.

14. Windows NT Server Setup prompts you enter a domain name. Type **LAB** as your domain name. Click Next to continue.

**PHASE 3**

1. Click Finish to continue the setup process.

2. Accept the defaults selected in the Microsoft Internet Information Server 2.0 Setup dialog box. Click OK to continue.

3. Click Yes to create the directory.

4. Accept the default directories in the Publishing Directories dialog box by clicking OK.

5. Click Yes to create the directories.

6. Click OK in the Microsoft Internet Information Server 2.0 Setup dialog box. (You won't be configuring the Gopher functionality in this course.)

7. Click SQL Server in the Install Drivers dialog box to highlight it. Click OK to continue.

8. In the drop-down list box under the Time Zone tab, click your time zone to highlight it. Optionally, click the Date & Time tab and set the correct date and time. When you are finished, click Close to continue.

9. Setup displays a screen indicating that it has found your video display adapter. Click OK in the Detected Display dialog box to continue.

10. Adjust the display settings to suit your preferences. Click Test. The Testing Mode dialog box appears. Click OK to test. When the Testing Mode dialog box reappears, click Yes if you saw the test bitmap. When the Display Settings dialog box appears, click OK to continue. Click OK in the Display Properties dialog box to complete the installation. (This takes a few minutes.)

11. When prompted, label and insert a blank 3.5-inch floppy disk into drive A:. Setup formats and makes this disk into your Emergency Repair Disk. Click OK to continue. (This takes a couple of minutes.)

12. Windows NT Setup displays a window indicating that Windows NT 4.0 is successfully installed. Remove your newly created Emergency Repair Disk from drive A: (and save it for future use). Also remove the compact disc from your CD-ROM drive. Then click Restart Computer to reboot and start Windows NT Server. The setup is complete.

At the completion of Labs 2.1 and 2.2, both Windows NT Workstation and Windows NT Server are installed on your computer, and your computer is configured to dual boot between the two operating systems.

### Lab 3.3 *Managing Partitions*

The objective of this hands-on lab exercise is for you to gain experience using Disk Administrator to manage partitions.

Follow the steps carefully to successfully partition and format the remaining 10MB of your computer's hard drive with an NTFS partition.

Workstation
Server
Enterprise

note

**If you didn't leave enough space on your hard disk to perform this, I recommend that you reinstall NT Workstation and NT Server to accommodate this lab. If this is not possible, you should create an NTFS partition somewhere on one of your hard disks so that you can perform the file security labs later in this book.**

caution

**Don't delete or reformat any partition that contains data that you don't want to lose. As always, make sure you back up all important data and programs *before* you do the lab exercise.**

1. Boot your computer to either Windows NT Server or Windows NT Workstation. Log on as Administrator. (Remember the password? It's *password*.)

2. Close the Welcome to NT dialog box if it appears. (Hint: If you never want to see this dialog box again, the second time it appears, you are given a check box to select if you don't want this box to appear each time you run NT.)

3. Select Start ⇒ Programs ⇒ Administrative Tools (Common) ⇒ Disk Administrator.

4. Disk Administrator displays a dialog box indicating that this is the first time Disk Administrator has been run. Click OK to update the system configuration.

5. If this is the first time Disk Administrator has been run, a Confirm dialog box appears, indicating that no signature is found on Disk 0. Click Yes to write a signature on Disk 0.

6. Click the box that indicates a drive with a 10MB partition (to highlight it), and select Partition ⇒ Delete. (Caution! If this partition is displayed as Free Space, don't do this step. Instead, skip to Step 11.)

7. Click Yes in the Confirm dialog box to delete the partition.

8. Select Partition ⇒ Commit Changes Now.

9. Click Yes in the Confirm dialog box to save the changes to your disk.

10. Click OK to return to the Disk Administrator main dialog box.

11. Click the box that indicates the drive with 10MB of free space (to highlight it), and then select Partition ⇒ Create.

12. A Confirm dialog box appears. Click Yes to continue to create the partition.

13. Click OK in the Create Primary Partition dialog box to create a new partition.

14. Select Partition ⇒ Commit Changes Now.

15. Click Yes in the Confirm dialog box to save the changes to your disk.

16. Click OK to return to the Disk Administrator main dialog box.

17. Click the box that indicates the drive with a 10MB partition (labeled Unknown) to highlight it.

18. Select Tools ⇒ Format.

19. Choose NTFS in the File System drop-down list box, accept all the other defaults, and then click Start.

20. A warning dialog box appears. Click OK to format the drive.

21. A dialog box appears indicating that the format is complete. Click OK.

22. Click Close to return to the Disk Administrator main dialog box.

23. Select Partition ⇒ Exit to exit Disk Administrator.

Congratulations! You have now formatted the 10MB partition on your computer with NTFS.

## Lab 3.4 *Updating the Emergency Repair Disk*

Server
Enterprise

The purpose of this hands-on lab exercise it to provide you with the skills required to update your Emergency Repair Disk, and to give you experience performing this task.

In order to do this lab, you need the Emergency Repair Disks you created in Labs 2.1 and 2.2 during the original installations of your Windows NT operating systems.

 note **The Emergency Repair Disks for Windows NT Workstation and Windows NT Server are different. If you have both operating systems on the same computer, you need to update both disks.**

Do this lab twice, once from each operating system.

1. Boot to Windows NT (either Workstation or Server).

2. Select Start ⇒ Run.

3. When the Run dialog box appears, type **RDISK** in the drop-down dialog box.

4. Click OK to run `Rdisk.exe`.

5. When the Repair Disk Utility dialog box appears, click Update Repair Info.

6. Click Yes to update your repair information.

7. `Rdisk.exe` saves your current configuration. This takes a couple of minutes. Click Yes to create the Emergency Repair Disk.

8. When prompted, place the Emergency Repair Disk you created in Lab 2.1 (if you are running Windows NT Workstation) or Lab 2.2 (if you are running Windows NT Server) in drive A:. Click OK to create the Emergency Repair Disk. (This process erases your original Emergency Repair Disk and creates a new Emergency Repair Disk with your current system configurations.) It takes a couple of minutes for the Repair Disk Utility to complete this process.

9. Click Exit to exit the Repair Disk Utility. Your Emergency Repair Disk is now updated. Remove it from drive A:. (Remember to do this lab again with your other NT operating system.)

## Lab 4.5 *Configuring directory replication*

Server
Enterprise

The purpose of this lab is to provide you with hands-on experience and the skills needed to configure and use the Directory Replicator service.

There are seven parts to this lab:

Part 1: Creating a logon script

Part 2: Creating a directory replication user account

Part 3: Configuring the startup type of the Directory Replicator service

Part 4: Configuring replication

Part 5: Stopping and restarting the Directory Replicator service

Part 6: Viewing the replication of the logon script

Part 7: Testing your logon script

Follow these steps carefully:

### Part 1: Creating a logon script

1. Boot your computer to Windows NT Server.

2. Select Start ⇒ Programs ⇒ Accessories ⇒ Notepad.

**3.** In the Untitled-Notepad dialog box, type the following:

**@echo This is the logon script I created in Lab 4.5.**
**@echo**
**@echo**
**@pause**

(Note: Make sure to type the text *exactly* as it is presented above.)

**4.** Select File ⇒ Save As. Edit the File name text box to read as follows:

**c:\winntsrv\system32\repl\export\scripts\logonscript.bat**

**5.** Click Save.

**6.** Exit Notepad.

## Part 2: Creating a directory replication user account

**1.** Select Start ⇒ Programs ⇒ Administrative Tools (Common) ⇒ User Manager for Domains.

**2.** Select User ⇒ New User in the User Manager dialog box.

**3.** In the New User dialog box, type in the username **Repluser**. Type in a password of **password** (remember that passwords are case sensitive in Windows NT). Confirm the password by retyping it in the Confirm Password box. Deselect the check box next to User Must Change Password at Next Logon. Select the check box next to Password Never Expires. Click the Groups command button at the lower left-hand corner of the dialog box.

**4.** The Group Memberships dialog box appears. In the "Not member of" text box, highlight Backup Operators and click the Add command button. In the "Not member of" text box, highlight Replicator and click the Add command button. There should be three groups listed in the Member of text box: Backup Operators, Domain Users, and Replicator. Click OK.

**5.** The New User dialog box reappears. Click Add. Then click Close.

**6.** The User Manager dialog box reappears. Exit User Manager.

## Part 3: Configuring the startup type of the Directory Replicator service

**1.** Select Start ⇒ Settings ⇒ Control Panel.

**2.** Double-click Services.

**3.** The Services dialog box appears. Highlight Directory Replicator. Click Startup.

**4.** The Service dialog box appears. In the Startup Type section, select the Automatic radio button. In the Log On As section, select the This Account radio button. Click the … command button at the end of the This Account text box.

**5.** The Add User dialog box appears. In the Names list box, highlight Repluser, and click Add. Click OK.

**6.** The Service dialog box reappears. Highlight the asterisks in the Password text box and type in **password**. In the Confirm Password text box, highlight the asterisks and type **password**. Click OK.

**7.** A Services dialog box appears indicating that the account LAB\Repluser has been granted the Log On As A Service right. Click OK.

**8.** The Services dialog box reappears. Click Close. The Control Panel dialog box reappears.

### Part 4: Configuring replication

**1.** In Control Panel, double-click Server.

**2.** In the Server dialog box, click Replication.

**3.** The Directory Replication dialog box appears. Click the Export Directories radio button. Click the Add command button at the bottom of the Export Directories section.

**4.** The Select Domain dialog box appears. In the Select Domain list box, click LAB. LAB should now appear in the Domain text box. Click OK.

**5.** The Directory Replication dialog box reappears. LAB should appear in the To List box. Click the Import Directories radio button. Click the Add command button at the bottom of the Import Directories section.

**6.** The Select Domain dialog box appears. In the Select Domain list box, double-click LAB. Click PDCLAB. \\PDCLAB should now appear in the Domain text box. Click OK.

**7.** The Directory Replication dialog box reappears. PDCLAB should appear in the From List box. Click OK to save the directory replication configuration and automatically start the Directory Replicator service.

**8.** In the Server dialog box, click OK. The Control Panel dialog box reappears.

### Part 5: Stopping and restarting the Directory Replicator service

**1.** In Control Panel, double-click Services.

**2.** The Services dialog box appears. In the Service list box, highlight Directory Replicator. Click Stop. A warning message appears, asking if you want to stop the Directory Replicator service. Click Yes.

**3.** A Service Control dialog box appears, indicating that NT is attempting to stop the Directory Replicator service.

**4.** The Services dialog box reappears. Note that the Status column no longer shows "Started" for the Directory Replicator service. Click Start.

**5.** A Service Control dialog box appears, indicating that NT is attempting to start the Directory Replicator service.

**6.** The Services dialog box reappears. Note that the Status column now shows "Started" for the Directory Replicator service. Click Close.

**7.** The Control Panel dialog box reappears. Exit Control Panel.

## Part 6: Viewing the replication of the logon script

**1.** Select Start ⇒ Programs ⇒ Windows NT Explorer.

**2.** Maximize the Exploring dialog box. In the All Folders column on the left, click the + sign next to the Winntsrv folder. Then click the + sign next to the system32 folder. Click the + sign next to the Repl folder. Click the + sign next to the Export folder. Click the Scripts folder. Notice that the logonscript.bat file you created in the first part of this lab appears in the Contents window. (Remember that you saved this file in the c:\winntsrv\system32\repl\export\scripts folder in the first part of this lab.)

**3.** Click the + sign next to the Import folder (in the All Folders column on the left). Click the Scripts folder beneath the Import folder. Notice that the logonscript.bat file has been replicated from the Export\Scripts folder to the Import\Scripts folder. The Directory Replicator service is now fully functional. Exit Windows NT Explorer.

## Part 7: Testing your logon script

**1.** Select Start ⇒ Programs ⇒ Administrative Tools (Common) ⇒ User Manager for Domains.

**2.** In the User Manager dialog box, select User ⇒ Properties.

**3.** The User Properties dialog box appears. Click the Profile command button.

**4.** The User Environment Profile dialog box appears. In the Logon Script Name text box, type **logonscript.bat**. (Don't type the period at the end.) Click OK.

**5.** The User Properties dialog box reappears. Click OK.

6. Close User Manager.

7. Select Start⇒Shut Down. The Shut Down Windows dialog box appears. Click the "Close all programs and log on as a different user" radio button. Then click Yes.

8. In the Begin Logon dialog box, press Ctrl + Alt + Delete to log on.

9. The Logon Information dialog box appears. Type in your password in the Password text box. Click OK.

10. A command prompt window should appear. The logon script you created in part one of this lab has run and appears like the following:

```
This is the logon script I created in Lab 4.5.
ECHO is on.
ECHO is on.
Press any key to continue . . .
```

11. Press spacebar to complete this lab.

tip    **This logon script will appear every time you log on from this point. If you'd like to remove it, start User Manager for Domains, then double-click the Administrator user. Click Profile. Highlight** logonscript.bat **in the User Environment Profile dialog box, and press Delete. Click OK. In the User Properties dialog box, click OK. Exit User Manager for Domains.**

### Lab 4.6 *Exploring Control Panel*

Workstation
Server

The purpose of this hands-on lab exercise is to provide you with the skills required to use Control Panel applications.

This lab is divided into three parts. You'll use the following Control Panel applications in the following three parts:

Part 1: Add/Remove Programs

Part 2: Using System

Part 3: Becoming familiar with Display,

Keyboard, Modems, Mouse,

Ports, SCSI Adapters,

Tape Devices, and UPS

Begin this lab by booting your computer to Windows NT Server.

## Part 1: Using Add/Remove Programs

In this part, you use Add/Remove Programs to install an optional Windows NT component.

### TO INSTALL MAIL, FOLLOW THESE STEPS:

**1.** Select Start ⇒ Settings ⇒ Control Panel.

**2.** Double-click Add/Remove Programs.

**3.** In the Add/Remove Programs Properties dialog box, click the Windows NT Setup tab. Scroll to the bottom of the Components list box. Click in the check box next to Windows Messaging. Click the Details command button. Ensure that the Internet Mail, Microsoft Mail, and Windows Messaging check boxes are all selected. Click OK.

**4.** In the Windows NT Setup tab in the Add/Remove Programs Properties dialog box, click OK.

**5.** NT copies files to your hard disk. If prompted, supply the path to your Windows NT installation source files (usually on your Windows NT compact disc). This process takes a few minutes.

**6.** The Control Panel dialog box reappears. Windows Messaging (Mail) is now installed. Exit Control Panel.

**7.** Optional: If you want, you can install games on your computer by using the same steps, except click on the check box next to Games (instead of Windows Messaging) in the Windows NT Setup tab. (Try Pinball if you have a sound card—it's really fun!)

## Part 2: Using System

In this part, you use System to create an additional paging file and create a hardware profile.

### TO CREATE AN ADDITIONAL PAGING FILE, FOLLOW THESE STEPS:

**1.** Select Start ⇒ Settings ⇒ Control Panel.

**2.** Double-click System.

**3.** Click the Performance tab in the System Properties dialog box. In the Virtual Memory section, click Change.

**4.** The Virtual Memory dialog box appears. Click D: in the Drive list box. In the Paging File Size for Selected Drive section, type **5** in the Initial Size (MB) text box, and type **5** in the Maximum Size (MB) text box. Click Set. Notice that Drive D: now shows a Paging File Size of 5-5 in the list box at the top of the screen. Click OK.

**5.** On the Performance tab click Close.

**6.** Click Yes to restart your computer so the new settings can take effect.

**TO CREATE A HARDWARE PROFILE, FOLLOW THESE STEPS:**

Hardware profiles were originally designed to handle the unique needs of laptop computers. In this lab, you create two hardware profiles: docked (connected to the network) and undocked (not connected to the network) to simulate the use of a laptop computer at work and at home.

**1.** Select Start ⇒ Settings ⇒ Control Panel.

**2.** Double-click System.

**3.** Click the Hardware Profiles tab. Highlight Original Configuration (Current) in the Available Hardware Profiles list box. Click the Rename command button.

**4.** In the Rename Profile dialog box, edit the To: text box to read as follows: **Docked**. (Don't type the period at the end.) Click OK.

**5.** The Hardware Profiles tab reappears. Highlight Docked (Current) in the Available Hardware Profiles list box. Click Copy.

**6.** In the Copy Profile dialog box, edit the To: text box to read as follows: **UnDocked**. (Don't type the period at the end.) Click OK.

**7.** The Hardware Profiles tab reappears. Notice that two profiles now appear in the Available Hardware Profiles list box: Docked (Current) and UnDocked. Highlight UnDocked and click the Properties command button.

**8.** In the UnDocked Properties dialog box, click the Network tab. Click the check box next to Network-disabled hardware profile. Click OK.

**9.** The Hardware Profiles tab reappears. Click OK. Exit Control Panel.

**10.** Select Start ⇒ Shut Down. Click the "Restart the computer" radio button in the Shut Down Windows dialog box. Click Yes.

**11.** After you select Windows NT Server 4.0 from the boot loader menu, press the spacebar when `"Press spacebar now to invoke the Hardware Profile/Last Known Good menu"` appears.

**12.** A Hardware Profile/Configuration Recovery Menu is displayed. You can select a Docked or UnDocked hardware profile at this point. (Select Docked if you are connected to a network; select UnDocked if you are not connected to a network.) Press Enter to continue booting Windows NT Server.

### Part 3: Becoming familiar with Display, Keyboard, Modems, Mouse, Ports, SCSI Adapters, Tape Devices, and UPS

In this part, you explore several Control Panel applications. (You may even use a few of these applications to install devices that you have but which may not yet be installed.)

#### DISPLAY

**1.** Select Start ⇒ Settings ⇒ Control Panel.

**2.** Double-click Display.

**3.** In the Display Properties dialog box, click the Screen Saver tab.

**4.** In the Screen Saver drop-down list box, select 3D Pipes (OpenGL). Click the Settings command button.

**5.** In the 3D Pipes Setup dialog box, click the Textured radio button in the Surface Style section. Click the Choose Texture command button.

**6.** In the Choose Texture File dialog box, double-click `1 arimarint.bmp`.

**7.** The 3D Pipes Setup dialog box reappears. Click OK.

**8.** The Screen Saver tab reappears. Click Apply. (Your screen saver now consists of 3D Pipes that say "Windows NT Server" on them.)

**9.** Click the Settings tab. In the Desktop Area section, click and hold the slide bar and move it to the right until the display reads "800 by 600 pixels." Note: if your computer does not support a display setting larger than "640 by 480 pixels," you can click the slide bar, but it won't move. Continue on to Step 10.

**10.** Click the Test command button. Click OK in the Testing Mode dialog box.

**11.** A test screen appears for about five seconds. When the Testing Mode dialog box appears, click Yes if you saw the test bitmap.

**12.** The Settings tab reappears. Click OK to apply your new display settings.

note 🖉 **If you do not like the appearance of an 800 by 600 display, or your computer can't accommodate this setting, you can change your display settings to any resolution you desire. Follow Steps 9 through 12 above to change your display settings.**

### KEYBOARD

**1.** Select Start ⇒ Settings ⇒ Control Panel.

**2.** Double-click Keyboard.

**3.** In the Keyboard Properties dialog box, click the Input Locales tab. Click the Properties command button. Click the drop-down arrow in the Keyboard layout drop-down list box to view the optional keyboard layouts. Notice that US, several Dvorak options, and US-International are listed. Click US, then click OK.

**4.** In the Input Locales tab in the Keyboard Properties dialog box, click Cancel.

### MODEMS

(You don't have to have a modem to complete this section. If you have already installed a modem in your computer by using the Modems application in Control Panel, skip this section.)

**1.** Select Start ⇒ Settings ⇒ Control Panel.

**2.** Double-click Modems.

**3.** The Install New Modem dialog box appears. Select the check box next to Don't detect my modem; I will select it from a list. Click the Next command button.

**4.** The Install Modem dialog box appears. Select your modem's manufacturer from the Manufacturers list box. If your manufacturer is not listed, or if you don't have a modem, highlight (Standard Modem Types). Select your modem speed or model in the Models list box, or select Dial-Up Networking Serial Cable between 2 PCs if you don't have a modem. Then click Next.

**5.** The Install New Modem dialog box appears. Click the Selected ports radio button.

**6.** Highlight the COM port your modem is connected to, or any available COM port (that your mouse or another device isn't connected to) if you don't have a modem. Click Next. Windows NT installs your modem.

**7.** A dialog box may appear at this point requesting the area code you are in and other information. If this box appears, enter the requested information and continue. If a dialog box does not appear, skip to Step 8.

**8.** Click the Finish command button.

**9.** In the Modems Properties dialog box, click the Dialing Properties command button.

**10.** In the Dialing Properties dialog box, configure the dialing properties for your location. Then click OK.

**11.** In the Modems Properties dialog box, click Close.

### MOUSE

**1.** Select Start ⇒ Settings ⇒ Control Panel.

**2.** Double-click Mouse.

**3.** In the Mouse Properties dialog box, click each tab and view the configuration options available. Customize your mouse to suit your personal preferences. Click OK to return to Control Panel.

### PORTS

**1.** Select Start ⇒ Settings ⇒ Control Panel.

**2.** Double-click Ports.

**3.** In the Ports dialog box, highlight a COM port, and click Settings.

**4.** In the Settings dialog box, notice the settings that you can configure for your COM port. Customize your COM port settings as desired. Click Advanced.

**5.** In the Advanced Settings dialog box, notice the settings that you can configure. Click OK.

**6.** In the Settings dialog box, click OK.

**7.** In the Ports dialog box, click Close.

### SCSI ADAPTERS

**1.** Select Start ⇒ Settings ⇒ Control Panel.

**2.** Double click SCSI Adapters.

**3.** View the configuration options available on both the Devices tab and the Drivers tab by clicking on each of the tabs. (If you have a SCSI adapter but have not yet installed drivers for it, you may want to do so now. You can do this by clicking the Add command button on the Drivers tab and then selecting the appropriate manufacturer and SCSI adapter from the lists displayed. Click OK.) Click OK.

### TAPE DEVICES

**1.** Select Start ⇒ Settings ⇒ Control Panel.

**2.** Double-click Tape Devices.

**3.** View the configuration options available on both the Devices tab and the Drivers tab by clicking each of the tabs. (If you have a tape drive but have not yet installed drivers for it, you may want to do so now. You can do this by clicking the Add command button on the Drivers tab and then selecting the appropriate manufacturer and tape device from the lists displayed. Click OK.) Click OK.

**UPS**

**1.** Select Start ⇒ Settings ⇒ Control Panel.

**2.** Double-click UPS.

**3.** In the UPS dialog box, view the configuration options available. Click Help.

**4.** Read through the UPS help topics. Exit Windows NT Help.

**5.** If you do not have a UPS, skip to Step 6 now. If you have a UPS but have not yet configured it, you may want to do so now. Configure the settings in the UPS dialog box to match your UPS. Click OK. Stop here if you have a UPS (don't do Step 6).

**6.** Click Cancel in the UPS dialog box. Exit Control Panel.

## Lab 5.7 *Creating an answer file by using Setup Manager*

Workstation
Server

The purpose of this lab is to familiarize you with the use of Setup Manager to create Unattend.txt files.

There are two parts to this lab:

Part 1: Creating an Unattend.txt file using Setup Manager

Part 2: Viewing the contents of the Unattend.txt file

Begin this lab by booting your computer to Windows NT Server.

Insert your Windows NT Server (or Windows NT Workstation) compact disc in your CD-ROM drive.

Follow the steps below carefully.

**Part 1: Creating an Unattend.txt file using Setup Manager**

**1.** Select Start ⇒ Programs ⇒ Windows NT Explorer.

**2.** In the All Folders list box (on the left side of your screen) in Windows NT Explorer, scroll down to My Computer, and then click the + sign next to your CD-ROM drive.

**3.** Click the + sign next to Support, and then click the + sign next to Deptools.

**4.** Click the i386 folder (not the + sign next to it).

**5.** In the Contents of 'i386' box (on the right side of your screen), double-click Setupmgr.exe.

**6.** The Windows NT Setup Manager dialog box appears. Click General Setup.

**7.** The General Setup Options dialog box appears. Type in your user name (use **your name**). Press Tab. Type in the name of your organization (use any name . . . how about **MCSE Candidates Company**?). Press Tab. Type in your computer name (use **NTW2** for this lab). Press Tab. For the product ID number, type in **123-4567890**. (Don't type in the period at the end.) Click the General tab.

8. Notice the configuration options available in the General tab. Do not select any check boxes. Click the Computer Role tab.

9. In the Select the role of the computer drop-down list box, select Workstation in domain. In the "Enter the domain name" text box, type **LAB**. Leave the "Enter the computer account" text box blank. Click the Install Directory tab.

10. Notice the configuration options available in the Install Directory tab. Do not change any of the options. Click the Display Settings tab.

11. Notice the configuration options available in the Display Settings tab. In the Settings section, change the Horizontal Resolution to 800, and change the Vertical Resolution to 600. Click the Time Zone tab.

12. In the drop-down list box in the Time Zone tab, select your time zone. Click the License Mode tab.

13. A warning message appears, stating that if you want to configure the License Mode, the computer role must be a server. Click OK.

14. The General Setup Options dialog box appears. Click OK.

15. The Windows NT Setup Manager dialog box reappears. Click Networking Setup.

16. The Networking Options dialog box appears. On the General tab, select the radio button next to "Automatically detect and install first adapter." Click the Protocols tab.

17. On the Protocols tab, click the Add command button.

18. The Adding Protocols dialog box appears. In the drop-down list box, select TCP/IP. Click OK.

19. The Networking Options dialog box reappears. Click the Parameters command button.

20. The TCP/IP Protocol Parameters dialog box appears. Click the check box next to Do Not Use DHCP. Type an IP Address of **192.168.59.11**. (Don't type the period at the end.) Type a Subnet of **255.255.255.0**. (Don't type the period at the end.) Type a Gateway of **192.168.59.1**. (Don't type the period at the end.) Click OK to continue.

21. The Protocols tab reappears. Click the Services tab.

22. The Services tab appears. Click the Add command button.

23. The Adding Services dialog box appears. In the drop-down list box, select Remote Access Service (RAS). Click OK.

**24.** The Services tab reappears. Click the Parameters command button.

**25.** The Remote Access Service Parameters dialog box appears. Click the Ports tab.

**26.** On the Ports tab, click the Add command button. (Notice that PortSection1 has moved from the top list box to the bottom list box.)

**27.** Click the Parameters command button.

**28.** The Port Parameters dialog box appears.

**29.** Notice the configuration options available. Do not change any of the options. Click OK.

**30.** The Ports tab reappears. Click OK.

**31.** The Services tab reappears. Click the Modem tab.

**32.** In the COM drop-down list box on the Modem tab, select 1. In the Modem Description list box, type **STANDARD 28800 bps Modem**. (Don't type the period at the end.) In the Manufacturer text box, type **(Standard Modem Types)**. (Don't type the period at the end.) In the Provider text box, type **Unimodem Service Provider**. (Don't type the period at the end.) Click the Add command button. Click OK.

**33.** The Windows NT Setup Manager dialog box reappears. Click Advanced Setup.

**34.** The Advanced Options dialog box appears. On the General tab, check the check boxes next to Skip Welcome wizard page and Skip Administrator Password wizard page.

**35.** Click the File System tab.

**36.** Notice the configuration options available on the File System tab. Click the Mass Storage tab.

**37.** Notice the configuration options available on the Mass Storage tab.

 **You only need to specify mass storage devices whose drivers do *not* ship with Windows NT. All other mass storage devices are automatically detected by Windows NT. If you are using an SCSI adapter whose drivers do not ship with NT, click on the Add command button and follow the onscreen directions to add and configure the driver.**

**38.** Click the Display tab.

**39.** Notice the configuration options available on the Display tab. As with mass storage devices, you only need to modify this tab if your display adapter's drivers do not ship with Windows NT. (See the note above.) Click OK.

**40.** The Windows NT Setup Manager dialog box reappears. Select File ⇒ Save As.

**41.** In the File Name text box, type **C:\Unattend.txt.** (Don't type the period at the end.) Click the Save command button.

**42.** The Windows NT Setup Manager dialog box reappears. Click Exit.

**43.** The Windows NT Explorer dialog box reappears. The `Unattend.txt` file is now created. Continue to Part 2, where you'll view the contents of this file.

### Part 2: Viewing the contents of the `Unattend.txt` file

**1.** In the Windows NT Explorer dialog box, in the All Folders box (on the left side of the screen), click drive C: (not the + sign next to drive C:). In the Contents Of '(C:)' box (on the right side of the screen), scroll down to the bottom. Double-click `Unattend.txt`.

**2.** The `Unattend.txt` file is displayed in Notepad. Examine the contents of this file. (You can print the contents of this file if you desire.) Notice the formatting of the various sections.

**3.** When you are finished, select File ⇒ Exit.

**4.** Exit Windows NT Explorer.

## Lab 6.8 *Creating and sharing a local printer*

Workstation
Server
Enterprise

The purpose of this lab is to familiarize you with the Windows NT `Printers` folder and its user interface, and to provide you with the skills necessary to create and share a local printer.

To begin this lab, boot your computer to Windows NT Server.

There are two parts to this lab:

Part 1: Creating a local printer

Part 2: Sharing a local printer

### Part 1: Creating a local printer

**1.** Select Start ⇒ Programs ⇒ Windows NT Explorer.

**2.** Highlight (single-click) the `Printers` folder in the All Folders list box. (You might have to scroll down to find this folder.)

**3.** Double-click the Add Printer icon in the Contents of 'Printers' list box.

**4.** The Add Printer Wizard appears. Ensure that the radio button next to My Computer is selected. Click Next.

5. Select the check box next to LPT1: in the Available ports list box. Click Next.

6. If you have a print device, select your print device's manufacturer from the Manufacturers list box, and then select your print device's model from the Printers list box. Then click Next. (If you don't have a print device, accept the defaults in the Add Printer Wizard dialog box and click Next.)

7. Type in a name for the new printer in the text box, or accept the default name that Windows NT presents. (If your computer has any additional printers installed, you are presented with another option to configure: Select the radio button next to Yes if you want this to be your default printer. Otherwise, select the radio button next to No.) Click Next.

8. Ensure that the radio button next to Not shared is selected in the Add Printer Wizard dialog box. Click Next.

9. In the Add Printer Wizard dialog box, select the radio button next to Yes to print a test page. Click Finish.

10. Windows NT copies files. (Respond to any prompts requesting the location of your Windows NT source files.)

11. A dialog box appears indicating that the printer test page is completed. Click Yes.

12. The printer is now created. The Windows NT Explorer dialog box reappears. (If you do not have a print device connected to LPT1, an error message eventually appears, indicating that there was an error printing the test page and that the print device is not ready. Click Cancel.) Continue on to Part 2 to share the printer.

### Part 2: Sharing a local printer

1. In the Windows NT Explorer dialog box, with the Contents of 'Printers' list box displayed on the right, right-click the printer you just created. Select Sharing from the menu that appears.

2. A dialog box with your printer's properties appears. Select the radio button next to Shared. Edit the text box next to Share Name to read: **My Shared Printer**. (Don't type the period at the end.) Don't select any alternate drivers at this time. Click OK.

3. A warning message appears (because the share name you typed is longer than eight characters and has spaces in it) indicating that the share name you entered may not be accessible from MS-DOS workstations. Click Yes.

4. The Windows NT Explorer dialog box reappears. In the Contents of 'Printers' list box, right-click on your printer. Select Properties from the menu that appears.

5. In your printer's Properties dialog box, click the Security tab.

6. Click Permissions.

7. In the Printer Permissions dialog box, notice the default permissions for a newly created printer. Click OK.

8. The Printer Permissions dialog box reappears. Click OK. Exit Windows NT Explorer.

### Lab 6.9 *Installing and configuring Microsoft TCP/IP Printing*

**Workstation**
**Server**
**Enterprise**

The purpose of this lab is to give you hands-on experience in installing and configuring Microsoft TCP/IP Printing.

Begin this lab by booting your computer to Windows NT Server.

There are two parts to this lab:

Part 1: Installing Microsoft TCP/IP Printing
Part 2: Configuring Microsoft TCP/IP Printing

#### Part 1: Installing Microsoft TCP/IP Printing

1. Select Start ⇒ Programs ⇒ Windows NT Explorer.

2. Click Control Panel in the All Folders list box on the left. In the Contents of 'Control Panel' list box on the right, double-click Network.

3. The Network dialog box appears. Click the Services tab.

4. On the Services tab, click the Add command button.

5. The Select Network Service dialog box appears. Click Microsoft TCP/IP Printing in the Network Service list box. Click OK.

6. A Windows NT Setup dialog box appears, requesting the location of Windows NT source files. Type in the path to your Windows NT source files on your Windows NT compact disc (for example, d:\i386) and place your Windows NT compact disc in your CD-ROM drive. Click Continue.

7. Windows NT copies the files to your hard drive. The Services tab reappears. Click Close.

8. Several dialog boxes appear while Windows NT configures the new network service. When the Network Settings Change warning dialog box appears, click Yes to restart your computer.

### Part 2: Configuring Microsoft TCP/IP Printing

1. Select Start ⇒ Programs ⇒ Windows NT Explorer.

2. Click Control Panel in the All Folders list box on the left. In the Contents of 'Control Panel' list box on the right, double-click Services.

3. Select TCP/IP Print Server from the Service list box. Click the Startup command button.

4. In the Startup Type section of the Service dialog box, select the radio button next to Automatic. Click OK.

5. The Services dialog box reappears. Click the Start command button.

6. A Service Control dialog box appears, indicating that Windows NT is attempting to start the service. The Services dialog box reappears. Notice in the Status column that the TCP/IP Print Server service is started. Click Close.

7. The Windows NT Explorer dialog box reappears. Exit Windows NT Explorer. Microsoft TCP/IP Printing is now installed and configured.

## Lab 7.10 *Creating and managing user and group accounts*

Workstation
Server
Enterprise

The purpose of this lab is to give you hands-on experience creating user accounts, assigning home directories, managing user account properties, creating group accounts, and assigning user accounts to groups. You will also create user account templates to help simplify the creation of user accounts.

This lab consists of four parts:

Part 1: Creating the Users folder

Part 2: Creating group accounts

Part 3: Creating user account templates

Part 4: Creating and managing user accounts

In this lab, you'll create users and groups for the local office of a sales organization. Within this organization, there are several employees. The following table shows the organization's employees and their job titles.

| SALES ORGANIZATION EMPLOYEES | |
| --- | --- |
| EMPLOYEE | JOB TITLE |
| Pam Rhodes | District Manager |
| John Spencer | Sales Manager |
| Robert Jones | Accounting Manager |
| Colleen Green | Sales Representative |

| EMPLOYEE | JOB TITLE |
|----------|-----------|
| Bill Tracy | Sales Representative |
| Mike Calhoun | Sales Representative |
| Nancy Yates | Accounting Staff |
| Mike Cook | Accounting Staff |

The users will select their own passwords when they first access their user accounts. Each user will have a home folder on the primary domain controller (named PDCLAB).

Begin this lab by booting your computer to Windows NT Server. Log on as Administrator. (Remember: the password is *password*.)

Follow the steps below carefully:

## Part 1: Creating the Users folder

In this section, you create and share a Users folder in Windows NT Explorer. The Users folder will eventually contain a home directory for each user account.

**1.** Select Start ⇒ Programs ⇒ Windows NT Explorer.

**2.** In the All Folders list box, highlight the drive on which your NTFS partition is located. (This is probably drive D:.) Select File ⇒ New ⇒ Folder.

**3.** A folder named New Folder is created and appears in the "Contents of D:." Edit the folder's name so that it is called **Users**. Press Enter.

**4.** Highlight the Users folder in the Windows NT Explorer dialog box. Select File ⇒ Sharing.

**5.** In the Users Properties dialog box, select the radio button next to Shared As. Accept the default Share Name of Users. Click OK.

**6.** Exit Windows NT Explorer. Continue to Part 2.

## Part 2: Creating group accounts

In this section, you create three new global groups: Managers, Sales, and Accounting.

**1.** Select Start ⇒ Programs ⇒ Administrative Tools (Common) ⇒ User Manager for Domains.

**2.** Highlight any of the groups listed in the Groups list box. (The reason for this is that the first user in the Username list box is highlighted by default, and if this user is not unhighlighted, the user will automatically become a member of the new global group you create.) Select User ⇒ New Global Group.

**3.** The New Global Group dialog box appears. In the Group Name text box, type in **Managers**. In the Description text box, type in **Managers of the Sales Organization**. Click OK.

**4.** The User Manager dialog box reappears. Select User ⇒ New Global Group.

**5.** The New Global Group dialog box appears. In the Group Name text box, type in **Sales**. In the Description text box, type in **Sales Representatives**. Click OK.

**6.** The User Manager dialog box reappears. Select User ⇒ New Global Group.

**7.** The New Global Group dialog box appears. In the Group Name text box, type in **Accounting**. In the Description text box, type in **Accounting Staff**. Click OK.

**8.** The User Manager dialog box reappears. You have now created three new global groups: Managers, Sales, and Accounting. Continue to Part 3.

### Part 3: Creating user account templates

In this section, you create two user account templates one that will be used to create user accounts for sales representatives, and another that will be used to create user accounts for accounting staff.

**1.** In the User Manager dialog box, select User ⇒ New User.

**2.** The New User dialog box appears. Type the bolded information below in the appropriate text boxes:

- User Name: **Sales_User**
- Full Name: (leave this box blank)
- Description: **Sales Representative**
- Password: **newuser**
- Confirm Password: **newuser**

Select the check box next to User Must Change Password at Next Logon. Select the check box next to Account Disabled. Click the Groups command button.

**3.** The Group Memberships dialog box appears. In the "Not member of" list box, highlight Sales. Click the Add command button. (Notice that the Sales group, along with Domain Users, is now listed in the "Member of" list box.) Click OK.

**4.** The New User dialog box reappears. Click the Dialin command button.

**5.** The Dialin Information dialog box appears. Select the check box next to Grant dialin permission to user. Accept the default of No Call Back in the Call Back section. Click OK.

**6.** The New User dialog box reappears. Click the Profile command button.

**7.** The User Environment Profile dialog box appears. In the Home Directory section, select the radio button next to Connect. Accept the Z: in the drop-down list box. In the To text box, type: **\\PDCLAB\USERS\ %USERNAME%**. Click OK.

**8.** The New User dialog box reappears. Click the Add command button.

**9.** The New User dialog box reappears. Type the following bolded information in the appropriate text boxes:

- o User Name: **Acct_User**
- o Full Name: (leave this box blank)
- o Description: **Accounting Staff**
- o Password: **newuser**
- o Confirm Password: **newuser**

Select the check box next to User Must Change Password at Next Logon. Select the check box next to Account Disabled. Click the Groups command button.

**10.** The Group Memberships dialog box appears. In the "Not member of" list box, highlight Accounting. Click the Add command button. (Notice that the Accounting group, along with Domain Users, is now listed in the "Member of" list box.) Click OK.

**11.** The New User dialog box reappears. Click the Hours command button.

**12.** The Logon Hours dialog box appears. Using your mouse, highlight the entire graph. Click the Disallow command button. Using your mouse, highlight the area on the graph that represents 6:00 a.m. to 9:00 p.m., Monday through Friday. Click the Allow command button. Click OK.

**13.** The New User dialog box reappears. Click the Profile command button.

**14.** The User Environment Profile dialog box appears. In the Home Directory section, select the radio button next to Connect. Accept the Z: in the drop-down list box. In the To text box, type: **\\PDCLAB\USERS\ %USERNAME%**. Click OK.

**15.** The New User dialog box reappears. Click the Add command button. Click the Close command button. Notice that your two new user account templates, Sales_User and Acct_User, now appear in the Username list box within the User Manager dialog box. Continue to Part 4.

## Part 4: Creating and managing user accounts

In this section, you create user accounts from scratch and also use the user account templates to create user accounts. You assign some of the new user accounts to groups.

**1.** In the User Manager dialog box, select User ⇒ New User.

**2.** The New User dialog box appears. Type the following bolded information in the appropriate text boxes:

- o User Name: **PamR**
- o Full Name: **Pam Rhodes**
- o Description: **District Manager**
- o Password: **newuser**
- o Confirm Password: **newuser**

Select the check box next to User Must Change Password at Next Logon. Click the Groups command button.

**3.** The Group Memberships dialog box appears. In the "Not member of" list box, highlight Accounting. Then press and hold Ctrl while you scroll down and click Managers and Sales. Click the Add command button. (The Accounting, Managers, and Sales groups, along with Domain Users, should now be listed in the "Member of" list box.) Click OK.

**4.** The New User dialog box reappears. Click the Add command button.

**5.** The New User dialog box reappears. Type the following bolded information in the appropriate text boxes:

- o User Name: **JohnS**
- o Full Name: **John Spencer**
- o Description: **Sales Manager**
- o Password: **newuser**
- o Confirm Password: **newuser**

Select the check box next to User Must Change Password At Next Logon. Click the Groups command button.

**6.** The Group Memberships dialog box appears. In the "Not member of" list box, highlight Managers. Then press and hold Ctrl while you click Sales. Click the Add command button. (The Managers and Sales groups, along with Domain Users, should now be listed in the "Member of" list box.) Click OK.

**7.** The New User dialog box reappears. Click the Add command button.

**8.** The New User dialog box reappears. Type the following bolded information in the appropriate text boxes:

- ○ User Name: **RobertJ**
- ○ Full Name: **Robert Jones**
- ○ Description: **Accounting Manager**
- ○ Password: **newuser**
- ○ Confirm Password: **newuser**

Select the check box next to User Must Change Password at Next Logon. Click the Groups command button.

**9.** The Group Memberships dialog box appears. In the "Not member of" list box, highlight Accounting. Then press and hold Ctrl while you scroll down and click Managers. Click the Add command button. (The Accounting and Managers groups, along with Domain Users, should now be listed in the "Member of" list box.) Click OK.

**10.** The New User dialog box reappears. Click the Add command button. Click the Close command button.

**11.** The User Manager dialog box reappears. Notice that the three users you just created are in the Username list box. Highlight JohnS, and then press and hold Ctrl while you click PamR and RobertJ. Select User ⇒ Properties.

**12.** The User Properties dialog box appears. Notice the three users you selected are listed in the Users list box. Click the Dialin command button.

**13.** The Dialin Information dialog box appears. Select the check box next to Grant dialin permission to user. Accept the default of No Call Back in the Call Back section. Click OK.

**14.** The User Properties dialog box reappears. Click the Profile command button.

**15.** The User Environment Profile dialog box appears. In the Home Directory section, select the radio button next to Connect. Accept the Z: in the drop-down list box. In the To text box, type: **\\PDCLAB\USERS\ %USERNAME%**. Click OK.

**16.** The User Properties dialog box reappears. Click OK. You have now granted dialin permission and assigned home folders to JohnS, PamR, and RobertJ.

**17.** The User Manager dialog box reappears. Highlight Sales_User. Select User ⇒ Copy.

**18.** The Copy of Sales_User dialog box appears. Type the following bolded information in the appropriate text boxes:

- User Name: **ColleenG**
- Full Name: **Colleen Green**
- Description: (already filled in)
- Password: **newuser**
- Confirm Password: **newuser**

Select the check box next to User Must Change Password at Next Logon. Click Groups. Notice that the Sales group, as well as Domain Users, is listed in the "Member of" list box. Click OK.

**19.** In the Copy of Sales_User dialog box, click the Dialin command button. In the Dialin Information dialog box, notice that the check box next to "Grant dialin permission to user" is selected. Click OK.

**20.** In the Copy of Sales_User dialog box, click the Add command button.

**21.** The Copy of Sales_User dialog box reappears. Type the following bolded information in the appropriate text boxes:

- User Name: **BillT**
- Full Name: **Bill Tracy**
- Description: (already filled in)
- Password: **newuser**
- Confirm Password: **newuser**

Select the check box next to User Must Change Password at Next Logon. Click the Add command button.

**22.** The Copy of Sales_User dialog box reappears. Type the bolded information below in the appropriate text boxes:

- User Name: **MikeC**
- Full Name: **Mike Calhoun**
- Description: (already filled in)
- Password: **newuser**
- Confirm Password: **newuser**

Select the check box next to User Must Change Password at Next Logon. Click the Add command button. Click the Close command button.

**23.** The User Manager dialog box reappears. Notice that your new users now appear in the Username list box. Highlight the Acct_User. Select User ⇒ Copy.

**24.** The Copy of Acct_User dialog box appears. Type the following bolded information in the appropriate text boxes:

- User Name: **NancyY**
- Full Name: **Nancy Yates**
- Description: (already filled in)
- Password: **newuser**
- Confirm Password: **newuser**

Select the check box next to User Must Change Password at Next Logon. Click the Groups command button. Notice that the Accounting group, in addition to Domain Users, appears in the "Member of" list box. Click OK.

**25.** In the Copy of Acct_User dialog box, click the Hours command button. In the Logon Hours dialog box, notice that this user will be able to log on between 6:00 a.m. and 9:00 p.m., Monday through Friday. Click OK.

**26.** In the Copy of Acct_User dialog box, click the Add command button.

**27.** The Copy of Acct_User dialog box reappears. Type the following bolded information in the appropriate text boxes:

- User Name: **MikeCo**
- Full Name: **Mike Cook**
- Description: (already filled in)
- Password: **newuser**
- Confirm Password: **newuser**

Select the check box next to User Must Change Password at Next Logon. Click the Add command button. Then click the Close command button.

**28.** The User Manager dialog box reappears. Notice that the new users you created appear in the Username list box. Exit User Manager.

## Lab 8.11  *Implementing auditing*

**Server
Enterprise**

The purpose of this lab is to provide you with hands-on experience in using the Windows NT auditing feature.

This lab consists of three parts:

Part 1: Implementing auditing

Part 2: Creating audited events

Part 3: Viewing the security log in Event Viewer

Begin this lab by booting your computer to Windows NT Server. Log on as Administrator.

Perform the following steps carefully.

### Part 1: Implementing auditing

In this part you implement auditing on a Windows NT Server computer.

**1.** Select Start⇒Programs⇒Administrative Tools (Common)⇒User Manager for Domains.

**2.** In the User Manager dialog box, select Policies⇒Audit.

**3.** In the Audit Policy dialog box, select the radio button next to Audit These Events, and then select the Success and Failure check boxes for *all* audit events *except* Process Tracking. Click OK.

**4.** Auditing is now implemented. Exit User Manager for Domains. Proceed to Part 2.

### Part 2: Creating audited events

In this part you cause a user to create audited events.

**1.** Select Start⇒Shut Down.

**2.** In the Shut Down Windows dialog box, select the radio button next to Restart the computer. Click the Yes command button. The computer shuts down and restarts.

**3.** Reboot the computer to Windows NT Server. Press Ctrl+Alt+Delete to log on. When the Logon Information dialog box appears, type in a user name of **PamR** (replacing Administrator) and a password of **wrongo**. Click OK.

**4.** An error message appears, stating the system could not log you on. Click OK.

**5.** The Logon Information dialog box reappears. Type in a password of **newuser**. Click OK.

**6.** A message appears, indicating you are required to change your password at first logon. (You may recall you set this configuration when you created this user in Lab 7.10.) Click OK.

**7.** Type in a new password of **password**. Confirm the new password by retyping it. Click OK.

**8.** A dialog box appears, indicating your password has been changed. Click OK.

**9.** Another dialog box appears, indicating the local policy of this system does not enable you to log on interactively. Click OK.

**10.** The Logon Information dialog box reappears. Type in a user name of **Administrator**, and a password of **password**. Click OK. You have now created several audited events. Continue to Part 3.

**Part 3: Viewing the security log in Event Viewer**

In this part you view the security log in Event Viewer to see the audited events you created in Part 2.

**1.** Select Start⇒Programs⇒Administrative Tools (Common)⇒Event Viewer.

**2.** Select Log⇒Security.

**3.** Scroll down the list and double-click the first event marked with a lock (not a key) in the left margin. (A lock marks a failure audit event. A key marks a success audit event.)

**4.** The Event Detail dialog box appears. Notice the event is a logon failure for PamR, because she was not allowed to log on interactively (locally). Click the Close command button.

**5.** Scroll down and double-click the next event marked with a lock in the left margin.

**6.** The Event Detail dialog box reappears. This is also a failure audit event. Notice an unexpected error occurred during PamR's attempted logon. Click the Close command button.

**7.** Scroll down and double-click the next event marked with a lock in the left margin.

**8.** The Event Detail dialog box appears. This is a logon failure event for PamR, because an incorrect password (wrongo) was entered. Click the Close command button.

**9.** Double-click various other events, as desired, and view their event details.

**10.** Exit Event Viewer.

## Lab 8.12 *Managing account policy and user rights*

Server
Enterprise

The purpose of this lab is to provide you with hands-on experience in setting account policy and user rights in Windows NT.

This lab consists of three parts:

Part 1: Setting account policy

Part 2: Creating users and configuring user rights

Part 3: Auditing revisited—clearing the security log in Event Viewer

Begin this lab by booting your computer to Windows NT Server. Log on as Administrator.

Follow the steps below carefully.

### Part 1: Setting account policy

In this section, you set account policy that affects all users in the domain.

1. Select Start ⇒ Programs ⇒ Administrative Tools (Common) ⇒ User Manager for Domains.
2. In the User Manager dialog box, select Policies ⇒ Account.
3. The Account Policy dialog box appears. Configure the following:
   - Configure the Maximum Password Age Expires in **30** Days.
   - Configure the Minimum Password Age to Allow Changes in **5** Days.
   - Configure the Minimum Password Length to be At Least **8** Characters.
   - Configure Password Uniqueness to Remember (the last) **6** Passwords.
   - Select the radio button next to Account lockout.
   - Set Lockout after **3** bad logon attempts.
   - Set Reset count after **30** minutes.
   - Configure Lockout Duration to Forever (until admin unlocks).
   - Select the check box next to Users must log on in order to change password.

     The following figure shows the Account Policy dialog box as correctly configured at the close of this step. You can check the configurations you have made against this figure. Click OK.

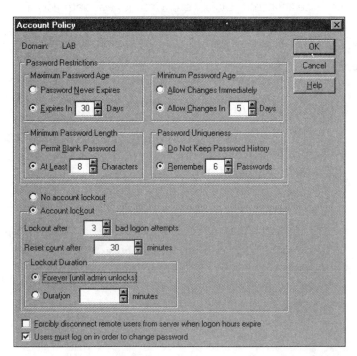

Account Policy dialog box as correctly configured in Lab 8.12

**4.** In the User Manager dialog box, select Policies ⇒ User Rights.

**5.** The User Rights Policy dialog box appears. In the Right drop-down list box, select Log on locally. Click the Add command button.

**6.** The Add Users and Groups dialog box appears. In the Names list box, double-click the Everyone group. (Everyone appears in the Add Names list box.) Click OK. (Granting the Log on locally right to the Everyone group enables all users to log on interactively at the Windows NT Server.)

**7.** In the Users Rights Policy dialog box, click OK.

**8.** Exit User Manager.

**9.** Select Start ⇒ Shut Down. In the Shut Down Windows dialog box, select the radio button next to Close all programs and log on as a different user. Click the Yes command button.

**10.** Press Ctrl+Alt+Delete to log on.

**11.** In the Logon Information dialog box, type in a user name of **JohnS** and a password of **newuser**. Click OK.

**12.** A dialog box appears, indicating you are required to change your password at first logon. (You may recall you set this configuration when you created this user in Lab 7.10.) Click OK.

**13.** The Change Password dialog box appears. Type in a new password of **password**. Confirm the new password by retyping it. Click OK.

**14.** A warning message appears, indicating you do not have permission to change your password. (This is because in the Account Policy dialog box you selected the check box next to Users must log on in order to change password **and**, when you created this user, you selected the option for User Must Change Password at Next Logon. *These two options do not work together.*) Click OK.

**15.** The Change Password dialog box appears. Click the Cancel command button.

**16.** The Logon Information dialog box appears. Type in a user name of **PamR** and a password of **wrongo**. Click OK. (Note: In this part of the lab, you will attempt to log PamR on several times with an incorrect password to experience the account lockout feature.)

**17.** A warning message appears, indicating the system could not log you on. Click OK.

**18.** Repeat Steps 16 and 17 until a warning message appears, indicating NT is unable to log you on because your account has been locked out. You must contact your network administrator to unlock your account. Click OK. (Next, you will log on as administrator and unlock PamR's user account.)

**19.** In the Logon Information dialog box, type in a user name of **Administrator** and a password of **password**. Click OK.

**20.** Select Start ⇒ Programs ⇒ Administrative Tools (Common) ⇒ User Manager for Domains.

**21.** In the User Manager dialog box, double-click the user account PamR in the Username list box.

**22.** The User Properties dialog box appears. Notice the check box next to Account Locked Out is checked. Deselect this check box. Click OK.

**23.** Double-click PamR again in the Username list box.

**24.** The User Properties dialog box appears. Notice the check box next to Account Locked Out is cleared and grayed out. (The Administrator can't lock out a user account—only the system can.) Click the Cancel command button.

**25.** In the User Manager dialog box, select Policies ⇒ Account.

**26.** In the Account Policy dialog box, deselect the check box next to Users must log on in order to change password. (This will enable users to change their passwords during logon.) Click OK.

**27.** Continue to Part 2.

### Part 2: Creating users and configuring user rights

In this section, you create two special-use user accounts and configure user rights for these new user accounts.

**1.** In the User Manager dialog box, select User ⇒ New User.

**2.** The New User dialog box appears. Type the following bolded information in the appropriate text boxes:

User name: **Admin2**

Full name: **Administrator's Helper**

Description: **User account with limited admin privileges**

Password: **password**

Confirm password: **password**

Deselect the check box next to User Must Change Password at Next Logon. Select the check box next to Password Never Expires. Click the Add command button.

**3.** The New User dialog box reappears. Type the following bolded information in the appropriate text boxes:

User name: **Backuponly**

Full name: **Backup Operator's Helper**

Description: **Only able to back up files, not restore**

Password: **password**

Confirm password: **password**

Deselect the check box next to User Must Change Password at Next Logon. Select the check box next to Password Never Expires. Click the Add command button. Click the Close command button.

4. In the User Manager dialog box, select Policies ⇒ User Rights.

5. The User Rights Policy dialog box appears. In the Right drop-down list box, select Log on locally. Click the Add command button.

6. The Add Users and Groups dialog box appears. Click the Show Users command button. Double-click Backup only. Click OK.

7. In the Right drop-down list box, select Back up files and directories. Click the Add command button.

8. The Add Users and Groups dialog box appears. Click the Show Users command button. Scroll down and double-click Backuponly. Click OK. (The Backuponly user is now able to log on to the Windows NT Server and is able to back up the server's files.)

9. The User Rights Policy dialog box reappears. Using the sequence you used in the previous Steps 7 and 8, grant the following rights to the Admin2 user:

   o Add workstations to domain

   o Back up files and directories

   o Change the system time

   o Log on locally

   o Manage auditing and security log

   o Restore files and directories

   o Shut down the system

   o Take ownership of files or other objects

   Note: You must go through all the steps for each user right you want to assign. No shortcuts exist here.

   Click OK in the User Rights Policy dialog box when you finish.

10. Exit User Manager for Domains. Continue to Part 3.

### Part 3: Auditing revisited—clearing the security log in Event Viewer

In this section, you explore the capabilities of the "Manage auditing and security log" user right, and clear the security log in Event Viewer.

1. Press Ctrl + Alt + Delete. Click the Logoff command button. Click OK to close all programs and log off.

2. Press Ctrl + Alt + Delete. In The Logon Information dialog box, type in a user name of **Admin2** and a password of **password**. Click OK. (If a Welcome to Windows NT screen is displayed, click the Close command button.)

3. Select Start ⇒ Programs ⇒ Administrative Tools (Common) ⇒ User Manager for Domains.

4. In the User Manager dialog box, select Policies. Notice all the options in the Policies menu are grayed out. These options are only available to members of the Administrators group—The "Manage auditing and security log" user right does *not* give you the rights needed to set account policy, to configure user rights, or to enable auditing. Exit User Manager for Domains.

5. Select Start ⇒ Programs ⇒ Administrative Tools (Common) ⇒ Event Viewer.

6. In the Event Viewer dialog box, select Log ⇒ Security.

7. Select Log ⇒ Clear All Events.

8. Click Yes in the Clear Event Log dialog box.

9. In the Save As dialog box, type **old security log** in the File name text box. Click the Save command button.

10. Click the Yes command button to clear the security log. (The "Manage auditing and security log" user right authorizes a user to view and change the security log in Event Viewer, and enables a user to configure auditing of files, directories, and printers [in Windows NT Explorer, or in a printer's Properties dialog box, and so forth]. But this user right does *not* enable a user to access the Audit Policy dialog box in User Manager or User Manager for Domains.)

11. Exit Event Viewer.

## Lab 9.13 *Implementing user profiles*

Workstation
Server
Enterprise

The purpose of this lab is to give you hands-on experience in creating and copying user profiles, and experience in configuring roaming and mandatory user profiles.

This lab consists of five parts:

> Part 1: Creating and sharing a profile's folder
>
> Part 2: Configuring a user profile
>
> Part 3: Copying a user profile
>
> Part 4: Configuring server-based profiles
>
> Part 5: Testing profiles

Begin this lab by booting your computer to Windows NT Server. Log on as Administrator.

Follow the steps below carefully.

## Part 1: Creating and sharing a profile's folder

In this section, you create a shared folder on the PDC that contains users' profiles.

**1.** Select Start ⇒ Programs ⇒ Windows NT Explorer.

**2.** In the All Folders section of the Exploring dialog box, highlight the NTFS volume on your computer—this is most likely drive D:. Select File ⇒ New ⇒ Folder.

**3.** In the Contents of the NTFS Volume section, type the new folder name: **Profiles**.

**4.** Right-click the newly created `Profiles` folder. Select Sharing from the menu that appears.

**5.** In the Profiles Properties dialog box, select the radio button next to Shared As. Accept the default Share Name of Profiles. Click OK.

**6.** Notice that a hand appears under the `Profiles` folder in the Exploring dialog box, indicating that it is a shared folder. Exit Windows NT Explorer. Continue to Part 2.

## Part 2: Configuring a user profile

In this section, you configure a profile that will be used by all sales representatives.

**1.** Select Start ⇒ Programs ⇒ Administrative Tools (Common) ⇒ User Manager for Domains.

**2.** In the User Manager dialog box, double-click Sales_User in the Username list box. (You will use this user account to create the profile that you will copy to the user account of each sales representative.)

**3.** In the User Properties dialog box, clear the check boxes next to User Must Change Password at Next Logon and Account Disabled. Select the check box next to Password Never Expires. Click OK.

**4.** Exit User Manager for Domains.

**5.** Select Start ⇒ Shut Down.

**6.** In the Shut Down Windows dialog box, select the radio button next to Close all programs and log on as a different user. Click the Yes command button.

**7.** Press Ctrl + Alt + Delete to log on.

**8.** In the Logon Information dialog box, type in a user name of **Sales_User** and a password of **newuser**. Click OK.

**9.** If the Welcome to Windows NT dialog box appears, click the Close command button.

**10.** Right-click the desktop. Select Properties from the menu that appears.

**11.** In the Display Properties dialog box, click the Appearance tab.

**12.** In the Scheme drop-down list box, select the Red, White, and Blue (VGA) scheme. Click the Background tab.

**13.** In the Pattern drop-down list box, select the Scottie pattern. Click OK.

**14.** Right-click the desktop. Select New ⇒ Shortcut from the menus that appear.

**15.** In the Create Shortcut dialog box, type **calc.exe** in the Command line text box. Click the Next command button.

**16.** In the Select a name for the shortcut text box, type **Calculator**. Click the Finish command button.

**17.** Right-click the desktop. Select New ⇒ Shortcut from the menus that appear.

**18.** In the Create Shortcut dialog box, type **notepad.exe** in the Command line text box. Click the Next command button.

**19.** In the Select a name for the shortcut text box, type **Notepad**. Click the Finish command button.

**20.** Right-click the desktop. Select Arrange Icons ⇒ Auto Arrange from the menus that appear. Notice that the new shortcuts are neatly arranged on your desktop.

**21.** Select Start ⇒ Shut Down.

**22.** In the Shut Down Windows dialog box, select the radio button next to Close all programs and log on as a different user. Click the Yes command button.

**23.** Press Ctrl + Alt + Delete to log on.

**24.** In the Logon Information dialog box, type in a user name of **Administrator** and a password of **password**. Click OK. Continue to Part 3.

### Part 3: Copying a user profile

In this section, you copy the user profile you created in Part 2 to a profile folder for each sales representative. You also configure one of the sales representative's user profiles as a mandatory user profile.

**1.** Select Start ⇒ Settings ⇒ Control Panel.

**2.** In the Control Panel dialog box, double-click the System icon.

**3.** In the System Properties dialog box, click the User Profiles tab.

**4.** Scroll down the Profiles stored on this computer list box. Select the LAB\Sales_User profile. Click the Copy To command button.

**5.** In the Copy profile to text box, type **\\pdclab\profiles\BillT**. (Don't type the period at the end.) Click the Change command button.

**6.** In the Choose User dialog box, click the Show Users command button. Scroll down the Names list box and select BillT. Click the Add command button. Click OK.

**7.** In the Copy To dialog box, click OK.

**8.** The System Properties dialog box reappears, with LAB\Sales_User highlighted. Click the Copy To command button.

**9.** In the Copy profile to text box, type **\\pdclab\profiles\MikeC**. (Don't type the period at the end.) Click the Change command button.

**10.** In the Choose User dialog box, click the Show Users command button. Scroll down the Names list box and select MikeC. Click the Add command button. Click OK.

**11.** In the Copy To dialog box, click OK.

**12.** The System Properties dialog box reappears, with LAB\Sales_User highlighted. Click the Copy To command button.

**13.** In the Copy profile to text box, type **\\pdclab\profiles\ColleenG**. (Don't type the period at the end.) Click the Change command button.

**14.** In the Choose User dialog box, click the Show Users command button. Scroll down the Names list box and select ColleenG. Click the Add command button. Click OK.

**15.** In the Copy To dialog box, click OK.

**16.** In the System Properties dialog box, click OK.

**17.** Exit Control Panel.

**18.** Select Start⇒ Programs⇒ Windows NT Explorer.

**19.** In the All Folders section of the Exploring dialog box, click the + sign next to the NTFS volume (probably drive D:). Click the + sign next to the Profiles folder. Highlight the BillT folder. In the Contents of BillT section of the dialog box, highlight the Ntuser.dat file. Select File⇒ Rename. Rename the Ntuser.dat file as **Ntuser.man**. Press Enter. (Renaming BillT's Ntuser.dat file as Ntuser.man causes BillT's profile to be a mandatory user profile.)

**20.** Exit Windows NT Explorer. Continue to Part 4.

**Part 4: Configuring server-based profiles**

In this section, you configure the user accounts of the sales representatives to use the server-based profiles you created for them in Parts 2 and 3. Additionally, you configure the user accounts of the accounting staff to use roaming user profiles.

**1.** Select Start⇒ Programs⇒ Administrative Tools (Common)⇒ User Manager for Domains.

**2.** In the User Manager dialog box, highlight BillT, and then press and hold Ctrl while you click ColleenG and MikeC in the Username list box. Select User⇒ Properties.

**3.** In the User Properties dialog box, click the Profile command button.

**4.** In the User Environment Profile dialog box, type **\\pdclab\profiles\ %USERNAME%** in the User Profile Path text box. Click OK. (This step assigns a copied profile to each selected user account.)

**5.** In the User Properties dialog box, click OK.

**6.** In the User Manager dialog box, double-click Sales_User in the Username list box.

**7.** In the User Properties dialog box, select the check box next to Account Disabled. (Remember that in Part 2, you deselected this check box so that you could use the account to create a profile. Now you want to disable the account again so that no one can use it to log on.) Click OK.

**8.** In the User Manager dialog box, highlight MikeCo, and then press and hold Ctrl while you click NancyY. Select User⇒ Properties.

**9.** In the User Properties dialog box, click the Profile command button.

**10.** In the User Environment Profile dialog box, type **\\pdclab\profiles\%USERNAME%** in the User Profile Path text box. Click OK. (This step assigns a roaming user profile to MikeCo and NancyY.)

**11.** In the User Properties dialog box, click the Hours command button.

**12.** In the Logon Hours dialog box, highlight the entire chart, so that all hours are selected. Click the Allow command button. (You are changing the hours now in case you're doing this lab during nonbusiness hours. This change enables you to log on as MikeCo or NancyY anytime.) Click OK.

**13.** In the User Properties dialog box, click OK.

**14.** In the User Manager dialog box, select Policies⇒ User Rights.

**15.** In the User Rights Policy dialog box, select Shut down the system from the Right drop-down list box. Click the Add command button.

**16.** In the Names list box (in the Add Users and Groups dialog box), double-click the Everyone group. Click OK.

**17.** In the User Rights Policy dialog box, click OK.

**18.** Exit User Manager for Domains. Continue to Part 5.

### Part 5: Testing profiles

In this section, you try out the sales representatives' profiles, including the mandatory user profile. Additionally, you try out the roaming user profiles for one of the accounting staff.

**1.** Select Start ⇒ Shut Down.

**2.** In the Shut Down Windows dialog box, select the radio button next to Close all programs and log on as a different User. Click the Yes command button.

**3.** Press Ctrl + Alt + Delete to log on.

**4.** In the Logon Information dialog box, type in a user name of **ColleenG** and a password of **newuser**. Click OK.

**5.** A message appears indicating that you are required to change your password at first logon. Click OK.

**6.** In the Change Password dialog box, type in a new password of **password**, and confirm the new password by retyping it. Click OK.

**7.** A message is displayed, indicating that your password has been changed. Click OK.

**8.** If a Welcome to Windows NT screen appears, deselect the check box next to Show this Welcome Screen next time you start Windows NT, and then click the Close command button.

**9.** Notice that the background pattern (Scottie dogs) and color scheme (Red, white, and blue) that you configured for the Sales_User profile and copied to ColleenG's profile appear on the desktop. Right-click the desktop. Select Properties from the menu that appears.

**10.** In the Display Properties dialog box, select (None) from the Pattern drop-down list box. Select a Wallpaper of lanmannt. Click the Appearance tab.

**11.** In the Scheme drop-down list box, select Rose. Click OK.

**12.** Select Start ⇒ Shut Down.

**13.** In the Shut Down Windows dialog box, select the radio button next to "Close all programs and log on as a different User." Click the Yes command button.

**14.** Press Ctrl + Alt + Delete to log on.

**15.** In the Logon Information dialog box, type in a user name of **ColleenG** and a password of **password**. Click OK.

**16.** Notice that the changes you made to ColleenG's desktop (the rose scheme and the lanmannt wallpaper) appear on the desktop. These settings have been successfully saved to ColleenG's user profile, because her profile is not a mandatory user profile.

**17.** Select Start ⇒ Shut Down.

**18.** In the Shut Down Windows dialog box, select the radio button next to "Close all programs and log on as a different User." Click the Yes command button.

**19.** Press Ctrl + Alt + Delete to log on.

**20.** In the Logon Information dialog box, type in a user name of **BillT** and a password of **newuser**. Click OK.

**21.** A message appears indicating that you are required to change your password at first logon. Click OK.

**22.** In the Change Password dialog box, type in a new password of **password**, and confirm the new password by retyping it. Click OK.

**23.** A message is displayed, indicating that your password has been changed. Click OK.

**24.** If a Welcome to Windows NT screen appears, deselect the check box next to Show this Welcome Screen next time you start Windows NT. Click the Close command button.

**25.** Notice that the background pattern (Scottie dogs) and color scheme (Red, white, and blue) that you configured for the Sales_User profile and copied to BillT's profile appear on the desktop. Right-click the desktop. Select Properties from the menu that appears.

**26.** In the Display Properties dialog box, select Critters from the Pattern drop-down list box. Click the Appearance tab.

**27.** In the Scheme drop-down list box, select Pumpkin (large). Click OK.

**28.** Select Start ⇒ Shut Down.

**29.** In the Shut Down Windows dialog box, select the radio button next to Close all programs and log on as a different user. Click the Yes command button.

**30.** Press Ctrl + Alt + Delete to log on.

**31.** In the Logon Information dialog box, type in a user name of **BillT** and a password of **password**. Click OK.

**32.** If a Welcome to Windows NT screen appears, deselect the check box next to "Show this Welcome Screen next time you start Windows NT." Click the Close command button.

**33.** Notice that the desktop changes that you made for BillT's desktop in Steps 26 and 27 were *not* saved to BillT's profile. (This is because in an earlier part of this lab, you configured BillT to have a mandatory user profile.) Select Start ⇒ Shut Down.

**34.** In the Shut Down Windows dialog box, select the radio button next to "Close all programs and log on as a different user." Click the Yes command button.

**35.** Press Ctrl + Alt + Delete to log on.

**36.** In the Logon Information dialog box, type in a user name of **NancyY** and a password of **newuser**. Click OK.

**37.** A Logon Message is displayed, indicating that you are required to change your password at first logon. Click OK.

**38.** In the Change Password dialog box, type in a new password of **password**, and confirm the new password by retyping it. Click OK.

**39.** A message indicating that your password has been changed appears. Click OK.

**40.** If a Welcome to Windows NT screen appears, click the Close command button.

**41.** Right-click the desktop. Select New ⇒ Shortcut from the menus that appear.

**42.** In the Create Shortcut dialog box, type **calc.exe** in the Command line text box. Click the Next command button.

**43.** In the Select a name for the shortcut text box, type **Calculator**. Click the Finish command button.

**44.** Right-click the desktop. Select Arrange Icons ⇒ Auto Arrange.

**45.** Select Start ⇒ Shut Down.

**46.** In the Shut Down Windows dialog box, select the radio button next to "Close all programs and log on as a different user." Click the Yes command button.

**47.** Press Ctrl + Alt + Delete to log on.

**48.** In the Logon Information dialog box, type in a user name of **Administrator** and a password of **password**. Click OK.

**49.** Select Start ⇒ Programs ⇒ Windows NT Explorer.

**50.** In the All Folders section of the Exploring dialog box, click the + sign next to the NTFS volume (probably drive D:). Click the Profiles folder. Notice that a profile folder has been created for NancyY. (It is displayed in the Contents Of Profiles section.) Also notice that there is not a folder for MikeCo, because he has not logged on since you assigned him a roaming profile. Exit Windows NT Explorer.

### Lab 9.14 *Configuring a system policy*

Server
Enterprise

The purpose of this lab is to give you hands-on experience in creating and configuring a Windows 95 system policy; and experience in creating, configuring, and testing a Windows NT system policy.

This lab consists of three parts:

> Part 1: Creating a system policy and configuring load balancing for all
> Windows 95 computers
>
> Part 2: Creating a system policy for all Windows NT computers
>
> Part 3: Testing the Windows NT system policy

Begin this lab by booting your computer to Windows NT Server. Log on as Administrator.

Follow these steps carefully.

#### Part 1: Creating a system policy and configuring load balancing for all Windows 95 computers

1. Select Start ⇒ Programs ⇒ Administrative Tools (Common) ⇒ System Policy Editor.

2. In the System Policy Editor dialog box, select Options ⇒ Policy Template.

3. In the Policy Template Options dialog box, click the Add command button.

4. In the Open Template File dialog box, type **\winntsrv\inf\windows.adm** in the File Name text box. Click the Open command button.

5. The Policy Template Options dialog box reappears. Highlight the C:\WINNTSRV\INF\Winnt.adm file. Click the Remove command button. Click OK.

6. In the System Policy Editor dialog box, select File ⇒ New Policy.

7. Double-click Default Computer.

8. On the Policies tab, click the + sign next to Network. Then click the + sign next to System policies update. Select the check box next to Remote update. In the Settings For Remote Update section, select Automatic (use default path) in the Update Mode drop-down list box. Scroll to the bottom of the section, and select the check box next to Load balancing.

9. On the Policies tab, click the + sign next to Windows 95 Network. Then click the + sign next to Microsoft Client for Windows networks. Select the check box next to Log on to Windows NT. In the Settings for Log on to Windows NT section, select the check boxes next to Display domain logon confirmation and Disable caching of domain password. Type **LAB** in the Domain name text box.

**10.** On the Policies tab, click the + sign next to Windows 95 System. Then click the + sign next to Profiles. Select the check box next to Enable user profiles. Click OK.

**11.** In the System Policy Editor dialog box, double-click Default User.

**12.** On the Policies tab, click the + sign next to Shell. Then click the + sign next to Restrictions. Then select the check boxes next to "Remove Run command from Start menu" and "Don't save settings at exit."

**13.** On the Policies tab, click the + sign next to System. Then click the + sign next to Restrictions. Next, select the check box next to Disable Registry editing tools. Click OK.

**14.** In the System Policy Editor dialog box, select File⇒Save As. In the File name text box, type **\\pdclab\repl$\scripts\config**. (Don't type the period at the end.) Click the Save command button.

**15.** In the System Policy Editor dialog box, select File⇒Close. Continue to Part 2.

### Part 2: Creating a system policy for all Windows NT computers

**1.** In the System Policy Editor dialog box, select Options⇒Policy Template.

**2.** In the Policy Template Options dialog box, click the Add command button.

**3.** In the Open Template File dialog box, double-click the `Winnt.adm` file.

**4.** In the Policy Template Options dialog box, highlight `C:\WINNTSRV\INF\windows.adm`. Click the Remove command button. Click OK.

**5.** In the System Policy Editor dialog box, select File⇒New Policy.

**6.** Double-click Default Computer.

**7.** On the Policies tab, click the + sign next to Windows NT System. Click the + sign next to Logon. Then select the check box next to Logon banner.

**8.** On the Policies tab, click the + sign next to Windows NT User Profiles. Then select the check box next to "Delete cached copies of roaming profiles."

**9.** On the Policies tab, click the + sign next to Windows NT Network. Then click the + sign next to Sharing. Then select the check box next to "Create hidden drive shares (Server)." Then select the same check box again, so it turns white (not gray), *without* a check in it. Click OK.

**10.** In the System Policy Editor dialog box, double-click Default User.

**11.** On the Policies tab, click the + sign next to Windows NT System. Then select the check box next to Parse `Autoexec.bat`. Click OK.

**12.** In the System Policy Editor dialog box, select File⇒Save As.

**13.** In the Save As dialog box, type **\\pdclab\repl$\scripts\ntconfig** in the File name text box. Click the Save command button.

**14.** Exit System Policy Editor.

**15.** Select Start ⇒ Programs ⇒ Windows NT Explorer.

**16.** In the All Folders section of the Exploring dialog box, click the + sign next to the `Winntsrv` folder. Then click the + sign next to the `System 32` folder. Next, click the + sign next to the `Repl` folder, and then click the + sign next to the `Export` folder. Highlight the `Scripts` folder. Notice in the Contents of Scripts section that both the policy files you created (`config.POL` and `ntconfig.POL`) are listed. Click the + sign next to the `Import` folder. Highlight the `Scripts` folder under `Import`. Wait until the `ntconfig.POL` file appears (is replicated) to the Contents of Scripts section.

**17.** Exit Windows NT Explorer. Continue to Part 3.

### Part 3: Testing the Windows NT system policy

**1.** Select Start ⇒ Shut Down.

**2.** In the Shut Down Windows dialog box, select the radio button next to Close all programs and log on as a different user. Click the Yes command button.

**3.** Press Ctrl + Alt + Delete to log on.

**4.** In the Logon Information dialog box, type in a user name of **Administrator** and a password of **password**. Click OK. (Logging on has implemented the Default Computer and Default User policies. These policies will take effect the next time you log on.)

**5.** Select Start ⇒ Shut Down.

**6.** In the Shut Down Windows dialog box, select the radio button next to Close all programs and log on as a different user. Click the Yes command button.

**7.** Press Ctrl + Alt + Delete to log on.

**8.** Notice that a logon banner (Important Notice) is displayed. (Remember: you configured a logon banner in Part 2 of this lab.) Click OK.

**9.** In the Logon Information dialog box, type in a user name of **Administrator** and a password of **password**. Click OK. This step completes Lab 9.14.

## Lab 10.15 *Implementing a trust relationship*

note ▼ This lab is optional, but *only* because it requires an additional Intel-based computer with a 486/33 processor, 16MB of RAM, and 500MB–1GB available hard disk space. You will also need a VGA monitor and graphics card and mouse. A CD-ROM drive for the second computer would be nice, but it's not absolutely necessary if you don't mind taking the CD-ROM drive out of your first computer and installing it in the second for the NT installation portion of this lab. This lab also requires that you use two network adapters and the appropriate cabling to connect the two computers.

I can't suggest strongly enough that you go through whatever pain is necessary to beg, borrow, rent, or purchase a second computer to use in this lab—a 486 can be obtained fairly inexpensively, and the benefit you'll receive from experiencing trusts and groups in a multiple domain environment will pay off big when you take the Enterprise exam.

Enterprise

The objective of this lab is to give you hands-on experience with implementing and testing one-way and two-way trust relationships between two domains.

This lab consists of the following five parts:

Part 1: Installing Windows NT Server 4.0 on a second computer

Part 2: Configuring a one-way trust

Part 3: Testing a one-way trust

Part 4: Configuring a two-way trust

Part 5: Testing a two-way trust

### Part 1: Installing Windows NT Server 4.0 on a second computer

First install MS-DOS on the second computer's hard drive, and load the drivers for the CD-ROM drive. Make sure that the Windows NT Server compact disc is in the CD-ROM drive.

You will need one blank, 3.5-inch high-density floppy disk for this lab exercise.

Follow the steps below carefully to perform the installation of Windows NT Server 4.0.

### Precopy phase

**1.** Change the default drive to your CD-ROM drive by typing in the CD-ROM drive letter followed by a colon (for example, **D:**), then press Enter.

**2.** Type **cd i386**, then press Enter.

**3.** Type **winnt /b**, then press Enter. (This command instructs Setup to perform the `Winnt.exe` installation without creating the Setup Boot Disk set.)

**4.** When Windows NT Setup asks you to enter the path where NT files are located, press Enter.

**5.** Setup copies files to your hard disk. (This process takes a few minutes. How about a stretch break or a fresh cup of coffee?)

**6.** When the Windows NT Server Setup screen appears, press Enter to restart your computer and continue Windows NT Setup.

### Phase 0

**1.** After a minute or two, when the Windows NT Server Setup screen appears, press Enter to set up Windows NT now.

**2.** Setup displays a screen showing any mass storage devices, such as SCSI adapters, CD-ROM drives, and so on. Some older IDE controllers will not be displayed here, but they will still function and be recognized by NT. Specify additional devices by making changes on this screen if you need to. When you have completed all necessary changes, press Enter to continue.

**3.** The Windows NT Licensing Agreement screen appears. Read the licensing agreement, pressing PgDn to view additional screens of the agreement. When you reach the bottom of the agreement, press F8 to continue setup.

**4.** Windows NT Server Setup displays a screen listing your computer's hardware and software components. Make any changes necessary. When you are finished, highlight "The above list matches my computer," and press Enter.

**5.** If you have a previous version of Microsoft Windows installed on your computer, Setup displays a screen stating that it detected a previous version. If this screen appears, press **N** to install Windows NT Server in a different directory.

**6.** Windows NT Server Setup displays a screen showing your computer's hard disk partitions. Highlight the partition on which you want to install Windows NT Server, then press Enter. (Make sure the partition you choose has at least 124MB free.)

**7.** Windows NT Server Setup asks you to select the type of file system you want on this partition. Highlight "Leave the current file system intact <no changes>," and press Enter.

**8.** Windows NT Server Setup displays the location where it will install the NT Server files. In the highlighted area, edit the text so that it reads: **\WINNTSRV.** (Don't type in the period at the end.) Then press Enter.

**9.** Windows NT Server Setup offers to examine your hard disk for corruption. Press Enter to enable this. (This takes a few minutes.)

**10.** Windows NT Server Setup displays a screen that indicates this portion of Setup is complete. If you have a floppy disk inserted in drive A:, remove it now. Then press Enter to restart your computer and to continue with setup.

## Phase 1

**1.** After your computer reboots and the Windows NT Server Setup dialog box finally appears, click Next to continue.

**2.** Type in your name, press Tab, then type in the name of your organization. Click Next to continue.

**3.** Type in the 10-digit CD key number from the back of your Windows NT Server compact disc case (press Tab after you enter the first three digits). Click Next to continue.

**4.** Select a Licensing Mode for the server. Select Per Server for: and enter the number of client licenses you purchased. Click Next to continue.

**5.** When prompted to type in a name for your computer, type **PDCMAINOFFICE**. Click Next to continue.

**6.** Select Primary Domain Controller in the Server Type window. Click Next to continue.

**7.** Type **password** when prompted to enter an administrator password. Press Tab. Confirm the password by retyping it. Click Next to continue.

**8.** Windows NT Server Setup asks you if you want to create an Emergency Repair Disk. Accept the Yes default. Click Next to continue.

**9.** Windows NT Server Setup displays a screen prompting you to Select Components. Add any components that you want to install, but do *not* deselect any components that are selected by default. Click Next to continue.

**Phase 2**

1. Windows NT Server Setup displays a window indicating that Phase 2, Installing Windows NT Networking, is about to begin. Click Next to continue.

2. Accept the default check in the box next to "Wired to the network." Click Next to continue.

3. Accept the default check in the box next to "Install Microsoft Internet Information Server." Click Next to continue.

4. Windows NT Server Setup displays the Network Adapters box. Click Start Search. Your network adapter should then appear in the Network Adapters box.

   If your network adapter did not appear, click Select from list. If your network adapter is shown in the list, highlight it and click OK.

   If your network adapter is not on the list, and you have a driver disk from its manufacturer, highlight any network adapter and click Have Disk. Setup then prompts you to insert this disk. Insert the disk and click OK. Highlight your network adapter from the list and click OK.

   You should now have your network adapter displayed in the Network Adapters box. Click Next to continue.

5. Windows NT Server Setup displays the Network Protocols list box. Deselect NWLink IPX/SPX Compatible Transport. Ensure that the TCP/IP Protocol is the only protocol selected (it will have a gray check in the check box). Click Next to continue.

6. Windows NT Server Setup displays the Network Services list box. Accept all of the defaults selected in this window. Click Next to continue.

7. Click Next to continue and to have Setup install the selected components.

8. Setup prompts you to enter your network adapter card settings. (This screen may not appear for some network adapters.) Verify that the settings shown match the ones that you used when you installed and configured your network adapter. Make changes only as needed. Click Continue to continue.

9. A TCP/IP Setup warning screen appears. If you are on a network that has a DHCP server, click Yes. Otherwise, click No.

10. The Microsoft TCP/IP Properties dialog box appears if you clicked No in the previous step. *If you are on a network that uses TCP/IP, or if you are connected to the Internet, obtain an IP address, subnet mask, and default gateway from your network administrator.* Otherwise, type an IP address of: **192.168.59.6** and a subnet mask of: **255.255.255.0**.

caution

**Do *not* use this IP address if you are on a network that uses TCP/IP, or if you are connected to the Internet.**

**11.** Leave the Default Gateway blank. Click OK to continue.

**12.** Windows NT Server Setup displays a screen showing network binding information. Click Next to continue.

**13.** Click Next to start the network.

**14.** Windows NT Server Setup prompts you enter a domain name. Type **MAINOFFICE** as your domain name. Click Next to continue.

### Phase 3

**1.** Click Finish to continue the setup process.

**2.** Accept the defaults selected in the Microsoft Internet Information Server 2.0 Setup dialog box. Click OK to continue.

**3.** Click Yes to create the directory.

**4.** Accept the default directories in the Publishing Directories dialog box by clicking on OK.

**5.** Click Yes to create the directories.

**6.** Click OK in the Microsoft Internet Information Server 2.0 Setup dialog box.

**7.** Click SQL Server in the Install Drivers dialog box to highlight it. Click OK to continue.

**8.** In the drop-down list box under the Time Zone tab, click your time zone to highlight it. Optionally, you may also click the Date & Time tab and set the correct date and time. When you are finished, click Close to continue.

**9.** Setup displays a screen indicating that it has found your video display adapter. Click OK in the Detected Display dialog box to continue.

**10.** Adjust the display settings to suit your preferences. Click Test. The Testing Mode dialog box appears. Click OK to test. When the Testing Mode dialog box reappears, click Yes if you saw the test bitmap. When the Display Settings dialog box appears, click OK to continue. Click OK in the Display Properties dialog box to complete the installation. (This takes a few minutes.)

**11.** When prompted, label and insert a blank 3.5-inch floppy disk into drive A:. Setup formats and makes this disk into your Emergency Repair Disk. Click OK to continue. (This takes a couple of minutes.)

**12.** Windows NT Setup displays a window indicating that Windows NT 4.0 is successfully installed. Remove your newly created Emergency Repair Disk from drive A: (and save it for future use). Also remove the compact disc from your CD-ROM drive. Then click Restart Computer to reboot and start Windows NT Server. The setup is complete. Continue on to Part 2.

**Part 2: Configuring a one-way trust**

In this section, you create users in the MAINOFFICE domain, and configure the LAB domain to trust the MAINOFFICE domain.

Boot both of your computers to Windows NT Server. Log on as Administrator to each one.

Perform the following steps on the computer you named PDCMAINOFFICE (the second computer):

1. Select Start ⇒ Programs ⇒ Administrative Tools (Common) ⇒ User Manager for Domains.

2. Select User ⇒ New User.

3. In the New User dialog box, type the following bolded information in the appropriate text boxes:

   User name: **CarmenM**

   Full name: **Carmen Martinez**

   Description: **Corporate Sales Manager**

   Password: **password**

   Confirm password: **password**

   Clear the check box next to User Must Change Password at Next Logon. Select the check box next to Password Never Expires. Click the Add command button.

4. In the New User dialog box, type the following bolded information in the appropriate text boxes:

   User name: **HansS**

   Full name: **Hans Schmidt**

   Description: **Corporate Accounting Manager**

   Password: **password**

   Confirm password: **password**

   Clear the check box next to User Must Change Password at Next Logon. Select the check box next to Password Never Expires. Click the Add command button. Click the Close command button.

5. In the User Manager dialog box, select Policies ⇒ Trust Relationships.

6. In the Trust Relationships dialog box, click the Add command button next to the Trusting Domains list box (this is the text box at the *bottom* of the dialog box).

7. In the Add Trusting Domain dialog box, type the following bolded information in the appropriate text boxes:

Trusting domain: **LAB**

Initial password: **password**

Confirm password: **password**

Click OK.

**8.** In the Trust Relationships dialog box, PDCLAB appears in the Trusting Domains list box. Click the Close command button.

**9.** Exit User Manager for Domains.

Perform the following steps on the computer named PDCLAB (the first computer):

**1.** Select Start ⇒ Programs ⇒ Administrative Tools (Common) ⇒ User Manager for Domains.

**2.** In the User Manager for Domains dialog box, select Policies ⇒ Trust Relationships.

**3.** In the Trust Relationships dialog box, click the Add command button next to the Trusted Domains list box (this is the list box toward the top of the dialog box).

**4.** In the Add Trusted Domain dialog box, type the following bolded information:

Domain: **MAINOFFICE**

Password: **password**

Click OK.

**5.** A message appears, indicating that a trust relationship with MAINOFFICE has been successfully established. Click OK.

**6.** In the Trust Relationships dialog box, notice that MAINOFFICE appears in the Trusted Domains list box. Click the Close command button.

**7.** Exit User Manager for Domains. Continue on to Part 3.

**Part 3: Testing a one-way trust**

In this section, you verify that the LAB domain trusts the MAINOFFICE domain by assigning a user from the MAINOFFICE domain permissions to a printer in the LAB domain, and by logging on to the PDC in the LAB domain by using a user account from the MAINOFFICE domain. In addition, you attempt to log on to the PDC in the MAINOFFICE domain by using a user account from the LAB domain, but fail, verifying that the MAINOFFICE domain does *not* trust the LAB domain.

Perform these steps on the computer named PDCLAB (the first computer):

1. Select Start ⇒ Settings ⇒ Printers.

2. In the Printers dialog box, highlight the printer you created in Lab 6.8. Select File ⇒ Properties.

3. In the printer's Properties dialog box, click the Security tab.

4. On the Security tab, click the Permissions command button.

5. In the Printer Permissions dialog box, click the Add command button.

6. In the Add Users and Groups dialog box, click the down arrow in the List Names From drop-down list box. Select MAINOFFICE from the list that appears. Click the Show Users command button. Scroll down the list in the Names list box and highlight CarmenM. Click the Add command button. Click OK.

7. In the Printer Permissions dialog box, notice that MAINOFFICE\CarmenM now appears in the Name list box. She has permissions to print to the printer. (You have just verified that the LAB domain trusts the MAINOFFICE domain by successfully assigning CarmenM, a user in the MAINOFFICE domain, permissions to a printer in the LAB domain.) Click OK.

8. In the printer's Properties dialog box, click OK.

9. Close the Printers dialog box.

10. Select Start ⇒ Shut Down.

11. In the Shut Down Windows dialog box, select the radio button next to "Close all programs and log on as a different user." Click the Yes command button.

12. Press Ctrl + Alt + Delete to log on.

13. Click OK in the Important Notice dialog box.

14. In the Logon Information dialog box, type the user name, **HansS,** and the password, **password**. Select MAINOFFICE in the Domain drop-down list box. Click OK.

15. If the Welcome to Windows NT screen appears, click the Close command button.

16. Because HansS, a user in the MAINOFFICE domain, is successful in logging on at the PDC in the LAB domain, you have verified that the LAB domain trusts the MAINOFFICE domain.

17. Select Start ⇒ Shut Down.

18. In the Shut Down Windows dialog box, select the radio button next to "Close all programs and log on as a different user." Click the Yes command button.

Perform the following steps on the computer named PDCMAINOFFICE (the second computer):

1. Select Start ⇒ Shut Down.

2. In the Shut Down Windows dialog box, select the radio button next to Close all programs and log on as a different user. Click the Yes command button.

3. Press Ctrl + Alt + Delete to log on.

4. In the Logon Information dialog box, click the down arrow in the Domain drop-down list box. Notice that only the MAINOFFICE domain is listed. (This is because the MAINOFFICE domain does *not* trust the LAB domain.) Click the Cancel command button. You have verified that the MAINOFFICE domain does *not* trust the LAB domain. Continue on to Part 4.

### Part 4: Configuring a two-way trust

In this section, you configure the MAINOFFICE domain to trust the LAB domain. (This completes the creation of a two-way trust between the LAB and MAINOFFICE domains.)

Perform these steps on the computer named PDCLAB (the first computer):

1. Press Ctr + Alt + Delete to log on.

2. Click OK in the Important Notice dialog box.

3. In the Logon Information dialog box, type in a user name of **Administrator**, a password of **password**, and select the LAB domain from the Domain list box. Click OK.

4. Select Start ⇒ Programs ⇒ Administrative Tools (Common) ⇒ User Manager for Domains.

5. In the User Manager dialog box, select Policies ⇒ Trust Relationships.

6. In the Trust Relationships dialog box, click the Add command button next to the Trusting Domains list box (the list box toward the bottom of the dialog box).

7. In the Add Trusting Domain dialog box, type the following bolded information in the appropriate text boxes:

   Trusting domain: **MAINOFFICE**

   Initial password: **password**

   Confirm password: **password**

   Click OK.

8. In the Trust Relationships dialog box, notice that MAINOFFICE appears in the Trusting Domains list box. Click the Close command button.

9. Exit User Manager for Domains.

Perform the following steps on the computer named PDCMAINOFFICE (the second computer):

**1.** Press Ctrl + Alt + Delete to log on.

**2.** In the Logon Information dialog box, type in a user name of **Administrator**, a password of **password**, and select the MAINOFFICE domain. Click OK.

**3.** Select Start ⇒ Programs ⇒ Administrative Tools (Common) ⇒ User Manager for Domains.

**4.** In the User Manager dialog box, select Policies ⇒ Trust Relationships.

**5.** In the Trust Relationships dialog box, click the Add command button next to the Trusted Domains list box (this list box is located near the top of the dialog box).

**6.** In the Add Trusted Domain dialog box, type in a domain of **LAB** and a password of **password**. Click OK.

**7.** After a few moments, a dialog box appears, indicating that a trust relationship with the LAB domain has been successfully established. Click OK.

**8.** In the Trust Relationships dialog box, notice that the LAB domain appears in the Trusted Domains list box. The MAINOFFICE domain is now configured to trust the LAB domain. Click the Close command button.

**9.** In the User Manager dialog box, select Policies ⇒ User Rights.

**10.** In the User Rights Policy dialog box, select Log on locally from the Right drop-down list box. Click the Add command button.

**11.** In the Add Users and Groups dialog box, double-click the Everyone group in the Names list box. Click OK. (This step enables all users from both the LAB and MAINOFFICE domains to log on locally to this computer.)

**12.** In the User Rights Policy dialog box, click OK.

**13.** Exit User Manager for Domains. Continue on to Part 5.


### Part 5: Testing a two-way trust

In this section, you verify that the MAINOFFICE domain trusts the LAB domain by logging on to the PDC in the MAINOFFICE domain by using a user account from the LAB domain. (You already verified that the LAB domain trusts the MAIN-OFFICE domain.)

Perform the following steps on the computer named PDCMAINOFFICE (the second computer):

1. Select Start⇒Shut Down.

2. In the Shut Down Windows dialog box, select the radio button next to "Close all programs and log on as a different user." Click the Yes command button.

3. Press Ctrl + Alt + Delete to log on.

4. In the Logon Information dialog box, type in a user name of **MikeCo**, a password of **newuser**, and select the LAB domain. Click OK.

5. A Logon Message appears, indicating that you are required to change your password at first logon. Click OK.

6. In the Change Password dialog box, type in a new password of **password** and confirm the new password. Click OK.

7. A Change Password dialog box appears, indicating that your password has been changed. Click OK.

8. If a Welcome to Windows NT dialog box appears, click the Close command button.

   Because you were able to log on successfully to the PDC in the MAINOFFICE domain by using a user account from the LAB domain (MikeCo), you verified that the MAINOFFICE domain trusts the LAB domain.

## Lab 10.16 *Planning a Directory Services architecture*

Enterprise

The objective of this lab is to give you hands-on experience in planning a Directory Services architecture and trust relationships in given situations.

In each of the following exercises, your job is to:

1. Plan the appropriate Directory Services architecture for the given scenario (single domain model, single master domain model, multiple master domain model, or complete trust domain model).

2. Plan the appropriate trust relationships for the scenario.

**Exercise 1**   An international marketing firm called Worldwide Promotions, Inc., based in New York City, is planning to roll out Windows NT 4.0 in all of its offices worldwide.

The following table lists Worldwide Promotions' offices, and the number of users at each office.

| WORLDWIDE PROMOTIONS, INC. | |
|---|---|
| *OFFICE LOCATION* | *NUMBER OF USERS* |
| New York City | 500 |
| Paris | 150 |
| London | 100 |
| Seattle | 100 |
| Mexico City | 50 |
| Total Users | 900 |

A Windows NT network will be installed at each location, and all offices will be connected to the New York City office via a high-speed, digital leased line. The company plans to standardize by using Windows NT Server on all of its servers, and by using Windows NT Workstation on all client computers.

The company's MIS (Management Information Systems) department is located in the New York City office, and wants to manage all of the user accounts in all five locations. On-site network managers at each of the other four offices will manage the security for local network resources at their own respective offices.

Worldwide Promotions maintains a critical database in the New York City office that all users from all locations need to be able to access.

**1.** Which Directory Services architecture would you choose for this situation?

**2.** What trust relationships would you use in this situation, if any?

(You might want to draw out your Directory Services architecture design and trust relationships on a piece of scratch paper.)

**Exercise 2**    An international import company called Import International, Ltd., based in Toronto, Canada, is planning to roll out Windows NT 4.0 in all of its offices worldwide.

The following table lists Import International, Ltd.'s offices, and the number of users at each office.

| IMPORT INTERNATIONAL, LTD. | |
| --- | --- |
| **OFFICE LOCATION** | **NUMBER OF USERS** |
| Toronto | 9,000 |
| Los Angeles | 8,000 |
| Tokyo | 7,000 |
| Rio de Janeiro | 6,000 |
| Miami | 6,000 |
| Bombay | 3,000 |
| Johannesburg | 3,000 |
| Sydney | 2,000 |
| Hong Kong | 1,000 |
| Bangkok | 1,000 |
| Total Users | 46,000 |

High-speed, digital leased lines connect the locations, as shown in the following figure.

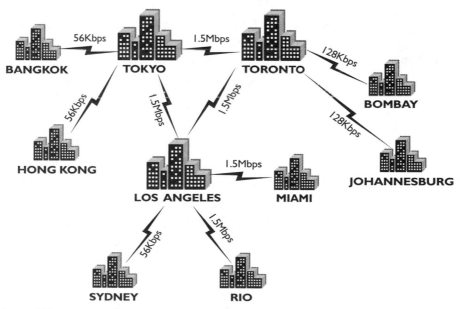

Leased lines connecting Import International, Ltd.'s ten offices

A Windows NT network will be installed at each location. Import International plans to standardize by using Windows NT Server on all of its servers, and by using Windows NT Workstation on all client computers.

The company's Data Processing and Computer Services department is located in the Toronto office and wants to manage all of the user accounts for all ten locations. On-site network managers at each of the other nine offices will manage the security for local network resources at their own respective offices.

Personnel travel frequently and log on to computers in various offices when traveling. Users must be able to log on using a single user account from a computer in any Import International office.

Import International maintains three critical databases: one in Toronto, one in Los Angeles, and one in Tokyo. All users from all locations need to be able to access all three of these databases.

**1.** Which Directory Services architecture would you choose for this situation?

**2.** What trust relationships would you use in this situation, if any?

(You might want to draw out your Directory Services architecture design and trust relationships on a piece of scratch paper.)

### Lab 11.17 *Optimizing WAN link performance by the appropriate placement of BDCs*

Enterprise

The purpose of this lab is to provide you with hands-on experience in planning the optimization of WAN link performance by determining the appropriate number and placement of BDCs throughout a master domain model.

Your goal, in optimizing WAN link performance, is to optimize for efficient local user logon and authentication.

**Scenario:**   You are planning to implement a master domain model for your company's multilocation Windows NT network. You have chosen to implement the master domain model that is shown in the following figure. Notice that the LAS_VEGAS, SALT_LAKE_CITY, and ALBUQUERQUE domains trust the DENVER domain. Also note that the DENVER domain contains all of the user accounts.

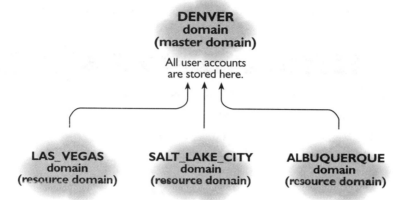

Your company's domain model

Your company's three remote locations (Las Vegas, Salt Lake City, and Albuquerque) are connected to the Denver office by various speed WAN links, as shown in the following figure.

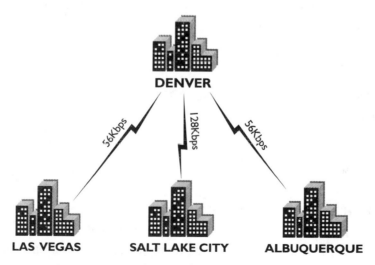

WAN connections between your company's four locations.

Your company has a different number of users at each of its four locations. The following table shows the number of users at each location.

| NUMBER OF USERS, BY LOCATION | |
|---|---|
| *LOCATION* | *# OF USERS* |
| Denver | 4,500 |
| Las Vegas | 2,700 |
| Salt Lake City | 3,800 |
| Albuquerque | 1,200 |

Your company's minimum hardware standard for BDCs is a 486/66 CPU with 32MB of RAM. The BDCs will be used *only* for user logon and authentication purposes.

The PDC will be located in the Denver office.

How many BDCs for the DENVER domain are required in each location to optimize your company's network for efficient local user logon and authentication? (Record your answers below).

| Location | # of BDCs |
|---|---|
| Denver | _____ |
| Las Vegas | _____ |
| Salt Lake City | _____ |
| Albuquerque | _____ |

## Lab 12.18 *Sharing and securing resources*

Workstation
Server
Enterprise

The purpose of this lab is to provide you with hands-on experience in planning a strategy for sharing and securing resources, and in performing the tasks of sharing and securing resources in Windows NT.

This lab consists of three parts:

> Part 1: Planning a strategy for sharing and securing resources
> Part 2: Sharing and securing folders
> Part 3: Establishing NTFS permissions

Begin this lab by booting your computer to Windows NT Server. Log on as Administrator.

Follow the steps below carefully.

### Part 1: Planning a strategy for sharing and securing resources

In this section, you plan a strategy for sharing and securing folders on a Windows NT Server computer given a particular scenario.

**Scenario:**   SalesPros, Inc. is a sales organization. (It's the same company you created users and groups for in Lab 7.10). The following table shows some of SalesPros, Inc.'s employees, their user names, job titles, and respective group membership(s):

| SALESPROS, INC.'S USER AND GROUP ACCOUNTS | | | |
| --- | --- | --- | --- |
| EMPLOYEE | USER NAME | JOB TITLE | GROUP MEMBERSHIP(S) |
| Pam Rhodes | PamR | District Manager | Managers, Sales, Accounting, Domain Users |
| John Spencer | JohnS | Sales Manager | Managers, Sales, Domain Users |
| Robert Jones | RobertJ | Accounting Manager | Managers, Accounting, Domain Users |
| Colleen Green | ColleenG | Sales Rep | Sales, Domain Users |
| Bill Tracy | BillT | Sales Rep | Sales, Domain Users |
| Mike Calhoun | MikeC | Sales Rep | Sales, Domain Users |
| Nancy Yates | NancyY | Accounting Staff | Accounting, Domain Users |
| Mike Cook | MikeCo | Accounting Staff | Accounting, Domain Users |

The resources to be shared are located on two partitions on a Windows NT Server computer. The C: drive is a FAT partition that contains applications, and the D: drive is an NTFS partition that contains data folders. The following resources exist:

| **C: Drive - FAT Partition** | **D: Drive - NTFS Partition** |
|---|---|
| C:\Apps\Word | D:\Data\Managers |
| C:\Apps\Excel | D:\Data\Accounting |
| C:\Apps\Access | D:\Data\Sales |
| | D:\Data\AllUsers |

Use the following criteria for determining your strategy to share and secure resources:

1. All employees need to be able to access all three applications: Word, Excel, and Access. However, employees should *not* be able to save data files to the application folders or to change or delete files in the application folders.

2. Employees should be able to access (create, read, write, and delete files) only the data folders that correspond to the groups to which they belong. For example, only members of the Accounting group should be able to access the D:\Data\Accounting folder. Furthermore, members of the Accounting group should *not* be able to access data folders that correspond to groups of which they are *not* members.

3. All employees need to be able to access (create, read, write and delete files) the D:\Data\AllUsers folder.

4. Members of the Administrators group require Full Control to all shared resources on the NTFS partition.

Plan a strategy for sharing and securing folders by assigning a share name to each resource (folder), and then choosing the appropriate share and/or NTFS permissions for each resource listed.

Use the following worksheet for your answers:

| Resource:<br>(Include path) | Share<br>Name: | Share Permissions<br>Applied: | | NTFS Permissions<br>Applied: | |
|---|---|---|---|---|---|
| | | User/Group | Permission | User/Group | Permission |
| (Example)<br>D:\Data\Sales | SalesData | Domain<br>Users<br><br>(Remove<br>Everyone<br>group) | Full<br>Control | Sales<br><br>Adminis-<br>trators | Change<br><br>Full<br>Control |
| C:\Apps\Word | | | | | |
| C:\Apps\Excel | | | | | |
| C:\Apps\Access | | | | | |
| D:\Data\Managers | | | | | |
| D:\Data\Accounting | | | | | |
| D:\Data\AllUsers | | | | | |

Continue to Part 2.

### Part 2: Sharing and securing folders

In this section, you create several folders to share, then apply appropriate share permissions to each of the folders.

**1.** Select Start ⇒ Programs ⇒ Windows NT Explorer.

**2.** In the Exploring dialog box, highlight the C: drive (or the drive that contains your FAT partition—this is the drive that you installed Windows NT Server and Windows NT Workstation on). Select File ⇒ New ⇒ Folder.

**3.** The new folder appears in the Name list box. Type in a new folder name of **Apps**. Press Enter. Double-click the Apps folder.

**4.** Select File ⇒ New ⇒ Folder.

**5.** The new folder appears in the Name list box. Type in a new folder name of **Word**. Press Enter.

**6.** Select File ⇒ New ⇒ Folder.

**7.** The new folder appears in the Name list box. Type in a new folder name of **Excel**. Press Enter.

**8.** Select File ⇒ New ⇒ Folder.

**9.** The new folder appears in the Name list box. Type in a new folder name of **Access**. Press Enter.

**10.** Highlight the Word folder in the Name list box. Select File ⇒ Properties.

**11.** In the Word Properties dialog box, click the Sharing tab. Select the radio button next to Shared As. In the Share Name text box, accept the default name of Word. Click the Permissions command button.

**12.** The Access Through Share Permissions dialog box appears. Click the Add command button.

**13.** The Add Users and Groups dialog box appears. Double-click the Domain Users group. In the Type of Access drop-down list box, select Change. Click OK.

**14.** In the Access Through Share Permissions dialog box, highlight the Everyone group. Click the Remove command button. Click OK.

**15.** In the Word Properties dialog box, click OK.

**16.** In the Exploring dialog box, highlight the Excel folder in the Name list box. Select File ⇒ Properties.

**17.** In the Excel Properties dialog box, click the Sharing tab. Select the radio button next to Shared As. In the Share Name text box, accept the default name of Excel. Click the Permissions command button.

**18.** The Access Through Share Permissions dialog box appears. Click the Add command button.

**19.** The Add Users and Groups dialog box appears. Double-click the Domain Users group. In the Type of Access drop-down list box, select Change. Click OK.

**20.** In the Access Through Share Permissions dialog box, highlight the Everyone group. Click the Remove command button. Click OK.

**21.** In the Excel Properties dialog box, click OK.

**22.** In the Exploring dialog box, highlight the Access folder in the Name list box. Select File ⇒ Properties.

**23.** In the Access Properties dialog box, click the Sharing tab. Select the radio button next to Shared As. In the Share Name text box, accept the default name of Access. Click the Permissions command button.

**24.** The Access Through Share Permissions dialog box appears. Click the Add command button.

**25.** The Add Users and Groups dialog box appears. Double-click the Domain Users group. In the Type of Access drop-down list box, select Change. Click OK.

**26.** In the Access Through Share Permissions dialog box, highlight the Everyone group. Click the Remove command button. Click OK.

**27.** In the Access Properties dialog box, click OK.

**28.** The Exploring dialog box reappears. Notice that all three folders (Word, Excel, and Access) appear in the Name list box, and that all three appear with a hand under the folder, indicating that they are shared folders.

**29.** Highlight the D: drive (or the drive that contains your NTFS partition). Select File ⇒ New ⇒ Folder.

**30.** The new folder appears in the Name list box. Type in a new folder name of **Data**. Press Enter. Double-click the Data folder.

**31.** Select File ⇒ New ⇒ Folder.

**32.** The new folder appears in the Name list box. Type in a new folder name of **Managers**. Press Enter.

**33.** Select File ⇒ New ⇒ Folder.

**34.** The new folder appears in the Name list box. Type in a new folder name of **Accounting**. Press Enter.

**35.** Select File ⇒ New ⇒ Folder.

**36.** The new folder appears in the Name list box. Type in a new folder name of **Sales**. Press Enter.

**37.** Select File ⇒ New ⇒ Folder.

**38.** The new folder appears in the Name list box. Type in a new folder name of **AllUsers.** Press Enter.

**39.** In the Exploring dialog box, highlight the Managers folder in the Name list box. Select File ⇒ Properties.

**40.** In the Managers Properties dialog box, click the Sharing tab. Select the radio button next to Shared As. In the Share Name text box, type in **ManagersData**. Click the Permissions command button.

**41.** The Access Through Share Permissions dialog box appears. Notice that the Everyone group is listed and has the Full Control share permission. (Since this folder is located on an NTFS partition, you will use NTFS permissions to secure this folder, and accept the default share permission.) Click OK.

**42.** In the Managers Properties dialog box, Click OK.

**43.** A warning message appears, indicating that the new share name may not be accessible from some MS-DOS workstations. (This is because the name you assigned is longer than eight characters). Click the Yes command button.

**44.** In the Exploring dialog box, highlight the Accounting folder in the Name list box. Select File ⇒ Properties.

**45.** In the Accounting Properties dialog box, click the Sharing tab. Select the radio button next to Shared As. In the Share Name text box, type in **AccountingData**. Click OK.

**46.** In the Sharing warning dialog box, click the Yes command button.

**47.** In the Exploring dialog box, highlight the Sales folder in the Name list box. Select File ⇒ Properties.

**48.** In the Sales Properties dialog box, click the Sharing tab. Select the radio button next to Shared As. In the Share Name text box, type in **SalesData**. Click OK.

**49.** In the Sharing warning dialog box, click the Yes command button.

**50.** In the Exploring dialog box, highlight the AllUsers folder in the Name list box. Select File ⇒ Properties.

**51.** In the AllUsers Properties dialog box, click the Sharing tab. Select the radio button next to Shared As. In the Share Name text box, type in **AllUsersData**. Click OK.

**52.** In the Sharing warning dialog box, click the Yes command button.

**53.** The Exploring dialog box reappears. Notice that all four folders (Managers, Accounting, Sales, and AllUsers) appear in the Name list box, and that all four appear with a hand under the folder, indicating that they are shared folders.

In the next section, you assign NTFS permissions to these folders. Continue on to Part 3.

### Part 3: Establishing NTFS permissions

In this section, you assign the appropriate NTFS permissions to the Managers, Accounting, Sales, and AllUsers folders that you created and shared in Part 2.

**1.** In the Exploring dialog box, highlight the Managers folder in the Name list box. Select File ⇒ Properties.

**2.** In the Managers Properties dialog box, click the Security tab. Click the Permissions command button.

**3.** In the Directory Permissions dialog box, click the Add command button.

**4.** In the Add Users and Groups dialog box, double-click the Managers group. In the Type of Access drop-down list box, select Change. Click OK.

**5.** Click the Add command button.

6. In the Add Users and Groups dialog box, double-click Administrators. In the Type of Access drop-down list box, select Full Control. Click OK.

7. In the Directory Permissions dialog box, highlight the Everyone group. Click the Remove command button. Click OK.

8. In the Managers Properties dialog box, click OK.

9. In the Exploring dialog box, highlight the Accounting folder in the Name list box. Select File ⇒ Properties.

10. In the Accounting Properties dialog box, click the Security tab. Click the Permissions command button.

11. In the Directory Permissions dialog box, click the Add command button.

12. In the Add Users and Groups dialog box, double-click the Accounting group. In the Type of Access drop-down list box, select Change. Click OK.

13. Click the Add command button.

14. In the Add Users and Groups dialog box, double-click Administrators. In the Type of Access drop-down list box, select Full Control. Click OK.

15. In the Directory Permissions dialog box, highlight the Everyone group. Click the Remove command button. Click OK.

16. In the Accounting Properties dialog box, click OK.

17. In the Exploring dialog box, highlight the Sales folder in the Name list box. Select File ⇒ Properties.

18. In the Sales Properties dialog box, click the Security tab. Click the Permissions command button.

19. In the Directory Permissions dialog box, click the Add command button.

20. In the Add Users and Groups dialog box, double-click the Sales group. In the Type of Access drop-down list box, select Change. Click OK.

21. Click the Add command button.

22. In the Add Users and Groups dialog box, double-click Administrators. In the Type of Access drop-down list box, select Full Control. Click OK.

23. In the Directory Permissions dialog box, highlight the Everyone group. Click the Remove command button. Click OK.

24. In the Sales Properties dialog box, click OK.

25. In the Exploring dialog box, highlight the AllUsers folder in the Name list box. Select File ⇒ Properties.

26. In the AllUsers Properties dialog box, click the Security tab. Click the Permissions command button.

27. In the Directory Permissions dialog box, click the Add command button.

28. In the Add Users and Groups dialog box, double-click the Domain Users group. In the Type of Access drop-down list box, select Change. Click OK.

29. Click the Add command button.

30. In the Add Users and Groups dialog box, double-click Administrators. In the Type Of Access drop-down list box, select Full Control. Click OK.

31. In the Directory Permissions dialog box, highlight the Everyone group. Click the Remove command button. Click OK.

32. In the All Users Properties dialog box, click OK. This completes the assigning of NTFS permissions. Exit Windows NT Explorer.

### Lab 12.19 *Establishing file and folder auditing*

Server
Enterprise

The purpose of this lab is to provide you with hands-on experience in establishing file and folder auditing.

This lab consists of two parts:

> Part 1: Establishing file and folder auditing
> Part 2: Testing file and folder auditing

Begin this lab by booting your computer to Windows NT Server. Log on as Administrator.

Follow these steps carefully.

#### Part 1: Establishing file and folder auditing

In this section, you establish file and folder auditing on the Managers, Accounting, Sales, and AllUsers subfolders in the D:\Data folder that you created and shared in Lab 12.18.

In Lab 8.11, you implemented success and failure auditing for File and Object Access by using User Manager for Domains. That was the first step in auditing files and folders. This lab completes the process of establishing auditing on files and folders.

1. Select Start ⇒ Programs ⇒ Windows NT Explorer.

2. In the All Folders section of the Exploring dialog box, click the plus sign next to the drive that contains your NTFS partition (usually this is the D: drive). Highlight the Data folder. In the Name list box in the Contents of 'Data' section, highlight the Accounting folder. Select File ⇒ Properties.

3. In the Accounting Properties dialog box, click the Security tab. Click the Auditing command button.

**4.** In the Directory Auditing dialog box, click the Add command button. Double-click the Domain Users group. Click OK.

**5.** In the Directory Auditing dialog box, select the Success and Failure check boxes next to Read, Write, and Execute. Click OK.

**6.** In the Accounting Properties dialog box, click OK.

**7.** In the Name list box in the Contents of 'Data' section, highlight the AllUsers folder. Select File ⇒ Properties.

**8.** In the AllUsers Properties dialog box, click the Security tab. Click the Auditing command button.

**9.** In the Directory Auditing dialog box, click the Add command button. Double-click the Domain Users group. Click OK.

**10.** In the Directory Auditing dialog box, select the Success and Failure check boxes next to Delete. Click OK.

**11.** In the AllUsers Properties dialog box, click OK.

**12.** In the Name list box in the Contents of 'Data' section, highlight the Managers folder. Select File ⇒ Properties.

**13.** In the Managers Properties dialog box, click the Security tab. Click the Auditing command button.

**14.** In the Directory Auditing dialog box, click the Add command button. Double-click the Domain Users group. Click OK.

**15.** In the Directory Auditing dialog box, select the Success and Failure check boxes next to Read, Write, Execute, Delete, Change Permissions, and Take Ownership. Click OK.

**16.** In the Managers Properties dialog box, click OK.

**17.** In the Name list box in the Contents of 'Data' section, highlight the Sales folder. Select File ⇒ Properties.

**18.** In the Sales Properties dialog box, click the Security tab. Click the Auditing command button.

**19.** In the Directory Auditing dialog box, click the Add command button. Double-click the Domain Users group. Click OK.

**20.** In the Directory Auditing dialog box, select the Success and Failure check boxes next to Read, Write, and Execute. Click OK.

**21.** In the Sales Properties dialog box, click OK. Exit Windows NT Explorer. Continue on to Part 2.

### Part 2: Testing file and folder auditing

In this section, you clear the security log in EventViewer, then log on as NancyY and attempt to access each of the data folders you created and shared in Lab 12.18. Then you use Event Viewer to view the results of the auditing that you established in Part 1.

**1.** Select Start ⇒ Programs ⇒ Administrative Tools (Common) ⇒ Event Viewer.

**2.** In the Event Viewer dialog box, select Log ⇒ Security. Select Log ⇒ Clear All Events. (You are clearing the security log to make room for new auditing events.)

**3.** In the Clear Event Log dialog box, click the No command button, so as to not save the log to a file.

**4.** In the Clear Event Log dialog box, click the Yes command button to clear the security log.

**5.** Exit Event Viewer.

**6.** Select Start ⇒ Shut Down.

**7.** In the Shut Down Windows dialog box, select the radio button next to "Close all programs and log on as a different user." Click the Yes command button.

**8.** Press Ctrl + Alt + Delete to log on.

**9.** Click OK in the Important Notice dialog box.

**10.** Type in a user name of **NancyY**, and a password of **password.** Click OK.

**11.** A warning message may appear, indicating that your password will expire in *xx* days. Click the No command button.

**12.** If a Welcome to Windows NT dialog box appears, clear the check box next to "Show this Welcome Screen next time you start Windows NT." Click the Close command button.

**13.** Select Start ⇒ Programs ⇒ Windows NT Explorer.

**14.** In the Exploring dialog box, click the plus sign next to the drive that contains your NTFS partition (usually this is the D: drive). Click the plus sign next to the Data folder on this drive. Highlight the Accounting folder. Notice that there are no files in this folder.

**15.** Highlight the AllUsers folder. Notice that there are no files in this folder.

**16.** Highlight the Managers folder. A dialog box appears, indicating that access has been denied. (This is because NancyY is not a member of the Managers group and does not have the appropriate permission to access this folder.) Click the Cancel command button.

**17.** Highlight the Sales folder. A dialog box appears, indicating that access has been denied. (This is because NancyY is not a member of the Sales group and does not have the appropriate permission to access this folder.) Click the Cancel command button. Exit Windows NT Explorer.

**18.** Select Start⇒Shut Down.

**19.** In the Shut Down Windows dialog box, select the radio button next to "Close all programs and log on as a different user." Click the Yes command button.

**20.** Press Ctrl + Alt + Delete to log on.

**21.** Click OK in the Important Notice dialog box.

**22.** Type in a user name of **Administrator**, and a password of **password**. Click OK.

**23.** Select Start⇒Programs⇒Administrative Tools (Common)⇒Event Viewer.

**24.** In the Event Viewer dialog box, select Log⇒Security. Scroll down the log and double-click the first event that lists NancyY in the User column *and* Logon/Logoff in the Category column.

**25.** The Event Detail dialog box appears. Notice that this is a Success audit of the Logon/Logoff event. Click the Close command button.

**26.** Scroll down and double-click the event that has a lock (rather than a key) in the left-hand margin, lists NancyY in the User column, *and* Object Access in the Category column. (This should be approximately eleven events down from the one you just viewed.)

**27.** The Event Detail dialog box appears. Notice that this is a Failure audit event of the Object Access type. (This audit event occurred when NancyY attempted to access the D:\Data\Sales folder and was denied access.) Click the Next command button to view the next audit event.

**28.** Continue clicking on the Next command button to view several more audit events. When you are finished viewing audit events, click the Close command button.

**29.** Exit Event Viewer.

## Lab 12.20 *Troubleshooting resource access and permission problems*

The purpose of this lab is to provide you with hands-on experience in troubleshooting some common resource access and permission problems.

For each problem presented, consider the troubleshooting information provided and determine:

Workstation
Server
Enterprise

**1.** The cause of the problem, and

**2.** What steps you would take to resolve the problem.

**Problem 1**  A user, NancyY, reports that she can't save files to the AccountingData share located on an NTFS volume on a Windows NT computer. You begin the troubleshooting process by using User Manager for Domains and Windows NT Explorer to obtain NancyY's group memberships, and the share and NTFS permissions assigned to the AccountingData share.

The following figure shows the Group Memberships dialog box, which lists NancyY's group memberships.

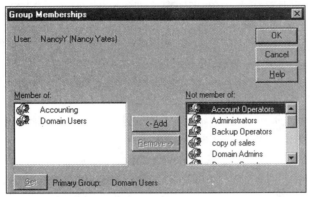

**Group memberships for NancyY**

The following figure shows the Access Through Share Permissions dialog box, which lists the share permissions assigned to the AccountingData share.

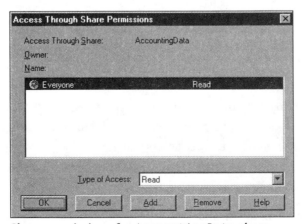

**Share permissions for** AccountingData **share**

The following figure shows the Directory Permissions dialog box. This dialog box lists the NTFS permissions assigned to the `D:\Data\Accounting` folder, which is shared as `AccountingData`.

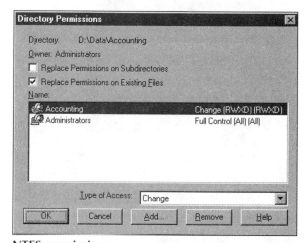

**NTFS permissions**
**for** `AccountingData` **share**

What is the cause of the problem?

What would you do to resolve the problem?

**Problem 2**   A user, JohnS, reports he can't access the `ManagersData` share located on an NTFS volume on a Windows NT computer. You begin the troubleshooting process by using User Manager for Domains and Windows NT Explorer to obtain JohnS's group memberships, and the share and NTFS permissions assigned to the `ManagersData` share.

The following figure shows the Group Memberships dialog box, which lists JohnS's group memberships.

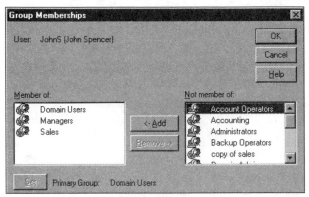

**Group memberships for JohnS**

The following figure shows the Access Through Share Permissions dialog box, which lists the share permissions assigned to the `ManagersData` share.

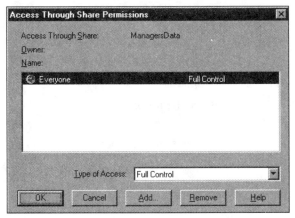

**Share permissions for** `ManagersData` **share**

The following figure shows the Directory Permissions dialog box. This dialog box lists the NTFS permissions assigned to the `D:\Data\Managers` folder, which is shared as `ManagersData`.

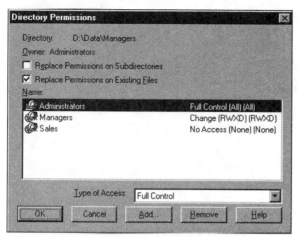

**NTFS permissions for** ManagersData **share**

What is the cause of the problem?

What would you do to resolve the problem?

## Lab 13.21 *Configuring the Computer Browser service*

Workstation
Server
Enterprise

The purpose of this lab is to give you hands-on experience in configuring the Windows NT Computer Browser service. You will edit the Registry to configure your Windows NT Computer to force an election when it is booted, in an attempt to become the master browser for its subnet.

Begin this lab by booting your computer to Windows NT Server. Log on as Administrator.

### FOLLOW THESE STEPS CAREFULLY:

**1.** Select Start ⇒ Run.

**2.** In the Run dialog box, type **Regedt32** in the Open drop-down list box. Click OK.

**3.** In the Registry Editor dialog box, select Window ⇒ HKEY_LOCAL_MACHINE on Local Machine.

**4.** Maximize the HKEY_LOCAL_MACHINE on Local Machine window.

**5.** Double-click the SYSTEM folder. Under the SYSTEM folder, double-click the CurrentControlSet folder. Double-click the Services folder. Scroll down and double-click the Browser folder. Click the Parameters folder.

**6.** In the right-hand window, double-click the IsDomainMaster value.

**7.** Edit the String Editor dialog box to read **TRUE**. Click OK. (This step configures the computer to force an election on startup, and to attempt to become the master browser for its subnet.)

**8.** Notice in the right-hand window that the IsDomainMaster value is changed to TRUE.

**9.** The MaintainServerList value should be Yes. (If it isn't, double-click MaintainServerList and change the value to **Yes** in the String Editor dialog box.)

**10.** Exit Registry Editor. These changes will become effective the next time you boot the computer.

## Lab 13.22 *Accessing network resources*

 note ⓘ **This lab is optional, because it requires an additional networked computer. Additionally, Lab 10.15 must be completed prior to performing this lab. (See Lab 10.15 for specific computer hardware requirements.)**

Workstation
Enterprise

The purpose of this lab is to give you hands-on experience in accessing shared network resources. You will create and then access shared folders by using Windows NT Explorer, and also connect to shared folders from the command line.

This lab consists of three parts:

> Part 1: Configuring shares on the second computer (PDCMAINOFFICE)
> Part 2: Connecting to shared folders by using Windows NT Explorer
> Part 3: Connecting to a shared folder from the command line

Follow the steps in each part carefully.

### Part 1: Configuring shares on the second computer (PDCMAINOFFICE)

Perform these steps on your second computer (PDCMAINOFFICE) after you have booted the computer to Windows NT Server and logged on as Administrator.

**1.** Select Start⇒ Programs⇒ Windows NT Explorer.

**2.** In the Exploring dialog box, highlight the Program Files folder. Select File⇒ Properties.

**3.** In the Program Files Properties dialog box, click the Sharing tab.

**4.** On the Sharing tab, select the radio button next to Shared As. Edit the Share Name text box so that it appears as **Programs**. Click OK.

**5.** Highlight the C: drive under My Computer. Select File⇒ New⇒ Folder.

**6.** Rename the new folder as **Projects**. Press Enter.

**7.** Select File⇒ Properties.

**8.** In the Projects Properties dialog box, click the Sharing tab.

**9.** On the Sharing tab, select the radio button next to Shared As. Accept the default share name of Projects. Click OK.

**10.** Highlight the C: drive under My Computer. Select File⇒ New⇒ Folder.

**11.** Rename the new folder as **Public**. Press Enter.

**12.** Select File⇒ Properties.

**13.** In the Public Properties dialog box, click the Sharing tab.

**14.** On the Sharing tab, select the radio button next to Shared As. Accept the default share name of Public. Click OK.

**15.** Exit Windows NT Explorer. Continue on to Part 2.

## Part 2: Connecting to shared folders by using Windows NT Explorer

Perform these steps on your main computer (NTW40) after booting it to Windows NT **Workstation** and logging on as Administrator.

**1.** Select Start⇒ Programs ⇒ Windows NT Explorer.

**2.** In the Exploring dialog box, right-click Network Neighborhood. Select Map Network Drive from the menu that appears.

**3.** In the Map Network Drive dialog box, double-click MAINOFFICE in the Shared Directories list box. Double-click PDCMAINOFFICE. Double-click the Programs folder.

**4.** Notice that Programs on 'Pdcmainoffice' appears with a drive letter under My Computer in the All Folders section of the Exploring dialog box. You have successfully connected a network drive to the Programs share on PDCMAINOFFICE (the second computer.)

**5.** Select Tools⇒ Map Network Drive.

**6.** In the Map Network Drive dialog box, type **\\pdcmainoffice\public** in the Path drop-down list box. Click OK.

**7.** Notice that Public on 'Pdcmainoffice' appears with a drive letter under My Computer in the All Folders section of the Exploring dialog box. You have successfully connected a network drive to the Public share on PDCMAINOFFICE (the second computer.)

**8.** Exit Windows NT Explorer. Continue on to Part 3.

**Part 3: Connecting to a shared folder from the command line**

Perform these steps on your main computer (NTW40) that is running Windows NT Workstation.

**1.** Select Start⇒Programs⇒Command Prompt.

**2.** At the C:\> command prompt, type **net use p:\\pdcmainoffice\projects**

**3.** Press Enter. Windows NT should indicate that the command completed successfully. This means that you have successfully connected to the Projects share on PDCMAINOFFICE (the second computer).

**4.** At the C:\> command prompt, type **exit** and press Enter.

## Lab 14.23    *Installing Windows NT Server tools and using NT Server tools to administer a remote server*

Server
Enterprise

The purpose of this lab is to give you hands-on experience in installing Windows NT Server tools, and experience in using NT Server tools to administer a remote server. You install Windows NT Server tools on a Windows NT Workstation computer, and then (optionally) use Windows NT Server tools to administer your second Windows NT Server computer remotely.

This lab consists of two parts:

> Part 1: Installing Windows NT Server tools on a Windows NT Workstation computer
>
> Part 2: (Optional) Administering a remote Windows NT Server computer

**Part 1: Installing Windows NT Server tools on a Windows NT Workstation computer**

Perform these steps on your first or primary computer.

**1.** Boot your computer to Windows NT Workstation. Log on as Administrator. Place your Windows NT Server 4.0 compact disc in your CD-ROM drive.

**2.** Select Start⇒Programs⇒Windows NT Explorer.

**3.** In the Exploring dialog box, click the + sign next to your CD-ROM drive. Under your CD-ROM drive, click the + sign next to the Clients folder. Click the + sign next to the Srvtools folder. Highlight the Winnt folder.

**4.** In the "Contents of Winnt" section in the right-hand window, double-click Setup.bat.

**5.** A window appears, indicating that the Client-Based Network Administration Tools are being installed. When you are prompted to press any key to continue, do so.

**6.** The Exploring dialog box reappears. The Windows NT Server tools are now installed. Continue to Step 7 to create icons for the various server tools.

**7.** In the Exploring dialog box, click the + sign next to the drive on your computer on which you originally installed Windows NT Workstation (if it is not already expanded). Normally, this is the C: drive. Click the + sign next to the `Winntwks` folder. Click the + sign next to the `Profiles` folder. Click the + sign next to the `All Users` folder. Click the + sign next to the `Start Menu` folder. Click the + sign next to the `Programs` folder. Highlight the `Administrative Tools (Common)` folder.

**8.** Select File ⇒ New ⇒ Shortcut.

**9.** In the Create Shortcut dialog box, type **c:\winntwks\system32\usrmgr.exe** in the Command line text box. (If you installed Windows NT Workstation on a different drive than C:, substitute the correct drive letter in this path.) Click the Next command button.

**10.** In the Select a Title for the Program dialog box, type **User Manager for Domains** in the Select a name for the shortcut text box. Click the Finish command button.

**11.** The Exploring dialog box reappears. Select File ⇒ New ⇒ Shortcut.

**12.** In the Create Shortcut dialog box, type **c:\winntwks\system32\srvmgr.exe** in the Command line text box. (If you installed Windows NT Workstation on a different drive than C:, substitute the correct drive letter in this path.) Click the Next command button.

**13.** In the Select A Title For The Program dialog box, type **Server Manager** in the Select a name for the shortcut text box. Click the Finish command button.

**14.** The Exploring dialog box reappears. Select File ⇒ New ⇒ Shortcut.

**15.** In the Create Shortcut dialog box, type **c:\winntwks\system32\poledit.exe** in the Command line text box. (If you installed Windows NT Workstation on a different drive than C:, substitute the correct drive letter in this path.) Click the Next command button.

**16.** In the Select a Title for the Program dialog box, type **System Policy Editor** in the Select a name for the shortcut text box. Click the Finish command button.

**17.** The Exploring dialog box reappears. Notice the three shortcuts you have just created are listed in the Contents of Administrative Tools (Common). Exit Windows NT Explorer. The icons you have just created will now appear in the Start ⇒ Programs ⇒ Administrative Tools (Common) menu.

Continue to Part 2.

**Part 2: (Optional) Administering a remote Windows NT Server computer**
Part 2 of this lab is optional, because it requires an additional networked computer. Additionally, Lab 10.15 and Lab 13.22 must be completed before performing this lab. See Lab 10.15 for specific computer hardware requirements.

Begin Part 2 by booting your second computer to Windows NT Server. It is not necessary that you log on.

In the first eight steps of Part 2, you use User Manager for Domains (an NT Server tool that you just installed on your Windows NT Workstation computer) to view users remotely and to add a new user to the MAINOFFICE domain on your second computer.

(Perform these steps from your first or primary computer, booted to Windows NT Workstation. Log on as Administrator.)

1. Select Start ⇒ Programs ⇒ Administrative Tools (Common) ⇒ User Manager for Domains.

2. The User Manager dialog box appears. Select User ⇒ Select Domain.

3. In the Select Domain dialog box, type **MAINOFFICE** in the Domain text box. (This is the domain name of your second computer.) Click OK.

4. The User Manager dialog box reappears, this time listing users from the MAINOFFICE domain. Notice that the two users you created in Lab 10.15, CarmenM and HansS, appear in the User Name list box. Select User ⇒ New User.

5. Type in your first name and last initial in the User Name text box. (Don't leave a space between the two.) Type in your full name in the Full Name text box. Type in a password of **password**, and confirm the password by retyping it. Clear the check box next to User Must Change Password at Next Logon. Select the check box next to Password Never Expires. Click the Groups command button.

6. In the Group Memberships dialog box, highlight Administrators in the Not member of list box. Click the Add command button. Click OK.

7. In the New User dialog box, click the Add command button. Click the Close command button.

8. The User Manager dialog box reappears. Notice that your name now appears in the list of users in the MAINOFFICE domain. Exit User Manager for Domains.

In the remaining steps in Part 2, you use Server Manager to share the CD-ROM drive on your second computer remotely from your Windows NT Workstation computer.

9. Select Start ⇒ Programs ⇒ Administrative Tools (Common) ⇒ Server Manager.

10. In the Server Manager dialog box, select Computer ⇒ Select Domain.

11. In the Select Domain dialog box, type **MAINOFFICE** in the Domain text box. Click OK.

12. The Server Manager dialog box reappears, this time displaying PDCMAINOFFICE, your second computer, in the Computer list box. Select Computer ⇒ Shared Directories.

13. In the Shared Directories dialog box, click the New Share command button.

    In the New Share dialog box, type **CDROM** in the Share Name text box, and type the drive letter of the CD-ROM drive on your second computer in the Path text box, for example, **D:\**. Click OK.

14. (Note: If you don't have a CD-ROM drive on your second computer, select any other drive letter to share.)

15. The Shared Directories dialog box reappears. Note that CDROM appears in the Shared Directories on \\PDCMAINOFFICE list box, with a hand under it, indicating that it is shared. Click the Close command button.

16. Exit Server Manager.

## Lab 15.24 *Performing a backup*

 **This lab is optional because it requires a tape drive.**

Server
Enterprise

The purpose of this lab is to give you hands-on experience using Windows NT Backup to back up files and folders on a Windows NT computer. You will also view the detailed log created during the backup by using Windows NT Explorer and Notepad.

Begin this lab by booting your computer to Windows NT Server. Log on as Administrator. If you haven't already done so, install a driver for your tape drive by using the Tape Devices application in Control Panel. Place a tape in the tape drive.

**FOLLOW THE STEPS BELOW CAREFULLY:**

1. Start ⇒ Programs ⇒ Administrative Tools (Common) ⇒ Backup.

2. The Backup dialog box appears. Select Window ⇒ Drives.

3. Maximize the Drives dialog box. Double-click the C: drive (or the drive that you have installed Windows NT Server on). Select the check box next to the Winntsrv folder. (If you wanted to back up the entire C: drive instead of selected folders only, when the Drives dialog box first appears, select the check box next to the C: drive instead of double-clicking it.)

    Click the Backup command button.

**4.** The Backup Information dialog box appears. Select the check boxes next to the following: Verify After Backup, Hardware Compression (if the box is not grayed out), and Backup Local Registry.

In the Operation section, ensure that the radio button next to Replace is selected.

In the Description text box, type **Winntsrv folder *current_date* normal backup.**

In the Backup Type drop-down list box, select Normal.

In the Log Information section, select the radio button next to Full Detail.

Click OK.

**5.** The Backup Status dialog box appears. If the tape has been used before, a Replace Information dialog box appears. Click the Yes command button to have Windows NT Backup replace the data on the tape with the backup you are preparing to perform.

**6.** Windows NT Backup performs the backup. (This process takes several minutes.)

**7.** The Verify Status dialog box appears. Windows NT Backup verifies that all files and folders were backed up correctly. (This process also takes several minutes.) After the verify is completed, click OK.

**8.** The Backup –(Drives) dialog box appears. Select Window ⇒ Tapes.

**9.** The Backup–(Tapes) dialog box appears. Double-click the + sign next to the C: in the right-hand window (or the letter of the drive on which you installed Windows NT Server).

**10.** Double-click the Winntsrv folder in the left-hand window.

**11.** Windows NT Backup displays the contents of the Winntsrv folder from the tape backup that you just created. Notice that, for restore purposes, you can select individual files and subfolders by selecting the check boxes next to the files and subfolders that you want to restore.

Exit Windows NT Backup.

**12.** To view the log for the backup you just created, select Start ⇒ Programs ⇒ Windows NT Explorer.

**13.** In the Exploring dialog box, click the + sign next to the C: drive (or the drive on which you installed Windows NT Server). Highlight the Winntsrv folder. In the 'Contents of Winntsrv', double-click Backup.log.

**14.** View the backup log that is displayed in Notepad. Exit Notepad.

**15.** Exit Windows NT Explorer.

## Lab 16.25  *Implementing WINS and Microsoft DNS Server*

Enterprise

The purpose of this lab exercise is to give you hands-on experience in installing WINS and DNS Server, and configuring DNS Server to interact with WINS.

This lab consists of two parts:

Part 1: Installing WINS and Microsoft DNS Server

Part 2: Configuring Microsoft DNS Server to interact with WINS

Begin this lab by booting your computer to Windows NT Server. Log on as Administrator. Place your Windows NT Server compact disc in your CD-ROM drive. Complete the following steps carefully.

### Part 1: Installing WINS and Microsoft DNS Server

In this section, you install Windows Internet Name Service (WINS) and Microsoft Domain Name Service (DNS) Server on a Windows NT Server computer.

**1.** Select Start ⇒ Settings ⇒ Control Panel.

**2.** In the Control Panel dialog box, double-click Network.

**3.** In the Network dialog box, click the Services tab.

**4.** On the Services tab, click the Add command button.

**5.** In the Select Network Service dialog box, highlight Microsoft DNS Server. Click OK.

**6.** A Windows NT Setup dialog box appears. Ensure the correct source file location is displayed in the text box at the bottom of the dialog box. (This is probably the i386 folder on your Windows NT Server compact disc.) Edit this text box if necessary. Click the Continue command button.

**7.** Windows NT copies and installs Microsoft DNS Server. The Network dialog box reappears. Click the Add command button.

**8.** The Select Network Service dialog box appears. Scroll down and highlight Windows Internet Name Service. Click OK.

**9.** A Windows NT Setup dialog box appears. Ensure the correct source file location is displayed in the text box at the bottom of the dialog box. Click the Continue command button.

**10.** Windows NT copies and installs WINS. The Network dialog box reappears. Click the Close command button.

**11.** Windows NT performs various bindings operations. A Network Settings Change warning dialog box appears, asking if you want to restart your computer now for the new settings to take effect. Click the Yes command button.

**12.** Boot your computer to Windows NT Server and log on as Administrator. Continue on to Part 2.

**Part 2: Configuring Microsoft DNS Server to interact with WINS**

In this section, you configure Microsoft DNS Server to use WINS to resolve host names to IP addresses.

**1.** From the desktop, select Start ⇒ Programs ⇒ Administrative Tools (Common) ⇒ DNS Manager.

**2.** In the Domain Name Service Manager dialog box, select DNS ⇒ New Server.

**3.** The Add DNS Server dialog box appears. Type **192.168.59.5** in the DNS Server text box. Click OK.

**4.** Your server appears (indicated by its IP address) in the Server List on the left side of the Domain Name Service Manager dialog box. Right-click your server's IP address. Select Refresh from the menu that appears. Right-click again on your server's IP address. Select New Zone from the menu that appears.

**5.** The "Creating new zone for 192.168.59.5" dialog box appears. Select the radio button next to Primary. Click the Next command button.

**6.** Type **lab.com** in the Zone Name text box. Type **lab.com.dns** in the Zone File text box. Click the Next command button.

**7.** Click the Finish command button in the "Creating new zone for 192.168.59.5" dialog box. The `lab.com` zone appears in the Domain Name Service Manager dialog box under the Server List for your Windows NT Server computer. Right-click `lab.com`, and then select Properties from the menu that appears.

**8.** The "Zone Properties–lab.com" dialog box appears. Click the WINS Lookup tab.

**9.** On the WINS Lookup tab, select the check box next to Use WINS Resolution. In the uppermost WINS Servers text box, type **192.168.59.5** and click the Add command button. Click OK.

**10.** Your DNS Server is now configured to use WINS for host name resolution. Exit DNS Manager.

## Lab 16.26 *Configuring Internet Information Server and installing and configuring Peer Web Services*

Workstation
Enterprise

The purpose of this lab exercise is to give you hands-on experience in configuring Microsoft Internet Information Server and in installing and configuring Peer Web Services.

This lab consists of two parts:

Part 1: Configuring Microsoft Internet Information Server

Part 2: Installing and configuring Peer Web Services

Begin this lab by booting your computer to Windows NT Server. Log on as Administrator.

Complete the following steps carefully.

### Part 1: Configuring Microsoft Internet Information Server

In this section, you configure Microsoft Internet Information Server on your Windows NT Server computer.

**1.** Select Start ⇒ Programs ⇒ Microsoft Internet Server (Common) ⇒ Internet Information Server Setup.

**2.** The Microsoft Internet Information Server 2.0 Setup dialog box appears. Click OK.

**3.** In the next Microsoft Internet Information Server 2.0 Setup dialog box that appears, click the Add/Remove command button.

**4.** Ensure the correct source file location is displayed in the text box. (This is probably the `C:\WINNTSRV\system32\inetsrv` folder on your Windows NT Server computer.) It should be unnecessary to edit this text box. Click OK.

**5.** In the Microsoft Internet Information Server 2.0 Setup dialog box, *deselect* the check box next to Gopher Service. (This will deinstall the Gopher Service, which is not used in most NT installations.) Click OK.

**6.** The Microsoft Internet Information Server 2.0 Setup dialog box appears. Click the Yes command button to stop the Gopher Publishing Service.

**7.** In the Microsoft Internet Information Server 2.0 Setup dialog box, click OK.

**8.** Select Start ⇒ Programs ⇒ Microsoft Internet Server (Common) ⇒ Internet Service Manager.

**9.** In the Microsoft Internet Service Manager dialog box, double-click the first computer listed in the Computer list box.

**10.** The "WWW Service Properties for pdclab" dialog box appears. Notice the configuration options available on the Service tab. Click the Directories tab.

**11.** On the Directories tab, notice the configuration options available. Click the Logging tab.

**12.** On the Logging tab, notice the configuration options available. Click the Advanced tab.

**13.** Notice the configuration options available. Click OK.

**14.** In the Microsoft Internet Service Manager dialog box, highlight the first computer listed in the Computer list box. Select Properties ⇒ Stop Service.

**15.** Notice the state of the WWW service has changed to Stopped. Select Properties ⇒ Start Service.

**16.** Notice the state of the WWW service has changed to Running. Exit Microsoft Internet Service Manager.

**17.** Double-click Internet Explorer on your desktop.

**18.** The Microsoft Internet Explorer Home Page dialog box appears. Edit the Open text box so it reads **pdclab** and press Enter.

**19.** The Microsoft Internet Information Server home page is displayed. You have successfully configured and accessed the Microsoft Internet Information Server. Exit Internet Explorer.

**20.** Shut down your computer, reboot to Windows NT Workstation, and log on as Administrator. Place the Windows NT Workstation compact disc in your CD-ROM drive. Continue to Part 2.

### Part 2: Installing and configuring Peer Web Services

In this section, you install and configure Peer Web Services on your Windows NT Workstation computer.

**1.** Select Start ⇒ Settings ⇒ Control Panel.

**2.** In the Control Panel dialog box, double-click Network.

**3.** In the Network dialog box, click the Services tab.

**4.** On the Service tab, click the Add command button.

**5.** In the Select Network Service dialog box, highlight Microsoft Peer Web Services. Click OK.

**6.** The Internet Information Server Installation—Files Needed dialog box appears. Ensure the correct source file location is displayed in the text box. (This is normally the i386 folder on your Windows NT Workstation compact disc.) Edit this text box if necessary. Click OK.

**7.** The Microsoft Peer Web Services Setup dialog box appears. Click OK.

**8.** In the Microsoft Peer Web Services Setup dialog box, *deselect* the check box next to Gopher Service. *Select* the check box next to Internet Service Manager (HTML). Click OK.

**9.** When a dialog box appears prompting you to do so, click the Yes command button to create the installation directory.

**10.** The Publishing Directories dialog box appears. Click OK to accept the default publishing directories.

**11.** Windows NT copies and installs Peer Web Services. This process takes a few minutes.

12. If a Microsoft Peer Web Services Setup dialog box appears, indicating you must close Control Panel before you can install the ODBC drivers, click OK to close Control Panel.

    The Install Drivers dialog box appears. Highlight SQL Server, and then click OK.

13. A dialog box appears, indicating Microsoft Peer Web Services has been installed and set up. Click OK.

14. The Network dialog box reappears. Click the Close command button.

15. Exit Control Panel if it is still open.

16. Double-click Internet Explorer.

17. The Microsoft Internet Explorer Home Page appears. Edit the Address text box so it reads: **ntw40** and press Enter.

18. The Microsoft Peer Web Services home page is displayed. Scroll down to the Administrative Tools heading, and click the blue text that reads *click here* in the description under that heading.

19. Internet Service Manager for Peer Web Services appears. This an HTML version of Internet Service Manager. Exit Internet Explorer.

## Lab 16.27 *Installing and configuring an Internet (TCP/IP) router*

The purpose of this lab exercise is to give you hands-on experience in installing and configuring an Internet (TCP/IP) router on a Windows NT Server computer.

Begin this lab by booting your computer to Windows NT Server. Log on as Administrator. Place your Windows NT Server compact disc in your CD-ROM drive. Complete the following steps carefully.

**MCSE**

Server
Enterprise

1. Select Start ⇒ Settings ⇒ Control Panel.

2. In the Control Panel dialog box, double-click Network.

3. In the Network dialog box, click the Adapters tab.

4. On the Adapters tab, click the Add command button.

5. In the Select Network Adapter dialog box, highlight MS Loopback Adapter. Click OK. (You already installed a network adapter when you initially installed Windows NT Server. This step installs a second network adapter that will allow your computer to function as a TCP/IP router.)

6. The MS Loopback Adapter Card Setup dialog box appears. Click OK.

7. The Windows NT Setup dialog box appears. Ensure the correct source file location is displayed in the text box. (This is probably the i386 folder on your Windows NT Server compact disc.) Edit this text box if necessary. Click the Continue command button.

8. The Network dialog box reappears. Click the Services tab.

9. On the Services tab, click the Add command button.

10. In the Select Network Service dialog box, highlight RIP for Internet Protocol. Click OK.

11. The Windows NT Setup dialog box appears. Ensure the correct source file location is displayed in the text box. Click the Continue command button.

12. The Network dialog box reappears. Click the Close command button.

13. Windows NT performs various bindings operations, and then displays the Microsoft TCP/IP Properties dialog box. In the Adapter drop-down list box, select the MS Loopback adapter you installed in Steps 5–7 in this lab. (This is the second adapter in the list.) In the IP Address text box, type **192.168.60.1** and press Tab. In the Subnet Mask text box, type **255.255.255.0** and then click the Routing tab.

14. On the Routing tab, notice the check box next to Enable IP Forwarding is checked. Windows NT automatically selects this check box when RIP for Internet Protocol is installed. Click OK.

15. A Network Settings Change dialog box appears. Click the Yes command button to restart your computer so the new settings can take effect.

 caution

**If your computer is connected to a network that uses TCP/IP, you should remove RIP for Internet Protocol after the computer reboots. If you don't do this, it can cause routing problems on your network. (To remove RIP for Internet Protocol, use the Services tab in the Network application in Control Panel.) You will have to reboot your computer again after you remove RIP for Internet Protocol.**

## Lab 16.28 *Identifying and resolving TCP/IP connectivity problems*

Server
Enterprise

The purpose of this lab exercise is to give you hands-on experience in identifying and resolving common TCP/IP connectivity problems.

In each of the following situations:

1. Identify the TCP/IP connectivity problem (for example, an invalid or duplicate IP address).

2. Describe what you would do to resolve the problem.

**Situation 1**   Several components on a network subnet are configured as shown in the following figure.

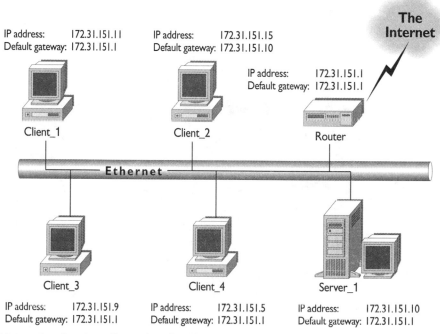

IP address:       172.31.151.11
Default gateway: 172.31.151.1

IP address:       172.31.151.15
Default gateway: 172.31.151.10

The Internet

IP address:       172.31.151.1
Default gateway: 172.31.151.1

Client_1

Client_2

Router

Ethernet

Client_3

Client_4

Server_1

IP address:       172.31.151.9
Default gateway: 172.31.151.1

IP address:       172.31.151.5
Default gateway: 172.31.151.1

IP address:       172.31.151.10
Default gateway: 172.31.151.1

**Network subnet configuration for Situation 1**

What is the TCP/IP connectivity problem in this situation?
What would you do to resolve the problem?

**Situation 2**   Several components on a network subnet are configured as shown in the following figure.

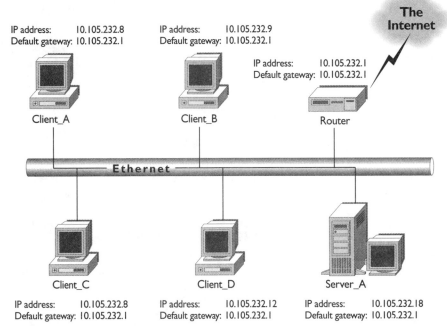

IP address:       10.105.232.8
Default gateway: 10.105.232.1

IP address:       10.105.232.9
Default gateway: 10.105.232.1

IP address:       10.105.232.1
Default gateway: 10.105.232.1

Client_A

Client_B

Router

The Internet

Ethernet

Client_C

Client_D

Server_A

IP address:       10.105.232.8
Default gateway: 10.105.232.1

IP address:       10.105.232.12
Default gateway: 10.105.232.1

IP address:       10.105.232.18
Default gateway: 10.105.232.1

**Network subnet configuration for Situation 2**

What is the TCP/IP connectivity problem in this situation?

What would you do to resolve the problem?

### Lab 17.29  *Installing and configuring NWLink and Client Service for NetWare*

Workstation

The purpose of this lab exercise is to give you hands-on experience in installing and configuring NWLink IPX/SPX Compatible Transport, and also in installing and configuring Client Service for NetWare on a Windows NT Workstation computer.

This lab consists of two parts:

Part 1: Installing NWLink and Client Service for NetWare

Part 2: Configuring Client Service for NetWare and NWLink

Begin this lab by booting your computer to Windows NT Workstation. Log on as Administrator. Place your Windows NT Workstation compact disc in your computer's CD-ROM drive.

Follow these steps carefully.

### Part 1: Installing NWLink and Client Service for NetWare

In this section, you install NWLink IPX/SPX Compatible Transport and Client Service for NetWare on a Windows NT Workstation computer.

1. Select Start ⇒ Settings ⇒ Control Panel.
2. In the Control Panel dialog box, double-click Network.
3. In the Network dialog box, click the Protocols tab.
4. On the Protocols tab, click the Add command button.
5. In the Select Network Protocol dialog box, highlight NWLink IPX/SPX Compatible Transport in the Network Protocol list box. Click OK.
6. A Windows NT Setup dialog box appears. Ensure that the correct path to your Windows NT Workstation source files (usually the i386 folder on your Windows NT Workstation compact disc) is listed in the text box. Edit the text box as necessary. Click the Continue command button.
7. Windows NT installs NWLink IPX/SPX Compatible Transport. The Network dialog box reappears. Click the Services tab.
8. On the Services tab, click the Add command button.
9. In the Select Network Service dialog box, highlight Client Service for NetWare. Click OK.
10. A Windows NT Setup dialog box appears. Ensure that the correct path to your Windows NT Workstation source files (usually the i386 folder on your Windows NT Workstation compact disc) is listed in the text box. Click the Continue command button.
11. Windows NT installs Client Service for NetWare. The Network dialog box reappears. Click the Close command button.
12. Windows NT performs various bindings operations.
13. A Network Settings Change dialog box appears, indicating that you must shut down and restart the computer in order for the new settings to take effect. Click the Yes command button to restart the computer. Continue to Part 2.

### Part 2: Configuring Client Service for NetWare and NWLink

In this section, you configure Client Service for NetWare and NWLink IPX/SPX Compatible Transport on a Windows NT Workstation computer.

1. When the computer restarts, reboot to Windows NT Workstation. Log on as Administrator.
2. When the Select NetWare Logon dialog box appears, click OK.

3. Select Start ⇒ Settings ⇒ Control Panel.

4. In the Control Panel dialog box, double-click the CSNW icon.

5. The Client Service for NetWare dialog box appears.

   o If your computer is connected to a network that has a NetWare server, configure the Select Preferred Server option, or Default Tree and Context option, as appropriate. (Obtain the appropriate configuration settings from your network administrator.) Configure the Print Options and Login Script Options as desired or as instructed by your network administrator.

   o If your computer is *not* connected to a network that has a NetWare server, ensure that the radio button next to Preferred Server is selected, and accept the default Select Preferred Server option of <None>.

   Click OK.

6. The Control Panel dialog box reappears. Double-click Network.

7. In the Network dialog box, click the Protocols tab.

8. On the Protocols tab, double-click NWLink IPX/SPX Compatible Transport.

9. An NWLink IPX/SPX Properties dialog box appears. In the Frame Type drop-down list box, select Ethernet 802.2. In the Network Number text box, type **12345678** (if you are connected to a network that uses IPX, obtain an appropriate network number from your network administrator). Click OK.

10. The Network dialog box reappears. Click the Close command button.

11. A Network Settings Change dialog box appears, indicating that you must shut down and restart the computer in order for the new settings to take effect. Click the Yes command button to restart the computer.

## Lab 17.30 *Installing and configuring NWLink and Gateway Service for NetWare*

Server
Enterprise

The purpose of this lab exercise is to give you hands-on experience in installing and configuring NWLink IPX/SPX Compatible Transport, and also in installing and configuring Gateway Service for NetWare on a Windows NT Server computer.

This lab consists of two parts:

Part 1: Installing NWLink and Gateway Service for NetWare

Part 2: Configuring Gateway Service for NetWare

Begin this lab by booting your computer to Windows NT Server. Log on as Administrator. Place your Windows NT Server compact disc in your computer's CD-ROM drive.

Follow the steps below carefully.

## Part 1: Installing NWLink and Gateway Service for NetWare

In this section, you install NWLink IPX/SPX Compatible Transport and Gateway Service for NetWare on a Windows NT Server computer. Additionally, you configure NWLink IPX/SPX Compatible Transport.

**1.** Select Start ⇒ Settings ⇒ Control Panel.

**2.** In the Control Panel dialog box, double-click Network.

**3.** In the Network dialog box, click the Protocols tab.

**4.** On the Protocols tab, click the Add command button.

**5.** In the Select Network Protocol dialog box, highlight NWLink IPX/SPX Compatible Transport in the Network Protocol list box. Click OK.

**6.** A Windows NT Setup dialog box appears. Ensure that the correct path to your Windows NT Server source files (usually the i386 folder on your Windows NT Server compact disc) is listed in the text box. Edit the text box as necessary. Click the Continue command button.

**7.** Windows NT installs NWLink IPX/SPX Compatible Transport. The Network dialog box reappears. Click the Services tab.

**8.** On the Services tab, click the Add command button.

**9.** In the Select Network Service dialog box, highlight Gateway (and Client) Services for NetWare. Click OK.

**10.** A Windows NT Setup dialog box appears. Ensure that the correct path to your Windows NT Server source files (usually the i386 folder on your Windows NT Server compact disc) is listed in the text box. Click the Continue command button.

**11.** Windows NT installs Gateway Service for NetWare. The Network dialog box reappears. Click the Close command button.

**12.** Windows NT performs various bindings operations.

**13.** An NWLink IPX/SPX warning dialog box appears, indicating that you need to configure your computer's internal network number. Click the Yes command button.

**14.** The NWLink IPX/SPX Properties dialog box appears. Change the Internal Network Number to **87654321**. Select the radio button next to Manual Frame Type Detection, and click the Add command button.

**15.** In the Manual Frame Detection dialog box, select Ethernet 802.2 from the Frame Type drop-down list box. Type in a Network Number of **12345678**. (If you are connected to a network that uses IPX, obtain an appropriate network number from your network administrator.) Click the Add command button.

**16.** In the NWLink IPX/SPX Properties dialog box, click OK.

**17.** A Network Settings Change dialog box appears, indicating that you must shut down and restart the computer in order for the new settings to take effect. Click the Yes command button to restart the computer. Continue to Part 2.

**Part 2: Configuring Gateway Service for NetWare**

In this section, you configure Gateway Service for NetWare on a Windows NT Server computer.

**1.** When the computer restarts, reboot to Windows NT Server. Log on as Administrator.

**2.** When the Select NetWare Logon dialog box appears, click OK.

**3.** Select Start ⇒ Settings ⇒ Control Panel.

**4.** In the Control Panel dialog box, double-click the GSNW icon.

**5.** The Gateway Service for NetWare dialog box appears.

   o If your computer is connected to a network that has a NetWare server, configure the Select Preferred Server option, or Default Tree and Context option, as appropriate. (Obtain the appropriate configuration settings from your network administrator.) Configure the Print Options and Login Script Options as desired or as instructed by your network administrator.

   o If your computer is *not* connected to a network that has a NetWare server, ensure that the radio button next to Preferred Server is selected, and accept the default Select Preferred Server option of <None>.

   Click the Gateway command button.

**6.** The Configure Gateway dialog box appears. Notice the various options in this dialog box. Click OK.

**7.** The Gateway Service for NetWare dialog box reappears. Click OK.

**8.** The Control Panel dialog box reappears. Exit Control Panel.

**Lab 17.31** *Installing and configuring RIP for NWLink IPX/SPX Compatible Transport*

Enterprise

The purpose of this lab exercise is to give you hands-on experience in installing and configuring RIP for NWLink IPX/SPX Compatible Transport.

Begin this lab by booting your computer to Windows NT Server. Log on as Administrator. Place your Windows NT Server compact disc in your computer's CD-ROM drive.

Follow the steps below carefully.

1. Select Start ⇒ Settings ⇒ Control Panel.

2. In the Control Panel dialog box, double-click Network.

3. In the Network dialog box, click the Services tab.

4. On the Services tab, click the Add command button.

5. In the Select Network Service dialog box, highlight RIP for NWLink IPX/SPX Compatible Transport. Click OK.

6. A Windows NT Setup dialog box appears. Ensure that the correct path to your Windows NT Server source files (usually the i386 folder on your Windows NT Server compact disc) is listed in the text box. Edit this text box if necessary. Click the Continue command button.

7. The RIP for NWLink IPX Configuration dialog box appears, asking if you want to enable NetBIOS Broadcast Propagation. Click the Yes command button.

8. The Network dialog box reappears. Click the Protocols tab.

9. On the Protocols tab, double-click NWLink IPX/SPX Compatible Transport.

10. The NWLink IPX/SPX Properties dialog box appears. Click the Routing tab.

11. On the Routing tab, notice that the check box next to Enable RIP Routing is selected. Windows NT automatically enables RIP routing when it installs RIP for NWLink IPX/SPX Compatible Transport. Click OK.

12. The Network dialog box reappears. Click the Close command button.

13. Windows NT performs various bindings operations.

14. A Network Settings Change dialog box appears, indicating that you must shut down and restart the computer in order for the new settings to take effect. Click the Yes command button to restart the computer.

caution  If your computer is connected to a network that uses IPX, you should remove RIP for NWLink IPX/SPX Compatible Transport after the computer restarts unless you want your computer to function as a RIP router. If you don't remove RIP for NWLink IPX/SPX Compatible Transport, it will create additional broadcast traffic on your network. (To remove RIP for NWLink IPX/SPX Compatible Transport, use the Services tab in the Network application in Control Panel.) You will have to reboot your computer again after you remove RIP for NWLink IPX/SPX Compatible Transport.

## Lab 19.32 *Installing and configuring RAS and Dial-Up Networking*

Workstation
Server
Enterprise

The purpose of this lab is to give you hands-on experience in installing and configuring RAS on a Windows NT Server computer, and in installing RAS and configuring Dial-Up Networking on a Windows NT Workstation computer.

This lab consists of two parts:

Part 1: Installing and configuring RAS (on a Windows NT Server computer)

Part 2: Installing RAS and configuring Dial-Up Networking (on a Windows NT Workstation computer)

Begin this lab by booting your computer to Windows NT Server. Log on as Administrator. Place your Windows NT Server compact disc in your CD-ROM drive. Follow the steps below carefully.

### Part 1: Installing and configuring RAS (on a Windows NT Server computer)

In this section, you install and configure RAS on your Windows NT Server computer.

**1.** Select Start ⇒ Settings ⇒ Control Panel.

**2.** In the Control Panel dialog box, double-click Network.

**3.** In the Network dialog box, click the Services tab.

**4.** On the Services tab, click the Add command button.

**5.** In the Select Network Service dialog box, highlight Remote Access Service. Click OK.

**6.** A Windows NT Setup dialog box appears. Ensure that the correct path to your Windows NT Server source files (usually the i386 folder on your Windows NT Server compact disc) is listed in the text box. Edit this text box if necessary. Click the Continue command button.

**7.** Windows NT copies source files. The Add RAS Device dialog box appears. Select the modem that you installed in Lab 4.6 from the RAS Capable Devices drop-down list box. Click OK.

**8.** The Remote Access Setup dialog box appears. Click the Configure command button.

**9.** The Configure Port Usage dialog box appears. Select the radio button next to "Dial out and Receive calls." Click OK.

**10.** The Remote Access Setup dialog box reappears. Click the Network command button.

**11.** The Network Configuration dialog box appears. Select the check box next to Enable Multilink at the bottom of the dialog box. Click the Configure command button next to the TCP/IP option in the Server Settings section.

**12.** The RAS Server TCP/IP Configuration dialog box appears. Click the radio button next to "Use static address pool." In the Begin text box, enter an IP address of **192.168.58.1**, and in the End text box, enter an IP address of **192.168.58.255**. Click OK.

**13.** The Network Configuration dialog box reappears. Click the Configure command button next to the IPX option in the Server Settings section.

**14.** The RAS Server IPX Configuration dialog box appears. Notice that IPX clients are configured, by default, to access the entire network. Click OK.

**15.** The Network Configuration dialog box reappears. Click OK.

**16.** The Remote Access Setup dialog box reappears. Click the Continue command button.

**17.** Windows NT installs and configures RAS. If the RIP for NWLink IPX Configuration dialog box appears, asking if you want to enable NetBIOS Broadcast Propagation, click the Yes command button.

**18.** A Setup Message dialog box appears, indicating that RAS has been successfully installed. Click OK.

**19.** The Network dialog box reappears. Click the Close command button.

**20.** Windows NT performs various bindings operations.

**21.** A Network Settings Change dialog box appears, indicating that you must shut down and restart the computer in order for the new settings to take effect. Click the Yes command button to restart the computer.

**22.** Reboot your computer to Windows NT Server. Log on as Administrator. If the Control Panel dialog box appears, close it.

**23.** Select Start ⇒ Programs ⇒ Administrative Tools (Common) ⇒ Remote Access Admin.

**24.** The Remote Access Admin dialog box appears. Notice that RAS is running on your server. Select Users ⇒ Permissions.

**25.** The Remote Access Permissions dialog box appears. Click the Grant All command button to assign the dialin permission to all user accounts.

**26.** The Remote Access Admin warning dialog box appears, asking you to confirm that you want to grant the dialin permission to all users. Click the Yes command button.

**27.** The Remote Access Permissions dialog box reappears. Click OK.

**28.** The Remote Access Admin dialog box reappears. Close Remote Access Admin. Continue on to Part 2.

**Part 2: Installing RAS and configuring Dial-Up Networking (on a Windows NT Workstation computer)**

In this section, you install RAS and configure Dial-Up Networking on your Windows NT Workstation computer.

Begin this section by booting your computer to Windows NT Workstation. Log on as Administrator. Place your Windows NT Workstation compact disc in your CD-ROM drive.

**1.** Select Start ⇒ Settings ⇒ Control Panel.

**2.** In the Control Panel dialog box, double-click Network.

**3.** In the Network dialog box, click the Services tab.

**4.** On the Services tab, click the Add command button.

**5.** In the Select Network Service dialog box, highlight Remote Access Service. Click OK.

**6.** A Windows NT Setup dialog box appears. Ensure that the correct path to your Windows NT Workstation source files (usually the i386 folder on your Windows NT Workstation compact disc) is listed in the text box. Edit this text box if necessary. Click the Continue command button.

**7.** Windows NT copies source files. If you have already installed a modem using Windows NT Workstation, skip to Step 13.

If you haven't installed a modem, the Remote Access Setup dialog box appears, indicating that there are no RAS capable devices to add. Click the Yes command button to invoke the modem installer.

**8.** The Install New Modem dialog box appears. Select the check box next to "Don't detect my modem; I will select it from a list." Click the Next command button.

**9.** The Install New Modem dialog box appears. Ensure that (Standard Modem Types) is highlighted in the Manufacturers list box, and that Dial-Up Networking Serial Cable between 2 PCs is selected in the Models list box. Click the Next command button.

**10.** The next Install New Modem dialog box appears. Ensure that the radio button next to "Selected ports" is selected. Highlight a serial port from the list box (such as COM1 or COM2). Click the Next command button.

**11.** The Location Information dialog box appears. Type in your area code in the "What area (or city) code are you in now" text box. Click the Next command button.

**12.** Click the Finish command button in the Install New Modem dialog box.

**13.** The Add RAS Device dialog box appears. Select a modem from the RAS Capable Devices drop down list box. Click OK.

**14.** The Remote Access Setup dialog box appears. Click the Configure command button.

**15.** The Configure Port Usage dialog box appears. Select the radio button next to "Dial out and Receive calls." Click OK.

**16.** The Remote Access Setup dialog box reappears. Click the Continue command button.

**17.** The RAS Server TCP/IP Configuration dialog box appears. Click the radio button next to "Use static address pool." In the Begin text box, enter an IP address of **192.168.58.1**, and in the End text box, enter an IP address of **192.168.58.255**. Click OK.

**18.** The RAS Server IPX Configuration dialog box appears. Click OK.

**19.** Windows NT installs and configures RAS. If the RIP for NWLink IPX Configuration dialog box appears, asking if you want to enable NetBIOS Broadcast Propagation, click the Yes command button.

**20.** A Setup Message dialog box appears, indicating that RAS has been successfully installed. Click OK.

**21.** The Network dialog box reappears. Click the Close command button.

**22.** Windows NT performs various bindings operations.

**23.** A Network Settings Change dialog box appears, indicating that you must shut down and restart the computer in order for the new settings to take effect. Click the Yes command button to restart the computer.

**24.** Reboot the computer to Windows NT Workstation. Log on as Administrator.

**25.** If the Control Panel dialog box appears, close it.

**26.** Select Start ⇒ Programs ⇒ Accessories ⇒ Dial-Up Networking.

**27.** A Dial-Up Networking dialog box appears, indicating that the phonebook is empty. Click OK.

**28.** The New Phonebook Entry Wizard appears. Accept the default of MyDialUpServer in the "Name the new phonebook entry" text box. Click the Next command button.

**29.** The Server dialog box appears. Select the check boxes next to "I am calling the Internet" and "Send my plain text password if that's the only way to connect." Click the Next command button.

**30.** The Phone Number dialog box appears. Type **555-5425** in the "Phone number" text box. Click the Next command button.

**31.** Click the Finish command button in the New Phonebook Entry Wizard dialog box.

**32.** The Dial-Up Networking dialog box reappears. Exit Dial-Up Networking.

## Lab 20.33    *Installing and configuring Services for Macintosh*

Enterprise

The purpose of this lab exercise is to give you hands-on experience in installing and configuring Services for Macintosh on a Windows NT Server computer.

This lab consists of two parts:

Part 1: Installing and configuring Services for Macintosh

Part 2: Configuring a Macintosh-accessible volume

Begin this lab by booting your computer to Windows NT Server. Log on as Administrator. Place your Windows NT Server compact disc in your computer's CD-ROM drive.

Follow the steps below carefully.

### Part 1: Installing and configuring Services for Macintosh

In this section, you install and configure Services for Macintosh on a Windows NT Server computer.

**1.** Select Start ⇒ Settings ⇒ Control Panel.

**2.** In the Control Panel dialog box, double-click the Network application.

**3.** In the Network dialog box, click the Services tab.

**4.** On the Services tab, click the Add command button.

**5.** In the Select Network Service dialog box, highlight Services for Macintosh. Click OK.

**6.** A Windows NT Setup dialog box appears. Ensure that the correct path to your Windows NT Server source files (usually the I386 folder on your Windows NT Server compact disc) is listed in the text box. Edit this text box if necessary. Click the Continue command button.

**7.** Windows NT copies source files and installs Services for Macintosh.

**8.** The Network dialog box reappears. Click the Close command button.

**9.** Windows NT performs various bindings operations.

**10.** The Microsoft AppleTalk Protocol Properties dialog box appears. Click OK to continue.

**11.** A Network Settings Change dialog box appears, indicating that you must shut down and restart the computer for the new settings to take effect. Click the Yes command button to restart the computer.

**12.** Reboot your computer to Windows NT Server. Log on as Administrator. If the Control Panel dialog box appears, close it.

Continue to Part 2.

**Part 2: Configuring a Macintosh–accessible volume**

In this section, you configure a Macintosh-accessible volume on an NTFS partition on a Windows NT Server computer.

**1.** Select Start ⇒ Programs ⇒ Windows NT Explorer.

**2.** The Exploring dialog box appears. Highlight your D: drive (or the drive where your NTFS volume is located) in the All Folders list box. Select File ⇒ New ⇒ Folder.

**3.** In the Contents of D: list box, rename the New Folder **Macfiles** and press Enter.

**4.** Exit Windows NT Explorer.

**5.** Select Start ⇒ Programs ⇒ Administrative Tools (Common) ⇒ Server Manager.

**6.** The Server Manager dialog box appears. Highlight your server in the list box and select MacFile ⇒ Volumes.

**7.** The Macintosh-Accessible Volumes dialog box appears. Click the Create Volume command button.

**8.** The Create Macintosh-Accessible Volume dialog box appears. Type the following bolded information in the appropriate text boxes:

Volume Name—**MACFILES**

Path—**D:\MACFILES** (Or if your NTFS volume is located on another drive, use the drive letter for your NTFS volume.)

Password—Leave this text box blank.

Confirm Password—Also leave this text box blank.

Click OK.

**9.** The Macintosh-Accessible Volumes dialog box reappears. Notice that MACFILES appears in the Volumes list box as a shared Macintosh volume. Click the Close command button.

**10.** The Server Manager dialog box reappears. Exit Server Manager.

## Lab 21.34 *Starting applications at various priorities*

Workstation

The purpose of this lab exercise is to give you hands-on experience in configuring foreground application responsiveness and in starting applications at various priorities on a Windows NT Workstation computer.

This lab consists of two parts:

> Part 1: Using the System application to configure foreground application responsiveness

Part 2: Using the Start command and Task Manager to start applications at various priorities

Begin this lab by booting your computer to Windows NT Workstation. Log on as Administrator. Place your Windows NT Workstation compact disc in your computer's CD-ROM drive.

Follow the steps below carefully.

### Part 1: Using the System application to configure foreground application responsiveness

In this section, you use the System application in Control Panel to change foreground application responsiveness on a Windows NT Workstation computer. Additionally, you install games on your computer (if you haven't already done so).

**1.** Select Start ⇒ Settings ⇒ Control Panel.

**2.** The Control Panel dialog box appears. Double-click the System icon.

**3.** The System Properties dialog box appears. Click the Performance tab.

**4.** The Performance tab appears. Notice the Application Performance section on this tab. Move the Boost slide bar to the middle, halfway between None and Maximum. (This configures a performance boost of one point for the foreground application.) Move the Boost slide bar back to Maximum. (This configures a performance boost of 2 points for the foreground application.) Click OK.

**5.** The Control Panel dialog box reappears. If you have already installed games (including Pinball) on your Windows NT Workstation computer, close Control Panel, skip the remaining steps in this section, and continue on to Part 2. If you haven't yet installed games on your Windows NT Workstation computer, double-click the Add/Remove Programs icon, and continue on to step 6.

**6.** The Add/Remove Programs Properties dialog box appears. Click the Windows NT Setup tab.

**7.** The Windows NT Setup tab appears. Select the check box next to Games in the Components list box. Click OK.

**8.** The Add/Remove Programs Properties—Copying Files dialog box appears. If the Files Needed dialog box appears, ensure that the correct path to the source files (usually the i386 folder on your Windows NT Workstation compact disc) is presented in the "Copy files from" text box. Edit this text box as necessary. Click OK.

**9.** Windows NT Workstation copies files.

**10.** The Control Panel dialog box reappears. Close Control Panel. Continue on to Part 2.

## Part 2: Using the Start command and Task Manager to start applications at various priorities

In this section, you use the `Start` command and Windows NT Task Manager to start applications at various priorities on a Windows NT Workstation computer.

**1.** Select Start ⇒ Programs ⇒ Command Prompt.

**2.** The Command Prompt dialog box appears. At the command prompt, type **cd \winntwks\system32** and press Enter.

**3.** At the `C:\WINNTWKS\system32>` command prompt, type **start /low usrmgr.exe** and press Enter.

**4.** User Manager starts. Press Ctrl + Alt + Delete.

**5.** The Windows NT Security dialog box appears. Click the Task Manager command button.

**6.** The Windows NT Task Manager dialog box appears. Click the Processes tab.

**7.** The Processes tab appears. Select View ⇒ Select Columns.

**8.** The Select Columns dialog box appears. Deselect the check boxes next to PID (Process Identifier) and CPU Usage. Select the check box next to Base Priority. Click OK.

**9.** The Processes tab in the Windows NT Task Manager dialog box reappears. Find `USRMGR.EXE` in the list box. Notice that `USRMGR.EXE` has a Base Priority of Low. Click the Applications tab.

**10.** The Applications tab appears. Highlight User Manager and click the End Task command button at the bottom of the dialog box. (This action stops User Manager). Minimize (*don't* close) Windows NT Task Manager.

**11.** At the `C:\WINNTWKS\system32>` command prompt, type **start /realtime usrmgr.exe** and press Enter.

**12.** User Manager starts. Maximize Task Manager, and click the Processes tab.

**13.** The Processes tab appears. Notice that `USRMGR.EXE` now has a base priority of Realtime. Highlight `USRMGR.EXE` and click the End Process command button.

**14.** A Task Manager Warning dialog box appears. Click the Yes command button. (This action stops User Manager.)

**15.** Minimize (*don't* close) Windows NT Task Manager.

**16.** At the `C:\WINNTWKS\system32>` command prompt, type **start /realtime perfmon.exe** and press Enter.

**17.** Performance Monitor starts. Maximize Task Manager.

**18.** The Processes tab appears. Notice that `perfmon.exe` has a base priority of High. (The `/realtime` switch does *not* always work with all applications. Performance Monitor always starts with a base priority of High, no matter which priority is assigned with the `Start` command.)

Right-click `perfmon.exe`. Select Set Priority ⇒ Realtime from the menu that appears.

**19.** A Task Manager Warning dialog box appears. Click the Yes command button.

**20.** In the Windows NT Task Manager dialog box, notice that `perfmon.exe` now has a Base Priority of Realtime. (This is how you can change the priority of applications that don't respond correctly to the priority setting specified by the `Start` command.)

Highlight `perfmon.exe` and click the End Process command button.

**21.** A Task Manager Warning dialog box appears. Click the Yes command button.

**22.** Minimize (*don't* close) Windows NT Task Manager.

**23.** At the `C:\WINNTWKS\system32>` command prompt, type **cd "\program files\windows nt\pinball"** and press Enter.

**24.** At the `C:\Program Files\Windows NT\PINBALL>` command prompt, type **start /realtime pinball** and press Enter.

**25.** The Pinball game starts. Notice that your computer is locked up and won't respond to keyboard or mouse input. As you can see, not all programs should be run at real-time priority. In this case, when Pinball is set at real-time priority, it utilizes all available system resources, so that even the operating system is unable to function properly. Press the Restart button on your computer, or power off your computer.

### Lab 22.35 *Using Performance Monitor*

Workstation
Server
Enterprise

The purpose of this hands-on lab exercise is to provide you with experience in using Performance Monitor on a Windows NT computer.

This lab consists of four parts:

> Part 1: Adding objects and counters by installing Network Monitor Agent and SNMP Service, and enabling the PhysicalDisk and LogicalDisk objects and their counters using `Diskperf.exe`
>
> Part 2: Using Performance Monitor Chart view and Alert view
>
> Part 3: Creating a Performance Monitor log file

Part 4: Importing a Performance Monitor log file into Report view and
Chart view

Begin this lab by booting your computer to Windows NT Server. Log on as
Administrator. Place your Windows NT Server compact disc in your computer's
CD-ROM drive.

 **note** **If you are preparing *only* for the NT Workstation exam, you might
want to perform this lab on your Windows NT Workstation computer (instead of your Windows NT Server computer). The steps are
the same regardless of whether you use Windows NT Server or
Windows NT Workstation.**

Follow these steps carefully.

### Part 1: Adding objects and counters by installing Network Monitor Agent and SNMP Service, and enabling the PhysicalDisk and LogicalDisk objects and their counters by using Diskperf.exe

In this section, you check for the existence of Performance Monitor objects. Then
you install Network Monitor Agent and SNMP Service on your Windows NT Server
computer. Finally, you use Diskperf.exe to enable the PhysicalDisk and
LogicalDisk objects and their counters on your Windows NT Server computer.

1. Select Start ⟹ Programs ⟹ Administrative Tools (Common) ⟹ Performance Monitor.
2. The Performance Monitor dialog box appears. Select View ⟹ Chart.
3. Click the **+** command button located in the toolbar at the top of the dialog box.
4. The Add to Chart dialog box appears. Click the down arrow in the Object drop-down list box. Look for each of the following objects: ICMP, IP, Network Segment, TCP, and UDP. Notice that *none* of these objects appear in the Object drop-down list box. Click the Cancel command button.
5. The Performance Monitor dialog box reappears. Exit Performance Monitor.
6. Select Start ⟹ Settings ⟹ Control Panel.
7. The Control Panel dialog box appears. Double-click the Network icon.
8. The Network dialog box appears. Click the Services tab.
9. The Services tab appears. Click the Add command button.
10. The Select Network Service dialog box appears. Highlight Network Monitor Agent. Click OK.

**11.** A Windows NT Setup dialog box appears. Ensure that the correct path to your Windows NT Server source files (usually the i386 folder on your Windows NT Server compact disc) is listed in the text box. Edit this text box if necessary. Click the Continue command button.

**12.** Windows NT copies source files and installs Network Monitor Agent.

**13.** The Network dialog box reappears. Click the Add command button.

**14.** The Select Network Service dialog box appears. Highlight SNMP Service. Click OK.

**15.** A Windows NT Setup dialog box appears. Ensure that the correct path to your Windows NT Server source files (usually the i386 folder on your Windows NT Server compact disc) is listed in the text box. Edit this text box if necessary. Click the Continue command button.

**16.** Windows NT copies source files and installs the SNMP Service.

**17.** The Microsoft SNMP Properties dialog box appears. Click OK.

**18.** The Network dialog box reappears. Click the Close command button.

**19.** Windows NT performs various bindings operations.

**20.** A Network Settings Change dialog box appears. Click the No command button.

**21.** The Control Panel dialog box reappears. Exit Control Panel.

**22.** Select Start ⇒ Programs ⇒ Command Prompt.

**23.** The Command Prompt dialog box appears. At the command prompt, type **diskperf -y** and press Enter.

Notice that Windows NT indicates that disk performance counters on your computer are now set to start at boot, and will become effective after the computer is restarted.

**24.** At the command prompt, type **exit** and press Enter.

**25.** The Windows NT desktop reappears. Select Start ⇒ Shut Down.

**26.** In the Shut Down Windows dialog box, select the radio button next to "Restart the computer." Click the Yes command button.

**27.** Reboot the computer to Windows NT Server. Log on as Administrator. Continue to Part 2.

### Part 2: Using Performance Monitor Chart view and Alert view

In this section, you install games (if you haven't already done so) on your Windows NT Server computer, and use Performance Monitor Chart view and Alert view to chart server performance and to create an alert.

1. If you have already installed games (including Solitaire and Pinball) on your Windows NT Server computer, skip to Step 8.

   If you have *not* already installed games on your Windows NT Server computer, select Start ⇒ Settings ⇒ Control Panel, and continue to Step 2.

2. The Control Panel dialog box appears. Double-click the Add/Remove Programs icon.

3. The Add/Remove Programs dialog box appears. Click the Windows NT Setup tab.

4. The Windows NT Setup tab appears. Select the check box next to Games. (Or if you have one or two games installed but Solitaire or Pinball is *not* yet installed, deselect and then reselect this check box.) Click OK.

5. The Add/Remove Programs Properties—Copying Files dialog box appears.

   If the Files Needed dialog box appears, ensure that the correct path to your Windows NT Server source files (usually the i386 folder on your Windows NT Server compact disc) is listed in the "Copy files from" text box. Edit the text box as necessary. Click OK.

6. Windows NT installs games.

7. The Control Panel dialog box reappears. Exit Control Panel.

8. Select Start ⇒ Programs ⇒ Administrative Tools (Common) ⇒ Performance Monitor.

9. The Performance Monitor dialog box appears. Select View ⇒ Chart.

10. Click the + command button located in the toolbar at the top of the dialog box.

11. The Add to Chart dialog box appears. Click the down arrow in the Object drop-down list box. Look for each of the following objects: ICMP, IP, Network Segment, TCP, and UDP. Notice that after installing Network Monitor Agent and the SNMP Service (which you did in Part 1), all of these objects now appear in the Object drop-down list box.

    Click Memory in the Object drop-down list box. Select Pages/sec from the Counter list box. Click the Add command button.

12. Click the down arrow in the Object drop-down list box. Click Processor in the Object drop-down list box. Select % Processor Time from the Counter list box. Click the Add command button.

13. Click the down arrow in the Object drop-down list box. Click PhysicalDisk in the Object drop-down list box. Select % Disk Time from the Counter list box. Click the Add command button.

**14.** Click the down arrow in the Object drop-down list box. Click Server in the Object drop-down list box. Select Bytes Total/sec from the Counter list box. Click the Add command button. Click the Done command button.

You have just configured the four most commonly used Performance Monitor counters that monitor server performance.

**15.** The Performance Monitor dialog box reappears. In the list box at the bottom of the dialog box, highlight % Processor Time in the Counter column. Note the color assigned to the % Processor Time counter.

**16.** Move your mouse rapidly in a sweeping circular pattern on your mouse pad for several (at least five) seconds. Notice the increase in % Processor time usage, as depicted on the graph, from just moving your mouse.

**17.** Minimize (*don't* close) Performance Monitor.

**18.** Select Start ⇒ Programs ⇒ Accessories ⇒ Games ⇒ Solitaire.

**19.** Play Solitaire for a minute or two.

(If you've never played Solitaire before, select Help ⇒ Contents to find out how to play.)

When you finish playing, exit Solitaire, and quickly select Performance Monitor from the taskbar.

**20.** The Performance Monitor dialog box appears. Notice the counters and their levels during your Solitaire game, as depicted on the Performance Monitor chart.

**21.** Highlight Pages/sec (in the Counter column). Press Delete.

Highlight % Disk Time (in the Counter column). Press delete.

Highlight Bytes Total/sec (in the Counter column). Press Delete.

Highlight % Processor Time (in the Counter column). Press Delete.

**22.** Select Edit ⇒ Add To Chart.

**23.** The Add to Chart dialog box appears. Click the down arrow in the Object drop-down list box. Click LogicalDisk in the Object drop-down list box. Select % Free Space from the Counter list box. Highlight 0 ⇒ C: in the Instance list box. Click the Add command button. Click the Done command button.

**24.** The Performance Monitor dialog box reappears. Write the number that appears in the Last box here: _____

**25.** Add 5 to the number that you entered in Step 24, and write the resulting number here: _____

**26.** Highlight % Free Space (in the Counter column), and press Delete.

**27.** Select View ⇒ Alert.

**28.** The Alert View appears. Select Edit⇒Add To Alert.

**29.** The Add to Alert dialog box appears. Click the down arrow in the Object drop-down list box. Click LogicalDisk in the Object drop-down list box. Select % Free Space from the Counter list box. Select 0⇒C: in the Instance list box. Select the radio button next to Under in the Alert If section. Type the number you entered in Step 25 in the text box in the Alert If section. Click the Add command button. Click the Done command button.

**30.** The Performance Monitor dialog box reappears. Every five seconds, an alert should appear in the Alert Log list box, indicating that the % Free Space on your C: drive has fallen below the level that you entered in the previous step.

Press Delete to stop logging this alert.

Continue to Part 3.


### Part 3: Creating a Performance Monitor log file

In this section, you create a Performance Monitor log file. (You will view the data in this Performance Monitor log file in Part 4.)

**1.** In the Performance Monitor dialog box, select View⇒Log.

**2.** Select Edit⇒Add To Log.

**3.** The Add To Log dialog box appears. Highlight Memory in the Objects list box. Click the Add command button.

**4.** Highlight PhysicalDisk in the Objects list box. Click the Add command button.

**5.** Highlight Processor in the Objects list box. Click the Add command button.

**6.** Highlight Server in the Objects list box. Click the Add command button. Click the Done command button.

**7.** The Performance Monitor dialog box reappears. Select Options⇒Log.

**8.** The Log Options dialog box appears. In the File Name text box, type **practice.log**. Select **1** from the Interval (Seconds) drop-down list box. Click the Start Log command button.

**9.** Minimize (*don't* close) Performance Monitor.

**10.** Select Start⇒Programs⇒Accessories⇒Games⇒Pinball.

**11.** Play one game of Pinball.

(Hold down the space bar for a couple of seconds and then release it to launch the ball. The z key on the keyboard controls the left flipper. The ? key on the keyboard controls the right flipper.)

When you finish playing, exit Pinball, and quickly select Performance Monitor from the taskbar.

**12.** The Performance Monitor dialog box reappears. Select Options ⇒ Log.

**13.** The Log Options dialog box appears. Click the Stop Log command button. Continue to Part 4.

### Part 4: Importing a Performance Monitor log file into Report view and Chart view

In this section, you import the Performance Monitor log file you created in Part 3 into Performance Monitor Report view and Chart view.

**1.** In the Performance Monitor dialog box, select View ⇒ Report.

**2.** Select Options ⇒ Data From.

**3.** The Data From dialog box appears. Select the radio button next to Log File. Type **practice.log** in the text box. Click OK.

**4.** Select Edit ⇒ Add To Report in the Performance Monitor dialog box.

**5.** The Add to Report dialog box appears. Click the down arrow in the Object drop-down list box. Notice that only four objects appear in this list, because you only chose to log four objects when you created the log file. Click Memory. Select Pages/sec in the Counter list box. Click the Add command button.

**6.** Click the down arrow in the Object drop-down list box. Click PhysicalDisk. Select % Disk Time in the Counter list box. Click the Add command button.

**7.** Click the down arrow in the Object drop-down list box. Click Processor. Select % Processor Time in the Counter list box. Click the Add command button.

**8.** Click the down arrow in the Object drop-down list box. Click Server. Select Bytes Total/sec in the Counter list box. Click the Add command button. Click the Done command button.

**9.** The Performance Monitor dialog box reappears.

The report displayed shows the last value measured for each of the four counters you selected, from the time you initially created the log file until after you finished your Pinball game and clicked on the Stop Log command button in Performance Monitor.

Now let's look at the same four counters (for the same time period) in a Chart view (instead of a Report view).

**10.** Select View ⇒ Chart.

**11.** Select Options ⇒ Data From.

**12.** The Data From dialog box appears. Select the radio button next to Log File. Ensure that **practice.log** appears in the text box. Click OK.

**13.** Select Edit⇒Add To Chart in the Performance Monitor dialog box.

**14.** The Add to Chart dialog box appears. Click the down arrow in the Object drop-down list box. Click Memory. Select Pages/sec in the Counter list box. Click the Add command button.

**15.** Click the down arrow in the Object drop-down list box. Click PhysicalDisk. Select % Disk Time in the Counter list box. Click the Add command button.

**16.** Click the down arrow in the Object drop-down list box. Click Processor. Select % Processor Time in the Counter list box. Click the Add command button.

**17.** Click the down arrow in the Object drop-down list box. Click Server. Select Bytes Total/sec in the Counter list box. Click the Add command button. Click the Done command button.

**18.** The Performance Monitor dialog box reappears.

The chart displayed shows the values for each of the four counters you selected, from the time you initially created the log file until after you finished your Pinball game and clicked on the Stop Log command button in Performance Monitor.

**19.** Exit Performance Monitor.

## Lab 23.36  *Installing and using Network Monitor*

The purpose of this hands-on lab exercise is to provide you with the experience of installing and using Network Monitor on a Windows NT Server computer.

Enterprise

note **This lab is optional** because it requires that a network adapter be installed in your Windows NT Server computer. Also, if you have a second computer that is network-connected to your first computer, you can use this computer in Part 2 of this lab.

This lab consists of two parts:

Part 1: Installing Network Monitor

Part 2: Using Network Monitor

Begin this lab by booting your computer to Windows NT Server. Log on as Administrator. Place your Windows NT Server compact disc in your computer's CD-ROM drive.

Complete the following steps carefully.

**Part 1: Installing Network Monitor**

In this section, you install Network Monitor on your Windows NT Server computer. Then you edit the Registry to force the network adapter in your computer to operate in promiscuous mode.

1. Select Start⇒Settings⇒Control Panel.

2. In the Control Panel dialog box, double-click the Network icon.

3. In the Network dialog box, click the Services tab.

4. On the Services tab, highlight Network Monitor Agent in the Network Services list box. Click the Remove command button.

5. A warning dialog box appears. Click the Yes command button to continue. Windows NT removes Network Monitor Agent.

6. On the Services tab, click the Add command button.

7. In the Select Network Service dialog box, highlight Network Monitor Tools and Agent. Click OK.

8. A Windows NT Setup dialog box appears. Ensure the correct path to your Windows NT Server source files (usually the i386 folder on your Windows NT Server compact disc) is listed in the text box. Edit this text box if necessary. Click the Continue command button.

9. Windows NT copies source files and installs Network Monitor Tools and Agent.

10. The Network dialog box reappears. Click the Close command button.

11. Windows NT performs various bindings operations.

12. A Network Settings Change dialog box appears. Click the No command button.

13. Close Control Panel.

14. Select Start⇒Run.

15. The Run dialog box appears. Type **regedt32** in the Open drop-down list box. Click OK.

16. The Registry Editor dialog box appears. Select Windows⇒ HKEY_LOCAL_MACHINE on Local Machine.

17. Double-click the + sign next to SYSTEM. Double-click the + sign next to CurrentControlSet. Double-click the + sign next to Services. Double-click the + sign next to bh. Highlight the Linkage folder.

18. Find the Bind value (located in the right-hand part of the dialog box). In the space provided, write the entry for the Bind value that directly *follows* the *first* \Device\ portion of the entry. (For example, Elnk31.)

_____

19. Highlight the Parameters folder.

**20.** Select Edit ⇒ Add Key.

**21.** The Add Key dialog box appears. Type **ForcePmode** in the Key Name text box. Leave the Class text box blank. Click OK.

**22.** The Registry Editor dialog box reappears. Click the ForcePmode folder.

**23.** Select Edit ⇒ Add Value.

**24.** The Add Value dialog box appears. In the Value Name text box, type the value you wrote in Step 18. For example, elnk31. In the Data Type drop-down list box, select REG_DWORD. Click OK.

**25.** The DWORD Editor dialog box appears. In the Data text box, type **1**. (Don't type the period at the end.) Click OK.

**26.** The Registry Editor dialog box reappears. Close the Registry Editor.

**27.** Select Start ⇒ Shut Down.

**28.** In the Shut Down Windows dialog box, click the radio button next to "Restart the computer." Click the Yes command button.

**29.** Reboot your computer to Windows NT Server. Log on as Administrator. Continue to Part 2.


## Part 2: Using Network Monitor

In this section, you use Network Monitor on your Windows NT Server computer to capture and view packets.

 **If you have a second computer and it is network-connected to your first computer, boot both computers before you do this part of the lab. (Boot the first [primary] computer to Windows NT Server, and boot the second computer to Windows NT Workstation.)**

**If you don't have a second computer, you can still do this part of the lab, but you won't be able to capture as much data.**

**1.** Select Start ⇒ Programs ⇒ Administrative Tools (Common) ⇒ Network Monitor.

**2.** The Network Monitor dialog box appears. Maximize this dialog box. Also maximize the Capture Window (Station Stats) within the Network Monitor dialog box.

**3.** Select Capture ⇒ Filter.

**4.** A Capture Filter dialog box appears. Click OK.

**5.** The Capture Filter dialog box appears. Highlight the entry *under* AND (Address Pairs). Click the Line command button in the Delete section of this dialog box. (This allows Network Monitor to capture all packets transmitted on the local network segment.) Click OK.

6. The Network Monitor dialog box reappears. Select Capture⇒Start to start capturing packets.

7. Wait approximately 1-2 minutes to allow Network Monitor time to capture data. While this process is taking place, notice the % Network Utilization, Frames Per Second, and Bytes Per Second bar graphs in the Network Monitor dialog box.

8. Select Capture⇒Stop to stop capturing packets.

9. Select Capture⇒Find All Names.

10. A Find All Names dialog box appears. Click OK.

11. To determine which computer is sending the most packets on the network segment, right-click Frames Sent (the Frames Sent column header) in the bottom section of the Network Monitor dialog box. Select Sort Column from the menu that appears. The computer on the network segment that sent the most packets during the capture period should appear at the top of the list in this section of the dialog box.

12. Right-click each of the other column headers (Frames Rcvd, Bytes Sent, Bytes Rcvd, Directed Frames Sent, Multicasts Sent, and Broadcasts Sent) and sort each column, one at a time. Notice the results of each sort.

13. Select Capture⇒Display Captured Data.

14. The Capture (Summary) dialog box appears. Select Display⇒Filter.

15. The Display Filter dialog box appears. Double click Protocol == Any.

16. The Expression dialog box appears. Notice you can filter the display of captured packets by address, by protocol, or by protocol property. Click OK.

17. The Display Filter dialog box reappears. Click OK.

18. The Capture (Summary) dialog box reappears. Double-click any packet displayed in this dialog box to view its details. Do this several times.

19. When you are finished viewing packet details, exit Network Monitor.

20. A Save File dialog box appears. Click the No command button.

21. A Save Address Database dialog box appears. Click the No command button.

## Lab 25.37 *Finding and resolving bottlenecks*

Workstation
Server
Enterprise

The purpose of this lab exercise is to give you experience in analyzing Performance Monitor statistics in order to identify the bottleneck in a system, and also to give you experience in making recommendations to resolve a bottleneck.

Each problem below presents a situation and a set of statistics. In the space provided, supply the requested response to the problem.

**Problem 1**   Users of your network report slow response times when accessing files from a Windows NT Server computer. The server has a 486/66MHz processor with 20MB of RAM and a 2GB IDE hard disk. You run Performance Monitor on that server and obtain the statistics shown in the following table:

| Object | Counter | Statistic |
|---|---|---|
| Processor | % Processor Time | 55% |
| Memory | Pages/sec | 125 |
| PhysicalDisk | % Disk Time | 85% |
| Network Segment | % Network utilization | 15% |

There is enough money left in your annual equipment budget to allow you to do any *one* of the following:

o Upgrade the processor to a Pentium 166MHz processor

o Upgrade memory to 64MB of RAM

o Upgrade to a faster hard disk and a faster hard disk controller

o Install a second network adapter in the server and segment the network

Which upgrade would you perform, and why?

_____

_____

_____

_____

**Problem 2**   Users of your network report slow response times when accessing files from a Windows NT Server computer. The server has a Pentium 100MHz processor with 64MB of RAM and a 4GB SCSI hard disk. You run Performance Monitor on that server and obtain the following statistics:

| Object | Counter | Statistic |
|---|---|---|
| Processor | % Processor Time | 15% |
| Memory | Pages/sec | 4 |
| PhysicalDisk | % Disk Time | 90% |
| Network Segment | % Network utilization | 15% |

There is enough money left in your annual equipment budget to enable you to do any *one* of the following:

- Upgrade to a multiprocessor system with 2 Pentium PRO 200MHz processors

- Upgrade memory to 128MB of RAM

- Upgrade to a hardware-based RAID 5 (disk striping with parity) disk subsystem

- Install a second network adapter in the server to segment the network

    Which upgrade would you perform, and why?

_____

_____

_____

_____

## Lab 25.38 *Optimizing Windows NT performance*

Enterprise

The purpose of this lab exercise is to give you experience in analyzing a Windows NT Server network, and to make recommendations to optimize server and/or network performance for a given situation.

Assume that you are an outside consultant, hired to optimize server/network performance for a company. Each problem below presents a situation and what your customer wants to accomplish. In the space provided, supply the requested response to each problem.

**Problem 1**   Your client has three networks, each located in a different city. The three networks are connected by WAN links, as shown in the following figure.

The company uses a master domain model for its Windows NT network. The master domain is located in London, and resource domains are located in Paris and Munich.

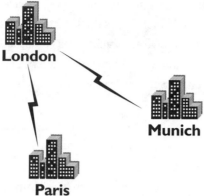

**WAN configuration for Problem 1**

Servers are currently installed as follows:

**London:**    PDC for LONDON domain

7 BDCs for LONDON domain

1 BDC for PARIS domain

1 BDC for MUNICH domain

4 WINS servers

**Paris:**    PDC for PARIS domain

3 BDCs for PARIS domain

**Munich:**    PDC for MUNICH domain

2 BDCs for MUNICH domain

The company wants you to make recommendations for minimizing the amount of logon authentication and NetBIOS name resolution traffic sent across their WAN links. What recommendations would you make to accomplish these two tasks?

_____

_____

_____

**Problem 2**   Your client wants you to optimize the Server service on a Windows NT Server computer. The computer functions as the PDC for a large network. The PDC is used primarily to manage the Directory Services database, and also functions as a DHCP server for clients on its local network segment.

How would you optimize the Server service on this Windows NT Server computer?

---

**Lab 27.39**   *Troubleshooting Windows NT*

Workstation
Enterprise

The purpose of this lab exercise is to give you experience in using advanced Windows NT troubleshooting techniques.

This lab consists of four parts:

Part 1: Using Windows NT Diagnostics

Part 2: Using the Registry editors

Part 3: Configuring a memory dump

Part 4: Starting and configuring Dr. Watson for Windows NT

Begin this lab by booting your computer to Windows NT Server. Log on as Administrator.

Follow these instructions carefully.

### Part 1: Using Windows NT Diagnostics

In this section, you use Windows NT Diagnostics to examine your Windows NT Server system configuration and to view service dependencies and group dependencies.

**1.** Select Start ⇒ Programs ⇒ Administrative Tools (Common) ⇒ Windows NT Diagnostics.

**2.** The Windows NT Diagnostics dialog box appears. Click the System tab.

**3.** The System tab appears. Notice the BIOS and CPU information displayed on this tab. Click the Display tab.

**4.** The Display tab appears. Notice the display adapter and driver settings. Click the Drives tab.

**5.** The Drives tab appears. Click the + sign next to Local hard drives. Highlight drive D: (or the letter of your NTFS drive, if not D:). Click the Properties command button.

**6.** The Properties dialog box appears. Notice the statistics on the number of bytes free, used, and total that are presented. Click OK. Click the Memory tab.

**7.** The Memory tab appears. Notice the memory and pagefile statistics displayed. Click the Network tab.

**8.** The Network tab appears. Notice the various network information that is displayed. Click the Statistics command button. Notice the statistics that are displayed. These statistics are not updated automatically—you must click the Refresh command button to update these statistics. Click the Resources tab.

**9.** The Resources tab appears. Notice that you can obtain Interrupt (IRQ), I/O Port, DMA, and memory information on this tab. Click the Devices command button. Double-click Floppy in the Device list box.

**10.** The Floppy Properties dialog box appears. Notice the resource settings displayed. Click OK. Click the Services tab.

**11.** The Services tab appears. Click the Devices command button.

**12.** In the Device list box, scroll down and double-click Parallel.

**13.** The Parallel Properties dialog box appears. Click the Dependencies tab.

**14.** The Dependencies tab appears. Notice the Service Dependencies and Group Dependencies listed. In the space provided, write down the following, as shown on your monitor:

Service Dependencies: _____

Group Dependencies:  _____

Click OK.

**15.** The Services tab reappears. Click the Services command button.

**16.** Double-click the Server service.

**17.** The Server Properties dialog box appears. Click the Dependencies tab.

**18.** The Dependencies tab appears.

In the space provided, write down the following, as shown on your monitor:

Service Dependencies: _____

Group Dependencies:  _____

Click OK.

**19.** The Services tab reappears. Click OK. Proceed to Part 2.

### Part 2: Using the Registry editors

In this section, you use the `Regedit.exe` and `Regedt32.exe` Registry editors to search the Registry, and to view service dependencies and group dependencies.

**1.** Select Start ⇒ Run.

**2.** The Run dialog box appears. In the Open drop-down list box, type **regedit** and click OK. (This starts the Windows 95 Registry Editor.)

**3.** The Registry Editor dialog box appears. Select Edit⇒Find.

**4.** The Find dialog box appears. In the Find what text box, type **WINS Client**. Ensure that the check boxes next to Keys, Values, and Data are checked. Click the Find Next command button.

**5.** Registry Editor searches the Registry. (This may take a few minutes.) The Registry Editor dialog box reappears. Notice that the Title value is highlighted on the right-hand side of the screen. Also notice that the Registry location of the highlighted value is displayed across the bottom of the dialog box.

**6.** Select Edit ⇒ Find Next.

**7.** Registry Editor searches the Registry. The Registry Editor dialog box reappears. Notice that a different value, DeviceDesc, is highlighted. Again, notice that the Registry location of this value is displayed across the bottom of the dialog box.

**8.** Exit Registry Editor.

**9.** Select Start⇒Run.

**10.** The Run dialog box appears. In the Open drop-down list box, type **regedt32** and click OK. (This starts the Windows NT Registry Editor.)

**11.** The Registry Editor dialog box appears. Select Window⇒HKEY_LOCAL_ MACHINE on Local Machine.

**12.** Maximize the Registry Editor dialog box and the HKEY_LOCAL_MACHINE on Local Machine window.

**13.** Double-click the `SYSTEM` folder.

**14.** Double-click the `CurrentControlSet` folder.

**15.** Double-click the `Services` folder.

**16.** Scroll down and highlight the `Parallel` folder. Notice the DependOnGroup and DependOnService entries on the right-hand side of the dialog box.

In the space provided, write down the entries that follow these values: (You can ignore the REG_MULTI_SZ: portion of the entries—this just identifies the type of data that will be placed in the Registry; in this case, multiple string values.)

DependOnGroup: _____

DependOnService: _____

Notice that the DependOnGroup and DependOnService values are the same as the Group Dependencies and Service Dependencies that you found using Windows NT Diagnostics in Step 14 in Part 1 of this lab.

**17.** On the left side of the Registry Editor dialog box, scroll up and highlight the `LanmanServer` folder. Notice the DependOnGroup and DependOnService entries on the right-hand side of the dialog box.

In the space provided, write down the entries that follow these values: (You can ignore the REG_MULTI_SZ: portion of the entries.)

DependOnGroup: _____

DependOnService: _____

Notice that the DependOnGroup and DependOnService values are the same as the Group Dependencies and Service Dependencies that you found using Windows NT Diagnostics in Step 18 in Part 1 of this lab.

Also notice the DisplayName value on the right-hand side of the dialog box. The LanmanServer service is the same as the Server service.

**18.** Exit Registry Editor. Proceed to Part 3.

## Part 3: Configuring a memory dump

In this section, you use the System application in Control Panel to ensure that Windows NT Server is correctly configured to automatically dump memory when a STOP error occurs.

Then you use the System application to configure Windows NT Workstation to automatically dump memory when a STOP error occurs.

**1.** Select Start ⇒ Settings ⇒ Control Panel.

**2.** The Control Panel dialog box appears. Double-click the System icon.

**3.** The System Properties dialog box appears. Click the Startup/Shutdown tab.

**4.** The Startup/Shutdown tab appears. In the Recovery section of the dialog box, ensure that all check boxes are selected. Also ensure that the text box reads as follows: `%SystemRoot%\MEMORY.DMP`. Click OK.

**5.** Exit Control Panel.

**6.** Select Start ⇒ Shut Down.

**7.** In the Shut Down Windows dialog box, click the radio button next to "Restart the computer." Click the Yes command button.

**8.** Reboot your computer to Windows NT Workstation. Log on as Administrator.

**9.** Select Start ⇒ Settings ⇒ Control Panel.

**10.** The Control Panel dialog box appears. Double-click the System icon.

**11.** The System Properties dialog box appears. Click the Startup/Shutdown tab.

**12.** The Startup/Shutdown tab appears. In the Recovery section of the dialog box, select all of the check boxes. Also ensure that the text box reads as follows: `%SystemRoot%\MEMORY.DMP`. Click OK.

**13.** A System Control Panel Applet dialog box appears, indicating that the Alerter service is not running. Click OK.

**14.** A System Settings Change dialog box appears. Click the No command button (don't reboot your computer at this time).

**15.** The Control Panel dialog box reappears. Double-click the Services icon.

**16.** The Services dialog box appears. Highlight the Alerter service. Click the Startup command button.

**17.** The Service dialog box appears. In the Startup Type section, select the radio button next to Automatic. Click OK.

**18.** In the Services dialog box, click the Close command button.

**19.** Exit Control Panel. Proceed to Part 4.

### Part 4: Starting and configuring Dr. Watson for Windows NT

In this section, you manually start Dr. Watson for Windows NT, and verify that Dr. Watson is configured to automatically dump application memory when an application fails.

**1.** Select Start ⇒ Run.

**2.** The Run dialog box appears. In the Open drop-down list box, type **drwtsn32** and click OK.

**3.** The Dr. Watson for Windows NT dialog box appears. Notice that, by default, Dr. Watson is configured to create a log file and to dump application memory to a file named `user.dmp` when an application fails.

Ensure that the Crash Dump text box reads as follows: `%windir%\user.dmp`

Ensure that the check boxes next to: Dump All Thread Contexts, Append To Existing Log File, Visual Notification, and Create Crash Dump File are selected.

Click OK. Windows NT closes Dr. Watson for Windows NT automatically.

# Exam Preparation Tips

concept link

*This appendix contains material from the Microsoft Certified Professional Program Exam Study Guide (Microsoft Corporation, 1997), reprinted with permission. The complete version of this study guide is included on the compact disc accompanying this book. To view it, follow the instructions contained in Appendix H.*

The Microsoft Certified Professional Exams are *not* easy, and require a great deal of preparation. The exam questions measure real-world skills. Your ability to answer these questions correctly will be greatly enhanced by as much hands-on experience with the product as you can get. Appendix F provides some practical and innovative ways for you to prepare for the Microsoft Certified Professional Exams for Windows NT Workstation 4.0, Windows NT Server 4.0, and Windows NT Server 4.0 in the Enterprise.

# ABOUT THE EXAMS

An important aspect of passing the MCP Certification Exams is understanding the big picture. This includes understanding how the exams are developed and scored.

Every job function requires different levels of cognitive skills, from memorization of facts and definitions to the comprehensive ability to analyze scenarios, design solutions, and evaluate options. To make the exams relevant in the real world, Microsoft Certified Professional exams test the specific cognitive skills needed for the job functions being tested. These exams go beyond testing rote knowledge—you need to *apply* your knowledge, analyze technical solutions, solve problems, and make decisions—just like you would on the job.

## How the Certification Exams Are Developed

To help ensure the validity and reliability of the certification exams, Microsoft adheres to an eight-phase exam development process:

1. Job analysis
2. Objective domain definition
3. Blueprint survey
4. Item development
5. Alpha review and item revision
6. Beta exam
7. Item selection and cut-score setting
8. Exam live

The following paragraphs describe each phase of exam development.

### Phase 1: Job analysis

Phase 1 is an analysis of all the tasks that make up the specific job function, based on tasks performed by people who are currently performing the job function. This phase also identifies the knowledge, skills, and abilities that relate specifically to the performance area to be certified.

### Phase 2: Objective domain definition

The results of the job analysis provide the framework used to develop objectives. The development of objectives involves translating the job function tasks into a comprehensive set of more specific and measurable knowledge, skills, and abilities. The resulting list of objectives, or the objective domain, is the basis for the development of both the certification exams and the training materials.

## Phase 3: Blueprint survey

The final objective domain is transformed into a blueprint survey in which contributors—technology professionals who are performing the applicable job function—are asked to rate each objective. Contributors may be selected from lists of past Certified Professional candidates, from appropriately skilled exam development volunteers, and from within Microsoft. Based on the contributors' input, the objectives are prioritized and weighted. The actual exam items are written according to these prioritized objectives. Contributors are queried about how they spend their time on the job, and if a contributor doesn't spend an adequate amount of time actually performing the specified job function, his or her data is eliminated from the analysis.

The blueprint survey phase helps determine which objectives to measure, as well as the appropriate number and types of items to include on the exam.

## Phase 4: Item development

A pool of items is developed to measure the blueprinted objective domain. The number and types of items to be written are based on the results of the blueprint survey. During this phase, items are reviewed and revised to ensure that they are:

- Technically accurate
- Clear, unambiguous, and plausible
- Not biased for any population subgroup or culture
- Not misleading or tricky
- Testing at the correct level of Bloom's Taxonomy
- Testing for useful knowledge, not obscure or trivial facts

Items that meet these criteria are included in the initial item pool.

## Phase 5: Alpha review and item revision

During this phase, a panel of technical and job function experts reviews each item for technical accuracy and then answers each item, reaching consensus on all technical issues. Once the items have been verified as technically accurate, they are edited to ensure that they are expressed in the clearest language possible.

## Phase 6: Beta exam

The reviewed and edited items are collected into a beta exam pool. During the beta exam, each participant has the opportunity to respond to all the items in this beta exam pool. Based on the responses of all beta participants, Microsoft performs a statistical analysis to verify the validity of the exam items and to determine which items will be used in the certification exam. Once the analysis has been completed, the items are distributed into multiple parallel forms, or versions, of the final certification exam.

### Phase 7: Item selection and cut-score setting

The results of the beta exam are analyzed to determine which items should be included in the certification exam based on many factors, including item difficulty and relevance. Generally, the desired items are those that were answered correctly by anywhere from 25 to 90 percent of the beta exam candidates. This helps ensure that the exam consists of a variety of difficulty levels, from somewhat easy to extremely difficult.

Also during this phase, a panel of job function experts determines the cut score (minimum passing score) for the exam. The cut score differs from exam to exam because it is based on an item-by-item determination of the percentage of candidates who answered the item correctly and who would be expected to answer the item correctly. The cut score is determined in a group session to increase the reliability among the experts.

### Phase 8: Exam live

Microsoft Certified Professional exams are administered by Sylvan Prometric™, an independent testing company. The exams are made available at Sylvan Prometric testing centers worldwide.

## Exam Items and Scoring

Microsoft certification exams consist of three types of items: multiple-choice, multiple-rating, and enhanced. The way you indicate your answer and the number of points you can receive differ depending on the type of item.

### Multiple-choice item

A traditional multiple-choice item presents a problem and asks you to select either the best answer (single response) or the best set of answers (multiple response) to the given item from a list of possible answers.

For a multiple-choice item, your response is scored as either correct or incorrect. A correct answer receives a score of 1 point and an incorrect answer receives a score of 0 points.

In the case of a multiple-choice, multiple-response item (for which the correct response consists of more than one answer), the item is scored as being correct only if all the correct answers are selected. No partial credit is given for a response that does not include all the correct answers for the item.

For consistency purposes, the question in a multiple-choice, multiple-response item is always presented in singular form, regardless of how many answers are correct. Always follow the instructions displayed at the bottom of the window.

## Multiple-rating item

A multiple-rating item presents a task similar to those presented in multiple-choice items. In a multiple-choice item, you are asked to select the best answer or answers from a selection of several potential answers. In contrast, a multiple-rating item presents a task, along with a proposed solution. Each time the task is presented, a different solution is proposed. In each multiple-rating item, you are asked to choose the answer that best describes the results produced by one proposed solution.

concept link

**To view an example of a multiple-rating item, follow the instructions in Appendix H to access the entire *Microsoft Certified Professional Program Exam Study Guide* on the compact disc accompanying this book. See the "Multiple-rating item" section.**

## Enhanced item

An enhanced item is similar to a multiple-choice item because it asks you to select your response from a number of possible responses. However, unlike the traditional multiple-choice item that presents you with a list of possible answers from which to choose, an enhanced item may ask you to indicate your answer in one of three ways:

- Type the correct response, such as a command name.
- Review an exhibit (such as a screen shot, a network configuration drawing, or a code sample), and then use the mouse to select the area of the exhibit that represents the correct response.

○ Review an exhibit, and then select the correct response from the list of possible responses.

As with a multiple-choice item, your response to an enhanced item is scored as either correct or incorrect. A correct answer receives full credit of 1 point and an incorrect answer receives a score of 0 points.

# PREPARING FOR A MICROSOFT CERTIFIED PROFESSIONAL EXAM

The best way to prepare for an exam is to study, learn, and master the job function on which you'll be tested. For any certification exam, you should follow these important preparation steps:

1. Identify the objectives on which you'll be tested.
2. Assess your current mastery of those objectives.
3. Practice tasks and study the areas you haven't mastered.

This section describes tools and techniques that may be helpful as you perform these steps to prepare for the exam.

## Exam Preparation Guides

For each certification exam, an Exam Preparation Guide provides important, specific information about what you'll be tested on and how best to prepare. These guides are essential tools for preparing to take certification exams. You'll find the following types of valuable information in the exam preparation guides:

○ **Tasks you should master:** Outlines the overall job function tasks you should master

○ **Exam objectives:** Lists the specific skills and abilities on which you should expect to be measured

○ **Product resources:** Tells you which products and technologies with which you should be experienced

- **Suggested reading:** Points you to specific reference materials and other publications that discuss one or more of the exam objectives

- **Suggested curriculum:** Provides a specific list of instructor-led and self-paced courses relating to the job function tasks and topics in the exam

You'll also find pointers to additional information that may help you prepare for the exams, such as *Microsoft TechNet*, *Microsoft Developer Network* (MSDN), online forums, and other sources.

By paying attention to the verbs used in the "Exam Objectives" section of the Exam Preparation Guide, you can get an idea of the level at which you'll be tested on that objective.

 web links **To view the most recent version of the Exam Preparation Guides, which include the exam's objectives, check out Microsoft's Training and Certification Web site at** www.microsoft.com/train_cert.

## Assessment Exams

When preparing for the exams, take lots of assessment exams. Assessment exams are self-paced exams that you take at your own computer. When you complete an assessment exam, you receive instant score feedback so you can determine areas in which additional study may be helpful before you take the certification exam. Although your score on an assessment exam doesn't necessarily indicate what your score will be on the certification exam, assessment exams give you the opportunity to answer items that are similar to those on the certification exams. And the assessment exams use the same computer-based testing tool as the certification exams, so you don't have to learn the tool on exam day.

An assessment exam exists for almost every certification exam.

 concept link **The compact disc accompanying this book contains one Microsoft Windows NT 4.0 self-administered assessment exam, and two Microsoft NT 4.0 Core Technologies exam preparation practice exams (one for NT Workstation, one for NT Server). See Appendix H for details on how to install and access these exams.**

# Test-Taking Tips

Here are some tips that may be helpful as you prepare to take a certification exam.

**Before the exam:**

- Be sure to read "What to Expect at the Testing Center" in this guide for important information about the sign-in and test-taking procedures you'll follow on the day of your exam.

- Do the hands-on labs and review activities for each chapter in this book as you read it. Remember, the exams measure real-world skills that you can't obtain unless you use the product.

- Review the Key Point Summary sections *and* answer the Instant Assessment questions at the end of the chapters in this book just before taking an exam.

- Pay special attention to the exam preparation pointers scattered throughout this book—these pointers will help you focus on important exam-related topics.

- When you've finished reading all of the chapters (and have done all the labs) that pertain to a particular exam, take one or more practice tests to assess your readiness for the exam. Most practice tests will tell you what your weak areas are. Use this information to go back and study.

- Take as many practice exams as you can get your hands on before taking the exam. This will help you in two ways. First, some practice exam questions are quite similar to the real thing, and if you do enough practice exams, some of the questions you see on the exam might look familiar. Second, taking practice exams will make you more comfortable with the computer-based testing environment/process. This will reduce your stress when you take the actual exam. You can't take too many practice exams. It's virtually impossible to be *too* prepared for the exam.

- Take the exam preparation process seriously. Remember, these exams weren't designed to be easy—they were designed to recognize and certify professionals with specific skill sets.

- Consider joining (or becoming an associate member of) a professional organization or user group in your area that focuses on Windows NT. Some user groups have a computer lab and/or lending library that can help you with your exam preparation. The meetings are a great place to meet people with similar interests, and potential employers, too.

- Consider subscribing to *Microsoft Certified Professional Magazine*. This magazine, which is an independent publication that is not associated with Microsoft, features an Exam Spotlight section where new Microsoft Certified Professional exams are critically reviewed as they are released. For more information about this magazine or to subscribe, visit the magazine's Web site at www.mcpmag.com.

- If possible, talk to friends or colleagues who have taken the exam for which you're preparing. Or check out the Internet for newsgroups or forums where people sometimes share their exam experiences. The experiences of others can shed some light on your potential weak areas that might benefit from further study. The MCSE list server at saluki.com is one example. Don't share (or ask friends to share with you) specific exam questions. However, it's fair game to share general topics that were strongly emphasized on the exam, and/or areas that had particularly detailed or tough questions.

- Consider forming a study group with friends or coworkers who are also preparing for one or more of the NT exams. As a group, you can share hardware and software resources, thus reducing your out-of-pocket costs for exam preparation.

- Check out the Internet. From time to time, Microsoft offers free 120-day evaluation copies of Windows NT on their Web site at www.microsoft.com. These evaluation copies are often offered in conjunction with a new product release, such as Internet Information Server, and so on. A free evaluation copy is a great study tool.

- Don't study all night before the test. A good night's sleep is often better preparation than the extra studying.

- Try to schedule the exam during your own "peak" time of day. In other words, if you're a morning person, try not to schedule the exam for 3:00 p.m.

- Know your testing center. Call ahead. Ask about the hardware they use for their testing computers. If some computers are faster than others, ask for the seat numbers of the faster computers and request one of those seat numbers when scheduling your testing appointment with Sylvan Prometric. Consider visiting a testing center before you schedule an exam there. This will give you an opportunity to see what the testing environment will be like.

**On exam day:**

- Arrive ten to fifteen minutes early, and don't forget your picture ID.

- Dress comfortably. The more comfortable you are, the more you'll be able to focus on the exam.

- If you have any questions about the rules for the exam, ask the exam administrator before the exam begins. The exams are timed, so avoid using valuable test time for questions you could have asked earlier.

- Don't drink a lot of coffee or other beverage before taking an exam. Remember, these tests last ninety minutes, and you don't want to spend precious exam time running back and forth to the restroom.

**During the exam:**

- Answer the easy items first. The testing software enables you to move forward and backward through the exam. Go through all the items on the test once, answering those items you are sure of first; then go back and spend time on the harder items.

- Remember, no trick items exist. The correct answer will always be among the list of choices.

- Eliminate the most obvious incorrect answers first. This will make it easier for you to select the answer that seems most right to you.

- Answer all the items before you quit the exam. An unanswered item is scored as an incorrect answer. So if you're unsure of an answer, it can't hurt to make an educated guess.

- Try to relax. People often make avoidable, careless mistakes when they rush.

- When taking the actual exam, pause every few minutes and take a couple of deep breaths—this will bring more oxygen into your body, and, hopefully, help you to think more clearly. More importantly, this should help you relax and relieve some of the tension of the testing environment.

**After the exam:**

- Remember, if you don't pass the first time, you can use your score report to determine the areas where you could use additional study and take the exam again later (for an additional fee).

- Don't get discouraged if you don't pass the test your first time — or second time. Many intelligent, seasoned professionals fail a test once, twice, or more times before eventually passing it. If at first you don't succeed, try, try again . . . perseverance pays.

# TAKING A MICROSOFT CERTIFIED PROFESSIONAL EXAM

This section contains information about registering for and taking a Microsoft Certified Professional exam, including what to expect when you arrive at the Sylvan Prometric testing center to take the exam.

## How to Find Out Which Exams Are Available

You can find a complete list of MCP exams and their registration costs on the Microsoft Training and Certification Offline CD-ROM, which is included on the compact disc accompanying this book. To get the latest schedule information for a specific exam, contact Sylvan Prometric at (800) 755-EXAM.

## How to Register for an Exam

Candidates may take exams at any of more than seven hundred Sylvan Prometric testing centers around the world. For the location of a Sylvan Prometric testing center near you, call (800) 755-EXAM (755-3926). Outside the United States and Canada, contact your local Sylvan Prometric Registration Center.

To register for a Microsoft Certified Professional exam:

1. Determine which exam you want to take and note the exam number.
2. Register with the Sylvan Prometric Registration Center nearest to you. A part of the registration process is advance payment for the exam.

**3.** After you receive the registration and payment confirmation letter from Sylvan Prometric, call a Sylvan Prometric testing center to schedule your exam.

When you schedule the exam, you'll be provided instructions regarding the appointment, cancellation procedures, and ID requirements, and information about the testing center location.

Exams must be taken within one year of payment. You can schedule exams up to six weeks in advance, or as late as one working day prior to the date of the exam. You can cancel or reschedule your exam if you contact Sylvan Prometric at least two working days prior to the exam.

Although subject to space availability, same-day registration is available in some locations. Where same-day registration is available, you must register a minimum of two hours before test time.

## What to Expect at the Testing Center

As you prepare for your certification exam, it may be helpful to know what to expect when you arrive at the testing center on the day of your exam. The following information gives you a preview of the general procedure you'll go through at the testing center:

- You will be asked to sign the log book upon arrival and departure.

- You will be required to show two forms of identification, including one photo ID (such as a driver's license or company security ID), before you may take the exam.

- The test administrator will give you a Testing Center Regulations form that explains the rules you will be expected to comply with during the test. You will be asked to sign the form, indicating that you understand the regulations and will comply.

- The test administrator will show you to your test computer and will handle any preparations necessary to start the testing tool and display the exam on the computer.

- You will be provided a set amount of scratch paper for use during the exam. All scratch paper will be collected from you at the end of the exam.

- The exams are all closed-book. You may not use a laptop computer or have any notes or printed material with you during the exam session.

- Some exams may include additional materials, or exhibits. If any exhibits are required for your exam, the test administrator will provide you with them before you begin the exam and collect them from you at the end of the exam.

- Before you begin the exam, the test administrator will tell you what to do when you complete the exam. If the test administrator doesn't explain this to you, or if you are unclear about what you should do, ask the administrator before beginning the exam.

- The number of items on each exam varies, as does the amount of time allotted for each exam. Generally, certification exams consist of about fifty to one hundred items and have durations of sixty to ninety minutes. You can verify the number of items and time allotted for your exam when you register.

Because you'll be given a specific amount of time to complete the exam once you begin, if you have any questions or concerns, don't hesitate to ask the test administrator before the exam begins.

As an exam candidate, you are entitled to the best support and environment possible for your exam. In particular, you are entitled to following:

- A quiet, uncluttered test environment

- Scratch paper

- The tutorial for using the online testing tool, and time to take the tutorial

- A knowledgeable and professional test administrator

- The opportunity to submit comments about the testing center and staff or the test itself

For more information about how to submit feedback about any aspect of your exam experience, see the section "If You Have Exam Concerns or Feedback" in this appendix. The Certification Development Team will investigate any problems or issues you raise and make every effort to resolve them quickly.

# Your Exam Results

Once you have completed an exam, you will be given immediate, online notification of your pass or fail status. You will also receive a printed Examination Score Report indicating your pass or fail status and your exam results by section. (The test administrator will give you the printed score report.) Test scores are automatically forwarded to Microsoft within five working days after you take the test. You do not need to send your score to Microsoft.

If you pass the exam, you will receive confirmation from Microsoft, typically within two to four weeks.

# If You Don't Receive a Passing Score

If you do not pass a certification exam, you may call Sylvan Prometric to schedule a time to retake the exam. Before retaking the exam, you should review the appropriate Exam Preparation Guide and focus additional study on the topic areas where your exam results could be improved. Please note that you must pay again for each exam retake.

One way to determine areas where additional study may be helpful is to carefully review your individual section scores. Generally, the section titles in your score report correlate to specific groups of exam objectives listed in the Exam Preparation Guide.

Here are some specific ways you can prepare to retake an exam:

- Go over the section-by-section scores on your exam results, noting objective areas where your score could be improved.

- Review the Exam Preparation Guide for the exam, with a special focus on the tasks and objective areas that correspond to the exam sections where your score could be improved.

- Increase your real-world, hands-on experience and practice performing the listed job tasks with the relevant products and technologies.

- Consider taking or retaking one or more of the suggested courses listed in the Exam Preparation Guide.

- Review the suggested readings listed in the Exam Preparation Guide.

- After you review the materials, retake the corresponding Assessment Exam.

# IF YOU HAVE EXAM CONCERNS OR FEEDBACK

To provide the best certification preparation and testing materials possible, we encourage feedback from candidates. If you have any suggestions for improving any of the Microsoft Certified Professional exams or preparation materials, please let us know.

The following sections describe what to do if you have specific concerns or feedback about the certification exams.

## If You Encounter a Problem with the Exam Software or Procedures

Although Microsoft and Sylvan Prometric make every effort to ensure that your exam experience is a positive one, if any problems should occur on the day of the exam, inform the Sylvan Prometric test administrator immediately. The Sylvan Prometric personnel are there to help make the logistics of your exam run smoothly.

## If You Have a Concern About the Exam Content

Microsoft Certified Professional exams are developed by technical and testing experts, with input and participation from job function and technology experts. Through an exhaustive process, Microsoft ensures that the exams adhere to recognized standards for validity and reliability, and are considered by candidates to be relevant and fair. If you feel that an exam item is inappropriate or if you believe the answer shown is incorrect, write or send a fax to the Microsoft Certification Development Team, using the address or fax number listed in "For More Information."

Although Microsoft is unable to respond to individual questions and issues raised by candidates, all input from candidates is thoroughly researched and taken into consideration during development of subsequent versions of the exams. Microsoft is committed to ensuring the validity and reliability of these exams, and your input is a valuable resource.

# FOR MORE INFORMATION

To find out more about Microsoft Education and Certification materials and programs, to register with Sylvan Prometric, or to get other useful information, check the following resources. Outside the United States or Canada, contact your local Microsoft office or Sylvan Prometric testing center.

- **Microsoft Certified Professional Program: (800) 636-7544.** Call for information about the the Microsoft Certified Professional program and exams, and to order the *Microsoft Certified Professional Program Exam Study Guide* or the Microsoft Training and Certification Offline CD-ROM.

- **Sylvan Prometric Testing Centers: (800) 755-EXAM.** Call to register to take a Microsoft Certified Professional exam at any of more than seven-hundred Sylvan Prometric testing centers around the world, or to order the *Microsoft Certified Professional Program Exam Study Guide*.

- **Microsoft Sales Fax Service: (800) 727-3351.** Call for Microsoft Certified Professional Exam Preparation Guides, Microsoft Official Curriculum course descriptions and schedules, or the *Microsoft Certified Professional Program Exam Study Guide*.

- **Education Program and Course Information: (800) SOLPROV.** Call for information about Microsoft Official Curriculum courses, Microsoft education products, and the Microsoft Solution Provider *Authorized Technical Education Center* (ATEC) program, where you can attend a Microsoft Official Curriculum course, or to order the *Microsoft Certified Professional Program Exam Study Guide*.

- **Microsoft Certification Development Team: Fax#: (425) 936-1311.** Use this fax number to volunteer for participation in one or more exam development phases or to report a problem with an exam. Address written correspondence to: Certification Development Team, Microsoft Education and Certification, One Microsoft Way, Redmond, WA 98052.

- **Microsoft TechNet Technical Information Network: (800) 344-2121.** Call for support professionals and system administrators. Outside the United States and Canada, call your local Microsoft subsidiary for information.

- Microsoft Developer Network (MSDN): (800) 759-5474. MSDN is the official source for software development kits, device driver kits, operating systems, and information about developing applications for Microsoft Windows and Windows NT.

- Online Services: (800) 936-3500. Call for information about Microsoft Connection on CompuServe, Microsoft Knowledge Base, Microsoft Software Library, Microsoft Download Service, and Internet.

- Microsoft Online Institute (MOLI): (800) 449-9333. Call for information about Microsoft's new online training program.

- Microsoft Press: (800) MSPRESS. Call for information about books published by Microsoft Press.

# Windows NT Planning Forms

Windows NT planning forms in this appendix include:

- Form 1: Preinstallation Checklist. This form is designed to be used for gathering the information required to install Windows NT.

- Form 2: Sharing and Securing Resources. This form is designed to help you plan how to apply share and/or NTFS permissions to shared resources on your network.

concept link

**Regarding Form 1:**

**If you need a detailed explanation of any of the items in the Preinstallation Checklist, see the expanded version in the "Preinstallation Checklist" section in Chapter 2.**

**Regarding Form 2:**

**For more information on share and NTFS permissions, see Chapter 12.**

# FORM 1: PREINSTALLATION CHECKLIST

**Mass storage devices — SCSI, IDE, and CD-ROM adapter information**

SCSI/IDE/CD-ROM adapter          IRQ          I/O port          DMA channel

_____          ____          ____          _____

_____          ____          ____          _____

_____          ____          ____          _____

_____          ____          ____          _____

**Hardware and software components**

Computer type     _____

Display     _____

Keyboard     _____

Keyboard layout     _____

Pointing device     _____

**Upgrade**

Upgrade previous version of Windows?     Yes _____     No _____

**Hard disk partition information**

| Disk partition number | Type of partition (primary, extended, FAT, NTFS, HPFS, and so on) | Available disk space |
|---|---|---|
| 1 | _____ | _____ |
| 2 | _____ | _____ |
| 3 | _____ | _____ |

Partition number to be used for installation of Windows NT _____

**File system to be used for installation (choose one)**

FAT _____     NTFS _____

**Installation directory**

Installation directory for new install _____

**Setup options—Windows NT Workstation only (choose one)**

Typical _____    Portable _____

Compact _____    Custom _____

**Registration**

Ten-digit CD key # _____ - _____ (from back of compact disc case)

**Licensing mode — Windows NT Server only**

(Select either per server or per seat)

Per server _____    Per Seat _____

Number of client access licenses _____

**Computer name** _____

**Server type — Windows NT Server only**

Choose one of the following: primary domain controller, backup domain controller, member server, or stand-alone server. Then fill in all information requested for that choice.

Primary domain controller _____

Domain name _____

Backup domain controller _____

Domain name _____

Administrator's account name _____

Administrator's password _____

Member server            _____

Domain name  _____

Administrator's account name  _____

Administrator's password  _____

Stand-alone server     _____

Workgroup name    _____

### Administrator password

Although you may not want to write down the password on this worksheet, you need to enter an administrator password during the installation process.

### Emergency Repair Disk

Will an Emergency Repair Disk be created during installation?

Yes ____  No ____

### Select components

(Choose the components you want to install.)

Accessibility options   Yes ____  No ____

### Accessories

Calculator              ____

Character Map           ____

Clipboard Viewer        ____

Clock                   ____

Desktop Wallpaper       ____

Document Templates      ____

Imaging                 ____

Mouse Pointers          ____

Object Packager         ____

Paint                   ____

Quick View     ____

Screen Savers     ____

Wordpad     ____

## Communications

Chat     ____

HyperTerminal     ____

Phone Dialer     ____

## Games

Freecell     ____

Minesweeper     ____

Pinball     ____

Solitaire     ____

## Multimedia

CD Player     ____

Jungle Sound Scheme     ____

Media Player     ____

Musical Sound Scheme     ____

Robotz Sound Scheme     ____

Sample Sounds     ____

Sound Recorder     ____

Utopia Sound Scheme     ____

Volume Control     ____

## Windows messaging

Internet Mail     ____

Microsoft Mail     ____

Windows Messaging     ____

**Participation on a network**

Participate on a network (Windows NT Workstation only)?   Yes \_\_\_ No \_\_\_

Wired to the network \_\_\_

Remote access to the network \_\_\_

**Microsoft Internet Information Server (Windows NT Server Only)**

Install Microsoft Internet Information Server?   Yes \_\_\_   No \_\_\_

**Network adapter**

Network adapter manufacturer (if applicable)   _____

Network adapter name (if applicable)   _____

Interrupt _____   I/O port _____

**Network protocols**

TCP/IP   Yes \_\_\_ No \_\_\_

(If Yes, then Windows NT Setup offers you an opportunity to configure TCP/IP by using DHCP.)

DHCP   Yes \_\_\_ No \_\_\_ (If No, fill in information below.)

IP address   _____

Subnet mask   _____

Default gateway   _____

DNS server #1   _____

DNS server #2   _____

WINS server #1   _____

WINS server #2   _____

NWLink IPX/SPX Compatible Transport   Yes \_\_\_ No \_\_\_

(If Yes) frame type _____

NetBEUI   Yes \_\_\_ No \_\_\_

**Network services**

Network services to add  _____

_____

**Network bindings**

Network bindings to disable  _____

**Make this computer a member of**

(This section applies only to NT Workstation, and to NT Server when installed as a stand-alone server.)

You must choose to participate in either a workgroup or a domain.

Workgroup   Yes ____   No ____    If Yes, workgroup name _____

Domain   Yes ____   No ____    If Yes, domain name _____

Create a computer account in the domain?   Yes ___   No ___

Administrator's account name   _____

Administrator's password   _____

**Internet Information Server (Windows NT Server only)**

Select the publishing directories you want to install:

World Wide Web publishing directory _____

FTP publishing directory _____

Gopher publishing directory _____

**Time zone**  _____

**Video adapter display settings**

Video adapter type  _____

Display settings desired  _____

# Form 2: Sharing and Securing Resources

Consider using this form to help you plan how to apply share and/or NTFS permissions to shared resources on your network.

| Resource (Include path) | Share Name | Share Permissions Applied | | NTFS Permissions Applied | |
|---|---|---|---|---|---|
| | | User/Group | Permission | User/Group | Permission |
| **(Example)** D:\Data\Sales | SalesData | Domain Users (Remove Everyone group) | Full Control | Sales | Change |
| | | | | | |
| | | | | | |
| | | | | | |
| | | | | | |
| | | | | | |
| | | | | | |
| | | | | | |
| | | | | | |

# What's on the CD-ROM?

## CD-ROM Contents

The CD-ROM included with this book contains the following materials:

- Adobe Acrobat Reader

- An electronic version of this book, *Windows NT®  4.0 MCSE Study Guide* in Adobe Acrobat format

- An electronic version of three chapters of *MCSE Career Microsoft®!* (IDG Books Worldwide, 1997) in Adobe Acrobat format

- Microsoft Internet Explorer version 3.01

- Validate! Windows NT 4.0 Workstation and Server practice exams

- Microsoft Training and Certification Offline CD-ROM, including:

  - www.microsoft.com/train_cert (entire contents of Web site)

  - Microsoft Windows NT 4.0 self-administered assessment exam

  - Supporting Microsoft Windows NT 4.0 Core Technologies (for Windows NT Workstation) exam prep practice exam

- Supporting Microsoft Windows NT 4.0 Core Technologies (for Windows NT Server) exam prep practice exam
- Microsoft Certified Professional Program Exam Study Guide

- *Micro House Technical Library* (evaluation copy)
- Diskeeper Lite (evaluation copy)

# INSTALLING AND USING THE CD-ROM

The following sections describe each product and include detailed instructions for installation and use.

## Adobe Acrobat Reader and the Adobe Acrobat Version of This Book

The Adobe Acrobat Reader is a helpful program that will enable you to view the electronic version of this book in the same page format as the actual book.

**TO INSTALL AND RUN ADOBE ACROBAT READER AND VIEW THE ELECTRONIC VERSION OF THIS BOOK, FOLLOW THESE STEPS:**

**1.** Start Windows Explorer (if you're using Windows 95) or Windows NT Explorer (if you're using Windows NT), and then open the `Acrobat` folder on the CD-ROM.

**2.** In the `Acrobat` folder, double-click `ar32e30.exe` and follow the instructions presented onscreen for installing Adobe Acrobat Reader.

**3.** To view the electronic version of this book after you have installed Adobe Acrobat Reader, start Windows Explorer (if you're using Windows 95) or Windows NT Explorer (if you're using Windows NT), and then open the `Books\MCSE WINDOWS NT 4.0` folder on the CD-ROM.

**4.** In the `MCSE WINDOWS NT 4.0` folder, double-click the chapter or appendix file you want to view. All documents in this folder end with a `.pdf` extension.

## *MCSE Career Microsoft®!* (Sample Chapters in Adobe Acrobat Format)

Most books covering the Microsoft Certified Professional program focus entirely on practice exams and their subject matter. *MCSE Career Microsoft®!* focuses on the professional characteristics involved with obtaining a Microsoft Certification, as well as maintaining and advancing your career once you are certified. This book also provides many practical and essential references to information, training, and tools available to information technology professionals, including Microsoft Certified Professionals (MCPs) and MCP candidates. Included here are excerpts from *MCSE Career Microsoft®!*, Chapters 1, 2, and 5. These chapters should give you a good impression of how useful and valuable this book can be. No other computer book on the market today provides a comprehensive approach to MCPs and their careers as does *MCSE Career Microsoft®!*

### TO INSTALL AND RUN ADOBE ACROBAT READER TO VIEW *MCSE CAREER MICROSOFT®!*, FOLLOW THESE STEPS:

**1.** If you've already installed the Adobe Acrobat Reader to view the electronic version of this book, skip to Step 3.

If you haven't installed Adobe Acrobat Reader, start Windows Explorer (if you're using Windows 95) or Windows NT Explorer (if you're using Windows NT), and then open the `Acrobat` folder on the CD-ROM.

**2.** In the `Acrobat` folder, double-click `ar32e30.exe` and follow the instructions presented onscreen for installing Adobe Acrobat Reader.

**3.** To view the **MCSE Career Microsoft®!** sample chapters after you have installed Adobe Acrobat Reader, start Windows Explorer (if you're using Windows 95) or Windows NT Explorer (if you're using Windows NT), and then open the `Books\Career Microsoft` folder on the CD-ROM.

**4.** In the `Career Microsoft` folder, double-click the chapter you want to view. All documents in this folder end with a `.pdf` extension.

# Microsoft Internet Explorer Version 3.01

This is a complete copy of Microsoft Internet Explorer. With Internet Explorer you'll be able to browse the Internet if you have an Internet connection, and view the contents of the Microsoft Training and Certification Offline CD-ROM (included on this CD-ROM).

**TO INSTALL AND RUN MICROSOFT INTERNET EXPLORER, FOLLOW THESE STEPS:**

**1.** Start Windows Explorer (if you're using Windows 95) or Windows NT Explorer (if you're using Windows NT), and then open the `Mscert\Ie` folder on the CD-ROM.

**2.** In the `Mscert\Ie folder`, double-click `Msie301r.exe` and follow the instructions presented onscreen for installing Microsoft Internet Explorer.

**3.** To run Microsoft Internet Explorer, double-click the Internet Explorer icon on the desktop.

# Validate! Certification Preparation Tool and the Validate! Windows NT 4.0 Workstation and Server Practice Exams

These practice exams help you to assess your readiness for the actual Microsoft Certified Professional exams. They will also help you to determine the areas in which you need more preparation. USE THESE EXAMS...You'll be glad you did.

**TO INSTALL AND ACCESS THE VALIDATE! CERTIFICATION PREPARATION TOOL AND THE VALIDATE! WINDOWS NT WORKSTATION 4.0 PRACTICE EXAM, FOLLOW THESE STEPS:**

**1.** Start Windows Explorer (if you're using Windows 95) or Windows NT Explorer (if you're using Windows NT), and then open the `NT WORKSTATION 4.0 VALIDATE! DEMO` folder on the CD-ROM.

2. In the `NT WORKSTATION 4.0 VALIDATE! DEMO` folder, double-click `Setup.exe` and follow the instructions presented onscreen for installing the Validate! Certification Preparation Tool and the Validate! Windows NT 4.0 Workstation practice exam.

3. After the installation is complete, you can access the practice exam by selecting Start ⇒ Programs ⇒ Windows NT Workstation 4.0 Validate! Demo ⇒ Validate CertPrep.

To install and access the Validate! Windows NT Server 4.0 practice exam, follow the same steps as those presented above, using the `NT SERVER 4.0 VALIDATE! DEMO` folder instead of the `NT WORKSTATION 4.0 VALIDATE! DEMO` folder.

## Microsoft Training and Certification Offline CD-ROM

This offline CD-ROM includes the entire contents of a key Microsoft Web site where you can obtain MCSE certification requirements and view Microsoft Certified Professional exam objectives and Microsoft course information. In addition, you can view the most current version of this Web site by connecting to `www.microsoft.com/train_cert/` on the Internet.

### TO INSTALL AND ACCESS THE OFFLINE VERSION OF THE MICROSOFT TRAINING AND CERTIFICATION WEB SITE, FOLLOW THESE STEPS:

1. Start Windows Explorer (if you're using Windows 95) or Windows NT Explorer (if you're using Windows NT), and then open the `Mscert` folder on the CD-ROM.

2. In the `Mscert` folder, double-click `Setup.exe` and follow the instructions presented onscreen for installing the Microsoft Train_Cert Offline Web site.

3. After the installation is complete, you can view the Web site by selecting Start ⇒ Programs ⇒ Microsoft Train_Cert Offline ⇒ Microsoft Train_Cert Offline.

 note  **You must have Microsoft Internet Explorer installed before you can view this Web site.**

## Microsoft Self-Administered Assessment Exam: Administering Microsoft Windows NT 4.0

This self-test is designed to measure your basic Windows NT administration skills, including administering users and groups, backing up and restoring a server, securing and sharing resources, configuring printers, and performing basic auditing. I recommend you take this self-administered assessment exam as part of your preparation just before you take the actual exam. It should give you a good indication of whether or not you're ready to tackle the real thing.

---

**TO INSTALL AND ACCESS THE ADMINISTERING MICROSOFT WINDOWS NT 4.0 SELF-ADMINISTERED ASSESSMENT EXAM, FOLLOW THESE STEPS:**

**1.** Start Windows Explorer (if you're using Windows 95) or Windows NT Explorer (if you're using Windows NT). Create a folder named `AdminTst` on your computer's hard drive.

**2.** Use Explorer to copy the `Mscert\Download\Training\Nt4asm.zip` file from the CD-ROM to the `AdminTst` folder you just created.

**3.** Use your favorite zip utility to unzip the `Nt4asm.zip` file's contents to the `AdminTst` folder.

 **web links**   **If you don't have a utility that will unzip the assessment test file, you can download an evaluation copy of a program called "Winzip" from** `www.winzip.com`. **Winzip is a Windows-based zip and unzip utility.**

**4.** To start the self-administered assessment exam, double-click `Lnchtst.exe` in the `AdminTst` folder. Follow the instructions that appear onscreen and take the test.

---

## Microsoft Certification Personal Exam Prep Practice Exams

There are two Microsoft Certification Personal Exam Prep Practice Exams on the CD-ROM: Supporting Microsoft Windows NT 4.0 Core Technologies (for Windows NT Workstation) and Supporting Microsoft Windows NT 4.0 Core Technologies (for Windows NT Server). These two practice exams should be used in conjunction with the Microsoft Self-Administered Assessment Exam for Administering Microsoft Windows NT 4.0 to determine your readiness for the Workstation and Server exams. These practice exams will help identify any weak areas you might have, so you can put in some additional study time in these specific areas prior to taking the actual exams.

---

**TO INSTALL AND ACCESS THE MICROSOFT NT 4.0 CORE TECHNOLOGIES PRACTICE EXAMS, FOLLOW THESE STEPS:**

**1.** Start Windows Explorer (if you're using Windows 95) or Windows NT Explorer (if you're using Windows NT). Create a folder named `CoreTest` on your computer's hard drive.

**2.** Use Explorer to copy the `Mscert\Download\Cert\Pep.zip` file from the CD-ROM to the `CoreTest` folder you just created.

**3.** Use your favorite zip utility to unzip the `Pep.zip` file's contents to the `CoreTest` folder.

 web links **If you don't have a utility that will unzip the assessment test file, you can download an evaluation copy of a program called Winzip from** `www.winzip.com`**. Winzip is a Windows-based zip and unzip utility.**

**4.** To install the Microsoft NT 4.0 practice exams, double-click `Gopep.exe` in the `CoreTest` folder, and follow the instructions that appear onscreen to install the practice exams.

**5.** To start either of the Microsoft NT 4.0 practice exams, select Start ⇒ Programs ⇒ Microsoft Personal Exam Prep ⇒ Personal Exam Prep Multi Demo.

**6.** Follow the instructions that appear onscreen to select and start the practice exam you want to take.

---

## *Microsoft Certified Professional Program Exam Study Guide*

This study guide presents interesting and valuable information about the Microsoft Certified Professional exams, including how the exams are developed, a description of the types of questions asked on exams, and some exam preparation tips.

**TO VIEW THE *MICROSOFT CERTIFIED PROFESSIONAL PROGRAM EXAM STUDY GUIDE*, FOLLOW THESE STEPS:**

1. Start Windows Explorer (if you're using Windows 95) or Windows NT Explorer (if you're using Windows NT). Open the `Mscert\Download\Cert` folder.

2. In the `Cert` folder, double-click `Studgde4.doc`.

 You must have Microsoft Word, WordPad, or Word Viewer installed *before* you can view this study guide.

# *Micro House Technical Library* (Evaluation Copy)

*Micro House Technical Library* is a useful CD-ROM-based set of encyclopedias that contains hardware configuration information. This evaluation copy of *Micro House Technical Library* includes only the Encyclopedia of I/O cards. Use this evaluation copy to determine whether or not you want to purchase the full version of the *Micro House Technical Library*.

**TO INSTALL AND ACCESS THE *MICRO HOUSE TECHNICAL LIBRARY*, FOLLOW THESE STEPS:**

1. Start Windows Explorer (if you're using Windows 95) or Windows NT Explorer (if you're using Windows NT), and then open the `Micro House` folder on the CD-ROM.

2. In the `Micro House` folder, double-click `Install.exe` and follow the instructions presented onscreen for installing the *Micro House Technical Library*.

3. To run the *Micro House Technical Library* from Windows NT, select Start⇒ Programs⇒ MH Tech Library⇒ IO Cards Library.

   To run the *Micro House Technical Library* from Windows 95, select Start⇒ Programs⇒ MH Tech Library⇒ MTL Demo Edition.

# Diskeeper Lite (Evaluation Copy)

Diskeeper is the premier defragmentation utility for use on Windows NT NTFS partitions.

 caution **Diskeeper Lite runs *only* on Windows NT. Don't attempt to install or run this program on a Windows 95 computer.**

**TO INSTALL AND RUN DISKEEPER LITE, FOLLOW THESE STEPS:**

**1.** Start Windows Explorer (if you're using Windows 95) or Windows NT Explorer (if you're using Windows NT), and then open the `Diskeeper` folder on the CD-ROM.

**2.** In the `Diskeeper` folder, double-click `Setup.exe` and follow the instructions presented onscreen for installing Diskeeper Lite.

**3.** To run Diskeeper Lite, select Start ⇒ Programs ⇒ Diskeeper Lite ⇒ Diskeeper Lite.

# Glossary

**access control list (ACL)**   The ACL is a list that contains user and group security identifiers (SIDs), with the associated privileges of each user and group. Each object, such as a file or folder, has an access control list associated with it. *See also* security identifier (SID).

**account policy**   The account policy is the set of rules indicating how passwords and account lockout are managed in Windows NT. Account policy is managed by using the Account Policy dialog box in User Manager or User Manager for Domains.

**active partition**   The active partition is a primary partition on the first hard disk in a computer that has been marked active by a partitioning program, such as Fdisk or Disk Manager. A computer loads its operating system from the active partition.

**answer files (Unattend.txt)**   Answer files are text files that contain stylized responses to the queries posed by the Windows NT setup program during installation. You can use an answer file, in conjunction with a network installation startup disk, to fully automate the installation of Windows NT on a single computer (in other words, perform an unattended installation). The default name for an answer file is Unattend.txt, but you can use any file name you want for your answer files.

**AppleTalk**   AppleTalk is a routable network protocol developed by Apple Computer, Inc. This protocol is associated with Macintosh computers.

**application programming interface (API)**    An API is a set of operating system functions that can be called by an application running on the computer. Windows NT supports the Win32, Win16, POSIX, MS-DOS, and OS/2 1.*x* APIs.

**archive bit**    The archive bit is a file attribute that indicates that the file or folder has been modified since the last backup. The archive bit is applied by the operating system when a file or folder is saved or created, and is commonly removed by backup programs after the file or folder has been backed up. This file attribute is not normally changed by the administrator.

**auditing**    Auditing is a Windows NT feature that enables you to collect and view security-related information concerning the success and failure of specified events, such as: file access, printer access, logon and logoff, and security policy changes. File auditing is only available on NTFS partitions. File and printer auditing require that auditing of File and Object Access be selected in the Audit Policy dialog box.

**authentication**    Authentication is the verification of a user account name and password by Windows NT. Authentication can be performed by the local Windows NT computer or by a Windows NT Server domain controller.

**Backup**    *See* Windows NT Backup.

**backup browser**    A backup browser is a computer that maintains a backup copy of the browse list. The backup browser receives the browse list from the master browser, and then makes the browse list available to any computer that requests it. All computers on the network, when they request a copy of the browse list, do so from a backup browser. A backup browser updates its browse list by requesting an update from the master browser every twelve minutes. There can be more than one backup browser on each subnet. Any Windows NT Server, Windows NT Workstation, Windows 95, or Windows for Workgroups computer can perform the role of the backup browser. *See also* Computer Browser service and master browser.

**backup domain controller (BDC)**    A BDC is a Windows NT Server computer that is configured to maintain a backup copy of the domain Directory Services database (SAM). The BDC receives updates to the Directory Services database from the primary domain controller (PDC) via a process called synchronization. *See also* primary domain controller and synchronization.

**binary tree**   A binary tree is the type of search used by the NTFS file system to quickly locate files and folders on an NTFS partition. A binary tree search is much faster than a sequential read or search. *See also* sequential read.

**bindings**   Bindings are associations between a network service and a protocol, or between a protocol and a network adapter.

**BIOS**   BIOS stands for *Basic Input/Output System*. The BIOS is a program which is stored in ROM (read-only memory) on a computer's motherboard. The BIOS contains instructions for performing the Power On Self Test (POST).

**blue screen**   A blue screen is displayed by Windows NT when it encounters a STOP error that it cannot recover from. A blue screen contains information about the type of error that occurred, a list of loaded drivers, and a processor stack dump.

**boot loader**   Boot loader is a program that is used to load a computer's operating system. In Windows NT, the boot loader is a program called `ntldr`, and it creates a menu (the boot loader menu) by parsing the contents of the `Boot.ini` file. Once the user selects an operating system from this menu (or the default time period expires), `ntldr` begins the process of starting the selected (or default) operating system.

**boot partition**   The boot partition is the partition that contains the Windows NT system files. The boot partition contains the folder that Windows NT is installed in.

**boot sequence**   The Windows NT boot sequence consists of a series of steps, beginning with powering on the computer and ending with completion of the logon process. The boot sequence steps vary according to the hardware platform you are using.

**bottleneck**   A bottleneck is the component in the system that is slowing system performance. In a networking environment, the bottleneck is the part of the system that is performing at peak capacity while other components in the system are not working at peak capacity. In other words, if it weren't for the limiting component, the rest of the system could go faster.

**browsing**   Browsing is the process of viewing a list of computers and their available shared resources, or viewing a list of files and folders on a local or network-connected drive.

**built-in groups**    Built-in groups are the default groups created by the operating system during a Windows NT installation. Different groups are created on Windows NT domain controllers than are created on non-domain controllers.

**C2 secure environment**    C2 is a designation in a range of security levels identified in the computer security specifications developed by the National Computer Security Center. If installed and configured correctly, Windows NT meets the C2 level of security.

**cache**    Cache is a section of memory used to temporarily store files from the hard disk.

**capacity planning**    Capacity planning is the process of determining current usage of server and/or network resources, as well as tracking utilization over time, in order to predict future usage and the additional hardware that will be required to meet the projected levels of utilization.

**CDFS**    CDFS stands for *Compact Disc Filing System*. CDFS supports access to compact discs, and is only used on CD-ROM devices.

**client**    A client is a computer that is capable of accessing resources on other computers (servers) across a network. Some computers are configured with both client and server software. *See also* server.

**Client Service for NetWare (CSNW)**    CSNW is a Windows NT Workstation service that enables a Windows NT Workstation computer to access files and print queues on NetWare 3.*x* and 4.*x* servers.

**complete trust domain model**    This is a decentralized domain model that consists of two or more domains that contain both user accounts and shared resources. In the complete trust domain model, a two-way trust relationship must be established between each and every domain. Because of the excessive number of trusts required for this model, the complete trust domain model is not often implemented. *See also* trust relationship and two-way trust.

**Computer Browser service**    This Windows NT service is responsible for the process of building a list of available network servers, called a browse list. The Computer Browser service is also responsible for determining the role a computer will play in the browser hierarchy: domain master browser, master browser, backup browser, or potential browser. *See also* backup browser, domain master browser, master browser, and potential browser.

**computer name**   A computer name is a unique name, up to fifteen characters in length, that is used to identify a particular computer on the network. No two computers on the same internetwork should have the same computer name.

**computer policy**   A computer policy is a collection of Registry settings created in System Policy Editor that specify a local computer's configuration. A computer policy enforces the specified configuration on all users of a particular Windows NT (or Windows 95) computer.

**Control Panel**   Control Panel is a group of mini applications that are used to configure a Windows NT computer.

**Default Computer policy**   The Default Computer policy is a computer policy that applies to all computers that don't have an individual computer policy. *See also* computer policy.

**default gateway**   A default gateway is a TCP/IP configuration setting that specifies the IP address of the router on the local network segment.

**Default User policy**   The Default User policy is a user policy that applies to all users that don't have an individual user policy. *See also* user policy.

**Default User profile**   The Default User profile is a user profile folder created during the Windows NT installation process. The settings in the Default User profile are applied, by default, to new user profiles as they are created. The Default User profile can be modified by using the Registry Editors or by using Windows NT Explorer. *See also* user profile.

**demand paging**   Demand paging is a process used by the Windows NT Virtual Memory Manager that involves reading pages of memory from the paging file into RAM, and writing pages of memory from RAM into the paging file as required by the operating system. *See also* paging file.

**desktop**   The desktop is the screen that is displayed after Windows NT 4.0 boots and you log on. The desktop replaces the Program Manager interface from earlier versions of Windows and Windows NT.

**desktop operating system**   A desktop operating system is an operating system that is designed to be used by an individual user on his or her desktop. A desktop operating system is not designed to be used on a network server.

**DHCP**    DHCP stands for *Dynamic Host Configuration Protocol*. This protocol is used to dynamically assign IP addresses to client computers on a network.

**DHCP Relay Agent**    The DHCP Relay Agent is a Windows NT Server service that forwards client computers' DHCP requests to a DHCP server on another subnet. *See also* DHCP.

**Dial-Up Networking**    Dial-Up Networking is a Windows NT service that enables a computer to use its modem to make a network connection over a telephone line to another computer. Dial-Up Networking is installed during the installation of the Remote Access Service (RAS) on a Windows NT computer. *See also* Remote Access Service (RAS).

**directory**    A directory is a folder. In Windows NT terminology, the terms *directory* and *folder* are synonymous. The two terms are used interchangeably throughout Windows NT documentation and the Windows NT user interface.

**directory replication**    Directory replication was designed to copy logon scripts from a central location, usually the PDC, to all domain controllers, thus enabling all users to execute their own logon scripts no matter which domain controller validates their logon. Replication involves copying subfolders and their files from the source folder on the source server to the destination folder on all Windows NT computers on the network that are configured as replication destinations.

**Directory Replicator service**    The Directory Replicator service is a Windows NT service that copies (replicates) files from a source Windows NT computer to a destination Windows NT computer. *See also* directory replication.

**Directory Services**    *See* Windows NT Directory Services.

**Directory Services database**    *See* Security Accounts Manager (SAM) database.

**disk duplexing**    Disk duplexing is a fault tolerance method that involves duplication of a partition from one hard disk onto a second hard disk. In disk duplexing, each hard disk must be on a different hard disk controller.

**disk mirroring**    Disk mirroring is a fault tolerance method that involves duplication of a partition from one hard disk onto a second hard disk. In disk mirroring, each hard disk can be on the same or a different hard disk controller.

**DNS** *See* Microsoft DNS.

**domain** A domain is a logical grouping of networked computers in which one or more of the computers has shared resources, such as a shared folder or a shared printer, and in which all of the computers share a common central domain Directory Services database that contains user account and security information.

**domain controller** A domain controller is a Windows NT Server computer that maintains a copy of the domain Directory Services database (also called the SAM). *See also* backup domain controller, primary domain controller, and Security Accounts Manager database (SAM).

**domain master browser** The domain master browser is a computer that maintains a list of available network servers located on all subnets in the domain. Additionally, the domain master browser maintains a list of available workgroups and domains on the internetwork. The domain master browser is the primary domain controller. *See also* Computer Browser service.

**domain name** A domain name is a unique name, up to fifteen characters in length, assigned to identify the domain on the network. A domain name must be different than all other domain names, workgroup names, and computer names on the network.

**Dr. Watson for Windows NT** Dr. Watson is a Windows NT tool that is used to debug application errors.

**dual boot** Dual boot refers to the capability of a computer to permit a user to select from more than one operating system during the boot process. (Only one operating system can be selected and run at a time.)

**dynamic routing** In dynamic routing, a router automatically builds and updates its routing table. In a dynamic routing environment, administrators don't have to manually configure the routing table on each individual router. As changes are made to the network, dynamic routers automatically adjust their routing tables to reflect these changes. Periodically, each dynamic router on the network broadcasts packets containing the contents of its routing table. Dynamic routers that receive these packets add the routing table information received to their own routing tables. In this way, dynamic routers are able to recognize other routers as they are added to and removed from the network.

**Emergency Repair Disk**    The Emergency Repair Disk is a floppy disk created during (or after) the Windows NT installation process that is used to repair Windows NT when its configuration files have been damaged or corrupted.

**enhanced metafile (EMF)**    An enhanced metafile is an intermediate print job format that can be created very quickly by the graphic device driver interface. Using an EMF enables Windows NT to process the print job in the background while the foreground process continues.

**Event Log service**    The Event Log service is a Windows NT service that writes operating system, application, and security events to log files. These log files can be viewed by an administrator using Event Viewer. *See also* Event Viewer.

**Event Viewer**    Event Viewer is a Windows NT administrative tool that enables an administrator to view and/or archive the operating system, application, and security event logs.

**exabyte**    An exabyte is a billion gigabytes (1,152,921,504,606,846,976 bytes).

**Executive Services (Windows NT Executive)**    Executive Services is the entire set of services that make up the kernel mode of the Windows NT operating system.

**extended partition**    An extended partition is a disk partition that can be subdivided into one or more logical drives. An extended partition can't be the active partition. *See also* active partition.

**fault tolerance**    Fault tolerance refers to the ability of a computer or operating system to continue operations when a severe error or failure occurs, such as the loss of a hard disk or a power outage.

**file allocation table (FAT) file system**    FAT is a type of file system that is used by several operating systems, including Windows NT. Windows NT does not support security or auditing on FAT partitions. The maximum size of a FAT partition is 2GB.

**file attributes**    File attributes are markers assigned to files that describe properties of the file and limit access to the file. File attributes include: Archive, Compress, Hidden, Read-only, and System.

**file system**    A file system is an overall architecture for naming, storing, and retrieving files on a disk.

**folder**   A folder is a directory. In Windows NT terminology, the terms *directory* and *folder* are synonymous. The two terms are used interchangeably throughout Windows NT documentation and the Windows NT user interface.

**frame type**   A frame type (also called a *frame format*) is an accepted, standardized structure for transmitting data packets over a network.

**fully qualified domain name (FQDN)**   An FQDN is a fancy term for the way computers are named and referenced on the Internet. The format for an FQDN is: `server_name.domain_name.root_domain_name`. For example, a server named `wolf` in the `alancarter` domain in the `com` root domain has a Fully Qualified Domain Name of `wolf.alancarter.com`. Fully qualified domain names always use lowercase characters.

**gateway**   A gateway is a computer that performs protocol or data format translation between two computers that use different protocols or data formats.

**Gateway Service for NetWare (GSNW)**   Gateway Service for NetWare (GSNW) is a Windows NT Server service that, when installed and configured on a Windows NT Server computer, provides all of the functionality of Client Service for NetWare (CSNW). Additionally, GSNW enables the Windows NT Server computer to transparently share resources (files, folders, and printers) located on a NetWare server to client computers of the Windows NT Server computer. GSNW accomplishes this by converting the Server Message Blocks (SMBs) from the client computers of the Windows NT Server computer into NetWare Core Protocol (NCP) requests that are recognized by the NetWare server. *See also* Client Service for NetWare.

**gigabyte (GB)**   A gigabyte is 1,024 megabytes (MB), or 1,073,741,824 bytes.

**global group**   A global group is a Windows NT Server group that can only be created in the domain Directory Services database. Global groups are primarily used to organize users that perform similar tasks or have similar network access requirements. In a typical Windows NT configuration, user accounts are placed in a global group, then the global group is made a member of one or more local groups, and each local group is assigned permissions to a network resource. The advantage of using global groups is ease of administration—the network administrator can manage large numbers of users by placing them in global groups. Global groups are only available in Windows NT Server domains—they are not available in workgroups or on a stand-alone server. *See also* local group.

**Graphics Device Interface (GDI)**    The GDI is a specific Windows NT device driver that manages low-level display and print data. The GDI used to be part of user mode in Windows NT 3.51, but is now part of the kernel mode (Executive Services) in Windows NT 4.0.

**group dependencies**    Group dependencies are groups of services or drivers that must be running before a given service (or driver) can start.

**group policy**    A group policy is a policy that applies to a group of users. Group policies apply to all users that are members of a group (that has a group policy), and that do not have individual user policies.

**Hardware Compatibility List (HCL)**    The HCL is a list of hardware that is supported by Windows NT. The HCL is shipped with Windows NT. You can access the latest version of the HCL at `www.microsoft.com/ntworkstation` or `www.microsoft.com/ntserver`.

**hertz (Hz)**    Hz is a unit of frequency measurement equivalent to one cycle per second.

**hive**    A hive is a group of Windows NT Registry keys and values that are stored in a single file. *See also* key, Registry, and value.

**host**    A host is a computer that is connected to a TCP/IP network, such as the Internet.

**HPFS**    HPFS stands for *high performance file system*. This is the file system used by OS/2. Windows NT used to support HPFS, but HPFS support was dropped for NT version 4.0.

**Internet Information Server (IIS)**    Internet Information Server is a Microsoft Windows NT Server service that provides World Wide Web (WWW), File Transfer Protocol (FTP), and Gopher publishing services.

**internetwork**    An internetwork consists of multiple network segments connected by routers and/or WAN links.

**interrupt (IRQ)**    An interrupt is a unique number between two and fifteen that is assigned to a hardware peripheral in a computer. No two devices in the computer should have the same interrupt, unless the devices are capable of (and correctly configured to) share an interrupt.

**intranetwork**     An intranetwork is a TCP/IP internetwork that is not connected to the Internet. For example, a company's multi-city internetwork can be called an intranetwork as long as it is not connected to the Internet. *See also* internetwork.

**kernel**     A kernel is the core component of an operating system.

**kernel mode**     Kernel mode refers to a highly privileged mode of operation in Windows NT. "Highly privileged" means that all code that runs in kernel mode can access the hardware directly, and can access any memory address. A program that runs in kernel mode is always resident in memory—it can't be written to the paging file. *See also* user mode.

**key**     A key is a component of the Registry that is similar to a folder in a file system. A key can contain other keys and value entries. *See also* Registry and value.

**kilobyte (KB)**     A kilobyte is 1,024 bytes.

**line printer daemon (LPD)**     LPD is the print server software used in TCP/IP printing. LPD is supported by many operating systems, including Windows NT and UNIX.

**local group**     A local group is a Windows NT group that can be created in the domain Directory Services database on a domain controller or in the SAM on any non-domain controller. Local groups are primarily used to control access to resources. In a typical Windows NT configuration, a local group is assigned permissions to a specific resource, such as a shared folder or a shared printer. Individual user accounts and global groups are then made members of this local group. The result is that all members of the local group then have permissions to the resource. Using local groups simplifies the administration of network resources, because permissions can be assigned once, to a local group, instead of separately to each user account. *See also* global group.

**local print provider**     A local print provider is a Windows NT kernel mode driver that manages printing for all print devices managed by the local computer.

**LocalTalk**     LocalTalk is a specification for the type of network cabling, connectors, and adapters developed by Apple Computer, Inc. for use with Macintosh computers.

**logging on**     Logging on is the process of supplying a user name and password, and having that user name and password authenticated by a Windows NT computer. A user is said to "log on" to a Windows NT computer.

**logical drive**    A logical drive is a disk partition (or multiple partitions) that has been formatted with a file system and assigned a drive letter.

**logon hours**    Logon hours are the assigned hours that a user can log on to a Windows NT Server domain controller. The logon hours configuration only affects the user's ability to access the domain controller—it does not affect a user's ability to log on to a Windows NT Workstation computer or to a non-domain controller.

**logon script**    A logon script is a batch file that is run when a user logs on. All MS-DOS 5.0 (and earlier versions) batch commands can be used in logon scripts.

**mandatory user profile**    A mandatory user profile is a user profile that, when assigned to a user, can't be modified by the user. A user can make changes to desktop and work environment settings during a single logon session, but these changes are not saved to the mandatory profile when the user logs off. Each time the user logs on, the user's desktop and work environment settings revert to those contained in the mandatory user profile. A mandatory user profile is created by renaming the user's `ntuser.dat` file to `ntuser.man`. *See also* user profile.

**master browser**    A master browser is the computer on the subnet that builds and maintains the browse list for that subnet. The master browser distributes this browse list to backup browsers on the subnet and to the domain master browser. *See also* backup browser, Computer Browser service, and domain master browser.

**Maximum Password Age**    The Maximum Password Age is the maximum number of days a user may use the same password.

**megabyte (MB)**    A megabyte is 1,024 kilobytes, or 1,048,576 bytes.

**member server**    A member server is a Windows NT Server computer that is not installed as a domain controller, and that has joined a Windows NT Server domain.

**memory dump**    The term memory dump refers to the process of Windows NT copying the contents of RAM into a file (the `memory.dmp` file) when a STOP error or blue screen occurs.

**Microsoft DNS**    Microsoft DNS is a Windows NT Server service. This service is a TCP/IP-based name resolution service. It is used to resolve a host name or an FQDN to its associated IP address.

**Migration Tool for NetWare**   Migration Tool for NetWare is a Windows NT Server administrative tool that makes it possible for an administrator to migrate a NetWare server's user accounts and files to a Windows NT Server computer. Migration Tool for NetWare requires that Gateway Service for NetWare and NWLink IPX/SPX Compatible Transport be installed in the Windows NT Server computer. *See also* Gateway Service for NetWare and NWLink IPX/SPX Compatible Transport.

**million bits per second (Mbps)**   Mbps is a measurement of data transmission speed that is used to describe WAN links and other network connections.

**Minimum Password Age**   The Minimum Password Age is the minimum number of days a user must keep the same password.

**Minimum Password Length**   Minimum Password Length specifies the minimum number of characters required in a user's password.

**MS-DOS**   MS-DOS is a computer operating system developed by Microsoft. MS-DOS stands for *Microsoft Disk Operating System*.

**multihomed**   A computer is said to be multihomed when it has more than one network adapter installed in it.

**multiple master domain model**   This domain model consists of two or more master domains that contain user accounts, and any number of resource domains that contain shared resources. In this model, a two-way trust is used between each of the master domains, and a one-way trust is used from each resource domain to each and every master domain. *See also* trust relationship, one-way trust, and two-way trust.

**multiprocessing**   Multiprocessing refers to the capability of an operating system to use more than one processor in a single computer simultaneously.

**NetBEUI**   NetBEUI is a nonroutable protocol designed for use on small networks. NetBEUI is included in Windows NT 4.0 primarily for backward compatibility with older Microsoft networking products.

**network access order**   The network access order specifies which protocol or service Windows NT will use first when it attempts to access another computer on the network.

**network adapter**    A network adapter is an adapter card in a computer that enables the computer to connect to a network.

**Network Client Administrator**    Network Client Administrator is a Windows NT Server tool you can use to create an installation disk set to install network clients or services on client computers. You can also use Network Client Administrator to create a network installation startup disk. A network installation startup disk, when run on a computer that needs to be set up (the target computer), causes the target computer to automatically connect to the server and to start an interactive installation/setup routine.

**network device driver**    A network device driver is a Windows NT kernel mode driver that is designed to enable Windows NT to use a network adapter to communicate on the network.

**Network Monitor**    Network Monitor is a Windows NT Server administrative tool that allows you to capture, view, and analyze network traffic (packets).

**network number**    Network numbers are 32-bit binary numbers that uniquely identify an NWLink IPX/SPX Compatible Transport network segment for routing purposes. Because network numbers uniquely identify a network segment, they are used by IPX routers to correctly forward data packets from one network segment to another.

**non-browser**    A non-browser is a computer that is not capable of maintaining a browse list either because it was configured not to do so, or because the operating system on this computer is incapable of maintaining a browse list. *See also* Computer Browser service.

**NT Hardware Qualifier (NTHQ)**    The NT Hardware Qualifier (NTHQ) is a utility that ships with Windows NT. NTHQ examines and identifies a computer's hardware configuration, including the hardware settings used by each adapter.

**NTFS**    *See* Windows NT file system.

**NTFS permissions**    NTFS permissions are permissions assigned to individual files and folders on an NTFS partition that are used to control access to these files and folders. NTFS permissions apply to local users as well as to users who connect to a shared folder over-the-network. If the NTFS permissions are more restrictive than share permissions, the NTFS permissions will be applied. *See also* share permissions.

**NWLink IPX/SPX Compatible Transport**    NWLink IPX/SPX Compatible Transport is a routable transport protocol typically used in a combined Windows NT and NetWare environment. NWLink IPX/SPX Compatible Transport is Microsoft's version of Novell's IPX/SPX protocol. (IPX/SPX is the protocol used on most Novell NetWare networks.) NWLink provides protocol compatibility between Windows NT and NetWare computers. In addition to its functionality in a NetWare environment, NWLink also fully supports Microsoft networking.

**ODBC**    ODBC stands for *Open Database Connectivity*. ODBC is a software specification that enables ODBC-enabled applications (such as Microsoft Excel) to connect to databases (such as Microsoft SQL Server and Microsoft Access).

The ODBC application in Control Panel is used to install and remove ODBC drivers for various types of databases. Additionally, this application is used to configure ODBC data sources.

**$OEM$ subfolder**    The $OEM$ subfolder is used to store source files that are used to install applications, components, or files that do not ship with Windows NT. This subfolder is used during an automated setup of Windows NT.

**one-way trust**    When a single trust relationship exists between two domains, it is called a one-way trust. Both domains must be configured by an administrator in order to establish a trust relationship. Trusts are configured in Windows NT by using User Manager for Domains. The trusted domain should be configured first, and then the trusting domain. *See also* trust relationship, trusted domain, and trusting domain.

**packet**    A packet is a group of bytes sent over the network as a block of data.

**paging file**    A paging file (sometimes called a page file or a swap file) is a file used as a computer's virtual memory. Pages of memory that are not currently in use can be written to a paging file to make room for data currently needed by the processor. *See also* virtual memory.

**partition**    A partition is a portion of a hard disk that can be formatted with a file system, or combined with other partitions to form a larger logical drive. *See also* logical drive.

**pass-through authentication**    Pass-through authentication is a process in which one Windows NT computer passes a user name and password on to another

Windows NT computer for validation. Pass-through authentication makes it possible for a user to log on to a Windows NT Workstation computer by using a user account from a Windows NT Server domain.

**Password Uniqueness**    Password Uniqueness specifies how many different passwords a user must use before a previous password can be reused.

**Peer Web Services**    Peer Web Services is a Windows NT Workstation Internet publishing service that supports World Wide Web (WWW), File Transfer Protocol (FTP), and Gopher services. Peer Web Services is optimized to serve a small number of clients, such as might be found on a small company intranet.

**Performance Monitor**    Performance Monitor is a Windows NT tool that is used to gather statistics on current performance of a Windows NT computer. Performance Monitor statistics can be displayed in a Chart, Alert, or Report view; or can be saved to a log file for later viewing.

**permissions**    Permissions control access to resources, such as shares, files, folders, and printers on a Windows NT computer.

**Plug and Play**    Plug and Play is a specification that makes it possible for hardware devices to be automatically recognized and configured by the operating system without user intervention.

**Point-to-Point Multilink Protocol**    Point-to-Point Multilink Protocol is an extension of the Point-to-Point Protocol. Point-to-Point Multilink Protocol combines the bandwidth from multiple physical connections into a single logical connection. This means that multiple modem, ISDN, or X.25 connections can be bundled together to form a single logical connection with a much higher bandwidth than a single connection can support. *See also* Point-to-Point Protocol.

**Point-to-Point Protocol (PPP)**    Point-to-Point Protocol (PPP) is a newer connection protocol that was designed to overcome the limitations of the Serial Line Internet Protocol (SLIP). PPP is currently the industry standard remote connection protocol, and is recommended for use by Microsoft. PPP connections support multiple transport protocols, including: TCP/IP, NWLink IPX/SPX Compatible Transport, and NetBEUI. Additionally, PPP supports dynamic server-based IP addressing (such as DHCP). PPP supports password encryption, and the PPP connection process does not usually require a script file. *See also* Serial Line Internet Protocol (SLIP).

**Point-to-Point Tunneling Protocol (PPTP)**   Point-to-Point Tunneling Protocol (PPTP) permits a virtual private encrypted connection between two computers over an existing TCP/IP network connection. The existing TCP/IP network connection can be over a local area network or over a Dial-Up Networking TCP/IP connection (including the Internet). All standard transport protocols are supported within the Point-to-Point Tunneling Protocol connection, including NWLink IPX/SPX Compatible Transport, NetBEUI, and TCP/IP. A primary reason for choosing to use PPTP is that it supports the RAS encryption feature over standard, unencrypted TCP/IP networks, such as the Internet.

**POSIX**   *Portable Operating System Interface for Computing Environments* (POSIX) was developed as a set of accepted standards for writing applications for use on various UNIX computers. POSIX environment applications consist of applications developed to meet the POSIX standards. These applications are sometimes referred to as POSIX-compliant applications. Windows NT provides support for POSIX-compliant applications via the POSIX subsystem. Windows NT supports the POSIX subsystem on all hardware platforms supported by Windows NT. To fully support POSIX-compliant applications, at least one NTFS partition is required on the Windows NT computer. POSIX applications are source compatible across all supported hardware platforms. This means that POSIX applications must be recompiled for each hardware platform in order to be run on that platform.

**potential browser**   A potential browser is a computer that does not currently maintain or distribute a browse list, but is capable of doing so. A potential browser can become a backup browser at the direction of the master browser. *See also* backup browser, Computer Browser service, and master browser.

**preemptive multitasking**   In preemptive multitasking, the operating system allocates processor time between applications. Because Windows NT, not the application, allocates processor time between multiple applications, one application can be preempted by the operating system, and another application enabled to run. When multiple applications are alternately paused and then allocated processor time, they appear to run simultaneously to the user.

**primary domain controller (PDC)**   A PDC is a Windows NT Server computer that is configured to maintain the primary copy of the domain Directory Services database (also called the SAM). The PDC sends Directory Services database updates to backup domain controllers (BDCs) via a process called synchronization. *See also* backup domain controller, Security Accounts Manager database (SAM), and synchronization.

**primary partition**   A primary partition is a disk partition that can be configured as the active partition. A primary partition can only be formatted as a single logical drive. *See also* active partition.

**print device**   In Windows NT, the term print device refers to the physical device that produces printed output—this is what most people refer to as a printer.

**print device driver**   A print device driver is a Windows NT kernel mode driver that formats print jobs into a RAW format. (The RAW format is ready to print, and no further processing is required.) A print device driver can also convert EMF formatted print jobs into a RAW format. *See also* enhanced metafile (EMF).

**print job**   A print job is all of the data and commands needed to print a document.

**print monitor**   A print monitor is a software component that runs in kernel mode. A print monitor sends ready-to-print print jobs to a print device, either locally or across the network. Print monitors are also called port monitors.

**print processor**   A print processor is a kernel mode driver that manages printer device drivers and the process of converting print jobs from one format into another.

**print queue**   In Windows NT terminology, a print queue is a list of print jobs for a specific printer that are waiting to be sent to a print device. The print queue is maintained by the Windows NT Spooler service. *See also* Spooler service.

**print server**   A print server is a software program on a computer that manages print jobs and print devices. The Windows NT Spooler service functions as a print server. The term print server is also used to refer to a computer used primarily to manage multiple print devices and their print jobs. *See also* Spooler service.

**printer**   In Windows NT, the term printer does not represent a physical device that produces printed output. Rather, a printer is the software interface between the Windows NT operating system and the device that produces the printed output. In other operating systems, what Windows NT calls a printer is often referred to as a print queue.

**printer pool**   When a printer has multiple ports (and multiple print devices) assigned to it, this is called a printer pool. Users print to a single printer, and the printer load-balances its print jobs between the print devices assigned to it.

**RAM**   *Random access memory*, or RAM, is the physical memory installed in a computer.

**Rdisk.exe**   `Rdisk.exe` is a Windows NT utility that is used to update the Emergency Repair Disk. Using `Rdisk /s` causes this utility to back up the SAM and Security hives in the Registry. (If the `/s` switch is not used, the SAM and Security hives in the Registry are not backed up.) *See also* Emergency Repair Disk.

**refresh**   The term refresh means to update the display with current information.

**Registry**   The Windows NT Registry is a database that contains all of the information required to correctly configure an individual Windows NT computer, its user accounts, and applications. Registries are unique to each computer—you shouldn't use the Registry from one computer on another computer. The Registry is organized in a tree structure consisting of five subtrees, and their keys and value entries. *See also* key and value.

**Registry editors**   Registry editors are tools that enable you to search and modify the Windows NT Registry. There are two primary tools for editing the Windows NT Registry: the Windows NT Registry Editor (`regedt32.exe`), and the Windows 95 Registry Editor (`regedit.exe`). Additionally, you can use the Windows NT System Policy Editor (`poledit.exe`) to modify a limited number of settings in the Registry. However, you can't use System Policy Editor to search the Registry.

**Remote Access Admin**   Remote Access Admin is a Windows NT administrative tool that is primarily used to start and stop the Remote Access Service (RAS), to assign the dialin permission to users, and to configure a call back security level for each user. Remote Access Admin can also be used to view COM port status and statistics, to disconnect users from individual ports, and to remotely manage RAS on other Windows NT computers.

**Remote Access Service (RAS)**   Remote Access Service (RAS) is a Windows NT service that enables dial-up network connections between a RAS server and a Dial-Up Networking client computer. RAS includes software components for both the RAS server and the Dial-Up Networking client in a single Windows NT service. RAS enables users of remote computers to use the network as though they were directly connected to it. Once the dial-up connection is established, there is no difference in network functionality, except that the speed of the link is often much slower than a direct connection to the LAN.

**RIP**    *Routing Information Protocol* (RIP) is the software that enables routers to dynamically update their routing tables. Windows NT ships with two versions of RIP: RIP for Internet Protocol, and RIP for NWLink IPX/SPX Compatible Transport. *See also* dynamic routing, RIP for Internet Protocol, and RIP for NWLink IPX/SPX Compatible Transport.

**RIP for Internet Protocol**    RIP for Internet Protocol is a Windows NT service that enables Windows NT to dynamically update its routing tables when it is configured as a TCP/IP router. *See also* dynamic routing and RIP.

**RIP for NWLink IPX/SPX Compatible Transport**    RIP for NWLink IPX/SPX Compatible Transport is a Windows NT service that enables Windows NT to dynamically update its routing tables when it is configured as an IPX router. *See also* dynamic routing and RIP.

**roaming user profiles**    Roaming user profiles are user profiles that are stored on a server. Because these profiles are stored on a server instead of a local computer, they are available to users regardless of which Windows NT computer on the network they log on to. The benefit of using roaming user profiles is that users retain their own customized desktop and work environment settings even though they may use several different Windows NT computers.

**router**    A router is a network device that uses protocol-specific addressing information to forward packets from a source computer on one network segment across one or more routers to a destination computer on another network segment.

**routing**    Routing is the process of forwarding packets from a source computer on one network segment across one or more routers to a destination computer on another network segment by using protocol-specific addressing information. Devices that perform routing are called routers.

**SAP Agent**    The *Service Advertising Protocol* (SAP) Agent is a Windows NT service that advertises a Windows NT computer's services (such as SQL Server and SNA Server) to NetWare client computers. The SAP Agent requires the use of NWLink IPX/SPX Compatible Transport. The SAP Agent should be installed when NetWare client computers will access services on a Windows NT computer.

**SCSI**   SCSI stands for *Small Computer System Interface*. SCSI is a hardware specification for cables, adapter cards, and the devices that they manage, such as: hard disks, CD-ROMs, and scanners.

**Security Accounts Manager (SAM) database**   The SAM is a Windows NT Registry hive that is used to store all user account, group account, and security policy information for a Windows NT computer or a Windows NT domain. On a domain controller, the SAM is also referred to as the domain Directory Services database.

**security identifier (SID)**   A security identifier (SID) is a unique number assigned to a user account, group account, or computer account in the Security Accounts Manager (SAM) database. *See also* Security Accounts Manager (SAM) database.

**security log**   The security log is a file that is managed by the Windows NT Event Log service. All auditing of security events is written to the security log. An Administrator can view the security log by using Event Viewer.

**segment**   In network terminology, a segment refers to a network subnet that is not subdivided by a bridge or a router. The term segment can also be used as a verb, describing the process of dividing the network into multiple subnets by using a bridge or a router.

**sequential read**   A sequential read is a read performed (normally by the operating system) from the beginning of a file straight through to the end of the file. No random access to different parts of the file can occur during a sequential read.

**server**   A server is a computer on a network that is capable of sharing resources with other computers on the network. Many computers are configured as both clients and servers, meaning that they can both access resources located on other computers across-the-network, and they can share their resources with other computers on the network. *See also* client.

**Server Manager**   Server Manager is a Windows NT Server administrative tool that allows remote management of shared folders, remote starting and stopping of services, remote management of Directory Replication, remote viewing to determine which users are currently accessing shared resources, and remote disconnection of users from shared resources on a Windows NT Server computer.

**Server service**   The Server service is a Windows NT service that enables Windows NT computers to share their resources with other computers on the network.

**service dependencies**    Service dependencies are services and drivers that must be running before a particular service (or driver) can start.

**Services for Macintosh**    Services for Macintosh is a Windows NT Server service that enables Macintosh client computers to connect to Macintosh-accessible volumes on a Windows NT Server computer, enables Macintosh client computers to access shared printers on a Windows NT Server computer, enables a Windows NT Server computer to connect to network-connected print devices that support the AppleTalk protocol, and enables a Windows NT Server computer to function as an AppleTalk router.

**Setup Manager**    Setup Manager is a Windows NT tool that is used to create an answer file (`Unattend.txt`) for use in automating the installation of Windows NT. *See also* answer files.

**share name**    A share name is a name that uniquely identifies a shared resource on a Windows NT computer, such as a shared folder or printer.

**share permissions**    Share permissions control access to shared resources, such as shared folders and shared printers on a Windows NT computer. Share permissions only apply to users who access a shared resource over-the-network.

**shared folder**    A shared folder is a folder on a Windows NT computer that can be accessed by other computers on the network because the folder has been configured to be shared and has been assigned a share name.

**single domain model**    This domain model consists of one domain, and does not use trust relationships. All user accounts and shared resources are contained within one domain.

**single master domain model**    This domain model consists of one master domain that contains all user accounts, and one or more resource domains that contain shared resources. This domain model uses one-way trusts from each resource domain to the master domain. *See also* trust relationship and one-way trust.

**Serial Line Internet Protocol (SLIP)**    The Serial Line Internet Protocol (SLIP) is an older connection protocol, commonly associated with UNIX computers, that only supports one transport protocol—TCP/IP. SLIP connections don't support NWLink IPX/SPX Compatible Transport or NetBEUI. The version of SLIP supported by Windows NT 4.0 requires a static IP address configuration at the client computer—dynamic IP addressing is not supported. Additionally, password encryption is not supported by this version of SLIP. A script file is usually required to automate the connection process when SLIP is used.

**SNMP**   SNMP stands for *Simple Network Management Protocol*. The Windows NT SNMP service, once installed on a Windows NT computer, gathers TCP/IP statistics on the local computer and transmits those statistics to any SNMP management station on the network that is correctly configured to receive them. Additionally, installing the SNMP service enables various TCP/IP counters within Windows NT Performance Monitor.

**special groups**   Special groups are groups created by Windows NT during installation that are used for specific purposes by the operating system. These groups don't appear in User Manager or User Manager for Domains. Special groups are only visible in Windows NT utilities that assign permissions to network resources, such as a printer's Properties dialog box, and Windows NT Explorer. You can assign permissions to and remove permissions from special groups. You can't assign users to special groups, and you can't rename or delete these groups. Special groups are sometimes called system groups. There are five special groups: Everyone, Interactive, Network, System, and Creator Owner.

**Spooler service**   The Windows NT Spooler service manages the entire printing process on a Windows NT computer. The Spooler service performs many of the tasks that are associated with a print server.

**stand-alone server**   A stand-alone server is a Windows NT Server computer that is not installed as a domain controller, and that has not joined a Windows NT Server domain.

**static routing**   Static routing is basic, no-frills IP routing. No additional software is necessary to implement static routing in multihomed Windows NT computers. Static routers are not capable of automatically building a routing table. In a static routing environment, administrators must manually configure the routing table on each individual router. If the network layout changes, the network administrator must manually update the routing tables to reflect the changes.

**stripe set**   A stripe set is a disk configuration consisting of two to thirty-two hard disks. In a stripe set, data is stored, a block at a time, evenly and sequentially among all of the disks in the set. Stripe sets are sometimes referred to as disk striping. Disk striping alludes to the process wherein a file is written, or striped, one block at a time, first to one disk, then to the next disk, and then to the next disk, and so on, until all of the data has been evenly distributed among all of the disks.

**stripe set with parity**    A stripe set with parity is similar to a stripe set, but a stripe set with parity provides a degree of fault tolerance that a stripe set cannot. In a stripe set with parity, data is not only distributed a block at a time, evenly and sequentially among all of the disks in the set, but parity information is also written across all of the disks in the set. A stripe set with parity is made up of three to thirty-two hard disks. Like stripe sets, stripe sets with parity are created from identical amounts of free space on each disk that belongs to the set. *See also* stripe set.

**subfolder**    A subfolder is a folder that is located within another folder. Subfolders can contain other subfolders, as well as files.

**subnet mask**    A subnet mask specifies which portion of an IP address represents the network ID and which portion represents the host ID. A subnet mask enables TCP/IP to correctly determine whether network traffic destined for a given IP address should be transmitted on the local subnet, or whether it should be routed to a remote subnet. A subnet mask should be the same for all computers and other network devices on a given network segment. A subnet mask is a 32-bit binary number, broken into four 8-bit sections (octets), that is normally represented in a dotted decimal format. Each 8-bit section is represented by a whole number between 0 and 255. A common subnet mask is 255.255.255.0. This particular subnet mask specifies that TCP/IP will use the first three octets of an IP address as the network ID, and use the last octet as the host ID.

**synchronization**    Synchronization is a process performed by the NetLogon Service. In this process, domain Directory Services database update information is periodically copied from the primary domain controller (PDC) to each backup domain controller (BDC) in the domain.

**Sysdiff.exe**    Sydiff.exe is a Windows NT utility that is used to automate the installation of applications that don't support scripted installation and that would otherwise require user interaction during the installation process.

**system partition**    The system partition is the active primary partition on the first hard disk in the computer. (This is usually the C: drive.) The system partition contains several files that are required to boot Windows NT, including: ntldr, Ntdetect.com,

Boot.ini, and sometimes Bootsect.dos, and Ntbootdd.sys, depending on the installation type and hardware configuration. *See also* boot partition.

**system policy**    The Windows NT system policy file is a collection of user, group, and computer policies. System policy restricts the user's ability to perform certain tasks on any Windows NT computer on the network that the user logs on to. System policy can also be used to enforce certain mandatory display settings, such as wallpaper and color scheme. You can also create a system policy file that applies to users of Windows 95 computers. System policy gives the administrator far more configurable options than a mandatory profile. Administrators can use system policy to provide a consistent environment for a large number of users, or to enforce a specified work environment for "problem users" who demand a significant amount of administrator time.

**System Policy Editor**    System Policy Editor is a Windows NT Server tool that is used to edit Windows NT and Windows 95 system policy files. *See also* system policy.

**Task Manager**    Windows NT Task Manager is a Windows NT administrative utility that can be used to start and stop applications; to view performance statistics, such as memory and CPU usage; and to change a process's base priority.

**TCP/IP**    The *Transmission Control Protocol/Internet Protocol* (TCP/IP) is a widely used transport protocol that provides robust capabilities for Windows NT networking. TCP/IP is a fast, routable enterprise protocol. TCP/IP is the protocol used on the Internet. TCP/IP is supported by many other operating systems, including: Windows 95, Macintosh, UNIX, MS-DOS, and IBM mainframes. TCP/IP is typically the recommended protocol for large, heterogeneous networks.

**TechNet**    *Microsoft TechNet* is an invaluable knowledge base and troubleshooting resource. *TechNet* is published monthly by Microsoft on multiple compact discs. *TechNet* includes a complete set of all Microsoft operating system Resource Kits (currently in a help file format), the entire Microsoft Knowledge Base, and supplemental compact discs full of patches, fixes, and drivers (so you don't have to spend time downloading them).

**terabyte**    A terabyte is 1,024 gigabytes, or 1,099,511,627,776 bytes.

**terminate-and-stay-resident (TSR) program**    A terminate-and-stay-resident program is an MS-DOS program that stays loaded in memory, even when it is not running.

**thread**    A thread is the smallest unit of processing that can be scheduled by the Windows NT Schedule service. All applications require at least one thread.

**trust relationship**    A trust relationship, or *trust*, is an agreement between two Windows NT Server domains that enables authenticated users in one domain to access resources in another domain. A trust relationship enables users from the trusted domain to access resources in the trusting domain. *See also* one-way trust, trusted domain, trusting domain, and two-way trust.

**trusted domain**    The trusted domain is the domain that contains the user accounts of users who want to access resources in the trusting domain. The trusted domain is said to be trusted by the trusting domain. When graphically displaying a trust relationship, an arrow is used to point from the trusting domain to the trusted domain. *See also* trust relationship and trusting domain.

**trusting domain**    The trusting domain is the domain that has resources to share with users from the trusted domain. The trusting domain is said to trust the trusted domain. When graphically displaying a trust relationship, an arrow is used to point from the trusting domain to the trusted domain. *See also* trust relationship and trusted domain.

**two-way trust**    A two-way trust consists of two one-way trusts between two domains. *See also* one-way trust and trust relationship.

**Unattend.txt**    *See* answer files.

**UNC (universal naming convention)**    UNC is an accepted method of identifying individual computers and their resources on the network. A UNC name consists of a server name and a shared resource name in the following format: `\\Server_name\Share_name`. `Server_name` represents the name of the server that the shared folder is located on. `Share_name` represents the name of the shared folder. A UNC name in this format can be used to connect to a network share. For example, a shared folder named `Public` located on a server named `Server1` would have the following UNC name: `\\Server1\Public`.

**Uniqueness Database Files (*.UDF)**    Uniqueness Database Files (UDFs) are text files, similar to answer files, that make it possible for one answer file to be used for the installation of many computers that have different identifying characteristics. For example, each computer has a different computer name and user name. A UDF, used in conjunction with a network installation startup disk and an answer file, enables you to fully automate the installation of Windows NT on multiple computers on a network. The UDF is structured like an answer file, and uses the same types of entries that an answer file uses. The UDF has an additional section, named `UniqueIds`. When the appropriate command-line switch is used, selected entries in the UDF replace entries with the same name in the answer file. *See also* answer files.

**UPS**    UPS stands for *uninterruptible power supply*. A UPS is a fault-tolerance device that enables a computer to continue operations for a short period of time after a power outage.

**user account**    A user account is a record in the Security Accounts Manager (SAM) database that contains unique user information, such as user name, password, and logon restrictions.

**user account database**    *See* Security Accounts Manager (SAM) database.

**User Manager**    User Manager is a Windows NT Workstation administrative tool that is used to administer user accounts, group accounts, and security policy on a Windows NT Workstation computer.

**User Manager for Domains**    User Manager for Domains is a Windows NT Server administrative tool that is used to administer user accounts, group accounts, security policy, and trust relationships for the Windows NT Server domain or for an individual Windows NT Server computer.

**user mode**    Within the Windows NT architecture, user mode is referred to as a less privileged processor mode because it does not have direct access to hardware. Applications and their subsystems run in user mode. User mode applications are limited to assigned memory address spaces and can't directly access other memory address spaces. User mode uses specific application programming interfaces (API's) to request system services from a kernel mode component. *See also* application programming interface (API) and kernel mode.

**user name**    A user name is the name assigned to a user account in the Security Accounts Manager (SAM) database.

**user policy**    A user policy is a collection of Registry settings that restricts a user's program and network options, and/or enforces a specified configuration of the user's work environment.

**user profile**    A user profile is a series of Registry settings and folders in the user's profile folder that define a user's work environment. The contents of a user profile include user-specific settings for: Windows NT Explorer, Notepad, Paint, HyperTerminal, Clock, Calculator, and other built-in Windows NT applications; screen saver, background color, background pattern, wallpaper, and other display settings; applications written to run on Windows NT; network drive and printer connections; and the Start menu, including program groups, applications, and recently accessed documents.

**user rights**    User rights authorize users and/or groups to perform specific tasks on a Windows NT computer. User rights are not the same as permissions—user rights enable users to perform tasks; whereas permissions enable users to access objects, such as files, folders, and printers. *See also* permissions.

**value**    A value is an individual entry in the Windows NT Registry. A value cannot contain keys or other values. *See also* key and Registry.

**verbose mode**    Verbose mode refers to running an application in such a way that the application returns the maximum amount of information and detail to the user. The verbose mode is initiated on many applications by using the / v switch.

**virtual device driver**    A virtual device driver is a 32-bit protected mode device driver that is used in Windows 95 and Windows for Workgroups. Virtual device drivers are not supported by Windows NT.

**virtual memory**    Virtual memory is the physical space on a hard disk that Windows NT treats as though it were RAM. *See also* paging file.

**Virtual Memory Manager**    Virtual Memory Manager is a Windows NT kernel mode component that manages memory in a Windows NT environment by using demand paging. *See also* demand paging and virtual memory.

**volume**    A volume is a logical drive. *See also* logical drive.

**volume set**    A volume set is a combination of two to thirty-two partitions that are formatted as a single logical drive. A volume set does not use disk striping to store data on its partitions. *See also* logical drive and stripe set.

**Windows 95**    Windows 95 is a 32-bit desktop operating system. This operating system requires the least amount of hardware of all of the Microsoft Windows 4.0

operating systems. Windows 95 is the only Windows 4.0 operating system that fully supports the Plug and Play architecture.

Windows 95 is compatible with many existing software applications. It supports 16-bit and 32-bit Windows-based applications (including legacy applications designed to run on previous Windows operating systems) and MS-DOS-based applications. You can also run applications that require direct access to the hardware on the Windows 95 operating system.

**Windows NT Backup**    Windows NT Backup (simply called Backup in the user interface) is a Windows NT administrative tool that is used to back up and restore files, folders, and the Registry on a Windows NT computer. Windows NT Backup requires the use of a tape drive device.

**Windows NT Diagnostics**    Windows NT Diagnostics is a Windows NT administrative tool that allows you to view detailed system configuration information and statistics. This tool can help you troubleshoot system configuration problems. Windows NT Diagnostics can also be very useful in determining service and device driver dependencies.

**Windows NT Directory Services**    Windows NT Directory Services is a Microsoft catchall phrase that refers to the architecture, features, functionality, and benefits of Windows NT domains and trust relationships. Windows NT Directory Services (often referred to as Directory Services), as implemented in Windows NT 4.0, is not X.500 compliant. However, Microsoft plans on releasing a new version of Windows NT Directory Services, called the Active Directory, that will be X.500 compliant in a future release of Windows NT.

**Windows NT file system (NTFS)**    NTFS is the most powerful file system supported by Windows NT. Only Windows NT (both Windows NT Workstation and Windows NT Server) supports NTFS—no other operating systems currently support this file system. Windows NT auditing and security are only supported on partitions that are formatted with NTFS.

**Windows NT Server**    Windows NT Server is a powerful 32-bit operating system that is optimized to run on a network file, print, or applications server.

Windows NT Server supports the same software applications as Windows NT Workstation. Additionally, Windows NT Server is the operating system of choice for the Microsoft BackOffice products, including SQL Server, Exchange

Server, and SNA Server. An NT Server computer can support several processors to provide powerful multiprocessing capability.

**Windows NT Server tools**    Windows NT Server tools are a collection of Windows NT Server utilities that, when installed on a Windows 95 or Windows NT Workstation client computer, enable a user at the client computer to remotely manage an NT Server computer on the network. The NT Server tools make remote administration of an NT Server computer practical and convenient for many administrators. Windows NT Server tools are also referred to as client-based network administration tools.

**Windows NT Workstation**    Windows NT Workstation is a 32-bit operating system that is optimized to run as a desktop operating system. It can also be used on personal computers that are networked in a peer-to-peer workgroup configuration, or on a workstation computer that is part of a Windows NT Server domain configuration.

Windows NT Workstation supports most MS-DOS-based applications, most 16-bit and 32-bit Windows-based applications, POSIX 1.*x* applications, and most OS/2 1.*x* applications. It does not support any application that requires direct hardware access because this could compromise Windows NT Workstation's security. It also does not support software applications that require a terminate-and-stay-resident program or a virtual device driver. Windows NT Workstation is a high-end, powerful operating system that supports multiple processors for true multiprocessing.

**WINS**    *Windows Internet Name Service* (WINS) is a Windows NT Server service that provides NetBIOS name resolution services to client computers. A Windows NT Server computer that has WINS installed on it is called a WINS server.

**workgroup**    A workgroup is a logical grouping of networked computers in which one or more of the computers has shared resources, such as a shared folder or a shared printer. In a workgroup environment, the security and user accounts are maintained individually on each separate computer.

**Workstation service**    The Workstation service is a Windows NT service that enables a Windows NT computer to access shared resources on other computers across the network.

# Index

*(continued)*

*(continued)*

*(continued)*

*(continued)*

*(continued)*

*(continued)*

## P

*(continued)*

# U

*(continued)*

# Y

# Z

# IDG BOOKS WORLDWIDE, INC. END-USER LICENSE AGREEMENT

**READ THIS.** You should carefully read these terms and conditions before open-ing the software packet(s) included with this book ("Book"). This is a license agreement ("Agreement") between you and IDG Books Worldwide, Inc. ("IDGB"). By opening the accompanying software packet(s), you acknowledge that you have read and accept the following terms and conditions. If you do not agree and do not want to be bound by such terms and conditions, promptly return the Book and the unopened software packet(s) to the place you obtained them for a full refund.

1. **License Grant.** IDGB grants to you (either an individual or entity) a nonexclusive license to use one copy of the enclosed software program(s) (collectively, the "Software") solely for your own personal or business purposes on a single computer (whether a standard computer or a workstation component of a multiuser network). The Software is in use on a computer when it is loaded into temporary memory (RAM) or installed into permanent memory (hard disk, CD-ROM, or other storage device). IDGB reserves all rights not expressly granted herein.

2. **Ownership.** IDGB is the owner of all right, title, and interest, including copyright, in and to the compilation of the Software recorded on the disk(s) or CD-ROM ("Software Media"). Copyright to the individual programs recorded on the Software Media is owned by the author or other authorized copyright owner of each program. Ownership of the Software and all proprietary rights relating thereto remain with IDGB and its licensers.

3. **Restrictions on Use and Transfer.**

   **(a)** You may only (i) make one copy of the Software for backup or archival purposes, or (ii) transfer the Software to a single hard disk, provided that you keep the original for backup or archival purposes. You may not (i) rent or lease the Software, (ii) copy or reproduce the Software through a LAN or other network system or through any computer subscriber system or bulletin-board system, or (iii) modify, adapt, or create derivative works based on the Software.

**(b)** You may not reverse engineer, decompile, or disassemble the Software. You may transfer the Software and user documentation on a permanent basis, provided that the transferee agrees to accept the terms and conditions of this Agreement and you retain no copies. If the Software is an update or has been updated, any transfer must include the most recent update and all prior versions.

4. **Restrictions on Use of Individual Programs.** You must follow the individual requirements and restrictions detailed for each individual program in Appendix H, "What's on the CD-ROM?" in this Book. These limitations are also contained in the individual license agreements recorded on the Software Media. These limitations may include a requirement that after using the program for a specified period of time, the user must pay a registration fee or discontinue use. By opening the Software packet(s), you will be agreeing to abide by the licenses and restrictions for these individual programs that are detailed in Appendix H, "What's on the CD-ROM?" and on the Software Media. None of the material on this Software Media or listed in this Book may ever be redistributed, in original or modified form, for commercial purposes.

5. **Limited Warranty.**

**(a)** IDGB warrants that the Software and Software Media are free from defects in materials and workmanship under normal use for a period of sixty (60) days from the date of purchase of this Book. If IDGB receives notification within the warranty period of defects in materials or workmanship, IDGB will replace the defective Software Media.

**(b)** IDGB AND THE AUTHOR OF THE BOOK DISCLAIM ALL OTHER WARRANTIES, EXPRESS OR IMPLIED, INCLUDING WITHOUT LIMITATION IMPLIED WARRANTIES OF MERCHANTABILITY AND FITNESS FOR A PARTICULAR PURPOSE, WITH RESPECT TO THE SOFTWARE, THE PROGRAMS, THE SOURCE CODE CONTAINED THEREIN, AND/OR THE TECHNIQUES DESCRIBED IN THIS BOOK. IDGB DOES NOT WARRANT THAT THE FUNCTIONS CONTAINED IN THE SOFTWARE WILL MEET YOUR REQUIREMENTS OR THAT THE OPERATION OF THE SOFTWARE WILL BE ERROR FREE.

**(c)** This limited warranty gives you specific legal rights, and you may have other rights that vary from jurisdiction to jurisdiction.

## 6. Remedies.

**(a)** IDGB's entire liability and your exclusive remedy for defects in materials and workmanship shall be limited to replacement of the Software Media, which may be returned to IDGB with a copy of your receipt at the following address: Software Media Fulfillment Department, Attn.: *Windows NT 4.0 MCSE Study Guide*, IDG Books Worldwide, Inc., 7260 Shadeland Station, Ste. 100, Indianapolis, IN 46256, or call 1-800-762-2974. Please allow three to four weeks for delivery. This Limited Warranty is void if failure of the Software Media has resulted from accident, abuse, or misapplication. Any replacement Software Media will be warranted for the remainder of the original warranty period or thirty (30) days, whichever is longer.

**(b)** In no event shall IDGB or the author be liable for any damages whatsoever (including without limitation damages for loss of business profits, business interruption, loss of business information, or any other pecuniary loss) arising from the use of or inability to use the Book or the Software, even if IDGB has been advised of the possibility of such damages.

**(c)** Because some jurisdictions do not allow the exclusion or limitation of liability for consequential or incidental damages, the above limitation or exclusion may not apply to you.

## 7. U.S. Government Restricted Rights.
Use, duplication, or disclosure of the Software by the U.S. Government is subject to restrictions stated in paragraph (c)(1)(ii) of the Rights in Technical Data and Computer Software clause of DFARS 252.227-7013, and in subparagraphs (a) through (d) of the Commercial Computer—Restricted Rights clause at FAR 52.227-19, and in similar clauses in the NASA FAR supplement, when applicable.

## 8. General.
This Agreement constitutes the entire understanding of the parties and revokes and supersedes all prior agreements, oral or written, between them and may not be modified or amended except in a writing signed by both parties hereto that specifically refers to this Agreement. This Agreement shall take precedence over any other documents that may

be in conflict herewith. If any one or more provisions contained in this Agreement are held by any court or tribunal to be invalid, illegal, or otherwise unenforceable, each and every other provision shall remain in full force and effect.

# Have You Looked into Your Future?

Step into the future of computer books at ➤ *www.idgbooks.com* — IDG Books' newly revamped Web site featuring exclusive software, insider information, online books, and live events!

**Visit us to:**

- **Get freeware and shareware** handpicked by industry-leading authors found at our expanded *Free and Downloadable* area.

- **Pick up expert tips** from our online *Resource Centers* devoted to Java, Web Publishing, Windows, and Macs. Jazz up your Web pages with free applets, get practical pointers, use handy online code, and find out what the pros are doing.

- **Chat online** with in-the-know authorities, and find out when our authors are appearing in your area, on television, radio, and commercial online services.

- **Consult electronic books** from *Novell Press*. Keep on top of the newest networking technologies and trends presented by the industry's most respected source.

- **Explore Yahoo! Plaza,** the gathering place for our complete line of Yahoo! books. You'll find the latest hand-picked selection of hot-and-happening Web sites here.

- **Browse our books conveniently** using our comprehensive, searchable title catalog that features selective sneak-preview sample chapters, author biographies, and bonus online content. While you're at it, take advantage of our online book-buying—with free parking and overnight delivery!

**Don't wait—visit us now. The future is here!**

➤ www.idgbooks.com

IDG BOOKS WORLDWIDE™

# CD-ROM Installation Instructions

Each software item on the *Windows NT 4.0 MCSE Study Guide* CD-ROM is located in its own folder. To install a particular piece of software, begin by opening its folder with My Computer or Internet Explorer. What you do next depends on what you find in the software's folder:

- Look first for a ReadMe.txt file or a .doc or .htm document. If this is present, it should contain installation instructions and other useful information.

- If the folder contains an executable (.exe) file, this is usually an installation program. Often it will be called Setup.exe or Install.exe, but in some cases the filename reflects an abbreviated version of the software's name and version number. Run the .exe file to start the installation process.

- In the case of some simple software, the .exe file probably is the software— no real installation step is required. You can run the software from the CD-ROM to try it out. If you like it, copy it to your hard disk and create a Start menu shortcut for it.

The ReadMe.txt file in the CD-ROM's root directory and Appendix H, "What's on the CD-ROM?" contain additional installation information, so be sure to check these.

Also see Appendix H for a listing of the software on the CD-ROM.